Psychological Science

SECOND EDITION

Michael S. Gazzaniga

DARTMOUTH COLLEGE
UNIVERSITY OF CALIFORNIA, SANTA BARBARA

Todd F. Heatherton

DARTMOUTH COLLEGE

Psychological Science

SECOND EDITION

W. W. Norton & Company
New York • London

W. W. Norton & Company has been independent since its founding in 1923, when William Warder Norton and Mary D. Herter Norton first published lectures delivered at the People's Institute, the adult education division of New York City's Cooper Union. The Nortons soon expanded their program beyond the Institute, publishing books by celebrated academics from America and abroad. By mid-century, the two major pillars of Norton's publishing program—trade books and college texts—were firmly established. In the 1950s, the Norton family transferred control of the company to its employees, and today—with a staff of four hundred and a comparable number of trade, college, and professional titles published each year—W. W. Norton & Company stands as the largest and oldest publishing house owned wholly by its employees.

Editor: Jon Durbin
Managing Editor, College: Marian Johnson
Project Editor: Kim Yi
Electronic Media Editor: Denise Shanks
Editorial Assistant: Kelly Rolf
Copy Editor: Barbara Gerr
Director of Manufacturing, College: Roy Tedoff
Book Designer: Rubina Yeh
Photo Researchers: Neil Hoos and Kelly Rolf
Illustrations: Frank Forney
Composition by GGS Book Services
Layout Artist: Paul Lacy
Manufacturing by Von Hoffmann

PRINTED IN THE UNITED STATES OF AMERICA.
Second Edition.

The text of this book is composed in Benton Modern Two with the display type in Polymer.

Library of Congress Cataloging-in-Publication Data
Gazzaniga, Michael S.
    Psychological science / Michael S. Gazzaniga, Todd F. Heatherton.—2nd ed.
        p. cm.
Includes bibliographical references and indexes.
                        ISBN 0-393-92497-1
    1. Psychology. I. Heatherton, Todd F. II. Title.

BF121.G393 2005
150—dc22
                                                    2005048246

W. W. Norton & Company, Inc., 500 Fifth Avenue, New York, NY 10110
www.wwnorton.com
W. W. Norton & Company Ltd., Castle House, 75/76 Wells Street, London W1T 3QT

2 3 4 5 6 7 8 9 0

Michael S. Gazzaniga (Ph.D., California Institute of Technology) is the David T. McLaughlin Distinguished Professor at Dartmouth College and Distinguished Visiting Professor at the University of California, Santa Barbara. He founded and presides over the Cognitive Neuroscience Institute and is founding editor-in-chief of the *Journal of Cognitive Neuroscience*. He is President of the American Psychological Society and a member of the American Academy of Arts and Sciences. His research focuses on split-brain patients. He has held positions at the University of California, Santa Barbara; New York University; the State University of New York, Stony Brook; Cornell University Medical College; and the University of California, Davis.

Todd F. Heatherton (Ph.D., University of Toronto) is the Champion International Professor of Psychological and Brain Sciences at Dartmouth College. His research examines processes related to self, in particular self-regulation, self-esteem, and self-referential processing. This research is grounded in the traditions of personality and social psychology although the guiding theories, as well as the techniques and methodologies that he uses, are strongly influenced by research in cognitive neuroscience. He has been on the executive committees of the Society of Personality and Social Psychology (SPSP), the Association of Researchers in Personality, and the International Society of Self & Identity. He is Associate Editor of the Journal of Cognitive Neuroscience, and on several editorial boards. He has served as Head Tutor and chair of the undergraduate program in Psychology at Harvard University and department chair at Dartmouth College. He received the Petra Shattuck Award for Teaching Excellence from the Harvard Extension School in 1994. In 2005, he received the award for Distinguished Service on Behalf of Social and Personality Psychology from SPSP for his role in creating the annual SPSP meeting.

We dedicate this book to Francesca and Zachary Gazzaniga and Sarah and James Heatherton.

CONTENTS IN BRIEF

CONTENTS

1 INTRODUCTION TO PSYCHOLOGICAL SCIENCE   3

2 RESEARCH METHODOLOGY   37

3 GENETIC AND BIOLOGICAL FOUNDATIONS 73

6 LEARNING AND REWARD 209

7 MEMORY   249

9 MOTIVATION   341

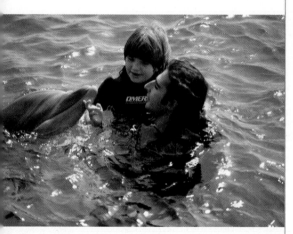

15 SOCIAL PSYCHOLOGY 607

Psychological Science *in Action* ◐ ◉ ○

Thinking Critically

Profiles in Psychological Science

J ust over seven years ago we joined forces with W. W. Norton to create an introductory psychology textbook that would capture the excitement of twenty-first-century psychological science. Our vision for the book was bold, as we sought to break the mold of the homogenized and encyclopedic textbooks that focus on classic themes and standard topics. Thanks to an editorial team that shared our vision, the First Edition of *Psychological Science* achieved our principal goals, the most important of which was to produce a readable book that focused on cutting-edge psychological and brain sciences. This approach resonated with faculty and students alike, as it captured the excitement of contemporary research being conducted in labs around the world. Instructors were especially enthusiastic about the levels-of-analysis approach to studying human behavior, which has become the cutting-edge way to investigate behavior in the fields of psychology and neuroscience. It is clear that there is an eager audience for a rigorous and scientific treatment of psychology that is accessible for the majority of students.

We frankly were thrilled with the response our First Edition received. We tried a lot of new approaches and most of them worked. Many of our colleagues told us that they especially liked the declarative writing style that focused on answers to current scientific questions driving psychological research. The "ask and answer" approach that serves as the pedagogical foundation of the book captured students' interest and kept the material engaging. It helped students take home the idea that psychological scientists are addressing big questions and making progress in solving them.

Even though the book received considerable praise, as authors we felt that some features and material didn't quite satisfy what we were trying to achieve. For instance, we sometimes went into too much technical detail and occasionally our coverage was a bit unbalanced. As we noted in the preface to the First Edition, our greatest challenge was in deciding what not to include rather than what to include. In retrospect, we sometimes included material that was unnecessary and other topics needed to be included or covered in more depth. Our core goal for *Psychological Science* in its current and future editions is to provide students with what they really need to know to be informed about psychological science. As we prepared this revision we spent considerable time addressing that very question. We sought advice from many colleagues, even repeatedly asking some of you, "Do students really need to know this at the introductory level?" If the answer was no, we eliminated that material so that we could more thoroughly treat essential topics that required greater attention. We thank all our colleagues and reviewers who helped us sort out these issues and provided good advice on how to improve the text.

Everything we tried to do in the First Edition was first and foremost for the benefit of students, and they continue to be our primary audience in the Second Edition. In response to their comments, we now include even more vivid examples and case histories, especially in the *Profiles in Psychological Science* units in each chapter, as well as descriptions of how psychological scientists are having an impact on their daily lives. Each chapter's *Psychological Science in Action* unit introduces students to how knowledge from psychological research is used in various professions (e.g., marketing, forensics, sports, robotics) and how it has helped answer important policy questions, such as how young children should be taught to read. In developing these units, we place psychological science in a human context by emphasizing the extent to which it applies to students' everyday lives. We have expanded the number of citations to the research literature, but we have avoided overloading the text with unnecessary citations—the focus remains on the words and ideas. We believe students will respond favorably to the changes we have made in this edition. We look forward to their responses to our efforts.

This Second Edition also includes changes that will appeal to instructors. Building on the "ask and answer" approach, we sought to have one or two broad themes drive each chapter. The themes reflect overarching questions that have played prominent roles throughout the history of psychological science, such as Chapter 3's discussion of the role of environment in gene expression, which provides new insights to longstanding questions about nature and nurture, and Chapter 4's discussion of whether psychological functions are localized in specific brain regions and which regions are involved in conscious experience. This strategy demonstrates the cumulative nature of psychological science as well as the multiple perspectives that researchers and teachers bring to the subject matter. Another good example of this occurs in Chapter 15, where we highlight the idea that people consistently underestimate the power of situations to affect human behavior, including their own, and discuss how much social cognition occurs automatically and without conscious awareness or intent, as people quickly evaluate and categorize others. Each chapter is now more tightly conceived and unified; each has its own unique emphasis. The chapter conclusions then take up these themes to provide students with a take-home message. When students finish a chapter, they should have a clear sense of the big questions and issues driving contemporary research in that area, as well as an understanding of what is known and what remains to be discovered.

Given the popularity of our levels-of-analysis approach, we worked hard to integrate more social and cultural examples throughout the first half of the book. We have streamlined our discussion to the three essential levels (biological, individual, social), but also expanded coverage within each level. We believe that the Second Edition balances social and cultural psychology with the biological. This increased emphasis on culture throughout the book begins in Chapter 1 with a foundational discussion on how culture is adaptive. We also increased the prominence of critical thinking throughout the book. Based on reviewer and instructor suggestions, we have made it a centerpiece of the new edition. To each chapter we added a *Thinking Critically* unit that takes on a controversial topic and demonstrates the value of critical analysis. We have also added short-answer critical thinking questions in the margins of each chapter. Finally, at the end of each chapter, we introduce a study feature called Applying the Principles that asks students to answer a series of questions designed to see if they can apply the chapter concepts to the real world. Recognizing that introductory psychology is the only exposure to the subject that many students will have, we believe it to be vitally important that students understand what it means to be consumers of psychological research, including recognizing the value of good, solid science.

In response to comments by reviewers and instructors and our own sense of the strengths and weaknesses of the First Edition, we made both major and minor changes throughout the book. We scrutinized each chapter and in a few cases decided that they needed to be reconsidered altogether. The chapters on cognition (Chapter 8) and sensation and perception (Chapter 5) have been completely reconceptualized and rewritten. The material in these chapters is both more student-friendly, in terms of the level of technical detail, and more applicable to students' lives. In Chapter 4, we introduced an innovative and appealing discussion of functional neuroanatomy and how it gives rise to consciousness. This is a fresh approach that really brings the anatomy home to the students and helps them see how understanding the brain helps with understanding the mind, both when it is awake and when it is in an altered state of consciousness, such as sleep. In the previous edition there were two developmental chapters and two social chapters. In this edition we consider these as unified areas, no longer separating, for example, cognitive and social development. In each case we took the best material from the two chapters, reframed the major themes and issues, and built a more concise and integrated chapter. We now have one unified development chapter (Chapter 11), with a greater lifespan emphasis, and one unified social chapter (Chapter 15), which focuses more on how context shapes behavior. In keeping with our levels-of-analysis approach, we moved the social chapter to the end of the book, where we use it to summarize many of the accomplishments of psychological science in understanding what it means to be humans.

We noted in the preface to the First Edition that writing this book had changed us as scientists and inspired us to more fully cross levels of analysis in our own research, including collaborating on using neuroscience methods to understand the self. The cross-fertilization of our interests has continued. Mike's most recent book, *The Ethical Brain*, considers the fundamental social nature of human existence. Todd has become even more interested in understanding the neural basis of social and personality phenomena. While continuing to keep busy on the research and administrative fronts, we truly enjoy teaching both graduate and undergraduate students. They keep us energized and teach us new ideas as we move forward with our own lives and careers. We hope that our own enthusiasm for the science of psychology inspires students to think about the big issues and questions that fascinate those of us who have dedicated our lives to understanding the mind and behavior.

Tour of *Psychological Science*

CHAPTER 1 (*Introduction to Psychological Science*) sets the stage for the book. We introduce students to psychological science by providing engaging examples of psychological questions and answers. We continue to emphasize the four guiding themes that characterize psychological science: (1) It is a cumulative science, with principles established through incremental advances in knowledge obtained through research. (2) A biological revolution has energized psychological research. (3) The human mind is adaptive, which means that the brain has evolved to solve everyday problems and also that culture provides adaptive solutions. (4) Psychological science crosses different levels of analysis and perspectives, from the biological to the social, from genes to culture. In the new edition, we have simplified our levels-of-analysis approach so that it now focuses on three broad levels of analysis: biological, individual, and social. Our first discussion from this perspective explores the psychological aspects of music. There is also a much greater emphasis on culture throughout the book. In this chapter, we present a foundational discussion that considers differences between how people in eastern and western cultures view and reason about the physical world. We then briefly trace the intellectual origins and historical background of psychological science and go on to describe how psychological knowledge is applied to solving real-world problems, such as treating mental disorders. We end the chapter by emphasizing the importance of critical thinking for consumers of psychological research.

In CHAPTER 2 (*Research Methodology*), we lay the foundations for understanding the methods of psychological science. We cover the major methods in sufficient detail so that students understand the techniques and strategies used to examine psychological questions. In the new edition we place a stronger emphasis on the role of critical thinking in testing theories about the mind, brain, and behavior. We also expand the description of how research with animals, including manipulating their genes, is an important tool for addressing fundamental psychological questions. As part of the emphasis on critical thinking, we highlight the need for researchers to pay attention to potential cultural differences when drawing conclusions about human nature. We also offer a unified presentation of the methods for assessing the working brain (i.e., electrophysiology, imaging, neuropsychology). Pulling the descriptions of these methods together will

help allow students understand the full range of tools available to psychological scientists.

In CHAPTER 3 (*Genetic and Biological Foundations*) we have substantially reconsidered the role of genes in psychological processes. For years, psychologists focused on whether people possessed certain types of genes, such as genes for psychological disorders or intelligence, with an emphasis on the extent to which human traits were hardwired. Recent cutting-edge research is emphasizing gene expression, what turns genes "on" and "off." The major lesson is that the environment, including social factors, plays an important role in gene expression, and therefore in how the environment affects the mind, brain, and behavior. It is as much gene expression as gene possession that makes us who we are as human beings. We provide a compelling example of how antisocial behavior results from the interaction of genes and environment. We also describe cutting-edge research on how gene expression can be modified, such as through small RNA activity. Throughout the chapter we have reduced the level of technical difficulty by focusing on what students really need to know in order to understand basic human physiology. For example, we eliminated the in-depth description of metabotropic receptors as well as distinctions between peptide and steroid hormones. We continue to enliven the discussion of the nervous system by focusing on the influence of neurotransmission on everyday mental activity and behavior.

CHAPTER 4 (*The Brain and Consciousness*) has been transformed in ways that we believe will excite teachers and students alike. Rather than focusing solely on the brain, we now explore how brain activity gives rise to the unique human capacity of consciousness. After briefly discussing evolving views of the localization of function, we emphasize that mental activity results from the integrated actions of specific and localized structures that are distributed throughout the brain. We also discuss the idea that we are not conscious of much of our mental activity, with social psychologists such as Dan Wegner and John Bargh demonstrating that much of human behavior occurs automatically and without intention. This raises interesting philosophical questions for students, such as the degree to which we are able to consciously will our actions. In keeping with the idea that the brain gives rise to conscious experience, we then discuss sleep in the context of brain activity. After all, many regions of the brain are more active when we sleep than when we are awake. Our goal with this fresh approach is to emphasize the importance of brain function to human experience.

CHAPTER 5 (*Sensation, Perception, and Attention*) provides a foundation for understanding how the brain senses and perceives the world. This chapter has been revised substantially to make the material more accessible to students. The section on psychophysics and signal detection now emphasizes basic concepts and methodological approaches rather than mathematical equations of difference thresholds. We reorganized the discussion of the five senses, beginning with taste and building up to vision, which helps students appreciate the commonalities in the various perceptual systems. A theme that runs throughout the chapter is that perception is an active constructive process that occurs in the brain. Our goal for this chapter is to foster an appreciation for how the brain takes in ambiguous sensory information and constructs rich and meaningful experiences that allow us to navigate the world around us. Because perception is important to social interaction, we discuss face perception in this chapter. Finally, we consider how attentional processes influence how people perceive the world around them, emphasizing that the ability to selectively attend to important sensory stimuli is crucial for survival.

CHAPTER 6 (*Learning and Reward*) covers the foundations of principles of learning and the role of learning in solving adaptive challenges. We emphasize that the study of learning has been a powerful force in psychological science for more than a century, and that the principles of classical and operant conditioning are important throughout psychology and allied sciences. This chapter provides a good demonstration of our theme that psychological science is cumulative, with researchers responding to and expanding on their predecessors to understand the complexities of learning. We have expanded the discussion of how economic principles can inform the understanding of reinforcement as well as how learning can be passed on through cultural transmission. In keeping with our goal of limiting technical jargon, we removed the discussion of the various subcomponents of the mesolimbic dopamine pathway, instead focusing more directly on the importance of dopamine to reward. We also describe new studies that use genetic manipulation to explore how long-term potentiation works.

CHAPTER 7 (*Memory*) continues to provide a cutting-edge treatment of how people encode, store, and retrieve different types of information. We have included new findings on emotional memory, on reconsolidation, and on H.M.'s recently discovered acquisition of new semantic knowledge. A central focus of the chapter is the neurological basis of memory, with classic and contemporary examples of how brain injury interferes with explicit recall. We also continue to emphasize the practical aspects of human memory, such as the ability to serve as eyewitnesses and the role of motivation and social context in shaping what we remember.

CHAPTER 8 (*Thinking and Intelligence*) has been completely reconceptualized and expanded. It now incorporates a much greater emphasis on the intelligent use of information and the idea that for the most part thinking is adaptive. We present a more streamlined discussion of representational knowledge and emphasize how knowledge structures, such as scripts and schemas, guide our behavior, often without our conscious awareness. The idea that unconscious processes play prominent roles in cognition is an important theme throughout the chapter. We have significantly modified the discussion of problem solving and decision making to emphasize more recent research on heuristic processes. We have expanded the discussion of deductive and inductive reasoning and provided more detail on how people solve problems in everyday life. We also consider at some length the idea that more thought does not necessarily make for better decisions. The revised chapter has a much more thorough discussion of what it means to be intelligent, with an increased focus on fluid intelligence and the prominent role it plays in dealing with modern society. We describe recent research on the neural and cognitive bases of intelligence and discuss the role that genes and environment play in shaping intelligence.

CHAPTER 9 (*Motivation*) presents an overview of the factors that motivate behavior. This chapter demonstrates the need to consider biological, psychological, and social factors in order to develop a satisfactory understanding of why people "choose" to engage in specific behaviors. We consider motivation in its adaptive context, with an interpretation based on evolutionary principles. The section on sleep, which was moved to Chapter 4, has been replaced by expanded discussions of addiction, sexual behavior, and the human need to belong. Each of these is considered across the multiple levels of analysis. The chapter invites students to reflect on what motivates them from day to day, how they deal with competing motives, and how setting and achieving goals can help them lead meaningful lives.

CHAPTER 10 (*Emotions and Health*) explores how emotions influence the human experience, including where they come from and how they are experienced, as well as how people cope with stress and handle negative events. In this revised chapter, we consider behaviors that significantly influence physical health, particularly those that lead to healthy living. We also include more discussion of how stress affects the heart and the immune system. In a new section, we look at how daily behaviors, such as eating, exercising, and smoking, play an important role in the most common causes of death in our society, and we consider evidence that emotional states often encourage people to develop bad habits.

CHAPTER 11 (*Human Development*) provides a thorough discussion of physical, cognitive, and social development. We have merged the two development chapters from the previous edition into one unified treatment of developmental issues across the life span. The driving idea behind this merger is that in looking at the factors that shape us, it is impossible to separate the cognitive from the social. We emphasize the multiple forces, from genes to culture, that interact to produce unique humans. Taking a life span approach, we consider how humans change as they grow, from infancy to old age. We now offer greater coverage of middle age and old age, examining the important roles that family and career have in our lives. The message of the final section is that, although physical and cognitive declines are an inevitable part of the aging process, contemporary research finds that older people are surprisingly satisfied with their lives.

CHAPTER 12 (*Personality*) remains a somewhat radical departure from historical treatments of personality. Most textbooks describe the area of personality as it existed more than 40 years ago, with an emphasis on unconscious Freudian processes and social learning experiences. Yet recent research has provided compelling evidence that human personality is determined to a large extent by genetic and physiological mechanisms. This chapter focuses on research by contemporary psychologists who have made considerable strides in understanding the development and structure of human personality. We cover traditional topics, such as Freudian and trait theory, but we emphasize more current research on the cognitive and biological factors involved in personality.

CHAPTER 13 (*Disorders of Mind and Body*) introduces students to the best-known forms of psychological disorders, especially those that we know to be of interest to students. In this revised chapter we have streamlined the discussion of legal issues and expanded the discussion of assessment techniques, such as interviews and behavioral assessments. Following a brief review of the issues surrounding determining whether a condition reflects a psychological disorder, we describe the essential features of each major disorder and discuss various etiological theories. We provide a thorough discussion of the biological, psychological, and social factors that have been implicated in the development of schizophrenia. We describe recent evidence that some indications of schizophrenia and other forms of adult psychopathology can be observed in childhood, such as in home movies. Vivid case studies are used throughout to illustrate symptoms and assessment. We include expanded coverage of childhood disorders, such as ADHD and autism, which are typically ignored in introductory textbooks; it is our experience that students find these disorders especially interesting. The overall theme of the chapter is that to really understand psychopathology we need to recognize the social, psychological, and biological factors that contribute to the expression of mental illness in those who are susceptible.

CHAPTER 14 (*Treating Disorders of Mind and Body*) examines the theoretical basis of psychotherapy, as well as typical treatments and outcomes. Following a discussion of treatment goals, we introduce students to the most common types of therapy. Although we mention classic psychological treatments, we emphasize the types of treatments most widely used by contemporary therapists. We consider treatments for anxiety disorders, depression, and schizophrenia in detail, with special attention to the empirical evidence for successful outcomes. One theme running through the chapter is that treatments are tailored specifically for a client with specific psychological symptoms. That is, there is no overall grand theory that guides treatment, but rather treatment is based on evidence of its effectiveness, which is established through rigorous research. Another important point is the preference for psychological treatments over pharmacological treatments when both are effective, as psychological treatments have fewer side effects and are longer lasting. We also discuss evidence that both psychological and pharmacological treatments lead to changes in brain functioning. As in the previous chapter, we include discussion of issues specifically related to children, such as how behavior therapy can be used to treat autism. The take-home message of the chapter is that although we have a ways to go, psychological scientists have discovered a great deal about how to improve the quality of life for people with serious disorders of mind and body.

CHAPTER 15 (*Social Psychology*) is a new chapter that merges the best sections from the two social chapters in the previous edition. An important theme that guides the chapter is that people have evolved as social animals and that much of human behavior and experience is shaped by social context; cultural rules and norms determine a great deal of our behavior. Another important theme of the chapter is that people reliably underestimate the power of situations in affecting human behavior. Numerous vivid examples, such as the prisoner abuse at Abu Ghraib, help students appreciate the effect of social context on behavior. We also emphasize that a great deal of social cognition occurs automatically and without conscious awareness or intent, especially in how we think about others and ourselves. In this chapter we have narrowed our focus to the social self, with an increased emphasis on self-relevant motives and the extent to which these motives are true across cultures. We discuss research that crosses levels of analysis from the social to the biological, as we explore recent neuroimaging studies on the self, attitudes, and stereotyping. And we expand the section on relationships, with a greater emphasis on romantic relationships. This unified chapter describes many of the important studies that have been conducted by social psychologists and demonstrates how the principles that developed out of these studies are relevant to students' everyday lives.

A Pedagogical Program That Reinforces *Psychological Science*'s Core Principles

I. Overview

Psychological Science's chapters are built around 4 to 6 major principles that are addressed through the "ask and answer" approach. Each is first raised in the form of a question ("ask"). Each major section then discusses one of these questions ("answer").

OUTLINING THE PRINCIPLES: At one level, this feature serves as a simple outline or road map for the chapter. At another level, it clarifies the major principles that will be covered in the chapter. Major heads are questions. Minor heads are declarative statements that reveal the current state of knowledge about the larger principles and concepts.

CHAPTER TIMELINES: Psychological science is built on cumulative knowledge and experience. This is one of the major themes of the text. Basic principles, both new and old, inspire and guide thinking and research in the field. The timelines highlight major developments within the various domains of psychology.

CRITICAL THINKING QUESTIONS: These questions are designed to encourage students to think integratively and beyond the text. Appearing in the margins throughout each chapter, they selectively highlight core principles and are ideal as short-answer questions on quizzes or for discussion in small groups.

"ASK AND ANSWER" RUNNING HEADS: *Psychological Science*'s left-hand running heads emphasize the larger topics, with the right-hand running heads repeating the questions that are explored in each section. The heads help students stay focused on the larger issue as they try to see the forest for the trees.

REVIEWING THE PRINCIPLES: These boxes are a critical component of the "ask and answer" approach and appear at the end of each major section. They repeat the question that governed the section and provide a basic answer that highlights key points for students to remember.

DEFINING THE PRINCIPLES: *Psychological Science* has a marginal glossary running throughout each chapter as well as a glossary at the end of the book and on the companion Web site. Many books highlight too many key terms for students to memorize. In keeping with this book's focus on core principles and concepts, *Psychological Science* highlights approximately 30 key terms per chapter.

CONCLUSION: *Psychological Science*'s brief chapter conclusions sum up the big ideas and concepts and remind students how the book's four key themes wove their way through the chapter.

SUMMARIZING THE PRINCIPLES: Designed to follow the outline for each chapter, this feature provides a detailed review. Students are reminded again of the major questions that governed each section and the key pieces of research-based knowledge that provide insight into those questions.

APPLYING THE PRINCIPLES: *Psychological Science* encourages students to apply core principles to real-world settings. Multiple-choice Applying the Principles questions at the end of each chapter highlight core principles students need to learn. Answers appear at the end of the section.

II. *Psychological Science*'s Art and Citations

A DYNAMIC ART PROGRAM: The visual materials in *Psychological Science* add substantially to the students' experience. The book contains a variety of visual materials, from photographs to tables and charts to drawn art. The emphasis in *Psychological Science*, however, is clearly on the drawn art. Having used many general psychology books ourselves, we wanted to take our text in a new direction. By featuring drawn art, *Psychological Science* is able to convey precisely, accurately, and meaningfully what the students need to gain from every image. This high level of precision can't be achieved with the stock photographs common in many texts.

SELECTIVE USE OF CITATIONS: *Psychological Science* embraces the notion that students should be introduced to material in a narrative style that focuses on ideas, concepts, and empirical findings rather than on specific researchers. At the same time, the text includes enough citations that students can pursue topics of interest and appreciate that psychological science is based on published empirical research. We have selected essential citations that we hope most teachers would agree are central to a first-year student's exploration of psychological science, and we have cited them in a way that should not distract from the narrative voice.

III. *Psychological Science*'s Special Topic Units

Special Topic Units amplify the text's basic strengths by challenging students to think critically and to understand the impact that the field of psychology has on their lives and world. Because each unit is seamlessly integrated into the narrative rather than set off like traditional feature boxes, it remains an important part of the learning experience.

PSYCHOLOGICAL SCIENCE IN ACTION units highlight major areas of applied research and possible careers in fields such as organizational psychology, sports psychology, consumer psychology, forensic psychology, and clinical psychology. Among these units are "Sports Psychologists Help Athletes Find the Zone," "Motivation on the Job," and "Forensic Assessment and Profiling."

PROFILES IN PSYCHOLOGICAL SCIENCE units focus on the human perspective, thereby broadening the book's rich presentation of science and research. Each of these units offers an individual case study to show how people's lives can intersect with science. Among these units are "One Boy's Journey out of Autism's Grasp," "Making Marriage Last," and "What Makes Killers Kill?"

THINKING CRITICALLY units contain stories from newspapers and magazines on controversial topics that enable students to formulate their own conclusions based on the information available. Among these units are "Should Drugs Be Used to Treat Adolescent Depression?" "Should Memory Be Altered by Drugs?" and "Are Self-Serving Biases Universal?"

Psychological Science, Second Edition, eBook—Same Great Content, Half the Price
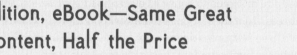

The eBook version of *Psychological Science*, Second Edition, offers the full content of the print version at half the price. Accessible at any time on the Web, the eBook is directly linked to the Student Web site's resources and incorporates many of its interactive elements.

Psychological Science's Ancillaries Focus on Research in Action

ZAPS: The Norton Psychology Labs
wwnorton.com/zaps

ZAPS: THE NORTON PSYCHOLOGY LABS give students a firm understanding of fundamental concepts by allowing them to experience psychological phenomena firsthand, taking the role of either subject or researcher in engaging, diverse experiments and demonstrations. Ideal for introductory psychology courses, these groundbreaking online labs allow students to see the significance of psychological research.

A **class results** feature allows instructors to collect aggregate ZAPS data for their class in real time.

Visit the free ZAPS demo site at wwnorton.com/zaps.

The Norton Psychology Reader edited by Gary Marcus (New York University)

0–393–92712–X / paper / 375 pages / November 2005

The Norton Psychology Reader offers a diverse collection of popular readings (8–10 pages in length) sure to enliven classroom discussion and inform student research, most of them written in the last decade. Available alone or as an ideal complement to *Psychological Science*, Second Edition, this engaging reader highlights the most exciting ideas in the field today. Authors range from Steven Pinker to Natalie Angier, from Malcolm Gladwell to Robert Cialdini.

Norton Psychology DVD created by Patrick Carroll (University of Texas, Austin)

With over 60 minutes of video footage, this useful classroom resource illustrates the exciting possibilities of psychological research through a diverse video-clip collection of research being performed. Free to qualified adopters.

Student Web site to accompany *Psychological Science*, Second Edition
wwnorton.com/psychsci

This innovative online learning tool offers a wealth of resources for study and review. In addition to timelines, vocabulary flashcards, and detailed chapter reviews, the site includes:

- **Diagnostic Quizzes** with smart feedback that allow students to pinpoint strengths and weaknesses
- **Activities**
- The **Norton Gradebook** feature, which allows students and instructors to effectively track quiz results
- **Animations** that clarify difficult psychological concepts
- **Psychology in the News**, a unique section, updated weekly, that gathers relevant news coverage and analysis

Study Guide to accompany *Psychological Science*, Second Edition

by Brett Beck and Eileen Astor-Stetson (both of Bloomsburg University)

Created by two highly successful instructors of large lecture classes, this carefully crafted study aid offers a guide to each chapter of the textbook, with helpful study advice, completion questions, key-figure exercises, multiple-choice self-tests, and thought questions.

Instructor's Resource Manual to accompany *Psychological Science*, Second Edition

by Margaret Forgie (Lethbridge University) and George Spilich (Washington College)

Prepared by two master teachers who cultivate active learning environments in their own classrooms, the Instructor's Resource Manual provides teaching suggestions from Professors Heatherton and Gazzaniga; Chapter Overviews by Professor Heatherton; Chapter Objectives; Ticket-In, Ticket-Out Assignments; Five-Minute Lecture Launchers; Classroom Demonstrations and Activities; Discussion Topics; and a substantial Link Library. Available to all adopters.

Test-Item File and Computerized Test-Item File

by Robert Kleck (Dartmouth College) and Margaret Lynch (San Francisco State University)

These Test-Item Files provide over 2,000 test questions, classified by chapter topic and question type (factual, vocabulary, applied, and conceptual). Available to all adopters.

Norton Media Library

The Norton Media Library features Web-ready teaching materials for WebCT, Blackboard, or personal–course page formats. Ideal for both classroom learning and distance education, this comprehensive online resource offers tools for instructors such as test-item files, problem sets, lecture outlines, PowerPoint slides of textbook art and figures, and glossaries.

Norton Gradebook— wwnorton.com/college/nrl/gradebook

The Norton Gradebook is an online resource that allows instructors and students to store and track their online quiz results effectively. Student results from each quiz are uploaded to the password-protected Gradebook, where instructors can access and sort them by section, chapter, book, student name, and date. Students can access the Gradebook to review their personal results. Registration for the Gradebook is instant and no setup is required.

Studying the Mind DVD

Filmed at Dartmouth College's Summer Institute for Cognitive Neuroscience, and featuring original footage exclusive to Norton, this DVD was created to bring examples of current brain-science research into the introductory psychology lecture. These five-to- seven-minute segments feature such well-known neuroscientific researchers as Marcus Raichle, Robert Knight, Mark D'Esposito, Michael Gazzaniga, John Gabrieli, Elizabeth Phelps, Marcia Johnson, Morris Moscovitch, Helen Neville, Denise Parks, and Patricia Reuter-Lorenz. Free to qualified adopters.

Norton Resource Library (wwnorton.com/nrl)

A Web site designed to house all electronic *Psychological Science* resources, from the test bank to PowerPoint slides to video clips. All of these resources are readily uploadable into WebCT and Blackboard environments. Available to all adopters.

Norton Video Library

A collection of first-rate documentary films focusing on psychological science drawn from the Films for Sciences and Humanities catalog and other fine video collections. Available to qualifying adopters.

Transparencies to accompany *Psychological Science*, Second Edition

These four-color transparencies include all the drawn art, tables, and charts from the book.

ACKNOWLEDGMENTS

We begin once again by thanking our families, who have put up with us spending long hours away from them for the past three years. We are both very fortunate to have unwavering family support. We also are grateful to the many colleagues who gave us constructive feedback and advice. Special acknowledgment needs to be made to six individuals: Elizabeth Phelps, for helping us develop a clear vision for the cognition chapter, Peter Tse and Howard Hughes for their suggestions for making the sensation and perception chapter clear and accessible, Jay Hull for assisting us in making hard decisions regarding how best to merge the social chapters, Gary Marcus for pushing us to think about gene expression in new ways, and Steven Heine for doing the same for us about culture. We also benefited from the astute guidance of John Cacioppo, Jamie Pennebaker, Fernanda Ferreira, Tara Callaghan, Margaret Lynch, Jim Enns, Wendi Gardner, Lauretta Reeves, and many others who were willing to discuss their teaching goals for introductory psychology and their beliefs about what works and doesn't work in introductory textbooks.

Producing a psychology textbook is a team enterprise and relies on the efforts of many individuals, especially those who help with the ancillaries. We are grateful to Margaret Lynch for her work on the Applying the Principles questions and on the Test-Item File. Beginning with the First Edition, Margaret has pushed us to make sure that the book speaks clearly to the students while never taking them for granted. Robert Kleck also deserves special mention for overseeing the development of the test-item file. Our colleagues from Bloomsburg University, Brett Beck, Eileen Astor-Stetson, and Connie Schick, provided key advice about the First Edition and also developed the Study Guide. Patrick Carroll from the University of Texas, Austin, was masterful in identifying video material for the DVD that accompanies the book. We thank Lauretta Reeves from University of Texas, Austin, for her key role in helping to develop ZAPS: The Norton Psychology Labs, Margaret Forgie from the University of Lethbridge for bringing many fresh new teaching insights to the Instructor's Manual for the Second Edition, and, finally, Gary Marcus of NYU for creating *The Norton Psychology Reader*, a wonderful new companion text for introductory psychology courses. All of these individuals have lent their talent and time to create a strong support package for the Second Edition.

Once again, many people at Norton served critical roles in supporting and publishing the Second Edition. Chief among them is Jon Durbin, editor extraordinaire. Jon brings unflagging energy and incredible focus to his books. He is building an exciting psychology list at Norton that captures trends in the field like neuroscience and culture, while pushing the envelope hard to build a strong list across the subfields of psychology. Through his persistence and insight, Jon has become a true insider in the field. He is one in a million: the Lance Armstrong of editors.

Kim Yi, the project editor, did a superb job of keeping the entire project on track, once again with good humor and amazing attention to detail. She has a knack for identifying troublesome sentences, and best of all for fixing them. She sure knows how to keep the authors happy. Barbara Gerr did a great job in copy editing the manuscript, including making sure the meaning was clear and the level of writing was consistent across chapters. Marian Johnson provided excellent advice on writing style throughout. Kelly Rolf was a godsend in keeping everything organized and on schedule and also is to be recognized for her ability to find interesting photos and cartoons. Rubina Yeh developed a striking new design for the book that holds to our original vision for an uncluttered text in which all of the elements have strong pedagogical value. Her clean design helps students focus on what is important. It is also extremely attractive. Roy Tedoff shepherded the book very effectively through the production process. We thank Denise Shanks for taking charge of the ancillaries to make sure we have the strongest possible support package. Many of the Norton sales representatives have also been especially helpful, including Peter Ruscitti, Peter McCullough, Chris Curcio, Scott Berzon, Kym Silvasy-Neale, Jason Flippen, Andrea Haver, Gordon Lee, John Darger, John Kelly, and Annie Stewart. We also offer special thanks to Steve Dunn (Director of Sales and Marketing) and Nicole Albas (National Sales Manager) for their sound insights and unflagging support of the text through its first two editions. Finally, we continue to be grateful to Roby Harrington and Drake McFeely for their faith in us.

Consultants and Reviewers for the Second Edition

Consultants

Tara Callaghan, St. Francis Xavier University
Fernanda Ferreira, Michigan State University
James Enns, University of British Columbia
Steven Heine, University of British Columbia
Howard Hughes, Dartmouth College
Jay Hull, Dartmouth College
Margaret Lynch, San Francisco State University
Gary Marcus, New York University
James Pennebaker, University of Texas, Austin
Elizabeth Phelps, New York University
Lauretta Reeves, University of Texas, Austin
Peter Tse, Dartmouth College

Reviewers

Rahan Ali, Pennsylvania State University
Caroyln Barry, Loyola College
Scott Bates, Utah State University
Joe Bilotta, Western Kentucky University

Tom Capo, University of Maryland
Graham Cousens, Macalester College
Dale Dagenbach, Wake Forest University
Suzanne Delaney, University of Arizona
Wendy Domjan, University of Texas, Austin
Valerie Farmer-Dougan, Illinois State University
Greg Feist, University of California, Davis
Holly Filcheck, Louisiana State University
Joseph Fitzgerald, Wayne State University
Trisha Folds-Bennett, College of Charleston
Margaret Forgie, University of Lethbridge
David Funder, University of California, Riverside
Margaret Gatz, University of Southern California
Katherine Gibbs, University of California, Davis
Bryan Gibson, Central Michigan University
Laura Gonnerman, Lehigh University
Tom Guilmette, Providence College
Erin Hardin, Texas Tech University
John Henderson, Michigan State University
Sarah Hodges, University of Oregon
Cynthia Hoffman, Indiana University
Don Hoffman, University of California, Irvine
Steve Joordans, University of Toronto, Scarborough
Mark Lamaukis, San Diego State University
Lori Lange, University of North Florida
Ting Lei, Borough of Manhattan Community College
Carol Lemley, Elizabethtown College
Liang Lou, Grand Valley State
Margaret Lynch, University of California, San Francisco
Karl Maier, Salisbury University
Leonard Mark, Miami University (Ohio)
Paul Merritt, George Washington University
Paul McCormack, St. Francis Xavier University
David McDonald, University of Missouri Columbia
Patricia McMullen, Dalhousie University
Hal Miller, Brigham Young University
Joe Morrissey, SUNY-Binghamton
Todd Nelson, Cal State-Stanislaus
Jackie Pope-Tarrance, Western Kentucky University
Gabriel Radvansky, Notre Dame University
Patty Randolph, Western Kentucky University
William Rogers, Grand Valley State University
Sharleen Sakai, Michigan State University
Heather Schellink, Dalhousie University
Richard Schiffman, Rutgers University
Jeniffer Siciliani-Pride, University of Missouri, St. Louis
Sheldon Solomon, Skidmore College
Sue Spaulding, University of North Carolina, Charlotte
Faye Steur, College of Charleston
Dawn Strongin, Cal State-Stanislaus
George Taylor, University of Missouri, St. Louis

Lee Thompson, Case Western Reserve University
Rob Tigner, Truman State College
Shaun Vecera, University of Iowa
Gordon Whitman, Tidewater Community College
Nicole Wilson, University of California, Santa Cruz
Al Witkofsky, Salisbury University
Dahlia Zaidel, University of California, Los Angeles

Consultants and Reviewers for the First Edition

Consultants

Alan Baddelay, Bristol University
Lori Badura, State University of New York, Buffalo
Mahzarin Banaji, Harvard University
Colin Blakemore, Oxford University
Randy Buckner, Washington University
Tara Callaghan, St. Francis Xavier University
Jennifer Campbell, University of British Columbia
Jonathan Cheek, Wellesley College
Dennis Cogan, Texas Tech University
Martin Conway, Bristol University
Michael Corballis, University of Auckland
James Enns, University of British Columbia
Raymond Fancher, York University
Fernanda Ferreira, Michigan State University
Vic Ferreira, University of California, San Diego
Christine Gancarz, Southern Methodist University
Wendi Gardner, Northwestern University
Rick O. Gilmore, Penn State University
James Gross, Stanford University
John Hallonquist, University of the Caribou
Mikki Hebl, Rice University
Mark Henn, University of New Hampshire
Don Hoffman, University of California, Irvine
James Hoffman, University of Delaware
Jake Jacobs, University of Arizona
Thomas Joiner, Florida State University
Dacher Keltner, University of California, Berkeley
Marke Leary, Wake Forest University
Monica Luciana, University of Minnesota
Neil Macrae, Bristol University/Dartmouth College
Julie Norem, Wellesley College
Lauretta Reeves, Rowan University
Jennifer Richeson, Dartmouth College
Paul Rozin, University of Pennsylvania
Constantine Sedikedes, University of Southhampton
Allison Sekuler, McMaster University

Andrew Shatte, University of Pennsylvania
Diane Tice, Case Western Reserve University
David Uttal, Northwestern University
Elaine Walker, Emory University

Reviewers

Gordon A. Allen, Miami University of Ohio
Ron Apland, Malaspina College
John P. Broida, University of Southern Maine
Katherine Cameron, Washington College
Timoth Cannon, University of Scranton
Charles Carver, University of Miami
Stephen Clark, Keene State College
Joseph Dien, Tulane University
Jack Dovidio, Colgate University
Margaret Forgie, University of Lethbridge
David Funder, University of California, Riverside
Peter Gerhardstein, Binghamton University
Peter Graf, University of British Columbia
Leonard Green, Washington University
Norman Henderson, Oberlin College
Terence Hines, Pace University
Sara Hodges, University of Oregon
Mike Kerchner, Washington College
Rondall Khoo, Western Connecticut State University
Charles Leith, Northern Michigan University
Margaret Lynch, San Fransisco State University
James Gross, Stanford University
Dan McAdams, Northwestern University
Doug McCann, York University
Bill McKeachie, University of Michigan
Judy Miller, Oberlin College
Zehra Peynircioglu, The American University
Brady Phelps, South Dakota State University
Alex Rothman, University of Minnesota
Juan Salinas, University of Texas, Austin
Margaret Sereno, University of Oregon
Arthur Shimamura, University of California, Berkeley
Rebecca Shiner, Colgate University
Reid Skeel, Central Michigan University
Dennison Smith, Oberlin College
Mark Snyder, University of Minnesota
George Taylor, University of Missouri
Robin R. Vallacher, Florida Atlantic University
Benjamin Walker, Georgetown University
Brian Wandell, Stanford University
Kevin Weinfurt, Duke University
Doug Whitman, Wayne State University
Maxine Gallander Wintre, York University
Claire Wiseman, Trinity College

Dear Student:

Our most important overarching goal for this textbook was to write it first and foremost for you, the student reader. We know that many of you are drawn to psychology to find out more about what makes you and those you know tick. We also know from our own recent teaching experiences that many of you are highly interested in learning more about how the human mind works and what that means for you in everyday life. Thus, as you search for insights into the human experience, we have made every effort to focus on core psychological principles and ideas to provide a starting point (and sometimes an end point) for your quest. Our focus on principles is reinforced by the "ask and answer" approach that serves as the pedagogical foundation for the book. Each chapter consists of a series of "big questions" that focus on major psychological principles and concepts. Each section of a chapter answers one of these questions. Our use of declarative headings reflects our belief that psychological scientists have made headway in providing answers to these questions—perhaps not the final answers, as new research helps shape our thinking, but answers that summarize what psychological scientists have discovered about mind, brain, and behavior.

Psychological Science is intended both for those of you who wish to pursue careers in psychology and for those of you for whom this course will be your only exposure to psychology as a science. While using this text, you will gain an integrated grounding in traditional psychology as well as an introduction to new approaches within psychological science. The material is by nature intellectually challenging, but we have tried to make it accessible and enjoyable for you as well as directly applicable to your life. We hope that *Psychological Science* spurs on your curiosity about psychological phenomena and that you will learn to think critically about issues and themes in psychological science. In the end (or the beginning!), we hope that you will also develop greater self-understanding and understanding of others.

Before you begin, please take a few minutes to study the following pages so that you can gain a full understanding of how to get the most out of reading *Psychological Science*.

Overview—A Focus on the Principles

Psychological Science's chapters are built around core principles. The "ask and answer" approach serves as the structure and foundation for every chapter. Each chapter focuses on approximately 4 to 6 major principles, which are first raised in the form of questions ("ask"). Each major section in a chapter then looks to "answer" one of these questions. Here is how it works in action.

A Chapter Opening Vignette begins each chapter. The vignettes are drawn from a variety of sources, including news media, research journals, and history. They highlight a major theme, issue, or tension point that will be discussed throughout the chapter.

An Outlining the Principles box appears on the second page of every chapter opener. At one level, this feature serves as a simple outline or road map for the chapter. At another level, it reveals the major principles that will be discussed in the chapter. By studying the major headings, you can see which questions ("ask") will drive the chapter. The subheadings appear in the form of declarative statements ("answer") that reveal our current state of knowledge about the question.

A Chapter Timeline appears on the bottom of the page in the opening section of every chapter. Psychological science is built on cumulative knowledge and experience. This is one of the major themes of the text. Basic principles, both new and old, inspire and guide thinking and research in the field. The timelines highlight major developments within the various domains of psychology. By studying them, you will see more clearly how various principles have been established, challenged, and modified.

the hair. Other receptors are capsules in the skin that respond to continued vibration, sudden movements, and steady pressure. In terms of temperature, there appear to be separate receptors for hot and cold, although both can be triggered at the same time by intense stimuli. The simultaneous activation of hot and cold receptors can produce strange sensory experiences, such as a feeling of wetness. The integration of these various signals produces haptic experiences. For instance, stroking multiple pressure points can produce a tickling sensation, which can be pleasant or unpleasant depending on the mental state of the person being tickled. This raises the age-old question of why you can't tickle yourself. Indeed, recent imaging research finds that the brain areas involved in touch sensation respond less to self-produced tactile stimulation than to external tactile stimulation (Blakemore, Wolpert, & Frith, 1998).

TWO TYPES OF PAIN Pain is part of a warning system that stops you from continuing activities that may harm you. Whether the message is to remove your hand from a hot burner or to stop running when you have damaged a tendon, pain signals that you should quit doing whatever you are doing. Children born with a rare genetic disorder that leaves them insensitive to pain usually die young, no matter how carefully they are supervised. They simply do not know how to avoid activities that harm them or to report when they are not feeling well (Melzack & Wall, 1982). As with other sensory systems, the actual experience of pain is created by the brain. For instance, as you recall from Chapter 4, people with amputated limbs sometimes feel phantom pain in the nonexistent limb. The person really feels pain, but the pain occurs because of a misinterpretation of neural activity.

Most experiences of pain result from damaging the skin, which activates haptic receptors. The nerve fibers that convey pain information are thinner than those for temperature and touch and are found in all body tissues that sense pain: skin, muscles, membranes around bones and joints, organs, and so on. Two kinds of nerve fibers have been identified for pain: fast fibers for sharp, immediate pain, and slow fibers for chronic, dull, steady pain. An important distinction between these fibers is the myelination of their axons that travel from the pain receptors to the spinal cord. Recall from Chapter 3 that myelination speeds up neural signals; fast-acting axons are myelinated, whereas the axons of slow-acting receptors are not. Think of when you touch a hot pan. You feel two kinds of pain: a sharp, fast, localized pain at the point where your skin touches the pan, followed by a slow, dull, more diffuse burning pain. The fast-action receptors are activated by strong physical pressure and temperature extremes, whereas the slow-acting receptors are activated by chemical changes in tissue when skin is damaged. From an adaptive perspective, fast pain leads to recoil from harmful objects and therefore is protective, whereas slow pain keeps us from using the affected body part and therefore helps in recuperation.

GATE-CONTROL THEORY The brain regulates the experience of pain, sometimes producing it, sometimes suppressing it. The *gate-control theory of pain*, formulated by Ronald Melzack and Patrick Wall (1982), states that in order for us to experience pain, pain receptors must be activated and a neural "gate" in the spinal cord must allow these signals through to the brain. One way to close the gate is to stimulate other haptic receptors, which overwhelms the signals from pain receptors. This is why rubbing an aching muscle helps to reduce pain or why scratching an itch is so satisfying. Experienced nurses often vigorously rub the skin surrounding the injection site, which overwhelms the haptic signals and reduces the sting of the needle. A number of cognitive states can also close the gate, such as when people are distracted by more pressing concerns. Athletes sometimes can play through pain because of

Can we override pain?

169

"Ask and Answer" Running Heads help you stay focused on the larger issue as you try to see the forest for the trees. *Psychological Science*'s left-hand running heads emphasize the larger topics, with the right-hand running heads repeating the questions that are explored in each section.

Critical Thinking Questions are designed to encourage you to think integratively and beyond the text. Appearing in the margins throughout each chapter, they selectively highlight core principles and are ideal for discussion in small groups.

REVIEWING THE PRINCIPLES boxes are a critical component of the "ask and answer" approach and appear at the end of each major section. They repeat the question that governed the section and provide a basic answer that highlights key points for you to remember.

DEFINING THE PRINCIPLES refers to the marginal glossary that runs throughout each chapter. Many books highlight an overabundance of key terms for students to memorize. In keeping with this book's focus on core principles and concepts, *Psychological Science* highlights approximately 30 key terms per chapter. The full glossary appears at the end of the book and on the companion Web site.

REVIEWING
the Principles | How Do We Sense Our Worlds?

The study of sensation focuses on how our sense organs respond to and detect external stimulus energy. Stimuli need to be transduced in order for the brain to use that information. Sensory coding for quantitative factors, such as intensity and loudness, depends on the number of neurons firing and how frequently they fire. Qualitative aspects, such as color or bitterness, are coded by the integration of activation across specific receptors. The development of psychophysical methods allowed psychological scientists to study psychological reaction to physical events. Psychophysical methods can be used to determine thresholds for detecting events and for noticing change. These thresholds can be influenced by situational factors and by biases in human judgment.

What Are the Basic Sensory Processes?

How does information about the world get into the brain? Helen Keller's perceptual experience was restricted because her sensory systems were damaged. The neurons in her brain that construct visual and auditory perceptions did not receive any sensory signals. As you learned in Chapter 3, no neuron beyond the sensory organs responds directly to events in the world. All that a neuron in the brain receives is signals from other neurons. In other words, a neuron in the brain does not respond to events in the world, it responds to its input from other neurons. As a result, you could say that your experience is a construction of your brain and resides inside your skull, despite the illusion that your experience is of objects or events out in the space around you. Neurons are talking to neurons in total darkness, and yet from this emerges our conscious experience of the outside world. How is this information transmitted to the brain? In this section, we will review the first step in this process, how stimuli are detected and sent to the brain for each of the five primary senses: taste, smell, touch, hearing, and vision.

In Gustation, Taste Buds Are Chemical Detectors

The job of our sense of taste, or *gustation*, is to keep poisons out of our digestive systems while allowing good food in. The stimuli for taste are chemical substances from food that dissolve in saliva, though how these stimuli work is still largely a mystery. The taste receptors are part of the **taste buds** of the tongue and mouth. People differ greatly in how many taste buds they have, ranging from 500 to 10,000, mostly located on the tongue, but also spread throughout the mouth and even the throat. Each taste bud has about 50 receptor cells. *Microvilli*—short, hairlike structures at the tip of each taste bud—come into direct contact with saliva. When stimulated, they send electrical signals to a brainstem region called the medulla and from there to the thalamus and cortex, which ultimately produces the experience of taste.

We have several different kinds of taste receptors. These taste buds each respond most strongly to one of four "primary" taste sensations: sweet, sour, salty, and bitter. Every taste experience is composed of a mixture of these four qualities. This experience reflects a general principle of sensory experiences, in that a near-infinite variety of perceptual experiences arises from the activation of unique combinations

taste buds Sensory receptors that transduce taste information.

A Brief Conclusion sums up the big ideas and concepts and reminds you how the book's four key themes wove their way through the chapter.

The Summarizing the Principles section provides a more detailed review. Designed to follow the outline for each chapter, you are reminded again of the major questions that governed each section and the key pieces of research-based knowledge that provide insight into those questions.

Further Readings represent psychological writing at its best. If any of the topics in a chapter interested you, we encourage you to follow up with one of the suggested reading titles. There are many wonderful popular psychology books that provide keen insights and pleasurable excursions into human behavior.

Applying the Principles questions highlight the core principles that you need to learn. These multiple-choice questions at the end of each chapter encourage you to apply these principles to real-world settings. The answers appear at the end of the section.

A Focus on Critical Thinking and Applications

SPECIAL TOPIC UNITS apply psychological science to your life. These units amplify the text's basic strengths by challenging you to think critically and to understand the impact that the field of psychology has on your life and world.

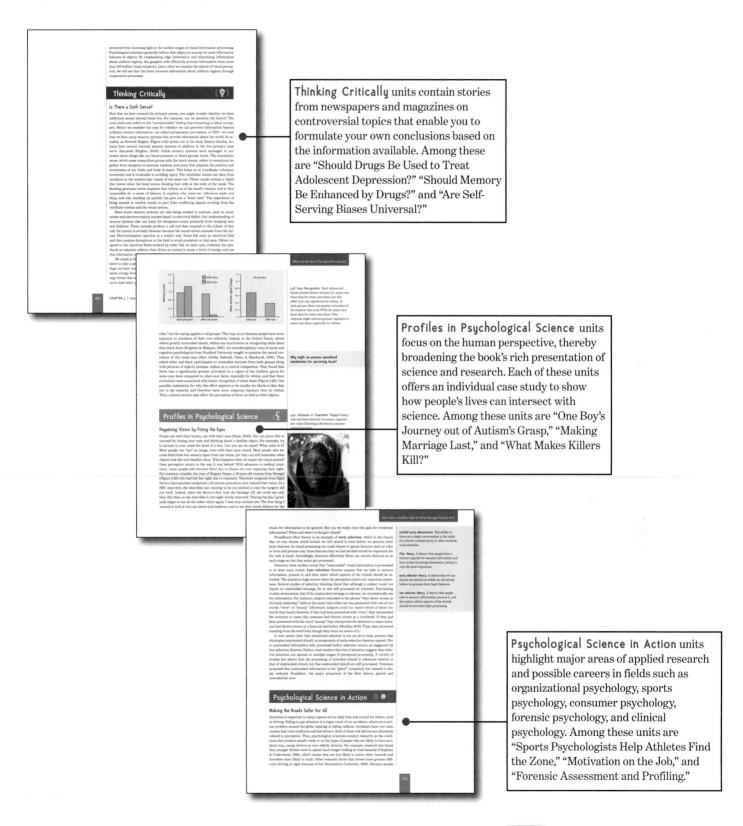

Thinking Critically units contain stories from newspapers and magazines on controversial topics that enable you to formulate your own conclusions based on the information available. Among these are "Should Drugs Be Used to Treat Adolescent Depression?" "Should Memory Be Enhanced by Drugs?" and "Are Self-Serving Biases Universal?"

Profiles in Psychological Science units focus on the human perspective, thereby broadening the book's rich presentation of science and research. Each of these units offers an individual case study to show how people's lives can intersect with science. Among these units are "One Boy's Journey out of Autism's Grasp," "Making Marriage Last," and "What Makes Killers Kill?"

Psychological Science in Action units highlight major areas of applied research and possible careers in fields such as organizational psychology, sports psychology, consumer psychology, forensic psychology, and clinical psychology. Among these units are "Sports Psychologists Help Athletes Find the Zone," "Motivation on the Job," and "Forensic Assessment and Profiling."

A Dynamic Art Program

The Art in *Psychological Science* enhances your reading experience. The text contains a variety of visual materials, from photographs to tables and charts to drawn art. The emphasis, however, is clearly on the drawn art. By featuring drawn art, *Psychological Science* is able to convey precisely, accurately, and meaningfully what you need to gain from every image. This high level of precision can't be achieved with the stock photographs common in many texts.

Psychological Science, Second Edition, eBook—Same Great Content, Half the Price

The eBook version of *Psychological Science*, Second Edition, offers the full content of the print version at half the price. Accessible at any time on the Web, the eBook is directly linked to the Student Web site's resources and incorporates many of its interactive elements.

Psychological Science's Student Supplements Will Help You Succeed

Study Guide to Accompany Psychological Science

by Brett Beck and Eileen Astor-Stetson (both of Bloomsburg University)

Created by two highly successful instructors of large lectures classes, this carefully crafted study aid offers a guide to each chapter of the textbook, with helpful study advice, completion questions, key-figure exercises, multiple-choice self-tests, and thought questions.

Student Web site to accompany *Psychological Science*

wwnorton.com/psychsci

This innovative online learning tool offers a wealth of resources for study and review. In addition to timelines, vocabulary flashcards, and detailed chapter reviews, the site includes:

- **Diagnostic Quizzes** with smart feedback that allow students to pinpoint strengths and weaknesses
- **Activities**
- The **Norton Gradebook** feature, which allows students and instructors to effectively track quiz results
- **Animations** that clarify difficult psychological concepts
- **Psychology in the News**, a unique section, updated weekly, that gathers relevant news coverage and analysis

Psychological Science

SECOND EDITION

Exploring the Mind and Brain

Throughout the history of psychology, there has been debate about whether psychological characteristics are due more to *nature* or *nurture*. It is now clear that culture, social environment, and biology all play important roles in the development of one's behavior and mental life. Individuals who share genes, such as these quadruplets, are particularly interesting to psychological scientists studying the impact of biology and environment.

Introduction to Psychological Science

1

Around midnight on February 4, 1999, four members of a special police Street Crime Unit drove down Wheeler Avenue in the Bronx, looking for a rape suspect. They saw 22-year-old Amadou Diallo (Figure 1.1), a West African immigrant, standing in the doorway to his apartment building. The officers say they told Diallo to "freeze" but then saw him reach into his pants pocket. The officers, believing that Diallo was reaching for a weapon, opened fire. Within approximately 5 seconds, the four officers fired a total of 41 shots at the unarmed Diallo, 19 of which struck him. Diallo died at the scene. Neighbors say that Diallo probably didn't understand the word "freeze," since English was not his first language. Others suggest that Diallo might have been reaching for his wallet to prove his identity. No one will ever know. The four officers were tried for murder, and all were acquitted.

Psychologists are interested in understanding how people perceive, think, and act in a wide range of situations. A situation such as the killing of Amadou Diallo is especially interesting to psychologists because it allows them to consider thought and behavior in the context of a real-life event. The Diallo case involves psychological phenomena such as emotion, memory, visual perception, decision making, social interaction, cultural differences, prejudice, group behavior, and mental trauma. Within this menu of topics, psychologists would be interested in knowing, for example, how the emotional state of the officers affected their decision making at the scene. They would also want to study the accuracy of the defendants' and eyewitnesses' accounts of the shooting. In addition, they would want to examine group behavior. Did the fact that many officers arrived at the scene simultaneously affect individual behavior? Did the high-profile demonstrations outside the courthouse influence the trial? Finally, psychologists would also want to know if prejudice played a role. Did prejudice affect the way the officers identified and approached the suspect? Did being the target of prejudice affect Diallo's reaction to the police? Did prejudice affect the jury's decision? Many Bronx residents charged that the Diallo shooting was motivated by racism. The defense lawyers asserted that race had little to do with the shooting. How can we know?

Studying the factors underlying racial attitudes is difficult, since most people deny holding beliefs that are not socially acceptable. How, then, can we "peek inside" the mind to discover what people are thinking and feeling? ■

1.1 Amadou Diallo Diallo, a native of West Africa, was shot by police officers who were searching for a serial rapist. The innocent Diallo died at the scene. Did racism play a part in this tragic death?

Over the decades, psychology has offered many powerful insights into prejudice. Employing a range of strategies—from self-reports to observational studies to experiments—researchers have discovered a number of important findings about prejudice. For instance, prejudice influences people's beliefs and expectations about others, which leads to racist behavior. Racism has strong negative psychological effects on the targets of prejudice, whose behavior is shaped in part by others' beliefs about them. Perhaps most important, however, psychologists have also discovered methods for reducing stereotyping and prejudice. These findings have given us glimpses inside the human mind, but they have not provided a complete picture of how the mind works and its relevance to our own behavior.

A number of important developments over the past few years have opened new doors for studying mental life that should really deepen our understanding of the

Timeline

1637

Cartesian Dualism René Descartes proposes that mind and body are interrelated but separate entities, with each affecting the other. This idea challenges the long-held belief that the mind, or soul, is master of the body.

1859

The Mind Evolved Charles Darwin's groundbreaking theory of natural selection lays the foundation for a biological basis of behavior and the notion that the human mind has evolved along with physical characteristics and behaviors.

1879

Psychology Adopts the Tools of Science Wilhelm Wundt sets up the first psychological laboratory and starts to measure behavior. His first methods involve asking people to reflect on their mental experiences.

1890

Principles of Psychology Influenced by Darwin's theory, William James argues in his groundbreaking *Principles of Psychology* that there is a need to understand the adaptive functions of behavior.

human mind and behavior. We now have methods for observing the working brain in action. A collection of techniques known as *brain imaging* involves assessing changes in metabolic activity in the brain, such as noting where blood flows as people process information. These changes in blood flow represent changes in brain activity that indicate which parts of the brain are involved in certain behaviors or mental activities. For instance, the cognitive neuroscientist Elizabeth Phelps and the social psychologist Mahzarin Banaji and their colleagues used brain imaging to study racial attitudes. They showed white college students pictures of familiar and unfamiliar black and white faces while they used a technique known as *functional magnetic resonance imaging (fMRI)* to scan the brain (Phelps et al., 2000). For some of the research participants, the unfamiliar black faces activated a structure in the brain called the *amygdala*, which is involved in detecting threat; this activation indicates a fear response. This does not mean that the white students who responded in this way are necessarily afraid of unfamiliar black people, but it does indicate that those faces activate the brain region that detects threat.

It is important to point out that this response did not occur in all student participants. Rather, it occurred only in those who also showed signs of holding negative attitudes about blacks, as measured by a computer program called the *implicit attitudes test (IAT)*. This test indirectly assesses how people associate positive and negative words with certain groups of people. Those who were found to hold negative attitudes on the computer test were the most likely to show activation of the amygdala when observing unfamiliar black faces (Figure 1.2). In a second study, the researchers showed a new group of white students pictures of familiar black and white faces; this time activation of the amygdala did not occur. This is encouraging news. It suggests that increasing familiarity reduces the fear response, which may indicate a reduction in the likelihood of prejudice and discrimination.

The research just described reveals a great deal about the current state of psychology and touches on a number of issues that are central to this book. Psychology has formally been around as a discipline of study for just over 100 years, and in that time we've learned a great deal about such basic mental processes as learning, memory, emotion, and perception. Psychologists have documented changes in individuals from birth to old age and have developed elaborate theories about how humans do things such as acquire language and solve difficult problems. They have explored the importance of the social world in which we live, such as how people are influenced by the presence of others and the circumstances that lead them to prefer some types of

1.2 Composite Maps of the Brain
Composite maps displaying brain regions in which greater activation in response to black versus white faces is associated with an indirect measure of racial attitudes. The areas indicate activation of the amygdala, especially on the left half of the brain, as well as another area, the anterior cingulate, which is also associated with emotional responses.

1900	1912	1925	1940s	1944
The Role of the Unconscious Sigmund Freud introduces the idea of the unconscious and the role it plays in our everyday mental life. His theory of psychoanalysis captures clinicians and scientists alike for almost half a century.	**Gestalt Psychology** German psychologist Max Wertheimer proposes that perception is a subjective experience that cannot be understood by looking at its elementary components. That is, the whole is different from the sum of its parts.	**Behaviorism** John B. Watson and later B. F. Skinner argue that all behaviors can be understood as a result of learning, and that to predict behavior one has to look at environmental forces.	**Physiological Psychology** Karl Lashley and Roger Sperry conduct systematic brain research using animals as a way to gain insight into how the human mind works.	**Social Dynamics** Kurt Lewin introduces field theory, in which he argues that situational dynamics play an important role in predicting human behavior.

people to others. Psychologists have also examined how the environment helps shape each person in a unique way that produces what we call "personality." The goal for psychology today is to understand people by considering both individual factors, such as how a person's brain processes information about others, and contextual factors, such as how societal beliefs shape how we behave toward those other people. You will learn what has been discovered about each of these topics in this book and about the future directions of research. You will learn too about how genes and biology influence human mental life, an area of research that has deepened psychology over the last few years.

The ultimate ambition of psychologists is to explain effectively the most important human behaviors in real-life contexts. To do this, we need to study behavior from its most fundamental aspects: biological, individual, and social. It's precisely for this reason that it is so exciting on a daily basis to learn more about how the brain works. New technologies and methods have allowed our understanding to move forward in ways that were unimaginable even 20 years ago. These technologies have allowed psychological scientists to begin examining which parts of the brain are involved when we perform certain tasks and interact with our social worlds. For instance, did you know that your brain chemistry is being altered with each concept or story that you remember while reading this chapter? Every time we remember a story or a joke or feel an intense emotion, that experience is processed and stored in our brains. One major challenge for psychologists is to figure out what brain mechanisms are involved when we interact with our environment, as well as how the environment influences our brain mechanisms. Of course, understanding people in their real lives requires more than just studying the activity of their brains. People live in societies in which they interact regularly with others in multiple and complex ways. Another major challenge for psychologists is to understand how people are shaped by the cultures in which they live.

Psychological science is the study of mind, brain, and behavior. Let's explore each of these terms. *Mind* refers to mental activity, such as your thoughts and feelings. The perceptual experiences that you have while interacting with the world (sight, smell, taste, hearing, and touch) are examples of the mind in action, as are memories, thinking about what you want to have for lunch, and how you feel about kissing someone you find attractive. Mental activity results from biological processes within the *brain*, such as the action of nerve cells and associated chemical reactions. You will read later about the long-standing controversy among scholars about the nature of the relationship between the brain and the mind. For now it is sufficient to note that the "mind is what the brain does" (Kosslyn & Koenig, 1995, p. 4). In other words, it is the physical brain that enables the mind.

The term *behavior* is used to describe a wide variety of actions, from the subtle to the complex, that occur in organisms from ants to humans. For many years psychologists tended to focus mainly on behavior rather than on mental states. They did this

psychological science The study of mind, brain, and behavior.

What is mind?

1957	1960s	1980s	1990s	1990s
The Cognitive Revolution At Harvard University, George A. Miller launches the field of cognitive psychology, which will later be formalized by Ulric Neisser in his integrative 1967 book, *Cognitive Psychology*.	**Biology of Mental Disorders** Advances in drug-treatment trials support theories of a biological basis for many types of mental disorders. Disorders such as depression and schizophrenia are linked to neurochemical abnormalities.	**The Return of Darwin** David Buss, Leda Cosmides, John Tooby, and Steve Pinker are among those who develop evolutionary psychology, which reintroduces Darwinian thinking into understanding mind and behavior.	**The Brain Enables Mind** A number of fields including neuroscience, cognitive psychology, computer science, and neurology forge a new interdisciplinary field, cognitive neuroscience.	**The Rise of Culture** Scholars such as Hazel Markus, Shinobu Kitayama, and Richard Nisbett are among those whose work helps increase recognition that culture shapes mental processes.

in large part because they had few objective techniques for assessing the mind. The advent of technology to observe the working brain in action has allowed psychological scientists to study mental states such as consciousness, which in turn allows us to develop a fuller understanding of human behavior.

What Are the Themes of Psychological Science?

For as long as people have been thinking, they've been thinking about other people. We have a strong desire to figure out other people, to understand their motives, thoughts, desires, intentions, moods, actions, and so on. We want to know why they remember some details and conveniently forget others, or why they engage in behaviors that are self-destructive. We want to know whether others are friends or foes, leaders or followers, likely to spurn us or fall in love with us. Our social interactions require us to use our impressions of others to categorize them, to make predictions about their intentions and actions. Essentially, people are constantly trying to figure out what makes other people tick. People who do this for a living are known as *psychological scientists*. They use the methods of science to understand how people think, feel, and act. This crucial point will be emphasized throughout this book. As you will read in Chapter 2, the scientific method refers to the use of objective, systematic procedures that lead to an accurate understanding of what is being studied. It involves careful observations of the natural world to examine how things work. Psychological scientists typically conduct experiments to understand human behavior. For instance, they might study prejudice by looking at how interracial interactions affect people's thoughts, feelings, or behaviors compared with interactions between those of the same race. Through the application of the scientific method, psychological scientists have learned a great deal about the mind, brain, and behavior.

Throughout this book we will highlight four major themes that have defined this field in the past and present. These themes guide and direct the way psychological scientists study the mind, brain, and behavior.

The Principles of Psychological Science Are Cumulative

The first theme is that research on mind, brain, and behavior has accumulated over time to produce the *principles* of psychological science. Throughout history there have been occasional leaps in scientific knowledge, such as the recognition of gravitational forces, the discovery of penicillin, and the recent mapping of the human genome. But more typically, science progresses in smaller, incremental steps, as knowledge accumulates based on systematic study of questions raised by what is already known. In this way, science builds on the foundation of shared knowledge. Understanding the human mind and behavior is no different.

So that you can appreciate the questions that drive contemporary research, we will describe the basic principles that make up the foundation of psychological knowledge. In doing so, we focus on what is *known* in psychological science. For example, the behavioral properties of memory are quite well known, and today no psychologist has to demonstrate that it is easier to *recognize* old information than it is to *recall* old information. We've known that for more than half a century; it is one of the many principles we will use in this book. As scientists expand the outer edge of knowledge, their search for the unknown is still rooted in the basic principles of psychological science. To demonstrate this, we will describe cutting-edge research that is building on these principles, focusing on the research that we believe will establish the future foundations of psychological science. In Chapter 7 you will see that our modern understanding of memory builds on findings that have accumulated over the past century.

One consequence of focusing on principles is that it can at times make things seem simpler than they really are. Most psychological phenomena involve complexities that we do not have the space to discuss. Complexity is inherent in science as ideas and theories are modified by new information that describes the conditions under which phenomena exist. Consider gravity, a basic force that has been recognized for hundreds of years. Gravity does not work in a uniform fashion; its force depends on the properties of the earth itself. On earth if you drop an apple, it falls to the ground. That is the principle. Likewise, when we say that recognition is easier than recall, there are certainly conditions under which this is not true. But these complexities are of greater interest to the scientific researcher than to the student learning the material for the first time. So if you enjoy your introductory psychology course, and this book, then by all means consider taking advanced psychology courses in which you will explore the complexities of the field in greater depth. For now, it is time to focus on the principles.

A New Biological Revolution Is Energizing Research

The second theme is this: A new biological revolution of profound significance is in progress at the dawn of the twenty-first century, bringing with it a deeper understanding of the human mind and behavior. Since the time of Aristotle, philosophers and other scholars have asked questions about basic psychological phenomena, but they lacked the methods to examine scientifically many of these fundamental questions, such as *What is consciousness? Where does emotion come from, and how does it affect cognitive processes? How are memories stored in the brain?* In the end, they were left with philosophical speculation. This began to change around the beginning of the twentieth century, and in the last 20 years or so there has been a tremendous growth in understanding of the biological bases of these mental activities. This interest in biology permeates all areas of psychological science, from locating the neural, or brain, correlates of how we identify friends to discovering the neurochemical problems that produce various psychological disorders. Three developments have set the stage for a new biological revolution contributing to our understanding psychological phenomena.

BRAIN CHEMISTRY The first major development in the biological revolution is an understanding of brain chemistry. The brain works through the actions of chemicals known as *neurotransmitters,* which communicate messages between nerve cells. Over the last 30 years psychological scientists have made tremendous progress in identifying these chemicals and their functions. Although it was long believed that no more than a handful of neurotransmitters were involved in brain activity, it is now known that hundreds of different substances play critical roles in mental activity and behavior. For instance, we now know that people have better memories for events that happen when they are aroused than when they are calm, because chemicals involved in responding to stimuli influence the neural mechanisms involved in memory. Understanding the chemical processes of the brain has provided many new insights into mental activity and behavior and has also been useful for developing treatments to help people with various psychological disorders.

THE HUMAN GENOME The second major development in the biological revolution is the enormous progress in understanding the influence of genetic processes. Not only have scientists been able to map out the *human genome,* the basic genetic code or blueprint for the human body, but they have also developed various techniques that allow them to discover the link between genes and behavior. For instance, to study the effects of a gene on memory, researchers have been able to breed mice that either lack a specific gene or have new genes inserted. These mice subsequently show either impaired memory or improved memory, respectively. By identifying the genes that are involved in memory, researchers may soon be able to develop therapies based on genetic manipulation that will assist people who have memory problems, such as those who have Alzheimer's disease.

Of course, the idea that a single gene causes a specific behavior is overly simplistic. Almost all psychological and biological activity is affected by the actions of multiple genes. No one specific gene is solely responsible for memory, or racist attitudes, or shyness. Nonetheless, evidence is accumulating that genes are involved in many of these various processes. You will see in Chapter 3 that many physical and mental characteristics are to some degree inherited. You will also see that scientists are beginning to understand how situational contexts, such as the presence of other people, influence how genes are expressed and therefore how they affect behavior. It is the expression of genes that helps give rise to mind and behavior. Mapping the human genome has provided scientists with the foundational knowledge to study how specific genes affect thoughts, actions, feelings, and various disorders. Although many of the fantastic possibilities for correcting genetic defects are decades away, the methods used by scientists to study the influence of genetic processes have provided fresh insights into mental activity.

What role does genetics play in mind and behavior?

WATCHING THE WORKING BRAIN The development of methods for assessing the brain in action has provided the third major impetus to the biological revolution in psychology. The principles of how cells operate in the brain to influence behavior have been studied with increased effectiveness for more than a century, but only since the late 1980s have researchers been able to study the working brain as it performs its vital psychological functions. Using the methods of brain science, or *neuroscience,* psychological scientists have been able to address some of the most central questions of human experience, such as how different brain regions interact to produce perceptual experience, how various types of memory are similar or different, and how conscious experience involves changes in brain activity.

Knowing where in the brain something happens doesn't by itself tell you very much, but knowing that there are consistent patterns of brain activation associated with specific mental tasks provides evidence that the two are connected. Indeed, for more than 100 years scientists have disagreed about whether psychological processes are located in specific parts of the brain or distributed throughout the brain. We now know that there is some *localization* of function, but that many different brain regions participate to produce behavior and mental activity. The use of brain imaging has allowed psychological scientists to make tremendous strides in understanding mental states such as those involved in paying full attention to one thing while ignoring

THE FAR SIDE® BY GARY LARSON

Great moments in evolution

other things, the study of which has been central to psychology for more than a century (Posner & DiGirolamo, 2000). The progress in understanding the neural basis of mental life has been rapid and dramatic. This new knowledge is being used throughout psychology; for example, as demonstrated in the opening paragraphs of this chapter, social psychologists have been able to identify and better understand the neural correlates of racism. The 1990s were labeled the decade of the brain, for good reason.

The Mind Is Adaptive

The third theme of psychological science is that the mind has been shaped by evolution. Humans are products of both biological and cultural evolution, each of which exerts an influence over how people think and behave. From an **evolutionary theory** perspective, the brain is an organ that has evolved over millions of years to solve problems related to survival and reproduction. During the course of human evolution, those ancestors who were able to solve survival problems and adapt to their environments were most likely to reproduce and pass along their genes. That is, those who inherited characteristics that helped them survive in their particular environments had a selective advantage over those who did not, which is the basis of the process of **natural selection**. Random gene mutations endowed some of our ancestors with physical characteristics, skills, and abilities, known as **adaptations**, that increased their chances of survival and reproduction, which means that their genes were passed along to future generations. Of course, if the environment changes, what once was adaptive might become maladaptive. The ability to store fat in the body may have been adaptive when the food supply was scarce, but it may be maladaptive when food is abundant. Further complexities in the process of natural selection are discussed in Chapter 3.

Modern evolutionary theory has driven the field of biology for years. Only recently, however, have psychologists taken it up. Rather than being a specific area of scientific inquiry, evolutionary theory represents a way of thinking that can be used to understand many different aspects of mind and behavior (Buss, 1999). Three aspects of evolutionary theory are particularly helpful in this regard.

SOLVING ADAPTIVE PROBLEMS Over the last five million years that humans have been evolving, adaptive behaviors have been built into our bodies and brains. A corollary to this notion is the idea that the body contains specialized mechanisms that have evolved to solve problems that required adaptation. For instance, a mechanism that produces calluses has evolved to protect the skin from the abuses of hard work, and these calluses are useful when humans need to engage in physical labor to survive. Likewise, the brain has evolved specialized circuits or structures that solve adaptive problems (Cosmides & Tooby, 2001).

Evolutionary theory is especially useful for thinking about adaptive problems that occur regularly and have the potential to affect whether one survives and reproduces, such as mechanisms for eating, sex, language and communication, emotions, and aggression. Accordingly, the evolutionary approach is particularly relevant to social behavior. For decades we have known that situational and cultural contexts are influential in the development of social behaviors and attitudes. Now evidence is accumulating that many of these behaviors can also be considered adaptive solutions to recurring human problems. For example, humans have a fundamental need to belong to their group, and therefore behaviors that lead to possible social exclusion are discouraged in all societies (Baumeister & Leary, 1995). People who lie, cheat, or steal drain group resources and thereby possibly decrease survival and

evolutionary theory In psychological science, a theory that emphasizes the inherited, adaptive value of behavior and mental activity throughout the entire history of a species.

natural selection Darwin's theory that those who inherit characteristics that help them adapt to their particular environment have a selective advantage over those who do not.

adaptations In evolutionary theory, the physical characteristics, skills, or abilities that increase the chances of reproduction or survival and are therefore likely to be passed along to future generations.

Why is evolutionary theory important to understanding mental activity?

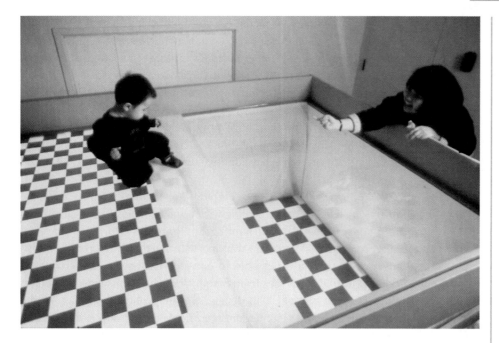

1.3 Infants and Height Although there is a glass covering the visual cliff, infants will not crawl onto the glass, even if encouraged by their mothers. Infants become wary of heights at about the same age they learn to crawl.

reproduction for other group members. Some evolutionary psychologists believe that humans have "cheater detectors" that are on the lookout for this sort of behavior in others (Cosmides & Tooby, 2000).

Evolutionary theory can be applied to many topics in psychology. The capacity to see well, remember where food was abundant, recognize dangerous objects, understand the basic laws of physics (such as the effects of gravity if one walks off a cliff), and so on were also critical to survival and therefore can be considered from an evolutionary perspective. According to evolutionary theory, solutions to these adaptive problems are built into the brain and therefore require no special training. Young infants develop a fear of heights at about the same time they learn to crawl, even though they have little personal experience with heights or gravity (Figure 1.3). Such built-in mechanisms assist in solving recurring problems that faced our ancestors over the course of human evolution.

MODERN MINDS IN STONE AGE SKULLS According to evolutionary theory, we must seek to understand the challenges that faced our early ancestors to understand much of our current behavior, whether adaptive or maladaptive. To provide perspective on this, consider the following: The human brain evolved slowly over millions of years, and many of the adaptive problems faced by early humans no longer exist, or at least no longer present the threat they once did. Humans began evolving about five million years ago, but modern humans (*Homo sapiens*) can be traced back only about 100,000 years, to the Pleistocene era. If we compare the history of the earth to a 24-hour timescale, the arrival of humans has occurred in the last 30 seconds. The fact that the human brain adapted to accommodate the needs of Pleistocene hunter-gatherers means we should be looking at what life was like then, and look to understand how the brain works within the context of the environmental pressures that the brains of Pleistocene-era humans faced. For instance, people like sweet foods, especially those that are high in fat. These foods are highly caloric and eating them would have provided substantial survival value in prehistoric times. In other words, a preference for fatty-sweet foods would have been adaptive. Today, many societies have an abundance of foods that are high in fat and sugar. That we still enjoy them and eat them, sometimes to excess, may now be maladaptive in that it can produce obesity. Nonetheless, our evolutionary heritage encourages us to eat foods that had survival value when food was relatively scarce.

Many of our current behaviors, of course, do not reflect our evolutionary heritage. Reading books, driving cars, using computers, talking on telephones, and watching television are behaviors that have only very recently become part of human experience. Rather than being adaptations, such behaviors can be considered *by-products* of adaptive solutions to earlier adaptive problems.

CULTURE PROVIDES ADAPTIVE SOLUTIONS For humans, many of the most demanding adaptive challenges involve dealing with other humans. These challenges include selecting mates, cooperating in hunting and gathering, forming alliances, competing for scarce resources, and even warring with neighboring groups. Unlike many animal species, humans are not able to care for themselves at birth; they require substantial effort and resources from caregivers, who themselves are reliant on other group members for survival. This dependency on group living is not unique to humans, but the nature of relations among and between ingroup and outgroup members is especially complex in human societies. The complexity of living in groups gives rise to **culture**, which refers to the beliefs, values, rules, norms, and customs that exist within a group of people who share a common language and environment, the assumption being that the various aspects of culture are transmitted from one generation to the next through learning. For instance, our musical and food preferences, our ways of expressing emotion, our tolerance of body odors, and so on are strongly affected by the culture in which we are raised. Many of these cultural rules reflect adaptive solutions that have been worked out by previous generations. Successful methods of hunting and gathering, beliefs about supernatural forces that shape behavior, and the capacity to communicate with other group members reflect knowledge that is handed down through the generations, helping future generations solve recurring adaptive problems.

In contrast to biological evolution in humans, which has taken place over several million years, cultural evolution has occurred over a much shorter period, with the most dramatic changes coming in the last few thousand years. Although humans have changed only modestly in physical terms in the last two or three thousand years, they have changed profoundly in terms of how they live together; even within the last century there have been dramatic changes in how human societies interact. The flows of peoples, commodities, and financial instruments, often referred to as globalization, have increased in velocity and scale in the past century in ways that were unimaginable nearly 500 years ago, when explorers from Europe and China first set out on their global journeys. Some commentators have suggested that we may indeed be witnessing the rise of a global culture as a result of this newest form of globalization. Most recently, the Internet has created a worldwide network of humans, in essence creating a new form of culture with its own rules, values, and customs.

Over the past decade there has been a growing recognition that culture plays a foundational role in shaping how people view and reason about the world around them and that different cultures possess strikingly different minds. Research by the social psychologist Richard Nisbett has demonstrated that people from most Asian countries have a view of the world that is quite different from the worldview of people from most European and North American countries. The work of Nisbett has suggested that Westerners tend to miss the forest for the trees, focusing on single elements in the forefront, whereas those from Eastern cultures tend to overlook sin-

Are all behaviors adaptive?

culture The beliefs, values, rules, and customs that exist within a group of people who share a common language and environment and that are transmitted through learning from one generation to the next.

CHAPTER 1 | Introduction to Psychological Science

gle trees, focusing on the entire forest in the background. Nisbett and his colleagues (2001) have documented numerous ways in which the thinking styles of these groups differ. The general pattern is that Westerners are much more analytic, breaking complex ideas into simpler components, categorizing information, and using logic and rules to explain behavior, whereas Easterners tend to be more holistic in their thinking, seeing everything in front of them as an inherently complicated whole, with all elements affecting all other elements.

In his book *The Geography of Thought,* Nisbett (2003) argues that these essential cultural differences date back to ancient Greek and Chinese societies, from roughly the eighth through the third centuries B.C.E., with the Greeks focusing on personal freedom, logic, and debate and the Chinese focusing on harmonious relationships with family and other villagers. To this day, the general findings from cultural psychologists are that Westerners tend to be "independent" and autonomous, stressing their individuality, whereas Easterners tend to be more "interdependent" on each other, stressing their sense of being part of a collective. Moreover, Canadian psychologist Steven Heine (2003) has found that Westerners are more likely to emphasize their personal strengths whereas Easterners are more likely to emphasize their need for self-improvement.

The culture in which we live shapes many aspects of daily life. Pause for a moment and think about the following questions: How do we decide what is most important in our lives? How do we want to relate to members of our families? Our friends? Our colleagues at work? How should we spend our leisure time? How do we define ourselves in relationship to our own cultures—or across cultures? For instance, the increased participation of women in the work force has changed the nature of contemporary Western culture in numerous ways, from a fundamental change in how women are viewed to more practical changes such as people marrying and having children later in life, a greater number of children in day care, and a greater reliance on convenient, fast foods. Culture shapes beliefs and values, such as the extent to which people should emphasize their own interests versus the interests of their families or the group. As we've already seen, this is magnified even more when we compare phenomena across cultures. Cultural rules are learned as *norms,* which specify how people ought to behave in different contexts, such as not laughing at funerals and keeping quiet in libraries. There are also material aspects of culture, such as media, technology, health care, and transportation. Many of us find it hard to imagine life without cars, televisions, and telephones, yet we recognize that each of these inventions has changed the fundamental ways in which people interact. Psychological scientists have played a significant role in providing a better understanding of the relationship between culture and behavior, showing that it's important to consider behavioral phenomena in their cultural context.

The accumulating evidence indicates that the human mind is adaptive in both biological and cultural terms, providing solutions to survival and reproductive challenges as well as a strong framework for a shared social understanding of how the world works. A true understanding of mind, brain, and behavior requires careful consideration of the evolution of biology and culture.

How does culture shape the way we interact with the world?

Psychological Science Crosses Levels of Analysis

The fourth theme of psychological science is that the mind and behavior can be studied on many levels of analysis. As we'll see throughout this book, psychological researchers working on the same problem often ask different questions and work at different levels. Indeed, many times psychologists collaborate with researchers from

CATEGORY	LEVELS	WHAT IS STUDIED?
Social	Cultural	Norms, beliefs, values, symbols, ethnicity
	Interpersonal	Groups, relationships, persuasion, influence, workplace
Individual	Individual Differences	Personality, gender, developmental age groups, self-concept
	Perception and Cognition	Thinking, decision making, language, memory, seeing, hearing
	Behavior	Observable actions, responses, physical movements
Biological	Brain Systems	Neuroanatomy, animal research, brain imaging
	Neurochemical	Neurotransmitters and hormones, animal studies, drug studies
	Genetic	Gene mechanisms, heritability, twin and adoption studies

1.4 Categories of Analysis Psychological scientists study three basic categories of behavior and mental life: social, individual, and biological.

How can the same problem be studied at multiple levels?

other sciences, such as biology, computer science, physics, anthropology, and sociology. This *interdisciplinary* effort shares the common goal of understanding the mind and behavior. Using the principles of the scientific method, psychological scientists must break down behavioral phenomena into their component parts in order to understand them. Only then can we begin to develop a full understanding of how the biological, individual, and social components influence our specific behaviors.

Three broadly defined categories of analysis will be evident throughout this book, reflecting research methods that emphasize the various aspects of studying mind and behavior. These categories can be further broken down in terms of levels of analysis; the most common levels are shown in Figure 1.4. *Social* aspects involve an examination of how cultural and social contexts affect the ways people interact and influence each other. *Individual* aspects concern individual differences in personality and mental processes that concern how we perceive and know our worlds. The *biological* aspects deal with how the physical body contributes to mind and behavior, such as the neurochemical and genetic processes that occur with the body and brain. Within these broader categories, psychological scientists typically focus on a certain level of analysis, such as at the cultural or neurochemical level (see Figure 1.4).

To understand how different types of psychological scientists work at each of these levels, let's look at the study of music. What type of music do you like? The enjoyment of music is a fascinating aspect of human life. Music is present in many aspects of daily life and is important to most people (Renfrow & Gosling, 2003). There are many questions to be asked about the musical experience, such as how preferences vary among individuals and across cultures, how music affects emotional states and thought processes, and even how the brain perceives sound as music rather than noise. For instance, suppose you wanted to know how often people listen to music. One survey of 2,465 English adolescents found that they reported listening to 2.45 hours of music each day, and they said they did so because it allowed them to project a desired "image" to the world and helped them to satisfy emotional needs (North, Hargreaves, & O'Neill, 2000). In a study conducted at the *behavioral* level of analysis, researchers used a computerized tape recorder to sample students' activities throughout the day and found that they listened to music during 14 percent of their waking hours (Mehl & Pennebaker, 2003)

What effect does listening to music have on people? At the *cognitive* level of analysis, researchers have used laboratory experiments to study the effects of music on mood, memory, decision making, and a variety of other mental states and processes

(Krumhansl, 2002). For instance, "Russia under the Mongolian Yoke" from Prokofiev's *Field of the Dead,* played at half speed, reliably puts people into negative moods. Mood may be affected not only by the tempo of the music, but also by whether it is in major or minor mode. At least for Western music, major mode is typically associated with positive moods and minor mode is associated with sad moods. This emotional response appears to be learned rather than innate, since very young children do not discriminate between modes, but by age seven or eight, children can reliably distinguish the mood effects of major and minor modes (Gregory, Worrall, & Sarge, 1996). Why does music affect mood? One way to study this is to go to the *neurochemical* level of analysis and look at the effect of music on brain chemistry. Indeed, it appears that pleasant music may be associated with increased activation of one brain chemical, serotonin, that is known to be relevant to mood (Evers & Suhr, 2000). These mood effects of music can even change how people behave. In one field study, shoppers were more likely to purchase expensive wine while listening to classical music than while listening to Top 40 music (Areni & Kim, 1993).

Researchers can also examine the effects of music at a *brain-systems* level of analysis (Peretz & Zatorre, 2005). Does perceiving music use the same brain circuits as, say, perceiving the sound of cars or spoken language? It turns out that the processing of musical information is similar to general auditory processing, but it likely also uses different brain mechanims. Case reports of patients with certain types of brain injury indicate that some lost the ability to hear tones and melody but not speech or environmental sounds. One 35-year-old woman who had brain damage lost the ability to recognize even familiar tunes, a condition known as *amusia*, even though other aspects of her memory and language systems were intact (Peretz, 1996). There are also case studies of so-called musical savants, who can play piano concertos by ear or sing elaborate songs but who otherwise show gross intellectual impairments, such as being unable to communicate with others or even respond to their own names. Such findings suggest that there are specific brain regions responsible for the processing of music. Researchers are using methods such as brain imaging to understand which parts of the brain are involved in perceiving and enjoying music, and how the perception of music might differ from the perception of other sounds (Blood & Zatorre, 2001).

Finally, some researchers have examined aspects of music at the *genetic* level of analyis. One study of attitudes in 800 British twins (Martin et al., 1986) revealed that about half the variability in the liking of jazz is determined by genetic influence. Moreover, there are anecdotal reports of musical expertise running in families, such as the Bach family, which might be due to an inborn ability to develop absolute pitch, also called perfect pitch. The evidence suggests that the ability to identify or produce the pitch of a sound with any reference point appears to depend both on genes and on musical experience during childhood (Levitin & Rogers, 2005; Zatorre, 2003). Only some people develop absolute pitch, and people who do not receive formal music training before age 9 or 10 are never able to develop it.

As these examples show, researchers are crossing different levels of analysis to gain a greater understanding of music. Throughout the text, we will include more examples of this kind of effort. Of course, each of the levels can be studied independent of the others. Throughout the history of psychology, this has been the favored approach. Only recently have researchers started to explain behavior in terms of several levels of analysis. It is this crossing of the levels of analysis that many modern-day psychological scientists find so captivating because it helps provide an increasingly complete picture of important behavioral and mental processes.

the Principles | What Are the Themes of Psychological Science?

Psychological science is the study of mind, brain, and behavior. Four themes characterize psychological science. (1) It is cumulative, in that principles are established on the basis of incremental advances in knowledge obtained through research. (2) A biological revolution has been energizing psychological research. Increasing knowledge of the neurochemistry of mental disorders, the mapping of the human genome, and the invention of imaging technologies that allow researchers to observe the working brain in action have provided psychological scientists with the methods to examine how the brain enables the mind. (3) Psychological science has also been heavily influenced in recent years by evolutionary psychology, which argues that the brain has evolved to solve adaptive problems. (4) Finally, although psychological scientists share the common goal of understanding mind, brain, and behavior, they do so by focusing on the same problems at different levels of analysis.

What Are the Intellectual Origins of Psychology?

Psychology is a young science that addresses questions that have challenged great minds for millennia. Many of these issues reflect long-standing philosophical questions about the nature of human experience. Psychology's roots are in philosophy and medicine, and many of the earliest psychologists were trained in one of these disciplines. In this section we will consider some of the "grand" questions and issues that have shaped psychological debate over centuries.

The Nature–Nurture Debate Considers the Impact of Biology and Environment

From the time of the ancient Greeks, there has been a debate about whether psychological characteristics are more due to *nature* or *nurture,* that is, whether they are biologically innate or acquired through education, experience, or culture. The **nature-nurture debate** has taken one form or another throughout psychology's history and will likely continue as researchers explore how thoughts, feelings, and behaviors are influenced by genes and by the culture or society in which one lives. It is now widely recognized that both nature and nurture are important, but more significant, recent advances in scientific knowledge have allowed researchers to specify *when* either nature or nurture is important, as well as how they interact. It is the relative importance of nature and nurture in determining mind and behavior that captivates the interest of psychological scientists.

As an example of the changing influences of nature and nurture, consider just two mental disorders—schizophrenia and bipolar disorder (you will read much more about them in Chapter 13). *Schizophrenia* is a disorder in which people have unusual thoughts, such as believing they are God, or experience unusual sensations, such as hearing voices. In *bipolar disorder* a person has dramatic mood swings, from feeling extremely sad (depressed) to feeling euphoric (manic). Prior to the 1950s, it was gen-

nature–nurture debate The arguments concerning whether psychological characteristics are biologically innate or acquired through education, experience, and culture.

How do we disentangle nature and nurture?

erally believed that these two mental disorders, among others, resulted from bad parenting or other environmental circumstances—that is, the causes were all nurture. But in the late 1950s and 1960s a variety of drugs were discovered that could alleviate the symptoms of these disorders; more recent research showed that these conditions are also heritable. Psychological scientists now believe that many mental disorders result as much from the way the brain is "wired" (nature) as from the way people are treated (nurture). Rapid advancements in understanding the biological basis of mental disorders have led to effective treatments that allow people to live normal lives. So is it all nature rather than nurture? Of course not. Both schizophrenia and bipolar disorder are more likely in certain environments, suggesting that they can be triggered by the situation. Many mental disorders result from events that happen in people's lives, such as combat soldiers who develop *posttraumatic stress disorder* (*PTSD*), in which people have intrusive and unwanted memories of their traumatic experiences. But recent research also indicates that some people inherit a genetic predisposition to develop PTSD, so nurture activates nature. Thus, nature and nurture are tightly interwoven and inseparable. Moreover, the social environment also plays an important role in whether treatment is successful; negative comments from family members predict poor outcomes. Psychological science depends on understanding both the genetic basis of human nature and the environment that shapes it.

The Mind-Body Problem Has Challenged Philosophers and Psychologists

Close your eyes and think about yourself for a second. Where do your thoughts reside? If you are like most people, you have a subjective sense that your mind is floating somewhere around your head, perhaps a few inches inside your skull, or perhaps even a few inches above or in front of your forehead. But why do you feel like your mind is in your head? The mind has been viewed throughout history as residing in many organs of the body, especially the liver or the heart. What is the relationship between the mental activity of your mind and the physical workings of your body? The **mind-body problem** is perhaps the quintessential psychological issue: whether the mind and body are separate and distinct, or whether the mind is simply the subjective experience of the physical brain.

For most of human history, scholars have believed that the mind and body are separate entities, with the mind very much in control of the body. This belief was held, in part, because of strong theological beliefs that the existence of a *divine and immortal soul* is what separates humans from animals. Even early theorists who challenged church doctrine were careful to avoid being too controversial. Leonardo da Vinci conducted experiments around 1500 to make his anatomical drawings more accurate, which offended the church because they violated the presumed sanctity of the human body. His dissections led him to many conclusions about the workings of the brain, including the idea that all sensory messages, such as vision, touch, and smell, arrived at one location in the brain (Figure 1.5), the *sensus communis,* which he believed to be the home of thought and judgment. (This is possibly why we call using good judgment *common sense* [Blakemore, 1983].)

mind-body problem A fundamental psychological issue that considers whether mind and body are separate and distinct or whether the mind is simply the subjective experience of the physical brain.

1.5 da Vinci and the Brain This drawing by Leonardo da Vinci dates from around 1506. He used a wax cast to study the brain. He found that the various sensory images arrived in the middle region of the brain, which he referred to as the *sensus communis,* or common sense.

It was René Descartes, the great French philosopher, who promoted the first influential theory that mind and body were separate yet intertwined (the theory known as **dualism**). The notion that the mind and body were separate was not novel, of course, but how Descartes connected them was at the time quite radical. The body, he argued, was nothing more than an organic machine, governed by "reflex," which Descartes defined as a "unit of mechanical, predictable, deterministic action" (Figure 1.6). For Descartes, many mental functions, such as memory and imagination, were the result of bodily functions. Linking some mental states with the body was a fundamental departure from the earlier views of dualism, in which all mental states were separate from bodily functions. In keeping with prevailing religious beliefs, however, Descartes concluded that the rational mind, which controlled volitional action, was divine and separate from the body. Thus, his view of dualism kept the distinction between mind and body, but he assigned to the body many of the mental functions previously considered the sovereign domain of the mind.

Descartes's most radical idea was to suggest that although the mind could affect the body, the body could also affect the mind. For instance, he believed that passions such as love, hate, and sadness arose from the body and influenced mental states, although the body acted on these passions through its own mechanisms. In this way, Descartes brought mind and body closer together by focusing on their interactions.

1.6 Descartes's "Reflex" Theory A woodcut illustrating Descartes's "reflex" theory of biological function.

Evolutionary Theory Introduces Natural Selection

One of the major intellectual events that shaped the future of psychological science was the publication of Charles Darwin's *On the Origin of Species* in 1859. In the book he outlined a theory of evolution that relied on the process of natural selection (as described earlier). Earlier naturalists and philosophers, including his own grandfather Erasmus Darwin, had all discussed the possibility that species might evolve, but it wasn't until Charles Darwin came along that the mechanism of evolution became clear. How did Darwin develop his theory of natural selection?

Charles Darwin (Figure 1.7) attended Cambridge and traveled as a naturalist aboard the *Beagle* from 1832 to 1837, collecting information about finches on the Galápagos Islands. When he later analyzed this information, he discovered that each island had slightly different species of finches (Figure 1.8). It seemed clear to him that these different finches must have descended from the same species, but he wondered what could account for the small variations. His famous notebooks from this era trace his thinking about how this must have occurred. He found a suitable explanation in Thomas Malthus's essay on population:

> I happened to read for amusement "Malthus on population," and being well prepared to appreciate the struggle for existence which everywhere goes on from long-continued observation of the habits of animals and plants, it at once struck me that under these circumstances favourable variations would tend to be preserved and unfavourable ones to be destroyed. The result of this would be the formation of a new species. (Darwin, 1887, p. 68)

1.7 Charles Darwin Darwin's theory of natural selection has had a huge impact on how psychologists think about the mind. This portrait is reported to be his favorite picture of himself.

Darwin called this mechanism for evolution *natural selection,* the process by which random mutations in organisms that are adaptive are passed along and mutations that hinder reproduction are not. Thus as species struggle to survive, those that are better adapted to their environment will leave more offspring, and those offspring will produce more offspring, and so on (i.e., the notion of *survival of the fittest*).

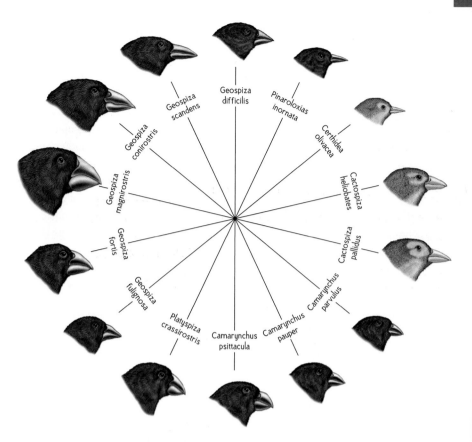

1.8 Finches on the Galápagos Islands The variation in these different species of finches on the Galápagos Islands was powerful evidence for some kind of selection process working on a common ancestor.

A further implication of Darwin's theory was that inheritable *individual differences* provide the basis of evolutionary development. This idea was seized on by his cousin Francis Galton, who proposed that some differences were psychological in nature (e.g., intelligence), and that they could be measured and tested. The *mental testing movement* followed in Galton's wake. Ultimately, the idea of natural selection has had a profound impact on science, philosophy, and society.

REVIEWING
the Principles | What Are the Intellectual Origins of Psychology?

The origins of psychological science can be found in the major philosophical questions that have endured for centuries. For instance, the nature-nurture debate involves determining the extent to which mind and behavior are predetermined by biology or are developed and shaped by environment. The mind-body problem tackles the question of how mental activity is related to brain functioning. Darwin's theory of evolution set the stage for a new understanding of the origins of mind and behavior.

How Did the Scientific Foundations of Psychology Develop?

How can we study mental activity?

introspection A systematic examination of subjective mental experiences that requires people to inspect and report on the content of their thoughts.

structuralism An approach to psychology based on the idea that conscious experience can be broken down into its basic underlying components or elements.

What are the problems with the method of introspection?

In 1843, John Stuart Mill published *System of Logic,* in which he declared that psychology should leave the realm of speculation and philosophy and become a science of observation and experiment. Indeed, he defined psychology as "the science of the elementary laws of the mind" and argued that only through the methods of science would the processes of the mind be understood. As a result, throughout the 1800s there was a growing emphasis on studying mental activity through careful scientific observation. Besides shifting from philosophy to experimentation, early psychologists were also heavily influenced by rapid increases in knowledge about basic physiology. Although these two approaches were not originally as intertwined as they are now, both were central to the development of psychological science.

Experimental Psychology Begins with Structuralism

In 1879 Wilhelm Wundt (Figure 1.9) established the first psychology laboratory and institute in Leipzig. There students could earn higher degrees in the new discipline. Accordingly, Wundt is widely regarded as the founder of experimental psychology as an academic discipline. He trained many of the great early psychologists, such as Edward Titchener, many of whom then established psychological laboratories throughout Europe, Canada, and the United States.

Through his training, Wundt realized that psychological processes, as the products of physiological actions in the brain, take time to occur. Thus, to study the mind he would present a subject with two psychological tasks: one that was simple and one that was more complex. He would then measure the speed at which subjects completed the tasks. By subtracting the easier task from the complex task, Wundt could infer how much time a particular mental event took to occur. Wundt was not satisfied with simply studying mental reaction times: he wanted to measure conscious experiences. To do this, he developed the method of **introspection**, a systematic examination of subjective mental experiences that required people to inspect and report on the content of their thoughts, such as describing the "blueness" of the sky. Using introspection, Wundt asked people to compare their subjective experiences as they contemplated a series of objects, such as by stating which one they found more pleasant.

Edward Titchener used methods such as introspection to develop a new school of thought that became known as *structuralism*. The basic idea of **structuralism** is that conscious experience can be studied when it is broken down into its underlying components or elements. Just as when you know the ingredients and recipe you can bake a cake, Titchener believed that understanding the basic elements of consciousness would provide the scientific basis for understanding the mind. Titchener argued that one could take a stimulus such as a musical tone and by introspection analyze its "quality," "intensity," "duration," and "clarity." Wundt ultimately rejected this particular use of introspection, but Titchener relied on the method throughout his career. The problem with this approach is that experience is subjective. Each person brings to introspection a unique perceptual system, and it is difficult to determine whether subjects are using the criteria in a similar way. Accordingly, over the course of time introspection was largely abandoned in psychology. Nonetheless, Wundt, Titchener, and other structuralists

1.9 Wilhelm Wundt Wundt (far right), the founder of modern experimental psychology, at work with his collaborators in his later years.

were important because of their goal to develop a pure science of psychology with its own self-contained vocabulary and set of rules.

Functionalism Addresses the Purpose of Behavior

One of the main critics of structuralism was William James (Figure 1.10), a brilliant scholar whose work has had an enormous, enduring impact on psychology. James abandoned a career in medicine to teach physiology at Harvard University in 1873. He was an excellent lecturer and was among the first professors at Harvard to openly welcome questions from students. His personal interests were more philosophical than physiological; he was captivated by the nature of conscious experience. He gave his first lecture on psychology in 1875, which he later quipped was also the first lecture on psychology he had ever heard. James's charm and brilliance were best expressed in his classic *Principles of Psychology,* published in 1890. Good genes perhaps contributed to his writing skills; his brother was the famous novelist Henry James. *Principles of Psychology* was an immediate hit with students and became the most influential book in the early history of psychology. To this day psychologists find rich delight in reading James's penetrating analysis of the human mind; it is amazing how many of his central ideas have held up over time.

James criticized structuralism's failure to capture the most important aspects of mental experience. He believed that the mind could not be broken down into its elements because the mind was much more complex than its elements. For instance, he noted that the mind consisted of a continuous series of thoughts that are ever-changing. This **stream of consciousness** could not be frozen in time, according to James, and so the strategies used by the structuralists were sterile and artificial. He likened psychologists who used the structural approach to someone who tried to understand a house by studying each of its bricks individually. More important to James was that the bricks worked together to form a house, and that a house has a particular function. James stressed that the important point was not the elements that made up the mind, but rather the mind's usefulness to people.

James was also heavily influenced by Darwinian thinking, and he argued that psychologists ought to examine the *functions* served by the mind. His approach to psychology, which became known as **functionalism**, was more concerned with how the mind operates than with what the mind contains. According to functionalism, the mind came into existence over the course of human evolution, and it works the way it does because it is useful for preserving life and passing along genes to future generations. In other words, it helps organisms adapt to environmental demands.

Many of the functionalists were concerned with applying psychological research to the real world. After all, if behavior served a purpose, the purpose ought to be reflected in daily human life. Thus, for example, John Dewey, the great educator, tested functionalist theories in his classrooms, where he stressed teaching students according to how the mind processed information rather than simply through repetitive drill learning. This *progressive* approach to education emphasized divergent thinking and creativity rather than the rote learning of conventional knowledge that might be incorrect anyway (Hothersall, 1995). William James was also interested in applying the functional approach to the study of real-world phenomena, such as the nature of religious experience. Yet the broad-ranging subjects to which functionalism was applied led to criticism that it was not sufficiently rigorous, and therefore functionalism slowly lost steam as a movement within psychology. However, the functional approach has returned to psychological science within the past few decades, as more and more researchers consider the adaptiveness of the behaviors and mental processes they study.

1.10 William James James was highly influenced by Darwin and is credited with "naturalizing" the mind. His book *The Principles of Psychology* remains a classic.

stream of consciousness A phrase coined by William James to describe one's continuous series of ever-changing thoughts.

functionalism An approach to psychology concerned with the adaptive purpose, or function, of mind and behavior.

Early Women Pioneers

William James also contributed to psychology in another important way, namely championing the rights of women to become scholars. As in many scientific fields, the contributions of women to psychological science were long underappreciated and for many years even ignored. Consider Mary Whiton Calkins (Figure 1.11), the oldest of five children born in Hartford, Connecticut in 1863. The daughter of a Protestant minister, Calkins attended Smith College, where she studied philosophy and classics. Initially employed as a temporary Greek instructor at Wellesley College, she was invited to become a professor of the new field of philosophical psychology, contingent on completing advanced training in psychology. At the time, her options were quite limited, as psychology was relatively new to North America. After canvassing the possibilities, she decided that studying with William James at Harvard University would provide her with the best training. James was enthusiastic to have her as a student. Unfortunately, Harvard president Charles Eliot did not believe in coeducation, and it was only after great pressure from James, Calkins's father, and the president of Wellesley College that Eliot relented and let her enroll in the seminar as a guest. The male students withdrew from the seminar in protest, leaving Calkins with a private tutorial "at either side of a library fire," as she describes in her autobiography.

Calkins continued her psychological studies with a number of other mentors at Harvard, including the famous German psychophysicist Hugo Munsterberg. With him, she completed all of the requirements for a Ph.D., including scoring higher than her male classmates on the qualifying exam, but Harvard denied her the degree, offering instead a Ph.D. from Radcliffe, the women's school affiliated with Harvard. Calkins refused the degree, bristling at the unequal treatment she received, describing differential education of men and women as artificial and illogical. Efforts to have Harvard overturn its earlier decision continue to this day, as does Harvard's refusal to grant her the degree that she earned (Harvard did not grant a Ph.D. to a woman until 1963).

Mary Whiton Calkins had an enormously productive career as a professor at Wellesley College, including writing an introductory psychology textbook in 1901, being the first woman to set up a psychology laboratory, publishing more than 100 articles, and being elected in 1905 the first woman president of the American Psychological Association. Her major research interest focused on the "self," which she believed could be studied using the methods of science. She made a number of other important contributions to the early science of psychology, although in her later years she became somewhat disenchanted by the rise of behaviorism and its dismissal of concepts such as "self." Professor Calkins retired from Wellesley in 1927 and died in 1930.

Margaret Flay Washburn was the first woman to be officially granted a Ph.D. in psychology. She was awarded her doctorate in 1921 at Cornell University, where she studied with Edward Titchener. She spent most of her career at Vassar College, which she had attended as an undergraduate. Her passion for teaching was rewarded by her students, who raised $15,000 as a gift to celebrate her 25 years at Vassar. In keeping with her devotion to students, Washburn used the gift to set up a scholarship fund for women.

1.11 Mary Whiton Calkins Calkins was a pioneer of psychological science.

Gestalt theory A theory based on the idea that the whole of personal experience is different from simply the sum of its constituent elements.

Of course, many other women contributed to the history of psychology, and thankfully their contributions are now readily acknowledged. Today, women make up approximately three-quarters of psychology majors and nearly half of all psychology doctorates in the work force (Frincke & Pate, 2004). ■

Gestalt Psychology Emphasizes Patterns and Context in Learning

Another of the schools of thought that arose in opposition to structuralism was the *Gestalt* school, founded by Max Wertheimer in 1912 and further expanded by Wolfgang Köhler, among others. According to **Gestalt theory**, the whole of personal experience is different from simply the sum of its constituent elements, or *the whole is different from the sum of the parts*. If you show people a triangle, they see a triangle, not three lines on a piece of paper, as would be the case for the trained observers in one of Titchener's structuralist experiments. So, for instance, look at Figure 1.12. What do you see? The elements of the picture are organized by the mind, automatically and with little effort, to produce the percept of a dog sniffing the ground. The picture is processed and experienced as a unified whole. Experimentally, the Gestalt psychologists relied not on trained observers but on the observations of ordi-

1.12 What Do You See? If you look carefully, you will see that these fragments make up a picture of a dog.

nary people in investigating subjective experience. This unstructured reporting of experience was called the *phenomenological* approach, referring to the totality of subjective conscious experience.

The Gestalt movement reflected an important idea that was at the heart of criticisms of structuralism: The perception of objects is subjective and dependent on context. Two people can look at an object and see different things. Indeed, one person can look at an object and see it in completely different ways, as in Figure 1.13. Note that you can alternate between seeing the face, the profiles, or the candlestick, but that it is difficult to perceive the image in all three ways at the same time. Thus, your mind organizes the scene into a perceptual whole, so that you see the picture in a specific way. The important lesson of Gestalt psychology is that the mind perceives the world in an organized fashion that cannot be broken down into its constituent elements. The Gestalt perspective has had an impact on many areas of psychology, such as the study of vision and our understanding of human personality.

The Unconscious Influences Everyday Mental Life

Twentieth-century psychology was profoundly influenced by one of its most famous thinkers, Sigmund Freud (Figure 1.14). Freud was trained in medicine and began his career working with people who had neurological disorders, such as paralysis of various body parts. He found that many of his patients had few medical reasons for their paralysis, and he soon came to believe that their conditions were caused by psychological factors.

1.13 Face(s)? This drawing by Stanford psychologist Roger Shepard can be viewed as either a face behind a candlestick or two separate profiles.

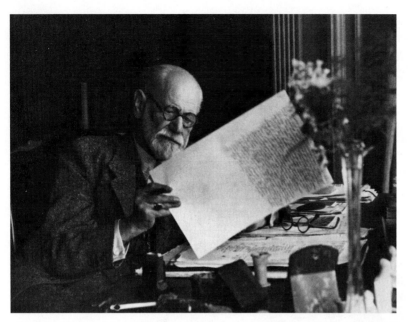

1.14 Sigmund Freud The father of psychoanalytic theory had a huge influence in the early days of psychology. Today his theories have largely been abandoned.

At the end of the nineteenth century, the structuralists and functionalists were focusing on conscious experience, but Freud made the deduction that much of human behavior is determined by mental processes that operate below the level of conscious awareness, at the level of the **unconscious**. Freud believed that these unconscious mental forces were often in conflict, which produced psychological discomfort and in some cases even apparent psychological disorders.

From his theories, Freud pioneered the clinical case study approach and developed the therapeutic method of **psychoanalysis**, which involves trying to bring the contents of the patients' unconscious into conscious awareness so that their conflicts could be dealt with in a constructive manner. For example, he analyzed the apparent symbolic content in his patients' dreams in search of hidden conflicts. He also used a technique called *free association,* in which people would simply talk about whatever they wanted to for as long as they wanted to. Freud believed that through free association people would eventually reveal the unconscious conflicts that were causing them problems. He eventually extended his theories to account for general psychological functioning.

Freud's influence was considerable, not only on the psychologists who followed him but also on the public's view of psychology. Many people unfamiliar with psychology imagine that most psychologists have patients lie on couches and probe their innermost thoughts. In fact, today relatively few psychologists follow Freudian thinking. The basic problem with many of Freud's original ideas, such as the meaning of dreams, is that they are extremely difficult to test using the methods of science (as you will see in the next chapter). And although Freud's idea that mental processes occur below the level of conscious awareness is now widely accepted in psychological science, the unconscious processes studied by contemporary scientists share only a passing resemblance to the unconscious sexual conflicts that permeated Freudian theorizing.

Most Behavior Can Be Modified by Reward and Punishment

Psychology's focus on mental processes, both conscious and unconscious, was soon challenged as inherently unscientific by John B. Watson (Figure 1.15), an American psychologist who developed the approach known as **behaviorism**, which emphasizes the role that environmental forces have on producing behavior. Watson believed that if psychology was to be a science, it had to stop trying to study mental events that could not be directly observed, and he therefore was scornful of methods such as introspection and free association.

The intellectual question that was most central to Watson and his followers was the nature-nurture question. For Watson and other behaviorists, it was all nurture. Heavily influenced by the work of Russian physiologist Ivan Pavlov, Watson believed that all behavior was caused by environmental factors: Understanding the environmental *stimuli,* or triggers, was all one needed to predict a behavioral *response.* Watson's behaviorism was mainly concerned with how animals acquired new behaviors, which is known as learning (discussed in Chapter 6). Psychologists greeted Watson's approach with great enthusiasm. Many had grown dissatisfied with the ambiguous

unconscious A term that identifies mental processes that operate below the level of conscious awareness.

psychoanalysis A method developed by Sigmund Freud that attempts to bring the contents of the unconscious into conscious awareness so that conflicts can be revealed.

behaviorism A psychological approach that emphasizes the role of environmental forces in producing behavior.

methods used by those studying mental processes; they longed to be taken more seriously as scientists, which they believed would happen if they focused on studying only observable behaviors.

It was B. F. Skinner who became famous for taking up the mantle of behaviorism. Like Watson, Skinner denied the existence of mental states, writing in his provocative *Beyond Freedom and Dignity* (1971) that concepts referring to mental processes were of no scientific value for explaining behavior. Rather, Skinner believed that mental states were nothing more than an illusion. Skinner was interested in how repeated behaviors were shaped or influenced by the events or consequences that followed them. For instance, an animal would learn to perform a behavior if doing so in the past had led to a positive outcome, such as receiving food.

Behaviorism dominated psychological research well into the early 1960s. In many ways, these were extremely productive times for psychologists. Many of the basic principles established by behaviorists continue to be viewed as critical to understanding the mind, brain, and behavior. At the same time, sufficient evidence has accumulated to show that thought processes do influence outcomes, and few psychologists today describe themselves as strict behaviorists.

How People Think Affects Behavior

While much of psychology was focused on studying observable behavior, during the first half of the twentieth century evidence slowly emerged showing that how humans perceived situations could influence behavior and that learning was not as simple as the behaviorists believed. In the late 1920s, the Gestalt theorist Wolfgang Köhler found that chimpanzees could solve a problem in their efforts to reach a banana. The chimpanzees had to figure out how to connect two sticks, which would then allow them to reach the banana and draw it close. The animals tried various things until suddenly they seemed to have insight, as evidenced by their reaching the banana and using the strategy perfectly on subsequent tasks. At around the same time, learning theorists such as Edward Tolman were showing that animals could learn by observation, which made little sense (according to behaviorist theory) given that the observing animals were not being rewarded—it was all going on in their heads. Other psychologists conducting research on memory, language, and child development showed that the simple laws of behaviorism could not explain such things as why cultural influences alter how people remember a story, why grammar develops in a systematic fashion, and why children go through stages of development in which they interpret the world in different ways. All of this suggested that mental functions were important for understanding behavior.

In 1957, George A. Miller (Figure 1.16) and colleagues established the Center for Cognitive Studies at Harvard University and launched the *cognitive revolution* in psychology. Ulric Neisser integrated a wide range of cognitive phenomena in his classic 1967 book, which named and defined the field. *Cognitive psychology* is concerned with higher-order mental functions, such as intelligence, thinking, language, memory, and decision making (you will read more about cognitive psychology in Chapter 8). Cognitive research has shown that the way people think about things influences their behavior. A number of events occurring in the 1950s set the stage for the rise of cognitive science, with perhaps the growing use of computers leading the way. Computers operate according to software programs, which dictate rules for how information is processed. Cognitive psychologists such as Alan Newell and the Nobel laureate Herbert Simon applied this process to their explanation of how the mind works. These *information-processing* theories of cognition viewed the brain as the hardware that ran the mind as software; the brain takes in information as a

1.15 John B. Watson Watson, who spent most of his adult life in advertising, was a proponent of behaviorism. His views were amplified by thousands of psychologists, including B. F. Skinner.

How might a computer analogy be useful for thinking about the mind?

1.16 George A. Miller Miller launched the cognitive revolution by establishing the Center for Cognitive Science at Harvard University in 1957.

code, processes it, stores relevant sections, and retrieves stored information as required. There was an early recognition that the brain was important to cognition, but many cognitive psychologists preferred to focus exclusively on the software, with little interest in the specific brain mechanisms involved. In the early 1980s, cognitive psychologists joined forces with neuroscientists, computer scientists, and philosophers to develop an integrated view of mind and brain. The field of *cognitive neuroscience* emerged during the 1990s as one of the most exciting fields of science.

Social Situations Shape Behavior

While tracing the origins of the field of psychology, we have focused a great deal on the relationship between the mind and the brain, and the role of evolution and learning on human behavior. After World War II, psychologists broadened their efforts to better understand human behavior in the real world. In particular, the atrocities committed in World War II led a number of psychologists and thinkers to begin researching topics such as authority, obedience, and group behavior. These topics are the province of *social psychology,* which focuses on the power of situation and how people are shaped through their interactions with others.

In 1962 Adolf Eichmann, one of Hitler's chief lieutenants, was hanged for "causing the killing of millions of Jews." Shortly before his death, Eichmann claimed, "I am not the monster I am made out to be. I am the victim of a fallacy." The atrocities committed in Nazi Germany compelled psychologists to consider whether evil is an integral part of human nature. Why had apparently normal Germans willingly participated in the murder of innocent men, women, and children? Researchers, many influenced by Freudian ideas, initially sought to understand what types of people would commit evil acts. They concluded that certain types, especially those raised by unusually strict parents, did display a slightly greater willingness to follow orders. But social psychology shows that almost all people are strongly influenced by social situations. Indeed, as you will read in Chapter 15, people will send painful electric shocks to innocent others if directed to do so by someone in apparent authority. Although it does not excuse anything, Eichmann was correct that people were overlooking the power of the situation in explaining his heinous actions.

Kurt Lewin (Figure 1.17), who was trained as a Gestalt psychologist, can be credited with bringing a scientific, experimental approach to the field of social psychology. His *field theory* emphasized the interplay between people—their biology, habits, and beliefs—and their environment, such as social situations and group dynamics. This perspective allowed psychologists to begin examining some of the most complex forms of human mental activity, such as how people's attitudes shape behavior, why they are prejudiced against other groups, how they are influenced by other people, and why they are attracted to some people and repelled by others. As we saw so vividly in the case of Amadou Diallo, human beings navigate through the social world, and psychological science recognizes the importance of fully considering the situation in order to predict and understand behavior.

Psychological Therapy Is Based on Science

Earlier we mentioned that the physician Sigmund Freud developed psychoanalysis to treat people with psychological disorders. Although credit must be given to Freud for recognizing the impact of psychological factors on human functioning, his method of therapy is no longer widely used. In the middle of the twentieth century, a humanistic approach to the treatment of psychological disorders, led by Carl Rogers and Abraham Maslow, stressed how people can come to know and accept themselves in order to reach their unique potentials. Some of the techniques developed by Rogers, such as specific ways of questioning and listening during therapy, are staples of modern treatment. Only in the last four decades, however, has a scientific approach to the study of psychological disorders emerged.

Throughout psychology's history, the methods developed to treat psychological disorders mirrored advances in psychological science. For instance, the rise of behaviorism led to a group of therapies designed to modify behavior rather than deal with underlying mental conflicts. Behavioral modification methods continue to be highly effective in a number of situations, from training those with intellectual impairments to treating patients who are especially anxious and fearful. The cognitive revolution in scientific thinking led therapists to recognize the important role of thought processes in mental disorders. Pioneers such as Aaron T. Beck developed therapies to correct faulty cognitions. These cognitive therapies are especially effective for treating conditions such as depression and eating disorders. For some mental disorders, such as schizophrenia, the only truly effective treatments are drugs that alter brain chemistry. For those with these disorders, the biological revolution in psychological science has been a godsend. But drug therapy is less preferable than cognitive and behavioral therapies for other disorders because of the potential for side effects and for patients to develop a reliance on the drugs. In many situations, a combination of drug and cognitive-behavioral therapy may be the best treatment plan. Today, most therapeutic approaches to dealing with psychological disorders consist of two key factors that reflect the origins of the field: adopting a widely recognized treatment of choice that scientific research has demonstrated to be clinically effective and recognizing that each person is a unique individual with specific issues and needs. Probably the greatest change in the field of clinical psychology over the course of the twentieth century comes from our realization, via scientific research, that there is no universal treatment or approach for all psychological disorders—contrary to the thinking of the early giants such as Freud, Rogers, and Skinner. Instead, as you will see in Chapter 14, different treatments are most effective for different disorders.

1.17 Kurt Lewin Lewin is the founder of modern social psychology. He pioneered the use of theory, using experimentation to test hypotheses.

REVIEWING

the Principles | How Did the Scientific Foundations of Psychology Develop?

The foundations of psychological science emerged from philosophy and physiology. Early experimental psychologists included some who believed it necessary to reduce mental processes into their constituent, "structural" parts, and others who argued that it was more important to understand how the mind functions than what it contains. During this period, most research was aimed at understanding the subjective mind, such as Freud's emphasis on the unconscious and the Gestalt movement's focus on perception. It was the behaviorists who claimed that the study of mind was too subjective and therefore unscientific. Accordingly, for the first half of the twentieth century most psychologists studied only observable behaviors. The cognitive revolution in the 1960s returned the mind to center stage, and research on mental processes such as memory, language, and decision making blossomed. Throughout the last century, some psychologists have emphasized the social context of behavior and mental activity. Advances in psychological science have informed the treatment of psychological disorders.

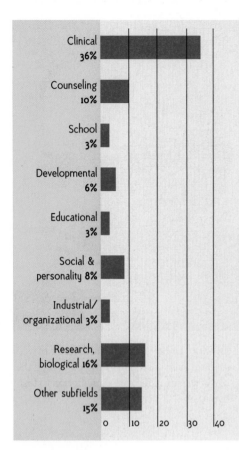

1.18 How Psychology Is Applied
Psychologists pursue their interests by studying a variety of topics within different settings.

psychological scientist One who uses the methods of science to study the interplay between brain, mind, and behavior and how the social environment affects these processes.

psychological practitioners Those who apply findings from psychological science in order to assist people in their daily lives.

Why does crossing levels of analysis provide better insights about the mind?

How Can We Apply Psychological Science?

As you will discover, psychological science covers broad ground. Many different types of researchers study the mind, brain, and behavior at different conceptual levels. This diversity means that psychological scientists pursue research on topics that touch all aspects of human life.

Subdisciplines Focus on Different Levels of Analysis

The term *psychologist* is used broadly to describe people whose careers involve predicting behavior or understanding mental life (Figure 1.18). We use the term **psychological scientist** to refer to those who use the methods of science to study the brain, the mind, and behavior. Psychological scientists work in many settings, such as clinics, schools, businesses, universities, and colleges. There are also **psychological practitioners**, who apply the findings of psychological science in order to do such things as help people in need of psychological treatment, design safe and pleasant work environments, counsel people on career paths, or help teachers design better classroom curricula. The distinction between science and practice can be fuzzy, since many psychological scientists are also practitioners. For example, many *clinical psychologists* both study and treat people with psychological disorders.

As we discussed earlier in this chapter, psychological scientists pursue their research interests at different levels of analysis; not surprisingly, the different levels of analysis tend to be associated with different subdisciplines. Let's apply these levels of analysis to the example of music, which we looked at earlier in this chapter, and examine how different types of psychological scientists might study it. *Social psychologists* focus on the influences that other situations and people have on how we act, think, and feel. Thus, researchers in this area might look at how cultural values or peer groups shape musical preferences. *Personality psychologists* are interested in individual preferences, such as how certain types of people might prefer certain types of music, whereas *developmental psychologists* address changes in mind and behavior over the life span and so they might study how children learn the basic structure of music or how musical preferences change as one grows older.

Cognitive psychology is concerned with mental processes such as thinking, perceiving, remembering, and decision making, and so researchers in this area might be interested in how people perceive various aspects of music as well as how music changes the way people think. Those in *cognitive neuroscience* would seek to understand the brain systems involved in the perception of music and how they might differ from the parts of the brain involved in ordinary auditory processing. *Behavioral neuroscientists* study the biological mechanisms responsible for behavior, and therefore might be interested in how music affects the body and brain. Music changes our physical state: classical music may soothe us, rock music might rev us up. As mentioned earlier, music also changes brain chemistry in a way that affects mood. Finally, *experimental psychopathologists,* who study abnormal or disordered behavior, might use music to induce a sad mood in people in order to examine the mental processes associated with feeling depressed.

Many of the chapters of this book reflect the work of the different subdisciplines of psychological science and consequently show the use of different levels of analysis. The choice of which level to study is based on the scientists' particular interests, as well as their general theoretical approaches and how they were trained. But more and more, psychological science emphasizes examining behavior across multiple levels in an integrated fashion. Thus, psychologists interested in understanding the hormonal basis of obesity interact with geneticists who explore the heritability of obesity, as well as social psychologists who study human beliefs about eating. Crossing the levels of analysis provides more insights than working within one level. The Gestalt psychologists were right in asserting that the whole is different from the sum of its parts. Throughout this book, you will see how this multilevel approach has led to breakthroughs in understanding psychological activity.

Psychological Science *in Action*

Sports Psychologists Help Athletes Find the Zone

As we have seen, psychological practitioners apply what is known from psychological science to help people perform at their best. A good example of a popular applied area is sports psychology. Elite athletes work for years to perfect physical skills necessary to excel at their sports. Their daily practices hone their skills so that they can perform at peak competitive levels. Yet many professionals go through slumps in which they can look like blundering amateurs. Consider David Duval, a golfer who within recent years was on the leaderboard at every tournament, yet has fallen out of contention for the last few seasons, finishing nearly last in the 2005 British Open at St. Andrews. Golf analysts have suggested that he has not lost his skills but rather his mental edge. Elite performances require not only physical prowess, but also a mind-set that one is a champion. Helping elite athletes think of themselves as winners is part of the job of sports psychologists, professionals who study the behavioral factors that influence and are influenced by participation in sports and exercise. Sports psychologists help athletes do a number of things, such as maintaining focus during competition, communicating with teammates, building feelings of confidence, motivating themselves to achieve their goals, and dealing with the intensity of their emotions. Specific exercises help athletes to overcome doubts, use relaxation to calm their minds, and develop strategies for focusing solely on the task at hand. In other words, they help athletes get into "the zone."

1.19 Bob Rotella

Many athletes work with a sports psychologist as part of their regular training. But sometimes athletes going through slumps require stronger assistance. Golfers like David Duval often seek out the assistance of the sports psychologist Bob Rotella, known affectionately as "Doc" on the PGA Tour (Figure 1.19). Rotella, a native of Vermont who earned his doctorate in psychology from the University of Connecticut, has worked with many PGA golfers as well as professional athletes in baseball, hockey, and basketball, and with members of the U.S. Olympic ski and equestrian teams. He is considered one of the pioneers in sports psychology, conducting research on exercise and sports at the University of Virginia. He now is a best-selling author and frequent television commentator. Rotella helps athletes train their minds to focus on their goals and teaches them to deal with their doubts, worries, and frustrations. Like many sports psychologists, he emphasizes relaxation as a key to preparing for competition. One of his favorite psychologists is William James, who often espoused the view that people by and large become what they think about themselves. For Rotella, this means that how athletes view themselves, their beliefs, and their performance expectations shapes how they actually perform. His approach to working with athletes, therefore, is to help them learn to think of themselves as champions.

Sports psychologists receive extensive training to be able to help their clients. To be certified, they need to demonstrate expert knowledge in the research base of psychological principles that apply to sports, which include understanding motor behavior, human physiology, principles of learning, motivation, and counseling skills. More than 50 programs around the world specialize in training practitioners of sports psychology, one of the fastest-growing areas of applied psychology. Information on career opportunities in sports psychology can be found on the following Web sites:

Sports psychology at the American Psychological Association
www.psyc.unt.edu/apadiv47
The Association for the Advancement of Applied Sports Psychology
www.aaasponline.org
The International Society of Sports Psychology
www.issponline.org ∎

Psychological Knowledge Is Used in Many Professions

Psychology is one of the most popular majors in many colleges. Not only is the subject material fascinating and personally relevant, but psychological science serves as excellent training for many professions. For instance, physicians need to know a lot more than anatomy and chemistry. They need to know how to relate to their patients, how the patients' behaviors are linked to health, and what motivates or discourages patients from seeking medical care or following treatment protocols. Understanding the aging brain and how it affects visual perception, memory, and motor movement is vital for those who treat elderly patients. Psychological scientists make major contributions to research on human physical and mental health, which is why the National Institute of Health funds research in the field. Much of the psychological research you will read about in this book is being applied today to make people's lives better.

Psychological science is equally useful for anyone whose career involves needing to understand people. In order to persuade jurors, lawyers need to know how groups make decisions. Advertisers need to know how attitudes are formed or changed, and to what extent people's attitudes predict their behavior. Politicians use psychological techniques of impression management to make themselves attractive to voters. The general usefulness of understanding mental activity may also explain psychology's popularity on campuses. It can help you understand your motives, your personality, even why you remember some things and forget others.

Of course, some of you will be so fascinated by psychological science that you will devote your lives to studying the mind and behavior. We, the authors, understand

S. GROSS

"For God's sake, think! Why is he being so nice to you?"

How do we use knowledge acquired from psychological science?

how you feel. There is tremendous excitement in psychological science as we unravel the very nature of what it means to be a human being. Although the foundations of psychological science are growing and established scientific principles of mind, brain, and behavior exist, there is still a tremendous amount to learn about issues such as how nature and nurture interact and how the brain enables the mind. Indeed, contemporary psychological science is providing new insights into problems and issues that the great scholars of the past struggled to solve.

People Are Intuitive Psychological Scientists

By our very nature, we humans are intuitive psychological scientists who develop hypotheses about and try to predict the behavior of others. People choose marriage partners they expect will best meet their emotional, sexual, and support needs. Defensive driving relies on an intuitive understanding of when other people are likely to make mistakes while driving. People are also pretty good at predicting whether others are kind, would make good teachers, or are trustworthy. But people can't intuitively know if taking certain herbs will increase memory, or whether playing music to newborns makes them more intelligent, or whether mental illness results from too much or too little of a certain brain chemical.

One of the most important goals of our textbook is to provide a basic education about the methods of psychological science for those students whose only exposure to psychology is through this introductory course. Although psychologists make important contributions to understanding and treating mental illness, most of psychological science has little to do with couches or dreams. Instead, it has everything to do with understanding mental activity, social interactions, and how people acquire behaviors. To understand what makes you tick and what makes other people tick, you will need to be introduced to the basic operating manual for the human mind and behavior. This is found in the psychological sciences.

Psychological Sciences Require Critical Thinking

One of the hallmarks of science is skepticism. You should be skeptical of dramatic new findings reported in science until you have convincing evidence to support the claims. Science progresses carefully and often slowly, and good science takes time. The ability to think skeptically is often referred to as **critical thinking**, a systematic way of evaluating information in order to reach reasonable conclusions. Being a critical thinker involves considering alternative explanations, looking for holes in evidence, and using logic and reasoning to see whether the information makes sense. It also involves considering whether the information might be biased, such as by personal or political agendas. Mostly, critical thinking involves healthy questioning and keeping an open mind. This doesn't mean just questioning information that doesn't fit in with your worldviews, but also thinking critically about all information, and perhaps especially that which fits your preconceptions. After all, this is where you may be least motivated to think critically.

Suppose, for instance, you read about a study that purports to demonstrate that people who share your political views are much more intelligent than those with a different political orientation. As a critical thinker, you would want to know whether the political affiliation of the researchers influenced the study as well as how they measured intelligence, such as whether they measured knowledge about events that matter more to one political group than to others. Before you take solace in the findings, it is important to make sure that those findings are real. The only way to do so

critical thinking A systematic way of evaluating information in order to reach reasonable conclusions.

is to evaluate the findings using critical thinking. Developing critical thinking skills will be useful to you not only in your other classes but also in any career that you choose. Being a critical thinker means making good decisions based on reasonable and logical conclusions about evidence.

Does Listening to Mozart Make You Smarter?

As you read this book you will learn how to separate the believable from the incredible. You will learn to spot badly designed experiments, and you will develop the skills necessary to critically evaluate claims made in the popular media. The information in this book will also provide a state-of-the-art background in psychological science so that you will know whether or not a claim is consistent with what we know about psychology. The media love a good story, and findings from psychological research are often very provocative. Unfortunately, media reports can be distorted or even flat-out wrong. You will be consumers of psychological science throughout your lives, and you will need to be skeptical of overblown media of "brand-new" findings obtained by "groundbreaking" research. For instance, a study conducted by a cognitive psychologist found that playing Mozart to research participants led them to score slightly higher on a test that is loosely related to intelligence. The media jumped onto the so-called Mozart effect with abandon; the result has been that many parents are determinedly playing Mozart to young infants, and even to fetuses (Figure 1.20). Indeed, governors of two U.S. states instituted programs that provided free Mozart CDs to every newborn. Web sites make bold claims about the power of Mozart, including fantastical assertions that listening to Mozart can cure neurological illness and other maladies. What is the power of Mozart for the developing mind?

Let's step back and critically evaluate the research underlying the Mozart effect. In 1993, researchers played the first 10 minutes of the Mozart Sonata for Two Pianos in D Major (K. 448) to a group of college students. Compared with students who listened to relaxation instructions or who sat in silence, those who heard Mozart performed slightly better on a task that involved folding and cutting paper, a task that is part of a larger overall measure of intelligence. This modest increase lasted for about 10 to 15 minutes (Rauscher, Shaw, & Ky, 1993).

Unfortunately, subsequent research largely failed to replicate the findings. Following a careful review of the studies testing the "Mozart effect," Christopher Chabris and his colleagues (1999) have concluded that the effect of listening to Mozart is quite trivial and certainly unlikely to increase intelligence among listeners. According to Chabris and his team, listening to Mozart appears to enhance only certain types of motor skills but does not influence measures more commonly associated with intelligence. Thus, it is unclear whether the effects have anything to due with intelligence. Another important question from a critical thinking perspective is whether it was the music or some other aspect of the situation that led to better performance on the folding and cutting task. A team of Canadian researchers has shown that the effect may be due simply to the fact that the music is more uplifting than sitting in silence or relaxing, and thus it is the increase in positive mood that is largely responsible for better performance (Thompson, Schellenberg, & Husain, 2001). Recall from earlier in this chapter that music has many effects on mood and cognition.

What is critical thinking?

1.20 The Mozart Effect A much publicized research study done in the early 1990s concluded that infants benefited from the "Mozart effect," but subsequent findings have been extremely critical of this theory.

It is also critical to note that all of the studies to date have been conducted on college students, yet all of the publicity concerns whether playing Mozart to infants increases their intelligence. Most likely it does not. John Bruer, in his important book *The Myth of the First Three Years* (1999), notes that people have taken leaps past the data in suggesting that experiences during the first three years shape or alter the developing brain in any meaningful or permanent way. Now that you are a bit more informed, what do you think? Does listening to Mozart increase your intelligence? Does it have any positive impact on your physical or mental health? ■

REVIEWING
the Principles | How Can We Apply Psychological Science?

Psychological scientists study the mind, brain, and behavior across different levels of analysis and often identify themselves within various subdisciplines of psychology. However, there is a growing tendency for researchers to cross traditional areas to collaborate with researchers from different subdisciplines. The content of psychological science is of interest and value to many professions, which may explain why psychology is one of the most popular majors on most college campuses. Using critical thinking skills and understanding the methods of psychological science are important for evaluating research that is reported in the popular media.

Conclusion

The rich history of psychology is clear. Its founders grappled with the most important and interesting issues there are. Who are we? How does the brain get the job done? How much of us is predetermined by our genes? How does our personality affect our lives? What are the social forces that influence our personal decisions?

As Darwin predicted over a century ago, the concept of natural selection is becoming an integral part of psychological science. In general terms, psychologists have come to appreciate that to understand behavior, they first must understand what it is designed for. Did this behavior solve a problem for our human ancestors? Once we have a sense of what something is for, then we can ask, "How does it work?" These questions remain at the forefront of research today as psychological scientists seek to unravel the mysteries of mind, brain, and behavior. These basic questions apply to all levels of analysis: biological, individual, and social. Furthermore, research across the multiple levels of analysis is invigorating psychological science and providing new insights into age-old questions. In the chapters ahead, you will learn not only how psychological science operates but also many remarkable things about the mind, brain, and behavior. It might just be one of the most fascinating explorations of your life.

Summarizing the Principles of Psychological Science

What Are the Themes of Psychological Science?

1. **The principles of psychological science are cumulative:** Psychological science relies on empirical evidence and builds on previous discoveries in a dynamic way.

2. **The new biological revolution is energizing research:** Discoveries in brain activity have been enhanced by the discoveries of neurotransmitters. Mapping of the human genome has furthered the role of genetics in analyzing disease and behavior. Tremendous advances in brain imaging have revealed the working brain.

33

3. **The mind is adaptive:** The brain has evolved to solve survival problems and adapt to environments. Many modern behaviors are by-products of adaptation.

4. **Psychological science crosses levels of analysis:** Psychological scientists examine behavior from a variety of levels of analysis: social (culture and interpersonal behavior), individual (personality, and perception and cognition), and biological (brain systems, neurochemistry, and genetics).

What Are the Intellectual Origins of Psychology?

5. **The nature-nurture debate considers the impact of biology and environment:** Historically, philosophy and science have been concerned with the relative influence of biology and environment on behavior.

6. **The mind-body problem has challenged philosophers and psychologists:** A persistent challenge exists in reconciling the relationship of the mind to the physical activity of the brain.

7. **Evolutionary theory introduces natural selection:** Darwin's theory of evolution assumes that behaviors that promote reproductive success and survival are passed on and, therefore, that individual differences are the basis of evolutionary change.

How Did the Scientific Foundations of Psychology Develop?

8. **Experimental psychology begins with structuralism:** Using the technique of introspection, scientists attempted to understand conscious experience by reducing it to its basic elements, its structure. This brings about a strong scientific approach.

9. **Functionalism addresses the purpose of behavior:** Functionalists argued that the mind is best understood by examining the functions or purposes it serves, not its structure.

10. **Gestalt psychology emphasizes patterns and context in learning:** The assertion that the whole experience (the Gestalt) is different from the sum of its parts led to an approach emphasizing the subjective experience of perception.

11. **The unconscious influences everyday mental life:** The psychoanalytic assumption that unconscious processes not readily available to our awareness influence behavior had an enormous impact on psychology.

12. **Most behavior can be modified by reward and punishment:** Discoveries that behavior is changed by its consequences caused behaviorism to dominate psychology until the 1960s.

13. **How people think affects behavior:** The computer analogy of the brain and the cognitive revolution led to the information processing perspective.

14. **Social situations shape behavior:** Work in social psychology has highlighted how other people and situations are powerful forces in shaping behavior.

15. **Psychological therapy is based on science:** Scientific research over the course of the twentieth century taught psychological scientists that there is no universal treatment for psychological disorders. Instead, different treatments are effective for different disorders.

How Can We Apply Psychological Science?

16. **Subdisciplines focus on different levels of analysis:** Different approaches to understanding behavior are the focus of the various areas of psychology and are often combined.

17. **Psychological knowledge is used in many professions:** Because psychology focuses on human behavior, it is of interest to many students and professionals.

18. **People are intuitive psychological scientists:** Humans naturally explain and predict the behavior of others.

19. **Psychological sciences require critical thinking:** Skepticism is an important element of science and requires critical thinking and the evaluation of evidence and conclusions.

Applying the Principles

1. You are watching a baseball game and comment that the pitching expertise accounts for the score; someone else says it's the hitting; and a third person asserts that it is the payroll. This is similar to what theme of psychological science?

_____ a) science is cumulative
_____ b) the biological revolution
_____ c) the brain is adaptive
_____ d) there are different levels of analysis

2. It is freezing outside, so you slip on a heavy coat before heading out. Your cousin visiting from Hawaii has never even owned a heavy coat and decides to stay in. He complains that he is cold even in your apartment, which is heated to 68 degrees. Your different behaviors and the ability to think about and solve the problem of how to deal with cold temperatures demonstrate which of the following basic principles of psychological science?

_____ a) the role of both the brain and the environment in shaping behaviors for survival
_____ b) the influence of environmental experience alone on survival
_____ c) the ability of the brain alone to determine survival behaviors
_____ d) the belief that nature has a greater influence on behavior than nurture

3. If you attempt to understand a behavior—for example, bowling a perfect strike or solving a puzzle—by breaking it down into empirical evidence defined by the stimulus (the pins; the puzzle pieces), the response (perfect release of the ball; fitting together pieces), and the consequence (the strike score; the completed puzzle); you would be using the scientific approach of _____, which has its roots in _____.

_____ a) Gestalt; psychoanalysis
_____ b) behaviorism; functionalism
_____ c) psychoanalysis; structuralism
_____ d) behaviorism; structuralism

4. Having been a student for some time, you have an intuitive sense for what a course will be like from watching the professor during the first couple of sessions. The accuracy of your judgment could be the focus of all but which of the following psychologists?

_____ a) cognitive psychologist
_____ b) personality psychologist
_____ c) social psychologist
_____ d) psychopathologist (clinician)

ANSWERS: 1.d 2.b 3.b 4.d

Key Terms

adaptations, p. 10
behaviorism, p. 24
critical thinking, p. 31
culture, p. 12
dualism, p. 18
evolutionary theory, p. 10
functionalism, p. 21

Gestalt theory, p. 23
introspection, p. 20
mind-body problem, p. 17
natural selection, p. 10
nature-nurture debate, p. 16
psychoanalysis, p. 24
psychological practitioners, p. 28

psychological science, p. 6
psychological scientist, p. 28
stream of consciousness, p. 21
structuralism, p. 20
unconscious, p. 24

Further Readings

Aronson, E. (2003). *The social animal* (9th ed.). New York: Freeman.

Bruer, J. (1999). *The myth of the first three years: A new understanding of early brain development and lifelong learning*. New York: Free Press.

Darwin, C. (1964). *On the origin of species*. Cambridge, MA: Harvard University Press. (Original work published 1859)

Gazzaniga, M. S. (1998). *The mind's past*. Berkeley, CA: University of California Press.

Hothersall, D. (2003). *History of psychology* (4th ed.). Boston, MA: McGraw-Hill.

James, W. (1983). *Principles of psychology*. Cambridge, MA: Harvard University Press. (Original work published 1890)

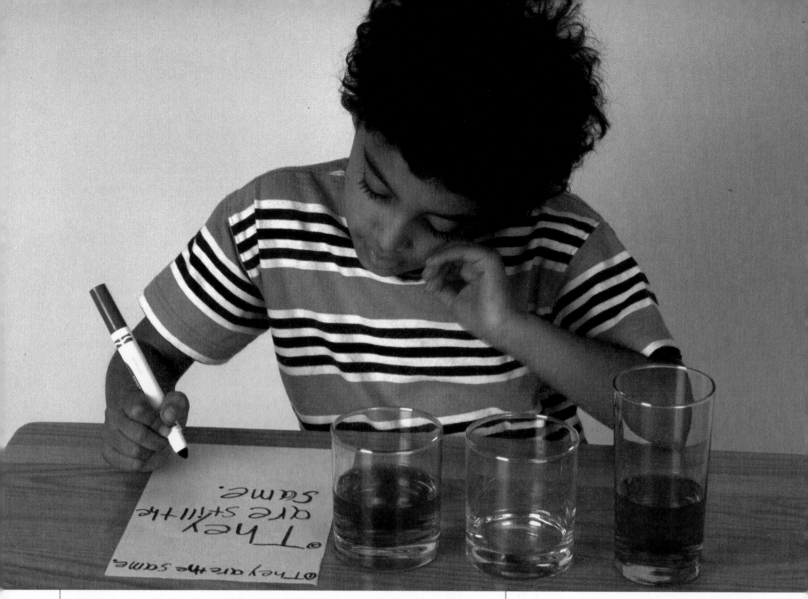

Creative Approaches to Psychological Research

A good theory is one that produces a wide variety of testable hypotheses. In the early twentieth century, psychologist Jean Piaget theorized that cognitive development occurs in a fixed series of "stages" from birth to adolescence. He designed experiments to test his theory. In one such test, similar to the one shown here, children of different ages were asked to compare the volume of equal amounts of liquid poured into different-sized glasses. Piaget found that the responses were consistent within an age group, and only children at a certain age, or "stage," were able to grasp that the volume of liquid in each glass was equal. Studies in psychological science have subsequently shown that some aspects of this theory were wrong.

Research Methodology

In the late 1800s, the Italian physiologist Angelo Mosso began studying the relationship between mind and brain by examining how mental activity affects the flow of blood to the brain. He was working on the assumption that because the brain is the organ responsible for generating thoughts, feelings, and emotions, mental activity should affect how the brain functions. In one interesting experiment, Mosso had his participant lie on a table that was carefully balanced on a fulcrum. Remarkably, as soon as the subject engaged in emotional or intellectual activity, such as being afraid or doing mental arithmetic, the table began to tilt down toward the head! Mosso concluded that because mental activity increases the physiological activity of the brain, the tilt in the table was due to an increase in the amount of blood that was flowing into the subject's brain.

Mosso's experiment was a harbinger of the modern experimental techniques that allow us today to visually image mental activity. For example, by injecting subjects with small doses of radioactively labeled water, scientists

Outlining the Principles

What Is Scientific Inquiry?

- Scientific Questions Can Be Objectively Answered
- The Empirical Process Depends on Theories, Hypotheses, and Research

What Are the Types of Studies in Psychological Research?

- An Experiment Involves Manipulating Conditions
- Correlational Designs Examine How Variables Are Related
- Descriptive Studies Observe and Classify Behavior

What Are the Data-Collection Methods of Psychological Science?

- Observing Is an Unobtrusive Strategy
- Asking Takes a More Active Approach
- Case Studies Examine Individual Lives
- Response Performance Measures Stimulus Processing
- Body and Brain Activity Can Be Directly Measured
- Research with Animals Provides Important Data
- There Are Ethical Issues to Consider

How Are Data Analyzed and Evaluated?

- Good Research Requires Valid, Reliable, and Accurate Data
- Descriptive Statistics Provide a Summary
- Correlations Describe the Relationships between Variables
- Inferential Statistics Predict Chance Results

can now track changes in the flow of blood in the brain during mental tasks, such as trying to remember what you ate for breakfast or looking at a picture of someone who is afraid.

Although dramatic improvements have been made in the research technology since Mosso's table experiment, his study does share many of the goals of modern psychological research. Research always begins with a question that intrigues the researcher, who then designs and conducts a study to answer the question. Whether the study provides a useful answer depends on how well it is designed. In this chapter we will examine the different ways researchers study the questions of psychological science. You will learn the qualities that separate good studies from bad, as well as the types of questions that can be addressed through psychological research. ■

During the last century psychologists have made a number of important discoveries about the mind, brain, and behavior. These discoveries have emerged through careful scientific research. Throughout your life you have observed people and developed your own explanations for why they think and act the way they do. Unfortunately, many commonsense explanations for behavior are either inadequate or flat-out wrong. For example, most people believe that brainstorming leads to creative solutions, that opposites attract, that venting anger is a good idea, that children with low self-esteem are especially aggressive, and that there are shooting streaks in basketball. None of these intuitions is supported by scientific research. In the previous chapter, we noted the importance of using critical thinking, which is a systematic way of scrutinizing evidence to see if it makes sense. A key aspect of critical thinking is maintaining skepticism, which means being wary of subjective beliefs, such as intuition, that can be biased and are often based on limited information. Intuition and hunches help guide scientific questions rather than answers. To answer the questions, scientists use objective, systematic procedures so that they can develop an accurate understanding of the phenomena they study.

So how do psychologists use the methods of science to study behavior? Let's suppose you are concerned about drunk driving. Thus, you decide you want to conduct a study that examines the effects of alcohol on driving skills. You begin with an idea that alcohol probably impairs motor skills and coordination. Thus, you are testing the hypothesis that alcohol affects behavior in a specific way. You then set up a study in which you give people alcohol and measure some behavioral response that you believe is related to driving skill, such as how long they can balance on one leg or how quickly they can respond to a command to press a brake pedal. Basically, you have designed an *experiment* in which you altered, or *manipulated,* the situation in order to see how the change affects mental state or behavior. Of course, you must also mea-

Timeline

CHAPTER 2 | Research Methodology

1861
Neuropsychological Assessment Paul Broca's autopsy of his patient Tan reveals frontal lobe damage, which supports the idea that mental functions are localized in the brain.

1879
Reaction Times Wilhelm Wundt and others at the University of Leipzig use reaction-time measures to study mental processes. These measures assume the time it takes to respond to a stimulus corresponds to the time it takes for mental activity.

1880
Case Studies Josef Breuer, a Viennese physician, treats a young patient who is suffering from a psychological affliction. Sigmund Freud develops many of his ideas about psychoanalysis by analyzing the case of Anna O.

1896
Correlation Coefficient Karl Pearson, an English statistician, builds on Galton's ideas and develops the correlation coefficient, a statistic that measures the degree of association between two variables; it is still widely used in psychological science.

Steps in research	Example
Formulate hypothesis	People who are intoxicated will show less motor coordination than people who have not drunk alcohol.
Design study	Plan an experiment in which you give alcohol to one group and no alcohol to a control group. Alternatively, compare people before and after drinking alcohol.
Collect the data	Give people alcohol and measure motor coordination and balance. Select tasks that are appropriate to collect this information.
Analyze data	Use statistical techniques to assess whether the results are genuine or probably due to chance.
Disseminate the results	Report on the findings in a research journal or at a conference.

2.1 The Methods of Psychological Science
A flowchart showing the normal progression of psychological science.

sure the same behaviors when your research participants have not been drinking to see if the manipulation changed behavior. Alternatively, you could compare your group's behavior after drinking to that of another group of people who did not consume alcohol, known as a *control group.*

Once you have collected the performance information, or *data,* you use *statistical procedures* to assess whether the results you obtained were due to drinking alcohol or simply due to chance. The results of your statistical analysis will provide an answer to your research question, which you can then share with the world. Although this example provides a general overview of scientific research (Figure 2.1), you need to address many important details to make sure your study adequately tests your question.

What Is Scientific Inquiry?

Science assumes that the world works in an orderly fashion based on physical laws: Gravity causes apples to fall to the ground, and the Bernoulli principle explains how aircraft can fly. Although the various fields of science differ somewhat in the particular techniques and strategies they use, all share a general approach known as the *scientific method,* which is an objective examination of the natural world. Scientific

---

1897

First Social Psychology Experiment The first observational study of social behavior is undertaken by Norman Triplett, who discovers that bicycle racers pedal more quickly in the presence of other cyclists than when on their own.

1924

The Electrical Brain Hans Berger records the first electrical signals of the brain from the intact skull of a human. The electroencephalogram is used to measure the activity of the brain during mental processes.

1925

The Foundation of Experimental Design Sir Ronald Fisher publishes *Statistical Methods for Research Workers,* which establishes the foundation for contemporary experimental design.

1933

Testing Hypotheses Jerzy Neyman and Egon Pearson, the son of Karl Pearson, detail the central concepts behind statistical hypothesis testing in a paper presented to the Cambridge Philosophical Society.

1950S

Recording Individual Neurons Experimenting on cats, David Hubel and Torsten Wiesel make the first recordings from individual neurons in the cerebral cortex.

inquiry has four basic goals, which correspond to describing *what* happens, *when* it happens, *what causes* it to happen, and *why* it happens.

Let's apply these goals to the study of alcohol intoxication. The first goal of science is *description* (what), which asks, what is the behavior? The description stage leads us to make observations in a systematic fashion. For instance, a scientist interested in alcohol intoxication might watch restaurant patrons to see whether they consume alcohol. The second goal is *prediction* (when), which asks when the behavior occurs. Observation can reveal that two events tend to happen together, which means that one can be used to predict the occurrence of the other. A researcher might find that people who drink alcohol tend to stumble, have impaired language, and show poor social judgment. Thus, the researcher might predict that drinking alcohol is associated with those behaviors. The third goal of science is *causal control* (what causes), which involves systematically varying the situation to produce a change in behavior or mental state. Scientists seek cause-effect relationships between variables. Thus, the researcher interested in intoxication might provide people with alcohol or tonic water to see if they produce different effects. The final goal of science is *explanation* (why), understanding why something happens. For instance, do people act the way they do because of the physiological effects of alcohol or because of their beliefs about the effects of alcohol? Fully understanding a phenomenon requires examining it at many different levels of analysis, which is the essence of scientific inquiry.

Scientific Questions Can Be Objectively Answered

What defines an empirical question?

Scientific inquiry is the study of empirical questions—questions that can be answered by observing and measuring the world around us. Can some psychics communicate with the dead? Well, perhaps, but this is impossible to study because it would require the ability to assess what dead people were saying, assuming that dead people can speak, which itself is impossible to investigate using the methods of science. Does alcohol impair the ability to drive? This is a question that can be answered by measurement. And the answer is yes: A review of 112 studies found that the skills necessary to drive a car can become impaired after people consume even small amounts of alcohol (Moskowitz & Fiorentino, 2000). The key point is that scientific questions are those that can be tested and either confirmed or shown to be false. The answer to an empirical question does not depend on what the respondent or scientist *thinks* about the question. Whether a researcher believes that consuming alcohol is a good or bad thing is irrelevant.

replication Repetition of an experiment to confirm the results.

Because empirical questions can be answered by objective means, the same answer should be attained by any and all individuals willing to take the trouble, at least in theory. That is, studies that are properly designed and conducted can be repeated, by the same researcher or by others, and produce the same findings. **Replication**, in

CHAPTER 2 | Research Methodology

1960s	1969	1970s	1986	1990s
Experimenter Expectancy Robert Rosenthal shows that the outcome of an experiment can be influenced by the researcher's beliefs or expectancies, and others develop techniques to minimize bias in research.	**Identifying Cognitive Operations** Saul Sternberg updates how to use reaction-time measures to infer the sequence of cognitive processing stages employed during a task, laying the groundwork for human brain-mapping techniques.	**Understanding Relationships** Elaine Hatfield and Ellen Berscheid pioneer the scientific study of love. Their research provides important insights into the study of interpersonal relationships.	**Brain Imaging** Peter Fox and others lay out the theoretical foundation for tracking changes in blood flow in the brain. This leads to the development of brain-imaging technologies that associate brain regions with specific mental processes.	**Gene Manipulation** Methods are rapidly developed that allow researchers to delete (knock out) or substitute (knock in) genes with great specificity. These techniques provide experimental methods for determining how genes influence psychological processes such as learning and memory.

pecially if friends or family report that the person was different before the brain damage, the lack of control over the situation makes it difficult to draw firm conclusions. For instance, in 1966 a man named Charles Whitman climbed a tower at the University of Texas and began firing a rifle at passersby, killing 14 and wounding many more in a 90-minute spree. The night before, he had killed his wife and mother and had composed a letter trying to explain his actions. His case history, including his visits to a psychiatrist and the letter he wrote, indicate that Whitman might have had a brain tumor, and an autopsy did turn up evidence consistent with this assessment. But was a brain tumor responsible for Whitman's murderous actions? We will never know.

Profiles in Psychological Science

What Makes Killers Kill?

The subjective nature of case studies means that we need to be cautious in deciding how to interpret them. One of the hallmarks of critical thinking is to avoid relying on anecdotal cases that seem to prove a point, such as when someone proclaims, "I know smoking doesn't cause cancer because my uncle smokes and he is still alive." Anecdotal cases can be exceptions to general rules of behavior and therefore must be critically examined. However, if you have a good theory and can accumulate evidence from multiple case studies, then the conclusions that are drawn are more persuasive. Let's look at how such an approach was used to test a novel hypothesis about why people become murderers.

Lee Boyd Malvo was 17 years old when he began killing people. His participation in the 2002 Washington-area sniper killings came as a tremendous surprise to teachers and school officials who had known him years earlier and described him as a polite, hard-working, and intelligent student. Indeed, his grade-school teacher Beverly Clark described his personality as striking: "You look at the kid and you know he's cut out to be something great in life" (Kovaleski & Sheridan, 2003, p. C.01). How did this religious and studious young boy become a mass murderer?

In May 1998, Kip Kinkel shot and killed his parents. Earlier in the day, the 15-year-old had been arrested for purchasing a stolen gun at school. His father picked him up at the police station and then berated Kip for bringing shame on the family. A few hours later, Kip approached his father from behind in the kitchen and shot him in the head, using one of the father's many guns. He then waited two hours for his mother to come home, at which point he shot her repeatedly: "I shot her again so she wouldn't know that I killed her. . . . I loved my mom." The next morning he walked into the cafeteria at Thurston High School in Springfield, Oregon, and sprayed the room with semi-automatic gunfire, killing two students and wounding 25 others.

According to the neurologist Jonathan Pincus, both Malvo and Kinkel are typical of murderers, albeit younger than most (Figure 2.6). Pincus has examined more than 150 murderers, including Kinkel, and has found a combination of early childhood abuse, psychiatric disorders such as paranoia, and frontal-lobe dysfunction in more than 90 percent of these violent killers. None of these problems appears to be sufficient on its own, but when all three combine in an individual, serious trouble often results. Kinkel fits this pattern well. His parents were verbally abusive, and he displayed many mental health problems, such as depression and paranoid thoughts; apparently he heard voices telling him he was worthless. These same voices

2.6 Lee Boyd Malvo and Kip Kinkel
Psychologists think that immature brain development, in combination with other factors, contributes to violent behavior. Lee Boyd Malvo and Kip Kinkel were both convicted of murder in their teens.

commanded him to kill his parents and shoot at students in his school. Importantly, brain imaging showed evidence of abnormalities in several brain regions, especially the frontal lobes. This is relevant because the frontal lobes are crucial in helping people inhibit their impulses and control their behavior. The cause of Kinkel's abnormalities is not known, but the consequences of having impaired frontal lobes have been well established in psychological research.

The immaturity of frontal lobes in adolescent killers raises perplexing policy issues regarding punishment; should they be treated as adults or as children? The psychologist Lawrence Steinberg and his colleagues (e.g., Steinberg & Scott, 2003) argue that adolescent cognitive capacities for self-control and decision making are not fully developed and lessen the extent to which adolescents can be held responsible for criminal behaviors. Making plans or decisions, thinking about their consequences, controlling impulses, and resisting social pressure all are functions of the frontal lobes. Although scientists once believed that the frontal lobes were pretty well developed in early childhood, overwhelming evidence from the past decade has established that frontal brain regions continue to develop well into early adulthood (Giedd, 2004). This means that adolescents are typically more impulsive and more easily influenced by others than are adults. Indeed, although laboratory research indicates that adolescents perform adequately on decision-making tasks, even comparable to adults, the sterile lab environment does not reflect the real world. This is especially true in situations in which crimes are committed, when decisions are made under great emotional arousal and are often accompanied by strong pressure from peers or accomplices. There is considerable evidence that Lee Malvo was coerced, even brainwashed by his father figure, John Allen Muhammad. Malvo's lawyer based his closing argument on psychological evidence suggesting that immature brain development makes adolescents less culpable for their crimes. The jury apparently was persuaded by this science, since it did not impose the death penalty, as another jury had for the older Muhammad. ■

Response Performance Measures Stimulus Processing

In Chapter 1 we noted that Wilhelm Wundt established the first laboratory in psychology in 1874. Wundt and his students pioneered many of the methods for studying how the mind works by examining how people respond on psychological tasks. The typical goal of measuring **response performance** is to quantify how a perceptual or cognitive process responds to a specific stimulus. Specifically, researchers infer how a stimulus is processed from how a person responds to it. Response performance is quantified in three basic ways. First, a researcher can measure **reaction time**, the speed of a response—which has been the workhorse method of cognitive psychology. The interpretation of reaction times is based on the idea that processing in the brain

response performance A research method in which researchers quantify perceptual or cognitive processes in response to a specific stimulus.

reaction time A quantification of performance behavior that measures the speed of a response.

red blue green red blue yellow red blue

blue red green yellow red blue green red

green yellow red yellow blue red green blue

2.7 The Stroop Effect Quickly name the color of ink that each of these words is printed in. Name the color for each word in the row as quickly as you can. Notice how it took you longer to name the colors for the last row. This is called the Stroop effect, in which it takes longer to name the color of words printed in conflicting colors. The interference from your automatic reading of the word slows you down.

takes time; the more processing a stimulus requires, the longer the reaction time to that stimulus will be. By manipulating what a subject has to do with a stimulus and measuring reaction times, researchers can gain much information regarding the different operations involved in stimulus processing. For example, suppose you have a theory that it takes longer to determine the shape of an object than it does to determine its size. Your theory generates the hypothesis that reaction times should be longer when people are asked to discriminate the shape of an object compared with when they have to discriminate the size of the object. Why? The assumption is that the longer the process takes, the longer the corresponding reaction time will be. An example of a reaction-time task is presented in Figure 2.7.

Researchers can also measure *response accuracy,* which usually concerns how well a stimulus was perceived. For example, does paying attention to a stimulus actually improve its perception? One way to study this in the visual domain would be to ask participants to pay attention to just one side of a computer screen while keeping their eyes focused on the center of the screen. We can then present a stimulus requiring a discrimination response (to a question such as, Was the shape a hexagon or an octagon?) to either the attended or the unattended side of the screen. If the accuracy of responses is greater for stimuli presented on the attended side, then the implication is that attention is improving the perception of the stimulus.

Finally, researchers can measure response performance by asking people to make *stimulus judgments* regarding the different stimuli with which they are presented. Typical examples would be asking subjects to indicate whether a faint stimulus was noticed, or asking them to compare two objects and judge whether they are the same on some parameter, such as color, size, or shape (Figure 2.8). The benefit of using response performance as a methodology is that it can be a relatively simple way to study cognition and perception.

2.8 Stimulus Judgments A common method for studying questions at the cognitive/perceptual level is to ask participants to make judgments about stimuli. In this case, the participant is required to decide whether the two letters on the screen are the same or different.

Body and Brain Activity Can Be Directly Measured

The activity of the body and the brain can be directly measured in different ways. For instance, it is now well established that certain emotional states influence the body in predictable ways. When people are frightened their muscles become tense, and their hearts start beating faster. Other bodily systems influenced by mood and mental states include blood pressure, blood temperature, rate of perspiration, pupil size, breathing rates, and so on. These various measures are examples of **psychophysiological assessment**, in which researchers examine how changes in bodily functions are associated with behavior or mental state. For example, police investigators often use *polygraphs,* popularly known as lie detectors, which assess these bodily states, under the assumption that people who are lying are experiencing more arousal and therefore are more likely to show physical signs of stress. It should be noted that the correspondence between bodily response and mental state is not perfect. For instance, some stressful events lead to increased heart rate whereas others

psychophysiological assessment A research method that examines how changes in bodily functions are associated with behavior or mental state.

lead to reduced heart rate. Nonetheless, these methods allow researchers to study bodily responses that circumvent the problems inherent in self-report, such as people being unwilling or unable to report on their thoughts or feelings.

ELECTROPHYSIOLOGY **Electrophysiology** is a method of data collection that measures electrical activity in the brain to see how it is related to cognitive and perceptual tasks. A researcher fits electrodes onto the participant's scalp; they act almost like small microphones to pick up the electrical activity of the brain (Figure 2.9). The device that measures brain activity is an *electroencephalogram,* or *EEG,* which provides a record of overall brain activity. This method is useful because different behavioral states produce predictable EEG patterns. As we will explore in Chapter 4, the EEG shows specific and consistent patterns as people fall asleep, and it reveals that the brain is very active even when the body is at rest, especially during dreams. As a measure of specific cognitive states, the EEG is limited because the recordings reflect all brain activity and therefore are too noisy to isolate specific responses to particular stimuli. A more powerful method of examining how brain activity changes in response to a specific stimulus involves conducting many trials and averaging across the trials. Researchers are thus able to observe patterns associated with specific events, hence the name *event-related potential* or *ERP.* The real advantage of the EEG and the ERP is not that they provide information about *where* in the brain an electrical event comes from, but that they determine exactly *when* it happens. They provide maps of approximate origins of various electrical signals and give insight into how the brain processes information on the basis of which regions are activated and when.

Electrophysiological measures can be used with other methods to assess complex behaviors, such as drinking and driving. Working across levels of analysis, researchers have measured EEGs and ERPs in relatives of alcoholics and found that their brain responses appear to be muted overall (Bierut et al., 2002). Interestingly, the researchers have linked these brain responses to genes that are believed to predispose people to alcoholism. Over the past decade, researchers have made significant advances in the use of genetic methods to predict alcoholism, and although there is unlikely to be a specific gene, we now have compelling evidence that many

electrophysiology A method of data collection that measures electrical activity in the brain.

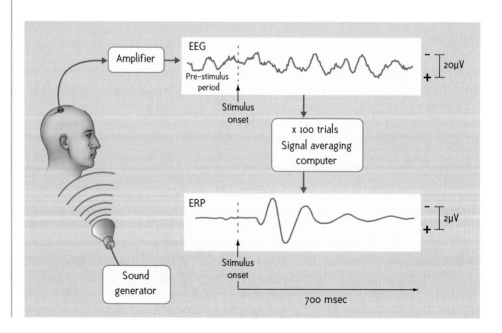

2.9 Measuring the Brain's Electrical Activity The relatively small electrical responses to specific events can be observed only by averaging the EEG traces over a series of trials. The large background oscillations of the EEG trace make it impossible to detect the evoked response to the sensory stimulus from a single trial. However, averaging across tens or hundreds of trials removes the background EEG and leaves the event-related potential (called ERP).

CHAPTER 2 | Research Methodology

aspects of alcoholism have a strong genetic component. For instance, evidence indicates that children of alcoholics report needing to consume much greater quantities of alcohol than most people before feeling alcohol's effects and are therefore much more likely to report drinking large amounts of alcohol (Schuckit et al., 2001). In cases of drunk driving, some individuals may consume large amounts of alcohol to obtain subjective effects, and these large amounts of alcohol may interfere with their motor skills and reaction times without their awareness. This suggests that some individuals may fail to notice that they are impaired in their motor and cognitive abilities because they do not feel as though alcohol has had much effect.

BRAIN IMAGING The electrical activity of the brain is associated with changes in the flow of blood as it carries oxygen and nutrients to the active brain regions. Brain-imaging methods measure such changes in the flow, and by keeping track of these changes, researchers can monitor which brain areas are active during a study. Imaging is a powerful tool for uncovering where different systems reside in the brain and the manner in which different brain areas interact in order to process information. For example, research has shown that certain brain regions become active whenever people look at pictures of faces, whereas other brain regions are active when people try to understand what other people are thinking. In another example of drinking and driving, one study found that alcohol leads to a one-third reduction in activity in areas of the brain concerned with vision, which suggests that alcohol may impair drivers by directly affecting their sight (Levin et al., 1998). We will discuss the two major imaging technologies.

Positron emission tomography, or **PET**, was developed in the late 1980s. It is the computer-aided reconstruction of the brain's metabolic activity through the use of a relatively harmless radioactive substance injected into the bloodstream. The research participant lies in a special scanner that detects the radiation, and a three-dimensional map of the density of radioactivity within the participant's brain is produced (Figure 2.10). This map is useful because as the brain performs a mental task, blood flow increases to the most active regions, leading to more emitted radiation. The amount of radioactivity emitted by a brain region roughly corresponds to the amount of electrical activity in the local neurons. By scanning participants as they perform some psychological task (for example, looking at pictures of faces expressing fear), researchers obtain a map of brain metabolic activity during the task. However, since the entire brain is extremely metabolically active all of the time, scans must also be made while the participant performs another, closely related task (for example, looking at pictures of faces with neutral expressions). By subtracting one image from the other, experimenters obtain a "difference image" of which brain regions are most active during the task in question. In this way, regions of the brain can be correlated with specific mental activities.

positron emission tomography (PET) A method of brain imaging that assesses metabolic activity by using a radioactive substance injected into the bloodstream.

2.10 Positron Emission Tomography (PET) A PET scan of blood flow in a subject's brain under different conditions.

2.11 Magnetic Resonance Imaging (MRI)
MRI provides very high quality images of intact human brains.

Magnetic resonance imaging, or **MRI**, is the newest and perhaps most powerful of imaging techniques. It relies on the fact that protons contained in hydrogen, a major component of water and fat, behave like tiny magnets. In MRI, which is not dangerous, a research participant lies in a scanner that produces a powerful magnetic field. The field causes the protons in the participant's brain to line up with it, just as a magnetized needle turns to point north. Radio waves are then sent through the magnetic field and cause the protons to briefly align to a different orientation. As they return to the direction of the MRI magnetic field, energy is released in a form that can be measured by detectors surrounding the head. Since the protons in fat and water release this energy differently, researchers can discriminate between them, which results in a high-resolution image of the brain (Figure 2.11).

MRI images are extraordinarily valuable for determining the location of brain damage, for example, but they can be even more profitable when used to create an image of the working brain. This is what **functional magnetic resonance imaging**, or **fMRI**, can do; like PET, it makes use of the brain's blood flow to map its activity, scanning the participant during the performance of several tasks. Whereas PET works by measuring the flow of blood directly, fMRI works by assessing changes in the oxygen level of blood, which is an indirect measure of blood flow. In all brain-imaging methods, including fMRI, the tasks used should differ in only one way, which reflects the particular mental function of interest. The images are then compared to examine differences in blood flow and therefore brain activity (Figure 2.12).

The value of measuring brain activity is that clear links can be made between actual activity in the brain and aspects of personality, social behavior, cognition, and the like. Thus, many different types of researchers are now using brain imaging. For instance, both cognitive and social psychologists have used fMRI to study how people interpret facial expressions. Brain imaging is also widely used to help diagnose psychological disorders, especially those that may result from brain injury or disease. However, research in this domain can be prohibitively expensive—the cost of imaging machines, their upkeep, and their attendant personnel runs in the millions of dollars.

magnetic resonance imaging (MRI) A method of brain imaging that produces high-quality images of the brain.

functional magnetic resonance imaging (fMRI) An imaging technique used to examine changes in the activity of the working human brain.

Research with Animals Provides Important Data

Throughout the history of psychological science, many of the most important research findings have been obtained by studying the behavior of animals. For instance, watching animals—usually rats—run through mazes or press levers to earn rewards led to the development of many of the principles of learning. Indeed, Pavlov's observation of a salivating dog inspired John B. Watson to launch the behaviorist movement

2.12 Functional Magnetic Resonance Imaging (fMRI)
Activity maps showing changes in blood oxygenation, obtained by fMRI while the subject performed a task (and subtracted from another "control" image), superimposed on higher-resolution MRI images taken of the same brain. This procedure allows precise determination of which brain areas are active during different mental activities.

(see Chapter 6). One of the central assumptions underlying Watson's behaviorism was that humans are subject to the same laws of nature as other animals. Although the behaviors displayed by humans might seem more complex than those of rats, the forces that control the behaviors of rats and humans are in many ways the same.

Besides in learning studies, animals have also been used in research that examines the physiological basis of behavior. For example, psychological scientists manipulate levels of a certain chemical in the brain or body and then observe the effects on behavior. Another method involves selectively removing specific brain regions and observing whether behavior is impaired. Researchers also use electrophysiological methods to measure the activity of single neurons in the brains of animals. This method has helped us begin to uncover the different kinds of information single neurons code in different parts of the brain, something that can't be done by recording from the scalp. Recall the study by Hubel and Wiesel in which the stuck slide led to the serendipitous finding that cells in a cat's primary visual cortex respond to moving lines. Without the ability to measure directly the activity of single neurons in animals, the questions raised by Hubel and Wiesel could not have been answered.

Psychological scientists working at the biological level of analysis manipulate genes directly to examine their effects on behavior. For instance, *transgenetic* mice are produced by inserting or manipulating the genes in a developing embryo, for example, by inserting strands of foreign DNA. The inserted gene is integrated into every cell of the body. As you will read in greater detail in Chapter 3, specific natural genes can also be targeted for genetic manipulations. Researchers can delete genes to eliminate their effects or replace genes in other locations to enhance their effects.

These genes are known respectively as *knock-outs* or *knock-ins*. There has been rapid growth in the use of transgenetic and knock-out/knock-in models to study psychological activity, with the hope that these methods will help in the development of new therapies for psychological disorders.

There Are Ethical Issues to Consider

When scientists select a method of research, it is imperative that they make decisions with full knowledge of the ethical issues involved. Are the participants being asked to do something unreasonable? Is there a risk of physical or emotional harm from the study? Some ethical concerns are specific to the kind of method used, while other concerns apply across all methods. Therefore, to ensure the well-being of study participants, all colleges and universities have strict guidelines in place regarding both human- and animal-based research. **Institutional Review Boards (IRBs)** consisting of trained scholars, administrators, and legal advisers are given the task of reviewing proposed research to ensure that it meets the accepted standards of science.

One of the more prominent ethical concerns with research is the reasonable expectation of *privacy*. If behavior is going to be observed, is it okay to observe people without their knowledge? This question obviously depends on what sorts of behaviors one might be looking at. If the behaviors occur in public, then the concerns may be less than if one is interested in behaviors that are considered more private. For example, it would be okay to observe the behavior of couples saying good-bye in an airport, as this is a public place, but it would be inappropriate to examine the private mating behaviors of couples—at least without their knowledge. The concern over privacy is compounded by the growing technology available for remotely monitoring people. Although someone might like to compare the behavior of men and women in public bathrooms, would it be okay to install a discreet video camera to monitor people in restrooms? Likely not.

When asking people for information, are there topics that should not be raised because they may be insensitive or inappropriate? For example, many researchers would like to understand how physical and emotional trauma affect people in the months and years after a traumatic event. Although exploring such issues is necessary to develop strategies for overcoming anguishing and difficult experiences, researchers exploring such topics must *always* remain sensitive to how their line of questioning is affecting the individuals they are studying.

No matter what kind of method is employed, it is critical to consider who will have access to the data that have been collected. Participant *confidentiality* should always be carefully guarded so that personal information is not publicly linked to the behavioral findings of the study. Often the quality and accuracy of data directly depend on how confident the subjects are that their responses will be kept confidential, especially when emotionally or legally sensitive topics are involved. For extremely sensitive topics, it is preferable that the participants' responses be anonymous.

INFORMED CONSENT Research with human participants is a partnership based on mutual respect and trust. People who volunteer for psychological research, whether compensated or not, have the right to know what will happen to them during the course of the study. Ethical standards require providing people with all relevant information that would affect their willingness to become partici-

---

How do ethical issues constrain psychological research?

Institutional Review Boards (IRBs) Groups of people responsible for reviewing proposed research to ensure that it meets the accepted standards of science and provides for the physical and emotional well-being of research participants.

pants. This **informed consent** means that participants make a knowledgeable decision to participate. Typically, informed consent is obtained in writing; in the case of observational studies of public behavior, to protect privacy, individuals are treated anonymously. Minors, the intellectually incapacitated, and the mentally ill cannot legally provide informed consent, and therefore the permission of a legal guardian is necessary.

It is not always possible to inform participants fully about details of a study. Sometimes researchers must use *deception,* which involves either misleading participants about the goals of the study or not fully revealing what will take place, because knowing the specific goals of the study may alter the participants' behavior, thereby rendering the results meaningless. Deception is used only when other methods are not appropriate, when the goals of the research are important, or when the deception does not involve situations that would strongly affect the people's willingness to participate. If deception is used, a careful *debriefing,* or explanation of the study after its completion, must take place to fully inform participants of the goals of the study and the need for deception, and to eliminate or counteract any negative effects produced by the deception.

informed consent A process in which people are given full information about a study, which allows them to make a knowledgeable decision about whether to participate.

RELATIVE RISKS OF PARTICIPATION Another ethical issue is the *relative risk* to mental or physical health. Researchers must always be aware of what they are asking participants to do in the name of data collection. People cannot be asked to endure unreasonable amounts of pain or discomfort, either from stimuli or from the manner in which data measurements are taken. Fortunately, in the vast majority of research being conducted, these types of concerns are not an issue. However, although risk is low, researchers have to think carefully about the potential for risk to specific participants. For example, fMRI involves placing participants in powerful magnetic fields. As a result, participants must be carefully screened to ensure they have no metal in or on their bodies, even if it's only a tattoo with metal-based inks. Again, it is important to note that all research now conducted at colleges and universities must be approved by an IRB that is familiar with the various rules and regulations that protect research participants from possible physical or psychological harm. Most IRBs look at the relative trade-off between risk and benefit. There is much to be gained from the scientific enterprise, and sometimes it requires asking participants to expose themselves to some risk in order to obtain important findings. The *risk-benefit ratio* asks whether the research is important enough to warrant placing participants at risk. Poorly designed studies have little benefit to science, and therefore no element of risk is justified by them. Thus, scientists have an ethical obligation to conduct carefully designed research.

RESEARCH WITH ANIMALS Many of the major medical and scientific discoveries of the past century have involved the use of animals as research subjects. The use of animals allows researchers to examine biological mechanisms that cannot be studied in humans. Obviously, animal research should be undertaken only when the potential benefits outweigh the costs and when the studies are well designed. In addition, researchers have a responsibility to treat the animals as humanely as possible. Indeed, government regulations require a careful monitoring of animals used in research, and potential animal studies are screened for problems before they are conducted. Fortunately, the majority of those who conduct animal research are compassionate and do their best to minimize stress or discomfort in the animals they study.

REVIEWING

the Principles | What Are the Data-Collection Methods of Psychological Science?

There are five basic data-collection methods in psychological science; the choice of which to use is generally dictated by the research question. First, we can observe behavior as it is taking place and either write down general descriptions of the behaviors or check off a tally sheet of prespecified behavior categories. Second, we can ask people for information about their thoughts, feelings, and preferences by using surveys, questionnaires, interviews, and self-reports. Third, we can measure how quickly and accurately people respond to a stimulus. Fourth, we can directly measure electrical activity and blood flow in the brain, techniques that are increasingly being combined with the other three methods. Finally, researchers can use animal models in which genes, neurochemicals, or brain structures are altered to study the effects on behavior. Regardless of the method chosen, it is essential always to consider the ethical consequences associated with the method of data collection; attention must be given to the relative risks and benefits associated with the study.

How Are Data Analyzed and Evaluated?

How do we ensure that our measurements are accurate?

Up to this point, we have examined the essential elements of scientific inquiry in psychology. In particular, we have examined how to frame an empirical question within the realm of theories, hypotheses, and research; discussed what type of study to run; and looked at the different methods of collecting data. This section focuses more closely on the issue of data, such as the characteristics that make for good data and the statistical procedures that are used to analyze them.

Good Research Requires Valid, Reliable, and Accurate Data

If data are to properly answer a hypothesis, they must actually address it. **Validity** refers to whether the data you collect address your question; valid data provide clear and unambiguous information from which to evaluate the theory or hypothesis. Suppose a theory predicts that children who are physically abused by their parents are more likely than nonabused children to use drugs in high school. The obvious hypothesis generated by this theory is that if we compare the childhoods of high school drug users and non–drug users, we should find that a greater percentage of the drug users were abused by their parents. In this case, examining the medical records of all the students might be one way to document whether abuse had occurred. Regardless of whether the hypothesis is supported, the data would be considered valid on the reasonable assumption that in children, abuse often leads to suspicious medical problems. The key here is that the validity of data depends on the question being studied. Data that might be invalid for one question may be perfectly valid for a different question.

validity The extent to which the data collected address the research hypothesis in the way intended.

reliability The extent to which a measure is stable and consistent over time in similar conditions.

Another important aspect of data is **reliability**, or the stability and consistency of a measure over time. If the measurement is reliable, the data collected will not vary because of changes over time in the measurement device. Suppose that you have a theory that people in their twenties are more likely to channel surf than are people in their fifties. To test your theory you would need to study television-watching behavior and, in particular, the average length of time people stay tuned to each station. One option for measuring the duration of each channel stay would be to have an observer use a handheld stopwatch. However, there will likely be some variability in when the stopwatch is started and stopped, relative to when the surfer actually changes channels. As a consequence, the data in this scenario would be relatively unreliable in comparison to data collected by a computer that was linked to the television remote.

A third and final characteristic of good data is **accuracy**, or the extent to which the measure is free from *error*. While this may seem obvious, the problem is that although a measure may be both valid and reliable, this does not guarantee that the measure is *accurate*. The way psychological scientists think about this problem is by turning it on its head and asking, How do errors creep into a measure? There are two basic types of error, *random* and *systematic*. Take the channel-surfing study. The problem with using a stopwatch to measure the duration of each channel stay is that each measurement will tend to either overestimate or underestimate the actual duration (because of human error). This is known as a *random error,* because although an error is introduced into each measurement, the actual value of the error is different each time. But suppose that the stopwatch has a glitch, such that it always overstates the actual time measured by two seconds. This is known as a *systematic error,* because the amount of error introduced into each measure is a constant. Generally, systematic error is more problematic than random error because the latter tends to average out over time and therefore is less likely to lead to inaccurate results (Figure 2.13).

What kinds of statistics are used to analyze data?

accuracy The extent to which an experimental measure is free from error.

Actual correct time

Random error: notice that the final average is correct

Systematic error: notice that the final average is incorrect

2.13 Systematic versus Random Errors
Systematic errors occur when the measurement has the same degree of error on each occasion, whereas random errors occur when the degree of error varies each time.

central tendency A measure that represents the typical behavior of the group as a whole.

mean A measure of central tendency that is the arithmetic average of a set of numbers.

median A measure of central tendency that is the value in a set of numbers that falls exactly in the halfway point between the lowest and highest values.

mode A measure of central tendency that is the most frequent score or value in a set of numbers.

variability In a set of numbers, how widely dispersed the values are from each other and from the mean.

standard deviation A statistical measure of how far away each value is on average from the mean.

Descriptive Statistics Provide a Summary

The first step in evaluating data is simply to inspect the raw values. This allows researchers to familiarize themselves with the data and to detect possible errors in data recording. For instance, you would assess whether any of the responses seemed especially unlikely, such as finding someone with a blood alcohol content of 50 percent. Once you are satisfied that the data make sense, you summarize the basic patterns using *descriptive statistics,* which provide an overall sense of the results of the study, such as how people performed in one condition compared to another. The simplest descriptive statistic is the **central tendency**, which is a single value that describes a typical response, or the behavior of the group as a whole. Perhaps the most intuitive measure of central tendency is the **mean**, which is the arithmetic average of a set of numbers. The class average on an exam is an example of a mean score. Consider the hypothetical study of alcohol and driving performance. A basic way to summarize the data would be to calculate the mean driving performance across all participants for when they were (1) sober and (2) intoxicated. If alcohol affects driving, then we would expect to see a difference in the mean between sober and intoxicated driving performance.

A second measure of central tendency is the **median**, which is the value in a set of numbers that falls exactly halfway between the lowest and highest values. For instance, if you received the median score on a test, then half the people in your class scored lower than you and half the people in the class scored higher. Sometimes researchers will summarize data using a median instead of a mean because if one or two numbers in the set are dramatically larger or smaller than all the others, the mean will give either an inflated or deflated summary of the actual "average." This occurs when we try to examine average income. Perhaps only 50 percent of Americans make more than $30,000 per year, but some make so much more that the *mean* income is much higher. The median provides a better estimate of how much money the average person makes.

A third measure of central tendency encountered in psychological research is the **mode**, or the most frequent score or value in a set of numbers. For instance, the modal number of children in a family is two, which means that most families have two children. Examples of all three central tendency measures are shown in Figure 2.14.

In addition to measures of central tendency, another important characteristic of data is the **variability** in a set of numbers, or how widely dispersed the values are about the mean. For instance, the *range* tells you the distance between the largest and smallest value, which is often not of much use because it only uses two scores. The most common measure of variability is the **standard deviation**, which refers to how far away each value is, on average, from the mean. For instance, if the mean of an exam is 75 percent and the standard deviation is 5, this tells you that most people scored between 70 and 80 percent on the exam.

Number of children in 31 selected families

0 0 0 0 1 1 1 1 1 1 2 2 2 2 2 2 2 2 2 2 3 3 3 3 3 4 4 5 6 8 9

Total children in the sample = 77

Mean = 77/31 = 2.48
Median = 2
Mode = 2

2.14 Central Tendency Measures The mean, median, and mode are different measures of central tendency; each reveals important information on a set of numbers. The graph here shows that for some data sets, all three measures can be the same; however, for other data sets, the values may be quite different.

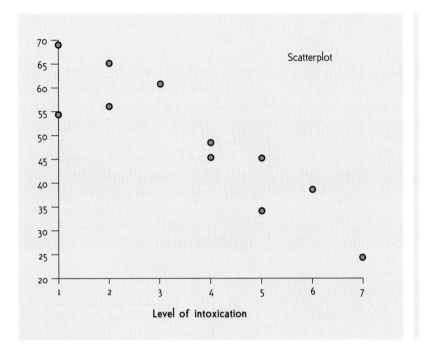

Level of intoxication

2.15 Scatterplots Scatterplots illustrate the relationship between two variables. Note that it appears that the more intoxicated people are, the fewer seconds they can maintain their balance.

Correlations Describe the Relationships between Variables

The descriptive statistics discussed thus far pertain to summarizing the central tendency and variability in a set of numbers. Descriptive statistics can also be used to summarize how two variables relate to each other. As shown in Figure 2.15, the first step in comparing two variables is to create a graph known as a *scatterplot,* which provides a convenient picture of the data. A scatterplot represents each participant's measure on two different variables—in this case, the level of intoxication—on an eight-point scale (with higher numbers meaning more intoxicated) and the ability to balance on one leg as measured in seconds. By looking at the scatterplot we can determine that the people who were more intoxicated also were less able to maintain balance.

In analyzing the relationship between two dependent variables, researchers are not limited to creating a scatterplot. They can also compute a **correlation**, which is a descriptive statistic that provides a numerical value (between +1.0 and −1.0) indicating the strength of the relationship between two variables. If two variables have a strong relationship, knowing how people measure on one variable becomes a good predictor of how they might measure on the other variable.

What signifies a strong relationship? Consider the different scatterplots in Figure 2.16 (on p. 66). Two variables have a *negative correlation*: as one *increases* in value, the other *decreases* in value. For example, as people become more intoxicated, they are less able to balance on one foot. In terms of values, a correlation of −1.0 indicates a perfect negative correlation. Two variables can also have a *positive correlation,* in which the variables increase or decrease together—for example, taller people often weigh more than shorter people. In this case, the correlation is positive, and a perfect positive correlation is indicated by a value of +1.0. If two variables show no apparent relationship, then the value of the correlation will be a number close to zero.

correlation A statistical procedure that provides a numerical value, between +1 and −1, indicating the strength and direction of the relation between two variables.

"I think you should be more explicit here in step two."

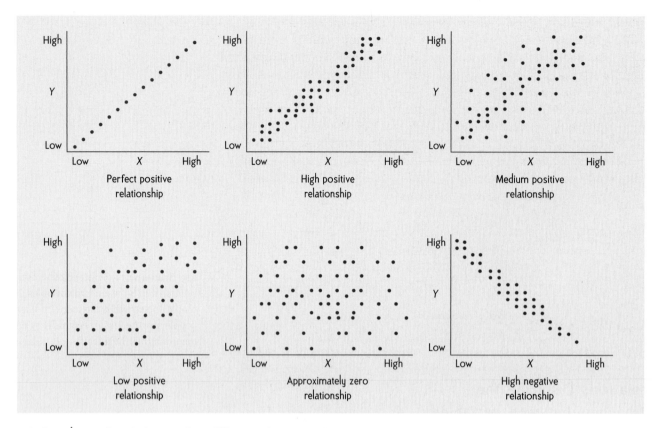

2.16 Correlation Correlations can have different values, which in turn reveal different kinds of relationships between two variables. The greater the scatter of values, the lower the correlation. A perfect correlation occurs when all of the values fall on a straight line.

Inferential Statistics Predict Chance Results

Whereas researchers use descriptive statistics to summarize data sets, they use **inferential statistics** to decide whether differences actually exist between different sets of numbers. For instance, suppose you find that the mean driving performance for intoxicated drivers is lower than the mean driving performance for sober drivers. How different do these two means need to be in order for you to conclude that drinking alcohol does in fact reduce people's ability to drive?

To answer this kind of question, you can use inferential statistics to compute the probability that a difference between means was actually due to chance rather than a causal effect of one variable on another. How does this work? Pretend for a moment that intoxication doesn't influence driving performance. Even so, if you go out and measure the driving performance of sober and drunken drivers, just by chance there will be some degree of variability in the mean performance of the two groups. Most of the time the difference in means will be small, but sometimes the difference may happen to be large. The key is that if alcohol does not actually affect driving performance, then the *probability* of showing a large difference between the two means is relatively small. The principle is the same as for how many heads are obtained when flipping a coin ten times: on average, the number will usually be five or close to it, but every now and then we may get either no heads or ten heads, just by chance.

Therefore, when you are comparing two means, inferential statistics tell you how probable the outcome would be if in fact there were no actual difference between the variables measured. If the probability is small enough, then you can feel reasonably certain that your result was more likely due to an actual difference (or an effect of one variable on another) rather than due simply to chance. How small is small enough? Although the question has long been contentious, a 5 percent chance of concluding there is a difference, when there is really not, tends to be the most liberal value encountered in psychological research. Regardless, the critical thing when deciding to use inferential statistics is to determine beforehand what probability level will be accepted as "small enough." If the results of the study fall below this predetermined probability value, then the difference in means can be labeled as *statistically significant.* If not, the alternative is to report the effect as *nonsignificant,* meaning that the observed difference is likely due to chance.

Psychological Science *in Action*

Understanding Consumers

Have you ever wondered why the managers of grocery stores put daily necessities like milk and eggs at the back of the store and sweets like candy near the checkout stand? They do so because it increases sales. Forcing people to walk to the back of the store ensures that they pass many items along the way, perhaps remembering their need to purchase one or two of them. Nearer to the cash register are items that people buy on impulse. The study of how people relate to the products and services they buy is a growing field known as *consumer psychology*: using the principles and methods of psychological science to understand how people spend their money.

Consumer psychologists receive training in research methods and often complete advanced coursework in topics such as marketing, advertising, and management. They work in a variety of settings, such as advertising agencies, automobile manufacturers, airlines, food manufacturers, and universities. For instance, a consumer psychologist might study how someone's personality predicts whether they will purchase one product over another. This information can then be used to target certain types of people with advertising. Because psychological scientists understand a great deal about how the mind works, they can also help devise strategies to increase sales. There are a number of ways that consumers can be influenced to purchase products, such as being invited to try a product at home without any obligation to purchase it—people come to think of the product as their own and are unlikely to return it.

A variety of methods are used to understand consumer behavior. Researchers use observational studies to watch how people interact with products, such as observing children playing with toys. Consumers are also surveyed about their attitudes, sometimes with other people in focus groups in which the manufacturer is present as people discuss their thoughts and feelings about a product. Interestingly, simply asking questions can affect subsequent consumer behavior. For instance, do you plan to buy a Krispy Kreme doughnut today? According to research by Patti Williams and colleagues (2004), simply being asked that question, no matter how you answer it, makes you more likely to actually buy a doughnut. So, go ahead and have one (any brand you like). You can blame it on us.

One of the most common methods of consumer research is to assess people's memory for products that have been advertised. For example, researchers have

2.17 Understanding Consumer Psychology Consumer psychologists use the methods of psychological science to understand how and why people spend their money. The results of their research have had a big effect on how advertisers devise sales strategies and target their advertising.

studied what type of advertisements are most likely to capture attention and be remembered. In one study, researchers created a magazine that contained a number of interesting articles as well as advertising. The researchers were interested in comparing memory for ads that used pictures to those that used only verbal descriptions. Participants were told that the study was about either the quality of the articles or the quality of the ads. Research participants were much more likely to remember the ads that contained pictures, especially when they had not been instructed to pay attention to the ads (McQuarrie & Mick, 2003). Perhaps a picture really is worth a thousand words.

As the methods of psychological science have evolved, so has their use in consumer research (Figure 2.17). For instance, some years ago the popular Pepsi Challenge ad campaign showed people taking a blind taste test of Coca-Cola against Pepsi. Pepsi was usually the winner. But Coke outsells Pepsi in most countries around the world, and if they know which brands they are tasting, Coke drinkers prefer Coke. How does knowing the brand affect taste perception? In a recent brain-imaging study, participants tasted Pepsi or Coke while they were in the brain scanner, but they were told the brand only on some trials (McClure et al., 2004). In a previous session, the participants had made blind taste ratings on Coke and Pepsi. Interestingly, about half preferred Coke and half Pepsi, and their blind ratings did not match their stated preference. In the scanner, an area of the brain that has been found to be involved in rewarding experiences was more active when participants tasted the drink that they preferred in the behavioral tasks. It was not more active when they tasted their stated preference. But when the products were labeled, brain activity changed when participants drank Coke. When they knew it was Coke, a number of other brain regions, many of them involved in emotion and decision making, became active. Thus, brand preferences are determined by not only our sensory experience, but also our beliefs and expectations regarding the product.

The use of techniques such as imaging to study consumer behavior has been labeled neuromarketing. The idea that corporations can peek inside your head to study your purchasing habits makes some people nervous. But marketing specialists argue that people are not aware of many of the factors that influence buying, so they can't report them during focus groups or other traditional data-collection methods. They also point out that these methods will help businesses understand how people decide which products they prefer, which ultimately will benefit consumers. As with psychological science, the ultimate goal of consumer research is to understand the factors that guide behaviors that are important to our everyday lives. ■

REVIEWING
the Principles | How Are Data Analyzed and Evaluated?

Data analysis begins with descriptive statistics, which summarize the data. Measures of central tendency indicate statistical averages across sets of numbers, whereas standard deviations and variances indicate how widely numbers in a set are distributed about an average. Correlations in turn are used to describe the relationship between two variables: positive, negative, or none. Inferential statistics are used to decide whether the results of a study were due to an effect of one variable on another or whether the results were more likely due to chance.

Conclusion

Throughout this chapter we have emphasized the major issues involved in designing and conducting research in psychological science. However, the ideas we have discussed have another important application as well: evaluating research. Understanding the quality of research is important whether you go on to conduct experiments yourself or not. Each day the media report some new major finding, such as the link between smoking marijuana and heart attacks that was discussed earlier. Should you believe a report and perhaps change how you lead your daily life as a result, or should you ignore new and potentially important data, because they came from a flawed study? To make educated decisions in this domain requires understanding how good psychological science is performed, which in turn requires the use of critical thinking.

So what determines good science? A number of factors need to be considered. Is there a theoretical basis for the work? Were the method and level of analysis appropriate for the question of interest? Does the study have adequate operational definitions of the variables involved? Are the researchers presenting their results as showing a causal relationship between two variables even though an experiment was not performed?

If an experiment was performed, was it carefully designed and well controlled, or are there potential confounds that might have been overlooked? Do the results of the study apply to everyone or just to the population (e.g., the elderly, teenage males) that was actually studied? These fundamental questions underscore the necessity of being a critical, well-informed research evaluator. If you can't answer these questions when reading about a study, then you can't properly evaluate whether you should believe the results or how those results have been interpreted.

Quality research stems from both sound methodology *and* good questions. What defines a good question? Although it may be a subjective issue, there are certainly things to think about. Does the question address something fundamental or something relatively minor? If you obtain the results you predict, what impact will it have on the specific field of study? Will the results establish new understanding between different levels of analysis, or will they simply confirm a minor aspect of an old and arcane theory? We can't all be doing research that places us in the running for a Nobel prize, but at the same time, we shouldn't shy away from focusing our efforts on important rather than trivial issues.

Summarizing the Principles of Research Methodology

What Is Scientific Inquiry?

1. **Scientific questions can be objectively answered:** Scientific inquiry relies on objective methods and empirical evidence to answer testable questions.

2. **The empirical process depends on theories, hypotheses, and research:** Interconnected ideas or models of behavior (theories) yield testable predictions (hypotheses), which are tested in a systematic way (research) by collecting and evaluating evidence (data). Unexpected (serendipitous) discoveries sometimes occur.

What Are the Types of Studies in Psychological Research?

3. **An experiment involves manipulating conditions:** In experiments, researchers control the variations in the conditions that the participant experiences (independent variables) and measure the outcomes (dependent variables), which lead to an understanding of causality.

4. **Correlational designs examine how variables are related:** Correlational studies are used to examine how variables are naturally related in the real world but cannot be used to establish causality or the direction of the relationship.

5. **Descriptive studies observe and classify behavior:** Researchers observe and describe naturally occurring behaviors in order to provide a systematic and objective analysis.

What Are the Data-Collection Methods of Psychological Science?

6. **Observing is an unobtrusive technique:** Data collected by observation must be clearly defined and systematically collected. Bias in the data may occur because the participant is aware they are being observed or because of the expectations of the observer.

7. **Asking takes a more active approach:** Using surveys, questionnaires, and interviews, we can directly ask people

about their thoughts and behaviors. These self-report data may be biased by the respondents' needs to present themselves in a particular way.

8. **Case studies examine individual lives:** An intensive examination of an individual is useful for examining unusual participants and research questions. But interpretation of case studies can be subjective.

9. **Response performance measures stimulus processing:** Measuring reaction times and accuracy, and asking people to make stimulus judgments are methods used to examine how people respond to psychological tasks.

10. **Body and brain activity can be directly measured:** Electrophysiology (EEG and ERP) measures the brain's electrical activity. Brain imaging is done using positron emission tomography (PET), magnetic resonance imaging (MRI), and functional magnetic resonance imaging (fMRI).

11. **Research with animals provides important data:** Animal research provides useful, albeit simpler, models of behavior and genetics.

12. **There are ethical issues to consider:** Ethical research is governed by a variety of principles, which ensures fair and informed treatment of participants.

How Are Data Analyzed and Evaluated?

13. **Good research requires valid, reliable, and accurate data:** Data must be meaningful (valid) and its measurement consistent and stable (reliable) and accurate.

14. **Descriptive statistics provide a summary:** Measures of central tendency and variability are used to describe data.

15. **Correlations describe the relationship between variables:** A correlation is a descriptive statistic that describes the strength and direction of the relationship between two variables.

16. **Inferential statistics predict chance results:** Inferential statistics evaluate the variability and difference between sets of data to determine if they are due to chance or truly represent real change.

Applying the Principles

1. Philosophers, theologians, and psychological scientists are concerned with human behavior. What separates psychological science from other areas of inquiry, such as philosophy and theology?

____ a) Philosophers only ask "why" and do not seek the answer.
____ b) Psychological science deals with theories and the others deal with facts.
____ c) Philosophy and theology do not require scientific objectivity.
____ d) Psychological science is a subjective science.

2. A hypothesis states that television violence causes children to be violent. A researcher tests this hypothesis by using a television-viewing behavior questionnaire and then observing how children behave during recess at school. This type of study is

____ a) correlational and therefore cannot establish if TV causes violence, because of a potential third variable.
____ b) experimental because the researcher has control over the setting in which the behavior is observed.
____ c) descriptive, only because there is observation involved.

____ d) able to clearly establish that viewing violence on television causes violence at school.

3. In Gordon's introductory psychology class, students earn credit for participating in research. Gordon takes part in three research activities. In the first, he completes a questionnaire that asks about racial attitudes. Next, he is shown a video of various people (of different ethnicities) at their jobs and later measured on his speed and accuracy in matching the inividuals with their occupations. Finally, physiological measures (i.e., heart rate and brain activity) are recorded while he views screen images of individuals. Which type of data might have the most bias?

____ a) the questionnaire response
____ b) the speed and accuracy measures
____ c) the physiological measures
____ d) all are unbiased measures

4. A researcher is investigating the likelihood of success of entering college freshmen. She has existing data about the accuracy of GPA and SAT scores. She next uses a variety of measures, including GPA and SAT scores, and examines whether or not students complete their undergraduate degrees. Her research reveals that GPA has more predictive value of college success than SAT scores. She concludes

that SAT scores in relationship to predicting college success are

_____ a) reliable and valid measures.
_____ b) stable but unreliable measures.
_____ c) reliable but not valid measures.
_____ d) valid but not reliable measures.

ANSWERS: 1c 2a 3a 4c

Key Terms

accuracy, p. 63
case study, p. 52
central tendency, p. 64
confound, p. 43
correlation, p. 65
correlational study, p. 44
data, p. 41
dependent variable, p. 43
descriptive study, p. 47
electrophysiology, p. 56
experiment, p. 43
experimenter expectancy effect, p. 50
functional magnetic resonance imaging (fMRI), p. 58
hypothesis, p. 41
independent variable, p. 43

inferential statistics, p. 66
informed consent, p. 61
Institutional Review Boards (IRBs), p. 60
magnetic resonance imaging (MRI), p. 58
mean, p. 64
median, p. 64
mode, p. 64
naturalistic observation, p. 47
observational technique, p. 49
observer bias, p. 50
operational definition, p. 42
participant observation, p. 47
positron emission tomography (PET), p. 57

psychophysiological assessment, p. 55
random assignment, p. 44
reaction time, p. 54
reactivity, p. 50
reliability, p. 62
replication, p. 40
research, p. 41
response performance, p. 54
self-report method, p. 51
socially desirable responding, p. 51
standard deviation, p. 64
theory, p. 41
third-variable problem, p. 45
validity, p. 62
variability, p. 64
variable, p. 42

Further Readings

Fossey, D. (1988). *Gorillas in the mist.* New York: Houghton Mifflin.

Huff, D. (1993). *How to lie with statistics.* New York: Norton.

Martin, P., & Bateson, P. (1993). *Measuring behaviour: An introductory guide.* New York: Cambridge.

Stanovich, K. E. (2003). *How to think straight about psychology* (7th ed.). Boston: Allyn &Bacon.

Zechmeister, J. S., Zechmeister, E. B., & Shaughnessy, J. J. (2000). *Essentials of research methods in psychology.* Boston: McGraw-Hill.

Investigating Our Genetic Heritage

A visitor at the American Museum of Natural History examines a digital representation of the human genome. As technology has advanced, psychological scientists have developed more sophisticated tools to study the biological bases of mind and behavior. Recent research has focused less on whether specific genes cause specific outcomes, and more on how genes are expressed—turned "on" and "off"—by environmental factors. Changing the expression of even a single gene can have remarkable effects on complex behaviors such as social interaction.

Genetic and Biological Foundations

3

They were a happy couple in their early thirties, with three healthy young children. When their infant son died during a routine surgical procedure, they understandably were devastated. Although many people in this situation might have wanted to have another child, this couple did not; they wanted to bring their dead son back to life. To do so, they decided to finance—using money from a malpractice settlement with the hospital where he died—an attempt to clone their son. Welcome to the twenty-first century.

The idea of human cloning moved from the realm of science fiction to remote plausibility with the announcement in 1997 that Scottish researchers had created a successful sheep clone named Dolly. If sheep could be cloned, why not humans? Aghast at the idea, many governments around the world

Outlining the Principles

What Is the Genetic Basis of Psychological Science?

- Heredity Involves Passing along Genes through Reproduction
- Genotypic Variation Is Created by Sexual Reproduction
- Genes Affect Behavior
- Social and Environmental Contexts Influence Genetic Expression
- Gene Expression Can Be Modified

How Does the Nervous System Operate?

- Neurons Are Specialized for Communication
- Action Potentials Cause Neuronal Communication

- Changes in Electrical Potential Lead to Action
- Action Potentials Spread along the Axon
- Neurotransmitters Bind to Receptors across the Synapse

How Do Neurotransmitters Influence Emotion, Thought, and Behavior?

- Acetylcholine Affects Motor Control and Mental Processes
- Monoamines Are Involved in Affect, Arousal, and Motivation
- Amino Acids Are General Inhibitory and Excitatory Transmitters in the Brain
- Peptides Modulate Neurotransmission

How Are Neural Messages Integrated into Communication Systems?

- The Central Nervous System Consists of the Brain and Spinal Cord
- The Peripheral Nervous System Includes the Somatic and Autonomic Systems
- The Endocrine System Communicates through Hormones
- Actions of the Nervous System and Endocrine System Are Coordinated

banned research on human cloning. However, in 2001 separate teams of researchers confirmed that they were actively attempting to clone a human using the methods pioneered in Scotland. Ethicists, religious leaders, and scientists are locked in debate about whether human cloning is viable and ethical, with most agreeing that it is neither. In the midst of this debate, psychological scientists can't help wondering what cloning might tell us about what it means to be a human being.

In the cloning debate, it is important to separate efforts to clone human cells to be used for basic medical research from reproductive cloning. Most scientists want to use cloning to study genetic processes, not to grow a human being. In England, the team that cloned Dolly received permission to conduct human cloning research to study amyotrophic lateral sclerosis (ALS), known in America as Lou Gehrig's disease. Although ALS usually leads to death within five years, some people with the disease, such as the physicist Stephen Hawking, live much longer. These researchers want to take a cell from an ALS patient and, through cloning, create embryonic stem cells. From these, nerve cells can be extracted and the genes responsible for ALS can be studied. This technique could be a valuable research method for understanding many genetic outcomes, including psychological disorders. The approach is completely different from using cloning to create a human being, which is unlikely to occur any time soon. But let's imagine for a second that you could clone a person, because that allows us to consider fundamental and profound questions about what it means to be a human being. What if we could clone a person, so that the clone and the person contained identical genes? Would the clone be the same person? Are we so hard-wired that our clone would share our favorite foods, our work habits, and even our ethical views of cloning?

Nature already clones people, in the form of identical twins. As you will read in this chapter, such twins have many remarkable similarities, even if they are raised apart. But would "clones" be as similar to their gene donors as identical twins are to each other? There are many reasons to believe they would not. Consider the infant boy whom the young couple wants to re-create, assuming again that it was even possible. The clone's natural environment would be similar but not identical to that of his predecessor. Among other things, the clone would have a different uterine environment and would be raised by parents who are now older and who have undergone a major transformative experience; he would also be interacting with sib-

Timeline

1817

Parkinson's Disease The physician James Parkinson identifies this major neurological disorder, which affects muscular control and results from depletion of the dopamine system.

1866

Mendel's Peas Gregor Mendel, a monk, conducts studies on heredity in pea plants. His results provide the basis of genetics, including the idea of dominant and recessive genes.

1870s

Golgi Stain Italian physician Camillo Golgi invents what becomes known as the "Golgi stain," a method of tissue preparation that allows the examination of single neurons.

1880s

Neuron Doctrine The Spanish anatomist Santiago Ramón y Cajal uses the Golgi stain to chart the microscopic anatomy of different regions of the brain. He correctly argues that the nervous system is composed of distinct cells.

lings who are older. Moreover, even though identical twins grow up to be quite similar in many respects, they still differ from each other in multiple ways, as we'll see in our discussions on twin studies. There would be similarities, but also substantial differences. This clone would be a unique individual, just like his predecessor. Thus, much of the debate over the morality of cloning should be muted by Mother Nature's near-perfect clones, identical twins. Science can only hope to improve on the "identicalness" of identical twins by cloning two or more individuals from the same cell donor and developing them in the same environment at the same time.

As a thought experiment, human cloning raises issues of great interest to psychological scientists. Would a cloned child develop at the same rate as the first child, or might his development be affected by the parents' expectations? How much of who we are is determined by our genes and how much by the environment? If two clones were raised in different cultures, how different might they be? What if they were raised ten years apart, and therefore exposed to different cultural environments? Every person is unique. What determines this uniqueness?

For many years, geneticists focused on whether people possessed certain types of genes, such as genes for psychological disorders or even genes for intelligence. The emphasis was on the extent to which human traits were genetically hard wired, a formulation that left little room for environmental factors. Recent research is approaching the study of genes by trying to understand not only the possession of certain genes, but also gene expression, how genes are turned "on" and "off." The major lesson emerging from this research is that the environment plays an important role in how genes are expressed and therefore in how they influence mind and behavior. Although there is evidence that people might possess specific genes that have specific effects, it is the expression of those genes ("turning on and off") as much as mere possession that makes us who we are. This chapter begins our examination of the genetic and biological foundations of psychological science. To understand fully what makes us who we are, we need to understand how basic physiological processes affect behavior, thought, and emotion. We also need to understand how those physiological processes are shaped by the environment—how nurture influences nature. Along the way, we will look at some of the exciting new genetic research that is reshaping the way we think about the human mind and behavior. ■

1897	1921	1936	1950s	1950s
The Synapse Sir Charles Sherrington proposes that neurons communicate with each other across the synapse through electrical means. A few years later, Thomas Renton Elliott suggests that synapses are chemical rather than electrical.	**Neurotransmission Is Chemical** Otto Loewi shows that neurons communicate through the release of neurotransmitters, chemicals released from one neuron that signal other neurons. He is awarded a Nobel prize.	**First Neurotransmitter Identified** Sir Henry Dale identifies acetylcholine as the neurotransmitter that operates in the control of muscles.	**Sodium-Potassium Pump** Alan Hodgkin and Andrew Huxley show that there are active components within the neuron that stabilize the concentration of sodium and potassium, the main chemicals involved in action potentials.	**Pharmacology** Researchers show that chemicals that bind to neurotransmitter receptors can be used in therapies for various forms of mental illness, setting the stage for modern-day drug therapy.

Over the past three decades, scientific understanding of the genetic and physiological foundations of psychological activity has increased dramatically. As technology has advanced, sophisticated tools have been developed to explore the biological bases of mind and behavior. Researchers can now examine DNA to predict who will develop specific disorders and to understand how certain diseases are passed from one generation to the next. Researchers have also identified genes that predispose people to be, among other things, outgoing, sociable, and intelligent. Most recently, researchers have developed techniques that allow them to turn specific genes on and off. Remarkably, changing the expression of a single gene can have profound effects even on complex behaviors such as social interaction (Insel & Young, 2001). Research at the biological level of analysis has led to great strides in understanding the various biological processes that occur within the brain and body to produce experience, thought, emotion, memory, and behavior. By building across the levels of analysis, we plan to demonstrate how psychological scientists conduct research to understand different questions related to mind, brain, and behavior. This chapter examines psychological activity at the genetic and neurochemical levels; in Chapter 4 we will describe the functions of various brain regions at the brain-systems level of analysis.

What Is the Genetic Basis of Psychological Science?

One of the major outgrowths of the new biological revolution occurred in February 2001, when two groups of scientists published separate articles detailing the results of the first phase of the *Human Genome Project,* an international research effort to map the entire structure of human genetic material. This achievement represents the coordinated efforts of hundreds of scientists around the globe. To understand their goals it is important to have a basic understanding of genetic processes.

Within nearly every cell in the body is the genome for making the entire organism: It is the master recipe that provides detailed instructions for everything from how to grow a gall bladder to where to place the nose on your face. Whether a cell becomes part of a gall bladder or a nose is determined by which genes are turned "on" or "off" within the cell, and this is determined by cues from outside the cell. The genome provides the option, and the environment determines which option is taken (Marcus, 2004). As you will learn, recent discoveries about how genes are turned on or off have provided important insights into not only how physical bodies develop but also how the mind works. The term *genetics* is typically used to describe how characteristics, such as height, hair color, and weight, are passed along through inheritance, but it also refers to those processes that are involved in turning genes off and on.

1974	1977	1980s	1998	2001
Endogenous Opiates Scottish researchers Hans Kosterlitz and John Hughes discover that endorphins are important for reward and for the natural control of pain.	**Releasing Hormones** Roger Guillemin, Andrew Shally, and Rosalyn Yalow share a Nobel prize for their work showing the existence of releasing factors that regulate hormonal function.	**Behavioral Genetics of Personality** Researchers at the University of Minnesota study identical twins who have been raised apart, demonstrating that genetics plays an important role in human personality.	**Gene Silencing** Researchers discover that modified RNA causes a shutdown in gene expression, effectively silencing genetic instructions. This discovery might allow treatments for genetic disorders.	**Human Genome Project** An international collaboration of genetics researchers maps the basic gene sequence of human DNA, setting the stage for the more complex task of figuring out how genes interact to produce illness and influence behavior.

3.4 **Two Couples, Four Children** Shown in the top row are two couples. Below are four children. Try to match which child comes from which parents. The answer is revealed at the bottom of the page.*

even identical twins do not have the exact same environment (and in rare circumstances might even have different genes due to random mutations), and therefore they have different phenotypes, but they are typically more similar than dizygotic twins, who differ both in genotype and phenotype.

Adoption studies compare the similarities between biological relatives and adoptive relatives. Adopted siblings have similar home environments but different genes. Therefore, the assumption is that similarities among adopted siblings have more to do with environment than genes. Interestingly, it turns out that growing up in the same household has relatively little influence on many traits, such as personality. Indeed, after we control for their genetic similarity, even biological siblings raised in the same household are no more similar than two strangers plucked at random off the street. This point will be examined in greater detail in the development and personality chapters, but for now it is sufficient to understand the basic logic of the different types of studies.

One interesting behavioral genetic study is to compare monozygotic twins who have been *raised together* or *raised apart*. This would seem the ideal way to test the relative contributions of genes and the environment. Thomas Bouchard and his colleagues at the University of Minnesota have identified more than 100 pairs of identical and nonidentical twins who were either raised together or raised apart (1990; Figure 3.5). They examined a variety of traits and characteristics, including intelligence, personality, sense of well-being, achievement, alienation, and aggression. The general finding was that identical twins were likely to be similar, whether raised together or not. The "Jim Twins" are perhaps the most famous case study to emerge from the Minnesota Twin Project. How is it possible that two boys separated from birth and raised by different families had the same first name, had each married and divorced women named Linda, had each remarried women named Betty, had named their sons James Alan and James Allen, and had each named their dogs Toy? In addition, both were part-time law-enforcement officers who drove Chevrolets and vacationed in Florida. Just to complete the circle, they were the same height and weight, chain-smoked the same brand of cigarettes, and drank the same brand of

How do studies of twins help us understand genetics?

*The boy and the girl on either end of the bottom row are children of the parents at the top right. The two girls in the middle of the bottom row are children of the parents at top left.

3.5 Gerald Levey and Mark Newman
Participants of Dr. Bouchard's study, Levey and Newman are identical twins who were separated at birth. Reunited at age 31, they discovered that they were both firefighters and had similarities in personality traits.

beer. Although no one suggests that there are genes for naming dogs Toy or for marrying and divorcing women named Linda, the obvious similarities in many aspects of the Jim Twins' lives point to the importance of genetic influences in shaping personality and behavior.

Some critics have argued that most of the adopted twins were raised in relatively similar environments, in part because adoption agencies try to match the child to the adoptive home. However, this argument doesn't explain the identical twins Oskar Stohr and Jack Yufe (Bouchard et al., 1990). Oskar was raised a Catholic in Germany and even joined the Nazi party. Jack was raised a Jew and lived for a while in Israel. What twins could be more different? Yet when they met at an interview, they were wearing similar clothes, exhibited similar mannerisms, and had the same odd habits, such as flushing the toilet before using it, dipping toast in coffee, storing rubber bands on their wrists, and surprising people by sneezing in the elevator. Critics have suggested that nothing more than coincidence is at work in these case studies, but it is clear that twins share similarities other than just behavior quirks, such as intelligence and personality. Indeed, some evidence suggests that twins raised apart are more similar than twins raised together. This would likely occur if parents encouraged individuality in twins raised together by emphasizing different strengths and interests. In effect, the parents would actively create a different environment for each twin. Continued research using the methods of behavioral genetics is needed to provide additional insight into the relative influence of heredity and environment on individual behavior.

UNDERSTANDING HERITABILITY *Heredity* is the transmission of characteristics from parents to offspring by means of genes. A term that is often confused with heredity, but that means something else altogether, is **heritability**, which is a statistical estimate of the portion of observed variation in a population that is caused by differences in heredity. *Variation* is the measure of the overall amount of difference among people. This variation is estimated based on studies of twins and other methods.

It is important to understand that heritability refers to differences in a certain trait among individuals, not to the trait itself. If a trait such as height has a heritability of .60, it means that 60 percent of height variation among individuals is genetic, not that you get 60 percent of your height from genetics and 40 percent from your environment. Heritability refers to populations, not to individuals. The heritability for a trait depends on variability within a population. For instance, almost everyone has two legs, and more people lose legs through accidents than are born without them. Thus, the heritability value for having two legs is nearly zero, in spite of the obvious fact that the human genome contains instructions to grow two legs. Herein lies a key lesson: Estimates of heritability are concerned only with the extent that people differ in terms of their genetic makeup. For example, how shy you are compared to others is determined in part by genes, and about half of the variability in shyness among different people is determined by genetic variation. Thus, the heritability for shyness is approximately 50 percent. It's important to point out that although there is genetic variation among us, the vast majority of genes work nearly identically in all people, and, indeed, across many species of other animals.

It is also important to point out that the population used to estimate total variation can affect the estimate obtained for heritability. Typically, the more diverse

heritability A statistical estimate of the fraction of observed measure of the overall amount of difference among people in a population that is caused by differences in heredity.

Why is heritability lower when the population is more diverse?

the population, the lower the estimate of heritability. This occurs because of the increased variability that comes from diversity and because the estimates of the genetic variation do not consider such diversity. The important point is that heritability is an estimate that is not precise and that can be affected by a number of factors. Still, it helps behavioral geneticists in clarifying the interaction between the environment and genes, so that they can understand the circumstances in which genes operate.

Social and Environmental Contexts Influence Genetic Expression

Let's examine how social and environmental contexts can influence genetic processes. For instance, African Americans typically have higher rates of hypertension. According to some researchers, the dismal conditions of the slave trade may have led to a change in the genetic constitution of African Americans (Wilson & Grim, 1991). As many as one in four slaves died during transportation, and approximately the same number died within the first few years of arrival in America. Wilson and Grim argue that the horrific conditions imposed a strong selection factor in determining the type of individual who was able to survive. Those slaves who were able to maintain high blood pressure on low levels of salt might have been more likely to survive. In contemporary times, however, with salt readily available, a greater sensitivity to salt may cause African Americans to become salt hypertensive. The theory is provocative and difficult to test, but it highlights one possible way in which social context can affect genetic constitution.

Another strong example of how social environment interacts with gene expression is found in a longitudinal study of criminality conducted by Avshalom Caspi and his colleagues. These researchers followed a group of more than 1,000 New Zealanders from their births in 1972–1973 until adulthood, collecting enormous amounts of information about the participants and their lives each few years. When the participants were 26 years old, the investigators were able to examine which factors predicted who became a violent criminal. Prior research had demonstrated that children who are mistreated by their parents are more likely to become violent offenders. But not all mistreated children become violent. These researchers wanted to know why. They developed the hypothesis that differences in a gene that controls a certain enzyme (monoamine oxidase, or *MAO*) may be important in determining susceptibility to the effects of maltreatment. You will read about MAO in Chapter 13; for now it is sufficient to know that low levels of MAO have been implicated in aggressive behaviors. The gene for MAO comes in two forms, one of which leads to higher levels of MAO and one of which leads to lower levels. Caspi and colleagues (2002) found that boys with the low-level MAO gene appeared to be especially susceptible to early childhood maltreatment. Those children who were mistreated and had the low-activity MAO gene were much more likely to be convicted of a violent crime than those with the high-activity gene. Indeed, although only 1 in 8 boys was mistreated and had the low MAO gene, they were responsible for nearly half of all violent crimes committed by the group (Figure 3.6). The New Zealander study is a good example of how the combination of nature and nurture can work together to affect human behavior—unfortunately, in this case, violent behavior.

3.6 MAO Activity and Violent Crimes Those who had the gene for low MAO activity were much more likely than others to have been convicted of violent crimes if they had been maltreated. The effects of maltreatment had less influence on those with the high MAO gene.

Finally, there is also evidence that genes and the social context interact to affect the phenotype. Sandra Scarr (Scarr & McCarthy, 1983) proposed a theory of development that stresses the interactive nature of genes and environment. According to Scarr, early environments influence young children, but children's genes also influence the experiences they receive. For instance, children exposed to the same environment interpret and react to it in different ways. Some children who are teased withdraw; others shrug it off without concern. Similarly, different sorts of children evoke different responses from others. A well-mannered, cuddly child cues more nurturing from parents and others than a baby who is irritable and fussy. Finally, as children become older they can choose their social situations. Some children prefer to spend time outdoors engaged in vigorous physical pursuits; others prefer the tranquility of a good book in a comfortable setting. Thus, genes predispose certain behaviors that elicit different responses, and these subsequent interactions then shape the phenotype. Because genes and social contexts interact, it can be very difficult to separate their independent effects.

Gene Expression Can Be Modified

What can we learn and ultimately achieve through the manipulation of our genes? Throughout this section, we have highlighted the new emphasis on gene expression—what causes genes to turn on and off—in addition to the heritability of particular traits or behaviors. In Chapter 2 we described methods that researchers use to study gene expression. A variety of gene-manipulation techniques are employed to enhance or reduce the expression of genes, or even to insert genes into a different animal species. Animals with genetic modifications are then compared with animals without such modifications to test theories about the genes' function. For instance, genes can be removed from or disrupted within the genome to create knock-outs; if the gene is important for a specific function, then disrupting it should interfere with that function. These gene-manipulation techniques have led to dramatic increases in understanding how gene expression influences mind and behavior.

One remarkable finding so far is that changing even a single gene can lead to dramatic changes in behavior. Using gene-manipulation techniques, researchers have created anxious mice, hyperactive mice, mice that can't learn or remember, mice that groom themselves to the point of baldness, mice that fail to take care of their offspring, and even mice that progressively increase alcohol intake when stressed (Marcus, 2004; Ridley, 2003). Consider a study in which a gene from the highly social prairie vole was inserted into normally antisocial mice. These transgenic mice exhibited social behavior more typical of prairie voles than of mice (Insel & Young, 2001). Another study found that knocking out specific genes led mice to lose the ability to remember mice they had previously encountered. These mice also failed to investigate new mice placed in their cages when normal mice would do so readily. In essence, knocking out one gene led to multiple impairments in social recognition (Choleris et al., 2003). This indicates not that there is a specific gene for being social, but rather that changing the expression of one gene leads to the expression of a cavalcade of other genes, which ultimately influences even complex behaviors. A major lesson from recent research is that genes seldom work in isolation to influence mind and behavior; rather, the complex interaction among thousands of genes gives rise to the complexity of human experience.

Efforts to manipulate genes in humans have so far proven difficult and in some cases even dangerous. But there is new hope for altering gene expression with a method that focuses on RNA rather than on DNA. Recall that gene expression involves DNA sending instructions via RNA to create specific proteins. Although RNA was once viewed as little more than a messenger, recent dramatic discoveries have indicated that RNA might be more important than ever imagined. These findings are so amazing that the most influential research journal, *Science,* labeled them the number one scientific breakthrough for the year 2002. In 1998, researchers discovered that injecting a slightly modified form of RNA into worms led to a dramatic shutdown in gene expression in the very genes that were associated with producing that RNA in the first place (Fire et al., 1998). The modified RNA is broken down by other gene expression processes into tiny segments called small RNA. This process, now referred to as *RNA interference* (RNAi), prevents gene expression by silencing the DNA instructions to make proteins. Researchers view the potential of RNAi as astounding, and the race is on among various laboratories around the world to use RNAi as therapy for a variety of diseases and disorders ranging from cancer, to AIDS, to schizophrenia (Shankar, Manjunath, & Lieberman, 2005). Recall Nancy Wexler, the psychologist who has devoted her life to understanding Huntington's disease. Her team has discovered that the gene for Huntington's produces a protein that attacks the brain. We already know that knock-out methods will not work to prevent Huntington's because the gene serves many important functions. But what if RNAi could be used to silence the production of the specific brain-damaging protein? Indeed, using a mouse model of Huntington's disease, researchers recently have demonstrated that RNAi can dramatically reduce signs of brain damage and improve behavioral symptoms of the disease (Harper et al., 2005). The hope of being able to control such gene expression opens the possibility of bold new advances in our understanding of how genes influence mind and behavior.

REVIEWING the Principles | What Is the Genetic Basis of Psychological Science?

Human behavior is influenced by genetic processes. People inherit both physical characteristics and personality traits from their parents. Only recently have scientists developed the tools to measure genetic processes and the roles that various genes play in psychological activity. The Human Genome Project has succeeded in mapping the basic sequence of DNA, but a great deal more needs to be accomplished before that information can be translated into medical treatments or a greater understanding of individual differences among people. Within the last few years, researchers have begun to focus more on how and when genes are expressed in addition to the heritability of particular traits. Methods have been developed to enhance or interrupt gene expression, and most recently scientists are looking at how modified RNA can be used to silence gene expression entirely.

How Does the Nervous System Operate?

Many of the genes in the human genome direct the development and ongoing functions of the *nervous system,* a communication network that serves as the foundation for all psychological activity. Comprising billions of specialized cells known as nerve cells, the nervous system takes in a variety of information from the external world, evaluates that information, and subsequently produces behaviors or makes bodily adjustments to adapt to the environment. At the biological level of analysis, the essence of life—from smelling a rose, to thinking, to moving your big toe—comes down to communication among the billions of nerve cells throughout the body. So how do nerve cells operate? How do they communicate with each other? How do communicating networks function to produce behaviors, thoughts, and feelings? Before we get to the workings of the nervous system as a whole, we begin by describing how cells within this system communicate with each other to produce psychological activity.

Neurons Are Specialized for Communication

Neurons, the basic units of the nervous system, are cells that specialize in communication. Neurons differ from most other cells because they are excitable: They operate through electrical impulses and communicate with other neurons through chemical signals. They have three functions: to take in information from neighboring neurons (reception), integrate those signals (conduction), and pass signals to other neurons (transmission).

Neurons come in a wide assortment of shapes and sizes, but they typically share four structural regions that assist the neuron's communication functions (Figure 3.7). The first region is the **dendrites**—short outgrowths that increase the neuron's receptive field. These branchlike appendages detect chemical signals from neighboring neurons.

The second region of the neuron is the **cell body**, where information from thousands of other neurons is collected and integrated. The cell body is also the site of metabolism and genetic action. Like all cells in the body, neurons contain DNA, the recipe for action for the neuron. Once the incoming information has been integrated in the cell body, electrical impulses are transmitted along a long narrow outgrowth known as the **axon**. Axons, the third region of the neuron, vary tremendously in

neuron The basic unit of the nervous system that operates through electrical impulses, which communicate with other neurons through chemical signals. Neurons receive, integrate, and transmit information in the nervous system.

dendrites Branchlike extensions of the neuron that detect information from other neurons.

cell body In the neuron, where information from thousands of other neurons is collected and processed.

axon A long narrow outgrowth of a neuron by which information is transmitted to other neurons.

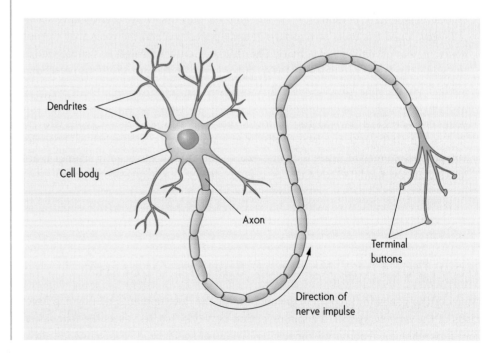

3.7 A Neuron Messages are received by the dendrites, processed in the cell body, transmitted along the axon, and sent to other neurons via chemical substances released from the terminal buttons.

CHAPTER 3 | Genetic and Biological Foundations

length, from a few millimeters to more than a meter. The longest axons stretch from the spinal cord to the big toe. You have probably heard the term *nerve,* as in a pinched nerve. Used in this context, a nerve refers to a bundle of axons that carry information between the brain and the body.

Terminal buttons, small nodules at the ends of axons, are the fourth region of the neuron. Terminal buttons receive the electrical impulses and release chemical signals from the neuron to an area called the synapse. The **synapse** is the site for chemical communication between neurons. Chemicals leave one neuron, cross the synapse, and then pass signals along to the dendrites of other neurons.

The boundary of a neuron is defined by its membrane, a double layer of fatty molecules called *lipids*. As you will see, the membrane plays an important role in communication between neurons by regulating the concentration of electrically charged molecules that are the basis of the neuron's electrical activity.

TYPES OF NEURONS The three basic types of neurons are *sensory neurons, motor neurons,* and *interneurons*. **Sensory neurons** detect information from the physical world and pass that information along to the brain, usually via the spinal cord. You know from hitting your funny bone that sensory neurons can transmit fast-acting signals that trigger a nearly instantaneous bodily response and sensory experience. Sensory neurons are often called *afferent* neurons, because they send their signals from the body to the brain. Signals that travel from the brain to the body are known as *efferent* (Figure 3.8).

Motor neurons direct muscles to contract or relax, thereby producing movement. Motor neurons are efferent neurons, in that signals *from* the brain are transmitted *to* the body. **Interneurons** communicate within local or short-distance circuits. That is, interneurons integrate neural activity within a single area rather than transmitting information to other brain structures or to the body organs.

Together, sensory and motor neurons control movement. For instance, when you use your pen your brain sends a message via motor neurons to the muscles in your fingers to move in specific ways. Receptors in your skin and muscles send back

terminal buttons Small nodules at the ends of axons that release chemical signals from the neuron to an area called the synapse.

synapse The site for chemical communication between neurons.

sensory neurons One of the three types of neurons, these afferent neurons detect information from the physical world and pass that information along to the brain.

motor neurons One of the three types of neurons, these efferent neurons direct muscles to contract or relax, thereby producing movement.

interneurons One of the three types of neurons, these neurons communicate only with other neurons, typically within a specific brain region.

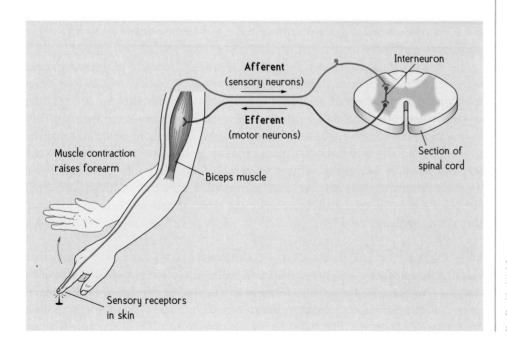

3.8 Afferent and Efferent Signals
Receptors send afferent signals to the brain for processing. An efferent signal is then sent from the brain to the body via the spinal cord to produce a response.

messages through sensory neurons that help to determine how much pressure is needed to hold the pen. The nerves that provide information from muscles are referred to as *somatosensory,* which is the general term for sensations experienced from within the body.

Even the tiniest actions require the integration and coordination of multiple brain and body systems. Writing requires brain mechanisms that initiate the desire to use the pen, motor messages that direct the arm, hand, and fingers to reach for and hold the pen, and somatosensory messages that provide feedback necessary for successful use of the pen. If any of the components fail to work, you will have great difficulty even writing your name.

Complex networks of thousands of neurons sending and receiving signals are the functional basis of all psychological activity. Although the actions of single neurons are simple to describe, human complexity is a result of billions of neurons, each making contact with tens of thousands of other neurons. Neurons don't communicate randomly or arbitrarily; they selectively communicate with other neurons to form circuits or *neural networks.* These networks develop through maturation and experience, forming permanent alliances among groups of neurons.

Action Potentials Cause Neuronal Communication

Neuronal communication depends on the ability of the neuron to respond to incoming stimulation by changing electrically and subsequently passing along signals to other neurons. An **action potential**, also called *neuronal firing,* is the electrical signal that passes along the axon and causes release of chemicals that transmit signals to other neurons. Let's examine some of the factors that contribute to the firing of an action potential.

THE RESTING MEMBRANE POTENTIAL IS NEGATIVELY CHARGED
When not active, the inside and outside of a neuron differ electrically because of the balance of *ions* in the intracellular fluid. This electrical difference is referred to as the **resting membrane potential**. As with all salty solutions, the salts in intracellular fluid consist of particles called *ions* that have negative or positive charges. The ratio of negative to positive ions is greater inside the neuron than outside the neuron. Thus, the electrical charge inside the neuron is slightly more negative than that outside the neuron.

Scientists measure a neuron's resting membrane potential with *microelectrodes,* extremely tiny devices that register electric currents. The result is displayed on an oscilloscope, a monitor that shows voltage changes over time (Figure 3.9). Placing one microelectrode in the fluid inside the neuron and one microelectrode in the fluid surrounding the neuron registers a steady voltage of approximately -70 millivolts (mV). The negative sign indicates that the inside is negative in comparison to the outside, which is arbitrarily defined as zero voltage. This differential electrical charge inside and outside of the neuron is a condition known as *polarization.* The polarization across the cell membrane creates the electrical energy necessary to power the action potential.

THE ROLES OF SODIUM AND POTASSIUM IONS
Two types of ions that contribute to a neuron's resting membrane potential are *sodium ions* and *potassium ions.* Ions pass through the cell membrane at specialized pores referred to as *ion channels,* each of which is structured to match a specific type of ion. The flow of ions through their channels is controlled by a gating mechanism. When the gate is open,

action potential The neural impulse that passes along the axon and subsequently causes the release of chemicals from the terminal buttons.

resting membrane potential The electrical charge of a neuron when it is not active.

(a)
Axon terminals of other neurons

Cell body

Chart recorder indicates response to stimulation by other neurons

−mV

Electrical potential

Pen

+mV

Time

Axon

Intracellular microelectrode

Reference microelectrode

Amplifier

Oscilloscope

(b)

3.9 **Resting Membrane Potential** (a) The neuron's resting membrane potential can be recorded by placing one microelectrode in the fluid inside the neuron and one micro-electrode in the fluid surrounding the neuron and measuring the difference in voltage, approximately −70 millivolts (mV). (b) A microelectrode being placed into a neuron.

ions flow freely past, but when closed the gate prevents passage of ions through the cell membrane (Figure 3.10). The flow of ions also is affected by the fact that the cell membrane is *selectively permeable*—it allows some types of ions to cross more easily than others, much like a bouncer at an exclusive nightclub. Partially as a result of the selective permeability of the cell membrane, there is more potassium inside the neuron than sodium, which contributes to polarization.

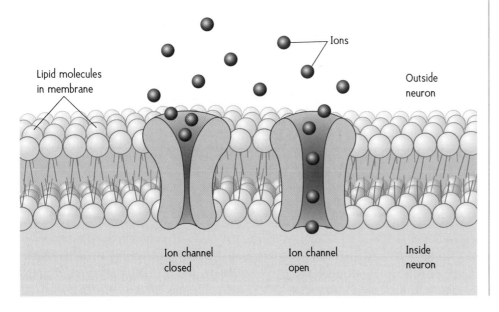

Ions

Lipid molecules in membrane

Outside neuron

Ion channel closed

Ion channel open

Inside neuron

3.10 **Cell Membrane Permeability** The cell membrane is selectively permeable. Ions can travel into the neuron when ion channels are open but not when ion channels are closed. The channels are specialized for specific ions. Thus, the sodium channel controls only the passage of sodium.

Changes in Electrical Potential Lead to Action

Earlier you read that the dendrites receive chemical signals from nearby neurons, which then signal the neuron to fire or not. "Firing" means passing a signal along the axon and releasing chemicals from the terminal buttons. The signals arrive at the dendrites by the thousands and are of two types: *excitatory* or *inhibitory*. Excitatory signals stimulate the neuron to fire, whereas inhibitory signals reduce the likelihood of the neuron's firing. Signals work by affecting polarization. Each signal either *depolarizes* or *hyperpolarizes* the cell membrane. Excitatory signals lead to depolarization, which increases the likelihood that the neuron will fire; inhibitory signals lead to hyperpolarization, which decreases the likelihood that the neuron will fire. Let's look at this in more detail.

DEPOLARIZATION AND HYPERPOLARIZATION Neurons fire when the cell membrane is depolarized past a certain threshold. Depolarization causes a change in the permeability of the cell membrane, which opens the gates of the sodium channels and allows sodium to rush into the neuron. This influx of sodium causes the inside of the neuron to become slightly more positively charged than the outside (approximately 50 mV), as shown in Figure 3.11. This change from a negative to a positive charge inside the neuron is the basis of the action potential.

Signals that are inhibitory lead to hyperpolarization of the cell membrane, in which sodium channels become even more resistant to the passage of sodium. This hyperpolarization means that it will be more difficult for excitatory signals to cause neuronal firing.

Action Potentials Spread along the Axon

Inhibitory and excitatory signals received by the dendrites are integrated within the neuron. If the total amount of depolarization surpasses the neuron's threshold, which occurs when there are more excitatory than inhibitory signals, an action potential is generated. When the neuron fires, the depolarization of the cell membrane moves along the axon like a wave, which is called *propagation*. Sodium rushing through its ion channels leads to further depolarization, causing adjacent sodium channels to

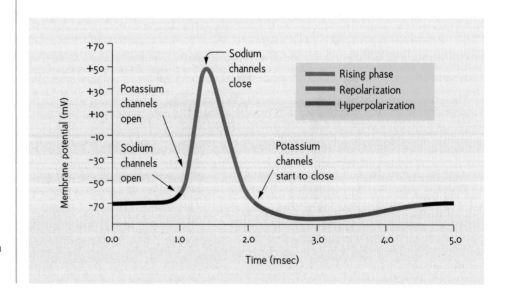

3.11 Membrane Potential In the resting state, sodium ion channels are closed. Depolarization opens the sodium channels, which allows sodium to flow into the neuron and changes the electrical charge of the neuron.

open. Thus, like toppling dominoes, sodium ion channels open successively along the cell body to the end of the axon. At any point along the axon, the sudden influx of sodium repels the potassium ions, which are forced out of the neuron. This influx of sodium and outflow of potassium continues until a state of near equilibrium is reached, at which point other forces take over to shut the sodium ion channel gates and stop the influx of sodium. All this occurs within about 1/1,000 of a second.

ABSOLUTE AND RELATIVE REFRACTORY PERIODS Once the gating mechanism stops the flow of sodium into the neuron, potassium stops leaving. However, this takes 1 to 2 milliseconds, during which a decreased concentration of potassium in the cell body momentarily creates a state of hyperpolarization. During this brief period, known as the *absolute refractory period,* it is impossible for the neuron to fire, which keeps the action potential from repeating up and down the axon in a kind of ripple effect (McCormick, 1999). As each section of the axon depolarizes, the preceding section enters its absolute refractory state. Hence, under natural conditions, action potentials move along the axon in only one direction. The signal can't travel backward because the preceding axonal section is in its refractory period and its sodium ion channels are blocked.

As potassium stops exiting the neuron and the cell membrane is returning to its resting membrane potential, the neuron can fire, but only in response to an especially strong signal, such as might occur if the neuron were bombarded by excitatory signals. This brief period of time is called the *relative refractory period*. Until the neuron returns to its resting potential, it is somewhat hyperpolarized and requires a stronger signal to become depolarized.

ALL-OR-NONE PRINCIPLE Any one signal received by the neuron has little influence on whether it fires. Normally, the neuron is barraged by thousands of inhibitory and excitatory signals, and its firing is determined by the number and frequency of those signals. The firing criterion is the total electrical voltage produced by the signals at a given time. If the sum of the depolarizations and hyperpolarizations leads to a drop in voltage that exceeds the neuron's firing threshold, then an action potential is generated. It is as if you decided to change your major from English to psychology because five of the eight friends you asked said to go for it.

The firing of the neuron is all or none—a neuron cannot partially fire. The **all-or-none principle** dictates that a neuron fires with the same potency each time, but at intervals of different frequency depending on the strength of stimulation. Suppose you are playing a video game in which you fire missiles by pressing a button. Every time you press the button, a missile is launched at the same velocity as the last. It makes no difference how hard you press the button. But if you keep your finger on the button, additional missiles fire in rapid succession. Thus, the strong stimulus—your finger holding down the button—controls the firing frequency.

THE MYELIN SHEATH The propagation of action potentials along the axon happens quickly, which permits the fast and frequent adjustments required for coordinating motor activity. However, the action potential moving along the axon by depolarizing adjacent sodium channels does not occur rapidly enough to explain the precision of fine motor movements. So what permits rapid firing? Signals can travel quickly down the axon because it is insulated by a **myelin sheath**, a fatty material that encases axons (Figure 3.12). Made up of *glial cells* (Greek, "glue"), myelin, like the plastic tubing around wires in an electrical cord, insulates sections of the axon and facilitates the passage of electrical impulses.

all-or-none principle The principle whereby a neuron fires with the same potency each time, although frequency can vary; it either fires or not, it cannot partially fire.

myelin sheath A fatty material, made up of glial cells, that insulates the axon and allows for the rapid movement of electrical impulses along the axon.

3.12 The Myelin Sheath and the Nodes of Ranvier The myelin sheath surrounds the axon, except at the nodes of Ranvier. The electrical signal jumps from node to node.

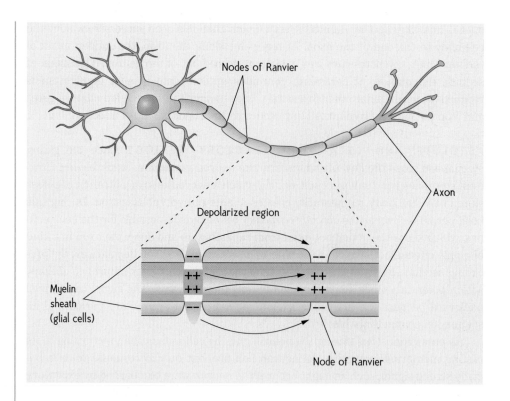

nodes of Ranvier Small gaps of exposed axon, between the segments of myelin sheath, where action potentials are transmitted.

3.13 The Brain of an MS Patient The arrows point to areas of sclerosis.

As shown in Figure 3.12, the myelin sheath grows along axons in short segments. Between these segments are small gaps of exposed axon known as the **nodes of Ranvier**, named for Louis A. Ranvier, the researcher who first described them. It is only at these unmyelinated gaps that ion channels can transmit action potentials. Thus, action potentials skip quickly along the axon, pausing only briefly at each node of Ranvier to get recharged. This method of conduction, known as *saltatory conduction* (from Latin *saltare,* "to jump"), enables signals to move through the nervous system extraordinarily fast. Deterioration of the myelin sheath leads to *multiple sclerosis (MS)*, an especially tragic neurological disorder that mostly affects young adults. The symptoms result from decay of the myelin sheath surrounding axons. The earliest symptoms are often numbness in the limbs and blurry vision. Since the myelin insulation helps messages move quickly along axons, demyelination slows down neural impulses. The axons essentially short-circuit, and normal neuronal communication is interrupted. Motor actions become jerky, and victims lose the ability to coordinate motor movements. Over time, movement, sensation, and coordination are severely impaired. As the myelin sheath disintegrates, axons are exposed and may themselves start to break down. The term *sclerosis* means "hardening," which is noticeable from the scarring in the brains of patients with MS, as shown in Figure 3.13.

This progressive disease appears to have both genetic and environmental causes. Evidence for a genetic influence includes that it is more common among identical twins than nonidentical twins and that it is more common among Caucasians than Asians. However, it is also more common in cold climates than in warm climates. Although the connection between cold weather and MS is unclear, growing up in a cold climate seems more relevant than moving to one as a young adult; moving from a cold climate to a warmer one after childhood does not seem to reduce the risk of developing MS. Some theories suggest that MS may be an autoimmune disorder in which the body views myelin as an intruder, triggering an immune reaction that attacks and kills the myelin sheath. This autoimmune disorder may have its origins in a slow-acting infection that is contracted early in childhood. There is currently no known cure for multiple sclerosis.

Neurotransmitters Bind to Receptors across the Synapse

Neurons do not touch one another; they are separated by a small space known as the **synaptic cleft**, which is the site of chemical communication between neurons. Action potentials cause neurons to release from their terminal buttons chemicals that travel across the synaptic cleft and are received by the dendrites of other neurons. The neuron that sends the signal is called *pre*synaptic, and the one that receives the signal is called *post*synaptic.

How do these chemical signals work? Inside the terminal buttons are small packages, or *vesicles,* that contain chemical substances known as neurotransmitters. The term **neurotransmitter** is a generic word used for chemical substances that carry signals across the synaptic cleft. After an action potential travels to the terminal button, it causes the vesicles to spill their neurotransmitters into the synaptic cleft. These neurotransmitters then spread across the synaptic cleft and attach themselves, or *bind,* to receptors on the postsynaptic neuron (Figure 3.14).

Receptors are specialized protein molecules. The binding of neurotransmitter to receptor causes ion channels to open, which changes the membrane potential at that location, thus affecting the probability that the neuron will fire. If a neurotransmitter binds with a receptor and depolarizes the membrane, it is excitatory and increases the likelihood that the receiving neuron will fire. By contrast, if the neurotransmitter's binding hyperpolarizes the membrane, it is inhibitory and makes the receiving neuron less likely to fire.

synaptic cleft The small space between neurons that contains extracellular fluid.

neurotransmitter A chemical substance that carries signals from one neuron to another.

receptors In neurons, specialized protein molecules on the postsynaptic membrane that neurotransmitters bind to after passing across the synaptic cleft.

How do nerve cells communicate with each other to influence mind and behavior?

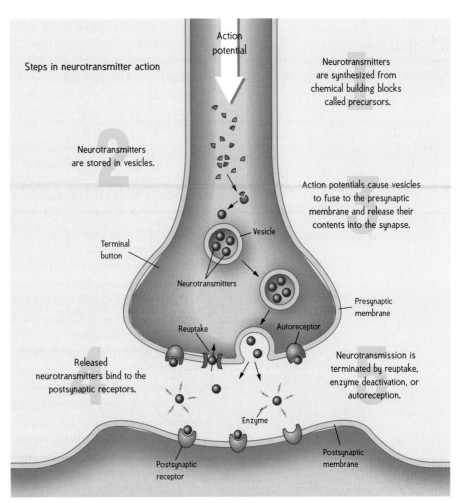

3.14 Neurotransmitters An overview of how neurotransmitters work.

RELATIONSHIP BETWEEN RECEPTORS AND NEUROTRANSMITTERS In much the same way as a lock opens only with the correct key, each receptor can be influenced by only one type of neurotransmitter. Yet drugs and toxins can mimic neurotransmitters and bind with their receptors as if they were the real thing. Addictive drugs such as heroin and cocaine, for example, have their effects because they are structurally similar to naturally occurring neurotransmitters; the receptors cannot differentiate between the ingested drug and the real neurotransmitter. Through knowledge of how neurotransmitters bind with receptors, researchers have been able to develop effective pharmacological therapies for many psychological and medical disorders.

TERMINATING SYNAPTIC TRANSMISSION The three events that terminate the influence of transmitters in the synaptic cleft are *reuptake, enzyme deactivation,* and *autoreception.* Unless one of these processes occurs, once a neurotransmitter is released into the synaptic cleft it continues to bind with receptors and blocks new signals from getting through. This would lock up the brain and prevent new activity. For change to occur, the signals have to be interrupted. The most common termination process is **reuptake**, when the neurotransmitter molecules are taken back into the presynaptic terminal buttons. The cycle of reuptake and release repeats continuously. An action potential prompts terminal buttons to release the transmitter into the synaptic cleft and then take it back for recycling. Another process that terminates the actions of a neurotransmitter occurs when an enzyme destroys the transmitter substance in the synaptic cleft, which is appropriately called **enzyme deactivation**. Different enzymes break down different neurotransmitters. Neurotransmitters can also bind with their own receptors. These **autoreceptors** monitor how much neurotransmitter has been released into the synapse. When excess is detected, the autoreceptors signal the neuron to stop releasing the neurotransmitter. All three methods of termination serve to regulate the activity of neurotransmitters in the synapse.

reuptake The process whereby the neurotransmitter is taken back into the presynaptic terminal buttons, thereby stopping its activity.

enzyme deactivation The process whereby the neurotransmitter is destroyed by an enzyme, thereby terminating its activity.

autoreceptors A neuron's own neurotransmitter receptors, which regulate the release of the neurotransmitters.

REVIEWING the Principles | How Does the Nervous System Operate?

Neurons are the basic units of the nervous system. The neuron's primary task is to take in information, integrate that information, and pass a signal to other neurons. Neurons receive information at the dendrites and process that information in the cell body. An action potential results from the depolarization of the cell membrane, which causes sodium channels to open and allows sodium ions to rush into the neuron. Whether or not a neuron fires depends on the integration of inhibitory and excitatory signals received at the dendrites. Summation of excitatory signals affects the frequency of neuronal firing but not the strength—neurons fire all-or-none. The myelination of axons allows action potentials to propagate rapidly. Action potentials cause vesicles to release neurotransmitters into the synaptic cleft. Neurotransmitters diffuse across the synaptic cleft and bind with specific postsynaptic receptors. Neurotransmitters that depolarize the postsynaptic membrane are excitatory, whereas those that hyperpolarize the postsynaptic membrane are inhibitory. These excitatory and inhibitory signals are terminated through reuptake, enzyme deactivation, and autoreception.

CHAPTER 3 | Genetic and Biological Foundations

How Do Neurotransmitters Influence Emotion, Thought, and Behavior?

Before the 1970s, most researchers believed that communication in the brain took place through the actions of just five or so narrowly defined neurotransmitters. Now we know that more than 60 chemicals transmit information in the brain and body, and that different transmitters are responsible for influencing emotion, thought, and behavior.

As you have learned, all neurotransmitters act to enhance or inhibit action potentials, by depolarizing or hyperpolarizing postsynaptic cell membranes. Many substances, such as drugs and toxins, can alter the actions of neurotransmitters in several ways. This fact is important because much of what we know about neurotransmitters has been learned through the systematic study of the effects of drugs and toxins on emotion, thought, and behavior. For instance, drugs and toxins can alter how the neurotransmitter is synthesized, they can raise or lower the amount of neurotransmitter released from the terminal buttons, and they can change the way the neurotransmitter is deactivated in the synaptic cleft by blocking reuptake or preventing enzyme deactivation. Drugs that enhance the actions of neurotransmitters are known as **agonists**; drugs that inhibit action are **antagonists** (see Figure 3.15).

Researchers often inject neurotransmitter agonists or antagonists into the brains of animals to assess the behavioral effects of a neurotransmitter. For instance,

How do drugs alter neural activity?

agonist Any drug that enhances the actions of a specific neurotransmitter.

antagonist Any drug that inhibits the action of a specific neurotransmitter.

Agonistic drug effects

Drugs increase the synthesis of neurotransmitters.

Drugs increase the release of neurotransmitters.

Drugs bind to autoreceptors and block their inhibitory effect.

Drugs block the deactivation or reuptake of drugs from the synapse.

Drugs bind to postsynaptic receptors and either activate them or increase the effect of the neurotransmitter.

Antagonistic drug effects

Drugs block the synthesis of neurotransmitters.

Drugs block the release of neurotransmitters.

Drugs activate autoreceptors so that they inhibit release of neurotransmitters.

Drugs destroy the neurotransmitter in the synapse.

Drugs bind to postsynaptic receptors thereby blocking neurotransmitter binding.

Action potential

Drug molecule

Vesicle

Neurotransmitter

Reuptake

Auto-receptor

Enzyme

Postsynaptic receptor

3.15 How Drugs Work The typical mechanisms of drug action.

TABLE

3.1 | Common Neurotransmitters and Their Major Functions

NEUROTRANSMITTER	FUNCTIONS
Acetylcholine	Motor control over muscles Learning, memory, sleeping, and dreaming
Monoamines	
Norepinephrine	Arousal and vigilance Eating behavior
Dopamine	Reward and motivation Motor control over voluntary movement
Serotonin	Emotional states and impulsiveness Dreaming
Amino Acids	
GABA (gamma-aminobutyric acid)	Inhibition of action potentials Anxiety and intoxication
Glutamate	Enhances action potentials Learning and memory
Peptide Modulators	
CCK (cholecystokinin)	Learning and memory Satiety
Endorphins	Pain reduction Reward
Substance P	Pain perception

researchers can test the hypothesis that a certain neurotransmitter in a specific brain region leads to increased feeding behavior by injecting an agonist into that brain region, which should increase feeding; in contrast, injecting an antagonist should decrease feeding. By understanding agonistic and antagonistic properties of drugs, researchers have developed effective pharmacological treatments for many psychological and medical disorders.

An important point to keep in mind about neurotransmitters is that their effects are not a property of the chemicals themselves, but rather a function of the receptors to which they bind. The same neurotransmitter can be excitatory or inhibitory, or produce radically different effects, depending on the properties of the receptor. For convenience, we will describe neurotransmitters in four categories: *acetylcholine* (by itself), *monoamines, amino acids,* and *peptides* (Table 3.1).

Acetylcholine Affects Motor Control and Mental Processes

acetylcholine (ACh) The neurotransmitter responsible for motor control at the junction between nerves and muscles; also involved in mental processes such as learning, memory, sleeping, and dreaming.

The neurotransmitter **acetylcholine** (ACh) is responsible for motor control at the junction between nerves and muscles. Terminal buttons release acetylcholine into the synapse, and it binds with the receptors on muscle cells and makes them contract or relax. For instance, ACh both excites skeletal muscles and inhibits heart muscles. Whether its effects will be inhibitory or excitatory depends on the receptors. This difference reinforces the rule that the receptor controls the process.

Acetylcholine is also involved in complex mental processes such as learning, memory, sleeping, and dreaming. Because ACh affects memory and attention, drugs that are ACh antagonists inhibit its activity and can cause temporary amnesia. In a similar way, Alzheimer's disease, a condition characterized primarily by severe memory deficits, is associated with diminished ACh functioning (Geula & Mesulam, 1994). Drugs that are ACh agonists may enhance memory and decrease other symptoms, although so far there has been only marginal success in the pharmacological treatment of Alzheimer's.

Toxins that mimic ACh can bind to its receptors and cause temporary paralysis. For example, curare, an herbal poison used by South American Indians, competes with ACh for receptor binding and inhibits the mechanisms that produce muscle movement. Administration of curare paralyzes the limbs and lungs of its victims, asphyxiating them. Botulism, a form of food poisoning, inhibits the release of ACh from terminal buttons in a similar fashion and leads to trouble with breathing, difficulty in chewing, and often death. Because of its ability to paralyze muscles, botulism is now used in cosmetic surgery in smaller, much less toxic doses. Physicians inject botulism into the eyebrow region, paralyzing muscles that produce some wrinkles. Because the effects wear off over time, a new dose of botulism needs to be injected every two to four months.

NICOTINE One substance that excites ACh receptors is nicotine, the addictive drug found in tobacco leaves. Given the role of ACh in memory and sleeping, it may not surprise you that the ingestion of nicotine has several cognitive effects. For instance, people who wear the nicotine patch often have extremely vivid dreams, probably because of the activation of ACh neurons known to affect the stage of sleep associated with dreaming. Studies demonstrate that smoking a cigarette can heighten attention, improve problem solving, and facilitate memory (Warburton, 1992). But before you rush out to buy a pack, some evidence suggests that nicotine may produce these effects only for current smokers (Heishman, Taylor, & Henningfield, 1994). When nonsmokers are given nicotine gum, they perform more poorly on cognitive tasks, as do former smokers who have not had nicotine for a while. Thus, smoking or chewing tobacco alters how the mind works, and over time users suffer deficits in cognitive performance *unless* they ingest nicotine. This is one of the many reasons why giving up nicotine is so difficult; recent ex-smokers find it hard to think or concentrate.

Monoamines Are Involved in Affect, Arousal, and Motivation

The **monoamines** are a group of neurotransmitters synthesized within the neuron from single amino acids—*mono* means "one." Although the monoamines are involved in a variety of psychological activities, their major functions are to regulate states of arousal and affect (feelings) and to motivate behavior. Earlier we noted that men who had a gene that produced low levels of monoamine oxidase (MAO) and who had been mistreated as children were much more likely to be convicted of violent crimes. MAO is an enzyme that interrupts the activity of all monoamines. The four monoamines are *epinephrine, norepinephrine, serotonin,* and *dopamine.*

EPINEPHRINE AND NOREPINEPHRINE **Epinephrine** is found primarily in the body, although small amounts are in the brain. It was initially called *adrenaline*

monoamines A group of neurotransmitters synthesized from a single amino acid that are involved in a variety of psychological activities.

epinephrine A monoamine, found primarily in the body, which causes a burst of energy after an exciting event.

norepinephrine A monoamine neurotransmitter involved in states of arousal and vigilance.

serotonin A monoamine neurotransmitter important for a wide range of psychological activity, including emotional states, impulse control, and dreaming.

dopamine A monoamine neurotransmitter involved in reward, motivation, and motor control.

Parkinson's disease A neurological disorder that seems to be caused by dopamine depletion, marked by muscular rigidity, tremors, and difficulty initiating voluntary action.

and is the basis for the phrase "adrenaline rush," a burst of energy caused by its release in the body. **Norepinephrine** is involved in states of arousal and alertness. Norepinephrine is especially important for vigilance, a heightened sensitivity to what is going on around you. Norepinephrine appears to be useful for fine-tuning the clarity of attention; it inhibits responsiveness to weak synaptic inputs and strengthens or maintains responsiveness to strong synaptic inputs.

SEROTONIN **Serotonin** is a monoamine neurotransmitter involved in many different behaviors; it is especially important for emotional states, impulse control, and dreaming. Low levels of serotonin are associated with sad and anxious moods, food cravings, and aggressive behavior. Drugs that block the reuptake of serotonin are now used to treat a wide array of mental and behavioral disorders, including depression, obsessive-compulsive disorders, eating disorders, and obesity (Tollesfson, 1995).

The drug LSD is structurally similar to the neurotransmitter serotonin; when ingested, LSD enters the brain and binds with serotonin receptors. When LSD binds with serotonin receptors normally involved in dreaming, it causes hallucinations, a dreamlike state of mind people experience while they are awake.

DOPAMINE **Dopamine** serves many significant brain functions, especially motivation and motor control. Many theorists believe dopamine is the primary neurotransmitter that communicates which activities may be rewarding. Eating when hungry, drinking when thirsty, or having sex when aroused all lead to activation of dopamine receptors and therefore are experienced as pleasurable. At the same time, dopamine activation is involved in motor control and planning, thereby guiding behavior toward objects and experiences that will lead to additional reward. One theory of drug addiction is that certain drugs are dopamine agonists; people self-administer these drugs because they activate dopamine receptors and cause pleasure (Wise & Rompre, 1989). For example, cocaine blocks the reuptake of dopamine into presynaptic vesicles and allows dopamine to have a longer-lasting effect on postsynaptic receptors, leading to heightened arousal and feelings of euphoria. Rats quickly learn to self-administer cocaine, which supports the idea that it has rewarding qualities.

Dopamine also is involved in controlling voluntary muscle movements. Research in the past few decades implicates dopamine depletion in **Parkinson's disease**, a neurological disorder marked by muscular rigidity, tremors, and difficulty initiating voluntary action. With Parkinson's disease, the dopamine-producing neurons slowly die off. In the later stages of the disorder, people suffer from cognitive and mood disturbances. Parkinson's is a slow and degenerative disease that eventually leads to death.

From a treatment standpoint, drugs that enhance dopamine production can compensate for the lack of dopamine-producing neurons. For instance, injections of one of the chief building blocks of dopamine, L-DOPA, help the surviving neurons produce more dopamine. When used to treat Parkinson's disease, L-DOPA often produces a remarkable, though temporary, recovery. However, L-DOPA does nothing to stop the underlying disease that is destroying dopamine neurons in the first place. Fewer and fewer neurons work harder and harder to provide enough dopamine for fine motor movement; eventually, too many neurons die, and L-DOPA's effect diminishes.

A promising development in Parkinson's research is the transplanting of fetal tissue into human brains in the hope that the new fetal cells will produce dopamine. The first American to undergo fetal neural transplantation, Donald Wilson, regained the ability to walk and was able to return to his hobby of woodworking. Brain scans showed increased release of dopamine one year following implantation (Figure 3.16).

Although case studies indicate that fetal transplants have promise for treating Parkinson's disease, clinical studies using random assignment have not found large differences between patients receiving fetal-cell transplants and those undergoing sham surgery, which mimics the surgery but does not involve transplantation (Olanow et al., 2003). Nonetheless, these methods are still being developed, and researchers are continuing to explore how fetal-cell transplants might be used to treat brain disorders. As discussed in Chapter 4, there is also hope that implanting stem cells, which might be more potent than fetal cells, might aid in the treatment of disorders such as Parkinson's.

3.16 Dopamine Activity PET scans showing dopamine activity before (left) and after (right) fetal transplant surgery. This increase suggests that the transplant was successful and that the new neurons are producing dopamine.

Profiles in Psychological Science

Frozen Addicts

Although the cause of Parkinson's disease is not known, there is evidence that ingestion of certain drugs and toxins can produce symptoms that mimic the disease, as was dramatically demonstrated in the mysterious case of the "frozen addicts." Every now and then a patient baffles emergency-room physicians, challenging their years of medical training and practical experience. In July 1982, six patients ranging in age from 26 to 42 showed up at hospitals in San Jose, California, with symptoms unlike any the ER physicians had previously encountered. The patients' eyes were open and they appeared to be conscious; their limbs were stuck in place and their faces were frozen into hideous masks. Unable to speak, the six could not give any clues about the cause of their condition.

That all six patients had the same unusual symptoms could mean they had been exposed to a common toxic substance, but interviews with friends and family allowed the doctors to dismiss that possibility. The interviews did reveal, however, that each was a frequent heroin user. Still, the doctors remained uncertain about the role of heroin in their condition, since none of them bore any resemblance to the usual heroin overdose victim. Heroin depresses the body's nervous system, so a typical overdose is associated with lethargy and lax muscles; it was obvious that they had not taken real heroin. This was confirmed through interviews with their friends, who told of injecting what they believed to be heroin but experiencing sensations and bodily movements that were nothing like what they had come to expect from the drug. Most heroin users report a warm glow that comes almost immediately after injection; the warmth spreads throughout the body and leads to orgasmic sensations. Those who took the tainted heroin felt a stinging, burning sensation at the site of the injection, their vision became blurry, they experienced a metallic taste in the backs of their mouths, and their limbs starting jerking uncontrollably. This was certainly not the sought-after high associated with intravenous heroin injection. Drug users are accustomed to unanticipated side effects, since most street drugs are mixtures of narcotics and a wide array of fillers, some of which are poisons, used by dealers to increase profits.

The patients' symptoms persisted over many days. Doctors began to suspect brain damage, but no signs of it could be identified using CT scans or MRI. The six

3.17 MPTP and Parkinson's Disease These people developed symptoms of Parkinson's disease after ingesting the substance MPTP, which they mistakenly believed to be a synthetic form of heroin.

had undoubtedly ingested the same drug, but what was the drug and why was it causing these symptoms? William Langston, a brain scientist from Stanford University, examined the patients and was struck by the similarity between their symptoms and those of patients with Parkinson's disease. The six patients (five of whom are shown in Figure 3.17) were unlikely candidates for Parkinson's disease, which rarely affects people under age 45. And the chance that it would strike six young people from the same basic area at the same time is outside the realm of possibility. Dr. Langston suspected that the six might have injected a synthetic drug that was supposed to act like heroin, and that this drug had led to a condition similar to Parkinson's. His diagnosis turned out to be correct. The drug (later called MPTP) taken by these patients damaged a region of the brain that is normally involved in communicating with muscles to produce voluntary movements. The drug MPTP is now used to study Parkinson's disease, since it can be used to create animal models of the disease.

Whatever happened to the frozen addicts? Dr. Langston has tried a variety of experimental procedures on them over the two decades since their poisoning, including implanting new dopamine neurons in their brains, which produced modest improvement. Of the original six, some have died, one is in jail, and only one is completely able to take care of herself. In spite of this sad outcome, the finding that MPTP damages specific brain regions has allowed scientists to explore methods that might cure Parkinson's disease or at least delay the development of its symptoms in those with the disease. ■

Amino Acids Are General Inhibitory and Excitatory Transmitters in the Brain

For much of the past century, the monoamines and acetylcholine were considered to be the only neurotransmitters. In the past 40 years, however, it has become apparent that many other substances are also involved in neuronal communication. For instance, although the monoamines are made up of amino acids, some amino acids serve as neurotransmitters all by themselves. More recent research has established important roles for amino acids in general levels of inhibition and activation of the nervous system. Here we will look at two amino acids, *GABA* and *glutamate*.

GABA **GABA** (gamma-aminobutyric acid) is the primary inhibitory transmitter in the nervous system and works throughout the brain to hyperpolarize postsynaptic membranes. Without the inhibitory effect of GABA, synaptic excitation might get out of control and spread through the brain in a reverberating circuit. Epileptic seizures may happen because of an abnormality in GABA functioning (Upton, 1994).

Drugs that affect the GABA system are widely used to treat anxiety disorders. For instance, people with nervous disorders commonly use benzodiazepines, which include drugs such as Valium. Benzodiazepines assist GABA in binding with one of its primary receptors, an action that inhibits neuronal connections and reduces symptoms of anxiety. These drugs also treat insomnia and other stress-related disorders. Ethyl alcohol—the type that people drink—has similar effects on GABA re-

GABA (gamma-aminobutyric acid) The primary inhibitory transmitter in the nervous system.

ceptors, which is why alcohol typically is experienced as relaxing. GABA reception also may be the primary mechanism by which alcohol interferes with motor coordination. Drugs that block the effects of alcohol on GABA receptors also prevent alcohol intoxication. However, drugs that prevent the effects of alcohol are not used to treat alcoholics because reducing the symptoms of being drunk could easily lead to even greater alcohol abuse.

GLUTAMATE **Glutamate** is the primary excitatory transmitter in the nervous system and is involved in fast-acting neuronal transmission throughout the brain. It opens sodium gates in postsynaptic membranes and causes depolarization. Glutamate receptors aid learning and memory by strengthening synaptic connections.

In addition to being released by neurons, glutamate is also released by *astrocytes,* which are a type of glial cell. Until very recently, glial cells were believed to play primarily a support role in neuronal communication, such as being the building blocks of the myelin sheath. However, within the last few years it has become apparent that astrocytes play an important role in the nervous system. The release of neurotransmitters into the synapse causes a change in the activity of *calcium ions* in astrocytes, which causes the release of glutamate into the synapse. In this way, astrocytes contribute to the activity of neurons, such as by modifying their levels of polarization. Philip Haydon (2001) has described astrocytes as being analogous to stagehands and directors in the theater; they may not be center stage, but they are nonetheless important for the performance. How this alternative mode of communication within the nervous system affects higher brain processes, such as psychological activity, is currently unknown.

Peptides Modulate Neurotransmission

Peptides are chains of two or more amino acids that are found in the brain and the body. Often, neurotransmitters and peptides are released simultaneously into the synaptic cleft, and the peptide modifies the effect of the neurotransmitter with which it is paired. Some peptides, for example, prolong or shorten the action of neurotransmitters; others influence postsynaptic receptors. An analogy of the effects of peptides on neurotransmitters is the sound controls on a stereo. Peptide *modulation* can turn the volume up or down and alter the tone, but it cannot change the tune. As such, peptides help to explain the vast subtleties and nuances of human experience. There are more than 30 known peptides that act as neurotransmitters or modulators. Three examples are *cholecystokinin (CCK)*, *endorphins,* and *Substance P.*

CCK **Cholecystokinin (CCK)** is the peptide found in highest concentration in the cerebral cortex. It plays a role in learning and memory, pain transmission, and exploratory behavior. The administration of CCK triggers panic attacks in people who suffer from panic disorder, creating intense anxiety, a feeling of impending doom, and often feelings of suffocation (Bourin, Baker, & Bradwejn, 1998). CCK may also contribute to social anxiety. In one experiment, two rats are placed together in a novel or brightly lit setting. The amount of time they interact, grooming and sniffing, measures their social behavior, which usually declines under stress. Administration of CCK antagonists leads to more social interaction whereas administration of CCK agonists has the opposite effect (Woodruff & Hughes, 1991). CCK is also found in the gastrointestinal system, where it promotes *satiety,* the feeling of fullness that terminates feeding. Administration of CCK before a meal leads people to feel full more quickly and decreases the amount they eat (Woods & Stricker, 1999). As you might

glutamate The primary excitatory transmitter in the nervous system.

peptides Chains of two or more amino acids found in the brain and the body; they can act like classic neurotransmitters or modify the quality of the neurotransmitter with which they are released.

cholecystokinin (CCK) The peptide found in highest concentration in the cerebral cortex; it plays a role in learning and memory, pain transmission, and exploratory behavior.

imagine, research is currently under way to see whether CCK can be used to help treat human obesity.

endorphins Peptides involved in natural pain reduction and reward.

substance P A peptide that acts as a neurotransmitter and is involved in pain perception.

ENDORPHINS **Endorphins** are peptides involved in natural pain reduction and reward. In the early 1970s Candace Pert and Solomon Snyder established that opiate drugs such as heroin and morphine bind to receptors in the brain, which led to the discovery of naturally occurring substances that bind to those sites. These substances were called endorphins (short for "endogenous morphine").

Endorphins are part of the body's natural defense against pain. Pain is useful because it signals that an animal is hurt or in danger and therefore should try to escape or withdraw, but pain can also interfere with adaptive functioning. If pain prevented animals from engaging in behaviors such as eating, competing, and mating they would fail to pass along their genes. The analgesic effects of endorphins help animals perform these behaviors even when they are in pain. In humans, administration of drugs that bind with endorphin receptors, such as morphine, reduces the subjective experience of pain. People still feel pain but report detachment; they know about the pain but do not experience it as aversive (Foley, 1993). Apparently morphine alters the way pain is experienced rather than blocking the nerves that transmit pain signals.

Endorphins may account for the *placebo effect*. A placebo is a neutral substance, such as water, that has no pharmacological effect. Yet people being treated for pain with a placebo might report relief just because they expect relief. In a classic report published in the 1950s, 4 out of 10 surgical patients reported satisfactory relief from pain after the injection of salt water (Lasagna, Mosteller, von Felsinger, & Beecher, 1954). Placebo effects are real; administration of a placebo leads to physiological changes in heart rate and digestion. When people take a medication and expect to gain relief, mechanisms release endorphins, which confirm their expectations.

Endorphins are associated with euphoric moods; this may explain why drugs such as heroin or morphine, which mimic endorphins by binding with their receptors, are so addictive. Endorphins may also explain "runner's high," the experience that runners get when they push their bodies beyond endurance, and pain turns to pleasure. One theory is that the body produces endorphins to cope with anticipated pain; when pain fails to materialize or is less than expected, the result is pleasure. Skydiving and other high-risk activities may be pleasurable for similar reasons (Jones & Ellis, 1996).

SUBSTANCE P **Substance P** is another peptide that functions as a neurotransmitter and is involved in pain perception. This mysterious-sounding stuff was first identified in 1931 by von Euler and Gaddum, who referred to it in their notes simply by the initial "P," and this simple name stuck. Substance P helps transmit signals about pain to the brain. Probably the best evidence for it can be found at your local Mexican restaurant, where you can conduct your own experiment. Chili peppers, especially jalapeño peppers, contain a substance known as capsaicin, which releases Substance P. Once released, Substance P makes your tongue and mouth burn, your eyes water, and your hand reach for the nearest pitcher of water—a bad idea, because water spreads capsaicin around and releases more Substance P, which only intensifies the pain.

Over-the-counter liniments also contain capsaicin; when rubbed on your skin they release Substance P, which transmits pain signals to the brain, causing a burning sensation. Used in sufficient quantity, the capsaicin in these ointments depletes reserves of Substance P, preventing the neurons from transmitting other pain messages to the brain. This analgesic effect lasts until more Substance P is produced.

REVIEWING the Principles | How Do Neurotransmitters Influence Emotion, Thought, and Behavior?

Neurotransmitters are chemical substances that carry signals across the synaptic cleft and act to enhance or inhibit action potentials by depolarizing or hyperpolarizing postsynaptic cell membranes. Substances that enhance the actions of neurotransmitters are known as agonists; those that inhibit action are antagonists. Acetycholine is involved in motor movement as well as complex thought. The monoamines are involved in arousal and motivation, such as dopamine's role in reward. GABA and glutamate are related to general inhibiion and excitation. The number of known substances that act as neurotransmitters is now over 60 and growing. In addition to the classic neurotransmitters, other amino acids and peptides also affect neurotransmission.

How Are Neural Messages Integrated into Communication Systems?

A number of communication systems operate together to regulate all psychological activity. The most important communication system is the nervous system, made up of networks of neurons throughout the body. The nervous system is divided into two functional units: the **central nervous system (CNS)**, which consists of the brain and spinal cord, and the **peripheral nervous system (PNS)**, which consists of all other nerve cells in the body. The two systems are anatomically separate, but their functions are highly interdependent. The PNS transmits a variety of information to the CNS, which organizes and evaluates that information and then directs the PNS to perform specific behaviors or make bodily adjustments. In addition, the CNS receives information from the *endocrine system,* which uses a different mode of communication. This section describes the interaction of the nervous system and the endocrine system in the production of psychological activity.

The Central Nervous System Consists of the Brain and Spinal Cord

Nearly all the functions of the CNS are performed by the brain, and there has recently been dramatic growth in scientific knowledge about how the brain works. For our purposes of understanding how neural messages are integrated into communication systems, remember that behavior and mental activity are produced within specific locations in the brain. For example, some brain regions are involved with emotional states, others with the ability to see, and others with the ability to speak. The brain has developed specialized mechanisms over millions of years to solve problems related to survival and reproduction. Using methods such as brain imaging, psychological scientists have been able to map the functions of many structures in the brain, and you will learn about these in the next chapter.

The other part of the CNS is the spinal cord. Although the spinal cord is capable of reflex action, its main job is to receive sensory signals from the body and transmit them to the brain, and to receive signals from the brain and relay them to the body

How does the brain communicate with the body?

central nervous system (CNS) The brain and spinal cord.

peripheral nervous system (PNS) All nerve cells in the body that are not part of the central nervous system. The PNS includes the somatic and autonomic nervous systems.

to control muscles, glands, and internal organs. When the spinal cord is damaged, the brain loses both sensory input from and control over the body. The severity of feeling loss and paralysis depends on where the spinal cord is damaged. The higher up on the spine the damage is, the greater the number of nerve connections between the brain and the body that are severed.

The CNS is separated from the rest of the body by the *blood-brain barrier,* which refers to the selectively permeable nature of blood vessels throughout the CNS that prevents certain toxins and poisons in the blood from entering the brain or spinal cord. The extent to which chemical substances have an influence on the brain depends on the ease with which they pass through the blood-brain barrier. Many drugs, such as cocaine and heroin, cross the blood-brain barrier easily and therefore are able to bind with receptors and affect neurotransmitter functioning.

The Peripheral Nervous System Includes the Somatic and Autonomic Systems

The PNS has two primary components, which themselves are referred to as nervous systems: the *somatic nervous system* and the *autonomic nervous system* (Figure 3.18). The **somatic nervous system** transmits sensory signals to the CNS via nerves (bundles of axons). Specialized receptors in the skin, muscles, and joints send sensory information to the spinal cord, which relays it to the brain. In addition, signals are sent from the CNS to muscles, joints, and skin to initiate, modulate, or inhibit movement.

The second major component of the PNS is the **autonomic nervous system (ANS)**, which regulates the body's internal environment by stimulating glands (such as sweat glands) and by maintaining internal organs such as the heart. Nerves in the ANS carry *somatosensory* signals to the CNS, providing information about, for example, the fullness of your stomach or bladder, and how anxious you feel.

somatic nervous system A major component of the peripheral nervous system, which transmits sensory signals to the CNS via nerves.

autonomic nervous system (ANS) A major component of the peripheral nervous system, which regulates the body's internal environment by stimulating glands and by maintaining internal organs such as the heart, gall bladder, and stomach.

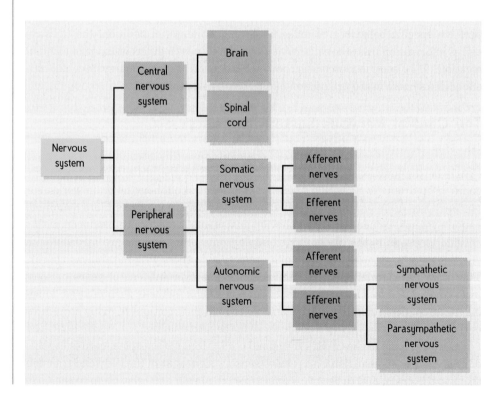

3.18 The Nervous System The major divisions of the nervous system.

CHAPTER 3 | Genetic and Biological Foundations

SYMPATHETIC AND PARASYMPATHETIC DIVISIONS Two types of signals travel from the CNS to organs and glands in the PNS. To understand them, imagine that as you are studying, a fire alarm goes off. In the second after hearing the alarm, signals have been sent out to parts of your body to tell it to prepare for action: blood flows to skeletal muscles, epinephrine is released to increase heart rate and blood sugar, your lungs start taking in more oxygen, you stop digesting food to conserve energy, your pupils dilate to maximize visual sensitivity, and you start perspiring to keep cool. These actions are the result of the **sympathetic division** of the autonomic nervous system, which prepares the body for action. Should there be a fire, you will be physically prepared to flee. As often happens, the fire bell is a false alarm. Now your heart returns to its normal steady beat, your breathing slows, you resume digesting food, and you quit perspiring. This return to a normal state results from the action of the **parasympathetic division** of the ANS (Figure 3.19). Parasympathetic signals return your body to a resting state after sympathetic activation. Most of your internal organs are controlled by inputs from sympathetic and parasympathetic systems. The more aroused you are, the greater the dominance of the sympathetic system.

It doesn't take a fire alarm to activate your sympathetic nervous system. When you meet someone you find attractive, your heart starts beating quickly, you start

sympathetic division of ANS A division of the autonomic nervous system that prepares the body for action.

parasympathetic division of ANS A division of the autonomic nervous system that returns the body to its resting state.

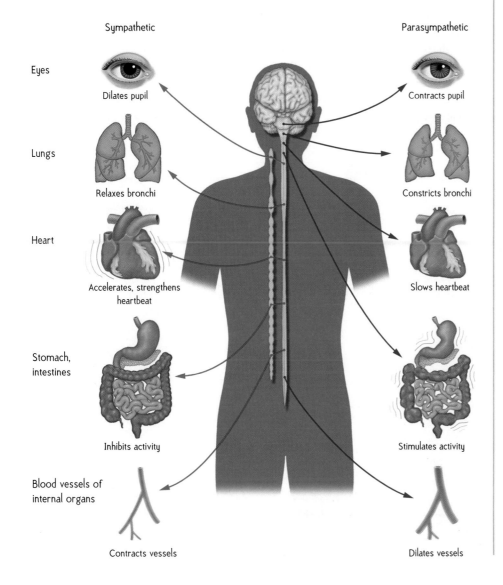

3.19 **The Sympathetic and Parasympathetic Systems** The sympathetic division of the nervous system prepares the body for action, whereas the parasympathetic returns it to a resting state.

perspiring, you may start breathing heavily, and although you may not know it, your pupils widen. These are all signs of sexual arousal, which relies on activation of the sympathetic division of the ANS, and they provide nonverbal cues during social interaction.

The sympathetic nervous system is also activated by psychological states such as anxiety or unhappiness. Certain people worry a great deal or cannot cope with stress; their are bodies in a constant state of arousal. Chronic activation of the sympathetic nervous system is associated with medical problems that include ulcers, heart disease, and asthma (Davison & Pennebaker, 1996).

The Endocrine System Communicates through Hormones

Like the nervous system, the **endocrine system** is a communication system that influences thoughts, behaviors, and actions. The main distinction between the two is their mode of communication: The endocrine system uses hormones, whereas the nervous system uses electrochemical signals. **Hormones** are chemical substances released into the bloodstream by *endocrine glands,* ductless glands such as the pancreas, thyroid, and testes or ovaries (Figure 3.20). Once released by a gland or an organ, hormones travel through the bloodstream until they reach their target tissues, where they bind to receptor sites and influence the tissue. Because they travel through the bloodstream, hormones can take from seconds to hours to exert their effects; once hormones are in the bloodstream, their effects can last for a long time and affect multiple targets.

The endocrine system and the nervous system work together to regulate psychological activity. For instance, the brain interprets potential physical threats and

endocrine system A communication system that uses hormones to influence thoughts, behaviors, and actons.

hormones Chemical substances, typically released from endocrine glands, that travel through the bloodstream to targeted tissues, which are subsequently influenced by the hormone.

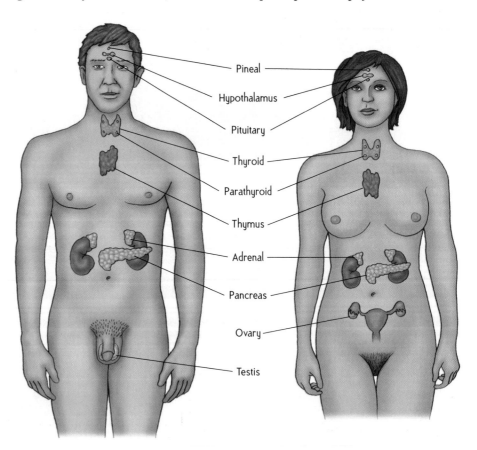

- Pineal
- Hypothalamus
- Pituitary
- Thyroid
- Parathyroid
- Thymus
- Adrenal
- Pancreas
- Ovary
- Testis

3.20 Glands The major endocrine glands.

CHAPTER 3 | Genetic and Biological Foundations

directs action in the endocrine system to prepare for battle or to deal with possible injury.

EFFECTS OF HORMONES ON SEXUAL BEHAVIOR An example of hormonal influence is evident in sexual behavior. The main endocrine glands in sexual behavior are the **gonads**, which for males are testes and for females are ovaries. The two major gonadal hormones are identical in males and females, although the quantity differs: *androgens* such as testosterone are more prevalent in males, whereas *estrogens* such as estradiol are more prevalent in females. Gonadal hormones influence both the development of secondary sex characteristics and adult sexual behavior.

For males, successful sexual behavior depends on having at least a minimum amount of testosterone. Surgical removal of the testes diminishes the capacity for developing an erection and lowers sexual interest. Yet a castrated male who receives an injection of testosterone will be able to perform sexually. Do injections of testosterone increase sexual behavior among healthy men? The answer is no, which implies that as long as a minimum amount of testosterone is available, the healthy male will be able to perform (Sherwin, 1988).

The influence of gonadal hormones on females is much more complex. In many nonhuman animals there is a finite period called *estrus* when the female is sexually receptive and fertile. During estrus the female displays behaviors designed to attract the male. Surgical removal of the ovaries terminates these behaviors and the female is no longer receptive. However, injections of estrogen reinstate estrus. What does this mean for women? Apparently not very much. The sexual behavior of women is not particularly linked to their menstrual cycle, and surgical removal of the ovaries has a minimal effect on sexual interest or behavior (Dennerstein & Burrows, 1982). Moreover, sexual behavior in women may have more to do with androgens than estrogens (Morris, Udry, Khan-Dawood, & Dawood, 1987). Women with higher levels of testosterone report greater interest in sex, and injections of testosterone increase women's sexual interest after surgical removal of the uterus (Sherwin, 1994).

"You have been charged with driving under the influence of testosterone."

How does hormonal communication differ from neurotransmission?

gonads The main endocrine glands involved in sexual behavior: in males, the testes; in females, the ovaries.

Thinking Critically

Does Taking Steroids Lead to Violence?

Imagine that you have been asked to serve on a jury deliberating the case of 16-year-old Jamie Fuller, who in August 1991 killed his 14-year-old girlfriend, Amy Carnevale. Fuller, who reportedly was angry that Amy had gone to the beach the day before with some other boys, repeatedly stabbed her and then dumped her body in a pond. Those are the facts. But why did he kill her?

According to the prosecutors, Fuller was a troubled youth who had planned the murder for months and discussed it with his friends. Afterward, he even bragged about killing her. According to the defense attorneys, however, Fuller had been taking steroids at the time of the crime, and the effects of steroids caused him to become enraged and lose control. Let's examine some of the issues involved in the defense claim.

According to the defense, steroids can produce violent outbursts in those who take them, so-called "roid rage." The particular steroid that Fuller ingested was a synthetic form of the male sex hormone testosterone, which enhances muscle growth. Although steroids are banned in most sports, some athletes use them to become stronger, faster, and more competitive. Steroid use is reputed to be widespread in some sports, such as weightlifting, but it is apparently on the rise in others, such as baseball, and even among high school athletes who want to be more muscular. There is little doubt that steroids can enhance performance, but can they create killers?

Given that the steroid that Fuller was taking was a synthetic form of testosterone, is there any evidence that testosterone itself is associated with aggression? Let's critically examine the evidence. Males have more testosterone than females, and males carry out the vast majority of aggressive and violent acts in this world. Boys play more roughly than girls at an early age. They become especially aggressive during early adolescence, a time when their levels of testosterone rise tenfold (Mazur & Booth, 1998). But this could just as easily be because increases in testosterone coincide with other maturational changes that promote aggression, such as physical growth.

The overall picture suggests only a modest correlation between testosterone and human aggression. Particularly aggressive men, such as violent criminals, and particularly physical athletes, such as hockey players, have been found to have higher levels of testosterone than other males (Dabbs & Morris, 1990). This relationship, however, is not large, and it is unclear how testosterone is linked to greater aggressiveness. For instance, it may be that testosterone changes are the result of rather than the cause of aggressive behavior. A number of studies have shown that testosterone rises just prior to athletic competition; it remains high for the winners of competitive matches and drops lower for the losers. Even those who simply watch a competition can be affected. Testosterone increased in Brazilian television viewers who watched Brazil beat Italy in the 1994 World Cup soccer tournament, but decreased for Italian television viewers (Bernhardt, Dabbs, Fielden, & Lutter, 1998). This suggests that testosterone might not play a direct role in aggression, but rather may be related to dominance, the results of having greater power and status (Mazur & Booth, 1998). If this is true, the question then is how feelings of dominance are related to aggression.

It remains possible that taking large doses of some steroids might increase testosterone to such a level that it produces an extreme need for dominance and control, thereby provoking violent behavior when a male is challenged. Jamie Fuller had been a skinny, introverted teen who often was picked on by bigger kids. After he took steroids for many months, his appearance and personality changed dramatically: he gained some 30 pounds of muscle and became more socially assertive, as well as increasingly short-tempered and belligerent. According to testimony by the Harvard psychiatrist Harrison Pope, steroids caused these changes in Jamie Fuller, which should mitigate his guilt in the murder of Amy Carnevale. Pope claims there have been a number of case studies of steroid users becoming extremely violent. Athletes themselves report becoming more aggressive and even committing violent crimes after steroid use. In self-report studies, those who admit taking large quantities of steroids also report experiencing grandiose beliefs and frenzied mental states and engaging in reckless and aggressive behavior (Figure 3.21). Should we believe these anecdotal reports? Isn't it possible that the athletes are simply repeating what they have heard on television or that they are using this possible link to excuse their aggressive actions?

It is important to remember that correlation does not prove causation. In self-report studies, researchers cannot determine whether it is the steroids or some other factor that is responsible for aggressive outbursts. Perhaps the social environment of athletes encourages aggressive behavior; emotionally intense practices and demanding coaches can't be discounted. Alternatively, perhaps male athletes who are susceptible to violence or who have other psychological problems are more likely to use steroids to enhance athletic performance (Yates, Perry, & Murray, 1992). A study by Pope and his colleagues found that weightlifters who used steroids were much more likely to be substance abusers, as was Fuller, than those who had never taken steroids (Kanayama, Pope, Cohane, & Hudson, 2003). Which causes which?

An effective research strategy to understand the effect of steroids is to administer randomly either steroids or placebos to research participants, without anyone knowing which participants received which, and then examine changes in mood and behavior. Pope and his colleagues (2000) conducted such a study and found that those subjects who took steroids experienced overall increases in aggression and frenzied emotions. But they also found that these effects were highly variable, with 16 percent of the participants showing quite dramatic changes and the remainder showing minimal effects. One limitation of this kind of research is that it is unethical to give research participants the massive doses of steroids that athletes often take, since serious health consequences are associated with such use. Maybe if higher doses were used, all of the participants would have shown increased aggression. It is impossible to know. But the preponderance of evidence suggests that chronic high doses of steroids may promote aggressive outbursts, at least among some users. Still, is this a sufficient explanation of why Jamie Fuller killed Amy Carnevale? Obviously there are many details about the crime that you do not know. But how would knowing about Fuller's steroid use affect your willingness to convict him? Do you think his changes in personality and aggressiveness were caused by steroid use?

The actual trial jury didn't accept the steroid defense; Fuller was convicted and sentenced to life in prison. What evidence would you require in order to determine whether steroids could ever be responsible for violent behavior? ∎

3.21 "Roid Rage" Some athletes report that they become more aggressive and violent after taking steroids, but psychological research has been unable to determine the exact relationship between steroids and aggression.

Actions of the Nervous System and Endocrine System Are Coordinated

Throughout this chapter, we have described communication systems that link neurochemical and physiological processes to behaviors, thoughts, and feelings. These systems are fully integrated and interact to facilitate survival. The nervous and endocrine systems use information from the environment to direct behavioral responses that are adaptive. Ultimately, the endocrine system is under the control of the central nervous system. External and internal stimuli are interpreted in the brain, and signals are sent from the brain to the endocrine system, which then initiates a variety of effects on the body and on behavior.

Most of the central control of the endocrine system is accomplished by a small brain structure called the *hypothalamus,* which is located just above the roof of the mouth. As you will learn in the next chapter, the hypothalamus plays an extremely important role in behaviors related to survival and reproduction, such as feeding and sex. How does this central control work? At the base of the hypothalamus is the **pituitary gland**, which controls the release of hormones from the rest of the endocrine glands. Based on some sort of neural activation, a *releasing factor* is secreted from the hypothalamus. This releasing factor causes the pituitary to release a specific

pituitary gland Located at the base of the hypothalamus, the gland that sends hormonal signals that control the release of hormones from endocrine glands.

hormone, which then travels to endocrine sites throughout the body. Once the hormone is at the target sites, it touches off the release of other hormones, which subsequently affect bodily reactions or behavior.

It is fascinating how finely tuned this integration can be. For example, consider the case of physical growth. *Growth hormone (GH)* is an extract from the pituitary gland that affects bone, cartilage, and muscle tissues, helping them to grow or regenerate after injury. External administration of GH can increase body size, something known since the 1930s. A common and effective therapy for children with medical conditions such as dwarfism is a synthetic version of GH. How does it work? To build body tissues, GH requires dietary protein. A lack of protein in the diet is associated with a lack of normal growth.

GH is released in bursts throughout the day. Its release is triggered by the *growth hormone releasing factor (GRF)*. GRF neurons are connected to an area of the hypothalamus that is involved in sleep-wake cycles. Thus, the bursts of GH are controlled by the body's internal clock.

Once GH is available, it needs protein. GRF also plays a role in the control of feeding behavior. Injections of GRF into the area of the brain that controls the body clock increase consumption of protein but not fats or carbohydrates (Dickson & Vaccarino, 1994). Consider the whole picture: GRF selectively stimulates eating protein, perhaps by making protein especially enjoyable. At the same time, it also releases GH, which relies on the higher intake of dietary protein to help build strong bones and muscles. Hence, the CNS, PNS, and endocrine system are clearly integrated to ensure that behaviors provide the body with substances it needs for survival at the times they are required.

REVIEWING the Principles | How Are Neural Messages Integrated into Communication Systems?

The central nervous system, consisting of the brain and spinal cord, attends to the body and the environment, initiates actions, and directs the peripheral nervous system and endocrine system to respond appropriately. All three systems use chemicals to transmit their signals, but transmission in the nervous system occurs across synapses whereas transmission in the endocrine system uses hormones that travel through the bloodstream. The hypothalamus controls the endocrine system by directing the pituitary to release specific hormones. The various communication systems are integrated and promote behavior that is adaptive to the environment.

Conclusion

The human body is a biological machine, produced by a genome that has been shaped by millions of years of evolution. Some 30,000 genes provide instructions for producing proteins, and this modest process builds a brain that thinks, feels, and acts. The biological revolution has revealed that these genes not only build the common structures of the human body, but they are also partially responsible for differences among individuals, such as physical appearance, personality, and mental abilities. So far, we only have a minimal understanding of the complexity of our mental lives at the genetic level of analysis. Only now are we beginning to understand the relationship between our environments and our genes. There are more neuronal connections in the human brain than there are stars in our galaxy (Kandel, Schwartz, & Jessell, 1995), and the messages that are transmitted are modulated by subtle variations in the actions of dozens of chemicals in the synapses. Not only do we need to understand how these mechanisms work, but we also need to know how our environment causes our genes to "turn on and off." Understanding the inner workings of genetic expression may well lead to profound insights into what makes us human and how our minds work.

Summarizing the Principles of Genetic and Biological Foundations

What Is the Genetic Basis of Psychological Science?

1. **Heredity involves passing along genes through reproduction:** The Human Genome Project has mapped the approximately 30,000 genes that make up the 23 chromosomal pairs in humans. Variations of genes (alleles) are either dominant or recessive. The genome represents the genotype and the observable characteristics are the phenotype. Many characteristics are polygenetic.

2. **Genotypic variation is created by sexual reproduction:** Because one half of each chromosome comes from each parent and is randomly joined, there is enormous variation in the genome of the resulting zygote. Mutations also give rise to variations.

3. **Genes affect behavior:** Behavioral geneticists are able to examine the similarity and variation in shared characteristics in a population, based on genetic and environmental similarity; this assessment is termed heritability.

4. **Social and environmental contexts influence genetic expression:** Though genes guide the development of characteristics, their final expression is a complex interaction between genetic makeup and environmental context.

5. **Gene expression can be modified:** Genetic manipulation has been achieved in other mammals (e.g., mice) but has proven difficult in humans. However, studies focusing on RNA offer new hope.

How Does the Nervous System Operate?

6. **Neurons are specialized for communication:** Neurons are the basic building blocks of the nervous system that receive and send chemical messages. The structure of all neurons is the same but vary by function and location in the nervous system.

7. **Action potentials cause neuronal communication:** Changes in the electrical charge of neurons results in an action potential (neural firing). This is the means of communication within networks of neurons.

8. **Changes in electrical potential lead to action:** Neural firings either continue the message to other neurons or halt it. Neurons fire due to a change in the electrical balance of positive and negative sodium and potassium ions inside and outside the neuron.

9. **Action potentials spread along the axon:** The dendrites receive a signal that spreads the changes in the exchange of positive and negative ions to reach a threshold, which generates an action potential. The firing of a neuron is all or none—a neuron does not partially fire. This electrical signal travels along the axon. The myelin insulation on the axon speeds transmission.

10. **Neurotransmitters bind to receptors across the synapse:** Neurons do not touch; they release chemicals (neurotransmitters), which bind with receptors of other neurons thus changing the charge in that neuron. The effect of neurotransmitters is halted by a variety of actions.

How Do Neurotransmitters Influence Emotion, Thought, and Behavior?

11. **Acetylcholine affects motor control and mental processes:** Acetylcholine acts on neurons directing muscle movement.

12. **Monoamines are involved in affect, arousal, and motivation:** Epinephrine and norepinephrine are involved in arousal and alertness. Serotonin is involved in impulse control, emotion, and dreaming. Dopamine affects motor control and motivation.

13. **Amino acids are general inhibitory and excitatory transmitters in the brain:** The amino acid GABA is the transmitter for inhibiting neuronal transmission. Glutamate does the opposite; it is involved in neuronal transmission and aids learning and memory.

14. **Peptides modulate neurotransmission:** Peptides change the effect of other transmitters. Cholecystokinin (CCK), endorphins, and substance P affect satiation and pain.

How Are Neural Messages Integrated into Communication Systems?

15. **The central nervous system consists of the brain and spinal cord:** The central nervous system is made up of the structures and functions of the brain and spinal cord.

16. **The peripheral nervous system includes the somatic and autonomic systems:** The structures and functions that regulate the body's internal environment is the autonomic system, which has the complementary division of the alarm response (sympathetic) and the return-to-normal-state response (parasympathetic). The somatic system relays sensory information.

17. **The endocrine system communicates through hormones:** Endocrine glands and organs produce and release chemical substances, which travel to tissues in the body through the bloodstream and influence a variety of processes, including sexual behavior.

18. **Actions of the nervous system and endocrine system are coordinated:** The endocrine system is controlled by the central nervous system. Most of the central control of the endocrine system occurs through the action of the hypothalamus and the pituitary gland, which controls the release of hormones from the rest of the endocrine glands.

Applying the Principles

1. You've just made two new friends at school today, Jack and Jim, who happen to be identical twins. They look physically alike, but you're more curious about whether they will behave exactly alike. Because of what you know about the role of genes and the environment in shaping the psychological characteristics of an individual, you would expect that Jack and Jim will be

   _____ a) identical in most characteristics.
   _____ b) very different in all characteristics if their parents make a special effort to treat them differently.
   _____ c) different only if separated and raised in different families.
   _____ d) very similar in most characteristics.

2. As you read this question, how is your nervous system responding?

   _____ a) The neurons in the brain plug into each other and fire all at once.
   _____ b) An action potential causes the release of neurotransmitters, which affect whether other neurons fire.
   _____ c) The strength of the action potential changes as you understand the words.
   _____ d) A different chemical messenger is released for every neuron that fires and the sum of these chemical messages is the response.

3. As you sit in a large lecture hall listening to the professor, your ability to stay alert and effectively remember the material is due to

   _____ a) the action of only one class of neurotransmitters.
   _____ b) the actions of a variety of different classes of neurotransmitters.
   _____ c) the actions of peptides (for memory response) and neurotransmitters (for arousal).
   _____ d) the continuous availability of excitatory neurotransmitters for memory and inhibitory neurotransmitters to suppress sleep.

4. On the television show *24,* Jack Bauer, played by Kiefer Sutherland, spends an entire day in unbelievably stressful situations as an agent for the Counter Terrorism Unit. Throughout Jack's day, his _____ controls his planning; his _____ executes behaviors such as running and shooting; and his _____ releases chemicals into the bloodstream to respond to stress.

   _____ a) PNS; CNS; endocrine system
   _____ b) endocrine system; CNS; PNS
   _____ c) CNS; PNS; endocrine system
   _____ d) CNS; endocrine system; PNS

ANSWERS: 1. d 2. b 3. d 4. c

Key Terms

acetylcholine (ACh), p. 98	enzyme deactivation, p. 96	parasympathetic division of ANS, p. 107
action potential, p. 90	epinephrine, p. 99	Parkinson's disease, p. 100
agonist, p. 97	GABA (gamma-aminobutyric acid), p. 102	peptides, p. 103
all-or-none principle, p. 93	gene, p. 77	peripheral nervous system (PNS), p. 105
antagonist, p. 97	genotype, p. 79	phenotype, p. 79
autonomic nervous system, p. 106	glutamate, p. 103	pituitary gland, p. 111
autoreceptors, p. 96	gonads, p. 109	receptors, p. 95
axon, p. 88	heritability, p. 84	recessive gene, p. 79
cell body, p. 88	hormones, p. 108	resting membrane potential, p. 90
central nervous system (CNS), p. 105	interneurons, p. 89	reuptake, p. 96
cholecystokinin (CCK), p. 103	monoamines, p. 99	sensory neurons, p. 89
chromosomes, p. 77	monozygotic twins, p. 82	serotonin, p. 100
dendrites, p. 88	motor neurons, p. 89	somatic nervous system, p. 106
dizygotic twins, p. 82	myelin sheath, p. 93	substance P, p. 104
dominant gene, p. 79	neuron, p. 88	sympathetic division of ANS, p. 107
dopamine, p. 100	neurotransmitter, p. 95	synapse, p. 89
endocrine system, p. 108	nodes of Ranvier, p. 94	synaptic cleft, p. 95
endorphins, p. 104	norepinephrine, p. 100	terminal buttons, p. 89

Further Readings

Carlson, N. R. (2003). *Physiology of behavior* (8th ed.). Needham Heights, MA: Allyn & Bacon.

Gazzaniga, M. S., Ivry, R. B., & Mangun, G. R. (2002). *Cognitive neuroscience: The biology of the mind* (2nd ed.). New York: Norton.

Kandel, E. R., Schwartz, J. H., & Jessell, T. M. (2000). *Principles of neural science* (4th ed.). New York: McGraw-Hill.

Marcus, G. (2004). *The birth of the mind.* New York: Basic Books.

Marshall, L. H., & Magoun, H. W. (1998). *Discoveries in the human brain: Neuroscience prehistory, brain structure, and function.* Totowa, NJ: Humana Press.

Pinel, J. P. J. (2005). *Biopsychology* (6th ed.). Needham Heights, MA: Allyn & Bacon.

Ridley, M. (2003). *Nature versus nurture: Genes, experience, and what makes us human.* New York: HarperCollins.

Zigmond, M. J., Bloom, F. E., Landis, S. C., Roberts, J. L., & Squire, L. R. (2002). *Fundamentals of neuroscience* (2nd ed.). San Diego, CA: Academic Press.

115

Focusing on the Physical Brain

Former heavyweight boxing champion Muhammad Ali and actor Michael J. Fox, both of whom suffer from Parkinson's disease, pose for the cameras before the start of a congressional subcommittee hearing on Parkinson's. Specific parts of the brain control specific mental and physical capabilities. Parkinson's patients, for example, have difficulty learning tasks that require repetition because of damage to their basal ganglia, which is crucial for planning and producing movement.

The Brain and Consciousness

I t was the 1940s, and a patient lay on the operating table, fully conscious, with part of her skull temporarily removed to expose the surface of her brain. Her surgeon at the Montreal Neurological Institute, Dr. Wilder Penfield, delicately touched a small electrode to her brain, and the patient announced that she had the sudden experience *"of being in her kitchen listening to the voice of her little boy who was playing outside in the yard. She was aware of the neighborhood noises, such as passing motor cars, and understood that might mean danger to him."*

The patient suffered from *epilepsy,* the debilitating affliction in which *seizures,* uncontrolled "storms" of electrical activity, begin in some part of the brain and spread throughout much of it, often causing violent, life-threatening convulsions of the entire body. As a last resort, she had agreed to undergo surgery to try to find and remove the part of her brain in which the seizures began.

Outlining the Principles

What Are the Basic Brain Structures and Their Functions?

- The Spinal Cord Is Capable of Autonomous Function
- The Brainstem Houses the Basic Programs of Survival
- The Cerebellum Is Essential for Movement
- Subcortical Structures Control Basic Drives and Emotions
- The Cerebral Cortex Underlies Complex Mental Activity

How Does the Brain Change?

- The Interplay of Genes and the Environment Wires the Brain
- The Brain Rewires Itself throughout Life
- The Brain Can Recover from Injury

How Is the Brain Divided?

- The Hemispheres Can Be Separated
- The Separate Hemispheres Can Be Tested
- The Hemispheres Are Specialized
- The Mind Is a Subjective Interpreter

Can We Study Consciousness?

- Definitions of Consciousness Allow Its Empirical Study

- Unconscious Processing Influences Awareness
- Awareness Has Many Seats in the Brain

What Is Sleep?

- Sleep Is an Altered State of Consciousness
- Sleep Is an Adaptive Behavior
- Sleep and Wakefulness Are Regulated by Multiple Neural Mechanisms
- People Dream while Sleeping

4.1 Direct Stimulation One of Wilder Penfield's patients undergoing direct stimulation of the brain. Left: the patient immediately before surgery. A local anesthetic has been applied to her scalp; Penfield's patients remained fully conscious throughout the procedures. Right: the exposed surface of her cortex. Numbered tags denote electrically stimulated locations.

Penfield was electrically stimulating points on the surface of her brain in an effort to set off the beginning of a seizure, to determine exactly which part of the brain should be excised (Figure 4.1). He was also mapping out the functions of specific brain areas to determine which ones could be removed without damaging the patient's ability to speak. The small electric current interfered with the local area of brain tissue that it flowed through, temporarily deactivating it. If the patient stopped speaking during one of these stimulations, Penfield would know that that area was vital to speech and should not be removed.

Interestingly, the current, while *deactivating* the region in the immediate vicinity of the electrode, *reactivated* more distant brain regions that were connected to neurons in the stimulated area. The result was the vivid reawakening of specific memories in the patient.

Although Penfield repeated this demonstration many times, it is now believed that the specific memory phenomena may have resulted from the patients' disorders, thus not necessarily reflecting a normal brain. However, electrical inductions of experiences, sensations, movements, emotions, and even beliefs, have been reproduced countless times since then. These physical reawakenings of mental events demonstrate the physical nature of the mind. Far from existing as an incomprehensible substance distinct from the physical world, the mind is very much a part of it, consisting of the electrical and chemical activity of our brains. ∎

You learned in the last chapter that mental activities and behaviors are produced by biological processes within the brain, such as the action of nerve cells and associated chemical reactions. In this chapter we will make connections across levels of analy-

Timeline

Fourth century B.C.E.	1650s	1800s	1848
Locating the Mind Although Greek philosophers such as Aristotle believed the mind was located in the heart, Hippocrates describes the brain as the location of the mind, a view supported in the second century C.E. by the influential Roman physician Galen.	**Mind–Body Dualism** French philosopher René Descartes proposes a dualistic theory of the mind and body in which the body's movements are controlled by mechanical reflexes interacting with a nonphysical soul located in the brain's pineal gland.	**Phrenology** German physiologist Franz Joseph Gall develops phrenology, arguing that personality traits and mental abilities are housed in distinct areas of the brain, and can be assessed by measuring the external dimensions of the skull.	**Frontal Lobe Pathology** In Vermont, railroad worker Phineas Gage is accidentally lobotomized by an iron rod. Major changes are observed in his personality and impulse control, but he is otherwise unimpaired.

sis, from the biological level to the level of individual personal experience. We will consider a number of intriguing questions about how the brain enables the mind: How do different regions of the brain contribute to our mental experience of the world? What role do genes and the environment play in shaping individual brains? Can the brain recover following injury? Following this physical consideration of the brain, we will probe its most distinguishing capacity—the ability to have a sense of consciousness. The coordinated action of a number of different brain regions contributes not only to consciousness, but also to variations in conscious experience, from being highly aware of our surroundings to being fast asleep and dreaming. Throughout it all, the brain is active, functioning at every moment to keep us alive as it processes information from the external world—and in doing so creating our mental worlds.

The brain wasn't always recognized as the home of the mind. The Egyptians, for example, viewed the heart as more important; they elaborately embalmed the hearts of their deceased, but the brains they simply threw away. The heart was to be weighed in the afterlife to determine the deceased's fate. But in the ensuing centuries, there was a growing recognition that the brain was essential for normal mental functioning. Much of this came from observing those with brain injuries—at least since the time of the Roman gladiators it was apparent that a blow to the head often produced disturbances in mental activity, such as unconsciousness or loss of the ability to speak.

By the beginning of the nineteenth century, anatomists had a reasonably good understanding of the basic structure of the brain. But debates raged over how the brain worked to produce mental activity. Did different parts do different things or did the entire brain act in unison? In the early nineteenth century, Franz Gall and Johann Spurzheim proposed their theory of *phrenology,* based on the idea that the brain operates on a principle of functional localization. **Phrenology** is the practice of assessing personality traits and mental abilities by measuring bumps on the human skull (Figure 4.2). Although an influential theory in its day, its validity could not be tested scientifically. One of its most vigorous critics was French scientist Pierre Flourens, who believed that the brain functions as a single unit, with all parts working together. To test his theory, Flourens conducted experiments in the 1820s on birds and rodents, in which he removed brain regions and observed the effects on behavior. In the first half of the twentieth century, the psychologist Karl Lashley used a similar method to identify the places in the brain where learning occurred. Unlike Flourens, who did not believe in brain specialization, Lashley conceded that specific brain regions were involved in motor control and sensory experiences. Yet Lashley believed that all parts of the cortex contributed equally to mental abilities, such as problem solving and memory, a concept called *equipotentiality*. Today, his theory has been discredited, and we now know that the brain consists of a patchwork of highly specialized areas.

How does the brain enable the mind?

phrenology An early method of assessing personality traits and mental abilities by measuring bumps on the skull.

4.2 Phrenology One of Johann Spurzheim's phrenological maps of the skull. Each numbered region corresponds to a different characteristic.

1861

Broca's Area French physician Paul Broca presents the first widely accepted and rigorously substantiated assignment of a specific function to a particular cortical area. "Broca's area" is still recognized today as important for speech.

1920s

Equipotentiality American experimental psychologist Karl Lashley removes pieces of a rat's cortex in an effort to locate the memory trace. He wrongly concludes that much of the cortex can contribute equally to most mental functions.

1940s

Stimulating the Awake Brain Canadian neurologist Wilder Penfield experiments with electric current applied to different brain areas to examine the functions of these areas. He later founds the Montreal Neurological Institute.

1949

Reticular Formation and Arousal Giuseppe Moruzzi and Horace Magoun discover that stimulating the reticular formation in the brainstem leads to arousal, a state of heightened physical and brain activity.

1950s

Recording Neurons David Hubel and Torsten Wiesel make the first recordings from individual neurons in the cerebral cortex, characterizing the response properties of neurons in a cat's primary visual cortex using visual displays.

unused brains. Nonetheless, this experiment does demonstrate at a minimum that environment is important for normal development. We will consider enriched environments and their effects on gene expression in Chapter 8.

The Brain Rewires Itself throughout Life

Although plasticity decreases with age, the brain retains the ability to rewire itself throughout life. This is the biological basis of learning.

CHANGE IN THE STRENGTH OF CONNECTIONS UNDERLIES LEARNING

With every moment of life, we gain new memories: experiences and knowledge instantaneously acquired that can later be recalled and habits that gradually form. All these forms of memory consist of physical changes in the brain.

It is now widely accepted by psychological scientists that these changes are most likely not in the brain's gross wiring or arrangement, but simply in the strength of preexisting connections. One possibility is that two neurons firing at the same time strengthens the synaptic connection between them, making them more likely to fire together in the future, and that, conversely, *not* firing at the same time tends to weaken two neurons' connection. Known technically as *Hebbian learning* (discussed in Chapter 6), this theory is summarized by the catchphrase "Fire together, wire together," and it is consistent with a great deal of experimental evidence and many theoretical models. It accounts for both the "burning in" of an experience—a pattern of neuronal firing is made more likely to recur, leading us to recall an event—and for the ingraining of habits: Merely repeating a behavior makes us tend to perform it automatically.

Another possible method of plasticity is the growth of entirely new connections; this takes much longer but appears to be a major factor in recovery from injury. Until very recently, it was believed that, uniquely among bodily organs, adult brains produced no new cells—presumably to avoid obliterating the connections that had been established in response to experience. However, Fred Gage and his colleagues at the Salk Institute demonstrated that new neurons *are* produced in the adult brain, a process known as *neurogenesis* (Eriksson et al., 1998). There appears to be a fair amount of neurogenesis in the hippocampus. Recall that memories are retained within (or at least require) the hippocampus initially but are eventually transferred to the cortex, with the hippocampus being continuously overwritten. It may be that lost neurons can be replaced without disrupting memory.

Princeton University psychologist Elizabeth Gould and her colleagues have demonstrated that environmental conditions play an important role in neurogenesis. For example, they have found in their tests with rats, shrews, and marmosets that stressful experiences, such as being confronted by strange males in their home cages, interfere with neurogenesis both during development and adulthood (Gould & Tanapat, 1999). When animals are housed together, they typically form dominance hierarchies that vary along social status. Dominant animals—those who possess the highest social status—show greater increases in new neurons than do subordinate animals (Kozorovitskiy & Gould, 2004). This demonstrates that the social environment can exert important effects on brain plasticity. Although we are at the earliest stages of understanding this dynamic process, it is possible that neurogenesis underlies the entire basis of neural plasticity. Another implication is that neurogenesis may be able to reverse the loss of neurons and slow down the rate of decline as we age. Imagine how quality of life would improve for all of us if our minds remained nimble throughout our lives.

How might environment affect brain development in young children?

4.12 Skin Regions Changes in cortical representations of skin regions in monkeys that were trained or not trained to detect certain touch stimulation. Repeated training led to an increased representation in cortical areas (as shown in a). In (b), the filled circles indicate where the fingers were touched for the trained (blue) and untrained (green) fingers. The circles show the regions of the finger that became sensitive to the stimulation. More of the finger becomes sensitive to the stimulation after training.

Trained skin

Untrained skin

D5

D4

D3

D2

D1

(a)

D3

D2

D4

D5

D1

(b)

Does the brain rewire itself during learning, aging, and repair?

CHANGES IN USE DISTORT CORTICAL MAPS All the maps in the cerebral cortex shift in response to their activity. Recall the homunculus (Figure 4.9), in which more cortical tissue is devoted to body parts that receive more sensation or that are used more. Again, wiring in the brain is affected by underuse or overuse. If a monkey's finger is repetitively stimulated, for example, that finger's cortical representation will expand (Figure 4.12). However, such plasticity apparently does not take place if the brain is not paying attention: *distract* the monkey during the stimulation and this effect will not occur. The finding that the hippocampus was much larger in experienced London taxi drivers is another example of changes in cortical maps.

Cortical reorganization can also have bizarre results. Amputees are often afflicted with *phantom limbs,* the intense sensation that the amputated body part still exists. Some phantom limbs are experienced as moving normally, being used to gesture in conversation as if they really existed, for example, whereas some are frozen in position. Unfortunately, phantom limbs are often accompanied by sensations of pain, which may result from the misgrowth of the severed pain nerves at the stump, with the pain being interpreted by the cortex as coming from the place those nerves originally came from (Figure 4.13). This would suggest that the brain had *not* reorganized in response to the injury, and that the cortical representation of the arm was still intact. However, V. S. Ramachandran of the University of California, San Diego, discovered that some of these people, when their eyes were closed, perceived a touch on the cheek as if it were on their missing hand! Apparently, the hand is represented next to the face in our somatosensory homunculus. Following the loss of the limb, the patient's unemployed cortex assumed to some degree the function of the closest group, which was to represent the skin of the face. Touching the face then activated these neurons. Somehow, the rest of the brain had not kept pace with the somatosensory area enough to figure out these neurons' new job.

Amputee

4.13 Cortical Remapping Following Amputation A cotton swab touching the subject's cheek was felt as touching his missing hand.

Psychological Science *in Action*

Manipulating Objects with the Mind

Let's consider an example of how brain plasticity might allow researchers to improve the lives of those with spinal injuries. In our daily interactions with the world, we use our arms and hands to manipulate objects around us, as we type on keyboards, play computer games with joysticks, change television channels with remotes, and control our cars with steering wheels. Imagine being able to manipulate these objects simply by thinking about using them. How amazing this would be for the more than 40,000 Americans who do not have use of their arms or legs because of spinal cord injuries or disease, who could perhaps be taught to control prosthetic limbs with their minds. In groundbreaking research that provides hope for those with paralysis, neuroscientists at Duke University have taught monkeys how to control a robot arm using only their thoughts (Carmena et al., 2003). As the media have quipped, "Monkey see, robot do."

How did the researchers accomplish this remarkable feat? The first step was to implant small electrodes in the frontal and parietal lobes of two rhesus monkeys and then record impulses from those electrodes while the monkeys learned to play a simple computer game. These brain areas were chosen because they are known to be involved in controlling complex movement. In the computer game, the monkeys used a joystick that allowed them to perform actions such as steering a cursor and squeezing a trigger to achieve a goal, which involved moving a robotic arm that they could see but not touch. By examining the recordings from various brain regions, the research team was able to determine which patterns of brain activity led to specific motor actions. At this point, scientists unplugged the joystick so that it no longer controlled the movement of the robotic arm and then made movements of the robotic arm directly dependent on the pattern of neuronal firing from the monkeys' motor cortices. At first, the monkeys moved their arms wildly as if controlling the joystick, but it was not their arm movements that controlled the robot; it was their thoughts. "The most amazing result, though, was that after only a few days of playing with the robot in this way, the monkey suddenly realized that she didn't need to move her arm at all," says the lead neuroscientist, Miguel Nicolelis, describing one of the experiment's subjects (Figure 4.14). "Her arm muscles went completely quiet, she kept the arm at her side and she controlled the robot arm using only her brain and visual feedback. Our analyses of the brain signals showed that the animal learned to assimilate the robot arm into her brain as if it were her own arm" ("Gazette: Monkeys Move Matter, Mentally," 2004).

This experiment reveals an amazing property of brain plasticity: The brain learns to use tools as natural extensions of our physical bodies. Watch young children who have learned to play computer games; they aren't thinking about using the mouse to control the action on the monitor—the mouse becomes part of their physical being. In many ways, this is no different from the way our brains control our biological appendages; sensory information is received by the brain, and motor commands control physical action. When you drive, your arms don't control the steering wheel; your brain turns the wheel. Researchers have been able to tap into the motor command signals from the brain and use those signals to control an external device.

Is the brain activity identical in the two situations? According to Nicolelis, it is not. When the researchers removed the joystick, the physiological properties of the

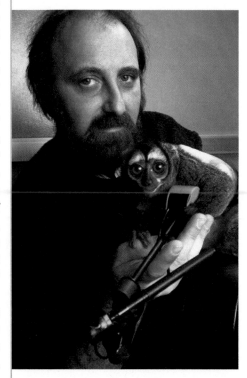

4.14 Advances in Motor Control
Neurobiologist Miguel Nicolelis with one of the owl monkeys used in his study of the brain's motor command signals. Dr. Nicolelis's research revealed new information on brain plasticity and the brain's capabilities to adapt.

neurons changed immediately, and they changed a second time when the monkeys were once again required to use the joystick. The methods used in this study will allow neuroscientists to study brain plasticity, because they can modify subtle aspects of the robot arm (such as building in a short delay between thought and action) and watch how the brain adapts.

How soon might this research help those who are paralyzed? A team of researchers led by John Donoghue at Brown University, in collaboration with a private company, received permission from the U.S. Food and Drug Administration to implant a small computer chip into five quadriplegic individuals. The chip reads signals from 20 to 100 neurons in the motor cortex. The first human to benefit from this technology was 25-year-old Matthew Nagle, who had been paralyzed from the neck down following a knife attack in 2001. The implanted device, called BrainGate, has allowed him to use a remote control to perform physical actions such as change television channels and open and close curtains, entirely with his thoughts. As in the Duke research, this firing pattern is translated into signals that control the movement of a robotic arm. The longer-term goals are to allow paralyzed individuals to control prosthetic devices that will assist them in all aspects of daily living. Possibly within the next few years we will witness quadriplegics doing things that are now unimaginable, and in doing so we will learn a great deal about how brain plasticity allows the mind to control behavior. ∎

The Brain Can Recover from Injury

The converse of the brain's reorganization in response to overuse or underuse is its reorganization in response to brain damage. Following a lesion in the cortex, the surrounding gray matter assumes the function of the damaged area, with the map distorting everywhere around it to recover the lost capability, like local businesses scrambling to pick up the customers of a newly bankrupt store. Some of this remapping seems to occur immediately and to continue for years. Such plasticity involves all levels of the nervous system, from the cortex down to the spinal cord.

This reorganization is much more prevalent in children than adults, in accordance with the critical periods of normal development. Young children afflicted with severe and uncontrollable epilepsy sometimes undergo "radical hemispherectomy": the surgical removal of one entire cerebral hemisphere. This procedure is not possible in adults because of the inevitable and permanent paralysis and loss of function that results. Young children, however, eventually regain almost complete use of the initially paralyzed arm and leg, as well as the other functions of the lost hemisphere: These are simply taken up by the remaining one. But even in adults, recovery from brain injury can be quite dramatic. Stroke patients with a paralyzed arm, for example, very often recover its use within a few months.

Finally, one of the most exciting areas of current neurological research is the transplantation of stem cells into the brain to repair damage. *Stem cells* are "master" cells that not only are able to regenerate themselves, but also have the capacity to develop into any type of tissue, such as muscles or nerve cells. This procedure, using stem cells typically obtained from human fetal tissue, is beginning to be explored as a possible treatment for degenerative diseases such as Parkinson's or Huntington's, and also for strokes. The significant challenge is to get the newly introduced cells to make the proper connections and regrow the damaged circuits. These techniques are still in their earliest days, and they pose obvious ethical dilemmas, but they may well soon become very important treatment methods.

Thinking Critically

Is Stem Cell Research Ethical?

One of the most exciting areas of current neurological research is the transplantation of stem cells into the brain to repair damage. It is also extremely controversial. Let's critically examine the promise and the controversy.

When the actor Christopher Reeve was paralyzed in a horseback riding accident, he vowed to walk again some day. Until recently, such vows would be dismissed as wishful thinking, since paralysis from spinal injuries was believed to be permanent. Within the last decade, however, the discovery of stem cells has provided new hope for the treatment of many diseases. *Stem cells* are special "master" cells that have the ability to develop into any type of tissue, such as muscles or nerve cells. They have another amazing property: They can renew themselves through cell division, perhaps indefinitely. The hope is that injecting stem cells into damaged tissue will allow the stem cells to repair the damage and restore function. Findings from animal studies provide tantalizing evidence that stem cells might reverse the effects of spinal injuries, repair damage following heart attacks, cure diabetes, and provide effective treatments for many neurological disorders. Brain diseases such as Huntington's, Parkinson's, and Lou Gehrig's disease may soon go the way of polio and smallpox and become diseases of the past.

Using stem cells to cure diseases seems an obvious choice, but some ethicists and religious leaders have raised moral objections to stem cell research (Figure 4.15). Their concerns revolve around the obtaining of stem cells from embryos because the process actually destroys the embryos. They argue that in destroying embryos, we

4.15 The Stem Cell Controversy Stem cell research is a highly controversial and divisive subject. Stem cell researchers, such as cell biologist Lesley Young from the UK Stem Cell Bank in London (left), work to develop treatments that could save millions of lives. Political and religious leaders, such as President George W. Bush and the late Pope John Paul II (right), have publicly criticized such research on moral and ethical grounds.

are destroying life. Stem cells can be harvested from various sources, but scientists prefer embryonic stem cells because they are the purest and therefore likely to be most useful for medical treatment. There is also a potentially huge supply of embryos from which stem cells can be obtained. When people undergo in vitro fertilization, dozens of embryos are created. Once the treatment is successful, the leftover embryos are destroyed or frozen for later use. Researchers want to use these "spare" embryos to obtain stem cells.

But are embryos people? At the heart of the ethical debate is whether these clumps of 100 or so cells really deserve the same degree of respect and protection given to adults and children. Are we humans from the moment of fertilization, or do we become humans with the development of a nervous system capable of sensation and conscious experience? The government of the United Kingdom considered the available evidence and decided that embryos can be used as long as they have not developed beyond 14 days. In the first 14 days following fertilization, the embryo can go through many changes, such as splitting into twins or recombining back into one embryo, that make it difficult to accord to it the status of an individual human being. From this perspective, conception of a person does not happen in an instant but occurs over 14 days. Moreover, during this period there is no trace of a nervous system, and the possession of a nervous system is considered an important determinant of whether someone is alive. Following birth, a person whose brain stops working is considered dead for all practical purposes, even if other bodily systems function. The question of when life begins can be addressed from scientific, religious, or other philosophical perspectives; the implications of how this question is addressed for stem cell research are enormous.

In the United States, President George W. Bush's administration enacted rules in 2001 that severely restrict the use of federal research grant dollars to fund stem cell research. This raises other important ethical questions. Should moral values be considered in federal funding decisions? Is it ethical to block the development of treatments that might save millions of lives? Should political leaders be allowed to shape medical research according to their religious beliefs—beliefs that others might not share? In response to the federal restrictions, New Jersey and California passed legislation supporting stem cell research. In addition, a number of private companies and universities, such as Harvard and Stanford, have begun their own stem cell initiatives. Research conducted by private industry also raises critical questions, such as whether the findings will be made available to other scientists and whether treatments that are developed will be available to the public.

History has taught us that science marches on, one way or the other. Even if stem cell research is banned in the United States, or dramatically slowed down, other countries, such as Great Britain and South Korea, will forge ahead, and a more practical set of issues will emerge. If stem cells and the treatments that emerge from the research are not available in the United States, those with limited economic means could die from diseases while wealthier Americans could be treated in countries that have active stem cell programs. Perhaps someone like Christopher Reeve could have raised millions of dollars to receive treatment in another country to restore his ability to walk. Could you? More important, should we make it impossible for someone like Christopher Reeve to walk again? Sadly, Reeve died in October 2004 and did not live to see the promise of stem cell research fulfilled. But, should we make it impossible for someone with Huntington's disease to live a full and meaningful life? How should ethical values shape research? Should our government reduce the limits currently placed on stem cell research? ■

the Principles | How Does the Brain Change?

Though neural connections are intricate and precise, they are malleable. The human genome is the blueprint for normal development, but it is affected by environmental factors, such as injury or sensory stimulation or deprivation. During development, and throughout our lifetimes of learning, the circuitry is reworked and updated. Reorganization also occurs following brain injury, with recovery ability far greater in children than in adults.

corpus callosum A fiber of axons that transmits information between the two cerebral hemispheres of the brain.

split brain A condition in which the corpus callosum is surgically cut and the two hemispheres of the brain do not receive information directly from each other.

Does each half of the brain possess the same capacities?

How Is the Brain Divided?

As we have seen, studying humans whose brains were damaged by accidents or surgically altered has been a rich source of insight into the mechanics of the mind. Many of these surgeries were attempts to treat epilepsy by specifically removing the part of the brain in which the seizures begin. Another strategy, pioneered in the 1940s and still practiced on occasion when other interventions have failed, is to cut connections within the brain to try to isolate the site of seizure initiation, so that a seizure that begins there will be less able to spread throughout the cortex. This surgical procedure has provided many important insights into the basic organization of each hemisphere of the brain and the specialized functions they perform. But this procedure also raises another interesting question: "If you split the brain, do you split the mind?"

The Hemispheres Can Be Separated

The only connection between the hemispheres that may readily be cut without damaging the gray matter itself is the massive fiber bundle called the **corpus callosum** (Figure 4.16). To treat epilepsy, the corpus callosum may be cut only partway through, sparing some of the connecting axons, or it may be completely severed. Most epilepsy patients, and all of those on whom the initial operations were performed and who provided the first striking results, have had the corpus callosum completely cut. This leaves the two halves of the forebrain almost completely isolated from each other, and the two hemispheres connected only back to the brainstem, hence only indirectly to each other. This condition is known as the **split brain**.

Perhaps the most obvious thing about the split-brain patients after their operations was how very normal they were. Unlike patients following other types of brain surgery, split-brain patients had no major problems that were immediately apparent. In fact, some early investigation suggested that the surgery had not affected the patients in any discernible way. They could walk and talk normally, think clearly, and interact socially.

However, work with animals had shown that this could not be the full story. One of the authors (M.S.G.), working with the eventual Nobel laureate Roger Sperry, conducted a series of tests on the first split-brain participants. The results were stunning: Just as the brain had been split in two, so had the mind!

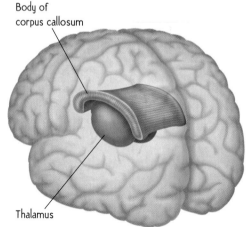

Body of corpus callosum

Thalamus

4.16 The Corpus Callosum A massive bundle of millions of axons connect the two cerebral hemispheres.

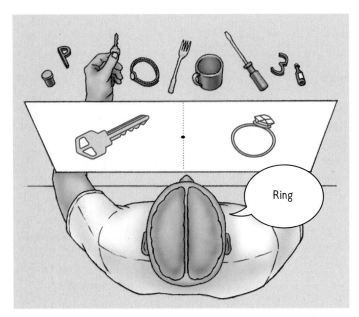

4.17 An Experiment with a Split-brain Subject When asked what he sees, the left hemisphere responds that he sees a "ring," because that is what is shown on the right side of the screen. The right hemisphere sees the left side of screen, and although not able to verbalize what it sees, it can pick the correct object using the left hand.

The Separate Hemispheres Can Be Tested

Recall from earlier in this chapter that images from the left side of the visual field go to the right hemisphere, and those from the right side go to the left. Remember also that the left hemisphere controls the right hand, and the right hemisphere controls the left hand. These divisions allow researchers to provide information to and get information from only a single hemisphere at a time.

Figure 4.17 shows a typical experimental setup. The split-brain patient sits in front of a screen, staring at a central dot. Two images are flashed simultaneously, one on each side of the dot. Because each hemisphere sees only the contents of the opposite side of the visual field, the right hemisphere sees the image on the left, and the left hemisphere the image on the right.

It has long been known that the left hemisphere is dominant for language in most people. If a split-brain patient, having just been flashed two pictures in the manner just described, is asked to report what was shown, he or she will announce that only one picture was shown and will describe the one on the right. Why is this? Because the left hemisphere, with its control over speech, saw only the picture on the right side. The mute right hemisphere (or "right brain"), having seen the picture on the left, is unable to articulate a response. It can be shown, though, that the right brain indeed saw the picture. If the picture on the left was, for example, of a spoon, the right hemisphere can easily pick out an actual spoon from a selection of objects, using, of course, the left hand. The left hemisphere has no knowledge whatsoever of what the right one saw. Splitting the brain, then, produces two half brains, each with its own independent perceptions, thoughts, and consciousness!

The Hemispheres Are Specialized

Further explorations revealed much more about the division of labor within the brain. In all the patients studied, the left hemisphere was far more competent at language than the right, so much so that in most patients the right hemisphere had no discernable language capacity at all. In some patients, though, the right hemisphere did have some rudimentary language comprehension. Interestingly, such right-hemisphere language capabilities tend to improve in the years following the split-brain operation, presumably as the right hemisphere attains communication skills that were unnecessary when the hemisphere was fully connected to the fluent left brain.

The right hemisphere, however, has its own competencies, which complement those of the left. The left brain is generally hopeless at spatial relationships. In one experiment, a split-brain participant is given a pile of blocks and a drawing of a simple arrangement in which to put them—for example, a square. If the participant is using his or her left hand, controlled by the right hemisphere, the blocks are arranged effortlessly. If, however, the left brain is doing the arranging via the right hand, the result is a meandering, incompetent attempt. During such a dismal performance, the idle left hand will attempt to slip in and help out, as the right brain presumably looks on in frustration!

Split-brain patients have provided insight into not only the functional specializations of the left and right sides, but also the organization within each hemisphere. When the corpus callosum was not cut along its entire length, the relative contributions of its different ends to the transfer of different kinds of information could be explored. Figure 4.18 shows the reaction of one such patient, who had enough right-hemisphere language capability to comprehend words flashed in the left visual field. His operation was done in two parts, with the back half of the corpus callosum cut first. He was tested following the first operation. Since the visual cortex occupies the back of the brain, the cut rear half of the corpus callosum prevented any direct transfer of visual information. The left brain, then, was unable to see the word "knight." Fascinatingly, though, the left brain was nevertheless able to visualize what the right brain was thinking about! Evidently, more "meaningful" information *could* be transferred, through the axons in the front half of the corpus callosum connecting the two front halves of the brain.

The Mind Is a Subjective Interpreter

Another interesting dimension to the relationship between the brain's hemispheres is how they work together to reconstruct our experiences. This can be demonstrated by asking a disconnected left hemisphere what it thinks about previous behavior that has been produced by the right hemisphere. In one such experiment, different images are flashed simultaneously to the left and right visual fields and the patient is asked to point with both hands to the pictures that seem most related to the images on the screen (Figure 4.19). As one example, a picture of a chicken claw was flashed to the left hemisphere and a picture of a snow scene to the right hemisphere. In response, the left hemisphere directed the right hand to point to a picture of a chicken head, and the right hemisphere pointed the left hand at a snow shovel. The participant was then asked why he chose

4.18 Information Transfer in the Brain
Different kinds of information are transferred by different parts of the corpus callosum. If the back half is severed but the front half left intact, meaning transfers from one hemisphere to the other, but visual information does not.

4.19 The Left-Brain Interpreter Mechanism
The left hemisphere attempts to explain the behavior of the right hemisphere on the basis of limited information.

those items. Clearly, the speaking left hemisphere could have no idea what the right hemisphere had seen. However, the patient (or rather his left hemisphere) calmly replied, "Oh, that's simple. The chicken claw goes with the chicken, and you need a shovel to clean out the chicken shed." The left hemisphere had evidently interpreted the left hand's response in a manner consistent with the left brain's knowledge. This left-hemisphereic propensity to construct a world that makes sense is called the *interpreter* (Gazzaniga, 2000).

The interpreter strongly influences the way we view and remember the world. Shown a series of pictures that form a story and asked later to choose which of another group of pictures they had seen previously, normal participants have a strong tendency to falsely "recognize" pictures that are consistent with the theme of the original series and to reject those that are inconsistent with the theme. The left brain, then, tends to "compress" its experience into a comprehensible story and reconstructs remembered details based on the gist of the story. The right brain seems simply to experience the world and remember things in a manner less distorted by narrative interpretation. Given the finite capacity of the brain, the advantages of compression seem clear, though it appears the right hemisphere may check the left hemisphere's potentially unwarranted speculations. Many of our thoughts reflect the processes of the interpreter. Thus, our sense of consciousness, to which we turn in the next section, is influenced greatly by our left hemisphere interpreter.

Can We Study Consciousness?

Arguably, the brain's greatest expression is that it gives rise to the consciousness of ourselves as thinking and feeling beings. Despite our subjective *experience* of being self-aware humans, consciousness has long been a difficult phenomenon to study from a scientific perspective. On the one hand, it is the very mechanism by which we experience thoughts and feelings. In this sense consciousness is a very tangible thing, as there is a clear delineation for most of us between being "conscious" and being "unconscious." On the other hand, perhaps the greatest unanswered question in the biological sciences today is how neural activity in the brain gives rise to the phenomenal awareness of the world that we associate with the state of being conscious.

Consciousness has long been a topic of debate among philosophers, ever since René Descartes asserted that the mind is physically distinct from the brain. As you will recall from Chapter 1, this view of consciousness, called dualism, posits a clear separation between what we call mind and the brain. As an alternative to dualism, *materialism* is based on the belief that the brain and mind are inseparable, that the brain directly enables the mind. According to materialism, it is the activity of neurons in the brain that produces the contents of consciousness, such as cognition and perception. When we drink too much, our decision making becomes impulsive and confused because alcohol is affecting the synaptic transmissions between neurons. When we have strokes or traumatic brain injuries, we may lose our ability to feel empathy because brain tissue has been damaged. Therefore, we can study consciousness only through studying the brain.

Definitions of Consciousness Allow Its Empirical Study

As discussed in Chapter 2, the methods of psychological science dictate that in order to study a phenomenon, we need to be able to define operationally exactly what it is we're studying. In this regard, consciousness has proven difficult to define in scientifically practical terms. In recent years the solution that researchers have converged on is to break down consciousness into more basic issues that are easier to study, which include:

Subjectivity: This is the unique perspective each of us has on our own conscious experience. What we see, hear, feel, and think can be discussed with other people, but the actual *experience* of these things can never be shared in a manner resembling our own internal awareness of them. How can we explain to others what the color red looks like to us? These aspects of consciousness—the properties of our subjective experience—are referred to as **qualia**, and perhaps the most difficult aspect of a scientific study of consciousness concerns understanding how qualia arise from neural activity (Figure 4.20).

Access to Information: Mental experience presupposes that we have knowledge of the contents of our consciousness, at least when we are in a normal, unaltered mind state. However, that content is the by-product of the actions of a number of different

qualia The properties of our subjective, phenomenological awareness.

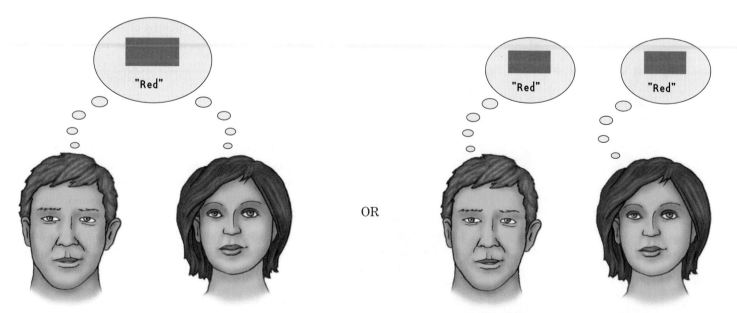

4.20 Seeing Red One of the difficult questions of consciousness is how to account for "qualia," or the phenomenological percepts of the world. For instance, does the color red appear the same to everyone who has normal color vision?

unconscious Those processes that are outside the realm of conscious awareness.

underlying processes, of whose workings we have no direct knowledge. We see the products of the visual system, not the computations upon which they are based. What does this mean? Information processing in the brain can be divided into two classes: processes that are accessible to consciousness and processes that are not. The processes that we are not conscious of we label **unconscious,** or outside our mental awareness.

A Unitary Experience: Consciousness brings together the fruits of our sensory systems into a unified phenomenal experience that remains continuous over time. Our awareness of the world is based on a melding of these sensations into a single, multimedia event.

The goal of breaking down consciousness is to facilitate empirical study. For instance, now that we have defined qualia, we may be able to design studies that begin to investigate what parts of the brain are active and what parts are inactive when experiencing specific qualia. We now turn to several different definitions of consciousness and the different empirical approaches they have spurred.

Unconscious Processing Influences Awareness

One of the properties of consciousness is the idea that we are aware of some mental processes and not aware of others. Over the last several decades, one of the more fruitful areas of consciousness research has explored different ways in which unconscious or *subliminal perception* can influence cognition. Subliminal perception refers to stimuli that our sensory systems respond to but that because of their short duration or subtle form never reach the threshold of entering into consciousness (Figure 4.21).

THE CASE FOR UNCONSCIOUS INFLUENCE There is no doubt that stimuli can influence our thoughts and actions even though they stay outside the realm of consciousness (Gladwell, 2005). One often-used illustration of this point involves priming test subjects by flashing before them a picture of a boy who appears either mean or kind. Subjects remain unaware that they have been shown the initial picture. For the main test, subjects are shown a picture of the boy wearing a neutral expression on his face, and the subjects are asked whether the boy appears to have a "good" or a "bad" character. Subjects who were previously presented with the kind picture rate the boy's character much higher than those who saw the mean picture (Figure 4.22).

Other kinds of effects have been observed as well. In a classic experiment by Richard Nisbett and Timothy Wilson (1977), participants were asked to examine word pairs such as "ocean-moon" that had obvious semantic associations between the words. They were then asked to free associate on other, single words, such as "detergent." Nisbett and Wilson were interested in finding to what degree, if any, the word pairs would influence free associations, and if they did, whether the participants would have any awareness that the pairs had indeed influenced their thoughts. What they found was that when given the word "detergent" after the word pair "ocean-moon," participants'

4.21 Seeing the Subliminal This design contains a subliminal message that is dramatically obvious when you discover it. Can you find it?

typical free association was the word "Tide." Interestingly, they would usually give reasons such as "My mom used Tide when I was a kid"; they had no awareness that they were being influenced by the word pairs. Here again we see the effects of the left hemisphere interpreter at work, making sense of a situation and providing a plausible explanation for cognitive events when complete information is not available. What this reveals is that we are frequently unaware of the different things that can affect our decisions about what we say and do. Similar effects underlie the classic *Freudian slip*, in which unconscious thoughts are suddenly expressed at inappropriate times, often to inappropriate people.

Another example comes from the work of John Bargh and his colleagues (1996), who had subjects make sentences out of words that were jumbled up. Some of the words were associated with the elderly. For instance, the subjects were asked to construct a sentence using "old," "Florida," and "wrinkles." After research participants had made up a number of such sentences, they were told the experiment was over. But instead, what Bargh and his colleagues were interested in was whether the unconscious activation of beliefs about old people would influence the participants' behavior. They found that participants primed with the elderly stereotype walked much more slowly down the hall than those who performed a sentence task that did not activate beliefs about elderly people. When questioned later, the participants had no awareness that the concept of elderly had been activated or that it had changed their behavior. Other researchers have obtained similar findings. For instance, Ap Dijksterhuis and Ad van Knippenberg (1998) at Nijmegen University in the Netherlands found that people better answered trivial questions when they were unconsciously presented with information about "professors" than when they were presented with subliminal information about "soccer hooligans." Even how hard people work can be influenced by unconscious cues. Students who receive incidental information that emphasizes "achievement" perform better than those who do not have achievement primed. What these findings indicate is that much of our behavior occurs without our constant awareness or intention (Ferguson & Bargh, 2004).

THE ILLUSION OF CONSCIOUS WILL Many of our behaviors occur automatically and without much conscious awareness. You walk along without thinking about how to move your legs or swing your arms, you drive home without paying much specific attention to what you are doing, and you engage in breezy conversation even though you are not consciously aware of how you know what to say or how to say it. On other occasions, however, we consciously choose to engage in a specific behavior— we feel that we willed the action. This usually happens when we are aware of the action before we perform it. In his book *The Illusion of Conscious Will* (2002), Harvard social psychologist Daniel Wegner presents examples of situations in which people have a feeling of will. According to Wegner, our sense of will occurs in part because brain activity causes both the feeling of will and the action that is associated with the feeling of will, even when they did not cause the action. You may have thought that you are thirsty and then have a drink of water. Did your thought cause you to drink? Or did feeling thirsty lead to both the thought of drinking and the action? When letters are chosen on a Ouija board, is it because of supernatural forces or because your fingers are responding to unconscious choices in your mind? According to

4.22 Subliminal Perception If asked to judge the character of the boy in panel B, subliminal perception of panel A1 beforehand will bias people to give a negative report. Alternatively, subliminal perception beforehand of panel A2 will bias people toward a positive report.

Wegner, even though people using a Ouija board do not experience a conscious sense of will, it can be shown that they are in fact providing the answers.

Awareness Has Many Seats in the Brain

How does the brain give rise to awareness?

As we have stated, perhaps the greatest challenge in the psychological sciences today is to understand how neural activity gives rise to the conscious awareness we associate with cognition and perception. However, to approach this issue, we need to ask: What exactly is *awareness*? Although there are a host of definitions, they all converge on the notion that to be aware of information is to be able to report that information is being—or has been—perceived. Based on this general definition, a great deal of research over the last several decades has focused on identifying the brain areas involved in *awareness*. By studying awareness in individuals with damage to specific regions of the brain, researchers hope to link selective losses of awareness—that is, awareness for specific forms of information—to the damaged brain areas.

blindsight A condition in which people who are blind have some spared visual capacities in the absence of any visual awareness.

BLINDSIGHT One of the most fascinating areas of study in cognitive neuroscience has concerned the neural basis of visual awareness. In particular, researchers have focused on the phenomenon of **blindsight**, a condition in which people suffer blindness due to damage to their visual cortex but continue to have some visual capacities in the absence of any visual awareness. Although blindsighted patients are exceedingly rare, they typically have loss of vision in only a small portion of their visual field. Researchers have discovered that if these patients are presented with a stimulus in their blind field, they can unconsciously perceive important aspects of the stimulus. For example, patients might be presented with a moving dot in their blind spot, and their task is to indicate in which direction the dot is moving. The typical scenario will have patients declaring that they have seen nothing and thus have nothing to report. However, when pressed to guess the direction of motion, more often than not patients will guess correctly.

A fascinating example of blindsight was recently found in a 52-year-old physician who had become blind following two consecutive strokes that destroyed the primary visual cortices in both hemispheres of his brain (Pegna, Khateb, Lazeyras, & Seghier, 2005). Although there was nothing wrong with his eyes, the visual regions of his brain were unable to process any information they received from them. So although alert and aware of his surroundings, the patient reported being unable to see anything, even the presence of intense light. Visual information also goes to other brain regions, such as the amygdala. As you will learn in Chapter 10, one theory suggests that the amygdala processes visual information very crudely and quickly, which helps identify potential threats. The amygdala, for example, becomes activated in imaging studies when people observe subliminal presentations of faces expressing fear (Whalen et al., 2005). When our blind patient was shown a series of faces and simply asked to guess the expression, although he had no sense of having seen an object, he was able to correctly identify the expression at a much better than chance level. He did not respond to other stimuli (such as shapes, animal faces, or other scary stimuli). When this patient was placed in a brain scanner, his amygdala became activated when presented with emotional faces but not to faces with neutral expressions. Thus, his amygdala may well have been processing the emotional content of the faces, in spite of his lack of awareness of seeing anything at all. This raises intriguing questions of whether the patient is "seeing" the faces, as well as how visual information reaches the amygdala when primary visual areas are damaged.

Many of our responses to events around us occur without our conscious awareness of them.

NEURONAL WORKSPACE How does activity within the brain relate to awareness? An influential model of consciousness known as the *neuronal workspace model* posits that consciousness arises as a function of which brain regions are active. When one region is more highly activated than another, the image that reaches consciousness is the one associated with that region's functional activity. A study by Frank Tong and colleagues (1998) looked at the relationship between consciousness and neural responses in the brain. Participants were shown images with houses superimposed on faces (Figure 4.23). The researchers found that the fusiform face area increased activity when participants reported seeing a face, but that when participants reported seeing a house, temporal cortex regions associated with object recognition became active. This finding suggests that the neural correlates of awareness depend on the activity of brain regions that process certain types of sensory information. In the case of rivalry between faces and houses, if the fusiform face area is more highly activated than areas associated with objects, the participant's conscious experience is that of seeing a face, rather than a house.

Work with brain-injured patients reveals a pattern that supports the neuronal workspace model, in which the output of active brain regions is experienced as conscious awareness. If one of these systems is damaged or not working, then there is no output to consider and nothing is noted as being wrong. This can be seen with the phenomenon of hemineglect discussed earlier in the chapter. People with hemineglect are not aware that part of their visual world is missing. In one patient's words: "I knew the word 'neglect' was a sort of medical term for whatever was wrong but the word bothered me because you only neglect something that is actually there, don't you? If it's not there, how can you neglect it?" (Halligan & Marshall, 1998). Cooney and Gazzaniga (2003) explain this phenomenon by arguing that our left hemisphere interpreter can make sense only of information that is available, so even though we might find the behavior of the hemineglect patients bizarre, they see the state of their world as perfectly normal. Studies like these show us that the experience of the patient with hemineglect does not include awareness of the deficit, which supports the idea that consciousness arises as a result of the brain processes that are active at any point in time.

The importance of the neuronal workspace model is that it demonstrates that there appears to be no single area in the brain responsible for general "awareness." Rather, different areas of the brain deal with different types of information, and each of these systems in turn is responsible for awareness of that type of information (Figure 4.24). Taken from this perspective, consciousness can be viewed as the mechanism that is actively "aware" of information, and which serves the important role of prioritizing what information we need or want to deal with at any moment.

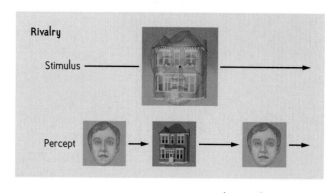

4.23 Consciousness and Neural Responses The picture at the top can be viewed as a face or a house; how it is perceived activates different brain regions.

4.24 Areas of Awareness The central theme emerging from cognitive neuroscience is that awareness of different aspects of the world is associated with functioning in different parts of the brain.

What Is Sleep?

At regular intervals the brain does a strange thing—it goes to sleep. A common misperception is that the brain shuts itself down during sleep, and is no longer processing information from the external world; nothing could be further from the truth. As you will discover, many regions of the brain are more active during sleep than during wakefulness. It is even possible that complex thinking, such as working on difficult problems, occurs while people are asleep. In one study, people had to learn a task at which they slowly got better with practice. Unbeknownst to participants, there was a hidden rule that once discovered led to much better performance. The researchers found that people were more likely to figure out the rule after sleep than after wakefulness, independent of the time of day (Wagner, Gals, Haider, Verleger, & Born, 2004).

Rather than the brain shutting off, it's the conscious experience of the outside world that is apparently turned off during sleep. Even then people are aware to some extent of their surroundings, as when a sleeping mother is aware of her baby rustling in his crib. Many psychological scientists view sleep as an *altered state of consciousness,* one sharing many properties with other altered mental states, such as when people consume drugs or alcohol, meditate, or are under hypnosis. These altered states are associated with unusual subjective experiences, diminished or enhanced levels of self-awareness, and often disturbances in control over physical actions. In this section we focus on sleep as the prototypical altered state of consciousness (we discuss other altered states throughout the text).

Given that all animals sleep, and that people can't go without sleep for more than a few days, most researchers believe that sleep serves some biological purpose. However, as you will see, it isn't clear exactly *why* sleep is important.

The average person sleeps around eight hours per night, although there is tremendous variability, both in terms of individual differences and in terms of age. Infants sleep most of the day, whereas elderly individuals may need only a few hours of sleep per night. Some adults report needing 9 or 10 hours of sleep to feel rested, whereas others report needing only an hour or two a night. One 70-year-old retired nurse, Miss M., reported sleeping only an hour a night. Perhaps, like the researchers who studied Miss M., you find this hard to believe. But after spending two sleepless nights in a sleep laboratory, apparently because of the excitement, she slept for only 99 minutes on the third night, awaking refreshed, cheerful, and full of energy (Meddis, 1977). Imagine having all those extra hours of spare time!

Sleep Is an Altered State of Consciousness

When you are asleep, your brain is still processing information. People who sleep with pets or children tend not to roll over and smother them. Most people also don't fall out of bed while sleeping, indicating that the brain is still aware of the environment, such as the relative position of the edge of the bed. Indeed, even though you are not conscious when asleep, your mind is at work, analyzing potential dangers, controlling body movements, and shifting body parts to maximize comfort. The difference between sleep and awake states has as much to do with conscious experience as biological processes.

Before the discovery of objective methods to assess brain activity, most people believed that the brain went to sleep along with the rest of the body. However, the invention of the electroencephalogram (EEG), a machine that measures the electrical activity of the nervous system, revealed that a great deal goes on in the brain during sleep. The fact that there are different psychophysiological states during sleep has been described as one of the first major discoveries of neuroscience (Hobson, 1995). When people are awake, the neurons in their brains are extremely active, as evidenced by short, frequent, desynchronized brain signals known as *beta waves* (Figure 4.25). When people close their eyes and relax, brain activity slows down and becomes more synchronized, a pattern that produces *alpha waves.*

4.25 Brain Activity during Sleep Patterns of electrical brain activity during different stages of sleep.

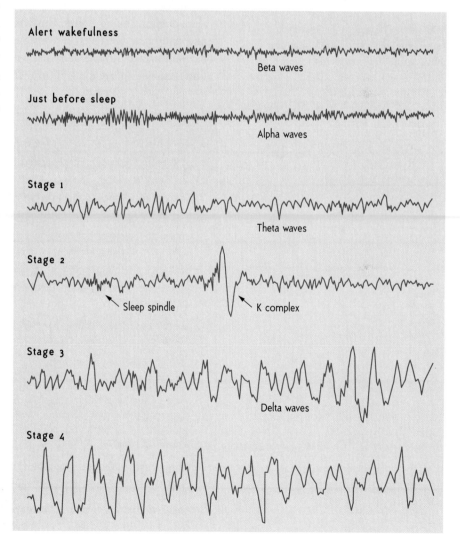

Alert wakefulness
Beta waves

Just before sleep
Alpha waves

Stage 1
Theta waves

Stage 2
Sleep spindle   K complex

Stage 3
Delta waves

Stage 4

STAGES OF SLEEP Sleep occurs in stages, as evidenced by changes in EEG readings. As you drift off to sleep, you enter stage 1, characterized by *theta waves,* from which you can be easily aroused. Indeed, if you are awakened you will probably deny that you were sleeping. In this light sleep you might see fantastical images, such as geometric shapes, or have the sensation that you are falling or that your limbs are jerking. As you progress to stage 2, your breathing becomes more regular and you become less sensitive to external stimulation. You are now really asleep. Interestingly, although the EEG continues to show theta waves, there are occasional bursts of activity known as *sleep spindles* and large waves called *k-complexes*. Some researchers believe that these are signals of brain mechanisms involved with shutting out the external world and keeping people asleep (Steriade, 1992). Abrupt noise can trigger k-complexes, and as people age they show fewer sleep spindles and sleep much more lightly. This is interesting because it suggests that the brain actually has to work to keep you sleeping. For some people, getting to sleep and staying asleep is difficult. **Insomnia** is a sleep disorder in which people's mental health and ability to function are compromised by their inability to sleep. Ways to deal with insomnia are listed in Table 4.1.

The progression to deep sleep occurs through stages 3 and 4, which are marked by large, regular brain patterns referred to as *delta waves*. This period of sleep is often referred to as *slow-wave sleep*, reflecting the presence of delta waves. It is extremely hard to wake people up if they are in slow-wave sleep, and when they do wake up they are often very disoriented. However, people still process some information in stage 4. Parents can be aroused by crying children but blissfully ignore sirens or traffic noise. The mind continues to evaluate the environment for potential danger.

REM SLEEP After about 90 minutes of sleep, a very peculiar thing happens. The sleep cycle reverses, returning to stage 3 and then to stage 2. At this point, the EEG suddenly indicates a flurry of beta-wave activity that usually indicates an alert, awake mind. At the same time, the eyes start darting back and forth rapidly beneath closed eyelids. This is called **REM sleep** for the *rapid eye movements* that occur during this stage. It is sometimes called *paradoxical sleep* because of the paradox of a sleeping body with an activated brain. Indeed, some neurons in the brain, especially in the occipital cortex and brainstem regions, are more active during REM sleep than during waking hours. But while the brain is active, most muscles in the limbs and body are paralyzed during REM episodes. At the same time, the body shows signs of arousal in the genitals, with most males of all ages developing an erection and females experiencing clitoral engorgement.

How would you define sleep?

insomnia A disorder characterized by an inability to sleep.

REM sleep The stage of sleep marked by rapid eye movements, dreaming, and paralysis of motor systems.

TABLE 4.1	Sleeping through the Night

HOW TO DEVELOP GOOD SLEEPING HABITS

1. Go to bed and wake up at the same time every day, including weekends. Establish a routine to help set your biological clock. Changing the time you wake up each day can alter sleep cycles and disrupt other physiological systems.

2. Never have alcohol or caffeine just before going to bed. Alcohol might help you get to sleep more quickly, but it will interfere with your sleep cycle and cause you to wake up early the next day.

3. Regular exercise will help your sleep cycles, but do not do it immediately before going to sleep.

4. Use your bed only for sleeping and sex. Do not spend time in your bed reading, eating, or watching television. You want your mind to associate your bed with sleeping.

5. Relax. Don't worry about the future. Have a warm bath or listen to soothing music. Learning relaxation techniques, such as imagining you are on the beach, with the sun shining on your back and radiating down your hands, may assist in dealing with chronic stress.

6. If you have trouble sleeping, get up and do something else. Don't force yourself to lie there trying to get to sleep. Remember that one sleepless night won't affect your performance very much and worrying about how you will be affected by not sleeping only makes it more difficult to sleep.

The psychological significance of REM sleep is that about 80 percent of the time that people are awakened during REM sleep they report dreaming, compared to less than half of the time during non-REM sleep (Solms, 2000). As you will see below, the dreams themselves are quite different during the two types of sleep.

Over the course of the night, the sleep cycle repeats, with progression from slow-

wave sleep to REM sleep and then back to slow-wave sleep. As morning approaches, the sleep cycle becomes shorter and relatively more time is spent in REM sleep (Figure 4.26). People also briefly awaken many times during the night but do not remember these awakenings in the morning. As people age, they sometimes have more difficulty going back to sleep after awakening.

4.26 Stages of Sleep Stages of sleep over the course of the night.

Sleep Is an Adaptive Behavior

Why do we sleep? It can be dangerous to tune out the external world. If nothing else, it might seem like a huge waste of time that you could spend in more productive ways. But people cannot override indefinitely the desire to sleep; the body shuts down whether we like it or not. Sleep must do something important, because nearly all animals sleep. Some animals have peculiar sleeping styles. Some species of dolphins have *unihemispherical sleep,* in which the cerebral hemispheres take turns sleeping! Researchers do not yet know exactly why animals sleep, but there are three general explanations that are used to describe the adaptiveness of sleep: restoration, circadian cycles, and facilitation of learning.

RESTORATION AND SLEEP DEPRIVATION The *restorative theory* of sleep emphasizes that the brain and body need to rest and that sleep allows the body to repair itself. Indeed, growth hormone is released during deep sleep, and one of its functions is to facilitate repair of damaged tissue. Additional evidence that sleep is a time of restoration is that people who have engaged in vigorous physical activity, such as running marathons, seem to sleep longer. But people sleep even if they spend the day being physically inactive. In addition, it appears that sleep allows the brain to replenish glycogen stores and strengthen the immune system (Hobson, 1999).

Numerous laboratory studies have examined the effects of sleep deprivation on physical and cognitive performance. Surprisingly, most studies find that two or three days of deprivation have little effect on strength, athletic ability, or cognitive performance on complex tasks. Performing boring or mundane tasks when sleep deprived, however, is nearly impossible. A brain-imaging study of sleep-deprived people found increased activation of the prefrontal cortex, suggesting that some brain regions may compensate for the effects of deprivation (Drummond et al., 2000). Over long periods, however, sleep deprivation eventually causes problems with mood and cognitive performance. Indeed, studies using rats have found that extended sleep deprivation compromises the immune system and leads to death.

People who suffer from chronic sleep deprivation, such as many college students, may experience lapses in attention, reduced short-term memory, and **microsleeps**, in which they fall asleep during the day for brief periods of time ranging from a few seconds to as long as a minute. These microsleeps may lead to disastrous results if the person is driving a car or performing a dangerous task.

microsleeps Brief, unintended sleep episodes, ranging from a few seconds to a minute, caused by chronic sleep deprivation.

Interestingly, sleep deprivation might serve one very useful purpose, which is helping people overcome depression. Consistent evidence has emerged over the past decade demonstrating that depriving depressed people of sleep sometimes alleviates their depression. This effect appears to occur because sleep deprivation leads to increased activation of serotonin receptors, as do drugs used to treat depression (Benedetti et al., 1999).

CIRCADIAN RHYTHMS The *circadian rhythm* theory of sleep proposes that sleep has evolved to keep animals quiet and inactive during times of the day when there is greatest danger, which for most is when it is dark. Physiological and brain processes are regulated into regular patterns known as **circadian rhythms** (*circadian* roughly translates to "about a day"). Body temperature, hormone levels, and sleep-wake cycles are all examples of circadian rhythms, which operate like biological clocks. Circadian rhythms are themselves controlled by cycles of light and dark, although animals continue to show these rhythms when light cues are removed.

According to the circadian rhythm theory, animals need only so much time in the day to accomplish the necessities of survival, and it is adaptive to spend the remainder of the time inactive, preferably hidden away. Accordingly, the amount an animal sleeps depends on how much time it needs to obtain food, how easily it can hide, and how vulnerable it is to attack. Small animals sleep a great deal, whereas large animals vulnerable to attack, such as cows and deer, sleep little. Large animals that are not vulnerable, such as lions, also sleep a great deal. After a fresh kill, a lion may sleep for days on end. Humans, who depend greatly on vision for survival, adapted to sleeping at night, when the lack of light put them in possible danger.

FACILITATION OF LEARNING It has been proposed that sleep may be important because it is involved in the strengthening of neuronal connections that serve as the basis of learning. The general idea is that circuits that have been wired together during the waking period are consolidated, or strengthened, during sleep (Wilson & McNaughton, 1994). Robert Stickgold and colleagues (2000) conducted a study in which they required participants to learn a complex task. They found that participants improved at the task only if they had slept for at least six hours following training. Both slow-wave sleep and REM sleep appeared to be important for learning to take place. The researchers argued that learning the task required neuronal changes that normally occur only during sleep. Indeed, some evidence indicates that students have more REM sleep during exam periods, when it might be expected that greater consolidation of information is taking place (Smith & Lapp, 1991).

The argument that sleep, especially REM sleep, promotes development of brain circuits for learning is also supported by the changes in sleep patterns that occur over the life course. Infants and the very young, who learn an incredible amount in a few short years, sleep the most and also spend the most time in REM sleep.

Sleep and Wakefulness Are Regulated by Multiple Neural Mechanisms

Multiple neural mechanisms are involved in producing and maintaining circadian rhythms and sleep. For instance, the biological clock is located in the suprachiasmatic nucleus (SCN) of the hypothalamus. Light-sensitive photoreceptors in the eye send signals to the SCN. These photoreceptors are different from those that provide visual information, and they may even work for people who are otherwise blind. Individual neurons within the SCN seem to be the neural basis of the biological clock, as

circadian rhythms The regulation of biological cycles into regular patterns.

they show a peak in firing activity about once a day (Welsh, Logothetis, Meister, & Reppert, 1995). The SCN also signals a tiny structure called the *pineal gland* (Figure 4.27) to secrete melatonin, a hormone that travels through the bloodstream and affects various receptors in the body and the brain. Bright light suppresses production of melatonin, whereas darkness triggers its release. It has recently been noted that taking melatonin can help people cope with jet lag and shift work, both of which interfere with circadian rhythms. Taking melatonin also appears to help people get to sleep, although it is presently unclear why this happens.

Hypothalamus

Suprachiasmatic nucleus

Pineal gland

BRAINSTEM AND AROUSAL Sleep involves alterations in states of arousal, thereby implicating brain mechanisms that produce aroused states. In 1949, Giuseppe Moruzzi and Horace Magoun found that stimulating the *reticular formation* in the brainstem leads to increased arousal in the cerebral cortex. If you cut the fibers from the reticular formation to the cortex, animals fall asleep and stay asleep until they die. Accordingly, Moruzzi and Magoun proposed that low levels of activity in the reticular formation produce sleep, and high levels lead to awakening.

4.27 The Biological Clock The suprachiasmatic nucleus houses the biological clock. It signals the pineal gland to secrete melatonin, which affects bodily states related to being tired.

It is now known that multiple regions within the reticular formation participate in the control of sleep-wake cycles. For instance, one region sends the neurotransmitter norepinephrine to many regions of the brain, thereby increasing cortical arousal. Research has demonstrated that this region is highly active when animals are awake, less active during non-REM sleep, and almost completely inactive during REM sleep (Figure 4.28). The system is also involved in sleep.

What triggers sleep? There is some evidence that a small area of the forebrain, just in front of the hypothalamus, is involved in inducing non-REM sleep. Neurons in this region become more active during non-REM sleep, and lesioning this region leads to insomnia. Once this area is activated, inhibitory signals are sent to the reticular formation, thereby reducing arousal and triggering sleep.

REM SLEEP During REM sleep, various neural processes are activated, of which some lead to paralysis of motor systems whereas others lead to activation of mental circuits related to motivational states. For instance, neurons in the *pons,* a region of the brainstem, send signals to the spinal cord that block movement during REM sleep. Surgical lesioning of the pons causes animals to become very active while in REM sleep, as if acting out scenes from their dreams. People who have strokes that damage the brainstem sometimes develop *REM behavior disorder,* in which the normal muscle paralysis that accompanies REM is absent. Unfortunately for their sleeping partners, these individuals can become quite violent during REM episodes. In contrast, people with *cataplexy* experience REM muscle paralysis while awake; their muscles can suddenly become flaccid and they collapse to the floor.

4.28 Neuronal Activity Activity of neurons in one regional reticular formation during wakefulness and stages of sleep.

REM sleep is triggered by acetylcholine neurons in the pons. In the minute before REM episodes, these neurons become increasingly active, eventually producing

4.29 PET Scans Patterns of activation using PET, comparing REM to slow-wave sleep and waking. Note that there is greater activation (indicated by yellow and red) in limbic regions during REM than during slow-wave sleep. There is also less activation (indicated by purple) of much of the prefrontal cortex.

REM. Signals from this region are transmitted to the thalamus and the occipital lobes and also appear to trigger the eye movements that give REM sleep its name.

Brain-imaging studies show activation of limbic structures, such as the amygdala and certain regions of prefrontal cortex (i.e., the middle region behind the eyes), during REM sleep. This activation occurs along with a lessening of activity of other regions of prefrontal cortex, areas typically involved in rational thought and decision making. Surprisingly, the primary visual areas seem to be inhibited during REM sleep, whereas visual association areas are activated (Braun et al., 1998; Figure 4.29). These patterns of activation may produce one of the hallmark associations of REM sleep, vivid imagery in dreaming.

People Dream while Sleeping

Dreaming is one of life's great mysteries, as the mind conjures up images and stories that make little sense and sometimes scare the dreamer awake. **Dreams** are the products of this altered state of consciousness in which images and fantasies are confused with reality. Usually, people realize they were dreaming only when they

dreams The product of an altered state of consciousness in which images and fantasies are confused with reality.

wake up. Some people claim not to remember their dreams, but unless a person has a specific brain injury or is taking medication, everyone dreams. Indeed, the average person spends six full years of his or her life dreaming. People who have trouble remembering their dreams can be taught to do so, mostly by trying to write down their dreams as soon as they wake up.

Dreams occur both in REM and non-REM sleep, although the contents of dreams differ in the two types of sleep. Non-REM dreams are often very dull, such as deciding what clothes to wear or thinking about taking notes in class. In contrast, REM dreams are often bizarre. They involve intense emotion, visual and auditory hallucinations (but rarely taste, smell, or pain), illogical content, and an uncritical acceptance of events. Rules of time and space and physical laws are ignored in dreams.

When researchers first noticed rapid eye movements in the 1950s, they initially believed that dreams were mainly a product of REM sleep. Initially, non-REM dreams were dismissed as trivial or as based on faulty recollection. However, it is now clear that REM sleep can occur without dreaming and dreams can occur without REM sleep. Moreover, REM and dreaming appear to be controlled by different neural signals (Solms, 2000). Activation of different brain regions during REM and non-REM sleep may be responsible for their different types of dreams. The content of REM dreams is a result of the activation of brain structures associated with motivation, emotion, and reward along with the visual association areas. This closed loop allows the brain's emotion centers and visual association areas to interact without self-awareness, reflective thought, or input from the external world.

WHAT DO DREAMS MEAN? Sigmund Freud, in one of the first major theories of dreams, argued that dreams contain hidden content that represents unconscious conflicts. According to Freud, the **manifest content** is the dream the way the dreamer remembers it, whereas the **latent content** is what the dream symbolizes, or the material that is disguised to protect the dreamer. However, there is virtually no support for Freud's idea that dreams represent hidden conflicts or that objects in dreams have special symbolic meanings. What is true is that daily life experiences influence the content of dreams. That is, you may be especially likely to have anxiety dreams while studying for exams. The dreams themselves have a thematic structure, in that they unfold as events or stories rather than as jumbles of disconnected images, but there is apparently no secret meaning to the way the story is told.

ACTIVATION-SYNTHESIS HYPOTHESIS The sleep researcher Alan Hobson proposed an influential theory that has dominated thinking about dreaming for the past two decades. Hobson's **activation-synthesis hypothesis** proposes that neural stimulation from the pons activates mechanisms that normally interpret visual input. The sleeping mind tries to make sense of random neuronal firing by synthesizing apparent activity in visual and motor neurons with stored memories. From this perspective, then, dreams are *epiphenomenal*—they are the experienced side effects of mental processes. Hobson and his colleagues (2000) have recently revised the activation-synthesis model to take into account recent findings in cognitive neuroscience. For instance, they have included amygdala activation as the source of the emotional content of dreams, and they propose that deactivation of the frontal cortices contributes to the delusional and illogical aspect of dreams. By its nature, the activation-synthesis hypothesis is more concerned with REM than non-REM dreams.

manifest content The plot of a dream; the way a dream is remembered.

latent content What a dream symbolizes, or the material that is disguised in a dream to protect the dreamer.

activation-synthesis hypothesis A theory of dreaming that proposes that neural stimulation from the pons activates mechanisms that normally interpret visual input.

What do dreams really mean?

"Look, don't try to weasel out of this. It was my dream, but you had the affair in it."

EVOLVED THREAT-REHEARSAL STRATEGIES Antti Revonsuo (2000) has proposed an evolutionary account wherein dreams simulate threatening events to allow people to rehearse coping strategies. Although Revonsuo does not believe that all dreams perform this function, he does suggest that dreams that provided people with solutions to adaptive problems helped them to survive and reproduce; thus dreaming is a result of natural selection. That the majority of dreams reported by people involve negative emotions, such as fear and anxiety, supports the evolved threat-rehearsal theory. Dreaming is associated with the activation of limbic structures, such as the amygdala, that are also activated during real threat encounters. Moreover, people tend to dream about real threats in their lives and to have nightmares about past traumas for long periods of time.

REVIEWING

the Principles | What Is Sleep?

All animals experience sleep, an altered state of consciousness in which the sleeper loses most contact with the external world. Sleep has a number of stages that can be identified by different patterns on EEG recordings. There is a basic distinction between non-REM and REM sleep, and different neural mechanisms are responsible for producing each type, although the brainstem figures prominently in the regulation of sleep-wake cycles. Dreams occur in REM and non-REM sleep, although the content of those dreams differs. This may be due to differential activation of brain structures associated with emotion and cognition. Although a number of theories have been proposed to explain sleeping and dreaming, their biological function is currently unclear.

Conclusion

The brain is a unique and remarkable set of structures that have collectively evolved to control the organism as it goes about the business of survival and reproduction. In humans, this evolutionary adaptiveness has led to the development of complex communication, culture, and thought. Our knowledge about the brain has expanded rapidly and dramatically over the past few decades, drawing on research from all the levels of analysis. For more than 100 years scholars debated whether psychological processes were located in specific parts of the brain or distributed throughout it. Along the way, they also built a formidable base of knowledge and principles. It was not until the 1990s, with the results of brain-imaging studies, among other methods, that it became clear that many mental processes are localized to specific regions of the brain that work together to produce behavior and mental activity. Research on the brain has revealed many fascinating phenomena, such as phantom limbs, split brains, and a left brain interpreter that struggles to make sense of the world. Brain-imaging techniques have also allowed psychological scientists to begin investigating consciousness, the personally familiar but scientifically elusive mental process that in some sense defines our entire experience with the world. Similarly, being able to watch the working brain has taught us an incredible amount about altered states of consciousness such as sleep and dreaming. Although much remains to be discovered, scientists using the tools of the biological revolution are making great and rapidly accelerating progress in understanding how the circuits of the brain enable the mind.

Summarizing the Principles of the Brain and Consciousness

What Are the Basic Brain Structures and Their Functions?

1. **The spinal cord is capable of autonomous function:** The spinal cord is a bundled rope of neurons that responds to sensory inputs and directs muscle responses (reflexes).

2. **The brainstem houses the basic programs of survival:** The top of the spinal cord at the base of the skull forms the brainstem, which is involved in basic functions and general arousal.

3. **The cerebellum is essential for movement:** The cerebellum, the bulging structure connected to the back of the brainstem, is essential for balance and movement.

4. **Subcortical structures control basic drives and emotions:** The subcortical structures play a key part in psychological functions because they control vital functions (the hypothalamus), sensory relay (the thalamus), memories (the hippocampus), emotions (the amygdala), and planning and producing movement (the basal ganglia).

5. **The cerebral cortex underlies complex mental activity:** The lobes of the cortex play specific roles in controlling vision (occipital), touch (parietal), hearing and speech comprehension (temporal), and planning and movement (frontal).

How Does the Brain Change?

6. **The interplay of genes and the environment wires the brain:** Chemical signals influence the growth and function of cells. Environmental experiences, especially during critical periods, are necessary for cells to develop properly and for them to make more detailed connections.

7. **The brain rewires itself throughout life:** Although plasticity decreases with age, the brain retains the ability to rewire itself throughout life. This ability is the biological basis of learning.

8. **The brain can recover from injury:** The brain can reorganize the function of areas in response to brain damage, although this capacity decreases with age. Transplanted stem cells may be able to grow to replace damaged neurons.

How Is the Brain Divided?

9. **The hemispheres can be separated:** A bundle of axons (the corpus callosum) connects the two sides of the brain; the connection can be cut, resulting in two independently functioning sides.

10. **The separate hemispheres can be tested:** Testing of split-brain patients has revealed the functions of each hemisphere.

11. **The hemispheres are specialized:** The left hemisphere is primarily responsible for language and the right hemisphere is competent in images and spatial relations.

12. **The mind is a subjective interpreter:** Our left hemisphere interprets and strives to make sense of our experiences, influencing the way we view and remember the world.

Can We Study Consciousness?

13. **Definitions of consciousness allow its empirical study:** To better study consciousness, researchers have divided the topic into basic issues, including subjectivity, access to information, and the unitary aspect of experience.

14. **Unconscious processing influences awareness:** Research findings indicate that much of our behavior occurs automatically, without our constant awareness.

15. **Awareness has many seats in the brain:** Blindsight demonstrates visual ability without awareness. The neuronal workspace model of consciousness demonstrates how awareness depends on activity in a variety of different cortical areas.

What Is Sleep?

16. **Sleep is an altered state of consciousness:** The stages of sleep vary by brain and respiration activity. REM sleep activates the brain and produces body paralysis and genital stimulation.

17. **Sleep as an adaptive behavior:** Sleep restores the body and circadian rhythms control changes in body function and sleep. Learning is consolidated during sleep.

18. **Sleep and wakefulness are regulated by multiple neural mechanisms:** The brainstem structures are involved in arousal (the reticular formation) and REM sleep (the pons).

19. **People dream while sleeping:** REM and non-REM dreams involve activation of different areas of the brain. Sigmund Freud thought dreams revealed unconscious conflicts. The activation-synthesis hypothesis posits that dreams are side effects of brain activity. Antti Revonsuo has theorized that dreaming is adaptive.

Applying the Principles

1. You are <u>riding</u> your mountain bike, <u>listening</u> to your iPod, and <u>thinking</u> about your plans for spring break, when suddenly you <u>are frightened</u> by a barking dog that starts chasing you. What parts of the central nervous system would be primarily responsible for each of these underlined behaviors?

   _____ a) cerebellum; temporal lobes; prefrontal cortex; amygdala

   _____ b) reticular formation; parietal lobe; occipital lobe; hippocampus

   _____ c) frontal lobes; temporal lobes; cerebellum; amygdala

   _____ d) occipital lobe; amygdala; prefrontal cortex; cerebellum

2. In your sociology class, while watching a video that deals with the conditions of infants in institutional care in Romania, you are struck by the limited interaction the children have with others, and by the complete lack of stimulating materials in their environment. The children appear listless and withdrawn. Based on what you have learned about the development of the brain, you correctly conclude that

   _____ a) their brains will not develop, leaving them like newborns.

   _____ b) their development will be significantly slowed, since the brain is "wired" by experience rather than genetics.

   _____ c) their brain development can catch up later in life, when they are placed in more stimulating environments.

   _____ d) their brains will develop normally since genes, not experiences, control development.

3. You are right-handed, but after breaking your right hand you are forced to use your left hand for several months. Initially you are able to do very little with your left hand, but with practice, you develop adequate skills. This is an example of

   _____ a) the human brain's preference that most motor skills be done by the right hand.

   _____ b) the simultaneous damage that occurs in the left cortex when the right hand is damaged.

   _____ c) the opposite-side control of the body by the brain and the ability of each hemisphere to specialize and to assume new functioning.

   _____ d) the left side of your brain, which controls the left hand, rewiring itself for the new skills.

4. You stayed up studying all night right before an exam on formal logic for your philosophy class. When you get back the graded exam, you discover that you performed poorly compared to your roommate, who had hit the sack at midnight. Which of the following reasons might account for this difference in performance?

   _____ a) One of the roles of sleep is consolidation of memories and learning.

   _____ b) The horizontal position during sleep enabled a beneficial blood flow pattern for the brain.

   _____ c) The lack of sleep made it hard for you to have enough motor control to write your exam responses.

   _____ d) The lack of sleep made your mind drift into REM activity, thus interfering with conscious thought.

ANSWERS: 1.a 2.b 3.c 4.a

Key Terms

activation-synthesis hypothesis, p. 153
amygdala, p. 124
basal ganglia, p. 125
blindsight, p. 144
brainstem, p. 121
Broca's area, p. 120
cerebellum, p. 122
cerebral cortex, p. 125
circadian rhythms, p. 150
corpus callosum, p. 137
critical period, p. 130
dreams, p. 152

frontal lobes, p. 127
gray matter, p. 121
hippocampus, p. 124
hypothalamus, p. 123
insomnia, p. 148
latent content, p. 153
manifest content, p. 153
microsleeps, p. 149
occipital lobes, p. 125
parietal lobes, p. 126
phrenology, p. 119

plasticity, p. 129
prefrontal cortex, p. 127
qualia, p. 141
REM sleep, p. 148
reticular formation, p. 122
spinal cord, p. 121
split brain, p. 137
temporal lobes, p. 127
thalamus, p. 123
unconscious, p. 142
white matter, p. 121

Further Readings

Brodal, P. (1998). *The central nervous system.* Oxford, U.K.: Oxford University Press.

Finger, S. (1994). *Origins of neuroscience.* Oxford, U.K.: Oxford University Press.

Gazzaniga, M. S., Ivry, R. B., & Mangun, G. R. (2002). *Cognitive neuroscience: The biology of the mind* (2nd ed.). New York: Norton.

Gladwell, M. (2005). *Blink.* New York: Little, Brown.

Kolb, B., & Whishaw, I. Q. (1998). *Fundamentals of human neuropsychology.* New York: Freeman.

McConnell, S., Roberts, J., Spitzer, L., Zigmond, M., Squire, L., & Bloom, F. (2002). *Fundamental neuroscience* (2nd edition). San Diego, CA: Academic Press.

Ramachandran, V. S., & Blakeslee, S. (1998). *Phantoms in the brain: Probing the mysteries of the human mind.* New York: William Morrow.

Sacks, O. (1985). *The man who mistook his wife for a hat.* New York: Summit Books.

Wegner, D. M. (2002). *The illusion of conscious will.* Cambridge, MA: MIT Press.

Sensation and Perception

Sensation and perception bridge the physical and psychological worlds. The museum visitors pictured here experience stimuli (e.g., the colors of the painting, the sounds of the crowds in the gallery room), which are first detected by sensory organs (such as the eyes or ears) before they are processed by the brain to produce a conscious, internal experience. The way in which our sensory organs convert information about the physical environment into signals that the brain can understand is an adaptive system developed over the course of human evolution.

Sensation, Perception, and Attention

5

I magine yourself to be Helen Keller at the age of six. Ever since you were 19 months of age, your life has proceeded in complete darkness and perpetual silence. For you the world exists only through touch, smell, and taste. You can recognize your parents by the feel of their skin and clothing, and you can tell where you are by smell and by touching objects that are around you. But you are otherwise completely isolated. You realize that others can communicate, but you are locked out. You are so enraged and frustrated by your mental prison that you throw daily tantrums. Your parents seek assistance from Alexander Graham Bell, the inventor of the telephone who has worked with deaf children, and he puts them in touch with the Perkins school for the blind in Watertown, Massachusetts. Through the school, they hire a teacher, Anne Sullivan, to teach you to communicate with signs. She makes strange sequences of hand motions in your hands. You mimic them, but they make no sense. Then one day she runs cool well water

5.1 Keller and Sullivan Helen Keller (left) with her teacher, Anne Sullivan.

over one hand while spelling w-a-t-e-r in the other. You finally make the connection. You then grab some dirt and ask for that to be spelled. By evening you have learned your first 30 words, and have begun a life of passionate learning and social activism (Figure 5.1).

Now imagine that you are not only blind and deaf but also unable to experience touch, or smell, or taste. You still feel hunger and other bodily sensations, such as fatigue, but for you there is no world beyond this. You have no way of knowing about the existence of other people or an environment outside your body. You are truly alone and no one can reach you, and you can reach no one. What can you do without perception?

Perception is the only bridge we have to the world. Without it we would be prisoners in the loneliest of solitary confinements. In order to perceive the world, we rely on information provided by our sense organs—our eyes, ears, skin, nose, and tongue. Each of these organs is sensitive to different physical stimuli, and each contributes different information. Ultimately, our perceptual representation of the environment is limited by the kinds of stimuli to which we are sensitive, and by the limits of our sensory systems in responding to those stimuli. And yet, we are sensitive to only a tiny fraction of the stimulus energy surrounding us. What we call light is far less than 1 percent of the electromagnetic spectrum, which also includes radio and television waves, x-rays, ultraviolet and infrared light, cosmic rays, and microwaves. We cannot sense magnetic fields, for example, or experience the world with sonar, as do bats and dolphins, or see the polarization of light, as do certain insects, or experience objects at a distance using electric fields, as do some fish. Even with fully functioning sensory organs we are blind to the vast majority of energy, events, and information surrounding us. If we are blind to most of what surrounds us, why does this not bother us? How would we know we are blind? Unless we have instruments, such as radios and televisions, that can convert these "invisible" forms of energy into forms that we can detect, it is for us as if this energy and information did not exist. Yet evolution has bestowed on us a system that allows us to flourish in our particular environment, providing rich sensory experiences of the world around us. ■

sensation How sense organs respond to external stimuli and transmit the responses to the brain.

perception The processing, organization, and interpretation of sensory signals that result in an internal representation of the stimulus.

Psychological scientists often divide the way we experience the world into two distinct phases: sensation and perception. **Sensation** refers to how our sense organs respond to and detect external stimulus energy (lights, air vibrations, odors, and so

Timeline

c. 1500

Art and Perception Leon Alberti describes the use of linear perspective and other depth cues to create the impression of depth in representational art.

1672

The Nature of Light Sir Isaac Newton performs his prism experiment, demonstrating that white light is in fact composed of a mixture of the spectral colors.

1709

The Empiricist View of Perception In his *New Theory of Vision* George Berkeley outlines the Empiricist view that perception is learned through experience with the world.

1838

The Stereoscope Charles Wheatstone invents the stereoscope and documents the role of binocular vision in spacial perception.

160   **CHAPTER 5** | Sensation, Perception, and Attention

on), and how those responses are transmitted to the brain. **Perception** refers to the brain's further processing of these detected signals that ultimately results in an internal representation of stimuli and a conscious experience of a world. Whereas the essence of sensation is detection, the essence of perception is construction of useful and hopefully meaningful information about the environment. For example, a green light emits photons that are detected by specialized neurons in the eyes, which transmit signals to the brain (sensation). The brain processes those neural signals and the observer experiences a green light (perception).

The study of sensation and perception, our focus in this chapter, is the study of those bodily systems that convert stimulus energy into useful information. We will study how various types of stimulus energy are detected by the sense organs, how the brain constructs information about the world on the basis of what has been detected, and how we use this constructed information to guide ourselves through the world around us. Many times, perception is based on our prior experience, which shapes our expectations during identification of sensory experiences. Thus, you are unlikely to see a blue, apple-shaped object as an apple, because you know from past experience that apples are not blue. An important lesson that will emerge in this chapter is that our perception of the world does not work like a tape recorder or camera, faithfully and passively capturing the physical properties of stimuli we encounter. Rather, what we *see* or *hear* is the result of brain processes that actively construct perceptual experiences to allow adaptation to the environment. This system can get the details wrong, such as filling in information that doesn't exist, but it does so in an intelligent and efficient way that produces a meaningful understanding of what is going on in the world around us.

How is information from stimuli in the world transformed into neural activity in the brain?

How Do We Sense Our Worlds?

Our sensory organs gain information about the environment by converting forms of physical energy into signals that the brain can understand. This system has been shaped over the course of evolution to solve adaptive problems, such as providing information on potential dangers or assisting in the identification of items that are vital for survival, such as edible foods and fresh water. Because they faced different adaptive challenges, each animal species is sensitive to different types of physical energy. Animals that hunt at night have poor vision but superb hearing. Unlike humans, many insects can perceive ultraviolet light, which is useful because such light reveals their primary food source. This is important to keep in mind as we focus mainly on human sensation and perception. We sense and perceive energy information that has solved adaptive problems for humans over the course of evolution.

1860	1867	1907	1950	1961
Psychophysics Gustav Theodor Fechner publishes *Elements of Psychophysics*, laying the foundations for the systematic investigation of sensory processes.	**Searching for Biological Foundations** Hermann von Helmholtz publishes his seminal *Handbook of Physiological Optics*, integrating the physics, physiology, and psychology of visual perception.	**Birth of the Gestalt School** Max Wertheimer's experiments with Phi motion mark the beginning of the Gestalt movement in perceptual psychology.	**Sensation and the Brain** Wilder Penfield and Theodore Rasmussen publish *The Cerebral Cortex of Man*, describing cortical stimulation experiments during neurosurgery that evoke sensory experiences.	**A Theory of Hearing** Georg von Békésy is awarded the Nobel prize for his research into the mechanisms of hearing. His theory articulates how sound waves are transformed into neuronal information.

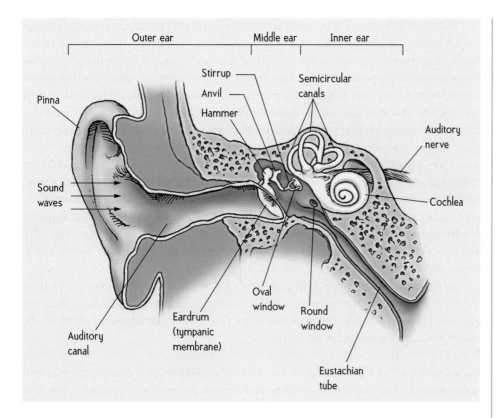

5.5 The Human Ear **5.5 The Human Ear** Sound waves enter the auditory canal, causing the eardrum to vibrate. These vibrations are carried along as waves in the liquid of the inner ear.

waves stimulate the *hair cells* located on the surface of the basilar membrane. These hair cells are primary auditory receptors; the oscillations of the basilar membrane prompt the hair cells to generate action potentials. Thus, the mechanical signal of the oscillations produced by sound waves is converted into a neural signal that travels down the auditory nerve to the brain.

TIME AND PLACE CODING FOR PITCH How does the firing of auditory receptors signal different frequencies of sound, such as high notes and low notes? In other words, how is pitch coded by the auditory system? Two mechanisms for encoding the frequency of an auditory stimulus operate in parallel in the basilar membrane: temporal coding and place coding.

temporal coding A mechanism for encoding low-frequency auditory stimuli in which the frequency of the sound wave is encoded by the frequency of firing of the hair cells.

Temporal coding is used to encode relatively low frequencies, such as the sound of a tuba. The firing rates of cochlear hair cells match the frequency of the pressure wave, so that a 1,000 Hz tone causes hair cells to fire 1,000 times per second. Physiological research has shown that this strict matching between the frequency of auditory stimulation and firing rate of the hair cells can occur only for relatively low frequencies—up to about 4,000 Hz. At higher frequencies, temporal coding can be maintained only if hair cells fire in volleys, in which different groups of cells take turns firing, so that the overall temporal pattern matches the sound frequency.

5.6 Path of Transduction in the Inner Ear When sound waves hit the fluid of the inner ear, the fluid causes the basilar membrane to move up and down, activating electrical potentials in the hair cells (the receptor cells for hearing).

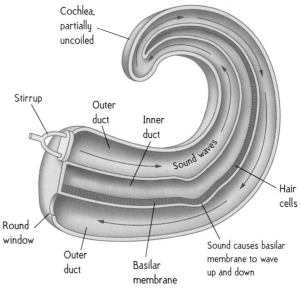

place coding A mechanism for encoding high-frequency auditory stimuli in which the frequency of the sound wave is encoded by the location of the hair cells along the basilar membrane.

The second mechanism for encoding frequency is **place coding**. During the nineteenth century, Hermann von Helmholtz proposed that different receptors in the basilar membrane respond to different frequencies, so that low frequencies would activate a different type of receptor than would high frequencies. Later, the perceptual psychologist Georg von Békésy discovered that Helmholtz's idea was theoretically correct, but wrong in the details. Békésy (1957) discovered that different frequencies activate receptors at different *locations* on the basilar membrane. Thus, the receptors were similar, but just located in different places. This membrane responds to sound waves like a clarinet reed, vibrating in resonance with the sound. Because its stiffness decreases along its length, higher frequencies vibrate better at the membrane's base, while lower frequencies vibrate more toward its tip. Thus, hair cells at the base of the cochlea are activated by high-frequency sounds; hair cells at the tip are activated by low-frequency sounds (Culler, Coakley, Lowy, & Gross, 1943). The frequency of a sound wave, therefore, is encoded by the receptors on the area of the basilar membrane that vibrates the most.

Both temporal and place coding are involved in our perception of pitch. Most of the sounds we hear—from conversations to concerts—are made up of many frequencies and activate a broad range of hair cells. Our perception of sound relies on the integrated activities of many neurons.

CONCURRENT PROCESSING TO LOCATE SOUNDS Locating the origin of a sound is another significant problem in auditory perception. In audition, the sensory receptors do not code where in the world events occur. Instead, the brain integrates the different sensory information coming from each of our two ears. Much of our understanding of auditory localization has come from examining barn owls, which use a fine-tuned sense of hearing to locate their prey. These nocturnal animals can locate a mouse in a dark laboratory using their sense of hearing alone. Barn owls use two cues to locate a sound: the difference in timing between its arrival in each ear, and the difference in its intensity in the ears. Unless a sound is coming from a point exactly in front or in back of the owl, it will reach one ear before the other. Likewise, if sound comes from the right, it will be softer on the left because the head acts as a barrier. These differences in timing and magnitude are minute—but not too small for the owl's brain to detect and act on. The neurobiologist Mark Konishi (1993) has discovered that separate neural pathways process the timing cue and the intensity cue. Whether similar neural mechanisms are responsible for sound localization in humans is unknown, but the concept that such functions are likely to be segregated is a key to understanding how and what we perceive.

In Vision, the Eye Detects Light Waves

If knowledge is acquired through our senses, then vision is by far our most important source of knowledge. Consider how much of what we know comes from what we see. Is a place safe or dangerous? Does that person look friendly or hostile? Even our metaphors for knowledge and understanding are often visual: "I see," "the answer is clear," "I'm fuzzy on that point." It should come as no surprise, then, that most of the scientific study of sensation and perception is concerned with vision. In this section we focus (so to speak) on how energy is transduced in the visual system. It is important to keep in mind, however, that what is commonly called *seeing* is much more than transducing energy; it is an intelligent process that occurs in the brain to produce useful information about the environment. In his book *The Thinking Eye, the Seeing Brain,* James Enns (2005) notes that very little of what we call seeing actually

How do we know where sound is coming from?

takes place in the eyes; rather, what we see results from active constructive processes that occur throughout much of the brain to produce our visual experiences. When you open your eyes and look around, nearly half your brain springs into action to make sense of the energy arriving in your eyes. It seems so effortless and automatic that we often take it for granted, but our ability to see results from a cascade of neural processes that occur when light hits our eye. Of course, although the brain sees, it does so based on sensory signals from the eyes. If the eyes are damaged, then the sensory system fails to process new information. Here we examine how this energy is processed in the visual system.

The human eye works like a rather crude camera, focusing light to form an image on the retina (Figure 5.7). Light first passes through the *cornea,* a thick, transparent outer layer of the eye. The cornea focuses incoming light in a process called refraction. Light rays then enter and are bent farther inward by the lens, which focuses the light to form an image on the **retina**, the inner surface of the back of the eyeball. Although more refraction (bending of light) happens at the cornea than at the lens, the lens is adjustable, whereas the cornea is not. The *pupil,* a small opening in the front of the lens, contracts or dilates to alter how much light enters the eye. The *iris,* an opaque, circular muscle, controls the size of the pupil and gives eyes their color. Behind the iris, muscles change the shape of the lens—flattening it to focus on distant objects and thickening it to focus on closer objects. This is called **accommodation**. The lens and cornea work together to collect and focus light rays reflected from an object to form an inverted image of the object on the retina.

RODS AND CONES The retina has two types of receptor cells: rods and cones, so called because of their distinctive shapes. Rods respond at extremely low levels of illumination and are primarily responsible for night vision; they do not support color vision, and they are poor at resolving fine detail. This is why everything on a moonless night appears as shades of gray. Cones, in contrast, are less sensitive to low levels of light; they are primarily responsible for vision under high illumination, and for color and detail. Within the rods and cones, light-sensitive chemicals called *photopigments* initiate the transduction of light waves into electrical neural impulses.

There are approximately 120 million rods and 6 million cones in each retina. Cones are densely packed in a small region near the center of the retina called the **fovea**. Although cones are spread throughout the remainder of the retina (except in the blind spot, as you will see shortly), they become increasingly scarce near the outside edge (Figure 5.8). Rods are all located at the edges of the retina; none are located in the fovea. You can prove this to yourself at night by looking at a very dim star on a moonless night. If you look directly at the star it appears to vanish, because its light falls on the retina, where there are no rods. However, if you look just to the side of the star, it becomes visible again, because now its light is falling just outside the fovea, where there are rods.

TRANSMISSION FROM THE EYE TO THE BRAIN Shine a light in someone's eyes so that you can see their retina, and you are in fact looking at the only part of their brain that is visible to us from outside the skull. It is the one part of the central nervous system that is located where you can see it. The generation of electrical signals by the photoreceptors in the retina begins the visual process. Immediately after light is transduced into neural impulses by the rods and cones, other cells in the retina (*bipolar, amacrine, horizontal;* see Figure 5.8) perform a series of sophisticated computations on those impulses that help the visual system process incoming information. The outputs from these cells converge on about 1 million retinal *ganglion* cells. These cells are the first in the visual pathway to generate action potentials.

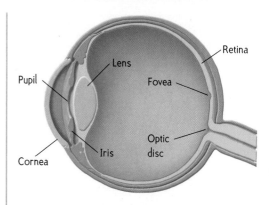

5.7 The Eye The cornea is a clear protective layer covering the lens, which focuses images on the retinal surface. Receptors in the retina send information to the visual cortex via the optic nerve.

retina The thin inner surface of the back of the eyeball. The retina contains the photoreceptors that transduce light into neural signals.

accommodation A process by which muscles change the shape of the lens by flattening it to focus on distant objects or by thickening it to focus on closer objects.

fovea The center of the retina where cones are densely packed.

Ganglion cells

Middle layer

Receptor cells

Light

Bipolar cells

Amacrine cell

Horizontal cell

Rod

Cone

Optic nerve fibers →

Cornea
Iris
Lens
Fovea
Retina

Optic nerve

Toward periphery:
% of rods increase

Near fovea:
cones predominate

**5.8 A Schematic Cross Section of the
Retina** Light passes through the cornea and
is focused on the retina by the lens. It passes
through the ganglion cell layer and middle
layer before it is transduced into neural
impulses by the receptor cells. There are
two types of receptors in the retina: rods
and cones. The cells in the middle layer
transduce the neural impulses, which form
a synapse with the ganglion cells. The
ganglion cells, in turn, transmit neural
impulses to the brain.

A surprising fact about the structure of the eye is that ganglion and other retinal
cells and blood vessels lie in front of the cones and rods, potentially blocking light from
being detected. Try this: hold a penlight near the outside corner of one eye (being careful not to touch your eye or burn yourself) and gently wiggle this light back and forth
while looking at a blank wall. If you do this, you may be able to see shadows cast by the
blood vessels in your eye. These will typically look like a large river delta as seen from
the sky. The brain normally discounts these shadows. But when light enters the eye
from a sharp angle, shadows are cast on cones that usually do not have this shadow
cast on them. The brain fails to discount these shadows, and they are seen as if they
were "out there" in the world.

Because the ganglion cells are inside the eye, they must leave it in order to send
their signals to higher areas of the brain. Axons from ganglion cells are gathered into
a bundle called the *optic nerve* that exits the eye at the back of each retina like a cable
leaving a room. The point at which the optic nerve exits the retina has no rods or
cones at all, resulting in a blind spot in each eye that is about the size of a fist held at
arm's length. This blind spot can be isolated, as demonstrated in Figure 5.9, but we
are generally not aware of it. Each optic nerve carries information to the central nervous system. The optic nerve splits into two parts that cross at the *optic chiasm*,
causing all information from the left side of visual space (i.e., everything visible to

CHAPTER 5 | Sensation, Perception, and Attention

5.9 The Blind Spot The optic nerve creates the blind spot we all have—a small point at the back of the retina. To find your blind spot, hold this book in front of you and look at the dot, closing your left eye. Move the book toward and away from your face until the rabbit disappears. You can repeat this for your right eye by turning the book upside down.

the left of the point of gaze) to be projected to the right hemisphere of the brain and vice versa, as shown in Figure 5.10. The first synapse of the majority of ganglion cells lies within the visual areas of the thalamus, and visual information is transmitted from there to cortical areas at the back of the head called the *primary visual cortex* (see Figure 5.10). The pathway from the retina to this region carries all the information that we consciously experience as seeing.

THE DETECTION OF VISUAL PRIMITIVES Sensory neurons are generally picky about what they respond to in the world. Scientists say that sensory neurons have a particular "tuning." This can be understood by thinking of a tuning fork tuned to, say, middle C. If the air around this tuning fork vibrates at the frequency of middle C, then this will make our tuning fork vibrate, resonating with the energy around it. However, if the air vibrates at a different frequency, our tuning fork will not resonate. Similarly, visual sensory neurons can be thought to be tuned to particular types of information in light. Some visual neurons respond best to particular colors, shape orientations, or directions of motion. This tuning property of a given visual neuron specifies its receptive field. A **receptive field** is the population of sensory receptors that influences activity in a sensory neuron, the region within which the cell

receptive field The region of visual space to which neurons in the primary visual cortex are sensitive.

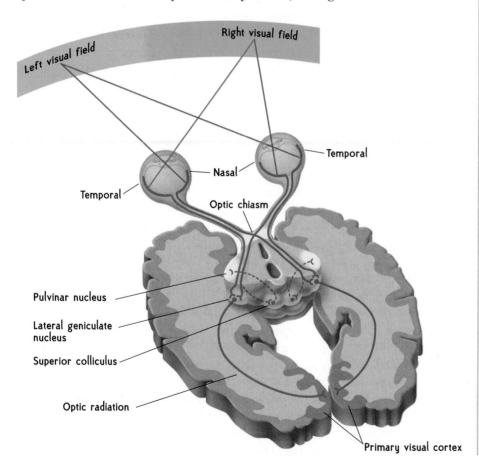

5.10 Visual Pathways The pathways along which information from the left visual field projects to the right visual cortex and the information from the right visual field projects to the left visual cortex.

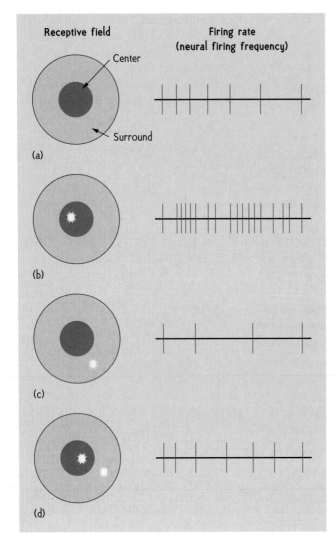

Receptive field

Center

Surround

(a)

(b)

(c)

(d)

Firing rate
(neural firing frequency)

5.11 Receptive Fields A typical receptive field consists of a center and a surround. When there is no light the cell fires at its baseline rate (a). When a light is shined in the center, the neural firing frequency increases (b); but when a light is shined in the surround, the cell decreases its firing (c). When a light shines in both the center and the surround, the cell's firing rate is similar to its baseline rate (d).

lateral inhibition A visual process in which adjacent photoreceptors tend to inhibit one another.

responds to a given stimulus. As in the tuning analogy, it responds best to some stimuli. Receptive fields are found for many sensory systems; the receptors can be in a region of skin or a set of photoreceptors in the retina. Since the eye projects an image of the visual scene onto the retina, *visual receptive fields* can be thought of as being located on a specific region of the retina or a specific location in visual space. To understand the nature of a receptive field, consider one of the most common types, consisting of a center region and a surrounding region (see Figure 5.11). In this type of receptive field, light that is directed towards the center region causes the cell to become more active, whereas light directed toward the surrounding region inhibits cell firing.

The processing of form information begins in the retina. Ganglion cells have receptive fields that make them especially sensitive to edges (abrupt changes in brightness or color) while at the same time relatively insensitive to uniform regions, such as large areas of the same color or brightness. In effect, the retina filters out uniform regions because they convey little useful information. The information that the retina transmits to the brain for further processing is a compressed version of the image that emphasizes information about borders.

LATERAL INHIBITION Another process that contributes to edge detection occurs because adjacent photoreceptors in neighboring regions of the retina tend to inhibit one another. If a cell is stimulated it sends information up to the brain, but it also sends information to its neighboring neurons, inhibiting their activity. The physiological mechanism that causes this effect is called **lateral inhibition**. If you look at Figure 5.12, you will see one consequence of lateral inhibition, which is the illusion of round grey dots appearing at the intersections of white lines against a dark background. Another consequence of lateral inhibition is that an object looks lighter againt a black background than against a white one, which is known as simultaneous contrast.

The effect of this lateral inhibition is to emphasize changes in visual stimuli, which once again makes the visual system especially sensitive to edges and contours. This is important because areas of changing visual stimulation are likely to correspond to the boundaries of objects in the physical world. From a very early stage of processing, then, the circuitry of the visual system is "wired" to make finding the boundaries of objects easier.

THE COLOR OF LIGHT IS DETERMINED BY ITS WAVELENGTH Visible light consists of electromagnetic waves ranging from about 400 to 700 nanometers (nm) in length. The color of light is determined by the wavelengths of the electromagnetic waves that it comprises. In the simplest terms, different wavelengths of light correspond to different colors (see Figure 5.13). It would be wrong, however, to equate physical wavelength with perceived color. How the brain coverts physical energy into the experience of color is quite complex, and it can be understood only by considering the response of the visual system to different wavelengths at the same time. White light, for example, contains the entire range of wavelengths in the visible spectrum.

Human beings can distinguish millions of shades of color, which can be categorized along three dimensions: hue, brightness, and saturation. *Hue* refers to the dis-

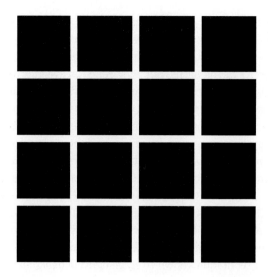

5.12 The Hermann Grid The Hermann grid is a demonstration of lateral inhibition at work. Look at the figure as a whole and you will immediately see darkened spots at the intersections of the white lines. However, if you look directly at the intersections, or cover all but one row of squares, you see that the dark spots are illusory. What is happening? Receptors coding information from the white lines are inhibited by their neighbors on two sides. Those receptors that code information from the intersections, however, are inhibited from four sides, so they respond less vigorously. This makes it look as though the intersections are darker than the lines.

tinctive characteristics of a color that place it in the spectrum; hue depends primarily on the light's wavelength when it reaches the eye. *Brightness* relates to the perceived intensity or luminance of a color, which is determined chiefly by the total amount of light reaching the eye. One should be careful not to confuse brightness—a physical dimension—and lightness—a psychological dimension. The *lightness* of an area is determined by its brightness relative to its surroundings. Because of simultaneous contrast, two grays with the same brightness can differ in lightness, depending on the surrounding levels of brightness. Although lightness is a more important variable than brightness for describing visual appearance, it has no simple physical correlate. The third dimension, *saturation,* refers to the purity of a color. Saturation varies according to the mixture of wavelengths present in a stimulus. Pure spectral colors have only a single wavelength, whereas pastels have a mixture of many wavelengths.

SUBTRACTIVE COLOR MIXING Color is determined not just by wavelength but also by the mixture of wavelengths (or spectral pattern) of a stimulus. There are two ways to produce a given spectral pattern: *subtractive* and *additive* mixture of wavelengths. Here we consider the subtractive process. In mixing, say, paints, the mixture occurs within the stimulus itself and is a physical process. This is an example of **subtractive color mixing**. Subtractive mixing of paints occurs because colors are determined by pigments—chemicals on objects' surfaces that absorb different wavelengths of light and prevent them from being reflected to the eye. The color of

subtractive color mixing A way to produce a given spectral pattern in which the mixture occurs within the stimulus itself and is actually a physical, not psychological, process.

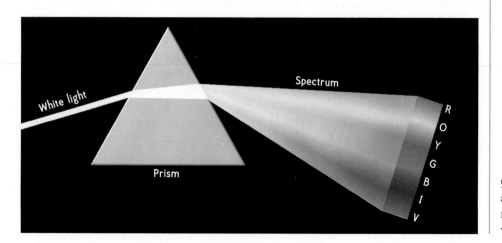

5.13 The Color Spectrum A prism breaks apart light rays into the spectrum of colors: red, orange, yellow, green, blue, indigo, and violet (ROYGBIV).

additive color mixing A way to produce a given spectral pattern in which different wavelengths of lights are mixed. The percept is determined by the interaction of these wavelengths with receptors in the eye and is a psychological process.

the pigment is determined by the wavelengths that are reflected. Thus blue paint contains pigments that absorb only long wavelengths (yellow and red); the paint appears blue because it reflects the shorter waves. Yellow pigments absorb shorter (blue) and longer (red) wavelengths, but they reflect wavelengths in the central yellow region of the visible spectrum. If we mix blue and yellow paint we get green because the yellow pigment absorbs the blue wavelengths and the blue pigment absorbs the red and yellow wavelengths. What remains is the wavelength corresponding to green. Thus the pigments mix to make green by subtraction. Red, yellow, and blue are the *subtractive primary colors*. Mix all three together and you get black, because together these pigments absorb nearly all the colors of the visible spectrum.

ADDITIVE COLOR MIXING When lights of different wavelengths are mixed, what you see is determined by the interaction of these wavelengths within receptors in the eye and is a psychological process. This is called **additive color mixing**. Additive color mixing is a technique known to stage lighting designers. For them, red, yellow, and blue are not the primary colors because they can aim red and green lights at the same point on a stage and create a yellow light. In fact, almost any color can be created by combining just three wavelengths, so long as one is from the long-wave end of the spectrum (red), one is from the middle (green-yellow), and one is from the short end of the spectrum (blue-violet). This phenomenon is called the *three primaries law of color*. Note that the exact colors of the three primaries in additive color mixing are more or less arbitrary. However, for reasons that will become clear soon, most psychologists consider the *additive primary colors* to be red, green, and blue. Whereas mixing red, green, and blue paint yields black paint, mixing red, green, and blue light yields white light. Isaac Newton discovered that white light is made up of many colors of light. You can see this for yourself with a prism (see Figure 5.13). Because different wavelengths of light bend (refract) at different angles when they pass through a prism, white light entering a prism leaves it with all the colors of a rainbow. Indeed, rainbows form in the sky because tiny water droplets in the air function as prisms, refracting sunlight in different directions.

EXPLAINING THE PHENOMENA OF COLOR VISION Whether color is created by subtracting hues from white light or mixing colors together, the result is the same: a certain combination of wavelengths striking the retina. However complicated this pattern is, it can be replaced with light of a single wavelength to yield the same perceived color.

If different wavelengths correspond to different colors, how is it that combining multiple wavelengths can create unique colors? This occurs because of the way light is transduced into neural impulses in the retina. Color vision begins in the retinal cone cells, which transduce light into neural impulses. There are actually three distinct types of cones in the retina, each of which responds best to a different wavelength of light. One type of cone is most sensitive to blue light (short wavelength), another is most sensitive to green light (medium wavelength), and the remaining population is most sensitive to red light (long wavelength). The three cone populations are therefore called "S," "M," and "L" cones because they respond maximally to short, medium, and long wavelengths, respectively. The color of a stimulus is determined by how much of each cone type it activates. Thus, yellow light looks yellow because it stimulates the L and M cones about equally and hardly stimulates the S cones at all. Similarly, we can create yellow light from red and green light because each stimulates the corresponding cone population. As far as the brain can tell, there is no difference between yellow light and a combination of red and green lights.

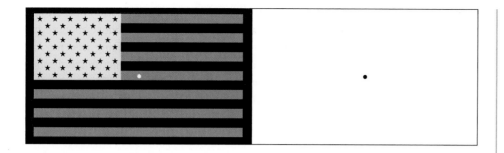

Ultimately, our perception of different colors is determined by the ratio of activity among the three cone receptors.

The initial coding of color information by just three types of retinal cone cells is one of the most important discoveries in the scientific study of visual perception. It illustrates how an essentially limitless variety of colors can be encoded by a small number of receptors. We've seen this integration property with other sensory systems. There are aspects of color vision, however, that are not predicted by the existence of three types of cones in the retina. For example, some colors seem to be "opposites" in some sense (Hering, 1878/1964). When we stare at a red image for some time, we see a green afterimage when we look away (and vice versa). Likewise, when we stare at a blue image for some time, we see a yellow afterimage when we look away (and vice versa) (Figure 5.14). We also have trouble visualizing certain color mixtures. For instance, it is easier to imagine reddish yellow or bluish green than reddish green or bluish yellow.

These phenomena cannot be explained by the responses of the different cones in the retina. To account for them, we must turn to the next stage of visual processing, in the retinal ganglion cells. As you have seen, the information from the cones converges on ganglion cells in the retina, some of which are sensitive to the color of a stimulus, and some of which are not. One class of color-sensitive ganglion cells receives excitatory input from L cones but is inhibited by M cones (or vice versa). These cells create the perception that red and green are "opposites." Other ganglion cells are excited by input from S cones, but inhibited by both L- and M-cone activity (or vice versa). These create the perception that blue and yellow are opposites.

A typical receptive field for a "color-opponent" ganglion cell is shown in Figure 5.15. A ganglion cell with this receptive field structure will respond well when red light is shined in its center, but will respond less when red light is shined in both its center and surround. It will respond even less when green light is shined in its inhibitory surround. Cells with color-opponent receptive fields respond most to color boundaries, and less to uniform regions of color. Edge information is therefore

5.15 Color-Opponent Ganglion Cell A ganglion cell with this receptive field structure will respond well when red light is shined in its center, but will respond less when red light is shined in both its center and surround. It will respond even less when green light is shined in its inhibitory surround.

extracted from incoming light at the earliest stages of visual information processing. Psychological scientists generally believe that edges are among the most informative features of objects. By emphasizing edge information and minimizing information about uniform regions, the ganglion cells efficiently process information from more than 100 million visual receptors. Later, when we examine the nature of visual perception, we will see that the brain recovers information about uniform regions through constructive processes.

Thinking Critically

Is There a Sixth Sense?

Now that we have covered the primary senses, you might wonder whether we have additional senses beyond these five. For instance, can we perceive the future? The term *sixth sense* refers to the "unexplainable" feeling that something is about to happen. Before we consider the case for whether we can perceive information beyond ordinary sensory information—so-called extrasensory perception, or ESP—we note that we have many sensory systems that provide information about the world. In actuality, as Howard Hughes (Figure 5.16) points out in his book *Sensory Exotica,* humans have several internal sensory systems in addition to the five primary ones we've discussed (Hughes, 2000). Subtle sensory systems send messages to our brains about things like our blood pressure or blood glucose levels. The kinesthetic sense, which some researchers group with the touch senses, refers to sensations we gather from receptors in muscles, tendons, and joints that pinpoint the position and movements of our limbs and body in space. This helps us to coordinate voluntary movement and is invaluable in avoiding injury. The vestibular senses use data from receptors in the semicircular canals of the inner ear. These canals contain a liquid that moves when the head moves, bending hair cells at the ends of the canal. The bending generates nerve impulses that inform us of the head's rotation and is thus responsible for a sense of balance. It explains why inner-ear infections make you dizzy, and why standing up quickly can give you a "head rush." The experience of being seasick or carsick results in part from conflicting signals arriving from the vestibular system and the visual system.

More exotic sensory systems are also being studied in animals, such as sonar senses and electroreception (senses based on electrical fields). Our understanding of sensory systems that use sonar for navigation comes primarily from studying bats and dolphins. These animals produce a call and then respond to the echoes of that call; the system is actually biosonar because the sound waves emanate from the animal. Electroreception operates in a similar way: Some fish emit an electrical field and then analyze disruptions in the field to avoid predators or find prey. Others respond to the electrical fields emitted by other fish. In each case, evolution has produced an adaptive solution that allows an animal to sense a form of energy and use that information to interact with its environment.

We noted at the beginning of this chapter that the human sensory system is sensitive to only a small range of the energy available in the environment. For instance, dogs can hear much higher frequencies than humans, and many insects are able to sense energy forms that we cannot detect. You might wonder, then, if there are energy forms that scientists have not yet discovered, such as energy that would allow us to read other people's minds, predict the future by examining the stars, or communicate with ghosts. Many reports of ESP are based on anecdotal cases. Psychological scientists tend to reject such claims because they are difficult to prove and because ordinary thought processes can explain many of them. For instance, if you see a couple fighting all the time, you might predict accurately that they will break up, but that doesn't make you a psychic. Much of social perception requires us to be sensitive to the subtle cues that guide behavior in a situation. Although this form of perception is beyond our basic senses, it cannot be considered ESP.

Perhaps the best evidence for ESP was obtained by the Cornell social psychologist Daryl Bem and his collaborator Charles Honorton. In these studies, a "sender" in a soundproof booth focuses on a randomly generated image and a receiver in another room tries to sense the sender's imagery. The receiver is then asked to choose among four alternatives, one of which is correct. By chance, the receivers should be correct 25 percent of the time, but across 11 studies, Bem and Honorton (1994) found that receivers were right about 33 percent of the time. Is this evidence of ESP? Many psychological scientists say that other factors in the experiments might have affected the results. A statistical review of many such studies found little support for ESP (Milton & Wiseman, 2001). Moreover, numerous scientific organizations and government agencies have reviewed decades of research and have concluded that no such phenomenon exists.

Perhaps you are a believer because you've seen a stage performer accomplish amazing feats. Be warned: Many magic tricks are designed to fool your basic senses; they can be viewed as elaborate examples of other visual illusions you will encounter in this chapter. They rely on the fact that our sensory system is far from perfect, and that our expectations shape much of what we perceive. These are tricks, not evidence of psychic abilities. But does any of this prove that ESP does not exist? An important quality of critical thinking is to keep an open mind and not to conclude that something doesn't exist just because it hasn't yet been demonstrated. The only reasonable thing to conclude is that the evidence for ESP is currently weak and that healthy skepticism demands better evidence.

What kinds of evidence would it take to convince you that ESP does or does not exist? What social factors might psychics use to *read* information from their clients? What might explain how some dogs can be trained to predict when their owners will have an epileptic seizure? ∎

5.16 Howard Hughes Hughes describes several sensory systems in humans and other animals in addition to the five primary systems of touch, taste, smell, sight, and hearing.

REVIEWING

the Principles | What Are the Basic Sensory Processes?

Each of our sensory systems has receptors that respond to different physical or chemical stimuli by transducing them into some pattern of brain activity. Typically, different receptors respond to different types of stimuli, and most sensory systems use coarse coding to integrate signals from these different receptors into an overall sensation. This allows a relatively small number of receptors to code a wide variety of stimuli. For example, the visual system can interpret the entire range of colors with only three cone types. These various sensory receptors help the perceptual system receive important information that assists in solving adaptive problems. Sensory information, although obtained from the outside world, is processed entirely in the brain to produce sensory experience through perception.

What Are the Basic Perceptual Processes?

The perceptual system is stunningly intelligent in its ability to guide us through the world around us. Every minute, our brains make millions of calculations—all in milliseconds—producing a coherent experience of our environment. For instance, as you stare at a computer screen, you are aware of one image, not the thousands that dance across your retina to create that constant, static scene. What you perceive, then, is vastly different from the pattern of stimulation your retina is taking in. How does the brain extract a stable representation of the world from the information the senses provide? This is what perception research is about.

If we were aware every moment of what our brain was doing, we would be paralyzed by the overload of information. Most of the computations the brain performs never reach our conscious awareness—only important new outcomes do. Perceptual psychology has drawn on many disciplines to understand how we represent our world. They have made many advances by noting how perception is disrupted following some injury to the brain, working backward to infer how the intact brain processes information. In addition, modern psychophysicists have developed clever techniques to describe the perceptual functions of the brain. Areas as diverse as art, computer science, music, philosophy, anatomy, and physiology have also informed our understanding of perception. Recall our discussion of music perception in Chapter 1, in which we saw how music can be used to explore various aspects of perception, from how genes predispose perfect pitch to how music can affect our moods. It is truly an interdisciplinary study that crosses the levels of analysis.

Perception Occurs in the Brain

So far, you have seen how sensory stimuli are transduced into electrical impulses and transmitted to the brain via nerves. These electrical impulses are all that the brain has to work with to create our rich variety of perceptual experiences. With the exception of olfaction, all sensory information is relayed to the brain via the thalamus. From the thalamus, information from each sense is projected to specific regions of the cerebral cortex, called *primary sensory areas* (Figure 5.17). It is in these areas that the perceptual process begins in earnest. This section considers perceptual processing in audition, touch, and vision. The brain regions involved in taste and smell are less well understood, and therefore we will not consider them here.

HEARING Auditory neurons in the thalamus extend their axons to the *primary auditory cortex* (called A1, for the *first* auditory area) in a region of the temporal lobe.

5.17 Primary Sense Regions These are the primary sense regions for the five primary senses. From the primary visual cortex, the dorsal stream codes for "where" objects are, whereas the ventral stream codes for "what" objects are.

Single-cell recording experiments have shown that neurons in A1 code the frequency (or pitch) of auditory stimuli. These studies have also revealed that A1 has a *tonotopic organization.* That is, neurons at the rear end of A1 respond best to lower frequencies, such as the sound of a fog horn, whereas neurons at the front end respond best to higher frequencies, such as a train whistle. Thus, the encoding of frequency in A1 is primarily by location. Several secondary auditory areas in the temporal and parietal lobes surround A1. Although we have little information about the organization of these secondary areas, it appears that they are also organized tonotopically.

TOUCH Touch information from the thalamus is projected to the *primary somatosensory cortex* (called S1) in the parietal lobe. In a classic series of studies of patients undergoing brain surgery, described in Chapter 4, the neurosurgeon Wilder Penfield discovered that electrical stimulation of S1 could evoke the sensation of touch in different regions of the body. Penfield found that neighboring body parts tended to be represented next to one another in the primary somatosensory cortex. That is, S1 has a *somatotopic* organization: The body is effectively mapped out according to physical proximity, such that connected areas of the body tend to be next to each other in the cortex. Remember that the drawing of the homunculus from Chapter 4 (see Figure 4.9) showed that more sensitive body parts have relatively larger amounts of S1 dedicated to them. The most sensitive regions of the body, such as lips and fingers, have a great deal of cortical tissue devoted to them. Other areas, such as the back or the calves, have very little. You can confirm this by having someone touch your back at adjacent locations. How far apart do the two points have to be before you notice that they are different? It turns out that this distance is much larger for the back than for, say, the cheek. The cheek has many more receptors in the skin and much more cortex devoted to it than does the back.

VISION The study of perception has focused to a large extent on the visual cortex and the multiple areas in which the retinal image is processed. The complexity of visual perception is underscored by the amount of cortical real estate that is dedicated to processing visual information. Some estimates suggest that up to half of the cerebral cortex may participate in visual perception in some way. By now you are aware that the **primary visual cortex**, also called area **V1**, is in the occipital lobe of the brain. The neuronal pathway from the retina to the occipital lobe preserves spatial relationships, so that adjacent areas of the retina correspond to adjacent areas in V1. This systematic ordering is known as **retinotopic organization**. The more forward we go along V1, the more the peripheral (away from the center) portion of the visual field is represented.

Early cortical processing consists of a rough description of various image properties and their locations within the scene. This description is a processed version of the original retinal image, but it is still a long way from identification of the three-dimensional structure of the visible world; a great deal of additional computation is required. A keystone in thinking about the neural mechanisms of visual perception is the concept of *hierarchical processing* of the details of the visual image. A widely held view is that this processing occurs in a number of stages, the first of which performs an analysis of the retinal image by extracting different elementary features (called *primitives*), such as lines, angles, colors, curves, and motion. It has been argued that relatively independent modules that specialize in extracting and interpreting

"Great! O.K., this time I want you to sound taller, and let me hear a little more hair."

primary visual cortex (V1) The largest area in the occipital lobe, where the thalamus projects the image.

retinotopic organization The systematic ordering of the neuronal pathway from the retina to the occipital lobe; this organization preserves spatial relationships, so that adjacent areas of the retina correspond to adjacent areas in the primary visual cortex.

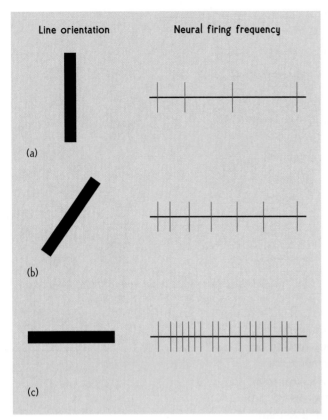

Line orientation **Neural firing frequency**

(a)

(b)

(c)

5.18 Simple Cells This neuron responds minimally to the vertical bar (a) and maximally to the horizontal bar (c). A slanted bar produces an in-between response (b).

particular classes of visual information may process different primitive features.

In the 1960s, the neurophysiologists David Hubel and Torsten Wiesel (1962) began exploring the properties of neurons in V1 by recording activity from single cells—work for which they were awarded a Nobel Prize. They discovered that some neurons in the primary visual cortex respond more to lines of particular orientations; for example, some neurons increase their firing rate when a vertical line segment is presented in their receptive field (Figure 5.18). The firing rate of these cells—termed *simple cells* by Hubel and Wiesel—decreases as the orientation of the line segment is rotated away from the preferred orientation. Further studies by Hubel and Wiesel and others have also found neurons that specialize in detecting the ends of lines, corners, and colors, as well as more complex visual features.

WHAT VERSUS WHERE One of the core discoveries of the past few decades has been that neurons in different parts of the brain tend to have different types of receptive fields. Besides V1, visual information is processed in a cascade of other visual areas many of which are also organized retinotopically. These visual areas appear to process specific aspects of a visual stimulus, such as color or motion. One important theory proposes that visual areas beyond V1 form two parallel processing streams—a lower ventral pathway that includes occipital and temporal lobe regions, and a higher dorsal pathway involving occipital and parietal lobe regions (see Figure 5.17). The *ventral stream* appears to be specialized for object perception and recognition, such as color and shape, whereas the *dorsal stream* seems to be specialized for spatial perception—determining where an object is and relating it to other objects in a scene. These two processing streams therefore are known as the *"what" pathway* and the *"where" pathway* (Ungerleider & Mishkin, 1982). Subsequent studies using brain imaging of humans have confirmed that brain regions in the dorsal stream are activated by tasks that require decisions about spatial relationships between objects, whereas regions in the ventral stream are activated by tasks that require identifying objects.

Damage to certain regions of visual cortex provides support for distinguishing between ventral and dorsal streams. Consider the case of D.F. (Goodale & Milner, 1992), who at 34 years of age suffered carbon monoxide poisoning that damaged her visual system, in particular regions involved in the "what" pathway. She was no longer able to recognize the faces of her friends and family, common objects, or even a drawing of a square or circle. She could recognize people by their voices, however, and if you placed objects in her hands, she could tell you what they were. Her condition—*object agnosia,* the inability to recognize objects—is striking in what she can and cannot do. When presented with a drawing of, say, an apple, she cannot identify or reproduce it. But if asked to "draw an apple," she can do so from memory. Despite major deficits in object perception, she can use visual information about the size, shape, and orientation of objects to control visually guided movements—her "where" pathway appears intact. For instance, she can walk across a room and step around things adeptly. She can reach out and shake your hand. Most confounding, in laboratory tests, she can reach out and grasp a block, with the exact right distance between her fingers, even though she cannot tell you what she is going to pick up, or how big it is. Thus, her conscious perception of objects is impaired—she has no awareness that she is taking in any visual information about objects she sees. However, other aspects of visual processing are unaffected. The intact regions of her visual cortex allow her to use information about the size and location of objects despite her lack of awareness. These systems operate independently to help us understand the world around us.

VISUAL FILLING-IN The central characteristic of perception is the construction of information about the world based on sensory information. A process known as *filling-in* offers a fascinating example of the constructive nature of perception. Earlier in this chapter you learned that the information sent from the ganglion cells to V1 is compressed in the sense that it emphasizes information about brightness and color boundaries and deemphasizes information about regions that are more uniform, such as large swaths of similar color. Yet our perception includes the whole scene, with an equal emphasis on edges and areas that are more uniform. When you look at a wall you do not only see the corners, you notice the vast expanse of the wall inside its edges. Most perceptual psychologists assume that the early visual areas, such as area V1, actually fill in the constant region information that was thrown out at the level of the ganglion cells. An example of perceptual filling-in is your blind spot, as you might have discovered in Figure 5.9. When the gap falls on your blind spot, your brain fills in the portion of the area that it assumes is missing because of the blind spot. Note that filling-in happens automatically. It is "cognitively impenetrable" because your thought cannot change the perceptual experience. Even though you know that there is a gap out there in the world, you cannot help but see a continuous line when the image of the gap falls on your blind spot (Pylyshyn, 1999). Now that we have seen that perception occurs in the brain, let's see how we actually construct our perceptual worlds.

Object Perception Requires Construction

The neural computations required for object perception begin early in visual processing. We have already seen how lateral inhibition among neurons in the retina helps to accentuate areas of changing stimulation—which are likely to correspond to the boundaries of objects. In addition, the work of Hubel and Wiesel on the properties of neurons in the primary visual cortex strongly suggests that one of the most important roles for V1 is extracting the edges and contours that define the boundaries of objects. Thus it appears that one of the first steps in processing a form is encoding the features that compose it.

The psychologist Anne Treisman and her colleagues developed a clever technique to reveal how these feature detectors can be used (Treisman, 1988). They employed a **visual search task** in which an observer tries to detect a target stimulus among an array of identical distracter stimuli. For example, the display might consist of one vertical line in a crowd of horizontal ones. The observer's job was to respond as soon as he or she saw the target. Treisman and her coworkers found that, for simple stimuli, subjects took no more time to find the target when it was buried in a large number of distracters than when it appeared with only one or two. They termed this phenomenon **pop-out**. The experimenters concluded that these simple scene elements are processed all at once, with oddballs standing out automatically from the crowd. These and other behavioral studies suggest that a vast amount of low-level visual information is automatically detected at the same time. We will see later that Treisman's visual search tasks have provided important information about how we pay attention to objects around us.

How do we identify objects?

visual search task An experiment used to study form perception, in which an observer tries to detect a target stimulus among an array of distracter stimuli.

pop-out The phenomenon whereby, when simple stimuli are used, subjects take the same amount of time to find the target, whether there are a few or many distracters.

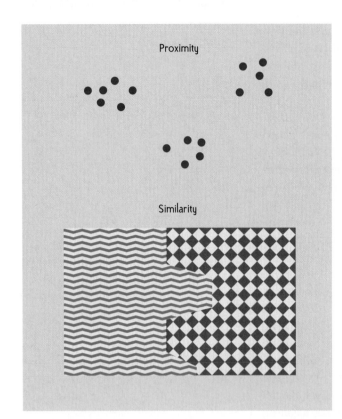

Proximity

Similarity

5.19 Proximity and Similarity Proximity and similarity are two powerful organizing principles identified by Gestalt psychologists.

GESTALT PRINCIPLES OF PERCEPTUAL ORGANIZATION

So what do we do with the information we take in about an object's features? How do we organize that information? As you will recall from Chapter 1, in the years prior to World War I, psychologists in Germany and the United States began theorizing that perception is more than the result of accumulating sensory data. This *Gestalt school* of perceptual psychology, founded by Max Wertheimer along with the experimental psychologists Wolfgang Köhler and Kurt Koffka, contributed much to the study of perception and other fields of psychology. The Gestalt psychologists believed that our perceptions are different from the sum of their constituent sensations. The German word *gestalt* means "shape" or "form," but as used in psychology it means "organized whole." Gestalt psychology holds that our brains use certain built-in (innate) organizing principles to organize sensory information; that is why we perceive, say, "car" as opposed to "metal, tires, glass, door handles, hubcaps, fender." The founders of Gestalt psychology postulated a series of laws to explain how perceived features of a visual scene are grouped into organized wholes.

PROXIMITY AND SIMILARITY Two of the most important Gestalt laws are the principles of proximity and similarity. The *principle of proximity* states that the closer two figures are to each other, the more likely we are to group them together and see them as part of the same object. The principle of similarity is illustrated by the *Sesame Street* song/game "One of These Things Is Not Like the Others." We tend to group figures according to how closely they resemble each other, whether it is in shape, color, or orientation (Figure 5.19). Both of these principles tend to clump elements of the visual scene into clusters, enabling us to consider them as a whole rather than as their individual parts. For example, we often perceive a flock of birds as a single entity because all the elements—the birds—are similar and in close proximity.

THE "BEST" FORMS Other organizing principles of Gestalt psychology describe how we perceive a form's features. *Good continuation* is the tendency to interpret intersecting lines as being continuous, rather than as changing direction radically. Good contour continuation appears to play a role in completing objects behind *occluders*. For example, in Figure 5.20 the bar appears to be completely behind the

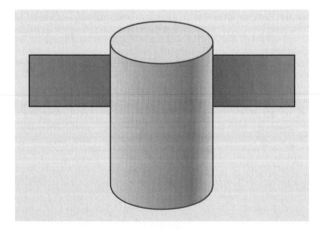

5.20 Bar Behind Occluders We perceive the bar to be continuous.

occluder. However, good continuation may operate over more complex representations than contour information. For example, the apparently very long cat in Figure 5.21 appears to wrap around the pole, yet there are no continuous contours permitting this completion to take place. Completion behind the occluder must happen at a level where three-dimensional surfaces are completed. *Closure* refers to the tendency to complete figures that have gaps (Figure 5.22).

A phenomenon that illustrates several Gestalt principles is *illusory contours,* which we perceive even though they don't exist. Illusory contours appear when stimulus configurations suggest that contours ought to be present—for example, when depth transitions are implied or useful in interpreting a pattern (Figure 5.23).

FIGURE AND GROUND One of our most basic organizing principles is distinguishing between figure and ground. A classic illustration of this is the *reversible figure illusion,* an example of which is in Chapter 1 (see Figure 1.13). In the figure, we see either a full face or two faces looking at each other—but not both at the same time. This illusion shows that our visual perceptual system divides scenes into figure and ground. When we identify a figure, we assign the rest of the scene as the background. In reversible figures, the "correct" assignment of figure and ground is ambiguous, so they periodically switch back and forth as the visual system strives to make sense of the stimulation. This illustrates the dynamic and ongoing nature of visual perception.

In Chapter 1, we described the work of Richard Nisbett and his colleagues (2001), who have demonstrated that there are cultural differences in how people from the East and West perceive the world. Westerners focus on single elements in the forefront, whereas those from Eastern cultures focus on the entire scene more holistically. From this perspective, Westerners are more likely to extract figure from ground, whereas Easterners are more likely to be influenced by both the figure and the ground.

5.21 Cat Occluder In this drawing by vision scientist Peter Tse, two cats appear to be one cat wrapped around the bar. You have the illusion of one continuous cat even though you know a cat is unlikely to be so long.

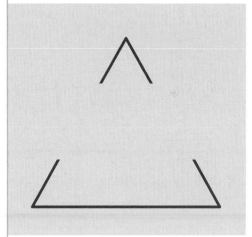

5.22 Closure We tend to complete figures even when gaps exist.

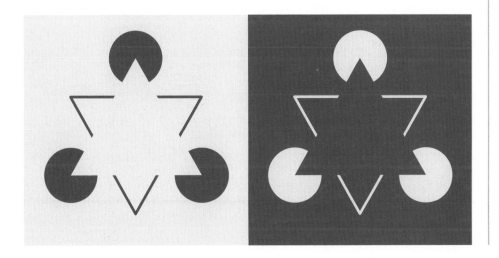

5.23 Illusory Contours Related to closure, we tend to see contours even when they don't exist.

RECOVERING SHAPE FROM IMAGE CUES In visual perception, an object's form (shape) seems to be the most salient cue for the brain to identify it. A square of any size or color is still a square. The ability to recognize objects by their shape develops at an early age. The psychologist Barbara Landau studied 3-year-olds and found that when scientists showed the children a shape and told them it was a "dax," the children accepted this definition (Landau, 1994). When they were shown other objects, some with the same shape as the "dax" but made of different materials, sizes, or colors, they still identified each object of the same shape as a "dax." It is perhaps no surprise, then, that we recognize a Granny Smith, a Red Delicious, or a Macintosh as an "apple."

While it is clear that form is the most important cue for object recognition, how we are able to extract an object's form from the image on our retina is still somewhat mysterious. We are able to recognize objects from different perspectives and in unusual orientations. We generally have little trouble telling where one object ends and another begins. Consider how we know that a horse and rider are two distinct beings, and not some strange animal.

Psychologists have described several shape-formation models. One of the main ones, *geon theory* (Biederman, 1987; see also Marr, 1982), is built on the idea that objects can be represented as an assemblage of primitive parts called *geons,* which is an abbreviation of the term "geometric ions." Geons are constructed by sweeping a basic two-dimensional shape like a circle or square through space to define a volume. This theory claims that all objects can be represented as a combination of geons, which function as a sort of shape alphabet from which more complex objects can be constructed (Figure 5.24). Some researchers have objected to this theory because they feel that a solution to the problem of shape formation should not be limited to combinations of primitive volumes. They pointed out that many shapes lack a distinct form entirely, such as the surface of the ocean, stalagmites, or swirls of smoke.

Even if the visual system does not use a geon description for recognition, it is likely that some other similar process is used. In general, the visual system attempts to recover the internal properties of objects (surface reflectance, material substance, three-dimensional shape) because these are more or less constant, whereas external properties (lighting, shading, shadows, distance, orientation) are constantly changing.

5.24 Geons The geon theory proposes that object recognition is based on identifying patterns of geons. (a) Twelve geons that differ by shape and the extent to which the lines are parallel. (b) A set of common objects with their component geons marked, using the geons from panel a.

CHAPTER 5 | Sensation, Perception, and Attention

Both internal and external information can be derived from an image, and probably both types are stored and used for various tasks, including recognition. Once even a part of an unfamiliar object has been recognized, the object's representation in memory can be used to provide information about other, still unrecognized parts. For example, in the image shown in Chapter 1 (Figure 1.12), it is hard to discern a Dalmatian standing among many black spots scattered on a white background because the part of the image corresponding to the dog lacks contours that define the edges of the dog, and the dog's spotted texture resembles that of the background. Many observers find that they first recognize one part of the dog, say the head, which then makes the whole dog's shape apparent. This is an example of how our model of a dog's shape in memory informs shape processing.

BOTTOM-UP AND TOP-DOWN INFORMATION PROCESSING How do we assemble the information about parts into a perception of a whole object? Most models of pattern recognition are hierarchical, using **bottom-up processing**. This means that data are relayed from lower to higher levels of processing. But perception is actually a combination of both bottom-up and **top-down processing**, in which information at higher levels of processing can influence lower, "earlier" levels in the processing hierarchy, such as helping us perceive the Dalmatian's body once we recognize its head. One illustration of this is the effect of context on perception: What we expect to see influences what we perceive. Consider, for example, the incomplete letter in Figure 5.25; the two lines in the center of each word are perceived as either "H" or "A" depending on which interpretation would make sense in the context of the word.

If expectations are faulty, it can lead to faulty perceptions. On November 28, 1979, Air New Zealand Flight 901 crashed into the slopes of Mount Erebus on Ross Island in Antarctica, with the loss of all 257 passengers and crew. Several factors contributed to this disaster. The aircraft's flight computer had been incorrectly programmed, so the plane was badly off course. In addition, the pilot had descended below the minimum altitude allowed for the flight. These factors don't explain, however, why the flight crew failed to notice the 12,000-foot volcano looming in front of them until moments before impact.

Psychologists testifying at the commission of inquiry offered a possible, if startling, explanation—the pilots saw what they expected to see. One of the unique hazards of Antarctic aviation is "white out," in which the sky and the snow-covered terrain appear to merge, and pilots are unable visually to distinguish the ground or the horizon. The pilots believed they were hundreds of miles away, flying over the Ross Ice Shelf, so they had no expectation that there would be mountains anywhere near their flight path. The psychologists argued that the few visual cues available to the pilots were sufficiently consistent with what they expected to see that in their minds their expectations were confirmed. Since there appeared to be no danger, the pilots decided—fatally—to reduce altitude to give the passengers a better view of the spectacular Antarctic landscape. The combination of an unusually sparse visual environment and the pilots' own beliefs had conspired to fool their visual systems into seeing terrain that wasn't there—and failing to see the mountain that was. This story conveys the importance of expectation in determining what we perceive. Recall the killing of Amadou Diallo described at the beginning of Chapter 1. The police officers expected Diallo to pull out a gun possibly in part because of stereotypical expectations, as well as the context they were in. We will see in Chapter 15 that the chances of an object being perceived as a gun rather than as a tool are higher when the object is held by a black person than when it is held by a white person (Payne, 2001).

How do expectations affect perception?

TAE CAT

5.25 Context Context plays a role in object recognition.

bottom-up processing A hierarchical model of pattern recognition in which data are relayed from one processing level to the next, always moving to a higher level of processing.

top-down processing A hierarchical model of pattern recognition in which information at higher levels of processing can also influence lower, "earlier" levels in the processing hierarchy.

5.26 Perceiving Faces Faces presented within an array of (a) nonobjects or (b) objects activated the fusiform gyrus. This occurred more strongly for the right hemisphere (c and d), especially when faces were presented among objects (d). Note that the right side of the brain (in c and d) is presented on the left side of the image.

5.27 Thatcher Illusion These two inverted pictures of former British prime minister Margaret Thatcher look normal. Turn your book upside down to reveal a different perspective.

FACE PERCEPTION One special class of object that the visual system cares about is faces, and psychological scientists have studied face perception across multiple levels of analysis, from how different brain regions seem to be especially responsive to anything that resembles a face, to how people determine a face's identity (i.e., who it is), to how various characteristics of the face determine whether we find it attractive. As highly social animals, humans have a well-developed ability to perceive and interpret facial expressions. At the biological level of analysis, faces are so important that certain brain regions appear to be dedicated solely to perceiving them. As part of the "what" stream, certain cortical regions, and even specific neurons, seem to be specialized to perceive faces. For example, neurons in the temporal lobes of monkeys became active only when the monkeys are looking at faces (Gross, Rocha Miranda, & Bender, 1972; Perrett, Mistlin, & Chitty, 1987). A number of brain-imaging studies have identified an area of the right hemisphere that seems particularly active during the observation of faces. As mentioned in Chapter 4, researchers such as Gregory McCarthy, James Haxby, and Nancy Kanwisher, working in separate laboratories, have found that a region of the *fusiform gyrus* may be specialized for perceiving faces (see Figure 5.26; Grill-Spector, Knouf, & Kanwisher, 2004; McCarthy, Puce, Gore, & Allison, 1997). Indeed, this brain area responds most strongly to upright faces, as we would perceive them in the normal environment (Kanwisher, Tong, & Nakayama, 1998).

Although some have argued that faces are simply a specialized category of object, there are people who have selected deficits in the ability to recognize faces (a condition known as *prosoagnosia*) but not in the ability to recognize other objects (Farah, 1996). In general, it appears that some areas of the brain, especially the fusiform gyrus, are important for the identification of faces, whereas other areas are sensitive to changes in faces, such as in facial expression and gaze direction. The emotional significance of a face appears to activate the amygdala, which is involved in calculating the potential danger of objects (Adams, Gordon, Baird, Ambady, & Kleck, 2003; Adolphs, 2003). Overall, the evidence suggests that many brain regimes contribute to the perception of faces, which aids in survival.

Interestingly, people have a surprisingly hard time recognizing faces that are upside down. We are much worse at this than we are at recognizing other inverted objects. People have difficulty with inverted faces, especially unknown faces, because such faces interfere with how people perceive the relations between various facial features (Hancock, Bruce, & Burton, 2000). For instance, if the eyebrows are bushier—the change is obvious if the face is upright, but not detectable when the face is inverted. One interesting example of the perceptual difficulties associated with inverted faces is evident in the Thatcher illusion (Thompson, 1980). When you view the faces upside down (see Figure 5.27), they both look pretty normal. However, if you turn your textbook upside down you will notice that one of the faces looks grotesque. Inversion of the whole face interferes with the perception of the individual components. This implies that we pay most attention to the eyes and mouth, and as long as they are in the right orientation the rest of the face appears normal, even if it actually is not.

At the social level, people are better at recognizing members of their own ethnic group than members of other ethnic groups. There is some truth to the old saying "They all look

5.28 Face Recognition Both whites and blacks showed better memory for same-race faces than for other-race faces, but this effect was only significant for whites. In both groups, there was greater activation of the fusiform face area (FFA) for same-race faces than for other-race faces. This response might indicate greater exposure to same-race faces, especially for whites.

alike," but the saying applies to all groups. This may occur because people have more exposure to members of their own ethnicity. Indeed, in the United States, where whites greatly outnumber blacks, whites are much better at recognizing white faces than black faces (Brigham & Malpass, 1985). An interdisciplinary team of social and cognitive psychologists from Stanford University sought to examine the neural correlates of this same-race effect (Golby, Gabrieli, Chiao, & Eberhardt, 2001). They asked white and black participants to remember pictures from both groups along with pictures of objects (antique radios) as a control comparison. They found that there was a significantly greater activation in a region of the fusiform gyrus for same-race faces compared to other-race faces, especially for whites, and that these activations were associated with better recognition of those faces (Figure 5.28). One possible explanation for why this effect appears to be smaller for blacks is that they are in the minority and therefore have more outgroup exposure than do whites. Thus, cultural context may affect the perception of faces, as well as other objects.

Why might we possess specialized mechanisms for perceiving faces?

Profiles in Psychological Science

Regaining Vision by Fixing the Eyes

People see with their brains, not with their eyes (Enns, 2005). You can prove this to yourself by closing your eyes and thinking about a familiar object. For example, try to picture in your mind the head of a lion. Can you see its mane? What color is it? Most people can "see" an image, even with their eyes closed. Most people who become blind have lost sensory input from the retina, yet they can still remember what objects look like and visualize them. What happens when we repair the visual system? Does perception return to the way it was before? With advances in medical treatment, many people who became blind due to illness are now regaining their sight. For instance, consider the case of Nogaye Gueye, a 58-year-old woman from Senegal (Figure 5.29) who had lost her sight due to cataracts. Volunteer surgeons from Sight Savers International conducted a 20-minute procedure that restored her vision. In a BBC interview, she describes not wanting to be too excited in case the surgery did not work. Indeed, when the doctors first took the bandage off, she could see only blue. But then, as she describes it, her sight slowly returned: "During the day, I gradually began to see all the other colors again. I was very excited now. The first thing I wanted to look at was my nieces and nephews, and to see their small children for the

5.29 Advances in Treatment Nogaye Gueye, who had been blind for two years, regained her vision following a 20-minute cataract-removal surgery.

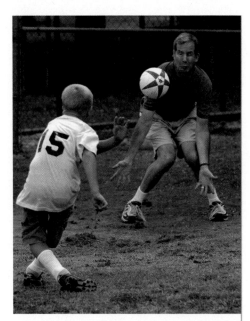

5.30 Recovering Vision Michael May, pictured here playing soccer with his son, became blind at age three; his vision in one eye was partially restored by corneal and stem cell implants.

binocular depth cues Cues of depth perception that arise from the fact that people have two eyes.

monocular depth cues Cues of depth perception that are available to each eye alone.

binocular disparity A cue of depth perception that is caused by the distance between a person's eyes.

first time." While traveling home she was able to make out objects, such as palm trees and cars. Her return to normal vision occurred quickly, but she had been blind for only two of her 58 years. What if a person had been blind for a much longer time and then had sight restored? What would that be like?

Michael May lost his eyesight in a chemical explosion when he was 3½ years old. In March 2000, at age 43, he underwent an experimental cornea and stem cell transplant into his right eye (the other eye was lost entirely in the explosion). Prior studies had found that people whose sight was restored after many years had great difficulty using visual information. The psychological scientists Ione Fine, Donald MacLeod, and their colleagues followed May's progress and tested his visual capacities (Fine et al., 2003). Two years after the surgery, May (Figure 5.30) was able to detect color and motion, but he still had great difficulty with other visual tasks, especially those that required higher-level constructive processes, such as using depth cues and identifying objects. Indeed, he had special difficulty recognizing faces; he could not recognize his wife or children by sight alone, and he had a hard time even judging gender from faces. A brain-imaging study showed that brain areas that normally react robustly to faces and objects were not at all active for May. But the brain regions that process motion reacted similarly to the same brain regions in typical research participants. Motion, however, is still a strange experience for him. May was an expert skier, having learned through verbal instructions. After the surgery he skied with his eyes closed because the overwhelming sensation of motion gave him a frightening sense that he was going to crash. He also became more nervous about crossing roads, which he used to do without much thought. So was having his sight restored a good or bad experience for May? According to May, not a day goes by that he doesn't appreciate the return of his sight.

The case of Michael May provides some interesting insights about visual perception. The brain is fine-tuned through experience; if a cortical region is not used in perception, it ceases to develop normally. Perhaps most interesting is how his brain had adapted to his loss of vision, so that he was highly successful in navigating his environment using his other senses. Regaining his sight added new joys, but his way of interacting with the world was thrown into turmoil by the addition of the novel experience of vision. Even though progress is slow, May continues to develop better vision with hard work. This demonstrates that brain plasticity continues well into adulthood. It will be interesting to observe May's progress over the coming years as his brain continues to learn how to use effectively the sensory cues it receives. ■

Depth Perception Is Important for Locating Objects

One of the most important tasks for our visual systems is to locate objects in space. Without this capacity we would find it difficult to navigate in and interact with the world. One of the most enduring problems in psychological research is how we are able to construct a three-dimensional mental representation of the visual world on the basis of two-dimensional retinal input. The fact that we can see depth in a photograph illustrates this point. A three-dimensional array of objects creates exactly the same image on the retina as a photograph of the array of objects. Despite this inherent ambiguity, we seldom have trouble understanding the arrangement of objects in the world. We actually make use of the ambiguous nature of depth perception when we look at photographs, movies, and television images. We are able to perceive depth in these two-dimensional patterns because the brain is able to apply the same rules or mechanisms that it uses to work out the spatial relations between objects in the (three-dimensional) world. To do this, the brain must rapidly and automatically ex-

CHAPTER 5 | Sensation, Perception, and Attention

ploit certain prior assumptions it has about the nature of the relationship between two-dimensional image cues and three-dimensional world structure. To understand this process, let us begin by considering the cues that are available to help the visual system perceive depth. These depth cues can be divided into those that arise from the fact that we have two eyes, called **binocular depth cues**, and those that are available to each eye alone, called **monocular depth cues**.

BINOCULAR DEPTH PERCEPTION One of the most important cues to depth perception is the **binocular disparity** (or *retinal disparity*) caused by the distance between your two eyes. Because each eye has a slightly different view of the world, your brain has access to two different but overlapping retinal images. The brain uses the disparity between these two retinal images to compute distances to nearby objects (see Figure 5.31).

Try this simple demonstration: hold your finger out in front of you and close first one eye and then the other. Your finger appears to move because each eye, due to its position relative to the object in question, has a unique retinal image.

The ability to determine the depth of an object on the basis of its different projections to each eye is called stereoscopic vision. In 1838 the physicist and inventor Charles Wheatstone devised the stereoscope, a device that enables a viewer to perceive depth by presenting a pair of two-dimensional pictures—each taken from a slightly different perspective. Wheatstone used this device to demonstrate that depth perception was influenced by binocular disparity, and thus that stereoscopic vision was an important cue for the depths of objects. In 1849 David Brewster, the Scottish physicist who invented the kaleidoscope, discovered the autostereogram—an optical illusion in which you can turn specially designed pairs of two-dimensional images into three-dimensional images by looking at them in an unfocused manner (see Figure 5.32).

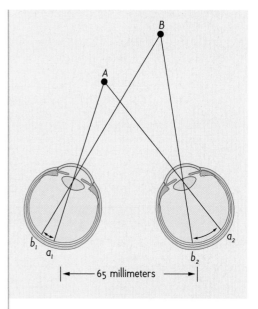

5.31 Binocular Disparity Our two eyes cause us to see every object from two distinct vantage points, resulting in two slightly different retinal images. The distance between the images for objects A and B is different for each eye. This disparity is an important cue for depth.

5.32 Autostereogram Hold the picture on the left close to your eyes and stare straight ahead. Try to relax your eyes and let them look through the book to an imaginary point in the distance. Slowly move the book away from you, still fixating on that imaginary point. Try to allow the doubled images to fall on top of each other and keep them there. The result of superimposing the images should be a three-dimensional effect. The picture on the right is the embedded image. If you don't see it in a few minutes, stop and try again later.

MONOCULAR DEPTH PERCEPTION Although binocular disparity is an important cue for depth perception, it is useful only for objects that are relatively close to us. Furthermore, we can still perceive depth with one eye closed. Monocular depth cues allow us to do this. Because artists routinely use these cues to create a sense of depth, they are also called pictorial depth cues. Leonardo da Vinci first identified many of these cues, which include:

- *occlusion:* A near object occludes (blocks) an object that is farther away.
- *relative size:* Far-off objects project a smaller retinal image than close objects.
- *familiar size:* We know how large familiar objects are, so we can tell how far away they are from the size of their retinal images.
- *linear perspective:* Parallel lines appear to converge in the distance.
- *texture gradient:* There is a continuous change in uniformly textured surfaces. As a surface recedes, its texture becomes denser, as shown in Figure 5.33.
- *position relative to horizon:* All else being equal, objects below the horizon that appear higher in the visual field are perceived as being farther away. Objects above the horizon that appear lower in the visual field are perceived as being farther away.

MOTION CUES FOR DEPTH PERCEPTION Motion is also a cue for depth. *Motion parallax* is the relative movement of objects at varying distances from the observer. Imagine sitting in a moving car and watching the scenery. Near objects seem to pass quickly, far objects more slowly (Figure 5.34). If we fixate on a point farther away, such as the moon, it appears to match our speed. If we fixate on an object at an intermediate distance, anything closer moves opposite our direction relative to that object, whereas anything farther moves in our direction relative to the object. Motion cues such as these help the brain to calculate which objects are closer and which are farther away.

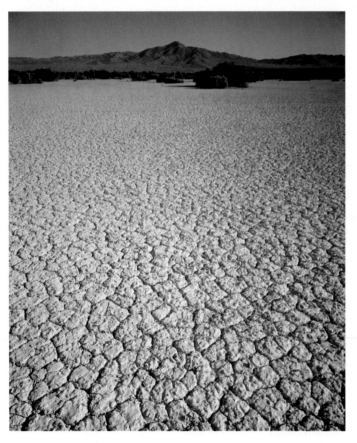

5.33 Texture Gradients Texture gradient is another important depth cue. Uniformly textured surfaces appear denser as objects recede. When texture disappears, it indicates a drop-off.

5.34 Motion Parallax Near objects seem to pass us more quickly in the opposite direction of our movement. Objects farther away seem to move more slowly.

Size Perception Depends on Distance Perception

The size of the retinal image of an object depends on the distance of the object from the observer; the farther away it is, the smaller its retinal image. In order to determine the size of an object, then, the visual system needs to know how far away it is. Most of the time enough depth information is available for the visual system to work out the distances of objects, and thus how big they are. However, in some circumstances size perception fails, and objects look bigger or smaller than they really are (see Figure 5.35). These optical illusions arise when normal perceptual processes result in an incorrect representation of the distal stimulus. Optical illusions are some of the favorite tools perceptual scientists have for understanding the way the brain uses information. Researchers rely on these tricks to reveal automatic perceptual systems that, in most circumstances, result in accurate perception. Optical illusions rely on depth cues to fool us into seeing depth when it is not really there. There are many such illusions. We will concentrate on just three: Ames boxes (also called Ames rooms), the Ponzo illusion, and the moon illusion.

AMES BOXES Ames boxes, crafted in the 1940s by Adelbert Ames, a painter turned psychologist, are a powerful example of depth illusions. His boxes elaborated on the Victorian trick in which a person looking through a peephole would see a furnished room and then open the door and find the room empty—with a dollhouse room nailed to the door. He built rooms that played with linear perspective and other distance cues. One such perspective illusion was a room that made a far corner appear to be the same distance away as a near corner. Normally, a nearby child projects a larger retinal image than a child farther away but does not appear larger because the perceptual system takes depth into account when assessing size. If the depth cues are wrong, so that the child appears to be farther away than he is—as in the Ames box—the disproportionate size of his image on your retina makes him look huge (see Figure 5.36).

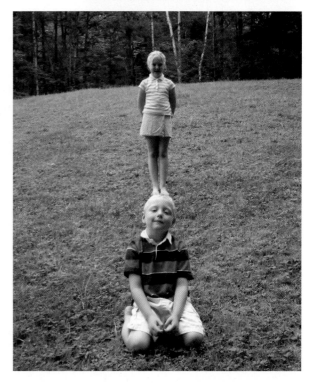

5.35 Distance Perception This picture was taken by 14-year-old babysitter Rebecca Robinson, who captured what appears to be a tiny Sarah Heatherton standing on James Heatherton's head. This illusion occurs because the photo does not capture the hill on which Sarah is standing and so fails to convey depth information.

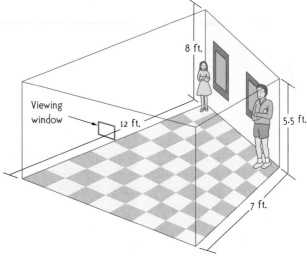

5.36 An Example of the Ames Box Ames played with depth cues to create size illusions. He made a diagonally cut room appear rectangular by using crooked windows and floor tiles. When one child stands in a near corner and another (of similar height) stands in a far corner, the room creates the illusion that they are both equidistant from the viewer; therefore the closer child appears as a giant compared to the child farther away.

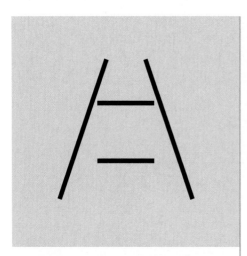

5.37 The Ponzo Illusion A classic size illusion caused by misleading cues of depth perception. The two horizonal lines appear to be different sizes because of the law of perspective that tells us that parallel lines converge in the distance. In fact, the two lines are the same length.

What causes perceptual illusions?

THE PONZO ILLUSION The Ponzo illusion, shown in Figure 5.37, was first described by Mario Ponzo in 1913 and is another classic example of a size-distance illusion. The common explanation for this illusion is that monocular depth cues make the two-dimensional figure seem three-dimensional (Rock, 1984). As noted earlier, parallel lines appear to converge in the distance. The two lines drawn to look like a railroad track receding in the distance trick your brain into thinking that the lines are parallel. Therefore, you perceive the two parallel lines in the center as if they are at different distances, and thus different in size when they actually are the same exact size. This shows how much we rely on depth perception to gauge size—your brain defaults to using depth cues even when there is no depth present.

THE MOON ILLUSION You may have noticed that a full moon looks much larger when it is near the horizon than when it is overhead (Figure 5.38). This is an illusion—the moon (obviously) remains the same size and distance from the earth, and the image of the moon on your retina is the same size whether it is on the horizon or overhead. The most common explanation for this illusion is that when the moon is near the horizon, several depth cues indicate that it is really very far away. When the moon is overhead, no such cues are available so the moon looks as if it is closer to the earth. The logic of this explanation is similar to that offered for the Ponzo illusion. The horizon moon looks farther away than the overhead moon, yet since they are really the same distance away, they create identical images on the retina. The only way for the brain to reconcile this discrepancy is to assume that the horizon moon is larger than the overhead moon. The mechanism responsible for the apparent difference in distance between horizon and overhead moon is still disputed, but all current theories of the moon illusion agree that perceived distance is the source.

Many perceptual psychologists believe that illusions reveal the operation of the mechanisms that help our visual systems determine the sizes and distances of objects

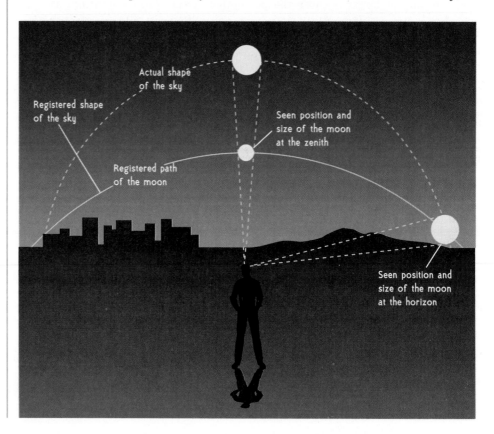

Registered shape
of the sky

Actual shape
of the sky

Seen position and
size of the moon
at the zenith

Registered path
of the moon

Seen position and
size of the moon
at the horizon

5.38 The Moon Illusion The moon looks larger when it is near the horizon than when it is overhead, due to various visual cues.

CHAPTER 5 | Sensation, Perception, and Attention

in the visual environment. In doing so, illusions illustrate the interdependence of size and distance perception in how we form accurate representations of the three-dimensional world.

Motion Perception Has Both Internal and External Cues

We know how motion can cue depth perception, but how does our brain perceive motion? One answer is that we have neurons that are specialized for detecting movement—they fire when movement occurs. But how does the brain then know what is moving? If you look out a window and see a car driving past a house, how does your brain know that the car is moving and not the house? Consider the dramatic case of M.P., a German woman who developed selective loss of motion perception following damage to secondary visual areas of the brain. She saw the world as a series of snapshots rather than as a moving image (Zihl, von Cramon, & Mai, 1983). Pouring tea, M.P. would see the liquid frozen in air and be surprised when her cup overflowed (Figure 5.39). Before crossing a street, she would spot a car far away, but when she tried to cross it would be right in front of her. M.P.'s unique deficit has been termed *akinetopsia*—the inability to perceive motion. She could perceive objects and colors, but why couldn't she perceive continuous movement? Unraveling mysteries such as these is the goal of researchers who study motion perception. We will consider three phenomena that offer some insight into how the visual system perceives motion. These are motion aftereffects, compensation for head and eye motion, and stroboscopic motion perception.

MOTION AFTEREFFECTS Motion aftereffects occur when you gaze at a moving image for a prolonged period and then look at some stationary scene. You experience a momentary illusion of seeing the new scene moving in the opposite direction from the moving image. This is also called the *waterfall effect,* because if you stare at a waterfall and then turn away, the rocks and trees will seem to move upward for a moment. Aftereffects are strong evidence that motion-sensitive neurons exist in the brain. The theory behind this illusion combines the phenomenon of sensory adaptation with neural specificity. The visual cortex has neurons that respond to movement in a given direction. When you stare at a moving stimulus for long enough, these direction-specific neurons begin to adapt to the motion, becoming less sensitive, or fatigued. If the stimulus is suddenly removed, the motion detectors that respond to all the other directions are more active than the fatigued motion detectors. This results in the impression that a new scene is moving in the other direction.

COMPENSATORY FACTORS The fact that we have motion-sensitive neurons doesn't completely explain motion perception. How do you know, for instance, whether an object is moving or whether you, or your eyes, are moving? Images move across your retina all the time and you don't always perceive them as moving. Each slight blink or movement of the eye creates a new image on the retina. Why is it that every time you move your eye, or your head, the images you see don't jump around? One explanation is that the brain calculates objects' perceived movement by monitoring the movement of the eyes or head as they track a moving object. In addition, motion detectors track the motion of an image across the retina, receptors in the retina firing one after the other (see Figure 5.40).

5.39 Motion Blindness Patients with motion blindness (akinetopsia) see the world as a series of snapshots rather than as a moving image. Even pouring a cup of tea becomes difficult because by the time they see the cup as full, it is overflowing.

Image movement system   Eye-movement system

5.40 Perceiving Movement There are two ways the visual system detects movement of objects: (1) if the eye is fixed, the image moves across the retina; (2) if the eye moves to follow the object, the retinal image stays in place.

5.41 Perceptual Constancy Depth cues make the man with the beard and tie look smaller in (b) than (a) but he isn't. The retinal image is the same, but depth cues in (a) make him look further away.

perceptual constancy People correctly perceive objects as constant in their shape, size, color, and lightness despite raw sensory data that could mislead perception.

Another explanation for movement perception is the *frame of reference effect:* The perceptual system establishes a stable frame of reference and uses it to assess the movement of other objects. Suppose you are sitting in the library reading, and around you are dozens of other students studying. While you are watching one student, he rises and moves down two seats. Since you were watching him move, you moved your head, or at least your eyes, prompting an array of images across your retina. However, your brain knows that it was the student who moved, and not the room around him, because it had established a frame of reference.

But when that frame of reference is the wrong one, you can be tricked into thinking that the wrong object is moving. Say you are on a train looking out the window at another stationary train. That train starts to move—and you think you are moving. This *induced movement illusion* also happens when you look up at the sky on a cloudy, windy night and it seems as if the moon is moving through the clouds.

STROBOSCOPIC MOVEMENT Movies are made up of still-frame images, presented one after the other to create the illusion of a "motion picture." This phenomenon is based on a perceptual illusion called *stroboscopic movement,* which occurs when two or more slightly different images are presented in rapid succession. The Gestalt psychologist Max Wertheimer conducted experiments in 1912 by flashing, at different intervals, two vertical lines placed close together. He discovered that when the interval was less than 30 milliseconds, subjects thought the two lines were flashed simultaneously. When the interval was greater than 200 milliseconds they saw two lines being flashed at different times. Between those times movement illusions occurred. When the interval was about 60 milliseconds the line appeared to jump from one place to another; at slightly longer intervals, the line appeared to move continuously—this is called *phi movement.*

Perceptual Constancies Are Based on Ratio Relationships

As we discussed earlier, illusions are inaccurate representations of stimuli. The opposite situation is called **perceptual constancy**, in which we correctly perceive objects as constant despite sensory data that could lead us to think otherwise. Consider the profile of Lincoln's head on an American penny. At first glance, it seems like a perfect representation of Lincoln's head. But if you were to meet someone with as flat a head as this, you might be shocked. The reason a profile can provide such a good likeness is that the relative positions and orientations of features on the head are the same as they would be for an actual head. Similarly, how does the brain know that a person is six feet tall when the retinal image of that person changes size according to how near or far he is (Figure 5.41)? How does the brain know that snow is white and a tire is black, even when snow at night or a tire in bright light might send the same luminance cues to the retina? For the most part, changing the angle, distance, or illumination of an object does not change our perception of that object's size, shape, color, or lightness. But to perceive any of these four *constancies,* we need to understand the relationship between at least two factors. For instance, for *size constancy* we need to know how far away the object is from us. For *shape constancy* we need to know from what angle we're seeing the object. For *color constancy* we need to compare the wavelengths of light reflected from the object with those from its background. Likewise, for *lightness constancy* we need to know how much light is being reflected from the object and from its background. In each case, the brain is computing a ratio based on the relative magnitude rather than relying on the absolute magnitude of each sensation. The ability of the perceptual system to make relative judgments is what allows constancy to be maintained across a variety of perceptual contexts. Although the precise mechanisms of the constancies are unknown, they illustrate that perceptual systems are tuned to detect change from some baseline condition, and not just to respond to sensory inputs.

HELMHOLTZ'S VS. GIBSON'S DIRECT-PERCEPTION THEORIES Broadly speaking, there are two approaches to the study of how we arrive at these ratio relationships. Classical perceptual theory, which originated with the nineteenth-century works of Hermann von Helmholtz, assumes that perceptual experience and perhaps innate knowledge provide the information about the ratio relationships that determine constancies. Thus, sensations create impulses to the brain, and the brain then interprets those impulses according to what it has learned in the past or had hard wired into it over the course of evolution. Earlier in this chapter we pointed out that the visual system must have prior assumptions in place about the relationship between two-dimensional retinal activation and the nature of events and objects in the three-dimensional world in order to be able rapidly to construct a representation of the world from the retinal image. These prior assumptions allow the brain to infer the correct state of the world from highly ambiguous retinal information. In this view, visual perception is always based on *unconscious inferences:* The brain is actively "connecting the dots" provided to it by sensation via automatic and unconscious Gestalt grouping procedures and prior assumptions that it has learned or inherited.

Studying how illusions work, many perceptual psychologists have come to believe that the brain has built-in prior assumptions that influence perceptions. The vast majority of visual illusions appear to be beyond our conscious control—we cannot make ourselves not see illusions. As an example, look at the two tables in Figure 5.42. Believe it or not, the tops of the tables are the exact same size and shape, not just the same surface area. Our brains will not allow us to accept that fact, however. Even if you trace one and place it on top of the other, your brain still cannot see it. The reason is that you have automatic perceptual processes that use perspective cues to tell you the size and shape of the tables are different.

Beginning in the 1940s, the perceptual psychologist James J. Gibson offered an alternative to classical perceptual theory, *direct perception*. Gibson (1966) approached the study of perception from an evolutionary perspective. He believed that to understand visual perception, the most important question to ask is: What is vision good for? In the most basic sense, the function of vision is to identify and locate predators and prey, find mates, avoid cliffs, and so on. The idea that our brains would have to rely on inference, on learning and memory, to form concepts that were basic to survival didn't make sense to him. In his view, the visual system is not built to enable us to see an exact copy of the real world; it is built to interpret cues that maximize its function. His direct-perception theory, then, stated that stimuli already have enough information for us to perceive them—we don't need additional memories or calculations to understand the sensory data. From this perspective, the brain does not have to construct representations of the three-dimensional world, it just needs to extract useful information from light. Whereas Helmholtz might have said that your brain effectively adds information that is not present in the retinal image when it "connects the dots" provided by sensation, Gibson simply rejected the notion that perception involves the construction of any information in addition to what is already available in the light itself.

Modern perceptual psychology has synthesized the ideas of Gibson and Helmholtz with Gestalt insights. Most perceptual psychologists now accept that the brain makes rapid inferences on the basis of prior assumptions about the relationship of the retinal image to the three-dimensional world, as Helmholtz first argued. Many of these

5.42 The Tabletop Illusion This unbelievable tabletop illusion of Roger Shepherd's demonstrates the automatic perceptual processes of the brain. Even when we know the two surfaces are the same, we cannot make ourselves "see" it.

inferences appear to arise from the global grouping procedures first discussed by the Gestalt psychologists. Yet there appears to be truth in Gibson's notion that much of perception is inaccurate but adequately useful. The big puzzle that occupies the minds of modern psychological scientists is unraveling the nature of the connection between electrochemical activity within neuronal circuits and the complex information processing that culminates in our perception of the world.

REVIEWING

the Principles | What Are the Basic Perceptual Processes?

The perceptual system is stunningly intelligent. It take ambiguous sensory information and constructs rich and meaningful experiences that allow us to navigate the world around us. All perception takes place in the brain, in which a variety of perceptual processes take incoming sensations and construct them into percepts. Information first arrives in primary sensory regions, such as V1 for vision and A1 for audition, but multiple brain regions contribute to our unified perceptual experience. The perceptual system uses cues from the environment to help interpret sensory information. For instance, visual cues help provide information about what objects are and where they are located, as well as other cues that provide information about depth and motion. Contemporary theorists emphasize that perceptions are not faithful reproductions of the physical world, but rather are constructed based on multiple processes that allow us to taste, smell, touch, hear, and see.

How Does Attention Help the Brain Manage Perceptions?

The brain is constantly receiving input from an enormous number of sources. How does the brain combine all this information into coherent, usually correct, perceptions? And how do we manage all of the sensory information that constantly bombards us? The study of attention is the study of how the brain selects which sensory stimuli to discard and which to pass along to higher levels of processing. Attention is important to our ability to function in our daily lives, as we try to focus attention on the task at hand and ignore all of the things that might distract us. Even having a decent conversation requires paying attention to the speaker, which might be difficult when the person has unusual facial features (such as a wandering eye) or if there is food hanging from the chin. In these cases, the unusual features capture our attention and make it difficult to comprehend what the person is saying. How does the brain know which features of the environment are most important and therefore are most deserving of our attention? In this section we consider the basic principles of how human attention works.

Visual Attention Is Selective and Serial

As you learned earlier, the psychologist Anne Treisman proposed that we identify "primitive" features automatically (color, shape, orientation, etc.). Her theory of the automatic recognition of these features has been a major development in the study of attention. Treisman proposed that different visual features of objects are ana-

Can we perceive something without attending to it?

lyzed by separate systems. These systems process information in parallel (at the same time), and we can attend selectively to one feature by effectively blocking the further processing of the others (Treisman & Gelade, 1980). Recall that in Treisman's visual search tasks (called feature search tasks), participants were looking for targets that differed in only one feature, and that these would pop out immediately, regardless of the number of distracters.

A very different picture emerges, however, if the participants are looking for a target that is harder to discriminate from the distracters. In conjunction search tasks, observers are asked to search for a target with two or more features. In Figure 5.43, for example, the subject might be asked to search for a green T among red Ts and green Xs. In this case the target can be distinguished from the distracters only by the conjunction of its features—it shares color with one half of the distracters and shape with the other half. In contrast to the immediate pop-out found in feature search, the presence of distracters markedly affected the participants searching for conjunctions. The time it takes to find the target increases linearly with the number of distracters—suggesting that subjects laboriously consider each distracter one by one.

These studies led Treisman to propose a two-stage theory of visual-image processing. According to this theory, visual processing begins with a rapid, parallel extraction of elementary features, whose distribution the visual system is simply mapping. Separate maps are created for each feature type—one for color, one for form, and so forth. The second stage of processing is slower and more effortful as this visual system combines the features from the various maps to form objects. This stage is not automatic—it requires the deployment of attention. Because of this, only selected regions of the feature maps get bound together. In feature searches, the average time it takes viewers to respond to targets is not affected by the number of distracters. This is the hallmark of preattentive searches (searches that do not require attention); the entire array is scanned in parallel, and the critical feature is rapidly registered if it is present. Conjunction searches, however, require attention and are processed serially, so the search time lengthens as more distracters are included.

SEGREGATION OF VISUAL FUNCTIONS Other evidence suggests that elementary visual processes proceed in parallel and are integrated relatively late in processing. For example, consider the versions of the Ponzo illusion shown in Figure 5.44. In the left red-on-green version, the illusion remains, but in the version on the right the illusion is much less effective. This is because in the right version the red and green have been set to the same approximate luminance, such that the figure and background are distinguished only by their color; in contrast, the left version has both color and brightness differences. Color and depth are processed in separate pathways in the visual cortex, so the depth information is lost in the right version. Without depth information, the parallel lines appear equal in length.

Cases in which people suffer visual deficits as a result of brain injuries also support the view that humans have distinct perceptual systems for processing different visual features. For instance, color-blind people do not have problems with depth and texture perception—they can still see and recognize objects. The akinetopsia patient described

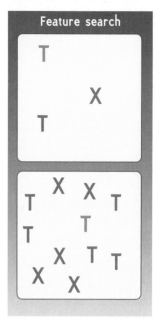

5.43 Visual Search Tasks In visual search tasks, subjects are asked to find the target—the thing unlike the others. In feature searches, in which the target has only one feature (color or shape) that differs from the distracters, this is simple. When the target has more than one feature that differs (for instance, the green T among red T's and green X's), it takes longer.

5.44 The Ponzo Illusion The Ponzo illusion is effective in all but the third panel. When the background and lines are the same brightness, depth cannot be perceived. This indicates that visual processing of brightness and depth are separate.

earlier apparently has normal processing of color and form, despite her profound impairment in processing motion.

BINDING If the brain processes features automatically and separately, how does it determine which features go with which objects? This is known as the binding problem. Treisman has shown that attention helps integrate features so that we correctly perceive objects. When a normal observer is given too many cues to pay attention to, errors in binding occur. For example, in tests in which people are briefly shown red Xs and blue Os and are asked to name a digit presented at the same time, they often report that they saw a blue X or red O. These illusory events happen because the observer's attention was divided and overextended between the colored letters and the digit-identification task. As a result, features from objects recombine to form an object that doesn't exist. The binding system breaks down.

Auditory Attention Allows Selective Listening

Because of attention, it is hard to do two tasks at the same time, especially if they rely on the same mechanisms. We easily can listen to music and drive at the same time but find it hard to listen to two conversations at once. Driving and listening to the radio at the same time can even be hazardous depending on what you're listening to—a sports broadcast may engage your visual system to imagine the game in progress, diverting attention away from the visual cues on the road ahead.

The **cocktail party phenomenon**, so called by the British psychologist E. C. Cherry (1953), refers to how you can focus on a single conversation in the midst of a chaotic cocktail party, yet a particularly pertinent stimulus, such as hearing your name mentioned in another conversation, can capture your attention. While proximity and loudness contribute, your selective attention can also determine which conversation you hear. Imagine you are having dinner with a friend at a crowded restaurant. Suddenly the conversation at the next table piques your interest. If you really want to hear that conversation, you can focus your attention on it rather than on what your (closer and therefore louder) friend is saying. When your friend notices the blank look on your face and protests, "You're not listening to me!" chances are you won't be able to tell your friend what he or she said—but you can relate the drama at the next table.

Cherry developed selective-listening studies to examine this aspect of attention. He used a technique called shadowing, in which a participant wears headphones, with one ear receiving one message, and the other ear receiving a completely different message. The person is asked to attend to one of the two messages and "shadow" it by repeating it aloud. In this situation, the subject will usually notice the unattended sound (the message given to the other ear), but will have no idea about the content of that message (Figure 5.45).

What captures attention?

Ignored inputs

The horses galloped across the field...

Attended inputs

President Lincoln often read by the light of the fire...

Headphones

Speech output

President Lincoln often read by the light of the fire...

5.45 Listening Inputs In shadowing experiments, subjects receive different auditory messages in each ear but are asked to "shadow" or say aloud only one.

Selective Attention Can Operate at Multiple Stages of Processing

The psychologist Donald Broadbent (1958) developed the **filter theory** to explain selective-listening findings. He assumed that we have a limited capacity for sensory information and thus screen incoming information, only letting in the most important. In this model, attention is like a gate that opens for important information and closes for information to be ignored. But can we really close the gate for irrelevant information? When and where is the gate closed?

Broadbent's filter theory is an example of **early selection**, which is the theory that we can choose which stimuli we will attend to even before we process their basic features. In visual processing we could choose to ignore features such as color or form and process only those features that we had decided would be important for the task at hand. Accordingly, attention effectively filters out certain features at an early stage so that they never get processed.

However, some studies reveal that "unattended" visual information is processed to at least some extent. **Late selection** theories assume that we take in sensory information, process it, and then select which aspects of the stimuli should be attended. The attention stage occurs when the perception enters our conscious awareness. Several studies of selective listening found that although a subject could not repeat an unattended message, he or she still processed its contents. Fascinating studies demonstrate that if the unattended message is relevant, we automatically use the information. For instance, subjects attended to the phrase "they threw stones at the bank yesterday," while at the same time either ear was presented with one of two words: "river" or "money." Afterward, subjects could not report which of these two words they heard; however, if they had been presented with "river," they interpreted the sentence to mean that someone had thrown stones at a riverbank. If they had been presented with the word "money," they interpreted the sentence to mean someone had thrown stones at a financial institution (MacKay, 1973). Thus, they extracted meaning from the word even though they were not aware of it.

It now seems clear that attentional selection is not an all-or-none process that eliminates unattended stimuli, as proponents of early-selection theories argued. Nor is unattended information fully processed before selection occurs, as suggested by late-selection theories. Rather, most modern theories of attention suggest that selective attention can operate at multiple stages of perceptual processing. A variety of studies has shown that the processing of attended stimuli is enhanced relative to that of unattended stimuli, but that unattended stimuli are still processed. Treisman proposed that unattended information is not "gated" completely but instead is simply reduced. Broadbent, the major proponent of the filter theory, agreed and amended his view.

cocktail party phenomenon The ability to focus on a single conversation in the midst of a chaotic cocktail party or other similarly noisy situation.

filter theory A theory that people have a limited capacity for sensory information and thus screen incoming information, letting in only the most important.

early selection theory A theory that we can choose the stimuli to which we will attend before we process their basic features.

late selection theory A theory that people take in sensory information, process it, and then select which aspects of the stimuli should be attended after processing.

Psychological Science *in Action*

Making the Roads Safer for All

Attention is important to many aspects of our daily lives and crucial for others, such as driving. Failing to pay attention is a major cause of car accidents, which are a serious problem around the globe, injuring or killing millions. Accidents have two main causes: bad road conditions and bad drivers. Both of these risk factors are ultimately related to perception. Thus, psychological scientists conduct research on the conditions that produce unsafe roads or on the types of people who are likely to have accidents (e.g., young drivers or very elderly drivers). For example, research has found that younger drivers tend to spend much longer looking at road hazards (Chapman & Underwood, 1998), which means they are less likely to notice other hazards and therefore more likely to crash. Other research shows that drivers have greater difficulty driving at night because of low illumination (Leibowitz, 1996). Because people

5.46 Making the Roads Unsafe Those who eat, talk, or read while they drive pose a serious safety risk to themselves and others because such distractions impair the visual processing necessary for them to navigate traffic conditions.

are not aware of this degradation of their perceptual abilities, they often drive as quickly at night as they do in the day, the result being an increased likelihood of crashing. Due to the effects of aging on the visual system, older drivers are likely to experience difficulty at night or when contrast is reduced, as in rain or fog.

Ultimately, many accidents are due to limitations of perception and attention. For instance, road glare can overwhelm the visual system. People can fail to notice sharp turns, or they can become confused by traffic signs or strange intersections. Human-factors researchers are psychologists who help road designers build safer roads and car makers build safer cars. On busy highways in Canada, for example, there are markers on the road at fixed distances that help drivers calculate how much space to leave between their car and the car in front of them. Signs advise drivers to keep two "chevrons" in distance, which works no matter how fast you are driving. As drivers exit from highways, some roads contain horizontal lines that get closer together near the end of the exit. This produces an illusion of speed that encourages drivers to slow down even more. Car makers also have worked with psychologists to build safer cars with new features, such as daytime running lights, larger and more prominent brake lights, and even sonar that warns drivers that they are too near to objects, and adaptive cruise control that keeps them multiple car lengths from vehicles in front of them.

Some psychologists focus on bad drivers, such as those who eat, talk, read, or put their makeup on while driving. Paying attention is an important aspect of safe driving. Indeed, being distracted or inattentive is one of the major causes of car accidents. As we saw earlier, attending to multiple things at the same time is difficult, as attention has a limited capacity (Figure 5.46). Simulated-driving experiments have shown that talking on a cell phone is especially dangerous, impairing driving skills nearly as much as alcohol. For instance, talking on a cell phone interferes with drivers' braking reactions to cars in front of them, possibly because talking impairs visual processing (Strayer, Drews, & Johnston, 2003). Interestingly, researchers from Spain have demonstrated that conversations in general may be dangerous. They found that talking either on a cell phone or to a passenger impaired visual processing in real traffic conditions (Recarte & Nunes, 2003).

Even when stressed, drivers need to be able to pay attention. One group that is especially likely to encounter stressful driving situations is police officers, who sometimes need to pursue fleeing suspects. Police chases have come under increased public scrutiny because of their risks to the general public. Some 40 percent of police chases end in crashes, with about 1 percent ending in a fatality (Hill, 2002). Psychologists help to train police officers to control their emotions while driving, in part by recognizing the adrenaline rush they feel as they start the chase. Police officers are also trained to pay attention to possible hazards during a chase. One study in England examined how police respond to the visual demands made on them during a chase (Crundall, Chapman, Phelps, & Underwood, 2003). The researchers found that police officers were more likely than other drivers to scan the horizon with quick visual fixations, allowing them to attend to more of the road and possible hazards.

The various types of research that we've just considered provide excellent examples of how psychological research in the laboratory can be applied to help solve real-world problems. At the same time, working in applied settings often enriches the questions that psychological scientists address. The goal of psychological research, as we mentioned in Chapter 1, is to explain the most important human behaviors in real-life contexts. Applying principles developed in perceptual psychology can help make the roads safer for all. ∎

REVIEWING the Principles | How Does Attention Help the Brain Manage Perceptions?

Attention is how the brain selects which sensory stimuli to ignore, and which to pass along to higher levels of perceptual processing. Visual search tasks indicate that we process visual information about primitive features along parallel pathways. Recombining information from these pathways may require attention. A key aspect of attention is that it is selective; we have the ability to choose the stimuli to which we attend. Despite this, we can still process some information contained in sensory stimuli to which we are not consciously attending. It is now clear that attention can operate on multiple stages of perceptual processing, and that unattended stimuli are reduced rather than eliminated from further processing.

Conclusion

Perceptual psychologists seek to understand how elementary sensations are translated into conscious perception. Our entire experience of the world relies on this process. Although it seems effortless, perceiving relies on numerous active processes that work together to construct our experience. Our senses gather information from relatively limited sources of physical energy. We hear few of the available sound waves and see only a small portion of the electromagnetic spectrum. But our experience does not feel limited, because these perceptual systems allow us to perform the tasks necessary for our survival and reproduction. After over a century of research, science still cannot state definitely how perception works. No single theory or model has yet successfully accounted for more than a fraction of perceptual phenomena. Despite this, the workings of our perceptual systems have begun to yield to the concerted efforts of psychological scientists working at many levels of analysis. With the advent of new technologies for studying the brain, these efforts have increased in their urgency. Perhaps the twenty-first century will finally yield answers to two of humankind's most enduring questions: How do we know our world? And how are mental events realized in the physical events of the brain?

Summarizing the Principles of Sensation, Perception, and Attention

How Do We Sense Our Worlds?

1. **Stimuli must be coded to be understood by the brain:** Stimuli reaching the receptors are converted to neural impulses through the process of transduction.

2. **Psychophysics relates stimulus to response:** By studying how people respond to different sensory levels, scientists can determine thresholds and perceived change (signal-detection theory). Our sensory systems are tuned to adapt to constant levels of stimulation and detect changes in our environment.

What Are the Basic Sensory Processes?

3. **In gustation, taste buds are chemical detectors:** The gustatory sense uses taste buds to respond to the chemical substances producing basic sensations of sweet, sour, salty, and bitter. The amount and concentration of taste buds vary individually.

4. **In smell, the nasal cavity gathers particles of odor:** Receptors in the olfactory epithelium respond to chemicals and send signals to the olfactory bulb in the brain. Pheromones are particular chemical signals linked to physiological responses in animals.

5. **In touch, sensors in the skin detect pressure, temperature, and pain:** The haptic sense relies on tactile stimulation to activate receptors for temperature, sharp and dull pain, and other sensations. Neural "gates" in the spinal cord also control pain.

6. **In hearing, the ear is a sound-wave detector:** The size and shape of sound waves activate hair cells in the inner ear. The receptors respond depending on frequency of the sound waves, timing, and the location of the activated receptors. Having two ears allows us to locate the source of a sound.

7. **In vision, the eye detects light waves:** Receptors (rods and cones) in the retina detect different forms of light waves. The lens helps the eye focus the stimulation on the retina for near versus far objects. Color is determined by wavelengths of light activating certain types of cones, by the absorption of wavelengths by objects, or the mixing of wavelengths of light.

What Are the Basic Perceptual Processes?

8. **Perception occurs in the brain:** The primary auditory cortex handles hearing. Touch is handled by the primary somatosensory cortex. Vision results from a complex series of events in a variety of areas of the brain but primarily in the occipital lobe.

9. **Object perception requires construction:** By using the Gestalt principles of stimulus organization, we are able to perceive our world. We use cues about similarity, proximity, form, figure and background properties, and shading. Perception involves the dual processes: bottom-up (sensory information) and top-down (brain organization).

10. **Depth perception is important for locating objects:** The pattern of stimulation of an object on each of the two retinas (binocular) informs the brain about depth. Pictorial (monocular) cues use information from the appearance of objects relative to their surroundings to inform about depth, as well as relative motion.

11. **Size perception depends on distance perception:** Illusions of size can be created when the retinal size conflicts with the known size of objects in the visual field, such as with the Ames, Ponzo, and moon illusions.

12. **Motion perception has both internal and external cues:** Motion detectors in the cortex respond to stimulation. The perceptual system establishes a stable frame of reference and relates object movement to it. Intervals of stimulation of repeated objects give the impression of continuous movement.

13. **Perceptual constancies are based on ratio relationships:** Hermann von Helmholz felt that experience provides ratio information about objects in their surroundings to achieve constancy. James Gibson felt the information was a primary, evolutionarily based aspect of perception. The contemporary view is a blend of the two theories.

How Does Attention Help the Brain Manage Perceptions?

14. **Visual attention is selective and serial:** We process the elements and features of visual stimulus simultaneously. Studies of brain-injured patients reveal that different areas of the brain process different information.

15. **Auditory attention allows selective listening:** The cocktail party phenomenon demonstrates how we readily shift attention to relevant auditory information.

16. **Selective attention can operate at multiple stages of processing:** The debate on selective attention centers on when information is filtered or passed on for further processing.

Applying the Principles

1. In grade school, most of us were given a hearing test. We wore headphones and were presented with tones in one ear and told to raise a hand whenever we heard a tone. Some of the time you may have raised your hand even though you were not certain if you heard something. Your uncertainty was the result of the _____ principle of signal-detection theory; and the lowest determined level of your hearing ability was your _____.

   _____ a) response and signal; difference threshold

   _____ b) response and noise; minimal threshold

   _____ c) noise and response bias; difference threshold

   _____ d) noise and response bias; absolute threshold

2. While studying in her room, Michiko hears a song she likes playing on her roommate's stereo in the living room. She then goes into the living room, turns up the stereo, and turns up the halogen lamp in order to read the CD case. What properties of the stimuli has she changed?

_____ a) light- and sound-wave frequency
_____ b) light- and sound-wave amplitude
_____ c) light-wave frequency; sound-wave amplitude
_____ d) light-wave amplitude; sound-wave timbre

3. Driving in the country, you notice in the distance something that appears to be a hawk on the side of the road. As you get closer to it, you realize it is only a bent county road marker. This change in visual perception is an example of

_____ a) the basic uncertainty of our visual experience.
_____ b) how motion affects depth perception.
_____ c) how our brain engages in an ongoing process of organization and identification of sensory information.
_____ d) how our sensory system picks up the wrong information.

4. In the movie *At First Sight,* actor Val Kilmer plays a man who, blind from birth, has his eyesight restored in adulthood and finds that he has incredible difficulty making sense of the visual information that bombards him. This scenario demonstrates

_____ a) the importance of attention in selecting which information to process.
_____ b) that seeing is solely a function of the visual system.
_____ c) that older people process visual information differently.
_____ d) that if you don't see something it is because the sensory system didn't process it.

ANSWERS: 1d 2b 3c 4a

Key Terms

absolute threshold, p. 163
accommodation, p. 173
additive color mixing, p. 178
binocular depth cues, p. 193
binocular disparity, p. 193
bottom-up processing, p. 189
cochlea (inner ear), p. 170
cocktail party phenomenon, p. 202
difference threshold, p. 164
eardrum (tympanic membrane), p. 170
early selection theory, p. 203
filter theory, p. 202
fovea, p. 173
haptic sense, p. 168

lateral inhibition p. 176
late selection theory, p. 203
monocular depth cues, p. 193
olfactory bulb, p. 167
ossicles, p. 170
outer ear, p. 170
perception, p. 161
perceptual constancy, p. 198
pheromones, p. 168
place coding, p. 172
pop-out, p. 185
primary visual cortex (V1), p. 183

receptive field, p. 175
retina, p. 173
retinoptic organization, p. 183
sensation, p. 160
sensory adaptation, p. 165
sound wave, p. 170
subtractive color mixing, p. 177
taste buds, p. 166
temporal coding, p. 171
top-down processing, p. 189
transduction, p. 162
visual search task, p. 185

Further Readings

Enns, J. (2005). *The thinking eye, the seeing brain.* New York: Norton.

Gazzaniga, M. S., Ivry, R. B., & Mangun, G. R. (2002). *Cognitive neuroscience: The biology of the mind* (2nd ed.). New York: Norton.

Gibson, J. J. (1979). *The ecological approach to visual perception.* Boston: Houghton Mifflin.

Hoffman, D. D. (1998). *Visual intelligence.* New York: Norton.

Hughes, H. C. (2000). *Sensory exotica.* Cambridge, MA: MIT Press.

Kandel, E. R., Schwartz, J. H., & Jessell, T. M. (2002). *Essentials of neural science and behavior.* New York: Appleton & Lange.

Rock, I. (1984). *Perception.* New York: Scientific American Books.

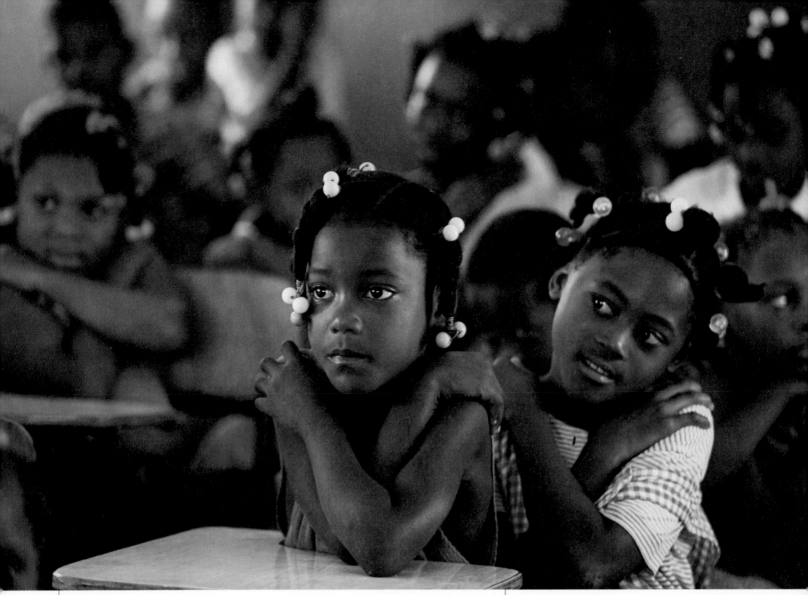

Learning through Conditioning

Children receive higher grades and positive reinforcement for studying and paying attention in class. In this way, children learn how to become good students.

Learning and Reward

6

The person who arguably had some of the greatest influence on contemporary psychological science started out as a novelist. Burrhus Frederick (B. F.) Skinner was inspired to pursue writing during his senior year in college after the poet Robert Frost read some of his work and provided encouraging comments. After many months spent toiling away in his parents' attic, with measly results, Skinner began to contemplate alternative careers. He originally had wanted to be a novelist so that he could explore big questions about the human condition, such as understanding why people act the way they do. Skinner, known as "Fred" to his friends, had always been a bit socially awkward and aloof and did not have great insight into other people's emotions. Unfortunately, the process of writing did not provide additional insights for him. As a novelist, he could describe people's actions, but this did not help him gain the true understanding of people that he was seeking. To pursue his intellectual interests in the human condition, particularly in human behavior, Skinner began to contemplate a career in psychology, though he had not taken a single psychology course in college. He became convinced that psychology was his calling after reading John B. Watson's *Behaviorism* (1924), and the novelist H. G. Wells's 1927 *New York Times Magazine* article in which he expressed admiration for the work of Ivan Pavlov, a Russian physiologist. Increasingly, the perspective of the behaviorists made sense to Skinner. Having made his decision, he enrolled in graduate school at Harvard University and began his explorations of human behavior. As they say, the rest is history—this time, to a large extent, a major part of the history of psychological science.

Skinner really came into his own at Harvard, in spite of the fact that he shared few interests with the faculty. Many faculty members were concerned about his apparent disdain for their efforts to analyze the inner mind through introspection, an approach that was common at Harvard at the time. Because of the influence of Pavlov and Watson on this thinking, Skinner became obsessed with the idea that he could dramatically change an animal's behavior simply by providing incentives to the animal for performing the behavior. For the next half century, Skinner conducted systematic studies of animals, often pigeons or rats, to discover the basic rules of learning. The importance of Skinner's work cannot be underestimated: Skinner discovered many of the most important principles that shape animal and human behavior. These principles are as relevant today as they were more than 50 years ago. As you'll see later in the chapter, we typically refer to this kind of approach to learning as operant conditioning and when it's applied to people as behavior modification.

Through his groundbreaking work, B. F. Skinner came to be radical in his beliefs about behaviorism, dismissing the importance of mental states and questioning philosophical concepts such as free will. He believed that the application of basic learning principles could create a better, more humane world for all, one that was free of poverty and violence. His best-selling novel *Walden Two* depicts a utopia in which children are raised only with praise and incentives, never with punishment. In his fictional community, behavioral engineers use principles of learning to create a world in which all people are well satisfied. *Walden Two* has inspired many people over the past 50 years; entire communities, such as Los Horcones in northern Mexico and Twin Oaks in rural Virginia, live according to the principles discovered in Skinner's research.

Timeline

1690

The Mind as a Blank Slate Building on ideas that can be traced back to Aristotle, the philosopher John Locke argues that all knowledge is acquired through contact with the environment.

1898

The Law of Effect Edward Thorndike proposes the Law of Effect, which shows that behaviors that lead to satisfying outcomes are likely to be repeated.

1906

Learning from Association Russian physiologist Ivan Pavlov provides the first empirical demonstration of simple associative learning, such as a dog associating the sound of a bell with the arrival of food.

1920s

The Rise of Behaviorism John B. Watson proposes the theory of behaviorism, which emphasizes that all behavior is determined by external forces and that only behaviors that can be manipulated and observed are of value to psychological science.

Skinner also used the ideas established through his research to raise his own children, especially in emphasizing reward over punishment. This was sometimes misinterpreted, as typified by the "baby in the box" incident. For his infant daughter Deborah, Skinner developed a sleeping chamber that kept an optimal temperature and provided a continuous supply of fresh linens. Unfortunately, the media portrayed this as the workings of a cold, mad scientist cruelly mistreating his child by locking her in a box, and rumors circulated that she was depressed and had killed herself. Nothing could be further from the truth. Deborah is an artist who is alive and well, and both daughters had excellent relationships with their father until his death in 1990.

B. F. Skinner's work has been enormously influential throughout society, from classrooms to clinics and beyond. During World War II, the U.S. military funded Skinner to conduct research on how animals might be trained to perform tasks such as guiding missiles. Although none of Skinner's animals were ever used as weapons, Skinner was able to demonstrate that animals could be trained to perform tremendously complex tasks, all via the selective administration of rewards for engaging in specific behaviors. These techniques continue to be used today, as in training dogs to serve as guides for people with handicaps; to sniff out drugs, bombs, or cadavers; or even to sense oncoming seizures in people with epilepsy. During the 2003 Iraq war, specially trained dolphins were used by the U.S. Navy to search for explosives in the Persian Gulf. Not surprisingly, these techniques are equally effective with humans. Skinner was especially interested in education, and many of his findings have been translated directly into the classroom, for example, the importance of self-paced computerized instruction. Many of the methods used to help people with mental limitations and disorders to lead healthy and productive lives are also based on the behavioral principles discovered by Skinner and other psychological scientists.

In this chapter, you will find out what Skinner and a number of other learning theorists have discovered about how learning takes place. This material is central to what psychology has contributed to our understanding of human and animal behavior and affects all the other major areas of psychology. It is therefore a cornerstone for a number of the foundational principles of psychological science. We will see how these findings have been used to improve quality of life and to train humans and animals to learn new tasks. We will also see how contemporary psychological scientists are discovering the brain mechanisms that support this learning and what new theories are emerging to explain how we learn. ■

1930s	1940s	1948	1960s	1960s
Learning from Reinforcement B. F. Skinner develops the theory of operant conditioning, which states that behaviors are controlled by reinforcement or punishment. The widely used method of behavior modification is based on this theory.	**Cognitive Learning Approach** Edward Tolman, among others, sets the groundwork for the cognitive revolution in psychology by arguing that learning is not the change in behavior as such but is instead the acquisition of new knowledge or cognitions.	**Learning by Synaptic Alteration** The Canadian psychologist Donald Hebb proposes that learning results from alterations in synaptic connections. Psychological science has since shown the basic tenets of this proposal to be accurate.	**Social Learning Theory** Concerned that behaviorism is ignoring the social context of learning, Albert Bandura shows that people learn behaviors by observing whether others are rewarded or punished for performing those behaviors.	**Learning as an Evolved Mechanism** John Garcia argues that certain types of learning involve special mechanisms that have evolved through natural selection.

learning An enduring change in behavior that results from experience.

6.1 John B. Watson Watson was the founder of behaviorism and one of its most ardent supporters.

Learning is a relatively enduring change in behavior that results from experience. It occurs when organisms benefit from experience so that their future behavior is better adapted to the environment. The ability to learn is crucial for all animals. To survive, animals need to learn such things as which types of foods are dangerous, when it is safe to sleep, and which sounds indicate potential dangers. Learning is central to almost all aspects of human existence, from learning such basic abilities as walking and speaking, to even more complex abilities, such as flying airplanes, performing surgery, or maintaining intimate relationships. Learning also shapes many aspects of daily life, from clothing and musical tastes, to cultural rules for how close we stand to each other, to our values about the environment.

The focus in this chapter is on how learning occurs. The essence of learning is in understanding how events are related, such as how you associate going to the dentist with being in pain or how you associate working with getting paid. These associations develop through a process known as *conditioning,* in which environmental stimuli and some sort of behavioral response become connected. We will see that psychologists have tended to focus on two types of conditioning. The first, known as *classical conditioning,* occurs when we learn that two types of events go together, such as walking in the rain and getting wet. The second, known as *operant conditioning,* occurs when we learn that a behavior leads to a particular outcome, such as that studying leads to better grades. This is the type of learning that was of greatest interest to B. F. Skinner. We will also consider other types of learning, such as by observing others—for example, learning about new fashions by paying attention to what movie actors and rock stars wear.

The study of learning has been central to psychological science since the early nineteenth century and is an excellent example of how the principles of psychological science are cumulative. As we read about the major learning theories, we'll see how great theorists such as Thorndike, Watson, Skinner, Hebb, Bandura, and Kandel were responding to and expanding on the ideas of their predecessors in an effort to understand the complexities of how people and animals learn. Let's now look at the different ways that we learn and the most recent efforts to understand the biological underpinnings of learning.

How Did the Behavioral Study of Learning Develop?

The rise of learning theory in the early twentieth century was due in part to the dissatisfaction among some psychologists with the widespread use of verbal reports to assess mental states. At the time, Freudian ideas were at the heart of psychological theorizing. To assess the unconscious mental processes that they believed were the

1972	1973	1980s	1990s	2000s
Expectancies and Learning Robert Rescorla and Allan Wagner propose that learning occurs when organisms develop expectancies that allow them to predict future events.	**Long-Term Potentiation** Working in Norway, Terje Lømo and Tom Bliss find that rapid stimulation of a synapse strengthens the synaptic connection. This potentiation is now known to be an important cellular process underlying learning.	**The Neural Basis of Learning** Eric Kandel studies the cellular and molecular mechanisms of learning in a type of invertebrate creature. This work earns him a Nobel Prize in 2000.	**Computer Models of Neural Networks** Superfast modern computers allow psychological scientists to develop neural-network models of learning.	**Mirror Neurons** Giacomo Rizzolatti and colleagues discover that neurons involved in performing an action become activated when monkeys simply observe others performing that action. These mirror neurons might support observational learning.

primary determinants of behavior, Freud and his followers used verbal report techniques such as dream analysis and free association. The American psychologist John B. Watson (Figure 6.1) scorned any form of psychological enterprise that focused on things that could not be observed directly, such as people's mental events. He argued that Freudian theory was unscientific and ultimately meaningless. According to Watson, overt behavior was the only valid indicator of psychological activity. Although he acknowledged that thoughts and beliefs existed, he denied that they could be studied using scientific methods.

Watson founded the school of behaviorism, which was based on the belief that animals and humans are born with the potential to learn anything. Based on philosopher John Locke's idea of *tabula rasa* (Latin, "blank slate"), which states that infants are born knowing nothing and that all knowledge is acquired through sensory experiences, behaviorism stated that the environment and its associated effects on organisms were the sole determinants of learning. Watson felt so strongly about the preeminence of the environment that he issued the following bold challenge: "Give me a dozen healthy infants, well formed, and my own specified world to bring them up in and I'll guarantee to take any one at random and train him to become any type of specialist I might select—doctor, lawyer, artist, merchant-chief, and yes, even beggar-man and thief, regardless of his talents, penchants, tendencies, abilities, vocations and race of his ancestors" (Watson, 1924, p. 82).

Behavioral Responses Are Conditioned

Watson had an incredible influence on the study of psychology in America. Behaviorism was the dominant psychological paradigm well into the 1960s, and it influenced the methods and theories of every area within psychology. Watson developed his ideas about behaviorism after he read the work of the Russian physiologist Ivan Pavlov (Figure 6.2), a distinguished scientist who had won a Nobel Prize for his work on the digestive system. Pavlov was interested in the *salivary reflex,* the automatic and unlearned response that occurs when the stimulus of food is presented to hungry animals, including humans. For his work on the digestive system, Pavlov had created an apparatus that collected saliva from dogs (Figure 6.3). He placed various types of food into a dog's mouth and measured differences in salivary output. Like so many major scientific advances, Pavlov's contribution to psychology started with a simple observation. One day he realized that the dogs were salivating well before they tasted the food. Indeed, the dogs started salivating the moment that a lab technician walked into the room, or whenever they saw the bowls that usually contained food. The genius of Pavlov was in recognizing that this behavioral response was a window to the working mind. Unlike inborn reflexes, salivation at the sight of a bowl is not automatic and therefore must have been acquired through experience. The insight that dogs could associate bowls and lab technicians with food led Pavlov to devote the rest of his life to studying the basic principles of learning.

6.2 Ivan Pavlov Pavlov conducted groundbreaking work on classical conditioning.

6.3 Pavlov's Apparatus for Collecting Saliva The dog was presented with a bowl containing meat. A tube from the salivary glands carried the saliva to a container that measured the amount of salivation.

PAVLOV'S EXPERIMENTS In a typical Pavlovian experiment, a *neutral stimulus* unrelated to the salivary reflex, such as a ringing bell, is presented together with a stimulus that reliably produces the reflex, such as food. This pairing, known as a *conditioning trial,* is repeated a number of times; then, on *critical trials,* the bell sound is presented alone and the salivary reflex is measured. Pavlov found that under these conditions, the sound of the bell on its own produced salivation. This type of learning is now referred to as *classical conditioning* or *Pavlovian conditioning.* **Classical conditioning** occurs when a neutral object comes to elicit a reflexive response when it is associated with a stimulus that already produces that response.

Pavlov called the salivation elicited by food the **unconditioned response** (**UR**), because it occurred without any prior training. Unconditioned responses are unlearned, automatic behaviors, such as any simple reflex. Similarly, the food is referred to as the **unconditioned stimulus** (**US**). In the normal reflex response, the food (US) leads to salivation (UR). Because the ringing bell produces salivation only after training, it is called the **conditioned stimulus** (**CS**); it stimulates salivation only after learning takes place. The salivary reflex that occurs when only the conditioned stimulus is presented is known as the **conditioned response** (**CR**); it is an acquired response that is learned. Note that both the unconditioned and the conditioned responses are salivation, but they are not identical: The bell produces less saliva than does the food. The conditioned response usually is less strong than the unconditioned response. The process of conditioning is outlined in Figure 6.4.

Consider this common reaction. Watching a frightening scene in a movie, such as someone being attacked, makes you feel tense, anxious, and perhaps even disgusted. In this scenario, the frightening scene, the stimulus, and your reaction, the response, are unconditioned—they occur naturally. Now imagine a piece of music that doesn't initially have much effect on you but that you hear in the movie just before each frightening scene. (Think of *Jaws*!) Eventually you will begin to feel tense and anxious as soon as you hear the music. You have learned that the music, the conditioned stimulus, predicts scary scenes, and therefore you feel anxious, which is the conditioned response. As in the Pavlov studies, the CS (music) produces a somewhat different emotional response than the US (the scary scene), perhaps less intense and more a feeling of apprehension than of being

How do events become associated?

6.4 Before and After Conditioning Initially, the US elicits UR. During acquisition, the formerly neutral CS is paired with the US. Eventually the CS elicits CR. Note that the UR is typically stronger than the CR.

US

UR

Conditioning

+

Neutral stimulus

US

After conditioning

CS

CR

afraid or disgusted. If you later hear this music in a different context, for example, on the radio, you will again feel tense and anxious even though you are not watching a movie. You have been classically conditioned to be anxious when you hear the music.

ACQUISITION, EXTINCTION, AND SPONTANEOUS RECOVERY Like many other scientists at the time, Pavlov was greatly influenced by Darwin's *On the Origin of Species*. Pavlov believed that conditioning was the basis for how animals learn to adapt to their environments. By learning to predict what objects bring pleasure or pain, animals acquire new behaviors that are adaptive to the environment. For instance, let's suppose that each time it rains, a delicious and nutritious plant blooms. An animal that learns this association will seek out this plant each time it rains. **Acquisition**, the initial learning of a behavior, is the gradual formation of an association between the conditioned and unconditioned stimuli. From his research, Pavlov concluded that the critical element in the acquisition of a learned association is that the stimuli occur together in time, which is referred to as *contiguity*. Subsequent research has shown that the strongest conditioning actually occurs when there is a very brief delay between the CS and the US. Thus, you will develop a stronger conditioned response to a piece of music if it comes just before a scary scene than if it occurs during the scary scene. As you will see later, the role of the music in predicting the frightening scene is an important part of classical conditioning.

Once a behavior is acquired, how long does it persist? For instance, what if the animal sought out the tasty blooms following rain, but they stopped appearing? Animals sometimes have to *unlearn* previous associations when they are no longer adaptive. Let's look at how this happens. After conditioning, the bell (CS) leads to salivation (CR) because the animal learns to associate the bell with the food (US). If the bell is presented many times and food does not arrive, the animal learns that the bell is not a good predictor of food, and therefore the salivary response gradually disappears. This process is known as **extinction**. The conditioned response is *extinguished* when the conditioned stimulus no longer predicts the unconditioned stimulus (Figure 6.5).

But suppose the delicious plant blooms only during a certain time of the year. The adaptive response is to check back once in a while to see if the plant blooms following rain. In the lab, an analogous situation occurs when the conditioned stimulus is presented a long time after extinction. Sounding the bell will once again produce the conditioned response of salivation (see Figure 6.5). This **spontaneous recovery**, in which the extinguished CS again produces a CR, is temporary and will quickly fade unless the CS is again paired with the US. Even a single pairing of the CS with the US will reestablish the CR, which will then again diminish if CS-US pairings do not continue. Thus, extinction inhibits but does not break the associative bond. It is a new form of learning that overwrites the previous association; what is learned is that the original association no longer holds true (Bouton, 1994; Bouton, Nelson, & Rosas, 1999).

GENERALIZATION, DISCRIMINATION, AND SECOND-ORDER CONDITIONING
In any learning situation, hundreds of possible stimuli can be associated with the unconditioned stimulus to produce the conditioned response. How does the brain determine which of these stimuli is relevant? For instance, suppose we classically condition a dog so that it salivates (CR) when it hears a 1,000 Hz (hertz) tone. After the CR is established, tones that are similar to 1,000 Hz will also produce it, but the farther the tones are from 1,000 Hz, the less the dog will salivate (Figure 6.6). **Stimulus generalization** occurs when stimuli that are similar but not identical to the CS

Why might a delay strengthen conditioning?

classical conditioning A type of learned response that occurs when a neutral object comes to elicit a reflexive response when it is associated with a stimulus that already produces that response.

unconditioned response (UR) A response that does not have to be learned, such as a reflex.

unconditioned stimulus (US) A stimulus that elicits a response, such as a reflex, without any prior learning.

conditioned stimulus (CS) A stimulus that elicits a response only after learning has taken place.

conditioned response (CR) A response that has been learned.

acquisition The gradual formation of an association between the conditioned and unconditioned stimuli.

extinction A process in which the conditioned response is weakened when the conditioned stimulus is repeated without the unconditioned stimulus.

spontaneous recovery A process in which a previously extinguished response reemerges following presentation of the conditioned stimulus.

stimulus generalization Occurs when stimuli that are similar but not identical to the conditioned stimulus produce the conditioned response.

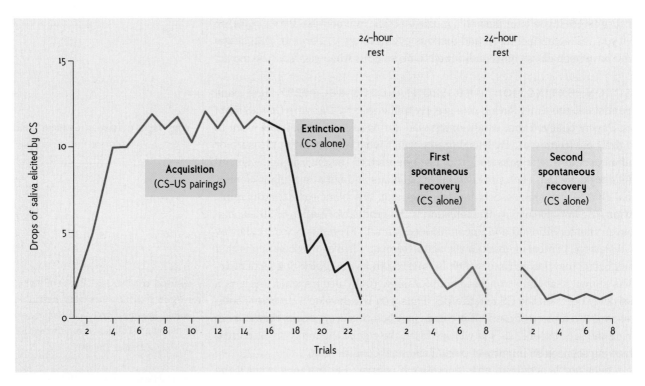

6.5 Extinction During acquisition, the CS-US pairings lead to increased learning such that the CS can produce the CR. However, if the CS is presented without the US, eventually the CR extinguishes. Later, if the CS is presented alone it will produce a weak CR, known as spontaneous recovery. This CR will quickly extinguish if the US does not appear.

produce the CR. Generalization is adaptive because in nature the CS is seldom experienced repeatedly in an identical fashion. Slight differences in variables such as background noise, temperature, and lighting lead to slightly different perceptions of the CS, so animals learn to respond to variations in the CS.

Of course, there are limits to generalization. Sometimes it is important for animals to distinguish among similar stimuli. For instance, two species of plants may look similar, but one might be poisonous. **Stimulus discrimination** means that animals learn to differentiate between two similar stimuli if one is consistently associated with the unconditioned stimulus and the other is not. In various studies, Pavlov and his students demonstrated that dogs could learn to make very fine distinctions between similar stimuli, such as subtle differences in shades of gray.

Sometimes a conditioned stimulus does not become directly associated with an unconditioned stimulus, but rather with other stimuli that themselves are associated with the US, a phenomenon known as *second-order conditioning*. In one of Pavlov's early studies, a CS-US bond was formed between a tone and food so that the tone (CS) led to salivation (CR). Following this conditioning, a second training session was conducted in which a black square was repeatedly presented at the same time as the tone. There was no US during this phase of the study. Following many trials, the black square was presented alone and it also produced salivation. Second-order conditioning helps to account for the complexity of learned associations, especially among

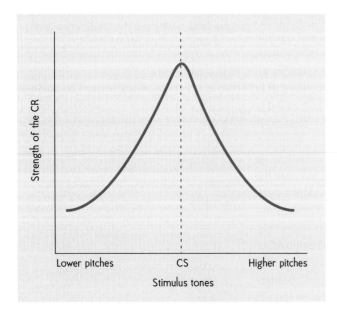

6.6 Generalization and Discrimination Maximal salivation occurs at the CS of 1,000 Hz, but stimuli that are similar to the CS also produce the CR. The strength of the CR diminishes as the tone diverges from 1,000 Hz.

people. For instance, money is usually just paper or cheap metal, but it means something entirely different to people. It is the association between paper and what it buys that makes us want to have it. As we will see later, second-order conditioning is why money is rewarding for those who receive it. Similarly, when we see our favorite actor drinking a particular brand of soda we develop more positive attitudes about that soda, which is why advertisers often seek out celebrities to endorse products. Even though it has a powerful influence over many of our beliefs and attitudes, most second-order conditioning occurs implicitly, without our awareness or intention.

Phobias and Addictions Have Learned Components

Classical conditioning helps explain a number of behavioral phenomena, including phobias and addictions.

PHOBIAS AND THEIR TREATMENT **Phobia** is an acquired fear that is out of proportion to the real threat, as you will learn more about in Chapter 13. Common phobias include fear of heights, dogs, insects, snakes, and the dark. According to classical-conditioning theory, phobias develop through the generalization of a fear experience, as when a person who is stung by a wasp develops a fear of all flying insects.

Animals can be classically conditioned to fear neutral objects, a process known as *fear conditioning.* For example, if an animal is repeatedly presented with a flash of light followed by a moderately painful electric shock, it will soon display physiological and behavioral responses indicating fear, such as change in heart rate, whenever it sees a flash of light. As you will read later in this chapter, psychological scientists now know a great deal about the biological basis of fear conditioning. Over the last decade, researchers have made enormous progress in understanding how the brain learns to fear an object or a situation, how these learned fears can help the animal learn to avoid danger, and how the experience of fear can strengthen learning for important events. The most important brain structure for fear conditioning is the amygdala. Without an amygdala, there is no fear conditioning.

Techniques from classical conditioning have been valuable for developing behavioral therapies to treat phobias. For instance, exposing people to small doses of the feared stimulus while having them engage in a pleasurable task, called *counterconditioning,* can help people overcome their fears. Joseph Wolpe, a behavioral therapist, developed a formal treatment based on counterconditioning known as *systematic desensitization* (Wolpe, 1997). Patients are taught how to relax their muscles, and when they are able to do so, they are asked to imagine the feared object or situation while continuing to use the relaxation exercises. Eventually the person is exposed to the feared stimulus while relaxing. The general idea is that the CS→CR$_1$ (fear) connection can be broken by developing a new CS→CR$_2$ (relaxation) connection. The behavioral treatment of phobias has proven to be very effective.

DRUG ADDICTION Classical conditioning also plays an important role in drug addiction. Conditioned drug effects are common. For example, the smell of coffee can become a conditioned stimulus, leading coffee drinkers to feel activated and aroused. Likewise, because the needle becomes a CS, heroin addicts will sometimes inject themselves with water, when heroin is not available, to reduce their cravings. These learned associations demonstrate the power of conditioning and the potential for problems. When former heroin addicts are exposed to environmental cues associated with their drug use, they often experience cravings and physiological sensations similar to those they experienced during *withdrawal,* the unpleasant state of

stimulus discrimination A learned tendency to differentiate between two similar stimuli if one is consistently associated with the unconditioned stimulus and the other is not.

phobia An acquired fear that is out of proportion to the real threat of an object or a situation.

6.7 PET Scans Showing Activation of Abstinent Limbic System Structures Cocaine addicts were shown videos of nature scenes or cocaine cues. Areas with greatest activation are shown in red.

tension and anxiety that occurs when addicts stop using drugs. Thus, addicts who quit using drugs in treatment centers often relapse when they return to their old environments. They experience conditioned withdrawal effects.

In the laboratory, presenting heroin or cocaine addicts with cues associated with drug ingestion leads to cravings and a variety of physiological responses associated with withdrawal, such as changes in heart rate and blood pressure. Brain-imaging studies have found that such cues lead to activation of the prefrontal cortex and various regions of the limbic system (Figure 6.7; Childress et al., 1999; see also Maas et al., 1998). Recall from Chapter 4 that the limbic system is involved in emotion and motivation. The role of the limbic system in addiction will be discussed in greater detail in Chapter 9.

The learning theorist Shepard Siegel has conducted fascinating research showing that drug-tolerance effects are specific to certain situations. *Tolerance* is a process by which addicts need more and more of a drug to experience the same effects. According to research by Siegel, tolerance effects are greatest when the drug is taken in the same location as previous drug use. Tolerance can be so great that addicts regularly use drug doses that would be fatal for the inexperienced user. Conversely, Siegel's findings imply that if addicts take their usual large doses in a novel setting they are more likely to overdose (Siegel, 1984; Siegel, Hinson, Krank, & McCully, 1982).

Profiles in Psychological Science

Albert B.

An early case study demonstrating the role of classical conditioning in the development of phobias was John B. Watson's teaching of an infant named Albert B. to fear neutral objects. It is important to note Watson's motives for conditioning Albert. At the time, 1919, the prominent theory of phobia was based on Freudian ideas about unconscious repressed sexual desires. Watson thought that Freudian ideas were unscientific and unnecessarily complex. He proposed that phobias could be explained by simple learning principles, such as classical conditioning. To prove his point, Watson talked a woman he knew into having her son take part in a learning study. The child was chosen because he was emotionally stable and Watson believed the experiment would cause him little harm. When Albert was nine months of age, Watson and his lab assistant, Rosalie Rayner, presented him with a variety of neutral objects, including a white rat, a rabbit, a dog, a monkey, costume masks, and a ball of white wool. Albert showed a natural curiosity regarding these items, but displayed no overt emotional response.

6.8 Albert B. John B. Watson and Rosalie Rayner conducted a conditioning experiment on their infant subject, Albert B., in which they taught him to fear neutral objects.

When Albert was eleven months old, Watson and Rayner began the conditioning trials. This time, as they presented the white rat and Albert reached for it, Watson smashed a hammer into an iron bar, producing a loud clanging sound (Figure 6.8). The sound scared the child, who immediately withdrew and hid his face. Watson did this a few more times at intervals of five days until Albert would whimper and cringe when the rat was presented alone. Thus, the US (smashing sound) led to a UR (fear), and eventually the pairing of the CS (rat) and US (smashing sound) led to the rat producing fear (CR) on its own. The fear response generalized to other stimuli that Watson had presented along with the rat at the initial meeting, including the rabbit and the ball of wool, and Albert eventually became frightened of them all. Even a Santa Claus with a white beard produced a fear response. Thus, classical conditioning was shown to be an effective method of inducing phobia.

Although Watson had planned to conduct extinction trials to remove the learned phobias, Albert's mother removed him from the study before Watson could conduct those trials. Whatever became of Albert? No one knows. Watson's conditioning of Albert has long been criticized as unethical, and nowadays it is unlikely that an ethics committee would approve such a study. It is only fair to note that Watson had developed detailed plans to change the conditioning so that Albert no longer feared the items used in the study. For instance, he described a method of continually presenting the objects until the response habituated, while at the same time "reconditioning" the feared objects with more pleasant things, such as candy. Behavioral methods such as these have since been found to be effective for treating phobias. ■

Classical Conditioning Involves More Than Contiguity

Pavlov's original explanation for classical conditioning was that any two events presented at the same time, in contiguity, would produce a learned association. Pavlov and his followers believed that the strength of the association was determined by factors such as the intensity of the conditioned and unconditioned stimuli, with greater intensity associated with increased learning. In the mid-1960s a number of challenges suggested that some conditioned stimuli were more likely to produce learning than others, and that contiguity was not sufficient to create CS-US associations.

EVOLUTIONARY SIGNIFICANCE According to Pavlov, any object or phenomenon could be converted into a conditioned stimulus during conditioning trials. Thus, a light, tone, color, or odor could be associated with the unconditioned stimulus. The idea that all stimuli are equally capable of producing conditioning is known as *equipotentiality*. However, it appears that not all stimuli are equally potent. Research conducted by the psychologist John Garcia and his colleagues showed that certain pairings of stimuli are more likely to become associated than others. For instance, animals that are given poison in their food quickly learn to avoid the tastes or smells associated with the food (Garcia & Koelling, 1966). In these cases, just a few trials are enough to produce a long-lasting avoidance of the food item that was poisoned. These conditioned food aversions are easy to produce with taste or smell, but very difficult to produce with light or sound. This makes sense, since taste and smell are the main cues that guide eating behavior in animals. From an evolutionary viewpoint, animals that quickly associate a certain flavor with illness, and therefore avoid that flavor, are more likely to survive and pass along their genes.

Other research has shown that it is easier to condition monkeys to fear snakes than to fear objects such as flowers or rabbits (Cook & Mineka, 1989). Psychologist Martin Seligman (1970) argued that animals are genetically programmed to fear specific objects, which he refers to as **biological preparedness**. Preparedness helps to explain why animals tend to have phobias of things that have potential danger (e.g., snakes, fire, heights) rather than objects that pose little threat (e.g., flowers, shoes, babies).

At the most general level, contemporary researchers are interested in how classical conditioning helps animals learn adaptive responses (Hollis, 1997; Shettleworth, 2001). The adaptive value of a particular response varies according to the animal's evolutionary history. For example, taste aversions are easy to condition in rats, but difficult to condition in birds because they rely more on vision than taste to select food. However, birds quickly learn to avoid a visual cue that has been associated with illness. Rats freeze and startle if the CS is auditory, but rise on their hind legs when the CS is a visual cue (Holland, 1977). These differences in learned adaptive responses may reflect the meaning of, and potential danger associated with, auditory and visual stimuli in the environment.

THE COGNITIVE PERSPECTIVE Prior to the 1970s, most animal learning theorists were concerned only with observable stimuli and responses. In the past three decades, learning theorists have placed a greater emphasis on trying to understand the mental processes that underlie conditioning. An important principle that has emerged is that classical conditioning is a means by which animals come to *predict* the occurrence of events. This rise in consideration of mental processes, such as prediction and expectancy, is referred to as the cognitive perspective on learning (Hollis, 1997).

Robert Rescorla (1966) conducted one of the first studies highlighting the role of cognition in learning. He argued that for learning to take place, the conditioned stimulus needs to be an accurate predictor of the unconditioned stimulus. For instance, a stimulus that occurs *before* the US is more easily conditioned than one that comes *after* it. Even though the two are both contiguous presentations with the US, the first stimulus is more easily learned because it predicts rather than comes after the US. Indeed, as mentioned earlier, across all conditioning situations, some delay between the CS and the US is optimal for learning. The length of delay varies depending on the nature of the conditioned and unconditioned stimuli. For instance, eyeblink conditioning occurs when a sound

Why are some associations easier to learn than others?

biological preparedness The idea that animals are biologically programmed to learn to fear specific objects.

"Oh, not bad. The light comes on, I press the bar, they write me a check. How about you?"

(CS) is associated with a puff of air blown into the eye (US), which leads to a blink. Optimal learning for eyeblink conditioning is measured in milliseconds. By contrast, conditioned taste aversions often take many hours, since the ill effects of consuming poisons often take time to occur.

In 1972, Robert Rescorla and his colleague Allan Wagner published a cognitive model of classical conditioning that profoundly changed our understanding of learning (Rescorla & Wagner, 1972). The **Rescorla-Wagner model** states that the strength of the CS-US association is determined by the extent to which the US is unexpected or surprising. The greater the surprise of the US, the more effort an organism puts into trying to understand its occurrence so that it can predict it more accurately in the future. The end result is greater classical conditioning of the surprising event (CS) that predicted the US. According to the model, conditioning is a process by which organisms learn to expect the unconditioned stimulus based on the conditioned stimulus. Your pet wags its tail and runs around in circles when you start to open a can of food because it expects that it will soon be fed. According to Rescorla and Wagner, your pet has developed a mental representation in which the sound of the can opener (CS) predicts the appearance of food (US). When the US occurs unexpectedly, the animal attends to events in the environment that might have produced it. For example, say you use a manual can opener because the electric one is broken. Your pet finds itself presented with the food even though it did not hear the can being opened. Your pet soon will learn to anticipate being fed by the wrist movements you make with the new opener.

Consistent with the Rescorla-Wagner model, novel stimuli are more easily associated with the unconditioned stimulus than are familiar stimuli. For example, dogs can be conditioned more easily with the novel smell of almonds than with smells more familiar to their environments, like dog biscuits. Once learned, a conditioned stimulus can prevent the acquisition of a new conditioned stimulus, a phenomenon known as the *blocking effect*. For example, a dog that has acquired the smell of almonds (CS) as a good predictor of food (US) does not need to look for other predictors. Furthermore, a stimulus that is associated with a CS can act as an *occasion setter* or trigger for the CS (Schmajuk, Lamoureaux, & Holland, 1998). For example, a dog can learn that the smell of almonds predicts food only when the smell is preceded by a sound or a flash of light and not at other times. The smell or light indicates whether or not the association between the smell of almonds and food is active.

Rescorla-Wagner model A cognitive model of classical conditioning that states that the strength of the CS-US association is determined by the extent to which the unconditioned stimulus is unexpected.

Why does learning occur more readily for novel events?

REVIEWING the Principles | How Did the Behavioral Study of Learning Develop?

Behaviorism, founded by John B. Watson, focused on observable aspects of learning. Pavlov developed the classical-conditioning theory to account for the learned association between neutral stimuli and reflexive behaviors. Conditioning occurs when the conditioned stimulus becomes associated with the unconditioned stimulus. For learning to occur, the conditioned stimulus needs to be a reliable predictor of the unconditioned stimulus, not simply contiguous. A cognitive model that accounts for most conditioning phenomena is the Rescorla-Wagner model, which states that the amount of conditioning is determined by the extent to which the unconditioned stimulus is unexpected or surprising.

How Is Operant Conditioning Different from Classical Conditioning?

Classical conditioning is a relatively passive process in which subjects associate events that happen around them. This form of conditioning does not account for the many times that one of the events occurs because of some action on the part of the subject. We don't sit idly waiting for food to be presented to us; we go out and purchase it. Our behaviors often represent a means to an end. We buy food to eat it, we study to get good grades, and we work to receive money. Thus, many of our actions are *instrumental*; they are done for a purpose. We learn to behave in certain ways in order to be rewarded, and we avoid behaving in certain ways in order not to be punished; this is called *instrumental conditioning* or *operant conditioning*. B. F. Skinner, the psychologist most closely associated with this type of learning, selected the term *operant* to express the idea that animals operate on the environment to produce an effect. **Operant conditioning** is the learning process in which the consequences of an action determine the likelihood that it will be performed in the future.

The study of operant conditioning began in the basement of the psychologist William James's house in Cambridge, Massachusetts. A young graduate student working with James, Edward Thorndike, had been influenced by Darwin and was studying whether nonhuman animals showed signs of intelligence. As part of his research, Thorndike built an apparatus called a puzzle box, a small cage with a trapdoor (Figure 6.9). The trapdoor would open if the animal performed a specific action, such as pulling a string. Thorndike placed food-deprived animals, usually cats, inside the puzzle box to see if they could figure out how to escape. To motivate the cats, he would place food just outside the box. When a cat was first placed in the box, it usually engaged in a number of nonproductive behaviors in an attempt to escape. After 5 to 10 minutes of struggling, the cat would *accidentally* pull the string and the door would open. Thorndike would then return the cat to the box and repeat the trial. Thorndike found that the cats would pull the string more quickly on each trial, until they soon learned to escape from the puzzle box within seconds. From this line of research Thorndike developed a general theory of learning, known as the **law of effect**, which states that any behavior that leads to a "satisfying state of affairs" is more likely to occur again, and that those that lead to an "annoying state of affairs" are less likely to occur again.

6.9 The Puzzle Box Thorndike used a primitive puzzle box, such as the one depicted here, to assess learning in cats.

Reinforcement Increases Behavior

Thirty years after Thorndike, another Harvard graduate student in psychology, B. F. Skinner (Figure 6.10), developed a more formal learning theory based on the law of effect. As you read in the beginning of this chapter, Skinner had been greatly influenced by John B. Watson and shared his philosophy of behaviorism. He therefore objected to the subjective aspects of Thorndike's law of effect: states of "satisfaction" are not observable empirically. Skinner coined the term *reinforcer* to describe events that produced a learned response. A **reinforcer** is a stimulus that occurs following a response that increases the likelihood that the response will be repeated. Skinner believed that behavior, from studying to eating to driving on the proper side of the road, occurs because it has been reinforced.

THE SKINNER BOX Skinner developed a simple device for assessing operant conditioning called the *Skinner box,* a small chamber or cage in which a lever (or response

---

How is behavior shaped by rewards and punishments?

operant conditioning A learning process in which the consequences of an action determine the likelihood that it will be performed in the future.

law of effect Thorndike's general theory of learning, which states that any behavior that leads to a "satisfying state of affairs" is more likely to occur again, and that those that lead to an "annoying state of affairs" are less likely to recur.

reinforcer A stimulus following a response that increases the likelihood that the response will be repeated.

key) is connected to a food or water supply. An animal, usually a rat or a pigeon, is placed in the box; when it presses the lever, food or water becomes available. Skinner's earlier research used mazes in which a rat had to take a specific turn to get access to the reinforcer. After the rat completed the trial, Skinner had to get the rat and return it to the beginning. He developed the Skinner box, or *operant chamber,* as he called it, basically because he got tired of constantly fetching the rats. With the Skinner box, the rats could be exposed to repeated conditioning trials without the experimenter having to do anything but observe. Skinner later built mechanical recording devices that allowed trials to be conducted without the experimenter even being present.

SHAPING With little to do in a Skinner box, the animal typically presses the lever sooner rather than later. One of the major problems encountered with operant conditioning outside the Skinner box is that you need to wait until the animal emits an appropriate response before you can provide the reinforcer. Let's say you are trying to teach your dog to roll over. Rather than waiting for your dog to spontaneously perform this action, you can use an operant conditioning technique to teach your dog to do so. The process, called **shaping**, involves reinforcing behaviors that are increasingly similar to the desired behavior. You initially reward your dog for any behavior that even slightly resembles rolling over, such as lying down. Once this behavior is established you become more selective in which behaviors you reinforce. Reinforcing *successive approximations* will eventually produce the desired behavior, as your dog learns to discriminate which behavior is being reinforced (Figure 6.11). Shaping is a powerful procedure that can condition animals to perform amazing feats, such as pigeons playing table tennis, dogs playing the piano, and pigs doing housework such as picking up clothes and vacuuming. Shaping has also been used to teach mentally ill people appropriate social skills, autistic children language, and mentally retarded individuals basic skills such as dressing themselves. More generally, parents and educators often use subtle forms of shaping to encourage appropriate behavior in children, such as praising children for their initial—often illegible—attempts at handwriting.

REINFORCERS CAN BE CONDITIONED The most obvious reinforcers are those that are necessary for survival, such as food or water. Those that satisfy biological needs are referred to as **primary reinforcers**. From an evolutionary standpoint, the learning value of primary reinforcers makes a great deal of sense, since organisms that repeatedly perform behaviors reinforced by food and water are more likely to survive and pass along their genes. But many apparent reinforcers do not directly satisfy basic biological needs. For instance, as we noted already, money is only pieces of metal or paper, but many people work hard to receive it. Likewise, a compliment, a hug from a friend, or an "A" on a paper can be reinforcing. Events or objects that serve as reinforcers but that do not satisfy biological needs are referred to as **secondary reinforcers**. As mentioned earlier in this chapter, secondary reinforcers are established through classical conditioning. We learn to associate a neutral stimulus, such as paper money (CS), with, for example, food (US). Of course, money also takes on other meanings, such as power and security, but the essential point is that a neutral object becomes meaningful through its association with unconditioned stimuli.

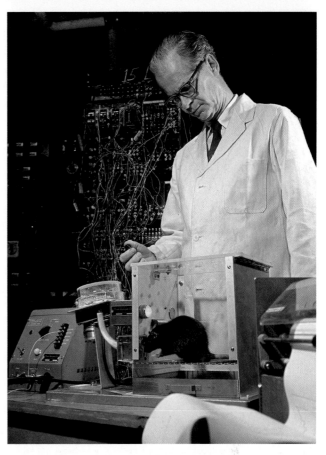

6.10 B. F. Skinner Skinner (seen here demonstrating the Skinner box) was one of the most influential psychologists of all time.

shaping A process of operant conditioning that involves reinforcing behaviors that are increasingly similar to the desired behavior.

primary reinforcers Reinforcers that are innately reinforcing, such as those that satisfy biological needs.

secondary reinforcers Events or objects that become reinforcers through their repeated pairings with primary reinforcers.

6.11 Shaping The process of shaping can be used to train extraordinary behaviors. Here, a trained dog water skis for a boat show.

REINFORCER POTENCY Some reinforcers are more powerful than others. An integrative theory of reinforcement was proposed by the psychologist David Premack, who theorized that the value of a specific reinforcer could be determined by the amount of time an organism engages in that behavior when free to choose anything. For instance, you could observe that most children choose to spend more time eating ice cream than spinach, indicating that ice cream is more reinforcing. One great advantage of Premack's theory is that it can account for individual differences in values. Undoubtedly some people prefer spinach to ice cream; therefore, spinach serves as a more potent reinforcer for them.

A logical extension of Premack's theory is that a more valued activity can be used to reinforce the performance of a less valued activity, which is referred to as the *Premack principle*. Parents use the Premack principle all the time: "Eat your spinach and then you'll get dessert"; "Finish your homework and then you can go out."

Both Reinforcement and Punishment Can Be Positive or Negative

Reinforcement and punishment have opposite effects on behavior. Whereas reinforcement increases behavior, punishment decreases behavior. Formally, **punishment** is the process by which the consequences of an action reduce the likelihood that the action will be repeated. For example, giving a rat an electric shock for pressing a lever will decrease the number of times that it presses the lever. Both reinforcement and punishment can be positive or negative.

POSITIVE AND NEGATIVE REINFORCEMENT **Positive reinforcement** increases the probability of a behavior's being repeated by administration of a pleasurable stimulus. Positive reinforcement often is referred to as *reward*. Behaviors that are rewarded increase in frequency, such as working hard because of praise or money. In contrast, **negative reinforcement** increases behavior through the *removal* of an aversive stimulus. For instance, a rat is negatively reinforced when required to press a lever to turn off an electric shock. Note how negative reinforcement is different from punishment, in which the rat receives a shock for pressing the lever. Negative reinforcement is not punishment. Reinforcement—positive or negative—*increases* whereas punishment *decreases* the likelihood of a behavior. Negative reinforcement is quite common in everyday life. You close the door to your room to shut out noise. You change the channel to avoid watching an awful program. In each case, you are trying to escape or avoid an unwanted stimulus, which is the negative reinforcer.

How does negative reinforcement differ from positive punishment?

POSITIVE AND NEGATIVE PUNISHMENT Punishment reduces behavior, but it can do so through positive or negative means. **Positive punishment** decreases the probability of a behavior's recurring by administration of an averse stimulus. A rat's getting a shock for pressing a lever is an example of positive punishment. **Negative punishment** decreases the probability of a behavior by removal of a pleasurable stimulus. Youths whose driving privileges are revoked for speeding are less likely to speed the next time they get behind the wheel. Although losing driving privileges is a form of negative punishment, getting a speeding ticket is a form of positive punishment. Figure 6.12 provides an overview of positive and negative reinforcement and punishment.

EFFECTIVENESS OF PARENTAL PUNISHMENT Parents who want their children to behave may use punishment as a means of discipline. But many contempo-

Response rate

		Increases	Decreases

Response causes stimulus to be

Presented
Positive reinforcement (lever press → food) | Positive punishment (lever press → shock)

Removed
Negative reinforcement (lever press → turns off shock) | Negative punishment (lever press → removes food)

6.12 An Overview of Negative and Positive Reinforcement and Punishment

rary psychologists believe that punishment is often applied ineffectively and that it may have unintended and unwanted consequences. Research has shown that for punishment to be effective, it must be reasonable, unpleasant, and applied immediately so that the relationship between the unwanted behavior and the punishment is clear (Goodall, 1984; O'Leary, 1995). Also, it must be applied only in direct response to unwanted behavior. But experience shows us that there is considerable potential for confusion here. Sometimes punishment is applied following a desired action, as when a student is punished after admitting to cheating on an exam. The student may then associate the punishment with being honest rather than with the original offense; the result may be that the student learns not to tell the truth. As Skinner once pointed out, one thing that people learn from punishment is how to avoid it; they learn not to get caught rather than how to behave appropriately.

Punishment can also be problematic because it can lead to negative emotions, such as fear or anxiety, which may become associated, through classical conditioning, with the person who administers the punishment. A child may learn to fear a parent or teacher rather than stop the undesired behavior, and this may damage the long-term relationship between adult and child (Gershoff, 2002). Another potential problem with punishment is that it often fails to offset the reinforcing aspects of the behavior. In real life, any behavior can be reinforced in multiple ways. For instance, thumb sucking may be reinforced because it makes a child feel good and provides relief from negative emotions and hunger. The threat of punishment may not be sufficient to offset the rewards of thumb sucking, though it may reinforce secrecy. For these and other reasons, most psychologists agree with Skinner's recommendation that reinforcement be used rather than punishment. A child who receives compliments for being a good student is likely to show better academic performance than one who is punished for doing poorly. After all, reinforcing a behavior tells the child what to do, whereas punishing a student for poor grades doesn't provide information about what the child should do to improve.

One form of punishment that most psychological scientists believe is especially ineffective is physical punishment, such as spanking. However, spanking is very common, with nearly three-quarters of American parents reporting spanking their children (Gallup, 1995), which indicates that many of them believe it is effective. As noted by Kazdin and Benjet (2003), beliefs about the appropriateness of spanking involve religious beliefs and cultural views, as well as legal issues. Many countries (e.g., Austria, Denmark, Israel, and Italy) have banned corporal punishment in homes or schools, and even the United Nations has passed resolutions discouraging it. Indeed, some researchers have provided evidence of numerous negative outcomes

punishment A stimulus following a response that decreases the likelihood that the response will be repeated.

positive reinforcement The increase in the probability of a behavior's being repeated following the administration of a pleasurable stimulus, referred to as a reward.

negative reinforcement The increase in the probability of a behavior's being repeated through the removal of an aversive stimulus.

positive punishment Punishment that occurs with administration of a stimulus that decreases the probability of a behavior's recurring.

negative punishment Punishment that occurs with removal of a stimulus that decreases the probability of a behavior's recurring.

associated with spanking, especially severe spanking. These include poor parent-child relations, weaker moral values, mental health problems, increased delinquency, and future child abuse. One concern is that the use of physical punishment teaches the child that violence is appropriate behavior for adults. (We consider imitation learning later in this chapter.) Although the extent to which mild forms of spanking cause problems is open to debate (Baumrind, Larzelere, & Cowan, 2002), the evidence does indicate that other forms of punishment are more effective for decreasing unwanted behaviors (Kazdin & Benjet, 2003). Time-outs, small fines, and grounding can effectively modify behavior. Yet many psychological scientists believe that any method of punishment is less effective than providing positive reinforcement for alternative behaviors. By rewarding the behaviors they wish to see, parents are able to increase those behaviors while building more positive bonds with their children.

Operant Conditioning Is Influenced by Schedules of Reinforcement

How often should a reinforcer be given? For fast learning, you might wish to reinforce the desired behavior each time it occurs, referred to as **continuous reinforcement**. In the real world, behavior is seldom reinforced continuously. Animals do not find food each time they look for it, and people do not receive praise each time they behave in an acceptable fashion. Most behavior is reinforced intermittently, which is referred to as **partial reinforcement**. The effect of partial reinforcement on conditioning depends on the reinforcement schedule.

RATIO AND INTERVAL SCHEDULES Partial reinforcement can be administered according to the number of behavioral responses or the passage of time. For instance, factory workers can be paid by the piece (behavioral response) or by the hour (passage of time). In a **ratio schedule**, reinforcement is based on the number of times the behavior occurs, such as reinforcing every third or tenth occurrence of the behavior. With **interval schedules**, reinforcement is based on a specific unit of time, such as once every minute or hour. In general, ratio reinforcement leads to greater responding than does interval reinforcement. Factory workers who are paid by the piece are usually more productive than those paid by the hour, especially if there are incentives for higher levels of productivity.

FIXED AND VARIABLE SCHEDULES Partial reinforcement also can be given on a *fixed* or *variable* schedule. In a **fixed schedule**, the reinforcer is consistently given following a specific number of occurrences or after a specific amount of time. Whether factory workers are paid by the piece or by the hour, they usually are paid according to a fixed rate, earning the same for each piece or for each hour. The rate of reinforcement is entirely predictable. In **variable schedules** of reinforcement, the reinforcer is applied at different rates or at different times. The responder does not know how many behaviors need to be performed or how much time needs to pass before reinforcement occurs. Variable reinforcement occurs when salespeople are paid only when a customer agrees to purchase a product.

The influence of reinforcement schedules on behavior can be observed in the study habits of students. Ideally, students will spread their studying out over the entire term, but the reality is that when exams are scheduled at fixed points, students tend to study a great deal just before the exam and not at all afterward. It is typical of *fixed-interval reinforcement* that the behavior is performed only when it is time for the reinforcer to be administered. When exams are on a *variable-interval schedule*—say,

Which reinforcement schedule would you use if you wanted a behavior to continue over time?

continuous reinforcement A type of learning in which the desired behavior is reinforced each time it occurs.

partial reinforcement A type of learning in which behavior is reinforced intermittently.

ratio schedule A schedule in which reinforcement is based on the number of times the behavior occurs.

interval schedule A schedule in which reinforcement is based on a specific unit of time.

fixed schedule A schedule in which reinforcement is consistently provided upon each occurrence.

variable schedule A schedule in which reinforcement is applied at different rates or at different times.

partial-reinforcement extinction effect The greater persistence of behavior under partial reinforcement than under continuous reinforcement.

with surprise quizzes—students tend to study more often and more consistently. The patterns of behavior typically observed under different schedules of reinforcement can be seen in Figure 6.13.

BEHAVIORAL PERSISTENCE The schedule of reinforcement also affects the persistence of behavior. Continuous reinforcement is highly effective for acquiring a behavior, but if the reinforcement is stopped, the behavior extinguishes quickly. For instance, typically when you put money in a vending machine it gives you a product. If it fails to do so, you will quickly stop giving it your money. In contrast, a slot machine pays out on a *variable-ratio schedule.* People continue to pour money into slot machines even if the machine rarely reinforces their behavior. The **partial-reinforcement extinction effect** describes the greater persistence of behavior under partial reinforcement, due to the difficulty of detecting a lack of reinforcement. During continuous reinforcement, it is easy to detect when reinforcement has ceased. But if the behavior is reinforced only some of the time, the subject needs to repeat the behavior comparatively more times to detect the absence of reinforcement. Thus, the less frequent the reinforcement during training, the greater the resistance to extinction. To condition a behavior that you wish to persist, reinforce it continuously during early acquisition and then slowly change to partial reinforcement. Parents naturally follow this strategy in teaching their children toilet training and other behaviors.

6.13 Learning Curves These curves show typical learning under different schedules of reinforcement. The steeper the line, the higher the response rate. The slash marks on the lines indicate when reinforcement is given. Note that ratio reinforcement leads to the highest rate of response.

Psychological Science *in Action*

Behavior Modification

Parents, teachers, and animal trainers widely use operant-conditioning strategies. *Behavioral modification* refers to using the techniques of operant conditioning to eliminate unwanted behaviors and replace them with desirable ones. The general rationale behind behavior modification is that most unwanted behaviors are learned and therefore can be unlearned. Through conditioning principles, people can be taught, for example, to be more productive at work, to save energy, and to drive more safely. These techniques can even be used to train children with profound learning disabilities to communicate and interact with their classmates. As we will see in Chapter 14, operant techniques are also effective for treating psychological conditions such as depression and anxiety disorders.

Because they are so successful, many businesses have embraced the use of behavior modification in the workplace. Consider the classic case of Emery Air Freight, a large company in the shipping industry. In the 1970s, Emery was losing a great deal of money because workers were not filling containers to capacity before shipping. Management instituted a program in which workers were monitored and rewarded for filling the containers completely. Within a matter of days the percentage of full containers more than doubled, saving the company millions of dollars. Other companies quickly took notice, and many developed programs—such as profit sharing, stock options, and bonuses—to reward productivity. These programs have to be used carefully, however, because if rewards are not given properly they can backfire, as happens when workers become overly competitive, when rewards undermine natural inclinations to work hard, or when rewards make people feel as if they are being bribed. Think about what you know regarding how schedules of reinforcement affect productivity. If a company used a reward program on a fixed schedule, it is likely that productivity would decline quickly when the rewards ceased. Thus, companies need to change rewards and offer them on a variable schedule to maintain productivity.

Another widespread behavior-modification method uses the principles of secondary reinforcement. Chimpanzees can be trained to perform tasks in order to receive tokens, which they can later trade for food. The tokens themselves thus reinforce behavior and the chimps work as hard to obtain the tokens as they do food. Using similar principles, many prisons, mental hospitals, and classrooms have established *token economies* in which people earn tokens for completing tasks and lose tokens for behaving badly. These tokens can be saved and later traded for objects or privileges. So, for instance, teachers can provide tokens to students for obeying class rules, turning in homework on time, and helping others. At some future point the tokens can be exchanged for rewards, such as extra recess time or fun activities. Token economies are often established in mental hospitals to encourage good grooming and appropriate social behavior and to discourage bizarre behaviors. The use of a token economy not only reinforces participants, but also gives them a sense of control over their environment.

You can use the principles of behavior modification to change your own behavior. To do this you must first select some target behavior you wish to change, such as swearing, not spending enough time studying or exercising, or spending too much time watching television—anything, as long as it is specific and you have a realistic goal for changing it. You then need to monitor the behavior to see how often you do it (or not do it), such as how many hours per day you spend productively studying. Simply noting the behavior is likely to move you toward your goal, since you will be more conscious of it, but keeping careful track will also allow you to assess your progress. By monitoring, you can also identify potential triggers of an unwanted behavior, such as time pressure or stress. Knowing what the triggers are will allow you to develop plans or strategies for dealing with them. Now you are ready to take charge. The first thing to do is pick a good reinforcer, something that you really want and that is reasonably attainable, such as going out to a movie, having a nice meal at a restaurant, or hanging out with friends. But remember: If you don't behave appropriately, you don't get the reinforcer! Over time, as you become more successful, phase out the reinforcer so that you are performing the behavior out of habit. Once you are used to exercising regularly, for example, you will do it regularly and it may even become reinforcing on its own. Give it a try—you might amaze yourself with the power of behavior modification. ■

Biology and Cognition Influence Operant Conditioning

Behaviorists such as B. F. Skinner believed that all behavior could be explained by straightforward conditioning principles. Recall that Skinner's *Walden Two* describes a utopia in which all of society's problems are solved through operant-conditioning principles. In reality, however, we know there are limits to explaining human behavior through schedules of reinforcement. Biology places constraints on learning, and reinforcement does not always have to be present for learning to take place.

BIOLOGICAL CONSTRAINTS Although behaviorists believed that any behavior could be shaped through reinforcement, it is now apparent that animals have a hard time learning behaviors that run counter to their evolutionary adaptation. A good example of biological constraints was obtained by the Brelands, a husband-and-wife team of psychologists who used operant-conditioning techniques to train animals for commercials (Breland & Breland, 1961). They discovered that many of their animals refused to perform certain tasks they had been taught. For instance, they trained a raccoon to place coins in a piggy bank, but, although the raccoon initially learned the task, it eventually refused to deposit the coins. Instead, it stood over the piggy bank and briskly rubbed the coins in its paws. The rubbing behavior was not reinforced; it actually delayed reinforcement. One explanation for the raccoon's behavior is that the task was incompatible with innate adaptive behaviors. The raccoon associated the coin with food and treated it the same way: rubbing food between the paws is hardwired for raccoons. Along similar lines, pigeons can be trained to peck at keys to obtain food or secondary reinforcement, but it is difficult to get them to peck at keys to avoid electric shock. However, they can learn to avoid shock by flapping their wings because it is their natural means of escape. Psychologist Robert Bolles argues that animals have built-in defense reactions to threatening stimuli (Bolles, 1970). Conditioning is most effective when the association between the behavioral response and the reinforcement is similar to the built-in predispositions of the animal.

The evolutionary perspective views the brain as a compilation of different domain-specific modules, each responsible for different cognitive functions. This suggests that learning is the result of many unique mechanisms that solve individual adaptive problems, not the result of general learning mechanisms (Rozin & Kalat, 1971; Shettleworth, 2001). As the evolutionary psychologist Randy Gallistel (2000) argues, people readily accept that the lungs are adapted for breathing and the ear is adapted for hearing. No one would argue that the lungs could be used to hear, or the ears to breathe. There is no general "sensing organ." Thus, it makes equal sense to postulate that a variety of learning mechanisms have evolved to solve specific problems. Consider an ant that leaves its nest to forage for food. Typically, the ant takes a circuitous and wandering path until it finds food, at which point it takes a direct path back to the nest, even over unfamiliar territory. This differs from what would be expected from traditional models of learning. The ant has never been rewarded for following the path, and there has been no classically conditioned association between the unfamiliar environmental objects and the most direct path back to the nest. Instead, mental processes that compute small changes in distance and direction provide a solution for the most direct path home. Gallistel's point is that learning consists of specialized mechanisms (rather than universal mechanisms) that solve the adaptive problems faced by animals in their environments.

ACQUISITION-PERFORMANCE DISTINCTION Another challenge to the idea that reinforcement is responsible for all behavior is that learning can take place without reinforcement. Edward Tolman, an early cognitive theorist, argued that reinforcement has more impact on performance than on learning. At the time, Tolman was conducting experiments in which rats had to learn to run through complex mazes to obtain food. Tolman believed that the rats developed **cognitive maps**, spatial representations of the maze that helped them learn to quickly find the food. To test his theory, Tolman and his students studied three groups of rats whose task was to travel through a maze to a "goal box" containing the reinforcer, usually food. The first group did not receive any reinforcement, and their performance was quite poor. With no food in the goal box, the rats wandered through the maze. A second group was reinforced on every trial, and they learned to find the goal box quickly. The critical group was the third group, which was not reinforced for the first ten trials but

cognitive map A visual/spatial mental representation of the environment.

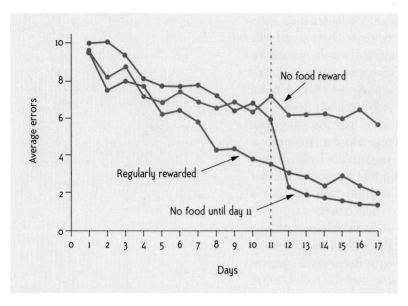

6.14 Reinforcement Rats that were regularly reinforced for correctly running through a maze showed improved performance over time compared to rats that did not receive reinforcement. Rats that were not reinforced for the first ten trials but were reinforced thereafter showed an immediate change in performance, indicating that they had learned a path through the maze, but that their learning was not revealed, or was latent, until it was reinforced. (Note that between days 11 and 12 their average number of errors decreased dramatically.)

was then reinforced on subsequent trials. Tolman found that this group showed an amazingly fast learning curve, so that they immediately caught up to the group that had been continuously reinforced (Figure 6.14). This result implies that the rats had learned a cognitive map of the maze and could use it when reinforcement became available. Tolman used the term **latent learning** to refer to learning that takes place in the absence of reinforcement.

Another form of learning that takes place in the absence of reinforcement is *insight learning*—a form of problem solving (discussed in Chapter 8) in which a solution suddenly emerges after a period of inaction or following contemplation of the problem. You probably have had this sort of experience, in which you mull over a problem for a while and then suddenly know the answer. Reinforcement does not provide an adequate account of the process of insight learning, although it does predict whether the behavior is subsequently repeated.

The Value of Reinforcement Follows Economic Principles

A relatively new approach to understanding operant conditioning considers the value of reinforcement in the context of basic economic principles, such as supply and demand. That which is in short supply is typically valued more, and therefore is a more potent reinforcer. Sometimes the economic considerations are more complicated. Which would you prefer, $100 today or $1,000 next year? Although it might appear that the larger payment would be more reinforcing, its value is discounted because there is a significant delay before it is received. But what if you really needed money right now? In that case, waiting has additional costs. Indeed, adults with lower incomes discount future payments more steeply than those with large incomes (Green, Myerson, Lichtman, Rosen, & Fry, 1996). At the heart of the behavioral economics approach is the idea that people and other animals often need to make choices between reinforcers. The personal worth of the reinforcer is affected by how long one has to wait to receive it as well as the likelihood that the payoff will actually be received. This approach has provided insights into a variety of behaviors, especially those associated with addiction. Warren Bickel and his colleagues (1999; Madden, Petry, Badger, & Bickel, 1997) found that both smokers and heroin addicts discounted future rewards more greatly than did nonaddicts, which may contribute to their problems with impulsivity and self-control. The issue of delaying immediate gratification to obtain long-term rewards is discussed more fully in Chapter 9.

Behavioral choice is also implicated in studies of animal foraging. Where animals choose to eat is dependent on the likelihood that food will be present, the energy costs associated with obtaining the food, and the risks associated with predators (Shettleworth, 2001). Should an animal eat all the berries in one patch and then search for a new patch, or should it save some for later and search for more patches? The new patches might have berries, but they might not. Researchers who study animals in their natural habitats find that animals are highly sensitive to the relative rates of reinforcement among different patches. The time they spend eating in one patch is influenced by the rate of reinforcement, the relative rate of reinforcement in other patches,

latent learning Learning that takes place in the absence of reinforcement.

and the time it takes to travel to those other patches. *Optimal foraging theory* describes how animals in the wild choose to provide their own schedules of reinforcement. It predicts that animals will sometimes act in apparently risky fashion. Consider an animal faced with the choice of feeding from two locations that have the same average amount of food, but one is much more variable, sometimes having no food and sometimes having lots. If an animal is facing starvation, its best chance for survival is to follow the apparently risky strategy of foraging in the more highly variable location. Animals also learn to vary how they eat according to the likelihood of being attacked by predators. Research at the University of Lethbridge in Canada found that rats eat very quickly when in the dark, especially when they are food deprived (Wishaw, Drigenberg, & Comery, 1992). Although eating quickly is optimal for consuming large amounts of food, it is not optimal for digestion. When in the light, rats eat more slowly, but they make frequent scans of the environment to check for predators. These variations reflect the fact that even a simple behavior such as eating requires a number of calculations to detect the costs and benefits associated with different behavioral options. The choices made by animals reflect specialized learning capacities that are adaptive to the environment.

REVIEWING the Principles | How Is Operant Conditioning Different from Classical Conditioning?

Whereas classical conditioning involves the learned association between two events, operant conditioning involves learning the association between a behavior and its consequences. Developed initially by B. F. Skinner, operant conditioning explains why some behaviors are repeated and others are not. The application of reinforcement increases the likelihood that a behavior will be repeated, whereas punishment reduces that likelihood. The extent to which a reinforcer increases behavior depends on whether it is positive or negative, its relative value, and on how it is provided. Although Skinner was confident that operant conditioning could ultimately explain all behavior, it has faced a number of challenges. Chief among these is that it is difficult to change instinctive behaviors and that learning can take place in the absence of reinforcement. Modern learning theorists recognize the important role of cognitive processes and biological constraints on behavior. Models based on economic theory have become increasingly useful for understanding how animals choose among reinforcers.

How Does Watching Others Affect Learning?

Suppose that you were trying to teach someone to fly an airplane. How might you apply learning principles discussed in this chapter to accomplish your goal? Reinforcing arbitrary correct behaviors obviously would be a disastrous strategy for training aspiring pilots. Similarly, teaching people to play football, eat with chopsticks, or perform complex dance steps requires more than simple reinforcement. For many behaviors, we learn not by doing but by observing the actions of others. We learn things such as social etiquette through observation, and we learn whether to be anxious in a situation by watching to see if others are anxious. Similarly, we acquire many of our attitudes about politics, religion, people, and objects from outside sources, such as parents, peers, teachers, and the media.

What is learned from observing others?

Learning Can Be Passed On through Cultural Transmission

Although humans around the world belong to the same species and share the vast majority of genes, there is enormous cultural diversity in what people think and how they behave. Would you be the same person if you were raised in a small village in China, or the jungles of South America, or the mountains of Afghanistan? Probably not, since your religious beliefs, personal values, and even your musical tastes are shaped by the culture in which you are raised. The term that evolutionary psychologists use for the transmission of cultural knowledge is **meme**. Memes are analogous to genes, in that they are selectively passed on from one generation to the next, with some, such as fads, dying out quite quickly.

A good example of cultural transmission of knowledge can be found in the case of Imo the monkey. In the 1950s, researchers who were studying monkeys in Japan threw some sweet potatoes onto the sandy beach for the monkeys to eat. Imo developed the habit of washing her sweet potato in the ocean to get the sand off. Within a short time, other monkeys copied Imo and soon all the monkeys washed their potatoes before eating them. This behavior has continued to be passed along from one generation to the next through social learning, and monkeys can still be observed washing their potatoes to this day (Dugatkin, 2004). Unlike natural selection, which typically occurs slowly over thousands of years, memes can spread quickly, such as the worldwide adoption of surfing the Internet. Although memes can be conditioned through association or reinforcement, many memes are learned from watching the behavior of others.

Learning Can Occur through Observation

Observational learning, which occurs when behaviors are acquired or modified following exposure to others performing the behavior, is a powerful adaptive tool both for humans and for other animals. Animals learn that food is safe by watching what their parents eat, and they learn to fear dangerous objects by watching their parents avoid those objects. Similarly, children acquire beliefs and basic skills by observing their parents and other role models. Any parent will tell you that young children are sponges, absorbing everything that goes on around them. They learn by watching as much as by doing.

BANDURA'S OBSERVATIONAL STUDIES The most thorough work on observational learning was conducted by Albert Bandura (Figure 6.15) in the 1960s. In a now-classic series of studies, preschool children were shown a film of an adult playing with a large inflatable doll called Bobo (Figure 6.16). In the film, the adult either played quietly with Bobo or attacked the doll furiously, whacking it with a mallet, socking it in the nose, and kicking it around the room. When the children were later allowed to play with a number of toys, including the Bobo doll, those who had seen the more aggressive display were more than twice as likely to act aggressively toward the doll (Bandura, Ross, & Ross, 1961). These results suggest that exposure to media violence may increase the likelihood that children will act aggressively.

OBSERVATIONAL LEARNING OF FEAR Observational learning also occurs in animals. For example, psychologist Susan Mineka explored whether rhesus monkeys could develop a phobia of snakes by observing other monkeys react fearfully to them. She had noticed that monkeys raised in the laboratory do not fear snakes, whereas

meme The knowledge transferred within a culture.

observational learning Learning that occurs when behaviors are acquired or modified following exposure to others performing the behavior.

6.15 Albert Bandura Bandura conducted important research showing that people could learn through observation.

6.16 **Scenes from the Classic Bobo Doll Studies** After viewing the adult act aggressively (top row), children (bottom two rows) imitated what they had seen.

those raised in the wild have an intense fear of them. Mineka and her colleagues set up an experiment with two groups of monkeys, one group reared in the wild and one group reared in the laboratory. The monkeys were required to reach beyond a clear box that contained either a snake or a neutral object to obtain food. When a snake was in the box, not only did the wild-reared monkeys not touch the food, but they also showed signs of distress, such as clinging to their cages and making threatening faces (Figure 6.17). The laboratory-raised monkeys reached past the box whether it contained a snake or not, and they showed no overt signs of fear. Mineka then showed the laboratory-raised monkeys the fearful response of the wild monkeys to see if it would affect their reaction to the snake. The laboratory monkeys quickly developed a fear of the snakes, and this fear was maintained over a three-month period (Mineka, Davidson, Cook, & Keir, 1984).

TEACHING THROUGH DEMONSTRATION Because humans can learn through observation, they can be taught many complex skills through demonstration. For instance, parents use slow and exaggerated motions to show their children how to tie their shoes. Do animals other than humans teach their offspring? Although the idea is somewhat controversial, there do appear to be instances in which animals teach their offspring through demonstration (Caro & Hauser, 1992). For instance, cheetahs appear to teach their young to hunt by injuring rather than killing their prey, which makes it easier for the cubs to knock down the prey. One chimpanzee who learned sign language (which you will read about in Chapter 11) was observed trying to demonstrate the proper use of signs to another chimpanzee.

6.17 **The Fear Response** In Susan Mineka's experiment, two sets of monkeys had to reach past a clear box to get food. When the clear box contained a snake, the wild-reared monkeys refused to reach across the box. By observing the actions of those monkeys, the laboratory-reared monkeys, who did not originally fear snakes, learned to become afraid of them. This suggests that fears can be learned through observation.

Animals and Humans Imitate Others

Animals and humans readily imitate the actions of others. In one study, pigeons observed other pigeons being reinforced at a feeder when they either stepped on a bar or pecked at the feeder directly. When the observing pigeons were themselves placed before the feeder, they tended to use the same technique they had seen (Zentall, Sutton, & Sherburne, 1996). Within a few days of birth, if not hours, human newborns will imitate facial expressions they observe, and they will continue to imitate gestures and other actions as they mature, just like the monkeys who copied the potato-washing behavior of Imo the monkey.

The imitation of observed behavior is commonly referred to as **modeling**, in that humans or animals reproduce the behaviors of *models*—those being observed. Modeling in humans is influenced by a number of factors. In general, we are more likely to imitate the actions of models who are attractive, have high status, and are somewhat similar to ourselves. In addition, modeling will be effective only if the observer is physically capable of imitating the behavior. Simply watching Tiger Woods blast 300-yard drives does not mean we could do so if handed a golf club.

The influence of models on behavior often occurs implicitly, without our being aware that our behavior is being altered. Indeed, who wants to admit that we change the way we speak or dress to act like some celebrity? But the evidence is overwhelming that we imitate what we see in others, especially those we admire. Adolescents whose favorite actors smoke in the movies are much more likely to smoke themselves (Tickle, Sargent, Dalton, Beach, & Heatherton, 2001), and the more that adolescents observe smoking in movies, the more positive their attitudes about smoking become and the more likely they are to begin smoking (Dalton et al., 2003). This effect is strongest among children whose parents do not smoke, which may be because what these children learn about smoking comes completely through the media, which tend to glamorize the habit. Smokers in movies are often presented as attractive, healthy, and wealthy, which does not really reflect the typical smoker. It isn't that adolescents watch a movie and decide to smoke, but rather that the images of smokers as mature, attractive, and cool—things that teenagers want to be—shape adolescent attitudes about smoking and subsequently lead to imitation.

VICARIOUS REINFORCEMENT Another factor that determines whether observers imitate a model is whether the model is reinforced for performing the behavior. In another study, Bandura and his colleagues showed children a film of an adult aggressively playing with a Bobo doll, but this time the film had one of three different endings (Bandura, Ross, & Ross, 1963). A control condition showed no consequences for the model's behavior, while the second film showed the adult being rewarded by being given candy and praise, and the third showed the adult being spanked and verbally reprimanded. When subsequently allowed to play with the Bobo doll, the children who observed the model being rewarded were much more likely to be aggressive toward the doll than those children in the control group. In contrast, those who saw the model being punished were less likely to be aggressive than the control group. Does this mean that those children did not learn the behavior? No. When the children later were offered small gifts to perform the model's actions, all of them could do so reliably. It is important to distinguish between the *acquisition* of a behavior and its *performance*. All of the children learned the behavior, but only those who saw the model being rewarded actually performed the behavior. **Vicarious learning** occurs when people learn about the consequences of an action by observing others being rewarded or punished for performing the action.

modeling The imitation of behavior through observational learning.

vicarious learning Learning that occurs when people learn the consequences of an action by observing others being rewarded or punished for performing the action.

MIRROR NEURONS What happens in the brain during imitation learning? An intriguing study found that special neurons in the brain called **mirror neurons** become activated when a monkey observes another monkey reaching for an object (Rizzolatti, Fadiga, Gallese, & Fogassi, 1996). These mirror neurons are the same neurons that would be activated if the monkey performed the behavior itself. Mirror neurons are especially likely to become activated when monkeys observe a target monkey engaging in movement that has some goal, such as reaching out to grasp an object. Neither the sight of the object on its own nor the mere sight of the target monkey leads to activation of these mirror neurons.

Brain-imaging techniques have identified similar mirror neurons in humans (Rizzolatti & Craighero, 2004). Thus, every time you observe another person engaging in an action, similar neural circuits are firing in both your brain and in the other person's. The function of mirror neurons is currently open to debate. This system may serve as the basis of imitation learning, but note that the firing of mirror neurons does not lead to imitative behavior in the observer. This has led some theorists to speculate that mirror neurons help us explain and predict the behavior of others. In other words, they allow us to step into the shoes of those we observe so that we can better understand their actions.

Humans also have mirror neurons for mouth actions, and these are stimulated when observers see a mouth move in a way that is typical of chewing or speaking (Ferrari, Gallese, Rizzolatti, & Fogassi, 2003). This has led to speculation that mirror neurons are important not only for imitation learning, but also for the human ability to communicate through language. Mirror neurons may be a brain system that creates a link between the sender and receiver of a message. Rizzolatti and Arbib (1998) proposed that the mirror neuron system evolved to allow language. Their theory relies on the idea that speech evolved mainly from gestures, and indeed people readily understand many nonverbal behaviors, such as waving or thrusting a fist in the air. If their theory is true, then speech sounds came to represent gestures, and this suggests a direct link between words that describe actions and the very actions themselves. Indeed, there is evidence that listening to sentences that describe actions activates the same brain regions that are active when those actions are observed (Tettamanti et al., 2005). Even reading words that represent actions leads to brain activity in relevant motor regions, such as the word *lick* activating brain regions that control tongue movements (Hauk, Johnsrude, & Pulvermüller, 2004).

mirror neurons Neurons in the premotor cortex that are activated during observation of others performing an action.

Thinking Critically

Does Watching Violence on Television Cause Aggression?

The average television set in the United States is on for five or six hours per day, and young children often spend more time watching television than doing any other activity, including schoolwork (Roberts, 2000). There is a great deal of violence in television programming. The average child witnesses more than 100,000 violent acts on TV before the end of elementary school; you probably witnessed over 18,000 murders on TV before you started college. What effect does this massive exposure to violence have on behavior? Do we imitate the violence we see on television?

Three decades of research have linked the viewing of violence with imitative violence, aggressive behavior, acceptance of violence as a solution, increased feelings of

6.18 What Causes Violent Behavior? Many scientists believe there is a direct correlation between exposure to violent television shows or video games (like the one seen here) and aggressive behavior in children. Still, it is problematic to generalize based on the interpretation of specific studies because correlation does not prove causation.

hostility, and willingness to deliver painful stimuli to others. Some researchers have conducted controlled laboratory studies in which they randomly assign children to watch either violent or neutral film clips and then measure subsequent aggressive behavior. In general, compared to those who watch neutral clips, children who watch the violent ones are more likely to act in an aggressive manner during subsequent tasks. A study by Leonard Eron and his colleagues found that television viewing habits at age 8 predicted violent behavior and criminal activity at age 30 (Eron, 1987). The average effect size (the magnitude of the association between independent and dependent variables), determined by statistically averaging across the hundreds of studies, is nearly as large as that linking smoking and cancer, and is larger than the effect size for condom nonuse and HIV transmission or for lead exposure and IQ in children (Bushman & Anderson, 2001).

There are, however, a number of problems with the studies on this topic. The social psychologist Jonathan Freedman (1984) notes that many of the so-called aggressive behaviors displayed by children could be interpreted as playful rather than aggressive. A more serious concern is whether the studies generalize to the real world. Viewing a violent film clip in a lab is unlike watching TV in one's living room. The film clips used in studies are often brief and extremely violent, and the child watches them alone. In the real world, violent episodes are interspersed with nonviolent material, and children often watch them with others who may buffer the effect.

Even the longitudinal studies that assess childhood television watching and later violent behavior fail to prove satisfactorily that TV caused the behavior. It could easily be that extraneous variables, such as personality, poverty, or parental negligence, have an effect on both television viewing habits and violent tendencies. After all, not all of those who view violence on television become aggressive later in life. Perhaps those who watch excessive amounts of TV, and who therefore have fewer opportunities to develop social skills, act aggressively. Correlation does not prove causation. Only through careful laboratory studies in which participants are randomly assigned to experimental conditions can we determine causality. Obviously, it isn't practical to assign children randomly to different types of media, and it is ethically questionable to expose any children to violence if we think it will make them more aggressive.

In spite of the problems with interpreting specific studies, most scientists believe that there is a direct relation between exposure to violence and aggressive behavior. Indeed, a recent joint statement by professional groups representing psychologists and pediatricians concluded that a plethora of studies "point overwhelmingly to a causal connection between media violence and aggressive behavior in some children" (Joint Statement, 2000, p. 1).

How might media violence promote aggression in children? One possibility is that exposure to massive amounts of violence in movies, which misrepresents the prevalence of violence in real life, leads children to believe that violence is both common and inevitable (Figure 6.18). Because few people are punished for acting violently in movies, children may come to believe that such behaviors are justified (Bushman & Huesmann, 2001). That is, the portrayal of violence in movies teaches children questionable social scripts for solving personal problems. By mentally rehearsing the script, or observing the same script enacted many times in different movies, a child might come to believe that engaging in brutality is an effective way to solve problems and dispense with annoying people (Huesmann, 1998).

What do you think? How much violence have you seen in movies or on television? Do you think it affected you? Should it be banned even if it only affects some children? What might parents do if they are concerned about what their children watch on television? ■

REVIEWING

the Principles | How Does Watching Others Affect Learning?

Thanks to psychological research, we now know that much of behavior is learned by observing the behavior of others. Children learn language, social skills, and political attitudes from observing their parents, peers, and teachers, and we teach complex skills, such as surgery and driving, by demonstration. Nonhuman animals also learn through observation, for example, which food is safe to eat and which objects should be feared. People imitate models that are attractive, high status, and somewhat similar to themselves. Modeling is more likely to occur when the model has been rewarded for the behavior, and less likely when the model has been punished. Vicarious conditioning influences whether a behavior is performed, but not whether it is learned. It is possible that mirror neurons, which fire when a behavior is observed, may be the neural basis of imitation learning.

What Is the Biological Basis of Reward?

Although people often use the term *reward* as a synonym for positive reinforcement, Skinner and other traditional behaviorists defined reinforcement strictly in terms of whether it increased behavior. They were relatively uninterested in *why* it increased behavior. Indeed, they carefully avoided any speculation about whether subjective experiences had anything to do with behavior, since they believed that mental states were impossible to study empirically. The biological revolution, however, has begun to provide new insights into how we learn. In this section we examine the biological basis of reinforcement and its application to understanding conditioned behaviors.

Self-Stimulation Is a Model of Reward

One of the earliest discoveries pointing to the role of neural mechanisms in reinforcement came about because of a small surgical error. In the early 1950s, Peter Milner and James Olds were testing whether electrical stimulation to a specific brain region would facilitate learning. To see whether the learning they observed was caused by the activity of the brain or by the aversive qualities of the electrical stimulus, Olds and Milner administered electrical stimulation to the brains of rats only while the rats were in one specific location in the cage. The logic was that if the application of electricity was aversive, the rats would selectively avoid that location. Fortunately for science, they administered the shocks to the wrong part of the brain, and instead of avoiding the area of the cage associated with electrical stimulation, the rats quickly came back, apparently looking for more.

PLEASURE CENTERS Olds and Milner then set up an experiment to see whether rats would press a lever to self-administer shock to specific sites in their brains, a procedure subsequently referred to as **intracranial self-stimulation (ICSS)** (Figure 6.19). The rats self-administered electricity to their brains with gusto, pressing the lever hundreds of times per hour (Olds & Milner, 1954). Olds and Milner referred to brain regions that support ICSS as *pleasure centers*. Although behaviorists might

intracranial self-stimulation (ICSS) A procedure in which animals are able to self-administer electrical shock to specific areas of the brain.

6.19 Intracranial Self-Stimulation A rat will self-administer electricity to pleasure centers in the brain.

Why are certain experiences rewarding?

have objected to the term *pleasure,* it was clear to everyone that ICSS was a powerful reinforcer. In one experiment, rats that had been on a near-starvation diet for ten days were given a choice between food and the opportunity to administer ICSS. They chose the electrical stimulation more than 80 percent of the time! Deprived rats also chose electrical stimulation over water or receptive sexual partners; they even crossed a painful electrified grid in order to receive ICSS. Rats will continue intracranial self-stimulation until they collapse from exhaustion. Monkeys tested in similar studies have been found to press a bar for electrical stimulation up to 8,000 times per hour (Olds, 1962).

ELECTRICAL STIMULATION AND NATURAL REINFORCEMENT Most psychologists believe that ICSS acts on the same brain regions as those activated by natural reinforcers, such as food, water, and sex. Electrical stimulation applied to pleasure centers in rats elicits naturally motivated behaviors, such as feeding, drinking, and copulating with an available partner. Also, depriving an animal of food or water leads to increased ICSS, which is taken to indicate that the animal is trying to obtain the same experience associated with natural reward. Finally, the neural mechanisms underlying ICSS and natural reward appear to use the same neurotransmitter system, namely dopamine. In terms of operant conditioning, this evidence suggests that dopamine serves as the neurochemical basis of positive reinforcement.

Dopamine Signals Reward

Recall from Chapter 3 that the neurotransmitter dopamine is involved in motivation and emotion. It also appears to be crucial for positive reinforcement. Research over the past 50 years has shown that dopamine plays an important role in the experience of reward (Wise & Rompre, 1989). For instance, intracranial self-stimulation activates dopamine receptors; interfering with dopamine eliminates self-stimulation as well as other naturally motivated behaviors, such as feeding, drinking, and copulating.

NUCLEUS ACCUMBENS ACTIVATION The *nucleus accumbens* is a subcortical brain region that is part of the limbic system. The experience of pleasure usually results from activation of dopamine neurons in the nucleus accumbens. For example, enjoying food depends on dopamine activity. Hungry rats that are given food have increased release of dopamine in the nucleus accumbens, and the greater the hunger, the greater the release of dopamine (Rolls, Murzi, Yaxley, Thorpe, & Simpson, 1980). Food tastes better when you are hungry and water is more rewarding when you are thirsty because more dopamine is released under deprived than nondeprived conditions. Even the enjoyable activity of looking at funny cartoons activates the nucleus accumbens (Mobbs, Greicius, Abdel-Azim, Menon, & Reiss, 2003).

In operant conditioning, the release of dopamine sets the value of a reinforcer. Drugs that block the effects of dopamine disrupt operant conditioning. For instance, Jim Stellar and his colleagues taught rats to run a maze in order to receive electrical stimulation, but when they injected a dopamine blocker into the rats, they had to turn up the electrical current in order to get the rats to run the maze (Stellar, Kelley, & Corbett, 1983). The blocker decreased the value of the electrical-stimulation reinforcement. As you might expect, drugs that enhance the activation of dopamine, such as cocaine and amphetamine, increase the reward value of stimuli.

SECONDARY REINFORCERS ALSO RELY ON DOPAMINE Natural reinforcers appear to signal reward directly through the activation of dopamine receptors in the nucleus accumbens. But what about secondary reinforcers, such as money or good grades? Through a process of classical conditioning, neutral stimuli that fail to stimulate a release of dopamine at first do so readily after they are paired with unconditioned stimuli. In one study, monkeys were presented with a trapdoor that opened occasionally. The door opening did not activate dopamine activity. The experimenters then placed apples in the doorway, such that the door opening was associated with the unconditioned stimulus of food. After many conditioning trials, the door opening led on its own to increased activation of dopamine (Ljungberg, Apicella, & Schultz, 1992). Thus, the sight of a loved one, or getting a good grade or a paycheck, may be conditioned to produce dopamine activation. As mentioned earlier, money is an excellent example of a secondary reinforcer, and indeed, anticipated monetary rewards have been found to activate dopamine systems (Knutson, Fong, Adams, Varner, & Hommer, 2001). Drugs that block the effects of dopamine appear to block the rewarding qualities of most activities. Individuals with *Tourette's syndrome,* a disorder of motor control, are given dopamine blockers to control their involuntary body movements. These individuals often have trouble staying on their drug regimens because they feel the drugs rob them of life's enjoyment. We will discuss this in greater detail in Chapter 14.

DRUG USE AND ADDICTION People take drugs to feel good. Therefore, it should come as no surprise that most drugs activate dopamine receptors. As with intracranial self-stimulation, food, water, and sex, most drugs that people use and sometimes abuse—including alcohol, nicotine, heroin, cocaine, and cannabis—are associated with increased dopamine activation in the nucleus accumbens. These drugs either increase dopamine release or prevent the normal termination of its neural signal, thereby prolonging its effects. Over time, the continued use of drugs can lead to addiction; most researchers have concluded that the release of dopamine is a necessary condition for reinforcement and drug addiction (Koob, 1999). The potential for addiction to a specific drug is determined by the speed of its rewarding effects. For instance, people are more likely to become addicted to crack cocaine, which they smoke, than to powdered cocaine, which they sniff, because cocaine arrives at the brain faster through smoking. Of course, people become addicted to drugs for many other reasons, such as the social environment, and we will consider these in greater detail in Chapter 9.

REVIEWING the Principles | What Is the Biological Basis of Reward?

Although the behaviorists avoided any reference to internal mental states, it is clear that positive reinforcement generally works because it provides the subjective experience of pleasure. The neural basis of this reinforcement is the release of dopamine. Engaging in naturally motivated behaviors, self-administering electricity to the brain, and taking drugs or alcohol all lead to increased activation of dopamine neurons in the nucleus accumbens, which is associated with the experience of pleasure. Understanding the neural basis of reinforcement helps to explain complex conditioning, such as the development of addiction.

How Does Learning Occur at the Neuronal Level?

From a biological perspective, scientists have long believed that learning involves relatively permanent changes in the brain that result from exposure to environmental events. The roots of this idea can be traced back to a number of scientists, including the German researcher Richard Semon, who in 1904 proposed that memories are stored through changes in the nervous system. Semon called the storage of learned material an *engram,* a term later popularized by the eminent psychologist Karl Lashley. In 1948, the Canadian psychologist Donald Hebb (Figure 6.20) proposed that learning results from alterations in synaptic connections. According to Hebb, when one neuron excites another, some change takes place such that the synapse between the two becomes strengthened. Subsequently, the firing of one neuron becomes increasingly likely to cause the firing of the other. Although there have been a number of different interpretations of Hebb's postulate, most of them can be summed up as "cells that fire together wire together." Hebb did not have the technology to examine whether his hypothesis was true or not, but we now know that his basic theory was correct.

Habituation and Sensitization Are Simple Models of Learning

What happens at the synapse that leads to learning? One answer is found in research using simple invertebrates such as the *aplysia,* a small marine snail that eats seaweed (Figure 6.21). The aplysia is an excellent species to use to study learning because it has a relatively small number of neurons, some of which are large enough to be seen without a microscope (Kandel, Schwartz, & Jessell, 1995). The neurobiologist Eric Kandel and his colleagues have used the aplysia to study the neural basis of two types of simple learning: *habituation* and *sensitization.* As a result of this research, Kandel received a Nobel Prize for medicine in 2000.

Habituation is a decrease in behavioral response following repeated exposure to nonthreatening stimuli. When an animal encounters a novel stimulus, it pays attention to it, behavior known as an *orienting response.* If the stimulus is neither harmful nor rewarding, the animal learns to ignore it. We constantly habituate to meaningless events around us. For instance, sit back and listen. Perhaps you can hear a clock, or a computer fan, or your roommates playing music in the next room. You didn't really notice these sounds in the background before because you had habituated to them. Habituation in the aplysia can be demonstrated quite easily by repeatedly touching it. The first few touches cause it to withdraw its gills, but after about 10 touches it quits responding, and this lack of response lasts about 2 to 3 hours. Repeated habituation trials can lead to a state of habituation that lasts several weeks.

Sensitization is an increase in behavioral response following exposure to a threatening stimulus. For instance, imagine that while you are studying you smell burning. You are unlikely to habituate to this smell. You might focus even greater attention on your

6.20 Donald Hebb Hebb proposed that learning results from changes in synaptic connections: *Cells that fire together wire together.*

What is the neural basis of learning?

6.21 Simple Models of Learning The aplysia is a marine invertebrate that is used to study the neurochemical basis of learning.

sense of smell in order to assess the possible threat of fire, and you will be highly vigilant for any indication of smoke or flames. In general, sensitization leads to heightened responsiveness to other stimuli. Giving a strong electrical shock to the tail of the aplysia leads to sensitization. Following the shock, a mild touch anywhere on the body will cause the aplysia to withdraw its gills.

Kandel's research on aplysia has shown that alterations in the functioning of the synapse lead to both habituation and sensitization. For both types of simple learning, presynaptic neurons alter their release of neurotransmitters. A reduction in neurotransmitter release leads to habituation; an increase in neurotransmitter release leads to sensitization. Knowing the neural basis of simple learning gives us the building blocks to understand more complex learning processes.

Long-Term Potentiation Is a Candidate for the Cellular Basis of Learning

To understand learning in the complex mammalian brain, researchers have investigated a phenomenon known as *long-term potentiation*. The word *potentiate* means to strengthen, to make something more potent. **Long-term potentiation (LTP)** is the strengthening of the synaptic connection so that postsynaptic neurons are more easily activated. To demonstrate LTP, researchers first establish the extent to which electrically stimulating one neuron leads to an action potential (the level of stimulation needed to activate or "fire") in a second neuron. They then provide intense electrical stimulation to the first neuron, perhaps giving it a hundred pulses of electricity in five seconds. Finally, a single electrical pulse is readministered to measure the extent of activation of the second neuron. As you can see in Figure 6.22, LTP occurs when the intense electrical stimulation increases the likelihood that stimulating one neuron leads to an action potential in the second neuron. Whereas habituation and sensitization in aplysia are due to changes in neurotransmitter release from the presynaptic neuron, LTP results from changes in the postsynaptic neuron that make it more easily activated. There is also evidence that a similar process can weaken synaptic connections, a situation referred to as *long-term depression*.

A number of lines of evidence support the idea that long-term potentiation may be the cellular basis for learning and memory (Beggs et al., 1999). For instance, LTP effects are most easily observed in brain sites known to be involved in learning and memory, such as the hippocampus. Moreover, the same drugs that improve memory also lead to increased LTP, and those that block memory also block LTP. Finally, behavioral conditioning produces neurochemical effects that are nearly identical to LTP.

The process of long-term potentiation also supports Hebb's contention that learning results from a strengthening of synaptic connections that fire together. Hebb's rule can be used

habituation A decrease in behavioral response following repeated exposure to nonthreatening stimuli.

sensitization An increase in behavioral response following exposure to a threatening stimulus.

long-term potentiation (LTP) The strengthening of a synaptic connection so that postsynaptic neurons are more easily activated.

6.22 Electric Pulses in Neurons A presynaptic neuron is given a brief electrical pulse, which causes a slight response in the postsynaptic neuron. Applying intense and frequent electricity leads to a greater response of the postsynaptic neuron. When a single brief pulse is subsequently applied, it results in a greater effect on the postsynaptic neuron than occurred originally.

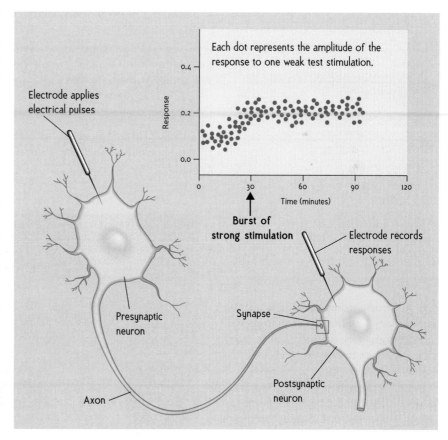

to explain a variety of learning phenomena, including classical conditioning. Neurons that signal the unconditioned stimulus are active at the same time as those that signal the conditioned stimulus. Over repeated trials, the synapses that connect these two events become strengthened, so that when one fires, the other fires automatically, producing the conditioned response.

FEAR CONDITIONING Although LTP was originally observed in the hippocampus, there is recent evidence that fear conditioning may induce LTP in the amygdala. In a typical fear-conditioning study, a rat is classically conditioned to produce a fear response to an auditory tone. Electric shock follows the tone, and eventually the tone produces fear responses on its own, which include specific physiological and behavioral reactions. One interesting response, *freezing*—standing still—is observed in many species, including humans. If you have seen video footage from the bombing at the Atlanta Summer Olympics in 1996, you probably noticed that most people froze in a crouch for the first few seconds after the bomb exploded. Immediately keeping still might be a hard-wired response that helped animals deal with predators, which often are attracted by movement (LeDoux, 2002). There is substantial evidence that the amygdala is crucial for fear conditioning. If one particular part of the amygdala is removed, animals are unable to learn that shock follows the tone (Davis, 1997). Joseph LeDoux and his students have demonstrated that both auditory fear conditioning and artificial LTP induction lead to similar changes in amygdala neurons, suggesting that fear conditioning might produce long-lasting learning through the induction of LTP (Rogan, Stäubli, & LeDoux, 1997).

LTP AND THE NMDA RECEPTOR Researchers have made considerable progress over the last decade in understanding how LTP works. A special receptor, called the *NMDA* receptor, is required for LTP. This receptor has a special property: It opens only if two nearby neurons fire at the same time, supporting the Hebb rule that cells that fire together wire together. The findings that NMDA receptors were involved in LTP led researchers to examine genetic processes that might influence learning. For instance, Joseph Tsien at Princeton University modified the genes in mice so that their NMDA receptors were more efficient. When tested in standard learning tasks, these transgenic mice performed amazingly well, learning novel tasks more quickly and showing increased fear conditioning (Tsien, 2000). The mice were such great learners that Tsien named them "Doogie mice" after the prime-time television character Doogie Howser, a boy doctor (Figure 6.23). Might we be able to modify genes so that people learn more quickly? This fascinating question raises all

6.23 A "Doogie" Mouse Used in a Learning and Memory Test Doogie mice and regular mice were given the chance to familiarize themselves with two objects. One of the objects was later replaced with a novel object. This change was quickly recognized by the Doogie mice but not by the normal mice. (Photo appeared in *Nature,* courtesy of Princeton University.)

sorts of ethical issues, but various pharmaceutical companies are exploring drugs that might enhance the learning process by manipulating gene expression or activating NMDA receptors. If successful, such treatments might prove valuable for treating patients with diseases such as Alzheimer's. This is an especially active area of research, and we will likely continue to hear of many discoveries about how genes, neurotransmitters, and the environment interact to produce learning.

Learning Can Be Simulated by Computerized Neural Networks

Psychological scientists have developed computer models of neural networks to understand how the brain learns. The computer is a widely used metaphor for the working mind. Both the brain and the computer receive information as input, process that information, and create output in the form of actions or behaviors. Computerized models of learning are often referred to as *connectionist models* because they are roughly based on the idea that neurons are connected or associated with each other. Instead of neurons, computer models have units, which are connected with each other in the computerized neural network.

A simple connectionist model is shown in Figure 6.24. Note that this model has three layers of units: It takes in information through the *input units,* processes that information in the *hidden units,* and generates an action through the *output units.* Just as one neuron can pass a message to another neuron to fire or not to fire, the computer units also can be excitatory or inhibitory, and the strength of their connections is modified through learning.

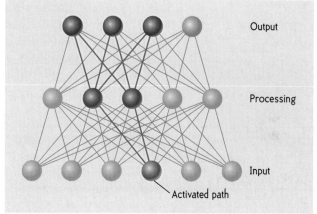

6.24 Neural Networks A simple network with three layers of units.

RULES FOR LEARNING The rule by which connectionist models operate is based on the degree to which a model's output matches the input. For instance, suppose you are trying to learn someone's name. When you see her face, you want to retrieve the correct name. When the output (i.e., the retrieved name) fails to match the input (i.e., the relevant face), you adjust the strength of association between the units so that the output becomes more similar to what it is supposed to be. For example, perhaps you recall the name as Karen when it is actually Kathy. To rectify the error, your neural network strengthens the association between the person's face and "Kathy" and weakens the association between her face and "Karen." After many trials, you call Kathy by her correct name. Subsequently, the connection between the person's face and the name Kathy is strengthened each time you associate them.

How connectionist models "learn" is similar to the Rescorla-Wagner model of classical conditioning discussed earlier. In both models, the greater the deviation from expectancy, the more learning takes place. If Kathy's face triggered an output of the name "Jake," you would need to learn a lot more! However, once the input matches the appropriate output, relatively little further learning takes place.

THE PARALLEL-DISTRIBUTED PROCESSING MODEL One of the best-known connectionist models of learning is the *parallel-distributed processing* (PDP) model developed by David Rumelhart and James McClelland. An important feature of the PDP model is that it is based on how neural networks actually operate. For instance, it views neuronal connections as richly distributed throughout the brain and it involves *parallel* processing, in which everything happens at the same time. This is an advance over serial models, in which learning was thought to occur in a fixed order, like the sequence of operations in a computer program.

The human brain is massively parallel, with millions of synapses within neural networks firing at the same time. In the PDP model, each unit in the network can be connected to all other units, and each is activated or inhibited by other units in the network. Essentially, each unit adds up the various inhibitory and excitatory messages from the other units, and it becomes activated when this sum passes a critical threshold. In this way, units in the PDP model operate as neurons do when they integrate information from other neurons to determine whether they will fire.

REVIEWING

the Principles | How Does Learning Occur at the Neuronal Level?

Researchers are rapidly identifying the neurophysiological basis of learning. Much of what has been learned supports Hebb's theories that neurons that fire together wire together. Kandel's work on aplysia has shown that habituation and sensitization, two simple forms of learning, occur through alteration in neurotransmitter release. The discovery of long-term potentiation shows that intense stimulation of neurons can strengthen synapses, increasing the likelihood that the activation of one neuron will increase the firing of other neurons in the network. Computerized models of neural networks have helped make predictions about how complex learning takes place.

Conclusion

Behaviorism has been a powerful force in psychological science since early in the twentieth century. The shift from subjective to empirical methods established psychology as a science. A renewed interest in mental processes eventually led many to abandon the strict principles of behaviorism, but basic conditioning and learning processes are still foundational principles in understanding mind and behavior. Psychological scientists use learning principles in studies across all levels of analysis, from synaptic connections in aplysia (cellular) to the cultural transmission of morals and values (cultural). With all its competing theories and sharing of ideas, the field of learning also serves as an excellent example of how psychological research is based on cumulative principles. We still see that dynamic in operation today. The principles of classical and operant conditioning are basic methodologies used by all neuroscientists to study brain mechanisms. In turn, recent advances in neuroscience techniques resulting from the biological revolution have allowed for a more complete understanding of learning processes. Learning occurs in the brain, and our relatively new access to brain-imaging techniques is reigniting interest in basic conditioning processes. Understanding the neurochemical basis of learning may help us to develop more effective treatments for a variety of psychological problems, including phobias and drug addictions.

Summarizing the Principles of Learning and Reward

How Did the Behavioral Study of Learning Develop?

1. **Behavioral responses are conditioned:** Pavlov established the principles of classical conditioning, a process that occurs when associations are made between stimuli and responses. This type of learning is reflex based and has many measurable aspects with regard to acquisition, discrimination, generalization, and extinction. Some emotional responses are learned through conditioning.

2. **Phobias and addictions have learned components:** Phobias are learned fear associations. Similarly, addiction involves a conditioned response, which results in withdrawal and tolerance.

3. **Classical conditioning involves more than contiguity:** Not all stimuli are equally potent in producing conditioning. Animals are biologically prepared to make connections between stimuli that are potentially dangerous. Animals are also predisposed to form predictions to enhance survival.

How Is Operant Conditioning Different from Classical Conditioning?

4. **Reinforcement increases behavior:** Positive consequences of a behavior will likely strengthen and reinforce the behavior. Shaping is a procedure where successive approximations of a behavior are reinforced, which leads to the desired behavior. Reinforcers are primary (those that satisfy biological needs) and secondary (those that do not directly satisfy biological needs).

5. **Both reinforcement and punishment can be positive or negative:** Positive reinforcement or punishment means the delivery of a stimulus after the response; negative reinforcement or punishment means the removal of a stimulus after the response. Positive and negative reinforcements increase the likelihood of a behavior; positive and negative punishments decrease the likelihood of the behavior.

6. **Operant conditioning is influenced by schedules of reinforcement:** Reinforcement is delivered at a fixed rate or a variable rate that depends on the number (ratio) or time (interval) of responses.

7. **Biology and cognition influence operant conditioning:** The biological makeup of an organism restricts the types of behaviors it can learn. Latent learning refers to learning that takes place in the absence of reinforcement.

8. **The value of reinforcement follows economic principles:** Animals are predisposed to calculate the relative cost and benefit of behaviors, thus aiding their survival.

How Does Watching Others Affect Learning?

9. **Learning can be passed on through cultural transmission:** Memes (knowledge transferred within a culture) are analogous to genes, in that behaviors are selectively passed on from generation to generation.

10. **Learning can occur through observation:** Observational learning is a powerful adaptive tool. Humans and other animals learn by watching others' behaviors and the consequences.

11. **Animals and humans imitate others:** Modeling occurs when the behavior of another is reproduced. Vicarious learning occurs when we see other people's behaviors reinforced or punished. Mirror neurons are activated when we watch a behavior, the same as when we actually perform the behavior.

What Is the Biological Basis of Reward?

12. **Self-stimulation is a model of reward:** The brain has specialized centers, which produce pleasure when stimulated. Behaviors that activate these centers are reinforced.

13. **Dopamine signals reward:** The nucleus accumbens (a part of the limbic system) has dopamine receptors, which are activated by pleasurable behaviors. Through conditioning, secondary reinforcers can also activate dopamine receptors. Drugs also increase actuation, which can lead to addiction.

How Does Learning Occur at the Neuronal Level?

14. **Habituation and sensitization are simple models of learning:** Repeated exposure to a stimulus results in habituation, a decrease in behavioral response. Sensitization is an increase in behavioral response to a new threatening stimulus.

15. **Long-term potentiation is a candidate for the cellular basis of learning:** Synaptic connections are strengthened when neurons fire together. This occurs in the hippocampus and, in fear responses, in the amygdala. The receptor NMDA is required for long-term potentiation.

16. **Learning can be simulated by computerized neural networks:** The connectionist model of neural networks is based on the idea that neurons are connected, which allows the brain to receive information (through input units), process the information (in hidden units), and generate an action (through output units). The strength of the connections is modified through learning. The parallel-distributed process (PDP) model is an advanced connectionist model that assumes learning involves parallel processing—it does not occur in a fixed order.

Applying the Principles

1. Imagine that in your experience, every time you saw a dog, it barked and frightened you; or each time you ate pepperoni pizza, you became ill; or perhaps your favorite grandmother always wore the same perfume. Now, whenever you see any kind of dog, it frightens you; the sight of a pizza makes you queasy; and the smell of that perfume always makes you smile. In all of these cases your response is due to

   _____ a) your ability to associate two different stimuli just because they happen together.
   _____ b) your ability to form contingencies between stimuli.
   _____ c) your intelligence.
   _____ d) your ability to override your reflexes with thought.

2. When your statistics instructor begins to sum up her main points and closes her lecture notes, you and the other students begin noisily packing your bookbags to get ready to leave. The instructor falls silent and glares at the class until the room is quiet again. What principles of learning are occurring with regard to your behaviors?

   _____ a) classical conditioning for both packing up and being quieted because two behavioral stimuli are being associated
   _____ b) operant conditioning with positive reinforcement for packing up and negative reinforcement for being quieted
   _____ c) classical conditioning for packing up; operant conditioning with negative reinforcement for being quieted
   _____ d) operant conditioning with negative reinforcement for the packing up; classical conditioning for being quiet

3. Amber is at a party, munching on some snacks while talking to Joe. Her friend Lisa, who is standing behind Joe, catches Amber's eye and brushes the right side of her face to signal that Amber has food on her cheek. Amber quickly raises a hand and brushes her cheek. What types of learning behaviors are occurring?

   _____ a) various conditioning responses in which Amber mimics Lisa

   _____ b) observational learning when Amber first brushes the left side of her face to mimic Lisa, and the likely firing of mirror neurons
   _____ c) observational learning that relies on species-specific responses
   _____ d) Amber is displaying a simple reflex response

4. German chocolate cake is your favorite dessert. You have many happy memories of eating a freshly made slice in your grandmother's kitchen after school. Your partner, knowing this, makes you a wonderful four-course birthday dinner with German chocolate cake for dessert prepared from your grandmother's recipe. At the biological level of analysis, what response in the nucleus accumbens of your brain may account for a less pleasurable experience than you had in the past?

   _____ a) the release of excess dopamine because you are older, which means you can't experience pleasure the same way
   _____ b) the communication of this area of the limbic system with the frontal cortex causing guilt for eating such a rich dessert
   _____ c) the big dinner has made you less hungry for dessert, so there is less dopamine activation
   _____ d) an activation of dopamine receptors due to thirst while consuming the cake results in a less pleasurable experience

5. Imagine that you've just bought a car. Initially, the key sticks in the lock and you have trouble opening the door, but after a while, the key goes in smoothly and you are able to unlock all the doors in a single turn of the key. This is similar to the effects of

   _____ a) long-term potentiation on the neuron.
   _____ b) dopamine on receptors.
   _____ c) long-term potentiation on the nucleus of the neuron.
   _____ d) genetic manipulation of neural receptors.

ANSWERS: 1 b   2 c   3 b   4 c   5 a

Key Terms

acquisition, p. 215
biological preparedness, p. 220
classical conditioning, p. 214
cognitive maps, p. 229
conditioned response (CR), p. 214
conditioned stimulus (CS), p. 214
continuous reinforcement, p. 226
extinction, p. 215
fixed schedule, p. 226
habituation, p. 240
interval schedule, p. 226
intracranial self-stimulation (ICSS), p. 237
latent learning, p. 230
law of effect, p. 222

learning, p. 212
long-term potentiation (LTP), p. 241
meme, p. 232
mirror neurons, p. 235
modeling, p. 234
negative punishment, p. 224
negative reinforcement, p. 224
observational learning, p. 232
operant conditioning, p. 222
partial reinforcement, p. 226
partial-reinforcement extinction effect, p. 227
phobia, p. 217
positive punishment, p. 224
positive reinforcement, p. 224

primary reinforcers, p. 223
punishment, p. 224
ratio schedule, p. 226
reinforcer, p. 222
Rescorla-Wagner model, p. 221
secondary reinforcers, p. 223
sensitization, p. 240
shaping, p. 223
spontaneous recovery, p. 215
stimulus discrimination, p. 216
stimulus generalization, p. 215
unconditioned response (UR), p. 214
unconditioned stimulus (US), p. 214
variable schedule, p. 226
vicarious learning, p. 234

Further Readings

Domjan, M. (2004). *The essentials of conditioning and learning.* Belmont, CA: Wadsworth.

Dugatkin, L. A. (2004). *Principles of animal behavior.* New York: Norton.

Kandel, E. R., Schwartz, J. H., & Jessell, T. M. (2000). *Principles of neural science* (4th ed.). New York: McGraw-Hill.

LeDoux, J. (2002). *Synaptic self.* New York: Viking.

McConnell, S., Roberts, J., Spitzer, L., Zigmond, M., Squire, L., & Bloom, F. (2002). *Fundamental neuroscience* (2nd ed.). San Diego, CA: Academic Press.

How and What We Remember

In the 2000 film *Memento,* Leonard Shelby (played by Guy Pearce, above) suffers from severe short-term memory loss. In search of his wife's killer, he tattoos words onto his body to remind himself of what he's discovered. Decades of study have revealed a great deal about memory and its importance to survival.

Memory

I magine what the world would be like if you lost the ability to remember new experiences. You wouldn't be able to remember meeting people, or what you did last night, or even what you had for breakfast this morning. In a few minutes, you would not even remember having contemplated this problem. Such is the fate of a man who received brain surgery to relieve his epilepsy.

Anticonvulsive drugs had proven ineffective at controlling H.M.'s seizures, and therefore in September 1953 his doctors performed a surgical technique in which they removed parts of his medial temporal lobes, including the hippocampus (Figure 7.1). The idea was to stop the seizures, which originated in the temporal lobes, from spreading throughout the brain. The surgery was

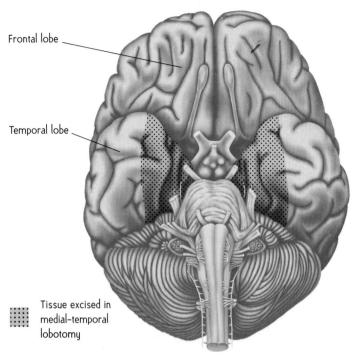

Frontal lobe

Temporal lobe

Tissue excised in medial-temporal lobotomy

7.1 A Sketch of H.M.'s Brain The portions of the medial temporal lobe removed from H.M.'s brain are indicated by the shaded regions.

memory The capacity of the nervous system to acquire and retain usable skills and knowledge, allowing living organisms to benefit from experience.

modal memory model The three-stage memory system that involves sensory memory, short-term memory, and long-term memory.

successful in quieting the seizures, but it also resulted in a most unfortunate side effect: H.M. lost the ability to form new long-term memories.

H.M.'s memory problems are profound. His world stopped in September 1953 when he was 27 years old. He can tell you about his childhood, explain the rules of baseball, and describe members of his family. According to neuropsychological testing, his IQ is slightly above average. Thus, his thinking abilities are perfectly fine, and he can hold a normal conversation as long as he is not distracted. Yet he cannot remember new information. Every moment is new and fresh. He never knows the day of the week, what year it is, or even his own age. The Canadian psychologist Brenda Milner, who has followed H.M.'s case for more than 40 years, and others who work with him continue to have to introduce themselves to him each time they meet. But he does seem to learn some new things . . . he just doesn't know it.

Most impressive is H.M.'s ability to learn new motor tasks. For instance, in one task he was required to trace the outline of a star while watching his hand in a mirror. This is a difficult task, and most people do poorly the first time they try it. H.M. was asked to trace the star 10 times on each of 3 consecutive days. As shown in Figure 7.2, H.M.'s performance improved over the 3 days, meaning that he had retained some information about the task; however, H.M. could not recall ever performing the task previously. H.M.'s ability to learn new motor skills allowed him to get a job at a factory, where he mounted cigarette lighters on cardboard cases. But he cannot give any description of the nature of his job or the place where he worked. The case of H.M. has contributed many clues to how memories are stored in the brain, and we will refer to his case throughout the chapter. ■

In this chapter we are concerned with **memory**, the capacity of the nervous system to acquire and retain usable skills and knowledge, allowing organisms to benefit from experience. We remember millions of pieces of information, from the trivial to the vital. Our entire sense of self is that which we know from our memories, from our recollection of personal experiences. What kind of person are you? Are you shy or outgoing? To answer such questions we rely on our memories of past experiences.

Timeline

1885

It Begins with Forgetting The psychologist Hermann Ebbinghaus studies how quickly people relearn nonsense syllables. He provides compelling evidence that forgetting occurs rapidly at first but then levels off over time.

1932

Reconstructive Memory Psychologist Frederic Bartlett suggests that human memory involves reconstruction and that people's memories are influenced by prior beliefs, challenging the view that memory is an objective recorder of experience.

1940s

Searching for the Engram While searching for the physical brain location of memory, called the engram, Karl Lashley concludes that the brain works as a whole to store memories.

1953

Amnesia and the Medial Temporal Lobes Brenda Milner publishes a landmark account of patient H.M., who underwent surgery for epilepsy and afterward experienced profound memory loss.

Yet as you will see, our memories are often incomplete, biased, and distorted. We are often surprised at how our memories for events differ vastly from those of others who experienced the identical event. There are many sides to every story because each person stores and retrieves memory for the event in distinctive ways. Memory is not like a video camera that faithfully captures objective images. Rather, memory is a story that can be subtly altered through tellings and retellings.

In this chapter we explore the mental processes involved in acquiring and retaining knowledge. Beginning with a discussion of the different stages of memory, we then discuss how different types of information are represented in memories that persist over time. Knowledge about memory has accumulated rapidly over the last decade through the use of brain-imaging techniques, as well as through case studies of those who have developed memory disorders through brain injury. We have also learned a great deal examining how people's memories of past events are selectively distorted. We then explain the basic processes of memory at the biological, individual, and social levels of analysis.

What Are the Basic Stages of Memory?

Since the late 1960s, most psychologists have viewed memory as a form of information processing, in which memory processes occur in much the same way as they do in a computer. A computer receives information through the keyboard or modem, processes it in software, stores it on the hard disk, and then retrieves that information when requested to by the user or another program. From an information-processing perspective, the common way to describe memory is through a three-stage memory system that involves *sensory memory, short-term memory,* and *long-term memory* (Figure 7.3). This general framework is referred to as the **modal memory model** because it is so widely used. The term *modal* refers to the model's being common or standard. Proposed by Richard Atkinson and Richard Shiffrin in

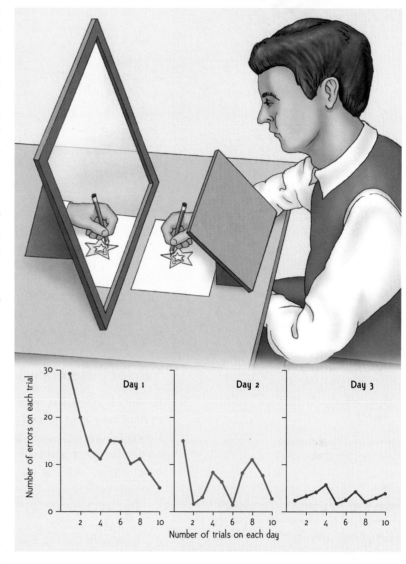

7.2 Tracing Task H.M. was required to trace a star figure while looking in a mirror. This is a difficult task, but H.M. improved in performance over time. However, he retained no conscious awareness that he had ever performed the task before.

1956

Memory Span George Miller, one of the intellectual founders of cognitive neuroscience, notes that short-term memory is limited, and demonstrates that people organize information into meaningful units, or chunks.

1960s

Stage Theories of Memory A number of memory researchers develop stage theories of memory. Most theories include a brief sensory memory buffer, short-term memory, and long-term memory.

1968–1970s

Neuropsychological Case Studies Researchers including Larry Squire, Stuart Zola-Morgan, Lawrence Weiskrantz, Elizabeth Warrington, and Tim Shallice report case studies of individuals with brain injury who have specific memory impairments.

1970s

Levels of Processing Fergus Craik, Robert Lockhart, and Endel Tulving emphasize that the way people process information determines how memory is stored and later retrieved. The more deeply people process information, the better they remember it.

1970s

Episodic Memory Endel Tulving introduces an important distinction between semantic memory of facts and knowledge and episodic memory of personal experiences.

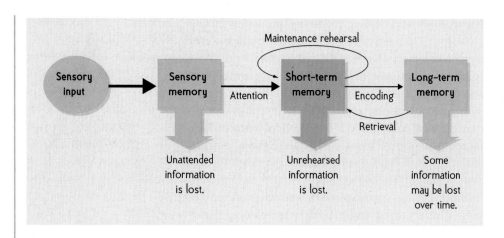

7.3 Three-Stage Memory System The modal memory model serves as a useful framework for thinking about the basic stages of memory.

1968, the modal model has dominated psychological thinking about memory, in spite of its being somewhat inaccurate and incomplete. For instance, many psychological scientists now believe that there are multiple memory systems that do not follow the three-stage sequence (we discuss these alternative views in the next section). However, the modal model is useful for introducing ideas about the memory system, and the vocabulary from this model remains widely used in memory research.

Sensory Memory Is Brief

Sensory information, such as lights, smells, and odors, leaves a trace on the nervous system for a split second and then vanishes. For instance, when you look at something and quickly glance away you can briefly picture the image and recall some of its details. When someone angrily proclaims, "you weren't listening to me," you can often repeat back the last few words the person spoke, even if you were thinking about something else. (Of course, this usually irritates the person further.)

This temporary sensory buffer is referred to as **sensory memory**. Visual sensory memory is also called *iconic memory,* whereas auditory sensory memory is also called *echoic memory.* George Sperling (1960) provided initial empirical support for sensory memory. In this classic experiment, three rows of letters were flashed on a screen for one-twentieth of a second, and then following various delay periods participants were asked to recall one of the rows. After very short delays people could perform this task quite well. But their performance became progressively worse with longer delay periods. Sperling concluded that the iconic memory persisted for about one-third of a second, after which the sensory-memory trace faded and was no longer accessible.

According to many theorists, iconic and echoic memories allow us to experience the world as a continuous stream rather than in discrete sensations, much the same way that a movie projector plays a series of still pictures that follow each other

sensory memory Memory for sensory information that is stored briefly in its original sensory form.

How are perceptual experiences transformed into memories?

1970S

Animal Models of Memory Researchers such as Mortimer Mishkin, Patricia Goldman-Rakic, and Howard Eichenbaum develop memory experiments that can be performed by nonhuman animals.

1970S–1980S

Spreading Activation Models Network models suggest that memories emerge from associations between items based on semantic meanings. Activation of one element in the network leads to activation of other elements that share similar meanings.

1978

Ecological Realism Ulric Neisser emphasizes that researchers need to pay attention to how memory works in the real world, outside of laboratories.

1980S

Multiple Memory Systems A variety of memory processes are identified that involve separate but interacting brain systems, challenging the view that memory is a unitary entity.

1990S–2000S

Imaging and Memory Researchers such as John Gabrieli, Lars Nyberg, Randy Buckner, Steven Petersen, and Barbara Knowlton use brain imaging to explore the neural basis of memory.

closely enough to look like continuous action. When you turn your head, the scene passes smoothly in front of you rather than in jerky bits.

Short-Term Memory Is Active

Information that is attended to is passed from sensory stores to **short-term memory (STM)**, a limited-capacity memory system that holds information in awareness for a brief period. Many contemporary researchers use the term *immediate memory* to emphasize the idea that this temporary buffer consists of our fleeting thoughts, feelings, and impressions of the world. A computer analogy for immediate memory is RAM, which can handle only a small amount of information compared with the vast amount stored in the computer's hard disk. The material in RAM is constantly replaced by new information, and it is lost forever if not saved.

Short-term or immediate memory can hold information for no longer than about 20 seconds; it then disappears unless you actively prevent that from happening by thinking about the information or rehearsing it. For instance, when you call directory assistance for a telephone number, you repeat the number over and over again until you dial it. If the number is busy, or if there is some delay before you can dial it, you may forget the number and have to seek out directory assistance again (and again!). Similarly, suppose you are trying to remember some novel information, such as the three-letter string of consonants X, C, J. As long as you keep repeating the string over and over, you will keep it in short-term memory.

Typically, however, you are bombarded with other events that try to capture your attention, and you may not be able to stay focused. To simulate this, try again to remember X, C, J, but this time as you do it count backward in threes from the number 309. If you are like most people, you will find it difficult to remember the consonants after a few seconds of backward counting. This procedure demonstrates that the longer you spend counting, the less able you are to remember the consonant string. By 18 seconds of counting, people have extremely poor recall for the consonants. This occurs because of interference from previous items in STM.

MEMORY SPAN AND CHUNKING Why do new items interfere with the recall of older items? Short-term memory is a limited resource that can hold only so much information. The cognitive psychologist George Miller noted that STM is generally limited to about seven items, plus or minus two, which is commonly referred to as *memory span*. Some recent work suggests that memory span may be limited to as few as four units on average (Cowan, 2001). Memory span also varies among individuals. Indeed, some tests of intelligence use memory span as a measure of IQ.

Because STM is limited, you might expect people to have great difficulty remembering a string of letters such as

UTUPHDNYUMAUCLABAMIT.

These 20 letters would tax even the largest memory span. But, what if we organized the information into smaller, meaningful units? For instance,

UT-PHD-NYU-MA-UCLA-BA-MIT.

Here we see that the letters can be separated to produce the names of universities or academic degrees. This organization makes them much easier to recall, for two reasons. First, memory span is limited to at most seven items, and probably fewer, but the items can be letters, numbers, words, or even concepts. Second, meaningful units are easier to remember than nonsense units. The process of organizing information

short-term memory (STM) A limited-capacity memory system that holds information in awareness for a brief period of time.

into meaningful units is known as *chunking,* as in breaking down the information into chunks. The more efficiently you chunk information, the more you can remember. Master chess players are able to glance at a chess scenario for a few seconds and then later reproduce the exact arrangement of pieces (Chase & Simon, 1973). They are able to do this because they can chunk the board into a number of meaningful sub-units based on their past experience with the game. Interestingly, if the game pieces are randomly placed on the chessboard so that the arrangement makes no "chess sense," experts are no better than novices at reproducing the board. In general, the greater your expertise with the material, the more efficiently you can chunk information, and therefore the more you can remember. The ability to chunk information efficiently relies on our long-term memory system, which we will discuss shortly.

WORKING MEMORY The initial conception of short-term memory was that it was simply a buffer in which verbal information was rehearsed until it was stored or forgotten. It became apparent, however, that STM is not a single storage system but rather an active processing unit that deals with multiple types of information, such as sounds, images, and ideas. The British psychologist Alan Baddeley and his colleagues developed an influential model of a three-part active memory system that they called working memory (Figure 7.4). **Working memory** is an active processing system that keeps information available so that it can be used for activities such as problem solving, reasoning, and comprehension (Baddeley, 2001). For instance, H.M., the patient described in the beginning of this chapter, is able to keep track of a conversation as long as he stays actively involved in it. The three components of working memory are the *central executive,* the *phonological loop,* and the *visuospatial sketchpad.*

The *central executive* presides over the interactions between the subsystems and long-term memory; it's the boss. It encodes information from the sensory systems and then filters information that is sufficiently important to be stored in long-term memory. It also retrieves information from long-term memory as needed. The central executive relies on two subcomponents that temporarily hold auditory or visual information.

The *phonological loop* encodes auditory information and is active whenever you read, speak, or repeat words to yourself in order to remember them. You've probably noticed this "inner voice" that reads along as your eyes process written material. If you haven't, try to read the next sentence without "speaking" the words in your head. It is difficult to obtain meaning simply by scanning your eyes across the text. Evidence for the phonological loop is found in studies in which people are shown lists of consonants and asked to remember them. People tend to make errors with consonants that sound alike rather than those that look alike, for instance, misremembering a G as a T rather than a Q. Recall is also poorer when many words on a list sound the same compared to when they sound dissimilar, even when the latter words are related to each other in meaning. These examples suggest that words are processed in working memory by how they sound rather than by what they mean.

The *visuospatial sketchpad* processes visual information, such as objects' features and where they are located. Suppose while walking along you see a dog. The visuospatial sketchpad allows you to keep track of both where the dog is located and

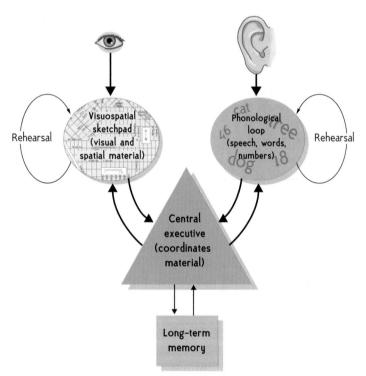

working memory An active processing system that keeps different types of information available for current use.

7.4 Baddeley's Working Memory System
The working memory system developed by Alan Baddeley includes the central executive, phonological loop, and visuospatial sketchpad.

whether it is the sort of dog that one needs to be especially careful to track. The distinction between phonological loop and visuospatial sketchpad has been demonstrated by studying patients with specific brain damage. Patients with some types of brain injury might have great difficulty remembering spatial layouts but have little difficulty remembering words, whereas others show the exact opposite pattern. These sorts of research findings demonstrate that short-term memory consists of much more than simply an all-inclusive buffer.

Long-Term Memory Is Relatively Permanent

When people talk about their memories, they are usually referring to the relatively permanent storage of information known as **long-term memory** (**LTM**). In the computer analogy, LTM is similar to information stored on a hard disk. Unlike computer storage, however, human LTM is nearly limitless. Long-term memory allows you to remember nursery rhymes from childhood, the meanings and spellings of rarely used words such as *aardvark,* and what you had for lunch yesterday.

DISTINGUISHING LONG-TERM MEMORY FROM SHORT-TERM MEMORY Long-term memory is distinct from short-term memory in two important ways, duration and capacity. A controversy exists, however, as to whether LTM represents a truly different type of memory storage from STM. Initial evidence that LTM and STM are separate systems came from research at the individual level of analysis that required people to recall long lists of words. The ability to recall items from the list depended on order of presentation, with items presented early or late in the list remembered better than those in the middle. This better recall of early and late items is known as the **serial position effect** (Figure 7.5), which actually involves two separate effects. The **primacy effect** refers to the better memory people have for items presented first, whereas the **recency effect** refers to our better memory for the most recent items.

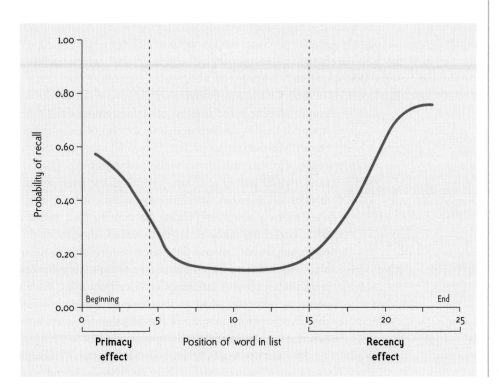

7.5 The Serial Position Effect After hearing a list of items, people typically remember more items from the beginning of the list (primacy effect) and the end of the list (recency effect) than from the middle of the list.

long-term memory (LTM) The relatively permanent storage of information.

serial position effect The ability to recall items from a list depends on order of presentation, with items presented early or late in the list remembered better than those in the middle.

primacy effect In a list, the better memory for items presented first.

recency effect In a list, the better memory for words presented later in the list.

One explanation for the serial position effect relies on a distinction between STM and LTM. As people study the long list, they rehearse the earliest items the most, and that information is transferred into LTM. The last few items, by contrast, are in STM. The idea that primacy effects are due to LTM whereas recency effects are due to STM is supported by studies in which there is a delay between the presentation of the list and the recall task. Such delays interfere with the recency effect, but not the primacy effect, just as you would expect if the former involves STM. However, it is questionable to attribute the recency effect entirely to STM. After all, you probably remember your most recent class better than the classes you had prior to that, even though you are not holding that material in STM. Indeed, studies show a recency effect even for information presented over days and weeks, which makes it unlikely that the material is being maintained in STM. Thus, the recency effect on its own does not prove that STM and LTM are really different types of memory storage.

Perhaps the best support for the distinction between STM and LTM can be found at the biological level of analysis in case studies such as that of H.M. His STM system was perfectly normal and much of his LTM system was intact, but he was unable to transfer new information from STM into LTM. In a different case, a 28-year-old accident victim with damage to the left temporal lobe had extremely poor STM, with a span of only one or two items. However, he had perfectly normal LTM—he had a fine memory for day-to-day happenings and reasonable knowledge of past events (Shallice & Warrington, 1969). Somehow, in spite of the bottleneck in his STM, a normal flow of information was getting into LTM. These case studies demonstrate that LTM can be dissociated from STM. However, the two memory systems are highly interdependent. For instance, to chunk information in STM, people need to form meaningful connections based on information stored in LTM.

WHAT GETS INTO LONG-TERM MEMORY Considering that we are bombarded with so much information and engaged in so many activities, it seems obvious that some type of filtering system or series of rules must constrain what goes into our LTM. Researchers have provided several possible explanations for this process. One possibility is that information enters permanent storage through rehearsal. When you study for exams you often go over the material many times to be sure that you have learned it. Memory researchers have even shown that *overlearning*, in which you keep rehearsing material that you already know pretty well, leads to improved memory, especially over longer periods of time. This is why studying that is spread out over time, known as *distributed practice,* is better remembered than material that is studied in a brief period of time, called *massed practice,* or cramming. The conclusion from many years of research is that studying for shorter periods of time, but spreading your study sessions out over several days or weeks, is the most efficient way to learn.

However, simply repeating or coming into contact with something many times does not mean that we develop long-lasting memory for the event or object. After all, sometimes we have extremely poor memory for objects that are highly familiar. Consider Figure 7.6. Which penny is accurate? Most people have difficulty choosing the correct penny, in spite of the fact that we encounter pennies almost every day.

Another possibility is that only information that helps us adapt to the environment is typically transferred from

EDY (DRAMA (VIDEOS YOU'VE FORGOTTEN YOU'VE SEEN ALREADY (ACTION

(a) (b) (c) (d) (e)

(f) (g) (h) (i) (j)

(k) (l) (m) (n) (o)

7.6 The Penny Quiz Can you tell which drawing of the penny is correct? See the bottom of the page for the correct answer.*

short-term to long-term memory. Out of the billions of sensory experiences and thoughts we have each day, we want to store only information that is useful. Our memory that a penny is money is much more useful to us than remembering its specific features. By storing information that is *meaningful,* organisms can benefit from experience.

Evolutionary theory helps explain how we decide in advance what information will be useful. Memory allows us to use information in a way that assists in reproduction and survival. For instance, animals that can use past experiences to increase their chances of survival have a selective advantage over animals that fail to learn from past experiences. Recognizing a predator and remembering the escape route will help an animal avoid being eaten in the future. Accordingly, remembering which objects are edible, which people are friends and which are enemies, and how to get home are typically not challenging for people with intact memory systems.

Psychological Science *in Action*

Strategies for Improving Memory

In this chapter we describe research indicating how and when people are more likely to remember or forget information. One of the central questions in psychological science is how people learn, and research over the past century has provided a wealth of information that is directly relevant to education. Much of what is found in psychological laboratories makes its way into classrooms, as teachers apply new techniques that have been found to enhance learning. Through research, psychological scientists have also developed specific strategies, called *mnemonics,* for improving memory. By using mnemonic strategies, most people are able to study and remember

*Answer to Figure 7.6: The correct penny is (a).

long lists of information. Let's examine some of the ways that findings from psychological science can help you study more effectively.

Practice. To become proficient you need to practice. The more times you repeat an action, the easier it is to do so on subsequent attempts. Motor skills, such as playing the piano, driving, and golf, become easier with practice.

Elaborate the Material. The deeper the level of processing, the more likely it is that you will remember the material later. This is another reason that critical thinking skills are important. Rather than just reading the material, think about its meaning and how it is related to other concepts. Try to organize the material in a way that makes sense to you, perhaps even putting the concepts into your own words. Indeed, making the material relevant to you is an especially good way to process material deeply, and therefore to remember it easily.

Overlearn. Rehearse material even after you think you have learned it. With the material in front of them, people are often overly confident that they will remember it later. But recognition is easier than recall. Test yourself by waiting a few hours after studying and then try to recall the material. Keep rehearsing until you can recall the material easily. Distributing your study over time rather than cramming will help you retain the information for longer periods of time. Three sessions of two hours each are much better for learning than one six-hour marathon.

Get Some Sleep. There is compelling evidence that sleep may help with the consolidation of memories and that disturbing sleep interferes with learning. How much sleep is necessary to promote learning and memory? A recent study found that a nap of 60 to 90 minutes is just as good as a full night of sleep (Mednick, Nakayama, & Stickgold, 2003). Chronic sleep deprivation, however, has its own costs that interfere with learning. Many students underestimate the importance of getting a good night's sleep.

Use Verbal Mnemonics. How many days are there in September? Most people can readily answer this because of the old saying that begins "Thirty days hath September . . ." Children also learn early that it is "*i before e except after c*" and that "*weird is weird.*" By memorizing such phrases, we more easily remember things that are difficult to remember. Students have long used acronyms to remember information, such as HOMES to remember the great lakes (Huron, Ontario, Michigan, Erie, and Superior). In Chapter 12, you will see the acronym OCEAN will help you remember the major personality traits (openness to experience, conscientiousness, extraversion, agreeableness, and neuroticism). Advertisers often create slogans or jingles that rely on verbal mnemonics so that consumers can't help but remember them. Even complex ideas can be understood through simple mnemonics, such as *cells that fire together wire together* as a way to remember long-term potentiation, discussed in the last chapter as the brain mechanism responsible for learning.

Use Visual Imagery. Creating a mental image of material is especially good for memory. Memory researchers have developed specific strategies that rely on imagery to help people remember long lists of information. One, the *method of loci,* involves visualizing placing objects in familiar locations so that when you have to retrieve the material you simply imagine going back to that location. Other similar techniques involve learning list of key words, or *pegs,* and then hanging new words onto those pegs by visualizing them together. Although these strategies may be useful for remembering long lists of items, they are typically not widely used in real life. For most of us, it is just as easy to keep lists of things we need on our computers or PDAs—or even to write important things down on a piece of paper (and don't forget where you put that!). ■

"You simply associate each number with a word, such as 'table' and 3,467,009."

the Principles | What Are the Basic Stages of Memory?

The information-processing approach to memory occurs in three basic stages: sensory memory, short-term memory, and long-term memory. Sensory memory consists of brief traces on the nervous system that reflect perceptual processes. Material is passed from sensory memory to short-term memory, a limited buffer that holds information in awareness for a brief period of time. An influential model of STM is working memory, which involves a central executive, a phonological loop, and a visuospatial sketchpad. STM is limited to fewer than seven chunks of information, probably around four. The rules for chunking are determined by the meanings provided from long-term memory. LTM is a limitless, relatively permanent store. Only information that is somehow meaningful is stored in LTM. The distinction between STM and LTM is best established by case studies of those with impairments to one but not to the other.

What Are the Different Memory Systems?

Until the last few decades, most cognitive psychologists thought long-term memory was a relatively unitary system. Memories were viewed as differing in terms of strength and accessibility, but generally they were considered to be of the same type. Cognitive psychologists such as Endel Tulving, Dan Schacter, and Larry Squire began to challenge this view in the late 1970s and early 1980s. They argued that memory is not just one monolithic entity, but rather a process that involves a number of interacting systems. Although the systems share a common function—to retain and use information—they encode and store different types of information in different ways. For instance, there are several obvious distinctions to be made between your memory for being able to ride a bicycle and your ability to recall what you ate for dinner last night or that the capital of Canada is Ottawa. The first task requires a behavioral component, an integration of motor and perceptual skills that you acquired over time during development. You are not consciously aware of your efforts to maintain balance or follow the basic rules of the road. By contrast, recalling a specific event or bit of knowledge has no behavioral component, and it sometimes requires a conscious effort to retrieve information from long-term memory.

Scientists do not yet agree on the number of human memory systems. For instance, some researchers have distinguished among memory systems based on how information is stored in memory, such as whether the storage occurs with or without deliberate effort. Other researchers have focused on the types of information stored, such as words and meaning versus particular muscle movements. Because the method of storage often differs depending on the type of information being stored, it is important to know whether reference is being made to process or content of memory. Understanding how different memory systems work has provided tremendous insight into memory, such as why it sometimes fails.

Are there different types of memories, or are all memories essentially the same?

Explicit Memory Involves Conscious Effort

The most basic distinction between memory systems is between those for which we consciously remember and use information and those for which memory occurs

explicit memory The processes involved when people remember specific information.

declarative memory The cognitive information retrieved from explicit memory; knowledge that can be declared.

episodic memory Memory for one's personal past experiences.

semantic memory Memory for knowledge about the world.

implicit memory The process by which people show an enhancement of memory, most often through behavior, without deliberate effort and without any awareness that they are remembering anything.

procedural memory A type of implicit memory that involves motor skills and behavioral habits.

without conscious effort or intention. **Explicit memory** involves the processes used to remember specific information. The information retrieved in explicit memory is known as **declarative memory**, which refers to cognitive information that can be brought to mind, that is, knowledge that can be declared. Many psychological scientists use the terms interchangeably, but explicit memory refers to the *process* of memory whereas declarative memory refers to the *content* of memory.

You use explicit memory when you try to recall what you had for dinner last night or what the word *aardvark* means. Declarative memories can involve words or concepts, visual images, or both. For instance, imagine earth's satellite. You are probably retrieving both the image and name of the moon. Most of the examples we have used so far in this chapter refer to explicit memories.

In 1972, Endel Tulving introduced a further distinction in explicit memory between episodic and semantic memory. **Episodic memory** refers to one's personal past experiences. **Semantic memory** represents one's knowledge of trivial or important facts independent of personal experience. For instance, people know the capitals of countries that they've never visited, and even those who have never played baseball know that three strikes mean you're out.

Evidence that episodic and semantic explicit-memory systems are separate can be found in cases of brain injury in which semantic memory is intact even though episodic memory is impaired. Such an instance was found in a group of British children who experienced brain damage during infancy or early childhood and developed poor memory for episodic information (Vargha-Khadem et al., 1997). They had trouble reporting what they had for lunch, what they were watching on television five minutes ago, or what they did during summer vacation. Their parents reported that the children had to be constantly monitored to make sure they remembered things such as going to school. Remarkably, these children attended mainstream schools and did reasonably well. Moreover, their IQs fell within the normal range. They learned to speak and read, and they could remember a great deal of facts. For instance, when given the question "Who is Martin Luther King Jr.?" one of the children responded, "An American; fought for Black rights, Black rights leader in the 1970 [*sic*]; got assassinated." These children, then, are capable of encoding and retrieving semantic information, but they do not remember how or when they learned the information.

Implicit Memory Occurs without Deliberate Effort

Implicit memory is the process by which people show without deliberate effort and without any awareness that they are remembering something. Implicit memory pervades daily experiences, such as brushing your teeth, or remembering how to get to class. Recall in Chapter 6 we described examples of classical conditioning; these are examples of implicit memory. You experience fear as you enter the dentist's office partially because of past associations (implicit memories) with pain. Implicit memory does not require attention. For instance, you may have had the experience while driving of realizing that you've been daydreaming and have no episodic memory of the past few minutes. However, during that time you *remembered* how to drive and where you were going. Implicit memory happens automatically and without deliberate effort.

An example of implicit memory is **procedural memory**, or *motor memory,* which involves motor skills, habits, and other behaviors that you employ to achieve a goal, such as coordinating muscle movements to ride a bicycle or following the rules of the road while driving. You remember to stop when you see a red light because you have learned to do so, and when you drive home, you follow a specific route without even thinking about it. Our procedural memories have an automatic, unconscious aspect to them. For instance, the next time you are walking try to think about each step involved in the process: first you lift your right foot off the ground and slightly bend the knee, then you extend the foot forward while transferring weight to the right leg, and so on. Most people find that consciously thinking about automatic behaviors, such as walking, interferes with the smooth production of those behaviors.

Implicit memory influences our lives in subtle ways. Many of our attitudes are formed through implicit learning. You might like someone because he or she reminds you of a favorite person, even if you are unaware of the connection. Advertisers rely on implicit memory to influence our purchasing decisions. Constant exposure to brand names makes us more likely to think of them when we buy a product.

At the social level of analysis, implicit attitude formation can even affect our beliefs about whether people are famous. Is Richard Shiffrin famous? Try to think for a second how you know him. You might recall that Richard Shiffrin was one of the psychologists who introduced the modal memory model (which might make him famous in scientific circles), or you might have known that you had read the name before but could not remember where, and therefore you assumed the person was famous. The psychologist Larry Jacoby called this the *false fame effect* (Jacoby, Kelley, Brown, & Jasechko, 1989). Jacoby had research participants read a list of made-up names as a test of pronunciation. The next day subjects completed an apparently unrelated study in which they were asked to read a list of names and decide whether each person was famous or not. Subjects misjudged some of the made-up names from the previous day as being famous. Why did this happen? Subjects knew they had heard the names before but couldn't remember where. Therefore, the implicit memory led them to assume the name was likely that of a famous person.

Implicit memory is also involved in **repetition priming**, the improvement in identifying or processing a stimulus that has previously been experienced. In a typical priming experiment, participants are exposed to a list of words and asked to do something, such as count the number of letters in the words. Following some brief delay, the participants are shown word fragments and asked to complete them with the first word that comes to mind. You can try this yourself. Count the letters in the following words: *appearance, chestnut, patent.* Now, complete the stems app_____, che_____, pat_____, with the first word that comes to mind. The participants in a typical experiment are much more likely to complete the fragments with the words they previously encountered, which were primed and therefore more easily accessible. In our example, you are much more likely to complete the stems as *appearance, chestnut,* and *patent* than, say, *application, cheese,* and *paternal.* This effect occurs even when participants cannot explicitly recall the words in the first task. Even many hours after viewing the primes, participants show implicit memory without explicit recall of the words.

repetition priming The improvement in identifying or processing a stimulus that has previously been experienced.

REVIEWING
the Principles | What Are the Different Memory Systems?

Memory researchers reject the idea that memory involves a single process or brain system. They now agree that there is a fundamental distinction between explicit and implicit memory systems. Explicit memory involves the conscious storage and retrieval of declarative memories, such as meanings of words or personal experiences. Implicit memory refers to an enhancement of memory without effort or awareness. Examples of implicit memory include procedural (or motor) memory, attitude formation, and repetition priming.

How Is Information Organized in Long-Term Memory?

Events that are sufficiently important to be remembered permanently need to be stored in a way that allows for later retrieval. Imagine if a video store just put each video or DVD onto a shelf, wherever there was empty space. What would happen if you wanted to find a certain movie? You would have to go through the entire inventory, film by film, until you encountered the right movie. Just as this system does not work for movies, it also does not work for memory. Rather, memories are stored in an organized fashion. In this section we examine the temporal and organizational principles of long-term memory.

Long-Term Memory Is a Temporal Sequence

In our computer analogy, memory is a process that involves storing new information so that it is available when it is later required. Memory can be divided temporally into three processes: *encoding, storage,* and *retrieval.* In **encoding**, our perceptual experiences are transformed into representations, or *codes,* which are then stored. For instance, when your visual system senses a shaggy, four-legged animal and your auditory system senses barking, you perceive a dog. The concept of "dog" is a *mental representation* for a category of animals that share certain features, such as barking and fur. The mental representation for "dog" differs from that for "cat," even though the two are similar in many ways. You also have mental representations for complex things, such as ideas, beliefs, and the feelings of falling in love. We will discuss representations in more detail in Chapter 8.

Whether simple or complex, information is stored in networks of neurons in the brain. **Storage** refers to the retention of encoded representations over time and corresponds to some change in the nervous system that registers the event. Stored representations are referred to as *memories*. Memories represent many different kinds of information, such as visual images, facts, ideas, tastes, or even muscle movements, such as memory for riding a bicycle. **Retrieval** is the act of recalling or remembering the stored information in order to use it. The act of retrieval often involves an explicit effort to access the contents of memory storage, such as when you try to remember the previous chapter or your fifth birthday. But many times you retrieve information implicitly, without any effort at all, as when you instantly remember the name of an acquaintance you encounter on the street. Thus, retrieval is involved in both explicit and implicit memory systems.

Long-Term Storage Is Based on Meaning

Books are stored by Library of Congress numbers, video stores tend to organize movies by type, and telephone books are organized alphabetically. Memories, however, are not stored by category, type, or number. Memories are stored by meaning. In the early 1970s, the psychologists Fergus Craik and Robert Lockhart developed an influential theory of memory based on depth of elaboration. According to their *levels of processing* model, the more deeply an item is encoded, the more meaning it has and the better it is remembered. Craik and Lockhart proposed that different types of rehearsal lead to differential encoding. **Maintenance rehearsal** involves simply repeating the item over and over again. **Elaborative rehearsal** involves encoding the information

encoding The processing of information so that it can be stored.

storage The retention of encoded representations over time that corresponds to some change in the nervous system that registers the event.

retrieval The act of recalling or remembering stored information in order to use it.

maintenance rehearsal A type of encoding that involves continually repeating an item.

elaborative rehearsal The encoding of information in a more meaningful fashion, such as linking it to knowledge in long-term memory.

Why is meaning important for long-term memory?

in more meaningful ways, such as thinking about the item conceptually or deciding whether it refers to oneself. In other words, we elaborate on the basic information by linking it to knowledge from long-term memory.

How does this model work? Suppose you showed participants a list of words and then asked them to do one of three things. You could ask them to make simple perceptual judgments, such as, "Is each word printed in capital or small letters?" Or you could ask them to judge the acoustics of the word, such as, "Does the word _____ rhyme with boat?" Or you could ask them about the semantic meaning of the words, such as, "Does the word fit the sentence 'They had to cross the _____ to reach the castle'?" Once they had processed the information, you might later ask them to recall as many words as possible (Figure 7.7). You would find that words that were processed at the deepest level, based on semantic meaning, were remembered the best. At the biological (brain systems) level of analysis, brain-imaging studies have shown that semantic encoding activates more brain regions than shallow encoding (Kapur et al., 1994). This greater brain activity is associated with better memory.

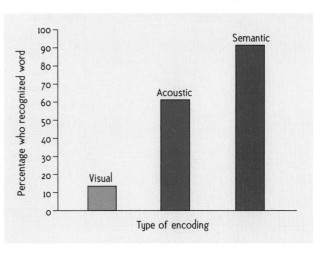

7.7 Encoding Participants are asked to consider a list of words: how the words are printed, how they sound, or what they mean. The more deeply the material is processed, the better it is remembered.

Schemas Provide an Organizational Framework

People store memories by meaning. But how is meaning determined? Earlier, we mentioned chunking as a good way to encode groups of items for easy memory. The more meaningful the chunks, the better they are remembered. Decisions about how to chunk information depend on previous organizational structures in long-term memory. **Schemas** are hypothetical cognitive structures that help us perceive, organize, process, and use information. They help us sort out incoming information and guide our attention to relevant features of the environment. People use their past memories and general knowledge about the world to shape incoming information. By doing so, they construct new memories. They fill in holes, overlook inconsistent information, and interpret meaning on the basis of past experience.

Existing schemas help us make sense of the world, but they can lead to biased encoding. In a classic demonstration conducted in the early 1930s, Frederick Bartlett asked British participants to listen to a Native American folk tale. After a 15-minute delay, Bartlett asked the participants to repeat the story exactly as they heard it. Bartlett found that the participants distorted the story a great deal, and they did so in a consistent way—they altered the story so that it made sense from their own cultural standpoint.

Schemas influence which information is stored in memory. Consider a study in which students read a story about a wild, unruly girl. Some of the participants were initially told that the girl was Helen Keller, whereas others were told it was "Carol Harris," a made-up name (Sulin & Dooling, 1974). One week later, the participants who were initially told the girl was Helen Keller were more likely to mistakenly report having seen the sentence "She was deaf, mute, and blind" than those who thought the story was about Carol Harris. Our schema for Helen Keller includes her various disabilities, and when we retrieve information about Helen Keller from memory, everything we know about her is retrieved along with the specific story we are trying to remember.

Read the following paragraph carefully.

schema A hypothetical cognitive structure that helps us perceive, organize, process, and use information.

The procedure is actually quite simple. First arrange things into different bundles depending on make-up. Don't do too much at once. In the short run this may not seem important, however, complications easily arise. A mistake can be costly. Next, find facilities. Some people must go elsewhere for them. Manipulation of appropriate mechanisms should be self-explanatory. Remember to include all other necessary supplies. Initially the routine will overwhelm you, but soon it will become just another facet of life. Finally, rearrange everything into their initial groups. Return these to their usual places. Eventually they will be used again. Then the whole cycle will have to be repeated. (Bransford & Johnson, 1972)

How easy did you find this to understand? If you had to recall the sentences from this paragraph could you do so? It might surprise you to know that researchers presented this paragraph to college students and that those students found it easy to understand and relatively straightforward to recall. How is that possible? It is easy if you know that the paragraph describes washing clothes. Go back and read the paragraph again. Notice how your schema for doing laundry helps you to understand and remember how the words and sentences are connected to one another.

Information Is Stored in Association Networks

One highly influential set of theories of memory organization is based on *networks of associations*. We can trace back to Aristotle the idea that our knowledge of the world is organized so that things that naturally go together are linked together in storage. Network models of memory emphasize the links between semantically related items. In a network model proposed by Allan Collins and Elizabeth Loftus (Figure 7.8), distinctive features of an item are linked together in such a way as to identify it. Each unit of information in the network is known as a *node*. Each node is connected to many other nodes. When you look at a fire engine, for example, all of the nodes that represent features of a fire engine are activated, and the resulting pattern of activation gives rise to the knowledge that the object is a fire engine rather than, say, a cat. An important feature of network models is that activating one node increases the likelihood that closely associated nodes will also be activated. In Figure 7.8, the closer the nodes, the stronger the association between them and therefore the more likely that activating one will activate the other. Seeing a fire engine activates nodes that indicate other vehicles, so that once your fire-engine nodes are activated, you are much quicker to recognize other vehicles than, for instance, fruits or animals. The idea that activating one node increases the likelihood that associated nodes become active is a central tenet of *spreading activation* models of memory. According to these views, stimuli in working memory activate specific nodes in long-term memory, which increases the ease of access to that material, thereby facilitating retrieval.

The overall organization of associative networks is based on categories that are hierarchically structured, providing a clear and explicit blueprint for where to look for needed information. Given the vast amount of material in memory, it is truly amazing how quickly we can search for and obtain needed memories from storage. Each time you hear a sentence, you not only have to remember what all the words mean, but you also have to recall all relevant information that helps you understand the meaning. For this to occur, the information needs to be organized in some logical fashion. Imagine trying to find a specific file on a full 40-gigabyte hard disk by opening one file at a time. Such a method would be hopelessly slow. Instead, most computer disks are organized into folders, and within each folder are more specialized folders, and so on. This hierarchical storage system allows us to find needed files quickly.

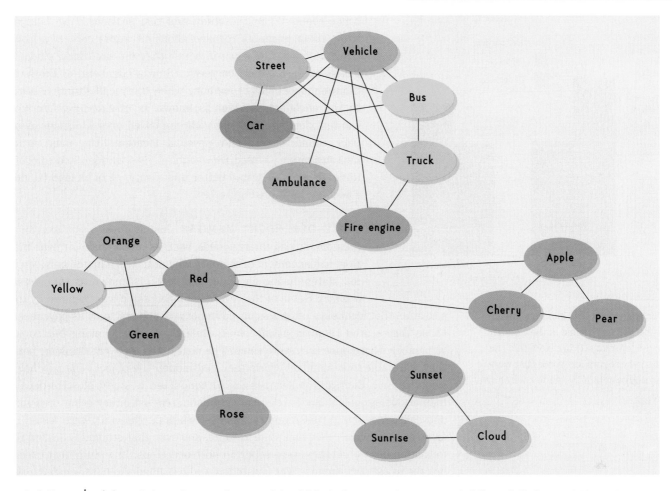

7.8 A Network of Associations A semantic network in which similar concepts are connected through their associations.

Retrieval Cues Provide Access to Long-Term Storage

Anything that helps people access information from long-term memory is known as a *retrieval cue*. Retrieval cues help us sort through the vast amount of data stored in LTM to identify the right information. The power of retrieval cues explains why it is easier to *recognize* than to *recall* information. For example, What is the capital of Vermont? You probably had to spend a moment or two thinking about this, even if you could retrieve the correct answer. Now consider the question, Is the capital of Vermont Concord, Montpelier, or Pierre? Most people find it easier now to remember that Montpelier is Vermont's capital. Seeing the word helps you to retrieve specific information that allows you to answer the question.

ENCODING SPECIFICITY Almost anything can be a retrieval cue, from the smell of turkey, to a favorite song from high school, to walking into a familiar building. Encountering these sorts of stimuli often triggers unintended memories. According to psychologist Endel Tulving's **encoding specificity principle**, any stimulus that is encoded along with an experience can later trigger the memory of the experience. In an interesting study with provocative findings, Steven Smith and his colleagues had students study 80 words in one of two different rooms. The rooms differed in a number of ways, including size, location, and scent in the room. The students were then tested for recall either in the room in which they studied or the

How are people able to retrieve specific memories?

encoding specificity principle Any stimulus that is encoded along with an experience can later trigger memory for the experience.

265

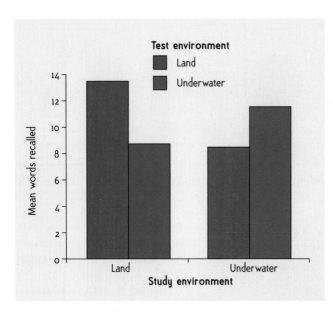

Test environment
■ Land
■ Underwater

7.9 Context-Dependent Memory Mean number of words recalled in the Godden and Baddeley study (1975). Note that the best memory occurs for words that were studied and tested in the same environment.

other room. When the study and test sessions were held in the same room, students recalled about 49 words correctly. However, when tested in the room in which they did not study, students recalled only 35 words correctly (Smith, Glenberg, & Bjork, 1978). Such enhancement of memory when the recall situation is similar to the encoding situation is known as *context-dependent memory*. Context-dependent memory can be based on such things as odors, background music, and physical location. The most dramatic demonstration showed that scuba divers who learned information underwater later tested better underwater than on land (Godden & Baddeley, 1975; see Figure 7.9).

STATE-DEPENDENT MEMORY Just as physical context can affect memory, so can internal cues, such as mood states or even inebriation. Enhancement of memory when there is a match between internal states during encoding and recall is known as *state-dependent memory*. Some of the research on this topic was inspired by the observation that alcoholics often misplaced important objects, such as paychecks, because they stored them in a safe place while they were drinking but could not remember where once they were sober. The next time they were drinking, however, they were able to remember where they had hidden the object. The psychological scientist Eric Eich and colleagues (1975) conducted a study of state-dependent memory using marijuana. Participants studied a test list either sober or high. Eich and colleagues found that memory was best when participants were tested in the same state in which they had studied. Note, however, that students recalled the information best when they were sober on both occasions. In a study that used alcohol, the worst performance was for students who studied when intoxicated and took the test sober. They did worse than students who studied sober and took the test intoxicated. Students who studied intoxicated and took the test intoxicated did much worse than students who were sober at both study and test (Goodwin, Powell, Bremer, Hoine, & Stern, 1969). State-dependent memory works because internal state is an additional retrieval cue that can facilitate the recovery of information from long-term memory.

REVIEWING
the Principles | How Is Information Organized in Long-Term Memory?

Memory is composed of a temporal sequence of encoding, storage, and retrieval. Encoding and storage are organized so that information can be quickly retrieved. Human memory is stored according to meaning, and the more that meaning is elaborated at time of storage, the better the later memory will be. Shallow encoding does not lead to long-term storage. Schemas help people perceive, organize, and process information, which is then stored if processed deeply. Hierarchical networks of associated nodes provide semantic links between related items. Activation of a node spreads throughout the rest of its network. Retrieval cues help access stored information. Contextual cues and internal states can be retrieval cues.

What Brain Processes Are Involved in Memory?

In the first part of this chapter, we focused on the cognitive dimensions of memory, including types of memory and the kinds of information that are stored in memory. Now we need to ask another fundamental question: What role does biology play in the formulation of our memories? In this section, we focus on the biological level of analysis to examine brain structures involved in memory, as well as some of the neurochemical processes that affect memory. As an outgrowth of the biological revolution, there has been tremendous progress over the past two decades in understanding what happens in the brain when we store and retrieve memories. Studies of patients with brain injuries have provided the basic foundations for understanding the neural basis of memory, and brain-imaging techniques have permitted an understanding of memory processes in the healthy brain.

There Has Been Intensive Effort to Identify the Physical Location of Memory

Locating where in the brain memories are stored has been one of the central goals of memory researchers during the twentieth century. As you learned in Chapter 4, the Harvard University professor Karl Lashley spent much of his career trying to localize memory. He used the term *engram* to refer to the physical site of memory storage. Lashley first trained rats to run a maze. He then removed different areas of their cortices to test how much of the learning they retained. Lashley found that the size of the area removed rather than its location was most important in predicting retention. Thus, he concluded that memory is distributed throughout the brain rather than in any specific location, an idea known as *equipotentiality*. It turns out that Lashley was partially right, but also quite wrong.

It is now well established that memories are not stored in any one specific brain location. Rather, memories are stored in multiple regions of the brain and linked together through memory circuits, as proposed by Donald Hebb's idea that neurons that fire together wire together (see Chapter 6). This is not to suggest that all areas of the brain are equally involved in memory. As you'll see below, a great deal of neural specialization occurs, with different brain regions responsible for storing different aspects of information. Indeed, different memory systems, such as declarative and procedural memories, use different brain regions. Lashley's failure to find critical brain regions for memory is due to at least two factors. First, the maze task involved multiple sensory systems (such as vision and smell), so the rats could compensate for the loss of one by using other senses. Second, Lashley did not examine subcortical areas, which are now known to be important for the retention of memories.

Over the past three decades, research at the biological (brain systems) level of analysis has identified a number of brain regions that contribute to learning and memory. For instance, we know from patient H.M. that the regions within the temporal lobes are important for the ability to encode new memories. It is clear that different brain regions are involved in different memory systems. You will see that the temporal lobes are important for declarative memory, but less important for implicit processes, such as motor learning, classical conditioning, and fear learning. We noted in Chapter 4 that the cerebellum plays a role in how motor actions are learned and remembered. Similarly, the basal ganglia, another brain region involved in motor actions, is important for classical conditioning, such as salivating at the sight of a tasty sandwich (Packard & Knowlton, 2002). One type of classical conditioning, fear learning, relies on the amygdala. You might recall from Chapter 6 that without an amygdala, animals cannot learn to fear objects that signal danger. In this section, we describe the most important brain systems involved in memory.

The Medial Temporal Lobes Are Important for Consolidation of Declarative Memories

The brain area that has been repeatedly identified as important for declarative memory is the middle section of the temporal lobes. Recall from Chapter 4 that Wilder Penfield, of the Montreal Neurological Institute, found that stimulating the temporal lobes led to reports of specific memories in some epilepsy patients. The medial temporal lobe consists of a number of structures relevant to memory, including the amygdala, hippocampus, and rhinal cortex, an area located around the front of the hippocampus (Figure 7.10). As was described earlier, H.M.'s brain surgery led to an inability to form new memories. Using brain imaging, Sue Corkin of MIT and her colleagues found that a large portion of H.M.'s hippocampus was removed, as well as a small section of nearby temporal lobe (Corkin, Amaral, Gonzalez, Johnson, & Hyman, 1997). It is now clear that damage to this region causes *anterograde amnesia,* which is the inability to store new explicit memories. However, it is *not* the case that the medial temporal lobes are the final repository of memory. After all, H.M. could remember things from before his surgery. Thus, damage to the medial temporal lobes interrupts storage of new material without impairing access to old material.

The transfer of contents from immediate memory into long-term memory occurs through a process known as **consolidation**. Consolidation results from changes in the strength of neural connections that support memory. Current thinking suggests that the medial temporal lobes are responsible for coordinating the strengthening between neuronal activations, but the actual storage most likely occurs in the particular brain regions engaged during perception, processing, and analysis of the material being learned. For instance, visual information is stored in the cortical areas involved in visual perception, whereas sound is stored in those areas involved in auditory perception. In one study, researchers exposed participants either to pictures of common objects (for example, dogs) or to their associated sounds (barking)

consolidation A hypothetical process involving the transfer of contents from immediate memory into long-term memory.

Rhinal cortex   Amygdala

Hippocampus

7.10 The Major Regions of the Medial Temporal Lobe

and asked the participants to become very familiar with the stimuli. Two days later, while the participants underwent brain imaging, they were reexposed to the pictures or sounds and then asked to recall the stimuli as vividly as possible. Thus, some participants tried to remember how the objects looked, whereas others tried to remember how they sounded. The same areas that became activated when participants were exposed to the stimuli became reactivated when the participants vividly recollected those stimuli (Figure 7.11; Wheeler, Petersen, & Buckner, 2000). Thus, memory for sensory experiences involves reactivating the cortical circuits involved in perceiving them. The medial temporal lobes form links or pointers between the different sites of storage and direct the gradual strengthening of the connections between these links (Squire, Stark, & Clark, 2004).

It has been proposed that once memories are activated they need to be consolidated again in order to be stored back in memory, a process known as *reconsolidation* (LeDoux, 2002). This is sort of like taking a book out of the library—the book must be returned to the shelf for permanent storage. Evidence for reconsolidation can be found by administering drugs that interfere with memory storage after a memory has been activated (Debiec, LeDoux, & Nader, 2002). This suggests that memories for past events can be affected by new circumstances once they are retrieved, so that the newly reconsolidated memories may differ from their original versions. In our library book analogy, this would be similar to what would happen if some pages were torn out of the book before it is returned. The book that is placed back on the shelf is slightly different from the one that was taken out; the information contained in those torn-out pages is no longer available for retrieval. The reconsolidation process repeats itself each time memory is activated and placed back in storage, which may explain why our memories for events can change over time. As you might imagine, this theory has received considerable attention, for it not only has implications for what it means to remember something but also opens up the intriguing possibility that bad memories could be erased by activating them and then interfering with reconsolidation.

LOCALIZING FUNCTION WITHIN MEDIAL TEMPORAL LOBES Which parts of the medial temporal lobes are most relevant to memory? Studies of primates with surgical lesions to the medial temporal lobes have given us a pretty good idea. In the 1970s, Mortimer Mishkin at the National Institute of Mental Health developed the first successful animal model of memory. In these studies, monkeys are placed in a box with a retractable door. In the first phase of the study, the monkey learns that a food reward is hidden under an object (Figure 7.12). Next, the door closes, then opens to reveal two objects: one that previously hid the reward and a new object. The rule is that the food reward is always under the novel object. This provides a good measure not only of learning, since the monkey has to learn the rule, but also of memory, since the monkey must remember which of the two objects was presented previously. The regions that are most important for this task are the hippocampus and surrounding rhinal cortex. Lesions to other areas of the medial temporal lobes do not interfere with this type of memory. Psychological scientists now view the hippocampus and surrounding regions as essential for declarative memory (Eichenbaum, 2001; Squire et al., 2004).

7.11 Brain Activation from Various Stimuli Four horizontally sliced brain images acquired using magnetic resonance imaging show regions of the brain active during perception of pictures (top left) and sounds (top right), and subsequently during retrieval of the same pictures (bottom left) and sounds (bottom right) from long-term memory. These data indicate that regions of sensory cortex are reactivated when we remember sensory-specific information.

Can old memories be changed by new circumstances?

(a)

Cue and response

Food reward

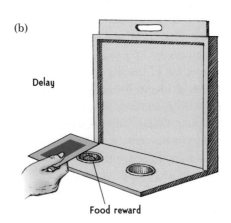

(b)

Delay

Cue and response

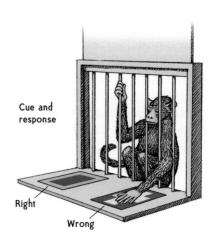

Right

Wrong

Food reward

7.12 Mishkin's Animal Model of Memory (a) The monkey is presented with a sample item, the red and yellow object. (b) After a delay, the monkey is presented with the same object and a new object. The monkey now has to select the new object, which implies it remembers the first object.

SPATIAL MEMORY Another important memory function of the hippocampus is **spatial memory**, which is memory for the physical environment and includes such things as direction, location of objects, and cognitive maps. A good example of this type of learning is the *Morris water maze test,* in which a rat is placed into a circular pool of murky water and learns to swim to an invisible platform that is just below the surface (Figure 7.13). Rats can learn this task quite readily, and they do so by using cues from the environment to remember where to find the platform. Rats with hippocampal damage are severely impaired at this task. The role of the hippocampus in spatial memory is supported by *place cells,* which are neurons that fire only when a rat returns to a specific location, such as one part of a maze. When rats are placed in novel environments, none of the place cells fire. But as the rat becomes familiar with the environment, its hippocampal place cells acquire a link to aspects of the surroundings. This suggests that the hippocampus helps animals to orient and find their way. Indeed, birds that rely on memory to find stored food, such as food-caching chickadees, have larger hippocampal regions than birds that do not store food. Patients with damage to the hippocampus also have trouble remembering the location of objects in pictures (Piggott & Milner, 1993), suggesting that the hippocampus is also important for spatial memory in humans.

7.13 The Morris Water Maze Test A rat is placed in the Morris water maze and must find the hidden platform. After many trials, the animal learns where the platform is hidden and swims directly to it.

Hidden platform

Before learning

After learning

The Frontal Lobes Are Involved in Many Aspects of Memory

It has long been known that the frontal lobes are important to many aspects of memory, including episodic memory, working memory, spatial memory, time sequences (see below), and various aspects of encoding and retrieval (Wager & Smith, 2003). Extensive neural networks connect the prefrontal cortex with other brain regions involved in memory, such as the medial temporal areas. Thus, the frontal lobes work together with other brain regions to coordinate the encoding, storage, and retrieval of memory.

Patients with damage to prefrontal regions typically do not develop profound memory loss, but they often have great difficulty remembering the time sequence of events, such as which of two events happened first. Moreover, they often can't tell you where or when they learned information. The inability to recall the circumstances under which learning took place has been reported for elderly individuals, who often experience signs of frontal lobe deficits, as well as for young children, who have immature frontal lobes.

Brain-imaging studies have provided compelling evidence that the frontal lobes are crucial for encoding (Buckner, Kelley, & Petersen, 1999). Moreover, deeper encoding tasks are more likely to lead to frontal activation than are shallow encoding tasks. Frontal activation is also a particularly good predictor for which events are later remembered or forgotten (Brewer, Zhao, Glover, & Gabrieli, 1998). For instance, during a memory task researchers compared words that were later remembered with words that were later forgotten. As you can see in Figure 7.14, words that were later remembered were associated with stronger activation of the frontal lobes (Wagner et al., 1998). Interestingly, brain activity in regions that are involved in processing specific types of information is associated with better memory for that type of information (Paller & Wagner, 2002). For example, the medial prefrontal cortex is selectively active when people think about themselves. As a result, activity in this region predicts memory for information encoded about the self, but not for information encoded about others (Macrae, Moran, Heatherton, Banfield, & Kelley, 2004).

7.14 Brain Activation in Memory Tasks This graph shows brain activation in the left prefrontal area during a memory task. Words that are later remembered elicit a larger response than words that are later forgotten.

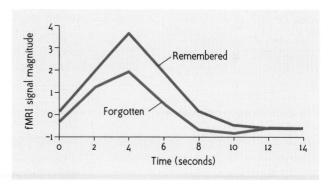

HEMISPHERICAL ASYMMETRIES IN ENCODING AND RETRIEVAL There is some evidence that encoding and retrieval occur in different hemispheres. The psychologist Endel Tulving and his colleagues analyzed a number of studies that used imaging to assess the encoding and retrieval of episodic experiences. When they looked at the brain-activation patterns, they found that the left frontal lobes were more active during encoding, whereas the right frontal lobes were more active during episodic retrieval (Habib, Nybert, & Tulving, 2003; Tulving, Kapur, Craik, Moscovitch, & Houle, 1994). They called this pattern the *hemispherical encoding retrieval asymmetry,* or *HERA.* William Kelley and his colleagues have argued that the pattern of left hemisphere activation might be due to the types of information used in the tasks. They argue that any stimulus that involves verbal information activates the left hemisphere, whereas objects that do not invoke verbal information (such as unfamiliar faces) activate the right hemisphere. Interestingly, nameable objects that contain both visual and verbal information (such as a picture of a frog; see Figure 7.15) activate both left and right frontal areas during encoding (Kelley et al., 1998). Thus, the asymmetry in memory applies more to the type of material studied than to memory processes themselves.

spatial memory Memory for the physical environment that includes such things as location of objects, direction, and cognitive maps.

7.15 Activation in Frontal Brain Regions
Frontal regions active during memory formation may depend on the material being memorized. Memorization of verbal material (words) activates the left frontal cortex, whereas memorization of nonverbal, pictorial material (unfamiliar faces) activates the right frontal cortex. Interestingly, memorization of objects (associated with both an image and a name) activates both the right and the left frontal cortices.

FRONTAL LOBES AND WORKING MEMORY So what do the frontal lobes do in memory? One hypothesis is that they play a role in working memory (Curtis & D'Esposito, 2003). Working memory holds information on line so that it can be used to solve problems, understand conversations, and follow plans. Patients with damage to the frontal areas often have difficulty following plans and goals, and monkeys given frontal lesions show impaired working memory (Goldman-Rakic, Scalaidhe, & Chafee, 2000). In one task, the monkey watches the experimenter hide a reward under one of two objects. After a delay, the monkey is allowed to reach for the object covering the reward. Monkeys with frontal lesions have difficulty with this task. Interestingly, human infants have trouble with a similar task. This further implicates the frontal lobes in working memory, since the frontal lobes are not fully matured until much later in development (Diamond & Doar, 1989).

Frontal regions become active when information is being either retrieved from long-term memory into working memory or encoded from working memory into long-term memory. For example, when you enter the classroom, the frontal lobes oversee retrieval of stored knowledge from neural networks that are spread throughout cortical and subcortical locations. This information helps you remember what to do when you enter the room (sit down), who the person is at the front of the class (the professor), and the meaning of the sounds emanating from the professor's mouth. The frontal lobes and medial temporal lobes then work together to consolidate long-term declarative memory storage for the lecture. The hippocampus helps strengthen associations between the events in working memory so that new experiences are consolidated into permanent storage.

Neurochemistry Influences Memory

It is known that memory involves alterations in connections across synapses. As memories are consolidated, distributed networks of neurons become linked together. Research has shown that a variety of neurotransmitters can weaken or enhance memory. Collectively, these neurotransmitters are known as *memory modulators,* because they modulate, or modify, the storage of memory.

NEUROCHEMISTRY INDICATES MEANINGFULNESS OF STIMULI Earlier we pointed out that animals store only information that is meaningful. Memory modulation is the system that evolution has bestowed on organisms to help determine whether something is important. Important events lead to neurochemical changes that produce emotional experiences. An animal that outruns a predator has experienced a fear reaction that helps to stamp in avoidance of that predator. A child who eats a good-tasting food experiences a rewarding sensation that is easily remembered, as parents who have watched their preverbal children point at cookie jars can readily attest. Events that produce emotional reactions are especially likely to be stored in memory.

So what are the neurochemical signals that indicate that an experience is meaningful? When animals are engaging in minimally arousing tasks, little memory is later shown for those tasks. However, animals injected with epinephrine, which induces a state of arousal, show significant memory enhancement for trivial events. It is as if the jolt of epinephrine gives the message "Remember me!" Of course, epinephrine is in the periphery of the body, not in the brain, and so it does not have a direct effect on memory. Researchers initially believed that this effect occurs because epinephrine causes a release of glucose, which then enters the brain and influences memory storage. The role of glucose is also implicated by a study in which elderly participants were given a memory test after consuming lemonade with either glucose (sugar) or saccharine (a sugar substitute). Those who had glucose had better memory for the studied items the next day (Gold, 1987). More recent studies suggest that epinephrine enhances memory because of its effect on norepinephrine activity in the amygdala, as we will see shortly. Other drugs, such as opiates, alcohol, and surgical anesthetics, may also interfere with memory through their effects on norepinephrine (McGaugh, 2002).

THE AMYGDALA AND THE NEUROCHEMISTRY OF EMOTION The amygdala is the prime candidate for the brain structure that controls the modulating effects of neurotransmitters on memory. It is the limbic structure closely tied to fear reactions, and it is located within the medial temporal lobe. Direct stimulation of the amygdala can enhance or impair memory, and damaging the pathways leading to or exiting it eliminates the effects of drugs on memory. As mentioned before, the modulation of memory occurs because of alterations in the activity of norepinephrine receptors in the amygdala. Any arousing event causes greater activity of norepinephrine receptors, which strengthens memory.

In humans, the amygdala is activated during recall of emotional film clips but not during recall of neutral film clips (Cahill et al., 1996). Interestingly, there appears to be a gender difference in this effect, such that emotional memory activates the right (but not left) amygdala in men and the left (but not right) amygdala in women (Cahill et al., 2001). Moreover, women have better memory than men for emotional events. For instance, Turhan Canli and colleagues (2002) showed men and women neutral and negative pictures and found that women not only reported greater emotional reactions to the negative pictures but also showed much better memory for those pictures. This may be because women process emotional information differently, such as rehearsing it and thinking about it more, or because they focus on different aspects of stimuli (Cahill, 2003). The effects of amygdala activity on memory are long lasting. Amygdala activity at encoding predicts increased memory for emotional pictures a year later (Dolcos, Labar, & Cabeza, 2005).

When people experience severe stress or emotional trauma—such as being in a serious accident, being raped, being in combat, or surviving a natural disaster—they often have negative reactions long after the threat has passed. In severe cases, people develop **posttraumatic stress disorder** (**PTSD**), a serious mental health disorder that involves frequent and recurring unwanted thoughts related to the trauma, including nightmares, intrusive thoughts, and flashbacks. Those with PTSD often have chronic tension, anxiety, and health problems, and they may experience memory and

posttraumatic stress disorder (PTSD) A mental disorder that involves frequent nightmares, intrusive thoughts, and flashbacks related to an earlier trauma.

273

attention problems in their daily lives. PTSD involves an unusual problem in memory, in that it is caused by the inability to forget. PTSD is associated with an attentional bias, such that people with PTSD are hypervigilant to stimuli associated with their traumatic event. For instance, soldiers with combat-induced PTSD show increased physiological responsiveness to pictures of troops, sounds of gunfire, and even words associated with combat. Exposure to stimuli associated with past trauma leads to activation of the amygdala (Rauch, van der Kolk, Fisler, & Alpert, 1996). It is as if the severe emotional event is "overconsolidated," burned into memory.

Knowing that neurochemistry can modify the formation of memory has led researchers to develop methods that may help people remember things they *want* to remember or forget things they *don't want* to remember.

Thinking Critically

Should Memory Be Altered by Drugs?

A paradox of memory is that many times we have trouble remembering things we want to remember, whereas we often have trouble forgetting things we want to forget. During an exam you might struggle to remember the answer to a question; at the same time you might feel anxious because you remember how it felt when you bombed on an exam in the past. The anxious memories might even be interfering with your ability to remember the relevant material. Or perhaps you witnessed a horrible car crash and you keep recalling gruesome details of the accident, causing you to relive your negative response over and over again. Wouldn't it be great if you could take a pill that would help you forget those unwanted memories? Equally desirable might be a pill that would help students better remember material for exams or aging baby boomers better remember where they left their car keys. We are now witnessing an explosion of drug therapies aimed at altering human memory capacities (Marshall, 2004). Let's consider some of these methods as well as their ethical implications.

In 1998, Eric Kandel, the Nobel laureate mentioned in Chapter 6, launched a company to develop drug treatments for learning and memory disorders associated with diseases such as Alzheimer's. Drawing on Kandel's own research into the molecular basis of memory, his company is developing drugs that alter gene expression to enhance learning and memory. Recall the transgenic "Doogie" mice that became fast learners. It is possible to alter gene expression, and indeed DNA itself, to produce better learners. But can we do the same to help people forget? Researchers at Emory University studied people who were trying to overcome their fear of heights through virtual reality training (Ressler et al., 2004). Those who received a drug that affected NMDA receptors (recall from Chapter 6 that this receptor is involved in long-term learning) responded much better than those given a placebo. In essence, the drug helped them to forget their fears. In other research, those given a type of beta blocker (drugs normally used to treat hypertension) right after experiencing a trauma had fewer emotional memories for that event months later (Pitman et al., 2002). Many other research efforts are underway to produce memory-altering drugs.

On the surface, the ability to enhance wanted memories and eliminate unwanted ones seems like a good idea (Figure 7.16). As with many recent neuroscientific advances, however, the possibility of altering basic psychological functioning raises important issues. One is whether in some contexts memory enhancement might be like athletic performance enhancement obtained through steroids or other muscle-building supplements. Knowing that an athlete performed some amazing feat while using drugs diminishes our appreciation of that performance. How is competition meaningful unless the playing field is level? If students could take a drug that would help them do better on exams, how should their performances be graded?

A critical issue about using drugs to increase forgetting is whether taking the emotional sting out of life will make us less human. Clearly such drugs are called for in treating conditions such as PTSD, but what about taking a pill to erase the memory of a recent breakup? Feeling sorrow, embarrassment, and fear is part of being human. If we could give people a pill after a loved one dies so that they do not feel grief, would that be a good thing? We grieve because we love; does love change if we don't grieve? If we wiped out negative memories, would that diminish our appreciation of life's positive events? Even if beta blockers might reduce long-term problems for some people, should we routinely give those drugs after traumatic events, even before knowing which people will go on to develop unwanted and persistent memories?

Some have argued that any drug that alters normal cognitive processes is unnatural and thus unethical. But is pharmacological treatment of traumatic memories really any different from medical treatments for any disorder? Throughout this book, we discuss how neuroscientific discoveries are providing ways to better understand and treat a number of psychological disorders, such as schizophrenia and depression. New medications have helped many afflicted individuals. How does using medicine to treat those with mental illnesses differ from using medicine to improve memory among those with Alzheimer's or to help sexual assault victims forget their traumatic experiences? Or are we concerned only about the potential for abuse among those who do not really suffer from memory impairments? Perhaps the critical question to resolve is where we draw the line between treatment and enhancement. ■

7.16 Altering Memories In the 2004 film *Eternal Sunshine of the Spotless Mind,* Joel Barish (played by Jim Carrey) tries to erase the painful memories of a recent breakup by undergoing an experimental procedure that eliminates unwanted memories. In real life, researchers struggle with the ethical implications of developing drugs that can alter memory.

REVIEWING
the Principles | What Brain Processes Are Involved in Memory?

Research during the past thirty years has demonstrated that memories are encoded in distributed networks of neurons in relatively specific brain regions. It is now known that damage to the medial temporal lobes, especially the hippocampus or rhinal cortex, causes significant memory disturbances. These medial temporal regions are important for the consolidation of declarative memories into storage. The sites of memory storage are the brain structures involved in perception. The frontal lobes are especially important for working memory, and a variety of neurotransmitters modulate memory storage. Fear causes activation of the amygdala, which is associated with the strengthening of memories.

When Do People Forget?

Up until now we have been focusing on remembering information. But along the way we have noted that failures of memory are extremely common. **Forgetting** is the inability to retrieve memory from long-term storage. Forgetting is an everyday experience that is perfectly normal. Ten minutes after you see a movie you might remember plenty of details, but the next day you probably remember mostly the plot

forgetting The inability to retrieve memory from long-term storage.

and the main characters. Years later you might remember the gist of the story, or you might not remember having seen the movie at all. We forget far more than we ever remember.

Most people bemoan forgetting, wishing that they could better recall information they study for exams, the names of childhood friends, or even the names of all the seven dwarfs. But imagine what life would be like if you couldn't forget. You would walk up to your locker and recall 10 or 20 different combinations. Consider the case of a Russian newspaper reporter who had nearly perfect memory. You could read him a tremendously long list of items, and as long as he could spend a few moments visualizing the items, he could recite them back, even many years later. But he was tortured by his condition and was eventually institutionalized. His memory was so cluttered with information that he had great difficulty functioning in normal society. Paradoxically, not being able to forget is as maladaptive as not being able to remember. It is therefore not surprising that memory tends to be best for meaningful and important points. We remember the forest rather than the individual trees. Normal forgetting helps us remember and use information that is important.

The study of forgetting has a long history in psychological science. Hermann Ebbinghaus, a German psychologist working at the individual level of analysis in the late nineteenth century, provided compelling evidence that forgetting occurs rapidly over the first few hours and days but then levels off. He used the so-called *methods of savings* to examine how long it took for people to relearn lists of nonsense syllables. Presumably, the more slowly people relearned the list, the greater evidence there was of forgetting. We've learned a great deal about forgetting over the last century. Harvard psychologist Daniel Schacter identifies what he calls *the seven sins of memory* (Schacter, 1999). These so-called sins are all too familiar for most people (Table 7.1 on p. 278). They are also characteristics that are useful or perhaps even necessary for survival. Schacter argues that the seven sins of memory are by-products of otherwise desirable aspects of human memory. The first three sins are related to forgetting: *transience, blocking,* and *absentmindedness* (we will consider some of the other sins later in this chapter).

Transience Is Caused by Interference

Do people really forget things, and if so, why?

Memory **transience** refers to the pattern of forgetting over time, such as was obtained by Ebbinghaus in his studies of nonsense syllables. What causes transience? Many early theorists argued that forgetting was the result of *decay* of the memory trace in our nervous system. Indeed, there is some evidence that forgetting occurs for memories that are not used. However, research over the last few decades has established that most forgetting occurs because of *interference* from other information. There are two ways that additional information can lead to forgetting. In **proactive interference**, prior information inhibits our ability to remember new information. For instance, if you have a new locker combination each year, you may have difficulty remembering it because you keep recalling the old one. Indeed, because the physical context provides retrieval cues for that earlier combination, it becomes especially difficult to remember the new one while standing in front of your locker. In **retroactive interference**, new information inhibits our ability to remember old information. Now that you finally know your new locker combination, you may find that you have forgotten the old one. Figure 7.17 shows the typical experimental tests that have been used to demonstrate proactive and retroactive interference. In both cases, we forget because competing information displaces the information we are trying to retrieve.

transience The pattern of forgetting over time.

proactive interference When prior information inhibits the ability to remember new information.

retroactive interference When new information inhibits the ability to remember old information.

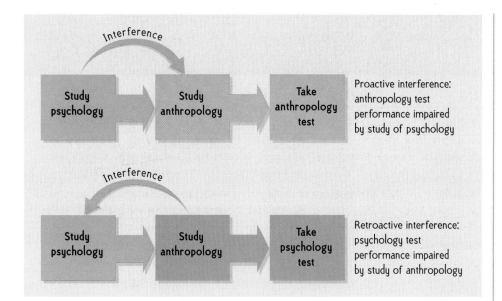

7.17 Proactive and Retroactive Interference Proactive interference occurs when material that is already known interferes with the ability to remember new information, whereas retroactive interference occurs when new material interferes with memory for old material.

Blocking Is Temporary

Blocking occurs when a person has a temporary inability to remember something that is known. Temporary blockages are common and frustrating, such as forgetting the name of a favorite CD, forgetting lines during a play, or forgetting someone's name when you introduce them. Another good example of blocking is the **tip-of-the-tongue phenomenon**, first described by Roger Brown and David MacNeill, in which people experience great frustration as they try to recall specific words that are somewhat obscure. The researcher Alan Brown (no relation to Roger) has shown that tip-of-the-tongue can be reliably produced in the laboratory (Brown, 1991). For instance, when asked to provide a word that means "patronage bestowed on a relative, in business or politics," people often struggle. Or how about "an astronomical instrument for finding position"? Sometimes people know which letter the word begins with, how many syllables it has, and even what it sounds like, but they can't pull the precise word into working memory. Did you know the words were *nepotism* and *sextant*? Blocking often occurs because of interference from words that are similar in some way, such as in sound or meaning. These similar words often keep recurring as we try to remember the target word.

Absentmindedness Results from Shallow Encoding

Absentmindedness describes the inattentive or shallow encoding of events—for instance, forgetting where you left your keys, the name of a person you met five minutes before, or whether you took your vitamins this morning. The major cause of absentmindedness is failing to pay sufficient attention to details. Consider the fascinating phenomenon of "change blindness." Imagine that you are standing around and someone walks up to you and asks directions. While you are answering, two workers, holding a door, cut between you, so you momentarily lose sight of the person asking for directions. Do you think you would notice if the person standing in front of you was switched? When Daniel Simons and Daniel Levin conducted this study, only half the participants noticed the change (Simons & Levin, 1998). Simons and Levin refer to the inability to detect changes to an object or a scene as *change blindness*. Interestingly, in the original study, older people were especially likely not to notice a change in the

blocking The temporary inability to remember something that is known.

tip-of-the-tongue phenomenon When people experience great frustration as they try to recall specific words that are somewhat obscure.

absentmindedness The inattentive or shallow encoding of events.

TABLE 7.1	Seven Sins of Memory		
ERROR	**TYPE**	**EXAMPLE**	
Transience	Forgetting	Reduced memory over time, such as forgetting the plot of a movie.	
Absentmindedness	Forgetting	Reduced memory due to failing to pay attention, such as losing your keys or forgetting a lunch date.	
Blocking	Forgetting	Inability to remember needed information, such as failing to recall the name of a person you meet on the street.	
Misattribution	Distortion	Assigning a memory to the wrong source, such as falsely thinking that Richard Shiffrin is famous.	
Suggestibility	Distortion	Altering a memory because of misleading information, such as developing false memories for events that did not happen.	
Bias	Distortion	Influence of current knowledge on our memory for past events, such as remembering our past attitudes as similar to our current attitudes even though they have changed.	
Persistence	Undesired	The resurgence of unwanted or disturbing memories that we would like to forget, such as remembering an embarrassing faux pas.	

SOURCE: Based on Schacter (2001).

person asking directions; college students were pretty good at noticing the change. Is this because older people are especially inattentive? Or is it that people process the gist of the situation rather than detail? Perhaps the older adults encoded the person as simply "a college student" and did not look for finer detail. To test this idea, Simons and Levin conducted an additional study in which college students were asked for directions by a construction worker. Sure enough, the college students failed to notice the replacement of one construction worker with another, proving the latter.

Amnesia Is a Deficit in Long-Term Memory

Sometimes we lose the ability to retrieve vast quantities of information from long-term memory. **Amnesia** refers to deficits in long-term memory that result from disease, brain injury, or psychological trauma. There are essentially two types of amnesia: retrograde and anterograde. In **retrograde amnesia,** people lose past memories for events, facts, people, or even personal information. Most portrayals of amnesia in the media are of retrograde amnesia, as when a character in a soap opera awakens from a coma and doesn't know who she is. By contrast, in **anterograde amnesia,** people lose the ability to form new memories. H.M. has a classic case of anterograde amnesia. He can remember old information about his past, but since his surgery he has lost the ability to form new memories. Interestingly, recent evidence suggests that H.M. has acquired some new semantic knowledge about people and events that have occurred since 1953. For instance, when he was given a list of people who became famous after 1953, H.M. was able to provide some information about them (O'Kane,

amnesia Deficits in long-term memory that result from disease, brain injury, or psychological trauma.

retrograde amnesia The condition in which people lose past memories, such as memories for events, facts, people, or even personal information.

anterograde amnesia An inability to form new memories.

Kensinger, & Corkin, 2004). Given the name Lee Harvey Oswald, H.M. described him as the man who "assassinated the president." This new learning may occur through extensive repetition of materials over a lengthy period of time.

Many cases of amnesia result from damage to the medial temporal lobes. Damage to other subcortical areas, such as around the thalamus, can also lead to amnesia. A common cause of this type of amnesia is *Korsakoff's syndrome,* a severe form of memory disturbance linked to chronic alcoholism. Long-term alcohol abuse can lead to vitamin deficiency that results in thalamic damage and, subsequently, amnesia.

Amnesia is a condition that can vary greatly. For instance, after getting hit in the head or losing blood flow to the brain, some people experience temporary memory loss that abates after a day or two. A serious blow to the head can cause a *concussion,* which involves a loss of consciousness that can range from moments to weeks. Trevor Rees-Jones, the bodyguard for Princess Diana, suffered a concussion during the car accident that claimed her life. He later was able to recall getting into the car but not the chase leading up to the crash. This is typical of amnesia following concussion. There is often a period of retrograde amnesia for events leading up to the incident and sometimes temporary anterograde amnesia. People visiting such patients in the hospital are often surprised that the person seems lucid during conversation but later fails to remember the visit. This occurs because working memory is not disrupted, but the memories are not consolidated to long-term memory.

REVIEWING
the Principles | When Do People Forget?

Forgetting is the inability to retrieve memory from long-term storage. The ability to forget is just as important as the ability to remember. Forgetting that occurs over time is often due to interference from competing stimuli. Blocking is a temporary inability to retrieve specific information, as exemplified by the tip-of-the-tongue phenomenon. It too is caused by interference. Absentmindedness is a result of shallow encoding, which occurs when people fail to pay sufficient attention to details. Amnesia is a deficit in long-term memory in which people forget past information (retrograde amnesia) or are unable to store new information (anterograde amnesia). Most amnesia is caused by injury to the brain.

How Are Memories Distorted?

Most people believe that human memory is a permanent storage, from which even minute and apparently forgotten details can be retrieved through hypnosis, truth drugs, or other special techniques. Research has clearly shown, however, that human memory is biased, flawed, and distorted. Memory illusions are common, as we described earlier in this chapter. However, not all memory distortions are so benign. In this section you will learn how the human memory systems provide a less than accurate portrayal of past events. Keep in mind, however, that simply because something doesn't work the way we think it works does not mean it is faulty. As Dan Schacter has argued, many of the seemingly flawed aspects of memory may be by-products of mechanisms that are beneficial. Let's examine some of the most striking examples of the apparent fallibility of human memory.

What causes people to have memories that are distorted, false, or inaccurate?

Flashbulb Memories Can Be Wrong

Do you remember where you were when you found out about the terrorist attacks on the World Trade Center and the Pentagon? Some events cause people to experience what Roger Brown and James Kulik termed **flashbulb memories**, which are vivid memories for the circumstances in which one first learned of a surprising and consequential or emotionally arousing event (Figure 7.18). When Brown and Kulik interviewed people about their memory of the death of President John Kennedy in 1963, they found that people described their memories in highly vivid terms that contained a great deal of detail, such as who they were with, what they were doing or thinking, who told them or how they found out, and what their emotional reaction was to the event.

7.18 Flashbulb Memories Many people report flashbulb memories for the destruction of the World Trade Center towers.

DO YOU REMEMBER WHERE YOU WERE WHEN YOU HEARD . . . ? Of course, the question is whether flashbulb memories are accurate. There is an obvious problem in conducting research on flashbulb memories—you have to wait for a "flash" to go off and then immediately conduct your study. The explosion of the space shuttle *Challenger* on January 28, 1986, at 11:38 EST provided a unique opportunity for research on this topic. Ulric Neisser and Nicole Harsch (1993) had 44 psychology students fill out a questionnaire the day the shuttle exploded and then tested their memory three years later. They found that the vast majority of students were incorrect about multiple aspects of the situation, and that only three students had perfect recall. However, other researchers have documented better memory for flashbulb experiences, such as where British participants were when they heard about Prime Minister Margaret Thatcher's resignation. Martin Conway and his colleagues (1994) showed that better memory for the flashbulb experience occurred among those who found the news surprising and felt that the event was important. Thus, students in the United Kingdom experienced stronger flashbulb memories for the Thatcher resignation than did students in the United States.

STRESS AND MEMORY REVISITED Although flashbulb memories are not perfectly accurate, this does not mean that they are less accurate than any other type of memory. It is indeed possible that flashbulb experiences are recalled more accurately than inconsequential or unsurprising events. To the extent that flashbulb memories contain an unusual number of incidental details, it is possible that this occurs because of the memory-modulating effects of stress hormones (Christianson, 1992). Thus, any event that produces a strong emotional response is likely to produce a vivid, although not necessarily accurate, memory. A second explanation is simply based on the well-known finding that distinctive events are recalled more easily than trivial events. This latter finding is known as the *von Restorff effect,* named after the researcher who first described it in 1933.

People Make Source Misattributions

Dan Schacter identified source misattributions as one of the "seven sins" of the memory system. **Source misattributions** occur when people misremember the time, place, person, or circumstances involved with a memory. A good example of

flashbulb memories Vivid memories for the circumstances in which one first learned of a surprising, consequential, and emotionally arousing event.

source misattributions Memory distortions that occur when people misremember the time, place, person, or circumstances involved with a memory.

this is the *false fame effect* described earlier, in which people mistakenly believe that someone is famous simply because they've previously encountered the person's name. Similarly, social psychologists have long known about the *sleeper effect,* in which strong arguments that are initially not very persuasive because they come from questionable sources become more persuasive over time. You would probably disbelieve a weekly tabloid if it claimed that scientists had discovered a way for people to learn calculus while sleeping. Yet over time you might remember the argument but fail to remember that the source was questionable; hence, you later believe that people can learn calculus while sleeping.

CRYPTOMNESIA An intriguing example of source misattribution is **cryptomnesia**, which is when people think they've come up with a new idea, when really they have retrieved an old idea from memory but have failed to attribute the idea to its proper source (Macrae, Bodenhausen, & Calvini, 1999). Students who take verbatim notes while conducting library research sometimes experience the illusion that they've written the sentences, which can later lead to an accusation of plagiarism. Thus students need to be especially vigilant to indicate verbatim notes while they are taking them. George Harrison, the former Beatle, was sued because his song "My Sweet Lord" is strikingly similar to the song "He's So Fine," recorded in 1962 by the Chiffons. Although he acknowledged having heard the song before, he vigorously denied that he plagiarized it. He argued that with a limited number of notes, and an even smaller number of chord sequences in rock and roll, some overlap was inevitable. In a controversial verdict, the judge ruled against Harrison.

cryptomnesia A type of misappropriation that occurs when people think they have come up with a new idea, yet have only retrieved a stored idea and failed to attribute the idea to its proper source.

People Make Bad Eyewitnesses

One of the most powerful forms of evidence is the eyewitness account. Early studies demonstrated that very few jurors are willing to convict an accused individual on the basis of circumstantial evidence alone. But add one person who says "That's the one!" and conviction rates shoot up, even if it is shown that the witness had poor eyesight or some other condition that raises questions about the accuracy of the testimony. The power of eyewitness testimony is troubling because it is so often in error. Indeed, Gary Wells and his colleagues studied 40 cases in which DNA evidence indicated that a person had been falsely convicted of a crime. In 36 of these cases, the person had been falsely identified by one or more eyewitnesses (Wells et al., 1998). No one knows this better than William Jackson (Figure 7.19), who served five years in prison after being wrongly convicted of a crime because of the testimony of two eyewitnesses. Let's look at some of the memory processes that contribute to eyewitness misidentification.

CROSS-ETHNIC IDENTIFICATION At the social level of analysis, people are particularly bad at accurately identifying individuals of other ethnicities. This effect occurs for Caucasians, Asians, African Americans, and Hispanics. The phrase "they all look alike" appears to be true of all people who are not members of our own ethnic group. In one recent brain-imaging study that crosses levels of analysis, both African American and Caucasian Americans showed better memory for same-race faces. The difference in performance by participants was associated with the degree of activity in the fusiform face area (Golby, Gabrieli, Chiao, & Eberhardt, 2001). As you recall from Chapter 4, this area responds more strongly to faces than to other objects. Apparently, the greater activation of this area to same-race faces accounts for the memory superiority for members of one's own racial group. One explanation

7.19 Eyewitness Accounts Can Be Unreliable William Jackson (left) served five years in prison because he was wrongly convicted of a crime based on the testimony of two eyewitnesses. The real perpetrator is shown on the right. Do these two men look the same to you?

suggestibility The development of biased memories when people are provided with misleading information.

for this effect is that people tend to have less frequent contact with members of other ethnicities; another is that people encode ethnicity according to gist rules of categorization, the way that older people in the change-blindness experiments saw "a college student" and students saw "a construction worker."

SUGGESTIBILITY AND MISINFORMATION Elizabeth Loftus (Figure 7.20) is one of the world's leading specialists in eyewitness memory. During the early 1970s, Loftus and her colleagues conducted a series of important studies demonstrating that people can develop biased memories when provided with misleading information—the "sin" of **suggestibility**. The general methodology of this research involves showing research participants an event and then asking them specific questions about it; the way the questions are worded alters the participants' memories for the event. For instance, in one experiment college students viewed a videotape of a car accident and then were asked, "How fast were the cars going when they _____ each other?" The following words were used in the question: contacted, hit, bumped, collided, or smashed. Loftus and John Palmer (1974) found that students estimated the cars to be traveling faster when the word "smashed" was used than when the other words were used. In a second study, groups of students saw videotapes of car accidents and were then asked about seeing the cars either "smash" into or "hit" each other. One week later they were asked if they had seen broken glass on the ground, an event that did not happen. Nearly one-third of those who heard the term "smashed" falsely recalled having seen the broken glass, whereas very few of those who heard the term "hit" did.

Not only did participants report an altered view of the car accident, in other experiments Loftus and her colleagues demonstrated that people could be induced to report having seen things that did not exist, such as barns, through the use of such questions as "How fast was the white sports car going when it passed the barn while traveling along the country road?" Participants who were asked this question were more likely to report having seen the nonexistent barn than participants who were not asked this question.

You might be wondering whether these sorts of laboratory analogues are appropriate for studying eyewitness accuracy. After all, the sights and sounds of a real traffic accident impress the event on our awareness. Wouldn't our memory be better in the real world? Some evidence supports this idea. A study in Vancouver examined reports of those who had witnessed a fatal shooting (Yuille & Cutshall, 1986). All observers had been interviewed by the police within two days of the shooting. When the researchers went back months later, they found that eyewitness reports were highly stable, including memory for details. Indeed, it makes sense that true eyewitness accounts might be more vivid than those in the laboratory, given the memory modulation effect of stress hormones. However, the real world differs in a number of ways from a controlled laboratory setting, and it is not clear whether the stable memories are accurate. For instance, it could be that by retelling the story over and over again to friends, the eyewitnesses inadvertently developed stronger memories for inaccurate details.

EYEWITNESS CONFIDENCE How good are observers such as jurors at judging whether eyewitnesses are accurate? Gary Wells and his colleagues conducted a number of studies at the University of Alberta and later at Iowa State University, and their general finding was that people cannot differentiate eyewitnesses who are accurate from those who are inaccurate. The problem is that eyewitnesses who are wrong are just as confident, often more confident, than eyewitnesses who are right. Eyewitnesses who report vivid details of all aspects of the scene are probably less credible than those who have poor memory for trivial details. After all, eyewitnesses to real crimes tend to be focused on the weapons or on the action—they fail to pay attention to minor details. Thus, strong confidence for minor details may be a cue that the memory is more likely to be inaccurate or perhaps even false. However, some people are just particularly confident, and whether they are correct or incorrect, jurors find them convincing.

7.20 Elizabeth Loftus Loftus has shown that memory is highly suggestible.

People Have False Memories

Source amnesia occurs when a person shows memory for an event but cannot remember where he or she encountered the information. Think back to your earliest childhood memory. Most people cannot remember specific memories before three years of age. The absence of prior memories is known as *childhood amnesia,* and it may be due to an early lack of linguistic capacity as well as immature frontal lobes. But let's consider that first memory. How vivid is it? How do you know you are not remembering something you saw in a photograph, or a story related to you by family members? When people recall childhood events, the memories are often partial and hazy. How do you know if the memory is real?

source amnesia A type of amnesia that occurs when a person shows memory for an event but cannot remember where he or she encountered the information.

CREATING FALSE RECOGNITION Recently, some powerful demonstrations have shown that people can be misled falsely to recall or recognize events that did not happen. Read the following list of words, saying each one out loud: sour, candy, sugar, bitter, good, taste, tooth, nice, honey, soda, chocolate, heart, cake, tart, pie. Now put your book aside and try to write down as many of the words as possible.

Henry Roediger and Kathleen McDermott used this experiment to see whether they could create false memories among normal, healthy people (Roediger & McDermott, 1995). For instance, without looking back, which of the following words did you recall? Candy, honey, tooth, sweet, pie. If you recalled "sweet," then you have experienced a false memory. If you look back, you will see that "sweet" was not one of the original words, but note that all of the words are related to the word *sweet.* This basic paradigm is extremely reliable for producing false recollections. Moreover, people are often extremely confident in their judgments of previously having seen or heard the critical word.

Mike Miller and George Wolford have argued that responses in the Roediger-McDermott task are due to change in the criteria by which people are willing to say they recognize the words, therefore representing a response bias rather than something that could be called a false memory (Miller & Wolford, 1999). They make the important point that errors are common in many memory tasks, and we should be careful before concluding that memory illusions are "false." After all, no one ever said that participants who misjudged made-up names as famous (in the false fame effect discussed earlier) were having a false memory. Nonetheless, there is a growing body of evidence that false memories can be implanted (Loftus, 2003).

CONFABULATION Some types of brain injury are associated with the false recollection of episodic memory, which is called **confabulation**. Morris Moscovitch has described confabulating as "honest lying" because there is no intent to deceive and the person is unaware of the falsehood of his or her story. Moscovitch (1995) provides an amazing example of confabulation. H.W. was a 61-year-old man who was the biological father of four children, all of them now grown. H.W. experienced severe frontal lobe damage following a cerebral hemorrhage. Here is part of the clinical interview:

> Q.   Are you married or single?
> H.W. Married.
> Q.   How long have you been married?
> H.W. About four months.
> Q.   How many children do you have?
> H.W. Four. (He laughs.) Not bad for four months!
> Q.   How old are your children?
> H.W. The eldest is 32, his name is Bob, and the youngest is 22, his name is Joe.
> Q.   How did you get those children in four months?
> H.W. They're adopted.
> Q.   Does this all sound strange to you, what you are saying?
> H.W. (He laughs.) I think it is a little strange.

Patients such as H.W. confabulate for no apparent purpose. They simply recall mistaken facts, and when questioned they try to make sense of their recollections by adding facts that make the story more coherent. Recall from Chapter 4 Gazzaniga's theory of the interpreter and how split-brain patients confabulate to make sense out of discrepant information fed to each cerebral hemisphere. A dramatic example of confabulation occurs in *Capgras syndrome,* in which patients have the delusional belief that their family members have been replaced by impostors. No amount of evidence can convince them that their siblings, parents, spouses, and children are real. Patients with Capgras often have damage to the frontal lobes and limbic brain regions.

Repressed Memories Are Controversial

One of the most vitriolic debates over the past few decades has centered on repressed memories. On one side are some psychotherapists and patients who claim that long-repressed memories for traumatic events can resurface during therapy. Recovered memories of sexual abuse are the most common repressed memories reported, and in the early 1990s there was a rash of celebrity reports of early childhood sexual abuse.

confabulation The false recollection of episodic memory.

On the other side are memory researchers, such as Elizabeth Loftus, who point out that there is little credible evidence indicating that recovered memories are genuine, or at least sufficiently accurate to be believable. Part of the problem is best summarized by the leading memory researcher Daniel Schacter (Figure 7.21): "I know that some traumatic events can be associated with temporary forgetting and subsequent memory recovery. I am convinced that child abuse is a major problem in our society. I have no reason to question the memories of people who have always remembered their abuse, or who have spontaneously recalled previously forgotten abuse on their own. Yet I am deeply concerned by some of the suggestive techniques that have been recommended to recover repressed memories" (Schacter, 1996, p. 251).

Schacter alludes to the frightening possibility that false memories for traumatic events were implanted by well-meaning but misguided therapists. There is convincing evidence that methods such as hypnosis, age regression, and guided recall can implant false memories. Likewise, a growing body of evidence from carefully controlled laboratory studies has demonstrated that children can be induced to remember events that did not occur (Ceci & Bruck, 1995). Indeed, one of the seven sins of memory identified by Schacter is *suggestibility,* which is illustrated by illusory memories that occur when people incorporate information provided by others into their own recollections. The Harvard psychologist Richard McNally (2003) has conducted research with people who had recovered memories of childhood abuse. In the laboratory, these individuals are more likely than control participants to develop false memories in general, as in the Roediger-McDermott method described earlier.

There have been a few infamous examples in which adults have accused their parents of abuse based on memories that they later realize were the products of therapy rather than reality. For instance, Diana Halbrook came to believe not only that she had been abused, but also that she had been involved in satanic ritualistic abuse and that she had herself killed a baby. When she expressed doubts to her therapist about the veracity of these events, the people in her "support" group and her therapist told her she was in denial and not listening to "the little girl" within. After all, all of the other members of the support group had recovered memories that they had been involved in satanic ritualistic abuse. After Diana left her therapy group she came to believe that she was neither abused nor a killer. It is interesting that so many people recover memories of satanic ritualistic abuse, since "though thousands of patients have 'remembered' ritual acts, not a single such case has ever been documented in the United States despite extensive investigative efforts by state and federal law enforcement" (Schacter, 1996, p. 269).

What is a reasonable person to conclude about repressed memories? The repressed-memory debate understandably involves strong and passionate beliefs on both sides. Research shows us that some therapeutic techniques seem especially likely to foster false memories, but it would be a mistake to simply dismiss all adult reports of early abuse. It is certainly possible that abuse occurs and is forgotten until some later period of time, and it is a disservice to actual victims of abuse to ignore their memories. It is interesting to note that in the latter half of the 1990s, the incidence of recovered memories fell dramatically. However, it is not clear whether this was because of less media attention to reports, or because people were less likely to seek therapy to uncover their past memories.

People Reconstruct Events to Be Consistent

The final example of memory distortion to consider is memory *bias,* in which people's memories for events are altered over time to be consistent with current beliefs

7.21 Daniel Schacter Schacter's research has provided numerous insights into the everyday "sins" of human memory.

or attitudes. One of psychology's greatest thinkers, Leon Festinger, when writing a tribute to his colleague Stanley Schachter, hit the nail on the head: "I prefer to rely on my memory. I have lived with that memory a long time, I am used to it, and if I have rearranged or distorted anything, surely that was done for my own benefit" (Festinger, 1987, p. 1).

Consider people who take study-skills courses. In spite of only modest evidence that such courses are beneficial, often because students fail to heed the advice they are given, most students who take them describe them as extremely helpful. How can something that often leads to only modest outcomes be so positively endorsed? To understand this, Michael Conway and Michael Ross randomly assigned students to a genuine study-skills course or to a control group that received no special training. Students who took the real course showed few signs of improvement; in fact, their final-exam performance was slightly poorer than the control group's. Still they reported the study-skills program as helpful. Why? The experiment had one feature that allows us to understand what is going on. At the beginning of the course, participants were asked to rate their studying skills. At the end of the course they once again rated themselves *and* they were asked to recall how they had originally rated themselves. In describing their earlier ratings, students in the study-skills course recalled themselves as significantly worse than they actually had been at the beginning of the course, thereby "getting what they want by revising what they had" (Conway & Ross, 1984).

People tend to recall their past attitudes and beliefs as being consistent with their current attitudes and beliefs, often revising their memories when they have a change in attitude. People also tend to remember an event so that it casts them in a prominent or favorable light. We tend to exaggerate our contribution to group efforts, to take credit for success and blame failure on others, and to remember our successes more than our failures, as you will discover in Chapter 15.

Not only individuals bias their recollection of past events; societies do so as well. The collective memory of groups can seriously distort the past, as expressed in the Orwellian idea that we can change only the past, not the future. Consider that the histories of most societies tend to downplay the unsavory, immoral, and even murderous behaviors of their pasts; perpetrators' memories are generally shorter than victims'. Is there an objective reality? As Leon Festinger observed, we construct our memories for our own purposes. Our memory for events tends to be highly consistent with our personal beliefs.

Profiles in Psychological Science

False Confessions and Memories

On September 11, 2001, Abdallah Higazy was sleeping in a hotel room when he was awoken by the attack on the World Trade Center across the street. He was quickly evacuated but had to leave his possessions behind. A few months later he was allowed to retrieve his belongings, but one of them did not belong to him—a radio scanner capable of intercepting airline communications. The FBI immediately arrested and interrogated Higazy. During the interrogation, Higazy felt threatened and believed his family would be at risk if he did not tell the FBI agents what they wanted to hear. In an interview on the television program *60 Minutes* in early 2004, he reported that he felt it would be better for his family if he confessed to owning the radio, even though it did not belong to him, and so he confessed. He told *60 Minutes,* "It was either I go to prison, or I go to prison and something happens to my family. So I chose I go to prison." Higazy was eventually released because it turned out that the radio belonged to an airline pilot and that a security guard had been confused about where the radio was originally located (Figure 7.22).

This case has a reasonably happy ending. But how often do people confess to crimes that they did not commit? Many researchers believe it happens more frequently than you might think. Even more surprising is that many times people come to believe their false confessions (Kassin, 2005; Kassin, Goldstein, & Savitsky, 2003). Can people really believe they committed a crime when they did not? How easy is it for people to develop false memories? Let's examine the evidence.

Think back to when you were five. Do you remember getting lost in a mall and being found by a kind old man who returned you to your family? No? Well, what if your family told you about this incident, including how panicked your parents were when they couldn't find you? According to research by Elizabeth Loftus, you may well remember the incident, even if it didn't happen.

In an initial study, a 14-year-old named Chris was told by his older brother Jim, who was part of the study, about the "lost in the mall" incident. The context was a game called "Remember when . . . ." All of the other incidents narrated by Jim were true. Two days later, when asked if he had ever been lost in a mall, Chris began reporting memories of how he felt during the mall episode; within two weeks he reported the following:

> "I was with you guys for a second and I think I went over to look at the toy store, the Kay-bee toy and uh, we got lost and I was looking around and I thought, 'Uh-oh. I'm in trouble now.' You know. And then I . . . I thought I was never going to see my family again. I was really scared you know. And then this old man, I think he was wearing a blue flannel shirt, came up to me. . . . [H]e was kind of old. He was kind of bald on top. . . . [H]e had like a ring of gray hair . . . and he had glasses" (Loftus, 1993, p. 532).

You might wonder if there was something special about Chris that made him susceptible to developing false memories, but in a later study, Loftus and her colleagues used the same paradigm to assess whether they could implant false memories in 24 participants. Seven of the 24 participants falsely remembered events that had been implanted by family members who were part of the study. Note that it is unlikely that false memories could be created for certain types of unusual events, such as receiving an enema (Pezdek & Hodge, 1999). However, a study by Saul Kassin and Katherine Kiechel (1996) found that people could even be induced to make false confessions of minor transgressions that they didn't actually commit. Moreover, their research participants truly believed that they had committed the transgressions. It is well established that children are particularly suggestible and that false memories, such as getting their fingers caught in mousetraps and having to go to the hospital, can easily be induced in them. When you ask people to imagine an event happening, they create of mental image of that event; it is possible that they later confuse their memory of their imagination with reality, and they come to believe that the imagined event really happened. Essentially, people have a source-monitoring problem: Did the event really happen, or did they imagine it? To Chris, the memory of being lost in the mall became as real as other events from childhood.

What about when people confess to crimes they did not commit? Police interrogation can be brutal; many times suspects are drunk or on drugs or otherwise have memory problems. In some instances, the police officers tell the suspects that there

7.22 False Confessions Abdallah Higazy was jailed during the investigation into the September 11, 2001 attacks on the World Trade Center because he falsely confessed to owning incriminating evidence. Higazy later told reporters he had lied because he feared that his family would be threatened if he didn't tell FBI agents what they wanted to hear.

are eyewitnesses or other evidence proving their guilt. In the United States, it is perfectly legal for police officers to make these false claims during interrogation. When confronted with evidence, suspects come to believe that it is possible that they actually committed the crime. It is apparent that with repeated questioning over many hours and extremely high stress levels, false memories can be formed. Ironically, *innocence* may put the innocent at risk because they fail to anticipate being accused of the crime, and so make decisions that are not in their best interests, such as not asking for a lawyer (Kassin, 2005). Over the last few years there have been a number of high-profile cases in which DNA analysis showed that a person who had confessed to a crime could not have been the perpetrator. Thus, just because someone confesses to a crime doesn't mean that he or she actually committed the crime. Sometimes confessions are motivated out of fear, such as Abdallah Higazy worrying about his family. But sometimes people confess even when they did not commit the crime because a false memory has been implanted. Confessions need to be treated skeptically unless there is corroborating evidence. Understanding the nature of false confessions may help the judicial system ensure that people are punished only for their genuine misdeeds. ■

REVIEWING
the Principles | How Are Memories Distorted?

Memory is far from a true and faithful recorder of objective facts and events. Rather, memory often includes a number of biases, distortions, and outright lies. People tend to make poor eyewitnesses because human memory is better for gist than for detail. Yet people maintain an unjustified confidence in their personal memories, such as flashbulb memories. Memories can be distorted or even implanted by false information, and there is a general bias toward maintaining consistency in our memories.

Conclusion

The brain is a wonderfully evolved instrument that has allowed humans to develop language, build civilizations, and visit the moon. However, we can't always remember where we left our keys, the faces of people whom we've witnessed commit crimes, whether a person is famous, or details from a book we read last year. It needs to be emphasized that memory has evolved to solve certain problems related to survival, such as remembering our friends and foes. Memory did not evolve to remember phone numbers, textbook definitions, or how to drive a car, but it does a pretty good job at all of these. Memory is a system that provides an organism with the ability to retain information and skills that are useful to survival. As such, it works pretty well, considering the amount of information that bombards the nervous system. Finally, as one of the most dynamic areas of research in psychological science, memory highlights our four fundamental themes, in particular the way that researchers are working at various levels of analysis to unwrap the mystery of the mind.

Summarizing the Principles of Memory

What Are the Basic Stages of Memory?

1. **Sensory memory is brief:** Visual (iconic) and auditory (echoic) memories are maintained at the sensory memory stage long enough to ensure a continuous sensory experience.

2. **Short-term memory is active:** Immediate active memory is limited. Chunking reduces information into meaningful units that are easier to remember. The three components of working memory are the central executive, the phonological loop, and the visuospatial sketchpad.

3. **Long-term memory is relatively permanent:** Long-term memory (LTM) is the potentially indefinite storage of all memories. Meaningful memories are stored in LTM.

What Are the Different Memory Systems?

4. **Explicit memory involves conscious effort:** Explicit, declarative memories that we consciously remember include personal events (episodic memory) and knowledge (semantic memory).

5. **Implicit memory occurs without deliberate effort:** Procedural (motor) memories of how to do things automatically are implicit.

How Is Information Organized in Long-Term Memory?

6. **Long-term memory is a temporal sequence:** Memory processes include encoding, storage, and retrieval. Elaborate rehearsal involves encoding information in more meaningful ways, and results in better memory than maintenance (repetition) rehearsal.

7. **Schemas provide an organizational framework:** Cognitive structures of meaning (schemas) aid the organization of memories.

8. **Information is stored in association networks:** Networks of associations are formed by nodes of information, which are linked together and are activated by spreading activation.

9. **Retrieval cues provide access to long-range storage:** According to the encoding specificity principle, any stimulus that is encoded along with an experience can later trigger the memory of the experience. The context of the memory is also activated.

What Brain Processes Are Involved in Memory?

10. **There has been intensive effort to identify the physical location of memory:** Unable to locate a specific site of memory storage (engram), Lashley concluded, somewhat inaccurately, that memory is distributed throughout the brain (equipotentiality). Research has revealed that a number of specific brain regions contribute to learning and memory.

11. **The medial temporal lobes are important for consolidation of declarative memories:** The hypothetical process of consolidation of new memories involves changes in neural connections. The hippocampus and rhinal cortex are regions of the medial temporal lobe that are important for declarative memories. Hippocampal place cells aid spatial memory.

12. **The frontal lobes are involved in many aspects of memory:** Frontal lobes activation occurs with deep encoding tasks. The medial prefrontal region is active for memories about the self. The left frontal region is more active during encoding and the right more active during retrieval. The frontal lobes may be especially important for working memory.

13. **Neurochemistry influences memory:** A group of neurochemicals modulate the storage of memories. Epinephrine enhances memory. The amygdala is probably responsible for memory modulation through activity in its norepinephrine receptors.

When Do People Forget?

14. **Transience is caused by interference:** Forgetting over time occurs because of interference from both old and new information.

15. **Blocking is temporary:** The tip-of-the-tongue phenomenon occurs when there is trouble retrieving the right word, usually from interference from a similar word.

16. **Absentmindedness results from shallow encoding:** Inattentive or shallow processing causes memory failure.

17. **Amnesia is a deficit in long-term memory:** Injury and disease can result in amnesia, the inability to recall past memories (retrograde amnesia) or the inability to form new memories (anterograde amnesia).

How Are Memories Distorted?

18. **Flashbulb memories can be wrong:** The strong emotional response that attends flashbulb memories may modulate the strength of a memory and affect accuracy.

19. **People make source misattributions:** People misremember the source of a memory (source misattributions). Cryptomnesia refers to when people think a new idea is theirs, when they have only retrieved an old memory.

20. **People make bad eyewitnesses:** Poor eyewitness recall occurs particularly with regard to ethnic identification. Suggestibility leads to misinformation.

21. **People have false memories:** Immature frontal lobes cause childhood amnesia. False memories can be implanted. Confabulation can occur due to brain damage.

22. **Repressed memories are controversial:** Some therapeutic techniques can result in false repressed memories.

23. **People reconstruct events to be consistent:** People try to maintain a consistency between past memories and their current attitudes and knowledge.

Applying the Principles

1. Frequently, people complain about problems with their "short-term memory" because they can't remember something that happened over the last few days. How does the information-processing model of short-term memory help us understand the problem?

    _____ a) The problem is not short-term memory but rather retrieval from long-term memory.
    _____ b) The problem is not short-term memory but rather a malfunctioning working memory.
    _____ c) The problem is that sensory memory is not picking up the information to transfer to short-term memory.
    _____ d) The problem is with the central executive function of long-term memory.

2. When you are studying for an exam, you are working with memories that are _____. When you are recalling this information while taking an exam, you are using the _____ memory system and the _____ memory sytem to fill in your response on the answer sheet.

    _____ a) implicit; declarative; declarative
    _____ b) explicit; procedural; motor
    _____ c) declarative; explicit; implicit
    _____ d) episodic; implicit; explicit

3. Is long-term memory simply stored in the logical manner of a library? To test this, think of the word *red*. Very quickly your mind will recall a variety of different associations, (for example, fire truck; crayon; "seeing red"; "red, white, and blue"; "red-letter day"). This demonstrates what important aspect of long-term memory?

    _____ a) semantic networks that link different memories in a hierarchy of personal familiarity

    _____ b) schema networks that connect general concepts
    _____ c) long-term scripts that connect all the different memories in a story
    _____ d) implicit memory networks

4. You are driving at high speed on the freeway you take home every day. Suddenly, a deer leaps from the side of the road and you hit it, resulting in a scary crash. After the accident, you are flooded with detailed memories about that section of the freeway, and you are able to recall details you had never remembered of that road before. This demonstrates

    _____ a) how motor memories are permanently processed by the hippocampus.
    _____ b) the role of the amygdala in tagging information so that we remember it better.
    _____ c) the role of high speed in memory processing.
    _____ d) the way the frontal lobe only processes the most important and emotional aspects of a memory.

5. Aaron is studying for an exam when his roommate mentions that Aaron's mom had called and asked to have Aaron call her later that day. Throughout the rest of the day, Aaron remembers he must call someone, but can't remember whom. The next morning, Aaron's mother calls, irate that he never returned her phone call. His response is "I forgot." It is likely that his memory failure occurred because of which of the following?

    _____ a) absentmindedness
    _____ b) blocking
    _____ c) transience
    _____ d) misattribution

ANSWERS: *1a 2c 3a 4b 5c*

Key Terms

absentmindedness, p. 277

amnesia, p. 278

anterograde amnesia, p. 278

blocking, p. 277

confabulation, p. 284

consolidation, p. 268

cryptomnesia, p. 281

declarative memory, p. 260

elaborative rehearsal, p. 262

encoding specificity principle, p. 265

encoding, p. 262

episodic memory, p. 260

explicit memory, p. 260

flashbulb memories, p. 280

forgetting, p. 275

implicit memory, p. 260

long-term memory (LTM), p. 255

maintenance rehearsal, p. 262

memory, p. 250

modal memory model, p. 251

posttraumatic stress disorder (PTSD), p. 273

primacy effect, p. 255

proactive interference, p. 276

procedural memory, p. 260

recency effect, p. 255

repetition priming, p. 261

retrieval, p. 262

retroactive interference, p. 276

retrograde amnesia, p. 278

schema, p. 263

semantic memory, p. 260

sensory memory, p. 252

serial position effect, p. 255

short-term memory (STM), p. 253

source amnesia, p. 283

source misattributions, p. 280

spatial memory, p. 270

storage, p. 262

suggestibility, p. 282

tip-of-the-tongue phenomenon, p. 277

transience, p. 276

working memory, p. 254

Further Readings

Bjork, E. L., & Bjork, R. A. (1996). *Memory.* San Diego, CA: Academic Press.

Gazzaniga, M. S. (2004). *The cognitive neurosciences III* (3rd ed.). Cambridge, MA: MIT Press.

LeDoux, J. E. (2002). *Synaptic Self.* New York: Viking.

Neath, I. (1998). *Human memory: An introduction to research, data, and theory.* Pacific Grove, CA: Brooks-Cole.

Schacter, D. L. (1996). *Searching for memory: The brain, the mind, and the past.* New York: Basic Books.

Schacter, D. L. (2001). *The seven sins of memory: How the mind forgets and remembers.* Boston: Houghton Mifflin.

Squire, L. R., & Kandel, E. R. (1999). *Memory: From mind to molecules.* New York: Scientific American Library.

Thinking and Intelligence

How do we define intelligence? Every week the cast of the popular TV show *The Amazing Race* face a series of mental and physical challenges designed to eliminate the slowest teams and reward the winners with a million dollars. Problem solving is a big part of life for everyone. We use our unique problem-solving abilities in conscious and unconscious ways all the time. The show dramatizes what psychologists already understand about intelligence: it is a combination of being able to learn quickly, make reasonable decisions, and adapt to diverse environments.

Thinking and Intelligence

I n the aftermath of 9/11, it was impossible not to think of the deaths of
the passengers in the hijacked planes and the office workers in the
World Trade Center and the Pentagon. After the two planes struck the
World Trade Center, footage of the results of the hijackings was repeatedly broadcast, resulting in vivid images that most of us will never forget.
Although the events of that day are unparalleled, there is another tragic
consequence of these highly publicized hijackings that has only rarely been
discussed.

The psychologist Gerd Gigerenzer of the Max Planck Institute proposed
that low-probability events that are publicized and have dire consequences,
such as the deaths associated with the hijackings of 9/11, can result in fears
he calls *dread risks* (Gigerenzer, 2004). These dread risks, although born of
uncommon events, can have a profound impact on reasoning and decision
making. For instance, after 9/11 many people felt some trepidation about
flying. In fact, in October, November, and December 2001 airline revenues

dropped by 20 percent, 17 percent, and 12 percent compared to those same months in 2000. Although fewer people were flying after 9/11, estimates for miles driven during those months increased by almost 3 percent, with the biggest increase (5.3 percent) on interstate rural highways, suggesting more interstate travel. It seems that Americans preferred to drive after 9/11.

For those who opted to drive, we can imagine that the images of the hijacked planes prompted an avoidance of being in a circumstance that could have the same horrible result. However, traveling by car is not without its risks. The number of people who die in car accidents every year far exceeds the number who die in airline disasters, much less in hijackings. Given that there were more people on the road after 9/11, was there an impact on traffic fatalities? The answer appears to be yes. The number of traffic fatalities in the three months following 9/11 was significantly above average. In fact, it is estimated that an additional 350 people may have died by avoiding flying during those months. The number of passengers and crew that died in all four hijackings on 9/11 was 266. Overall, it appears more people died by avoiding flying in the three months following 9/11 than died aboard airplanes on that fateful day. We can still see these effects four years later in the United States. Airfares are at historic lows and gasoline prices are at historic highs, yet more gasoline is being consumed on a monthly basis than ever before, while air travel still hasn't reached its pre–9/11 mark. Surely some of this is due to the growing popularity of sport utility vehicles, but at least part of it reflects people's preference for driving rather than flying.

When reasoning about the right choice to make, humans do not always weigh the actual probabilities of different actions. In fact, we can be heavily influenced by a number of factors that might not be considered rational, such as how prominent an event or image is in our mind. Psychologists are starting to identify some of the typical biases that enter into reasoning and decision making. Gerd Gigerenzer suggests that we should start educating the public about these biases in decision making after highly unlikely, tragic events. Publicizing some of the typical biases in reasoning that dread risks can create might prompt people to reconsider choices that could result in additional negative consequences. ■

In the preceding two chapters we discussed how we learn and remember information. Once we have that information, what do we do with it? This chapter is concerned with how we use information in the form of thinking as well as what it means

Timeline

1884

Defining Intelligence Sir Francis Galton opens his Anthropometric Laboratory, where people can measure the sensitivity of their sensory systems, the property that Galton proposes is the basis for intelligence.

1904

Spearman's G Charles Spearman proposed that one factor, known as general intelligence or g, underlies all mental abilities. Raymond Cattell subsequently differentiates fluid from crystallized general intelligence.

1905

Intelligence Quotient Alfred Binet and Théodore Simon of France develop the first intelligence test, which is later modified by the American Lewis Termin. Wilhelm Stern of Germany develops the concept of intelligence quotient, or IQ.

1925

Insight Wolfgang Köhler observes an ape, after long contemplation, join two sticks together in order to reach a banana, which suggests that animals are capable of insight.

to think intelligently. Our thoughts guide much of our behavior as we solve problems, make decisions, and try to make sense of events going on around us. Sometimes our thought processes lead to great ideas and creative discoveries, but sometimes they lead to bad decisions and regret. Yet even in the face of all these thought processes and biases, some people seem to be better at using information than others, which we can describe as being intelligent. In this chapter we consider the nature of thought, from how we represent it in our minds, to how we use it to solve problems and make decisions in our daily lives, to explaining differences in intelligence among people. We consider the central issue of whether there is one monolithic thing we can call intelligence or whether it is best considered as reflecting a range of possible talents. We will see that there are several different ways to think about what it means to be intelligent. For instance, some people are superb at math; others are gifted in language. Some people excel at artistic endeavors or athletics; others are smart in matters of business and everyday affairs. Yet overall there does appear to be some form of general intelligence in which people vary. We will see that being able to use information intelligently matters more and more as society becomes more complex. We will also see that cultural and environmental factors play important roles in determining people's levels of intelligence.

An important idea to keep in mind is that for the most part our thinking is adaptive. For instance, we develop rules for making fast decisions because daily life demands it. In his 2005 book *Blink* (subtitled *The Power of Thinking without Thinking*), science writer Malcolm Gladwell makes the case that the ability to use information rapidly is a critical human skill. When we encounter a person on a street who might pose a threat, we might change our route to avoid that person. Being able to instantly size up whether a person is trustworthy allows us to avoid harm. This can happen without our conscious awareness. Recall from Chapter 4 that unconscious cognitive processes can affect thought and behavior. We will see that this is also true for decision making and problem solving.

Sometimes snap judgments have important consequences. Gladwell describes a firefighter who was leading his colleagues in an effort to put out a kitchen fire. The fire did not respond in the expected way when they sprayed water on it. Feeling something was wrong, the firefighter quickly ordered everyone to leave the building, which was a good thing because the fire was under them in the basement and the kitchen floor on which they were standing collapsed moments after they left. If he had stopped to figure out the problem, he and his colleagues might have been killed. His intuitive decision saved him and the others. Sometimes, however, snap decisions can be disastrous—as in the case of the police shooting of Amadou Diallo, which we considered at the beginning of this book. Throughout this chapter we will see that just as thinking can solve important problems, it can also produce faulty outcomes. How do we use information intelligently so that it improves our lives?

1930s	1947	1956	1970s	1973
Problem Solving Researchers such as Abraham Luchins, Norman Maier, and Karl Duncker study cognitive factors involved in problem solving. They find that the inability to see a problem in new ways can prevent people from finding solutions.	**Decisions Are Rational** John von Neumann and Oskar Morgenstern publish the seminal book *Theory of Games and Economic Behavior*, which presents the central ideas underlying utility-based models of rational decision making.	**Decisions Are Less than Optimal** Nobel Laureate Herbert Simon introduces the notion of *satisficing*, the idea that human decision making is based on finding approximations to statistically optimal solutions.	**Genes and Intelligence** Researchers such as Arthur Jensen and Richard Herrnestein propose that intelligence has a genetic component. They spark controversy by suggesting that racial differences in intelligence may be due to genetics.	**Mental Representation** Through studies of how people mentally rotate objects, Roger Shepard shows that people form mental images, or representations, of objects.

name and a large price tag has convinced a great number of consumers to buy really expensive soap. Let's examine some of the most common heuristics that people use during inductive reasoning and decision making.

AVAILABILITY HEURISTIC Is it more common for the letter R to be the first letter in a word, or the third letter? If you were asked this question, how would you go about determining an answer? If you are like most people, you might try to think of as many words as you can with R as a first letter (for example, *right* or *read*) or R as a third letter (for example, *care* or *sir*) and come to the conclusion that R is more often the first letter in a word. However, R is much more likely to be the third letter of a word.

Why do people have difficulty with this type of reasoning? This error in reasoning occurs because it is much easier to think of words beginning with R than words with R as the third letter. When we try to determine an answer, the most readily available instances are those with R as a first letter. Making a decision based on the most available answer—the one that comes most easily to mind—is known as the **availability heuristic**. Although this heuristic can be useful because information that is important comes most easily to mind, it can also create a bias in reasoning and result in the wrong conclusion.

Using the availability heuristic in real-world circumstances can lead to significant consequences. As mentioned at the beginning of the chapter, when there is a major airplane disaster, such as the 9/11 hijackings, people who are planning to travel may be biased to drive rather than fly. Even though statistics indicate that the likelihood of dying in a car accident far exceeds that of dying in a plane crash, the salient and publicized examples of airline disasters make them more noticeable when people are reasoning about the relative safety of these two modes of travel. In the time period following 9/11 in particular, the availability heuristic created a bias in reasoning that led more people to drive on their vacations and trips. This ultimately resulted in an increase in the overall number of traffic fatalities.

REPRESENTATIVENESS HEURISTIC Helena is an intelligent, ambitious woman who describes herself as scientific-minded. She enjoys working on mathematical puzzles and talking with other people. She is an avid reader and gardener. Do you think that Helena is more likely a cognitive psychologist or a postal worker? If you are like most people, you would guess that Helena is a psychologist because these characteristics seem to be more representative of psychologists than of postal workers. Basing the selection on the extent to which Helena reflects what we believe about psychologists is an example of the **representativeness heuristic**. The problem with following this heuristic is that it can lead to faulty reasoning if you fail to take other information into account. For instance, overall there are many more postal workers in the world than cognitive psychologists. The frequency of an event's occurring is known as a *base rate;* in this case the base rate for postal workers is higher than that for cognitive psychologists. This base rate information should result in the guess that Helena is a postal worker, since there are millions of postal workers and only a few thousand cognitive psychologists. In other words, it is something like 200 times more likely that any given person is a postal worker, and surely many postal workers enjoy reading, math, and gardening. Although the traits listed for Helena may be more representative of cognitive psychologists overall, they also are likely to apply to a large number of postal workers. People tend to pay insufficient attention to base rates when they are reasoning, instead focusing on whether or not the information presented is representative of one conclusion or another.

---

availability heuristic Making a decision based on the answer that most easily comes to mind.

representativeness heuristic A rule for categorization based on how similar the person or object is to our prototypes for that category.

But what if postal workers don't like math problems or gardening? In that case you might wonder whether the base rate matters. Consider Ashley, whom you know to be an extremely reserved, sensitive, and literary person. Is it more likely that (a) Ashley is an engineering major, or (b) Ashley is majoring in engineering and minoring in English? When answering this question, people become distracted by information that is inconsistent with their stereotypes about engineers. Given that she is reserved and literary, it makes sense that if Ashley was an engineering major, she would also likely take courses in English. However, the probability of a *conjunction*— two events happening together—must always be less than the probability of either event. Thus, engineering majors who minor in English are a subset of engineering majors. The representativeness heuristic can be an important factor in racial stereotypes, such as when people constantly see black faces as crime suspects in the media, which alters their beliefs both about black people and about criminals. We will discuss stereotypes in greater detail in Chapter 15.

CONFIRMATION BIAS The tendency to focus selectively on some information and not use other information underlies the heuristic called **confirmation bias**. Have you ever tried to make a point by citing a single specific instance? For instance, a smoker, when trying to justify her choice to smoke, might point to an aunt who smoked every day and lived a healthy life until she died in her 90s. A politician arguing for welfare reform might try to gain support by providing an example of a specific individual who managed to cheat the current system. In general, people tend to seek out information that is consistent with whatever hypothesis, view, or theory they hold. At the same time, they tend to discount or ignore information that is inconsistent with their beliefs.

Confirmation bias is a natural tendency that can be difficult to guard against. Although scientists are trained to overcome inductive reasoning biases, a strong belief in the validity of a hypothesis can have an influence on their conclusions. For example, most scientists design experiments to confirm their hypotheses. Only rarely does a scientist conduct an experiment that is specifically designed to disconfirm his or her favored hypothesis. More often than not, scientists who have their own favorite alternative hypotheses conduct the studies that disconfirm others' hypotheses. An important component of critical thinking is to try to avoid confirming prior beliefs.

FRAMING EFFECTS Every weekend it seems that one of the local merchants is having a gigantic sale on jewelry, with bold advertisements proclaiming "80 percent off everything." Although this seems like a good deal, it turns out that the regular prices are substantially higher than any other store's. Thus, the sale simply lowers the price so it is more competitive. Nonetheless, people love to think they are getting a bargain. The way information is presented can alter how people perceive it, which is known as **framing**. Framing a decision to emphasize the losses or the gains when introducing alternatives can significantly alter the choice made. Consider the following problem: Imagine that the United States is preparing for the outbreak of a disease that is expected to kill 600 people. Two alternative programs are proposed to combat the disease. The scientific estimates of the consequences of the two programs are as follows:

> If Program A is chosen, 200 of these people will be saved.
> If Program B is chosen, there is a one-third probability that 600 people will be saved and a two-thirds probability that nobody will be saved.

confirmation bias A tendency to search for and believe evidence that fits our existing views.

framing The effect of presentation on how information is perceived.

Which would you choose? When asked this question, 72 percent of respondents chose program A (Kahneman & Tversky, 1984). Weighing the probabilities would result in 200 people saved for both programs, but people showed a clear preference for a sure gain as outlined in Program A, as opposed to a chance of a larger gain with the additional chance of no gain as outlined in Program B. Now consider these two alternatives:

If Program A is chosen, 400 people will die.
If Program B is chosen, there is a one-third probability nobody will die and a two-thirds probability that 600 people will die.

When asked this question, 78 percent of respondents chose program B. In this case, most people felt that the certain death of 400 people, outlined in Program A, was a worse alternative than the likely, but uncertain, death of 600 people outlined in Program B. The idea of a sure loss was less appealing than an uncertain, but possibly greater, loss. However, notice that the probabilities and outcomes are identical to those presented earlier, with the exception that the gains are emphasized in the first set of alternatives and the losses are emphasized in the second set of alternatives. Framing a decision so that the gains or losses are emphasized can have a clear impact on the ultimate choice. Research on the framing effect indicates that when people make choices, they may weigh losses and gains differently. Indeed, people are generally much more concerned with costs than with benefits, which is known as *loss aversion*. A schematic illustration of this concept is shown in Figure 8.8.

This tendency to view costs and benefits differently is exploited by companies that offer people the opportunity to test products on a trial basis before purchasing. These companies are banking on the probability that once their product is being used, the "cost" of giving it up at the end of the trial period will be perceived to be greater than the actual monetary cost of purchasing it. In this manner, the company has successfully changed the reference point from which the decision to purchase the product has been made: A cost that originally might have been viewed only in terms of dollars has now been juxtaposed with a cost viewed in terms of losing access to the product. If the latter is perceived as the greater cost, people will end up making a purchase they might not have made if they had considered only the cost in dollars.

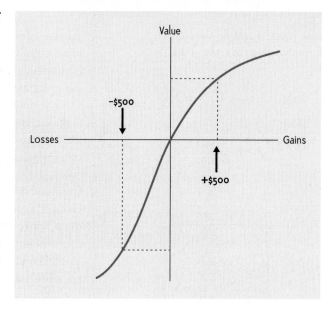

8.8 Loss Aversion The critical aspect of this figure is that with decision "value" plotted on the vertical axis, potential losses have a bigger impact on perceived value. That is, the potential loss of $500 has a greater effect on our decision making than a potential gain of $500.

AFFECTIVE HEURISTICS People often decide to do things that will make them happy, while they avoid doing things they will later regret. Expectation for how a decision will affect emotional state in the future is a powerful force in decision making. Unfortunately, people are not particularly good at *affective forecasting*—predicting how they will feel in the future. During the 2004 U.S. presidential election, many Americans claimed they would move to Canada if George W. Bush was reelected. As the Harvard psychologist Daniel Gilbert noted in the *New York Times,* "[M]y unofficial tally suggests that the number of disgruntled Democrats who actually emigrated northward is roughly zero, plus or minus none" (2005, p. 23). Gilbert and his colleague Timothy Wilson have found compelling evidence that people overestimate the extent to which negative events will affect them in the future. People mispredict how bad they will feel following a romantic breakup, losing a job, being diagnosed with a serious medical illness, or their favorite politician's losing an election (Gilbert, Pinel, Wilson, Blumberg, & Wheatley, 1998; Wilson & Gilbert, 2003).

According to Gilbert and Wilson, following a negative event people engage in a number of strategies that help them feel better, such as rationalizing why it happened and minimizing the event's importance. Essentially, they figure out a way that the event makes sense, which reduces its negative consequences. Humans have an amazing capacity for manufacturing happiness, and so even if a negative event causes them temporary anguish, most people adapt and return to their typical positive outlook. You will learn much more about the various biases that help people feel better about themselves in Chapter 15. Interestingly, people seem unaware that they have this capacity, and so when asked to predict how they will feel following an aversive event, they overestimate their pain and underestimate how well they will cope with the event (Gilbert, Morewedge, Risen, & Wilson, 2004). Even though the phrase "time heals all wounds" is familiar, people neglect to consider this idea when forecasting their future negative reactions. Knowing that we readily cope with most setbacks might help people keep their perspective when they face failure or other setbacks. Even when it seems as if you will never recover from failing an important test, being heartbroken, or receiving a devastating medical diagnosis, the fact is that most people will adapt and find new meaning in their lives. How emotions affect thought processes such as decision making is discussed in greater detail in Chapter 10.

Profiles in Psychological Science

The Tragedy of Winning Olympic Silver

The dream of any Olympic athlete is to a win a gold medal. As the American tennis player Mardy Fish prepared for his final match at the 2004 Athens Olympics, he fantasized about standing on the podium listening to "The Star-Spangled Banner" while a gold medal was placed around his neck. Instead, he stood a step down on the podium with a silver medal and tears of sadness rather than joy, as he listened to the national anthem of Chile. Following the match he spoke to reporters about his disappointment: "I think the most disappointing thing about it was that I just really wanted to hear the national anthem . . . I think that the Olympics is the biggest thing, and a gold medal is the biggest prize in sports. And I felt like if, you know, if I heard the national anthem, and I felt like some tears would come there as well. Sure enough, they came, but it was a song that I had never heard of" (as cited on www. usoc.org/11604_25477.htm). Fish's Olympic performance was amazing. He was an unseeded player who made it to the medal stand. Yet the experience was bittersweet as he reflected on what he might have done differently to win the gold (Figure 8.9).

Perhaps ironically, Fish might have been happier if he had won a bronze medal instead of silver. According to research by the social psychologists Victoria Medvec, Scott Madey, and Thomas Gilovich, the subjective outcome of winning a silver medal can be more negative than that of winning a bronze. To test their hypothesis, Medvec and her colleagues (1995) examined videotapes of Olympic athletes at the moment they found out about the finish. For instance, they watched tapes of the instant that Jackie Joyner-Kersee completed her last long jump to win the bronze medal. They also examined video footage of the awards ceremonies where the athletes received their various medals, as when Matt Biondi received the silver for the 50-meter freestyle and the Lithuanian men's basketball team received bronze medals (in tie-dye uniforms to honor the Grateful Dead, who provided sponsorship for the

8.9 Mardy Fish Even though this unseeded tennis player won the silver medal at the 2004 Olympics, he was disappointed with the outcome.

team). Students watched the tape and rated the emotions expressed in the faces on a 10-point scale "from agony to ecstasy." The researchers found consistent evidence that bronze medal winners were happier than those who won silver, both at the moment of finding out how they did and also later on the stand.

What explains these reactions? The difference in medalists' emotional responses can be explained by counterfactual thinking, which is the act of imagining an outcome that didn't happen. For instance, "What would the United States be like if President Kennedy had survived the assassination attempt?" is a counterfactual in that it considers something happening that did not. People use counterfactual reasoning to gauge how a decision may feel, basing the actual decision on which imagined outcome produced the greatest elation and least regret. For example, when game-show contestants have to decide whether to keep the winnings they have already earned and quit, or risk losing all in the hopes of gaining an even bigger prize, many will choose to "quit while they're ahead," for fear of experiencing the inevitable regret that would result if they failed to win the bigger prize and ended up with nothing.

Let's use the idea of counterfactuals to explain the thoughts of bronze and silver medalists. For the bronze medalists, the most salient alternative outcome was not winning any medal, so compared with that situation, they are pretty happy. By contrast, the silver medalists are focused on having just missed the gold medal, not on having just beaten the bronze-medal winner. Indeed, when Medvec and colleagues had students listen to statements the athletes made during subsequent interviews, it was clear that silver medalists made comments such as "I almost," whereas bronze medalists made comments such as "At least I," indicating a completely different reference for interpreting the value of their medal.

You have probably engaged in similar counterfactual reasoning in your life, for instance, when you are happy with a B in a course in which you are just getting by but are frustrated by a B in a course in which you have higher expectations. Similarly, people report that they would feel more upset if they missed a flight by five minutes than if they missed one by an hour, even though in both cases they missed the flight. This is because in both cases we focus on how we might have done something different to get an A or make the flight. This counterfactual thinking leads to the paradox of greater disappointment for those who come closest to success. ■

Problem Solving Achieves Goals

We have considered how reasoning leads to beliefs and conclusions and how this knowledge can aid decisions. Much of the time our thoughts are focused on our goals and how we might achieve them. What do you have to do to get an A in this course? How do you get into your car when you've locked the keys inside? How can you make enough money to spend your spring break somewhere nice? Problem solving explores how people use knowledge to achieve goals. For our purposes, a person has a problem when faced with a goal with no simple and direct means for attaining that goal. The task in problem solving is to determine how to move from the current initial state to the goal state, which often requires overcoming obstacles and devising strategies. In this section we examine some of the best ways to solve problems. We will see that how we think about problems can help or hinder our ability to find solutions. Sometime we think the wrong thing, and sometimes perhaps we think too much.

ORGANIZATION OF SUBGOALS One approach to the study of problem solving is to identify the steps people take to find a solution to a problem. The idea is that people can solve most problems in a number of different ways. In turn, each solution

8.10 The Tower of Hanoi Problem To solve this problem you need to break the task down into subgoals.

insight The realization of a solution to a problem.

can be broken down into a series of stages or steps. Researchers examine how people go from one step to the next, the typical errors people make when tricky or unintuitive steps must be negotiated, and how people converge on more efficient—or, in some cases, less efficient—solutions.

For example, in the classic "Tower of Hanoi" problem, participants are given a board that has a row of three pegs on it, with the peg on one end having three discs stacked on it in a descending order of size, such that the largest disc is on the bottom (Figure 8.10). The task is to move the ordered stack of discs to the peg on the other end, with the following constraints: Only one disc can be moved at a time, and a larger disc can never be placed on top of a smaller disc. Go ahead and try it. The easiest way to simulate this problem is to use a quarter, nickel, and penny to represent the different-sized disks. Solving the "Tower of Hanoi" problem requires you to break the task down into *subgoals*. For instance, your first subgoal is to move the largest ring to the farthest peg. You can do this by first moving the smallest ring to the farthest peg, the middle ring to the middle peg, and then the smallest ring to the middle peg on top of the middle ring. You can now move the large ring to the farthest peg. Your next subgoal is to get the middle ring on top of the large ring, which you can do by moving the small ring to the first peg. And then you are pretty much done.

Using subgoals is important for many problems. Imagine that Sarah, a high school senior, has decided she would like to become a doctor. In order to achieve this goal, she needs first to attain the more immediate subgoal of being admitted to a good college. In order to get into a good college, she needs to earn good grades in high school. This additional subgoal would require developing good study skills and paying attention in class. Breaking down a problem into subgoals is an important component of problem solving, although identifying the appropriate steps or subgoals and their order can be challenging for complex problems for which there is no obvious next step.

SUDDEN INSIGHT Problems are not often identified as problems until they seem unsolvable and the problem solver is, more or less, "stuck." It is when we spot the keys in the ignition when we encounter the locked door that we know we have a problem. As we stand helplessly trying to figure out a solution, sometimes one will just "pop" into our heads. How does this happen? **Insight** is the stereotypical mental lightbulb going on in one's head, a metaphor that is used to capture the phenomenon of suddenly realizing the solution to a problem. In 1925, the Gestalt psychologist Wolfgang Köhler conducted one of psychology's most famous examples of research on insight; perhaps ironically, he did not use humans as his research subjects. Köhler was convinced that some animals could behave in an intelligent fashion, and so he set out to study whether chimpanzees could solve problems. Köhler would place a banana out of reach outside the chimp's cage, while providing several sticks that, if used properly, could be used to move the banana within grabbing distance. In one situation there were two sticks, but neither was long enough to reach the banana. One chimpanzee, who sat looking at the sticks for some time, suddenly grabbed the sticks and joined them together. This longer stick did the trick and the chimp was able to capture the banana. Köhler argued that, after pondering the problem poised by the distant banana, the chimp had eventually had the insight to join the sticks in order to make a tool long enough to reach the banana. Once the chimp solved the problem, it was able to transfer this solution to other similar problems and solve them quickly.

In another classic study of insight, Norman Maier (1931) brought participants, one at a time, into a room that had two strings hanging from the ceiling and a table in the corner. On the table were several random objects, including a pair of pliers. The task given to each participant was to tie the two strings together. However, it was impossible to grab both strings at once—if a participant was holding one string, the other was too far away to grab as well. The solution to the problem was to tie the pliers onto one of the strings, so that the string could be used as a pendulum; one could then hold the other string and then grab the pendulum string as it swung by. Although a few participants eventually figured out this solution on their own, most people were stumped by the problem. After letting people ponder the problem for ten minutes, Maier casually crossed the room and brushed up against the string, causing it to swing back and forth. Maier reported that once the participants saw the brushed string swinging, most immediately solved the problem, as if they had had new insight. However, none of the subjects reported that Maier gave them the solution. They all believed that they had come up with it on their own. As Gladwell notes in *Blink,* Maier's hint was so subtle that it registered only at the unconscious level. As we will see a bit later, unconscious processes might be quite good at helping us solve certain types of problems.

The study by Maier also provides an example of how insight can be achieved when a problem initially seems unsolvable. In this case, the possible functions of the string and pliers needed to be reconsidered to solve the problem. How we view or represent a problem can have a significant impact on how easily we solve it. For example, Maier's "pendulum" experiment is based on the expectation that most people will fail to see the pliers as a pendulum weight; that is, participants initially think about the problem in ways that fail to consider the solution based on creating a pendulum. If our current view isn't working, are there other, less obvious ways we could structure the problem? Although terms such as "thinking out of the box" and "think different" have become recent clichés in our culture, the ideas they embody have been around for a long time and continue to be of great value.

CHANGING REPRESENTATIONS TO OVERCOME OBSTACLES

There are some common ways in which people become stuck in solving a problem, as well as common strategies that they can use to help overcome obstacles in problem solving. Insight into a problem can arise when we suddenly *restructure* a problem in a novel way, discovering a solution that was not available under the old problem structure. **Restructuring** the representation of a problem can lead to the sudden "aha!" moment that is characteristic of insight. In one now-famous study, Scheerer (1963) gave participants a sheet of paper that had a square of nine dots on it (Figure 8.11). The task was to connect all the dots using only four straight lines, without lifting the pencil off the page. As shown in Figure 8.11, the solution is to structure the problem such that it is permissible to draw the lines beyond the box formed by the dots. The difficulty most people have when first encountering this task is that their representation of the problem fails to consider solutions that do not keep all lines within the square. Although keeping the lines within the box formed by the dots was not a requirement of the problem, most people have a tendency to regard the problem this way. Solving the problem requires restructuring their representation of it. Thinking differently about the constraints of the problem and eliminating some assumed constraints allows for a solution.

restructuring A new way of thinking about a problem that aids its solution.

8.11 Scheerer's Nine-Dot Problem The problem (a) is solved by realizing that the lines can extend beyond the boundary formed by the dots (b).

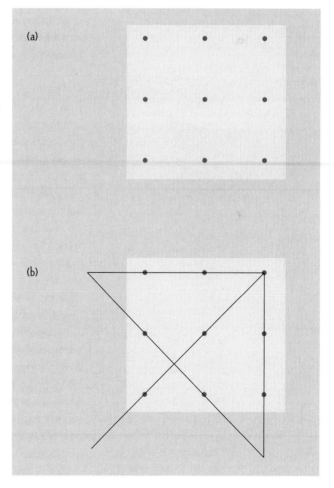

(a)

(b)

mental set A problem solving strategy that has worked in the past.

functional fixedness A tendency in problem solving to think of objects only as they are most commonly used.

8.12 Luchins's Mental Set Try to solve the water-jar problem. As described in the text, the solution for the early trials is B − A − 2(C). People fail to notice that later trials have an easier solution.

Desired water	Jar A	Jar B	Jar C
100	21	127	3
8	18	48	11
62	10	80	4
31	20	59	4
29	20	57	4
20	23	49	3
25	28	76	3

When we consider a solution to a problem, we commonly think back to how we solved similar problems in the past. Thus, we tend to persist with a previous strategy, known as a **mental set**, which sometimes makes it difficult to find the best solution. Abraham Luchins demonstrated a classic example of a mental set in 1942 (Figure 8.12). He gave participants three jars of different sizes and indicated that they had to use these jars to measure out specified amounts of water. For example, participants might be told that Jar A holds 21 cups, Jar B holds 127 cups, and Jar C holds 3 cups. Using these three jars, participants are asked to measure exactly 100 cups of water. The solution to this problems is to fill up Jar B with 127 cups, and then use Jar A to remove 21 cups of water, and use Jar C to remove 3 cups of water twice, which would leave 100 cups remaining in Jar B. The structure to the solution is B − A − 2(C). Participants are then given many similar problems in which the jar sizes and goal measurements differ, but in each the same formula applies. Participants are then given another problem, Jar A holds 23 cups of water, Jar B holds 49 cups of water, and Jar C holds 3 cups of water. Participants are asked to measure 20 cups of water. Luchins (1942) found that even though the simplest solution to the task would be to fill Jar A and remove 3 cups with Jar C, participants usually came up with the much more complicated solution using all three jars. Having developed a mental set of using three jars in combination to solve this type of problem, it was difficult for them to settle on the simpler solution using only two jars. Surprisingly, when given a problem that had a simple solution and for which the original formula did not work (see the last line of Figure 8.12), many participants failed to solve the problem.

Our mental representations about the typical functions of objects can also create difficulties in problem solving. Overcoming **functional fixedness** requires the problem solver to reinterpret the potential use or function of an object. For example, the candle problem, introduced by Karl Duncker (1945), gave people a candle, a box of matches, a bulletin board, and a box of tacks (Figure 8.13). Imagine how you would solve this problem: *Using only these objects, attach the candle to the bulletin board in such a way that the candle can be lit and burn properly.* Most people have difficulty in coming up with an adequate solution. However, if we reinterpret the function of the box, a solution emerges. Viewing the box not as a container for the matches but as a stand for the candle allows for an easy solution: The side of the box is tacked to the bulletin board so that it creates a stand; the candle is then placed on the box and lit. In general, it is difficult for subjects to view the box as a possible stand when it is being used as a container for the matches. When participants are shown representations of this problem with an empty box and the matches on the table next to it, it is somewhat easier to solve.

Restructuring the problem, breaking out of a mental set, and overcoming functional fixedness are all techniques that require the problem solver to view a problem differently and restructure the initial mental representations. Restructuring can lead to creative insights into how to solve difficult problems. It also forms the basis for a lot of humor. *Have you heard about the new restaurant that opened on the moon? It has great food, but no atmosphere!* Whether or not you found this joke amusing, a common thread in humor is that expectations based on common representations are often violated. The premise of this joke is that *atmosphere,* when interpreted in light of the restaurant schema, means one thing, but the fact that the restaurant is on the moon requires another interpretation. The ability to restructure representations not only leads to insight into problem solutions, but is also a key component of creativity and humor.

CONSCIOUS STRATEGIES Although restructuring mental representations is a valuable means to develop insight into solving a problem, it is often difficult to enact this as a conscious strategy when we are stuck. However, we can systematically apply strategies that may help lead to a solution. Two common heuristic strategies to overcome obstacles in problem solving are *working backward* and *finding an appropriate analogy.*

For complex problems, the appropriate steps to the solution are not always clear. One means of generating different strategies about how to solve a problem is to work backward from the goal state to the initial state. Consider the "water lily" problem (Sternberg & Davidson, 1983):

> Water lilies double in area every 24 hours. On the first day of summer there is only one water lily on the lake. It takes 60 days for the lake to be completely covered in water lilies. How many days does it take for half of the lake to be covered in water lilies?

One way to solve this problem is to figure that on day 1 there is one water lily, so on day 2 there are two water lilies, on day 3 there will be four water lilies, and so on, until you discover how many water lilies there are on day 60 and see which day had half that many. But if you work backward, you will realize that if the water lilies double every 24 hours and if on day 60 the lake is covered in water lilies, then on day 59 half of the lake must have been covered in water lilies. The natural tendency when problem solving is to focus on how to move from the initial state toward the goal state. However, at times it helps to consider working backward from the goal state to the initial state when trying to find the best solution.

Another common strategy to overcoming a problem-solving obstacle is to *find an appropriate analogy* (Reeves & Weisberg, 1994). For example, imagine that a doctor is dealing with a patient who has a tumor. The doctor has a laser that, when used at a high intensity, could destroy the tumor. However, an intensity high enough to destroy the tumor would also destroy the surrounding living tissue. How can the doctor safely use the laser without damaging the living tissue through which the rays must travel? The vast majority of people have a hard time when this type of problem is presented by itself (Duncker, 1945). However, when they are given an example of an analogous situation, their ability to solve this problem improves substantially.

Now imagine that the doctor reads a story about a general who wanted to capture a fortress. A large number of soldiers were needed to capture the fortress, but all the roads to the fortress were planted with mines. Small groups of soldiers could safely travel the roads, but the mines would be detonated by a larger group. In order to move all the soldiers he needed to the fortress, the general divided his army into smaller groups and had each group take a different road to the fortress where they would converge and attack together.

From reading this story about a problem with analogous constraints, the doctor might get the idea to aim several lasers at the tumor from different angles. Each laser by itself can be weak enough so that it does not destroy the living tissue in its path, but the combined intensity of all the lasers converging at the tumor could be strong enough to destroy it. When we are given analogous problems, the ability to find a solution is enhanced. According to some researchers, those participants who are given two or more analogous descriptions develop a schema for the solution, which helps them solve similar problems in the future (Gick & Holyoak, 1983). However, analogous solutions work only if people recognize that the problem they face is similar to those they have solved in the past (Keane, 1987; Reeves & Weisberg, 1994).

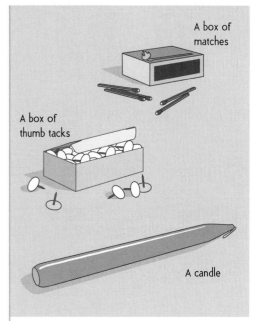

A box of matches

A box of thumb tacks

A candle

8.13 Overcoming Functional Fixedness
People are given the task of attaching a candle to the wall using only these materials. The solution requires restructuring our concept of the matchbox (see the following page for the solution).

Matchbox

Tacks

How might conscious thought interfere with problem solving?

We can also benefit from finding an appropriate analogy when trying to discover how to achieve life goals. For example, recent immigrants to the United States often have difficulty navigating the customs and expectations of the new culture and country. Other immigrants with a similar background who have succeeded in their new home can provide examples of paths that lead to success. We look to role models to provide examples of achieving certain goals because we believe that we may achieve a similar outcome if we follow an analogous path.

UNCONSCIOUS PROCESSING Common sense tells us that consciously thinking about a problem or deliberating about our options is the best strategy for solving problems and making decisions. We have noted, however, that insight and intuition seem to benefit from unconscious processing. In *Blink,* Gladwell makes the bold claim that fast decisions are often superior to those that follow deliberative thought. Clearly this is not always true. Which number is larger, the square root of 6724 or nine squared? You probably can't provide an immediate answer—you have to solve this problem consciously by doing the calculations. But does not consciously thinking sometimes produce superior outcomes to thinking? A recent study by Ap Dijksterhuis (2004) at the University of Amsterdam required people to evaluate complex information regarding real-world choices, for example, selecting an apartment. In each case they had to choose between various alternatives that had many negative and positive features, such as a nice landlord, cheap rent, bad location, and so on, but objectively, one apartment was a better choice. Participants were assigned to one of three conditions, which required them either to make an immediate choice (no thought), think for three minutes and then choose (conscious thought), or work for three minutes on a difficult, distracting task and then choose (unconscious thought). Across three separate studies, those in the unconscious thought condition made the best decisions. According to Dijksterhuis, unconscious processing is especially valuable for complex, difficult decisions in which it is difficult to weigh the pros and cons consciously. A similar phenomenon has also been reported in the creativity literature. Anecdotal reports suggest that allowing an idea to incubate over time helps in problem solving. Perhaps this is why for really important decisions people are often told to "sleep on it."

Can conscious thought undermine good decision making? Tim Wilson and Jonathan Schooler (1991) had research participants rate jam. When research participants simply tasted the jam, their ratings were very similar to ratings made by experts. However, when the participants had to explain their rating for each product, their ratings differed substantially from those of the experts. Having to talk about their reasons apparently altered their perception of the jam. Jonathan Schooler introduced the concept of *verbal overshadowing* to describe the impairment of performance that occurs when people try to explain verbally perceptual experiences that are not easy to describe (Schooler & Engslter-Schooler, 1990; Schooler, 2002). For example, participants who had to provide a verbal description of a person they saw in a simulated bank robbery were less able to pick the person out of a lineup than participants who did not provide a description. In another study, people who were asked to describe the taste of wines were less able to pick out the wine later than those who simply tasted the wine without describing it (Melcher & Schooler, 1996). The gist of these studies is that we really aren't good at using verbal labels to describe perceptual experiences, and so when we are forced to do so it impairs our processing of that perceptual information.

Consider one more example of how thinking too much can cause negative outcomes. Imagine looking at two lights, one red, the other green. Your job is to predict, on each trial, which light will come on. If you are correct you will receive some small reward. As you are performing this task, the lights flash in a random sequence, but overall the red light flashes 70 percent of the time. People are pretty quick to notice that the red light comes on more often. So to receive the most reward, what is the best strategy to follow? After doing this task a number of times, most nonhuman animals simply choose the most probable response 100 percent of the time; thereafter they are rewarded on 70 percent of the trials. This makes great sense in terms of adaptiveness. Humans do something much different. They appear to try to figure out patterns in the way the lights are presented, and they choose the red light about 70 percent of the time. That is, overall their choices match the frequency of how often red flashes, but because the lights are randomly presented, on any given trial they are often wrong. Indeed, in the 70 percent scenario, it turns out that they receive rewards on only 58 percent of the trials. Why don't humans follow the optimal strategy, which even rats can figure out? According to George Wolford and colleagues (2000), people search for patterns that might not even exist. These researchers attribute this human tendency to the workings of the left hemisphere *interpreter,* which as you recall from Chapter 4 tries to make sense out of the world. To test this idea, Wolford and colleagues had two split-brain patients perform a version of this task. They found that the patients' right hemispheres tended to respond in the optimal way that animals did (choosing the same thing 100 percent of the time), whereas the patients' left hemispheres matched that frequency but continued to guess both outcomes. The tendency of the left hemisphere interpreter to seek patterns and try to find relations between events may be adaptive in some contexts, but it can produce less-than-optimal outcomes when a pattern doesn't really exist. The greater reliance on verbal processes on the left hemisphere may also contribute to the impairments caused by verbal overshadowing (Schooler, 2002). Although exactly why thinking too much can impair memory and judgment is unclear, it appears that some things are best left unsaid, and that sometimes it is better to "sleep on it" before making important decisions. Unconscious processes may have a greater influence over our decisions that has previously been recognized.

"This isn't a hasty decision. A lot of daydreaming went into it."

Thinking Critically

Are More Choices Always Better?

In our modern society, people widely believe that the more choices we have, the better. But today we face an ever increasing array of choices for just about everything, from health-care plans to career options. Daily life requires deciding among countless options. Instead of ordering a cup of coffee, we now have to decide whether we want a latte, cappuccino, or mocha, as well as whether we want it hot or cold. Ice cream comes in dozens of flavors. We can choose from hundreds of different brands of breakfast cereal, and even numerous brands of bottled water. Although some choice is better than none, is there any downside to having too much choice? According to some scholars, too much choice can be frustrating, unsatisfying, and ultimately debilitating (Schwartz, 2004). Is there a tyranny of choice? What is the relation between choice and well-being? Are more choices always better?

317

Imagine if you were told which car to drive, which kind of food to eat, or what brand of shoes to wear. Not being able to choose violates our sense of freedom, at least in Western cultures. Indeed, having a sense of control in our lives and feeling free to choose how we act are generally viewed as beneficial to mental health. But when too many options are available, especially when all of them are attractive, people experience conflict and indecision. Consider a study in which shoppers were presented with a variety of gourmet jams (Iyengar & Lepper, 2000). In a grocery store, shoppers encountered a display containing either six or 24 varieties of jam to sample. They were also given a discount coupon to encourage them to make a purchase. Whereas the greater variety of jams attracted more shoppers, it failed to produce more sales; 30 percent of those with the limited choice bought jam compared with only 3 percent who did so with the greater variety. In a subsequent study, these investigators found that people choosing among a limited selection of chocolates were more satisfied with their selection than those who chose from a wider variety.

According to the psychologist Barry Schwartz, having too much choice can make some people miserable. He divides the world into groups he calls "satisficers" and "maximizers." Satisficers live according to a "good enough" philosophy. Schwartz borrowed the term from the late Nobel laureate psychologist Herbert Simon, who described satisficing as choosing an option that sufficiently satisfies needs. It isn't that satisficers lack standards, but they look around until they find something that most closely matches what they want and then buy it. They don't worry about whether there are better or cheaper products available. They like good things, but they don't care if those things are not the absolute best.

By contrast, maximizers always seek to make the best possible choices. They devote serious time and effort to reading labels, checking out consumer magazines, reading Internet reviews, considering alternatives, and comparing prices. They often feel frustrated by the countless options available to them and feel paralyzed by indecision, as they have to select between equally attractive choices. For maximizers, costs are associated with making the wrong choice. Choosing to order the fish special for dinner means that you won't have the pleasure of tasting the chicken special. What if the fish isn't good tonight? What if the chicken is a better choice? Not only do they hesitate in making decisions, but maximizers continue to evaluate options even after they have made their selection. As a result, they are generally more disappointed with their decisions and more likely to experience regret. They continue to analyze and question their choice, often ruminating about its negative features.

The paradox of choice might also be responsible for a cultural shift in the age at which people are settling into jobs and marriage. Historically, people were set in their career paths and often married and having children before age 25. A pattern emerging in industrialized nations is for young adults to delay all of this for many years, as they explore the vast number of options they have for working and seek a mate who matches their ideals (Grossman, 2005). In countries such as Canada, England, France, Germany, Italy, and Japan, the average age of marriage is now approaching 30. One possible explanation for this phenomenon is that young adults are trying to maximize their life choices. They want just the right job and just the right marriage. After all, picking badly in either of these areas can lead to serious consequences. The burden of making the right decision means that many young adults fail to make any decisions. The growth of options has turned more and more young adults into maximizers.

According to Schwartz, the consequence of nearly unlimited choice may explain the increase in clinical depression in modern countries. "If the experience of disappointment is relentless, if virtually every choice you make fails to live up to expectations and aspirations, and if you consistently take personal responsibility for the disappointments, the trivial looms larger and larger, and the conclusion that you can't do anything right becomes devastating" (2004, p. 215).

What can we do about the problem of maximizing? Schwartz suggests that people restrict their options when the decision isn't crucial and to settle for a choice that meets their needs even if it isn't the absolute best. He also encourages people not to dwell on their choices but instead to focus on the positive aspects of the decision they made. Does this sound to you as if Schwartz is advising people to strive for mediocrity? How much effort should you put into making good choices? Do you think you would be happier if you had fewer choices? Do you think having too many options is responsible for the recent increase in depression and other cultural changes, as when people put off careers and marriage? ■

REVIEWING
the Principles | How Do We Make Decisions and Solve Problems?

People use deductive and inductive reasoning to draw conclusions and then use decision making to choose among alternatives. Although normative models, such as the expected utility theory, have often been assumed to be accurate because they describe how decisions should occur if humans are performing optimally, it is increasingly clear that a number of factors that influence our choices are not completely rational. The descriptive approach to understanding reasoning, decision making, and problem solving shows that people often use heuristics that can lead to faulty outcomes, that they fail to take into account information such as base rates, and that their decisions tend to confirm that which they already believed. To solve problems, people often need to reconsider the problem and break out of their mental set. Working backward and finding an appropriate analogy are useful conscious strategies. Unconscious processes also play an important role in problem solving and decision making.

How Do We Understand Intelligence?

So far, we have considered the manner in which knowledge is represented in the mind and how we use this knowledge to make decisions and solve problems. One of the most hotly debated topics in psychological science concerns how knowledge and its application in everyday life translate into *intelligence,* and the relative degree to which intelligence is determined by our genes and our environment (Neisser et al., 1996). **Intelligence** is the human ability to use knowledge to solve problems, understand complex ideas, learn quickly, and adapt to environmental challenges. As modern society becomes more complex, with greater amounts of information available and greater demands on people to understand it all, being able to adapt to change and deal with increasing complexity is becoming more and more important (Gottfredson, 2004a; Lubinski, 2004). To succeed, people need to be innovative and "stay ahead of the curve." We are all intelligent beings. But there are individual differences among us in terms of intelligence, just as there are differences in our physical and psychological characteristics. So how do we know someone's level of intelligence?

intelligence The human ability to use knowledge, solve problems, understand complex ideas, learn quickly, and adapt to environmental challenges.

The earliest efforts to study intelligence were led by Sir Francis Galton in the late 1800s. Galton believed that intelligence was related to the speed of neural responses and the sensitivity of sensory/perceptual systems—the quicker our responses and the keener our perceptions, the smarter Galton believed us to be. Since that time researchers have taken numerous different approaches to defining and studying intelligence. Today three general approaches to understanding intelligence cross the major levels of analysis. The first focuses on how people perform on standardized achievement tests. This *psychometric* approach examines what people know and the skills they have for solving problems. The *cognitive* approach examines the particular mental abilities that allow people to operate in an intelligent fashion. In this approach researchers examine how information is processed, for instance, the speed at which people can react, the amount of information they can hold in memory, and the extent to which they can stay focused on a task. Finally, the *biological* approach is concerned with how the brain processes information and the extent to which differences in brain activity are affected by genes and the environment.

Intelligence Is Assessed by Psychometric Tests

For much of the last century, the psychometric approach to intelligence has been the most dominant and influential, especially in terms of how intelligence is viewed in everyday life. Tests that focus on *achievement* assess current levels of skill and knowledge. These are the kinds of exams that millions of American schoolchildren now take every three years as mandated by the federal government as part of the No Child Left Behind Act. *Aptitude* tests examine whether people will be good at various tasks in the future. Scores on aptitude tests such as the SAT and the GRE are widely used to predict how you will perform academically, which is why taking the tests makes most people very anxious. Aptitude tests also predict what kinds of jobs people might be good at, for example, whether they might make good accountants, pilots, or even spies. Performance on these tests can have a huge impact on people's lives. Given these high stakes, what do we know about intelligence testing?

The measurement of intelligence began in earnest just over a century ago. At the encouragement of the French government, Alfred Binet (Figure 8.14) developed the first method of assessing intelligence to identify children in the French school system who needed extra attention and instruction. Binet proposed that intelligence is best understood as a collection of high-level mental processes—in today's terms, attributes such as "verbal," "mathematical," and "analytical" abilities. Accordingly, with the help of his assistant Théodore Simon, Binet developed a test for measuring children's vocabulary, memory, skill with numbers, and other mental abilities—the *Binet-Simon Intelligence Scale*. One assumption underlying the test was that although students might do better on some of the specific components by chance, how they performed on average across the different components would be a good indicator of students' overall level of intelligence. Indeed, Binet found that scores on his tests were consistent with teachers' beliefs about children's abilities and the grades that they received.

A number of different intelligence tests have been developed since Binet's test. In the United States, the psychologist Lewis Terman of Stanford University modified the Binet-Simon test and established normative scores for American children. This test, revised for the fifth time in 2003, remains among the most widely used for children in the United States. In 1939 David Wechsler developed a test for use among adults, which is called the Wechsler Adult Intelligence Scale (WAIS), the most current version being the WAIS-III. The WAIS has two separate parts, each consisting

8.14 Alfred Binet Binet launched the psychometric approach to intelligence.

of several tasks. The *verbal* part measures such aspects as comprehension, vocabulary, and general knowledge. The *performance* part involves nonverbal tasks, such as arranging pictures in proper order, assembling parts to make a whole object, and identifying missing features from a picture.

INTELLIGENCE QUOTIENT An important concept introduced by Binet was the idea of **mental age**, which is an assessment of a child's intellectual standing compared with that of peers of the same age. Binet noticed that some children seem to think like normal children of a younger or older age. Thus, for instance, an eight-year-old who reads Shakespeare and performs calculus might score as well as the average 16-year-old, thus giving the eight-year-old a mental age of 16. Mental age is determined by comparing a given child's test score with the average score for children of each chronological age. For example, the **intelligence quotient (IQ)**, developed by the German psychologist Wilhelm Stern, is computed by dividing a child's estimated mental age by the child's chronological age and then multiplying this number by 100: For our child prodigy, this would mean an IQ of 200!

Although the term *IQ* continues to be used, it is no longer conceptualized in the same way, because using a strict ratio has serious flaws. For instance, consider a child who has a mental age of six. The day before his sixth birthday his IQ is 120, and then overnight his IQ drops to 100. Likewise, a 40-year-old professor would have to have an IQ of 230 just to be as smart as a typical undergraduate. Thus, the ratio concept of IQ does not apply equally to all different age groups. Today the average IQ is set at the value of 100, with norms for assessing where people stand relative to this average. Across large groups of people, the distribution of IQ scores forms a bell curve, which is known as a *normal distribution* (Figure 8.15). Most people are close to the average, with fewer and fewer people at the tails of the distribution. Recall from Chapter 2 the statistical concept of standard deviation, which indicates how far people are from the average. The standard deviation for most IQ tests is 15, such as that approximately 68 people fall within 1 standard deviation (they score from 85 to 115) and just over 95 percent of people fall within 2 standard deviations (they score from 70 to 130).

VALIDITY Are intelligence tests valid? That is, do they really measure what they claim to measure? The overall evidence indicates that IQ is a reasonably good predictor of grades at school and performance at work (Gottfredson, 2004b). For example, students who score high on tests such as the SAT tend to do better than those who score less well. In a recent analysis of more than 20,000 people who took the Millers Analogy Test, researchers found that high scores not only predicted graduate students' academic performance, but also their productivity, creativity, and job performance (Kuncel, Hezlett, & Ones, 2004). Similarly, people who have professional careers, such as attorneys, accountants, and physicians, tend to have high IQs. Those with jobs such as a miner, farmer, lumberjack, or barber tend to have lower IQs (Jencks, 1979; Schmidt & Hunter, 2004). Of course, this refers to averages rather than to individuals, but overall the data suggest a modest correlation between IQ and work performance as well as income. The relation between IQ and work performance also holds within professions, at least for those jobs requiring complex

mental age An assessment of a child's intellectual standing relative to that of his or her peers; determined by a comparison of the child's test score with the average score for children of each chronological age.

intelligence quotient (IQ) The number computed by dividing a child's estimated mental age by the child's chronological age, and then multiplying this number by 100.

8.15 The Distribution of IQ Scores Across the population, IQ is distributed in a bell-curve shape, such that most people score close to the mean. The height of the curve reflects the percentage of people scoring at each level of IQ. The mean IQ is set at 100 with a standard deviation of 15. Just over 68 percent of people have an IQ within one standard deviation of the mean, which means they will score between 85 and 115. Fewer than 3 percent of people have an IQ of more than 130, which is 2 standard deviations of the mean.

"I don't have to be smart, because someday I'll just hire lots of smart people to work for me."

Why might students with privileged backgrounds score especially high on IQ tests?

skills. Although IQ does not predict who will be a better truck driver, it does predict who will be a better computer programmer (Schmidt & Hunter, 2004).

We should note a number of things regarding these findings. First, IQ scores typically predict only about 25 percent of the variation in work or school performance, which means that other factors also matter (Neisser et al., 1996). Children who come from privileged backgrounds tend to have higher IQs, but it is possible that these students have other advantages that help them succeed, such as family contacts who can help them find good summer internships or access to better schools that can cater to their needs. Moreover, there are large individual differences in motivation, and some people are willing to spend more time working to get ahead. One 20-year follow-up study of nearly 2,000 gifted 13-year-olds (i.e., those with IQs in the top 1 - percent of their age group) revealed huge differences in how much people reported working as well as what they said they were willing to work. At age 33, some individuals refused to work more than 40 hours per week, whereas others reported regularly working more than 70 (Lubinski & Benbow, 2000). You can imagine how much more someone working 60 or 70 hours per week can accomplish compared with someone working 25 or 30, and therefore perhaps how such a person might be more likely to make partner in a law firm or earn a higher income (Lubinski, 2004). In other words, although IQ may be important, it is one among several factors that contribute to success in the classroom or the workplace.

CULTURAL BIAS One important criticism of intelligence tests is that they may unfairly penalize people from some cultures or groups. Doing well on many tests of intelligence requires intimate knowledge of mainstream culture and language. For instance, consider this analogy:

> STRING is to GUITAR as REED is to:
> (a) TRUMPET
> (b) OBOE
> (c) VIOLIN
> (d) TROMBONE

Being able to solve this analogy requires specific knowledge of these instruments, in particular knowing that an oboe uses a reed to make music. But unless you were exposed to this information, it is unlikely you could answer the question. Moreover, some words mean different things to different groups, and how a person answers a test item is determined by its meaning in his or her culture. When Randy Jackson on *American Idol* describes someone's performance as "da bomb," he doesn't mean she or he did badly. He means it was a *cool* performance, which also doesn't mean it was cold. And so on. A person's exposure to mainstream language and culture affects which meaning of a word comes most quickly to mind, if the person knows the meaning at all.

What it means to be intelligent also varies across cultures. Most measures of IQ reflect values of what is considered important in modern Western culture, such as being quick witted or speaking well. But what is adaptive in one society is not necessarily adaptive in others. One approach to dealing with cultural bias is to use items that do not depend on language, such as the performance measures of the WAIS. Other tests show series of patterns and asks the person to identify the missing pattern (Figure 8.16). Although these tests may be fairer than those that rely on understanding language, it is difficult to remove all forms of bias from the testing situation, which even includes the extent to which test takers are motivated to do well. Doing well on IQ tests matters more to some than to others, and therefore tests are biased to favor those who wish to do well.

General Intelligence Involves Multiple Components

Binet's original conception viewed intelligence as a general overall ability. However, we all know people who are especially talented in some areas but have weaknesses in others. Some of us feel more confident, for example, in our ability to write poetry than in our ability to solve difficult calculus problems. The question then is whether intelligence reflects one talent or many. One early line of evidence indicating that intelligence reflects a general capacity used a statistical procedure that analyzes the extent to which different test items are related to each other. By examining the correlations among all items, *factor analysis* creates clusters of items that are most similar to one another; these clusters are referred to as factors. Using this method, Charles Spearman (1904) found that most intelligence test items tended to cluster as one factor, and that people who scored high on one particular type of item also tended to score highly on other types of items; people who are very good at math are also good at writing, problem solving, and other mental challenges. Spearman viewed **general intelligence**, known as **g**, as a factor that contributed to performance on any intellectual task. In a sense, providing a single IQ score reflects the idea that one general factor underlies intelligence. Although most psychological scientists agree that some form of g exists, they also recognize different forms of intelligence, which we now examine.

FLUID VS. CRYSTALLIZED INTELLIGENCE Raymond Cattell (1971) agreed with Spearman but believed that g is made up of two different types of intelligence. **Fluid intelligence** involves information processing, especially in novel or complex circumstances, such as reasoning, drawing analogies, and thinking quickly and flexibly. It is often assessed in nonverbal culture-free intelligence tests, such as completing a series of complex patterns (see Figure 8.16). In contrast, **crystallized intelligence** concerns knowledge we acquire through experience, such as accumulated vocabulary and cultural information, and the ability to use this knowledge to solve problems. Distinguishing between fluid and crystallized is somewhat analogous to distinguishing between working memory (which is more like fluid intelligence) and long-term memory (which is more like crystallized intelligence). As would be expected because both intelligences are components of g, people who score high on one factor also score high on the other, which suggests that a strong crystallized intelligence is likely aided by a strong fluid intelligence.

MULTIPLE INTELLIGENCES Whereas Cattell argued that two different types of intelligence contribute to g, Howard Gardner (1983) proposed his theory of **multiple intelligences**, in which he identified different types of intellectual talents that are independent from one another. For example, he proposed that musical intelligence enables some people to discriminate subtle variations in pitch or timbre and also have a greater than average appreciation of music. Gardner also proposed bodily-kinesthetic intelligence, which is possessed by some individuals, such as athletes and dancers, who are highly attuned to their bodies and able to control their motions with exquisite skill. Gardner also described other intelligences, such as linguistic

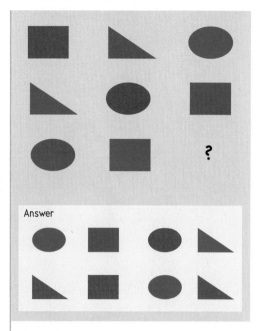

8.16 Removing Bias from Tests Test takers are asked to identify the missing pattern in the sequence. For instance, which of the eight objects completes the sequence? The ability to answer this question does not rely on verbal knowledge and is therefore not culturally biased. The correct answer is the first triangle in the second row.

general intelligence (g) The idea that one general factor underlies all mental abilities.

fluid intelligence Information processing in novel or complex circumstances.

crystallized intelligence Knowledge acquired through experience and the ability to use that knowledge.

multiple intelligences The idea that people can show different skills in a variety of different domains.

8.17 Multiple Intelligences Howard Gardner suggested that intelligence can take many different forms. Here, four different types of intelligence are represented by (a) athlete Mia Hamm, (b) musician Yo Yo Ma, (c) scientist Shirley Jackson, and (d) artist Diego Rivera.

(excellent verbal skills), mathematical/logical, spatial (thinking in terms of images and pictures), intrapersonal (or self-understanding), and interpersonal (or social understanding) (Figure 8.17).

One important feature of Gardner's theory is that it recognizes that people can be average or even deficient in some domains and outstanding in others. Consider the Juilliard School student Jay Greenberg, who by age 12 had written five full-length symphonies, including *The Storm,* which was commissioned by the New Haven Symphony and composed in just a few hours. Greenberg, a typical boy in all other regards, has been described as perhaps the greatest *prodigy* in the last two hundred years; his composing skills are said to rival those of historical greats such as Mozart and Beethoven. How does he do this? Greenberg told *60 Minutes* that he doesn't know where the music comes from, but he hears it fully written, as if it were being played by an orchestra in his head (*60 Minutes,* November 28, 2004).

We currently know very little about how prodigies come to be. Nor do we know much about another interesting group, known as *savants,* people with minimal intellectual capacities in most domains, but who at a very early age show an exceptional ability in some sort of "intelligent" process, such as math, music, or art. The talents of savants can be quite striking. Oliver Sacks (1995) recounts the story of an artistic savant named Stephen who could reproduce highly accurate drawings of buildings and places years after having only glanced at them (Figure 8.19). Further, his drawings were so remarkable that by the time he was a young teenager, he had a book of his artwork published. However, Stephen has *autism* (see Chapter 13), and it was only with the utmost effort that he was able to acquire language sufficient even for the simplest verbal communication.

According to Gardner, each person has a unique pattern of intelligences so that no one should be viewed as "smarter" than others, just differently talented. As appealing as this idea is, some psychological scientists have questioned whether being able to control body movements or compose music is truly a form of intelligence or whether such abilities should more appropriately be considered specialized talents. If a person is a bit of a klutz or tone deaf, does that make him unintelligent? To date we still have no standardized ways to assess many of Gardner's intelligences, in part because Gardner believes that the tests we do have fail to capture the true essence of intelligence. Instead, Gardner provides exemplars, such as the artist Pablo Picasso, the dancer Martha Graham, the physicist Albert Einstein, and the poet T. S. Eliot. There is no denying that each is especially talented in his or her field, but these individuals were likely talented in many respects, and all might be considered to have been high in general intelligence (Gottfredson, 2004b).

8.19 Stephen Wiltshire Although he has autism, Stephen Wiltshire can produce amazingly accurate drawings after glancing at something.

The Yale psychologist Robert Sternberg (1999) proposed a different type of theory that supports the notion of multiple intelligences. His theory involves three types of intelligence: analytical, creative, and practical. *Analytical intelligence* is similar to that measured by psychometric tests, such as being good in problem solving, analogies, puzzles, and other academic challenges. *Creative intelligence* involves the ability to gain insight and solve novel problems, to think in new and interesting ways. Finally, *practical intelligence* refers to understanding how people deal with everyday tasks, from knowing whether a parking space is large enough for your vehicle, to "reading" people, to becoming an effective leader. Each of these tasks is a challenge in daily life and people who are capable of performing them tend to get ahead. For instance, many successful business leaders and politicians received only marginal grades in college. Bill Gates dropped out of college, yet has developed one of the world's largest companies and now is the richest person alive. The current U.S. president, George W. Bush, was a mediocre student at best. The flamboyant British billionaire Richard Branson did not even attend college; neither did the cosmetic giant Estée Lauder. Each of these individuals clearly has talents that led to phenomenal success in spite of not doing well at traditional academics.

EMOTIONAL INTELLIGENCE Another type of intelligence is *emotional intelligence*. Conceived by the psychological scientists Peter Salovey and John Mayer, and subsequently popularized by the science writer Daniel Goleman, **emotional intelligence (EQ)** is a form of social intelligence that emphasizes the ability to perceive, understand, manage, and use emotions to guide thoughts and actions (Salovey & Mayer, 1990). Emotional intelligence involves such skills as being able to manage frustration, control one's emotions, and get along with other people. People high in EQ recognize emotional experiences in themselves and others and are able to respond to those emotions in a productive fashion. As you will discover in Chapters 9 and 10, emotions can sometimes overwhelm cognition and undermine motivation. When people are upset they sometimes act impulsively and thoughtlessly, for instance, lashing out at others, eating a cupboard full of chocolate, or doing other things they later regret. Being able to regulate mood, resist impulses and temptations, and control behavior are all important components of EQ. The idea of emotional intelligence

emotional intelligence (EQ) A form of social intelligence that emphasizes the ability to perceive, understand, manage, and use emotions to guide thoughts and actions.

has had a large impact in schools and industry, and programs have been designed to increase the emotional intelligence of students and workers. At the same time, some critics have questioned whether EQ really is a type of intelligence or whether it stretches the idea of intelligence too far. What the concept of emotional intelligence highlights is that many human qualities are important, and that independent of whether it is a type of intelligence, emotional intelligence is advantageous for those who have it.

IMPORTANCE OF G Even as intelligence may be defined in different ways, there is likely a general capacity that supports most of them, namely g. Some scholars have viewed g as a statistical anomaly that has no factual basis. Within the last few years, however, a growing number of psychological scientists have concluded that g exists and that it exerts an important influence over life's outcomes (Conway, Kane, & Engle, 2003; Deary, 2001; Garlick, 2002; Gray & Thompson, 2004; Haier, Jung, Yeo, Head, & Alkire, 2005; Plomin & Spinath, 2002). Research has shown that not only does g predict work and school performance, but it also predicts longevity. Indeed, low g is related to early death from a variety of causes, including heart disease, diabetes, stroke, Alzheimer's disease, traffic accidents, drownings, and other accidents (Gottfredson, 2004a; Gottfredson & Deary, 2004). Why might this occur? It may be the case simply because a number of different environmental forces are at work on each of us, such as differential access to health care, dangerous jobs, or other social factors. According to Linda Gottfredson, however, g may directly affect our own health. People who score high on psychometric measures of g may have greater health knowledge, be better able to follow medical advice, understand the link between behavior and health, and generally be more literate about health issues. As medical knowledge itself rapidly advances and becomes more complex, trying to keep up with and process all of this new information is a daunting challenge. From this perspective, people who are higher in g have an advantage in doing so. This is a provocative idea that warrants further investigation. But should it be true, it has a number of important implications for the medical system and how doctors communicate medical advice.

General intelligence, especially fluid intelligence, seems to be most important for predicting performance in jobs that require fast and creative thinking. Why is this? A number of theorists have proposed that the value of g is that it allows people to adapt quickly to environmental challenges, and the more complex the challenge, the greater the importance of g. Satoshi Kanazawa (2004) suggests that general intelligence is relevant only to evolutionarily novel situations. He notes that for most of human evolution, our ancestors on the savannah experienced few changes in their daily routines. Indeed, the life of a prehistoric hunting-gathering woman was pretty much the same as that of her mother, and of her grandmother, and of her great-grandmother, and so on for thousands of years. Only once in a while did some novel event occur, such as a drought or other natural disaster, and it was at these moments that those high in g had an advantage. According to Kanazawa, g does not matter for recurring adaptive challenges, and so it has little influence over many aspects of daily human life, such as figuring out what to eat, finding mates, recognizing our friends, and raising children. Indeed, people with high g have no advantage in these domains. For instance, there is no evidence that people with high g make better parents (Herrnstein & Murray, 1994). But today we encounter a multitude of phenomena that could scarcely be imagined even two hundred years ago, such as computers, wireless telephones, televisions, airplanes, automobiles, electric appliances, high-rise buildings, international conglomerates, and so on. With these new inventions

Why might people with high IQs live longer?

and institutions, there is great value in being able to adapt to novel challenges and to think creatively. The overall evidence is consistent with the idea that general intelligence is most valuable for tasks that require understanding novel, complex information (Lubinski, 2004). But what aspects of g provide these abilities? We now examine the evidence for the contribution of cognitive and brain processes to intelligence.

Intelligence Is Associated with Cognitive Performance

What cognitive processes are involved in producing intelligence? Being able to take a three-hour exam requires us to stay focused and pay attention, whereas recalling the definition of the word *heraldry* requires us to remember information about the Middle Ages. According to Galton, intelligence is related to the efficiency of how our brains work as well as the possession of keen perceptual skills. He speculated that intelligent people had larger, more efficient brains. Is there any evidence to support these ideas? Some psychological scientists believe that intelligence is supported by low-level cognitive processes, such as speed of mental processing, working memory, and attention. But can we equate these types of brain performance with our level of intelligence?

SPEED OF MENTAL PROCESSING People who are not very intelligent are sometimes described as being "a bit slow." Is that description accurate? Perhaps. On reaction-time tests, people who score high on intelligence tests respond more quickly and consistently than those who score lower on such tests; their responses are slower and more variable (Deary, 2000). One type of reaction-time task might require a person to press a button whenever a stimulus appears on the screen to test what is known as *simple reaction time*. A more difficult task requires a person to choose among various possible responses, again as quickly as possible, depending on the stimulus presented. Scores on intelligence tests are related even more strongly to this *choice reaction time* (Jensen, 1998). It is not simply being fast that explains this finding, because reaction times correlate with intelligence test items that do not require people to respond quickly.

Another line of evidence that supports a relation between general intelligence and speed of mental processing can be found in *inspection time* tasks. Note in Figure 8.20 that a stimulus can be shown in which either side *a* or side *b* is longer. If we present one of these quickly and then quickly cover it up, how much time do you need to inspect the stimulus to be able to identify correctly which side was longer? According to research by the psychologist Ian Deary and his colleagues, those people who need very little time for this task tend to score higher on psychometric tests of intelligence (Deary, 2001). Additional evidence that highly intelligent people's brains work faster is found in studies where the electrical activity of the brain is measured in response to the presentation of some stimulus (recall the psychophysiological methods described in Chapter 2). Brain event-related potentials to various stimuli occur more quickly for people high in intelligence, and the pattern of brain responses is somewhat different than for people low in intelligence (Deary & Caryl, 1997).

The relation between intelligence and mental speed appears to be involved in the greater longevity of people with high IQs. In a recent longitudinal study, those higher in intelligence and those who had faster reaction times at age 56 were much less likely to die in the next 14 years, even after controlling for factors such as smoking, social class, and education. The effect for reaction time was somewhat stronger than for scores on standardized intelligence tests (Deary & Der, 2005). Why people who are mentally quick live longer is uncertain, as is why they tend to be more intelligent.

8.20 Inspection Time Tasks A stimulus (a) is presented and then quickly followed by a mask (b). The participant is asked to decide whether side A or B is longer. Although easy when you have lots of time to examine the stimulus, the mask quickly covers it, making the task more difficult.

(a) Inspection time stimuli   (b) Mask

Although the various response-time measures lead to the same conclusion—that intelligence is associated with speed of mental processing—researchers are far from knowing what this actually means. Perhaps being able to process information quickly is just one of the many talents that people who are high in g possess. It may allow them to solve problems or make decisions quickly when doing so is advantageous. As the ultimate fictional example, think about someone such as agent Jack Bauer on the TV show *24*. Bauer is constantly forced to make snap judgments in life-and-death situations. In real life, think about soldiers in combat or emergency-room doctors and their support staff. People's lives hang on their abilities to make good snap judgments.

WORKING MEMORY Over the past decade, a growing number of researchers have noted that general intelligence scores are closely related to working memory (Conway et al., 2003), although the two are not identical (Ackerman, Beier, & Boyle, 2005). Recall from Chapter 7 that working memory is the active processing system that holds information on line so that we can use it for activities such as problem solving, reasoning, and comprehension. In that capacity, working memory might be related to intelligence (Kyllonen & Cristal, 1990; Süß, Oberauer, Wittman, Wilhelm, & Schulze, 2002). Many of the studies examining how working memory and intelligence are related differentiate between simple memory-span tests and those that require some form of secondary processing (Figure 8.21). Simple memory-span tasks require a person to listen to a list of words and then repeat them back in the same order; performance on this task is weakly related to general intelligence (Engle, Tuholski, Laughlin, & Conway, 1999). Working-memory tasks that have dual components, however, show a strong relation between working memory and general intelligence (Gray & Thompson, 2004; Kane, Hambrick, & Conway, 2005; Oberauer, Schulze, Wilhelm, & Süß, 2005). According to Randy Engle and his colleagues, the link between working memory and intelligence is due to the role of attention. In particular, being able to pay attention, especially while being bombarded with competing information or other distractions, allows people to stay on task until successful completion (Engle & Kane, 2004). Given our earlier discussion of how general intelligence is most important in the face of novel, complex tasks, the importance of being able to stay focused and ignore distracting information makes a great deal of sense. This raises the issue of whether brain regions that support working memory are involved in intelligence. We now consider this issue.

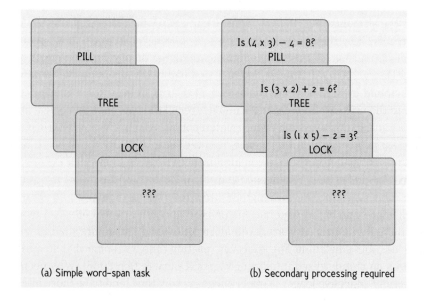

8.21 Memory-Span Tasks For simple memory-span tasks (a), a participant listens to a short list of words and then repeats them in order. In the more difficult tasks that involve secondary processing (b), the person has to solve simple mathematical operations at the same time the words are presented. Once again, the person has to repeat the words in the order they are presented (adapted from Conway et al., 2003).

BRAIN STRUCTURE AND FUNCTION What is the relation between the brain and intelligence? We sometimes call intelligent people "brainy." Maybe it won't surprise you, then, that many studies have documented a clear relationship between head circumference and scores on intelligence tests (Vernon, Wickett, Bazana, Stelmack, & Sternberg, 2000). Head circumference also predicts school performance, although the correlations are quite small (Ivanovic et al., 2004). What researchers are really trying to get at by measuring the circumference of the head is brain size. Studies using magnetic resonance imaging have found a small but significant correlation between brain size and scores on intelligence tests (Haier, Jung, Yeo, Head, & Alkire, 2004). A recent meta-analysis of 37 samples containing more than 1,500 people found that brain volume, as assessed by MRI, explained about 10 percent of the variability between people in general intelligence (McDaniel, 2005). You might wonder if the overall size of the brain matters or whether the sizes of some brain regions (those associated with working memory, planning, reasoning, and problem solving) are related to intelligence. Indeed, studies have found that a larger volume of neuronal cell bodies (gray matter) in the frontal lobes and other brain regions that support attentional control (the anterior cingulate) is related to measures of fluid intelligence (Frangou, Chitins, & Williams, 2004; Haier et al., 2005; Wilke, Sohn, Byars, & Holland, 2003), but not to crystallized intelligence (Gong et al., 2005). This is consistent with evidence that injury to the frontal lobes causes impairments in fluid intelligence, whereas crystallized intelligence remains intact (Duncan, Burgess, & Emslie, 1995).

Consistent with the anatomical and injury findings, studies using functional brain imaging have established that the frontal lobes are particularly important for fluid general intelligence. John Duncan and colleagues (2000) examined activity in people's brains as they performed three different cognitive tasks. Each of these tasks had two forms or levels, based on prior research: a high correlation with g and a low correlation with g. They found that regardless of the type of task, the high g version produced more frontal lobe activity. Jeremy Gray and colleagues (2003) used a working-memory task that on some trials required participants to ignore a distracting stimulus. As you might expect in light of the work on attention described above, the activity in frontal brain regions when the participants had to ignore the distracting information was strongly associated with scores on a measure of fluid intelligence. Considered together, the evidence is substantial that the frontal lobes play an important role in the components of intelligence involving reasoning and problem solving, namely fluid intelligence. Whether these or other brain regions support other components of intelligence, such as practical intelligence, is not yet known.

An obvious question is whether differences in brain structure and function are determined by genes or by the environment. Consider head circumference, which we noted was correlated with IQ. Correlation exists between parents and their children in the size of their heads. Yet, childhood nutritional status is highly related to head size, with malnourished children having smaller than expected head circumference and brain growth. Moreover, all of the findings linking brain size and structure to intelligence are correlational, and so it is possible that more education and frequent exposure to intellectual challenges lead to selective increases in some brain regions, just as we observed in Chapter 4 for London taxi drivers with larger hippocampuses. That is, perhaps more intelligent individuals seek out mental challenges, which in turn increase the volume of their frontal lobes (Gray & Thompson, 2004). One recent theory suggests that general intelligence reflects greater plasticity of the brain, such that some people more readily form neural connections during development. According to this view, general intelligence reflects the ability of the brain to adapt quickly to new environments (Garlick, 2002).

How might environmental factors affect brain development?

How much of our brain organization and cognitive capacity is due to genes and how much to environmental challenges? In the next section we consider the roles of genes and the environment in determining cognitive processing and intelligence.

Genes and Environment Both Influence Intelligence

One of the most contentious battles in psychological science has been over the role of genes in intelligence. This is especially true for the question of whether biological processes can explain IQ differences among groups. This is the quintessential nature-nurture debate: To what extent are individual differences in intelligence due to the effects of genes or to the environment? Throughout this book we have emphasized that both nature and nurture are important; this is especially so for intelligence. A key lesson in Chapter 3 was that gene expression is strongly influenced by external factors, and so to the extent that intelligence has a genetic basis, the environment will influence it. Thus, even if intelligence has a genetic component, how intelligence becomes expressed will be affected by various situational circumstances. The size of someone's vocabulary is considerably heritable, for example, but she has learned every word in it (Neisser et al., 1996). Moreover, which words she learns is also affected by the culture in which she is raised as well the amount of schooling that she receives. With both nature and nurture being crucial to intelligence, it becomes pointless to try to demonstrate which is more important. Instead, psychological scientists recognize that both are important, so they try to identify how genetic and environmental factors contribute to intelligence.

BEHAVIORAL GENETICS Recall from Chapter 3 that the field of behavioral genetics uses twin and adoption studies to estimate the extent to which traits are heritable, that is, the portion of variance in a trait that can be attributed to genes. Numerous studies have been conducted on the behavioral genetics of intelligence, and the conclusion is clear—genes matter. In studies of many thousands of twins, siblings, and adoptees, the evidence suggests that at least 50 percent of the variance in intelligence is because of genetic differences (Plomin & Spinath, 2004; Figure 8.22). Please remember that this doesn't mean that you received half of your intelligence from your genes! It means that genes account for half of the variation in intelligence among people.

Interestingly, the genetic contribution to intelligence becomes stronger over time, such that genes matter the least in childhood, when perhaps parents and teachers exert great influence, and matter the most in adulthood. Thus, adopted children raised in the same household show some similarity in intelligence as children, but as adults they are no more alike than strangers raised in different homes (McGue, Bouchard, Iacono, & Lykken, 1993). Likewise, correlations in IQ for dizygotic (nonidentical) twins drop off over time, whereas the correlations in IQ for identical twins remain strong throughout life (Figure 8.23). Why might gene effects grow stronger over time? One reason is that as children grow older, they are more in control of their environments, and it is possible that the environments people select as they get older are more in keeping with their genes, as when a very bright child spends time at the library rather than playing outside. This highlights the important role that people have in selecting, changing, and creating their own environments.

The quest now is to find the various genes that contribute to intelligence and to understand the conditions under which those genes are expressed. So, for instance, is there a genetic component to brain development? One research team examined monozygotic and dizygotic twins and found that the frontal lobes appeared to be under strong genetic influence, in that monozygotic twins were more similar in frontal lobe

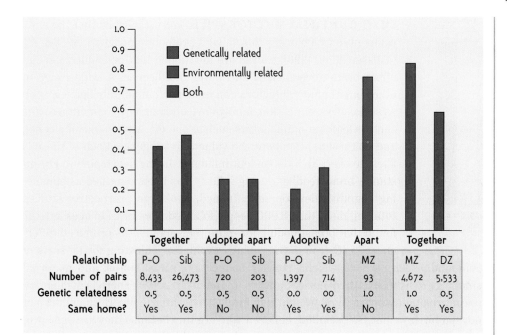

Relationship	Together		Adopted apart		Adoptive		Apart	Together	
	P-O	Sib	P-O	Sib	P-O	Sib	MZ	MZ	DZ
Number of pairs	8,433	26,473	720	203	1,397	714	93	4,672	5,533
Genetic relatedness	0.5	0.5	0.5	0.5	0.0	00	1.0	1.0	0.5
Same home?	Yes	Yes	No	No	Yes	Yes	No	Yes	Yes

8.22 Genes and Intelligence Shown are average IQ correlations for family, adoption, and twin study designs. What is clear is that the greater the degree of genetic relation, the greater the correlation in intelligence. The highest correlations are found among monozygotic twins, and this is so whether they are raised in the same household or not. What can also be observed is that siblings raised together show more similarity than siblings raised apart. A similar pattern occurs for the correlation between parent and child; they are more similar when the parent raises the child than when the child is raised by someone else. (P-O = parent, offspring; Sib = siblings; DZ = dizygotic twins; MZ = monozygotic twins)

brain volume than dizygotic twins were, and that for both types of twins there was a relation between the volume of the frontal lobes and intelligence (Thompson et al., 2001). Another approach is to seek specific genes that might contribute to intelligence, for example, by obtaining profiles of gene expression. Although attempts are under way to identify candidate genes that contribute to intelligence, so far researchers have been unsuccessful. One problem with this approach is that perhaps thousands of genes contribute to intelligence, and each gene might have only a small effect. In spite of these difficulties, researchers are actively pursuing efforts to identify these genes using large samples, and it is considered a promising area for future research (Plomin & Spinath, 2004). Finally, another method involves manipulating genes through knock-out or knock-in studies. Recall the Doogie Howser mice from Chapter 7 that became fast learners following genetic manipulation. Researchers have made great advances in understanding genes and their expression over the past few years. It is likely that we will make considerable progress moving beyond the demonstration of a genetic component to intelligence to understanding which genes work together to support cognition and intelligence.

8.23 The Effects of Genetic Influence over Time The correlations between monozygotic twins for intelligence remains stable over time, whereas correlations decrease for dizygotic twins. In other words, nonidentical twins become less similar to each other over time.

8.24 Birth Weight and Intelligence Among children of normal birth weight, mean IQ scores increase with weight.

ENVIRONMENTAL FACTORS It is well established that the environment in which one is raised has a profound impact on intelligence (Neisser et al., 1996). Earlier we mentioned that poor nutrition can affect brain development and lower intelligence. A wide range of other environmental factors can influence human intelligence, such as social class, education, family environment, environmental toxins such as lead, prenatal factors such as the mother's intake of alcohol, and cultural beliefs about the value of intelligence. Each of these is likely to exert an independent influence during development. For instance, breastfeeding during infancy has been identified as enhancing cognitive development. Indeed, two large prospective studies totalling more than 3,000 people followed from birth to ages 18 to 27 found that breastfeeding for more than six months produced differences in IQ from 5 to 7 points, even after adjusting for all sorts of confounds, such as birth weight, mother's education, social status, and maternal smoking (Mortensen, Michaelsen, Sanders, & Reinisch, 2002). There is also an apparent relation between birth weight and intellegence later in life. Even children of normal birth weight (so excluding children who are tiny because they are very premature) show a small positive association between birth weight and intelligence (Figure 8.24), although this effect is smaller than that of social class (Shenkin, Starr, & Deary, 2004).

The intellectual opportunities a child receives also affect intelligence. Stephen Ceci (1999) notes that schooling, for instance, makes an important contribution to intelligence. The longer that children remain in school, the higher their IQs will be. Students who start school early because of their birthdate have higher test scores than their same-age peers who start school later. It is clear that schooling not only builds knowledge but also teaches critical thinking skills such as being able to stay focused, think abstractly, and learn strategies for solving problems (Neisser et al., 1996). Considered together, the evidence is considerable that environmental factors contribute to intelligence. One sign of this is that IQ scores have risen quite dramatically during the last century of intelligence testing; this rise has been called the *Flynn effect* after James R. Flynn, the researcher who first described it (Flynn, 1981, 1987). Since genes cannot have changed much during this period, the increase must be due to environmental factors. Some possible explanations for the Flynn effect include better nutrition and health care, the refinement of education methods, longer school years, and smaller families with more intensive parenting, as well as exposure to technology and computers. The mean IQ score has not changed, however, because the various tests of intelligence have been re-standardized on a number of occasions over time so that the mean remains at 100.

In earlier chapters we noted that rats raised in enriched environments showed more synaptic connections and larger neurons than those raised in impoverished environments. Research from a number of different laboratories has shown that enriched environments enhance learning and memory as well, for example, by sustaining long-term potentiation (Lambert, Fernandez, & Frick, 2005; Tang, Wang, Feng, Kyin, & Tsien, 2001). The implication is that the environment influences how genes involved in brain development are expressed. In one study, genetically identical mice were split into groups that were exposed to different levels of an "enriched" environment—a cage with toys, tunnels, boxes, and the like. These researchers found that enrichment was associated with activation of genes involved in a number of brain functions, including forming new synapses (Rampon et al., 2000). These results present a clear affirmation that our environment can affect properties associated with intelligence by influencing—at least in part—the expression of our genes. Although it would be unethical to assign children randomly to enriched and impoverished environments, it is clear that humans as well as mice gain clear advantages from living in stimulating environments.

GROUP DIFFERENCES The most controversial aspect of intelligence testing over the last century has been the idea that genetics can explain overall differences in intelligence scores between different racial groups. In particular, one ongoing debate concerns differences in how American blacks and whites score on measures of intelligence. Multiple studies over the past 30 years have found that whites score about 10 to 15 points higher on average than blacks on most measures of intelligence. At issue is what causes the difference, not whether the difference exists. Given the importance of intelligence to educational and career attainment, claims that some groups are superior to others require close scrutiny because of the values of our society. This hotly debated topic will also challenge our critical thinking skills.

The first issue to be considered is whether "race" is a biologically meaningful concept. Many psychologists believe that it is not. Indeed, a recent special issue of the flagship journal of the American Psychological Association, *American Psychologist* (January 2005), was devoted to the subject. Various authors noted that the vast majority of genes are identical among people (perhaps as many as 99.9 percent). Although we differ in physical attributes (hair color, skin color, and so on), we do so to varying degrees depending on our entire ancestry, which raises troublesome issues of classification. Is Tiger Woods black or Asian? He has ancestors from both groups. Most methods of classifying race depend on self-report, in which people group themselves into categories. The rise in interracial families is making it harder for some people to select only one category. In regard to this discussion, it is clear that some genetically based biological differences do exist among people who identify themselves as black or white, such as skin color. What is not clear is whether these biological differences have any relevance for the mental capacities that underlie intelligence.

Whether race is real or not, it is not scientifically appropriate to conclude that genes cause differences among groups if there are any environmental differences among the groups. Richard Lewontin (1976) provided an excellent example of the difficulties of contrasting groups that differ in their circumstances. Consider seeds that are planted in two separate containers (Figure 8.25). In one, the soil is rich, and the seeds receive regular watering, nutrients, and sunlight. The other planter has poor soil, restricted water, and intermittent sunlight. Within both planters, differences

Why do minority group members score lower on IQ tests in different cultures around the world?

Field 1   Field 2

8.25 Variability in Fields Crops grown from similar seeds will vary in both fields, but on average, the crops will grow better when the soil is rich, as is the case in Field 2.

between the plants in their growth can be attributed to some genetic difference in the seeds. After all, the environment is identical, so only genes can explain the differences. But obviously the flowers in the separate containers will differ because of their different environments. The enriched environment helps the seeds reach their potential, whereas the impoverished environment will stunt growth.

There are many differences between black and white Americans. On average, blacks make less money and are more likely to live in poverty. On average, they also have fewer years of education and lower-quality health care, and they are more likely to face prejudice and discrimination. Around the world, minority groups that are the target of discrimination have lower intelligence scores on average, such as the Maori in New Zealand, the Burakumin in Japan, and the Dalits, or "untouchables," in India. John Ogbu (1994) argues that the treatment of minority-group members can make them pessimistic about their chances of success within their cultures. The potential result is that they are less likely to believe that hard work will pay off for them, which may lower their motivational levels in terms of performance. Although each of these explanations is plausible, at this time there is no clear-cut basis for understanding the differences in test scores between black and whites (Neisser et al., 1996). This does not mean, however, that we should not work to make adjustments in the way we measure intelligence to try to remove as much bias as possible against different groups of peoples.

Psychological Science *in Action* ◐ ● ○

Introducing the New SAT

On Saturday, March 12, 2005, many anxious college-bound students sat down to take a test that will play a vital role in determining which schools will admit them. The test takers were especially nervous because this was the first time that the new SAT was being administered (Figure 8.26). Doing well on the SAT is important, and many high school students spend considerable time and money preparing. Numerous SAT

8.26 The New SAT American high school students face considerable pressure to perform well on the SAT, a standard component of the college application process.

tutoring services are available for those who can afford them. This is not the first change for the SAT. Originally designed to measure innate intelligence and called the Scholastic Aptitude Test, it later became the Standardized Assessment Test. Now SAT doesn't stand for anything. The initials have no meaning—it is just the SAT, temporarily the *new* SAT. How did the old SAT become the new SAT?

In 2001, the psychologist Richard Atkinson launched a vigorous debate on the use of the SAT in college admission decisions. As president of the entire University of California system, Atkinson was in a powerful position to influence the makers of the SAT. Atkinson noted in a speech to the American Council on Education that his concerns about the SAT were sparked when he visited his 12-year-old granddaughter's private school and found the students practicing specific drills for the SAT. The 12-year-olds, he said, "spend hours each month—directly and indirectly—preparing for the SAT, studying long lists of verbal analogies such as 'untruthful is to mendaciousness' as 'circumspect is to caution.' " Atkinson believed not only that the SAT was distorting how children were being taught in schools, but also that it was not doing a good job of predicting how students would do in college, which raised doubts about its validity. As a good psychological scientist, he conducted research to examine how the SAT predicted student performance. His research found that high school grades and scores on tests of class material were better predictors than the SAT of first-year college grades.

In addition to his concern that the SAT was not a good predictor of college performance, Atkinson also believed that the current system of administering the tests may be unfair to those unable to pay for SAT preparation courses. Indeed, black and Hispanic students tend to score behind other groups on the SAT, and this might be attributable partly to their limited access to preparation programs. According to Stanford's Claude Steele, another problem affecting minority student performance on standardized exams is *stereotype threat,* anxiety that results from fears of doing badly and confirming societal stereotypes of racial inferiority in intelligence. According to Steele (1997), minority students who worry that they might confirm negative stereotypes become anxious and preoccupied, and this interferes with their ability to perform well on tests. For instance, when equally intelligent (as assessed by SAT scores) black and white Stanford students took a difficult test of verbal skills and were told that the test was unrelated to intelligence, black and white students performed at the same level. However, when the students were told the test was a measure of intelligence, black students did quite poorly (Figure 8.27; Steele & Aronson, 1995). Similarly, women do more poorly when taking an exam on which they believe men typically outscore women, but they do as well as men on the same test if they do not hold such a belief (Spencer, Steele, & Quinn, 1999). In an especially intriguing example of stereotype threat, researchers found that Asian American women did well on a math test when the "Asians are good at math" stereotype was primed and poorly when the "women are bad at math" stereotype was primed (Shih, Pittinsky, & Ambady, 1999). Stereotype threat is a problem because it contaminates the scores of minority test takers. The possible inaccuracy of these scores undermines the goal of the SAT, which is to provide a standardized assessment of all students taking the test. Recent research demonstrates that teaching test takers about stereotype threat may eliminate its negative effects (Johns, Schmader, & Martens, 2005). This provides another example of how research in psychological science contributes practical solutions to real-world problems.

8.27 Stereotype Threat When the test was described as diagnostic, stereotype threat led the black students to perform poorly.

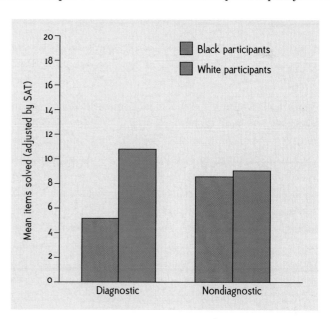

In response to various concerns about the SAT, many colleges and universities have placed more emphasis on school performance during the admissions process. In addition, the new SAT now includes an assessment of classroom learning and deemphasizes innate aptitude. According to the makers of the SAT, the reasoning component is now designed to assess critical thinking skills that students will need in college. It also emphasizes achievement more than aptitude. Through careful research documenting problems with using the SAT as the major determinant of college admission, Richard Atkinson was able to use his psychological training to instigate sweeping changes both in the admissions process and in how relevant learning skills are assessed in students. ■

REVIEWING

the Principles | How Do We Understand Intelligence?

Intelligence refers to human ability to reason, solve problems, think quickly and efficiently, and adapt to environmental challenges. The psychometric approach reveals multiple components to intelligence, but also a central dimension that has been called general intelligence, or g. Fluid intelligence is related to cognitive measures, such as working memory, as well as other measures of speed of mental processing. Crystallized intelligence reflects knowledge that we acquire. Other forms of intelligence have been identified, although there is debate regarding whether they reflect the same kind of intelligence as that which is more traditionally defined. Both genes and the environment influence intelligence, and researchers are now seeking to understand how environmental factors lead to differential gene expression. Finally, genes cannot be used to account for group differences in intelligence when there are environmental differences.

Conclusion

Being able to think has allowed humans to harness and use electricity, design technologies that simplify our lives, and even travel to the moon. The capacity for thought allows us to take in vast quantities of information and then use that information in our daily lives. As humans, we have many cognitive talents that allow us to reason, think critically, solve problems, and make important decisions. But much of the time our thought processes reveal biases that compromise the quality of our solutions and decisions. Although many of the earliest views in psychology considered humans to be rational, research over the past few decades has demonstrated that in their daily lives people misperceive base rates, use anecdotal

information, engage in counterfactuals, and fail to make accurate predictions about how future events will affect them. Much of the time people do not think deeply, but rather rely on heuristics, many of which are unconscious thought processes. Although heuristics are often adaptive and efficient, they can sometimes lead to unfortunate outcomes. People can also get caught in mental ruts that keep them from solving problems. We need to use knowledge effectively to solve problems and achieve goals, but doing so is not always easy.

Some people use information more effectively than others. Understanding the nature of intelligence has long been of interest to psychological scientists. We have vigorously debated most features of it, such as whether there is one monolithic way to be smart or whether there are multiple types of intelligence. The reality is likely in the middle ground. An underlying dimension—general intelligence, or g—predicts performance above and beyond our specific abilities, such as being good at algebra or poetry. Research in cognitive psychology and cognitive neuroscience has revealed new insights about general intelligence and its relation to working memory and attention. Throughout the chapter we have seen that living in the modern world places more and more emphasis on adapting to novelty, and therefore modern society places a premium on g.

How do we make people more intelligent? The answer appears to be that we are doing it already. By emphasizing early childhood and prenatal care and nutrition, by building good schools that stimulate and challenge, and by developing new technologies, society has made possible considerable gains in intelligence. An important goal, of course, is to ensure that each person, irrespective of race, ethnicity, or social group, can benefit from these circumstances, a goal that remains unfulfilled. Even very smart people fail to act rationally sometimes. That appears to be just as much a feature of human cognition as the talents that allow us to travel to the moon.

Summarizing the Principles of Thinking and Intelligence

How Does the Mind Represent Information?

1. **Mental images are analogical representations:** Thoughts can take the form of visual images. The primary visual cortex is activated proportionately to the size of an image in the mind's eye. Symbolic knowledge affects the ways in which we use visual imagery.

2. **Concepts are symbolic representations:** Concepts are mental representations of categories of subtypes and may be formed by defining attributes, prototypes, or exemplars. The boundaries of a category may be fuzzy.

3. **Schemas organize useful information about the environment:** We develop schemas based on our real-life experiences. Scripts are schemas that allow inferences about the sequence of events.

How Do We Make Decisions and Solve Problems?

4. **People use deductive and inductive reasoning:** Deductive reasoning follows from a general statement to specific applications. Syllogisms are formal structures of deduction. Inductive reasoning draws a general conclusion from specific instances.

5. **Decision making often involves heuristics:** Expected utility models assume normative, logical processes. Descriptive models highlight reasoning shortcomings—specifically the use of mental shortcuts (i.e., heuristics) that easily come to mind. We also select information to confirm our conclusions, avoid loss or regret, and to be consistent with the framing of a problem.

6. **Problem solving achieves goals:** Problem solving involves reaching a goal that is usually broken down into subgoals. Insights come suddenly by seeing elements of the problem in new ways. Restructuring aids solutions; mental sets and functional fixedness inhibit solutions. Unconscious processing (i.e., incubating) aids problem solving, and verbal overshadowing can confuse.

How Do We Understand Intelligence?

7. **Intelligence is assessed by psychometric tests:** The Binet-Simon was the first test of mental ability and lead to the concept of IQ as a ratio of mental age and chronological age. This was later normed to a distribution with a mean of 100 and standard deviation of 15; therefore average ability is from 85 to 115. The question of the validity of these tests persists, with cultural bias as a significant criticism.

8. **General intelligence involves multiple components:** Using the factor analysis of test performance, Charles Spearman concluded that a general intelligence component existed, known as g. Fluid intelligence involves problem-solving strategies whereas crystallized intelligence is accumulated knowledge. Howard Gardner has proposed a theory of multiple intelligences that include linguistic, mathematical/logical, spatial, bodily-kinesthetic, intrapersonal, and interpersonal abilities. Additionally, Robert Sternberg has proposed that there are three types of intelligence: analytical, creative, and practical. Finally, emotional intelligence is the ability to understand and use emotions.

9. **Intelligence is associated with cognitive performance:** Speed of mental processing is part of intelligence (i.e., choice reaction times and inspection times). The relationship of working memory to intelligence seems to be with

regard to attention. Various components of the brain (i.e., size and activity of the frontal lobes) have been found to relate to qualities of intelligence.

10. **Genes and environment both influence intelligence:** Behavioral genetics has revealed the substantial influence of genetics in setting the limits of the expression of intelli-

gence. Environmental factors, including breastfeeding, intellectual opportunities, nutrition, schooling, and parenting, seem to establish where within the genetic limits IQ falls. Assumed racial differences in intelligence based on genetics are invalid.

Applying the Principles

1. Think about what the brain looks like. Now rotate the image so that you are only examining the brain's left hemisphere. Your ability to do this demonstrates what type of mental representation? What is one region of your brain that is involved in processing this representation?

   _____ a) analogous representation; primary visual cortex
   _____ b) symbolic representation; temporal lobe
   _____ c) iconographic representation; right hemisphere of the cortex
   _____ d) virtual representation; frontal cortex

2. You want to go to a movie this weekend but you can't decide which one to see. If you ask a variety of friends if they have seen and liked a particular film and base your decision on their answers, you would be using _____. If you know the film stars an actor you like and therefore conclude that it will be a good movie, you are using _____.

   _____ a) inductive reasoning; deductive reasoning
   _____ b) the scientific method; the representative heuristic
   _____ c) loss aversion; confirmation bias
   _____ d) expected utility; the availability heuristic

3. Dave spent the weekend away from campus with his grandparents. He enjoyed discussing with his grandmother, who is a retired educator, what he has been studying in his psychology class. He was impressed by how much she knows. Furthermore, he found it interesting how quickly she understood the complexities of his new cell phone. His grandmother's general knowledge exemplifies her _____ intelligence, whereas her ability to figure out the cell phone exemplifies her _____ intelligence.

   _____ a) verbal; spatial
   _____ b) crystallized; fluid
   _____ c) fluid; spatial
   _____ d) g; multiple

ANSWERS: 1 a, 2 a, 3 b

Key Terms

analogical representation, p. 296
availability heuristic, p. 307
cognition, p. 296
concept, p. 299
confirmation bias, p. 308
crystallized intelligence, p. 323
deductive reasoning, p. 304
defining attribute model, p. 299
emotional intelligence (EQ), p. 325

fluid intelligence, p. 323
framing, p. 308
functional fixedness, p. 314
general intelligence (g), p. 323
heuristics, p. 306
inductive reasoning, p. 305
insight, p. 312
intelligence, p. 319

intelligence quotient (IQ), p. 321
mental age, p. 321
mental set, p. 314
multiple intelligences, p. 323
prototype model, p. 300
representativeness heuristic, p. 307
restructuring, p. 313
symbolic representation, p. 296

Further Readings

Deary, I. J. (2001). *Intelligence: A very short introduction.* Oxford: Oxford University Press.

Gladwell, M. (2005). *Blink: The power of thinking without thinking.* New York: Little, Brown.

Kosslyn, S. M. (1994). *Image and brain.* Cambridge, MA: MIT Press.

Medin, D. L., Ross, B. H., & Markman, A. B. (2005). *Cognitive psychology* (4th ed.). New York: Wiley.

Murphy, G. L. (2002). *The big book of concepts.* Cambridge, MA: MIT Press.

Neisser, U. (1976). *Cognition and reality: Principles and implications of cognitive psychology.* New York: Freeman.

Pinker, S. (1997). *How the mind works.* New York: Norton.

Schwartz, B. (2004). *The paradox of choice: Why more is less.* New York: Ecco.

Overcoming the Challenges of Life

Setting goals helps to motivate, or energize, our behavior. Many psychological scientists assert that we are more persistent when pursuing especially challenging goals than when we pursue less difficult ones. Here, breast cancer survivors gather for the Race for a Cure benefit, an event to mobilize people to raise money for cancer research.

Motivation

Oprah Winfrey is one of the most successful women in American history (Figure 9.1). Starting as a junior reporter in Nashville, Oprah rose through the ranks to become one of the most influential and important people in the entertainment industry. In 2004, *Time* magazine named her one of the 100 most influential people of the twentieth century. Her television show has changed daytime television; her power is so great that a single positive reference on her show can make any book a bestseller. Her many other successes include acting and producing, becoming one of the few women to own a thriving production company, and she is also a restauranteur, opening a popular restaurant in Chicago. Raised in poverty and bounced from house to house, she is now a wealthy humanitarian whose Angel Network has provided financial support to thousands.

Outlining the Principles

How Does Motivation Activate, Direct, and Sustain Behavior?

- Needs, Drives, and Arousal Motivate Behavior
- Pleasure Can Motivate Adaptive Behaviors
- Some Behaviors Are Motivated for Their Own Sake

Why Are Human Beings Social?

- Humans Have a Fundamental Need to Belong
- People Seek Others When They Are Anxious
- People Are Motivated to Detect and Reject Cheaters

How Do People Achieve Personal Goals?

- Good Goals Enhance Confidence
- Self-Regulation Requires Self-Awareness and Delay of Gratification
- The Frontal Lobes Are Important for Self-Regulation

What Determines How We Eat?

- Time and Taste Play Roles
- Culture Determines What We Eat
- Multiple Neural Processes Control Eating

What Is Addiction?

- Addiction Has Psychological and Physical Aspects
- People Use—and Abuse—Many Psychoactive Drugs
- Alcohol Is the Most Widely Abused Drug

What Factors Motivate Sexual Behavior?

- Biological Factors Influence Sexual Behavior
- Cultural Scripts and Rules Shape Sexual Interactions
- Mating Strategies Differ between the Sexes

9.1 Oprah Winfrey

Oprah Winfrey is the embodiment of the American dream. What has enabled this talented woman to achieve such success? It is clear from biographies of Oprah that she has been driven to succeed since childhood. She is a self-proclaimed workaholic, once stating about work: "This is all I do. I do this and I do it till I drop. I work, and on weekends I go as many places as I can to speak." Oprah's aspirations and goals are lofty, but she has attained many of them and then sought to achieve even more. By all accounts, she is as motivated as is humanly possible.

Yet Oprah faces ongoing personal battles in her everyday life. Like many of us, she has struggled throughout her life with her body weight. In 1988 Oprah slimmed down from nearly 220 pounds to 145 pounds, and exclaimed that doing so was the "greatest single achievement" of her life. Unfortunately, as is the case for most dieters, Oprah regained much of the weight. Over the past decade she has endured a constant struggle to control her eating and to maintain a body weight she finds acceptable. A self-described food addict, Oprah has found dieting success only when her eating and exercise habits are severely regimented and her actions supervised by personal trainers and chefs.

This raises a large question for many of us. How can we be so successful in some aspects of life and yet struggle so mightily in others? The simplest answer is that many different forces compel our behavior. We struggle even more when these forces conflict. Listen to what Oprah had to say in a recent interview on this very topic. When asked on America Online, "What keeps you motivated?" Oprah responded, "To work or to work out? To work—it is a mission for me, this show, more than just a talk show. I want people to see things on our show that make them think differently about their lives. That makes them better. For working out, my motivation is I don't want a fat butt!" Oprah's eating problems can be viewed as a basic conflict between her desire to eat good-tasting food and her desire to see herself as attractive. But why is this so difficult, especially for someone who has such an amazing capacity for success in other aspects of her life?

Oprah Winfrey is hardly alone in her quest to lose weight; indeed, more and more people in many Western countries are becoming overweight. The struggle to lose weight can sometimes seem a battle between body and mind—the mind trying to resist the body's urges to eat. As biological machines shaped by evolutionary forces, our bodies require certain things to

Timeline

1890

Instincts as Motives Greatly influenced by Darwin's ideas, William James proposes that human beings are endowed with behavioral instincts that require no experience or education, only environmental triggers to activate them.

1908

Yerkes-Dodson Law Robert Yerkes and John Dodson are the first to observe that there is an inverted U-shaped function between arousal and performance, with the best performance on learning tasks occurring at moderate levels of arousal.

1920s

Homeostasis In *The Wisdom of the Body*, Harvard physiologist Walter B. Cannon describes the process by which bodily systems, such as temperature and digestion, are regulated to maintain a steady state.

1940s

Drives Satisfy Needs Clark Hull proposes that states of biological deprivation, or drives, stimulate behaviors to satisfy needs. Drive theory becomes one of the most influential theories in the history of psychological science.

keep going, and to get those things the body encourages us to engage in specific behaviors. Many of these behaviors are things we enjoy, such as eating and having sex. As you will see, common brain systems make these behaviors rewarding. But modern living has provided new challenges that our bodies were not designed to handle, such as easily available food and substances such as drugs and alcohol that activate our basic reward circuitry. Each day we feel a tug between engaging in these behaviors that bring us pleasure and living up to the demands of society. William James noted that on a cold morning it takes an enormous amount of willpower to haul oneself out of a cozy bed. Throughout this chapter, we will consider how people struggle for self-control every day, how often we need to choose one action over another, forgoing immediate satisfaction to achieve our longer-term goals. Understanding motivation will provide insights into many aspects of our daily lives. ■

Motivation (from Latin, "to move") is the area of psychological science that studies the factors that energize, or stimulate, behavior. Specifically, it is concerned with how behavior is initiated, directed, and sustained. This concern leads to the study of physical factors such as the need for sleep and food, as well as the psychological factors that inspire people to set goals and try to achieve them. Many times people attempt to override their biological needs, as when they try to go without sleep or food, and often they find that doing so is difficult. How much can people prevail over their bodies in attempting to reach personal goals? As a student, you probably are highly motivated to succeed, and therefore you spend many of your waking hours reviewing notes, reading textbooks, and writing papers, perhaps resisting the temptation to meet with friends or have some fun. Although doing well in this course may not aid your immediate survival, it does help you achieve long-term aspirations.

This chapter explores different conceptions of the basis of motivation and discusses some of the most commonly motivated behaviors. These behaviors relate to immediate biological survival (such as responding to hunger and thirst), as well as to long-term social needs (such as affiliation and achievement). Issues of motivation are spread throughout the many levels of analysis of psychological science. For instance, the concepts of reward and reinforcement discussed in Chapter 6 and the physiological mechanisms discussed in Chapter 3 are central to theories of motivation. As you read through this chapter, keep in mind two important questions: What motivates me in my daily life? How can I manage, direct, and sustain those motivating forces so that I can live a meaningful life?

motivation Factors that energize, direct, or sustain behavior.

1948
Kinsey Reports Alfred Kinsey conducts landmark research on human sexuality, publishing *Sexual Behavior in the Human Male* in 1948 and *Sexual Behavior in the Human Female* in 1953.

1954
Dual-Center Theory Eliot Stellar proposes that motivated behavior is regulated by excitatory and inhibitory centers in the hypothalamus. The hypothalamus is later found to be crucial for many motivated behaviors.

1959
Affiliation and Anxiety Stanley Schachter examines how anxiety affects the human desire to affiliate with others. He concludes that the need for social comparison is an important motivator of affiliation.

1960
Plans and Goals George Miller, Eugene Gallanter, and Karl Pribram develop a cognitive model of self-regulation, in which people are motivated by discrepancies between their situation and an ideal state represented as a goal.

1960s
Delay of Gratification Walter Mischel and his students conduct research showing that children who are best able to delay gratification are later able to perform at a superior level in many domains.

The Frontal Lobes Are Important for Self-Regulation

Self-regulation requires us to control behaviors when they are not appropriate. This requires two things. First, it requires us to be aware of societal standards that tell us what is appropriate. This includes understanding how others will react to our actions, such as what will happen if we play our music very loud at 3:00 A.M. Second, it also involves the ability to inhibit doing those actions, such as overriding the impulse to turn up the music. The frontal lobes of our brains are important for both of these abilities. As you read in Chapter 4, people with damage to their frontal lobes often engage in inappropriate behavior. They are impulsive and have little self-control. If our dopamine system revs up the engine, our frontal lobes act as the brakes.

The frontal lobes are also involved in formulating goals, plans, and strategies. Studies using brain imaging have found significant activation of the prefrontal region during difficult tasks but not during simple recall tasks (Schacter & Buckner, 1998; Spence & Frith, 1999). The difficult tasks required effort, which links motivation to the prefrontal cortex. Damage to the prefrontal cortex is associated with difficulties in making plans and performing behaviors necessary to achieve goals. Patients with prefrontal damage often have intact intelligence and comprehension but lack the ability to put their knowledge to use. They might be able to tell you how to achieve a goal, but they seem incapable of following their own suggestions and are often unwilling even to try. It is possible that motivational deficits observed after brain injury occur because of damage to dopamine circuits that link the prefrontal cortex to the limbic system.

Scientists believe that people with prefrontal damage have difficulty focusing on a task because they are unable to ignore other stimuli in the environment (Knight & Grabowecky, 1995). For instance, if you sustained damage to your prefrontal region, you might be unable to study because you could not tune out background noise or other distractions. The prefrontal cortex also plays a critical role in working memory (see Chapter 7), which allows people to compare current performance with past standards and future goals. Working memory is important for the temporal organization of memory, which is often required for self-regulatory tasks. Consider the task of cooking a meal, which requires doing things in a certain order. People with frontal-lobe dysfunction often have difficulty following plans that require temporal ordering of behaviors. They might be able to tell you all the ingredients for a recipe but be incapable of following the steps of the recipe in the necessary order.

ADAPTIVENESS OF SELF-REGULATION Not only are the frontal lobes involved in inhibiting behavior, but they are also critical for living with other people. Living in social groups requires cooperation and the suppression of personal desires for the good of the group. Hunters and gatherers who returned to the group to share their bounty, rather than eating it immediately after the kill, would not only have increased the likelihood that their relatives received sufficient nutrition to survive and reproduce, but also would demonstrate their value as group members. Living in groups requires people to control their emotional reactions and violent urges as well as their appetites. Those who are unable to control their emotions or behavior are usually excluded from social groups and are therefore not likely to pass along their genes.

That we can consciously override biological urges is an important point to make about human nature. Some people object to evolutionary approaches to understanding behavior because of the assumption that genes are the sole determinant of behavior. This assumption implies that certain behaviors are inevitable and uncontrollable.

Research on self-regulation has established that people (and perhaps some nonhuman animals) have the capacity to override biology, at least within reason. You can choose to postpone eating, going to the bathroom, or breathing, albeit for brief periods of time—but you can do it. Socialization is an important mechanism that teaches group members the appropriate times and places to satisfy or inhibit various biological drive states.

REVIEWING the Principles | How Do People Achieve Personal Goals?

People are motivated to set and achieve goals and to control their behavior in pursuit of those goals. The best goals are challenging, concrete, and divisible into steps. The process by which people achieve goals is known as self-regulation, which depends on self-awareness of goals and behaviors. Self-regulatory strength allows people to delay immediate gratification in the service of long-term goals. The capacity for self-regulation depends on having intact frontal lobes. People who suffer damage to the frontal lobes often have trouble staying on task, making decisions, and inhibiting behavior. The ability to inhibit desires helps people live harmoniously with others.

What Determines How We Eat?

One of life's greatest pleasures is eating, and we do a lot of it: Most North Americans consume between 75,000 and 85,000 meals during their lives—more than 40 tons of food! Ingesting food is something everyone needs to do to survive, but eating is much more than simply survival. Special occasions often involve elaborate feasts, and much of the social world revolves around eating. With eating we can observe complex interactions between biology and cultural influences on cognition. Common sense dictates that most eating is controlled by hunger and *satiety*. People eat when they feel hungry and stop eating when they are full. However, some people eat a lot even when they are not hungry, whereas others avoid eating even though they are not full. What determines human eating behavior?

Time and Taste Play Roles

Eating is greatly affected by learning. Have you ever noticed that most people eat lunch at approximately the same time? This makes little sense, for people differ greatly in metabolic rate, the amount they ate for breakfast, and the amount of fat they have stored for long-term energy needs. Yet it occurs because people have been classically conditioned to associate eating with regular mealtimes. We eat not because we have deficient energy stores, but because it is time to eat. The clock indicating mealtime is much like Pavlov's bell, in that it leads to a number of anticipatory responses that motivate eating behavior and prepare the body for digestion. For instance, an increase in insulin promotes glucose utilization and increases short-term hunger signals. The sight and smell of tasty foods can have the same effect, and even the mere thought of fresh-baked bread, a favorite pizza, or a decadent dessert may initiate bodily reactions that induce hunger.

One of the main factors that determines feeding is flavor; good-tasting food motivates eating. When it comes to flavor, variety really is the spice of life. Animals presented with a variety of foods tend to eat a great deal more than animals presented with only one food type. For instance, rats who normally maintain a steady body weight when eating one type of food eat huge amounts and become obese when presented with a variety of high-calorie foods, such as chocolate bars, crackers, and potato chips (Sclafani & Springer, 1976; Figure 9.13). Humans show the same effect, eating much more when a variety of foods is available than when only one or two types of food are available.

One reason that rats and people eat more when presented with a variety of foods is because we quickly grow tired of any one flavor. *Sensory-specific satiety* is a phenomenon in which animals will become full relatively quickly if they just have one type of food to eat, but will eat more if presented with a different type of food. This may explain the behavior of people at times like Thanksgiving, when even though they couldn't imagine eating another bite of turkey they apparently can find room for a piece of pumpkin pie, or two, to finish the meal. From an evolutionary perspective, animals that ate a diversity of food types were more likely to satisfy nutritional requirements and survive than those that relied on a small number of foods. Sensory-specific satiety encourages consumption of varied foods, which increases the likelihood that nutritional needs will be met. It also encourages animals to eat a great deal, a behavior that may have been adaptive when the food supply was scarce or unpredictable.

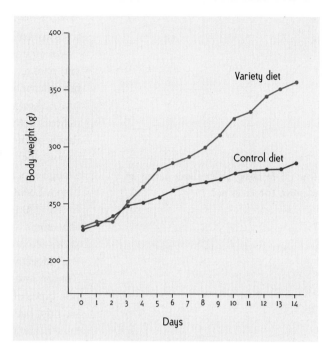

9.13 Tastes and Eating Behavior Rats eat a great deal more when given a variety of food and will become obese if given access to food such as marshmallows, salami, and cookies.

Culture Determines What We Eat

Would you eat bat? Bat is a delicacy in the Seychelles Islands—it tastes something like chicken. What we will eat has little to do with logic and everything to do with what our minds believe is food. Some of the most nutritious foods are not eaten in North America because they are viewed as disgusting. For instance, fried termites, a favorite in Zaire, have more protein than beef; spiders are considered tasty and nutritious treats in many countries. At the same time, people from other cultures might be nauseated by some of our favorite foods, such as hamburgers and ice cream. Even when people are starving to death, they will refuse to eat perfectly nutritious substances: People died in Naples in 1770 because they were suspicious of the potatoes sent to relieve their famine, whereas many of those who died in the potato famine in Ireland refused to eat corn that was sent over from America. Three million died in Bengal in 1943 in spite of being supplied with wheat, which they rejected because it was not familiar as food. What factors determine what is regarded as food?

What people will eat is determined by a combination of personal experience and cultural beliefs. Infants have an inborn preference for sweets, but they can learn to like just about anything. A general rule that determines preferences is familiarity: Animals like what is familiar and tend to avoid that which is unfamiliar. This makes great sense, because unfamiliar foods may be dangerous or poisonous, and therefore avoiding them is adaptive for survival. Getting children to like new foods often involves exposing them to small amounts at a time, until they get used to the taste. The avoidance of unfamiliar foods is an example of *neophobia,* the fear of novel things. Infants learn to try foods by observing their parents and siblings—if Mom eats something, it must be okay. Children are much more likely to eat a new food offered by their mothers than the same food offered by a friendly stranger. This also makes great sense from an evolutionary point of view, in that the rule "eat what my relatives are eating" would typically have been a good one.

Of course, what the mother prefers to eat is determined by her own upbringing and past experiences, and therefore families tend to like specific types of food. Ethnic differences in food preference often continue when a family moves to a new country. Although we may enjoy the occasional meal of some novel ethnic food, most people prefer the food of their own culture for their regular diet. Moreover, as Paul Rozin of the University of Pennsylvania has pointed out, there are cultural rules about which food is appropriate in different contexts. He gives the example that even though most Americans like chocolate and french fries, few people like them combined. Local norms of not only what to eat but also how to prepare it, part of what Rozin (1996) calls *cuisine*, reinforce many food preferences. Oprah Winfrey noted that some of her problems with food might have developed because of Southern styles of cooking: "I come from a culture of people where you cook a green in pork fat." Moreover, religious and cultural values often tell people which foods to avoid: Kosher Jews eat beef but not pork, and Hindus eat pork but not beef. Taboos on certain types of food may have been adaptive because those foods were likely to contain harmful bacteria. However, many food taboos and preferences are idiosyncratic and have nothing to do with harm avoidance. They simply reflect an evolved group preference for specific foods prepared and eaten in certain ways. The cultural transmission of food preferences is a powerful factor in choosing what foods to eat.

How might being picky about eating be adaptive for children?

Multiple Neural Processes Control Eating

The hypothalamus is the brain structure with the greatest influence on eating. Although it does not act alone to elicit eating behavior, the hypothalamus integrates the various inhibitory and excitatory feeding messages and organizes behaviors involved in eating. In the first half of the twentieth century, research revealed that damage to the hypothalamus leads to dramatic changes in eating behavior and body weight, depending on which specific area is damaged.

One of the first observations occurred in 1939, when researchers discovered that patients with tumors of the hypothalamus became obese. To examine whether obesity could be induced in normal-weight animals, researchers selectively damaged specific hypothalamic regions through lesioning. Experimentally lesioning the middle or *ventromedial* region (*VMH*) of the hypothalamus causes rats to eat great quantities of food, referred to as *hyperphagia*. Rats with VMH lesions grow extremely obese. In contrast, lesioning the outer or *lateral* area of the hypothalamus (*LH*) is associated with a condition known as *aphagia*, which is diminished eating behavior that leads to weight loss and eventual death, unless the animal is force fed.

Brain structures other than the hypothalamus are also involved in eating behavior. For instance, taste cues such as sweetness or saltiness are processed in part of the prefrontal cortex. This suggests that this region processes information about the potential reward value of food. Damage to either the limbic system or the right frontal lobes sometimes produces *gourmand syndrome,* in which people become obsessed with fine food and food preparation. One 48-year-old stroke patient who previously had shown little interest in food became preoccupied with food and eventually quit his job as a political correspondent to become a food critic (Regard & Landis, 1997). In spite of their fascination with good-tasting food, those who have gourmand syndrome do not necessarily become overweight; their obsession is not with eating but with the quality and variety of the food itself and how it is prepared.

INTERNAL SENSATIONS Earlier you learned how negative-feedback processes contribute to homeostasis, and for many years it was believed that eating was a classic homeostatic system. From this perspective, some sort of detector would notice deviations from the set-point and would signal an animal either to begin eating or to stop eating. But where do hunger signals come from? The search for energy-depletion detectors has led scientists from the stomach to the bloodstream to the brain.

The initial assumption, based on common sense, was that hunger derived from receptors in the stomach. Many people describe the subjective experience of hunger as emanating from their stomachs, and even our common descriptions of not being hungry refer to "feeling full." The first empirical test of the idea that hunger comes from the stomach was conducted by Walter Cannon and his research assistant Arthur Washburn. One day while working in the lab, Cannon noticed that Washburn's stomach was making rumbling sounds. Cannon theorized that perhaps it was doing so because Washburn was hungry, and so he quickly rigged up an experiment to test his hypothesis. Rather than let Washburn eat, Cannon had him swallow an empty balloon and then inflated the balloon so that he could register changes in the stomach walls caused by contractions. At the same time, he asked Washburn to report each time he felt a pang of hunger. Cannon found that Washburn reported feeling hungry at the end of each stomach contraction and therefore proposed that hunger was the subjective feeling associated with stomach contractions. Although these findings were intuitively appealing, it was quickly apparent that stomach contractions are not the only factors that determine hunger. Eating a small amount of food stops stomach contractions but is more likely to lead to additional eating than to terminate eating. Moreover, people who have had their stomachs removed continue to report being hungry. Research over the past few decades has established that stomach contractions and distensions are relatively minor determinants of hunger and eating.

In the 1940s and 1950s, a number of researchers postulated the existence of receptors in the bloodstream that monitor levels of vital nutrients. One of the best-known of these theories is the *glucostatic theory,* which proposes that specialized glucose receptors, called *glucostats,* monitor the extent to which glucose is taken up into cells so it can be used for energy. Because glucose is the primary fuel for metabolism and is especially crucial for neuronal activity, it makes sense for animals to be sensitive to deficiencies in glucose. Evidence supports the existence of glucoreceptors, and various experiments have demonstrated that injections of glucose in the bloodstream can postpone eating in hungry animals. Similarly, the *lipostatic theory* proposes a set-point for body fat in which deviations from set-point initiate compensatory behaviors to return to homeostasis. For instance, when an animal loses body fat, hunger signals motivate eating and a return to set-point.

The recently discovered hormone *leptin* is involved in fat regulation. Leptin is released from fat cells at a rate approximately equal to the amount of fat being stored in those cells. Leptin travels to the hypothalamus, where it acts to inhibit eating behavior. The message from leptin is slow acting, so it takes considerable time after eating before leptin levels change in the body. Thus, leptin is more important for long-term body-fat regulation than for short-term eating control. Animals that lack the gene necessary to produce leptin become extremely obese, and injecting leptin into these animals leads to a rapid loss of body fat. The extent to which leptin contributes to human obesity is unclear. As you will learn in the next chapter, many factors contribute to obesity. You will also learn why most of us who diet, like Oprah, have difficulty in losing weight and keeping it off.

the Principles | What Determines How We Eat?

The consumption of food is necessary for survival. A number of overlapping, redundant physiological systems motivate eating behavior to satisfy nutritional requirements. The motivation for variety helps animals achieve a nutritious diet, whereas fear of new foods and acquired taste aversions help animals avoid potential harm. People learn from those around them to like certain flavors. There is great variety in the types of substances that people consume as food.

What Is Addiction?

What motivates people to risk death or injury to achieve momentary pleasure? Throughout history, people have discovered that ingesting all sorts of substances can alter their mental state in desirable ways. Societal problems stemming from drug abuse are well known. Considering only the commonly abused substances, such as illegal drugs, alcohol, and prescription drugs, it is likely that most people know and care about someone who is an addict. If we include nicotine and caffeine, it is likely that addicts are in the majority in most countries in the world. The questions psychological science asks about addiction include, Why do people use drugs? Why do some people become addicted to drugs? Why do individuals with drug addiction continue to abuse drugs when doing so causes such personal turmoil and suffering? To gain a full understanding of addiction, it is necessary to address these questions on multiple levels, from the biological to the individual to the social.

Addiction Has Psychological and Physical Aspects

physical dependence Synonymous with addiction, the physiological state in which failing to ingest a specific substance leads to bodily symptoms of withdrawal.

psychological dependence Habitual substance use, despite consequences, and a compulsive need to continue using the drug.

The term **physical dependence** is synonymous with *addiction,* a physiological state in which failing to ingest a substance leads to symptoms of *withdrawal,* a state characterized by anxiety, tension, and cravings. Physical dependence is associated with *tolerance,* so that a person needs to consume more of the drug to achieve the same subjective effect. **Psychological dependence** refers to habitual and compulsive substance use despite the consequences. People can be psychologically dependent without showing tolerance or withdrawal. People can also show psychological dependence on other behaviors, such as gambling or shopping. Here we focus on addiction to substances.

As mentioned in Chapter 6, drug addiction has both negative and positive reinforcement aspects. Addicts habitually abuse drugs to escape withdrawal, thereby negatively reinforcing drug use. People also take drugs to forget their problems or to deal with stress, and this too involves negative reinforcement. Drug use is also positively reinforced. People take drugs to feel good, which occurs because drugs activate dopamine receptors. Recall that dopamine is the most important neurotransmitter for reinforcement and dependence (Koob, 1999).

How do people become addicted? Many theories related to the initiation of drug or alcohol use among children or adolescents focus on the social level of analysis. They explore social-learning processes that emphasize the role of parents, peers, and mass media. For example, the Joe Camel advertising campaign of the early 1990s heralded a tenfold increase in market share among adolescents for Camel cigarettes;

at one point more young children could identify Joe Camel than Mickey Mouse (Mizerski, 1995). Social-learning theories also emphasize self-identification with high-risk groups (e.g., "stoners" or "druggies") as central to the initiation of drug and alcohol use. Teenagers want to fit in somewhere, even with groups that society perceives as deviant. As you will recall from Chapter 6, children imitate the behavior of role models, especially those they admire or with whom they identify. For children whose parents smoke, the modeling of the behavior is continuous through early childhood and elementary school. It is not surprising then that multiple studies show that when parents smoke, it leads to positive attitudes about smoking and the early adoption of smoking behavior in their children (Rowe, Chassin, Presson, & Sherman, 1996).

At the individual level, some adolescents are especially likely to experiment with illegal drugs and to abuse alcohol. Children who are high in sensation seeking (a personality trait that involves attraction to novelty and risk taking) are more likely to associate with deviant peer groups and to use alcohol, tobacco, and drugs (Wills, DuHamel, & Vaccaro, 1995). These children also tend to have poor relationships with their parents, which, in turn promotes greater deviant-peer-group association, and so on. So does the family environment determine alcohol and drug use? Some theorists, operating at the biological level of analysis, turn this around and suggest that an inherited predisposition to sensation seeking may predict behaviors that increase the possibility of substance abuse, such as affiliating with drug users. Indeed, some evidence points to genetic components to addiction, especially for alcoholism. But it is important to point out that little direct evidence points to a *single* "alcoholism" or "addiction" gene. Rather, what might be inherited is a cluster of characteristics, including certain personality traits, a reduced concern about personal harm or injury, a nervous system that is chronically low in arousal, or a predisposition to find chemical substances pleasurable. In turn, these factors make some people more likely to explore drugs and to like them.

One of the most fascinating aspects of addiction is that only about 5 to 10 percent of those who use drugs other than tobacco or alcohol become addicted. Indeed, the vast majority of Americans have tried alcohol, and more than 90 million Americans have experimented with illicit drugs. Yet most either use alcohol or drugs in moderation (especially alcohol) or try them for a while and then give them up completely. In a major longitudinal study, Jonathan Shedler and Jack Block (1990) found that those who had experimented with drugs and alcohol as adolescents were better adjusted in adulthood than those who never tried them at all. Both complete abstainers and heavy drug users had adjustment problems compared with the experimenters. However, this does not mean that everyone should rush out to try drugs and alcohol, or that parents should encourage such behavior. After all, you have no way of knowing if you will become addicted or whether you are prepared to handle drugs' effects on your behavior.

In this section we examine some of the most commonly used drugs. One of the most common drugs—nicotine in cigarettes—is discussed in Chapter 10, along with a discussion of how addictions can be treated. Here we are concerned with the motivation to use drugs that alter mental state.

Why don't all drug users become addicts?

People Use—and Abuse—Many Psychoactive Drugs

Drugs are one of the most mixed blessings of our lives. Taking them when we have a severe injury or even a moderate headache can provide soothing relief. The right drugs, given to people who are depressed, can lift their moods and help them lead better lives. Other drugs given to children with attention deficits or hyperactivity disorders can help them settle down and be better classroom learners. But many of these same drugs can be used for recreational purposes—to alter physical sensations, levels of consciousness, thoughts, moods, and behaviors in ways that users believe to be desirable—and this recreational use can sometimes lead to severe negative consequences.

Psychoactive drugs are mind-altering substances that change the brain's neurochemistry by activating neurotransmitter receptors. The effects of a particular drug depend on which receptors are activated. Common psychoactive drugs include stimulants, depressants, narcotics, and hallucinogenics. In this section we consider drugs that often have legitimate medical uses, but are frequently abused outside of treatment. Later we will examine the most widely used legal drug that is seldom employed medically, namely alcohol.

STIMULANTS *Stimulants* are drugs that increase behavioral and mental activity and include substances such as cocaine, nicotine, caffeine, and amphetamines. These drugs activate the sympathetic nervous system (increasing heart rate and blood pressure), improve mood, cause people to become restless, and disrupt sleep. They are also highly reinforcing. Stimulants generally work by interfering with the normal reuptake of dopamine by the releasing neuron, which allows dopamine to remain in the synapse and thus prolongs its effects, although sometimes stimulants also increase the release of dopamine. Drugs that block the action of dopamine reduce the reinforcing properties of stimulants.

Cocaine is a stimulant that is often inhaled as a powder or smoked in the form of *crack cocaine.* However it is used, cocaine is derived from the leaves of the coca bush, which grows primarily in South America. After snorting or smoking cocaine, users experience a wave of confidence and good feeling. They are alert, energetic, sociable, and feel little need of sleep. These effects are especially intense for users of crack cocaine. Cocaine has a long history of use in America. A pharmacist from Georgia, John Pemberton, was so impressed with cocaine that in 1886 he added it to soda water for easy ingestion, thus creating *Coca-Cola* (Figure 9.14). In 1906, the U.S. government outlawed cocaine, so it was removed from the drink. To this day, however, coca leaves from which the cocaine has been removed are used in the making of Coca-Cola. In contrast to the positive effects of cocaine, habitual use of large quantities can lead to paranoia, as well as psychotic and even violent behavior (Ottieger, Tressell, Inciardi, & Rosales, 1992).

Amphetamines are stimulants synthesized using simple lab methods. Amphetamines go by street names such as *speed, meth, ice,* and *crystal.* Amphetamines have a long history of use for weight loss and staying awake. However, amphetamines have a number of negative side effects—such as insomnia, anxiety, and heart problems—and people quickly become addicted to them. They are seldom used for legitimate medical purposes.

MDMA One drug that has recently become very popular is *MDMA,* or *ecstasy,* which produces an energizing effect similar to that of stimulants, but also causes slight hallucinations. According to the National Institute of Drug Abuse, more than 10 million Americans age 12 or over report having tried ecstasy. The drug first became popular among young adults in nightclubs or at all-night parties known as raves. Compared with amphetamines, MDMA is associated with less dopamine

9.14 Everyday Stimulants
An early ad for Coca-Cola.

release and more serotonin release. The latter aspect may explain its hallucinogenic properties. As you might recall from Chapter 3, LSD's hallucinogenic effects are due to activation of serotonin neurons. Although many users believe it to be relatively safe, researchers have documented a number of impairments from long-term ecstasy use, especially memory problems and a diminishment of the ability to perform complex tasks. Because ecstasy also depletes serotonin, users often feel depressed when the rewarding properties of the drug wear off.

MARIJUANA The most widely used illegal drug in North America is marijuana, which is the dried leaves and flower buds of the hemp plant. The active psychoactive ingredient in marijuana is the chemical THC (tetrahydrocannabinol), which alters the working mind in a number of complex ways, but in particular leads to a relaxed mental state, uplifting or contented mood, and some perceptual and cognitive distortions. Users report that it makes perceptual experiences more vivid, with some extolling its effects especially on taste perception. Most first-time users of marijuana do not experience the "high" obtained by more experienced users. Part of this may be that novice smokers use inefficient techniques and may have trouble inhaling, but it is also appears that users need to learn how to *appreciate* the drug's effects. This makes marijuana different from most other drugs, which have stronger effects on first-time users, with subsequent usage leading to tolerance.

Although the brain mechanisms that marijuana affects remain somewhat mysterious, investigators have recently discovered a class of receptors that are activated by naturally occurring THC-like substances. Activation of these cannabinoid receptors appears to adjust and enhance mental activity, and perhaps alter the perception of pain. There is a large concentration of these receptors in the hippocampus, which may explain in part why marijuana impairs memory (Ilan, Smith, & Gevins, 2004).

OPIATES Heroin, morphine, and codeine belong to the family of drugs known as opiates. These drugs provide enormous reward value by increasing dopamine activation in the nucleus accumbens and binding with opiate receptors, producing feelings of relaxation, analgesia, and euphoria. Prior to the turn of the twentieth century, heroin was widely available without prescription and was marketed by the Bayer Aspirin Company. Heroin provides a rush of intense pleasure that most addicts describe as similar to orgasm, which then evolves into a pleasant, relaxed stupor. The dual activation of opiate receptors and dopamine receptors may explain why heroin and morphine are so highly addictive.

Profiles in Psychological Science

Soldiers Kick the Narcotics Habit

American soldiers who fought in Vietnam often took drugs to cope with the hellish conditions of war. By the late 1960s, estimates suggested that drug abuse among American soldiers, including the use of narcotics such as heroin and opium, had reached epidemic proportions. The widespread use of drugs was not surprising—the late 1960s were a time of youthful drug experimentation, soldiers in Vietnam had easy access to a variety of drugs, and drugs helped the soldiers cope temporarily with fear, depression, homesickness, boredom, and the repressiveness of army regulations.

The soldiers were also attracted to the euphoric and rewarding qualities of the drugs; they enjoyed getting "high." Although the military commanders were aware of drug use among soldiers, they mostly ignored it, viewing it as soldiers blowing off steam.

Beginning in 1971, the military began mandatory drug testing of soldiers in order to identify and detoxify drug users before they returned to the United States. More than 1 in 20 soldiers tested positive for narcotics, though they knew in advance that they would be tested. With speculation that many of these soldiers were unable to go without drugs for even a short time, concern grew that a flood of addicted soldiers returning from Vietnam would swamp treatment facilities back home. The White House asked a team of behavioral scientists to study a group of returning soldiers to assess the extent of the addiction problem.

Led by the behavioral epidemiologist Lee Robins, the research team examined a random sample of 898 soldiers who were leaving Vietnam in September 1971. Robins and her colleagues found extremely high levels of drug use among them (Robins, Helzer, & Davis, 1975). Over 90 percent reported drinking alcohol, nearly three-quarters smoked marijuana, and nearly half used narcotics such as heroin, morphine, and opium. About half of the soldiers who used narcotics either had symptoms of addiction or reported that they believed they would be unable to give up their drug habits. Robins's findings suggested that approximately 1 soldier in 5 returning from Vietnam was an addict. Given the prevailing view that addiction was a biological disorder with a low rate of recovery, these results indicated that tens of thousands of heroin addicts would soon be inundating American towns and cities. But this didn't happen.

Robins and her colleagues examined drug use among the soldiers after they returned to the United States. Of those who were apparently addicted to narcotics in Vietnam, only half sought out drugs when they returned to the States, and fewer still maintained their narcotic addictions. Approximately 95 percent of the addicts no longer used drugs within months of their return, which is an astonishing quit rate considering that the success rate of the best treatments is typically only 20 to 30 percent. A long-term follow-up study conducted in the early 1990s confirmed that only a handful of those who were addicts in Vietnam remained addicts.

Why did coming home help the addicts recover? One possible explanation comes from classical conditioning—all of the cues for drug use were connected to Vietnam and its associated military environment. When the soldiers returned home, their environment contained none of those cues, and therefore the soldiers did not experience conditioned withdrawal effects. But it is likely, too, that their motives for taking the drugs were also absent on their return. No longer needing the drugs to escape the horrors of combat, they focused on other needs and goals that became more important, such as family obligations and careers. An important lesson from this case study is that we cannot ignore the environment when we try to understand addiction. Knowing the physical actions of drugs in the brain may give us insights into the biology of addiction, but it fails to account for how these biological impulses can be overcome by other motivations. ■

Alcohol Is the Most Widely Abused Drug

Americans have a love-hate relationship with alcohol. On the one hand, moderate drinking is an accepted aspect of normal social interaction and may even be good for health. On the other, alcohol is a major contributor to many of our societal problems, such as spousal abuse and other forms of violence. Alcohol is a factor in over half of all fatal car accidents, killing over 20,000 people each year. Moreover, one-quarter of suicide victims and one-third of homicide victims have blood-alcohol levels that meet legal criteria for impairment. A recent study found that approximately one-third of college students reported having had sex during a drinking binge, and the heaviest drinkers were likely to have had sex with a new or casual partner (Leigh & Shafer, 1993). This places heavy college drinkers at great risk for exposure to AIDS. The overall cost of problem drinking in the United States, ranging from employee absence to health care, is estimated to be more than $100 billion annually.

Most individuals who drink do so in moderation, although the average American over age 14 consumes the equivalent of 2.5 gallons of pure alcohol per year, which corresponds to nearly 600 12-ounce cans of beer (USDHHS, 1993). It has been estimated that 10 percent of drinkers consume more than 50 percent of the total amount of alcohol consumed in the United States, and some 15 million Americans meet criteria for **alcoholism,** defined as abnormal alcohol seeking with some loss of control over drinking, accompanied by physiological effects of tolerance and withdrawal. Some 90 percent of high school seniors have tried alcohol, and in one recent survey almost one-third of seniors reported having had a bout of heavy drinking (five or more drinks) within the preceding two weeks.

alcoholism Abnormal alcohol seeking characterized by loss of control over drinking and accompanied by physiological effects of tolerance and withdrawal.

One reason people consume alcohol is the anticipated effects that alcohol will have on their emotions and behavior. Both light and heavy drinkers believe that alcohol reduces anxiety, and so many people regularly have a drink or two after a difficult day. Unfortunately, the available evidence does not support this belief; although moderate doses of alcohol are associated with temporarily increased positive mood, larger doses are associated with a worsening of mood. Also, although alcohol can interfere with cognitive processing of threat cues, such that anxiety-provoking events are less troubling when people are intoxicated, this occurs only if people drink *before* the anxiety-inducing event. According to this research, drinking after a hard day can actually increase people's focus on and obsession with their problems (Sayette, 1993).

Alan Marlatt, a leading researcher on alcohol and drug abuse, has commented that people view alcohol as the "magic elixir," capable of increasing social skills, sexual pleasure, confidence, and power (Marlatt, 1999). Expectations about the effects of alcohol are learned very early in life; children see that people who drink have a lot of fun and that drinking is an important aspect of many celebrations (Figure 9.15). Teenagers may view drinkers as sociable and grown up, two things that they desperately want to be. Thus, through observation, children learn to expect that consuming alcohol will have positive effects. It has been shown that children who have very positive expectations about alcohol are more likely to start drinking and to be heavy drinkers than children who do not share those expectations.

9.15 Alcohol and Behavior Many alcohol and beer companies promote the idea that good times will follow from drinking.

According to the social psychologists Jay Hull and Charles Bond, expectations have profound effects on behavior. To study the true effects of alcohol, researchers give individuals either tonic water or alcohol and then tell them that they are getting tonic water or alcohol, though not necessarily in correlation to the actual contents of the drink (Figure 9.16). This balanced-placebo design allows for a comparison of those who think they are drinking tonic water but are actually drinking alcohol with those who think they are drinking alcohol but are actually drinking tonic water. Researchers thus can separate drug effects from personal beliefs. This study has demonstrated that alcohol truly does impair motor processes, information processing, and mood, independent of whether people think they have consumed it. In contrast, the belief that one has consumed alcohol leads to

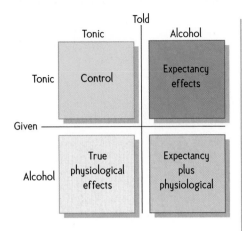

9.16 True Effects of Alcohol The consumption of alcohol typically includes both physiological and expectancy effects. The balanced-placebo design allows researchers to examine these influences on behavior separately.

disinhibition of a variety of social behaviors, such as sexual arousal and aggression, whether or not the person actually has consumed alcohol (Hull & Bond, 1986). Thus, some of people's behaviors when drunk are accounted for by learned beliefs about intoxication rather than by the pharmacological properties of alcohol. Sometimes the pharmacology and learned expectancies work in opposite ways. For instance, alcohol tends to increase sexual arousal, but it interferes with sexual performance.

Alcohol involves a number of different neurotransmitter systems and activates receptors for GABA, opiates, and dopamine (see Chapter 3). A variety of evidence suggests that the reinforcing aspects of alcohol are due to its activation of dopamine receptors, as is the case with other addictive drugs. Alcohol also interferes with the neurochemical processes involved in memory, which explains why memory loss can follow excessive alcohol intake. Heavy long-term alcohol intake can cause extensive brain damage. *Korsakoff's syndrome* is an alcohol-related disorder characterized by severe memory loss and intellectual deterioration.

REVIEWING

the Principles | What Is Addiction?

People have long ingested drugs that alter the way they think, feel, and act. Drug use and abuse has enormous societal costs, from impaired driving, to illness, to crime. Although moderate use of drugs such as alcohol and caffeine may have few consequences, excessive use can lead to physical or psychological dependence. The term *addiction* refers to physical dependence, in which not using the drug produces withdrawal and more of the drug is needed to obtain its effects. Psychoactive drugs affect a variety of neurotransmitter systems, but personal beliefs about a drug also affect the user's experience and behavior.

What Factors Motivate Sexual Behavior?

Sexual desire has long been recognized as one of humanity's most durable and powerful motivators because most human beings have a significant desire for sex. However, sex drives vary substantially across individuals and circumstances. This variation in sexual practices can be explained both in terms of individual differences and the fact that society has a dominating influence over how and when individuals engage in sexual activity.

For much of the history of psychological science, the study of sex was something of a taboo. The idea that women were motivated to have sex was almost unthinkable; many theorists believed that women were even incapable of enjoying the sexual act. The pioneering work of Alfred Kinsey and his colleagues in the 1940s provided—for the times—shocking evidence that women were in many ways similar to men in their sexual attitudes and behaviors. In Kinsey's surveys of thousands of Americans, he found that more than half of both men and women reported premarital sexual behavior, that masturbation was common in both sexes, that women enjoyed orgasms, and that homosexuality was much more common than most people expected. More than 50 years later, we know a great deal more about sexual behavior, although the topic still makes some people uncomfortable. Public discussion of sexual activity is rare, except perhaps on talk radio and daytime televison shows. In this section we describe what psychological science has learned about the motivation for sex.

Biological Factors Influence Sexual Behavior

Kinsey's research demonstrated how little most people knew about human sexual behavior. Despite Kinsey's eye-opening contributions, ignorance about the physiology of sex persisted into the 1960s, when William Masters and Virginia Johnson began to study sexual behavior in the laboratory. It needs to be acknowledged that their sample was a little bit unusual, in that only people who were willing to be filmed while having intercourse or masturbating served as research participants. Nonetheless, their work provided considerable insights into the physiological aspects of human sexual behavior. The most enduring contribution of this research was the identification of the **sexual response cycle**, consisting of a predictable pattern of physical responses that occur in four stages. The *excitement phase* occurs when people contemplate sexual activity or begin to engage in behaviors such as kissing and touching in a sensual manner. During this stage, blood flows to the genitals and they become aroused. The male penis begins to become erect. The female clitoris becomes swollen, the vagina expands and secretes fluids, and the nipples enlarge.

As excitement continues, people reach the *plateau phase,* during which pulse rate, breathing, and blood pressure increase, as do the various signs of arousal. For many people, this is the frenzied phase of sexual activity, in which inhibitions are lifted and passion takes control. The plateau phase culminates in the *orgasm phase,* which consists of involuntary muscle contractions throughout the body, dramatic increases in breathing and heart rate, rhythmic contractions of the vagina for females, and ejaculation of semen for males. Although orgasm nearly always occurs for healthy males, it is more variable for females. When it does occur, however, the pleasurable sensations are nearly identical to those experienced by males. Following orgasm there is dramatic release of sexual tension and a slow return to a normal state of arousal. In this *resolution phase,* the male enters a refractory period during which he is temporarily unable to maintain an erection or have orgasm. Females do not have such a refractory period and may experience multiple orgasms with short resolution phases between each one. This sexual response cycle involves both biological and psychological processes. Here we focus on the biological.

HORMONES As you recall from Chapter 3, hormones are involved in the production and termination of sexual behaviors. In nonhuman animals, hormones profoundly influence sexual activity. In many species, females are sexually receptive only when fertile, and estrogen is believed to control reproductive behaviors. As noted in Chapter 3, however, estrogen appears to play only a small role in human female sexuality. What role do hormones play for people?

Hormones influence human sexual behavior in two ways. First, they influence physical development of the brain and body. During the developmental phase of *puberty,* increases in hormones throughout the body stimulate bodily changes, such as the development of *secondary sexual characteristics,* including pubic hair, body hair, and, for females, breasts. In North America and Europe, puberty typically begins at age 11 or 12, and it typically begins earlier for females.

The second way hormones influence sexual behavior is through motivation; they activate reproductive behavior. Recall that sex hormones are released from the gonads (testes and ovaries) and that androgens are more commonly released in males and estrogens are more commonly released in females. As noted in Chapter 3, androgens appear to be much more important for reproductive behavior than estrogens, at least for humans. In both men and women, the androgen testosterone is involved in sexual functioning. Males need a certain amount of testosterone to be able to engage in sex, although they do not perform better if they have more testosterone. For women,

sexual response cycle A pattern of physiological responses during sexual activity.

it appears that the more testosterone they have, the more likely they are to have sexual thoughts and desires (Meston & Frohlich, 2000). Adolescent females with high testosterone levels are more likely to engage in sexual intercourse (Halpern, Udry, & Suchindran, 1997). Another hormone that is important for both men and women is *oxytocin*, which is released during sexual arousal and orgasm. Some researchers believe that oxytocin may promote feelings of love between partners; it also seems to be involved in social behavior more generally. Given the important role of the hypothalamus in controlling the release of hormones into the bloodstream, it should come as no surprise that the hypothalamus is the brain region considered most important for stimulating sexual behavior. Studies have shown that damaging the hypothalamus in rats interrupts sexual behavior, although the area that is most affected differs slightly for males and females.

NEUROTRANSMITTERS A variety of other neurotransmitters can affect various aspects of the sexual response. For instance, dopamine receptors in the limbic system are involved in the physical experience of pleasure. Serotonin has also been implicated in sexual behavior. The most common pharmacological treatments for depression enhance serotonin function, but they also cause serious reductions in sexual interest, especially for women. Why this happens is currently unclear, although small doses of drugs that enhance serotonin are useful for treating premature ejaculation.

One chemical that acts as a neurotransmitter in the brain and is also critical for sexual behavior is *nitric oxide*. Sexual stimulation leads to nitric oxide production, which then promotes blood flow to the penis and clitoris and subsequently plays an important role in the arousal of sexual organs, especially penile erections. When this system fails, males are unable to maintain an erection. Various drugs that enhance this system, such as Viagra, have been developed to treat erectile disorders. Although it is unknown whether drugs such as Viagra can be used to treat women's sexual disorders, they do appear to enhance the sexual experience for healthy women (Caruso, Intelisano, Farina, Di Mari, & Agnello, 2003).

VARIATIONS ACROSS THE MENSTRUAL CYCLE Women differ from men in how the hypothalamus controls the release of sex hormones. Whereas hormones for males are released at the same rate over time, the release of hormones for women varies according to a cycle that repeats itself approximately every 28 days— the menstrual cycle. Although research has found only minimal evidence that women's sexual behavior varies across the menstrual cycle, recent evidence indicates that women may process social information differently depending on whether they are in a fertile phase of the cycle or not. For instance, when researchers used a computer program to alter masculinity and femininity in male faces, they found that women preferred the more masculine faces during ovulation compared with other phases of the menstrual cycle (Pentok-Voak et al., 1999). Macrae and colleagues (2002) demonstrated that during ovulation women have an enhanced ability to identify faces as being male and are faster to judge behaviors as masculine, such as males being more athletic, decisive, and vulgar. In another recent study, women who watched videotapes of men competing to be lunch dates rated self-assured men as more desirable potential sex partners, but only if the woman were ovulating (Gangestad, Simpson, Cousins, Garver-Agar, & Christensen, 2004). These studies add to a growing literature suggesting that women evaluate men differently across the menstrual cycle.

PHEROMONES One interesting line of research examines the influence of pheromones, chemicals secreted from various glands throughout the body, on the initiation of sex. Recall from Chapter 5 that pheromones are detected through the olfactory system. Evidence from a variety of species suggests that pheromones can activate sexual behaviors. What about in humans? At this point some evidence suggests that pheromones might influence behavior, at least indirectly. In one study, female participants who overnight wore necklaces that contained male underarm sweat spent more time in social interactions with males the next day than did women who wore necklaces containing inert substances (Cowley & Brooksbank, 1991). In another study, men who mixed synthetic pheromone in their aftershave reported higher levels of sexual intercourse and other sexual behaviors, but no increase in masturbation. The authors concluded that the greater number of sexual encounters resulted because the pheromones increased the sexual attractiveness of the men to women (Cutler, Friedmann, & McCoy, 1998).

NEURAL CORRELATES OF VIEWING EROTICA Some recent imaging studies indicate that viewing erotica activates brain reward regions, such as various limbic structures. This effect was greatest for the men who had higher blood levels of testosterone (Stoleru et al., 1999). As noted in Chapter 4, Hamann and colleagues (2004) found that when men and women viewed sexually arousing stimuli, such as film clips of sexual activity or pictures of opposite-sex nudes, men showed more activation of the amygdala, which the authors suggest contributes to the arousing nature of the stimulus. Interestingly, men are typically more likely than women to report visual erotic stimulation as pleasurable (Herz & Cahill, 1997). However, this could be because much of erotica is produced for men. Research has shown that women prefer erotica produced specifically for women, which tends to emphasize more of the emotional factors of the sexual interaction. A recent study found that although both sexes prefer erotica that is aimed at their own sex, men were aroused by both types of movies (Janssen, Carpenter, & Graham, 2003).

Cultural Scripts and Rules Shape Sexual Interactions

In the movies, sexual relationships often start when one attractive young person meets another by chance, some exciting time is spent together, attraction develops, and sexual behavior ensues—often within a day or two. In real life, however, the course of action is often quite different. For one thing, most people rely on social networks to meet their sex partners. It is also apparent that people do not generally fall into bed together as fast as they do in the movies; most people know someone a long time before having sex. But the depiction of sexual behavior in movies and other media does shape beliefs and expectancies about what sexual behaviors are appropriate and when they are appropriate. *Sexual scripts* are cognitive beliefs about how a sexual episode should be enacted (see Chapter 8). For instance, the sexual script indicates who should make the first move, whether one should resist, the sequence of sexual acts, and even how one should act afterward. In North America, the sexual script involves initial flirtation through nonverbal actions, the male initiating physical contact, the female controlling whether sexual activity takes place, and refusals typically being verbal and direct (Berscheid & Regan, 2005).

DOUBLE STANDARDS At the social level, the double standard is a well-known pattern of cultural influence. It stipulates that certain activities (such as premarital or casual sex) are morally and socially acceptable for men but not for women. The sexual revolution of the late twentieth century entailed a large change in sexual behaviors, most of which must be attributed to changing cultural pressures and expectations. Although sexual customs and norms vary to some degree across cultures, all known cultures have some form of sexual morality, which indicates the importance to society of providing some regulation of sexual behavior. Cultures may seek to restrain and control sex for a variety of reasons, including maintaining control over the birth rate, establishing paternity, and reducing conflicts.

Perhaps because of the mixed messages that women receive, they tend to be higher than men in erotophobia, which is the disposition to respond negatively to sexual cues. Those high in erotophobia report parental strictness about sex, conservative attitudes, and the avoidance of masturbation (Fisher, Byrne, White, & Kelley, 1988). Paradoxically, those high in erotophobia may be at greater risk for unwanted pregnancies and sexually transmitted diseases, because they are less likely to carry condoms or take other precautions.

LOSING VIRGINITY The age at which people first lose their virginity has varied considerably across cultures and history. In recent decades in North America, this age has become younger. Miller and Benson (1999) concluded from multiple studies that about half of today's young American women and two-thirds of the men have had intercourse by their eighteenth birthdays. A substantial minority remain virgins longer than that, however—one out of five is still a virgin at age 20. Even so, the average can conceal wide variations. Interestingly, many people who start having sex at an early age express regret later on. Losing virginity is a major event in most lives, although the actual experience can be anticlimactic and disappointing. Sprecher, Barbee, and Schwartz (1995) found that men reported both more anxiety and more pleasure during the first experience than did women, and the men were also more likely to have an orgasm. Women were more likely to feel guilty. For both genders, alcohol use was correlated with lower enjoyment of the first sexual experience, whereas having the first sex in the context of a committed relationship was associated with having a better experience.

SEX DIFFERENCES IN SEXUAL MOTIVES A noticeable and consistent finding in nearly all measures of sexual desire is that men, on average, have a higher level of sexual motivation than women, although there are many individual exceptions. Research studies have found that in general men masturbate more frequently than women, want sex earlier in the relationship, think and fantasize about sex more often, spend more time and money (and other resources) in the effort to obtain sex, desire more different sexual activities, initiate sex more and refuse sex less, and rate their own sex drives as stronger than women's (Baumeister, Catanese, & Vohs, 2001). In one study, researchers asked college-age men and women how many sex partners they would ideally like to have in their lives, if they were unconstrained by fears about disease, social pressures, and the like (Miller & Fishkin, 1997). The majority of women wanted one or two, whereas the average answer by the men was several dozen. A large study of more than 16,000 people from 10 major regions around the world found that the greater male motive for sexual activity and sexual variety occurs in all cultures (Schmitt et al., 2003).

The relative influence of nature and culture on sexual motivation may vary with gender. Roy Baumeister (2000) used the term *erotic plasticity* to refer to the degree to which the sex drive can be shaped by social, cultural, and situational factors. Evidence suggests that women have higher erotic plasticity than men. A woman's sexuality may evolve and change throughout her adult life, whereas men's desires remain relatively constant (except for the gradual decline with age). Women's sexual desires and behaviors depend significantly on social factors such as education and religion, whereas men's sexuality shows minimal relationship to such influences.

How much of human sexual behavior is determined by biology?

sexual strategies theory Evolutionary theory that suggests men and women look for different qualities in their relationship partners due to the gender-specific adaptive problems they've faced throughout human history.

Mating Strategies Differ between the Sexes

All humans desire to enter into romantic relationships, and for the most part they want the same thing in their mates. Both men and women seek attractive mates who are kind, honest, and good-natured. In addition to liking the same set of features in a potential mate, both sexes avoid certain characteristics, such as showing insensitivity, displaying bad manners, speaking too loudly or in a shrill voice, and bragging about sexual conquests (Cunningham, Barbee, & Druen, 1996). In spite of these similarities, males and females have been found to differ in the relative emphasis they place on physical appearance and social status, with men being more concerned with appearance and women being more concerned with status. How does psychological science explain these differences?

According to the **sexual strategies theory** of the evolutionary psychologist David Buss (Figure 9.17), these differences are due to the different adaptive problems that have faced men and women throughout human history (Buss & Schmitt, 1993). From this perspective, women differ from men in how they maximize the passing along of their genes to future generations. Women's basic strategy is intensive care of a relatively small number of infants. Their commitment is to nurture rather than to simply maximize production. Once a woman is pregnant, additional matings are of no use, and once she has a small child, an additional pregnancy can put her current offspring at risk. Thus, biological mechanisms—for example, nursing typically prevents ovulation—ensure spacing between children. On purely reproductive grounds, men have no such interludes. For them, all matings may have a reproductive payoff, since they bear few of the personal costs of pregnancy.

Because having offspring is a much more intensive commitment for women, they will likely be more cautious about having sex. Indeed, there is evidence that women are much less willing than men to have sex with someone they don't know well. In one study, an attractive stranger approached people of the opposite sex and said, "I have been noticing you around campus. I find you attractive. Would you go to bed with me tonight?" Although not one woman said yes, three-quarters of the men agreed to the request (Figure 9.18). Indeed, the men were less likely to agree to go out on a date with the attractive woman than they were to agree to have sex with her (Clark & Hatfield, 1989). In another study, people were asked to state how long a couple should be together before it is acceptable to engage in sexual intercourse, given mutual desire. Women tend to think that couples should be together for a month or so before sex is appropriate, whereas males believe that even relatively short periods of acquaintanceship make having sex acceptable (Buss & Schmitt, 1993).

Although men and women value most of the same things in a relationship partner, men and women diverge in terms of which features they emphasize. Strictly in terms of maximizing reproduction, men primarily need to be concerned with whether a woman looks like she could bear healthy children. Conversely, women are better able to maximize reproduction by seeking mates who are likely to provide resources and assistance to help nurture offspring. In one study, Buss asked 92 married couples about which characteristics they valued in their spouse. Women generally preferred men who were considerate, honest, dependable, kind, understanding, fond of children, well liked by others, good earners, ambitious, career oriented, from a good family, and fairly tall. Men tended to value good looks, cooking skills, and sexual faithfulness. In general, men rate

9.17 David Buss Buss uses evolutionary theory to examine mating strategies. His research shows that there is great cross-cultural consistency in what men and women desire in their mates, and that mating strategies are adaptive.

9.18 Sexual Motives and Response When men and women were propositioned by an attractive stranger, men were much more willing than women to agree to have sex or to go home with the stranger. Note that not a single woman agreed to have sex.

"I'm rich, you're thin. Together, we're perfect."

physical attractiveness as much more important than do women, who demonstrate a preference for education and good earning capacity—in other words, status. Across some 37 cultures studied, females valued a good financial prospect to a greater extent than did men (Buss, 1989). In addition, women in all 37 cultures tended to marry older men, who are often more settled and financially stable. The relative male preference for attractiveness and the female preference for status can be observed in personal ads—studies show that males tend to seek out good looks and females tend to seek out maturity and financial stability. It is important to note, however, that both men and women value physical attractiveness highly. It is the relative emphases that conform to evolutionary predictions.

The evolutionary account of human mating is controversial. Some researchers believe that behaviors shaped by evolution have little impact on contemporary relationships. We must consider two important factors. First, the modern era is only a tiny fraction of human evolutionary history, and the modern mind resides in a Stone Age brain, solving adaptive problems that have faced our species for thousands of years. Thus, remnants of behaviors that were adaptive in prehistoric times may still linger even if they are not adaptive in contemporary society. What is more important, however, is that natural selection bestows not only biological urges, but also a strong sensitivity to cultural and group norms, so that instinctive behaviors are constrained by social context. The frontal lobes work to inhibit people from breaking social rules, which are determined to a great extent by culture. The current social context differs greatly from that of millions of years ago; human mating strategies are indeed influenced by these contemporary norms. For example, from a biological view, it might seem advantageous for humans to reproduce as soon as they are able. But many contemporary cultures discourage sexual behavior until people are older and better able to care for their offspring. The critical point is that human behavior emerges to solve adaptive problems, and to some degree the modern era introduces new adaptive challenges based on societal standards of conduct. These standards shape the context in which both men and women view sexual behavior as desirable and appropriate.

Thinking Critically

How Is Sexual Orientation Determined?

Why are some people homosexual? Homosexual behavior in various forms has been noted throughout recorded history. From an evolutionary perspective, homosexuality appears to make little sense; exclusive homosexuality would not lead to reproduction and therefore would not survive in the gene pool. Although there have been many theories of homosexuality, none to date has received conclusive support. Early theories of homosexuality regarded it as deviant, abnormal, and a psychological disorder; until 1973 it was officially viewed as a mental illness by psychiatrists. Classic psychoanalytic theories of homosexuality emphasized the importance of parenting practices. Families with a domineering mother and a submissive father were thought to cause the children to identify with the opposite-sex parent, which would translate into a sexual attraction toward the gender opposite of their identification—that is, a same-sex attraction. However, the overwhelming majority of studies have found little evidence that how parents treat their children has anything to do with sexual orientation. Likewise, no other environmental factor has been found to account for homosexuality. So does biology determine sexual orientation?

Remember that when we ask whether something is biological, we are really talking about the relative contribution of biological factors compared with that of environmental factors. Every behavior is the result of biological processes, such as gene expression, that are themselves influenced by events in the environment. A number of different approaches examine the extent to which biological factors contribute to sexual orientation. One such approach explores how much hormones affect the development of sexual orientation. For instance, early theorists speculated that lesbians had higher levels of testosterone and gay males had higher levels of estrogen, but those were wrong; the levels of circulating hormones do not differ. Rather, the best available evidence suggests that exposure to hormones, especially androgens, in the prenatal environment might play some role in sexual orientation (Mustanski, Chivers, & Bailey, 2002). For example, because of a mother's medical condition, some females are exposed to much higher levels of androgens than normal during prenatal development, and these women often have masculine characteristics, both physical and psychological, and are more likely to report being lesbians later in adulthood. An intriguing finding is that gay males are more likely to have older male siblings than are heterosexual males. One explanation for this is that the mother's body responds in some way to being pregnant with a boy and this response alters the level of hormones in the prenatal environment when the mother becomes pregnant with another boy (Blanchard & Ellis, 2001). But most males with older brothers are not homosexual, so why would this response affect only some males?

A second approach to understanding the biological contribution to sexual orientation is through behavioral genetics. The idea that gene expression might be involved in sexual orientation is supported by a recent study that used fruit flies. Researchers found that altering expression of a single "master" gene reversed the sexual orientation of both male and female flies (Demir & Dickson, 2005). But what about in humans? In 1993, the biologist Dean Hamer reported that he had found a link between a marker on the X chromosome and sexual orientation in males, which the media quickly dubbed "the gay gene." Is homosexuality inherited? Twin studies provide some support for the idea of a genetic component to homosexuality, particularly for males. In a review of previous studies, Mustanski and colleagues (2002) report the heritability of homosexuality as being greater for males than for females, but there was a significant genetic component for both. What is inherited? At this time it is unclear how human sexual orientation might be encoded in the genes.

Some research suggests that the hypothalamus may be related to sexual orientation. In postmortem examinations, neuroscientist Simon LeVay (1991) found that an area of the hypothalamus that typically differs between men and women was only half as large in homosexual men as heterosexual men. In fact, the size of this area in homosexual men was comparable to its size in heterosexual women. Likewise, in a recent brain-imaging study, heterosexual males showed greater activation of the hypothalamus when they sniffed a female pheromone substance than they did when they sniffed a male pheromone substance, whereas females showed greater activation when they sniffed a male rather than female pheromone substance (Savic, Berglund, & Lirdström, 2005). Male homosexuals showed a pattern more similar to women than to heterosexual men, with greater activation of the hypothalamus in response to the male pheromone substance. Although intriguing, both of these studies can be criticized on the grounds that correlation does not equal causation. That is, a size difference or activation difference in any one part of the brain cannot establish whether this area determines sexual orientation, whether being heterosexual or homosexual results in changes to brain structure or function, or whether a third variable is responsible for all these effects. For instance, some researchers believe that the size of the hypothalamus is determined by prenatal exposure to androgens. Thus, although the findings of these two studies are suggestive, we currently have insufficient evidence to establish a causal connection between brain regions and sexual orientation. Considered together, the evidence is consistent that biological processes do play some role in sexual orientation. The question now is how and when biology contributes and to what degree. It seems likely to many psychological scientists that multiple processes may affect one's sexual orientation in more than one subtle way.

How might biology interact with aspects of the environment to determine sexual orientation? Daryl Bem (1996) proposed that feeling different from opposite- or same-sex peers predicts later sexual orientation. A notable finding in the literature is that homosexuals report preferring the leisure activities of their opposite-sex peers, which Bem believes may be due to biological differences in temperament. As you will learn, children tend to play in same-sex groups, so that boys and girls are often segregated. In terms of sexual orientation, Bem believes that people are attracted to that which is different, so most girls are attracted to boys and vice versa. However, to some children, what seems different is peers of their own sex. According to Bem, that which is different creates arousal, and this arousal is the essence of sexual attraction. Because the opposite sex is different, it becomes attractive. Or, in Bem's words, "the exotic becomes erotic." For homosexuals, it is the same sex that is exotic, and that therefore becomes erotic. The interesting part of Bem's model is that it is based on the idea of initial biological differences, but then proposes that the social environment shapes what is sexually attractive. Although the theory is supported by a variety of anecdotal evidence, there is so far no concrete proof for it. But how can researchers ever really test such theories in humans?

What evidence is needed to conclude whether sexual orientation is determined or chosen? Are you pleased or troubled by evidence suggesting that homosexuality is biologically determined? How might your sexual orientation affect how you interpret these data and how you feel about them? ■

REVIEWING the Principles | What Factors Motivate Sexual Behavior?

Pioneering research by Alfred Kinsey launched the study of human sexual behavior and shattered many myths regarding the sexual lives of men and women. Masters and Johnson found that there were four stages to the sexual response cycle: excitement, plateau, orgasm, and resolution. Sexual behavior involves both physiological and psychological factors. Hormones influence the development of secondary sex characteristics as well as motivate sexual behavior. However, behaviors are constrained by sexual scripts, which dictate appropriate actions for men and women. Men and women look for different qualities in potential partners, which may be due in part to the different adaptive problems faced by the sexes over the course of human evolution. On average and across nearly all measures, men have a higher level of sexual motivation than women.

Conclusion

The study of motivation deals with explaining the occurrence of diverse behaviors, from composing poetry to working late to finish an important project to ingesting mind-altering chemicals. Motivation is concerned not only with immediate survival, but also with our efforts to achieve our loftiest goals. Many of our motivations arise to satisfy the basic biological needs of our bodies, such as drinking to quench our thirst or eating when we are hungry. But other needs are also important in our lives, such as the need for other people and the need to feel competent. An important principle in motivation is that over the course of human evolution, those things that brought pleasure were often adaptive, in that doing them increased survival and reproduction; sexual behavior is perhaps the most obvious example. However, evolution did not anticipate that people would be able to sit down one day and eat an entire box of cookies or order pizza delivery through the Internet, or that we would discover drugs that would artificially activate brain reward circuits that had been adaptive for millions of years. Now our efforts often require overriding the urge to seek pleasure, such as restricting our consumption of tasty foods or resisting the urge to use drugs. Maintaining a reasonable body weight is an example of a long-term goal, and long-term goals are another important part of motivation. Humans differ from other animals because we have the capacity to set personal goals and try to achieve them. All of this requires the ability to have some control over our biological urges as well as the ability to make choices, such as choosing to study rather than sleep or go out with friends. Each day brings new challenges in motivation as we try to satisfy our immediate needs, keeping in mind that we want to live meaningful and satisfying lives. The study of motivation helps us to make sense of why people desire to do certain things and why sometimes they need to inhibit those desires.

Summarizing the Principles of Motivation

How Does Motivation Activate, Direct, and Sustain Behavior?

1. **Needs, drives, and arousal motivate behavior:** Satisfying a need (a state of deficiency) motivates, with survival needs being the most motivating. According to the humanist perspective, we are compelled upwards in our needs hierarchy to achieve self-actualization. Drives are activated to satisfy needs and maintain homeostasis. Arousal affects performance, depending on the nature of the task and level of arousal.

2. **Pleasure can motivate adaptive behaviors:** The pleasure principle is central to motivation and pleasurable behaviors will be selected over satisfying biological needs. Satisfying pleasure needs may facilitate survival and reproduction. Dopamine activation may guide survival behaviors.

3. **Some behaviors are motivated for their own sake:** Extrinsically motivated behaviors emphasize external goals; intrinsically motivated behaviors are performed for their own sake, not biological needs. Curiosity, play, creativity, and problem solving are intrinsically motivated and are reduced by external reward.

Why Are Human Beings Social?

4. **Humans have a fundamental need to belong:** The formation of social bonds is adaptive because it aids survival and reproductive success. We experience anxiety at the prospect of rejection.

5. **People seek others when they are anxious:** Isolation causes anxiety and when anxious, we choose to be with others. Social comparison allows us to validate our self-perceptions.

6. **People are motivated to detect and reject cheaters:** A social dilemma arises when we experience a conflict between cooperating and being selfish. People act selfishly if they think others are as well, which threatens group stability. Therefore we are vigilant in detecting cheaters in the group and will stigmatize and reject them.

How Do People Achieve Personal Goals?

7. **Good goals enhance confidence:** Challenging, difficult, and specific goals are most productive. A sense of self-efficacy leads to success. Being motivated to achieve is a powerful influence on behavior.

8. **Self-regulation requires self-awareness and delay of gratification:** People use cognitive strategies to evaluate progress towards a goal. They act in accordance with their own goals when self-aware; deindividuation reduces that action. Avoiding self-awareness can lead to self-destructive behavior. Delay of gratification and self-regulatory strength are necessary to achieve goals.

9. **The frontal lobes are important for self-regulation:** The frontal lobes are involved in more complex tasks and therefore is involved in self-regulation. This is an adaptive function.

What Determines What We Eat?

10. **Time and taste play roles:** Eating schedules are conditioned. Sensory-specific satiety increases the likelihood of meeting nutritional needs during scarcity because it encourages consumption of a variety of foods but it can also account for over eating.

11. **Culture determines what we eat:** Specific food choices and how they are eaten are determined and vary by culture.

12. **Multiple neural processes control eating:** The hypothalamus influences eating behavior. Taste cues are processed in the prefrontal cortex. Receptors in the body also detect glucose and leptin levels as signals to eat.

What Is Addiction?

13. **Addiction has psychological and physical aspects:** Physical addiction involves the body's responses and tolerance. Psychological dependence involves habit and compulsion despite consequences.

14. **People use—and abuse—many psychoactive drugs:** Stimulants increase behavioral and mental activity. MDMA (ecstacy) produces energizing and hallucinogenic effects. THC (the active ingredient in marijuana) alters perception. Opiates provide high reward value by increasing dopamine activation.

15. **Alcohol is the most widely abused drug:** Though believed to reduce anxiety, alcohol consumption can increase anxiety and negative mood. A drinker's expectation can have significant effects on behavior.

What Factors Motivate Sexual Behavior?

16. **Biological factors influence sexual behavior:** The sexual response cycle includes excitement, plateau, orgasm, and resolution. Hormones determine physical development and they motivate sexual behavior. Neurotransmitters play a role in motivating sexual behavior. Women's sexual behavior varies across the menstrual cycle. Pheromones might play a role in sexual activity. Viewing erotica activates the amygdala.

17. **Cultural scripts and rules shape sexual interactions:** The cognitive sexual scripts inform sexual activity and are influenced by culture. A double standard of sexual behaviors exists for men verses women. Loss of virginity is culturally significant. Erotic plasticity is shaped by culture.

18. **Mating strategies differ between the sexes:** Female reproductive strategies revolve around intensive care of a few infants. Male strategies are less restrictive. Cross-cultural evidence support the different behaviors of males and females regarding reproductive imperatives.

Applying the Principles

1. Madison's third-grade teacher consistently tells the class that they are the best and smartest class ever. Madison's self-perception is that she is smart and she works hard on her school tasks. Mason's third-grade teacher gives students who do good work a sticker on their paper, but after a couple of months she notices the overall quality of Mason's work has leveled off to average. What difference in motivation may account for the difference in these two children's performance?

_____ a) Madison is intrinsically motivated; Mason is externally motivated

_____ b) Madison is responding to internally regulated drives; Mason to conditioning

_____ c) Madison needs approval; Mason does not need approval

_____ d) Madison needs no motivation; Mason needs increasing motivation

2. You have just received the results of the chemistry test you took last week. When class is over, you ask your classmates how they did. Why is this information useful in judging your performance?

_____ a) It really isn't useful since true academic accomplishments are internally driven.

_____ b) We are only able to determine satisfaction if it is shared by others.

_____ c) Social comparison offers us accurate information about ourselves.

_____ d) We are motivated to figure out who is truthful about their performance relative to our own.

3. Trang has just returned from the grocery store and is tempted to eat the chocolate that she bought to make brownies later in the day. Which of the following strategies might best enable her to resist?

____ a) putting a note on the chocolate that says "step away from the chocolate!"

____ b) thinking of herself as a good person

____ c) thinking of the chocolate as an unappetizing lump of brown clay

____ d) repeatedly saying out loud "I won't eat chocolate."

4. Ann says that she is addicted to chocolate. Her statement is most likely

____ a) true because she has a strong psychological need for chocolate.

____ b) false because chocolate is not a substance that leads to strong physical addiction.

____ c) true because chocolate has been found to create permanent changes in levels of neurotransmitters.

____ d) false because although she has a strong psychological desire for chocolate, she gives no indication of physical dependence.

5. The saying "women give sex to get love and men give love to get sex" exemplifies the idea

____ a) that we are attracted to what is different.

____ b) that men have greater sexual motivation.

____ c) that women and men have different reproductive scripts.

____ d) that men are only capable of love if it leads to sexual arousal.

ANSWERS: 1a 2c 3c 4d 5c

Key Terms

achievement motive, p. 356
alcoholism, p. 369
arousal, p. 345
creativity, p. 348
deindividuation, p. 357
delay of gratification, p. 358
drive, p. 345
extrinsic motivation, p. 348
goal, p. 355

homeostasis, p. 345
incentives, p. 346
intrinsic motivation, p. 348
motivation, p. 343
need, p. 344
need hierarchy, p. 344
need to belong theory, p. 352
physical dependence, p. 364
psychological dependence, p. 364

self-actualization, p. 344
self-efficacy, p. 355
self-regulation, p. 355
sexual response cycle, p. 371
sexual strategies theory, p. 375
social dilemma, p. 353
TOTE model, p. 356
Yerkes-Dodson law, p. 346

Further Readings

Berscheid, E., & Regan, P. (2005). *The psychology of interpersonal relationships*. New York: Prentice-Hall.

Capaldi, E. D. (1996). *Why we eat what we eat*. Washington, DC: American Psychological Association.

Franken, R. E. (1998). *Human motivation*. Pacific Grove, CA: Brooks-Cole.

Ilgen, D., & Pulakos, E. D. (1999). *The changing nature of performance*. San Francisco: Jossey-Bass.

381

Coping with Stress

Stress is a basic component of our daily lives, and a small amount of stress helps us to determine the boundaries of our emotional well-being. Extreme duress over an extended period of time, however, can lead to serious health problems. Combat soldiers often must use a combination of coping strategies to deal with the stress of their situation.

10

Emotions and Health

Elliot was in his early thirties when he began to suffer from severe headaches. He was happily married, a good father, and doing well professionally. His headaches increased until he could no longer concentrate, so he went to see his doctor. Sadly, it turned out that Elliot had a tumor the size of a small orange growing behind his eyes. As the tumor grew, it forced his frontal lobes upward into the top of his skull. A group of skilled surgeons removed the benign tumor, but in doing so they could not help but remove some of the surrounding frontal lobe tissue. Although the surgery appeared at first to be a great success—Elliot's physical recovery was quick and he continued to be an intelligent man with a superb memory—Elliot changed in a way that baffled his friends and family. He no longer experienced emotion.

Outlining the Principles

How Are Emotions Adaptive?

- Facial Expressions Communicate Emotion
- Emotions Serve Cognitive Functions
- Emotions Strengthen Interpersonal Relations

How Do People Experience Emotions?

- Emotions Have a Subjective Component
- Emotions Have a Physiological Component
- Emotions Have a Cognitive Component
- People Regulate Their Moods

What Is the Neurophysiological Basis of Emotion?

- Emotions Are Associated with Autonomic Activity
- The Amygdala and the Prefrontal Cortex Are Involved in Emotion
- Emotion Systems Are Lateralized in the Brain

How Do People Cope with Stress?

- There Are Sex Differences in Response to Stressors
- The General Adaptation Syndrome Is a Bodily Response to Stress

- People Encounter Stress in Daily Life
- Stress Affects Health
- Coping Is a Process

What Are Some of the Behaviors That Affect Physical Health?

- Obesity Results from a Genetic Predisposition and Overeating
- Restrictive Dieting Can Be Problematic
- Smoking Often Begins in Childhood
- People Do Not Get Enough Exercise

On the surface, Elliot seemed a reasonable, intelligent, and charming man, and yet his life fell apart. He lost his job; entered a doomed business venture with a sleazy character against the advice of his family and lost all his savings; divorced, remarried, and then quickly divorced again; and so on. He was incapable of making even trivial decisions, and he failed to learn from his mistakes. Though he had previously been a caring and compassionate man, he was now detached from his problems, reacting to them as if they had happened to someone else about whom he didn't care that much.

The neurologist Antonio Damasio was asked to examine Elliot to ascertain whether his emotional problems were real and whether they might have been due to the surgery. Damasio noted that Elliot displayed few emotional responses: "I never saw a tinge of emotion in my many hours of conversation with him: no sadness, no impatience, no frustration with my incessant and repetitious questioning" (Damasio, 1994, p. 45). Damasio's research team showed Elliot a series of disturbing pictures, such as severely injured bodies, and found that none of these elicited an emotional reaction from him. Elliot was not oblivious to his loss of emotion. He was able to report that he knew the pictures were disturbing, and that before the surgery he would have had an emotional response, but now he had none.

Imagine what your life would be like if you did not have any feelings. Like the android character from *Star Trek: The Next Generation,* Commander Data, you would be a rational being capable of sensation, perception, thought, memory, decision making, and so on, but you would not have any emotions. What sort of life would that be? For us human beings, every action and thought is colored by emotional reactions. As you read in the last chapter, emotions are a primary source of motivation, as we seek objects and activities that make us feel good and avoid doing or saying things that make us feel bad. Emotions permeate human life as we fall in love, achieve success, and enjoy friendships, but they also underlie painful episodes that many of us would just as soon forget.

Sometimes our emotions can overwhelm us, as when we become stressed by demands on our time. When people are stressed, they often act in ways that are bad for their health, such as eating too much or smoking cigarettes. People who feel time pressured to get things done, such as completing school or work projects, fail to get proper rest and exercise. We will learn that stress also directly affects physical health through its impact on various bodily systems, making people vulnerable to infection and disease. Even apparently minor daily hassles and frustrations can cause serious physical and mental health problems, especially if the frustration builds up over time. Learning to

Timeline

1872

Emotions Are Adaptive
Charles Darwin publishes *Expression of Emotion in Man and Animals,* in which he argues that for many species, emotions are adaptive and are hard wired through the processes of natural selection.

1884

Reactions Cause Emotions
William James and Carl Lange, working separately, assert that physical reactions can cause emotions.

1927

Emotions Cause Bodily Reactions Walter Cannon, in contrast to James, argues that people experience emotional states that subsequently lead to physiological responses.

1930s

General Adaptation Syndrome The endocrinologist Hans Selye proposes that stressors lead to bodily reactions and that prolonged stress could lead to deficiencies in the immune system. Selye's work launches the field of health psychology.

cope with negative emotional states is important for our health and well-being. People can use a number of constructive strategies to reduce the stress in their lives, from seeking the support of others to getting sufficient sleep and taking care of their bodies through exercise and good nutrition.

This chapter explores how emotions influence the human experience, including where they come from and how they are experienced, as well as how people cope with stress and handle negative events in their lives. We also consider the most important behaviors that influence physical health and describe ways to promote healthy living. We will see that daily habits—such as diet, exercise, and smoking—play an important role in the most common causes of death in our modern society, and that emotional states often encourage people to develop bad habits. Understanding how emotions influence cognition and behavior helps us to gain insight into what makes us mentally and physically healthy. ■

Emotions are a fundamental part of the human experience. They warn of danger, create bonds between people, and bring joy to life. However, they can also cause problems. People who feel overly anxious may be too afraid to meet new people or even to leave the house. People indulge in unhealthy behaviors trying to cope with stress and other negative feelings. For thousands of years, people have reflected on why we have emotions and what they do for us. Many scholars have viewed cognition and emotion to be separate, with emotion occasionally overwhelming reason and causing people to act in impulsive or inappropriate ways. However, an important lesson from Chapter 8 is that everyday cognition is far from cold and rational. Decisions and judgments are affected by how people feel. We now know that emotion and cognition are completely intertwined. There has been a growing emphasis in psychological science in understanding how emotion influences our daily lives. Important research is being conducted across all levels of analysis, and the biological revolution is producing exciting new findings about how neural and cognitive processes are involved in the experience of emotion. Case studies of people such as Elliot provide ample evidence about the role of various brain regions in producing and regulating emotional responses, as well as how people use emotional information.

Almost everyone has an intuitive sense of what is meant by the term *emotion*, but it has proven a difficult concept to define precisely. For psychological scientists, **emotion** (or *affect*) refers to feelings that involve subjective evaluation, physiological processes, and cognitive beliefs. Emotions are immediate responses to environmental events, such as being cut off in traffic or getting a nice gift. It is useful to distinguish emotion from mood, since the two are often used equivalently in everyday language. **Moods** are diffuse and long-lasting emotional states that influence rather

emotion Feelings that involve subjective evaluation, physiological processes, and cognitive beliefs.

mood A diffuse and long-lasting emotional state that influences rather than interrupts thought and behavior.

1937
Neural Basis of Emotions James Papez hypothesizes that emotional expression is mediated by several neural systems that form a circuit (known as the "Papez loop").

1962
Two-Factor Theory Stanley Schachter and Jerome Singer propose that emotions are the result of physical arousal and the attribution, or cognitive explanation, of the source of the arousal.

1963
Facial Feedback Hypothesis On the basis of Darwin's writings, Silvan Tomkins proposes that facial expressions trigger the experience of emotions.

1970S
Universal Emotional Expressions Paul Ekman and his colleagues find that people from diverse cultures recognize similar facial expressions. Carroll Izard demonstrates that infants also display basic emotions in their facial expressions.

1977
Health Psychology An interdisciplinary meeting of scientists at Yale University produces a vibrant new field of research that is focused on how behavioral and psychological factors affect physical health.

arousal, and a cognitive interpretation, or *emotion label*. When people experience arousal they initiate a search for its source. Although the search for a cognitive explanation is often quick and straightforward, since we generally recognize what event led to our emotional state, sometimes we are incorrect in our conclusions.

Schachter and his student Jerome Singer (1962) devised an ingenious experiment to test the two-factor theory. First, participants were injected with either a stimulant or a placebo. The stimulant was adrenaline, which produced symptoms such as sweaty palms, increased heart rate, and the shakes. Then either participants were told that the drug they took would make them feel aroused, or they were not given any information. Finally, each participant was left to wait with a confederate of the experimenter. In the euphoric condition, participants were exposed to a confederate who played with a hula hoop and made paper airplanes. In the angry condition, they were exposed to a confederate who asked them very intimate, personal questions, such as "With how many men (other than your father) has your mother had extramarital relationships?" [Making the question even more insulting were the three choices: (a) four or fewer, (b) five to nine, or (c) ten or more.] Note that those participants who received the adrenaline but were told what to expect would have an easy explanation for their arousal. However, those participants who received adrenaline but were not given information would be aroused but would not know why. Thus, they would look to the environment to explain or label their mood. Participants in the uninformed condition reported being happy with the euphoric confederate but less happy with the angry confederate (Figure 10.9).

10.8 Stanley Schachter Schachter emphasized the role of cognitive beliefs in the experience of emotion.

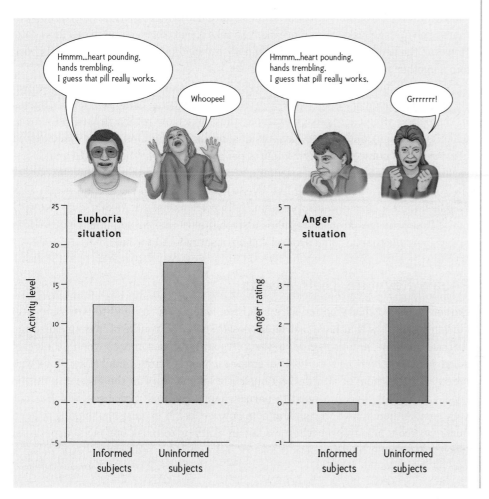

10.9 Testing the Two-Factor Theory The results of Schachter and Singer's experiment to test their theory of emotion showed that participants' subjective experience of emotion was a combination of the situation they were in, the physiological arousal of the stimulant pill, and whether they knew the purported effects of the pill.

PEOPLE CAN MISATTRIBUTE THE SOURCE OF EMOTIONAL STATES One interesting implication of the Schachter theory is that emotion can be mistakenly attributed to something that did not actually cause the arousal. *Misattribution of arousal* is a term used when an emotion label is derived from the wrong source. In one of the most amazing demonstrations of this phenomenon, researchers tried to see whether people could fall in love through misattribution (Dutton & Aron, 1974). Male participants were asked to meet an interviewer on one of two bridges over the Capilano River in British Columbia. One was a narrow suspension bridge with a low rail that swayed 230 feet above raging, rocky rapids (Figure 10.10); the other was a sturdy modern bridge just above the river. An attractive female research assistant approached the men and interviewed them in the middle of the bridge. She gave them her phone number and offered to explain the re-

10.10 Excitation Transfer Men who walked across a narrow and scary bridge (like the Capilano Bridge) displayed more attraction to a female experimenter than those who walked across a stable bridge.

sults of the study to them at a later date. According to the two-factor theory of emotion, the scary bridge would produce arousal that could possibly be misattributed to the interviewer. Indeed, this is what happened: Men who were interviewed on the scary bridge were more likely to call the interviewer and ask her for a date. It has to be noted that there could have been initial differences among the men who chose to cross the scary bridge and those who chose the safer bridge—perhaps men who were more likely to take risks were more likely to take a scary bridge and to call for a date. However, the general idea that people can misattribute arousal for affection has been found in other studies.

A similar form of misattribution is called **excitation transfer,** during which residual physiological arousal caused by one event is transferred to a new stimulus. In the period after exercise, for example, there is a slow return to baseline during which the person continues to have residual arousal symptoms, such as an elevated heart rate. Of course, after a few minutes people have caught their breath and do not realize their bodies are still aroused. If a second event occurs in this interim period, the residual excitation from the first event is transferred to the second event. This has an important practical application. It is perhaps best to take a date out to a movie that produces arousal, perhaps a strong tearjerker or action adventure. It is always possible that residual arousal will be misattributed to you.

excitation transfer A form of misattribution in which residual physiological arousal caused by one event is transferred to a new stimulus.

People Regulate Their Moods

Earlier we noted that emotions are adaptive, helping us respond to environmental challenges in ways that have proven successful over the course of human evolution. At the same time, emotions can be disruptive and troublesome, as when people feel so anxious that they can't study for exams, or when they are so mad at someone who raced ahead of them at an intersection that they want to run the other car off the road. In our daily lives we need to harness our emotional responses, which is not very easy. Although how we think affects how we feel, it is quite challenging to keep ourselves from being upset when we fail an exam or to mask our facial expression when we see something disgusting.

Why is it hard to control emotions?

Successfully regulating our emotional states depends on several strategies, some of which we can use to prevent or prepare for bad events and some of which we can use to deal with those events after they occur. James Gross (1999) outlined a number of strategies people use to regulate their emotions. For instance, we can try to put ourselves in certain situations and avoid others; if you want to feel romantic before proposing to your girlfriend, you are better off going to a quiet, intimate bistro than to a fast-food diner; if you don't want to feel jealous of your sister's athletic skill, you could choose not to attend her soccer, basketball, and softball games. People can also focus their attention on certain aspects of a situation that will help manage their emotional state. If you are scared of flying, you can distract yourself from your anxiety by helping the woman next to you entertain her restless toddler. People can also try to directly alter their emotional reactions to events by trying to change, or reappraise, the event in more neutral terms. If you get scared while watching a movie, you can remind yourself that it is all staged and that no one is actually being hurt. Recent studies have found that having people engage in reappraisal changes the activity of brain regions involved in the experience of emotion (Ochsner, Burge, Gross, & Gabrieli, 2002).

The way in which we think about an event, how we *cognitively frame it,* can contribute to the intensity of our emotional response as well as influence what label we place on it (Smith & Ellsworth, 1985). As an example, if the roof of your house is blown off during a storm and you attribute the situation to external forces, you will likely feel sad. However, if you see the outcome as having been under your personal control because you failed to replace what you knew to be a faulty roof, you will instead feel guilty and angry. How people appraise and frame events plays an important role in how they cope with the daily stress in their lives, which we consider later in this chapter.

"Next question: I believe that life is a constant striving for balance, requiring frequent tradeoffs between morality and necessity, within a cyclic pattern of joy and sadness, forging a trail of bittersweet memories until one slips, inevitably, into the jaws of death. Agree or disagree?"

HUMOR Humor is a simple and effective method of regulating negative emotions, one that has numerous mental and physical health benefits. Most obviously, humor increases positive affect. When we find something humorous, we smile, laugh, and enter a state of pleasurable, relaxed excitation. Research shows that laughter stimulates endocrine secretion; an improved immune system; and the release of hormones, catecholamines, and endorphins. When people laugh, they experience a rise in circulation, blood pressure, skin temperature, and heart rate, along with a reduction in perception of pain. All these responses are similar to those resulting from physical exercise, and they are considered beneficial to both short-term and long-term health.

People sometimes laugh in situations that do not seem very funny, such as at funerals or wakes. According to one theory, laughing in these situations helps people distance themselves from their negative emotions and strengthens their connections to other people. Dacher Keltner and George Bonanno (1997) interviewed 40 people who had recently lost a spouse. They found that genuine laughter during the interview was associated with positive mental health and fewer negative feelings, such as grief.

SUPPRESSION AND RUMINATION People make two common mistakes when trying to regulate mood. The first is *thought suppression,* in which they attempt not to respond or feel the emotion at all. Research by Daniel Wegner and his colleagues has

rumination Thinking about, elaborating, and focusing on undesired thoughts or feelings, which prolongs, rather than alleviates, a negative mood.

demonstrated that suppressing any thought is extremely difficult and often leads to a *rebound effect*, in which people think more about something after suppression than before. Thus, for example, those who try not to think of a white bear end up obsessed with thoughts of white bears (Wegner, Shortt, Blake, & Page, 1990). **Rumination,** the second mistake, involves thinking about, elaborating, and focusing on undesired thoughts or feelings, which prolongs the mood. Moreover, rumination impedes successful mood-regulation strategies, such as focused problem solving or distraction (Lyubomirsky & Nolen-Hoeksema, 1995).

Overall, distraction is the best way to avoid the problems of suppression or rumination, since it absorbs attention and temporarily helps people to stop thinking about their problems. But some distractions backfire, such as thinking about other problems or engaging in maladaptive behaviors. Watching a movie that captures your attention helps you to escape your problems, but watching a movie that reminds you of your troubled situation may lead you to wallow in mental anguish.

REVIEWING the Principles | How Do People Experience Emotions?

Emotions comprise a subjective experience, physiological changes, and cognitive interpretation. The three main theories of emotion differ in their relative emphasis on these components. The James-Lange theory states that specific patterns of physical changes give rise to the perception of associated emotions. The Cannon-Bard theory proposes two separate pathways, physical changes and emotion, occur at the same time. Schachter's two-factor theory emphasizes the combination of generalized physiological arousal and cognitive appraisals in determining specific emotions. People also use a number of strategies to alter their moods. The best methods for regulating negative affect include humor and distraction.

What Is the Neurophysiological Basis of Emotion?

There has been a recent increase in research that crosses levels of analysis to study emotion. Here we focus on the biological level. As was apparent in the three major theories discussed in the preceding section, the body plays an important role in emotional experience. People who have spinal-cord injuries report feeling less intense emotions than prior to injury, which occurs because the messages have difficulty reaching the brain. The closer the damage is to the brain, the greater the loss of sensation, and consequently, the greater the decrease in emotional intensity. As you will recall from Chapter 3, various hormones, neurotransmitters, and drugs affect mood states. For instance, drugs that increase the activity of serotonin receptors lead to a reduction in depressed mood; drugs that activate dopamine receptors lead to feelings of euphoria.

During the biological revolution at the end of the twentieth century, researchers found that specific emotional states are associated with unique patterns of brain activity, although many of the same brain structures are involved in multiple emotional experiences. For instance, imaging studies have shown that disgust, sadness, and happiness all activate the thalamus and prefrontal cortex. However, differential activation in surrounding structures can be distinguished among these three emotions. For example, happiness and sadness cause increased activity in the hypothalamus, whereas disgust does not (Lane, Reiman, Ahern, & Schwartz, 1997; Figure 10.11). Similarly, processing of faces showing fear and disgust may lead to differential patterns of brain activity. Fear activates the amygdala, whereas disgust activates another brain region that has previously been related to gustatory reactions to unpleasant tastes and smells (Phillips et al., 1997). We understand much about the neurophysiology of emotion, but we have a great deal still to learn. In this section we will examine several key issues regarding the link between physiology and emotion.

Emotions Are Associated with Autonomic Activity

Emotions tend to overlap in their pattern of autonomic nervous system activity, although there are some differences between emotional states. For instance, when a person is aroused, whether because of anger or sexual attraction, the face becomes flushed, but the pupils contract during anger and dilate during sexual arousal. As mentioned, actors who portrayed particular emotions showed differential heart-rate and blood-pressure patterns. These findings have been replicated with the Minangkabau people of West Sumatra (Levenson, Ekman, Heider, & Friesen, 1992), in spite of dramatic differences in culture, religion, lifestyles, and display rules. The Minangkabau people showed patterns of autonomic arousal similar to those of American actors: Heart rate increases with distress, fear, and anger, the last of which was also accompanied by higher skin temperature. However, the overlap in activity among emotions is so great that in most cases it is difficult to distinguish emotions based solely on autonomic responses (Cacioppo, Klein, Berntson, & Hatfield, 1993).

Robert Zajonc and colleagues described another link between physiological states and emotion. Zajonc hypothesized that facial expressions, through facial musculature, control the directional flow of air into the brain, warming or cooling the hypothalamus. This in turn affects the release of neurotransmitters that influence emotions. According to Zajonc, cooling the brain produces positive emotions, whereas warming the brain produces negative emotions. To test his theory, participants allowed air to be blown into their nasal passages. In support of his predictions, Zajonc found that people reported more negative emotions when the air was warm and more pleasant emotions when the air was cool (Zajonc, Murphy, & Inglehart, 1989).

10.11 Brain Activation and Emotions
Significant increases in regional brain activity occur during happiness, sadness, and disgust. Note that these emotions produce different patterns of brain activation.

Can Lies Be Detected from Physiological Responses?

We noted in Chapter 9 that people are motivated to detect liars and cheaters. But how do you catch a liar? For several decades, researchers have hoped that the methods of psychological science can be used to read bodily responses that indicate deception. Increasingly, applicants for certain types of jobs, such as those that involve classified documents, are asked to take a polygraph test, known informally as a lie-detector test. A *polygraph* is an electronic instrument that assesses the body's physiological response to questions. It records numerous aspects of arousal such as breathing rate, heart rate, and so on (Figure 10.12). The use of polygraphs is highly controversial. Most courts don't allow them as evidence, and few people understand what a lie detector can and cannot do. Let's examine some of the critical issues involved in using polygraphy to detect lies.

The goal of polygraphy is to determine a person's level of emotionality, as indicated by autonomic arousal, when confronted with certain information. For instance, criminals might be asked about specific illegal activities, whereas job applicants might be asked about drug use or previous job performance. Psychologists have long known that lying is stressful; therefore autonomic arousal should be higher when people are lying than when they are telling the truth. But can factors other than lying cause arousal? Of course, some people become nervous simply because the whole procedure is new and scary, or they are upset that someone thinks they are guilty when they are innocent. Even being attracted to the person giving the polygraph exam could produce arousal.

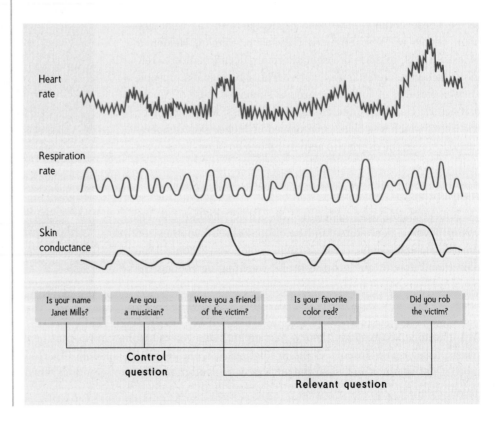

10.12 Lie Detection A polygraph measures autonomic systems such as respiration, skin conductance from sweating, and heart rate. Differences in autonomic reactions to critical questions, compared to control questions, indicate arousal, which in turn may indicate nervousness as a result of lying. However, the arousal might be due to general nervousness and may falsely indicate that the person is lying.

No absolute measure of autonomic arousal can indicate the presence or absence of a lie, because each person's level of autonomic arousal is different. So simply being highly aroused does not indicate guilt. Instead, to assess physiological arousal, polygraphers employ a control-question technique in which they ask a variety of questions, some of which are relevant to the critical information and some of which are not. Control questions, such as "What is your home address?" and "Have you ever been to Canada?" are selected with the assumption that they should not produce a strong emotional response. Critical questions, such as "Did you steal the money?" or "Do you use drugs?" are those of specific interest to the investigators. The difference between the physiological responses to the control and critical questions is the measure used to determine whether the person is lying. Sometimes the questions contain information that only a guilty party would know, such as how a person was killed or where the body was found. Thus, simply having guilty knowledge should produce arousal and therefore be detected by the polygraph.

How valid is the polygraph for detecting lies? How successful is it? Two researchers examined 50 criminal investigations in which a polygraph was administered to two suspects and later one of them confessed to the crime (Kleinmuntz & Szucko, 1984). When comparing the polygraph results with the suspects' true guilt or innocence, the researchers found that the polygraph correctly identified the guilty person 76 percent of the time but also wrongly accused someone of lying 37 percent of the time. Thus, polygraphy is far from infallible. Indeed, an expert panel convened by the National Academy of Sciences in 2002 found no scientific evidence to justify the regular use of polygraphs. The committee noted that although thousands of employees of the FBI, CIA, and other governmental agencies have been given polygraphs, not one person has been discovered to be a spy—including people such as Aldrich Ames and Robert Hansen, who passed polygraphs but subsequently were convicted of selling secrets to the Russians. Indeed, part of the reason that they were able to spy for so long was that they always passed the polygraph. It turns out that people can cheat the test in a number of ways. One method is to tense up on the control questions and try to relax on the critical questions, thus lessening the difference between one's physiological responses. Ways of increasing arousal include biting the tongue, pressing fingernails into the palms, or tightening the sphincter muscle for several seconds to increase blood pressure. Studies of college students who were taught these techniques found that they avoided detection by two expert polygraphers 50 percent of the time.

As you might expect, researchers are seeking new strategies to uncover deception. For instance, psychological scientists using event-related brain potentials have found that a brain-wave pattern typically associated with rare, meaningful stimuli, such as when a female name appears on a long list of male names, may indicate deception (Rosenfield, 2001). In a recent study using brain imaging, deceptive responses were associated with increased activation of specific frontal lobe regions (Langleben et al., 2002). However, the deception task in this study was relatively trivial, and the participants did not report feeling anxious about being deceptive. Whether the activation of the frontal lobe regions indicates genuine deception or simply reflects general inhibitory responses during the experimental task is unclear.

An important problem with polygraph tests is that most people who fail them are actually telling the truth. Polygraphy produces a high rate of false-positives (recall the discussion of signal detection in Chapter 5). Out of the many thousands of people who are required to take the test as part of their employment, many will be regarded as liars although they actually are not. As noted earlier, people who are especially anxious about the procedure or who are nervous in general may fail the test. Consider a person who doesn't use drugs but has a family member with a serious addiction. When asked about drug use, the person might start thinking of the relative and become upset, subsequently showing autonomic arousal. The basic problem is that the polygraph can't tell whether the response is due to lying, sexual fantasizing, or anything else arousing.

Given all this, why do you think that so many people remain convinced that the polygraph provides accurate information? Why do employers use it when it is unlikely to really tell them anything useful about their employees? What if a system could detect 99 percent of liars correctly, but falsely identified 5 percent of those telling the truth? Is that acceptable? Do you think the polygraph might be useful in scaring criminals into confessing to their crimes? Why or why not? ■

The Amygdala and the Prefrontal Cortex Are Involved in Emotion

In 1937, James Papez proposed that many different subcortical brain regions were involved in emotion. Fifteen years later, Paul MacLean expanded this list and called it the *limbic system.* (Recall from Chapter 4 that the word "limbic" refers to brain structures that border the cerebral cortex.) We now know that many brain structures outside the limbic system are involved in emotion and that many limbic structures are not central to emotion per se. For instance, the hippocampus is important mostly for memory and the hypothalamus mostly for motivation. Thus, the term *limbic system* is mainly used in a rough, descriptive way rather than in terms of directly linking brain areas to specific emotional functions (Figure 10.13). For understanding emotion, the two most important brain regions are the amygdala and the prefrontal cortex.

THE AMYGDALA The amygdala processes the emotional significance of stimuli and generates immediate emotional and behavioral reactions. According to Joseph LeDoux (Figure 10.14), affective processing in the amygdala is a circuit that has developed over the course of evolution to protect animals from danger. LeDoux (1996) has established the amygdala as the brain structure most important for emotional learning, such as the development of classically conditioned fear responses. Removal of the amygdala in animals produces a disorder known as *Kluver-Bucy syndrome,* after the scientists who first identified it in 1939. Animals with Kluver-Bucy syndrome engage in unusual behaviors, such as hypersexuality and putting objects into their mouths, and they are fearless.

Humans with damage to the amygdala do not develop the more severe symptoms associated with Kluver-Bucy syndrome, but they do experience a variety of deficits in processing and responding to emotional cues. More important, they show impairments in fear conditioning. They show fear when confronted with dangerous objects, but they do not develop conditioned fear of objects associated with dangerous objects (see Chapter 6). For instance, if you give people an electric shock each time they see a picture of a blue square, they will normally develop a conditioned response, evidenced by greater physiological arousal, when they see the blue square. But people with damage to the amygdala do not show classical conditioning of these fear associations. Consider patient S.P., who had damage to the amygdala (Anderson & Phelps, 2000). S.P. first showed signs of neurological impairment around age three and was later diagnosed with epilepsy. At age 48, she had her

10.13 The Limbic System The limbic system is important for assessing and responding to emotionally relevant stimuli. The two most important structures are the amygdala and prefrontal cortex.

Cingulate gyrus

Thalamus

Hippocampus

Prefrontal cortex

Hypothalamus

Amygdala

right amygdala removed to reduce the frequency of the seizures. The surgery was reasonably successful, and S.P. retained most of her intellectual faculties. She has a normal IQ, has taken college courses, and performs well on standardized tasks of visual attention. However, she does not show fear conditioning. Strangely, S.P. can tell you that the blue square is associated with shock, but her body shows no physiological evidence of having acquired the fear response.

Information reaches the amygdala along two separate pathways. The first path is a quick and dirty system that processes sensory information nearly instantaneously. Sensory information travels quickly through the thalamus to the amygdala for priority processing. The second pathway is somewhat slower, but it leads to evaluations that are more deliberate and thorough. Sensory material travels from the thalamus to the sensory cortex, where the information is scrutinized in greater depth before it is passed along to the amygdala. Contemporary thinking is that the fast system prepares the animal to respond should the slower pathway confirm the threat.

Recall from the earlier discussion that emotional events are especially likely to be stored in memory. Indeed, brain-imaging studies demonstrate that increased activity in the amygdala during an emotional event is associated with improved long-term memory for that event (Cahill et al., 2001; Hamann, Ely, Grafton, & Kilts, 1999). Researchers currently believe that the amygdala modifies how the hippocampus consolidates memory (Phelps, 2004). This idea is supported by research that shows a correlation between activity in the amygdala and the hippocampus for emotional stimuli but not for neutral stimuli (Dolcos, LaBar, & Cabeza, 2004).

Another role of the amygdala in emotion processing is its involvement in perceiving social stimuli, such as deciphering the affective meaning of facial expressions. For instance, fMRI studies demonstrate that the amygdala is especially sensitive to the intensity of fearful faces (Dolan, 2000; Figure 10.15). This effect occurs even if the participants are unaware that they have seen a face at all (Whalen et al., 1998).

10.14 Joseph LeDoux LeDoux has conducted important work showing that the amygdala is central to emotional learning.

10.15 Activation of the Amygdala As participants view these faces, the amygdala becomes more activated as the face displays more fear.

Perhaps surprisingly, the amygdala reacts more when people observe faces displaying fear than those displaying anger. On the surface, this doesn't make a great deal of sense, because a person looking at you with an angry expression may be more likely to be dangerous. According to some researchers, the greater activity of the amygdala when people look at a frightened face is due to the ambiguity of the situation (Whalen et al., 2001)—that is, not being sure about what the person fears. This is not to say that the amygdala reacts only to expressions of fear; rather, it responds to a variety of emotional expressions, even happiness, but generally the effect is greatest for fear. One recent study showed that the amygdala is activated even by neutral facial expressions, but only in people who are chronically anxious (Somerville, Kim, Johnstone, Alexander, & Whalen, 2004).

Given that the amygdala is involved in processing the emotional content of facial expressions, it is not surprising that damage to it leads to social impairments. Those with damage to the amygdala often have difficulty evaluating the intensity of fearful faces even though they do not show impairments in judging the intensity of other facial expressions, such as happiness. One interesting study suggests that those with damage to the amygdala fail to use information contained within facial expressions to make accurate interpersonal judgments (Adolphs, Tranel, & Damasio, 1998). For instance, those with damage to the amygdala have difficulty using photographs to assess people's trustworthiness, a task that most people can do without any trouble (Figure 10.16). People with amygdala damage can tell a smile from a frown, but they do not seem to use this information in making social judgments (Adolphs, Sears, & Piven, 2001). They also tend to be unusually friendly with people they don't know, which may mean they lack the normal mechanisms for caution around strangers and the feeling that some people should be avoided.

THE PREFRONTAL CORTEX Recall from the motivation chapter that the prefrontal cortex is involved in assessing the potential reward value of situations and objects. It is also involved in the processing of emotional cues, especially those related to interpersonal interactions. People with damage to this region often act inappropriately and are generally insensitive to the emotional expressions of others. Moreover, prefrontal damage is sometimes associated with excessive aggression and violence, suggesting difficulties with emotional control.

Antonio Damasio has found that patients, such as Elliot, with damage to the middle of the prefrontal region often fail to use somatic markers. When these regions are damaged, people still can recall information, but it has lost most of its affective meaning. They might be able to describe their current problems or talk about the death of

10.16 Amygdala Damage and Judgment
People with damage to the amygdala can tell a smiling face from a frowning face, but they have difficulty judging whether the person is trustworthy. Which of these people would you trust?

a loved one, but they do so without experiencing any of the emotional pain that normally accompanies such thoughts.

Emotion Systems Are Lateralized in the Brain

The psychological scientist Richard Davidson (Figure 10.17) has shown that unequal activation of the left and right hemispheres is associated with specific emotional states, a pattern known as **cerebral asymmetry.** In a series of studies, Davidson and his colleagues found that greater activation of the right prefrontal cortex is associated with negative affect, whereas greater activation of the left hemisphere is associated with positive affect. A study of responses to film clips found that people who were left-hemisphere dominant showed the most positive response to pleasant scenes, whereas those who were right-hemisphere dominant showed the most negative response to unpleasant scenes. Another study found that those who reported the strongest negative emotion showed the greatest activation of the right amygdala in response to unpleasant pictures (Davidson, 2000a; Figure 10.18).

Cerebral asymmetry is associated with general motivation (Davidson, 2000b). For instance, greater activation of the left hemisphere is associated with increased confidence and effort to achieve goals. A greater activation of the right hemisphere is associated with lack of motivation, a symptom of clinical depression. Imaging studies have shown diminished left-hemisphere activation among depressed patients, and depression is more common among those who have brain injuries to the left hemisphere. Remarkably, as early as three months of age, children of depressed mothers also show asymmetrical brain activation (Field, Fox, Pickens, & Nawrocki, 1995). Although the functional significance of cerebral asymmetry is not known, recent work by Davidson and his colleagues suggests it may have to do with the regulation of emotional states. For instance, anti-anxiety drugs decrease fearful behavior and increase left frontal activation in infant monkeys, suggesting that negative affective states such as anxiety may suppress the left frontal lobe and thus reduce motivation.

Research has demonstrated that the right hemisphere is more involved than the left in the interpretation and comprehension of emotional material. Neuroimaging studies have found that although emotional stimulation activates both hemispheres, activation is much greater on the right side. The right hemisphere is also more

10.17 Richard Davidson Davidson has proposed that affective style is influenced by cerebral asymmetry, with the right hemisphere associated with negative moods and the left hemisphere associated with positive moods.

cerebral asymmetry An emotional pattern associated with unequal activation of the left and right frontal lobes.

$$y = 2.33 + 0.64x$$
$$p = 0.63$$
$$p = 0.01$$

Rank of right amygdalar activation

Rank of negative affect (NA) score
Dispositional negative affect (PANAS)

(a)   (b)

10.18 Cerebral Asymmetry (a) The amygdala region is magnified in the bottom image and shows the greater activation of the right amygdala (on the left side of the image) during viewing of unpleasant pictures. (b) This activation corresponds with greater negative affect.

10.19 Divided Faces Divided faces have enabled psychologists to determine that the right hemisphere interprets the meaning of facial expressions.

accurate at detecting the emotional tone of speech (such as whether the voice sounds sad or happy), whereas the left hemisphere is more accurate at decoding semantic content. As an example, consider that when we look at facial expressions, the left half of the face is projected to the right hemisphere and the right half of the face is projected to the left hemisphere. Researchers who create divided faces, such as those shown in Figure 10.19, have found that the emotion "seen" by the right hemisphere heavily influences the interpretation of an emotional expression. Which face looks sadder to you? Which face looks happier? As researchers continue to conduct research at the biological level of analysis, it is likely that we will learn a great deal more about how the brain produces emotion.

REVIEWING
the Principles | What Is the Neurophysiological Basis of Emotion?

Emotions lead to specific autonomic reactions, but there is considerable overlap among emotions. A number of brain structures, especially the amygdala and the prefrontal cortex, are involved in emotion and social judgment. Research indicates that left-hemisphere activity is related to positive emotions and right-hemisphere activity to negative emotions.

How Do People Cope with Stress?

Stress is a common component of everyday emotional life, and it consists of a number of emotional responses. Although the term *stress* has negative connotations, a moderate level of stress is beneficial. Different levels of stress are optimal for different people, and learning how much stress you can handle is essential for recognizing its effects on your mental, physical, and emotional well-being.

Stress involves both physical and psychological factors. It has direct effects on the body, but how stressed people feel depends on factors such as how people perceive the stressful event, their emotional state, their tolerance for stress, and their personal beliefs about the resources they have to cope with the stressor. A **stressor** is an environmental event or stimulus that threatens an organism and that elicits a **coping response,** which is any response an organism makes to avoid, escape from, or minimize an aversive stimulus.

There Are Sex Differences in Response to Stressors

From an evolutionary perspective, our ability to deal effectively with stressors is important to survival. The physiological and behavioral responses that accompany stress help mobilize resources to deal with the danger, thereby facilitating survival and reproduction. The Harvard physiologist Walter Cannon coined the term **fight-or-flight response** to describe the physiological preparation of animals to deal with

stressor An environmental event or stimulus that threatens an organism.

coping response Any response an organism makes to avoid, escape from, or minimize an aversive stimulus.

fight-or-flight response The physiological preparedness of animals to deal with danger.

tend-and-befriend response The argument that females are more likely to protect and care for their offspring and form social alliances than flee or fight in response to threat.

any attack. This physical reaction includes increased heart rate, contraction of the spleen, redistribution of the blood supply from skin and viscera to muscles and brain, deepening of respiration, dilation of the pupils, inhibition of gastric secretions, and an increase in glucose released from the liver. This response to a stressor occurs within seconds or minutes and allows an organism to direct all energy to dealing with the threat at hand while postponing less critical autonomic activities.

The generality of the fight-or-flight response has been questioned by Shelley Taylor (Figure 10.20) and her colleagues, who point out that the vast majority of both human and nonhuman animal research has been conducted using males, which has distorted the scientific understanding of responses to stress. Most rat studies use male rats to avoid female hormonal cycles such as estrus. Although the reasons are unclear, a similar sex inequality exists for past human studies, with women representing fewer than 1 in 5 participants in laboratory stress studies.

Taylor and her colleagues argue that females respond to stress by protecting and caring for their offspring, as well as by forming alliances with social groups to reduce individual risk. They coined the phrase **tend-and-befriend response** to describe this pattern. Tend-and-befriend responses make great sense from an evolutionary point of view. Females typically bore a greater responsibility for the care of offspring, and responses that protected offspring as well as the self were maximally adaptive. When a threat appears, quieting the offspring and hiding may be more effective means of avoiding harm than trying to flee while pregnant or with a clinging infant. Furthermore, those females who selectively affiliate with others, especially other females, might acquire additional protection and support. Thus, Taylor's group proposes that women respond adaptively to stress by becoming more nurturing and by seeking out friendships.

A wide variety of evidence supports the tend-and-befriend hypothesis. At the biological level, females have low levels of testosterone, the male hormone that is implicated in physically aggressive behaviors, such as those used to fight predators or rivals. Rather, in response to stress, females tend to show greater release of the hormone oxytocin. Oxytocin plays an important role in maternal behavior, as well as in relaxation and feelings of love (Panksepp, 1992). Thus, a large release of oxytocin during stress may calm females as well as promote nurturing behavior toward offspring. At the behavioral level, mothers who are stressed by their jobs tend to pay more attention to their children, whereas stressed fathers tend to withdraw from their families. Indeed, children report receiving the most love and nurturance from their mothers on the days that their mothers report the highest levels of stress (Repetti, 1997, cited in Taylor et al., 2000). The tend-and-befriend stress response is an excellent example of how thinking about psychological mechanisms in terms of their evolutionary significance leads us to question long-standing assumptions about how the mind works. Females who responded to stress by nurturing and protecting their young and by forming alliances with other females apparently had a selective advantage over those who tried to fight or flee.

The General Adaptation Syndrome Is a Bodily Response to Stress

In the early 1930s, Hans Selye (Figure 10.21) began studying the physiological effects of sex hormones by injecting rats with samples from other animals. When he examined the rats, he found enlarged adrenal glands, decreased levels of lymphocytes in the blood, and stomach ulcers. Selye surmised that the foreign hormones must have been the cause of these changes, so he conducted further tests, using different types

10.20 Shelley Taylor Taylor has conducted important research in health psychology. She and her colleagues have revolutionized thinking about how animals respond to threat.

How do women and men differ in response to stress?

10.21 Hans Selye Selye popularized the term *stress* and demonstrated that stress could affect physical health. Although Hungarian, he spent most of his career in Montreal, Canada.

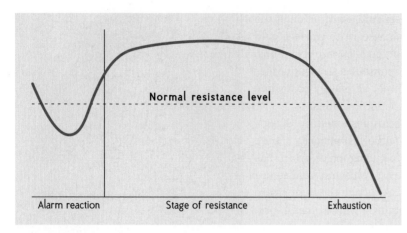

10.22 The General Adaptation Syndrome
Selye's general adaptation syndrome describes the three stages of physiological response to stress. Initially, resistance is reduced as the body prepares to fight or flee. However, the body eventually adapts and resistance increases. Eventually, the system becomes exhausted and resistance plummets.

general adaptation syndrome A consistent pattern of responses to stress that consists of three stages: alarm, resistance, and exhaustion.

of chemicals and even physically restraining the animals. He found slight variations in some physiological effects, but each manipulation produced this pattern of bloated adrenal glands, damaged lymphatic structures, and stomach ulcers. He concluded that these three responses were the hallmarks of *nonspecific stress response.* But these changes reduce the organism's potential ability to resist additional stressors. Selye borrowed the term *stress* from engineering, in which it is used to describe a force applied against resistance.

The **general adaptation syndrome,** a consistent pattern of responses that Selye identified, consists of three stages: the *alarm stage,* the *resistance stage,* and the *exhaustion stage* (Figure 10.22). It occurs in addition to specific physiological responses to particular stressors. The first stage is the *alarm stage,* an emergency reaction that prepares the body to fight or flee. In this stage, physiological responses are aimed at boosting physical abilities while reducing activities that make the organism vulnerable to infection after injury. This is the stage in which the body might be exposed to infection and disease, so the immune system kicks in and the body begins to fight back. During the *resistance stage,* the defenses are prepared for a longer, sustained attack against the stressor; immunity to disease continues to increase somewhat as the body maximizes its defenses. However, the body eventually reaches the *exhaustion stage,* during which a variety of physiological and immune systems fail. Bodily organs that were already weak before the stress are the first to fail. The general principles of this theory have been confirmed by scientific research.

Scientists now generally agree that the presence of a stressor leads to activation of the hypothalamic-pituitary-adrenal (HPA) system. During a stress response, the hypothalamus (H) secretes a hormone that triggers the pituitary (P) to release another hormone into the bloodstream, which in turn causes cortisol, still another hormone, to be released from the adrenal glands. Cortisol produces many of the bodily reactions to stress, such as breaking down protein and converting it to glucose, which helps meet immediate energy needs. Cortisol also helps the body deal with inflammation, which would occur if there were physical injuries. When cortisol levels are sufficiently high, a feedback loop is triggered that shuts down the HPA system. Because it takes 15 minutes to an hour to produce a feedback loop, cortisol continues to affect the body even after the stressor has ended. In addition to cortisol, the adrenal glands release norepinephrine and epinephrine, which activate the sympathetic nervous system, increasing blood pressure, heart rate, and other sympathetic responses (see Chapter 3). Thus, stress has a powerful effect on bodily systems and behavior.

People Encounter Stress in Daily Life

Stress occurs when aspects of the environment overwhelm people. That is, people feel stressed when too much is expected of them, or when events seem scary or worrisome. Stress occurs when we perceive a discrepancy—whether real or not—between the demands of the situation and the resources of our biological, psychological, and social systems. Psychologists typically think of stressors as falling into two categories: major life stressors and daily hassles. *Major life stressors* are changes or disruptions that strain central areas of people's lives. Positive events can be as stressful as, or even more stressful than, negative events. For instance, some parents report that having their first child is one of the most joyful—but also one of the most taxing—experiences of their lives. Major life stressors can be choices made by individuals, not just things that happen to them. Nonetheless, research has shown that unpredictable and uncontrollable catastrophic events (such as an earthquakes) are especially stressful. In general, life changes are stressful, whether it is moving to a new college or job, getting married, being fired, losing a parent, or winning a major award. The greater the number of changes, the greater the stress, and the more likely stress is to have an impact on physiological state.

Daily hassles are small, day-to-day irritations and annoyances, such as driving in traffic, dealing with unfair bosses or teachers, or having to wait in line. Daily hassles are stressful, and their effects can be comparable to those of major life changes. These low-level irritations are ubiquitous and, most important, pose a threat to coping responses by slowly wearing down personal resources. Studies that ask people to keep diaries of their daily activities consistently find that the more intense and frequent the hassles, the poorer the physical and mental health of the participant. People appear to habituate to daily problems, but some types, such as interpersonal difficulties, seem to have a cumulative effect on health. Living in poverty or working in a crowded city or in an area with noise or environmental pollution can also have detrimental effects on emotional well-being.

Stress Affects Health

One of Selye's central points was that the prolonged action of stress hormones, such as cortisol, has a negative impact on health. Indeed, although stress hormones are essential to normal health, over the long term they are associated with such problems as increased blood pressure, cardiac disease, diabetes, declining sexual interest, and dwarfism. People who have stressful jobs—air-traffic controllers, combat soldiers, firefighters—have numerous health problems, presumably in part due to the effects of chronic stress. Robert Sapolsky (1994) chronicles the multiple health problems attributable to chronic stress, especially psychosocial stress. He notes that chronic stress can even lead to memory impairments because cortisol damages neurons in the hippocampus. Recall from Chapter 7 that the hippocampus is involved in the consolidation of memory.

Overwhelming evidence suggests that stress is associated with the initiation and progression of a wide variety of diseases, from cancer to AIDS to cardiac disease. Not only does stress lead to specific physiological responses that affect health, but many people cope with stress by engaging in damaging behaviors. For instance, the number-one reason that problem drinkers give for abusing alcohol is to cope with negative stress in their lives. When people are stressed, they smoke cigarettes, eat junk food, use drugs, and so on. Most of the major health problems in Western society are attributable to unhealthful behaviors, many of which occur when people are stressed. We discuss some of these later in the chapter.

HEART DISEASE Coronary heart disease is the leading cause of death for adults in contemporary society. According to a World Health Organization report in 2002, more than 30 million people around the globe have heart attacks each year, of which more than 12 million are fatal. Heart disease is determined by many factors, including genetics, but two extremely important determinants are health behaviors and stress. Later in this chapter we describe three of the major risk factors for heart disease: a lack of exercise, obesity, and smoking. Here we are concerned with how stress affects the heart.

The heart pumps nearly 2,000 gallons of blood each day, on average beating more than 100,000 times. A vast network of blood vessels carries oxygen and nutrients throughout the body. As people age, the arteries leading from the heart become

Why is chronic stress harmful?

narrow because of the buildup of fatty deposits, known as plaque; this narrowing makes it more difficult for the heart to pump blood. The buildup of plaque leads to coronary heart disease. When pieces of plaque break off from the wall of the blood vessel, blood clots form around the plaque and interrupt blood flow. If a clot blocks a blood vessel feeding the heart, it causes a heart attack; if the vessel feeds the brain, the blockage causes a stroke.

Stress and negative emotions increase the risk of coronary heart disease (Sirois & Burg, 2003). Being stressed or depressed can cause heart problems in two ways. First, people often cope through behavioral strategies that are bad for health, such as overeating or smoking. But stress also produces direct physiological effects on the heart. Chronic stress leads to overstimulation of the sympathetic nervous system, causing higher blood pressure, the constriction of blood vessels, elevated levels of cortisol, increased release of fatty acids into the bloodstream, and greater buildup of plaque on arteries; all of these contribute to heart disease. Over time, then, being stressed causes wear and tear on the heart, making it more likely to fail.

Have you ever noticed that some people always seem to be stressed out, whereas others are more laid back? Given what we know about stress and the heart, those stressed-out people should be more likely to have heart disease. This assumption was first tested in 1960, when the Western Collaborative Group began what was to be an eight-and-a-half-year study of the effects of personality on coronary heart disease. Physicians recruited 3,500 men from northern California who were free of heart-disease symptoms and screened them annually for blood pressure, heart rate, cholesterol, and overall health practices. Personal details such as level of education, medical and family history, income, and personality traits were also assessed. The study results indicated that, adjusting for the presence of established risk factors (such as high blood pressure or high cholesterol), a pattern of personality traits predicted heart disease. This pattern, called the **Type A behavior pattern,** describes competitive, achievement-oriented, aggressive, hostile, time-pressed (constantly feeling hurried, restless, unable to relax), impatient, confrontational people. Men who exhibited these traits were much more likely to develop coronary heart disease than were those who exhibited the **Type B behavior pattern,** which describes a relaxed, noncompetitive, easygoing, accommodating person. In fact, this study found that Type A personality was as strong a predictor of heart disease as was smoking or high cholesterol or blood pressure (Rosenman et al., 1975).

Since the initial reports, numerous investigators have sought to understand the relation between personality and heart disease. Research over the past three decades has found that only certain components of the Type A behavior pattern are related to heart disease. Researchers at Duke University found that perhaps the most toxic factor was hostility (Williams, 1987). Hot-tempered people, who are frequently angry, cynical, and combative, are much more likely to die at an early age from heart disease (Eaker, Sullivan, Kelly-Hayes, D'Agostino, & Benjamin, 2004). Indeed, having a high level of hostility while in college predicts greater risk for heart disease later in life (Siegler et al., 2003). Evidence is also considerable that other negative emotional states, especially depression, also predict heart disease (Miller, Freedland, Carney, Stetler, & Banks, 2003). Of course, it could be that having a heart condition makes people feel depressed, but feelings of depression also predict worsening of heart disease, which creates a vicious cycle. In contrast, people who are optimistic about life tend to be at lower risk for

What aspects of personality are related to heart disease?

Type A behavior pattern A pattern of behavior characterized by competitiveness, achievement orientation, aggressiveness, hostility, restlessness, inability to relax, and impatience with others.

Type B behavior pattern A pattern of behavior characterized by relaxed, noncompetitive, easygoing, and accommodating behavior.

TYPE Z BEHAVIOR

heart disease (Maruta, Colligan, Malinchoc, & Offord, 2002). The take-home message from this research is that people who are frequently angry, depressed, or pessimistic are much more likely to die from coronary problems. Learning to manage stress and anger has been shown to improve outcomes for those who have heart disease (Sirois & Burg, 2003).

THE IMMUNE SYSTEM Stress alters the functions of the **immune system,** which is the physical mechanism that helps the body deal with infection. When foreign substances—such as viruses, bacteria, or allergens—enter the body the immune system launches into action to destroy the invaders. Stress interferes with this natural process. As Esther Sternberg (2000) has noted, "Stress can make you sick because the hormones and nerve pathways activated by stress change the way the immune system responds, making it less able to fight invaders" (p. 131). The field of *psychoneuroimmunology* studies the response of the body's immune system to psychological variables. Over the last 30 years, more than 300 studies have demonstrated that short-term stress boosts the immune system, whereas chronic stress weakens it, leaving the body less able to deal with infection (Segerstrom & Miller, 2004).

The immune system is made up of three types of specialized white blood cells known as **lymphocytes:** B cells, T cells, and natural killer cells. *B cells* produce *antibodies,* protein molecules that attach themselves to foreign agents and mark them for destruction. Some types of B cells are able to remember specific invaders, making for easier identification in the future; this is why you have lifelong immunity to some diseases once you've been exposed to them naturally or through inoculation. The *T cells* are involved in attacking the intruders directly and also with increasing the strength of the immune response. These so-called helper cells are incapacitated by infection with HIV, which eventually leads to the immune disorder AIDS. *Natural killer cells* are especially potent in killing viruses and also help attack tumors. The detrimental effects of both immediate and long-term stress on physical health are due, in part, to decreased lymphocyte production, which renders the body less capable of warding off foreign substances.

In a particularly clear demonstration that stress affects health, Sheldon Cohen and his colleagues (1991) paid healthy volunteers to be exposed to the common cold virus. Those who had reported the highest levels of stress in a questionnaire developed worse cold symptoms and higher viral counts than those who reported being less stressed (Figure 10.23). In another study, participants kept a daily diary for up to 12 weeks in which they recorded their moods and events in their lives. The participants also rated these events as desirable or undesirable. Each day, the participants took an antigen to challenge their immune systems and provided a saliva sample so that researchers could examine their antibody responses. The study revealed that the more desirable events a participant reported, the greater the antibody producton. Similarly, the more undesirable events reported, the weaker the antibody production. The effect of a desirable event on antibodies lasted for two days (Stone, Neale, Cox, & Napoli, 1994). These and subsequent findings provide substantial evidence that perceived stress influences the immune system. Chronic stress, especially when associated with changes in social roles or identity (such as becoming a refugee, losing a job, or getting divorced), has the greatest impact on the immune system (Segerstrom & Miller, 2004).

immune system The body's mechanism for dealing with invading microorganisms, such as allergens, bacteria, and viruses.

lymphocytes Specialized white blood cells known as B cells, T cells, and natural killer cells that make up the immune system.

10.23 Stress and the Immune System People who reported the greatest levels of stress were the most likely to catch colds.

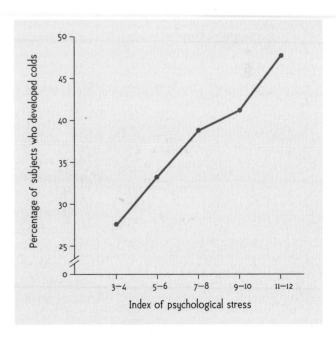

Coping Is a Process

Cognitive appraisals affect people's perception of and reactions to potential stressors. Coping that occurs before the onset of a future stressor is called *anticipatory coping,* as when parents rehearse what they will say when telling their children about plans to divorce. The psychologist Richard Lazarus (1993) conceptualized a two-part appraisal process. People use **primary appraisals** to decide whether the stimulus is stressful, benign, or irrelevant. If the stimulus is deemed stressful, people use **secondary appraisals** to evaluate response options and choose coping behaviors.

TYPES OF COPING A taxonomy of coping strategies developed by Folkman and Lazarus suggests that people use two general categories of coping style. **Emotion-focused coping** involves trying to prevent having an emotional response to the stressor. It includes strategies such as avoidance, minimizing the problem, trying to distance oneself from the outcomes of the problem, or doing things such as eating or drinking. People adopt these often passive strategies to numb the pain. They do nothing to solve the problem or prevent it from reoccurring in the future. By contrast, **problem-focused coping** involves taking direct steps to solve the problem. People generate alternative solutions, weigh them in terms of costs and benefits, and choose between them. People adopt problem-focused behaviors when they perceive the stressor as controllable and experience only a moderate level of stress. Conversely, emotion-focused behaviors enable people to continue functioning in the face of an uncontrollable stressor or a high level of stress.

Most people report using both problem- and emotion-focused coping. Usually, emotion-based strategies are effective only in the short run. For example, if someone in a bad mood is giving you a hard time, just ignoring him or her can be the best option. Yet ignoring your partner's drinking problem won't make it go away, and eventually you'll need a better coping strategy. However, for problem-focused coping strategies to work, people need to be able to do something about the situation. A fascinating study tested the best way to cope with an extremely threatening situation (Strentz & Auerbach, 1988). In this study, 57 airline workers were taken hostage by five "terrorists," who were actually FBI agents. Even though the participants volunteered to be hostages with full knowledge, the situation was very realistic and they were extremely stressed over the four days of the study. Half of the people were trained to use emotion-based coping whereas the other half were trained to use problem-based coping. Which strategy worked better? The emotion-based group experienced less stress because there was nothing the hostages could do that would not put them in greater danger. However, this study was done in 1988. Following the World Trade Center and Pentagon tragedies on September 11, 2001, it is no longer clear that a passive response would help people cope. The previous assumption that it is safer to cooperate with hijackers may no longer be true. Thus, the best way to cope with stress depends on personal resources and on the situation. Although problem-focused coping is usually more effective over the long run, emotion-focused coping might be a useful strategy in some circumstances over the short term, especially when people have little control over the situation.

Susan Folkman and Judith Moskowitz (2000) have demonstrated that in addition to problem-focused coping, two strategies can help people use positive thoughts to deal with stress. **Positive reappraisal** is a cognitive process in which people focus on possible good things in their current situation, the proverbial silver lining, as when people compare themselves to those who are worse off. These *downward comparisons* have been shown to help people coping with serious illnesses. *Creation of*

---

primary appraisal Part of the coping process that involves making decisions about whether a stimulus is stressful, benign, or irrelevant.

secondary appraisal Part of the coping process during which people evaluate their options and choose coping behaviors.

emotion-focused coping A type of coping in which people try to prevent having an emotional response to a stressor.

problem-focused coping A type of coping in which people take direct steps to confront or minimize a stressor.

positive reappraisal A cognitive process in which people focus on possible good things in their current situation.

CHAPTER 10 | Emotions and Health

positive events refers to a strategy of infusing ordinary events with positive meaning. Doing such things as taking note of a beautiful sunset, trying to find humor in a situation, or simply taking satisfaction in a recent compliment allows people to focus on the positive aspects of their lives, which helps them deal with their negative stress. For instance, caregivers of those with AIDS are under enormous stress. Folkman and Moskowitz have found that positive appraisal, creation of positive events, and problem-focused coping—which gave the caregivers some sense of control—were instrumental in successful coping.

INDIVIDUAL DIFFERENCES IN COPING People differ widely in the degree to which they perceive life events as being stressful. Some people could be termed "stress-resistant individuals" for their ability to adapt to life changes by viewing the events constructively. An idea that captures this personality characteristic is **hardiness,** developed by Suzanne Kobasa (1979), which has three components: *commitment, challenge,* and *control.* People who are high in hardiness are committed to their daily activities, view threats as challenges or opportunities for growth, and see themselves as being in control of their lives. People who are low in hardiness are typically alienated, view events as under external control, and fear or resist change. Numerous studies have found that people high in hardiness report fewer negative responses to stressful events. In a laboratory experiment in which participants were given difficult cognitive tasks, people high in hardiness exhibited higher blood pressure during the task, a physiological indicator of active coping. Moreover, a questionnaire completed immediately after the task revealed that participants high in hardiness boosted the number of positive thoughts about themselves in response to the stressor.

SOCIAL SUPPORT One of the most important factors for whether people effectively cope with stress is the level of social support they receive. **Social support** refers to having other people who can provide help, encouragement, and advice. Having social support is an essential component of positive mental and physical health. Ill people who are socially isolated are much more likely to die than those who are well connected to others (House, Landis, & Umberson, 1988), in part because isolation itself is associated with numerous health problems. Conversely, a recent review of more than 80 studies found strong evidence linking social support to fewer health problems (Uchino, Cacioppo, & Kiecolt-Glaser, 1996). For example, Janice Kiecolt-Glaser and Ronald Glaser (1988) found that people with troubled marriages and people going through divorce or bereavement all had compromised immune systems. In a study that categorized newlyweds on the basis of observed interactions, couples who fought more and showed more hostility toward one another exhibited decreased natural-killer-cell activity in the 24 hours after the interaction (Kiecolt-Glaser, Malarkey, Chee, & Newton, 1993).

Social support is important for people of all ages. Studies of children who seem *resilient,* meaning they have good outcomes in spite of being raised in deprived or chaotic situations, show the presence of parental or family support to be especially important (Masten, 2001). Because the elderly are particularly prone to social isolation, the effects of social support on health are particularly strong for this group. In keeping with the tend-and-befriend pattern mentioned earlier, women are much more affiliative under stress than men. They are more likely to seek out social support, to receive social support, and to be satisfied with the social support they receive. Interestingly, when stressed, women are especially likely to seek out other women. Thus, women are more connected to their social networks than are men.

hardiness A personality trait that enables people to perceive stressors as controllable challenges.

social support A network of other people who can provide help, encouragement, and advice.

Social support helps people cope with stress in two basic ways. First, people with social support experience less stress overall. Consider single parents who have to deal with job and family demands in isolation. The lack of a partner places more demands on them, which increases the likelihood that they will feel stressed. Second, social support aids coping because other people lessen the negative effects of the stress that occurs. The **buffering hypothesis** (Cohen & Wills, 1985) proposes that others can provide direct support in helping people cope with stressful events. Receiving emotional support is more important than just having others who provide information. Emotional support includes expressions of caring and willingness to listen to another person's problems. Social support can also take more tangible forms, such as providing material help or assisting with daily chores. But to be effective, social support needs to imply that people *care* about the recipient of the support.

REVIEWING

the Principles | How Do People Cope with Stress?

Stress occurs when people feel overwhelmed by the challenges they face, as when major change happens in their lives. Hans Selye proposed the general adaptation theory to conceptualize the stages of physiological coping. The stress of daily life includes both major life changes and daily hassles. However, cognitive appraisals, such as determining the relevance of the stressor or adopting a problem- versus emotion-focused approach, can alleviate stress or minimize its harmful effects. Perhaps the most important way people cope with stress is through their interactions with others who provide social support.

What Are Some of the Behaviors That Affect Physical Health?

We just looked at how stress affects our bodies, especially our hearts and immune system. We also learned some of the ways people cope with stress. We now look at the effect stress has on our everyday behavior. Before the twentieth century, most people died from infections and diseases that were transmitted from person to person. But the last century saw a dramatic shift in the leading causes of mortality. People now die from heart disease, cancer, accidents, diabetes, liver disease, and so on, all of which are at least partial outcomes of lifestyle. Our daily habits, such as smoking, poor eating, alcohol use, and lack of exercise, contribute to nearly every major cause of death in developed nations (Smith, Orleans, & Jenkins, 2004). Stress plays an important role in motivating each of these health-threatening behaviors. A study of more than 12,000 people from Minnesota found that high stress was associated with greater intake of fat, less frequent exercise, and greater smoking (Ng & Jeffrey, 2003). The field of *health psychology* was launched more than 25 years ago as psychologists, physicians, and other health professionals came to appreciate the extent to which lifestyle factors played important roles in physical health.

Psychological scientists who seek to understand health behaviors typically view them from a *biopsychosocial* perspective (Suls & Rothman, 2004) that emphasizes biological processes (e.g., the activation of reward circuits by neurotransmitters and the physiology of weight regulation); individual factors (e.g., level of stress, coping skills, personality traits); and social influences (e.g., friends, family, societal values, and environmental factors). Embodying one of our major themes for this book, research that crosses these levels of analyses helps scientists to identify strategies that prevent disease by helping people lead healthier lives. In this section we consider daily behaviors that have important health consequences.

Obesity Results from a Genetic Predisposition and Overeating

Obesity is a major health problem with both physical and psychological consequences. One factor that contributes to obesity is overeating, which some people are especially likely to do when stressed (Heatherton & Baumeister, 1991). Although there is no precise definition of obesity, people are considered obese if they are approximately 20 percent over ideal body weight, as indicated by various mortality studies. One of the most widely used measures of obesity in research is **body mass index (BMI)**, which computes a ratio of body weight to height. Figure 10.24 shows how to calculate BMI and how to interpret the value obtained. According to standard BMI cutoffs, more than one-third of Americans currently are medically obese. Researchers have spent the last 60 years trying to understand the causes of obesity. Although we have learned a great deal, obesity is clearly a multifaceted problem that is influenced both by genes and by the environment.

GENETIC INFLUENCE A trip to the local mall will immediately reveal one obvious fact about body weight: Obesity tends to run in families. Indeed, various family and adoption studies indicate that approximately half of the variability in body weight can be considered the result of genetics. One of the best and largest studies, carried out during the 1980s in Denmark, found that the BMI of adopted children was strongly related to the BMI of the biological parents and *not at all* to the BMI of the adoptive parents (Sorensen, Holst, Stunkard, & Skovgaard, 1992). Studies of identical and fraternal twins provide even stronger evidence of genetic control of body weight, with the heritability estimates (see Chapter 3) ranging from 60 to 80 percent. Moreover, the agreement for body weights of identical twins does not differ between twins raised together and twins raised apart, which suggests that environment has far less effect on body weight than genetics has.

If genes primarily determine body weight, why has the percentage of Americans who are obese doubled over the past few decades? Albert Stunkard, a leading researcher of human obesity, points out that genetics determine whether a person *can* become obese, but the environment determines whether that person will actually *become* obese (Stunkard, 1996). Consider an important study, conducted by the geneticist Claude Bouchard, in which identical twins were overfed by approximately 1,000 calories each day for 100 days. Most of the twins gained some weight, but there was great variability between pairs in how much was gained (ranging from 4.3 to 13.3 kg) (Bouchard et al., 1990). However, there was a striking degree of similarity within the twin pairs in terms of how much weight they gained and in which parts of the body they stored the fat. Some of the twin pairs were especially likely to put on weight. Thus, genetics determine sensitivity to environmental influences. Genes

body mass index (BMI) A ratio of body weight to height used to measure obesity.

10.24 A Nomogram for Determining Body Mass Index You can find your own BMI by drawing a straight line between your height and weight. A BMI under 20 suggests that you are underweight, between 20 and 25 is average, between 25 and 30 is overweight, and 30 and higher is considered obese. According to the latest guidelines from the Centers for Disease Control and Prevention, a healthy BMI for an adult is between 18.5 and 25. Beyond or below this optimal range, the more you are at risk for health problems.

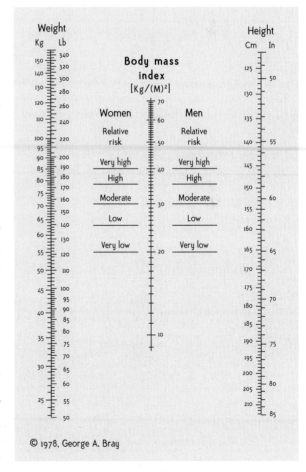

© 1978, George A. Bray

predispose some people to obesity in environments that promote overfeeding, such as contemporary Western societies. Many genes are involved in obesity, as you might expect in such a complex condition. Indeed, more than 300 different genetic markers or genes have been identified as playing some role in human obesity (Snyder et al., 2004).

THE STIGMA OF OBESITY Obesity is associated with a significant number of medical problems, including heart disease, high blood pressure, and gastric ailments. It can also give rise to a variety of psychological problems, primarily because of the extreme stigma associated with being overweight. In most Western cultures, obese individuals are viewed as less attractive, less socially adept, less intelligent, and less productive than their normal-weight peers (Dejong & Kleck, 1986). Moreover, perceiving oneself as overweight is linked to lower self-esteem, depression, and anxiety.

Not all cultures stigmatize obesity (Hebl & Heatherton, 1998). In some developing countries, such as many African nations, being obese is a sign of being upper class. Obesity may be desirable in developing countries because it helps prevent some infectious diseases, reduces the likelihood of starvation, and is associated with having more successful births. Obesity in developing countries may also serve as a status symbol, an indication that one can afford to eat luxuriously. In Pacific island countries such as Tonga and Fiji, being obese is a source of personal pride, and dieting is therefore not common. In most Western cultures, where food is generally abundant, being overweight is associated with lower socioeconomic status, especially for women. The upper classes in Western cultures have a clear preference for very thin body types. This preference can be verified by looking at high-fashion magazines. The typical woman presented by the fashion industry is 5 feet, 11 inches tall and weighs approximately 110 pounds, which is 7 inches taller and 30 pounds lighter than the average woman in the United States. Such an extreme standard of thinness reinforces body-weight ideals that are difficult for most people to obtain. Indeed, women report holding ideals for body weight that are not only lower than average weight, but also lower than what men find attractive *and* what women think men find attractive, as may be seen in Figure 10.25 (Fallon & Rozin, 1985).

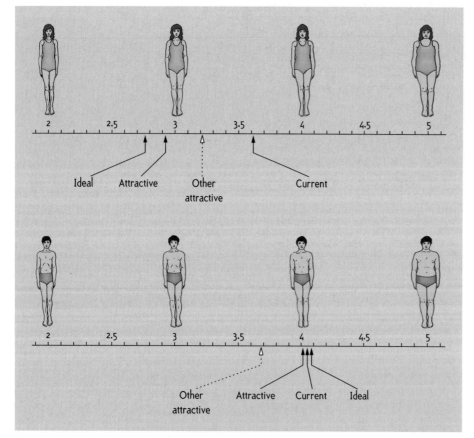

10.25 Rating Attractiveness Men and women were asked to choose which figures represent how they currently view their bodies, what their ideal body shape is, and what they believe is attractive to the opposite sex. Women chose a body-weight ideal that is thinner than what they believe men want and also thinner than what men actually say they want in women. Men chose an ideal that is closer to their current self-rating and close to what they believe women prefer, but heavier than what women say they want in men.

Restrictive Dieting Can Be Problematic

Dieting is a notoriously ineffective means of achieving permanent weight loss. Most individuals who lose weight through dieting eventually regain the weight; very often they gain back *more* than they lost. The primary reason that most diets fail has to do with the body's natural defense against weight loss. Body weight is regulated around a *set-point* that is determined primarily by genetic influence. Consider two examples. In 1966, several Vermont prisoners were given an interesting challenge: to try to increase their body weight by 25 percent (Sims et al., 1968). For six months these prisoners consumed more than 7,000 calories per day, nearly double their usual intake. Assuming each prisoner was eating about 3,500 extra calories a day (the equivalent of seven large cheeseburgers), simple math suggests each should have gained approximately 170 pounds over the six months. In reality, few gained more than 40 pounds, and most lost the weight when they went back to normal eating. Those who did not lose the weight had family histories of obesity, supporting the view that genetics predispose obesity when people are exposed to overfeeding.

At the other end of the spectrum, during World War II, more than 100 men volunteered to take part in a scientific study as an alternative to military service (Keys, Brozek, Henschel, Mickelsen, & Taylor, 1950). The researchers were interested in the short- and long-term effects of semistarvation. Over six months, the men lost an average of 25 percent of their body weight, but most found it very hard to do and some had great difficulty losing more than 10 pounds. The men underwent dramatic changes in emotions, motivation, and attitudes toward food. They became anxious, depressed, and listless; they lost interest in sex and other activities; and they became obsessed with eating. Interestingly, many of these outcomes are quite similar to those experienced by people with eating disorders.

Although it is possible to alter body weight, the body responds to weight loss by slowing down the metabolism and using less energy. Thus, after the body has been deprived of food, it takes less food to maintain a given body weight. Likewise, weight gain occurs much faster in previously starved animals than would be expected by caloric intake alone. In addition, repeated alterations between caloric deprivation and overfeeding have been shown to have cumulative metabolic effects, so that weight loss and metabolic functioning are slowed more each time the animal is placed on caloric deprivation, and weight gain occurs more rapidly with each resumption of feeding. Such patterns might explain why "yo-yo dieters" tend to become heavier over time.

RESTRAINED EATING A second reason that diets tend to fail is occasional, or not so occasional, bouts of overeating. Psychologists Janet Polivy and Peter Herman (1985) have demonstrated that chronic dieters, whom they call *restrained eaters,* are prone to excessive eating in certain situations. For instance, if restrained eaters believe they have eaten high-calorie foods, they abandon their diets (see Figure 10.26). The mindset of restrained eaters is "I've blown my diet, so I might as well just keep eating." Many restrained eaters diet all week only to lose control on the weekends when they are faced with increased food temptations at the same time that they are in a less-structured environment. Being under stress also leads restrained eaters to break their diets (Heatherton, Herman, & Poliny, 1991).

Binge eating by restrained eaters depends on their *perception* of whether their diet is broken or not. Dieters can eat 1,000-calorie Caesar salads and believe that their diets are fine, but if they eat 200-calorie chocolate bars they feel the diet is ruined and they become disinhibited. The problem for restrained eaters is that they rely on cognitive control of food intake, which is likely to break down when they eat

10.26 Restrained and Unrestrained Eating
Chronic dieters (called *restrained eaters*) and nondieters engaged in a supposed taste test, which was described as a test of perception (because the researchers did not want subjects to know that eating was being monitored). Prior to the taste test, some of the participants were asked to drink one or two obviously fattening milkshakes. The participants then were asked to taste and rate flavors of ice cream and were invited to help themselves to as much as they wanted. Nondieters (called unrestrained eaters) ate sensibly: Those who had drunk one or two milkshakes ate much less ice cream than those who had not. Restrained eaters, however, did just the opposite, eating much more ice cream if they had had the milkshakes. This has been called the "what the hell effect."

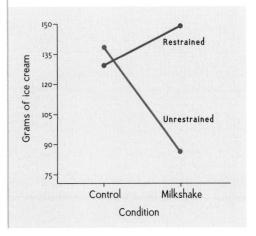

high-calorie foods or feel emotionally distressed. Rather than eating according to internal states of hunger and satiety, restrained eaters eat according to rules, such as time of day, number of calories, and type of food. Getting restrained eaters back in touch with internal motivational states is one goal of sensible approaches to dieting.

DISORDERED EATING When dieters fail to lose weight, they often blame their lack of willpower, vowing to redouble their efforts on the next diet. Repeated dietary failures may have harmful and permanent physiological and psychological consequences. In physiologic terms, weight-loss and weight-gain cycles alter the dieter's metabolism, which may make future weight loss more difficult. In psychological terms, repeated failures diminish body-image satisfaction and damage self-esteem. Over time, chronic dieters may begin to feel helpless and depressed. Some eventually engage in more extreme behaviors to lose weight, such as taking drugs, fasting, exercising excessively, or purging. For some vulnerable individuals, chronic dieting may promote the development of a clinical eating disorder.

The two best-known eating disorders are anorexia nervosa and bulimia nervosa (Wiseman, Harris, & Halmi, 1998). Individuals with **anorexia nervosa** have an excessive fear of becoming fat, and as a result they refuse to eat. Anorexia most often begins in early adolescence and mainly affects upper-middle- and upper-class Caucasian girls. Although many adolescent girls strive to be thin, fewer than 1 in 100 meet the clinical criteria of anorexia nervosa (Table 10.1). These criteria include both objective measures of thinness and psychological characteristics that indicate an abnormal obsession with food and body weight. Those who have anorexia view themselves as fat in spite of being at least 15 to 25 percent underweight. Issues of food and weight pervade their lives, controlling not only how they view themselves but also how they view the world. Initially, the results of their self-imposed starvation may draw favorable comments from others, although as the anorexic approaches her emaciated ideal, family and friends usually become quite concerned. In many cases, medical attention is required to prevent death from starvation. Anorexia is very difficult to treat, since patients maintain the belief that they are overweight, or not as thin as they would like to be, even when they are severely emaciated. This dangerous disorder causes a number of serious health problems, especially a loss of bone density, and about 15 to 20 percent of those with anorexia eventually die from the disorder (American Psychiatric Association, 2000).

Individuals with **bulimia nervosa** alternate between dieting and binge eating. Bulimia often develops during late adolescence. Like anorexia, bulimia is most common among upper-middle- and upper-class Caucasian women, but it is more common among minorities and men than anorexia. Approximately 1 to 2 percent of women in high school and college meet the definitional criteria for bulimia nervosa. These women tend to be of average weight or slightly overweight. They regularly binge-eat; feel that their eating is out of control; have excessive worries about body weight issues; and engage in one or more compensatory behaviors, such as self-induced vomiting, excessive exercise, or the abuse of laxatives. Unlike the starvation of anorexia, binge eating behavior tends to occur secretly. Although bulimia is associated with serious health problems, such as dental and cardiac disorders, it is seldom fatal (Keel & Mitchell, 1997). A variant of bulimia is *binge-eating disorder,* wherein individuals engage in binge eating but do not purge. Many of those with binge-eating disorder are obese.

Smoking Often Begins in Childhood

In spite of overwhelming evidence that smoking cigarettes leads to premature death, millions around the globe continue to light up (Carmody, 1993). Although smoking

anorexia nervosa An eating disorder characterized by an excessive fear of becoming fat and thus a refusal to eat.

bulimia nervosa An eating disorder characterized by dieting, binge eating, and purging.

| TABLE 10.1 | Diagnostic Criteria for Anorexia Nervosa and Bulimia Nervosa |

CRITERIA FOR ANOREXIA NERVOSA

A. Refusal to maintain body weight at or above a minimum normal for age and height (e.g., weight loss leading to maintenance of body weight less than 85 percent of that expected; or failure to make expected weight gain during period of growth, leading to body weight less than 85 percent of that expected).

B. Intense fear of gaining weight or becoming fat, even though underweight.

C. Disturbance in the way in which one's body weight or shape is experienced, undue influence of body weight or shape on self-evaluation, or denial of the seriousness of the current low body weight.

D. In postmenarcheal females, amenorrhea, i.e., the absence of at least three consecutive menstrual cycles. (A woman is considered to have amenorrhea if her periods occur only following hormone, e.g., estrogen, administration.)

CRITERIA FOR BULIMIA NERVOSA

A. Recurrent episodes of binge eating. An episode of binge eating is characterized by both of the following:
 (1) Eating, in a discrete period of time (e.g., within any 2-hour period), an amount of food that is definitely larger than most people would eat during a similar period of time and under similar circumstances.
 (2) A sense of lack of control over eating during the episode (e.g., a feeling that one cannot stop eating or control what or how much one is eating).

B. Recurrent inappropriate compensatory behavior in order to prevent weight gain, such as self-induced vomiting; misuse of laxatives, diuretics, enemas, or other medications; fasting; or excessive exercise.

C. The binge eating and inappropriate compensatory behaviors both occur, on average, at least twice a week for 3 months.

D. Self-evaluation is unduly influenced by body shape and weight.

E. The disturbance does not occur exclusively during episodes of anorexia nervosa.

SOURCE: *Diagnostic and Statistical Manual of the American Psychiatric Association,* 1994.

has declined over the past 40 years, the Centers for Disease Control report that in 2002 about 1 in 4 American adults was a current smoker. Most smokers begin in childhood or early adolescence. Every day nearly 5,000 Americans aged 11 to 17 have their first cigarette (Gilpin, Choi, Berry, & Pierce, 1999), and about half of these are likely to continue smoking into adulthood.

Smoking causes a number of health problems, such as heart disease, respiratory ailments, and a variety of cancers, and is blamed for over 440,000 deaths per year in the United States, decreasing the life of the typical smoker by more than 12 years (USDHHS, 2004). Cigarette smoke also causes health problems for nonsmoking bystanders, which has led to bans on smoking in numerous public and private places. It is not uncommon to see smokers huddled outside of office buildings or hospitals, braving both the elements and hostile looks from nonsmokers to satisfy their cravings for nicotine. Smokers also endure scoldings from physicians and loved ones who are concerned for their health and welfare, and in addition to spending money on cigarettes, they pay significantly more for life and health insurance. Why in the world does anyone smoke?

STARTING SMOKING It is hard to imagine any good reason to start smoking. First attempts at smoking often involve a great deal of coughing, watering eyes, a terrible taste in the mouth, and feelings of nausea. So why do kids persist? Most researchers point to powerful social influences as the leading cause of adolescent smoking (Chassin, Presson, & Sherman, 1990). Research has demonstrated that adolescents are more likely to smoke if their parents or friends are smokers (Biglan & Lichtenstein, 1984; Hansen et al., 1987). They often smoke their first cigarette in the company of other smokers, or at least with the encouragement of their peer group. Moreover, many adolescent smokers appear to show a false-consensus effect, in that they overestimate the number of adolescent and adult smokers (Sherman, Presson, Chassin, Corty, & Olshavsky, 1983). Thus, adolescents who incorrectly believe that smoking is common may take it up to fit in with the crowd.

The real reason dinosaurs became extinct

Others have pointed to the potential meaning of "being a smoker" as having a powerful influence. For instance, research has shown that smokers are viewed as having a number of positive qualities, such as being tough, sociable, and good with members of the opposite sex. Children take up smoking partially to look "tough, cool, and independent of authority" (Leventhal & Cleary, 1980, p. 384). Thus, smoking may be one way in which adolescents enhance their self-image as well as their public image (Chassin et al., 1990). Of course, it is hard to look tough while gasping and retching, so while most adolescents try one or two cigarettes, the majority do not become regular smokers. By grade 12, 70 percent of adolescents have some experience with tobacco products (Mowery, Brick, & Farrelly, 2000), but fewer than half of those who try cigarettes become established smokers.

Although many of the same factors that lead children to try cigarettes are involved in the establishment of regular smoking, additional factors are important for determining long-term, regular tobacco use. Over time, casual smokers become addicted. It is now widely acknowledged that the drug nicotine in tobacco is of primary importance in motivating and maintaining smoking behavior (Fagerström & Schneider, 1989; USDHHS, 2004). Once the smoker becomes "hooked" on nicotine, going without cigarettes will lead to unpleasant withdrawal symptoms, including heightened anxiety and distress (Russell, 1990). Some people appear to be especially susceptible to nicotine addiction, which may be due to genetics. Genes that control dopamine pathways are especially influential in determining whether individuals become addicted to nicotine (Sabol et al., 1999). Nicotine may lead to greater activation of dopamine neurons, which would be experienced as more rewarding. Positive reactions to the first smoking experience are associated with a greater likelihood of progression to regular smoking (Blitstein, Robinson, Murray, Klesges, & Zbikowski, 2003; Pomerleau, Pomerleau, & Namenek, 1998).

Profiles in Psychological Science

Success of a Fast-Food Dieter

One of the most unlikely recent celebrities is Jared Fogle, the formerly obese man who lost weight by walking every day and eating Subway sandwiches. Fogle shed a whopping 245 pounds and has maintained his weight loss for several years (Figure

10.27). His dramatic success stands in stark contrast to what might be expected from the more pessimistic research literature. A review of published weight loss studies by the National Institutes of Health found that nearly two-thirds of those who lose weight regain that weight within one year and that almost no one manages to maintain weight loss for five years (NIH Technology Assessment Conference Panel, 1993). Similarly, the research literature indicates that treatments of addictions are no more than 20 to 30 percent successful over the long term. So how do we explain it when people like Jared Fogle are able to defy the odds and lose weight, stop smoking, or give up other addictions?

Do you know someone who has quit smoking or lost a substantial amount of weight and kept it off? Chances are you do. Stanley Schachter (1982) interviewed 83 members of the Columbia University Psychology Department and 78 shopkeepers from Amagansett, New York. Schachter found that more than half of those who had tried to lose weight or quite smoking had done so successfully on their own, without professional treatment. What was impressive was that the average length of abstinence was close to seven years for smoking and that people had maintained weight loss for more than 10 years. How do we reconcile the clinical treatment literature with Schachter's finding? Perhaps people first try to resolve weight and addiction problems on their own, seeking therapy only after repeated failures. Success like Jared's is not counted in any published research because Jared did it on his own.

Even if we can be somewhat optimistic about people successfully changing a problem behavior, what factors predict whether a person will make the effort? Harald Klingemann (1991) studied the autobiographical accounts of ex-alcoholics and ex-heroin addicts to determine what factors led them to give up their addiction. Approximately three-quarters of the subjects reported extreme levels of stress associated with their addiction (e.g., family tensions, health problems, and feelings of helplessness). Many noted the occurrence of a critical event, such as losing a job or having a car accident. This is the proverbial "hitting rock bottom," what addicts describe as happening just before they realize that they have to do something about their behavior.

This sequence of hitting bottom and then making a change highlights the important role of thought processes in effecting behavioral changes. Psychologist David Premack provides the example of a man who quit smoking because of something that happened as he was picking up his children at the city library: "A thunderstorm greeted him as he arrived there; and at the same time a search of his pockets disclosed a familiar problem: he was out of cigarettes. Glancing back at the library, he caught a glimpse of his children stepping out in the rain, but he continued around the corner, certain that he could find a parking space, rush in, buy the cigarettes and be back before the children got seriously wet" (Premack, 1970). For the smoker, it was a shocking vision of himself "as a father who would actually leave the kids in the rain while he ran after cigarettes." The man quit smoking on the spot.

Similar critical incidents have been found in other studies of how and why some people are able to stop addictive behaviors. Consider the story of a young pregnant woman who recalls drinking a beer to cure a hangover: "I felt the baby quiver and I poured the rest of the beer out, and I said, 'God, forgive me. I'll never drink another drop.' And from that day to this I haven't" (Tuchfeld, 1981). Or the man who quit smoking after visiting an elderly friend at a cancer ward of a hospital: "While I was sitting a young woman who was approximately my age entered the lobby—she was walking with a walker. Although she was several yards from me I could hear every wheeze of her labored breathing. When she finally approached her friends, I heard her gasp, 'The doctors think I'm doing really well today.' Right then and there I decided to quit smoking. I guess I realized that it could happen to me" (Heatherton

10.27 Jared Fogle Fogle lost nearly 250 pounds from his obese frame, and has stayed slim against the odds.

& Nichols, 1994). In each of these cases the sudden realization of the extreme negative consequences associated with the behavior motivated the person to stop the behavior.

No particularly dramatic event motivated Jared Fogle; noticing a sign for low-fat sandwiches inspired him to try a new diet. In some unknown way, reading the sign led him to turn his life around. His success has inspired thousands of others to hope they might be able to lose weight. A Web site devoted to Jared contains many success stories. One woman who lost 75 pounds writes, "I was completely astonished when I learned of Jared's success. Seeing how you could completely change your life in a positive way was such a motivator. At first it was hard to believe that Jared could lose 245 pounds by eating two subs a day and walking, but it can definitely happen, because it happened to me as well. He was definitely an inspiration." Psychological scientists do not entirely understand these transformative experiences, but it is clear that many people can and do make major life changes to live healthier lives. ■

People Do Not Get Enough Exercise

The evidence is overwhelming that regular exercise profoundly affects physical and mental health. Modern society allows people to exert little physical energy, in comparison with what was required for most of previous human history. People drive to work, take the elevator, spend hours watching remote-controlled television, use various labor-saving devices, and complain about not having time to exercise. Once people are out of shape, it is very difficult for them to start regular exercise. According to the U.S. Health and Human Services Department, more than 60 percent of Americans do not exercise regularly, if at all. This is unfortunate: lifelong exercise yields both bodies and minds that deteriorate less radically with age.

In general, the more people exercise, the better their physical health. Aerobic exercise, that which momentarily increases breathing and heart rates, is especially good for cardiovascular health, lowering blood pressure and strengthening the heart and lungs (Lesniak & Dubbert, 2001). Other recent evidence indicates that exercise might help prevent certain cancers and improve the immune system. Because exercise also helps control appetite and metabolism, as well as burns calories, it is an essential element of any weight-control program.

> If exercise has so many benefits, why do so few people exercise regularly?

Exercise is important for the mind as well as the body. Research using animals demonstrates that exercise increases blood flow to the brain, the number of synaptic connections, and even the development of new neurons, all of which can lead to better learning and performance. Becoming fit has also been shown to increase human brain functioning. Older adults who had six months of cardiovascular training performed better on a measure of cognitive function and showed increased activation of brain regions involved in the ability to attend to an object and to ignore distractors (Colcombe et al., 2004).

Exercise is also good for mental health, as it has been found to reduce stress and improve mood. Indeed, as little as 10 minutes of exercise can improve feelings of vigor and enhance mood, although 30 minutes daily is associated with the most positive mental state (Hansen, Stevens, & Coast, 2001). The evidence is compelling that exercise can contribute to positive outcomes for the clinical treatment of depression (Craft & Perna, 2004) as well as of addiction and alcoholism (Read & Brown, 2003). How exercise exerts these positive effects is not currently known. It may provide a way for people simply to feel good, or it may build self-confidence and help people cope with stress. It might also affect neurotransmitter systems involved in reward, motivation, and emotion.

Psychological Science *in Action*

Taking Care of Mind and Body

Over the last quarter century, psychological science has learned a great deal about the complex relations between stress, behavior, and health. Fifty years ago people did not know how bad smoking was for the lungs, or that saturated fats and other dietary factors contribute to cardiovascular disease, or that being under stress could damage our bodies. We now know that people need to cope with stress, regulate their emotions, and control their daily habits to live healthy lives. Let's look at some of the behaviors that health psychologists have determined will improve physical and mental health.

- **Eat natural foods**   Various food fads go in and out of fashion, but the essential rules never change. You should eat a varied diet that emphasizes natural foods (e.g., whole grains, fruits, and vegetables) and avoid processed and fast foods. If you choose, various types of animal products can also be part of a natural, healthy diet. Try to avoid foods with trans fatty acids, artificial types of fat that prolong store shelf life. Some studies have found natural oils, such as olive oil, to have benefits for the heart.

- **Watch portion size**   Eat a varied diet in moderation—and eat only when you are hungry. Many prepared foods are sold in large portions, which encourage overeating. Many people eat for flavor or other reasons rather than to satisfy hunger. Over time, the extra calories from large portions contribute to obesity. Eating small snacks between meals can prevent people from becoming overly hungry and eating too much at their next meal.

- **Drink alcohol in moderation, if at all**   Some research indicates that two or so glasses of wine per day, or similar quantities of other alcohol-containing drinks, can produce cardiovascular benefits. However, excessive alcohol consumption can cause serious health problems, including alcoholism, liver problems, some cancers, heart disease, and immune-system deficiencies—and the list goes on.

- **Keep active**   Find a way to engage in moderate physical activity at least four times a week for at least 30 minutes. Ignore the mantra "no pain, no gain." Research shows not only that it is inaccurate, but that pain prevents people from exercising over the long run. Starting with moderate exercise that doesn't leave you breathless, and building up over time, is a safe way to ensure fitness. In addition, find opportunities throughout the day to be active, such as taking the stairs or walking.

- **Don't smoke**   This may seem obvious, yet many college students begin smoking each year. Smoking has no known benefits and eventually produces undesirable physical effects for all smokers, such as a hacking cough, unpleasant odor, and bad breath. The major way that smoking helps most people relax is that it reduces withdrawal symptoms in those who are addicted to nicotine. Going without nicotine makes people anxious.

- **Practice safe sex**   Numerous sexually transmitted diseases affect millions, including college students. A growing proportion of new HIV cases occurs among those under age 25 who are infected through heterosexual activity. In spite of the devastating consequences of many sexually transmitted diseases, many young adults engage in risky sexual practices, such as not using condoms.

425

This is especially likely to occur when alcohol or other drugs are involved. If you think that a sexual encounter is possible, be prepared and take appropriate precautions.

- **Learn to relax**   As we have seen, daily hassles and stress can cause numerous health problems, as well as conditions such as insomnia that can interfere with your ability to function in daily life. There are many relaxation exercises that can help people soothe their bodies and minds. Seek help from trained counselors who can teach you these methods, such as using biofeedback to measure your physiological activity so that you can learn to control it. You might also try an activity such as yoga.

- **Learn to cope**   Negative events are a part of life. You need to learn strategies for dealing with them, assessing them realistically so that you see what might be positive about them as well as accept the difficulties they pose. You can learn specific strategies for dealing with stressors, such as seeking advice or assistance, actively attempting new solutions, distracting yourself with more pleasant thoughts or activities, trying to reinterpret the situation in humorous ways, and so on. Different strategies are effective for different people, so you need to find out what works for you. The important thing is not to allow stress to consume your life. Remember that exercise helps reduce stress and is an excellent daily strategy for keeping it in check.

- **Build a strong support network**   Having supportive friends and family can help people deal with much of life's stress, from daily frustrations to serious catastrophes. Avoid people who encourage you to act in unhealthy ways or who are threatened by your efforts to be healthy. Instead, find people who share your values and understand what you want from life, who can listen and who can provide advice, assistance, or simply encouragement. ■

REVIEWING the Principles | What Are Some of the Behaviors That Affect Physical Health?

How people behave in their daily lives has a profound effect on their physical and mental health. With the advent of medical technologies to deal with infectious disease, many causes of mortality in Western culture are related to lifestyle factors, such as diet, lack of physical activity, substance use and abuse, and coping poorly with stress. People engage in many unhealthy behaviors when they are stressed, such as eating fatty foods or smoking. People who eat too much can become obese, especially if they have a genetic predisposition to put on weight, which poses a number of serious health risks. Smoking is especially bad for health and is one of the leading causes of death around the world. Unfortunately, smoking typically starts in adolescence, a time when people give little thought to long-term consequences. One of the best things that people can do for health is exercise. Regular physical activity helps people to cope with stress, enhances their emotional experiences, and builds a strong and healthy body. More recent evidence suggests that exercise can also improve mental functioning through its effects on the brain.

Conclusion

For many years scientists likened the brain to an information-processing device such as a computer. Humans are hardly like this. They react to environmental input with physiological reactions and cognitions, which together produce mental states that are perceived to be positive or negative, or shades in between. This response is known as emotion, and it is a primary force that motivates adaptive behaviors and discourages maladaptive behaviors. Thinking about emotions and stress from an evolutionary viewpoint provides novel perspectives for understanding them. For instance, emotions such as shame and guilt are often viewed as unnecessary emotional baggage. But guilt, embarrassment, and the like help to maintain and affirm social bonds and thereby serve adaptive functions. Similarly, the assumption that fight or flight was a uniform response to stress does not make complete sense from an evolutionary perspective. Scholars have recently shown that females of many species behave in a completely different manner—tending and befriending—that makes more adaptive sense. For both sexes, stress can have a number of negative consequences, beginning with high levels of stress hormones that can alter the brain to causing high levels of anxiety. Both of these effects can cause heart disease and interfere with the immune system. Stress also causes people to engage in the very behaviors that contribute to these health problems, such a eating large quantities of fattening foods, smoking cigarettes, and avoiding exercise. Learning to cope with stress, solve personal problems, develop strong social networks, and modify lifestyle can help people live healthier and more meaningful lives.

Summarizing the Principles of Emotions and Health

How Are Emotions Adaptive?

1. **Facial expressions communicate emotion:** The perception of the nonverbal communication of basic emotions in facial expression is cross culturally similar. However, culture governs the rules for the display of emotions.

2. **Emotions serve cognitive functions:** Emotions serve as heuristic guides in decision making. Emotions command attention and act as somatic markers in making choices. Emotions also aid memory.

3. **Emotions strengthen interpersonal relations:** In relationships, guilt can prevent harmful behavior, demonstrate caring, and can be used to manipulate. Interpersonal emotions develop out of socialization. Blushing is uniquely human and communicates apology. Jealousy signals commitment.

How Do People Experience Emotions?

4. **Emotions have a subjective component:** Primary emotions are adaptive; secondary emotions are a blend of primary ones. The circumplex model posits that emotions vary by valence and activation. There are neurochemical responses associated with emotions.

5. **Emotions have a physiological component:** The James-Lange theory of emotion states that physical changes are interpreted as specific emotions. According to the facial feedback hypothesis, facial expressions trigger the experience of emotions. The Cannon-Bard theory of emotion states that emotion-producing stimuli simultaneously activates physical and emotional reactions.

6. **Emotions have a cognitive component:** Stanley Schachter's two-factor theory of emotion proposes that a situation evokes a physiological response that is cognitively interpreted with an emotional label. Therefore, people may misattribute arousal states, and transfer their excitement to a new event.

7. **People regulate their moods:** People cognitively appraise and frame events in order to cope effectively. Humor is effective for regulating negative mood. Rebound may occur from emotional suppression. Rumination may prolong negative mood.

What Is the Neurophysiological Basis of Emotion?

8. **Emotions are associated with autonomic activity:** Emotions cause changes in heart rate, blood pressure, and skin temperature. Facial expressions, through facial musculature, may control the warming or cooling of the brain.

9. **The amygdala and the prefrontal cortex are involved in emotion:** The amygdala processes stimuli and generates an immediate emotional response. It deciphers the emotional content of facial expressions. The prefrontal cortex processes emotional cues related to interpersonal experiences.

10. **Emotion systems are lateralized in the brain:** Cerebral asymmetry exists with regard to emotions (i.e., the left brain processes positive emotions and the right brain processes negative ones).

How Do People Cope with Stress?

11. **The general adaptation syndrome is a bodily response to stress:** Hans Selye's general adaptation syndrome model consists of the alarm stage, resistance stage, and exhaustion stage—the three-stage response to stress. Stress has physiological components.

12. **People encounter stress in daily life:** Major life stressors are disruptions that strain people's lives. The more minor, but ubiquitous, daily hassles can have a cumulative effect on health.

13. **Stress affects health:** Stress and negativity increase the likelihood of heart disease. The Type A behavior pattern of personality traits is a strong predictor of heart disease. Stress compromises the immune system.

14. **Coping is a process:** People engage in primary appraisals of stressors before the secondary appraisal of coping strategies. Emotion-focused coping changes the emotional responses to stress; problem-focused coping seeks to solve the problem. Positive reappraisal helps people deal with stress. Hardiness is a personality characteristic that is helpful in stress resistance. Social support is a stress buffer.

What Are Some of the Behaviors That Affect Physical Health?

15. **Obesity results from a genetic predisposition and overeating:** Genetics sets body mass index range but the environment determines the final values. Culture determines whether obesity is stigmatized.

16. **Restrictive dieting can be problematic:** Set-point values regulate weight gain after restrictive dieting. Eating behavior that breaks a diet often leads to excessive eating. Disordered eating can lead to anorexia nervosa and bulimia nervosa.

17. **Smoking often begins in childhood:** Social influences are the leading cause of adolescent smoking. "Being a smoker" is associated with some positive qualities and these perceptions can influence smoking onset behavior. Genetics influence nicotine addiction.

18. **People do not get enough exercise:** In general, the more people exercise, the better their physical and mental health. Older adults who exercise regularly retain mental functioning longer.

Applying the Principles

1. While traveling to different, remote parts of the world, you notice that people display the same basic facial expressions as you do when feeling happiness, sadness, fear, and anger. This also happens to be true of infants from different cultures. Which of the following explains this phenomenon?

   _____ a) emotions are taught to everyone at birth
   _____ b) emotions are innate and adaptive because they signal information to others
   _____ c) there are only four basic emotions; all the others emotions are combinations
   _____ d) cultures have little influence on emotional display

2. You just found out that your essay on civil engagement on campus has been accepted for publication in your college paper! You are smiling and happy. Determining what accounts for the "happy" feeling involves which two components of emotional experience?

   _____ a) physical and cognitive
   _____ b) primary and secondary
   _____ c) emotion and appraisal
   _____ d) arousal and physiology

3. As you are walking home, you hear the sound of gunshots. You are startled and flee in fear. What neurological responses have occurred?

   _____ a) an autonomically governed startle response; a fast-path amygdala response that generated a fear response; a slow-path response that confirmed the fear, thus fleeing was warranted
   _____ b) the thalamus generated an autonomic startle response; a fast-path autonomic response caused you to flee
   _____ c) a sympathetic response generated by the amygdala created fear; a slow parasympathetic response evaluated the fear response and commanded your body to flee
   _____ d) a sympathetic response governed the startle response; the thalamus generated fear; the amygdala evaluated the fear and activated the flee response

4. You enter the classroom a bit late and find everyone is already seated, with a pencil and test form on each desk. You

realize that you forgot there is an exam today! After settling in your seat you calm down, gather your thoughts, and do your best to answer the exam questions. This response is consistent with which sequence of the general adaptation syndrome stages?

_____ a) alarm, avoidance, exhaustion
_____ b) resistance, exhaustion, termination
_____ c) alarm, resistance
_____ d) avoidance, termination

5. Jenna has just joined her junior high school's committee to develop a program to keep kids from smoking, and she asks her older sister Arlene for help. Based on what Arlene has learned from her psychology class, which of the following is likely to be the most effective recommendation?

_____ a) to tell kids how expensive it is to smoke
_____ b) to deliver a message showing that smokers are not cool because they are addicts
_____ c) to explain the health consequences of smoking and the physiological aspects of addiction
_____ d) to have the anti-smoking message delivered regularly by classroom teachers

ANSWERS: 1 b 2 a 3 a 4 c 5 b

Key Terms

alexithymia, p. 393	facial feedback hypothesis, p. 395	problem-focused coping, p. 414
anorexia nervosa, p. 420	fight-or-flight response, p. 408	rumination, p. 400
body mass index (BMI), p. 417	general adaptation syndrome, p. 410	secondary appraisal, p. 414
buffering hypothesis, p. 416	guilt, p. 391	secondary emotions, p. 394
bulimia nervosa, p. 420	hardiness, p. 415	social support, p. 415
Cannon-Bard theory of emotion, p. 396	health psychology, p. 386	somatic markers, p. 390
cerebral asymmetry, p. 407	immune system, p. 413	stress, p. 386
circumplex model, p. 394	James-Lange theory of emotion, p. 395	stressor, p. 408
coping response, p. 408	lymphocytes, p. 413	tend-and-befriend response, p. 409
display rules, p. 388	mood, p. 385	two-factor theory of emotion, p. 396
emotion, p. 385	positive reappraisal, p. 414	Type A behavior pattern, p. 412
emotion-focused coping, p. 414	primary appraisal, p. 414	Type B behavior pattern, p. 412
excitation transfer, p. 398	primary emotions, p. 394	

Further Readings

Damasio, A. R. (1999). *The feeling of what happens.* New York: Harcourt Brace.

Ekman, P., & Davidson, R. J. (1994). *The nature of emotion: Fundamental questions.* New York: Oxford University Press.

Glaser, R., & Kiecolt-Glaser, J. K. (1994). *Handbook of human stress and immunity.* San Diego: Academic Press.

Jenkins, J. M., Oatley, K., & Stein, N. L. (1998). *Human emotions: A reader.* Malden, MA: Blackwell Publishers.

Lane, R. D., Nadel, L., & Ahern, G. (1999). *Cognitive neuroscience of emotion.* New York: Oxford University Press.

LeDoux, J. E. (1996). *The emotional brain: The mysterious underpinnings of emotional life.* New York: Simon & Schuster.

Lewis, M., & Haviland, J. M. (1993). *Handbook of emotions.* New York: Guilford.

Panksepp, J. (1998). *Affective neuroscience: The foundations of human and animal emotions.* New York: Oxford University Press.

Sapolsky, R. M. (1995). *Why zebras don't get ulcers.* New York: Freeman.

Sternberg, E. M. (2000). *The balance within.* New York: Freeman.

Mysteries of Human Development

Developmental psychology is concerned with changes in physiology, cognition, and social behavior over the course of a person's life span. Social development refers to how we became social beings: how we learn to interact with others. As the excited (and messy) crowd shown here at the famous Tomatina Festival in Bunyol, Spain, demonstrates, many different factors can influence and dictate "appropriate" behavior.

Human Development

In 1970, a young girl walked into a welfare office in Los Angeles with her mother, who came seeking help after escaping an abusive husband. When a social worker saw the girl, who was later known as "Genie," she reported the situation to her supervisor, thinking the young girl suffered from autism. On closer examination they discovered that the girl was 13 years old, although at 4 feet 6 inches and 59 pounds she appeared much younger. Her physical state revealed that she had been severely neglected and abused. She could not hop, skip, climb, or do anything requiring the full extension of her limbs (Curtiss, 1977; Rymer, 1993). She was admitted to the hospital and then taken from her parents and placed in foster care.

Genie's early life had been a nightmare. She had been locked in a room for more than ten years, deprived of normal human contact (Figure 11.1). Her father, who was mentally ill, had kept her in a tiny, dark bedroom, tied to a chair, and caged in a crib at night. She had been beaten for making any noise

11.1 **Genie** A photo of Genie in 1971.

and poorly fed. She had no one to talk to and nothing to listen to or even look at in her barren room. She was raised with essentially no stimulation from the external world. When she was rescued, Genie had a strange gait, almost like a rabbit's, and held her hands out in front of her as if they were paws. She understood just a few words and could form only brief sentences, such as "Stop it" and "No more." Genie also showed few signs of emotion or interest in connecting with those around her.

For the next four years, scientists from Children's Hospital in Los Angeles cared for Genie as they sought to understand the consequences of her social isolation. For decades psychological scientists had struggled to understand the extent to which development was affected by nature and nurture, how much of who we are as humans is hard wired in our genes or is the result of early experience. What is human nature when it is stripped of society and culture? No ethical experiment could be conducted to answer these questions. Could Genie provide insight into what makes us human? Would Genie be able to learn? Could she develop normal social skills that would allow her to become a full member of society? Would a warm, nurturing environment help her recover from her tragic past? If the ability to acquire language is inborn, could she quickly learn how to speak so that she could describe what had happened to her?

In the first few years that Genie was cared for by the scientists, she made some progress in forming social relationships and acquiring minimal language. But as we will explore in greater detail later in the chapter, Genie was able to develop only the most rudimentary language skills. She learned many words, but she was not able to put them together properly in sentences. Sadly, when Genie turned 18 her mother was able to regain custody of her and immediately cut off all contact with the scientific community. Genie lived with her mother for only a short time before she was removed once again and sent to various foster homes. In at least one home she was again abused. She now lives in a small group home for adults who cannot look after themselves. ■

The case of Genie is tragic. We will never know what role her social and physical abuse played in the enduring difficulties that she had in interacting with others and acquiring language after age 13. Yet her case provides some tantalizing demonstrations of the role of experience in shaping brain development and psychological capacities. **Developmental psychology** is concerned with changes in physiology, cognition, and social behavior over the life span. For instance, to study how humans develop

developmental psychology The study of changes in physiology, cognition, and social behavior over the life span.

Timeline

1920s	1920s	1950s	1957
Cognitive Development View Swiss psychologist Jean Piaget proposes four distinct stages of how "thinking" develops in the brain. This theory guides research for nearly half a century.	**Cultural Context and Cognition** Russian psychologist Lev Vygotsky develops the first major theory of how cultural and social context influences cognitive and language development.	**Motherless Monkeys** Harry Harlow's experiments with infant rhesus monkeys and their artificial surrogate mothers demonstrate the importance of contact comfort in social development.	**The Psycholinguistic Revolution** Noam Chomsky transforms linguistics by positing that language must be governed by a universal grammar, a set of rules and principles built into the brain.

cognitive skills, scientists have focused on age-related changes in psychological capacities such as perception, language, and thinking. We will see that the mind develops in ways that are adaptive, as new, useful skills appear at appropriate times, even in the absence of specific training.

This chapter also examines how we develop as social beings. Social development refers to the maturation of skills or abilities that enable us to interact with others. In all cultures and across all time periods, every person's life is touched by the lives of others. Infants innately form bonds with others, an adaptive trait that provides protection and facilitates survival. As children grow, they learn how to communicate with and behave appropriately around others, and how to establish and maintain relationships. In this chapter, we consider how socialization affects human characteristics such as morality, gender, and identity. As we explore these specific aspects of development, we will also examine some of the most fundamental questions about humanity: How do we develop into members of society? How do we develop into who we are and come to value what we value? How do genes interact with early experiences to produce unique individuals? How do we grow and adapt within our own cultures? How do we change across the life span? These are the processes that shape us into who we become as human beings.

What Shapes a Child?

How does the human body grow and change to allow us to perform life's essential functions? How do our physical and social environments influence who we are as we develop over the course of childhood? For the most part, human development follows a predictable progression. Humans all do certain things, such as physically grow and mature at about the same period in the life span. During the prenatal period, the body develops in a fixed sequence, ultimately turning into a male or female infant based on genetic instructions. No newborns talk immediately, nor do any babies walk before they can sit up. Virtually all human babies make eye contact quickly after birth; display their first social smile at around six weeks; learn to roll over, sit up, crawl, stand, walk, and talk in that order (occasionally a step may be skipped or reversed) within a predictable range of ages (Figure 11.2). The consistency of this pattern suggests that our genes set the pace and order of development. However, the environment also influences what happens throughout the development process. For example, children raised in different cultures often achieve developmental milestones at a different pace. For instance, healthy children in Uganda tend to walk by 10 months, whereas those in France often do not walk before 15 months (Berger, 2004). These differences are due in part to different patterns of infant care across cultures, such as whether the infant is carried around during the day, whether the infant sleeps with the parents, or even whether the infant sleeps on her back or on

How does culture influence development?

1960s	1960s	1967	1968	1969
Infant Perception and Cognition Pioneering researchers such as Robert Fantz, Paul Eimas, Jacques Mehler, and Tom Bever demonstrate that many perceptual and cognitive abilities are hardwired.	**Attachment** John Bowlby proposes that infants are born with proximity-seeking behaviors that act to increase survival odds by keeping the child close to the mother.	**Critical Period Hypothesis** Eric Lenneberg proposes that there is a biological time period during which environmental input is necessary for a cognitive skill to develop. The term *sensitive periods* is now used for humans.	**Stages of Identity** Erik Erikson proposes a theory of identity development that considers development in eight stages, from infancy to old age.	**Moral Reasoning** Lawrence Kohlberg uses dilemmas to examine moral reasoning. His stage model is later criticized for not applying equally across genders and cultures.

Piaget Emphasized Stages of Development

Obviously, infants differ from adults. They can't read this book, for example. But are infants merely inexperienced humans who have not yet learned the skills they will develop over time? Or do their minds work in completely different ways from those of adults? Through careful observations of young children, Jean Piaget (Figure 11.12) devised an influential theory of how "thinking" develops in the brain. One critical aspect of Piaget's research is that he paid as much attention to how children made errors as to how they succeeded on tasks. These mistakes, although illogical by adult standards, provided insights into how the young mind makes sense of the world. By systematically analyzing children's thinking, Piaget developed the theory that children go through *stages* of cognitive development. These stages reflect different ways of thinking about the world. From this perspective, it is not that infants know less than adults, but rather that their view of how the world works is based on an entirely different set of assumptions than those held by adults. We will see later that others have challenged the idea of stages of development.

Piaget proposed four distinct stages of development (Figure 11.13), each characterized by a different way of thinking, which he referred to as *schemas*. According to Piaget, **schemas** are conceptual models of how the world works that children form at each stage of development. Piaget believed that each stage builds on the previous one through learning by assimilation and accommodation. **Assimilation** is the process through which a new experience is placed into an existing schema; **accommodation** is the process through which a schema is adapted or expanded to incorporate the new experience.

SENSORIMOTOR STAGE (BIRTH TO TWO YEARS) The first stage Piaget identified was the **sensorimotor stage**. Piaget's theory was that from birth until about age two, children acquire information about the world only through their senses—they react reflexively to objects. Thus, infants understand objects only when they reflexively react to those objects' sensory input—such as when they suck on a nipple, grasp a finger, or recognize a face. As they begin to control their movements, they develop their first schemas—conceptual models consisting of mental representations of the kinds of actions that can be performed on certain kinds of objects. For instance, consider the sucking reflex. This begins as a reaction to the sensory input from the nipple: The infant simply responds reflexively by sucking. Soon the child realizes it can suck other things—a bottle, a finger, a toy, a blanket. Piaget explained that sucking other objects is an example of assimilation to the schema of sucking. But sucking a toy or a blanket does not result in the same experience as the reflexive sucking of a nipple. This leads to accommodation with respect to the sucking schema—the child must adjust its understanding of sucking. Piaget believed that all of the sensorimotor schemas eventually merge into an exploratory schema. In other words, infants learn that they can act on objects—manipulate them in order to understand them—rather than simply react to them.

One of the cognitive concepts in this stage that Piaget explored was **object permanence**, the understanding that an object continues to exist even when it is hidden from view. Piaget noted that not until nine months of age will most infants search for objects that they have seen being hidden. Even at nine months, when infants will begin to snatch a blanket away to find a hidden toy, their search skills still have limits. For instance, suppose a child is given several trials in which an experimenter hides a toy under a blanket while the child watches, and the child then finds the toy. If the toy is then hidden under a different blanket, in full view of the child, the child will still look

11.12 Jean Piaget Piaget introduced the idea that cognitive development occurs in stages.

schemas Hypothetical cognitive structures that help us perceive, organize, process, and use information.

assimilation The process by which a new experience is placed into an existing schema.

accommodation The process by which a schema is adapted or expanded to incorporate a new experience that does not easily fit into an existing schema.

sensorimotor stage The first stage in Piaget's theory of cognitive development, during which infants acquire information about the world through their senses and respond reflexively.

object permanence The understanding that an object continues to exist even when it cannot be seen.

Stage	Characterization
Sensorimotor (birth–2 years) **1**	Differentiates self from objects Recognizes self as agent of action and begins to act intentionally; for example, pulls a string to set a mobile in motion or shakes a rattle to make a noise Achieves object permanence: realizes that things continue to exist even when no longer present to the senses
Preoperational (2–7 years) **2**	Learns to use language and to represent objects by images and words Thinking is still egocentric: has difficulty taking the viewpoint of others Classifies objects by a single feature; for example, groups together all the red blocks regardless of shape or all the square blocks regardless of color
Concrete operational (7–11 years) **3**	Can think logically about objects and events Achieves conservation of number (age 6), mass (age 7), and weight (age 9) Classifies objects according to several features and can order them in series along a single dimension, such as size
Formal operational (11 years and up) **4**	Can think logically about abstract propositions and test hypotheses systematically Becomes concerned with the hypothetical, the future, and ideological problems

11.13 Piaget's Stages of Cognitive Development

for the toy in the first hiding place. Full comprehension of object permanence was, for Piaget, one of the key accomplishments of the sensorimotor period.

PREOPERATIONAL STAGE (TWO TO SEVEN YEARS) In the **preoperational stage,** children can think about objects that are not in their immediate view and have developed various conceptual models of how the world works. During this stage, they begin to think symbolically—for example, taking a stick and pretending it is a gun. Piaget believed that what they cannot do yet is think "operationally"—they cannot imagine the logical outcome of certain actions on objects. They base their reasoning on immediate appearance, rather than logic. For instance, children at this stage have no understanding of the *law of conservation* of quantity: that the quantity of a substance remains unchanged, even if its appearance changes. For instance, if you pour a short, fat glass of water into a tall, thin glass, we all know that the amount of water has not changed. However, if you do this and ask a child in the preoperational stage which glass contains more, she will pick the tall, thin glass because the water is at a higher level. Children make this error even when they have seen someone pour the same amount of water into each glass—or even when they do it themselves (Figure 11.14).

CONCRETE OPERATIONAL STAGE (7 TO 12 YEARS) At about seven years of age, children enter the **concrete operational stage**, where they remain until adolescence. Piaget believed that humans do not develop logic until they begin to think about and understand *operations*. In other words, they can figure out the world by thinking about how events are related. A classic operation is an action that can be undone: A light can be turned on and off; a stick can be moved across the table and then moved back. He suggested that the ability to understand that an action is reversible enables children to begin to understand concepts such as conservation. Although this is the beginning of logic, Piaget believed that children at this stage reason only about concrete things—objects they can act on in the world. They do not yet have the ability to reason abstractly, or hypothetically, about what might be possible.

FORMAL OPERATIONAL STAGE (12 YEARS TO ADULTHOOD) The **formal operational stage** is Piaget's final stage of cognitive development. Formal operations involve abstract thinking, characterized by the ability to form a hypothesis about something and test it through deductive logic. For instance, at this stage teens can systematically begin to test a theory or solve a problem. Piaget used the example of giving students four flasks of colorless liquid and one flask of colored liquid. He told them that by combining two of the colorless liquids, they could obtain the colored liquid. Adolescents were able to try different combinations in a systematic fashion and obtain the correct result. Younger children, who just randomly combined liquids,

11.14 The Preoperational Stage and the Law of Conservation
In the preoperational stage, children cannot yet understand conservation tests. In this example, a six-year-old understands that the two short glasses contain the same amount of water (a). She carefully pours the water from one of the short glasses into a taller glass (b). Yet when asked "Which has more?" she points to the taller glass (c).

could not. If you think back to your school curricula, you will recall that subjects that require abstract reasoning, such as algebra or the scientific method, are not usually taught until around eighth grade. Here we see the influence of Piaget's research on education, providing an excellent example of psychological science in action.

Piaget revolutionized the understanding of cognitive development. His theories have dominated thinking for many years. However, many challenges have arisen to Piaget's views of how cognition develops. A key criticism disputes the idea that every person goes through the stages of development in the same order. Piaget believed that as children progress through each stage, they all use the same kind of logic to solve problems. This leaves little room for differing cognitive strategies or skills among individuals—or cultures. Some developmental psychologists have revised many of Piaget's theories while preserving his basic ideas. These theorists believe that different areas in the brain are responsible for different skills, and that the development of different skills therefore does not have to follow strict stages (Bidell & Fischer, 1995; Case, 1992; Fischer, 1980).

Infants Have Innate Knowledge

Earlier we asked if children are simply immature adults or whether their thinking styles are qualitatively different from the thinking styles of those who are older. Piaget suggested that children are not capable of understanding much of the world around them until they go through the various stages of cognitive development. However, recent research indicates that children understand much more and at much earlier ages than was previously believed.

Tests using the preferential looking technique have revealed that infants as young as three months of age are able to remember an object, even when it is no longer in plain sight, which seemingly contradicts Piaget's ideas about object permanence. Similarly, infants' reactions to novel stimuli indicate that they have cognitive skills quite early in life. For example, if you show three-month-old infants events that are impossible or unexpected, as if by magic (that is, that do not make rational sense), they will stare at the magic result longer than if you show them something that does make sense. For instance, suppose you show an infant an apple and then lower a screen. When you raise the screen again, the infant sees one of two situations: a possible event (the apple is still there) or an impossible event (a carrot has magically replaced the apple). If an infant looks longer at the impossible event, the experimenter deduces that the infant can tell the difference between the two scenes (Baillargeon, 1995). By responding differently to possible and impossible events, infants demonstrate some understanding that an object continues to exist when it is out of sight, even though they may not reach for a hidden object in Piaget's object-permanence test. Here we see that Piaget's task probably required too much of infants, especially in terms of having to reach for the object. Baillargeon's more implicit test revealed that object permanence occurs earlier than Piaget believed. In this section we consider some of the cognitive skills that appear to develop early in life.

preoperational stage The second stage in Piaget's theory of cognitive development, during which children think symbolically about objects, but reason is based on appearance rather than logic.

concrete operational stage The third stage in Piaget's theory of cognitive development, during which children begin to think about and understand operations in ways that are reversible.

formal operational stage The final stage in Piaget's theory of cognitive development; it involves the ability to think abstractly and to formulate and test hypotheses through deductive logic.

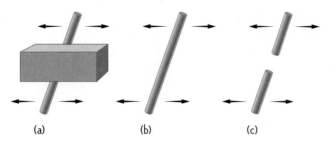

(a)   (b)   (c)

11.15 The Perceptual Effect of Occlusions in Early Infancy Four-month-olds were shown a rod that moved back and forth behind an occluding block as shown in (a). After being habituated to this stimuli they were shown two events, one in which a solid rod (b) moved behind the occluding block, another in which two separate rods (c) moved back and forth behind the block. The infants spent much more time looking at the unexpected event (c).

How can we test infants' innate knowledge?

11.16 Understanding the Laws of Nature In Baillargeon's test, infants looked longer during the impossible event, in which the box was placed in midair without any contact support but did not fall.

UNDERSTANDING THE LAWS OF NATURE: PHYSICS The developmental psychologist Elizabeth Spelke and her colleagues have conducted numerous studies indicating that infants have a primitive understanding of some of the basic laws of physics. Consider one such example. Humans are born with the ability to perceive movement: A newborn will follow moving stimuli with his or her eyes and head and prefer to look at a moving stimulus over one that is stationary. Experiments by Spelke and Philip Kellman indicate that as infants get older, they use movement information to determine if an object is continuous (Kellman, Spelke, & Short, 1986). In one experiment, the researchers showed four-month-old infants a rod moving back and forth behind a block. Once habituated, the infants were shown two scenes—one in which the block was removed and there was a single rod, and another in which the block was removed and there were two small rods (Figure 11.15). The infants looked longer at the scene with two smaller rods. This indicated that they expected the rod moving behind the block to be one continuous object rather than two smaller ones. If the experiment is conducted with the rod remaining stationary, the infants do not look longer at the two small rods. So infants appear to use movement to infer that objects that move together are continuous, whereas two stationary objects may or may not be continuous. Understanding the relation between movement and the physical properties of the rod requires cognitive skills. It requires the ability to see the rod as an object separate from the block, and to surmise that since the two ends are moving together, they must be part of the same whole rod, even though it is partially hidden from view.

In a series of studies that use impossible events, Renee Baillargeon has found that children begin to understand what is necessary to support an object in space very early. Working with infants of different ages, the experimenters determined how well they understand whether a box will be stable when it is released on a platform versus when it is released off the platform (Figure 11.16). They found that by three months of age, infants expect the box to be stable if it is released on the platform, but not if it is released off the platform. Thus, children seem to have an intuitive sense of the laws that govern the physical world.

Possible event

Impossible event

  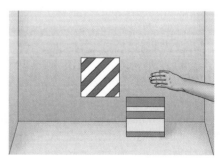

UNDERSTANDING THE LAWS OF NATURE: MATHEMATICS Research over the past 25 years has shown that we are born with certain numerical abilities, such as the ability to understand quantity. Piaget believed that young children do not understand numbers, and therefore must learn counting and other number-related skills through memorization. His experiments consisted of, for example, showing children four to five years old two rows of marbles (Figure 11.17). He found that if the marbles were spread out, then the child would usually say that the longer row had more marbles. Piaget concluded that children had no inherent sense of number—rather, their understanding of "more than" had to do with their perception of the length of the rows. This view was challenged by Jacques Mehler and Tom Bever (1967), who argued that children under three years old could understand the concept of more than or less than. To demonstrate their point, they repeated Piaget's experiment, but they used M&Ms candy (Figure 11.18). They showed the children the two rows of four M&Ms each and asked if the rows were the same. When the children said yes, the researchers then transformed the rows. For instance, they would add two candies to the second row, but they would compress that row so it was shorter than the row with fewer candies. Then they would tell the children to pick the row they wanted to eat. More than 80 percent picked the row with more M&Ms, even though it was the visually shorter row. Thus children do appear to understand the concepts of more than or less than, when properly motivated.

The growing evidence that infants have innate knowledge raises a serious challenge to Piaget's theory. Clearly, Piaget got many things right and his contributions to understanding cognitive development are enormous. The accumulation of scientific findings, however, indicates that Piaget underestimated the mental capacities of young children.

Memory Improves over Childhood

The development of memory also helps children learn about the world around them, as they use new information to build on what they already know. Once again, clever experiments have revealed that infants do possess some types of memory from an early age—though that memory is quite rudimentary. Carolyn Rovee-Collier and her colleagues devised two such experiments. In one, infants learn to move a mobile hanging over the crib by kicking. During the task, a ribbon attaches their ankle to the mobile so the infants learn that the mobile moves when they kick (Figure 11.19). The rate at which an infant kicks when the mobile is not attached serves as the baseline. When the infant is tested later, the ribbon is attached to the ankle but not to the mobile (so the kicks do not move the mobile). If the baby recognizes the mobile, it will presumably kick faster than the baseline rate to try to make the mobile move. Infants ranging in age from 2 to 18 months have been trained for two days on the mobile and then tested after different lengths of time have passed. Findings indicate that infants remember longer as they get older. By 18 months, they can remember the event for several weeks (Rovee-Collier, 1999).

INFANTILE AMNESIA For years it was believed that infants did not remember anything, primarily because adults can seldom remember events that occurred before they were three or four years old. Freud referred to this inability to remember events from early childhood as **infantile amnesia**. Psychologists have offered a variety of explanations for why adults cannot recall their earliest memories (Eacott, 1999). Some believe that memories are retained only when we have the ability to create autobiographical memory based on personal experience—for instance, recalling that "a cat scratched me" versus the fact that "cats scratch." Other psychologists

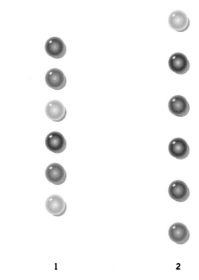

1   2

11.17 Piaget's Marble Test

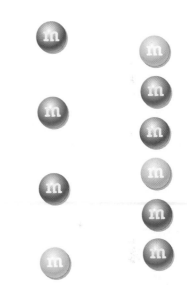

11.18 The M&M Version of Piaget's Marble Test Children who did not succeed on Piaget's marble test were able to choose the row that contained more items when those items were M&Ms and the test question was phrased as "Which row would you like to eat?"

infantile amnesia The inability to remember events from early childhood.

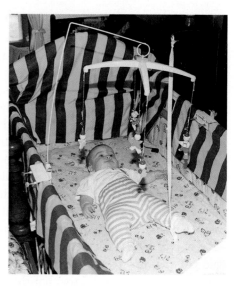

11.19 The Memory-Retention Test A three-month-old was trained in the mobile task and later given a retention test. During training (left), the infant's kicks move the mobile by means of the ankle ribbon attached to the mobile hook. During baseline and all retention tests (right), the ankle ribbon and the mobile are connected to different hooks so that kicks cannot move the mobile.

suggest that childhood memory increases with the acquisition of language because the ability to use words and concepts aids in memory retention.

INACCURATE MEMORY Young children often have difficulty knowing where they learned something, which is called **source amnesia**. Even when tested immediately after being presented with information, young children (age three) forget the source of the information faster than do older children (age five) (Gopnik & Graf, 1988). Evidence from investigations of source amnesia suggests that many of your earliest memories may come from watching home movies or hearing stories from your parents—not from an actual memory you have of the events.

Children are also known to confabulate—make things up. The fact that children have underdeveloped frontal lobes may explain why they are more likely than adults to engage in this behavior. Confabulation happens most when children are asked about personal experiences rather than general knowledge. In one study, preschool children were interviewed repeatedly and asked to think hard to remember if they had ever gotten their fingers caught in a mousetrap. They were asked to visualize the event, including thinking about the scene (who was with them, what they were wearing, etc.). After the children spent ten weeks thinking about the event, a new adult interviewed them and asked them if they had ever gotten their fingers caught in a mousetrap. Sixty percent of the children provided false narratives, telling a story about this happening to them and behaving as if it really had. Many of the children developed very elaborate stories with numerous details about why their fingers had been caught in a mousetrap and how it had felt (Bruck & Ceci, 1993).

Humans Learn from Interacting with Others

To protect ourselves and to succeed in life, we need to be aware of the intentions of other people. For example, defensive driving is based on the idea that you can predict the potential erratic actions of others. When people are deciding whether to go on a date or begin a physical relationship, they often want to know what the other person has in mind. According to contemporary thinking among developmental psychologists, the early social interactions between infant and caregiver are essential for understanding other people and being able to communicate with them through language. Knowing that other people have mental states and using that information to infer what another person is feeling or thinking is termed **theory of mind**.

source amnesia A type of amnesia that occurs when a person remembers an event but cannot remember where they encountered the information.

theory of mind The term used to describe the ability to explain and predict other people's behavior as a result of recognizing their mental state.

Piaget proposed that very young children are not good at understanding how others think. He characterized those in the preoperational stage as *egocentric:* They are not able to see another person's point of view, only their own. For instance, children at this stage might stand in front of a television and not understand that they are blocking the screen for others, because they can see the picture just fine. Evidence from the past two decades, however, has shown that young children are less egocentric than Piaget believed. Beginning in infancy, young children come to understand that other people's actions are performed for a reason—that the actions are intentional (Gergely & Csibra, 2003; Somerville & Woodward, 2005). Recognizing the intentionality of actions reflects the growing capacity for theory of mind. This is what allows us to understand, predict, and attempt to influence other people's behavior (Baldwin & Baird, 2001). In one recent study, infants watched as an adult handed them a toy. On some trials, the child did not receive the toy because the adult was unwilling to give it (e.g., she teased the child with the toy or played with it herself) or because she was unable to give it (e.g., she was distracted by a ringing telephone or accidentally dropped the toy). Children older than nine months showed greater signs of impatience (such as reaching for the toy) when the adult was unwilling than when she was unable (Behne, Carpenter, Call, & Tomasello, 2005). Consider another study in which 15-month-old children imitated the actions of an adult trying to pull apart two halves of a dumbbell. On some trials, the children watched the adult's hand slip off the end of the dumbbell before she was successful in separating it. However, the children imitated the goal of separating the dumbbells, rather than simply imitating the adult's actual movements, which included slipping (Meltzoff, 1995). These studies and others provide strong evidence that children begin to read intentions in the first year of life, and that they become very good at doing so by the end of their second year.

Understanding intentions helps children predict and understand other people's actions, but they do not develop the ability to take another person's perspective until they are around four or five years of age. For instance, children younger than four have difficulty understanding that others can have beliefs that are not true, or beliefs that differ from their own. Consider the *false belief test,* in which, in order to predict a person's actions, children are required to understand that people can sometimes act based on false information. In the classic example (Figure 11.20), Sally places a marble in a basket and then leaves the room. Ann comes in, removes the marble from the basket, and places it in a box. A child who has watched both actions take place is asked to guess where Sally will look for the marble when she comes back in the room. In order to do this correctly, the child must develop a theory: Sally put the marble in the basket; Sally doesn't know Ann moved the marble, so Sally will still look in the basket. Normally, developing children are able to solve this by age four.

Children's development of theory of mind and success at the false belief test appear to coincide with the frontal lobes becoming relatively mature. The importance of the frontal lobes is also supported by research with adults. In brain-imaging studies, prefrontal brain regions become active when people are asked to think about others' mental states. People with damage to this region have difficulty attributing mental states to others in stories (Stone, Baron-Cohen, & Knight, 1998). Futhermore, if the capacity for

How does theory of mind enable social interaction?

11.20 An Example of a Child's Theory of Mind When a child acquires theory of mind, she is able to understand that different individuals have different perspectives and knowledge based on their individual experiences.

Sally puts her marble in the basket.

Sally goes away.

Ann moves the marble.

"Where will Sally look for her marble?"

theory of mind is linked to brain development, then children in different cultures ought to solve the false belief test at about the same age. Indeed, a recent study comparing children from Canada, India, Peru, Samoa, and Thailand found that children crossed the false-belief milestone at around age five in each culture (Callaghan et al., 2005).

Finally, theory of mind, like math or physics, may develop independent of other brain functions, such as the ability to reason or general intelligence. Evidence for this comes from the study of children with the communications disorder autism. They are not able to solve the Sally/Ann problem. In contrast, children with Down syndrome can solve this problem, indicating that it is not a general intelligence or reasoning mechanism that governs theory of mind, since Down children are impaired in these areas. You will learn more about autism in Chapter 13.

Language Develops in an Orderly Fashion

The ability to communicate through language allows humans to learn a great deal more than can other animals. Through language we are able to communicate across cultures, sharing the new inventions and technologies that have shaped modern civilization. How does this remarkable ability develop?

As the brain develops, so does the ability to speak and form sentences. For the most part, the stages of language development are remarkably uniform across individuals, although the rate at which language develops does vary. We saw in the case of Genie that the ability to speak can be disrupted by social isolation and lack of exposure to language. According to Michael Tomasello (1999), the early social interactions between infant and caregiver are essential to understanding other people and being able to communicate with them through language. Research has demonstrated that infants and caregivers attend to objects in their environment together; this joint attention facilitates learning to speak (Baldwin, 1991). This capacity to share our mental actions with others and the motivation to do so makes humans unique in the animal kingdom. Language allows us to live in complex societies because it teaches us the history, rules, and values of our culture. We now examine how humans learn language.

FROM ZERO TO 60,000 Language is a system of using sounds and symbols to communicate. It can be viewed as a hierarchical structure (Figure 11.21) in which sentences can be broken down into smaller units consisting of phrases, which can be broken down further into groups of words, each of which consists of *morphemes* (the smallest units that have meaning, including suffixes and prefixes), which consist of *phonemes* (basic sounds). The system of rules that govern how words are combined into phrases and phrases are combined to make sentences is the *syntax* of a language. Here we describe how children learn the syntax of language. Babies may not be born talking, but experiments have revealed that they are born understanding the difference between their parents' language and another language. Babies can distinguish between different *phonemes,* which are the minimal speech sounds that signal a difference in meaning between words. For example, "cat" and "pat" mean different things in spite of /c/ and /p/ not carrying any meaning in themselves. The psychologists Peter Eimas and Peter Jusczyk devised a version of the habituation technique that allows experimenters to study when very young infants prefer to listen to one thing over another or note a difference between sounds. They inserted the switch for a tape recorder into a rubber nipple. When infants sucked on the nipple, the sucking turned on the recorder, which played a syllable such as "ba" each time the sucking occurred. Once the babies tired of the syllable, their sucking rate decreased.

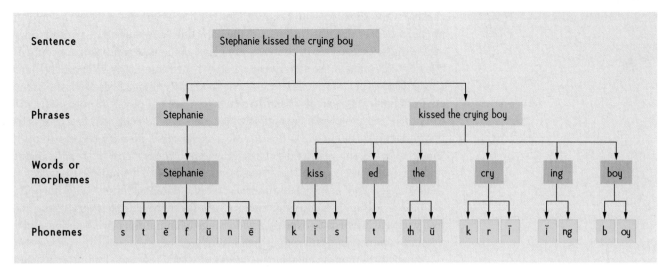

11.21 The Units of Language

Once the infants were habituated, the researchers changed the syllable, to "pa," for instance. The sucking rate increased when the babies heard the new sound (Eimas, Siqueland, Jusczyk, & Vigorito, 1971). Researchers used this same technique to show that French babies as young as four days old sucked more in response to French than to Russian, indicating that they had learned the sound of their native language in the womb or in the first days outside the womb (Mehler et al., 1988).

English has over 40 phonemes, and each phoneme has a distinct sound. For example, the distinction between /r/ and /l/ is important in English: "read" means something quite different than "lead." However, Japanese does not distinguish those two sounds and instead makes other distinctions that English does not make. After several months of exposure to their own language, infants lose the ability to distinguish between sounds that do not matter in their language (Kuhl, 2004; Werker, Gilbert, Humphrey, & Tees, 1981).

Given that babies can hear the difference between sounds immediately after birth and continue to learn the sounds of their own languages, how does this affect the development of spoken words? A normal adult knows about 60,000 words. Humans appear to go from babbling as babies to a full adult vocabulary without working very hard at it. Speech production follows a distinct path. During the first months of life, newborns' actions generate all of their sounds: crying, fussing, eating, and breathing. The sounds are cries, gurgles, or grunts. Cooing and laughing appear at three to five months. From five to seven months babies begin babbling, using consonants and vowels. From seven to eight months they babble in syllables (ba-ba-ba, dee-dee-dee). By the first year, the syllables are mixed (ba-dee, dah-dee), and those babbles begin to take on the sounds and rhythms of the infant's native language.

Babbling may be an infant's way of testing the system—checking that the basic parts exist and how they get tossed together. The onset of language is marked by the first words that a baby utters and appears to understand. Words consist of *morphemes,* which are, as mentioned, the smallest units of speech that have meaning. Sometimes a word is a morpheme, such as *cat,* but prefixes and suffixes are also morphemes, such as *-ed,* which changes a verb to past tense (See Figure 11.21).

First words tend to appear around age one. Babies most often first utter two types of words. One type is known as *performatives,* wordlike sounds that are learned in a context and that a baby may not be using to represent a meaning. For instance, a baby says, "Hello" or something that sounds like it when holding a phone. Does the baby know that "hello" is a greeting used to talk to someone on the other end of

Why do children lose the ability to discriminate sounds of foreign languages?

the line? Or is the baby simply imitating what it sees people do when they pick up the phone? Chances are it is the latter if the baby does not say "hello" in other appropriate settings. *True words,* in contrast, are clearly meant to represent concepts. For instance, "cat" names the family pet, "book" a bedtime story. When babies develop single words, they often use those words to identify things present in the immediate environment. They can also refer to things that are not physically present, as when a baby points to the cookie jar and says "cookie." It is curious that first words tend to be the same throughout the world. Most first words identify objects ("cat," "sky," "nose," "book"), the rest tend to be simple action words ("go," "up," "sit"), quantifiers ("all gone!" "more!"), qualities or adjectives ("hot"), socially interactive words ("bye," "hello," "yes," "no"), and even internal states ("boo-boo" after being hurt) (Pinker, 1984). Interestingly, as you might guess from these words, even very young children freely use early words to express a wide range of communicative functions, including naming, commenting, and requesting.

By about 18 months children begin to put words together, and their vocabularies start to grow rapidly. Rudimentary sentences of roughly two words or more emerge. The fascinating thing is that these minisentences, though missing words and grammatical markings, actually have a logic or "syntax." Typically the order of the words indicates what has happened or should happen: "Throw ball. All gone" roughly translates as "I threw the ball and now it's gone." In fact, the psychologist Roger Brown, often referred to as the father of child language for his pioneering research, called these utterances **telegraphic speech** because children speak as if they are sending a telegram—just bare-bones words without any frills but put together according to conventional rules.

As children begin to use language in more sophisticated ways, they make interesting errors in word formation and syntax. Sometimes children start to make mistakes at ages three to five with words they used correctly at age two or three. Psycholinguists believe this occurs because when children learn a new grammar rule, they tend to overapply it. For example, they learn that adding *-ed* to a verb in English makes something past tense. They then add *-ed* to every verb, including irregular verbs that do not follow that rule. For instance, they will say "runned" or "holded" even though they may have said "ran" or "held" at an earlier age. A similar pattern of errors is found with plurals. The rule to add *s* leads to errors such as "mouses" and "mans" when the rule is overapplied. Children do this despite having used the correct irregular plural at a younger age.

Although overgeneralizations are quite rare (Marcus, 1996; Marcus et al., 1992) in children's speech, they reflect an important aspect of language acquisition. Children are not simply repeating what they have heard others say, because they most likely have not heard anyone say "runned." Instead, these errors occur because children are able to use language in a generative way. Simply put, children have discovered a general rule of grammar, but they have not yet discovered that there are exceptions to the rule. Children make more errors with words that are used less frequently (such as "drank" and "knew") because they have heard the irregular form less often. Adults tend to do the same thing; we are more likely to make errors on the past tenses of words such as "trod," "strove," or "slew" (saying "treaded," "strived," or "slayed") because those are words we do not use often (Pinker, 1994).

UNIVERSAL GRAMMAR Much of the research by linguists and psycholinguists is aimed at breaking down language production and comprehension into detailed steps to understand how language is assembled, produced, and understood. The linguist Noam Chomsky (Figure 11.22) transformed the field when he argued that language

telegraphic speech The tendency for children to speak using rudimentary sentences that are missing words and grammatical markings but follow a logical syntax.

How Do Children Learn about Their Worlds?

must be governed by "universal grammar," or innate knowledge of a set of universal and specifically linguistic elements and relations that form the heart of all human languages.

Until Chomsky came on the scene in the late 1950s, linguists had focused on analyzing language and identifying basic components of grammar. In his early work, Chomsky argued that the way people combine these elements to form sentences and convey meaning is only the *surface structure* of a language. He introduced the concept of *deep structure:* the implicit meanings of sentences. For instance, "The fat cat chased the rat" implies that there is a cat, it is fat, and it chased the rat. "The rat was chased by the fat cat" implies the same idea even though on the surface it is a different sentence. Chomsky believed that we automatically and unconsciously transform surface structure to deep structure. Research has shown that the underlying meaning of a sentence is what we remember, not its surface structure. For example, in studies in which subjects are shown sentences with similar meanings but different syntax, like the examples above, they can remember the point of the sentences, but not which version they saw (Sachs, 1967). For Chomsky, humans are born with a "language acquisition device" that contains universal grammar, but exposure to one's native language narrows down which grammatical rules are learned. All languages contain similar elements, such as nouns and verbs, but how they are arranged varies considerably across languages. Chomsky's ideas are supported by research that shows young infants can understand simple grammatical rules. Gary Marcus and colleagues (1999) familiarized seven-month-old infants with sentences of an ABA design, such as "ga ti ga" or "li na li." Subsequently, they found that infants showed a preference for sentences that followed a new pattern (ABB), such as "wo fe fe," indicating that they noticed the inconsistency. This pattern suggests that young infants have a built-in readiness to acquire grammar.

There is little doubt that environment greatly influences a child's acquisition of language, such as fine-tuning which grammar is used. Indeed, the fact that you speak English rather than Swahili is determined entirely by your environment. The Russian psychologist Lev Vygotsky developed the first major theory that emphasized the role of social and cultural context in cognition and language development. According to Vygotsky, humans are unique because they use symbols and psychological tools, such as speech, writing, maps, art, and so on, through which they create culture. Culture, in turn, dictates what people need to learn and the sorts of skills they need to develop. For example, some cultures might value science and rational thinking, whereas others might emphasize supernatural and mystical forces. Some cultures emphasize keeping social distance, whereas others encourage people to be in close proximity. These cultural values shape how people think about and relate to the world around them. Vygotsky distinguished between elementary mental functions, such as innate sensory experiences, and higher mental functions, such as language, perception, abstraction, and memory. As children develop, their elementary capacities are gradually transformed, primarily through the influence of culture.

Central to Vygotsky's theories is the idea that social context influences language development, which in turn influences cognitive development. Children start by directing their speech toward specific communications with others, such as asking for food or toys. As children develop, they begin directing speech toward themselves, as when they give themselves directions or talk to themselves while they play. Eventually, children internalize their words into inner speech, which comprises verbal thoughts that direct behavior and cognition. From this perspective, your thoughts are based on the language that you acquire through your culture, and this ongoing inner speech reflects higher-order cognitive processes.

Is language hardwired?

11.22 **Noam Chomsky** The father of modern linguistic theory.

SENSITIVE PERIODS As we noted earlier in the chapter, there are critical learning periods for certain cognitive skills. But for humans, these periods are not rigid or inflexible but rather are sensitive periods in which skills such as language are easiest to learn. Cases such as those of Genie and other children raised in deprived environments indicate that humans are best able to acquire language prior to puberty. The extent to which individuals can become multilingual after adolescence also supports a sensitive learning period. People who are truly bilingual or multilingual have generally acquired multiple languages before the age of 12. Adults who move to a new country rarely become as fluent as their children (Zatorre, 1989).

Interaction across cultures can shape language. *Creole* describes a language that evolves over time from the mixing of existing languages. Creole languages develop, for example, when several different cultures colonize a new place, as when the French established themselves in southern Louisiana and acquired slaves who were not native French-speakers. Creoles, which follow formal grammatical rules, develop out of more rudimentary communications. Populations that speak several different languages develop a new means for communicating, often mixing words from each group's native language into what is called a *pidgin,* which is an informal creole that lacks consistent grammatical rules. The linguist Derek Bickerton has found that the pidgin is then fully developed by the children of the colonists into its own language—a creole language—as the children hear the pidgin spoken by their parents and impose rules on it. Bickerton argues that this is evidence for built-in, universal grammar: The brain takes a nonconforming language, applies rules to it, and changes it.

Bickerton also found that creole languages formed in different parts of the world, with different combinations of languages, are more similar to each other in grammatical structure than to long-lived languages. Although somewhat controversial, he sees this as further evidence for built-in grammar, arguing that older languages have evolved away from the grammatical constructions most natural for the brain to impose, whereas creole languages have not been around long enough for this to happen. Thus creole languages may be similar because the brain imposes the same basic rules on a new language (Bickerton, 1998).

ACQUIRING LANGUAGE ON THE HANDS What would happen if we stripped the human brain of sound and speech? If sound perception and production are the key neurological determinants of early language acquisition, then babies exposed to signed languages should acquire these languages in fundamentally different ways. If, however, what makes human language special is its highly systematic patterns and the human brain's sensitivity to them, then signing and speaking babies should acquire their respective languages in highly similar ways.

To test this hypothesis, Laura Ann Petitto and her students videotaped deaf babies of deaf parents in households using two entirely different signed languages—American Sign Language (ASL) and the signed language of Quebec, langue des signes quebecoise (LSQ). They found that deaf babies exposed to signed languages from birth acquire these languages on an identical maturational time table as hearing babies acquire spoken languages (Petitto, 2000). This research teaches us that speech cannot alone be driving all of human language acquisition. It provides an exciting glimpse into language and the brain by showing us that humans must possess a biologically endowed sensitivity to aspects of the patterns of language—a sensitivity that launches a baby into the course of acquiring language.

ANIMAL COMMUNICATION We know that animals have ways of communicating with each other. But no other animal uses language the way humans do. Scientists have tried for years to teach language to chimpanzees, one of our nearest living relatives (along with bonobos). Chimps lack the vocal abilities to speak aloud, so studies have used sign language or visual cues to determine whether they understand words or concepts such as causation. Although chimpanzees can learn some words and have some sense of causation, other research challenges the idea that this means they have innate language abilities. Consider the work of psychologists Herbert Terrace, Laura Ann Petitto, and Tom Bever, who set out to test Noam Chomsky's assertion that language was a uniquely human trait by attempting to teach a chimpanzee language. Hopeful of success, they named the chimp Neam Chimpsky (nicknamed Nim) (Figure 11.23). But after years of teaching Nim American Sign Language, the team had to admit that Chomsky might be right.

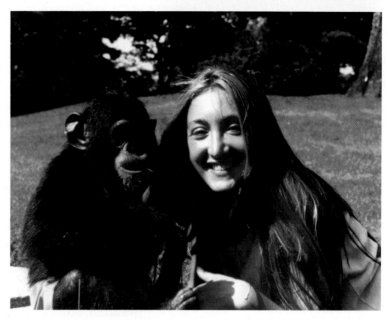

11.23 Laura Ann Petitto with Nim Chimpsky

Nim, like all other language-trained chimps, consistently failed to master key components of human language syntax. While Nim was quite adept at communicating with a small set of basic signs ("eat," "play," "more"), he never acquired the ability to generate creative, rule-governed sentences; he was like a broken record, talking about the same thing over and over again in the same old way. Crucially, unlike even the young child who names, comments, requests, and more with his or her first words, all the chimps used ASL almost exclusively to get something, to request. What the chimps seemed to appreciate was the power of language to obtain outcomes. In the end, the chimps could use bits and pieces of language only to get something from their caretakers (food, more food) rather than to truly express meanings, thoughts, and ideas by generating language (Petitto & Seidenberg, 1979).

How can we tell if animals use language?

Psychological Science *in Action*

Learning to Read

Reading, like speaking, is nearly effortless for most adults. When we look at letters, we see words and automatically derive meaning from them, even if they are misspelled. Try to look at the word *chocolate* without knowing what it means. But learning to read is challenging for most children, who struggle to figure out which symbols are letters, which letters clump together to make words, and which words go together to make meaningful sentences. So what are the best ways to teach children to read?

There are two major schools of thought regarding how to teach reading. Traditional methods use *phonics,* which teaches an association between letters and their phonemes (or sounds). Children learn to spell out words by how they sound. Because of the complexity of the English language, in which the sounds of letters can vary across words, some educators have advocated *whole-language* approaches, in which the emphasis is on meaning and understanding how words are connected in sentences. The whole-language approach has dominated in most American schools for the past two decades, perhaps in part because the philosophy that guides its instruction emphasizes student interest and enjoyment of reading. But does it do a better job than phonics in helping children learn to read? Across the United States, those who advocate whole-language instruction have vigorously debated those who argue that such methods are inferior to the traditional method of phonics. Let's look at the two methods in more detail.

Some form of the phonics method has been popular for teaching reading for over 200 years. In phonics, children learn the relation between letters of the alphabet and the sounds they make, including when they are combined. Thus a *t* is changed when it becomes *th* or *tr* or *st*. Children learn a small number of simple words that teach the sounds of letters across most words of the English language. Because of the irregularities in English, children first learn the general rules and then learn to recognize exceptions to those general rules. The emphasis with this approach is on memorizing the mappings between letters and their sounds, rather than on building vocabulary or processing the meaning of words.

The general idea behind whole-language instruction is that reading should follow the form of language, which requires deriving meaning from listening to a continuous stream of sound. Thus, children should learn to read the way they learn to talk. We do not process speech by breaking down the stream into phonemes; instead, we understand speech as a series of connected words that have meaning in the context of the entire sentence. According to this philosophy, people naturally and unconsciously learn to read by first learning individual words and then stringing them together. Proponents argue that breaking down words into sounds is unnatural, frustrating, and boring—therefore, using phonics is to be avoided.

Psychological science has made tremendous contributions to understanding not only how children learn to read, but also which educational practices work best for most children. A group of psychologists who are experts in reading reviewed the vast literature on how children learn to read and published a comprehensive report for the benefit of educators. From this research they conclude that some methods for teaching children to read are essential. Teachers who use these methods will be most effective in helping their students to become skilled readers (Rayner et al., 2001).

So, which is better? Classroom and laboratory research over the past three decades has consistently found evidence that phonics instruction is superior to whole-language methods in creating proficient readers (Rayneer, Foorman, Perfetti, Pesetsky, & Seidenberg, 2001). This is especially true for children who are at risk of becoming poor readers, such as those whose parents do not read to them on a regular basis. At the same time, the whole-language approach has clear benefits, with its emphasis on making reading fun and encouraging students to be creative and thoughtful. However, although whole-language approaches can motivate students to want to read, the students need the basic skills to do so, which are best provided through phonics. After all, reading is not fun when children struggle to identify words.

The phonics-versus-whole-language debate is an excellent example of how scientific research can contribute to figuring out important societal issues. The whole-language movement reflected a progressive philosophy that tried to foster a love of learning. Yet school districts that used this approach observed declines in national assessment tests, and a growing number of children developed reading problems. Parents responded by buying home reading programs that emphasized phonics and forming advocacy groups to change how reading is taught. The science of reading is clear—phonics works best (Figure 11.24). By sharing research with those who set education policy, psychological scientists are helping to make children more capable readers. ■

11.24 Phonics versus Whole-Language Approaches Although the whole-language method of teaching children to read has been popular in the last 20 years, researchers have found that phonics is a more effective way to create proficient readers.

the Principles | How Do Children Learn about Their Worlds?

Children acquire information through perception. Tests based on the fact that young infants look longer at novel stimuli than at familiar stimuli indicate that they are capable of learning very early. Piaget emphasized the consistent stages of cognitive development displayed by most young children. His influential theory suggested that each stage of learning builds on previous stages. However, recent evidence suggests that infants understand a great deal more about the physical properties of objects than was previously believed. For instance, infants can use the laws of physics and even perform simple arithmetic. An important part of learning occurs through social interaction, as young children develop the ability for theory of mind. This capacity allows people to survive in human society. A developing memory system helps children build a store of useful knowledge. The human capacity for language is innate, as there appear to be built-in methods of acquiring words and forming them into sentences. Although the development of language occurs in an orderly fashion, the specific language a child develops is influenced by environmental and cultural factors, such as exposure to the language spoken by caregivers and the creoles and pidgins that are used when groups who speak different languages interact. There are also sensitive periods during which language must be acquired in order to develop normally. These processes develop together to enable young children to learn and survive as they become members of society.

How Do Children and Adolescents Develop Their Identities?

As we go through childhood, we learn more about our worlds. We also begin to develop a sense of identity, of who we are. Identify formation is an important part of **social development**, which, as we described earlier, refers to the maturation of skills and abilities that enable us to interact with others. Many factors, including gender, play a role in shaping our sense of personal identify. What is amazing, however, is how unique each of us is even though we share so many genetic similarities and have so many common experiences. We each possess different habits, customs, personality characteristics, beliefs, skills, and even distinctive quirks. How people define themselves is influenced by the culture in which they are raised as well as the beliefs they hold about personal characteristics, such as race, sex, and age. The quest for identity is an important challenge during development. As children grow older and enter into **adolescence**, they seek to understand how they fit into the world and to imagine what kind of person they will become later in life. In this section we examine how a sense of identity develops.

social development The maturation of skills or abilities that enable people to live in a world with other people.

adolescence The transitional period between childhood and adulthood.

Gender Roles Are Determined by Cultural Norms

When people are asked to describe themselves, they often indicate whether they are female or male. Imagine for a second what you would be like if you were the same person but of the opposite sex—for many of us this is hard to do. Being a female or a

How does gender differ from sex?

"Do you know its sexual identity?"

male is central to how most people define themselves. But how different are men and women? Although the physical differences are obvious, such as in height and weight, how do women and men differ in psychological terms? Psychological scientists use the term *sex* to refer to biological differences between males and females, whereas the term **gender** is used for differences between males and females that result from socialization. According to evolutionary theory, sex differences ought to reflect different adaptive problems men and women face, and this is generally supported by research. But since men and women face similar adaptive problems, they are similar on most dimensions. Many of the differences between males and females have as much to do with socialization as with genetics.

Whether you think of yourself as a male or a female is part of your **gender identity**, which subsequently shapes how you behave. Children as young as one or two years old can tell you whether they are boys or girls. Once boys and girls discover that they are boys or girls, they seek out activities that are culturally sex appropriate. In North American culture, if not everywhere, most parents and teachers discourage girls from playing too roughly and boys from crying. The separation of boys and girls into different play groups is also a powerful socializing force.

Which behaviors boys and girls display is determined in part by cultural rules about sex-appropriate behavior. **Gender roles** are behaviors that differ between men and women because of cultural influences, expectancies, or learning. For instance, you may believe that it is more appropriate for men than for women to initiate sexual encounters or to repair cars for a living. Although many people now object to such beliefs, their existence is easy to observe. As mentioned in Chapter 8, when young children are asked to draw a picture of a scientist, most draw a man (Chambers, 1983). Children develop their expectations about gender through observing their parents, peers, and teachers, as well as through media. Cultural norms and media have a strong influence on the development of gender roles. Most news anchors are male, most firefighters are male, most nurses in films and on television are female, and so on. These portrayals help to develop and reinforce gender stereotypes, commonly held beliefs about men and women. We can find many examples of stereotyping in children's toys (Figure 11.25).

Gender schemas are cognitive structures that influence how people perceive the behaviors of females and males. They play a powerful role in establishing gender identity. A gender schema acts as a lens through which people see the world. People raised in environments that make clear distinctions between men and women become *gender typed*; that is, they expect large differences between males and females. The psychologist Sandra Bem measures degrees of gender typing by administering a questionnaire that asks people the extent to which traits that are typical of men and women describe them. People who rate themselves high on stereotypically masculine traits (e.g., competitiveness) and low on stereotypically feminine traits (e.g., tenderness) are labeled *masculine;* those who rate themselves high on feminine and low on masculine traits are labeled *feminine;* and those who rate themselves equally on both types of traits are *androgynous.* Bem believes that being androgynous is advantageous because it allows for more flexibility in social behavior. Conversely, her studies show that being sex typed can be cognitively efficient during tasks that benefit from encoding by gender, such as predicting whether a mechanic is likely to be male or female (Bem, 1975; Bem, Martyna, & Watson, 1976).

gender A term that refers to the culturally constructed differences between males and females.

gender identity Personal beliefs about whether one is male or female.

gender roles The characteristics associated with men and women because of cultural influence or learning.

gender schemas Cognitive structures that influence how people perceive the behaviors of men and women.

Situational factors also contribute to gender identity. According to a theory proposed by social psychologists Kay Deaux and Brenda Major (1987), the interaction between people and a specific situation *creates* gender-related behaviors. Deaux and Major accept the idea that people have beliefs and expectations about how men and women differ, but they emphasize that people of both sexes act differently depending on the situation. For instance, men may talk about football and cars around their male friends, but they are likely to change the topic when women are around.

A study of young women talking to either their boyfriends or their casual male friends on the telephone illustrates how situation alters gender-related responses. When the women talked to their boyfriends, their voices changed to a higher pitch and became softer and more relaxed, relative to the way they talked to their male friends. The way they spoke to their boyfriends was also more babylike, feminine, and absentminded, as rated by objective judges. When asked, the women said they knew they had taken on a different manner of speaking to their boyfriends relative to how they spoke to their male friends. The women reported doing this in order to communicate affection for their boyfriends (Montepare & Vega, 1988). Likewise, experiments have shown that heterosexual young men behave in a more masculine fashion when they think they are talking to a homosexual man versus when they talk to a heterosexual man (Kite & Deaux, 1986).

Although males and females are similar in many respects, there are sex differences based on biology and gender differences influenced by culture. Research in psychological science has identified some differences in how the brains of men and women differ, as when men show greater responsiveness to pictures of sexual imagery (see Chapter 4). However, research has not yet determined whether this is due to some inherent property of the male brain or to the way boys are treated during development. In terms of how we define ourselves as males and females, both nature and nurture play prominent roles.

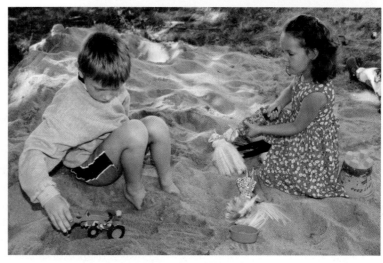

11.25 The Development of Gender Roles Many children's toys may promote gender stereotyping.

Profiles in Psychological Science

How Nature Made Him

How much of gender identity is determine by nature and nurture? On April 27, 1966, seven-month-old twin boys named Bruce and Brian Reimer were brought to St. Boniface Hospital in Winnipeg, Canada, for routine circumcision. Unfortunately, during the first operation, Bruce's penis was badly damaged. Its condition deteriorated over the next several days, and within the week it shriveled up and disappeared. (It should be noted that after what happened to Bruce, no attempt was made to circumcise Brian.) The accident and the events that followed changed not only the lives of the Reimer family but also psychologists' beliefs about the concept of gender.

As recounted in John Colapinto's 2000 book *As Nature Made Him: The Boy Who Was Raised as a Girl,* Bruce's parents, Janet and Ron, decided to investigate whether he should undergo sexual reassignment and be raised as a girl. The process had never been attempted on a child born with normal genitalia; previous sexual reassignment cases had involved hermaphrodite children, who were born with ambiguous genitalia. They contacted the world-renowned (and controversial) sexologist John Money at Johns Hopkins University, who convinced the Reimers that sexual reassignment was the best course of action for Bruce's psychological well-being. Bruce was castrated when he was 22 months old, renamed Brenda, and raised as a girl (Figure 11.26). Throughout the 1970s and 1980s, media accounts and psychology textbooks recounted the story as demonstrating that gender was the result of socialization rather than biology. Whether one was a boy or a girl was the result of how one was treated, not of genes or biology. Unfortunately, Colapinto's recent analysis indicates that Brenda's sexual reassignment was a failure from the start.

Brenda's life can be described as tumultuous at best, hellish at worst. Although her parents let her hair grow long, dressed her in feminine colors and clothing styles, and encouraged her to play with other girls, by all accounts Brenda was not comfortable or happy being a girl. She was teased incessantly for her rough and aggressive ways. It got worse when Brenda was given hormones at age 11 to initiate development of secondary sexual characteristics. The development of breasts was a source of intense embarrassment and horror for Brenda that did not fade with time.

As the years passed, Janet and Ron were finally forced to consider that Brenda was not—nor would ever truly be—a girl. After 15 years of family and peer problems and intense psychological troubles, Brenda was told the truth about what had happened. A flood of emotions welled up within her, but the most overwhelming feeling was relief. In her own words, Brenda recalled that day: "I was relieved. Suddenly it all made sense why I felt the way I did. I wasn't some sort of weirdo. I wasn't crazy."

Brenda immediately decided to return to being male. She stopped hormone therapy. She changed her name to David, which she chose because of the biblical story of David and Goliath. Although he had serious adjustment problems for a few years, David eventually sorted them out. New surgical techniques allowed physicians to provide David with a functional artificial penis that could be used for sexual intercourse. At the age of 23, he met a woman with three children. Jane and David fell in love. For many years, David lived a happy family life (Figure 11.27), but a series of financial setbacks and the death of his twin brother led him to become despondent. David killed himself in May 2004 at age 38. Whether the stress of being a boy raised as a girl contributed to problems with identity that troubled him throughout his adult life is unclear. What we learned from David's life is that one's gender identity is not shaped solely by whether one is treated as a boy or as a girl. ■

11.26 Brian and Bruce Reimer A photo of Brian (at left) and Bruce (Brenda) Reimer taken when they were children. The fact that they were identical twins made the situation ideal for studying the effects of culture on gender identity.

11.27 David (Bruce) Reimer

Friends Influence Adolescent Identity and Behavior

Developmental psychologists increasingly recognize the importance of peers in shaping identity. Children, regardless of their culture, tend to spend a large amount of their time interacting with other children, usually playing. Play takes numerous forms and helps children learn and practice skills that will be valuable in adulthood.

In developmental terms, attention to peers begins at the end of the first year of life, when infants begin to imitate other children and to smile and make vocalizations and other specific social signals to their peers (Brownell & Brown, 1992). Children of all ages learn how to behave from their friends, in part because they receive social rewards or punishments for behaving appropriately or inappropriately. Thus, early friends are both playmates and teachers.

How children compare themselves with peers also influences the development of identity as they come to know their personal strengths and weaknesses. Adolescence is a period of struggle to answer such essential questions as Who am I? and Where am I going? It is thought that adolescents often question who they are because of three changes: (1) changing physical appearance, which leads to examining self-image; (2) more sophisticated cognitive abilities, which prompt increased introspection; and (3) heightened pressure to prepare for the future and, in particular, to make career choices. Establishing a personal identity means breaking away from childhood beliefs by questioning and challenging parental and societal ideas (Erikson, 1968). Adolescents explore alternative belief systems and wonder what they would be like if they were raised in other cultures or in other times. The crisis is the search for an identity that "fits." As part of the search for identity, they may form friendships with other adolescents with similar values and worldviews. Interestingly, despite wide differences in geographic regions, peer groups tend to be described by a fairly small set of stereotypic names: jocks, brains, loners, druggies, nerds, and other not-so-flattering designations.

PARENTS AND PEERS In the last decade, the impact of parents versus peers on young people has become a controversial topic in developmental psychology. People often describe individuals as "coming from a good home" or as having "fallen in with the wrong crowd"; these clichés reflect the importance that is placed on both parents and peers in influencing an individual. In 1995, Judith Rich Harris suggested that beyond choosing where to live and what schools to send their children to, parents contribute surprisingly little to a child's social development in adolescence. Harris reviewed a number of psychological studies and concluded that parents have "no important long-term effects on the development of their child's personality" (p. 458). As mentioned in Chapter 3 and discussed in greater detail in Chapter 12, once you control for the genes they share, siblings raised in the same house are no more alike than strangers plucked off the street. Likewise, twin studies indicate that growing up with the same parents has only a small influence on personality. Harris posited that a child's peers are the most important influence when it comes to socialization. Harris's work is based largely on her *group socialization theory,* which proposes that children learn two sets of behaviors, one for inside the home and one for outside. The behaviors and responses children learn inside the home, such as those typically taught by the parents early in life, are not useful in outside social contexts. According to Harris, only those behaviors learned outside the home have long-term effects on personality and adult behavioral outcomes. Although Harris's theoretical stance has received a great deal of criticism, it has stimulated a fresh look at the social lives of children and the importance of peers.

Are parents or peers more important for social development?

In contrast to Harris's theory, a substantial amount of research has confirmed the influence of parents throughout the individual's life. Significantly, researchers have emphasized that neither the peer group nor the family can be assigned the primary role in a child's social development. Instead, the two contexts play complementary roles. B. Bradford Brown and his colleagues (1993) argue that the influence of parents is actually multifaceted. Parents not only contribute to specific individual behaviors but also affect social development indirectly by influencing the choices the child makes about what kind of crowd to join. In observations of 695 young people from childhood through adolescence, Robert and Beverly Cairns (1994) found that parents and teachers played a major role in realigning social groups so that they were consistent with family norms.

Identity Includes Moral Values

Do you view yourself as a moral person? Morality is an important component of social development because it involves choices people make that affect the lives of others, such as whether to take actions that may harm another or that may break implicit or explicit social contracts. Thus, moral development concerns the way in which people learn to decide between behaviors with competing social outcomes. Typically, morality has been divided into moral reasoning, which rests on cognitive processes, and moral emotions. Of course, cognition and affect are intertwined: Research has shown that if people lack adequate cognitive abilities, their moral emotions may not translate into moral behaviors; similarly, moral reasoning is enhanced by moral emotions.

Psychologists who study the cognitive processes of moral behavior have focused largely on Lawrence Kohlberg's stage theory. Kohlberg tested moral reasoning skills by asking people to respond to hypothetical situations in which a main character is faced with a moral dilemma, such as having to steal a drug to save his dying wife. Kohlberg was most concerned with the reasons children provided for their answers. He devised a theory of moral judgment that involved three levels of moral reasoning. Children in the *preconventional level* classify answers in terms of self-interest or pleasurable outcomes. For example, a child at this level may say, "He should steal the drug if he really likes his wife." At the *conventional* level responses conform to rules of law and order or focus on others' disapproval, such as "He shouldn't take the drug because it is wrong to steal, so everyone will think he is a bad person." At the highest, *postconventional* level, responses center around complex reasoning about abstract principles and values, such as "Sometimes people have to break the law if the law is unjust."

Moral reasoning theories have been faulted for emphasizing the cognitive aspects of morality. Some theorists contend that moral reasoning, as such, fails to predict moral behavior. These psychological scientists believe that moral actions, such as helping others in need, are influenced more by emotions than by cognitive processes.

MORAL EMOTIONS Research on the emotional components of moral behavior has focused largely on empathy, sympathy, guilt, and shame. These are called moral emotions because they relate to moral behaviors (as opposed to the cognitive processes, which predict moral reasoning). Along with embarrassment, they are considered "self-conscious" emotions, because they require comprehension of the self as a causal agent and an evaluation of one's own responses. Moral emotions form early in life, though they emerge later than primary emotions (such as happiness or anger), which is why they are also called secondary emotions.

Psychologists differentiate between empathy and sympathy. Empathy is an emotional state that arises from understanding another's emotional state in a manner similar to what the other person is feeling or would be expected to feel in a given situation. In contrast, sympathy arises from feelings of concern, pity, or sorrow for another (Eisenberg, 2000). When someone feels empathy, he feels *with* the other person, whereas when someone feels sympathy, she feels *for* the other person.

Recent research has asked whether parents' behaviors influence their children's level of moral emotions or prosocial behavior (see also Chapter 10). Parents of sympathetic children tend to be high in sympathy themselves, to allow their children to express negative emotions in a manner that does not harm others, to not express hostility in the home, to help their children cope with negative emotions, and to promote an understanding of and focus on others. In contrast, parents whose children were high in shame tended to show frequent anger, to be lax in discipline, and to not respond positively to appropriate behavior in the child (Ferguson & Stegge, 1995).

The interaction between the child and the parents is important in the development of moral emotions. Research has shown the value of reasoning with the child about his or her behavior, which involves inductive reasoning, as exemplified by the statements, "You made Chris cry. It's not nice to hit." Inductive reasoning on the part of the parents promotes sympathetic attitudes, feelings of guilt, and an awareness of others' feelings. One study reported that when mothers of four-year-olds commented on emotions and intentions ("you didn't mean to hurt him") and made evaluative statements ("you were good to do that for her"), their children were more likely to show appropriate forms of guilt and regret after misbehavior (Laible & Thompson, 2000). Attachment styles, too, have been linked to the presence of moral emotions. A secure attachment style between mother and child has been shown to promote appropriate guilt, empathy, and sympathy.

PHYSIOLOGICAL BASIS OF MORALITY Some evidence from the biological level of analysis indicates that moral emotions are based in physiological mechanisms that help people make decisions. Recall from Chapter 10 that Damasio's somatic-marker hypothesis states that people have a visceral response to real or imagined outcomes and that this response aids decision making. Damasio found that patients with damage to the prefrontal cortex fail to become emotionally involved in decision making because their somatic markers are not engaged. Damasio and colleagues (Anderson, Bechara, Damasio, Tranel, & Damasio, 1999) recently studied two people who had experienced prefrontal damage during infancy. Both of these individuals showed serious deficiencies in moral and social reasoning. When given Kohlberg's moral dilemma task, both patients scored at the preconventional level. These patients also neglected social and emotional factors in their life decisions. Both failed to express empathy, remorse, or guilt for wrongdoing, and neither had particularly good parenting skills. One engaged in petty thievery, was verbally and physically threatening (once to the point of physical assault), and frequently lied for no obvious reason. Thus, the frontal lobes appear to support the capacity for morality. However, it is also clear that children develop a sense of morality through socialization, especially from their parents. The development of a personal code of ethics plays a prominent role in how people define themselves.

People Define Themselves in Terms of Race and Ethnicity

There are approximately six billion people on earth. Given that these people fall into a variety of groups, how individuals develop a sense of their own and others' racial or ethnic identities is an important component of social development. Researchers have studied how children acquire the racial and ethnic categories prevalent in their community, identify their own race or ethnic group, and form stable attitudes toward their own and others' groups (Spencer & Markstrom-Adams, 1990).

Several studies have demonstrated that by the time children are four years old, they are already beginning to categorize others ethnically and racially. In one study, children demonstrated that they can sort dolls and pictures into racial categories (Bigler & Liben, 1993). These results, however, do not reveal how this ability contributes to the way a child develops ethnic stereotypes or self-concepts. Understanding how children come to form categories about race and ethnicity has been a controversial topic. The majority opinion to date is that shortly after children acquire the ability to make categorical distinctions about ethnicity and race, they become aware of their own ethnicity and form judgments about it. Their attitudes toward their own and other people's ethnicity depend on both the attitudes of their adult caregivers and their perceptions of the power and wealth of their own group in relation to other groups.

The process of identity formation in a country like the United States, where people of so many ethnicities live together, is particularly complicated. Due to prejudice and discrimination and the accompanying barriers to economic opportunities, children of ethnic minorities often face challenges with regard to the development of their ethnic identity. The factors that influence this process vary widely among individuals and groups. For example, Spencer and Markstrom-Adams (1990) have reported that skin color is more central to ethnic identity among African Americans and Native Americans than among Hispanic Americans. Children entering middle childhood have acquired an awareness of their ethnic identity to the extent that they know the label and attributes that the dominant culture applies to their ethnic group. Many researchers believe that during middle childhood and adolescence, children in ethnic minority groups often engage in additional processes aimed at ethnic identity formation (Phinney, 1990).

In this section we have examined how identity develops from childhood into adolescence. But development does not stop when people become adults. Psychologists now are interested in how people continue to develop across the life span. In the next section we will examine how cognition and social behavior change as people mature through adulthood.

REVIEWING **the Principles** | How Do Children and Adolescents Develop Their Identities?

How people define themselves is influenced by cultural beliefs about factors such as race, sex, and age. From an early age, children classify themselves on the basis of their biological sex, but how they come to understand the meaning of being a boy or a girl is largely determined through the socialization of gender roles, in which children adopt behaviors that are viewed as appropriate for their sex. Adolescents struggle for identity by questioning social values and personal goals, as they try to figure out who they are and what they want to become. Moral development helps adolescents define what they value and what is important to them. Finally, race and ethnicity shape our beliefs and attitudes regarding how we fit into the culture in which we are raised.

What Brings Meaning to Adulthood?

For many years developmental psychologists focused on childhood and adolescence, as if by age twenty most important aspects of development had occurred and little was left to consider. In recent decades, researchers working in a wide range of fields have demonstrated that important changes in physiology, cognition, and social behavior continue throughout adulthood into old age. Therefore many contemporary psychological scientists consider development from a *life-span perspective*, trying to understand how mental activity and social relations change over the entire course of life. It's worth noting here that the research shows that we should not automatically equate growing old with despair. In fact, there are many positive things that happen as we grow older. Although aging is associated with significant cognitive and physical decline, it remains an important part of life that can be very meaningful. As people live longer, understanding old age becomes especially important.

One of the first researchers to take this approach was Erik Erikson (Figure 11.28), who proposed a theory of development that emphasizes age-related psychological processes and their effects on social functioning across the life span. Erikson thought of development as composed of eight stages, ranging from an infant's first year to old age. Further, he conceptualized each stage as having a developmental "crisis" to be confronted, although the term refers more to a development challenge than to some form of emergency. Each challenge provides an opportunity for psychological progression, but if progress is not made, further psychosocial development is impaired (see Table 11.1). Three of Erikson's stages take place during adulthood and for our purposes we are going to focus on those stages exclusively.

11.28 Erik Erikson Erikson proposed a stage theory of identity development. This picture was taken in 1988, with his wife Joan.

TABLE 11.1	Erikson's Stages of Identity		
STAGE	AGE	IDENTITY CHALLENGE	SUCCESSFUL RESOLUTION OF CHALLENGE
Infancy	0–2	Trust vs. mistrust	Children learn that the world is safe and that people are loving and reliable.
Toddler	2–3	Autonomy vs. shame and doubt	Children are encouraged to explore the environment and gain feelings of independence and positive self-esteem.
Preschool	4–6	Initiative vs. guilt	Children develop a sense of purpose by taking on responsibilities, but also develop the capacity to feel guilty for misdeeds.
Childhood	7–12	Industry vs. inferiority	By working successfully with others, children learn to feel competent.
Adolescence	13–19	Ego identity vs. role confusion	Through exploration of different social roles, adolescents develop a sense of identity.
Young adulthood	20s	Intimacy vs. isolation	Young adults gain the ability to commit to long-term relationships.
Middle adulthood	30s to 50s	Generativity vs. stagnation	Adults gain a sense that they are contributing to the future and caring for future generations.
Old age	60s and beyond	Integrity vs. despair	Older adults feel a sense of satisfaction that they have lived a good life and developed wisdom.

Erikson's sixth stage involves close relationships and the challenge of *intimacy versus isolation,* which means the formation and maintenance of committed friendships and romantic relationships. Essentially, it involves finding someone with whom to share your life. The seventh stage takes place during middle life. Termed *generativity versus stagnation,* this stage involves producing or giving back to society, and usually includes parenthood or engaging in activities, such as volunteering, that bring additional meaning to life. Erikson's last stage, *integrity versus despair,* takes place in old age. In this stage, older adults reflect on their lives and respond either positively to having had a worthwhile life or with regret and sadness at what has passed. Erikson's theory highlights the importance of considering how people care about different things as they grow older. In this section we examine the physical, cognitive, and social changes that occur during adulthood and how they affect people's quality of life.

Adults Are Affected by Life Transitions

For many young people, college is a magical time of life. Meeting new friends, learning new ideas, having a good time, all occurring as adolescence emerges into adulthood. People in their twenties and thirties undergo incredible changes as they pursue career goals and make long-term commitments in relationships, such as getting married and raising children. All this corresponds to the Eriksonian idea that challenges face us as we mature through adulthood. In essence, the major challenges of adulthood reflect the need to find meaning in our lives. If life involved only getting up in the morning, working, eating, and sleeping, what would be the point? Most people seek more than that from life. They want jobs that fulfill them and they want family members to share their lives. Let's examine how the quest to satisfy these needs influences the course of human lives.

CAREER Children are commonly asked what they want to be when they grow up. Although some college students are committed to achieving specific career goals, as when someone has wanted to be a physician since age ten, many others struggle to find careers that they hope will be satisfying. You will work around 100,000 hours in your life. Imagine spending all that time on something you don't like. Career plays an important role in most people's lives. A good job not only provides material rewards, such as money to buy things you like, but also can bring a sense of accomplishment and purpose. The right career helps you feel that you contribute to society and that other people recognize you for doing so. It brings meaning to your life and helps you grow as a person and become better able to fulfill your life's goals. So how do you find the right job?

Although selecting a career path is rarely easy, one of the most important principles is to be honest with yourself. Although you don't necessarily need a specific plan upfront, you have to assess your strengths and weaknesses and try to develop some general ideas of what kind of career you can pursue effectively and what kind is likely to be fulfilling to you personally. Career counselors often advise people to follow their passions rather than the wishes of parents or family members. It is not uncommon for people who have been toiling away in corporate or professional jobs to have midlife crises in which they realize their jobs fail to bring them any meaningful satisfaction. Many times this happens because people

THE SEVEN AGES OF MAN

SLEEPY HAPPY DOPEY

BASHFUL DOC SNEEZY GRUMPY

focus on money rather than how the right job would allow them to be the type of parent, spouse, or community member they want to be. From an Eriksonian perspective, the motive for generativity inspires us to want to give something of ourselves to society. In the end, the right career allows you to pursue your interests and gain a sense of accomplishment as you balance family and other life goals.

MARRIAGE In adulthood, people devote a great deal of effort to achieving and maintaining satisfying relationships. Indeed, the vast majority of people around the world marry at some point in their lives or form some type of permanent bond with a relationship partner. The search for the right partner is an important feature in contemporary Western society, although in other cultures parents arrange marriages and decide whom their son or daughter will marry. Although it is hard for many Westerners to imagine, arranged marriages tend to be stable and the people within them quite satisfied.

One clear advantage to marriage is that married people tend to be healthier and to live longer (Berkman, 1984; Gottman, 1998). For example, unmarried heart patients are much more likely to die within five years of being diagnosed with heart disease (Williams et al., 1992). Men who are married survive much longer with prostrate cancer than those who are unmarried, divorced, separated, or widowed (Krongrad, Lai, Burke, Goodkin, & Lai, 1996). A number of theories try to explain why married people live longer, but most of them focus on how marital partners can support each other, as, for example, helping each other deal with stress or assisting each other in meeting life's demands. Married people may also influence the behavior of their partners by encouraging them to be healthy, such as by eating properly and getting exercise.

Given the likelihood that most people will marry, what are the chances that their marriages will be satisfying and stable? According to national surveys, at any given time the vast majority of married people report satisfaction with their marriages. The people who are most satisfied are those who have sufficient economic resources, share decision making, and together hold the view that marriage should be a lifelong commitment (Amato, Johnson, Booth, & Rogers, 2003). Yet in contemporary American society, approximately half of marriages end in divorce. Of those couples who stay together, a sizeable portion experience marital problems. It has been estimated that the chance of ending up in a happy and intact marriage is about 1 in 3 (Glenn, 1998). In Chapter 15 we will discuss ways to have a more satisfying relationship.

HAVING CHILDREN According to Erikson, one of the major ways that people satisfy the challenge of generativity is through having children. The arrival of a first child is a profound event for most couples. It changes their lives in almost every respect, from sleep being interrupted nightly to not being able to go out with friends at a moment's notice. First-time parents are also often anxious about how to respond to the child's cries and can be frustrated in trying to figure out why the child is distressed. But new parents also experience great joys—seeing a baby's first social smile, watching the first few tentative steps, and hearing a child proclaim "mama" or "dada" provide powerful reinforcement for becoming parents. Parents often become immersed in their children's lives, making sure the children have playmates, exposing them to new experiences, and trying to make sure they are happy and healthy. Being a parent is central to how many adults come to define themselves.

Although many people are eager to have children, research shows that children can be a strain on marriages, especially when time and money are tight. A consistent

Does having children bring meaning or happiness?

finding is that couples with children, especially adolescents, report less marital satisfaction than those who are childless (Belsky, 1990). Although satisfaction might be lower, the marriages of those with children appear to be more stable. For many people, having children is not about happiness, but about how they define their lives, reflecting the value they place on family. They look forward to coaching their kids in sports, encouraging them in school, and watching them grow up, have careers, get married, and provide grandchildren. In other words, along with career and marriage, children bring meaning to life.

Aging Can Be Successful

How do older adults seek out meaning in their lives? According to Erikson, older adults look back and evaluate what they have done with their lives. To the extent that they consider their time well spent, older adults are satisfied and able to live their final years gracefully. The crisis of this stage can be triggered by events that highlight the mortal nature of human life, such as the death of a spouse or close friend, or by changing social and occupational roles, such as retirement. Resolving such challenges allows people to come to terms with the reality of death. Although people of all ages are concerned with the meaning of life, it often becomes a preoccupation for the elderly. Here we examine the psychological processes that characterize the final years of life.

With the "graying" of the population in Western societies, much greater research attention has been given to the lives of people over age 60. By 2030, more than 1 in 5 Americans will be over age 65. People are living much longer these days, with the number of people over age 85 growing dramatically. Indeed, it is becoming commonplace for people to live beyond 100 years of age. Not only are there more elderly people, but within North America they are increasingly ethnically diverse, well educated, and physically fit.

Stereotypes regarding aging differ greatly across cultures. Just think of the mixed messages that are reflected in American popular culture. For example, films and television often depict older Native Americans as wise and knowing, whereas Anglo-American grandparents are often shown as doddering and senile. Yet the elderly contribute a great deal to modern society. For instance, nearly 40 percent of U.S. federal judges are over age 65, and they handle about 20 percent of the caseload (Markon, 2001). Many older adults continue to work productively well past their seventies. Consider Fred Hale, who died in November 2004, twelve days shy of his one hundred fourteenth birthday. He passed a driver's examination at age 104, and his grandson reported that he still found slower drivers annoying when he was 108. When he was 109, he traveled to Japan to visit a grandson. Our view of the elderly is likely to change a great deal as the baby boomer generation ages. Consider music stars, such as Bruce Springsteen, Tina Turner, and the Rolling Stones, who remain popular and vibrant well into their fifties, sixties, and beyond, certainly in defiance of most stereotypes of old people.

However, we cannot ignore the inevitable physical changes that accompany aging, even trivial changes such as graying hair and wrinkled skin. The brain also changes with age, with the frontal lobes shrinking proportionally more than other brain regions. Although scientists once believed that cognitive problems such as confusion and memory loss were an inevitable normal part of aging, they now recognize that most older adults remain alert as they grow older, although they do everything a bit more slowly. Older adults who experience a dramatic loss in mental ability often suffer from a brain condition called *dementia*, which is a progressive deterioration of thinking, memory, and behavior. Dementia has many causes, including excessive alcohol intake and HIV, but for older adults the major causes are Alzheimer's disease and small strokes that affect blood supply in the brain. After age 70, the risk of dementia increases with each year of life. Approximately 3 to 5 percent of people will develop Alzheimer's disease by age 70 to 75, and then the proportion of people with the disease doubles every five years. The disease is named after Dr. Alois Alzheimer, who in 1906 observed changes in the brain tissue of a woman who had died of an unknown mental illness. Upon inspection, Alzheimer noticed abnormal clumps and tangled bundles of fiber in the brain. The presence of such *plaques* and *tangles* is now considered telltale signs of Alzheimer's disease. Recall from Chapter 3 that acetylcholine neurons are damaged in Alzheimer's disease patients, which may explain the impairments in thought and memory. The cause of Alzheimer's is not currently known although there is evidence that genetics contributes to its development. One gene involved in cholesterol functioning has been shown to be predictive of Alzheimer's, although how this gene is related to the disease is not currently known (Corder et al., 1993). The initial symptoms of Alzheimer's disease are typically minor memory impairments, but the disease eventually progresses to more serious difficulties, such as forgetting daily routines. Eventually, the person loses all mental capacities, including memory and language (Figure 11.29).

Despite the physical, social, and emotional challenges of aging, most older adults are surprisingly healthy and happy. Indeed, some individuals thrive in old age, especially those with adequate financial resources and good health (Crosnoe & Elder, 2002). Although it is true that the body and mind do slowly deteriorate, starting at about age 50, the majority of older adults consider themselves to be in good health. Moreover, older adults report being just as satisfied with life as, if not more satisfied than, younger adults (Mroczek & Kolarz, 1998). Indeed, except for dementia, older adults have fewer mental health problems than younger adults, including depression.

11.29 Alzheimer's Disease A wife helps her husband, who is an Alzheimer's patient (left). PET scans comparing the brain of an Alzheimer's patient with a healthy brain (right).

According to psychologist Laura Carstensen's *socioemotional selectivity theory,* as people grow older they perceive time to be limited and therefore adjust their priorities to emphasize emotionally meaningful events and experiences (Carstensen, 1995; Fung & Carstensen, 2004). According to this theory, people focus more on emotional and rewarding goals as they near the end of life. For instance, they may choose to spend more time with a smaller group of close friends and avoid new people whom they might find annoying. They may spend an increasing amount of time reflecting on their lives and sharing memories with family members and friends. As they reminisce about their lives, older adults report more positive than negative emotions (Pasupathi & Carstensen, 2003). In essence, older adults want to savor their final years by putting their time and effort into having meaningful and rewarding experiences.

Cognition Changes during Aging

Cognitive abilities eventually decline with age, but it is difficult to pinpoint exactly what causes the decline. One of the most consistent and identifiable changes is a slowing of mental-processing speed. Experiments that test the time it takes to process a sensory input and react with a motor response show an increase in response time as early as an individual's mid-twenties (Era, Jokela, & Heikkinen, 1986). This increase becomes more rapid as the individual ages.

Some sensory-perceptual changes occur with age and may account for some of the observed decline. For instance, as we age our sensitivity to visual contrast decreases. Thus activities such as climbing stairs or driving at night may become more difficult and more dangerous. Sensitivity to sound also decreases with age, especially the ability to tune out background noise. This change may make older people seem confused or forgetful when they simply are not able to hear adequately. Here we examine two mental processes that change with age.

MEMORY Older people have difficulty with memory tasks that require the ability to juggle multiple pieces of information at the same time. Tasks in which attention is divided, such as driving while listening to the radio, also prove difficult. Some scientists believe these deficits reflect a decreased ability to store multiple pieces of information in working memory simultaneously (Salthouse, 1992). As you learned in Chapter 7, the frontal lobes play an important role in working memory. There is consistent evidence that the frontal lobes typically shrink as people grow older, and many of the cognitive skills that rely on the frontal lobes, such as working memory, show impairment with advancing age.

Generally speaking, long-term memory is less affected by aging than is short-term memory, although certain aspects of long-term memory do appear to suffer in advanced age. Older people often need more time to learn new information, but once they learn it, they use it as efficiently as younger subjects. It is also clear that elderly subjects are better at recognition than at retrieval tasks. For example, they have no trouble recognizing words that have been shown to them if they are asked, "Did you see the word *cat?*" But if they are asked what word they saw, or whether they saw an animal name, they do not do as well. Consistent with the socioemotional selection theory, older people also show better memory for positive than for negative information (Kennedy, Mather, & Carstensen, 2004), perhaps because older adults selectively ignore negative events (Mather & Carstensen, 2003).

Why do older adults show poor memory? Is it possible that they use less efficient strategies for encoding information to be remembered? In an intriguing study,

Jessica Logan and colleagues (2002) examined memory processes in younger (in their twenties) and older adults (in their seventies and eighties). The older adults performed worse than young adults. In terms of brain processes, they had less activation in left-hemisphere brain areas know to support memory and greater activation in right-hemisphere areas that do not aid memory. Next, these researchers sought to determine whether the memory deficit could be reduced if they gave the older subjects a strategy to improve memorization. Recall from Chapter 7 that the more deeply an item is encoded, the better it is remembered. Accordingly, in a second study the researchers asked older participants to classify words as concrete or abstract, a strategy that leads to deeper encoding. Undertaking this classification produced better memory and greater activation of the left frontal regions. These findings suggest that one reason for the decline in memory observed with aging is that older adults tend not to use strategies that facilitate memory, which raises the possibility that cognitive training might be useful for postponing age-related memory deficits.

INTELLIGENCE Research has consistently indicated that intelligence, as measured on standard psychometric tests, declines with advanced age. As we age, do we really lose IQ points? Or do older people just have a shorter attention span or lack the motivation to complete such tests? Some researchers have made a distinction between different forms of intelligence: fluid intelligence and crystallized intelligence (Horn & Hofer, 1992). As you will recall from Chapter 8, *fluid intelligence* is the ability to process new general information that requires no specific knowledge. Many standardized tests measure this kind of intelligence: the ability to recognize an analogy or to arrange blocks to match a picture. This type of intelligence is associated with speed of mental processing. Fluid intelligence tends to peak in early adulthood and decline steadily as we age. *Crystallized intelligence* refers to more specific knowledge that must be learned or memorized, such as vocabulary, or to knowledge of specialized information or reasoning strategies. This type of intelligence usually increases throughout life and breaks down only when declines in other cognitive abilities prevent new information from being processed (Figure 11.30).

These two different types of intelligence also seem to reflect the two different cultural views of aging. The decline in fluid intelligence is in keeping with the stereotype of the doddering old grandparent, whereas the continued increase in crystallized intelligence represents the respected elder to whom young people turn for guidance. So which is more accurate? The Seattle Longitudinal Study tracked adults from age 25 to 81 over seven years, administering tests of cognitive abilities such as verbal and mathematical skills (Schaie, 1990). They found that intellectual decline does not actually occur until the sixties or seventies. Further, people who were healthy and remained mentally active demonstrated less decline. Thus, although memory and the speed of processing may decline, the continued ability to learn new information may mitigate those losses in terms of daily functioning. Further, we can use alternative cognitive strategies to compensate. There has been a great deal of excitement lately about the possibility that active social engagement may help older adults maintain their cognitive abilities. For instance, older adults who have more extensive social contacts and remain active through leisure pursuits may be less susceptible to dementia and Alzheimer's disease (Fratiglioni, Paillard-Borg, & Winblad, 2004). With people now living much longer, it is likely that researchers will place even more emphasis on understanding how people can maintain their cognitive capacities to get the most out of their final years.

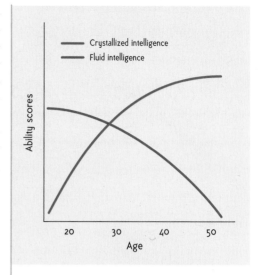

11.30 **Fluid and Crystallized Intelligence throughout the Life Span** Unlike fluid intelligence, which shows a steady decline with age, crystallized intelligence increases through at least the 40s and 50s and then levels off.

Does intelligence deteriorate with aging?

475

the Principles | What Brings Meaning to Adulthood?

Interest has been growing in studying humans across the entire life span, from conception to old age. Adulthood requires people to meet certain challenges, such as establishing a career, getting married, and raising a family. An overriding theme that emerges from studying life transitions is that people seek meaning in their lives and that they do so increasingly as they age. Although older adults are often characterized as feeble and senile, they are for the most part healthy, alert, and vital. Indeed, one of the biggest surprises in recent years is the finding that older people are often more satisfied than younger adults. In spite of declines in memory and speed of mental processing, older adults generally maintain their intelligence into very old age, especially if they engage in social and mental activities that help keep their mental skills in shape.

Conclusion

Born nearly helpless, infants blossom into inquisitive children, who later become questioning adolescents and stressed-out adults, and finally emerge by and large as satisfied older individuals. This is the journey of life for most of us. Throughout this journey, the interacting forces of nature and nurture work to shape our development as we emerge and grow as unique persons. As we mature, so do our mental processes. For centuries, people thought that children were born with blank minds. We now know that this is far from true. We now recognize that young children think about the world in completely different ways from adults, but now we also know that they are capable of incredible feats of cognition at very early ages, such as understanding the physical laws of the universe. As the brain develops, and especially as the frontal lobes become organized, we become social creatures, capable of sharing attention and communicating through language. Our capacity for theory of mind truly gives us a unique place in the animal kingdom as the most social of all species. Arising through development are the things that define us as people—our values, morals, and beliefs, as well as our hopes and dreams. Shaped by our interactions with parents and peers, who themselves are embedded within culture and society, we develop a sense of identity that recognizes our unique place in the world. This identity guides how we spend our lives. It shapes our career choices, helps us figure out whom to marry (if anyone), and guides us as we raise our children. And at some point we get old and our bodies and minds start to deteriorate. But there is good news: Older adults typically are much happier than we realized, which is a good thing because we are going to be spending increasingly long periods of our lives in what has traditionally been called old age. The cycle of birth, life, and death is remarkable. Even as psychological scientists explore the nature of physical and psychological development, we cannot help but marvel both at the vast amount of knowledge we acquire as children, and at how much we continue to learn throughout our lives.

Summarizing the Principles of Human Development

What Shapes a Child?

1. **Development starts in the womb:** Many factors in the prenatal environment (i.e., nutrition and hormones) can affect development. The most adverse consequences result from teratogens (i.e., drugs, alcohol, or viruses), exposure to which can result in death, deformity, or mental disorders.

2. **Brain development promotes learning:** Brain development proceeds in an interaction between maturation and experience. The plasticity of the brain allows changes in the development of connections and the synaptic pruning of unused neural connections. The timing of requisite experiences for brain development is particularly important in the early years.

3. **Attachment promotes survival:** The emotional bond that develops between a child and the caregiver aids the survival of the child. Attachment styles define the dynamic relationship between caregivers and infants, and are generally categorized as secure, avoidant, anxious-ambivalent, and disorganized. At the biological level, the hormone oxytocin facilitates attachment.

4. **Parental style can affect children's well-being:** Children's temperaments interact with their parents' behaviors and can result in a good "fit" or less optimal outcomes. Furthermore, parents influence attitudes, values, and beliefs and thus shape their childrens' views of themselves and others.

How Do Children Learn about Their Worlds?

5. **Perception introduces the world:** Experiments using the preferential looking technique and habituation have revealed the considerable perceptual ability of infants. Vision and hearing develop rapidly as neural circuitry develops.

6. **Piaget emphasized stages of development:** Jean Piaget proposed that through interaction with the environment, children develop mental schemas and proceed through stages of cognitive development. Initially, infants experience their world in a sensorimotor manner and develop object permanence; next they enter the preoperational stage, during which the appearance of objects dominates thinking; the third stage is marked by the logic of concrete operations; and finally, the formal operational stage is characterized by abstract, complex thinking.

7. **Infants have innate knowledge:** Experiments using the habituation paradigm have revealed that infants understand some of the basic laws of physics and mathematics.

8. **Memory improves over childhood:** Infantile memory is limited by a lack of language ability and autobiographical reference. Source amnesia is common in children. Confabulation, common in young children, may result from underdevelopment of the frontal lobes.

9. **Humans learn from interacting with others:** Being able to infer the mental states of others is known as theory of mind. Through socialization, children move from very egocentric thinking to being able to take another's perspective.

10. **Language develops in an orderly fashion:** Infants can discriminate phonemes. Language proceeds from making different sounds to words to telegraphic speech to sentences. Noam Chomsky asserts that language is governed by "universal grammar." According to Lev Vygotsky, social interaction is the force that develops language. Exposure to language in the sensitive period is required for its development. Interaction across cultures can shape language. Sign language develops like spoken language.

How Do Children and Adolescents Develop Their Identities?

11. **Gender roles are determined by cultural norms:** Gender identity develops in children and shapes their behaviors (i.e., gender roles). Gender schemas are the cognitive constructs of gender. People tend to rate themselves as masculine, feminine, or androgynous in stereotypic thinking. Situations affect gender-related response. Biology and culture shape gender differences.

12. **Friends influence adolescent identity and behavior:** Social comparisons shape children's identities. Parents and peers shape identity.

13. **Identity includes moral values:** Moral reasoning develops through a series of levels from self-interest to logical, rule-bound reasoning to abstract principles and values. Parents influence the understanding and expression of moral emotions (i.e., guilt, sympathy). There is evidence of a physiological and thus developmental component of morality.

14. **People define themselves in terms of race and ethnicity:** By age four, children begin to categorize themselves and others with regard to race or ethnicity. Ethnic identity is complicated by social prejudice.

What Brings Meaning to Adulthood?

15. **Adults are affected by life transitions:** Erikson considered development from a life-span perspective, and theorized that there are important social issues to be resolved at each stage of life. For adults, development focuses on generativity: being productive with regard to career and family. Marriage is a central issue, though about half of contemporary marriages fail.

16. **Aging can be successful:** With the "graying" of the population in western societies, more research has been done on aging. There are inevitable physical changes, but dementia is not normal and has many causes, including Alzheimer's disease. Most older adults are healthy and remain productive, and often become socioemotionally selective about their relationships and activities.

17. **Cognition changes during aging:** Short-term memory is affected by aging, thus complex memory and divided-attention tasks are affected. Crystallized intelligence increases; fluid intelligence declines in old age as speed in processing declines. Being mentally active and socially engaged preserves functioning.

Applying the Principles

1. While out jogging one day in a park near campus, you stop and rest on a bench at the playground. A group of mothers are seated on the benches, chatting with one another. You notice that most of the toddlers are happily playing and occasionally run to their moms for help or comfort. One girl seems totally independent and keeps some distance from her mother. Another girl is at one moment tugging on her mother to be picked up, and then almost immediately wants to be put down. What you are observing in these children is

____ a) the dual roles of temperament and attachment style in development.
____ b) the role of biologically based temperament alone in determining social interaction.
____ c) the importance of play groups for developing attachment.
____ d) different attachment styles.

2. Baby Jennie is sitting on the floor when an orange rolls toward her from the kitchen. She picks it up and puts it in her mouth. One of her tiny teeth pierces the orange rind, causing her to grimace from the bitter taste. She tosses the orange under the couch, out of sight. When a second orange rolls toward her, she picks it up, finds the other one under the couch, and takes both to her mother in the kitchen. Jennie has demonstrated a variety of cognitive functions. These are _____ for mouthing the object; _____ for locating it under the couch; and _____ for not mouthing the second one.

____ a) assimilation; object permanence; accommodation
____ b) sensorimotor; concrete operations; preoperations
____ c) egocentrism; orienting; conservation
____ d) source amnesia; theory of mind; egocentrism

3. When you were in high school, it was clear which kids were jocks, brainiacs, Goths, hippies, etc. Whatever group you belonged to, you had some certainty that despite various individual differences, there were great similarities in interests and attitudes among those in your clique. These similarities are important for

____ a) being sure that people called your group the right name.
____ b) defining who you were in comparison to others.
____ c) creating an identity that was distinctly different from anyone in your group.
____ d) having a distinct group identity different from your personal identity.

4. Like many college students, Annie often listens to music while studying. When she visits her grandparents, they complain when she does this, and even comment that the loud music makes it impossible for them to think. From what you know about changes in adulthood, how do you explain this difference?

____ a) older adults spend more time thinking about unpleasant things and the upbeat style of the music interferes
____ b) older adults have more difficulty with divided attention
____ c) older adults have more complex thoughts because of their increased crystallized intelligence
____ d) younger adults have better memory

ANSWERS: 1. b 2. a 3. b 4. b

Key Terms

accommodation, p. 447
adolescence, p. 461
assimilation, p. 447
attachment, p. 438
concrete operational stage, p. 448
critical period, p. 437
developmental psychology, p. 432
formal operational stage, p. 448

gender, p. 462
gender identity, p. 462
gender roles, p. 462
gender schemas, p. 462
infantile amnesia, p. 451
object permanence, p. 447
orienting reflex, p. 445
preoperational stage, p. 448

schemas, p. 447
sensorimotor stage, p. 447
social development, p. 461
source amnesia, p. 452
synaptic pruning, p. 436
telegraphic speech, p. 456
teratogens, p. 435
theory of mind, p. 452

Further Readings

Birren, J. E., & Schaie, K. W. (Eds.). (2001). *Handbook of the psychology of aging* (5th ed.). San Diego, CA: Academic Press.

Bloom, P. (2004). *Descartes' baby: How the science of child development explains what makes us human.* New York: Basic Books.

Colapinto, J. (2000). *As nature made him: The boy who was raised as a girl.* New York: HarperCollins.

Goldberg, S., Muir, R., & Kerr, J. (1997). *Attachment theory: Social, developmental, and clinical perspectives.* Hillsdale, NJ: Analytic Press.

Harris, J. R. (1998). *The nurture assumption: Why children turn out the way they do.* New York: Free Press.

Maccoby, E. E. (1998). *The two sexes: Growing up apart, coming together.* Cambridge, MA: Belknap Press/Harvard University Press.

Pinker, S. (1994). *The language instinct.* New York: Morrow.

Tomasello, M. (2001). *The cultural origins of human cognition.* Cambridge, MA: Harvard University Press.

Identifying Influences on Personality

On their MTV reality show, *The Osbournes,* Kelly and Jack Osbourne often seemed to be imitating the behavior of their notoriously wild father, rock musician Ozzy Osbourne. Cases like this one interest psychological scientists, who examine to what extent personality is inherited and to what extent it is subject to cultural and social influences. Recent evidence supports the idea that personality is rooted in genetics, although how personality traits are expressed also depends upon a person's environment.

Personality

T om Hanks is among the most likeable and talented actors of our time, winning Academy Awards for his performances in *Philadelphia* and *Forrest Gump*. Given everything that you know about Hanks, what kind of a person do you think he is? Do you think he is as nice off screen as he is on screen? Where does he get the confidence to act in movies that will be seen and judged by millions? The word *personality* comes from the Latin *persona,* a mask. In ancient Greece and Rome, actors would speak through masks, with each different mask representing a complete separate personality. So, who is the real Tom Hanks? We are constantly trying to figure other people out, so that we can understand why they behave the way they do and so that we can predict their future behavior. Many students report that one reason they take psychology courses is that they want to know what makes other people tick. We love to analyze people to figure

Outlining the Principles

How Have Scientists Studied Personality?

- Psychodynamic Theories Emphasize Unconscious and Dynamic Processes
- Humanistic Approaches Emphasize Integrated Personal Experience
- Type and Trait Approaches Describe Behavioral Dispositions
- Personality Reflects Learning and Cognitive Processes

How Is Personality Assessed, and What Does It Predict?

- Personality Refers to Both Unique and Common Characteristics

- We Can Use Objective and Projective Methods to Assess Personality
- Observers Show Accuracy in Trait Judgments
- People Sometimes Are Inconsistent
- Behavior Is Influenced by the Interaction of Personality and Situations

What Is the Biological Basis of Personality?

- Personality Is Rooted in Genetics
- Temperaments Are Evident in Infancy
- Personality Is Linked to Specific Neurophysiological Mechanisms
- Personality Is Adaptive

Can Personality Change?

- Traits Remain Stable over Time
- Characteristic Adaptations Change across Time and Circumstances
- Brain Injury and Pharmacological Interventions Affect Personality

out their personalities. One question that we will ask in this chapter is, "What do we need to know to know a person well?"

Would it surprise you to learn that Tom Hanks was painfully shy when he was growing up? He attributes this shyness to the frequent changes he experienced during childhood. By age 10, Hanks had had three different mothers, had attended five different schools, and had lived in 10 different houses, all of which hindered his chances for making lasting friendships. Lacking the social skills to make friends, Hanks found that he could get attention by being the class clown. He would take on different personas and make people laugh, which was excellent training for someone destined to become an actor.

Hanks soon found that he had a natural skill for changing his personality to suit any situation. In 1997 he told the *Guardian* newspaper that he had learned to adjust his behavior to what was expected: "If I was supposed to be repressed, I could repress myself; if I was supposed to be outgoing, I could be outgoing; if I was supposed to be raucous, I could be raucous. I think I still do that sometimes, I'm still good at it." So who is the real Tom Hanks?

One of the challenges of figuring people out is that they sometimes act differently, often depending on the situation. How much can a person's behavior tell us about his or her personality? What else do we need to know to really understand someone? Does knowing that Hanks moved around a lot as a child help us to understand his unique nature? Each person is unique. What determines this uniqueness? For instance, what factors during childhood affect personality? Have you ever wondered what makes you the person you are?

Does knowing that Hanks was shy as a child tell us anything about what he is like as an adult? An important question for researchers who study personality is the extent to which personality changes throughout a person's life. People who are shy spend a great deal of time worrying about what others think of them. Although most people feel shy on some occasions, some people feel shy all the time, so much so that it interferes with making friends or achieving their goals. If Hanks is still shy, how can he stand in front of thousands of people to give an acceptance speech at the Academy Awards? Did becoming involved in acting as a teenager allow Hanks to overcome his shyness? Can people just decide not to be shy? These are the sorts of questions that psychologists grapple with as they seek to understand what makes people unique. This chapter is concerned with the scientific understanding of human personality. ◼

Timeline

200 C.E.	1890s–1930s	1920s	1930s
Humoral Theory of Temperament The physician Galen formalizes Hippocrates' idea that personality is rooted in the body, arguing that it is determined by the relative amounts of different humors, or fluids.	**Freudian Psychodynamics** Sigmund Freud proposes that unconscious processes that originate in early childhood experiences determine much of human personality.	**Neo-Freudians** Some of Freud's followers, such as Carl Jung and Karen Horney, reject his emphasis on sex, although they share his belief in the importance of unconscious processes.	**Study of Lives** Henry Murray uses projective measures to examine unconscious needs and champions the scientific study of whole persons.

Understanding personality may be among the oldest quests in psychology. Since antiquity, an incredibly wide array of grand theories have been proposed to explain basic differences between individuals. **Personality** refers to an individual's characteristics, emotional responses, thoughts, and behaviors that are relatively stable over time and across circumstances. Personality psychologists study the basic processes that influence the development of personality on a number of different levels of analysis, such as the influence of culture, learning, biology, and cognitive factors. At the same time, those who study personality are most interested in understanding *whole persons*. That is, they try to understand what makes each person unique. People differ greatly in many ways, as you have no doubt noticed. Some are hostile, some are loving, and others are withdrawn. Each of these characteristics is a **personality trait**, a dispositional tendency to act in a certain way over time and across circumstances. What sort of person are you? More to the point, Why are you who you are?

personality Characteristics, emotional responses, thoughts, and behaviors that are relatively stable over time and across circumstances.

personality trait A characteristic; a dispositional tendency to act in a certain way over time and across circumstances.

How do we really know a person?

How Have Scientists Studied Personality?

Dan McAdams (Figure 12.1), a leading personality researcher, has posed the interesting question, "What must we know to know a person well?" The specific ways that psychologists try to answer this question vary greatly, often depending on their overall theoretical approach. Some psychological scientists emphasize the biological and genetic factors that predispose behaviors. Others might emphasize culture, patterns of reinforcement, or mental and unconscious processes. To really understand people is to understand everything about them, from their biological make-ups, to their early childhood experiences, to the way they think, to the cultures in which they were raised. All of these factors work together to shape a person in a unique way. Thus, personality psychologists approach the study of personality on many levels.

Gordon Allport (Figure 12.2), who published the first major textbook on personality, in 1937, gave perhaps the best working definition of personality: "the dynamic organization within the individual of those psychophysical systems that determine his characteristic behavior and thought" (1961, p. 28). This definition includes many of the concepts most important to a contemporary understanding of personality. The notion of *organization* indicates that personality is not just a list of traits but a coherent whole. Moreover, this organized whole is *dynamic*, in that it is goal seeking, sensitive to context, and adaptive to the environment. By emphasizing *psychophysical systems*, Allport highlights the psychological nature of personality while clearly recognizing that personality arises from basic biological processes. Finally, Allport's definition stresses that personality *causes* people to think, behave, and feel in relatively

12.1 Dan McAdams McAdams believes that to know people well, we need to know everything about them, including the personal narratives of their whole lives.

1937
Allport Defines Personality Gordon Allport publishes the first major textbook in personality psychology, helping to shape personality as the scientific study of the individual.

1950s
Humanism and Phenomenology Dissatisfied with deterministic views of personality, a number of psychologists emphasize personal experience and belief systems, focusing on the potential for individual growth.

1954
Locus of Control Julian Rotter helps establish the social-cognitive perspective on personality by showing that people's beliefs and expectancies play an important role in how they behave.

1960s
Biological Basis of Personality Hans Eysenck demonstrates physiological differences between introverts and extraverts, setting the foundation for contemporary research on the biological basis of personality.

1968
Trait Consistency Is Overrated Walter Mischel charges that personality traits are not predictive of behavior across different situations, which launches the person-situation debate.

12.2 Gordon Allport Allport published the first major textbook of personality psychology, which defined the field. He also championed the study of individuals and established traits as a central concept in personality research.

How much is personality influenced by unconscious processes?

psychodynamic theory Freudian theory that unconscious forces, such as wishes and motives, influence behavior.

consistent ways over time. Psychological researchers use diverse approaches to explore different aspects of personality.

Psychodynamic Theories Emphasize Unconscious and Dynamic Processes

Sigmund Freud, an Austrian physician whose theories dominated psychological thinking for many decades, developed one of the most influential theories of human personality. Focusing on the individual level of analysis, Freud developed many of his ideas about personality by observing people he was treating for various psychological disturbances, such as patients who experienced paralysis without any apparent physical cause. The central premise of Freud's **psychodynamic theory** of personality is that unconscious forces, such as wishes and motives, influence behavior. Freud referred to these psychic forces as *instincts* (although he used the term in a way slightly different from its contemporary use), defining them as mental representations arising out of biological or physical need. For instance, Freud proposed that people have a *life instinct* that is satisfied by following the *pleasure principle*, which directs people to seek pleasure and avoid pain. The energy that drives the pleasure principle is called *libido*. Although nowadays the term has a strong sexual connotation, Freud used it to refer more generally to the energy that promotes pleasure seeking. Instincts can be viewed as wishes or desires to satisfy libidinal urges for pleasure. These psychological forces can be in conflict, which was what Freud viewed as the essential cause of mental illness.

A TOPOGRAPHICAL MODEL OF MIND Freud believed that most of the conflict between various psychological forces occurred below the level of conscious awareness. In his *topographical model* (Figure 12.3), Freud proposed that the structure of the mind, the topography as it were, was divided into three different zones of mental awareness. At the *conscious* level, people are aware of their thoughts. The *preconscious* consists of content that is not currently in awareness but could be brought to awareness; it is roughly analogous to long-term memory. The *unconscious* contains material that the mind cannot easily retrieve. According to Freud, the unconscious mind contains wishes, desires, and motives that are associated with conflict, anxiety, or pain and are therefore not accessible to protect the person from distress. Sometimes, however, this information leaks into consciousness, such as occurs during a *Freudian slip*, in which a person accidentally reveals a hidden motive, such as the person who introduces her- or himself to someone attractive by saying "Excuse me, I don't think we've been properly seduced."

DEVELOPMENT OF SEXUAL INSTINCTS An important component of Freudian thinking was the idea that early childhood experiences had a major impact on the

1980s
The Big Five Building on earlier work by Warren Norman, researchers such as Lewis Goldberg, Paul Costa, Robert McCrae, and Oliver John argue that the universe of personality traits can be reduced to five basic factors.

1982
Inhibition and Approach Jeffrey Gray at Oxford University proposes that approach and inhibition motives, residing in distinct brain structures and processes, are the neural underpinnings of introversion and extraversion.

1990s
Behavioral Genetics Beginning with studies of twins, researchers demonstrate that personality traits are determined more by inheritance than by family environment.

1990s
Personology Led by Dan McAdams, researchers focus on how people's personal stories form coherent life narratives.

1990s
The Return of Temperaments Converging evidence indicates that basic temperaments, which can be observed in infancy and throughout childhood, are biologically based and have consequential impact on personality and behavior.

development of personality. Freud believed that children went through developmental stages that corresponded to their pursuit of satisfaction of libidinal urges. At each **psychosexual stage**, libido is focused on one of the *erogenous zones*: the mouth, anus, and genitals. The *oral stage* lasts from birth to approximately 18 months, during which time pleasure is sought through the mouth. Hungry infants experience relief when they breastfeed and come to associate pleasure with sucking. When children are two to three years old, toilet training leads them to focus on the anus; therefore learning to control the bowels is the key focus of the *anal phase*. From ages three to five, children enter the *phallic stage*, during which libidinal energies are directed toward the genitals. Children often discover the pleasure of rubbing their genitals during this time, although they have no sexual intent per se.

One of the most controversial Freudian theories applies to children in the phallic stage. According to Freud, children desire an exclusive relationship with the opposite-sex parent. Because the same-sex parent is therefore a rival, children develop hostility toward the same-sex parent, which for boys is known as the *Oedipus complex*, after the Greek legend in which Oedipus unknowingly kills his father and marries his mother. Freud believed that children develop unconscious wishes to kill the one parent in order to claim the other, and that they resolve this conflict through identification with the same-sex parent, taking on many of his or her values and ideals. This theory was mostly applicable to boys. Freud's theory for girls was more complex and even less convincing.

Following the phallic stage, children enter a brief *latency stage*, in which libidinal urges are suppressed or channeled into schoolwork or building friendships. Finally, in the *genital stage*, adolescents and adults work to attain mature attitudes about sexuality and adulthood. Libidinal urges are centered on the capacity to reproduce and contribute to society.

According to Freud, progression through these psychosexual stages has a profound impact on personality. For example, some people become *fixated* at a stage during which they have received excessive parental restriction or indulgence. Those fixated at the oral stage develop *oral personalities*; they continue to seek out pleasure via the mouth, such as by smoking, and they are excessively needy. Those fixated at the anal phase may have *anal-retentive* personalities, meaning they are stubborn and overly regulating. The latter may be due to overly strict toilet training, or overly rule-based rearing more generally.

STRUCTURAL MODEL OF PERSONALITY Freud proposed an integrated model of how the mind is organized, which consists of three theoretical structures that vary across the levels of consciousness. At the most basic level, and completely submerged in the unconscious, is the **id**, which operates according to the pleasure principle, acting on impulses and desires. The innate forces driving the id are sex and aggression. Acting as a brake on the id is the **superego**, which is the internalization of societal and parental standards of conduct. Developing during the phallic phase, the superego is a rigid structure of morality, or human conscience. Mediating between superego and id is the **ego**, which tries to satisfy the wishes of the id while being responsive to the dictates of the superego. The ego operates according to the *reality principle*, which involves rational thought and problem solving.

Conflicts between the id and superego lead to anxiety, which the ego copes with by employing a variety of **defense mechanisms**, unconscious mental strategies that the mind uses to protect itself from distress. For instance, people often *rationalize* their behavior by blaming situational factors over which they have little control, as when you explain that you didn't call your parents because you were too busy studying for

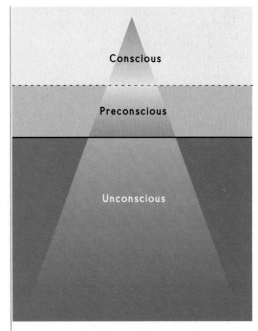

12.3 Levels of Consciousness Freud differentiated levels of consciousness into three zones. He believed that much of human behavior was influenced by unconscious processes.

psychosexual stages According to Freud, the developmental stages that correspond to the pursuit of satisfaction of libidinal urges.

id In psychodynamic theory, the component of personality that is completely submerged in the unconscious and operates according to the pleasure principle.

superego In psychodynamic theory, the internalization of societal and parental standards of conduct.

ego In psychodynamic theory, the component of personality that tries to satisfy the wishes of the id while being responsive to the dictates of the superego.

defense mechanisms Unconscious mental strategies the mind uses to protect itself from conflict and distress.

an exam. Much of the theoretical work on defense mechanisms can be credited to Sigmund's daughter, Anna Freud. Several common defense mechanisms are listed in Table 12.1. Research in psychology over the past 40 years has provided considerable support for the existence of many of these defense mechanisms (Baumeister, Dale, & Sommers, 1998), although contemporary researchers believe that these mechanisms protect self-esteem rather than relieve unconscious conflict over libidinal desires. For instance, *reaction formation* occurs when people ward off an uncomfortable thought about the self by embracing its opposite. In one study of homophobic men, those who expressed the most negative views of homosexuality showed greater physiological arousal when showed video depictions of homosexual sex than did men who were more accepting of homosexuality (Adams, Wright, & Lohr, 1996).

PSYCHODYNAMIC THEORY SINCE FREUD Although Freud is most closely identified with psychodynamic theory, a number of scholars, while rejecting certain aspects of Freudian thinking, embraced the notion of unconscious conflict. These *neo-Freudians* include Carl Jung, Alfred Adler, and Karen Horney, each of whom modified Freud through the development of their own psychodynamic theories. For instance, Adler and Horney strongly criticized Freud's view of women, believing many of his theories to be misogynistic. Many neo-Freudians rejected Freud's emphasis on sexual forces and instead focused on social interactions, especially the emotional attachments that children develop to their parents. This focus is embodied in *object relations* theory, in which the object of attachment is another person, such as a parent or spouse. In addition, some neo-Freudians, including Horney and Erik Erikson, emphasized the influence of culture, which Freud saw monolithically as "civilization."

TABLE 12.1	Common Defense Mechanisms	
MECHANISM	**DEFINITION**	**EXAMPLE**
Denial	Refusing to acknowledge source of anxiety	Ill person ignores medical advice
Repression	Excluding source of anxiety from awareness	Person fails to remember an unpleasant event
Projection	Attributing unacceptable qualities of the self to someone else	Competitive person describes others as supercompetitive
Reaction formation	Warding off an uncomfortable thought by overemphasizing its opposite	Person with unacknowledged homosexual desires makes homophobic remarks
Rationalization	Concocting a seemingly logical reason or excuse for behavior that might otherwise be shameful	Person cheats on taxes because "everyone does it"
Displacement	Shifting the attention of emotion from one object to another	Person yells at children after a bad day at work
Sublimation	Channeling socially unacceptable impulses into constructive, even admirable, behavior	Sadist becomes a surgeon or dentist

Psychological scientists have largely abandoned psychodynamic theories because of the lack of scientific evidence for Freud's central premises, since many of the ideas have not been amenable to empirical examination. However, Freud has to be understood in the context of the time in which he was working and the methods he had at his disposal. He was an astute observer of behavior and an amazingly creative theorist. His observations and ideas continue to have an important impact on personality psychology and have framed much of the research in personality over the last century (Westen, 1998).

Humanistic Approaches Emphasize Integrated Personal Experience

By the early 1950s, most psychological theories of personality were heavily deterministic; that is, personality and its associated behavioral characteristics were considered to be caused by forces beyond the person's control. As we have seen, Freud believed that personality was determined by unconscious conflicts. In a different vein, behaviorists such as B. F. Skinner argued that patterns of reinforcement determined response tendencies, which were the basis of personality. Against this backdrop emerged a view of personality that emphasized the uniqueness of the human condition. **Humanistic approaches** to personality emphasize personal experience and belief systems and propose that people seek to fulfill their human potential. At its core, humanism emphasizes subjective human experience, or *phenomenology*, and views each person as inherently good. Humanistic approaches to personality encourage people to fulfill their individual potential for personal growth through greater self-understanding; this process is referred to as *self-actualization*. Maslow's theory of motivation, discussed in Chapter 9, is an example of a humanistic approach to personality. Maslow believed that the desire to become self-actualized was the ultimate and most important human motive.

The most prominent humanistic psychologist was Carl Rogers (Figure 12.4), whose *person-centered* approach to personality emphasized people's personal understandings or phenomenology. As a therapeutic technique, Rogers focused on the need for the therapist to create a warm, supportive, and accepting environment and to deal with clients' problems and concerns as clients understood them.

Rogers's theory highlights the importance of how parents show affection for their children and how parental treatment affects personality development. Rogers speculated that although most parents provide love and support, it is often conditional. That is, parents love their children as long as the children do what the parent wants them to do. Parents who do not approve of their children's behavior often behave in ways that indicate they may withhold their love from the child. As a result, children quickly abandon their true feelings, dreams, and desires and accept only those parts of themselves that elicit parental love and support. Thus, people lose touch with their true selves in their pursuit of positive regard from others. By contrast, Rogers encouraged parents to raise their children with *unconditional positive regard*, in which children are accepted, loved, and prized no matter how they behave. Parents are to express disapproval with bad behavior, but in a context that ensures that children feel loved, as epitomized in the saying "Love the sinner, hate the sin." According to Rogers, a child raised with unconditional positive regard will develop a healthy sense of self-esteem and will be able to become, in Rogers's term, a *fully functioning person*.

By its nature, humanistic psychology has not been overly concerned with the scientific study of personality, since it emphasizes subjective personal experience. Recently, however, psychologists have begun to use the methods of science to study

humanistic approaches Approaches to studying personality that emphasize personal experience and belief systems, and propose that people seek personal growth to fulfill their human potential.

12.4 Carl Rogers Rogers emphasized people's subjective understandings of their whole lives.

the positive aspects of humanity. The *positive psychology movement* was launched by the clinical psychologist Martin Seligman when he was president of the American Psychological Association (Seligman & Csikszentmihalyi, 2000). Seligman and others have encouraged the scientific study of qualities such as faith, values, creativity, courage, and hope. For instance, Ed Diener (2000) has conducted more than three decades of research on *subjective well-being*, a general term for how much happiness and satisfaction people have in their lives. He has found that well-being varies across cultures such that the wealthiest countries often have higher levels of satisfaction, a finding that fits in well with Maslow's proposal that people need to satisfy basic needs (such as food, shelter, and safety) before they can focus on self-esteem needs. More recently, Michele Tugade and Barbara Frederickson (2004) found that people who are resilient, who are most able to bounce back from negative events, experience positive emotions even when under stress. According to the *broaden-and-build theory*, positive emotions prompt people to consider novel and creative solutions to their problems, which may in the end help resilient people to cope effectively with setbacks or negative life experiences (Frederickson, 2001).

Type and Trait Approaches Describe Behavioral Dispositions

Psychodynamic and humanistic approaches focus on explaining the mental processes that shape personality. The same underlying processes are thought to occur within each person, but people differ because they experience different conflicts, situations, parental treatment, and so forth. Other approaches to personality focus more on description than explanation, which is actually similar to the way most people intuitively view personality. For example, if asked to describe a friend, you would probably not delve into unconscious conflicts; rather, you would describe the person as a certain type, such as an *introvert* or an *extravert*. **Personality types** are discrete categories into which we place people. Subsequently, we fill in gaps in our knowledge with our beliefs about what behaviors and dispositions are associated with these types. Our tendency to assume that personality characteristics go together, and therefore to make predictions about people on the basis of minimal evidence, is referred to as *implicit personality theory*. For example, we think that introverts don't like to go to parties, that they like to read books, and that they are sensitive.

In addition to typologies, many personality psychologists are concerned with *traits*, defined earlier as behavioral dispositions that endure over time and across situations. Traits are on a continuum, with most people toward the middle and relatively few at the extreme ends. Thus, people range from being very unfriendly to very friendly, but most people are moderately friendly. The **trait approach** to personality provides a method for assessing the extent to which individuals differ in personality dispositions, such as sociability, cheerfulness, and aggressiveness (Funder, 2001).

How many traits are there? In the earliest stages of his career, Gordon Allport, along with his colleague Henry Odbert of Dartmouth College, went through the dictionary to count the number of words that could be used as personality traits. They counted nearly 18,000. Even weeding out synonyms and archaic words left 4,500 apparent traits.

During the 1950s, Raymond Cattell set out to ascertain the basic elements of personality. Cattell believed that by using statistical procedures he could take the scientific study of personality to a higher level and perhaps uncover the basic structure of

How do personality types differ from personality traits?

personality types Discrete categories based on global personality characteristics.

trait approach An approach to studying personality that focuses on the extent to which individuals differ in personality dispositions.

personality. Cattell had participants fill out personality questionnaires containing many trait items, which he reduced from the larger set produced by Allport and Odbert. Cattell then performed *factor analysis*, grouping items based on their similarities. For instance, all the terms that referred to friendliness ("nice," "pleasant," "cooperative," and so on) were grouped together. Through this procedure Cattell came to believe that there were 16 basic dimensions of personality, one of which was intelligence. The others were given rather unusual names to avoid confusion with everyday language; most personality psychologists no longer use these terms.

EYSENCK'S HIERARCHICAL MODEL Reducing the number of basic traits even further was the British psychologist Hans Eysenck, who in the 1960s proposed a hierarchical model of personality. As you can see in Figure 12.5, the basic structure begins at the *specific response level*, which consists of observed behaviors. For instance, a person buys an item because it is on sale. A person might then repeat the behavior on different occasions, which is the *habitual response level*. Some people find it hard to pass up sale items, whether they need them or not. If people are observed on many occasions to behave in same way, they are characterized as possessing a *trait*. Traits such as impulsiveness and sociability can then be viewed as components of *superordinate traits*, of which Eysenck proposed there were three: *introversion-extraversion, emotional stability,* and *psychoticism.*

The dimension of *introversion-extraversion*, terms originally coined by psychoanalyst Carl Jung, refers to the extent that people are shy, reserved, and quiet versus sociable, outgoing, and bold. As you will see later in this chapter, Eysenck believed that this dimension reflects differences in biological functioning. *Emotional stability* refers to the extent that people's moods and emotions change; people who are *neurotic* experience frequent and dramatic mood swings, especially toward negative emotions, relative to those who are more stable. People who are high in neuroticism report often feeling anxious, moody, and depressed, and they also tend to hold very low opinions of themselves. Finally, *psychoticism* describes a mix of impulse control, empathy, and aggression, with those who are high in psychoticism being more aggressive, impulsive, and self-centered than those low in psychoticism. The term "psychoticism" was perhaps not a wise choice, since it implies a level of psychopathology that Eysenck

12.5 Eysenck's Hierarchical Model of Personality Extraversion is a superordinate trait made up of sociability, dominance, assertiveness, activity, and liveliness at the trait level. Each trait is made up of habitual and specific responses.

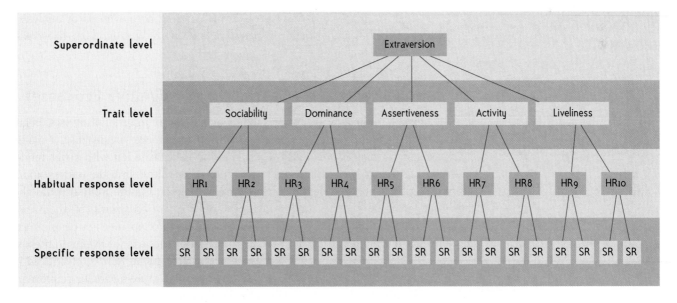

did not intend. More recent conceptions of this superordinate trait call it *constraint*, with people ranging from restrained to disinhibited (Watson & Clark, 1997).

THE BIG FIVE In the last 20 years, many personality psychologists have agreed that there are five basic personality traits, which is referred to as the **five-factor theory** (McCrae & Costa, 1999). The *Big Five*, as they are known, consist of *extraversion, neuroticism* (similar to Eysenck's model), *conscientiousness, agreeableness,* and *openness to experience*. A good way to remember the five is that they can be arranged to spell the acronym OCEAN. Each of these five factors is a higher-order trait comprising lower-order traits that are related to each other. For instance, as can be seen in Table 12.2, conscientiousness is determined by how careful and organized someone is, while agreeableness refers to the extent that a person is or is not trusting and helpful. Those high in openness to experience are imaginative and independent, whereas those low in this basic trait are down to earth and conformist.

five-factor theory The idea that personality can be described using five traits: openness to experience, conscientiousness, extraversion, agreeableness, and neuroticism.

TABLE **12.2** The Big Five	
OPENNESS TO EXPERIENCE	Imaginative vs. down to earth Variety vs. routine Independent vs. conforming
CONSCIENTIOUSNESS	Organized vs. disorganized Careful vs. careless Self-disciplined vs. weak-willed
EXTRAVERSION	Social vs. retiring Fun-loving vs. sober Affectionate vs. reserved
AGREEABLENESS	Softhearted vs. ruthless Trusting vs. suspicious Helpful vs. uncooperative
NEUROTICISM	Worried vs. calm Insecure vs. secure Self-pitying vs. self-satisfied

Considerable evidence supports the five-factor theory (John, 1990). The Big Five emerge across cultures, among adults and children, even when vastly different questionnaires are used to assess traits, and the same five traits appear whether people rate themselves or are rated by others. Nonetheless, some researchers have questioned whether the five-factor theory really helps us understand personality, since the trait terms are descriptive rather than explanatory, and because reducing all of human personality to five descriptions inevitably ignores human subtleties. For instance, evidence shows that many of these traits apply to animals as well as humans, as discussed later. However, one value of the five-factor theory is that it is an organizational structure for the vast number of traits that can be used to describe personality; by providing a common descriptive framework, the theory has helped integrate and invigorate the trait approach to personality (John & Srivastava, 1999). In addition, substantial evidence now indicates that personality traits have genetic components and are related to underlying neurophysiology. Thus, traits do exist at more than a descriptive level. Working across levels of analysis provides new ways to understand the basic traits (Clark & Watson, 1999), as we will discuss later in this chapter.

Personality Reflects Learning and Cognitive Processes

In contrast to those who saw personality as a result of internal processes, behaviorists such as B. F. Skinner viewed personality as little more than learned responses to patterns of reinforcement. However, growing dissatisfaction with strict models of learning theory led researchers to incorporate cognition into the understanding of personality. For instance, the early cognitive theorist George Kelly emphasized the importance of people's understandings, or *personal constructs*, of their circumstances. According to Kelly, personal constructs develop through people's experiences and represent their interpretations and explanations for events in their social worlds. Building further on the cognitive approach, Julian Rotter introduced in the 1950s the idea that behavior is a function of people's *expectancies* for reinforcement, as well as the *value* they ascribed to the reinforcer. Thus, if a person is deciding whether to study for an exam or go to a party, he or she will weigh the likelihood that studying will lead to a good grade, as well as how much that grade matters, against the likelihood that the party will be fun and the extent to which the person values having fun. Rotter proposed that people differ in the belief that their efforts will lead to positive outcomes, which he referred to as *locus of control*. People with an internal locus of control believe that they bring about their own rewards, whereas those with an external locus of control believe that rewards, and therefore their personal fate, are the result of forces beyond their control. These generalized beliefs have been shown to have a powerful effect on psychological adjustment.

The incorporation of cognition into learning theories led to the development of *cognitive-social theories* of personality, which emphasize how personal beliefs, expectancies, and interpretations of social situations shape behavior and personality. For instance, Albert Bandura (1977) accepts many of the tenets of learning theory but argues that humans possess mental capacities, such as beliefs, thoughts, and expectations, that interact with the environment to influence behavior. For Bandura, the extent to which people believe they can achieve specific outcomes, called *self-efficacy*, is an important determinant of behavior. Moreover, as discussed in Chapter 6, Bandura has proposed that people develop expectancies in part through *observational learning*, such as by noticing whether others are rewarded or punished for acting in certain ways.

One of the most influential cognitive-social theorists is Walter Mischel, who approached the study of personality at the social level of analysis. As you will read later in this chapter, Mischel sparked controversy by proposing that personality traits often fail to predict behavior across different circumstances. According to Mischel's *Cognitive-Affective Personality System* (*CAPS*) (Mischel & Shoda, 1995), people's responses in a given situation are influenced by how they encode or perceive the situation, their affective (emotional) response to the situation, the skills and competencies they have to deal with challenges, and their anticipation of the outcomes that their behavior will produce.

How do personal beliefs affect behavior?

Imagine, for instance, a person who walks into a party with an expectation of making a good impression, having done so many times in the past. This person will act very differently from a person whose past experiences of awkwardness, discomfort, and shyness lead to the expectation of rejection. Consider the personality style of *defensive pessimism*, studied by Julie Norem and Nancy Cantor. Defensive pessimists expect to fail and therefore enter test situations with dread. By contrast, optimists enter test situations with great expectations. You have probably encountered both of these types at your exams, with the pessimists predicting their imminent academic demise. And yet, both pessimists and optimists tend to perform similarly on exams (Norem, 1989). These two personality styles reflect different motivational strategies, with pessimists expecting the worst so they can be relieved when they succeed, and optimists focusing on positive outcomes.

The CAPS model also emphasizes *self-regulatory capacities*, in which people set personal goals, evaluate their progress, and adjust their ongoing behavior in pursuit of those goals. In addition, the values that people attach to goals, such as the importance of obtaining good grades, is part of the dynamic system. The pursuit of personal goals is an important component of cognitive-social theories of personality. Indeed, many personality psychologists believe that personal motives and strivings, such as those for achievement, power, or intimacy, are an essential aspect of personality (Snyder & Cantor, 1998). Personality, then, represents behavior that emerges from how people interpret their social worlds, and from the beliefs that they have about how they will affect and be affected by their social situations.

Thinking Critically

Do Animals Have Personality?

If you've ever owned a pet, you probably had the intuitive feeling that your pet had a personality of its own. For most of the history of psychological science, your intuition would have been regarded with skepticism, the assumption being that you were projecting your own sense of personality onto your pet. But if we are to take the principles of evolution seriously, there is continuity across species, raising the possibility that animals might display consistent behaviors across circumstances that reflect an underlying personality (Gosling, 2001). Developing animal models of personality may aid our understanding of general processes in personality perception. How do psychological scientists determine the personality of animals?

Sam Gosling studied the behavior of a group of 34 spotted hyenas at a field station of the University of California at Berkeley (Gosling, 1998). He created a personality scale consisting of 44 traits, applicable to both humans and hyenas. Four observers who knew hyenas well used the scale independently to rate the animals. It turned out that the agreement among the raters was as high as is typically found in personality studies of humans, suggesting that the raters could assess the hyenas reliably. Using factor analysis, Gosling found that the traits clustered into five factors, albeit not exactly the same five factors found for humans. Although there were rough similarities between humans and hyenas in traits related to agreeableness, neuroticism, and openness to experience, hyenas showed no evidence of a conscientiousness factor, and extraversion seemed to exist mainly in the form of assertiveness, which makes sense given that hyenas are a species that form dominance hierarchies.

What about other animals? Gosling and John (1999) summarized the findings of 19 studies that assessed multiple personality traits in modestly large samples of nonhuman animals, ranging from household pets to monkeys and other primates, to pigs and donkeys, and even to aquatic animals. They found evidence that traits similar to extraversion, neuroticism, and agreeableness could be seen in most species. Extraversion reflected different levels of energy, approach, and sociability. Neuroticism indicated differences in emotional reactivity, fearfulness, and excitability, whereas agreeableness reflected differences in aggression, hostility, and affinity for mates. What about openness and conscientiousness? In about half of the species, the animals did display individual differences in curiosity and play, and Gosling and John thought that openness in animals might be similar to behaviors one observes in young children. Conscientiousness, a core human trait, was found in a narrow form among only chimpanzees, with some showing more unpredictability and disorganized behavior. The finding that only chimpanzees showed any signs of conscientiousness is perhaps not surprising, since they are humans' closest relatives.

As a critical thinker, you might be wondering whether these judgments of personality in animals are accurate. Do they reflect true variations in personality or are they just stereotypes of certain species or breeds (Figure 12.6)? To test whether differences in personality traits among animals exist and can be measured, Gosling and his colleagues (2003) examined personality judgments for domestic dogs and compared those to judgments made for humans. How do you tell if personality ratings are accurate for animals? After all, they cannot answer for themselves and tell whether raters are correct. Gosling and his colleagues selected three measures of accuracy: (1) the extent to which ratings by the same judges were consistent for similar behaviors over time; (2) whether there was consensus, or agreement, among independent judges

12.6 Do Dogs Have Personality? Which is friendlier, a rottweiler or a golden retriever? How might you test your hypothesis?

viewing the same behavior; and (3) the extent to which the behavior corresponds to the definition of the trait, as when a dog is rated aggressive for baring its teeth in an angry fashion. To test these measures of accuracy, dog owners rated their own animals and provided the name of a friend who knew the dog well enough to rate it. Independent judges also assessed the behavior of the dog while it played in a park and performed a wide array of tasks. The dogs were assessed on four personality factors that roughly correspond to the Big Five without conscientiousness. In general, the findings indicated that the ratings of dogs were consistent over time, that the judges generally were in agreement, and that the trait behaviors displayed by the dogs corresponded to ratings of those traits made by independent judges. To rule out the possibility that breed stereotypes based solely on appearance influenced the ratings, another group of judges rated only pictures of the dogs. The personality ratings remained accurate even after statistically controlling for the ratings made of the pictures. This suggests that dogs can be rated with impressive accuracy. According to Gosling, knowing that animal personality can be assessed may permit studies of personality that could not be conducted with humans, such as breeding studies, altering the early environment, or manipulating neurotransmitter levels. Research might also address issues of animal welfare, such as matching pets to suitable owners.

Why do you think dogs of the same breed might have different personalities? What factors do you think are most important for raising a dog to be affectionate and calm around children? Do you believe that the observed differences in personality in dogs reflect the same sense of uniqueness that we assign to individual humans? Why or why not? ■

REVIEWING

the Principles | How Have Scientists Studied Personality?

According to the psychodynamic approach, unconscious motives and conflicts that are experienced throughout life, but especially in childhood, shape personality. Humanists believe that each person is unique and capable of fulfilling great potential. Trait theorists describe the behavior of people based on trait dispositions. Cognitive-social theorists focus on how cognitive interpretations and beliefs affect people's perceptions of their social environments. These varied approaches are not necessarily in opposition to each other. They share the common goal of trying to understand the ways in which people are similar to and different from one another.

How Is Personality Assessed, and What Does It Predict?

Personality researchers have yet to agree on the best method for assessing various aspects of personality. To understand people you need to examine them in some way. But unlike behavior or biological responses, personality cannot be directly assessed or observed. Psychological scientists measure personality by asking people to report on themselves, by asking people's friends or relatives to describe them, or by watching how people behave. Each of these methods has strengths and limitations. This section considers how psychological scientists assess personality, and how these different methods of assessment influence how we understand individuals.

Personality Refers to Both Unique and Common Characteristics

As differentiated by Allport, there are two approaches to studying personality: idiographic and nomothetic. **Idiographic approaches** are *person-centered* in that they focus on individual lives and how various characteristics are integrated into unique persons. If your classmates were to write down 10 personality traits that described them, although there would be some overlap, each person would probably have a unique list of traits. People like to be distinctive, and therefore they tend to choose traits that are particularly descriptive of them as compared to other people. These *central traits* are especially important for how individuals define themselves. In contrast, *secondary traits* are those that people consider less personally descriptive or not applicable at all. In general, central traits are more predictive of behavior than are secondary traits.

Researchers who use idiographic approaches often examine case studies of individuals, perhaps through interviews or biographical information. For example, many scholars have tried to account for Adolph Hitler's behavior in Nazi Germany by asking questions about his early childhood experiences, his physical stature, and his personal motivations. Henry Murray pioneered this approach at Harvard University. The study of people's lives emphasizes the idea that personality unfolds over the life course, as people react to their circumstances and come to define themselves.

There has recently been a resurgence of interest in the narrative approach to understanding human lives (McAdams, 1999, 2001). According to Dan McAdams, humans weave a *life story* that integrates self-knowledge into a coherent whole. Life stories help bring meaning to life and help people make sense of the world. Like all good stories, the ones people tell about their lives contain characters, settings, acts, plot twists, and themes. The life story is a reconstructive and imaginative process in which people link together personal motives, goals, and beliefs with events and people, and the circumstances in which they find themselves. People define themselves by creating *personal myths* that bind together past events and future possibilities. To study personality, then, we need to pay attention to the stories that people tell about their lives. The method of *psychobiography* uses personal life stories to develop and test theories about human personality.

Nomothetic approaches differ from idiographic approaches in that they focus on characteristics that are common among all people, but on which people vary—in other words, traits. For instance, every human can be rated along a continuum from very disagreeable to very agreeable. Researchers who follow this tradition tend to compare people by using common trait measures, such as questionnaires or other objective data. For example, they might give participants a list of 100 personality traits and ask them to rate themselves on each, on a scale from 1 to 10. From the nomothetic perspective, individuals are unique because of their unique combinations of common traits.

We Can Use Objective and Projective Methods to Assess Personality

Researchers use numerous methods to assess personality, ranging from self-reports to clinical interviews to observer reports. Aside from the manner by which the data are collected, how researchers choose to measure personality depends to a great extent on their theoretical orientations. For instance, trait researchers use personality

idiographic approaches Person-centered approaches to studying personality that focus on individual lives and how various characteristics are integrated into unique persons.

nomothetic approaches Approaches to studying personality that focus on characteristics that are common to all people, although there is individual variation.

projective measures Personality tests that examine unconscious processes by having people interpret ambiguous stimuli.

TAT (Thematic Apperception Test) A projective measure of personality where a person is shown an ambiguous picture and asked to tell a story about the picture.

objective measures Relatively unbiased assessments of personality, usually based on information gathered through self-report questionnaires or observer ratings.

descriptions to predict specific behaviors, whereas humanistic psychologists use more holistic approaches. At the broadest level, assessment procedures can be grouped into *projective* and *objective* measures.

PROJECTIVE MEASURES According to psychodynamic theory, personality is influenced by conflicts that people aren't aware of. So how can they tell you about something they don't know? **Projective measures** are tools that attempt to delve into the realm of the unconscious by presenting people with ambiguous stimuli and asking them to describe the stimulus items or tell stories about them. The general idea is that people will *project* their mental contents onto the ambiguous items, thereby revealing otherwise hidden aspects of personality, such as motives, wishes, and unconscious conflicts. Many of these procedures are used to assess psychopathology. One of the best-known projective measures is the *Rorschach inkblot test*, in which people look at an apparently meaningless inkblot and describe what it might be. How a person describes the inkblot is supposed to reveal unconscious conflicts and other problems. Unfortunately, many normal adults and children are found to be psychologically disturbed when they take the Rorschach, and it does a poor job of diagnosing specific psychological disorders (Wood, Garb, Lilienfeld, & Nezworski, 2002).

One classic projective measure used by personality psychologists is the **Thematic Apperception Test**, or **TAT**, developed by Henry Murray and Christiana Morgan, who used the TAT to study achievement motivation. In the TAT, a person is shown an ambiguous picture (Figure 12.7) and asked to tell a story about it. The story is then scored based on the motivational schemes that emerge, which are assumed to reflect the storyteller's personal motives. Many projective measures have been criticized for being too subjective and poorly validated. The TAT, however, has been shown to be useful for measuring motivational states, especially those related to achievement, power, and affiliation, and therefore continues to be used in contemporary research (McClelland, Koestner, & Weinberger, 1989). Indeed, evidence exists that the TAT, if used properly, reliably predicts behavior (Bornstein, 1999).

OBJECTIVE MEASURES **Objective measures** of personality are straightforward assessments, usually made by self-report questionnaires or observer ratings. For instance, the *NEO Personality Inventory* consists of 240 items designed to assess the Big Five personality traits (Costa & McCrae, 1992). Although called objective, the tests require people to make subjective judgments. Self-reports can be affected both by desires to avoid looking bad and by biases in self-perception that arise through self-relevant motives.

It can be difficult to compare self-reported objective measures directly, because individuals do not have objective standards against which to rate themselves. Just because two individuals report a "5" on a 7-point shyness scale does not mean they are equally shy. After all, the term can mean different things to different people.

One technique that assesses personal meanings of traits is the *California Q-sort*, which requires people to sort 100 statements printed on cards into nine piles according to what extent the statement is descriptive of them. These piles represent categories ranging from "not at all descriptive" to "extremely descriptive." A person is allowed to place only so many cards in each pile, usually with fewer cards allowed for the extreme ends of the scale. Because most of the cards must be piled in the moderately descriptive categories, the Q-sort has a built-in procedure for getting at

How might you confirm the validity of projective measures?

12.7 Thematic Apperception Test The type of picture used in a TAT.

central dispositions. The Q-sort, like most objective measures, can also be used by observers, such as parents, teachers, therapists, and friends.

Objective tests make no pretense of uncovering hidden conflicts or secret information. They measure only what the raters believe or observe. Personality researchers use them to compare people's responses and assess the extent to which the answers predict behavior. In addition to large personality inventories, personal researchers often use self-report questionnaires that target specific traits, such as how much excitement you seek out of life, a trait known as *sensation seeking*.

Observers Show Accuracy in Trait Judgments

Do you think other people know you pretty well? Imagine that you often feel a bit shy in new situations, as many people do. Would others know that shyness is part of your personality? Some shy people, such as Tom Hanks, force themselves to act in an outgoing manner in order to mask their inner feelings. Their friends might have no indication that they feel shy. Others react to the fear of social situations by remaining quiet and aloof. Observers might believe them to be cold, arrogant, and unfriendly. People are judged by others throughout their lives. How accurate are those judgments? That is, how well do the personality judgments people make predict the behavior of others?

An important study by the personality psychologist David Funder (1995) found a surprising degree of accuracy for trait judgments, at least under certain circumstances. For instance, it turns out that your close acquaintances may be more accurate at predicting your behavior than you are. In one study, ratings of assertiveness made by friends predicted assertive behavior in the lab better than did the person's own ratings (Kolar, Funder, & Colvin, 1996). The same was true for a variety of other traits. This may occur because friends observe how you behave in situations, whereas you may be preoccupied with evaluating other people. In other words, you may pay more attention to others than to yourself, and therefore you may fail to notice how you actually behave. Another possibility is that your subjective perception may diverge from your objective behavior. In either case, the study implies that there is some disconnect between how people view themselves and how they behave.

People Sometimes Are Inconsistent

How stable is personality across situations?

Imagine again that you are a shy person. Are you shy in all situations? Probably not. Shy people tend to be most uncomfortable in new situations in which they are being evaluated; they tend not to be shy around family and close friends. Walter Mischel (Figure 12.8) dropped a bombshell on the field of personality in 1968 by proposing that behaviors are determined as much by situations as by personality traits, a theory referred to as **situationism**. For evidence, working at the social level of analysis, he referred to studies in which people who are dishonest in one situation are completely honest in another. For instance, the student who is not totally honest with a professor in explaining why a paper is late is probably no more likely to steal from classmates or cheat on her taxes than is the student who admits he overslept. Mischel's critique of personality traits affected the field for more than a decade and caused considerable rifts between social psychologists, who tended to emphasize situational forces, and personality psychologists, who focused on individual dispositions. After all, the most basic definition of personality is that it is relatively stable

situationism The theory that behavior is determined as much by situations as by personality traits.

across situations and circumstances. If Mischel was correct and there was relatively little stability, then the whole concept of personality seemed empty.

As you might expect, there was a rather vigorous response to Mischel's critique. The basic argument made by personality researchers in the *person-situation debate* is that the extent to which traits predict behavior depends on the *centrality* of the trait, the *aggregation* of behaviors over time, and the type of trait being evaluated. People tend to be more consistent for central traits than for secondary traits, since the former are most relevant to them. In addition, if behaviors are averaged across many situations, then personality traits are more predictive of behavior. Shy people may not be shy all the time, but on average they are shy more often than not. Moreover, people who report being shy in college continue to report being shy many years later, which indicates that there is stability to the trait of shyness. Finally, some people may be more consistent than others. Consider the trait of *self-monitoring,* in which some people are highly sensitive to cues of situational appropriateness. Those who are high in self-monitoring alter their behavior to match the situation, so that they exhibit low levels of consistency. By contrast, those low in self-monitoring are less able to alter their self-presentations to match situational demands, and they tend to be much more consistent across situations.

Behavior Is Influenced by the Interaction of Personality and Situations

Considerable evidence now exists that personality traits are predictive of behavior. For instance, people who are high in neuroticism tend to be more depressed and have more illness, are more likely to have a midlife crisis, and so on. Indeed, being highly neurotic is the single best predictor of marital dissatisfaction and divorce (Karney & Bradbury, 1995). Likewise, those high in sensation seeking are more likely to smoke, use drugs, have sex, be impulsive, watch erotic movies, begin conversations, and engage in physically risky activities such as mountain climbing. The past three decades have found strong and compelling evidence that personality dispositions are meaningful constructs that predict people's behavior over time and across many circumstances. Yet people are also highly sensitive to social context, and most conform to situational norms. Few people would break the law right in front of a police officer or drive on the wrong side of the road just because they felt like it. The situation dictates behavior irrespective of personality.

Situational influences can be subtle. Consider your own behavior. Do you behave in the exact same way around your family, friends, and teachers? Although you remain the same person, you may reveal different aspects of your personality during your interactions with different people. Your goals for social interaction change, as do the potential consequences of your actions. For example, your family may be more tolerant of your bad moods than are your friends. Thus, you may feel freer to express your bad moods around your family.

Situations themselves differ in the extent to which they constrain the expression of personality (Kenrick & Funder, 1991). Consider two people, one highly extraverted, aggressive, and boisterous, and the other shy, thoughtful, and restrained. At a funeral, it would be hard to tell them apart just from their behavior. But at a party there would be obvious differences between them. Personality psychologists differentiate between *strong* situations (elevators, religious services, job interviews) and *weak* situations (parks, bars, your house); the former tend to mask differences in personality because of the power of the social environment. Most trait theorists are

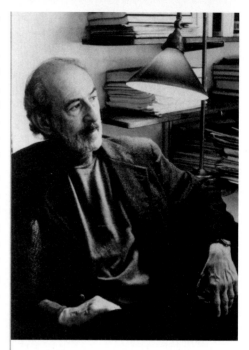

12.8 Walter Mischel Mischel proposed that situations are important in predicting behavior.

How might situations affect the display of personality traits?

interactionists, in that they believe that behavior is jointly determined by situations and underlying dispositions. In other words, you need to know something about both the person and the environment to predict behavior.

However, it is important to point out that people also have an impact on their environments. First, people choose their situations. Introverts tend to avoid parties or other situations in which they would feel anxious, whereas extraverts seek out social opportunities. Moreover, once they are in the situation, their behavior affects those around them. Some extraverts may draw people out and encourage them to have fun, whereas others might act aggressively and turn people off. Some introverts might create an intimate atmosphere and encourage people to open up and reveal personal concerns, whereas others might make people uncomfortable and anxious as both actors try to fill awkward gaps in the conversation. A reciprocal interaction occurs between the person and the environment so that they simultaneously influence each other. The important point is that personality is a dynamic system that reflects both underlying dispositions and the activation of goals and affective responses in given situations.

Psychological Science *in Action* ◐ ● ○

Finding the Right Career for Your Personality

Are scientists introspective, salespeople gregarious, and judges sober and responsible? Research by psychologists has demonstrated that some occupations seem better suited to certain personality types. What type of career suits you? Thousands of careers are possible today—some of them might bring you joy and fulfillment, whereas others may lead you to feel trapped or headed down a dead-end road. How can you find the career that is best for you? How can you determine what occupation best fits your unique abilities, interests, and personality?

Occupational psychologists help people find the right careers. Among their primary tools are psychological tests that identify personality factors indicating suitedness to specific careers. One of the most widely used personality measures for occupational counseling is the Myers-Briggs Type Indicator (MBTI). The scale of the MBTI is based on Carl Jung's theories about how people approach the world, how they perceive information, and how they make decisions. The MBTI assesses four dimensions: (1) whether people focus attention on the outside world of people and objects or on the inner world of ideas; (2) whether people prefer to rely on their objective senses or on intuition; (3) whether people make decisions based on logic or on feelings; and (4) whether their style of dealing with the world is planned and organized or flexible and spontaneous. On the basis of how a person is classified on each of these four dimensions, he or she is placed into one of sixteen possible personality types. More than three million people complete the MBTI each year, much of the time for corporations that use it for team building and management development (Gardner & Martinko, 1996). Although there are questions about the psychometric properties of the MBTI, it at least allows people to think about how they typically function in the world, and how this might make some jobs more satisfying than others. For example, people who base their decisions on intuition and feelings may be happier in business than in the more objective world of science.

Another tool widely used to assess vocational compatibility relies on the extent to which people in certain occupations tend to share similar preferences. The *Strong*

TABLE 12.3	Holland's Occupational Types		
OCCUPATION TYPE	PERSONALITY CHARACTERISTICS	PREFERRED ACTIVITIES	CAREER EXAMPLES
Realistic	Practical, stable, reliable, athletic, mechanical, honest, frank, humble	Repair things, enjoy physical activity, work outdoors, work with animals	Engineer, veterinarian, electrician, carpenter, farmer, mechanic, firefighter, geologist
Investigative	Curious, analytical, intellectual, reserved, independent, rational	Use computers, play chess, explore ideas, work alone, solve problems	Scientist, medical technician, systems analyst, software programmer, physician
Artistic	Creative, expressive, innovative, imaginative, impulsive, emotional	Attend music and dance events, write poetry, draw, take photographs	Artist, writer, musician, interior designer, reporter, actor, architect, photographer
Social	Helpful, kind, generous, friendly, responsible, concerned for others	Teach, volunteer, organize social events, engage in group activities, talking, entertaining	Teacher, social worker, nurse, clergy, speech therapist, aerobics instructor
Enterprising	Ambitious, confident, energetic, persuasive, enthusiastic, leader	Public speaking, managing others, promoting ideas, debating	Lawyer, sales and marketing, executive, public relations, manager, coach, stockbroker
Conventional	Efficient, organized, conscientious, precise, methodical, careful	Collect stamps or coins, build models, perform civic duties, organize things	Accountant, banker, secretary, financial analyst, statistician, computer operator

Interest Inventory measures an individual's interest in a broad range of occupations, leisure activities, and school subjects; those measurements are then compared with the measurements of people who are successfully employed in a variety of occupations. Thus, for example, you might find that people who like to engage in the same activities as you have fulfilling careers as artists or musicians but are miserable as accountants or investment bankers. Of course, career counselors need to take into account other personal factors because, for example, the relation between interests and occupation varies across cultures depending on how occupations are perceived (Fouad & Walker, 2005).

Among the most influential occupational psychologists was John Holland, who pioneered the scientific study of how careers match personality types. As a personnel clerk in the army during World War II, Holland noted that certain types of people had similar occupational histories. He examined this more formally while working on his doctorate in psychology at the University of Minnesota, which he obtained in 1952. During the next 20 years he conducted groundbreaking research demonstrating that certain personality types are best matched to particular work environments. His theoretical work has made a number of important contributions to occupational psychology, such as the core idea that occupational choice expresses one's personality (Gottfredson, 1999). After 40 years of research, Holland and his colleagues have identified six occupational personality types, each of which has distinctive key personal attributes and activity preferences (Table 12.3). These occupational types are associated with varying job satisfaction across different work settings (Holland, 1997). Holland's careful research has provided effective assessment tools that have helped millions of people around the world make successful career choices. ■

REVIEWING

the Principles | How Is Personality Assessed, and What Does It Predict?

Personality is assessed through either projective or objective measures, depending on the goals of the researcher. Sometimes personality psychologists examine individuals, for example, by examining personal myths that people use to explain their lives. Other times they examine many people using a common measure to assess whether individual differences in those measures predict behavior. People are relatively good at assessing personality traits in others, and some evidence suggests that observers might even be better at predicting people's behavior than are the people themselves. This occurs when observers are sensitive to environmental cues that might shape behavior. Indeed, traits interact with environments, such that situations sometimes constrain behavior, and personality sometimes influences situations.

What Is the Biological Basis of Personality?

Where does personality come from? Why are you the person that you are? Freud emphasized early childhood experiences in his theory of psychosexual stages. Certainly most people assume that the way parents treat their children will have a substantial impact on personality, for example, Rogers's belief that unconditional positive regard leads to positive mental health. But what role does biology play? Are you born with certain predispositions? How do the workings of your body and brain affect the sort of person you are?

Over the past few decades, evidence has emerged that biological factors—such as genes, brain structures, and neurochemistry—play an important role in determining personality. This is not to say that these factors are insensitive to experience. Recall from Chapter 3 that every cell in the body contains the genome, or master recipe, that provides detailed instructions for physical processes. Gene expression—whether the gene is turned off or on—underlies all psychological activity, such as how a person thinks or acts. Ultimately, genes have their effects only if they are expressed. The environment determines when or if this happens. In terms of personality, a person's genetic makeup may predispose certain traits or characteristics, but whether these genes are expressed depends on the unique circumstances that each child faces during development. For instance, we learned in Chapter 3 that children with a certain gene variation were more likely to become violent criminals as adults if they were abused during childhood. An important theme throughout this book is that nature and nurture work together to produce unique persons; this is particularly true for personality. In this section we consider the role of biological processes in personality.

Personality Is Rooted in Genetics

The evidence is overwhelming from researchers working at the biological level of analysis that nearly all personality traits have a genetic component (Plomin & Caspi, 1999). One of the earliest studies to document the heritability of personality was conducted by James Loehlin and Robert Nichols (1976). They looked at similarities in personality between more than 800 pairs of twins. Across a wide variety of traits they found that monozygotic twins were much more similar than dizygotic twins. Recall from Chapter 3 that this pattern reflects the actions of genes, since monozygotic twins share the same genes whereas dizygotic twins do not. Numerous twin studies have subsequently found that genetic influence accounts for approximately half of the variance (40–60 percent) between individuals in personality traits, including the Big Five (Figure 12.9). These genetic patterns can be found whether the twins rate themselves or whether friends, family, or trained observers rate them.

Of course, you might wonder whether identical twins are treated more similarly than other siblings and whether that explains the similarities in personality. The best evidence refuting this idea was obtained by Thomas Bouchard and his colleagues from the University of Minnesota. Their studies of twins raised apart (such as the twins described in Chapter 3) reveal that twins raised apart are often as similar, or even more similar, than twins raised together. Why might twins raised apart be more similar than twins raised together? One possibility is that parents strive to bring out individual strengths in each twin so that each feels unique and special. Thus, parenting style may foster differences rather than similarities. If this is true, one might expect that the correlations between personality traits would be stronger for older twins than for younger twins, since the effects of parenting would diminish over time. And indeed, identical twins become more alike as they grow older. By contrast, siblings and dizygotic twins do not.

ADOPTION STUDIES Further evidence for the genetic basis of personality can be found in adoption studies, although such studies usually yield lower estimates of gene influence than do twin studies. Siblings who are adopted (and not biologically related) and raised in the same household are no more alike in personality than any two strangers randomly plucked off the street (Plomin & Caspi, 1999). Moreover, the personalities of adopted children bear no significant relationship to those of the adoptive parents who raised them. These findings suggest that parenting style may have relatively little impact on personality. Is that true? The current evidence suggests that parental style has much less impact than has long been assumed. For instance, studies typically find only small correlations in personality between biological siblings or between children and their biological parents. Although small, however, these correlations are larger than for adopted children, suggesting that the similarities have a genetic component. Why are children raised together in the same household (who are not monozygotic twins) so different? One explanation is that the lives of siblings diverge as they establish friendships outside the home. Thus, siblings' personalities slowly grow apart as their initial differences become magnified through their interactions with the world.

Although the small correlations in personality between siblings might imply that parenting style has little effect, there are reasons to believe that caretakers matter a great deal. David Lykken (2000), a leading behavioral genetics researcher, has argued

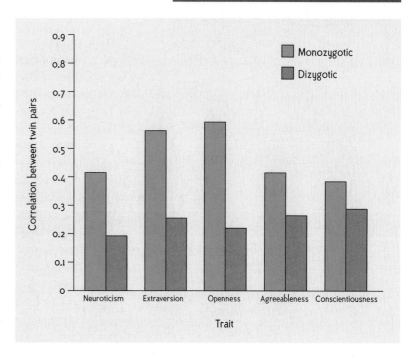

12.9 Correlation in Twins Researchers examined correlations between 123 pairs of identical twins (monozygotic) and 127 pairs of fraternal twins (dizygotic) in Vancouver, Canada. For each Big Five trait, the correlations for monozygotic twins were higher than for dizygotic twins, resulting in heritability estimates of 41 percent, 53 percent, 61 percent, 41 percent, and 44 percent of the variance in neuroticism, extraversion, openness, agreeableness, and conscientiousness.

"Oh, he's cute, all right, but he's got the temperament of a car alarm."

that children who are raised with inadequate parenting, such as those raised in poverty by single parents who are not able to spend time parenting, are not socialized properly and are therefore much more likely to become delinquent or display antisocial behavior. Thus, a minimum level of parenting is crucial, but the particular style of parenting does not appear to have a major impact on shaping personality.

ARE THERE SPECIFIC GENES FOR PERSONALITY? Research has revealed genetic components for particular behaviors such as television viewing and getting divorced, and even for specific attitudes, such as feelings about capital punishment and appreciation of jazz music. This does not mean, of course, that a gene lurking in your DNA determines the amount or type of television that you watch. Rather, genes predispose certain personality traits that are associated with behavioral tendencies. In most cases researchers are referring to the influence of multiple genes that each interact independently with the environment to produce general dispositions, such as a preference for quiet and passive activities over active outdoor pursuits.

Yet growing evidence indicates that genes can be linked with some specificity to personality traits. For instance, a gene that regulates one particular dopamine receptor has been associated with novelty seeking in a number of studies (Cloninger, Adolfsson, & Svrakic, 1996; Ekelund, Lichtermann, Jaervelin, & Peltonen, 1999). The theory is that people with one form of this gene are deficient in dopamine and seek out novel experiences to increase the release of dopamine. Research on the traits of neuroticism and agreeableness implicates a particular gene that regulates serotonin, although the effect is not large (Jang et al., 2001).

Within the last ten years, numerous studies have tested various candidate genes to assess their relation to personality. Although specific genes do seem to be involved in personality, it is likely that the measured effects will continue to be small. This is not surprising, as there are thousands of genes that could affect personality, and each one is likely to contribute to various personality traits in distinctive ways. For instance, some genes seem to work in opposite ways, such a making people more or less neurotic, and therefore they may cancel each other out (Savitz & Ramesar, 2004). David Lykken and his colleagues (1992) noted that it may be the chance aggregation of genes that produces unique persons. They provide the interesting analogy of a poker hand, in which you receive the ten and king of hearts from your mother and the jack, queen, and ace of hearts from your father. Although neither parent alone has a meaningful hand, together they pass you a royal flush. Thus, your personality reflects the resulting hand you were dealt from both of your parents. Moreover, each person lives in different circumstances that may cause the selective expression of certain genes. Given the complexity of most people's personalities, the complexity of their underlying physiology is hardly surprising. As we gain a greater understanding of the human genome in general, it is likely that we will continue to make progress in identifying how specific genes interact with the environment to produce various aspects of personality.

Temperaments Are Evident in Infancy

temperaments Biologically based tendencies to feel or act in certain ways.

Genes work by affecting biological processes. Thus, to the extent that genes influence personality, there ought to be corresponding biological differences, referred to as **temperaments**, in personality. Temperaments are considered much broader than traits and are described as general tendencies to feel or act in certain ways. Most of the research on temperaments focuses on infants, in that personality differences that exist very early in life indicate the actions of biological mechanisms. Although life experiences may alter personality traits, temperaments represent the basic innate biological structure of personality.

Arnold Buss and Robert Plomin (1984) argue that essentially three personality traits can be considered temperaments. *Activity level* refers to the overall amount of energy and behavior a person exhibits. For example, some children zoom around the house at great speeds whereas others are less vigorous and still others slow-paced. *Emotionality* describes the intensity of emotional reactions, or how easily and frequently people become aroused or upset. Children who cry often or become easily frightened and adults who are quickly angered are likely to be high in emotionality. Finally, *sociability* refers to the general tendency to affiliate with others. Those high in this temperament prefer to be with others rather than to be alone. According to Buss and Plomin, these three temperamental styles are the main personality factors influenced by genes. Indeed, evidence from twin studies, adoption studies, and family studies indicates a powerful effect of heredity on these core temperaments.

SHYNESS AND INHIBITION Throughout this chapter we have used the example of shyness, which refers to feelings of discomfort and inhibition during interpersonal situations (Henderson & Zimbardo, 1998). People who are shy are excessively self-focused and spend a great deal of time worrying about what others think of them. The extent to which people are shy has been linked to early differences in temperament. Research conducted at Harvard University by Jerome Kagan, Nancy Snidman, and their colleagues has shown that children as young as six weeks of age can be identified as likely to be shy (Kagan & Snidman, 1991). Approximately 15 to 20 percent of newborns react to new situations or strange objects by becoming startled and distressed, crying, and vigorously moving their arms and legs. Kagan refers to these children as *inhibited*, which he views as being biologically determined. Showing signs of inhibition at two months of age predicts later parental reports that the children are shy at four years of age, and such children are likely to be shy well into their teenage years. Indeed, measures of brainstem reactivity at ages 10 to 12 correspond to ratings made of these children when they were four months old (Woodward et al., 2001), with inhibited children showing greater reactivity. Similar genetic findings for inhibited behavior have been found in a variety of species, including dogs and monkeys. The biological evidence suggests that the amygdala is involved in shyness. For instance, in one study people who were socially phobic—extremely shy—had much greater amygdala activation when shown unfamiliar faces than did control participants (Birbaumer et al., 1998).

Although shyness has a biological component, it clearly has a social component as well: Approximately one-quarter of behaviorally inhibited children are not shy later in childhood. This development typically occurs when parents create supportive and calm environments in which children are able to deal with stress and novelty at their own pace. At the same time, these parents do not completely shelter their children from stress, so that the children learn to deal with their negative feelings in novel situations. Moreover, at the social level of analysis, shyness is related to being highly feminine in sex-role orientation and varies across cultures; it is quite common

"I could cry when I think of the years I wasted accumulating money, only to learn that my cheerful disposition is genetic."

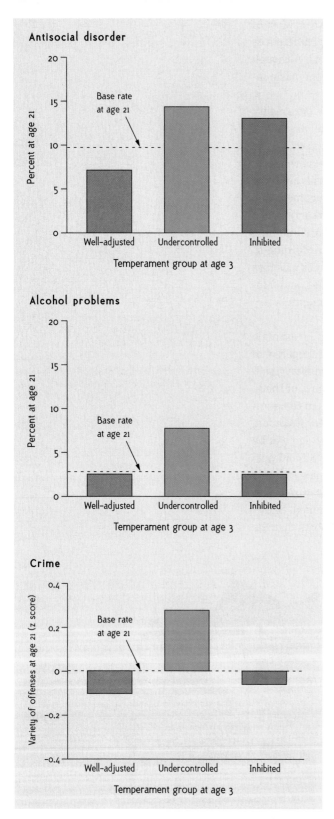

Antisocial disorder

Base rate at age 21

Percent at age 21

Well-adjusted | Undercontrolled | Inhibited

Temperament group at age 3

Alcohol problems

Base rate at age 21

Percent at age 21

Well-adjusted | Undercontrolled | Inhibited

Temperament group at age 3

Crime

Base rate at age 21

Variety of offenses at age 21 (z score)

Well-adjusted | Undercontrolled | Inhibited

Temperament group at age 3

12.10 Predicting Personality Temperament group at age 3 predicts antisocial personality disorder, alcohol problems, and criminal activity at age 21.

in Japan and less common in Israel, once again highlighting the interplay between nature and nurture.

LONG-TERM IMPLICATIONS OF TEMPERAMENTS To what extent do infant temperaments predict adult personality? If you were a fussy child, are you now a fussy adult? Recent research has documented compelling evidence that early childhood temperaments have a pervasive and powerful influence over behavior and personality structure throughout development (Caspi, 2000). In a particularly impressive study that we introduced in Chapter 3, a team of researchers in Dunedin, New Zealand, investigated the health, development, and personality of over 1,000 children born during a one-year period. These individuals were examined approximately every two years, with an impressive 97 percent remaining in the study through their twenty-first birthdays (Silva & Stanton, 1996). Children were classified at three years of age into temperamental types based on examiners' ratings. The classification of children at age three predicted personality structure and a variety of behaviors in early adulthood. For instance, those judged undercontrolled at age three were later more likely to have alcohol problems, to be criminals or unemployed, to attempt suicide, to be antisocial and anxious, and to have less social support (see Figure 12.10). Inhibited children were much more likely to become depressed. Early childhood temperaments do appear to be good predictors of later behaviors.

Personality Is Linked to Specific Neurophysiological Mechanisms

Genes act to produce temperaments, which affect how children respond to and shape their environments, which in turn interact with temperament to shape personality. But how do these genetic predispositions produce personality? That is, what neurophysiological mechanisms are linked to personality? Some theories focus on the underlying biological processes that produce the thoughts, emotions, and behaviors that make up personality. From this perspective, personality differences may reflect differences in the relative activation of different biological systems. Most research on the neurobiological underpinnings of personality has focused on the dimension of extraversion/introversion, and it is there that we focus as well.

AROUSAL AND EXTRAVERSION/INTROVERSION The intellectual founder of the modern biological approach to personality was Hans Eysenck (Figure 12.11). Eysenck believed that underlying differences in cortical arousal produce the observed behavioral differences between extraverts and introverts. Cortical arousal, or alertness, is regulated by the *ascending reticular activating system* (*ARAS*), and Eysenck proposed that this system differs between extraverts and introverts. Eysenck noted that extraverts seem constantly to be trying to seek out additional arousal—for example, by attending parties or seeking out new people. By contrast, introverts seem to avoid arousal by preferring solitary, quiet activities, such as reading. According to earlier psychological theories, each person prefers to operate, and operates best, at some *optimal level of arousal* (see Chapter 9). Eysenck proposed that the resting levels of the ARAS are higher for introverts than for extraverts, which places them above their optimal levels. In contrast, extraverts are typically below their optimal levels, which means that they are chronically underaroused. To operate efficiently, extraverts have to find arousal. Thus, they impulsively seek out new situations and new emotional experiences. Introverts don't want any additional arousal. They prefer quiet solitude with few incoming stimuli. So if you are an introvert, a noisy environment will distract you, whereas if you are an extravert, quiet places are boring. Consistent with Eysenck's theory, research has demonstrated that extraverts prefer to perform, and actually do perform better, in noisy settings (Geen, 1984).

If introverts are chronically more aroused than extraverts, they ought to be more sensitive to stimuli at all levels of intensity. This appears to be generally true. For instance, introverts are more sensitive to pain, and they salivate more than extraverts do if you place a drop of lemon juice on their tongues. However, evidence for baseline differences in arousal has been more difficult to produce. Thus, it appears that what differentiates introverts from extraverts is level of *arousability*, or reactivity to stimuli, with introverts being more arousable.

The psychologist Marvin Zuckerman describes the arousal-based trait of *sensation seeking* as similar to extraversion, but with an impulsive element that more closely matches Eysenck's psychoticism superordinate trait. According to Zuckerman, sensation seekers have a neurochemical deficiency that motivates them to seek arousal through adventures and new experiences. Moreover, those who are high in sensation seeking are easily bored and escape boredom through the use of drugs and alcohol.

12.11 Hans Eysenck Eysenck was one of the leading proponents of the idea that personality is rooted in biology.

NEUROPHYSIOLOGY OF EXTRAVERSION/INTROVERSION Since Eysenck's initial work on the biological underpinnings of personality, a number of theorists have offered refinements that reflect more recent understandings of functional neuroanatomy. Although a variety of theories have been proposed, they share common features, including a basic differentiation between approach and avoidance learning. Jeffrey Gray of Oxford University incorporated this distinction in his approach/inhibition model of learning and personality. Gray proposed that personality was rooted in motivational functions that had evolved to help organisms respond efficiently to reinforcement and punishment. In Gray's model, the **behavioral approach system (BAS)** consists of the brain structures that lead organisms to approach stimuli in pursuit of rewards. This is the *Go* system. There is also a *Stop* system, known as the **behavioral inhibition system (BIS)**, which is sensitive to punishment and therefore inhibits behavior that might lead to danger or pain (Figure 12.12). According to Gray, extraverts have a stronger BAS than BIS, so they are more influenced by rewards than by punishments. Indeed, extraverts tend to act impulsively in the face of strong rewards, even following punishment (Patterson & Newman, 1993). By contrast, introverts have a more active BIS. Their chronic anxiety often leads them to avoid social situations in which they anticipate possible negative outcomes.

The BIS is associated with activity in the frontal lobes, which are known to help inhibit inappropriate social behavior. Those with injury to the frontal lobes, especially the prefrontal cortex, exhibit social incompetence, disinhibition, impaired social judgment, and a lack of sensitivity to social cues. One imaging study found that introversion was associated with greater activation of the frontal lobes (Johnson et al., 1999), which supports Gray's model of BIS. The amygdala is another brain region involved in both social sensitivity and processing of cues related to possible punishment. Some researchers believe that personality traits such as fearfulness, anxiousness, and

behavioral approach system (BAS) The brain system involved in the pursuit of incentives or rewards.

behavioral inhibition system (BIS) The brain system that is sensitive to punishment and therefore inhibits behavior that might lead to danger or pain.

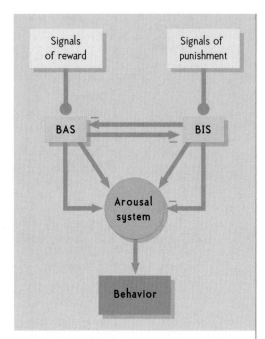

12.12 Behavioral Approach System (BAS)/ Behavioral Inhibition System (BIS) Signals of potential reward and punishment are processed by the BAS and the BIS. This information affects behavioral responses, with the BAS activating behavior and the BIS inhibiting behavior.

shyness are associated with excessive activation of the amygdala (Zuckerman, 1991). People who are usually anxious show a heightened amygdala response when observing pictures of neutral facial expressions, perhaps because they are especially sensitive to any signs of social rejection; faces looking at us with neutral expressions may trigger evaluation concerns (Somerville, Kim, Johnstone, Alexander, & Whalen, 2004).

Studies of the neurochemistry of the behavioral activation system implicate heightened activation of dopamine circuits for extraverts compared with introverts. Dopamine is involved in reward (as you will recall from Chapter 6), and extraversion appears to be associated with greater activation of dopamine receptors in the nucleus accumbens. Links between various brain regions that are rich in dopamine receptors process information about the reward value of objects and seem to be involved in extraversion (Depue & Collins, 1999). A second line of evidence for the role of dopamine in extraversion is that they are both associated with positive affect (Ashby, Isen, & Turken, 1999). Extraverts report high levels of energy, desire, and self-confidence. Indeed, the experience of positive affect may be the fundamental feature of extraversion (Lucas, Diener, Grob, Suh, & Shao, 2000). Finally, the link between dopamine and extraversion is also supported by the finding that a gene involved in dopamine reception is an indicator for novelty seeking, which itself is related to the greater willingness of extraverts to approach novel stimuli.

We still have much to learn about the biological bases of personality. As recently as three decades ago personality psychologists largely ignored the question of biology. Only with recent advances in technology have researchers started to explore the genetic and neurophysiological correlates of personality. We can anticipate many exciting new discoveries relevant to personality and temperament as the biological revolution spreads throughout psychological science (Canli, 2004). Consider a study in which only people possessing one particular form of a serotonin gene showed greater amygdala activity when looking at pictures of people showing emotional expressions than did those with the other form of the gene (Hariri et al., 2002). Interestingly, the first form of the gene has been associated with greater overall fearfulness and negativity. Using brain imaging and gene data together may become a powerful new way to assess the biological basis of personality.

Personality Is Adaptive

Natural selection has shaped the human genome over the course of evolution. Adaptive characteristics were likely to spread through the gene pool and have been passed along to increasing numbers in future generations. Thus, in terms of personality, we might expect that traits that were useful for survival and reproduction would have been favored. It is easy to imagine how being competitive might lead a person to obtain great rewards, or how being cooperative might increase a person's value to the group. But traits also provide important information about desirable and undesirable qualities in mates, such as whether a person is conscientious and agreeable or neurotic. David Buss (1999a) has argued that the Big Five personality traits emerged as foundational traits because they each provide important information regarding mate selection.

But if traits are adaptive, why are there such great individual differences among people? Natural selection ought to make people more similar rather than more different. After all, if a trait increased survival and reproduction, that trait should predominate in future generations. One possibility is that individual differences reflect characteristics that were of trivial importance over the course of evolution, perhaps resulting from random processes (Tooby & Cosmides, 1990). However, Buss and

Greiling (1999) have proposed that individual differences may reflect the inheritance of alternative strategies that become activated depending on situational context. For instance, consider a situation in which most people are honest and cooperative and therefore routinely trust others to be honest and cooperative as well. A dishonest person in such a system could do well by exploiting the basic trust of others. Of course, if too many people did this, then the system would change or collapse. However, the important point is that evolution has bestowed multiple strategies that are differentially adaptive depending on the environment, and that a built-in calibration system is sensitive to environmental demands. According to Buss and Greiling, the *early experiential calibration* system locks a person into the strategy chosen, to the exclusion of others that might have been pursued under different circumstances.

Another possible explanation for individual differences is that human groups whose members possess diverse skills have a selective advantage over other groups (Caporael, 2001). Members of successful groups and their relatives would all benefit from being members of a strong group, since they would be more likely to survive and reproduce. Consider the trait of novelty seeking. Having group members who seek out and explore new territory might lead to the discovery of new resources, such as an abundant food supply. At the same time, novelty seekers expose themselves to greater risks, and the group would suffer if all its members followed this strategy. Therefore it is to the advantage of the group to have cautious members in addition to bold members; these individuals may enhance the group in other ways, such as being more thoughtful or providing social support.

REVIEWING the Principles | What Is the Biological Basis of Personality?

Evidence from behavioral genetics has demonstrated that personality has a substantial genetic component explaining approximately half of the variance in most traits. Temperaments, the biological bases of traits, are evident in early childhood and have long-term implications for adult behavior. Temperamental styles reflect underlying differences in biological processes, suggesting that people are different in part because they have different underlying neurophysiology. Such differences may reflect adaptive advantages over the course of human evolution.

Can Personality Change?

The Jesuit maxim "Give me a child until he is seven, and I will show you the man" is the thesis of Michael Apted's well-known documentary series of films (the *Up* series), which follows the development of a group of British school children through interviews at ages 7, 14, 21, 28, 35, and 42. A striking aspect of these films is the apparent stability of personality over time. The child interested in the stars and science becomes a professor of physics; the boy who finds his childhood troubling and confusing develops an apparent schizo-affective personality; the reserved, well-mannered, upper-class girl at age 7 grows into the reserved, well-mannered woman in her pastoral retreat at age 35; a second-grader successfully predicts not only his future career, but also the schools that he will eventually attend. Are people really so stable? Is personality at age 70 preordained at age 7?

How should personality be stable?

From a functional perspective, it makes sense that personality should remain relatively stable over time. People need to predict the behavior of those they care about or rely on. When people choose friends or relationship partners, they do so with the general expectation that their interactions with these people will be somewhat predictable across time and situations. Yet people sometimes expect others to be able to change. Marital partners often hope that unfaithful spouses will change their wandering ways, and the penal system releases prisoners with the expectation that they will adopt less deviant roles in society. Are these expectations realistic?

Earlier you learned that childhood temperaments predict behavioral outcomes in early adulthood. But what about change during adulthood? If you are shy now, are you doomed to be shy forever? Indeed, the foundation of clinical psychology is the belief that people can and do change important aspects of their lives. People exert considerable energy trying to change—they attend self-help groups, read self-help books, buy time with therapists, and struggle with themselves and others. But how much do people really change over the course of their lives?

Traits Remain Stable over Time

How we define the essential features of personality has tremendous implications for whether it is fixed or changeable. Continuity over time and across situations is inherent in the definition of "trait," and accordingly it is not surprising that most research finds personality traits to be remarkably stable over the adult life span (Heatherton & Weinberger, 1994). For instance, over many years the relative rankings of individuals on each of the Big Five personality traits remain stable (McCrae & Costa, 1990). People who are very extraverted tend to stay very extraverted; people who are very introverted tend to remain that way as well. A recent meta-analysis of 150 studies consisting of nearly 50,000 participants who had been followed for at least one year found strong evidence for stability in personality (Roberts & Friend-DelVecchio, 2000). The rank orderings of individuals on any personality trait were quite stable over long periods of time across all age ranges. However, stability was lowest for young children and highest for those over age 50 (Figure 12.13). This suggests that personality does change somewhat in childhood, but that it becomes more stable by middle age. Such findings tend to support the contention of William James, who stated in 1890, "for most of us, by age 30, the character has set like plaster and will

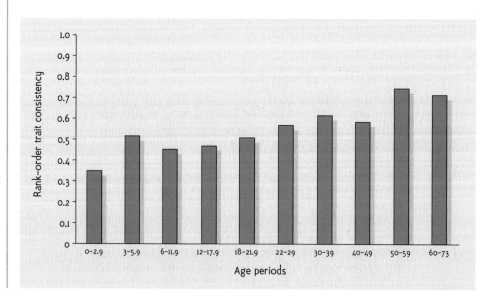

12.13 The Stability of Personality This graph shows consistency across time measures for personality at different ages. Consistency is lowest in childhood and highest after age 50.

CHAPTER 12 | Personality

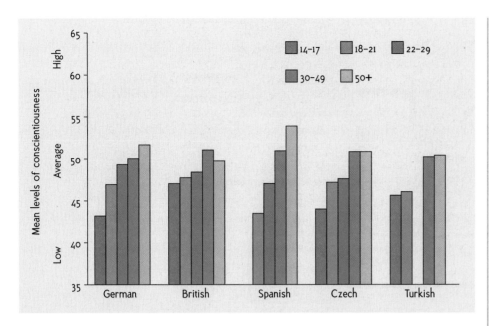

12.14 **Mean Levels of Conscientiousness at Different Ages in Five Cultures** Note that in all five cultures, conscientiousness increases as people age.

never soften again." According to the meta-analysis, James was right that personality becomes set, but this appears to happen a little later than age 30.

Stability in rank ordering means that individuals stay the same compared to others. However, is it possible that all people change in personality as they age, while retaining their relative rankings? For instance, consider the stereotype that people become wiser and more cautious as they get older. Is this true? In general, people do become less neurotic, less extraverted, and less open to new experiences as they get older. People also tend to become more agreeable and much more conscientious with age (Srivastava, John, Gosling, & Potter, 2003). These effects are not large, but they are consistent. What is most amazing is that the pattern holds in different cultures (Figure 12.14; McCrae et al., 2000). This suggests that age-related changes in personality occur independent of environmental influences, and therefore that personality change itself may be based in human physiology. Indeed, some evidence shows that personality change has a genetic component, such that the extent of change is more similar in monozygotic twins than in dizygotic twins (McGue, Bacon, & Lykken, 1993).

The reason personality is so stable, especially among adults, appears to be due to a number of factors. If personality is determined in part by biological mechanisms, then we can expect changes only to the extent that there are changes in biological makeup. The fact that the brain develops well into early adulthood may explain the greater evidence of personality change before age 30. Perhaps more important, environments tend to be relatively stable, especially after early adulthood. People tend to marry those who are similar in attitudes and personality, and people tend to have successive jobs that have the same level of status. It seems likely that the stability of situations contributes to the stability of personality.

Characteristic Adaptations Change across Time and Circumstances

In their research on potential change in personality, Robert McCrae and Paul Costa (1999) emphasize an important distinction between basic tendencies of personality and characteristic adaptations (Figure 12.15). *Basic tendencies* are dispositional traits

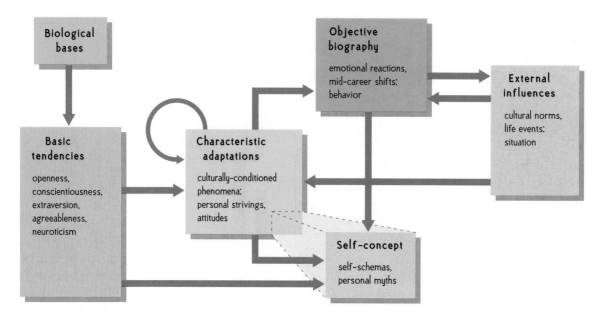

12.15 McCrae and Costa's Model of Personality Basic tendencies are biologically based, but characteristic adaptations are influenced by the situation and how the person behaves. The lines with arrows indicate some of the ways in which the different components interact. The important point is that basic tendencies do not change across situations, but observable behavior (objective biography) does because it is influenced by personal goals and motives as well as by the situation.

quantum change A transformation of personality that is sudden, profound, and enduring, and that affects a wide range of behaviors.

that are determined to a great extent by biological processes. As such, they are very stable. *Characteristic adaptations* are the adjustments people make to situational demands, which tend to be consistent because they are based on skills, habits, roles, and so forth. These changes in behavior do not indicate changes in the underlying core disposition. For instance, consider a young adult who is high in extraversion. She may go to a lot of parties, be a thrill seeker, and have multiple sexual partners. As she approaches 90, she is less likely to do these things, but she may still have many friends and enjoy traveling. Although the behaviors are different, they continue to reflect the underlying trait of extraversion.

Dan McAdams (1999; 2001) has proposed that some aspects of personality do change, depending on how you define personality. According to McAdams, personality can be examined at three levels (Table 12.4). At the basic level are *dispositional traits*, such as the Big Five, which by their nature are relatively stable. At the second level are *personal concerns*, which include goals, motives, and social roles; these reflect the tasks and challenges that people face within specific contexts or situations. Unlike dispositional traits, McAdams argues, personal concerns ebb and flow as people mature into new roles (such as career and family) and encounter new challenges. For instance, as people grow older they may express more concern with the well-being of future generations, for example, by making plans to educate their children or by donating to environmental charities. At the third level are *life narratives*, the personal myths and stories that people use to define their lives and identities. McAdams argues that life narratives evolve as people develop coherent stories from the different places, opportunities, and positions they encounter (Baver, McAdams, & Sakaeda, 2005).

Indeed, some people tell stories of sudden, dramatic changes in personality, much like the transformation of Ebenezer Scrooge in Charles Dickens's *A Christmas Carol*. William Miller and Janet C'de Baca (2001) describe these stories as examples of **quantum change**, which is a transformation of personality that is sudden, profound, and enduring. The people telling the stories claimed to remember the episodes vividly, down to the date and time of day when the change occurred. The quantum change experiences tended to be unexpected, often originating from some external source or event. The specific antecedents were amazingly varied and ranged from taking a walk to cleaning a toilet to having an abortion. Those who re-

LEVEL	DEFINITION	EXAMPLES
TABLE 12.4 Three Levels of Personality		
Dispositional traits	Broad dimensions of personality that describe assumed internal, global, and stable individual differences in behavior, thought, and feeling. Traits account for consistency in individual functioning across different situations and over time.	Friendliness Dominance Tendency toward depression Punctuality
Characteristic adaptations	More particular facets of personality that describe personal adaptations to motivational, cognitive, and developmental challenges and tasks. Characteristic adaptations are usually contextualized in time, place, situation, or social role.	Goals, motives, and life plans Religious values and beliefs Cognitive schemas Relational modes Psychosocial stages Developmental tasks
Life stories	Internalized and evolving narratives of the self that people construct to integrate the past, present, and future and provide life with some sense of unity, purpose, and meaning. Life stories address the problems of identity and integration in personality—problems especially characteristic of modern adulthood.	Earliest memory Reconstruction of childhood Perceptions of future self "Rags to riches" stories Imagery and theme in story

ported quantum change emphasized that everything about them changed, including their temperaments, perceptual styles, goals, and values. After the change, most people reported an increased sense of meaning and happiness, an increased sense of spirituality, and increased overall satisfaction. Of course, without an objective measure of personality before the experience it is hard to know whether the reported changes are accurate, but family members and friends substantiated the stories, which gives them some credence.

Brain Injury and Pharmacological Interventions Affect Personality

To the extent that biological processes determine personality, we might anticipate that physical changes would produce personality changes. Indeed, damage to specific regions of the brain is associated with dramatic changes in personality. For example, damage to the frontal lobes—such as in the case of the railroad worker Phineas Gage, described in Chapter 4, or Elliot, who had brain surgery, described in Chapter 10—has been found to produce a variety of changes in personality, including causing people to become more extraverted, impulsive, socially inappropriate, and moody (Stuss, Gow, & Hetherington, 1992). Patients with temporal-lobe damage also experience personality change, often becoming humorless, obsessive, paranoid, and rule bound. One sign of a possible brain tumor is a sudden and profound change in personality. Indeed, the whole point of psychosurgery, which was popular in the 1950s, was to alter the brain surgically to change abnormal aspects of personality (see Chapter 4). Some diseases that cause damage to the brain, such as Alzheimer's disease, also produce changes in personality that can be dramatic and surprising to family members.

NEUROCHEMISTRY AND PERSONALITY CHANGE In his 1993 book *Listening to Prozac*, Peter Kramer claimed that a drug used to treat depression could lead to changes in personality. His book includes stories of patients who underwent dramatic transformations after taking Prozac, a drug that treats depression by enhancing the activity of the neurotransmitter serotonin through selectively blocking its reuptake into the presynaptic neuron, thereby prolonging its effects in the synapse. In one story, a dour, shy, pessimistic woman suddenly became outgoing and sociable after she took Prozac. Her bubbly new personality, Kramer claimed, is a result of her altered serotonin levels.

Research has demonstrated that serotonin is related to some aspects of personality. For instance, low levels of serotonin are associated with hostility, aggressiveness, and criminality. Low levels of serotonin have also been linked to impulsivity and sensation seeking (Depue & Collins, 1999; Zuckerman, 1995). Thus, we might expect that drugs that enhance the activity of this neurotransmitter would lead to decreased impulsiveness. Indeed, evidence has been found that serotonin-enhancing drugs do cause significant changes in personality, such as increased social dominance and decreased hostility (Brody et al., 2000). One research team found that use of drugs that enhanced serotonin led to changes in two of the Big Five personality traits: neuroticism decreased and extraversion increased (Bagby, Levitan, Kennedy, Levitt, & Joffe, 1999). This effect apparently occurs independent of changes in mood or depression (Ekselius & von Knorring, 1999). That is, the personality change does not appear to occur simply because depression is lifted.

In perhaps the best empirical test of the effects of serotonin-based drugs, researchers had normal volunteers take a selective serotonin reuptake inhibitor (SSRI) and assessed its effects on social behavior and personality (Knutson et al., 1998). Animal research had previously shown that SSRIs led to decreased aggression and increased social affiliation among monkeys, and the researchers sought to examine whether it would produce similar effects in nondepressed humans. Following a careful screening for any psychiatric disorders, volunteers received either an SSRI or a placebo for four weeks. The results indicated that administration of the SSRI led to reductions in hostility and increases in cooperative behavior. Thus, altering brain neurochemistry can change personality even among normal, nondepressed individuals.

Profiles in Psychological Science

Reinventing the Material Girl

According to the 2005 *Guinness Book of World Records,* Madonna is the most successful female solo artist in the history of popular music, so far selling more than 250 million albums during a phenomenal 20-year career. Throughout it all, Madonna has been an extremely provocative entertainer, transforming her public image numerous times, from virgin bride and sex goddess to doting mother and author of children's books. Has Madonna's personality really changed or is it just her public behavior that has changed? Madonna has often been accused of redefining herself to stay in front of the camera and maintain her celebrity status. A key point we have made in trying to understand personality change is that changes in behavior do not necessarily reflect changes in core personality. As Madonna traveled the world in 2004 on her "Re-Invention" tour, to what extent was she reinventing herself and to what extent was she simply displaying an unchanging propensity to vary her public image?

Madonna Louise Ciccone was born in 1958 to working-class parents in a Detroit suburb. Following the death of her mother when she was six, she reportedly helped take care of her siblings and dedicated herself to doing well at school. She was a devout Catholic with passionate religious beliefs. But evidence from her childhood also indicates that she liked to perform in front of others, jumping onto tables to sing and dance when the mood struck her. In high school she became obsessed with dance and excelled at cheerleading. Indeed, her dancing was so good that she won a dance scholarship to the University of Michigan. Impatient for faster success, she dropped out of college after her first year and headed to New York City. Within six years she released two albums; the second, *Like a Virgin*, catapulted her to stardom.

12.16 Madonna In two of Madonna's recent incarnations, she is (left) a stylish follower of Eastern mysticism and (right) a mature, sophisticated children's book author.

During the ensuing 20 years, Madonna cemented her reputation as a celebrity icon. As each public persona began to fade, she reinvented herself in some jolting new way (Figure 12.16). In an early video she danced provocatively in a wedding dress; in subsequent videos and concerts, her costumes became more and more revealing until she finally exposed all in her book *Sex*, which contained pictures considered fairly graphic for the mainstream. Even into her forties, Madonna has continued to provide shocking moments, such as her open-mouthed kiss of Britney Spears at the 2003 MTV Video Music Awards. Once again, Madonna thrust herself into the limelight.

Over the years, Madonna has maintained a more serious and reflective side. She starred in a number of films, notably as Eva Peron in the film version of the musical *Evita*. During this period Madonna also became a mother, giving birth to a daughter in 1996. She subsequently had a child with her second husband, Guy Ritchie. Perhaps inspired by her new role as parent, Madonna has become a successful author of children's books. Her fifth book, *Lotsa de Casha*, was published in 2005.

All of Madonna's different personas have shared consistent themes that indicate little change in her core personality. First, she is relentlessly ambitious, excelling in dance as a teenager; in music and books as an adult; and in business, making a number of shrewd deals that have ensured her long-term financial success. Second, she has demonstrated an ability to reinvent her public image, each time capturing attention and fan support, even as the media have questioned her various publicity stunts. Finally, since childhood she has displayed a deeply spiritual side, first as a devout Catholic and more recently as a follower of Kabbalah, a branch of Jewish mysticism. Indeed, in 2004 Madonna announced she was adopting the name Esther in tribute to the ancient Hebrew queen of Persia who saved her people from annihilation. Many traditional followers of Kabbalah have expressed outrage at her adoption of a new-age form of their beliefs. And so Madonna's controversial life continues. What becomes apparent is that with each reinvention, Madonna is not changing at the core, but rather changing how she presents her basic personality, even to the point of affecting an English accent. Although the behaviors are different at the various stages of her life and career, the underlying confidence, intelligence, and charisma she possesses likely explain how she became one of the most famous celebrities of this era. ■

REVIEWING the Principles | Can Personality Change?

The evidence that personality is generally stable over the life course is considerable, especially for basic dispositions such as traits. People adapt to novel situations by altering behavior, but they tend to do so in ways that are consistent with their basic personalities. As shown by their life stories, people believe that they change, and such change narratives might help predict motives and behavior. Indeed, the story of change is itself a part of personality whether or not change occurs. Although it is unclear whether people can purposefully change, brain injury or disease and alterations in neurochemistry can transform personality. This supports the general idea that biological processes are important to personality.

Conclusion

Studying personality is complex because each person is unique. Researchers have contributed to the accumulated principles underlying personality by examining cognitive processes, both conscious and unconscious; behavioral dispositions; and people's own life narratives. Knowing a person well requires knowing a great deal about him or her. At the same time, it is now apparent—from research that crosses levels of analysis—that the basic blueprint for personality is genetically determined and is manifest through biologically based temperaments. Yet these temperaments do not predetermine personality; interaction between people and their social worlds creates unique individuals, perhaps by influencing brain processes that determine personality. What is clear is that personality is coherent and stable. Although people change jobs, relationships, and living circumstances, the fundamental core of their personalities stays with them throughout their lives.

Summarizing the Principles of Personality

How Have Scientists Studied Personality?

1. **Psychodynamic theories emphasize unconscious and dynamic processes:** Freud believed that personality was in part the result of unconscious conflicts. The personality is comprised of the id, ego, and superego. Stages of psychosexual development occur from birth to adolescence. The ego uses defense mechanisms to reduce the anxiety of the oppositional demands of the id and superego. Neo-Freudians have focused on relationships, especially the emotional

attachments that children develop to their parents, rather than sexual forces (libido).

2. **Humanistic approaches emphasize integrated personal experience:** Humanists view personality as the result of human experiences and beliefs. Humans strive to realize their full potential, and may be hampered in doing so if they do not receive unconditional positive regard from their parents. The positive psychology movement researches subjective well-being.

3. **Type and trait approaches describe behavioral dispositions:** Personality type theories focus more on description than explanation. Trait theories are based on the assumption that personality is a collection of traits that individually vary, and exist in a hierarchy of importance. Eysenck proposed a model of personality that showed that the biologically based traits (extraversion, emotional stability, psychoticism) are the important traits, under which lesser traits are organized. The Big Five theory considers personality to be the result of the composition of the basic traits: openness to new experience, conscientiousness, extraversion, agreeableness, and neuroticism.

4. **Personality reflects learning and cognitive processes:** Through interaction with their environment, people learn patterns of responding that are guided by expectancies and values. The extent to which people believe they can achieve specific outcomes, called self-efficacy, is an important determinant of behavior. The Cognitive-Affective Personality System (CAPS) emphasizes self-regulation.

How Is Personality Assessed, and What Does It Predict?

5. **Personality refers to both unique and common characteristics:** Idiographic approaches are person-centered; they evaluate personality from the perspective of assessing the unique pattern of characteristics of an individual. Nomothetic approaches focus on characteristics that are common among all people, but on which people vary (i.e., traits).

6. **We can use objective and projective methods to assess personality:** Projective measures (e.g., the Thematic Apperception Test, the Rorschach inkblot test) subjectively evaluate the unconscious issues a person projects onto ambiguous stimuli. Objective measures are straightforward assessments, usually made by self-report questionnaires or observer ratings.

7. **Observers show accuracy in trait judgments:** Your close acquaintances may be more accurate at predicting your behavior than you are.

8. **People sometimes are inconsistent:** Mischel proposed that situations are more important than traits in predicting behavior (situationism).

9. **Behavior is influenced by the interaction of personality and situations:** Situations vary in the extent to which they influence behavior and interact with personality to determine behavior.

What Is the Biological Basis of Personality?

10. **Personality is rooted in genetics:** Nearly all personality traits have a genetic component. Twin and adoptions studies have found that 40–60 percent of personality variation is due to genetics. Personality characteristics are polygenetic, and their expression is the result of interaction with the environment.

11. **Temperaments are evident in infancy:** Temperaments, the general tendencies of how we behave, are biologically mediated and observable in infants.

12. **Personality is linked to specific neurophysiological mechanisms:** Cortical arousal is regulated through the ascending reticular activating system (ARAS), and results in characteristics of introversion/extraversion. The behavioral approach system (BAS) and the behavioral inhibition system (BIS) affect variations in arousal and the behavioral responses. Dopamine pathway activation is greater in extraverts.

13. **Personality is adaptive:** Variations in personality and skills of individual members benefit a group, and provide an advantage for group survival.

Can Personality Change?

14. **Traits remain stable over time:** Trait consistency is lowest for young children and highest for those over age 50. Biological and environmental factors are more stable in adulthood.

15. **Characteristic adaptations change across time and circumstances:** Basic tendencies are dispositional traits that are determined to a great extent by biological processes,

and are therefore stable. Characteristic adaptations are contextualized by time, place, situation, and social role. Quantum-change events, as reported in life stories, are significant in changing personality.

16. **Brain injury and pharmacological interventions affect personality:** Drugs that affect the action of the neurotransmitter serotonin create changes in personality, particularly with regard to social dominance and reduced hostility.

Applying the Principles

1. After studying the different approaches to personality, Diane decides that multiple theories each partially explain her personality. She feels strongly that her childhood relationship with her mother has had an impact. She also realizes that she is basically introverted, conscientious, and cautious. Finally, she knows that she likes quiet situations and feels awkward around strangers. Which three theories of personality, respectively, correspond to Diane's three interpretations of her personality?

_____ a) psychodynamic; trait; social-cognitive
_____ b) humanistic; social-cognitive; behavioral
_____ c) behavioral; trait; psychodynamic
_____ d) humanistic; trait; behavioral

2. As part of the application process for becoming a police officer, candidates must have a personality evaluation. There are generally three parts to this evaluation. The first requires the candidates to decide which traits listed on a questionnaire apply to them; this is a(n) _____ measure. In the next part, the candidates report what they "see" when viewing some ink blots; this is a(n) _____ measure. Finally, the candidates undergo an extensive life history interview; this is a(n) _____ approach to personality.

_____ a) situationism; projective; objective
_____ b) objective; nomothetic; thematic apperception
_____ c) ideographic, objective; situationism
_____ d) objective; projective; ideographic

3. Bonita is a bit reckless, drives fast, and plunges into new situations without much forethought. Her sister Anna is almost the complete opposite. All but which of the following biological factors of personality are likely to vary between the two girls?

_____ a) temperament
_____ b) genotype
_____ c) cortical arousal
_____ d) natural selection

4. Your roommate Todd is very close to his older brother Jim, who is now married and whose wife is expecting a baby. Todd complains that his brother is not as much fun as he used to be and wonders if Jim has had a personality change. Based on what you have learned about the stability of personality, what would you say?

_____ a) It is likely that Jim has experienced some dramatic changes now that he is becoming a father; he will be his "old self" again soon.
_____ b) Jim's characteristic adaptations are consistent but his personal concerns have changed.
_____ c) Jim's dispositional tendencies are biological and have changed as he has aged.
_____ d) Jim has experienced a quantum change in personality because of an extraordinary life event.

ANSWERS: 1. a 2. d 3. d 4. b

Key Terms

behavioral approach system (BAS), p. 505
behavioral inhibition system (BIS), p. 505
defense mechanisms, p. 485
ego, p. 485
five-factor theory, p. 490
humanistic approaches, p. 487
id, p. 485

idiographic approaches, p. 494
interactionists, p. 498
nomothetic approaches, p. 494
objective measures, p. 495
personality, p. 483
personality trait, p. 483
personality types, p. 488
projective measures, p. 495
psychodynamic theory, p. 484

psychosexual stages, p. 485
quantum change, p. 510
situationism, p. 496
superego, p. 485
TAT (Thematic Apperception Test), p. 495
temperaments, p. 502
trait approach, p. 488

Further Readings

Funder, D. C. (2004). *The personality puzzle* (3rd ed.) New York: Norton.

Heatherton, T. F., & Weinberger, J. L. (1994). *Can personality change?* Washington, DC: American Psychological Association.

Hogan, R., Johnson, J., & Briggs, S. (1997). *Handbook of personality psychology.* San Diego: Academic Press.

McAdams, D. P. (2005). *The person: An integrated introduction to personality psychology* (4th ed.). Fort Worth: Harcourt.

Pervin, L. A., & John, O. P. (1999). *Handbook of personality: Theory and research.* New York: Guilford Press.

Living with Autism

Jay Jensen, 23, is a high-functioning person with autism who works a regular job doing data entry. Quite focused and indifferent to outside distractions, Jay is able to accomplish many tasks in a much shorter time than his nonautistic colleagues. Awareness of the symptoms of autism has increased so much in recent years that the number of children diagnosed with the disorder has risen dramatically.

Disorders of Mind and Body

13

Gertrude and Henry met in the 1930s. She found him annoying but eventually agreed to marry him after he threatened suicide. Gertrude became pregnant after three years of marriage, and in the fifth month of pregnancy, Gertrude's doctor predicted that she would have twins. In fact, she had quadruplets: Nora, Iris, Myra, and Hester. (Their names have been changed to protect their privacy.) Henry was frequently unemployed, so they could not afford to support four babies. A local newspaper raised money, and a house was donated to them. A steady stream of visitors wanted to see the babies, and Henry began charging admission. After a while, however, he became worried about the safety of his family and barred all visitors. At one point, he fired a pistol at his wife, mistaking her for an intruder.

13.1 The Genain Quadruplets as Adults

Henry and Gertrude both believed that the four girls really represented one person split into four. They consistently preferred the two larger babies, Nora and Myra, to the other two, and Gertrude took a particular dislike to Hester, especially after she caught her masturbating. Gertrude continued to worry excessively about masturbation. After she caught Hester and Iris engaging in mutual masturbation, she had a doctor amputate their clitorises. As the girls got older, Henry insisted on watching them dress and undress, and he even watched them changing their sanitary pads. In high school, Hester became irritable and depressed; her behavior was at times destructive and bizarre. She "admitted" to a series of sexual activities dating back to elementary school. Rather than fully exploring the causes for this behavior, her parents concluded that masturbation had made her mentally retarded. She was heavily sedated and kept at home. Although the other girls graduated from high school and even held jobs for a while, they all had psychotic episodes resulting in hospitalization. All four women were eventually diagnosed with schizophrenia. The National Institute of Mental Health offered free care in return for the opportunity to study them. To preserve their anonymity, the NIMH dubbed them the Genain quadruplets and assigned them first names beginning with the initials of NIMH (Figure 13.1; information from Rosenthal, 1963).

Although today the Genains are recognized as being mentally ill and receive appropriate treatment, the mentally ill have not always been viewed in a humane manner. In the Middle Ages, the Genain quadruplets might have been thought to be possessed by demons and been persecuted. In the 1700s, they would likely have languished in understaffed, overcrowded mental institutions. There would have been little attempt to understand their disorders and even less of an attempt to treat them. In the 1800s, the focus would have been on the environmental factors contributing to their illness, such as the physical abuse they suffered and their father's bizarre and inappropriate behavior. Although psychological factors probably contributed to the development of the quadruplets' mental disorders, we now understand that biological factors play a critical role in schizophrenia. Advances in research have demonstrated that most mental disorders are ultimately disorders of both mind and body, of both biological and psychological factors. ■

Timeline

460–377 B.C.E.
Humoral Imbalance Hippocrates explains abnormal behavior as the result of imbalances of four bodily fluids: blood, phlegm, black bile, and yellow bile.

130–200 C.E.
Psychological Factors Galen postulates that abnormal behavior could be due to imbalances in bodily fluids but also suggests psychological origins.

1400s
Demonic Possession During the Middle Ages, abnormal behavior is attributed to demonic possession.

1831
Unacceptable Impulses Johann Christian Heinroth states that mental disorders are the result of unconscious conflict arising from unacceptable impulses.

Over the course of human history, people have struggled with how best to understand **psychopathology**—literally, sickness or disorder of the mind. The prevailing view in the twenty-first century is that psychopathology has its origins in psychological turmoil and biological dysfunction. Philosophers as early as Plato and Aristotle suggested that mental illness might be the result of conflicts between thought and emotion. Sigmund Freud was the first to develop a theory of psychopathology and to propose specific treatment techniques based on his theory.

Understanding the role of both psychological and biological factors in the genesis of mental disorders is now known to be critical. Psychological scientists are working at all levels of analysis on many mental disorders so that we can understand and treat them effectively. The willingness of those who are afflicted with mental illness, such as the Genain sisters, to participate in scientific investigations has allowed researchers to make significant strides in understanding mental disorders. Advances in technology such as structural and functional neuroimaging have given us a window into the workings of the human brain. Our increased understanding of the effects of genes, neurotransmitters, and hormones on brain and behavior has resulted in remarkable advances in understanding both normal and abnormal human behavior. At the same time, longitudinal studies have demonstrated that children who are raised in certain types of environments, such as with abusive parents, are more likely than children not raised in such environments to develop some form of psychopathology later in life. In addition, we know that environment can trigger some mental disorders, as when combat leads to posttraumatic stress disorder or the death of a loved one triggers a bout of depression. This chapter examines how we think about mental illness and the circumstances that we believe produce mental disorders.

psychopathology A disorder of the mind.

How Are Mental Disorders Conceptualized and Classified?

How do you know if a person has a mental disorder? It can be quite challenging to decide if a given behavior is caused by psychopathology, because behavior, especially unusual behavior, always needs to be reviewed according to the situation. A person running through the streets, screaming hysterically, sobbing, grabbing people, and hugging them might have some form of mental illness—or could be celebrating following a phone call that told her she'd won a Nobel Prize. Many behaviors that are considered normal in one setting may be considered deviant in other settings. Some tribes in Africa spread feces in their hair as part of rituals. You can predict how this same behavior would be received in an industrialized society. In some Native American and Far Eastern cultures, having spirits talk to you is considered

1867

Brain Diseases Wilhelm Griesinger argues that "mental diseases are brain diseases," in that mental disorders result from brain dysfunction.

1883

Classifying Mental Illness Emil Kraepelin suggests a classification system based on a biological conception of abnormal behavior.

1893

The Unconscious Sigmund Freud and Josef Breuer develop the psychoanalytic approach, emphasizing that mental disorders result from unsatisfied drives and unconscious wishes.

1925

Behaviorism John B. Watson argues that mental illness results from basic principles of conditioning.

1930s

Psychological Testing Researchers develop the Minnesota Multiphasic Personality Inventory (MMPI), which is now widely used to assess various aspects of personality and psychopathology.

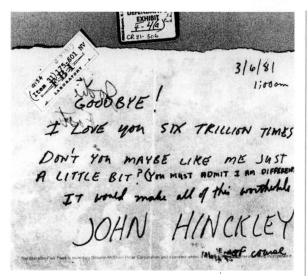

13.5 Hinckley and the Insanity Defense John Hinckley Jr. and a letter he wrote to actress Jodie Foster, with whom he was obsessed.

1981, Hinckley shot Reagan in the lung and Reagan's press secretary, James Brady, through the head. Both survived, but Brady sustained permanent severe physical and cognitive impairments. There was no doubt that Hinckley planned and committed the crime. The only question at the trial was whether he was legally insane at the time. After many hours of testimony, it became clear that Hinckley had had psychological problems beginning in early childhood. The two sides disagreed, however, about the severity of those problems and whether they met the criteria for legal insanity. According to the law at the time, the prosecution had to prove that the defendant was sane if the defense claimed that he was not. The jury in the Hinckley trial concluded that there was reasonable doubt about his sanity at the time of the crime and returned a verdict of "not guilty by reason of insanity." As a result of the public outrage following the verdict, the law was revised so that the burden of proof now falls on the defense to prove that a defendant was not sane at the time of a crime. For both the prosecution and the defense, psychologists are often called as expert witnesses regarding possible psychological problems that may have existed at the time a person committed a crime.

Psychological Science *in Action* ○ ● ○

Forensic Assessment and Profiling

The field of *forensic psychology* involves the application of psychological science to the criminal justice system. Forensic psychologists, who typically have a Ph.D. in clinical psychology, are called on to perform several different functions, ranging from assisting in child-custody disputes, to examining eyewitness testimony, to advising on jury selection, to improving interrogation techniques, to helping design correctional facilities. Another common duty is determining whether a defendant is mentally competent to stand trial—that is, whether the defendant can understand the legal proceedings and contribute to his or her own defense. The case of Theodore Kaczynski, referred to in the media as the Unabomber, hinged on his competence to stand trial (Figure 13.6). Kaczynski's lawyers planned to argue that he was insane at the time of the crimes (the planting of bombs at various locations around the United

13.6 Theodore Kaczynski Kaczynski, known as the Unabomber, shown here (top) as a young professor and (bottom) after his arrest. Kaczynski pled guilty rather than use the insanity defense.

States), but Kaczynski refused to consider this approach. Kaczynski then requested permission to act as his own attorney, but this request was denied. Forensic psychologists examined Kaczynski and still determined that although he met the DSM criteria for paranoid schizophrenia, he was still competent to stand trial. Faced with the choice of having his lawyers present a case for insanity or pleading guilty, Kaczynski pled guilty.

Another challenging task for forensic psychologists is predicting whether individuals are dangerous, such as whether they are likely to become violent in the workplace, be sexual predators, or stalk and kill their spouses. In many states, those predicted to be dangerous can be committed against their will to a mental health facility. However, determining whether a person is dangerous is fraught with ethical, legal, and clinical difficulties. Although forensic psychologists have worked hard to develop and refine ways of accurately predicting violent behavior, it remains virtually impossible to do so. Edmund E. Kemper III murdered his grandparents in 1964. At his trial, he was found not guilty by reason of insanity and was committed to a mental institution. Five years later, he was judged to be "cured" and was released. Three years later, he murdered six college students, his mother, and one of her friends. This time, the jury found him sane and guilty. As Kemper's case illustrates, patients mistakenly judged not dangerous can pose a considerable threat. Conversely, patients mistakenly judged dangerous can languish for years in mental institutions. In part because of the difficulty of predicting dangerousness, if a forensic assessment indicates that a person poses a danger to someone, the clinician has the obligation to warn that person. This duty to warn is one of the few situations in which clinicians are required to violate patient confidentiality (Anfang & Appelbaum, 1996).

Forensic psychologists also assist law enforcement officers in pursuing criminals. The Federal Bureau of Investigation's Behavioral Science Unit works to devise techniques for developing psychological profiles of criminals. For example, forensic psychologists sometimes examine murder scenes for clues to the relationship between the murderer and victim. Certain types of wounds indicate that the murderer was acting in a rage, suggesting some prior relationship with the victim. Compared with such *expressive* crime scenes, *instrumental* crime scenes are those in which the victim appears simply to have been used so that the murderer could achieve other aims, such as obtaining money or sex. Research indicates that the crime scene often provides basic information regarding the murderer, which helps law enforcement officers identify potential suspects (Salfati, 2000).

How accurate are criminal profilers? Psychologist Richard Kocsis and his colleagues in Australia have conducted thorough studies of criminal profiling (Kocsis, 2004; Kocsis, Hayes, & Irwin, 2002). Kocsis finds that profiling is most successful when it follows scientific principles, such as being objective and using critical thinking. Those who rely on gut instincts or hunches rarely develop successful profiles. In Kocsis's tests, undergraduate science students often outperform seasoned detectives in producing accurate profiles, perhaps because the students rely almost entirely on facts, while the detectives perhaps draw too much on past experience and intuition and pay too little attention to what actually happened. Through careful research like that conducted by Kocsis, forensic psychologists can help establish methods to develop psychological profiles of criminals. ■

Psychopathology takes many forms, and mental disorders are consequently difficult to define and categorize. Although the behavioral manifestations of mental disorders vary widely, those who are diagnosed with these disorders have two things in common: Their behavior is maladaptive, and it interferes with some important aspect of their lives. Diagnoses of specific mental disorders are based on the checklist system of the *DSM*. Clinical assessments typically consisting of interviews and psychological tests are used to examine a person's mental functions and psychological health. The specific cause of most mental disorders is unknown and may arise from a complex interaction of psychological, biological, and cognitive-behavioral factors. Psychopathology is conceptualized differently in the legal system than in the medical field: the former focuses on responsibility for one's actions, the latter on understanding and treating the disorder.

Can Anxiety Be the Root of Seemingly Different Disorders?

What does the fear of spiders have in common with the need to repeatedly check that the stove is turned off? They are both manifestations of anxiety disorders. Anxiety itself is normal and even useful. It can prepare us for upcoming events and motivate us to learn new ways of coping with life's challenges. For some people, however, anxiety can become debilitating and can interfere with every aspect of life. **Anxiety disorders** are characterized by excessive anxiety in the absence of true danger. It is normal to be anxious in stressful or threatening situations. It is abnormal to feel strong chronic anxiety without cause.

anxiety disorders Disorders characterized by the experience of excessive anxiety in the absence of true danger.

There Are Different Types of Anxiety Disorders

People suffering from anxiety disorders feel tense, anxious, and apprehensive. They are often depressed and irritable because they cannot see any solution to the anxiety they feel. Constant worry can make falling asleep and staying asleep difficult, and attention span and concentration can be impaired. Problem solving and judgment may suffer as well. Chronic anxiety also causes a variety of somatic symptoms, due to the arousal of the autonomic nervous system. Sweating, dry mouth, rapid pulse, shallow breathing, increased blood pressure, and increased muscular tension are all consequences of autonomic arousal. Chronic arousal can also result in hypertension, headaches, and intestinal problems and can even cause illness or tissue damage. Because of their high levels of autonomic arousal, those who suffer from anxiety disorders also exhibit restless and pointless motor behaviors. Exaggerated startle response is typical and behaviors such as toe tapping and excessive fidgeting are common. Recent research has shown that chronic stress can produce atrophy in the hippocampus, a brain structure involved in learning and memory (McEwen, 2000). It is not yet known whether the damage is reversible, or if there are functional implications of hippocampal atrophy. The fact that chronic stress can damage the body and brain, however, indicates the importance of identification and effective treatment of disorders that involve chronic anxiety. Although different anxiety disorders share some emotional, cognitive, somatic, and motor symptoms, the behavioral manifestations of these disorders are quite different (Barlow, 2002).

PHOBIC DISORDER A **phobia** is a fear of a specific object or situation. Fear can be adaptive, as it can lead us to avoid potential danger, such as poisonous snakes and rickety bridges. In phobias, however, the fear is exaggerated and out of proportion to the actual danger. Phobias are classified based on the object of the fear. *Specific phobias* (formerly known as simple phobias) involve particular objects and situations, such as snakes (ophidiophobia), enclosed spaces (claustrophobia), and heights (acrophobia). *Social phobia* is a fear of being negatively evaluated by others and includes fear of public speaking and of eating in front of others. Specific phobias are more common than social phobia, affecting about 10 percent of the population versus 2 to 5 percent for social phobia (Robins & Regier, 1991). Women are diagnosed with specific phobias at least twice as often as men, but with social phobia only slightly more often.

GENERALIZED ANXIETY DISORDER Whereas the anxiety in phobic disorders has a specific focus, the anxiety in **generalized anxiety disorder** is diffuse and omnipresent. People with this disorder are constantly anxious and worry incessantly about even minor matters (Sanderson & Barlow, 1990). Because the anxiety is not focused, it can occur in response to almost anything, and so the sufferer is constantly on the alert for problems. This hypervigilance results in distractibility, fatigue, irritability, and sleep problems, as well as headaches, restlessness, and muscle pain. Probably 3 to 4 percent of the population is affected by this disorder, with women more likely to be diagnosed than men (Kessler et al., 1994).

PANIC DISORDER It has been estimated that panic disorder affects about 3 percent of the population, with women twice as likely to be diagnosed as men (Kessler et al., 1994). **Panic disorder** sufferers experience attacks of terror that are sudden and overwhelming. The terror can seemingly come out of nowhere or can be cued by external stimuli or internal thought processes. Panic attacks typically last for several minutes. The victim of such an attack begins to sweat and tremble; her heart races, she begins to feel short of breath, and her chest hurts; she can feel dizzy and lightheaded with numbness and tingling in her hands and feet. People experiencing panic attacks often feel that they are going crazy or that they are dying, and people who suffer from persistent panic attacks attempt suicide much more frequently than those in the general population (Fawcett, 1992; Korn et al., 1992; Noyes, 1991). A related disorder is **agoraphobia**, a fear of being in situations in which escape is difficult or impossible, such as a crowded shopping mall. Being in those situations causes panic attacks. Those who experience panic attacks during adolescence are especially likely to develop other anxiety disorders, such as agoraphobia, PTSD, and general anxiety disorder, in adulthood (Goodwin et al., 2004).

OBSESSIVE-COMPULSIVE DISORDER **Obsessive-compulsive disorder** (OCD) involves frequent intrusive thoughts and compulsive actions, and affects 2 to 3 percent of the population. It is more common in women than men and generally begins in early adulthood (Robins & Regier, 1991; Weissman et al., 1994). Obsessions and compulsions plague sufferers of this disorder. *Obsessions* are recurrent, intrusive, and unwanted thoughts, ideas, or images. They often include fear of contamination, accidents, or one's own aggression. *Compulsions* are particular acts that the OCD patient feels driven to perform over and over again. The most common compulsive behaviors are cleaning,

phobia An irrational fear of a specific object or situation.

generalized anxiety disorder A diffuse state of constant anxiety not associated with any specific object or event.

panic disorder An anxiety disorder characterized by sudden, overwhelming attacks of terror.

agoraphobia An anxiety disorder marked by fear of being in situations in which escape may be difficult or impossible.

obsessive-compulsive disorder (OCD) An anxiety disorder characterized by frequent intrusive thoughts and compulsive actions.

checking, and counting. For instance, people may constantly check to make sure they locked the door because of their obsession that their home may be invaded, or they may engage in superstitious counting to protect against accidents. Those with OCD anticipate catastrophe and loss of control. However, as opposed to those who suffer from other anxiety disorders, who fear what might happen to them, those who suffer from OCD often fear what they might do or might have done:

> While in reality no one is on the road, I'm intruded with the heinous thought that I *might* have hit someone . . . a human being! God knows where such a fantasy comes from. . . . I try to make reality chase away this fantasy. I reason, "Well, if I hit someone while driving, I would have *felt* it." This brief trip into reality helps the pain dissipate . . . but only for a second. . . . I start ruminating, "Maybe I did hit someone and didn't realize it. . . . Oh my God! I might have killed somebody! I have to go back and check." Checking is the only way to calm the anxiety. (Rapoport, 1990, pp. 22–27)

Anxiety Disorders Have Cognitive, Situational, and Biological Components

Although the behavioral manifestations of anxiety disorders can be quite different, they share some causal factors (Barlow, 2002). When presented with ambiguous or neutral situations, anxious individuals tend to perceive them as threatening, whereas nonanxious individuals assume them to be nonthreatening (Eysenck, Mogg, May, Richards, & Matthews, 1991). The ambiguous sentence "The doctor examined little Emma's growth" is interpreted by anxious individuals as "The doctor looked at little Emma's cancer" and by nonanxious individuals as "The doctor measured little Emma's height." Anxious individuals also tend to focus excessive amounts of attention on perceived threats (Rinck, Reinecke, Ellwart, Heuer, & Becker, 2005). Threatening events are thus more easily recalled than nonthreatening events, increasing their perceived magnitude and frequency.

In addition to cognitive components, situational factors also play a role in the development of anxiety disorders. In Chapter 6 you learned that monkeys will develop a fear of snakes if they observe other monkeys responding to snakes in a fearful way. Similarly, a person could develop a fear of elevators by observing another person's reaction to the closing of the elevator doors. Such a fear might then generalize to other enclosed spaces, resulting in claustrophobia. Biological factors also seem to play an important role in the development of anxiety disorders; recent investigations have resulted in a number of exciting findings. For instance, children who have an inhibited temperamental style during infancy and childhood are more likely to have anxiety disorders later in life (Fox, Henderson, Marshall, Nichols, & Ghera, 2005). Recall from Chapter 12 that these children are usually shy and tend to avoid unfamiliar people and novel objects. These inhibited children are especially at risk for developing social phobia (Biederman et al., 2001). In one recent study, adults who were categorized as inhibited during their second year of life received brain scans while viewing pictures of familiar faces and of novel faces. Compared with adults who were categorized as uninhibited before age two, the inhibited group showed greater activation of the amygdala to the novel faces (Schwartz, Wright, Shin, Kagan, & Rauch, 2003). This suggests that some aspects of childhood temperament are preserved in the adult brain. Next we will consider some of the ways these three factors interact in the development of two anxiety disorders.

"Is the Itsy Bitsy Spider obsessive-compulsive?"

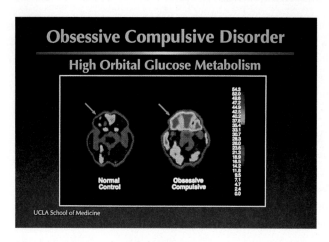

Obsessive Compulsive Disorder

High Orbital Glucose Metabolism

Normal Control — Obsessive Compulsive

UCLA School of Medicine

13.7 PET Scans of People with OCD The scans of people with OCD show greater activity in the frontal lobes, basal ganglia, and thalamus than do those of normal controls.

THE CAUSES OF OBSESSIVE-COMPULSIVE DISORDER A paradoxical aspect of OCD is that people are aware that their obsessions and compulsions are irrational and yet they are unable to stop them. One explanation is that the disorder results from operant conditioning. Anxiety is somehow paired to a specific event, and the person engages in behavior that reduces anxiety. This reduction of anxiety is reinforcing and increases the chance of engaging in that behavior again. For example, say you are forced to shake hands with someone who has a bad cold, and you have just seen that person wiping his nose with his right hand. Shaking that hand might cause you to be anxious or uncomfortable because you don't want to get sick yourself. As soon as the pleasantries are over, you run to the bathroom and wash your hands. You feel relieved. You have just paired hand washing with a reduction in anxiety, thus increasing the chances of hand washing in the future.

There is good evidence that the etiology of OCD is at least in part genetic (Crowe, 2000). Recently, it has been demonstrated that the caudate nucleus is dysfunctional in people with OCD (Baxter, 2000). The caudate is part of the basal ganglia, a region that helps to suppress impulses. In patients with OCD, the caudate is smaller and has structural abnormalities (Figure 13.7). In addition, patients with basal ganglia disease often manifest symptoms of OCD. Because this region is involved in impulse suppression, it is thought that dysfunction in this region results in the leak of mpulses into consciousness. The prefrontal cortex then becomes overactive in an effort to compensate (Whiteside, Port, & Abramowitz, 2004). It has been demonstrated that there are alterations in brain waves over the prefrontal cortex in OCD patients; severing the connections between the prefrontal cortex and the caudate can often result in dramatic improvement in the symptoms of the disorder.

There is also growing evidence that OCD can sometimes be triggered by environmental factors. In particular, it appears that a streptococcal infection can cause symptoms of OCD in some young children. Originally identified in 1998 by Susan Swedo and her colleagues at the National Institute of Mental Health, this syndrome strikes virtually overnight, with children suddenly displaying odd symptoms of OCD, such as engaging in repetitive behaviors, developing irrational fears and obsessions, and having facial tics. Researchers have speculated that an autoimmune response damages the caudate, thereby producing the symptoms of OCD (Snider & Swedo, 2004). Importantly, treatments that enhance the immune system have been found to diminish the symptoms of OCD in children with this syndrome. Why some children are susceptible to this autoimmune response is currently unknown.

It may be that biological and cognitive-behavioral factors interact to produce the symptoms of OCD. A dysfunctional caudate nucleus allows impulses to enter consciousness, and these impulses may give rise to the obsessions of OCD. The prefrontal cortex becomes overactive in an attempt to compensate, and this overactivity can establish associations between obsessions and behaviors that reduce the anxiety arising from the obsessions. These behaviors thus become compulsions through conditioning.

THE LINK BETWEEN PANIC DISORDER AND AGORAPHOBIA People who suffer from agoraphobia avoid going into open spaces or to places where there might be crowds. Specifically, they seem to fear being in places from which escape might be difficult or embarrassing. In extreme cases, sufferers of this type of phobia may feel unable to leave their homes:

Ms. Watson began to dread going out of the house alone. She feared that while out she would have an attack and would be stranded and helpless. She stopped riding the subway to work out of fear she might be trapped in a car between stops when an attack struck, preferring instead to walk the 20 blocks between her home and work. She also severely curtailed her social and recreational activities—previously frequent and enjoyed—because an attack might occur, necessitating an abrupt and embarrassing flight from the scene. (Spitzer, Skodol, Gibbon, & Williams, 1983)

This sort of description is typical of those with agoraphobia, and such descriptions have led many to explore the relationship between panic attacks and agoraphobia. The symptoms of sympathetic nervous system arousal that occur during a panic attack often lead victims to believe that they are having a heart attack. From a cognitive-behavioral perspective, a tendency to catastrophize (to expect the worst) paired with some kind of trigger stimulus can produce a panic attack. It has been speculated that agoraphobia is the result of untreated panic attacks (Barlow, 1988). People who have had panic attacks begin to fear having them again. This fear results in avoidance of situations in which it might be embarrassing to have an attack and difficult to escape. The fear then develops into a phobia.

Although agoraphobic symptoms are thought to arise from learned associations, panic attacks themselves seem more influenced by biological factors. Research suggests that panic disorder is in part genetic and linked to abnormalities that result in increased arousal of the central nervous system (Crowe, 2000). Studies show that infusions of lactate and inhalation of carbon dioxide, which heighten arousal, can produce panic attacks in those with a family history of panic disorder, but not in those without a family history (Rapee, Brown, Antony, & Barlow, 1992; Figure 13.8). Interestingly, although medication can be quite effective in reducing or eliminating panic attacks, it has no effect on agoraphobia. The fear of open or public places has been learned, and treating the neural basis for the fear has no effect. The conditioned response must be unlearned via cognitive-behavioral therapy.

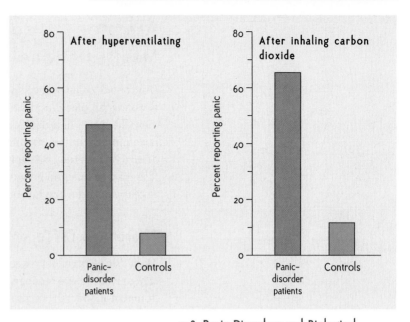

13.8 Panic Disorders and Biological Factors Research participants prone to panic attacks are more likely than normal controls to have a panic attack after hyperventilating or inhaling carbon dioxide.

REVIEWING
the Principles | Can Anxiety Be the Root of Seemingly Different Disorders?

On the surface, many of the anxiety disorders seem to be quite different. However, they share many of the same emotional, cognitive, somatic, and motor symptoms. All of the disorders in this category are associated with anxiety that is out of proportion with reality. This anxiety may arise from biological factors, but many of the behavioral and cognitive manifestations of the disorders are strongly influenced by psychological and environmental factors.

Are Mood Disorders Extreme Manifestations of Normal Moods?

Our moods color every aspect of our lives. When we are happy, the world seems like a wonderful place, and we are filled with boundless energy. When we are sad, we view the world in a decidedly less rosy light. Feelings of sadness, hopelessness, and isolation are all too common. Few of us, however, experience these symptoms day after day until they disrupt our ability to work, learn, and play. In addition, although it is easy to imagine how periods of sadness can interfere with daily life, periods of excessive elation can be equally devastating.

There Are Different Types of Mood Disorders

Mood disorders reflect extreme emotions, with depressive disorders featuring persistent and pervasive feelings of sadness, and bipolar disorders involving radical fluctuations in mood. Although some of their characteristics overlap, the two categories represent fundamentally different disorders.

major depression A disorder characterized by severe negative moods and a lack of interest in normally pleasurable activities.

dysthymia A form of depression that is not severe enough to be diagnosed as major depression.

DEPRESSIVE DISORDERS Within the category of depressive disorders are major depression and dysthymia. In order to be diagnosed with **major depression**, a person must have one of two symptoms: depressed (often irritable) mood or loss of interest in pleasurable activities. In addition, the person must have other symptoms such as appetite and weight changes, sleep disturbances, loss of energy, difficulty concentrating, feelings of self-reproach or guilt, and frequent thoughts of death and suicide. The following case study is of a 56-year-old woman diagnosed with depression:

> She described herself as overwhelmed with feelings of guilt, worthlessness, and hopelessness. She twisted her hands almost continuously and played nervously with her hair. She stated that her family would be better off without her and that she had considered taking her life by hanging herself. She felt that after death she would go to hell, where she would experience eternal torment, but that this would be a just punishment. . . . (Andreasen, 1984, p. 39)

Episodes of depression can last from a few weeks to many years. On average, depressive episodes last approximately six months. In many cases, the episodes are self-limiting and resolve without intervention. Although 90 percent of sufferers will recover from depression, they have a 50 percent chance of experiencing another depressive episode in the future (Keller, Shapiro, Lavori, & Wolfe, 1982).

Unlike major depression, **dysthymia** is of mild to moderate severity. Those diagnosed with dysthymia must have a depressed mood most of the day, more days than not, for at least two years. The depression is not, however, severe enough to merit a diagnosis of major depression. Periods of dysthymia last from 2 to 20 or more years, although the typical duration is about 5 to 10 years. Because the depressed mood is so long lasting, some psychological scientists consider it to be a personality disorder rather than a mood disorder. In fact, earlier editions of the *DSM* included a category of "affective personality" in the personality disorders section. In later editions, this term was dropped and dysthymia was added to the mood disorders category. The distinction between a depressive personality, dysthymic disorder, and major depression is unclear. They may be points along a continuum rather than distinct disorders. In support of this view, it has been found that dysthymia often precedes major depression (Lewinsohn, Allen, Seeley, & Gotlib, 1999; Lewinsohn, Rodhe, Seeley, & Hops, 1991).

Estimates of the likelihood of developing major depression in one's lifetime vary from as low as 7 percent to as high as 20 percent. One study found the lifetime prevalence of depression to be 13 percent in men and 21 percent in women (Kessler et al., 1994). These statistics are for major depression; the number of persons affected by less severe depression is much higher. A recent survey found that nearly half of Americans have experienced some form of depressive disorder.

BIPOLAR DISORDERS Although we all experience variations in our moods, normal fluctuations from sadness to exuberance seem minuscule in comparison to the extremes experienced by those with bipolar disorder. Bipolar disorder was previously known as manic depression, a term that captured the essence of the disorder. Those who are diagnosed with **bipolar disorder** have periods of major depression but also experience episodes of mania. *Manic episodes* are characterized by elevated mood, increased activity, diminished need for sleep, grandiose ideas, racing thoughts, and extreme distractibility. Kay Redfield Jamison, whom we will discuss in greater detail shortly, describes one of her own episodes of mania:

> With vibrissae twinging, antennae perked, eyes fast-forwarding and fly faceted, I took in everything around me. I was on the run. Not just on the run but fast and furious on the run, darting back and forth across the hospital parking lot, trying to use up a boundless, restless, manic energy. I was running fast, but slowly going mad. (Jamison, 1995, p. 3)

During episodes of mania, the heightened levels of activity and euphoria often result in excessive involvement in pleasurable but foolish activities—such as sexual indiscretions, buying sprees, and risky business ventures—that the individual will come to regret once the mania has subsided. Whereas some sufferers of bipolar disorder experience true manic episodes, others may experience less extreme mood elevations. These *hypomanic episodes* are often characterized by heightened creativity and productivity and can be extremely pleasurable and rewarding. People experiencing episodes of major depression and mania are diagnosed with *bipolar I* disorder, whereas people fluctuating between major depression and hypomania are diagnosed with *bipolar II*. A third category of bipolar disorder is **cyclothymia**, in which individuals experience hypomania and mild depression. Bipolar disorder is much less common than depression; the lifetime prevalence is estimated at 1 percent. In addition, whereas depression is more common in women, the prevalence of bipolar disorder is equal in women and men.

Mood Disorders Have Cognitive, Situational, and Biological Components

Mood disorders can be devastating. The sadness, hopelessness, and inability to concentrate that characterize major depression can result in the loss of jobs, friends, and family relationships. Because of the profound effects of this disorder, and the danger of suicide, a great deal of research has been focused on understanding the causes of and treating major depression. Suicide is also a risk with those with bipolar disorder. In addition, errors in judgment during manic episodes can have devastating effects on the lives of those who suffer from the disorder as well as on their families and friends.

DEPRESSION IS CAUSED BY A COMBINATION OF FACTORS Studies of twins, families, and adoptions support the notion that depression has a genetic

bipolar disorder A mood disorder characterized by alternating periods of depression and mania.

cyclothymia A less extreme form of bipolar disorder.

539

component. Although there is some variability among studies, concordance rates between identical twins are generally around four times higher than rates between fraternal twins (Gershon, Berrettini, & Goldin, 1989). The existence of a genetic component implies that biological factors are involved in depression, but there is as yet no consensus as to what these factors are. We know that medications that increase the availability of norepinephrine alleviate depression, whereas those that decrease levels of this neurotransmitter can cause depression. More recent medications, such as Prozac, selectively increase serotonin, so there is increased interest in understanding the role of this neurotransmitter in modulation of mood. Studies of brain function have suggested neural structures that may be involved in mood disorders. Damage to the left prefrontal cortex often leads to depression, but this is not true of damage to the right hemisphere. The brain waves of depressed persons show low activity in these same regions in the left hemisphere. Interestingly, this pattern persists in patients who have been depressed but are currently in remission. It therefore may be a kind of biological marker of predisposition to depression.

Biological rhythms have also been implicated in depression. Depressed patients enter REM sleep more quickly and have more of it. There is also evidence for abnormalities in a number of other biological rhythms, such as body temperature. Many people show a cyclical pattern of depression depending on the season. This disorder, known as **seasonal affective disorder** (**SAD**), results in periods of depression corresponding to the shorter days of winter in northern latitudes (Figure 13.9). Treatment with an artificial light source seems to alleviate the depression, possibly by resetting biological rhythms.

Although biological factors may play a role in depression, situational factors are also important. A number of studies have implicated life stressors in many cases of depression (Hammen, 2005). One source of stress seems to be particularly relevant for depression is interpersonal loss, such as having someone close die or getting divorced (Paykel, 2003). In one classic study, depression was especially likely in the face of multiple negative events (Brown & Harris, 1978; Figure 13.10). Another study found that depressed patients had more negative life events during the year before the onset of their depression (Dohrenwend, Shrout, Link, Skodol, & Martin, 1986). How an individual reacts to stress, however, can be influenced by interpersonal relationships, which play an extremely important role in depression (Joiner, Coyne, & Blalock, 1999). Regardless of any other factors, relationships contribute to the development of depression, alter people's experiences when depressed, and ultimately may be damaged by the constant needs of the depressed person. Many people report

seasonal affective disorder (SAD) A disorder in which periods of depression occur during the times of year with less sunlight.

How does the social environment affect depression?

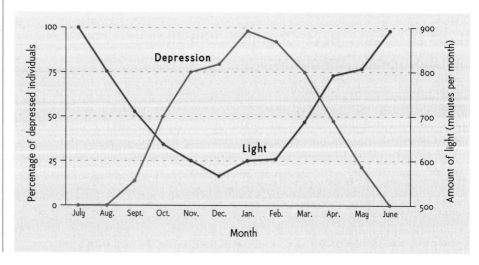

13.9 Depression and Light For some people, there is a direct correspondence between the amount of sunlight and their levels of depression.

CHAPTER 13 | Disorders of Mind and Body

negative reactions to depressed people, perhaps because of their poor social skills. Over time, people may avoid interactions with those who are depressed, which in turn makes them even more depressed, resulting in a downward spiral (Dykman, Horowitz, Abramson, & Usher, 1991). By contrast, a person who has a close friend or group of friends is less likely to become depressed when faced with stress. This protective factor is not related to the number of friends, but to the quality of the friendships. One good friend is more protective than a large number of casual acquaintances.

Cognitive processes also play a role in depression. Aaron T. Beck proposed that depressed people think about themselves, their situation, and the future in a negative manner, which he refers to as the *cognitive triad* (Beck, 1967, 1976; Beck, Brown, Seer, Eidelson, & Riskind, 1987; Beck, Rush, Shaw, & Emery, 1979). Misfortunes are blamed on personal defects, whereas positive occurrences are seen as the result of luck. Nondepressed people tend to do the opposite. Beck also notes that depressed people make *errors in logic,* such as overgeneralizing based on single events, magnifying the seriousness of bad events, and personalizing, or taking responsibility for, bad events in the world that have little to do with them.

A second cognitive model of depression is the **learned helplessness model** (Seligman, 1974, 1975), in which people see themselves as unable to have any effect on events in their lives. Seligman's model is based on years of research demonstrating that animals placed in aversive situations that they cannot escape eventually become passive and unresponsive, lacking the motivation to try new methods of escape when given the opportunity. People suffering from learned helplessness come to expect that bad things will happen over which they will have little control. The attributions, or explanations, they make for negative events tend to refer to personal factors that are stable and global, rather than to situational factors that are temporary and specific. This attributional pattern leads people to feel hopeless about making positive changes in their lives (Abramson, Metalsky, & Alloy, 1989). The accumulation of evidence suggests that dysfunctional cognitive patterns are a cause rather than a consequence of depression.

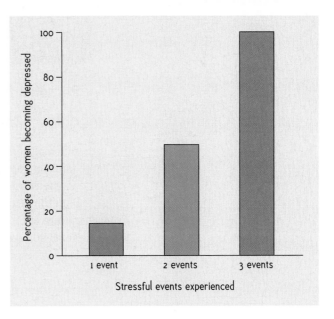

13.10 Depression and Stress In this study, the greater the number of stressors, the more likely it was that people felt depressed (Brown & Harris, 1972).

learned helplessness model A cognitive model of depression in which people feel unable to control events around them.

BIPOLAR DISORDER IS A BIOLOGICAL DISORDER Although depression may arise from a variety of factors, evidence is strong that bipolar disorder is predominantly a biological disorder. Twin studies reveal that the concordance for bipolar disorder in identical twins is upward of 70 percent, versus only 20 percent in fraternal or dizygotic twins (Nurnberger, Goldin, & Gershon, 1994). In the 1980s, a genetic research study was carried out on the Amish, an ideal population because they keep good genealogical records and few outsiders marry into the community. In addition, substance abuse is virtually nonexistent among adults, so mental illness is easier to detect. The results revealed that bipolar disorder ran in a limited number of families and that all of those afflicted had a similar genetic defect (Egeland et al., 1987).

Genetic research suggests that the hereditary nature of bipolar disorder is complex and not linked to a single gene. Current research is focusing on identifying genes that may be involved. In addition, it appears that in families with bipolar disorder, successive generations tend to have more severe illness and earlier age of onset (McInnis et al., 1993; Petronis & Kennedy, 1995). Focus on this pattern of transmission may help to reveal the genetics of the disorder, but the specific nature of the heritability of bipolar disorder remains to be discovered.

Personal Insight into Psychopathology

One of the world's foremost authorities on bipolar disorder has unique insight among psychological scientists—she has suffered from the disorder since childhood. For much of her professional career, Johns Hopkins University professor Kay Redfield Jamison kept this a secret, but eventually acknowledged her struggles with manic depression in her award-winning 1995 memoir *An Unquiet Mind.* It is possible that Jamison's experience with mania and depression helped guide her research into the nature of bipolar disorder. Her work has helped shape the study of the disorder, and her 1990 textbook on manic-depressive illness, coauthored with Frederick Goodwin, is considered the standard for the field. She has been cited as one of the "Best Doctors in the United States," was chosen by *Time* magazine as a "Hero of Medicine," has received numerous awards for her research and books, and won a MacArthur "genius grant" in 2001.

It is truly amazing that Jamison (Figure 13.11) has been so successful in spite of having bipolar disorder. In *An Unquiet Mind,* she details how she was intensely emotional and occasionally obsessive as a child. When she was 17, she had her first serious bout of what she describes as psychotic, profoundly suicidal depression, which seemed to strike out of the blue. Although she would later suffer even worse depression, at the time the experience was beyond anything she had ever imagined. In a recent essay she describes it this way: "The experience forever changed how I looked at myself, the gods, and the mentally ill; it was clear that the line between the mad and the not-mad had dissolved for me, and along with its dissolution went a packet of dreams and my faith in what the future might bring" (Jamison, 2004).

Jamison experienced deepening swings from nearly psychotic exuberance to paralyzing depression throughout her undergraduate years at the University of California at Los Angeles (UCLA). In part because of personal experiences, Jamison decided to pursue clinical psychology in graduate school. She was highly successful, being selected UCLA Graduate Woman of the Year and winning a National Science Foundation Research Fellowship. In 1975, after obtaining her Ph.D., she joined the UCLA Department of Psychiatry, where she directed the Affective Disorders Clinic. Within months after she began this job, her condition deteriorated dramatically. She began hallucinating and feared that she was truly losing her mind. This so terrified her that she sought out a psychiatrist with whom she felt safe, who quickly diagnosed Jamison as having manic-depressive illness and prescribed a drug called lithium. (You will read more about lithium and other treatments for bipolar disorder in Chapter 14.)

One of the unfortunate side effects of lithium is that it blunts positive feelings. Those who have bipolar disorder experience profoundly enjoyable highs during their manic phases. In a talk at the University of Melbourne, Jamison describes it this way: "But my manias, at least in their early and mild forms, were absolutely intoxicating states that gave rise to great personal pleasure, an incomparable flow of thoughts, and a ceaseless energy that allowed the translation of new ideas into papers and projects" (July 26, 2000). Even though patients with bipolar disorder know that lithium helps them, they resent the drug and often refuse to take it. Jamison took her medication only occasionally for the first few years and continued to experience episodes of mania, during which she made bad decisions and engaged in risky behaviors. These episodes were always followed by intense depression that left her

13.11 Kay Redfield Jamison Jamison was able to overcome her crippling bipolar disorder to succeed as a professor and researcher and an author.

unable to get out of bed. During one period of particularly severe depression, Jamison attempted suicide by taking an overdose of lithium. She survived only because she reflexively answered a phone call from a relative, who realized that something was wrong and called Jamison's psychiatrist. Left untreated, approximately 20 percent of those with bipolar disorder commit suicide.

Although lithium has helped Jamison, she also credits the psychological support she receives from her psychiatrist, as well as the general support of her family and friends. Jamison herself has made the point that lithium can rob people of creative energy. In her 1993 book *Touched With Fire,* she asks whether lithium would have dampened the genius of artists and writers who may have had mood disorders, such as Vincent van Gogh, Georgia O'Keeffe, Michelangelo, Ernest Hemingway, and Emily Dickinson. Jamison demonstrates that there is a strong association between manic depression and artistic genius, and she raises the disturbing question of whether eradicating the disease would rob society of much great art. Jamison herself embodies the type of a genius plagued by bipolar disorder. Her early career benefited from the energy and creativity of her manic phases even as her personal life was threatened by devastating depression. Her intelligent, beautiful writings have provided inspiration and hope to her fellow sufferers and have given the rest of us a glimpse into the lives of those suffering from mental illness. ■

REVIEWING
the Principles | Are Mood Disorders Extreme Manifestations of Normal Moods?

Although all people experience extreme moods and fluctuations in mood, mood disorders are qualitatively different from normal variations in emotion. Mood disorders disrupt the person's ability to function for significant lengths of time, and they are accompanied by a number of psychological and physiological elements. Depressive and bipolar disorders are included in the same *DSM* category and share some behavioral characteristics, but they are distinctly different disorders. Depressive disorders seem to result from a variety of psychological, cognitive, and biological factors, whereas bipolar disorders seem to arise from predominantly biological factors.

Is Schizophrenia a Disorder of Mind or Body?

Schizophrenia literally means "splitting of the mind" and refers to a split between thought and emotion. **Schizophrenia** is a *psychotic disorder,* which means that it is characterized by alterations in thoughts, perceptions, or consciousness. Current estimates are that about 1 percent of the population has schizophrenia (Keith, Regier, & Rae, 1991). This rate remains approximately the same in all countries of the world, although the prognosis tends to be better in developing than developed cultures (Kulhara & Chakrabarti, 2001), perhaps because there is more tolerance for symptoms or greater sympathy for unusual or different people in those countries. During the 1940s and 1950s, researchers and clinicians broadened the definition of schizophrenia by proposing new subtypes and suggesting that schizophrenia could sometimes masquerade as other disorders. Because of these changes, by 1952, 80 percent

schizophrenia A mental disorder characterized by alterations in perceptions, emotions, thoughts, or consciousness.

TABLE

13.3 | *DSM-IV Subtypes of Schizophrenia*

SUBTYPE	CHARACTERISTICS
Paranoid type	Preoccupation with delusion(s) or auditory hallucinations. Little or no disorganized speech, disorganized or catatonic behavior, or inappropriate or flat affect.
Disorganized type	All the following—disorganized speech, disorganized behavior, and inappropriate or flat affect—are prominent in behavior, but catatonic-type criteria are not met. Delusions or hallucinations may be present, but only in fragmentary or noncoherent form.
Catatonic type	At least two of the following: extreme motor immobility; purposeless excessive motor activity; extreme negativism (motionless resistance to all instructions) or mutism (refusing to speak); peculiar or bizarre voluntary movement; echolalia.
Undifferentiated type	Does not fit any of the subtypes above, but meets the symptom criteria for schizophrenia.
Residual type	Has experienced at least one episode of schizophrenia, but currently does not have prominent positive symptoms (delusions, hallucinations, disorganized speech or behavior). However, continues to show negative symptoms and a milder variation of positive symptoms (odd beliefs, eccentric behavior).

SOURCE: *Diagnostic and Statistical Manual of the American Psychiatric Association,* 1994.

of the patients in the New York Psychiatric Institute were diagnosed with schizophrenia, up from 20 percent in the 1930s. With more specific guidelines described in the recent editions of the *DSM,* the rate of schizophrenia diagnoses has stabilized (Manderscheid et al., 1985). Clinicians and researchers now rely on lists of symptoms to diagnose various subtypes of schizophrenia (Table 13.3).

Schizophrenia Has Positive and Negative Symptoms

Schizophrenia is arguably the most devastating of the mental disorders for the victim and for the family. It is characterized by a combination of motor, cognitive, behavioral, and perceptual abnormalities that result in impaired social, personal, and/or vocational functioning. Some researchers have grouped these characteristics into two categories: **Positive symptoms** are excesses, whereas **negative symptoms** are deficits in functioning.

POSITIVE SYMPTOMS OF SCHIZOPHRENIA Delusions and hallucinations are the symptoms most commonly associated with schizophrenia. **Delusions** are false personal beliefs based on incorrect inferences about external reality (Table 13.4). Delusional people will persist in their beliefs in spite of evidence to the contrary. An example of a *paranoid delusion* arose in response to the Domino's Pizza advertising campaign "Avoid the Noid." The Noid was depicted as an elflike creature who turned pizzas cold. In 1989, Kenneth Noid, a 22-year-old Georgia man, concluded that this ad campaign was directed at him, and in retaliation he took two Domino's employees hostage. The hostages escaped and Kenneth Noid surrendered to the police.

positive symptoms Symptoms of schizophrenia, such as delusions and hallucinations, that are excesses in behavior.

negative symptoms Symptoms of schizophrenia marked by deficits in functioning such as apathy, lack of emotion, and slowed speech and movement.

delusions False personal beliefs based on incorrect inferences about reality.

TABLE 13.4	Delusions and Associated Beliefs
Persecution	Belief that others are persecuting, spying on, or trying to harm them.
Reference	Belief that objects, events, or other people have particular significance to them.
Grandeur	Belief that they have great power, knowledge, or talent.
Identity	Belief that they are someone else, such as Jesus Christ or the president of the United States.
Guilt	Belief that they have committed a terrible sin.
Control	Belief that their thoughts and behaviors are being controlled by external forces.

Although delusions are characteristic of schizophrenia regardless of the culture, the type of delusion can be influenced by cultural factors (Tateyama et al., 1993). When the delusions of German and Japanese schizophrenia patients were compared, the two groups had similar rates of *delusions of grandeur*. However, there were significant differences between the two groups for other types of delusions. The German patients had delusions involving guilt and sin, particularly as these concepts related to religion. They also suffered from *delusions of persecution,* whereas the Japanese patients had delusions of harassment, such as the belief that they were being slandered by others.

Hallucinations, the other hallmark of schizophrenia, are perceptions with no clear external cause. Hallucinations are frequently auditory, although they can also be visual, olfactory, or somatosensory:

> I was afraid to go outside and when I looked out of the window, it seemed that everyone outside was yelling, "kill her, kill her." . . . Things continued to get worse. I imagined that I had a foul body odor and I sometimes took up to six showers a day. I recall going to the grocery store one day, and I imagined that the people in the store were saying "Get saved, Jesus is the answer." (O'Neal, 1984)

Auditory hallucinations are often voices giving a running commentary of what a person is doing. They can be accusatory, telling the person he is evil or inept, or they can command the person to do dangerous things. Sometimes the person hears a cacophony of environmental sounds with voices intermingled. Although the cause of hallucinations remains unclear, recent neuroimaging studies suggest that hallucinations are associated with activation in cortical areas that process external sensory stimuli. For example, auditory hallucinations accompany increased activation in brain areas that are also activated in normal subjects when they engage in inner speech (Stein & Richardson, 1999). This has led to speculation that auditory hallucinations might be caused by a difficulty in distinguishing inner speech from external sounds.

Loosening of associations is another characteristic associated with schizophrenia, in which patients shift between seemingly unrelated topics as they speak, making it difficult or impossible for the listener to follow their train of thought:

> "They're destroying too many cattle and oil just to make soap. If we need soap when you can jump into a pool of water, and then when you go to buy your gasoline, my folks always thought they could get pop, but the best thing to get is motor oil, and

hallucinations False sensory perceptions that are experienced without an external source.

loosening of associations A speech pattern among schizophrenic patients in which their thoughts are disorganized or meaningless.

money. May as well go there and trade in some pop caps and, uh, tires, and tractors to car garages, so they can pull cars away from wrecks, is what I believed in." (Andreasen, 1984)

In more extreme cases, *clang associations* become apparent—the stringing together of words that rhyme but that have no other apparent link. Speech problems make it very difficult for people with schizophrenia to communicate (Docherty, 2005).

DISORGANIZED AND INAPPROPRIATE BEHAVIOR Another common symptom of schizophrenia is bizarre behavior, such as wearing multiple layers of clothes even on hot summer days. Those with schizophrenia may walk along muttering to themselves, alternating between anger and laughter, or they might pace, wringing their hands as if extremely worried. Those who have *catatonic* schizophrenia might mindlessly repeat back words that they hear, a behavior called *echolalia;* or they might remain immobilized in one position for hours, with a rigid, masklike expression and eyes staring off into the distance. It has been speculated that catatonic behavior may be an extreme fear response—akin to how animals respond to sudden dangers—in which the person is literally "scared stiff" (Moskowitz, 2004).

NEGATIVE SYMPTOMS OF SCHIZOPHRENIA A number of behavioral deficits associated with schizophrenia result in patients' becoming isolated and withdrawn. People with schizophrenia often avoid eye contact and seem apathetic. They do not express emotion even when discussing emotional subjects, and they tend to use slowed speech, reduced speech output, and a monotonous tone of voice. This is characterized by such things as long pauses before answering, failing to respond to a question, or being unable to complete an utterance after initiating it. There is often a similar reduction in overt behavior; a patient's movements may be slowed and overall amount of movement reduced, with little initiation of behavior and no interest in social participation. These symptoms, though less dramatic than delusions and hallucinations, can be equally serious. Negative symptoms are more common in men than women (Raesaenen, Pakaslahti, Syvaelahti, Jones, & Isohanni, 2000) and are associated with a poorer prognosis.

Interestingly, although the positive symptoms of schizophrenia can be dramatically reduced or eliminated with antipsychotic medications, the negative symptoms often persist. The fact that negative symptoms are often intractable to medications has led researchers to speculate that positive and negative symptoms may result from different organic causes. Since positive symptoms do respond to antipsychotic medications that act on neurotransmitter systems, these symptoms are thought to be the result of neurotransmitter dysfunction. In contrast, it has been speculated that negative symptoms are associated with neuroanatomical factors, since structural brain deficits are not affected by changes in neurochemistry. Some researchers believe that schizophrenia with negative symptoms is a separate disorder from schizophrenia with positive symptoms (Messias et al., 2004).

Schizophrenia Is Primarily a Brain Disorder

Although schizophrenia runs in families, the etiology of the disorder is complex and not well understood. It has been established that genetics plays a role in the development of schizophrenia (Figure 13.12). If one twin develops schizophrenia, the likelihood of the other's also succumbing is almost 50 percent if the twins are identical, but only 14 percent if the twins are fraternal. If one parent has schizophrenia, the risk of the child's developing the disease is 13 percent. If, however, both parents have schizophrenia, the risk jumps to almost 50 percent (Gottesman, 1991). However, the genetic component of schizophrenia represents a predisposition rather than destiny. If schizophrenia was caused solely by genetic factors, concordance in identical twins would approach 100 percent. Although this is true of the Genains, the identical quadruplets introduced at the beginning of the chapter, there is a marked difference in the severity of the disorder among the four sisters (Mirsky et al., 2000). Because they are identical genetically, the difference in severity of the disorder cannot be accounted for by genetic factors.

We now know that there is no single gene for schizophrenia, but rather that multiple genes likely contribute in subtle ways to the expression of the disorder. Indeed, each of at least two dozen candidate genes might have a modest influence on the development of schizophrenia (Gottesman & Hanson, 2005).

It is also now well established that schizophrenia is a brain disorder (Walker, Kestler, Bollini, & Hochman, 2004). The advent of techniques that image both the

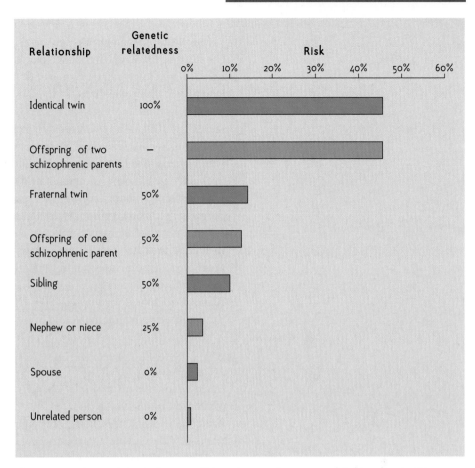

13.12 **Genetics and Schizophrenia** The more closely someone is genetically related to a person with schizophrenia, the greater is the risk that he or she will develop schizophrenia.

structure and the function of the brain have documented consistent abnormalities among those with schizophrenia. As noted earlier in the chapter, the first evidence of abnormality was that the ventricles, fluid-filled cavities in the brain, were enlarged in patients with schizophrenia, meaning that actual brain tissue is reduced. Moreover, greater reductions in brain tissue are associated with more negative outcomes (Mitelman, Shihabuddin, Brickman, Hazlett, & Buchsbaum, 2004), and longitudinal studies show continued reductions over time (Ho et al., 2003). This reduction of tissue occurs in many regions of the brain, especially the frontal lobes and medial temporal lobes. In functional brain imaging studies, typical results indicate reduced activity in frontal and temporal regions (Barch, Sheline, Csernansky, & Snyder, 2003).

Given that brain abnormalities occur throughout many regions of the brains of people with schizophrenia, some have speculated that schizophrenia is more likely a problem of connection between brain regions than the result of diminished or changed functions of any particular brain region (Walker et al., 2004). One possibility is that schizophrenia results from abnormality in neurotransmitters. Since the 1950s, scientists have believed that dopamine may play an important role in schizophrenia; drugs that block dopamine activity decrease symptoms, whereas drugs that increase the activity of dopamine neurons increase symptoms. However, evidence from the past two decades has implicated a number of other neurotransmitter systems in schizophrenia. More recently, researchers have suggested that schizophrenia might involve abnormalities in the glial cells that make up the myelin sheath (Davis et al., 2003; Moises & Gottesman, 2004). Such abnormalities would impair neurotransmission throughout the brain.

If schizophrenia is a disorder of the brain, when do brain abnormalities emerge? Because schizophrenia is most often diagnosed when people are in their 20s or 30s, it is hard to assess whether brain impairments occurred earlier in life. New evidence suggests that some neurological signs of schizophrenia can be observed long before the disorder is diagnosed. Psychologist Elaine Walker and her colleagues have analyzed home movies taken by parents whose children later developed schizophrenia. Compared with their siblings, those who developed the disorder displayed unusual social behaviors, more severe negative emotions, and motor disturbances (Walker et al., 2004). One study followed a group of children at risk for developing psychopathology because their parents suffered from a mental disorder. Those children who developed schizophrenia as adults were much more likely to display behavior problems as children, such as fighting or not getting along with others, than those who developed mood disorders or drug abuse problems or did not develop any disorders in adulthood (Amminger et al., 1999). Recently, Walker and her colleagues followed a group of high-risk children, aged 11 to 13, who were videotaped eating lunch in 1972. Those who developed schizophrenia showed greater impairments in social behavior and motor functioning than those who developed other mental disorders or those who developed no problems (Schiffman et al., 2004). These studies suggest that schizophrenia developed over the life course, with obvious symptoms sometimes emerging in childhood and often in late adolescence.

Environmental Factors Influence Schizophrenia

Why do urban environments have higher rates of schizophrenia?

Since genetics does not fully account for the onset and severity of schizophrenia, other factors must also be at work. Although the rate of schizophrenia tends to be similar across cultures, being born or raised in an urban area approximately doubles the risk of developing schizophrenia later in life (Torrey, 1999). Some have theorized that the increased stress of urban environments can trigger the onset of the disorder. In those at risk for schizophrenia, environmental stress does seem to contribute to its development (Walker et al., 2004). A study of adopted children whose biological mothers were diagnosed with schizophrenia found that if the adoptive families were psychologically healthy, none of the children became psychotic, but if the adoptive families were severely disturbed, 11 percent of the children became psychotic and 41 percent had severe psychological disorders (Tienari et al., 1990, 1994).

Others have speculated that there may be some kind of *schizovirus,* and that living in the close quarters of a big city increases the likelihood of the viruses spreading. In support of the virus hypothesis, some researchers have reported finding in the blood of schizophrenics antibodies that are not found in the blood of those without the disorder (Waltrip et al., 1997). Those diagnosed with schizophrenia are more likely to be born during the late winter and early spring (Mednick, Huttunen, & Machon, 1994; Torrey, Torrey, & Peterson, 1977). Mothers of children born in the late winter and early spring are in their second trimester of pregnancy during flu season. Retrospective studies suggest that the mothers of those with schizophrenia are more likely than other mothers to have contracted influenza during this critical period. Why is the second trimester so important? During this period a great deal of fetal brain development occurs. Trauma or pathogens in the second trimester have the potential of interfering with how brain regions are organized.

Studies of identical twins provide yet another piece of the puzzle. In identical twins, the embryo splits any time until the fifteenth day after conception. If the embryo splits by day 4, the twins are identical genetically and in every physical way. If the embryo splits later, the twins are more likely to be mirror images of each other, with opposite handedness. Early splitters have separate placentas, whereas late-splitting twins usually share the same placenta, which means they share the same blood supply as well as any viruses that pass through that blood supply. Therefore, if prenatal exposure to viruses does play a role in the etiology of schizophrenia, late-splitting twins should be more likely to be concordant for schizophrenia than early splitters. Evidence shows that this is true. For twins who have the same hand preference, the concordance rate for schizophrenia is approximately 10 to 30 percent. In contrast, for twins who have opposite handedness, and therefore likely shared the same placenta, the rate is 60 percent (Davis, Phelps, & Bracha, 1995). This shows not only that there is a strong genetic component to schizophrenia, but that the prenatal environment plays a significant role in the development of the disorder.

REVIEWING the Principles | Is Schizophrenia a Disorder of Mind or Body?

Schizophrenia consists of negative and positive symptoms, and it is at least in part a biological disorder. Twin and adoption studies have highlighted the critical role of genetics in the development of schizophrenia, and recent advances in genetic analysis have begun to yield more insights into the complexities of this disorder. In addition, research suggests the presence of neurochemical and neuroanatomical anomalies in the brains of those afflicted with schizophrenia. Despite all of this evidence, however, the specific ways in which genetics, neurochemistry, and neuroanatomy contribute to this disorder remain unclear. Also, most researchers would agree that environmental factors play a role in the development of schizophrenia, but little is known about how the environment interacts with biological factors.

Are Personality Disorders Truly Mental Disorders?

Personality is each person's unique way of responding to the environment. Although people do change somewhat over time (see Chapter 12), the ways we interact with the world and cope with events tend to be fairly fixed by the end of adolescence. Some people interact with the world in maladaptive and inflexible ways. When this style of interaction is long lasting and causes problems in work and social situations, it becomes a **personality disorder**. All of us at some point have likely exhibited at least some of the symptoms of personality disorders. We might be indecisive, self-absorbed, or emotionally unstable. Why isn't everyone diagnosed with a personality disorder? In general, those with true personality disorders consistently behave in maladaptive ways, whereas most people do so only on occasion. In addition, those with personality disorders show a more extreme level of maladaptive behavior and consequently experience more personal distress and more problems as a result of their behavior.

personality disorder A class of mental disorders marked by inflexible and maladaptive ways of interacting with the world.

Personality Disorders Are Maladaptive Ways of Relating to the World

Whereas the other disorders discussed in this chapter are classified on Axis I (see Table 13.1), personality disorders are classified on Axis II, along with mental retardation. Personality disorders and mental retardation are grouped together because they usually last throughout the life span with no expectation of significant change.

TABLE 13.5	Personality Disorders and Associated Characteristics

ODD OR ECCENTRIC BEHAVIOR

Paranoid	Tense, guarded, suspicious; holds grudges.
Schizoid	Socially isolated, with restricted emotional expression.
Schizotypal	Peculiarities of thought, appearance, and behavior that are disconcerting to others; emotionally detached and isolated.

DRAMATIC, EMOTIONAL, OR ERRATIC BEHAVIOR

Histrionic	Seductive behavior; needs immediate gratification and constant reassurance; rapidly changing moods; shallow emotions.
Narcissistic	Self-absorbed; expects special treatment and adulation; envious of attention to others.
Borderline	Cannot stand to be alone; intense, unstable moods and personal relationships; chronic anger; drug and alcohol abuse.
Antisocial	Manipulative, exploitive; dishonest; disloyal; lacking in guilt; habitually breaks social rules; childhood history of such behavior; often in trouble with the law.

ANXIOUS OR FEARFUL BEHAVIOR

Avoidant	Easily hurt and embarrassed; few close friends; sticks to routines to avoid new and possibly stressful experiences.
Dependent	Wants others to make decisions; needs constant advice and reassurance; fears being abandoned.
Obsessive-compulsive	Perfectionistic; overconscientious; indecisive; preoccupied with details; stiff; unable to express affection.

The personality disorders are generally divided into three groups, as listed in Table 13.5. People with the first group of disorders display odd or eccentric behavior. *Paranoid, schizoid,* and *schizotypal* personality disorders are included in this group. People with these personality disorders are often reclusive and suspicious. They have difficulty forming personal relationships because of their strange behavior and aloofness. The second group—*histrionic, narcissistic, borderline,* and *antisocial* personality disorders—is characterized by dramatic, emotional, and erratic behaviors. Borderline and antisocial personality disorders have been the focus of a great deal of research, and they are considered in more detail in the following sections. The third group of personality disorders—*avoidant, dependent,* and *obsessive-compulsive*—involves anxious or fearful behaviors.

Personality disorders remain controversial in modern clinical practice for a variety of reasons. First, personality disorders appear to be extreme or exaggerated versions of normal personality traits. For example, indecisiveness is characteristic of obsessive-compulsive personality disorder, but the *DSM* does not define the degree to which someone must be indecisive in order to be diagnosed as obsessive-compulsive. Second, there is overlap among the traits listed as characteristic of different personality disorders, so that the majority of people who are diagnosed with one personality disorder also meet the criteria for another personality disorder. This suggests that the categories may not be mutually exclusive and that there actually may be fewer types of personality disorders than are listed in the *DSM*.

It may seem that personality disorders do not have so large an impact on daily life as do some of the Axis I disorders discussed in this chapter. However, although people with personality disorders do not hallucinate or have radical mood swings, their ways of interacting with the world can have serious consequences. An in-depth consideration of borderline personality disorder and antisocial personality disorder will illustrate the devastating effect these disorders can have on the individual, family and friends, and society in general.

Borderline Personality Disorder Is Associated with Poor Self-Control

Borderline personality disorder, characterized by identity, affective, and impulse disturbances, was officially recognized as a diagnosis in 1980. The term *borderline* was initially used because these patients were considered to be on the border between normal and psychotic (Knight, 1953). The wide variety of clinical features of this disorder reflects its complexity (see Table 13.6). Approximately 1 to 2 percent of adults meet the criteria for borderline personality disorder (Swartz, Blazer, George, & Winfield, 1990; Torgerson, Kringlen, & Cramer, 2001); the disorder is more than twice as common in women than in men.

People with borderline personality disorder do not seem to have a strong sense of self. They cannot tolerate being alone and have an intense fear of abandonment. Because they desperately need an exclusive and dependent relationship with another person, they can be very manipulative in their attempts to control relationships, as shown in the following example:

> A borderline patient periodically rented a motel room and, with a stockpile of pills nearby, would call her therapist's home with an urgent message. He would respond by

borderline personality disorder A personality disorder characterized by identity, affective, and impulse disturbances.

TABLE 13.6	Clinical Features of Borderline Personality Disorder

A person having at least five of these characteristics might be considered to have borderline personality disorder.

1. Employment of frantic efforts to avoid real or imagined abandonment.

2. Unstable and intense interpersonal relationships.

3. Persistent and markedly disturbed, distorted, or unstable sense of self (e.g., a feeling that one doesn't exist or that one embodies evil).

4. Impulsiveness in such areas as sex, substance use, crime, and reckless driving.

5. Recurrent suicidal thoughts, gestures, or behavior.

6. Emotional instability, with periods of extreme depression, irritability, or anxiety.

7. Chronic feelings of emptiness.

8. Inappropriate intense anger or lack of control of anger (e.g., loss of temper, recurrent physical fights).

9. Transient, stress-related paranoid thoughts or severe dissociative symptoms.

SOURCE: *Diagnostic and Statistical Manual of the American Psychiatric Association,* 1994.

engaging in long conversations in which he "talked her down." Even as he told her that she could not count on his always being available, he became more wary of going out evenings without detailed instructions about how he could be reached. One night the patient couldn't reach him due to a bad phone connection. She fatally overdosed from what was probably a miscalculated manipulation. (Gunderson, 1984, p. 93)

In addition to problems with identity, borderline individuals also have affective disturbances. Emotional instability is paramount, with episodes of depression, anxiety, anger, and irritability that are often sudden and last from a few hours to a few days. Shifts from one mood to another usually occur with no clear precipitating cause.

Impulsivity is the third hallmark of borderline personality disorder. Impulsive behaviors can include sexual promiscuity, physical fighting, and binge eating and purging. The impulsive behavior most commonly associated with this disorder, however, is self-mutilation. Cutting and burning of the skin are typical behaviors for those with the disorder, who are also at high risk for suicide.

There is strong evidence from twin studies that borderline personality disorder has a genetic component (Skodol et al., 2002). Rates of mood disorders in the families of borderline patients also tend to be high, and these patients often show sleep abnormalities characteristic of depression. One possible reason that borderline personality disorder and affective disorders such as depression may be linked is that both appear to involve the neurotransmitter serotonin. Evidence has linked low serotonin levels to the impulsive behavior seen in borderline personality disorder (Skodol et al., 2002).

A strong relationship exists between borderline personality disorder and trauma or abuse (Lieb, Zanarini, Schmahl, Linehan, & Bohus, 2004). Some studies have reported that 70 to 80 percent of patients with borderline personality disorder have experienced physical or sexual abuse or observed some kind of extreme violence. Consider the following case of a young woman with borderline personality disorder:

[When Roberta was in fourth grade, her] oldest brother, Sam, turned fifteen and began babysitting his younger siblings two evenings a week while his mother went to Bingo and his father was out with "the boys." On one of these evenings, a few weeks after he'd started babysitting, Sam decided to "help" Roberta with her bath. Overriding her protests with the statement that he was in charge while their parents were gone, he demanded that she stand naked in front of him so that he could "make sure I was clean." Gradually, over the next several months, Sam's demands escalated. He watched her undress. He watched her urinate. By spring he had begun to masturbate as he watched her. (Bernheim, 1997, pp. 257–58)

Other theories implicate early interactions with caretakers. It has been suggested that borderline patients had caretakers who did not accept them or were unreliable or unavailable. The constant rejection and criticism made it difficult for the individual to learn to regulate emotions and understand emotional reactions to events (Linehan, 1987). An alternative theory is that caregivers may have encouraged dependence, and therefore individuals do not adequately develop a sense of self. They become extremely sensitive to the reactions of others, and if they are rejected, they reject themselves.

Antisocial Personality Disorder Is Associated with a Lack of Empathy

In the 1800s, the term "psychopath" was coined to describe people who seem willing to take advantage of and hurt others without any evidence of concern or remorse (Koch, 1891). The *DSM* dropped this pejorative label and adopted the term

antisocial personality disorder. This disorder is distinguished not so much by particular behaviors as by an approach to life, the most salient feature being a lack of remorse. Those with antisocial personality disorder tend to be hedonistic, seeking immediate gratification of wants and needs without any thought of others. Because they lack empathy, their interpersonal relationships tend to be shallow at best. They are very impulsive and engage in sensation-seeking behavior, as is illustrated in the case of Gary Gilmore (Figure 13.13), who was executed for the murder he describes here.

> "I went in and told the guy to give me the money. I told him to lay on the floor and then I shot him. I then walked out and was carrying the cash drawer with me. I took the money and threw the cash drawer in a bush and I tried to push the gun in the bush, too. But as I was pushing it in the bush, it went off and that's how come I was shot in the arm. It seems like things have always gone bad for me. It seems like I've always done dumb things that just caused trouble for me. I remember when I was a boy I would feel like I had to do things like sit on a railroad track until just before the train came and then I would dash off. Or I would put my finger over the end of a BB gun and pull the trigger to see if a BB was really in it. Sometimes I would stick my finger in water and then put my finger in a light socket to see if it would really shock me."
> (Spitzer et al., 1983, pp. 66–68)

CHARACTERISTICS OF ANTISOCIAL PERSONALITY DISORDER Antisocial personality disorder is surprisingly common, with an estimated lifetime prevalence of 4.5 percent in men and 0.8 percent in women (Robins & Regier, 1991). Interestingly, the disorder is most apparent in late adolescence and early adulthood, and it appears to remit around age 40 (Hare, McPherson & Forth, 1988). A diagnosis of antisocial personality disorder cannot be made before age 18, but the person must have displayed antisocial conduct before age 15. This stipulation ensures that only those with a lifetime history of antisocial behaviors can be diagnosed with antisocial personality disorder. They must also meet criteria such as repeatedly performing illegal acts, repeated lying or use of aliases, and reckless disregard for their own safety or the safety of others. Many of these individuals can be quite bright and highly verbal, and as a result many can talk their way out of bad situations. In any event, punishment seems to have very little effect on them (Lykken, 1957, 1995), and they often repeat the problem behavior a short time later.

It has been estimated that 40 to 75 percent of the prison population meet the criteria for antisocial personality disorder (Hare, 1993; Widiger & Corbitt, 1995), but not everyone with this disorder engages in criminal behavior. Because of the prevalence of the disorder in the prison population, much of the research on antisocial personality disorder has been conducted in this setting. One researcher, however, came up with an ingenious way of finding research participants outside of prison. She put the following advertisement in a counterculture newspaper:

> Wanted: charming, aggressive, carefree people who are impulsively irresponsible but are good at handling people and at looking after number one. Send name, address, phone, and short biography proving how interesting you are to . . . (Widom, 1978, p. 72)

Seventy-three people responded to the ad, about one-third of whom met the criteria for antisocial personality disorder. These individuals were then interviewed and given a battery of psychological tests. It was found that their characteristics were very similar to those of prisoners diagnosed with antisocial personality disorder, except that the group that responded to the ad had been able to avoid imprisonment.

Do people with antisocial personality disorder "suffer" from their condition?

13.13 Gary Gilmore after His Arrest Gilmore would have been given the diagnosis of antisocial personality disorder under the *DSM-IV*.

antisocial personality disorder A personality disorder marked by a lack of empathy and remorse.

THE CAUSES OF ANTISOCIAL PERSONALITY DISORDER In 1957, David Lykken reported that psychopaths did not become anxious when subjected to aversive stimuli. He and other investigators have continued this line of work, showing that such individuals do not seem to feel fear or anxiety (Lykken, 1995). EEG examinations have demonstrated that criminals who meet the criteria for antisocial personality disorder have slower alpha-wave activity (Raine, 1989). This indicates a lower overall level of arousal and may explain why these people often engage in sensation-seeking behavior. It also may explain why they do not learn from punishment—because of their low arousal, they do not experience punishment as particularly aversive. This pattern of reduced psychophysiological responding in the face of punishment has been found in adolescents who are at risk for developing psychopathy (Fung et al., 2005). There is also evidence of amygdala abnormalities in those with antisocial tendencies, which include the amygdala being smaller and less responsiveness to negative stimuli (Blair, 2003). Deficits in frontal-lobe functioning have also been found and may account for the lack of forethought and the inability to consider the implications of actions characteristic of antisocial personality disorder (Seguin, 2004).

To what can we attribute these biological correlates of antisocial personality disorder? There is good evidence for both genetics and the environment. Identical twins have a higher concordance of criminal behavior than do fraternal twins (Lykken, 1995), although this research did not rule out the role of shared environment. A large study of 14,000 adoptions (Mednick, Gabrielli, & Hutchings, 1987) found that adopted male children had a higher rate of crime if their biological fathers had criminal records. In addition, the more entrenched the criminal behavior of the biological father, the more likely it was that the adopted son had engaged in criminal behavior. Although genetics may be at the root of antisocial behaviors, such factors as low socioeconomic status, dysfunctional families, and childhood abuse may also play important roles. Indeed, malnutrition at age 3 has been found to predict antisocial behavior at age 17 (Liu, Raine, Venables, & Mednick, 2004). An enrichment program for children that included a structured nutrition component was associated with less criminal and antisocial behavior 20 years later (Raine, Mellingen, Liu, Venables, & Mednick, 2003). This raises the possibility that malnutrition or other similar environmental factors might contribute to the development of antisocial personality disorder.

REVIEWING the Principles | Are Personality Disorders Truly Mental Disorders?

Personality disorders are diagnosed along a different axis than are the other mental disorders discussed thus far. Personality disorders are not considered clinical disorders, yet they can have devastating effects on the individual, the family, and society. Borderline personality disorder is characterized by identity, affective, and impulse disturbances. Those with the disorder often have a history of abuse or rejection by caregivers. Those with antisocial personality disorder are hedonistic and sensation seeking, and they lack empathy for others. Although the outward symptoms of these disorders are not as severe as those of some of the clinical disorders, they are highly resistant to change, and the ways these individuals interact with others cause significant personal and societal problems.

Should Childhood Disorders Be Considered a Unique Category?

When Emil Kraepelin published his classic text on the classification of mental disorders in 1883, no mention was made of childhood disorders. The first edition of the *DSM,* published 70 years later, also considered children to be essentially mini versions of adults, and consequently disorders of childhood were not considered separately from disorders of adulthood. Currently, in response to the belief that cognitive, emotional, and social abilities should be considered in the context of the individual's developmental state, the *DSM* has a category in Axis I called "disorders usually first diagnosed in infancy, childhood, or adolescence." This category includes a wide range of disorders, from those affecting only circumscribed areas of a child's world, such as reading disorders and stuttering, to those affecting every aspect of a child's life, such as autism and attention-deficit/hyperactivity disorder (see Table 13.7). Despite the variety of disorders in this category, all should be considered within the context of knowledge about normal childhood development. Some symptoms of childhood mental disorders are extreme manifestations of normal behavior or are actually normal behaviors for children at an earlier developmental stage. Bedwetting, for example, is normal for two-year-olds but not for ten-year-olds. Other behaviors,

TABLE 13.7 Childhood Disorders

DISORDER	DESCRIPTION
Attention-Deficit/Hyperactivity	A pattern of hyperactive, inattentive, and impulsive behavior that causes social or academic impairment.
Autism	Characterized by unresponsiveness; impaired language, social, and cognitive development; and restricted and repetitive behavior.
Elimination Disorders	The repeated passing of feces or urination in inappropriate places by children from whom continence should be expected.
Learning Disorders	Marked by substantially low performance in reading, mathematics, or written expression with regard to what is expected for age, amount of education, and intelligence.
Mental Retardation	Characterized by below average intellectual functioning (IQ lower than 70) and limited adaptive functioning that begins before age 18.
Rumination Disorder	The repeated regurgitation and re-chewing of partially digested food, not related to nausea or gastrointestinal disorder.
Selective Mutism	Failure to speak in certain social situations, despite the ability to speak in other situations; interferes with social or academic achievement.
Tourette's Disorder	Recurrent motor and vocal tics that cause marked distress or impairment and are not related to a general medical condition.

however, deviate significantly from normal development. Two disorders of childhood, autism and attention-deficit/hyperactivity disorder, will be explored to illustrate this issue.

Autism Is a Lack of Awareness of Others

autism A developmental disorder involving deficits in social interaction, impaired communication, and restricted interests.

What factors might be responsible for the increased diagnosis of autism spectrum disorders?

Autism is characterized by deficits in social interaction, impaired communication, and restricted interests (Volkmar, Chawarska, & Klin, 2005). Autism was first described in 1943 by Leo Kanner, who was struck by the profound isolation of some children and coined the term "early infantile autism." Kanner described the syndrome in the following way: "There is from the start an extreme autistic aloneness that, whenever possible, disregards, ignores, shuts out anything that comes to the child from the outside." When people think of autism, they often imagine a beautiful, graceful child who seems tragically shut off from the world. Some autistic children are beautiful, and autistics tend to walk on their toes, which might have given rise to the myth of gracefulness. However, autistic children usually look the same as any other children, and they are often clumsier than normal children. Approximately 3 to 6 children out of 1,000 will show signs of autism, with males outnumbering females three to one (Muhle, Trentacoste, & Rapin, 2004). There has been a dramatic 556 percent increase in the number of children diagnosed with autism from 1991 to 1997 (Stokstad, 2001). This increase is likely due to greater awareness of the symptoms of autism by parents and physicians as well as a willingness to apply the diagnosis to a wider spectrum of behaviors (Rutter, 2005).

Autism varies in severity, from mild social impairments to severe social and intellectual impairments. *Asperger's syndrome* is high-functioning autism, in which children of normal intelligence have specific deficits in social interaction, such as having impoverished theory of mind (i.e., understanding other's intentions). Recall from Chapter 11 that theory of mind refers to understanding that other people have mental states and possessing the ability to predict their behavior accordingly. Perhaps the most famous person with Asperger's is Temple Grandin, an accomplished scientist who now designs humane animal facilities (Grandin, 1995). Although extremely intelligent, she has great difficulty understanding the subtle social motives and behaviors of other humans. She finds it easier to relate to animals. Grandin is able to understand the environment from an animal's point of view, which allows her to design facilities that are calming.

CORE SYMPTOMS OF AUTISM Autistic children are seemingly unaware of others. As babies, they do not smile at their caregivers, they do not respond to vocalizations, and they often actively reject physical contact with others. Autistic children do not establish eye contact and do not use gaze to either gain or direct the attention of those around them. One group of researchers had participants view video footage of autistic children's first birthdays to see if autistic characteristics could be detected before the child was diagnosed with autism (Osterling & Dawson, 1994). By considering only the number of times a child looked at another person's face, the participants correctly classified the children as either autistic or normal 77 percent of the time (see Figure 13.14).

Deficits in communication are the second major cluster of behaviors characteristic of autism. Autistic children show severe impairments in both verbal and nonverbal communication. Even if they do vocalize, it is often not with any intent to communicate. Autistics who develop language often exhibit odd speech patterns, such as echolalia and *pronoun reversal*. Echolalia, mentioned earlier as a symptom of catatonia, is the repetition of words or phrases, sometimes including an imitation of the intonation and sometimes using a high-pitched monotone. Pronoun reversal, in which autistic children may replace "I" with "you," may be related to echolalia. Even if a child ceases being echolalic, pronoun confusion often persists. Autistic children who develop functional language also often interpret words in a literal manner, use language inappropriately, and lack verbal spontaneity.

A third category of deficits is restricted activities and interests. Although autistic children appear to be oblivious to the people around them, they are acutely aware of their surroundings. Children with autism tend to focus on small details in their surroundings. Although most children automatically pay attention to the social aspects of a situation, those with autism may focus on seemingly inconsequential details (Klin, Jones, Schultz, & Volkmar, 2003; Figure 13.15). Any changes in the daily routine or in the placement of furniture or toys is very upsetting and can result in extreme agitation and tantrums. Autistic children also do not play in the same way as other children. Their play tends to be stereotyped and obsessive, and the focus is often on the sensory aspects of objects. They may smell and taste objects, or spin and flick them for the visual stimulation. Similarly, their own behavior tends to be stereotyped, with ritualistic hand movements, body rocking, and hand flapping. Self-abuse is common, and in some cases children must be forcibly restrained to keep them from hurting themselves.

AUTISM IS A BIOLOGICAL DISORDER Kanner believed autism was an innate disorder that was exacerbated by cold and unresponsive mothers, whom he called "ice box mothers" or "refrigerator mothers." He described the parents of autistic children as insensitive, meticulous, introverted, and highly intellectual. This view is given little credence today, as it is now well established that autism is the result of biological factors, the specific nature of which is still undetermined. Genetic studies of autism have been hampered by the rarity of the disorder and by the fact that autistic persons rarely marry and almost never have children. Despite the limited genetic research, there are indications that the disorder has a strong hereditary component (Muhle et al., 2004). If one child in a family is autistic, the probability of a second also being diagnosed is anywhere from 2 to 9 percent (Jorde et al., 1990; Szatzmari et al., 1993). Although this risk is relatively low, it is significantly higher than the estimated 0.4 percent prevalence of the disorder in the population at large. If two siblings are autistic, the chances of a third sharing the same diagnosis jumps to 35 percent. A number of studies have found concordance rates in twins to be 70 to 90 percent for monozygotic twins and 10 percent for dizygotic twins (Bailey et al., 1995; Steffenburg et al., 1989).

13.14 Scenes from Videotapes of Children's Birthday Parties The child in (a) focused more on objects than on people and was later diagnosed with autism. The child in (b) developed normally.

13.15 Toddler Viewer with Autism A two-year-old with autism focuses on the unimportant details in the scene rather than the social characters.

Research into the causes of autism points to prenatal and/or neonatal events that may result in brain dysfunction. The brains of children with autism grow unusually large during the first two years of life, and then growth slows until age five (Courchesne, Redcay, & Kennedy, 2004). Researchers are investigating both genetic and nongenetic factors that might explain this overgrowth-undergrowth pattern. In some cases, mothers of autistic children have experienced significant bleeding during the second trimester of pregnancy, suggesting some kind of trauma during the critical period for neuronal development. Autistic children also have a higher rate of neonatal complications such as apnea, seizures, and delay in breathing. Moreover, autistic children are more likely to have minor physical anomalies, to be the product of a first pregnancy, and to be born to older mothers (Gilberg, 1980).

Two exciting new research developments may help to focus the future of autism research. A deficit in oxytocin, a neuropeptide involved in social behavior (see Chapter 11), may be related to some of the behavioral manifestations of autism. It has been demonstrated that mice lacking oxytocin behave normally, except that they cannot recognize other mice or their mother's scent. A single dose of oxytocin cured them (Ferguson et al., 2000). In one study, autistic adults who received injections of oxytocin showed a dramatic improvement in their symptoms (Novotny et al., 2000). Injections of oxytocin seem particularly useful for reducing repetitive behaviors, such as repeating oneself, questioning, inappropriate touching, and self-injury (Hollander et al., 2003). A second recent finding suggests that levels of four proteins in the blood are elevated in 97 percent of autistic children and 92 percent of retarded children, but in none of the healthy controls. These elevated protein levels were found in blood samples taken at birth, and all four proteins are involved in brain development (Nelson et al., 2001). It is possible that these proteins may be involved in the pattern of overgrowth and undergrowth of the brain for those with autism. However, both whether these proteins are influenced by genetic or environmental factors and what role they play in the development of autism are matters for future research.

Attention–Deficit/Hyperactivity Disorder Is a Disruptive Behavior Disorder

> A hyperactive child's mother might report that he has difficulty remembering not to trail his dirty hand along the clean wall as he runs from the front door to the kitchen. His peers may find that he spontaneously changes the rules while playing Monopoly or soccer. His teacher notes that he asks what he is supposed to do immediately after detailed instructions were presented to the entire class. He may make warbling noises or other strange sounds that inadvertently disturb anyone nearby. He may seem to have more than his share of accidents—knocking over the tower his classmates are erecting, spilling his cranberry juice on the linen tablecloth, or tripping over the television cord while retrieving the family cat—and thereby disconnecting the set in the middle of the Super Bowl game. (Whalen, 1989)

We can laugh at this description, yet most of us have come into contact with such children. Although the symptoms can seem humorous in the retelling, the reality is a different story. Children with **attention–deficit/hyperactivity disorder (ADHD)** are restless, inattentive, and impulsive. They need to have directions repeated and rules explained over and over. Although these children are often friendly and talkative, they can have trouble making and keeping friends because they miss subtle social cues and make unintentional social mistakes. Note that many of these symptoms are exaggerations of the typical behavior of toddlers. This makes the line between

attention–deficit/hyperactivity disorder (ADHD) A disorder characterized by restless, inattentive, and impulsive behaviors.

normal and abnormal behavior hard to draw—as many as 50 percent of mothers of four-year-old boys believe their sons are hyperactive (Varley, 1984).

THE ETIOLOGY OF ADHD The American Psychiatric Association (1994) estimates that 3 to 5 percent of children have ADHD, although estimates from other sources vary widely, with some estimates as high as 20 percent (Gillis, Gilger, Pennington, & DeFries, 1992). The causes of the disorder are unknown; one of the difficulties in pinpointing the etiology is that ADHD is most likely a heterogeneous disorder. In other words, the behavioral profiles of children with ADHD vary, so it is likely that the causes of the disorder vary as well. There is some suggestion that children with ADHD are more likely than other children to grow up in disturbed families. This finding has led researchers to speculate that the disorder may have a psychological component. Factors such as poor parenting and social disadvantage may contribute to the onset of symptoms. Whether psychological factors are the cause or effect of the disorder, however, is not always clear. Most current research is focused on biological factors contributing to the development of ADHD.

ADHD clearly has a genetic component, with a 10 to 35 percent incidence of the disorder in families of those diagnosed with ADHD (Biederman, Faraone, Keenan, Knee, & Tsuang, 1990; Biederman, Faraone, & Lapey, 1992). Concordance is estimated at 55 percent in monozygotic twins and 32 percent in dizygotic twins (Goodman & Stevenson, 1989; Sherman, McGue, & Iacono, 1997). Although it is clear that something is inherited in ADHD, the question is what. In an imaging study, Zametkin and his colleagues (1990) found that adults who had been diagnosed with ADHD in childhood had reduced metabolism in brain regions involved in self-regulation of motor functions and attentional systems (Figure 13.16). These researchers postulated that the connection between the frontal lobes and the limbic system was impaired in ADHD patients. The symptoms of ADHD are similar to those seen in patients with frontal-lobe damage: problems with planning, sustaining concentration, using feedback, and thinking flexibly. Imaging studies have found prefrontal abnormalities when adolescents with ADHD perform tasks that require inhibiting a motor response. Greater impairments in performance on the task are associated with more activation of these prefrontal regions (Schulz et al., 2004). Current research continues to focus on underarousal of the frontal lobes (Barkely, 1997; Neidemeyer & Naidu, 1997) but also implicates subcortical structures. In particular, researchers have demonstrated differences in the basal ganglia in the brains of some

Section on Clinical Brain Imaging, LCM, NIMH

13.16 ADHD and the Brain During PET scanning, the brain of the person on the right, who has a history of ADHD, shows lesser overall activation, especially in frontal and limbic regions.

"Excuse me, Doc, my attention wandered. What type of deficit disorder did you say I had?"

What are the long-term prospects for children with ADHD?

ADHD patients (Aylward, Reiss, Reader, & Singer, 1996; Castellanos, Giedd, Eckberg, & Marsh, 1998; Fillipek et al., 1997; Hynd, Hern, & Novey, 1993). This region is involved in regulation of motor behavior and impulse control, and dysfunction in these structures could contribute to the hyperactivity characteristic of ADHD.

ADHD ACROSS THE LIFE SPAN Children are not generally given a diagnosis of ADHD until they enter a structured setting in which they are expected to conform to rules, get along with peers, and sit in a seat for long periods of time. In the past, this happened when children entered school, between the ages of five and seven. Now, with the increasing prevalence of structured day-care settings, the demands on children to conform are occurring much earlier. Although it is not unreasonable to expect a six-year-old to sit quietly and share crayons, it is probably unrealistic to expect the same of a three-year-old. Many preschoolers who are considered inattentive and overactive by their parents and teachers are simply going through a normal developmental stage that will not become the persistent pattern of ADHD. Some characteristics discriminate between children who go on to develop ADHD and those who do not. Infants who are later diagnosed with ADHD have difficulty establishing regular patterns for eating and sleeping (Ross & Ross, 1982). Toddlers exhibit excessive activity and temperamental behavior quite early in life (Hartsough & Lambert, 1985). They are very curious and engage in vigorous play, and consequently they tend to be quite accident prone. Older children do not generally demonstrate excess motor activity but are instead restless and fidgety (Pelham & Bender, 1982).

It was previously thought that children outgrew ADHD by the time they entered adulthood. More recent longitudinal studies, however, dispute this notion (McGough & Barkley, 2004). Between 30 and 80 percent of those with ADHD in childhood continued to show symptoms of this disorder in adulthood (Weiss & Hechtman, 1993). Adults with ADHD symptoms may struggle both academically and vocationally. They generally reach a lower-than-expected socioeconomic level and change jobs more frequently (Bellak & Black, 1992; Mannuzza et al., 1991). The impact of ADHD on society is apparently greater than previously believed. However, some ADHD patients do learn to adapt and are successful in their personal and vocational lives.

REVIEWING

the Principles | Should Childhood Disorders Be Considered a Unique Category?

Until recently, children were considered to be mini versions of adults, and mental disorders in children were classified using adult categories. Currently, it is understood that disorders in children should be considered in the context of normal development. In some cases, mental disorders identified in childhood have a lasting impact on the individual, and the problems apparent early in life continue throughout maturation. This is clearly the case for autism, in which the social and cognitive characteristics of the disorder deviate significantly from normal childhood development and continue to have a major impact throughout the life span. The impact of childhood ADHD on adult functioning is less certain.

Conclusion

Throughout this book, we have emphasized the adaptive nature of the human mind, as it solves problems of survival and performs complex functions such as perceiving and remembering. But sometimes minds fail to work properly, producing maladaptive thoughts, emotions, and behaviors. For instance, people can become too afraid to leave their houses, too depressed to get out of bed, or so manic that they take dangerous risks. Others hear voices or believe that their family members are trying to poison them. Sometimes people are incapable of interacting with others.

In this chapter, we have explored the nature and causes of psychopathology. From the time of Freud, most mental disorders were viewed as arising from mistreatment by caregivers; for instance, autism was considered the result of cold, uncaring mothers. The biological revolution has provided compelling evidence that many mental disorders involve a genetic predisposition, abnormalities in various neurotransmitter systems, or brains that do not function normally. It is now clear that biology plays an important role in psycho-

pathology. At the same time, psychological and social factors are implicated in the development and course of most mental disorders. An obvious example is the distorted thought patterns that afflict those with major depression and other mood disorders.

Various environmental factors also contribute to psychopathology. Parental maltreatment can damage children, as was the case with the Genain quadruplets and with those who report having multiple identities. Prenatal and early childhood factors, such as malnutrition, exposure to toxins and viruses, and poverty, seem to increase the risk that psychopathology will develop. The experience of loss or trauma can produce mood disorders among otherwise mentally healthy adults. Thus, to understand psychopathology thoroughly, we need to recognize the social, psychological, and biological factors that contribute to the expression of mental illness in those who are susceptible. Crossing levels of analysis to understand the causes of mental disorders is especially useful for determining the best ways to treat them, which is the topic of the next chapter.

Summarizing the Principles of the Disorders of Mind and Body

How Are Mental Disorders Conceptualized and Classified?

1. **Mental disorders are classified into categories:** The *Diagnostic and Statistical Manual of Mental Disorders (DSM)* has evolved from Kraeplin's categories of mental illness. It is a multiaxial system for diagnosing groups of symptoms in the context of related factors.

2. **Mental disorders must be assessed before diagnosis:** Assessment is the process of examining a person's mental functions and psychological health in order to make a diagnosis. Assessment is accomplished through interviews, behavioral evaluations, and psychological testing.

3. **Mental disorders have many causes:** Disorders may arise from psychological factors, such as the family system or sociocultural context. They may be the result of learned, maladaptive cognitions. Biological factors also underlie mental illness. The diathesis-stress model looks at mental disorders as an interaction among multiple factors. In this model, stressful circumstances may trigger a disorder in an individual with underlying vulnerabilities.

4. **The legal system has its own definition of psychopathology:** The legal system focuses on insanity as it relates to the issue of personal responsibility for actions.

Can Anxiety Be the Root of Seemingly Different Disorders?

5. **There are different types of anxiety disorders:** Phobias are exaggerated fears of specific stimulus. Generalized anxiety disorder is diffuse and omnipresent. Panic attacks cause sudden overwhelming terror, and may lead to agoraphobia. Obsessive-compulsive disorders involve anxiety-related thoughts and behaviors.

6. **Anxiety disorders have cognitive, situational, and biological components:** The etiology of OCD is at least in part genetic, and also involves brain dysfunction. The irrational thoughts that accompany panic attacks may lead to agoraphobia through cognitive-behavioral connections.

Are Mood Disorders Extreme Manifestations of Normal Moods?

7. **There are different types of mood disorders:** Depressive disorders may be unipolar or bipolar and are more severe than dysthymia. The less extreme form of bipolarity is cyclothymia.

8. **Mood disorders have cognitive, situational, and biological components:** The biological factors of depression

include genetics, frontal-lobe functioning, and serotonin modulation, as well as biological rhythms. Negative thinking and poor interpersonal relations also contribute to depression.

Is Schizophrenia a Disorder of Mind or Body?

9. **Schizophrenia has positive and negative symptoms:** Positive symptoms include excesses, such as delusions and hallucinations. Negative symptoms are deficits in functioning, such as social withdrawal and reduced movement.

10. **Schizophrenia is primarily a brain disorder:** The brains of schizophrenics have larger ventricles and less brain mass, with reduced frontal and temporal activation. A variety of neurochemical and neural structural abnormalities exist as well.

11. **Environmental factors influence schizophrenia:** Urban environments may trigger the onset of schizophrenia. Trauma or pathogens encountered by pregnant women may increase the likelihood of the disorder in their children.

Are Personality Disorders Truly Mental Disorders?

12. **Personality disorders are maladaptive ways of relating to the world:** Odd behaviors, extreme emotions, and fearful behaviors are characteristic of personality disorders. It is controversial whether some of these extremes are true psychopathologies.

13. **Borderline personality disorder is associated with poor self-control:** Borderline personality disorder involves disturbances in identity, affect, and impulse control. A strong relationship exists between the disorder and trauma and abuse.

14. **Antisocial personality disorder is associated with a lack of empathy:** Antisocial personality disorder is marked by lack of empathy and remorse, and a tendency to be manipulative. Both genetics and environment seem to be contributing factors.

Should Childhood Disorders Be Considered a Unique Category?

15. **Autism is a lack of awareness of others:** Autism emerges in infancy and is marked by avoidance of eye contact and impairment in verbal and nonverbal communication. Asperger's syndrome is a high-functioning variation of autism. Autism is a biological disorder. The biological factors may include abnormalities in oxytocin, brain growth, and blood proteins.

16. **Attention-deficit/hyperactivity disorder is a disruptive behavior disorder:** Children with ADHD are restless, inattentive, and impulsive. It is a heterogeneous disorder, so it is likely that the causes of the disorder vary. Environmental factors may include poor parenting and social disadvantages. Genetic factors and brain abnormalities, particularly with regard to activation of the frontal lobes and subcortical basal ganglia, may also play a part. ADHD continues into adulthood, presenting academic and career challenges.

Applying the Principles

1. Dr. Jones, a psychologist, is evaluating a client's negative mood and thoughts to decide if he is clinically depressed. Dr. Jones notes that the client has recently been in a serious car accident and suffered injuries that have left him unable to return to work. The financial stress on the client's family has been significant. Dr. Jones's consideration of the client's physical and mental health as a result of the accident and his concern about family circumstances represent the _____ approach of the *DSM*.

   _____ a) symptom check list
   _____ b) multiaxial
   _____ c) "pigeon hole"
   _____ d) labeling

2. Christina is constantly preoccupied with thoughts that she has left her car unlocked, and repeatedly returns to the parking structure to check. It is likely that she is suffering from _____, which is the result of the brain structure known as the _____ not functioning normally.

   _____ a) generalized anxiety; amygdala
   _____ b) phobia; hippocampus
   _____ c) panic disorder; motor cortex
   _____ d) OCD; caudate nucleus

3. Recently, Sam has started to think more about the nature of depression. First, his Uncle Joe seems depressed since his Aunt Becky passed away. Second, his good friend Mike

from high school always seems somewhat melancholy. Third, he's noticed that his good friend Alice seems to go through periods of deep, long-term depression. What do these examples tell us about the nature of depression, as well as many other mental disorders?

_____ a) There are unique symptoms in each patient.

_____ b) It is a disorder only if it has been preceded by a triggering event.

_____ c) Disorders vary along a continuum from mild to severe.

_____ d) Disorders are only apparent when observed in others, and difficult to recognize in ourselves.

4. Jason and David have both been diagnosed with schizophrenia. Jason has been hearing voices and feeling paranoid. David has become mute and catatonic. Jason's symptoms are _____ and likely due to _____; David's symptoms are _____ and likely due to _____.

_____ a) negative, neurochemistry; positive, neuroanatomy

_____ b) positive, environment; negative, neurochemistry

_____ c) positive, neurochemistry; negative, neuroanatomy

_____ d) negative, environment; negative, neurochemistry

5. Amber makes up a story of being mugged, in order to get the interest and sympathy of her boyfriend. She is emotionally volatile and manipulative. It is likely that Amber suffers from _____ and the prognosis for treatment is _____.

_____ a) borderline personality disorder; extremely poor

_____ b) antisocial personality disorder; excellent only with medication

_____ c) narcissistic personality disorder; excellent

_____ d) antisocial personality disorder; extremely poor

6. Shanea works at the campus daycare center. She has noticed a young boy who does not like to be held, avoids contact with others, does not use language, and gets very upset if the routine is changed. He has been diagnosed with _____, which is likely due to _____.

_____ a) extreme shyness; genetics

_____ b) autism; attachment and social factors

_____ c) Asperger's syndrome; biological factors

_____ d) autism; biological factors

ANSWERS: 1 b   2 d   3 c   4 c   5 a   6 d

Key Terms

agoraphobia, p. 534

antisocial personality disorder, p. 553

anxiety disorders, p. 533

assessment, p. 523

attention-deficit/hyperactivity disorder (ADHD), p. 558

autism, p. 556

bipolar disorder, p. 539

borderline personality disorder, p. 551

cognitive-behavioral approach, p. 528

cyclothymia, p. 539

delusions, p. 544

Diagnostic and Statistical Manual of Mental Disorders (*DSM*), p. 522

diathesis-stress model, p. 529

dysthymia, p. 538

family systems model, p. 528

generalized anxiety disorder, p. 534

hallucinations, p. 545

learned helplessness model, p. 541

loosening of associations, p. 545

major depression, p. 538

multiaxial system, p. 522

negative symptoms, p. 544

obsessive-compulsive disorder (OCD), p. 534

panic disorder, p. 534

personality disorder, p. 549

phobia, p. 534

positive symptoms, p. 544

psychopathology, p. 521

schizophrenia, p. 543

seasonal affective disorder (SAD), p. 540

sociocultural model, p. 528

Further Readings

Frith, C., & Johnstone, E. (2003). *Schizophrenia: A very short introduction.* New York: Oxford University Press.

Grandin, T. (1995). *Thinking in pictures.* New York: Doubleday.

Jamison, K. R. (1995). *An unquiet mind.* New York: Vintage Books.

Lezak, M. D. (2004). *Neuropsychological assessment* (4th ed.). New York: Oxford University Press.

Rapoport, J. (1990). *The boy who couldn't stop washing: The experience and treatment of obsessive-compulsive disorder.* New York: Penguin Books.

Sacks, O. (1985). *The man who mistook his wife for a hat.* New York: Harper & Row.

Styron, W. (1990). *Darkness visible: A memoir of madness.* New York: Random House.

Using Alternative Therapies

An animal trainer at Dolphin Reef Eilat in Israel holds an autistic child during a therapeutic session involving a bottlenose dolphin. Alternative therapies such as this one are sometimes useful, but their effectiveness must be established through careful research. Various disorders of mind and body require different kinds of treatments. The choice of treatment is based on rigorous scientific observation.

14

Treating Disorders of Mind and Body

D ennis was a 31-year-old insurance salesman. One day while shopping in a mall with his fiancée, Dennis suddenly felt very sick. His hands began to shake, his vision became blurred, and he felt a great deal of pressure in his chest. He began to gasp and felt weak all over. All of this was accompanied by a feeling of overwhelming terror. Without stopping to tell his fiancée what was happening, he ran from the store and sought refuge in the car. He opened the windows and lay down, and he started to feel better in about ten minutes. Later, Dennis explained to his fiancée what had happened and revealed that he had experienced this sort of attack before. Because of this, he would often avoid places like shopping malls. At the urging of his fiancée, Dennis agreed to see a psychologist. During his first several treatment sessions, Dennis downplayed his problems, clearly concerned that others might think him crazy. He was also reluctant to rely on medications because of the stigma attached. He

How Is Mental Illness Treated?

- Psychotherapy Is Based on Psychological Principles
- Biological Therapies Are Necessary for Some Disorders
- Common Factors Enhance Treatment

What Are the Most Effective Treatments?

- Treatments That Focus on Behavior and Cognition Are Superior for Anxiety Disorders
- Many Effective Treatments Are Available for Depression

- Lithium Is Most Effective for Bipolar Disorder
- Pharmacological Treatments Are Superior for Schizophrenia

Can Personality Disorders Be Treated?

- Dialectical Behavior Therapy Is Most Successful for Borderline Personality Disorder
- Antisocial Personality Disorder Is Difficult to Treat

How Should Childhood Disorders Be Treated?

- Children with ADHD Can Benefit from a Variety of Approaches
- Autistic Children Benefit from a Structured Treatment Approach

had read about cognitive-behavioral therapy and was interested in trying this approach to address his problem.

His therapist explained that Dennis was experiencing panic attacks combined with agoraphobia. The therapist believed Dennis's problems were the result of vulnerability to stress combined with thoughts and behaviors that exacerbated anxiety. The first step in treatment was therefore relaxation training, to give Dennis a strategy to use when he became anxious and tense. The next step was to modify his maladaptive thought patterns. Dennis kept a diary for several weeks to identify situations in which distorted thoughts might be producing anxiety, such as meeting with prospective clients. Before meeting with a client, Dennis would become extremely anxious because he felt that it would be catastrophic if he was unable to make the sale. With the help of his therapist, Dennis came to recognize that being turned down by a client was difficult but manageable, and that it was unlikely to have any long-term impact on his career. The final phase of treatment was to address Dennis's avoidance of situations that he associated with panic attacks. Dennis and his therapist constructed a hierarchy of increasingly stressful situations. The first was an easy situation, involving a short visit to a department store on a lightly crowded weekday morning. Dennis's fiancée accompanied him so that he would feel less vulnerable. After completing this task, Dennis moved on to increasingly difficult situations, using relaxation techniques as necessary to control his anxiety. After six months, therapy was discontinued. Dennis's anxiety levels were significantly reduced and he was able to make himself relax when he did become tense. In addition, he had not experienced a panic attack during that period and was no longer avoiding situations that he had previously found stressful (Oltmans, Neale, & Davison, 1999). ■

In the last chapter you learned about various mental disorders. What can be done about them? Psychologists use two essential techniques to treat mental illness, psychological and biological. Research findings show that there is more than one way to treat most mental disorders. The generic name given to formal psychological treatment is **psychotherapy**, although the particular techniques and methods used depend on the theoretical orientation of the practitioner. **Biological therapies** reflect the medical approach to illness and disease. For example, *psychopharmacology,* the use of medications that affect brain or bodily functions, has proven to be very effective in treating many mental disorders. The success of medication in the treatment of mental illness is largely responsible for the era of deinstitutionalization, in which scores of patients were discharged from mental hospitals and treated with drugs as

psychotherapy The generic name given to formal psychological treatment.

biological therapy Treatment based on the medical approach to illness and disease.

460–377 B.C.E.
Trepanning Fossil evidence indicates that holes were drilled into human skulls, possibly to cure mental illness.

1700s
Humane Treatment Phillipe Pinel in France is among the first to release supposedly dangerous and violent mental patients from chains and manacles.

1800s
Reform in the United States Dorothea Dix promotes reform of mental institutions in the United States, leading to the establishment of the state hospital system.

1900
Dreams in Therapy Sigmund Freud advocates dream interpretation as part of psychoanalytic therapy.

outpatients. In California during the 1980s, the number of hospital beds for mentally ill patients decreased from 40,000 to 5,000. The smaller number of inpatients meant that institutions could provide better treatment for those still under their care.

Both psychotherapy and biological therapies have proven to be beneficial to many of those who suffer from mental illness. The case of Dennis illustrates the effectiveness of cognitive-behavioral therapy, a form of psychotherapy. You will see throughout this chapter that this treatment is extremely effective for many mental disorders and that its effects are long-lasting. A limitation of biological therapies is that although they are often effective in the short term, long-term success requires the person to continue treatment, sometimes indefinitely. Recent focus has been on combining biological therapies with other therapeutic approaches to optimize treatment for each patient. This chapter explores the basic principles of therapy and describes the various treatment approaches to specific mental disorders.

How Is Mental Illness Treated?

As outlined in Chapter 13, a number of theories have been proposed to account for psychopathology. These approaches propose treatment strategies based on assumptions about the causes of mental disorders. However, even if we gain more understanding into the etiology of a mental disorder, this does not always give us further insights into how best to treat it. It is becoming clear that autism, for example, is caused by biological factors. Although this knowledge has helped parents accept that they are not responsible for their children's problems, it has not led to any significant advances in therapies for the disorder. In fact, the best available treatment at this point is based on behavioral, not biological, principles, as will discover later in this chapter.

Psychotherapy Is Based on Psychological Principles

Psychotherapy, regardless of the theoretical perspective of the treatment provider, is generally aimed at changing patterns of thought or behavior, though the ways in which such changes are effected can differ dramatically. It has been estimated that there are over 400 approaches to treatment (Kazdin, 1994). The discussion that follows highlights the major components of the most common approaches and describes how therapists use these methods to treat specific mental disorders. Today, many practitioners use an eclectic mix of techniques based on what they believe is best for the client's particular condition.

PSYCHODYNAMIC THERAPY FOCUSES ON INSIGHT Among the first to develop psychological treatments for mental illness was Sigmund Freud, who believed

---

1940s

Treatment of Mental Illness Loses Ground Many overcrowded mental hospitals return to the use of physical restraints, creating barbaric conditions.

1948

Behaviorism as Therapy B. F. Skinner pioneers behavior modification as a treatment for mental disorders.

1949

Lobotomies as Treatment Egas Moniz receives a Nobel Prize for his work on prefrontal lobotomies as a treatment for mental disorders, a technique later shown to cause further problems.

1950s

Drugs for Depression Antidepressant medications are discovered and revolutionize the treatment of depression, as their benefits outweigh some side effects.

1960s

The Cognitive Approach Aaron T. Beck and Albert Ellis develop cognitive therapy to treat dysfunctional thoughts and beliefs.

A study by David Barlow and his colleagues (2000) found that in the short term, both cognitive-behavioral therapy and imipramine were more effective than placebo for treatment of panic disorder and that they did not differ from one another in results. However, six months after treatment had ended, those who received psychotherapy were less likely to relapse than those who had taken medication. These findings indicate that cognitive behavioral therapy is the treatment of choice for panic disorder. For those who have panic disorder with agoraphobia, the combination of CBT and drugs is better than either treatment alone (Starcevic, Linden, Uhlenhuth, Kolar, & Latas, 2004).

OBSESSIVE-COMPULSIVE DISORDER Obsessive-compulsive disorder (OCD) is a combination of recurrent intrusive thoughts (obsessions) and behaviors that the client feels compelled to perform over and over (compulsions). Evidence that OCD is at least in part genetic and appears to be related to Tourette's syndrome, a neurological disorder characterized by motor and vocal tics, convinced many that OCD was a biological disorder that should respond to a biological treatment. However, traditional antianxiety drugs are completely ineffective for OCD. When SSRIs began to be used to treat depression, it was found that they were particularly effective in reducing the obsessional components of some depressions, such as constant feelings of worthlessness. Because of this, SSRIs were tried with clients suffering from OCD and found to be effective (Rapoport, 1989, 1991). The drug of choice for OCD is the potent serotonin reuptake inhibitor *clomipramine*. It is not a true SSRI, since it also blocks reuptake of other neurotransmitters, but its strong enhancement of the effects of serotonin appears to make it effective for OCD.

Researchers can learn a great deal about mental disorders by studying successful treatments. In obsessive-compulsive disorder, the effectiveness of SSRIs implicates the serotonin system. Despite the effectiveness of SSRIs, however, clinical studies have shown that 40 to 60 percent of patients with OCD do not improve when treated with these medications. For some of these patients, combining SSRIs with dopamine receptor blockers has been effective (Denys, Zohar, & Westenberg, 2004). It is interesting to note that the patients who benefit from this combination are those who also suffer from tics or who have a family history of tic disorders, such as Tourette's syndrome. Tic disorders are related to dopamine dysfunction; medications that block dopamine receptors are effective in suppressing tics (Shapiro et al., 1989). Genetic studies have hinted at a link between OCD and Tourette's syndrome, and it has been clinically observed that half to two-thirds of Tourette's patients also have OCD symptoms. Thus, this suggests dopamine plays a role in OCD.

Other research from a different angle implicates the hormone oxytocin in OCD. Researchers have found high levels of oxytocin in the cerebrospinal fluid of people with OCD (Leckman et al., 1994), but only those with no history of tic disorders; patients with tic-related OCD have normal oxytocin levels. Oxytocin receptors are found in a number of brain regions that have been implicated in OCD (Insel, 1992). Levels of oxytocin peak during the third trimester of pregnancy and remain high in breastfeeding women. Since higher levels of oxytocin are related to OCD, we might expect that pregnant and breastfeeding women would be prone to developing obsessive and compulsive symptoms. Anecdotal reports do suggest that women are more likely to develop OCD during these times, and for those who already have OCD, the higher levels of oxytocin during pregnancy and nursing can exacerbate symptoms (Epperson et al., 1995). Taken together, the findings on the roles of dopamine and oxytocin in OCD have an intriguing implication. There may be two distinct types of OCD: one tic related and one non–tic related. These two subtypes may well have

How might drug therapy inform us about the causes of mental disorders?

OCD Pre and Post Tx

SSRI - R_X

rCd

PRE   POST

Beh. - T_X

rCd

UCLA School of Medicine

14.9 PET Scans of OCD Patients Arrows point to locations in the basal ganglia that showed similar changes with psychotherapy and drug therapy.

different neural underpinnings, and their differential reactions to medications suggest that this is true. Thus, how people respond to treatment can help us understand the possible causes of a mental disorder.

Cognitive-behavioral therapy is also effective for OCD and is especially valuable for those who do not benefit from or who do not want to rely on medication. Behavioral therapy for OCD differs from therapy for panic disorder in that relaxation training is not typically part of treatment. The two most important components of behavioral therapy for OCD are exposure and response prevention. Clients are directly exposed to the stimuli that trigger compulsive behavior, but are prevented from engaging in the behavior. This treatment is based on the theory that a particular stimulus triggers anxiety, and that performing the compulsive behavior reduces that anxiety (see the hand-washing example in Chapter 13). For example, a client might compulsively wash his hands after touching a doorknob, using a public telephone, or shaking hands with someone. In exposure and response-prevention therapy, the client would be required to touch a doorknob and then would be instructed not to wash his hands afterward. As with exposure therapy for panic disorder, the goal is to break the conditioned link between particular stimuli and compulsive behavior. Some cognitive therapies are also useful for OCD, such as helping the client learn that most people experience unwanted thoughts and compulsions from time to time. The goal is to help clients recognized that having unwanted negative thoughts is not a catastrophe but rather a normal part of human experience.

In the 1990s, researchers imaged the brains of patients with OCD who were being treated either with Prozac or with cognitive-behavioral therapy. As Figure 14.9 illustrates, patients in both treatment groups showed the same changes in neural activity in the thalamus and basal ganglia (Baxter et al., 1992; Schwartz, Stoessel, Baxter, Martin, & Phelps, 1996). Recall the findings that the spider phobia treatment led to changes in brain activity. These studies provide further evidence that nonbiological therapies change how the brain functions. How does drug treatment compare with cognitive-behavioral therapy for OCD? In one recent study the use of exposure and ritual prevention was found to be superior to the use of clomipramine, the drug of choice for OCD, although both were better than placebo (Figure 14.10; Foa et al., 2005). Cognitive-behavioral therapy may thus be a more effective way of treating OCD than medication, especially over the long term (see also Foa et al., 2005).

Many Effective Treatments Are Available for Depression

Depression, characterized by low mood and loss of interest in pleasurable activities, is one of the most widespread mental disorders among adolescents and adults, and it has become more common over the past few decades (Hollon et al., 2002). Fortunately, a number of effective treatments have been validated through scientific research. There is no "best" way to treat depression; many treatment approaches are available to the depressed patient, and ongoing research is determining which type of therapy works best for individual clients.

PHARMACOLOGICAL TREATMENT In the 1950s, tuberculosis was a major health problem in the United States, particularly in urban areas. A common treatment was

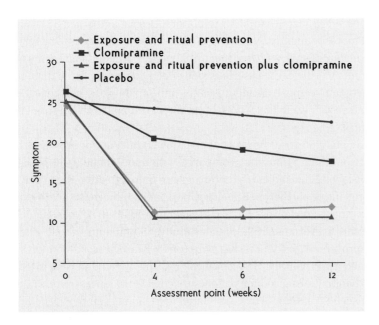

14.10 Treating Obsessive-Compulsive Disorder The most effective treatment for OCD in this study was exposure and ritual prevention. Adding the drug clomipramine did not reduce symptoms any further.

iproniazid, a drug that reduced tubercule bacilli in the sputum of patients. It also stimulated patients' appetites, increased their energy levels, and gave them an overall sense of well-being. In 1957, researchers who had noted the drug's effect on mood reported preliminary success in using it to treat depression. In the following year, nearly half a million depressed patients were given iproniazid, which is an MAO inhibitor. Although they can relieve depression, MAO inhibitors can be toxic because of their effects on a variety of physiological systems. Patients taking these drugs must avoid ingesting any substances containing tyramine, including red wine and aged cheeses, because they can experience severe, sometimes lethal elevations in blood pressure. Interactions with both prescription and over-the-counter medications can also be fatal, so MAO inhibitors are generally reserved for patients who do not respond to other antidepressants.

Another type of antidepressant, *tricyclics,* was also identified in the 1950s. The first tricyclic to be identified—imipramine, a drug developed as an antihistamine—was found to be effective in relieving clinical depression. This drug and others like it act on neurotransmitters as well as on the histamine system. Tricyclics are extremely effective antidepressants. However, as a result of their broad-based action, they have a number of unpleasant side effects. Because of their effect on the histamine system, patients often experience sedation and weight gain. Sweating, constipation, heart palpitations, and dry mouth can result from the effects of tricyclics on acetylcholine.

The discovery of these early antidepressants was largely serendipitous, but subsequently researchers began to search for antidepressants that did not affect multiple physiological and neurological systems and so would not have such troublesome side effects. In the 1980s, researchers discovered fluoxetine hydrochloride, better known as Prozac, which is an SSRI. Because this drug does not affect histamine or cholinergic systems it has none of the side effects associated with the tricyclic antidepressants, although it can occasionally cause insomnia, headache, weight loss, and sexual dysfunction. Because they have

"Before Prozac, she loathed company."

fewer serious side effects than MAO inhibitors, Prozac and other SSRIs began to be prescribed more frequently. A number of other drug treatments for depression have also been validated, such as *bupropion* (Wellbutrin), which affects many neurotransmitter systems but has far less serious side effects for most people than other drugs. For instance, unlike most antidepressants, bupropion does not cause sexual dysfunction. Interestingly, unlike SSRIs, bupropion is an ineffective treatment for panic disorder and OCD.

Approximately 60 to 70 percent of clients who take antidepressants will experience relief from their symptoms, compared with approximately 30 percent who respond to placebos. This indicates that drugs are quite effective, since placebo effects are a component of all therapeutic outcomes. Indeed, there is recent evidence that placebo treatment for depression leads to changes in brain activity (Leuchter, Cook, Witte, Morgan, & Abrams, 2002). In this study, 38 percent of those given placebos showed improvement in depressive symptoms. Those who responded to placebos had increased activity in the prefrontal cortex. This was a different pattern of brain activation than that observed for patients receiving antidepressants, but it does suggest that placebo treatments are associated with changes in neurochemistry, which supports the findings that they do alleviate symptoms for some people. Placebos may work by giving people hope that they will feel better, and these positive expectancies may alter brain activity.

Despite attempts to predict patient response to antidepressants, physicians must often resort to a trial-and-error approach in treating depressed patients. At this time no single drug stands out as being most efficacious. Some evidence suggests that tricyclics might be preferred for the most serious forms of depression, especially for patients who are hospitalized (Anderson, 2000), but SSRIs are generally considered first-line medications because they have the fewest serious side effects (Olfson et al., 2002). The decision of which drug to use often depends on the client's overall medical health and the possible side effects of each medication. Once the depressive episode has ended, should patients continue taking medication? Research has shown that patients who continue taking medication for at least a year have only a 20 percent relapse rate, whereas those who are maintained on a placebo have an 80 percent relapse rate (Frank et al., 1990).

COGNITIVE-BEHAVIORAL TREATMENT OF DEPRESSION Despite the success of antidepressant medications, not all patients benefit from these drugs. Moreover, others cannot or will not tolerate the side effects associated with drug therapy. Fortunately, the available evidence indicates that cognitive-behavioral therapy is just as effective as biological therapies in treating depression (Hollon et al., 2002). From a cognitive perspective, people who become depressed do so because of automatic, irrational thoughts. According to the cognitive distortion model of Aaron Beck, one of the most influential thinkers in this area, depression is the result of a cognitive triad of negative thoughts about oneself, the situation, and the future. The thought patterns of depressed patients are different from those of people with anxiety disorders. Whereas patients with anxiety disorders worry about the future, depressed people think about how they have failed in the past, how poorly they are dealing with the present situation, and how terrible the future will be.

The goal of the cognitive-behavioral treatment of depression is to help the patient think more adaptively, which in turn should improve mood and behavior. Although the specific nature of the treatment will be adapted to each individual patient, there are some general principles of this type of therapy for depression. Patients may be asked to recognize and record negative thoughts (Figure 14.11).

What factors need to be considered when deciding between drug treatments and psychological treatments?

Thinking about situations in a negative manner can become automatic, and recognizing these thought patterns can be difficult. Once the patterns are identified and monitored, the clinician can help the patient recognize that there are other ways of viewing the same situation—ways of thinking that are not so dysfunctional.

Although cognitive-behavioral therapy can be effective on its own, research shows that combining it with antidepressant medication is significantly more effective than either one of these approaches alone (McCullough, 2000). In addition, the response and remission rates of the combined-treatment approach were higher than any ever reported for depression (Keller et al., 2000; Kocsis et al., 2003). The issue is not drugs versus psychotherapy, but rather identifying the specific treatments from the available options that provide relief for individual clients. For instance, for clients who are suicidal, in acute distress, or unable to commit to regular attendance with a therapist, drug treatment may be most effective. For many others, especially those who have physical problems, psychotherapy may be the treatment of choice because it is long lasting and does not have the side effects associated with medications. As is the case with other mental disorders, treatment of depression with psychotherapy leads to changes in brain activation similar to those observed in drug treatments (Brody et al., 2001). However, one recent study found that although psychotherapy and drugs involved the same brain regions, activity in those regions was quite different during the two treatments, which suggests that they operate through different mechanisms (Goldapple et al., 2004).

Date	Event	Emotion	Automatic thoughts
April 4	Boss seemed annoyed.	Sad, anxious, worried	Oh, what have I done now? If I keep making him mad, I'm going to get fired.
April 5	Husband didn't want to make love.	Sad	I'm so fat and ugly.
April 7	Boss yelled at another employee.	Anxious	I'm next.
April 9	Husband said he's taking a long business trip next month.	Sad, defeated	He's probably got a mistress somewhere. My marriage is falling apart.
April 10	Neighbor brought over some cookies.	A little happy, mostly sad	She probably thinks I can't cook. I look like such a mess all the time. And my house was a disaster when she came in!

14.11 Recording Thoughts A record of automatic thoughts used in cognitive-behavioral therapy for depression.

14.12 Seasonal Affective Disorder Incidents of SAD vary by latitude, being much more common in areas that receive less sunlight during the winter.

ALTERNATIVE TREATMENTS In some patients, episodes of depression occur during the winter. The rate of this disorder, known as seasonal affective disorder (SAD), increases with latitude, with rates highest in regions with the fewest hours of daylight during the winter (Figure 14.12). Many of these patients respond favorably to phototherapy, in which patients are exposed to a high-intensity light source for a period of time each day (Figure 14.13). Patients who crave carbohydrates and sleep a great deal in the winter seem to respond better to phototherapy than do SAD patients who do not exhibit these symptoms.

For some depressed patients, regular aerobic exercise can reduce depression and prevent recurrence (Pollock, 2004). It has been

14.13 Phototherapy This woman sits in front of strong lighting for several hours each day to reduce her symptoms of SAD.

speculated that aerobic exercise reduces depression because it releases endorphins, which are chemically related to norepinephrine, a neurotransmitter implicated in depression. Release of endorphins can result in an overall feeling of well-being, which marathoners may recognize as the "runner's high." Aerobic exercise may also serve to regularize bodily rhythms, improve self-esteem, and provide social support if people exercise with others. For depressed patients, however, it may be difficult to find the energy and motivation to begin an exercise regime.

In addition to these somewhat benign interventions, more drastic treatments may be warranted for some depressed patients. In the 1930s, **electroconvulsive therapy (ECT)** was developed in Europe and tried on the first human in 1938. ECT involves placing electrodes on the patient's head and administering an electrical current strong enough to produce a seizure (Figure 14.14). Although ECT frequently results in an amelioration of depressed mood, the mechanism by which this occurs is unknown (Fink, 2001). ECT may affect neurotransmitters or the neuroendocrine system; it has been shown to increase levels of acetylcholine, and drugs that block the action of acetylcholine reverse the beneficial effects of ECT. However it works, ECT is the single most effective treatment for those who are severely depressed and do not respond to conventional treatments (Hollon et al., 2002).

The general public views ECT in a predominately negative manner. The 1975 film *One Flew over the Cuckoo's Nest* did a great deal to expose the abuses in mental health care and graphically depicted ECT as well as the tragic effects of lobotomy. Although care for the mentally ill is still far from perfect, many reforms have been implemented. ECT is now generally done under anesthesia with powerful muscle relaxants. This essentially eliminates the motor convulsions and confines the seizure to the brain. For a number of reasons, ECT might be preferable to other treatments for depression. Antidepressant medication can take weeks to be effective, whereas ECT works quickly. For a suicidal patient, waiting several weeks for relief can literally be deadly. In addition, ECT may be the treatment of choice for depression in pregnant women, since there is no evidence that the seizures harm the developing fetus. Many psychotropic medications, on the other hand, can cause birth defects. Most important, ECT has proven effective in clients for whom other treatments have failed, providing an effective last resort for those who would otherwise continue to suffer.

14.14 A Woman Being Prepared for Electroconvulsive Therapy To prevent her from possibly swallowing her tongue, a soft object is placed between her teeth.

ECT does, however, have some serious limitations, including a high relapse rate, often necessitating repeated treatments, and memory impairments (Fink, 2001). In most cases, memory loss is transient and is limited to the day of ECT treatment. Some patients, however, experience substantial memory loss that can be permanent (Donahue, 2000). Some centers perform unilateral ECT over only the hemisphere that is not dominant for language, which seems to reduce any memory disruption (Papadimitrious, Zervas, & Papakostas, 2001). New research suggests that the degree of memory and cognitive impairment resulting from ECT may be related to levels of cortisol, a hormone released in response to physical and psychological stress (see Chapter 10). Depressed patients with higher levels of cortisol show greater impairments in memory and cognitive functions (Neylan et al., 2001). This research may help to identify patients at risk for memory and cognitive losses due to ECT, and these potentially serious side effects can be weighed against the benefits of the treatment.

Recently, research has explored whether **transcranial magnetic stimulation (TMS)** can reduce depressive symptoms. In this procedure, an electromagnetic coil is placed on the scalp and transmits pulses of high-intensity magnetism. The rapid buildup and collapse of the magnetic field induces a momentary electrical current in the brain. The net result is that normal brain activity is disrupted in the brain region beneath the coil. In effect, the coil creates a brief, transient brain lesion. A series of studies has demonstrated that TMS over the left frontal regions results in a significant reduction in depression (Chistyakov et al., 2004; George, Lisanby, & Sackheim, 1999; George et al., 1995; Pascual-Leone, Catala, & Pascual-Leone, 1996). Because TMS does not involve anesthesia and does not have any major side effects (other than headache), it can be administered outside of hospital settings. It is not likely, however, that TMS will ever completely replace ECT, since the two methods may act via different mechanisms and may therefore be appropriate for different types of patients. TMS seems to be more effective for nonpsychotic depression, whereas ECT seems to be more effective for psychotic depression (George et al., 1999). The long-term value of TMS is that it is effective even for patients who have not responded to treatment with antidepressants (Fitzgerald et al., 2003). This highlights the idea that just as there are multiple causes of depression, so are there multiple effective treatments. The challenge for practitioners is to find the treatment that works best for a particular individual.

Lithium Is Most Effective for Bipolar Disorder

Although major depression and bipolar disorder are both disorders of mood, they are fundamentally different and require different treatments. Bipolar disorder, in which mood cycles between mania and depression, is one of the few mental disorders for which there is a clear optimal treatment. Psychotropic medications have been found to be the most effective way to treat this disorder, especially **lithium** (Geddes, Burgess, Hawton, Jamison, & Goodwin, 2004). Only about 20 percent of patients maintained on lithium experience relapses (Keller & Baker, 1991). The mechanisms by which lithium stabilizes mood are not well understood, but the drug seems to modulate neurotransmitter levels, balancing excitatory and inhibitory activities (Jope, 1999). As with other psychotropic drugs, the discovery of lithium for the treatment of bipolar disorder was serendipitous. In 1949, an Australian named John Cade found that the urine of manic patients was toxic to guinea pigs. He postulated that this effect might be due to uric acid. When he gave lithium urate, a salt in uric acid, to the guinea pigs, however, it was not toxic. To his surprise, it protected them against the toxic effects of the manic patients' urine and also sedated them. He next tried lithium salts on himself. When he was assured of their safety, he gave the salts to ten hospitalized manic patients, all of whom recovered rapidly. Lithium does, however, have unpleasant side effects, including thirst, hand tremors, excessive urination, and memory problems. These side effects often diminish after several weeks on the drug.

Although lithium is effective in stabilizing mood, it works better on mania than on depression, and patients are often treated both with lithium and with an antidepressant. In this regard, the available evidence indicates that selective serotonin reuptake inhibitors (SSRIs) are preferable to other antidepressants because they are less likely to trigger episodes of mania (Gijsman, Geddes, Rendell, Nolen, & Goodwin, 2004). Anticonvulsive medications, such as Depakote, also can stabilize

electroconvulsive therapy (ECT) A procedure used to treat depression that involves administering a strong electrical current to the patient's brain.

transcranial magnetic stimulation (TMS) A procedure that transmits pulses of high-intensity magnetism to the brain.

lithium A psychotropic medication used to treat bipolar disorder.

mood and may be effective for intense bipolar episodes. As with all psychological disorders, compliance with drug therapy can be a problem for a variety of reasons. Patients may skip doses or stop taking the medications completely in an effort to reduce the side effects of the drugs. Cognitive-behavioral therapy can be an effective way to increase compliance with medication regimes (Miller, Norman, & Keitner, 1989). Patients with bipolar disorder also may stop taking their medications because they miss the "highs" of their hypomanic and manic phases. Recall from Chapter 13 Kay Redfield Jamison's description of the intoxicating pleasure of mania. Psychological therapy can help patients accept their need for medication and understand the impact their disorder has on them and on those around them.

Pharmacological Treatments Are Superior for Schizophrenia

Freud's psychoanalytic theory and treatment were widely touted as the answer to many mental disorders in the early 1900s. Even Freud, however, admitted that his techniques were effective only for what he termed "neuroses" and were unlikely to benefit patients with more severe psychotic disorders such as schizophrenia. Because psychotic patients were difficult to handle and even more difficult to treat, they were generally institutionalized in large mental hospitals. By 1934, it was estimated that the physician-to-patient ratio in such institutions was more than 1 to 200 in New York State. This set up a situation in which the staff and administration of mental hospitals were willing to try any treatment that was inexpensive and had a chance of decreasing the patient population, or that at the very least might make the inmates more manageable.

Brain surgery was considered a viable option in the management of patients with severe mental illness. Although some brain surgeries were performed in the early 1880s, Egas Moniz is generally credited with bringing the practice to the attention of the medical world in the 1930s. His surgical procedure, later known as lobotomy, severed nerve-fiber pathways in the prefrontal cortex. Although Moniz initially reported that the operation was frequently successful, it soon became evident to him that the patients who benefited most from the surgery were those who were anxious or depressed. Schizophrenic patients did not seem to improve following the operation. With the introduction of psychotropic medications in the 1950s, lobotomies were virtually discontinued.

PHARMACOLOGICAL TREATMENT It had been known since the sixteenth century that extracts from dogbane, a toxic herb, could calm highly agitated patients. The critical ingredient was isolated in the 1950s and was named reserpine. When given to schizophrenic patients, it not only had a sedative effect, it also was an effective antipsychotic, reducing the positive symptoms of schizophrenia, such as delusions and hallucinations. Shortly afterward, a synthetic version of reserpine was created that had fewer side effects. This drug, called *chlorpromazine,* acts as a major tranquilizer. It reduces anxiety, sedates without inducing sleep, and decreases the severity and frequency of the positive symptoms of schizophrenia. Later, another antipsychotic, *haloperidol,* was developed that was chemically different and had less of a sedating effect than chlorpromazine.

Haloperidol and chlorpromazine revolutionized the treatment of schizophrenia and became the most frequently used therapy for the disorder. Schizophrenic patients who had been hospitalized for years were able to walk out of mental institutions and live independently. These antipsychotics are not without drawbacks, however. The medications have little or no impact on the negative symptoms of schizophrenia, such as apathy and social withdrawal. In addition, they have significant side effects. Chlorpromazine sedates patients, can cause constipation and weight gain, and causes cardiovascular damage. Although haloperidol does not cause these symptoms, both drugs have significant motor side effects that resemble Parkinson's disease. Immobility of facial muscles, trembling of extremities, muscle spasms, uncontrollable salivation, and a shuffling walk can all occur as a result of antipsychotic medication. **Tardive dyskinesia**, involuntary movements of the lips, tongue, face, legs, or other parts of the body, is another devastating side effect of these medications and is irreversible once it appears. Despite these debilitating side effects, chlorpromazine and haloperidol were essentially the only medications available to schizophrenia patients for many years.

In the late 1980s, clozapine was introduced. **Clozapine** was significantly different from the previous antipsychotic medications in a number of ways. First, it acted not only on dopamine receptors, but also on those for serotonin, norepinephrine, acetylcholine, and histamine. Second, it was beneficial in treating the negative symptoms of schizophrenia as well as the positive symptoms. Many patients who had not responded to the previously available neuroleptics improved on clozapine (Figure 14.15). Third, there was no evidence of Parkinsonian symptoms or of tardive dyskinesia in any of the patients taking the drug. Clozapine has fewer side effects than either chlorpromazine or haloperidol, but its side effects are serious. Clozapine is associated with seizures, heart arrhythmias, and substantial weight gain. Of even greater concern, clozapine can cause a fatal reduction in white blood cells. Although the risk of this is low, frequent blood tests are required for patients taking the drug. The cost of the blood tests, in addition to the high cost of the medication itself, has made this drug treatment prohibitively expensive for many patients. More recently, other medications similar to clozapine in structure and pharmacology have been introduced. These medications, such as risperidol and olanzapine, appear to be as effective as clozapine but do not reduce white blood cell counts. These new drugs, called second-generation antipsychotics, are now the first line in treatment for schizophrenia (Walker, Kestler, Bollini, & Hochman, 2004). A recent analysis of 11 separate studies containing 2,769 patients found that these second-generation antipsychotics had about one-fifth the risk of producing tardive dyskinesia as first-generation drugs (Correll, Leucht, & Kane, 2004).

tardive dyskinesia A side effect of some antipsychotic medications that produces involuntary movements of the lips, tongue, face, legs, or other parts of the body.

clozapine An antipsychotic medication that acts on multiple neurotransmitter receptors and is beneficial in treating both the negative and positive symptoms of schizophrenia.

14.15 The Effectiveness of Clozapine Clozapine is more effective than previously available antipsychotic medications in treating both the positive and the negative symptoms of schizophrenia.

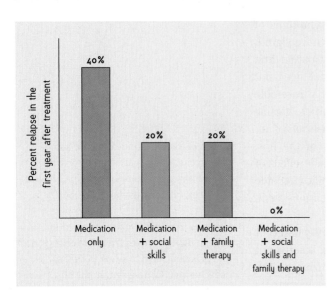

14.16 The Effectiveness of Antipsychotic Medications and Therapy Medication is the most effective way to reduce the rate of relapse for patients with schizophrenia, but adding psychosocial interventions, such as family therapy and social-skills training, improves outcome.

Why might social support enhance drug therapies for schizophrenia?

PSYCHOSOCIAL TREATMENTS It is well established that medication is essential in the treatment of schizophrenia. Without it, patients may deteriorate, experiencing more frequent and more severe psychotic episodes. When antipsychotic drugs became available, other types of therapies for schizophrenia were virtually dismissed. It became clear over time, however, that although medication is effective in reducing delusions and hallucinations, it does not have a substantial impact on patients' social functioning. A study of the clinical outcome of schizophrenia treatments over a 100-year period demonstrated that antipsychotic drugs improved the outcome for schizophrenic patients from just under 40 percent to about 50 percent (Hegarty, Baldessarini, Tohen, Waternaux, & Oepen, 1994). While this is an improvement, it falls far short of a cure.

Antipsychotic medication is most effective when used in combination with other treatment approaches. Social-skills training has been an effective way to address some of the deficits shown by those with schizophrenia. Schizophrenic patients can benefit from intensive training on regulating affect, recognizing social cues, and predicting the effects of their behavior in social situations (Figure 14.16). With intensive long-term training, schizophrenic patients can generalize the skills learned in therapy to other social environments. Self-care skills can be another area in which schizophrenic patients are deficient. Behavioral interventions can be focused on such areas as grooming and bathing, management of medications, and financial planning. Training in specific cognitive skills, such as modifying thinking patterns and coping with auditory hallucinations, has been less effective.

Recently, psychologist Aaron Beck has proposed that an intensive form of cognitive-behavioral therapy (CBT) is effective for treating schizophrenia (Beck & Rector, 2005). Beck believes that brain dysfunction gives rise to disordered beliefs and behaviors and that schizophrenia may be due in part to limited cognitive resources and an inability to inhibit the intrusion of inappropriate thoughts. From this perspective, delusions and hallucinations reflect biased information processing. In CBT for schizophrenia, a great deal of initial effort is made to get the client to trust the therapist as someone who will be nonjudgmental and who will try to understand the meaning of symptoms from the patient's perspective. Over time the therapy becomes more formal as the therapist seeks to help the client understand how stressful life circumstances contribute to the experience of disordered thoughts and how there might be alternative explanations for delusions and hallucinations. Initial studies using CBT for schizophrenia indicate that it is more effective than other psychological treatments in reducing symptoms such as delusions and hallucinations.

PROGNOSIS IN SCHIZOPHRENIA Most patients diagnosed with schizophrenia experience multiple psychotic episodes over the course of the illness. In some patients the disorder seems to be progressive, with each schizophrenic episode laying the groundwork for increasingly severe symptoms in the future. For this reason, it is thought to be in the patient's best interest to treat the disorder early and aggressively.

Although the disorder becomes progressively more severe in some affected individuals, this is not true for a majority of those diagnosed with schizophrenia. In fact, most schizophrenic patients improve over time. One long-term study that followed schizophrenic subjects for an average of 32 years showed that between half and two-thirds were recovered or had had considerable improvement in functioning on follow-up (Harding, Zubin, & Strauss, 1987). No one knows why most of those with schizophrenia seem to improve as they grow older. It may be that the patients who improve have found the treatment regimen that is most effective for them. Another theory is that the changes in the brain that occur with aging somehow result in fewer psychotic episodes. Dopamine levels may decrease with age and this may be related to the improvement in schizophrenic symptoms.

The prognosis for schizophrenic patients depends on a variety of factors, including age of onset, gender, and culture. Those diagnosed with schizophrenia later in life tend to have a more favorable prognosis than those who experience their first symptoms during childhood or adolescence (McGlashan, 1988). Women tend to have a better prognosis than men (Hambrecht, Maurer, Hafner, & Sartorius, 1992), perhaps because the onset of schizophrenia in women tends to be later than in men. Interestingly, culture also plays a role in prognosis. Schizophrenia in developing countries is often not so severe as in developed countries (Jablensky, 1989; Leff, Sartorius, Jablensky, Korten, & Ernberg, 1992). More extensive family networks in developing countries may provide more support in caring for schizophrenic patients.

Thinking Critically

Should Drugs Be Used to Treat Adolescent Depression?

Adolescent depression is a serious problem, affecting approximately 1 in 20 American adolescents at any one time (Angold & Costello, 2001). Untreated depression is associated with drug abuse, dropping out of school, and suicide. In the United States, approximately 5,000 teenagers kill themselves each year, making it the third leading cause of death for that age group (Arias, MacDorman, Strobino, & Guyer, 2003). For many years, depression in children and adolescents was ignored or viewed as a typical part of growing up. According to a report of the Surgeon General, fewer than 30 percent of children who have mental health problems receive any type of treatment (USDHHS, 1999). It is understandable, then, that many in the mental health community reacted favorably to the initial use of SSRIs such as Prozac to treat adolescent depression. Studies had found tricycle antidepressants were ineffective and dangerous for adolescents, but the first studies using SSRIs found them to be effective and safe (e.g., Emslie et al., 1997).

From the time that SSRIs were introduced as treatments for adolescent depression, some mental health researchers raised concerns that the drugs might cause some adolescents to become suicidal (Jureidini et al., 2004). These concerns were based in part on findings that SSRIs cause some adults to feel restless, impulsive, and suicidal. Following a report by one drug company of an increase in suicidal thoughts among adolescents taking its product, the Food and Drug Administration (FDA) asked all drug companies to analyze their records for similar reports. An analysis of reports on more than 4,400 children and adolescents found that about twice as many of them taking SSRIs reported having suicidal thoughts (4 percent) as those taking a placebo (2 percent), but none of the children or adolescents actually committed suicide. Given evidence of increased thoughts of suicide, the FDA voted in October 2004 to require manufacturers to add to their product labels a warning that antidepressants increase the risk of suicidal thinking and behavior in depressed children and adolescents, and that physicians prescribing these drugs need to balance risk with clinical need. Physicians were also advised to watch their patients closely, especially in the first few weeks of treatment. Suddenly many parents were wondering whether SSRIs were safe for their children.

Many issues concerning SSRIs and children need to be evaluated critically. First, are SSRIs effective for young people, and if so, are they more effective than other treatments? Second, do these drugs actually cause suicidal feelings, or are depressed adolescents generally likely to feel suicidal whether or not they take medication? Finally, how many adolescents would be suicidal if their depression was left untreated?

An ambitious study supported by the National Institutes of Health provides clear evidence that the SSRI Prozac is effective in treating adolescent depression. This study, called the Treatment of Adolescents with Depression Study (TADS, 2004), examined 429 patients aged 12 to 17 who had been depressed for an average of 40 weeks before the study began. Participants were randomly assigned to a type of treatment and followed for 12 weeks. The results indicated that 61 percent of participants taking Prozac showed improvement in symptoms, compared with 43 percent receiving cognitive-behavioral therapy, and 35 percent taking a placebo. The group that did best was the group receiving both Prozac and CBT, in which 71 percent improved; this is consistent with other studies showing that the combination of drugs and psychotherapy often produces the strongest results. In terms of suicidality, the results were more mixed. All treatment groups experienced a reduction in thoughts of suicide compared with the baseline. However, participants in the Prozac group were twice as likely to have serious suicidal thoughts or intentions compared with those undergoing other treatments, and of the 7 adolescents who attempted suicide during the study, 6 were taking Prozac. Critics of adolescents receiving drugs point out that these findings are consistent with other studies showing a risk from SSRIs (Antonuccio & Burns, 2004).

We need to keep a few things in mind as we analyze the use of SSRIs for adolescent depression. In the TADS study, suicide attempts were quite uncommon (7 of 429 patients). Indeed, this is consistent with the FDA finding that about 4 percent of adolescents taking Prozac will become suicidal. Moreover, only a small number of the 5,000 adolescents who kill themselves each year are taking antidepressants of any kind. The question is whether the millions of children who take antidepressants experience more benefits than risks. In addition, the rates of suicide have dropped since the use of SSRIs became widespread (Figure 14.17), which implies that the increased use of drugs such as Prozac may be lowering the overall rate of depression, thereby reducing suicide. The greater the increase in the number of SSRI prescriptions for adolescents within a region, the greater the reduction in teenage suicides (Olfson, Shaffer, Marcus, & Greenberg, 2003). This raises the possibility that not providing SSRIs to adolescents will raise the suicide rate (Brent, 2004).

14.17 Suicide Rates among People 15 to 24 Years of Age The rate of suicide among adolescents and young adults has been in decline for the past decade. This roughly corresponds to the period during which SSRIs have been used to treat depression.

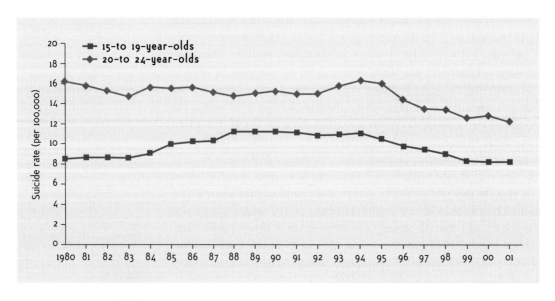

CHAPTER 14 | Treating Disorders of Mind and Body

According to some researchers, the relative success of psychotherapy for teenage depression makes it a better treatment choice. Indeed, considerable evidence shows that psychotherapy is effective on its own (Mufson et al., 2004) and also enhances drug treatment. Other psychological treatments, such as interpersonal psychotherapy, are also successful (Hollon et al., 2002). But getting adolescents to comply with psychotherapy can be challenging. Psychotherapy is also time consuming and expensive; many health insurance companies provide only minimal support (Rifkin & Rifkin, 2004). In addition, it is unrealistic to expect there to be sufficient resources to provide psychotherapy to all adolescents who need it in the near future. By contrast, it is relatively easy for pediatricians and family physicians to prescribe drugs. Unfortunately, the prescribing of such medications by general practitioners can be problematic because these individuals do not have specific training in treating psychological disorders.

What would you recommend? Do you think the FDA action was warranted by the data? Do you believe that it is acceptable to provide drugs that benefit many adolescents but place some at risk for suicide? The risk currently looks relatively small. How large a risk is acceptable, if any? ■

REVIEWING
the Principles | What Are the Most Effective Treatments?

Psychotherapy and biological therapy are used to treat mental disorders. When the two are equally effective, psychotherapy is preferred because it has fewer side effects and persists beyond treatment. Cognitive and behavioral therapies, especially exposure and response prevention, are particularly useful for anxiety disorders, although drug treatments are also used for panic disorder and OCD. There are a number of treatment strategies for mood disorders, including exercise, antidepressants, cognitive-behavioral therapy, electroconvulsive therapy, and transcranial magnetic stimulation. For mania, however, only lithium appears to be effective. Psychopharmacology is the recommended treatment for schizophrenia, and a variety of drugs are now known to be safe and effective. Pharmacological interventions for schizophrenia are most effective when used in combination with other treatment approaches. Training in social and self-care skills can help patients improve their ability to interact with others and to take care of themselves. Behavioral interventions can also help in improving self-care and in increasing compliance with medication.

Can Personality Disorders Be Treated?

Just as not much is known about the causes of personality disorders, little is known about how best to treat them. There is a growing literature of case studies describing treatment approaches for personality disorders, but few large well-controlled studies. The one thing about personality disorders that most therapists agree on is that they are notoriously difficult to treat. Individuals with personality disorders who are in therapy are usually also being treated for an Axis I disorder, which typically is the problem for which they sought therapy in the first place. People rarely seek therapy for personality disorders because one of the hallmarks of these disorders is that patients tend to see the environment rather than their own behavior as the cause of their problems. Individuals with personality disorders can be very difficult to engage in therapy since they do not see their behavior as a problem. We now consider two of the better-researched personality disorders.

Dialectical Behavior Therapy Is Most Successful for Borderline Personality Disorder

The impulsivity, affective disturbances, and identity disturbances that are characteristic of borderline personality disorder make therapy for those affected very challenging. Traditional psychotherapy approaches have been largely unsuccessful, so there have been efforts to develop approaches specific to borderline personality disorder.

The most successful treatment approach to date for borderline personality disorder was developed by Marsha Linehan (Figure 14.18) in the 1980s. **Dialectical behavior therapy (DBT)** combines elements of the behavioral, cognitive, and psychodynamic approaches (Lieb, Zanarini, Schmahl, Linehan, & Bohus, 2004). Clients are seen in both group and individual sessions, and the responsibilities of both the client and the therapist are made explicit. Therapy proceeds in three stages. In the first stage, the therapist targets the client's most extreme and dysfunctional behaviors. Often these are self-cutting and suicidal threats or attempts. The focus is on replacing these behaviors with others that are more appropriate. Clients are taught problem-solving techniques and more effective and acceptable ways of coping with emotions. In the second stage of the treatment, the therapist helps the client explore past traumatic experiences that may be at the root of emotional problems. In the third stage, the therapist helps the patient develop self-respect and independent problem solving. This is a crucial stage in therapy. Borderline patients are very dependent on others for support and validation, and they must be able to generate these things themselves or they will likely revert to their previous patterns of behavior.

Because of the depressive and sometimes psychoticlike symptoms experienced by individuals with borderline personality disorder, researchers previously believed that they would develop an Axis I disorder such as schizophrenia or depression. Studies that have followed these individuals over time, however, have demonstrated that this is not the case. Instead, they continue with their symptoms relatively unchanged over time (Plakun, Burkhardt, & Muller, 1985). The only group that does seem to show some long-term improvement is borderline patients of a high socioeconomic level who receive intensive treatment. These individuals show improvement in interpersonal relationships and often achieve full-time employment (Stone, Stone, & Hurt, 1987). In the remainder of borderline patients, however, interpersonal and occupational problems are the norm. Substance abuse is not uncommon, and many patients attempt suicide multiple times.

Therapeutic approaches specifically targeted at borderline personality disorder, such as DBT, may improve the prognosis for these patients. Studies have demonstrated that clients undergoing DBT are more likely to remain in treatment and less likely to be suicidal than are clients in other types of therapy (Linehan, Armstrong, Suarez, Allmon, & Heard, 1991; Linehan, Heard, & Armstrong, 1993). SSRIs are often prescribed along with DBT to treat feelings of depression. Although DBT was initially developed as an outpatient therapy, it has recently been adapted for use in an inpatient setting (Swenson, Sanderson, Dulie, & Linehan, 2001). Because borderline patients thrive on attention, inpatient settings that are not specifically designed for these patients can inadvertently reinforce dysfunctional behavior that brings them attention, such as self-injury and suicide attempts. The result is often a worsening of symptoms and long-term hospitalization (Rosenbluth & Silver, 1992). The DBT

14.18 Marsha Linehan Linehan developed dialectical behavior therapy, one of the few effective treatments for borderline personality disorder.

How do you treat people who thrive on attention or do not believe they have a problem?

program begins with a three-month inpatient stay followed by long-term outpatient therapy. It has been found to be very effective in reducing depression, anxiety, and suicidal gestures (Bohus et al., 2004, 2000).

Antisocial Personality Disorder Is Difficult to Treat

Although treating borderline patients may be very difficult, treating those with antisocial personality disorder often seems impossible. These patients lie without thinking twice about it, care little for the feelings of others, and live for the present without consideration of the future. All of these factors make development of a therapeutic relationship and motivation for change remote possibilities at best. Antisocial individuals are often more interested in manipulating their therapists than in changing their behavior. Therapists working with these patients must be constantly on guard.

THERAPEUTIC APPROACHES FOR ANTISOCIAL PERSONALITY DISORDER
A number of treatment approaches have been tried for antisocial personality disorder. Because antisocial individuals have been reported to have diminished cortical arousal, stimulants have been prescribed to normalize arousal levels. Evidence indicates that these drugs are beneficial in the short term, but they are not a long-term solution. Antianxiety drugs may lower hostility levels somewhat, and lithium has shown some promise in treating the aggressive, impulsive behavior of violent criminals. Overall, however, psychotropic medications have not proven effective in treating this disorder.

Similarly, traditional psychotherapeutic approaches seem to be of little use in treating antisocial personality disorder. Behavioral and cognitive approaches have met with somewhat more success. Behavioral approaches reinforce appropriate behavior and ignore or punish inappropriate behavior in an attempt to replace maladaptive behavior patterns with more socially appropriate behavior. This approach seems to work best when the therapist controls reinforcement, the client cannot leave treatment, and the client is part of a group. Individual therapy sessions rarely result in any change in antisocial behavior. Clearly, the behavioral approach cannot be implemented on an outpatient basis, since the client will receive reinforcement for his behavior outside of therapy and can leave treatment at any time. For these reasons, therapy for this disorder is most effective in a residential treatment center or correctional facility.

More recently, cognitive approaches have been tried for antisocial personality disorder. Beck and his colleagues (1990) have conceptualized this disorder as a series of faulty cognitions. The antisocial individual believes that his desire for something justifies any actions he takes to attain it. He believes his actions will not have negative consequences, or if they do that these consequences are not important. He also believes he is always right and that what others think is unimportant. Therapy is therefore focused on making the client aware of these beliefs and challenging their validity. Therapists try to demonstrate that the client's goals can be met more easily by following the rules of society than by trying to get around them, as in the following example (Beck et al., 1990):

Therapist: How well has the "beat-the-system" approach actually worked out for you over time?
Brett: It works great . . . until someone catches on or starts to catch on. Then you have to scrap that plan and come up with a new one.
Therapist: How difficult was it, you know, to cover up one scheme and come up with a new one?
Brett: Sometimes it was really easy. There are some real pigeons out there.

dialectical behavior therapy (DBT) A treatment for borderline personality disorder that combines elements of behavioral, cognitive, and psychodynamic approaches.

Therapist: Was it always easy?

Brett: Well, no. Sometimes it was a real bitch. . . . Seems like I'm always needing a good plan to beat the system.

Therapist: Do you think it's ever easier to go with the system instead of trying to beat it in some way?

Brett: Well, after all that I have been through, I would have to say yes, there have been times that going with the system would have been easier in the long run. . . . But . . . it's such a challenge to beat the system. It feels exciting when I come up with a new plan and think I can make it work.

This dialogue illustrates both the cognitive approach and why these patients are so difficult to work with. Even if they can understand that what they are doing is wrong, they don't care. They live for the thrill of getting away with something.

PROGNOSIS FOR ANTISOCIAL PERSONALITY DISORDER The prognosis that antisocial patients will change their behavior as a result of therapy is poor. Some of the more recently developed cognitive techniques show promise, but as yet there is no good evidence that the changes they produce are long-lasting or even real. Fortunately for society, however, most antisocial individuals improve after age 40 (Figure 14.19). The reasons for this are not known, but the improvement may be due to a reduction in biological drives. Alternative theories suggest that these individuals may gain insight into their self-defeating behaviors or may just get worn out and be unable to continue their manipulative ways. This improvement, however, is only in the realm of antisocial behavior. The egocentricity, callousness, and manipulativeness remain unchanged (Harpur & Hare, 1994). In fact, although criminal acts decrease among those with antisocial personality disorder after age 40, over 50 percent of these individuals continue to be arrested after age 40 (Hare, McPherson, & Forth, 1988).

Because of the limited effectiveness of therapy for this disorder, time and effort may be better spent in prevention. Conduct disorder is a childhood condition known to be a precursor to antisocial personality disorder. Some of the environmental and developmental risk factors for conduct disorder have been identified, and focusing on these may reduce the likelihood that a child with conduct disorder will grow up to have antisocial personality disorder.

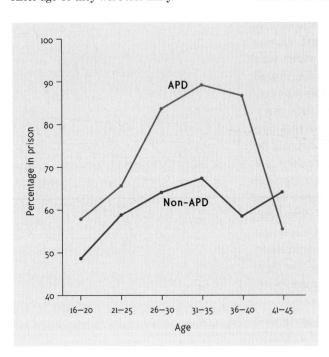

14.19 Antisocial Personality Disorder Of 521 prisoners studied by Robert Hare and his colleagues, those with antisocial personality disorder (APD) were more likely than other criminals to spend time in jail before age 40. After age 40 they were less likely.

REVIEWING

the Principles | Can Personality Disorders Be Treated?

Personality disorders are characterized by long-standing maladaptive ways of interacting with the world, and they are notoriously difficult to treat. Efforts have been made to develop treatment programs for both borderline and antisocial personality disorders because they can have devastating effects on the individual, the family, and society. Dialectical behavior therapy is the most successful method of treating borderline personality disorder. At this point, no treatment approach appears to be particularly successful in treating antisocial personality disorder.

How Should Childhood Disorders Be Treated?

It is estimated that more than 12 percent of children and adolescents in the United States suffer from mental disorders (Leckman et al., 1995). In 1990, the National Advisory Mental Health Council recommended that funding for research in childhood and adolescent mental disorders increase from $92 million to $283 million by 1995. The stated purpose of this increase was to "hasten the day when no child or adolescent need be too hard to handle, too sad to survive, too strange and angry to live among us, too ill to laugh, play and love." The recommendation reflected growing awareness of the scope and persistence of mental disorders in children. Childhood experience and development are critically important to adult mental health. Problems not addressed during childhood will still be there in adulthood and are likely to be more significant and more difficult to treat. Most theories of human development regard children as more malleable than adults and therefore more amenable to treatment. That would suggest that childhood disorders should be the focus of research into etiology, prevention, and treatment. To illustrate the issues involved in treating childhood disorders, we will consider treatment approaches for two of these disorders.

Children with ADHD Can Benefit from a Variety of Approaches

There is some dispute about whether attention-deficit/hyperactivity disorder is a mental disorder or simply a troublesome behavior pattern that children will eventually outgrow. Some children diagnosed with ADHD do grow out of it. Many more, however, continue to suffer from the disorder throughout adolescence and adulthood. Longitudinal studies show that 70 percent of individuals diagnosed with ADHD during childhood still meet the criteria for the disorder in adolescence. These individuals are more likely to drop out of school and to reach a lower socioeconomic level than expected. They continue to show a pattern of inattention, impulsivity, and hyperactivity, and they are at increased risk for other psychiatric disorders (Wilens, Faraone, & Biederman, 2004). Because of this somewhat bleak long-term prognosis, it is clear that effective treatment early in life is of great importance.

PHARMACOLOGICAL TREATMENT OF ADHD Currently, the most common treatment for ADHD is a central-nervous-system stimulant such as **methylphenidate** (*Ritalin*). The effects of this drug are similar to those of caffeine and amphetamines, but it is more potent than the former and less potent than the latter. Although the actions of methylphenidate are not fully understood, it is thought to affect multiple neurotransmitters, in particular dopamine. Based on the external behavior of children with ADHD, one might conclude that their brains are overly active, and it may seem surprising that a stimulant would improve their symptoms. In fact, functional brain imaging shows that children with ADHD have underactive brains; their hyperactivity may be a way of raising their arousal levels.

At appropriate doses, central-nervous-system stimulants decrease overactivity and distractibility and increase attention and the ability to concentrate. Children on stimulants are able to work more effectively on a task without interruption and are more academically productive. Even their handwriting seems to improve. They are less disruptive and noisy, and this likely has contributed to the large number of

How cautious should we be in prescribing drugs to children with ADHD?

methylphenidate A central-nervous-system stimulant medication used to treat ADHD.

14.20 The Effects of Ritalin The use of methylphenidate (Ritalin) for children with ADHD dramatically reduces negative behaviors while only slightly increasing the amount of positive behavior.

children who take this medication (Figure 14.20). Parents often feel pressured by the school system to medicate children who are an ongoing behavior problem in the classroom. Parents themselves can pressure physicians to prescribe the drug because it can make home life much more manageable. One study measured the effects of methylphenidate on the behavior of children during a baseball game (Pelham et al., 1990). Those children with ADHD who were taking the medication would assume the ready position in the outfield and could keep track of the game. Children with ADHD who were not taking the drug would often throw or kick their mitts even while the pitch was in progress.

Studies have shown that children taking methylphenidate are happier, more socially adept, and more academically successful. They also interact more positively with their parents, perhaps because they are more likely to comply with requests. The medication has its drawbacks, however. There is evidence that although stimulants are beneficial in the short term, their benefits do not seem to be maintained over the long term. In addition, there is a very real risk of abuse, with numerous cases of children and adolescents buying and selling these stimulants. Side effects include sleep problems, reduced appetite, bodily twitches, and temporary growth suppression. Perhaps most important, some children on medication may see their problem as beyond their control. They may not feel responsible for their behavior and may not learn coping strategies that they will need later if they discontinue their medication or if it ceases to be effective. Most therapists believe that medication should be supplemented by psychological therapies such as behavior modification, and some even urge that medication be replaced by other treatment approaches when possible. Nonetheless, the data are clear that treatment progresses much better if drugs are part of the overall treatment plan.

BEHAVIORAL TREATMENT OF ADHD Behavioral treatment of ADHD aims to reinforce positive behaviors and ignore or punish problem behaviors. The difficulties with this treatment approach are similar to those discussed in the following section on autism. Treatment is very intensive and time consuming. In addition, although it is often not difficult to improve behavior in a structured setting, the effects of therapy do not necessarily generalize beyond the clinic or classroom. Many therapists advocate combining behavioral approaches with medication. The medication is used to gain control over the behavior, and then behavioral modification techniques can be taught and the medication slowly phased out. Others argue that medication should be used only if behavioral techniques do not reduce inappropriate behaviors. Although this controversy is ongoing, recent research has shown that medication plus behavioral therapy is more effective than either approach alone.

The National Institute of Mental Health, in collaboration with teams of investigators, began the Multimodal Treatment of Attention-Deficit Hyperactivity Disorder (MTA) in 1992. The study involved 579 children who were randomly assigned to community care or to one of three treatment groups, each lasting 14 months. The treatment groups were: medical management (usually treatment with a stimulant such as methylphenidate), intensive behavioral treatment, and a combination of the two. Follow-up studies reveal that the children receiving medication and those receiving a combination of medication and behavioral therapy had greater improvement in their ADHD symptoms than did those in the other two groups (Jensen et al., 2001). Children who received both medication and behavioral therapy showed a slight advantage in areas such as social skills, academics, and parent-child relations over those who received only medication.

Autistic Children Benefit From a Structured Treatment Approach

The treatment of autistic children presents unique challenges to mental health professionals. The core symptoms of autism—impaired communication, restricted interests, and deficits in social interaction—make these children particularly difficult to work with. They often exhibit extreme behaviors as well as public self-stimulation. Although these behaviors must be reduced or eliminated before progress can be made in other areas, elimination is difficult because it is hard to find effective reinforcers. Although normal children respond positively to social praise and small prizes, autistic children are often oblivious to these things. In some cases, food is the only effective reinforcement in the initial stages of treatment. Another characteristic of autistic children is an overselectivity of attention. This tendency to focus on specific details while ignoring others interferes with generalizing learned behavior to other stimuli and situations. A child who learns to set the table with plates may be completely stymied when presented with bowls instead. Generalization of skills must be explicitly taught. For this reason, structured therapies are more effective for these children than unstructured interventions such as play therapy.

BEHAVIORAL TREATMENT FOR AUTISM One of the best known and perhaps most effective treatments for autistic children was developed by Ivar Lovaas and his colleagues at the University of California at Los Angeles. The program, called applied behavioral analysis, or ABA, is based on principles of operant conditioning. Behaviors that are reinforced should increase in frequency, while behaviors that are not reinforced should be extinguished. This very intensive approach requires a minimum of 40 hours of treatment per week. Preschool-age children with autism were treated by teachers and by their parents, who were given specific training. After more than two years of ABA treatment, the children had gained about 20 IQ points on average and most of them were able to enter a normal kindergarten program (Lovaas, 1987). In contrast, there was no change in IQ in a comparable control group of children who did not receive any treatment. A group of children who received ten hours of treatment per week fared no better than the control group. Initiating treatment at a younger age was also shown to yield better results, as did involving the parents and having at least a portion of the therapy take place in the home. Children with better language skills before entering treatment had better outcomes than those who were mute or echolalic.

Although Lovaas's ABA program has been demonstrated to be effective, it has its drawbacks. The most obvious is the time commitment. The therapy is very intensive and lasts for years. Parents essentially become full-time teachers for their autistic children. The financial and emotional drains on the family can be substantial. If the family has other children, they may feel neglected or jealous because of the amount of time and energy expended on the disabled child.

BIOLOGICAL TREATMENT FOR AUTISM Because there is good evidence that autism is caused by brain dysfunction, there have been many attempts to use this knowledge to treat the disorder. It is easy to find reports of children who benefited from alternative treatment approaches. These case studies are compelling, but when the treatments are assessed in controlled studies, there is little or no evidence that most of them are effective. However, a few biologically based treatment approaches have shown some promise, as we discussed in Chapter 13.

During the 1990s, it was noted that some autistic children had increased levels of peptides in their urine. These peptides were derived from gluten and were thought to have a negative pharmacological effect on learning, attention, brain maturation, and social interaction. Autistic children with elevated peptide levels were put on a special diet, and their progress was monitored for several years (Reichelt, Knivsberg, Lind, & Nodland, 1991). After one year, the level of peptides in their urine was normal. The children demonstrated reductions in odd behavior and improvements in social, cognitive, and communicative abilities. Four years later, they continued to improve, but their development lagged behind that of their neurologically normal peers. Findings like this are exciting and can provide hope to families with autistic children. However, this treatment was effective only for a subgroup of autistic children, and even within that group it was clearly not a cure.

Another approach to the treatment of autism involves serotonin. SSRIs such as Prozac have been found to reduce compulsions in patients diagnosed with obsessive-compulsive disorder. Because autism involves compulsive and stereotyped behavior, and because there is some evidence of abnormal serotonin metabolism in autistic children, SSRIs have been tried as a treatment for autism. It has been reported that in some autistic children the drug reduces stereotyped motor behavior and self-abuse and improves social interactions (McDougle, 1997). There is also evidence that medications that block the action of dopamine have similar effects. Still, at this point, the neurobiology of autism is not well understood, and although attempts to use psychopharmacology to treat the disorder have resulted in some improvements in behavior, such as by injections of oxytocin, a great deal remains to be learned.

PROGNOSIS FOR CHILDREN WITH AUTISM Despite a few reports of remarkable recovery from autism, the long-term prognosis is considered poor. A recent follow-up study of men in their early twenties revealed that they continued to show the ritualistic behavior typical of autism. In addition, nearly three-quarters had severe social difficulties and were unable to live and work independently (Howlin, Mawhood, & Rutter, 2000). Several factors affect prognosis for autistic individuals. Although it was once believed that the prognosis was particularly poor for children whose symptoms were apparent before age two (Hoshino et al., 1980), it is possible that only the most severe cases of autism were diagnosed prior to growing public recognition of the disorder. It is now clear that early diagnosis allows for more effective treatments (National Research Council, 2001). Still, severe cases—especially those with notable cognitive deficiencies—are less likely to benefit from treatment. Early language ability is associated with better outcome (Howlin et al., 2000), as is higher IQ. Autistic children have difficulty generalizing from the therapeutic setting to the real world, and this severely limits their social functioning (Handleman, Gill, & Alessandri, 1988). A higher IQ may mean a better ability to generalize learning and therefore a better overall prognosis.

Profiles in Psychological Science

One Boy's Journey out of Autism's Grasp

John O'Neil, a deputy editor at the *New York Times,* recently described what it is like to be the parent of an autistic child (O'Neil, 2004). O'Neil's son James, now eight, began to show signs of being "different" in early childhood. Although he had been an easy baby, as a toddler James seemed to have difficulty looking his parents in the eye, and there wasn't a strong sense of connection. James displayed little interest in objects, even toys, that were given or shown to him, instead repeating behaviors to the point of harming himself, for example, pulling on and off his cowboy boots until his feet were raw. He responded to loud noises by crying. James's behavior really started to deteriorate when he was two and a half, following the arrival of a baby brother and a move to a new house. His parents simply assumed he was overwhelmed. It took the director of James's new preschool to notice the telltale signs of autism. On her recommendation, a professional assessed James and determined that he did have autism.

The discovery of James's autism follows a familiar pattern. Although most diagnoses of autism are made by age three, the disorder can be detected earlier if parents or pediatricians know what to look for. Many children who will develop autism show abnormal social behavior in infancy. Other signs include such behaviors as staring at objects for long periods of time and not reaching developmental milestones, such as speaking. Sometimes autism appears to strike out of the blue in an otherwise normally developing child. The child suddenly withdraws from social contact, stops babbling, and may become self-abusive. Parents and pediatricians who notice symptoms of autism in such a child may write them off as quirks or feel that the child is just a little slow to develop. Luckily for James, the preschool teachers noticed his unusual behavior and recommended a professional evaluation. As we have seen, research has shown that the earlier treatment begins, the better the prognosis.

On finding out that treatments for autism did exist, the O'Neils were relieved. But then they heard the bad news: Treatment is expensive, difficult, and time consuming. As noted earlier, the recommended amount of treatment is over 40 hours per week. During their first visit to a speech therapist, James's mother learned just how much James needed treatment: he had forgotten his name. Although there are different versions of treatment, most are based on Lovaas's original therapy. Known as applied behavioral analysis (ABA), this therapy requires parents and teachers to spend hours helping children with autism learn basic skills, such as saying their names. It uses operant conditioning to reward even small behaviors.

14.21 James at Eight James O'Neil, center, the eight-year-old autistic son of John O'Neil, with, at left, his friend Larry, also eight, and his brother Miles, six.

As is the case with many school districts, resources were insufficient for James to receive full treatment in school. His mother, Marcia, a physician, gave up her full-time position in order to set up a home-based program for James. James spent up to eight hours every day performing tasks that most children would find extremely boring, such as repeatedly imitating the therapist's placing two blocks next to each other or touching her nose. The same behaviors, repeated over and over, for hours on end: that is the nature of ABA. It teaches each task as a series of simple steps, attempting to actively engage the child's attention in highly structured activities, and provides regular reinforcement of desired behavior. A day might begin with physical activities to strengthen coordination and build body awareness, followed by a snack break during which appropriate social behaviors are reinforced and language skills are stressed. Each part of the day is designed to work on a child's particular problem areas. Along the way progress is charted to guide subsequent sessions. At one point it became clear that James's language skills had to improve if he was going to be able to attend mainstream school. To accomplish this, James was encourage to talk by simply being given any treat he asked for, and it worked.

James was able to start school with the assistance of one of his full-time instructors, who attended class with him. Despite some rocky moments, James has made tremendous progress. Not that there still aren't problems, such as continued difficulties with reading comprehension, math, attention, social skills, and James's trying to understand why he has his disorder and why other kids do not. But James's journey is one of triumph. Perhaps his biggest accomplishments, especially for someone with autism, was making friends with a classmate named Larry, who was also eight (Figure 14.21). Why, O'Neil speculates, was Larry attracted to James as a friend? Perhaps they shared a love of potty humor or perhaps they were similarly warm and enthusiastic. One day O'Neil overhead the two friends engaged in silly conversation, telling stupid jokes and gossiping about their "girlfriends." In that moment, O'Neil realized just how many of his dreams for James had been realized. ■

REVIEWING the Principles | How Should Childhood Disorders Be Treated?

Medications such as methylphenidate can be quite effective in treating children with ADHD. However, side effects are associated with this type of medication, as well as ethical concerns. For these reasons, many parents and clinicians have turned to other approaches, such as behavioral therapy. Recent research suggests that the most effective management strategy for ADHD may be a combination of medication and behavioral therapy. In contrast, the most effective treatment for autism currently is structured and intensive behavioral therapy. Biological interventions, such as medication and restricted diet, have shown some promise in subgroups of children with autism but have been largely ineffective.

Conclusion

Although great strides have been made in identifying the etiology of mental disorders, this growing knowledge has not always given rise to new treatment approaches. Treatment of mental disorders is aimed at helping the individual think and behave in more adaptive ways, but the approaches can vary tremendously. For some disorders, several approaches are equally effective. For other disorders, some approaches are more effective than others. New understanding of the ways in which mental disorders affect neural functioning may lead to the discovery of more effective psychotropic medications. History teaches us, however, that medication is not the magic bullet for mental illness. Even with the creation of more effective medications, other interventions remain crucial. A pill may help relieve the symptoms of mental illness, but it cannot help the patient cope with the effects of the disorder, interact with others, or think and behave in more adaptive ways. Psychological, cognitive, and behavioral interventions can address these issues more effectively than any medication. Further research may help identify and implement the treatment approaches or combinations of approaches that are best for each disorder and for each individual.

Summarizing the Principles of Treating Disorders of Mind and Body

How Is Mental Illness Treated?

1. **Psychotherapy is based on psychological principles:** Psychotherapeutic treatments focus on insights. Psychodynamic forms focus on uncovering the unconscious. Humanistic approaches focus on clarifying feelings and motives. Behavioral approaches focus on modifying maladaptive behaviors, and include social skills training and systematic desensitization. Cognitive approaches restructure thinking. Group support is provided with group therapy, and a systems approach is part of family therapy.

2. **Biological therapies are necessary for some disorders:** Psychotropic medications change neurochemistry. Antianxiety drugs increase GABA activity. Antidepressants, in their various forms, affect serotonin availability. Antipsychotics reduce positive symptoms.

3. **Common factors enhance treatment:** Therapy helps, although different therapies are useful for different conditions. There are factors common to most successful therapies. Enhancement factors include a caring therapist and the benefit of unburdening one's problems.

What Are the Most Effective Treatments?

4. **Treatments that focus on behavior and cognition are superior for anxiety disorders:** Behavioral methods are effective in alleviating specific phobias. Cognitive restructuring is effecting in treating panic disorders. Obsessive-compulsive disorder (OCD) responds to medications that block serotonin reuptake and to cognitive-behavioral therapy.

5. **Many effective treatments are available for depression:** Pharmacological treatments include MAO inhibitors, tricyclics, and SSRIs. Cognitive-behavioral treatments are most effective when combined with antidepressants. Alternative therapies include phototherapy for seasonal affective disorder (SAD) sufferers and electroconvulsive therapy and transcranial magnetic stimulation for psychotic depression.

6. **Lithium is most effective for bipolar disorder:** The psychotropic medication lithium has been found to be the most effective in stabilizing mood in bipolar patients but has considerable side effects. Psychological therapy can help support compliance with drug treatment.

7. **Pharmacological treatments are superior for schizophrenia:** Antipsychotic medications are most effective for reducing the positive symptoms of schizophrenia. Tardive dyskinesia and other side effects are common with the older antipsychotic drugs. Clozapine acts specifically on dopamine receptors and reduces both positive and negative symptoms, with fewer side effects. The prognosis for patients depends on a variety of factors, including age of onset, gender, and culture.

Can Personality Disorders Be Treated?

8. **Dialectical behavior therapy is most successful for borderline personality disorder:** DBT combines elements of

603

behavioral, cognitive, and psychodynamic therapy. Therapy proceeds in three stages. First, the most extreme behaviors are targeted, and replaced with more appropriate behaviors. Next, the therapist explores past traumatic events. Finally, the therapist helps the patient develop self-respect and independence.

9. **Antisocial personality disorder is difficult to treat:** Psychotherapeutic approaches have not proven effective for treating antisocial personality disorder. Behavioral and cognitive approaches have been more effective, but most effectively in a controlled residential treatment environment. Generally, the prognosis is poor. Focusing on prevention by addressing conduct disorder in childhood may be the best strategy.

How Should Childhood Disorders Be Treated?

10. **Children with ADHD can benefit from a variety of approaches:** Methylphenidate, despite its side effects, is an effective pharmacological treatment, and works best as part of an overall treatment plan including psychotherapy, particularly behavioral treatment.

11. **Autistic children benefit from a structured treatment approach:** Behavioral approaches have been effective in improving language and social behavior. The treatment strategy is very time intensive and extends for years. Dietary restrictions of gluten, which result in elevated peptides, have been effective for some autistic children. Some children also improve with SSRIs. In general, the long-term prognosis is poor.

Applying the Principles

1. Imagine that your roommate is suffering from depression. She is listless, stays in all the time, skips classes, and focuses on sad memories. All but which of the following might be an appropriate approach to treatment?

   _____ a) antipsychotic medications that will stop her irrational depressive thoughts

   _____ b) client-centered therapy that will help clarify her feelings

   _____ c) cognitive-based therapy that will change the ways she thinks about things

   _____ d) psychopharmacology that will change the neurochemical activity in her brain

2. A recent study found that marriage therapy that focused on communication skills was ineffective in improving marriages and avoiding divorce. This finding is consistent with a(n) _____ view of treatment effectiveness. Teaching communication strategies, however, to empower an individual suffering from depression may be effective. This exemplifies that _____.

   _____ a) statistical; treatment must be tailored to the disorder

   _____ b) evidence-based; treatment must be tailored to the disorder

   _____ c) empirical; communication psychotherapies are only effective with individuals

   _____ d) behavioral; communication therapies are only effective for serious psychopathologies

3. Lisa has been caught in an elaborate web of lies about her misfortunes and about having a serious medical condition. These lies have gotten her considerable attention from her roommates, and kept her boyfriend from breaking up with her despite her impulsive and excessive behavior. What might you expect if you learned Lisa was diagnosed with borderline personality disorder?

   _____ a) She will respond very well to consistent behavioral therapies.

   _____ b) She will need to be institutionalized for effective therapy.

   _____ c) She will likely respond best to a three-step approach directed at behavioral change, insight, and cognitive restructuring.

   _____ d) She simply needs to experience intolerance and rejection by peers on a consistent basis in order to change her patterns of behavior.

4. When Edgar was in first grade, his teacher complained to his mother that he was "hyperactive" and not able to stay on task. The teacher recommended that Edgar should take medication, like the other children in the class who exhibited similar behavioral patterns. Edgar's mother instead moved him to a school with smaller classes and a more structured environment, and maintained a strict behavioral approach at home. Edgar's behavior improved and he was able to do well in the classroom. This demonstrates that

    a) medications mimic the effects of behavioral
       therapy strategies.

    b) ADHD is not a biologically based disorder.

    c) ADHD responds to any treatment because the
       child needs attention, which he gets with
       treatment.

    d) biological and psychological treatments may be
       equally effective when it comes to treating ADHD.

ANSWERS: 1.a 2.b 3.c 4.d

Key Terms

anti-anxiety drugs, p. 572
antidepressants, p. 572
antipsychotics, p. 572
behavior modification, p. 569
biological therapy, p. 566
client-centered therapy, p. 568
clozapine, p. 589
cognitive restructuring, p. 570
cognitive therapy, p. 570
cognitive-behavioral therapy (CBT), p. 570

dialectical behavior therapy (DBT), p. 594
electroconvulsive therapy (ECT), p. 586
exposure, p. 569
expressed emotion, p. 571
insight, p. 568
lithium, p. 587
MAO inhibitors, p. 572
methylphenidate, p. 597
psychotherapy, p. 566

psychotropic medications, p. 572
selective serotonin reuptake inhibitors (SSRIs), p. 572
systematic desensitization, p. 569
tardive dyskinesia, p. 589
transcranial magnetic stimulation, p. 587
tricyclic antidepressants, p. 572

Further Readings

Dawes, R. M. (1994). *House of cards: Psychology and psychotherapy built on myth.* New York: Maxwell Macmillan International.

Endler, N. (1982). *Holiday of darkness: A psychologist's personal journey out of his depression.* New York: John Wiley & Sons.

Kramer, P. D. (1993). *Listening to Prozac: A psychiatrist explores antidepressant drugs and the remaking of the self.* New York: Viking Penguin.

Linehan, M. M. (1993). *Cognitive-behavioral treatment of borderline personality disorders.* New York: Guilford Publications.

Maurice, C. (1994). *Let me hear your voice: A family's triumph over autism.* New York: Knopf.

Pennebaker, J. W. (1997). *Opening up: The healing power of confiding in others.* New York: William Morrow & Co., Inc.

Rosen, L. E., & Amador, X. F. (1997). *When someone you love is depressed: How to help your loved one without losing yourself.* New York: Free Press.

The Power of Situations

On October 2, 2001, the anniversary of Mahatma Gandhi's birth, children all across India dressed up as the late leader to join in national celebration. As this example shows, situations and cultural norms often dictate human behavior. As we explore social psychology further, we will learn just how powerful situational forces are in determining people's actions.

Social Psychology

According to the Geneva Convention, prisoners of war are to be treated with respect and dignity. Even amid the horrors of war, we expect the military to behave in a civilized and professional manner. This is why the events at Abu Ghraib prison in Iraq are so shocking to us. American soldiers brutalized and humiliated Iraqi detainees, threatening them with dogs, beating them with broom handles and chairs, and forcing them to lie on top of each other naked and simulate oral sex and masturbation. When photographs of these actions appeared on the Internet, outrage and condemnation of the deplorable conduct were immediate. Responding quickly to this fury, U.S. government officials stressed that these were isolated incidents carried out by a small group of wayward soldiers. The idea that only a few troubled individuals were responsible for torturing

Outlining the Principles

How Do We Know Ourselves?

- Our Self-Concept Consists of Self-Knowledge
- Perceived Social Regard Influences Self-Esteem
- We Use Mental Strategies to Maintain Our Views of Self

How Do Attitudes Guide Behavior?

- We Form Attitudes through Socialization and Experience
- Behaviors Are Consistent with Strong Attitudes
- Discrepancies Lead to Dissonance
- Attitudes Can Be Changed through Persuasion

How Do We Form Our Impressions of Others?

- Nonverbal Actions and Expressions Affect Our Impressions
- We Make Attributions about Others
- Stereotypes Are Based on Automatic Categorization
- Stereotypes Can Lead to Prejudice

How Do Others Influence Us?

- Groups Influence Individual Behavior
- We Conform to Social Norms
- We Are Compliant
- We Are Obedient to Authority

When Do We Harm or Help Others?

- Aggression Can Be Adaptive
- Aggression Has Social and Cultural Aspects
- Many Factors May Influence Helping Behavior
- Some Situations Lead to Bystander Apathy

What Determines the Quality of Relationships?

- Situational and Personal Factors Influence Friendships
- Love Is an Important Component of Romantic Relationships
- Making Love Last Is Difficult

and humiliating Iraqi prisoners is bizarrely comforting. Somehow we are relieved to know that their deviant behavior does not reflect on ordinary people. Surely we would not be willing to inflict such humiliation and pain on prisoners, many of whom were just teenagers and young men rounded up for questioning. Or would we?

Would you beat up or humiliate someone simply because you were ordered to do so or were in a situation where others were doing so? Or would you defy authority or resist peer pressure? Although we don't know whether or not they were ordered, how do we explain the actions of the guards at Abu Ghraib? The case of Abu Ghraib challenges many commonsense notions about human nature and forces us to consider questions about the dark side of humanity. People beat, rape, torture, and murder others. What is wrong with these people? What explains the violent side of human nature?

According to social psychologists, nothing is typically wrong with people such as the guards at Abu Ghraib. Rather, they are probably normal people caught up in overwhelming situations that shape their actions. Social psychologists point out a number of situational factors that likely influenced behavior at Abu Ghraib, such as the absence of any real authority in the prison and therefore a weakening of responsibility. Moreover, social psychologists know that people are typically obedient to authority, especially in times of war. Also, the working conditions promoted aggression. One of the Abu Ghraib units had expected to be in Iraq a short time working in traffic control; instead, they found themselves in an overcrowded prison where they worked long hours, six or seven days a week, in extremely hot temperatures while under frequent mortar attack. Finally, during wartime people are especially likely to view the world as consisting of "us" and "them." Members of the enemy group are viewed as being all the same and are treated in a dehumanized fashion, often portrayed as both evil and inferior. All of these factors contributed to the mistreatment of prisoners at Abu Ghraib.

One of the most important lessons of social psychology is that people consistently underestimate the power of situations in affecting human behavior. In a classic study, the social psychologists Philip Zimbardo and Chris Haney had male Stanford undergraduates play the role of prisoners and guards in a mock prison (Figure 15.1; Haney, Banks, & Zimbardo, 1973). The students, who had all been screened and found to be psychologically stable, were randomly assigned to their roles. What happened was unexpected and shocking. Within days, the guards became brutal and sadistic. They constantly harassed the prisoners, forcing them to engage in meaningless and tedious tasks

fundamental attribution error The tendency to overemphasize personal factors and underestimate situational factors in explaining behavior.

social psychology The branch of psychology concerned with how others influence the way a person thinks, feels, and acts.

Timeline

1898
Social Facilitation Norman Triplett conducts the first social psychology experiment by demonstrating that people ride their bicycles more quickly in the presence of others.

1930s
Attitude Measurement L. L. Thurstone and Rensis Likert develop attitude scales based on the principles of psychophysics. Carl Hovland at Yale University studies how attitudes are changed.

1945
Field Theory Kurt Lewin proposes a field theory based on physics that states behavior is a function of the person interacting with the environment.

1950s
People as Intuitive Scientists Fritz Heider argues that social psychologists need to understand "commonsense psychology." Heider's ideas form the basis of attribution theory.

and exercises. Although the study was scheduled to last two weeks, it became necessary to stop it after only six days. The Stanford prison study demonstrated the speed at which apparently normal college students could be transformed into the social roles they were playing. Similarly, the guards at Abu Ghraib believed it was their job to "soften up" the prisoners for interrogation, and their actions were strikingly similar to those of the Stanford participants. So is it the person? Or is it the situation?

When explaining other people's behavior, we tend to overemphasize the importance of personality traits and underestimate the importance of situation. This tendency is so pervasive that it has been called the **fundamental attribution error**. As you will learn in this chapter, attributions are explanations for behavior. We tend to attribute other people's behavior to their personalities. Even if they are just acting, we believe that their actions reflect their personal dispositions. People tend to think that the *Jeopardy!* host Alex Trebek is smart, that *Star Trek*'s Leonard Nimoy is cold and logical, and that *Friends'* Jennifer Aniston is ditzy and spoiled. We forget that they are actors playing roles and that Alex Trebek is given the answers in advance. Likewise, when people act in a brutal and sadistic way, we assume that they are brutal and sadistic people. We neglect to consider the situation in which they have acted brutally and sadistically and to assess how much power it had in shaping the behavior. In this chapter you will discover that situations and social rules guide much of our behavior. You will learn the basic principles of how people interact with each other. You will see that research in social psychology provides profound insights into situations such as Abu Ghraib, revealing to us not that humans are inherently flawed or evil, but rather that social context can be overpowering. Bear in mind that we still must take responsibility for our individual and collective actions, but we also need to learn from situations such as Abu Ghraib and work to create environments that allow individuals and groups to succeed in positive, constructive ways without harming themselves or others. ■

15.1 The Stanford Prison Study The basement of the psychology department at Stanford University was turned into a mock prison, with students randomly assigned to be guards or prisoners. The participants took on their roles with such vigor that the situation became overwhelming for many. The study was terminated early because of concerns for the well-being of the students.

Humans are social animals who live in a highly complex world. Some 6 billion people are right now talking with friends, forming impressions of strangers, arguing with family members, even falling in love with potential mates. Our regular interactions with others—even imagined others—shape who we are and how we understand the world. **Social psychology** is concerned with how people influence other people's

1954	1955	1957	1960s	1965
The Nature of Prejudice Gordon Allport provides a comprehensive review of the nature of stereotyping and prejudice. Allport points out that prejudice arises out of normal cognitive processes.	**Conformity to Group Norms** Solomon Asch demonstrates that people will conform to a group standard. Subsequent research verifies the importance of social influence on human behavior.	**Cognitive Dissonance** Leon Festinger argues that people want to maintain consistency between their attitudes and their behaviors, and that discrepancies create tension that needs to be resolved.	**Correspondence Bias and Attributions** Edward Jones demonstrates that people overemphasize the importance of personal factors when explaining others' behaviors, a tendency that is the fundamental attribution error.	**Obedience to Authority** Stanley Milgram shows that normal people will administer painful electric shocks when ordered to do so by an authority figure.

A number of cues influence the extent to which a message is persuasive. These include the *source* (who delivers it), the *content* (what the message says), and the *receiver* (who is processing the message). Sources who are both credible and attractive are the most persuasive. This is why television ads for medicines and medical services often feature unusually attractive people playing the roles of physicians. The message is effective because of peripheral processing. Even better, of course, is when a drug company ad uses a spokesperson who is both attractive *and* an actual doctor! In addition, credibility and persuasiveness are heightened when the receiver perceives similarity between the source and him- or herself.

Of course, the arguments in the message are clearly important for persuasion. Strong arguments that appeal to our emotions are the most persuasive. Advertisers also use the mere exposure effect, repeating the message over and over in the hopes that multiple exposures will lead to increased persuasiveness. As the old saying goes, "If you repeat a lie often enough people will believe it." This is why politicians often make the same statements over and over during campaigns. Those who want to persuade also have to decide whether to deliver a one-sided argument or to consider both sides. One-sided arguments are best if the audience is on the speaker's side or is gullible. When speaking to a more skeptical crowd, speakers who acknowledge both sides but argue that one is superior tend to be more persuasive than those who completely ignore the opposing view.

persuasion The active and conscious effort to change attitudes through the transmission of a message.

elaboration likelihood model A theory of how persuasive messages lead to attitude changes.

REVIEWING
the Principles | How Do Attitudes Guide Behavior?

Attitudes are evaluations of objects or ideas. They consist of affect, cognition, and behavior that become linked together. Attitudes are formed through socialization and direct experience and best predict behavior when they are strong and easily accessible. Discrepancies between attitudes, or between attitudes and behavior, lead to cognitive dissonance. Dissonance theory can be used to explain a wide range of human behavior. Attitudes can be changed through persuasion, by either central or peripheral means, depending on whether people think carefully about the issues or not.

How Do We Form Our Impressions of Others?

Social psychologists study attitudes because they are pervasive in our daily lives and influence many of our actions. Not surprisingly, attitudes that we hold about others are especially interesting to social psychologists. In addition to holding attitudes about other people, we also try to understand and predict them, to figure out why they act the way they do. We need to do this both to know how to relate to others and to ascertain whether they will help us or hurt us. Over the course of human evolution, one fact has remained constant: We are social animals who live in groups. Groups provide security from predators and competing groups, as well as mating opportunities and assistance in hunting and gathering food. At the same time, members within a group are essentially competitors for the same food and mates. Hence, mechanisms have evolved for distinguishing members of one's own group from members of other groups, as well as for detecting dangers from within the group, such as deception, coercion, and infidelity. We are constantly required to make social judgments, assessing whether a person is friend or foe, potential mate or potential challenger, honest or dishonest, trustworthy or unreliable, and so on. In this section, we examine how we form impressions of others, as well as how we understand and explain others' actions. We will see that we automatically classify people into social categories, which can have major implications for how we treat people.

Nonverbal Actions and Expressions Affect Our Impressions

Over the years, social psychology has confirmed the importance of first impressions on long-term evaluations of people. For instance, if a professor begins a course full of enthusiasm, humor, and energy, students will forgive the odd boring lecture later in the term. However, professors who give a monotonous, dry, dull lecture on the first day are unlikely to be viewed more positively as the course progresses, even if their lecture delivery improves. Many factors influence impression formation, ranging from the observer's expectations and attitudes to what the observed person says, as well as his or her nonverbal gestures and physical appearance.

Living in a social world requires that we understand and predict the behavior of others. Suppose someone is walking toward you. You make a number of quick judgments, such as whether you know the person, whether the person poses danger, or whether you might like to know the person better. How people initially feel about others is determined mostly by nonverbal behaviors. Facial expressions, gestures, walking style, and fidgeting are all examples of **nonverbal behavior**, sometimes referred to as body language.

What information is contained in nonverbal behavior?

nonverbal behavior The facial expressions, gestures, mannerisms, and movements by which one communicates with others.

FACIAL EXPRESSIONS The first thing people notice about others is usually the face. Human newborns less than an hour old prefer to look at and will track a picture of a human face over a drawing of a blank outline of a head (Morton & Johnson, 1991). The face communicates a great deal, such as emotional state, interest, and distrust. People use their eyes to indicate anger, to flirt, and to catch the attention of a passing waiter. When people won't meet our eyes, we assume, perhaps incorrectly, that they are embarrassed, ashamed, or lying, whereas we view people who look us in the eye as truthful and friendly. How we perceive this depends on our culture. For some groups, such as some Native American tribes, making direct eye contact, especially with the elderly, can be considered disrespectful. Social interactions can even be awkward when we can't see someone's eyes. People wearing sunglasses are often described as cold and aloof; police officers sometimes wear sunglasses partly to seem intimidating.

BODY LANGUAGE How much can be learned from nonverbal behavior? Nalini Ambady and Robert Rosenthal have found that people can make accurate judgments based on only a few seconds of observation, what they refer to as *thin slices of behavior*. For instance, videotapes of judges giving instructions to juries reveal that the nonverbal actions of judges can predict whether juries find defendants guilty or not guilty. Judges, perhaps unconsciously, may indicate their beliefs about guilt or innocence through their facial expressions, tone of voice, and physical gestures. In one study, participants were asked to view 30-second audioless film clips of college teachers lecturing. Based solely on nonverbal behaviors, the participants' ratings corresponded very highly to the ratings given by the instructor's actual students (Ambady & Rosenthal, 1993).

One important nonverbal cue is how people walk, known as gait. Gait provides information about affective state. People with a bounce in their step, who walk along swinging their arms, are seen as happy. By contrast, people who scurry along, taking short steps while stooped over, are perceived as hostile, while those taking long strides with heavy steps are perceived to be angry. In an intriguing study, researchers found that participants accurately judged sexual orientation at a better-than-chance rate after watching a 10-second silent video or a dynamic figural outline of someone walking or gesturing (Figure 15.12; Ambady, Hallahan, & Conner, 1999). These thin slices of behavior are powerful cues to impression formation.

We Make Attributions about Others

We constantly try to explain other people's motives, traits, and preferences. Why did she say that? Why is he crying? Why does she study so hard? and so on. As we learned earlier, **attributions** are people's causal explanations for why events or actions occur. People are motivated to draw inferences in part by a basic need for order and predictability in their lives. The world can be a dangerous place in which many unexpected things happen. People prefer to think that things happen for a reason, and that therefore they can anticipate future events. For instance, you might believe that you will do well if you study for an exam. Indeed, when events occur that don't seem to make any sense, such as when a person is brutally raped or murdered, people often make attributions about the victim, such as "she deserved it" or "he provoked it." Such attributions are part of what is referred to as the *just world hypothesis*. From this perspective, victims must have done something to justify what happened to them. People are applying the just world hypothesis when they say that the Iraqi detainees at the Abu Ghraib prison probably did something that led them to be arrested and therefore were in a sense responsible for and deserving of the abuse they received. Yet some of the prisoners were apparently innocent young men who were in the wrong place at the wrong time. It is much easier for us, however, to believe that they must be guilty of some criminal actions. Such attributions make their mistreatment seem more understandable, more justified.

ATTRIBUTIONAL DIMENSIONS In any situation, there are dozens of plausible explanations for specific outcomes. Doing well on a test could be due to brilliance, luck, intensive studying, or the test's being unexpectedly easy. Fritz Heider, the originator of attribution theory, drew the essential distinction between personal and situational attributions. **Personal attributions**, also known as internal or dispositional attributions, are explanations that refer to something within a person, such as abilities, traits, moods, or effort. By contrast, **situational attributions**, also known as external attributions, refer to outside events, such as the weather, accidents, or the actions of other people. Psychologist Bernard Weiner (1974) later noted that attributions can vary on other dimensions, such as whether they are stable over time versus variable, or controllable versus uncontrollable. For instance, weather is situational, variable, and uncontrollable. Good study habits are personal, stable, and controllable. Weiner's theory has also been used to explain psychological states such as depression. People who are not depressed tend to attribute their failures to personal, stable,

15.12 An Example of a Figural Outline In the study, participants watched a 10-second dynamic clip. Observers correctly guessed the person's sexual orientation at a better-than-chance rate.

attributions People's causal explanations for why events or actions occur.

personal attributions Explanations that refer to internal characteristics, such as abilities, traits, moods, and effort.

situational attributions Explanations that refer to external events, such as the weather, luck, accidents, or the actions of other people.

yet uncontrollable attributes. Depressed people attribute their failures to their own incompetence, which they believe is permanent.

ATTRIBUTIONAL BIAS Theorists such as Fritz Heider and Harold Kelly described people as intuitive scientists, trying to draw inferences about others and make attributions about events. However, unlike the objective scientist, people tend to be systematically biased in their social-information processing. The attributions they make are self-serving and consistent with preexisting beliefs, and they generally fail to take into account that other people are influenced by social circumstances. Recall the fundamental attribution error discussed in the context of Abu Ghraib prison, in which people overemphasize personal factors and underestimate the power of the situation. Edward Jones, who originated the idea of attribution error during the 1960s, actually called it the *correspondence bias*—he wanted to emphasize that people expect others' behaviors to correspond with their own beliefs and personalities. Interestingly, when people make attributions about themselves, they tend to focus on situations rather than on their personal dispositions, which, together with the fundamental attribution error, leads to the *actor-observer discrepancy*. For instance, people explaining their own lateness tend to attribute it to external factors, such as traffic or competing demands. When others are late, people tend to attribute it to personal characteristics, such as laziness or lack of organization. Hence, people are biased toward situational factors when explaining their own behavior, but toward dispositional factors when explaining the behavior of others.

Is the fundamental attribution error really fundamental? We saw earlier that there are cultural differences in the self-serving attributional bias. Might there also be differences in the attributional styles of Easterners and Westerners? Indeed, recall from Chapter 1 that Easterners tend to be more holistic in how they perceive the world, seeing the forest rather than individual trees. As you might expect, evidence indicates that people from Eastern cultures use much more information when making attributions than do people in Western cultures, and they also are more likely to believe that human behavior is the outcome of personal and situational factors (Choi, Dalal, Kim-Prieto, & Park, 2003; Miyamoto & Kitayama, 2002). This doesn't mean that Easterners are not susceptible to some of the same attributional biases as Westerners, but only that they are more likely to take situational forces into account, whereas people in the West place overriding emphasis on personal factors.

Stereotypes Are Based on Automatic Categorization

What are Italians like—do they all have fiery tempers? How about Canadians—do they all like hockey? Can white men jump? We hold attitudes and beliefs about groups because they allow us to answer these sorts of questions quickly. These attitudes and beliefs are **stereotypes,** cognitive schemas that organize information about people on the basis of their membership in certain groups. Stereotypes are mental shortcuts that allow for easy, fast processing of social information. Recall from Chapter 8 that heuristic processing allows us to make quick decisions. Stereotyping occurs automatically and, in most cases, outside of our awareness. In and of themselves, stereotypes are neutral and simply reflect efficient cognitive processes. Indeed, some stereotypes are true: Men tend to be more violent than women, and women are more nurturing than men. However, these are true on average; not all men are violent, nor are all women nurturing.

People construct and use categories to streamline impression formation in order to deal with the limitations inherent in mental processing. Rather than considering

stereotypes Cognitive schemas that allow for easy and efficient organization of information about people based on their membership in certain groups.

each person as unique and unpredictable, we categorize people as belonging to a group, a group about which we hold knowledge in long-term memory. As you walk through the hallways at your school, you might automatically categorize people on the basis of their clothing or hairstyles. Once you have categorized someone, you will have all sorts of beliefs about that person on the basis of your stereotypes of that category.

Stereotypes affect how we view and treat others (Kunda & Spencer, 2003). In Chapter 7, we discussed a study in which participants were asked to judge whether a person is famous or not. Recall that those who had seen the person's name in a prior task were likely to falsely remember the name as that of a famous person, in what is known as the *false fame effect*. However, such misremembering is much more likely to happen for male names than for female names, apparently because of the stereotype that men are more likely to be famous than are women (Banaji & Greenwald, 1995).

Once we form stereotypes, we maintain them by a number of processes. As schematic structures, stereotypes guide our attention toward information that confirms the stereotypes and away from disconfirming evidence. People's memories are also biased to match stereotypes. These biases lead to an illusory correlation in which people believe that a relationship exists when it actually does not. The professor who notices a single black student performing poorly but fails to notice other black students who are doing well will confirm a false belief relating race to performance. Similarly, the meaning of a behavior can be altered so that it is consistent with a stereotype. A white man's success may be attributed to hard work and determination, whereas a black man's success may be attributed to outside factors, such as luck or affirmative action. A lawyer described as aggressive conjures up different images from a construction worker described as aggressive. Moreover, when people encounter someone who does not fit a stereotype, rather than alter the stereotype they put that person in a special category, a process known as subtyping. Thus, a racist who believes that blacks are lazy categorizes Michael Jordan as an exception to the rule rather than as evidence for the invalidity of the stereotype. Forming a subtype that includes successful blacks helps racists maintain the stereotype that most blacks are unsuccessful.

INHIBITING STEREOTYPES Most people do not consider themselves prejudiced, and many are motivated to avoid stereotyping others. Yet according to many researchers in social cognition, categorization and stereotyping occur automatically, without awareness or intent (Bargh & Ferguson, 2000). Patricia Devine (1989) made the important point that people can override the stereotypes they hold and act in a nondiscriminatory fashion. For instance, most people in North America know the negative stereotypes associated with African Americans, and when a nonblack person encounters a black person, the information in the stereotypes becomes cognitively available. According to Devine, people who are low in prejudice override this automatic activation and act in a nondiscriminatory fashion. Clearly, then, simply categorizing people need not entail mistreating them. Unfortunately, some of the automatic consequences of stereotypes alter how we perceive and understand the behavior of those we stereotype.

You might wonder if automatic stereotyping can be changed. Indeed, numerous studies have shown that they can (Blair, 2002). For instance, Dasgupta and Greenwald

(2001) found that presenting positive exemplars of admired black individuals (e.g., Denzel Washington) produced more favorable attitudes toward African Americans on the IAT. In another study, training people to respond in a counter-stereotypical fashion, such as pressing a "no" key when they saw an elderly person paired with an elderly stereotype, led to reduced automatic stereotyping in subsequent tasks (Kawakami, Dovidio, Moll, Hermsen, & Russin, 2000). Telling people that their tests scores indicate that they hold negative stereotypes can motivate people to correct them, and the worse they feel about holding those attitudes, the harder they tried not to be biased (Monteith, 1993). These and other studies show that we can alter automatic stereotyping.

Inhibiting stereotyped thinking in everyday life is difficult and requires self-regulation (Monteith, Ashburn-Nardo, Voils, & Czopp, 2002). Recall from Chapter 9 that the mental functions that allow us to override habitual responses depend on the frontal lobes. In one recent brain-imaging study, showing white participants pictures of black faces produced amygdala activity if the faces were presented briefly. However, if the faces were presented for longer periods of time, the frontal lobes became active and the amygdala response decreased. This happened more for those whose IAT scores indicated negative stereotypes about blacks (Cunningham et al., 2004). In another study, frontal lobe activity when observing black faces was associated with poor performance on a subsequent task of mental function, which implies that controlling stereotypes is mentally taxing (Richeson et al., 2003). These studies and others demonstrate that college students today engage mental processes in order to inhibit their automatic stereotyping.

STEREOTYPES AND PERCEPTION We began Chapter 1 by describing the killing of Amadou Diallo by New York City police officers. How can social cognition help us understand this tragedy? In crossing levels of analysis, we find that these implicit social attitudes can influence basic perceptual processes. In two experiments that demonstrated this, Payne (2001) showed pictures of guns or tools to white participants and asked them to classify the objects as quickly as possible (Figure 15.13). Immediately before seeing a picture, the participants were briefly shown a picture of either a white or a black face. Priming by black faces led participants to identify guns more quickly and to mistake tools for guns. A more recent study found that the reverse is true: Priming people with pictures of criminal objects (e.g., guns and knives) leads them to pay greater attention to black faces than to white faces (Eberhardt, Goff, Purdie, & Davies, 2004). Such findings suggest that implicit bias may have been involved in the Diallo shooting. The officers were looking for individuals who fit a specific racial profile. When forced to make a split-second decision, they mistook Diallo's wallet for a weapon.

In a virtual reality simulation of the Diallo shooting, Greenwald, Oakes, and Hoffman (2003) required participants to respond to a simulated criminal holding a gun (by clicking a computer mouse to shoot him), a fellow police officer (by pressing the space bar), or a civilian holding a neutral object (by doing nothing). In some trials, white males holding guns were criminals and black males holding guns were police officers. In the other trials this was reversed—the

15.13 Sterotypes and Perception After being primed by black or white faces, white participants had to quickly classify pictures as tools or guns. Participants misidentified tools as guns when primed with black faces, suggesting that stereotypes alter perceptual processes.

black simulated persons were criminals. Blacks were more likely to be incorrectly shot in this study, in part because the objects they held were more likely to be identified as weapons. Fortunately, recent evidence suggests that computerized training, in which race is unrelated to the presence of a weapon, can eliminate this racial bias in shooting behavior among police officers (Plant & Peruche, 2005).

SELF-FULFILLING EFFECTS What effect does being treated as a member of a stereotyped group have on people? Stereotypes that are initially untrue can become true through **self-fulfilling prophecy**, in which people come to behave in ways that confirm their own or others' expectations. One of the most impressive early demonstrations of this process was conducted in the 1960s by Robert Rosenthal with a school principal, Lenore Jacobsen. In this study, elementary-school students took a test that supposedly identified some of them as being especially likely to show large increases in IQ during the school year. Teachers were given a list of the "bloomers" in their classes. At the end of the year, standardized testing revealed that the "bloomers" actually did show a large increase in IQ. As you might have guessed, students were chosen at random rather than through any test, and therefore their increase in IQ was attributed to the extra attention provided by the teachers. In effect, the teachers paid more attention to "bloomers," perhaps giving them extra encouragement. Thus, teacher expectations turned into reality. Of course, negative stereotypes can become self-fulfilling as well. Thus, teachers who expect certain students to fail—for example, minority students—might do things that subtly undermine students' self-confidence or motivation. For instance, offering unwanted help—even with the best of intentions—can send the message that the teacher does not believe the student has what it takes to succeed.

Stereotypes Can Lead to Prejudice

As we have seen, stereotypes are themselves neutral categories. However, negative stereotypes of groups lead to prejudice and discrimination. **Prejudice** refers to the affective or attitudinal responses associated with stereotypes, and it usually involves negative judgments about people on the basis of their group membership. **Discrimination** is the unjustified and inappropriate treatment of people due to prejudice. Prejudice and discrimination are major problems, responsible for much of the conflict and warfare around the world. Within nearly all cultures, some groups of people are treated negatively due to prejudice. Social psychologists have spent the last half century studying the determinants and consequences of prejudice as well as trying to find ways to reduce its pernicious effects.

Why do stereotypes so often lead to prejudice and discrimination? A variety of theories have been proposed over the years, including that only certain types of people are prejudiced, that people treat others as scapegoats to relieve the tensions of daily living, and that people discriminate against others to protect their own self-esteem. An explanation consistent with our theme that the mind is adaptive is that evolution has led to two processes that produce prejudice and discrimination. First, we have a tendency to favor our own groups over other groups. Second, we have a tendency to stigmatize those who pose threats to our groups.

INGROUP-OUTGROUP BIAS We are powerfully connected to the groups to which we belong. We cheer them on, we fight for them, and sometimes we are even willing to die for them. Those groups to which we belong are called *ingroups*; those to which we do not belong are called *outgroups*. People treat ingroup members much

self-fulfilling prophecy The observation that people may come to behave in ways that confirm their own or others' expectations.

prejudice The affective or attitudinal responses associated with stereotypes.

discrimination The inappropriate and unjustified treatment of people based solely on their group membership.

differently from outgroup members. For instance, in what is called the *outgroup homogeneity effect*, people tend to view outgroup members as less varied than ingroup members. University of Texas at Austin students may think Berkeley students are all alike, but when they think about UT students they can't help but notice the wide diversity of different student types. Of course, the reverse is true as well. Similarly, even as we recognize that people in our home countries differ in substantial ways, we tend to view Arabs, for example, as being very similar, sharing similar values and even attitudes about the West.

The consequence of categorizing people as ingroup or outgroup members is **ingroup favoritism**, in which people are more likely to distribute resources to members of the ingroup than to members of the outgroup. People are more willing to do favors, forgive mistakes or errors, and give tangible resources to ingroup members. The power of group membership is so strong that people will exhibit ingroup favoritism even if the groups are determined by arbitrary processes. British psychologist Henri Tajfel and his American collaborator John Turner (1979) randomly assigned volunteers to one of two groups, using totally meaningless criteria, such as flipping a coin. Participants were then given a task in which they divided up money. Not surprisingly, they gave more money to their ingroup members. But they also tried to prevent the outgroup members from getting any money, even when they were told that the basis of group membership was arbitrary and that giving money to the outgroup would not affect how much money their own group obtained!

Why do people value members of their own groups? We can speculate that over the course of human evolution, personal survival has depended on group survival. Especially when there was competition for scarce resources, those who worked together to keep resources within their group and deny resources to outgroup members had a selective advantage over those willing to share. At the psychological level, our group memberships are an important part of our social identity and contribute to our overall sense of self-esteem. Interestingly, women show a much greater automatic ingroup bias than men (Rudman & Goodwin, 2004). Why do women like women more than men like men? Rudman and Goodwin speculate that both men and women depend on women for nurturing and that both are threatened by male violence. Moreover, although women can freely express their affection for their female friends, American males appear to be less comfortable doing so, perhaps because it might threaten their sexual identity. Although men generally favor their ingroups, they fail to do so when the category is based on sex.

Psychological Science *in Action* ◯ ● ◯

Cooperation Promotes Harmony between Groups

The first half of this decade has witnessed widespread hostility and violence between various factions in many regions of the world. How might social psychologists use what we have learned in the laboratory to further the cause of world peace? Not surprisingly, we have reason to be pessimistic about whether this is possible. Over the past 50 years, a number of strategies for reducing prejudice and encouraging peace have been attempted, such as bringing people from different groups into contact. Most have failed. It is extraordinarily difficult to change cultural and religious beliefs, and attitudes toward ethnic groups are embedded deeply in both. Around the

ingroup favoritism The tendency for people to evaluate favorably and privilege members of the ingroup more than members of the outgroup.

world, groups clash over disputes that predate the births of most of the combatants, and sometimes people can't even remember the original source of conflict. Yet the global response to the deadly tsunami of late 2004 indicates that people can work together, and in doing so overcome intergroup hostilities if they have a greater purpose, such as dealing with natural catastrophes. What can social psychology tell us about strategies to promote intergroup harmony?

Social psychologists have uncovered a variety of strategies that are effective in producing greater tolerance for and liking of outgroups. The first study to provide evidence about what might work was conducted by Muzafer Sherif and his colleagues in the late 1950s. Sherif arranged for 22 well-adjusted and intelligent white fifth-grade boys from Oklahoma City to attend a summer camp. None of the boys had known each other before that summer. Prior to arriving at camp, the boys were divided into two groups that were essentially the same. During the first week, the boys lived in separate camps, unaware that a similar group of boys was across the lake.

Once the groups were established, Sherif started the experiment by having the groups compete over a four-day period in a number of athletic competitions, such as tug of war, football, and softball. Group pride was extremely strong, with the groups naming themselves the Rattlers and the Eagles. The stakes were high. The winning team would get a trophy, individual medals, and appealing prizes. The losers would receive nothing. Animosity between the groups quickly escalated. The Eagles burned the Rattlers' flag, and the Rattlers retaliated by trashing the Eagles' cabin. Eventually, there were confrontations and physical fights, which had to be broken up by the experimenters. All of the signs of prejudice emerged, including the outgroup homogeneity bias and ingroup favoritism.

Phase 1 of the study was complete. Sherif showed how easy it was to get people to hate each other. Simply divide them into groups and have the groups compete, and prejudice and mistreatment would result. The question in Phase 2 of the study was, Could the hostility be undone?

Sherif first tried what made sense at the time, simply having the groups come into contact with one another. This failed miserably. The hostilities were too strong and skirmishes continued. Sherif reasoned that if competition led to hostility, then cooperation should reduce hostility. The experimenters created situations in which members of both groups had to cooperate in order to achieve necessary goals. For instance, the experimenters rigged a truck to break down. Getting the truck moving required all the boys pulling together, ironically on the same rope used earlier in the tug of war. On success a great cheer arose from all, with plenty of backslapping all around. After a series of tasks that required cooperation, the walls between the two sides broke down and the boys became friends across the groups. From strangers, competition and isolation created enemies. From enemies, cooperation created friends.

Research over the past four decades has indicated that only certain types of contact between hostile groups are likely to reduce prejudice and discrimination. It is clear that having shared superordinate goals—those that require people to cooperate to succeed—reduces hostility between groups. Research has shown that people who work together to achieve a common goal often break down subgroup distinctions as they become one larger group (Dovidio et al., 2004). Athletes on multiethnic teams often have positive attitudes toward other ethnicities. Programs that require cooperation are most effective when they include members who challenge or defy the negative stereotypes of their groups.

The programs that are most successful involve person-to-person interaction. A good example is Eliot Aronson's jigsaw classroom, which he developed with his students in the 1970s. In this program, students work together in mixed-race or mixed-sex groups in which each member of the group is an expert on one aspect of the assignment. For instance, when studying Mexico, one group member might study its geography, another its history, and so on. The various geography experts from each group get together and master the material. They then return to their own groups and teach the material to their team members. Thus, cooperation is twofold: Each group member cooperates not only with members of other groups, but also within the group as well. More than 800 studies of the jigsaw classroom have demonstrated that it does lead to more positive attitudes toward other ethnicities and that students learn the material better and perform at a higher level. According to Aronson, children in jigsaw classrooms grow to like each other more and develop higher self-esteem than do children in traditional classrooms. The lesson is clear: Communal activities working toward superordinate goals can reduce prejudice.

Social psychology has shown us that we can work cooperatively toward reducing intergroup hostility, racism, and prejudice. Now we must take these lessons from the laboratory and the classroom and begin to study and apply them on a global scale. Certainly the outpouring of aid for the tsunami victims shows us that the heart is willing. Now the mind must be so too. ■

REVIEWING
the Principles | How Do We Form Our Impressions of Others?

Human social interaction requires people to form impressions of others. People are highly sensitive to nonverbal information and can develop accurate impressions of others on the basis of very thin slices of behavior. People also are motivated to figure out what causes other people to behave the way they do. People make attributions about others, which are often biased. They tend to attribute other people's behavior to dispositions rather than to situations, and they use heuristic processing, which biases social judgment. Stereotypes result from the normal cognitive process of categorization. However, negative stereotypes and prejudice lead to discrimination. Humans have a natural tendency to discriminate against those who are threatening, such as outgroup members.

How Do Others Influence Us?

What effect do groups have on self-awareness?

We humans have an overriding motivation to fit in with the group. One way we do this is by presenting ourselves in a positive way, such as being on our best behavior and trying not to offend others. But people also conform to group norms, obey direct commands by authorities, and are easily influenced by others in their social group. The desire to fit in with the group and avoid being ostracized is so great that under some circumstances people willingly engage in behaviors they would otherwise condemn. As we have noted throughout this chapter, the power of the social situation is much greater than most people believe—perhaps the single most important lesson from social psychology.

Groups Influence Individual Behavior

The first social psychology experiment was conducted by Norman Triplett in 1897 when he showed that bicyclists pedaled faster when riding with other people than when they were alone. This is due to **social facilitation**, in which the mere presence of others enhances performance. Social facilitation also occurs in other animals, including horses, dogs, rats, birds, fish, and even cockroaches. Robert Zajonc (1965) proposed a model of social facilitation that involves three basic steps (Figure 15.14). First, Zajonc proposed that all animals are genetically predisposed to become aroused by the mere presence of others of their own species, since they are associated with most of life's rewards and punishments. Zajonc then invoked Clark Hull's well-known learning principle that arousal leads animals to emit a dominant response, that is, the one that is most likely to be performed. In front of food, the dominant response is to eat, for example. Interestingly, Zajonc's model predicts that social facilitation can lead to either enhancement or impairment in performance, depending on whether the dominant response is the correct one. The presence of others improves performance of simple tasks for which the dominant response is well learned, such as adding single digits, but it interferes with performance of complex tasks for which the correct answer requires greater thought, such as differential calculus. As an example, think about the kind of work space that would enhance job performance. If a group of employees is performing a simple task such as database entry, it might be best to have them sit in a fairly open environment, either around a large common table or in cubicles where each employee is aware of the rate at which others are performing. If an employee is performing a more complicated task, such as editing a manuscript, a private office might ensure better performance since, presumably, the editor is the only person working on that particular manuscript, so an awareness of how others are performing is irrelevant to the complex work at hand.

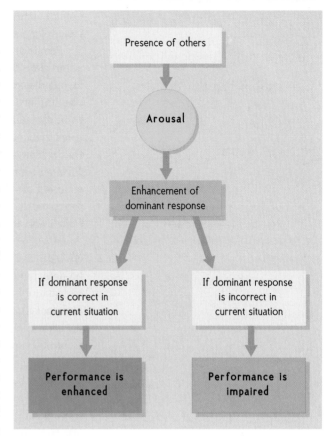

15.14 Social Facilitation The mere presence of other people leads to increased arousal, which in turn favors the dominant response. If this is the correct response, performance is enhanced, but if it is the incorrect response, performance suffers.

SOCIAL LOAFING In some cases, people work less hard when in a group than when working alone. This **social loafing** occurs when people's efforts are pooled so that no one individual is accountable or feels personally responsible for the group's output. In a classic study, six blindfolded people wearing headphones were told to yell as loudly as they could. Some were informed that they were shouting alone; others were told that they were yelling with other people. Participants did not shout so loudly when they believed others were shouting as well (Latané, Williams, & Harkins, 1979). Of course, making it clear that individual efforts can be monitored wipes out social loafing. Thus, for a group working on a class project, it is important to make each person feel personally responsible for some component of the project if you want her or him to exert maximum effort.

DEINDIVIDUATION People sometimes lose their individuality when they become part of a group. **Deindividuation** occurs when people are not self-aware and therefore are not paying attention to their personal standards. Recall that self-awareness typically causes people to act in accordance with their personal values and beliefs. When self-awareness disappears, so do restraints. Deindividuated people often do things they would not do if they were alone or self-aware. A good example is crowd behavior. Most of us like to think that we would try to help a person who was threat-

social facilitation When the mere presence of others enhances performance.

social loafing The tendency for people to work less hard in a group than when working alone.

deindividuation A phenomenon of low self-awareness, in which people lose their individuality and fail to attend to personal standards.

ening suicide. But people in crowds often not only fail to intercede, but also sometimes egg the person on, yelling, "Jump, jump" to someone teetering on a ledge.

People are especially likely to become deindividuated when they are aroused and anonymous, and when there is a diffusion of responsibility. Rioting by fans, looting following disasters, and other mob behaviors are the products of deindividuation. Recall the Stanford Prison Study mentioned at the beginning of this chapter. The study had to be stopped after just six days because the students became so immersed in their roles that many guards acted brutally and many prisoners became listless and apathetic. The situation was sufficiently powerful to radically alter people's behavior through a process of deindividuation. Not all deindividuated behavior is violent, of course. Gamblers in crowded casinos, fans doing the wave, and people dancing the funky chicken while inebriated in nightclubs are also most likely in deindividuated states, and accordingly they act in ways that they would not if they were self-aware.

GROUP DECISION MAKING It has been said that the intelligence of a group can be determined by averaging the IQs of its members and then dividing that average by the number of people in the group. In other words, groups are known for making bad decisions. Social psychologists have shown that being in a group does influence decision making, but in curious ways. For instance, you might think that groups would be especially cautious in making decisions. However, when James Stoner set out to study this assumption in the 1960s, he found that groups often made riskier decisions than individuals did, in what is known as the *risky-shift effect*. An obvious example is a group of children who decide to try something dangerous that none of them would have tried alone. Subsequent research has demonstrated that groups are sometimes riskier than individuals and sometimes more cautious, as groups tend to enhance the initial attitudes of members who already agree. This process is known as *group polarization*. For example, discussion tends to make people on juries believe more strongly in their initial opinions about guilt or innocence. When groups make risky decisions, it is usually because the individuals initially favor a risky course of action, and through mutual persuasion they come to agreement.

Sometimes group members are particularly concerned with maintaining the cohesiveness of the group, and so for the sake of cordiality, groups make bad decisions. Yale social psychologist Irving Janis coined the term *groupthink* in 1972 to describe this extreme form of group polarization. Examples of groupthink include the decision to launch the space shuttle *Challenger* despite there being clear evidence of a problem with one part and choices made by President Bill Clinton and his advisers following the allegations of his affair with Monica Lewinsky, which ultimately led to his impeachment. Groupthink typically occurs when a group is under intense pressure, is facing external threats, and is biased in a particular direction. The group does not carefully process all the information available to it, dissension is discouraged, and group members assure each other that they are doing the right thing. To prevent groupthink, leaders must refrain from too strongly expressing their opinions at the beginning of a discussion. The group should be encouraged to consider alternative ideas, either by having someone play devil's advocate or by purposefully examining outside opinions. Carefully going through alternatives, and weighing the pros and cons of each, can help people avoid groupthink.

We Conform to Social Norms

social norms Expected standards of conduct, which influence behavior.

Society needs rules. Imagine the problems if you woke up one morning and decided that you would henceforth drive on the wrong side of the road! **Social norms—**

expected standards of conduct—influence behavior in multiple ways, such as indicating which behavior is appropriate in a given situation. Standing in line is a social norm, and people who violate that norm by cutting in line are treated rudely and often directed to the back of the line. **Conformity**, the altering of one's behavior or opinions to match those of others or to match social norms, is also a powerful form of social influence.

How much do people conform to others? Muzafer Sherif was one of the first researchers to demonstrate the power of norms and conformity in social judgment. His studies, conducted in the 1930s, relied on a perceptual phenomenon known as the *autokinetic effect*, in which a stationary point of light appears to move when viewed in a totally dark environment. This effect occurs because people have no frame of reference and therefore cannot correct for small eye movements. Sherif had participants alone in a room estimate how far the light moved. Individual differences were considerable; some saw the light move only an inch or two, whereas others saw it move eight inches or more. In the second part of the study, Sherif put two or more participants in the room and had them call out their estimates. Although there were initial differences, participants very quickly revised their estimates until they agreed. In ambiguous situations, people often compare their reactions with others' reactions in order to judge what is appropriate.

Solomon Asch (1955) speculated that Sherif's effect probably occurred because the autokinetic effect is a subjective visual illusion. If there were objective perceptions, Asch thought, then participants would not conform. To test his hypothesis, Asch assembled participants to take part in a study of visual acuity. He had participants look at a reference line and then decide which of three other lines matched it (Figure 15.15). There were 18 trials, and each man said his answer aloud. This is an easy task, and normally people are able to do it with a high level of accuracy. But in these studies Asch had a naïve participant join a group of six confederates, people pretending to be participants but actually working for the experimenter. The actual participant always went sixth, giving his answer after five of the confederates gave theirs. On 12 of the 18 trials, the confederates deliberately gave the same wrong answer. After hearing five wrong answers, the participant then had to state his answer. Because the answer was obvious, Asch speculated that the participant would give the correct answer, but about one-third of the time, the participant went along with the confederates. More surprisingly, in repeated trials, three out of four people conformed to the incorrect response at least once (Figure 15.16).

Research has consistently demonstrated that people tend to conform to social norms. This can be seen outside the laboratory as well: Adolescents conform to peer pressure to smoke; jury members go along with the group rather than state their own opinions; people stand in line to buy tickets. In fact, you might be wondering when people don't conform to social norms. In a series of follow-up studies, Asch and others have identified factors that lessen or decrease the chances of conformity. One factor is group size. If there are only one or two confederates, the participant usually does not

conformity The altering of one's opinions or behavior to match those of others or to match social norms.

15.15 The Asch Task In the task, participants were shown a standard line (left) and then three comparison lines. Their task was simply to say which of the three lines matched the standard. When confederates gave false answers first, three-quarters of participants conformed by giving the wrong answer.

15.16 To Conform or Not to Conform The only true participant is number 6 (in the middle of each photo with glasses). He can't believe his eyes as the other participants, actually confederates of the experiment, give incorrect answers.

conform. But as soon as the confederates number three or more, conformity occurs. Interestingly, there seems to be a limit to conformity. Subsequent research has found that even groups as large as 16 do not lead to greater conformity than groups of 7.

Asch found that lack of unanimity is another factor that diminishes conformity. If even one confederate gave the correct answer, then conformity to the group norm decreased a great deal. Any dissent from majority opinion can diminish the influence of social norms. But dissenters are typically not treated well by groups. In 1951, Stanley Schachter conducted a study in which a group of students debated the fate of a juvenile delinquent, Johnny Rocco. A confederate deviated from the group judgment of how Johnny should be treated. When it became clear that the confederate would not be persuaded by group sentiment, the group began to ostracize him. When group members were subsequently given the opportunity to reduce group size, they consistently rejected the "deviant" confederate. The bottom line is that groups enforce conformity, and those who fail to go along are rejected. The need to belong, and the anxiety associated with the fear of social exclusion, gives a group powerful influence over its members. Indeed, a recent brain-imaging study that used a modified Asch conformity procedure found activation of the amygdala, perhaps a fear response, in participants whose answers did not conform to the group's incorrect answer (Berns et al., 2005).

We Are Compliant

Many times people influence the behavior of others simply by asking them to do something. When people do things requested by others, they are exhibiting **compliance**. A number of factors increase compliance. For instance, the Australian psychologist Joseph Forgas (1998) has demonstrated that people are especially likely to comply when they are in a good mood. This may be why people try to "butter up" others when they want something from them. According to the psychologist Robert Cialdini, people are often influenced by others because they fail to pay attention and respond without fully considering their options. For instance, if you give people a reason for a request, they are much more likely to comply, even if the request makes little sense. According to Cialdini, people often comply with requests because they really aren't thinking—they are simply following a standard mental shortcut to avoid conflict.

People can use a number of powerful strategies to influence others to comply. For instance, in the *foot-in-the-door effect*, people are more likely to comply with a large and undesirable request if they have earlier agreed to a small request. In 1962, Jonathan Freedman and Scott Fraser asked homeowners to allow a large, unattractive DRIVE CAREFULLY sign to be placed on their front lawns. As you might imagine, fewer than one in five people agreed to do so. However, another group of homeowners was initially asked to sign a petition to support legislation that would reduce traffic accidents. A few weeks later, these same people were approached about having the large sign placed on their lawns, and more than half of them agreed. Once people are committed to a course of action, they behave in ways consistent with that course.

The opposite influence technique is the *door in the face*, in which people are more likely to agree to a small request after they have refused a large request, because the second request seems modest in comparison and people want to seem reasonable. Salespeople often use influence techniques. One of their favorites is the *low-balling strategy*, which begins when a salesperson offers a product—for example, a car—for a very low price. Once the customer agrees, the salesperson may claim the manager didn't approve the price or that there are additional costs. Whatever the reason, once people are committed to buying the car, they often agree to pay the increased costs.

compliance The tendency to agree to do things requested by others.

obedience The willingness to follow an order given by an authority.

15.17 **Stanley Milgram** Milgram, pictured here with his infamous shock generator, demonstrated that average people will obey even hideous orders given by an authority figure.

We Are Obedient to Authority

One of the most famous and most disturbing psychology experiments was conducted in the early 1960s by Stanley Milgram (Figure 15.17), who wanted to understand how apparently normal German citizens would willingly obey orders to injure or kill innocent people during World War II. Milgram was interested in the determinants of **obedience**, why people follow orders given by an authority. Try to imagine yourself as a participant in his experiment. You have agreed to take part in a study of learning. On arriving at the laboratory, you meet another participant, a 50-year-old grandfatherly type (Figure 15.18). The study is described as one in which a teacher will administer electric shocks to a learner during a simple memory task in which word pairs are learned. Your role as the teacher is determined by an apparently random drawing of your name from a hat. On hearing that he may receive electric shocks, the learner reveals that he has a heart condition and expresses minor reservations. The experimenter says that although the shocks will be painful, they will not cause permanent tissue damage. You help the experimenter take the learner to a small room and hook him up to the electric shock machine. You then proceed to a nearby room and are seated at a table in front of a large shock generator with switches from 15 to 450 volts. Each voltage level carries a label, ranging from "Slight" to "Danger— Severe Shock," and finally, an ominous "XXX."

Your task is to give the learner a shock each time he makes a mistake, increasing the voltage with each subsequent error. So, whenever the learner errs, you dutifully

What types of people are obedient to authority?

15.18 **Testing Obedience** (a) The Milgram experiment required participants to "shock" the confederate learner (seated). The research participant (left) helped apply the electrodes that would be used to shock the learner. (b) An obedient participant shocks the learner in the "touch" condition. Fewer than one-third obeyed the experimenter in this condition. (c) After the experiment, all of the participants were introduced to the confederate learner so they could see he was not actually harmed.

(a)

(b)

(c)

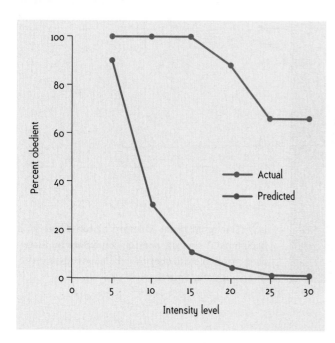

15.19 Predicting the Results Psychiatrists, college students, and middle-class adults predicted that fewer than one-tenth of one percent of participants in the Milgram experiment would be completely obedient and provide the maximum level of shock (each level = 15 volts). They believed that fewer than 10 percent of people would go beyond level 15 (225 volts). In fact, all of the participants were obedient at this level, and 65 percent were obedient to the highest level of shock.

administer a shock. When you reach 75 volts, the man yelps with pain, which you can hear over an intercom. At 150 volts, he starts screaming, banging on the wall, and demanding that the experiment be stopped. The man is clearly in agony as you apply additional stronger shocks, and at 300 volts he refuses to answer any more questions. After 330 volts, the learner is completely silent. All along you have wanted to leave, and you severely regret ever agreeing to participate in the study. You might have killed the man, for all you know. Indeed, you tried to stop the experiment, but each time you said you were quitting, the experimenter replied, "The experiment requires that you continue"; "It is essential that you go on"; "There is no other choice, you must go on!" So you do.

Does this sound crazy to you? How high do you think you would go in terms of shocking the learner? Do you think you would go up to 450 volts or do you think you would quit as soon as the man started to complain? A group of psychiatrists whom Milgram asked predicted that people would go no higher than 135 volts and that fewer than one in a thousand people would administer the highest level of shock. But that's not what happened. What actually happened would change how people viewed the power of authority.

Milgram found that although almost all the participants tried to quit, nearly two-thirds completely obeyed the directives of the experimenter (Figure 15.19), believing they were administering 450 volts to a nice old man with a heart condition (actually a confederate). These findings have been replicated by Milgram and others around the world. The conclusion of these studies is that ordinary people can be coerced into obedience by insistent authorities, even when what they're coerced into goes against the way they would usually behave.

You may wonder about the ethics of Milgram's study. It is important to recognize that Milgram himself was surprised by the results. Once he found that people were obedient, he set out to study how to reduce obedience. Milgram did find that some situations produced less compliance. For instance, if participants could actually see or had to touch the learner who was being shocked, obedience decreased. When the authority was more removed from the situation, giving the orders over the telephone, obedience dropped dramatically.

Throughout his study, Milgram was highly concerned with the mental state of his participants. He carefully revealed the true nature of the experiment to the participants in a systematic debriefing, and he made sure that they met the confederate learner and could see that he was not hurt in any way. Milgram also followed his participants over time to ensure that they experienced no long-term negative effects. Actually, many people were glad they had participated, feeling that they had learned something about themselves and about human nature. Most of us assume that only sadistic miscreants would willingly inflict injury on others when ordered to do so. Milgram's research, and that which followed, demonstrated that ordinary people may do horrible things when ordered to do so by an authority. Looking back on the prison guards at Abu Ghraib, it's interesting to consider them as ordinary people. We don't know exactly what they were ordered to do, but a number of social factors, from deindividuation, to social facilitation, to inappropriate norms and conformity, contributed to the situation and likely played prominent roles in the mistreatment of Abu Ghraib prisoners. As we stated earlier, it's important for all of us to be aware of situational influences when we evaluate our own behavior and that of others, particularly when our core beliefs and values are at risk.

the Principles | How Do Others Influence Us?

For the most part, people follow group norms, are influenced by others' opinions, and are obedient to authority. These effects are powerful, although most people underestimate their importance or do not believe that they themselves are affected by social influence. Yet the evidence is overwhelming that in many situations people will engage in behaviors quite inconsistent with their own standards. This sometimes occurs because people fail to attend to their internal beliefs and values, such as when they are in a state of deindividuation. Those who are aware of the power of social influence often use specific strategies to manipulate the behavior of others, such as foot-in-the-door, door-in-the-face, and low-balling techniques. Likewise, the more each of us is aware of our own values and beliefs, the more capable we are of upholding our own standards.

When Do We Harm or Help Others?

We have witnessed the extent to which obedience can lead people to commit horrible acts, yet we can also see how the need to belong to a group can lead us to acts of altruism and generosity. The turbulent events of the last few years reveal the extent of the human capacity for harming and helping others. We see terrorists beheading hostages, guards abusing prisoners, and the brutality of tribal warfare in the Darfur region of Sudan. Yet many people are kind, compassionate, and generous, as evidenced by the outpouring of support to the victims of the 2004 tsunami that killed hundreds of thousands and left millions homeless. Similarly, members of the group Doctors Without Borders travel to dangerous regions around the globe to care for those in need. This tension between our aggressive and altruistic sides is at the core of who we are as a species. Psychological scientists working at all the levels of analysis have provided much insight into the roles that nature and nurture play in these fundamental human behaviors.

Aggression Can Be Adaptive

Aggression refers to a variety of different behaviors, but basically it is any behavior or action that involves the intention to harm someone else. Aggression in animals often occurs in the context of fighting over a mate or defending territory from intruders. Sometimes just the threat of aggressive action is sufficient to dissuade invaders; at other times animals have to fight to defend their turf. Physical aggression, although common among young children, is relatively rare among adult humans; their aggressive acts more often involve words or actions designed to threaten, intimidate, or emotionally harm others. Aggression needs to be considered across the levels of analysis, from basic biology to cultural contexts.

aggression Any behavior or action that involves the intention to harm someone else.

BIOLOGICAL FACTORS At the biological levels of analysis, we see that stimulating certain brain regions or altering neurochemicals in animals can lead to substantial changes in behavior. Stimulating or damaging the septum, amygdala, or

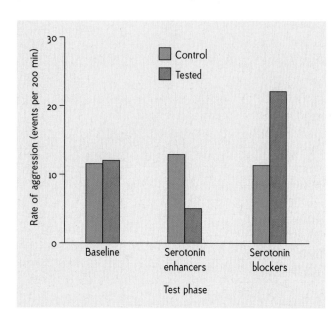

15.20 Serotonin and Aggression Male vervet monkeys were given either serotonin enhancers or serotonin blockers, and a corresponding change occurred in the number of aggressive acts against other members of the group.

hypothalamus regions in the brain leads to corresponding changes in the level of aggression that animals display. For example, stimulating a cat's amygdala with an electric probe causes the animal to attack, whereas damaging the amygdala leads to passive behavior. In 1937, researchers Heinrich Kluver and Paul Bucy produced a striking behavioral change by removing the amygdalas of normally very aggressive rhesus monkeys. Following the surgery, the monkeys were tame, friendly, and easy to handle. They began to approach and explore normally feared objects, such as snakes. They also showed unusual oral behavior, putting anything within reach into their mouths, including snakes, matches, nails, dirt, and feces. The behavior associated with damage to this region is now referred to as Kluver-Bucy syndrome.

In terms of neurochemistry, several lines of evidence suggest that serotonin is especially important in the control of aggressive behavior. Luigi Valzelli (1973) found increased aggression among mice with low levels of serotonin. Drugs that enhance the activity of serotonin lower aggression, whereas those that interfere with serotonin increase aggressive behaviors (Figure 15.20; Raleigh, McGuire, Brammer, Pollack, & Yuwiler, 1991). Low levels of serotonin in humans have been associated with reports of aggression in adults and hostility and disruptive behavior in children (Kruesi et al., 1992). In a large sample of men from New Zealand, low levels of serotonin were associated with violence, but not with criminal acts in general (Moffitt et al., 1998). Additionally, postmortem examinations of suicide victims have revealed extremely low levels of serotonin. Obviously, suicide is not the same as aggression, but many psychiatrists believe that suicide and violence toward others are manifestations of the same aggressive tendencies. Indeed, low serotonin levels were found among those who had killed themselves using violent means (such as shooting themselves or jumping from buildings) but not among those using nonviolent means (such as taking a drug overdose) (Asberg, Shalling, Traskman-Bendz, & Wagner, 1987).

Decreased serotonin levels may interfere with good decision making in the face of danger or social threat. For instance, monkeys with the lowest levels of serotonin are likely to pick fights with much larger monkeys. They also are the least socially skilled (Higley et al., 1996). This lack of social competence often leads the other monkeys to attack and kill them. Do these findings have implications for humans? Possibly. In one study, participants given a drug that enhances serotonin activity were found to be less hostile and more cooperative over time, compared with the control group (Knutson et al., 1998).

INDIVIDUAL FACTORS John Dollard and his colleagues proposed the first major psychological model of aggression in the 1930s. According to their **frustration-aggression hypothesis**, the extent to which people feel frustrated predicts the likelihood that they will be aggressive. The more that people's goals are blocked, the greater their frustration and therefore the greater their aggression. Thus, slow traffic is frustrating, and to the extent that it is impeding you from getting somewhere you really want to go or have to go—for instance, a concert you have been looking forward to or your first day in a new job—you may feel especially frustrated. If someone were to cut in front of you, you might feel especially angry and perhaps make some aggressive hand gesture. Indeed, road rage is most likely to occur where traffic is heavy and people feel frustrated.

According to Leonard Berkowitz's *cognitive-neoassociationistic model* (1990), frustration leads to aggression because it elicits negative affect. Thus, any situation that induces negative affect, such as being insulted, afraid, overly hot, or in pain, can trigger physical aggression even if it does not induce frustration. Berkowitz proposed that negative affect leads to aggression because it primes cognitive knowledge associated with aggression. From this perspective, negative events activate thoughts related to escaping or fighting, which prepare people to act in aggressive ways (see Chapter 10). Whether someone behaves aggressively depends on the situational context. If the situation also cues violence—for example, if the person has recently watched a violent movie or been in the presence of weapons—then the person is more likely to act in an aggressive fashion.

We can see the role of frustration and negative affect in the Abu Ghraib prison guards. Frustrated at being assigned to prison detail in Iraq for longer than expected, working in brutal, hot conditions, and being under the constant threat of attack easily primed the guards to be aggressive.

Aggression Has Social and Cultural Aspects

An evolutionary approach to aggression would dictate that similar patterns of aggressive behavior should exist in all human societies. After all, if aggression provided a selective advantage for human ancestors, then it should have done so for all humans. But an examination of the data shows us that violence varies dramatically across cultures and even within cultures at different points in time. For example, over the course of 300 years, Sweden went from being one of the most violent nations on earth to one of the most peaceable, which certainly did not correspond with a change in the gene pool. Moreover, murder rates in some countries are far higher than in others (Figure 15.21). In the United States, analysis of police statistics reveals that incidents of physical violence are much more prevalent in the South than in the North. Hence, although human nature might have an aggressive aspect, can culture exert a strong influence on the actual commission of physical violence?

Some cultures may be violent because they subscribe to a *culture of honor*, a belief system in which men are primed to protect their reputations through physical aggression. Men in the southern United States, for example, were (and perhaps still are) traditionally raised to be ready to fight for their honor and to respond aggressively to personal threats. To determine whether southern males are more likely to be aggressive than northern males, researchers conducted a series of studies at the University of Michigan (Cohen, Nisbett, Bowdle, & Schwarz, 1996). In each study, male participants walking down a narrow hallway had to pass a male confederate

15.21 Aggression across Cultures Murder rates vary dramatically in different countries.

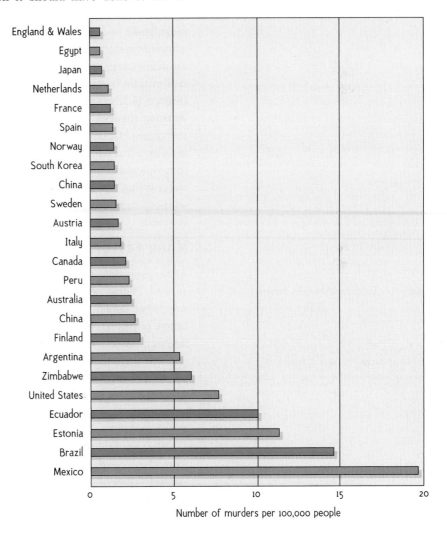

Number of murders per 100,000 people

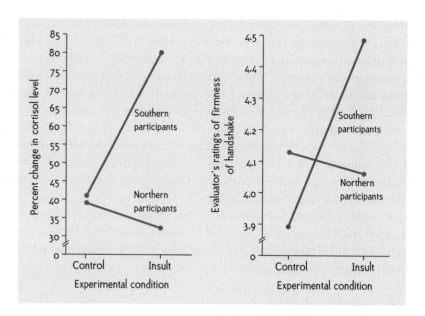

15.22 Cultural Aspects of Aggression When insulted, men from the southern United States had increased cortisol responses and shook hands more vigorously than northern men.

prosocial Tending to benefit others.

who was blocking the hallway at a filing cabinet. As the participant tried to edge past the confederate, the confederate responded angrily and insulted the participant. Compared with participants raised in the North, those raised in the South became more upset and were more likely to feel personally challenged, more physiologically aroused (measured by cortisol and testosterone increases), more cognitively primed for aggression, and more likely to act in an aggressive and dominant manner for the rest of the experiment, for instance, by vigorously shaking the experimenter's hand (Figure 15.22). The culture-of-honor theory of violence supports Bandura's social-learning theory (discussed in Chapter 6) that much aggressive behavior is learned through social observation of vicarious reward and punishment. People were traditionally admired for defending their honor in the South, and young men are taught that violence is an acceptable way to do so. The implications of this body of evidence suggest that our attitudes toward violence are determined by the cultural norms of our societies.

Many Factors May Influence Helping Behavior

Although people inflict harm on one another in many situations, the opposite is true as well. People often behave in ways that are **prosocial**, meaning that they act in ways that benefit others. Prosocial behaviors include doing favors, offering assistance, paying compliments, subjugating our egocentric desires or needs, resisting the temptation to insult or throttle another person, or simply being pleasant and co-operative. By providing benefits to those around us, prosocial behaviors promote positive interpersonal relationships. Group living, in which people necessarily engage in prosocial behaviors such as sharing and cooperating, may be a central human survival strategy. After all, a group that works well together is a strong group, and belonging to a strong group benefits the individual members.

Why are humans prosocial? Theories range from the selfless to the selfish, and from the biological to the philosophical. For instance, Daniel Batson and his colleagues (1988; 1995) argue that prosocial behaviors are motivated by empathy, in which people share the emotions of others. Conversely, Robert Cialdini and his colleagues (1987; Maner et al., 2002) have argued that most prosocial behaviors have selfish motives, such as wanting to manage one's public impression or relieve a negative mood. Others have proposed that people have an inborn disposition to help others. Young infants become distressed when they see other infants crying (Zahn-Waxler & Radke-Yarrow, 1990), and although their early attempts to soothe other children are generally ineffective (for instance, they tend initially to comfort themselves rather than the other children), this empathic response to the suffering of others suggests that prosocial behavior is hardwired.

Altruism is the providing of help when it is needed, without any apparent reward for doing so. The fact that people help others, and even risk personal safety to do so, may seem contrary to evolutionary principles; after all, those who protect themselves first would appear to have an advantage over those who risk their lives to help others. During the 1960s the geneticist William Hamilton offered an answer to this riddle; he proposed that natural selection occurs at the level of the gene rather than at the level of the individual. Thus, the "fittest" animals are those that pass along the most genes to future generations, through the survival of their offspring. Hamilton introduced the concept of *inclusive fitness* to describe the adaptive benefits of transmitting genes rather than focusing on individual survival. According to this model, people are altruistic toward those with whom they share genes, a process known as **kin selection**. A good example of kin selection occurs among insects such as ants and bees, whose workers feed and protect the egg-laying queen but never reproduce themselves. By protecting the eggs, they maximize the number of their common genes that will survive into future generations (Dugatkin, 2004).

Of course, sometimes animals help nonrelatives: For example, dolphins and lions will look after orphans. Similarly, a person who jumps into a lake to save a drowning stranger is probably not acting for the sake of genetic transmission. Robert Trivers (1971) proposed the idea of **reciprocal helping** to explain altruism toward nonrelatives. According to Trivers, one animal helps another because the other can return the favor in the future. Consider grooming, in which primates take turns cleaning each other's fur: "You scratch my back, and I'll scratch yours." For reciprocal helping to be adaptive, benefits must outweigh costs, and indeed people are less likely to help when the costs of doing so are high. Reciprocal helping is also much more likely to occur among animals—such as humans—that live in social groups, in which species survival depends on cooperation. This suggests that people will be more likely to help members of their ingroups than those of outgroups, and indeed the data generally supports this. From an evolutionary perspective, then, altruism does confer benefits, either by increasing the transmission of genes or by increasing the likelihood that others in the social group will reciprocate when needed.

Some Situations Lead to Bystander Apathy

In 1964, a young woman named Kitty Genovese (Figure 15.23) was walking home from work in a relatively safe area of New York City. An assailant savagely attacked her, eventually killing her during a 30-minute beating. There were 38 witnesses to the crime—all watched it happen from their windows. How many called the police or tried to intervene? None. In fact, it was reported that one of the couples pulled up chairs and turned out the lights so that they could better observe the action. As you might have guessed, when news of what had happened broke the next day, most people were outraged that 38 people could sit by and watch a brutal murder.

Why didn't these people help? Shortly after the Genovese murder, social psychologists Bibb Latané and John Darley conducted important research into the situations that produce the **bystander intervention effect,** or the failure to offer help to

altruism The providing of help when it is needed, without any apparent reward for doing so.

kin selection The tendency to be altruistic toward those who share a genetic bond.

reciprocal helping The tendency to help another because the recipient may return the favor.

bystander intervention effect The failure to offer help by those who observe someone in need.

15.23 Kitty Genovese Genovese was attacked and killed while 38 of her neighbors listened but did not try to stop the attack or even phone the police.

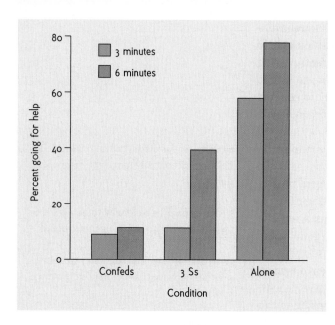

15.24 The Bystander Intervention Effect
Student participants waited alone, with two other naïve participants (3Ss), or with two apathetic confederates. When smoke started to fill the room, those who were on their own went for help quickly. Those with the apathetic confederates did not seek assistance.

How might we prevent diffusion of responsibility?

someone observed to be in need. Although common sense might suggest that the more people there are available to help the more likely it is that a person will be helped, Latané and Darley made the paradoxical claim that a person is less likely to help if there are other bystanders around. To test their theory, they conducted studies in which people were placed in situations that indicated that they should seek help. In one of the first situations (Latané & Darley, 1968), male college students filling out questionnaires in a room were exposed to pungent smoke puffing in through the heating vents. Participants were either alone, with two other naïve participants, or with two confederates who noticed the smoke, shrugged, and continued filling out the questionnaire. As can be seen in Figure 15.24, when participants were on their own, most went for help. However, with three participants, few initially went for help. With the two calm confederates, only 10 percent of participants went for help in the first six minutes. The other 90 percent "coughed, rubbed their eyes, and opened the window—but they did not report the smoke." Similar results were obtained in subsequent studies in which people were confronted with mock crimes, apparent heart-attack victims in subway cars, and people passed out in public places. The bystander intervention effect, also called bystander apathy, has been shown to occur in a wide variety of contexts—even among divinity students, who while rushing to give a lecture on the Good Samaritan failed to help a person in apparent need of medical attention (Darley & Batson, 1973).

Years of research have indicated four major reasons for the bystander intervention effect. First, a diffusion of responsibility occurs, with people expecting that others who are also around will offer help. Thus, the greater the number of people that witness the need for help, the less likely that someone will actually step forward. Second, people fear making social blunders in an ambiguous situation. All of the laboratory situations had some degree of ambiguity, and people may have worried that they'd look foolish if they sought help that was not needed. There is some evidence that people do actually feel less constrained from seeking help as the need for help becomes clearer. Third, people are less likely to help when they are anonymous and can remain so. If people are not anonymous, they are much more likely to help. Thus, if you need help, it is often wise to point to a specific person and request his or her help.

Fourth, a cost-benefit trade-off involves how much harm people risk by helping, or what benefits they would have to forgo if they stopped to help. Imagine you are walking to a potentially dull class on a sunny, warm day, and in front of you somebody falls down, twists an ankle, and needs transportation to the nearest clinic. You probably would be willing to help. Now imagine that you are trying to get to a final exam on time, and you are almost late, and the exam counts for 90 percent of your grade. In this case you probably would be much less likely to offer assistance.

There is evidence of bystander apathy in Abu Ghraib and other prisons. Government agents, such as FBI officers, apparently witnessed some of the mistreatment of prisoners. Although they reported these activities to their superiors, nothing formal was done to try to stop the mistreatment. Another factor that might have contributed to the diffusion of responsibility was the lack of a clear line of authority at Abu Ghraib, as prison guards received orders from various superiors representing various agencies. Thus, even though some people knew about the ongoing mistreatment, apparently little was done to stop it. Finally, one courageous soldier, Joseph Darby, grew disgusted with the abuse, took photographs, and shared them with his superiors. These photographs, subsequently leaked to the press, were concrete evidence of mistreatment that could not be ignored. Without doubt Abu Ghraib demonstrates the extent to which humans harm one another. Yet Darby's actions show humans have the capacity for goodness. Working across levels of analysis, psychological scientists have identified a number of important factors that contribute to how people treat one another. Although humans seem predisposed to act aggressively for personal gain, the world is surprisingly filled with acts of bravery and kindness.

REVIEWING

the Principles | When Do We Harm or Help Others?

Humans in all cultures engage in aggressive acts. Frustration can lead to aggression, as can other factors that induce negative affect. This may occur because negative emotion primes aggressive thoughts. Cultural norms and beliefs can alter the expression of aggressive behavior. People are likely to offer help to others in many situations, which is especially true if the person needing help is a relative. However, people are less likely to help when there are personal risks to doing so and when there is a diffusion of responsibility.

What Determines the Quality of Relationships?

Given the fundamental human need to belong (see Chapter 9) and the desire for social contacts, how do people select their friends and relationship partners? You might expect that studying relationships would be a high priority for psychological scientists. But until the last decade or so the topic was given little attention, perhaps due to the difficulty of developing rigorous experiments to test complex and fuzzy concepts such as love, a mysterious state that some think more appropriate for consideration by poets than by scientists. However, researchers have made considerable progress in identifying the factors that lead us to form friendships and close relationships (Berscheid & Regan, 2005). Many of these findings consider the adaptiveness of forming lasting affiliative bonds with others. In Chapter 9 we discussed evidence that humans have a strong need for social contact. We also discussed evidence for how people select mates. This section considers the factors that determine the quality of human relationships. We will first discuss the factors that promote friendships, and then we will look at why people fall in love and why love relationships sometimes fail. As you will see, many of the same principles are involved in choosing our friends and choosing our lovers.

Situational and Personal Factors Influence Friendships

Think for a second about your best friend. How is it that you came to be friends? Psychological scientists have discovered a number of factors that promote friendships. In 1950, Leon Festinger, Stanley Schachter, and Kurt Back examined friends in a college dorm. Because room assignments were random, the researchers were able to examine the effects of proximity, or how often people come into contact, on friendship. They found that the more often students came into contact, the more likely they were to become friends. Indeed, it is commonplace for friendships to form among those who are members of the same groups or clubs.

Proximity might have its effects because of familiarity. People like things that are familiar more than they like what is strange. Humans have a general fear of anything novel, known as neophobia. As discussed earlier in the attitudes section, simply being exposed to something repeatedly leads to increased liking. This mere exposure effect has been demonstrated in hundreds of studies using a variety of objects, including faces, geometric shapes, Chinese characters, and nonsense words (Zajonc, 2001).

BIRDS OF A FEATHER Another factor that increases liking is similarity. Birds of a feather really do flock together. People who are similar in attitudes, values, interests, backgrounds, and personalities tend to like each other. Roommates who are most similar at the beginning of the year are most likely to become good friends. Studies of high-school friendships have found that people tend to be friends with those of the same sex, race, age, and year in school. The most successful romantic couples also tend to be the most physically similar, which is called the matching principle (Bentler & Newcomb, 1978; Caspi & Herbener, 1990).

PERSONAL CHARACTERISTICS People tend especially to like those who have admirable personality characteristics and who are physically attractive, both as friends and as lovers. In a now-classic study conducted in the 1960s, Norman Anderson asked college students to rate 555 trait descriptions by how much they would like others who possessed those traits. Judging from the earlier discussion of who is rejected from social groups, you might expect that people dislike cheaters and others who drain group resources. Indeed, as can be seen in Table 15.1, the least likeable characteristics are dishonesty, insincerity, or lack of personal warmth. Conversely, people especially like those who are kind, dependable, and trustworthy. People like those whom they perceive to be competent much more than those they perceive to be incompetent or unreliable, perhaps because competent people make valuable group members. However, people who seem overly competent or too perfect make others feel uncomfortable or inadequate. In one study, a person who was highly competent but who spilled a cup of coffee on himself was rated more highly than an equally competent person who did not perform this clumsy act (Helmreich, Aronson, & LeFan, 1970). Small mistakes make people more human, and therefore more likeable. Generally, people like those who have personal characteristics valuable to the group.

PHYSICAL ATTRACTIVENESS Most people are also drawn to those who are physically attractive. Attractive people are typically judged to be happier; more intelligent, sociable, and successful; and less socially deviant. Taken together, these findings point to what Karen Dion and her colleagues in 1972 dubbed the "what is beautiful is good" stereotype. People who are physically attractive are less likely to be perceived as criminals, are given lighter sentences when convicted of crimes, are rated as more intelligent by teachers, are paid more for doing the same work, and have greater career opportunities. The preference for physical attractiveness begins early. Children as young as six months prefer to look at attractive faces, and young children prefer attractive over unattractive playmates (Rubenstein, Kalakanis, &

TABLE 15.1	The Ten Most Positive and Most Negative Personal Characteristics

MOST POSITIVE	MOST NEGATIVE
Sincere	Unkind
Honest	Untrustworthy
Understanding	Malicious
Loyal	Obnoxious
Truthful	Untruthful
Trustworthy	Dishonest
Intelligent	Cruel
Dependable	Mean
Thoughtful	Phony
Considerate	Liar

Langlois, 1999). Even mothers treat attractive children differently from unattractive children. In one study, researchers examined mothers of over 100 infants feeding and playing with their newborns just after birth (while the mothers were in the hospital) and then again three months later (Langlois, Ritter, Casey, & Sawin, 1995). Mothers of attractive children were much more affectionate and playful than mothers of unattractive children. Those mothers attended to other people more than to their infants. Mothers of attractive infants expressed slightly more positive attitudes about their children as well.

Given its importance, what determines physical attractiveness? Although some standards of beauty, such as preferences for body type, appear to change over time and across cultures, how people rate attractiveness is generally consistent across all cultures (Cunningham, Roberts, Barbee, Druen, & Wu, 1995). In terms of facial attractiveness, most people prefer symmetrical faces. This may be adaptive, in that a lack of symmetry could indicate poor health or a genetic defect. In a cleverly designed study of what people find attractive, Langlois and Roggman (1990) used a computer program to combine (or "average") a variety of faces, without regard to their individual attractiveness. They found that as more faces were combined together, participants rated the "average" as more attractive (Figure 15.25). People may view such "average" faces as attractive due to the mere exposure effect, in that such faces may be more familiar than unusual faces. However, other researchers contend that although average faces might be attractive, averaged attractive faces are rated more favorably than averaged unattractive faces (Perrett, May, & Yoshikawa, 1994). As you may notice in Figure 15.26, these female faces may be rated more attractive because they enhance feminine features, resulting in larger eyes, a smaller nose, plumper lips, and a smaller chin.

You might wonder, given this preferential treatment, whether people who are physically attractive actually possess characteristics consistent with the "what is beautiful is good" stereotype. The evidence on this issue is mixed. Among studies of college students, the correlation between objective ratings of attractiveness and other characteristics appears small. In one study that examined physical attractiveness, objectively rated by multiple judges, the researchers did not find any relation between appearance and self-esteem, grades, number of personal relationships, financial resources, or just about anything (Diener, Wolsic, & Fujita, 1995). However, evidence from more diverse settings indicates a robust effect of attractiveness on many outcomes. A meta-analysis of many hundreds of research studies of the effects of attractiveness on interpersonal evaluation and behavioral outcomes found that

(a)

(b)

(c)

15.26 **Which Average Is Preferred?** Which of these faces do you prefer? Image (a) represents the averaging of 60 women. Image (b) is the composite of the 15 most attractive faces. Given a choice between image (a) and (b), the vast majority of people prefer image (b). Image (c) exaggerates the subtle differences between images (a) and (b). Given a choice between image (b) and (c), 7 out of 10 participants prefer image (c).

(a)

(b)

(c)

(d)

(e)

15.25 **"Average" Is Attractive** The more faces that are averaged together (a–e), the more attractive the outcome. The face in (e), which has the most faces averaged together, is typically rated most attractive.

being attractive confers a number of benefits (Langlois et al., 2000). Not only are attractive people considered especially capable and gifted, but they also enjoy greater school and occupational success, and they are more popular, more socially skilled, and healthier. At the same time, they are similar to less attractive people in intelligence, life satisfaction, and self-esteem. Why does having all the benefits of attractiveness not lead to greater happiness? It is possible that attractive people learn to distrust attention from others, and especially from the opposite sex, because they assume that people like them simply for their looks. Believing that good things happen to them primarily because they are good looking may leave people feeling insecure, in that looks can fade or change with age.

Love Is an Important Component of Romantic Relationships

As noted earlier, psychological scientists have long neglected the study of love, in part because it seems a mysterious state that defies sensible comprehension. Thanks to the pioneering work of Elaine Hatfield and Ellen Berscheid (Figure 15.27), it is now clear that researchers can use scientific methods to examine this important interpersonal bond. Hatfield and Berscheid drew an important distinction between passionate love and companionate love. *Passionate love* is a state of intense longing and sexual desire, the kind of love that is often stereotypically portrayed in the movies. In passionate love people fall head over heels for one another, feel an overwhelming urge to be together, and are constantly sexually aroused in each other's presence. *Companionate love* is a strong commitment to care for and support a partner that develops slowly over time. It is based on friendship, trust, respect, and intimacy. Although people experience passionate love early in relationships, in most enduring relationships it often evolves into a more companionate love, in which intimacy and commitment dominate (Sternberg, 1986).

One theory of love is based on attachment theory. Recall from Chapter 11 that infants form different levels of attachment with their parents. According to Cindy Hazan and Phillip Shaver (1987), adult relationships, especially romantic relationships, also vary in their attachment style. The type of attachment style you have as an adult is assumed to relate to how your parents treated you as a child (Fraley & Shaver, 2000). Those who believe their parents were warm, supportive, and responsive report having *secure* attachments in their relationships. They find it easy to get close to others and they do not fear being abandoned. Just under 60 percent of adults report having this attachment style (Mickelson, Kessler, & Shaver, 1997). Those who found their parents were cold and distant, about 25 percent of the population, report having *avoidant* attachments. They find it hard to trust or depend on others, and they are wary of those who try to become close to them. Relationship partners make them uncomfortable. Those whose parents treated them in an inconsistent fashion—sometimes warm and sometimes not—have *anxious-ambivalent* attachments. This 11 percent of the population is best described as clingy. They worry that people do not really love them and are bound to leave them. Since people have to recollect how their parents treated them, it is possible that their memories are distorted. At the same time, this theory reinforces the importance of attachments throughout life.

Love is clearly a critical aspect of most people's social lives. Almost all of us enter into romantic relationships of one form or another. As we learned in Chapter 10, people in long-term, committed relationships tend to live longer, healthier lives. But if love is so important to people, why does it sometimes seem so elusive? Many people

15.27 Elaine Hatfield and Ellen Berscheid
Hatfield (top) and Berscheid (bottom) are pioneers in the study of human relationships.

struggle to find their "one true love," as they date and reject potential partners who fall short of the ideal. As mentioned in Chapter 8, nowadays people marry much later as they spend more and more time looking. Even when people fall in love and form committed relationships, they still encounter challenges to that relationship. What can social psychology tell us about the factors that make a relationship successful?

Making Love Last Is Difficult

An unfortunate aspect of contemporary Western marriages is that most of them fail. In North America, approximately half of marriages end in divorce or separation, many within the first few years. In addition, many couples who do not get divorced are unhappy and live together in a constant state of tension or as strangers sharing a house. The social psychologist Rowland Miller notes that "married people are meaner to each other than they are to total strangers" (1997, p. 12). People often take their relationship partners for granted, openly criticize them, and take out their frustrations on them by being cruel or cold. It is perhaps no surprise then that relatively few marriages meet the blissful ideals that newlyweds expect. What factors cause such dissatisfaction in relationships?

What factors cause marriages to be unhappy?

As mentioned in Chapter 9, passion typically fades over time. The long-term pattern of sexual activity within relationships shows a rise and then a decline. Typically, for a period of months or even years the two people experience frequent, intense desire for one another and have sex as often as they can arrange it. Past that peak, however, their interest in sex with each other wanes. Frequency of sex declines by about half from the first year of marriage to the second, and it continues to decline, although more gradually, thereafter. Not only does frequency of sex decline, but people typically experience less passion for their partners over time. Unless people develop other forms of satisfaction in their romantic relationships, such as friendship, social support, and intimacy, the loss of passion leads to dissatisfaction and often to the eventual dissolution of the relationship (Berscheid & Regan, 2005).

JEALOUSY AND POSSESSIVENESS Even when people lose some of their sexual desire for one another, however, they generally do not want their mates to have sex with anyone else. Some degree of sexual possessiveness and jealousy is found in all cultures, although with variation as to what makes people jealous and how they express it. Although people may disapprove of sexual infidelity in general, many eventually engage in it. Even so, infidelity is far less frequent than we might think. The best estimates are that one out of four husbands and one out of ten wives have had extramarital sex. Earlier estimates suggesting that half of married men and almost as many women were unfaithful may have reflected the more permissive patterns of the "sexual revolution" of the 1960s and seventies, and people may well be more faithful now than they were a couple of decades ago.

DEALING WITH CONFLICT Even in the best relationships, some conflict is inevitable, and couples need to constantly resolve strife. Confronting and discussing important issues is clearly an important aspect of any relationship. The way a couple deals with conflict often determines whether the relationship will last. John Gottman (1994) describes four interpersonal styles that typically lead to marital discord and dissolution. He calls these patterns of interacting the "Four Horsemen of the Apocalypse" to reflect their danger to relationships. These maladaptive strategies include being overly critical, holding the partner in contempt, being defensive, and mentally withdrawing from the relationship. When one partner launches a complaint, the other responds with his or her own complaints and often raises the stakes by recalling all of the other person's failings. People use sarcasm and sometimes insult or demean their partners. Inevitably, any disagreement, no matter how small, escalates into a major fight over the core marital problems, which often center around a lack of money or sex or both. Couples who are more satisfied tend to express concern for each other, even while disagreeing, try to see each other's point of view, and manage to stay relatively calm. Being able to deliver criticism in a lighthearted, playful fashion is also a strategy for relationship satisfaction (Keltner, Young, Heerey, Demig, & Monarch, 1998).

ATTRIBUTIONAL STYLE AND ACCOMMODATION Unhappy couples also differ from happy couples in attributional style, which refers to how one person explains another's behavior (Bradbury & Fincham, 1990). Unhappy couples make distress-maintaining attributions in which they view one another in the most negative way possible. In contrast, happy couples make partner-enhancing attributions in which they overlook bad behavior or respond constructively, a process referred to as accommodation (Rusbult & Van Lange, 1996). Essentially, happy couples attribute good outcomes to one another and bad outcomes to situations, whereas distressed couples do the opposite. If their partners bring them flowers, they wonder what ill deed their partners committed rather than thinking about what sweethearts they married.

Profiles in Psychological Science

Making Marriage Last

Many people were shocked when the Hollywood power couple Jennifer Aniston and Brad Pitt divorced in 2005. They seemed so perfect for each other. What happened? While wild rumors circulated about possible infidelity, different ideas about wanting children, and possibly some competition about whose career was more successful, one thing is clear: Celebrity marriages seem especially fragile. But despite the relationship implosions that daily feed the tabloids, there are many enduring marriages in Hollywood. Consider Danny DeVito and Rhea Perlman, Tom Hanks and Rita Wilson, or, most famously, Joanne Woodward and Paul Newman, who currently have been married for 47 years. As it turns out, marriages outside of Hollywood are fragile as well, with over half of them ending in divorce and only one quarter of them being identified as happy. Although popular culture and the media have focused on negative statistics and why marriages tend to fail—for example, because of infidelity, substance abuse, and money problems—they have ignored the factors responsible for lasting happiness in marriage.

Over the past two decades, a number of psychological scientists have conducted research to examine why marriages succeed or fail. Among the foremost of these researchers is John Gottman, who has studied thousands of married couples to understand what predicts marital outcomes (Gottman, 1998). In his 1994 book, *Why Marriages Succeed or Fail and How You Can Make Yours Last*, Gottman outlines a number of differences between couples who are happy and those who are not. He also dispels a number of commonly held myths, for instance that couples who have the most sex are the happiest. Actually, couples who agree on the *frequency* of sex are happiest. No matter the frequency, if one person thinks it is too often and the other thinks it is not often enough, that spells conflict. Furthermore, many people believe that conflict is a sign of a troubled marriage and that couples who never fight must be the happiest. But this isn't true either. According to research by Gottman and others, fighting, especially when it allows grievances to be aired, is one of the healthiest things a couple can do for their marriage. Conflict is inevitable in any serious relationship, but resolving such conflict in a positive way is the key to marital happiness.

Gottman asserts that the most successful type of couple is what he calls a *validating* couple, with each partner considering the other partner's opinions and emotions valid, even if they disagree. People in such relationships make statements like "I know that it makes you angry when I hang the toilet paper the wrong way, but it was never a big deal to me which way it should hang." Validating couples try to compromise and to demonstrate mutual respect. These couples manage to avoid the "Four Horsemen of the Apocalypse" we mentioned earlier, as their fights typically do not escalate to name-calling, contempt, or one partner fleeing the conflict. Quite simply, they do the hard work of working things out.

Based on his research, Gottman believes that as long as there are about five times more positive than negative interactions in a marriage, chances are good that the marriage will be stable. Couples headed for breakup fall below this level, and if there are as many negatives as positives in the marriage, the prognosis is pretty bleak. Thus, the task for any married couple is to seek opportunities for positive feelings within the relationship. Of course, the same principles apply to any long-term committed relationship, including those for gays and lesbians. According to Gottman and others, here are some ways to do that:

- Show interest in your partner. Listen to him or her describe the events of the day. Pay attention while the person is speaking and maintain eye contact. Try to be empathetic; show that you really understand and can feel what your partner is feeling. Such empathy and understanding can't be faked, but saying, "That must have been really annoying" conveys that you understand your partner's feelings.
- Be affectionate. You can show love in very quiet ways, such as simply touching the person once in a while. Reminisce about happy times together. Appreciate the benefits of the relationship. Couples who talk about the joys of their relationship, including comparing their partnership favorably to those of other people, tend to be happier with their relationships.
- Show you care. Many people take their partners for granted. Try to do something spontaneous like buying flowers or calling your partner at an unexpected time just to see how he or she is doing. Such actions let the partner know you think about him or her, even when you're not together. When we are dating people, we flirt with them, give them compliments, and display our best manners. Marriage doesn't mean you don't have to do any of these things. Be nice to your partner and try to make him or her feel that you value your mutual companionship. Praise your partner whenever possible. In turn, he or she will feel free to act in kind, which will help you feel good about yourself.
- Spend quality time together. It is easy for couples to drift apart and develop separate lives, especially in long-distance relationships. Be sure to share intimate details of your day on a regular basis. Find time to explore joint interests, such as hobbies or other activities. This doesn't mean that couples can't pursue independent interests (indeed, they should), but that having some activities and goals in common helps bring a couple closer. Having fun together is an

important part of any relationship. Share private jokes, engage in playful teasing, be witty. Enjoy each other.

- Maintain loyalty and fidelity. Outside relationships can be threatening to a marriage or intimate partnership. Believing your partner is emotionally or physically involved with another person can pose harm to even the healthiest relationship. At their core, relationship partners have to trust one another. Anything that threatens that basic sense of trust will harm the relationship.
- Handle conflict. Perhaps most important, learn how to handle conflict. Don't avoid it and pretend you have no serious issues. Rather, calm down, try to control your anger, and avoid name-calling, sarcasm, or excessive criticism. Validate your partner's feelings and beliefs even as you express your own feelings and beliefs. Look for areas of compromise.

Although much of this seems like common sense, many people lose sight of how to express love and commitment in their relationships. It is so easy for couples to get caught up in everything else in their lives, from work to raising children, that it becomes easier to focus on what is wrong in their marriages than on what is right. This is when you know the marriage has taken a wrong turn. To make a marriage stronger people must put considerable effort into recognizing and celebrating all that is good about the relationship. Those affirming experiences make marriages succeed rather than fail. ∎

REVIEWING the Principles | What Determines the Quality of Relationships?

People form friendships based on proximity, familiarity, similarity, and personal characteristics, such as personality traits and attractiveness. Love is an important component of romantic relationships. Relationships based solely on sexual passion may fail when that passion starts to wane, which often happens over time. How couples deal with conflict is an important determinant of whether the relationship will endure. Couples who are happy make positive attributions for their partners' behaviors, whereas unhappy couples tend to make negative attributions.

Conclusion

Social psychology teaches us a great deal about human existence. Even as we feel in control of ourselves and believe we can make sense of the actions of others, we often fail to take into account the powerful influence of social situations in shaping behavior. Throughout this chapter we have learned that situations influence our attitudes, beliefs, and behaviors. Moreover, much of how we think about others and ourselves occurs automatically, with relatively little thought, and is based on minimal information. These judgments are often biased in ways that make people feel good about themselves, frequently at the expense of others. Research that crosses levels of analysis has shown that stereotypes alter the way people perceive and process information about others. Many times brain activity indicates what people themselves do not report, or perhaps even know, such as negative attitudes about ethnic minorities. Using limited mental resources, human minds automatically categorize others, with the outcome that people fail to treat others individually and with respect. It is all too easy for people to develop ingroups and outgroups; all it takes is three people. Yet social psychologists have discovered that cooperative learning systems can benefit both the self and society. The challenge now is to adapt these systems to larger groups in society and to motivate these groups to use them.

Much of the strength of the social situation is that it capitalizes on the human need to belong. People favor their groups, go along with their leaders, and are motivated to avoid conflict to maintain group harmony. However, pressure to con-

form to the group leaves people susceptible to social influence and causes them to act in ways that conflict with their personal standards. Learning about the power of social situations allows a partial understanding of the long and tragic history of inhumane acts, such as genocide, prisoner abuse, and other organized forms of brutality. The lesson from social psychology is that we need to be aware of the power in a situation in order to understand how it affects our behavior as well as the behavior of others. Recognizing social forces provides us with a much greater understanding of how humans behave in their everyday lives—one of the key goals of psychological science.

Summarizing the Principles of Social Psychology

How Do We Know Ourselves?

1. **Our self-concept consists of self-knowledge:** Self-schemas are the cognitive aspects of self-knowledge and the working self-concept is what is activated and processed at any given time. Interdependent and independent self-construals are culture-based.

2. **Perceived social regard influences self-esteem:** Self-esteem is influenced by reflected appraisal. In sociometer theory, the basic need to belong influences social anxiety relative to self-esteem. Self-esteem may also be influenced by death anxiety.

3. **We use mental strategies to maintain our views of self:** Positive illusions of self are common. Self-esteem is influenced by our comparisons to others. A self-serving bias helps maintain positive self-esteem and may be culturally influenced.

How Do Attitudes Guide Behavior?

4. **We form attitudes through socialization and experience:** Attitudes are influenced by familiarity (the mere exposure effect), and can be shaped by conditioning and socialization by others.

5. **Behaviors are consistent with strong attitudes:** Implicit attitudes (those that are automatic and easily activated from memory) influence behavior and may differ from explicit attitudes (those that we profess).

6. **Discrepancies lead to dissonance:** A mismatch between attitudes or an attitude and a behavior cause cognitive dissonance, which is often resolved by a change in attitude. A behavioral change is possible but more difficult to accomplish. To justify discrepant behavior, many people often inflate the positive aspects of the experience.

7. **Attitudes can be changed through persuasion:** Persuasion often works by either focusing on the message (the central route) or the feelings the message generates (the peripheral route).

How Do We Form Our Impressions of Others?

8. **Nonverbal actions and expressions affect our impressions:** Nonverbal behavior (body language) is quickly interpreted and provides valuable information.

9. **We make attributions about others:** We use personal dispositions and situational factors to explain the behavior of others. Fundamental attribution error is when the personal attributions are favored over the situational attributions in explaining behavior.

10. **Stereotypes are based on automatic categorization:** Stereotypes are cognitive schemas that allow for fast, easy processing of social information, and can lead to bias and illusory correlations. Self-fulfilling prophecies occur when people behave in a way that confirms the biases of stereotypes.

11. **Stereotypes can lead to prejudice:** Prejudice occurs when the associated attitude is negative. Having a negative bias can lead to discriminatory actions. We show a preference for members of our ingroup versus those in the outgroup.

How Do Others Influence Us?

12. **Groups influence individual behavior:** The presence of others can improve performance (social facilitation) or create laziness (social loafing). Loss of personal identity

and self-awareness (deindividuation) can occur in groups. Group decisions can be extreme.

13. **We conform to social norms:** Socially determined influences on behavior occur through awareness of social norms. Lack of unanimity diminishes conformity.

14. **We are compliant:** A variety of factors influence the likelihood of compliance including what mood we are in and whether we've previously agreed to a lesser request (foot-in-the-door effect).

15. **We are obedient to authority:** People readily behave in ways directed by authorities even to the extent of harming others.

When Do We Harm or Help Others?

16. **Aggression can be adaptive:** Brain structures, neurochemistry, and hormones influence aggression. Biologically based responses can be adaptive. Frustration can lead to aggression.

17. **Aggression has social and cultural aspects:** Aggression is not entirely adaptive and is influenced by the social and cultural experiences we have.

18. **Many factors may influence helping behavior:** Prosocial behaviors maintain social relations. Altruism toward kin may favor inclusive fitness. Reciprocal helping is more likely in social groups in which survival depends on cooperation.

19. **Some situations lead to bystander apathy:** The presence of others in an emergency may create a diffusion of responsibility causing individual inaction.

What Determines the Quality of Relationships?

20. **Situational and personal factors influence friendships:** People affiliate with those who are similar and possess valued characteristics, including attractiveness.

21. **Love is an important component of romantic relationships:** In romantic relationships, passionate love evolves into companionate love.

22. **Making love last is difficult:** As passion fades, couples must develop other areas of satisfaction. Jealousy arises out of fears of infidelity. How couples deal with conflict influences the stability of the relationship. Generally, happy couples have positive views of their partners and their relationships.

Applying the Principles

1. In the movie *Harold and Kumar Go to White Castle*, Harold feels strongly that jaywalking is wrong but does it anyway. He tells himself it's okay since it is 2 A.M. and there are no cars around. This is an example of

   _____ a) cognitive dissonance and justification.
   _____ b) implicit and explicit attitudes.
   _____ c) persuasion and elaboration likelihood.
   _____ d) positive self-concept and maintenance.

2. Rex has met Cassie a few times and sees her as a not-very-bright but fun-loving blonde. When she excitedly tells him that she just got an A on her physics exam, he is surprised, and then wonders if perhaps it was an easy exam. What social cognition factor (or factors) account for his attitude?

   _____ a) self-fulfilling prophecy
   _____ b) ingroup-outgroup bias
   _____ c) stereotyping and fundamental attribution error
   _____ d) stereotyping and discrimination

3. Hazing is part of the tradition of fraternity pledging. Along with several of your frat brothers, you make the pledges strip down, stand out in the snow, and drink a vile concoc-

tion. This activity occurs with everyone cheering—and results in the near-death of one pledge. In hindsight, you are shocked by your behavior. Which of the following is a probable explanation?

   _____ a) transient deviant personality behavior
   _____ b) authoritarian personality attributional style
   _____ c) conformity and group processes
   _____ d) compliance behaviors

4. At the end of your English composition class, a student collapses at the front of the room. Although you notice the collapsed student, you rush out without helping because you have an exam to take in your next class. What may explain your behavior?

   _____ a) bystander intervention effect and hostility
   _____ b) time pressure and bystander intervention effect
   _____ c) anonymity and time pressure
   _____ d) lack of reciprocity and ambiguity

5. The first day conservative, "preppy" Jenna moved into the dorm, she was shocked and disappointed that her roommate was a liberal, "granola" type. Now at midsemester

they have become close friends. What is the most likely explanation for this change?

_____ a) proximity and familiarity
_____ b) opposites attract
_____ c) the effects of crowding
_____ d) one changed to be more similar to the other

ANSWERS: *1a 2c 3c 4b 5a*

Key Terms

aggression, p. 641
altruism, p. 645
attitude, p. 620
attributions, p. 627
bystander intervention effect, p. 645
cognitive dissonance, p. 622
compliance, p. 638
conformity, p. 637
deindividuation, p. 635
discrimination, p. 631
elaboration likelihood model, p. 624
frustration-aggression hypothesis, p. 642
fundamental attribution error, p. 609

implicit attitudes, p. 621
independent self-construals, p. 614
ingroup favoritism, p. 632
interdependent self-construals, p. 614
kin selection, p. 645
nonverbal behavior, p. 626
obedience, p. 639
personal attributions, p. 627
persuasion, p. 624
prejudice, p. 631
prosocial, p. 644
reciprocal helping, p. 645
self-awareness, p. 611

self-concept, p. 611
self-esteem, p. 614
self-fulfilling prophecy, p. 631
self-schema, p. 612
self-serving bias, p. 618
situational attributions, p. 627
social comparison, p. 617
social facilitation, p. 635
social loafing, p. 635
social norms, p. 636
social psychology, p. 609
sociometer, p. 615
stereotypes, p. 628

Further Readings

Berscheid, E., & Regan, P. (2005). *The psychology of interpersonal relationships.* New York: Prentice-Hall.

Cialdini, R. (2001). *Influence: Science and practice.* Boston: Allyn & Bacon.

Franzoi, S. (2005). *Social psychology* (4th edition). Boston: McGraw-Hill.

Gilovitch, T., Keltner, D., & Nisbett, R. E. (2006). *Social psychology.* New York: Norton.

Gottman, J. (1994). *Why marriages succeed or fail.* New York: Simon & Schuster.

Higgins, E. T., & Kruglanski, A. W. (1996). *Social psychology: Handbook of basic principles.* New York: Guilford Press.

Kunda, Z. (2000). *Social cognition.* Cambridge, MA: MIT Press.

Zebrowitz, L. A. (1997). *Reading faces: Window to the soul?* Boulder, CO: Westview Press.

absentmindedness The inattentive or shallow encoding of events.

absolute threshold The minimum intensity of stimulation that must occur before one can experience a sensation.

accommodation (1) A process by which muscles change the shape of the lens of the eye by flattening it to focus on distant objects or by thickening it to focus on closer objects. (2) The process by which a schema is adapted or expanded to incorporate a new experience that does not easily fit into an existing schema.

accuracy The extent to which an experimental measure is free from error.

acetylcholine (ACh) The neurotransmitter responsible for motor control at the junction between nerves and muscles; also involved in mental processes such as learning, memory, sleeping, and dreaming.

achievement motive The desire to do well relative to standards of excellence.

acquisition The gradual formation of an association between the conditioned and unconditioned stimuli.

action potential The neural impulse that passes along the axon and subsequently causes the release of chemicals from the terminal buttons.

activation-synthesis hypothesis A theory of dreaming that proposes that neural stimulation from the pons activates mechanisms that normally interpret visual input.

adaptations In evolutionary theory, the physical characteristics, skills, or abilities that increase the chances of reproduction or survival and are therefore likely to be passed along to future generations.

additive color mixing A way to produce a given spectral pattern in which different wavelengths of lights are mixed. The percept is determined by the interaction of these wavelengths with receptors in the eye and is a psychological process.

adolescence The transitional period between childhood and adulthood.

affiliation The tendency to be in social contact with others.

aggression Any behavior or action that involves the intention to harm someone else.

agonist Any drug that enhances the actions of a specific neurotransmitter.

agoraphobia An anxiety disorder marked by fear of being in situations in which escape may be difficult or impossible.

alcoholism Abnormal alcohol seeking characterized by loss of control over drinking and accompanied by physiological effects of tolerance and withdrawal.

alexithymia A disorder involving a lack of the subjective experience of emotion.

all-or-none principle The principle whereby a neuron fires with the same potency each time, although frequency can vary; it either fires or not, it cannot partially fire.

altruism The providing of help when it is needed, without any apparent reward for doing so.

amnesia Deficits in long-term memory that result from disease, brain injury, or psychological trauma.

amygdala A brain structure that serves a vital role in our learning to associate things with emotional responses and for processing emotional information.

analogical representation A mental representation that has some of the physical characteristics of an object; it is analogous to the object.

anorexia nervosa An eating disorder characterized by an excessive fear of becoming fat and a refusal to eat.

antagonist Any drug that inhibits the action of a specific neurotransmitter.

anterograde amnesia An inability to form new memories.

anti-anxiety drugs A class of psychotropic medications used for the treatment of anxiety.

antidepressants A class of psychotropic medications used to treat depression.

antipsychotics A class of drugs used to treat schizophrenia and other disorders that involve psychosis.

antisocial personality disorder A personality disorder marked by a lack of empathy and remorse.

anxiety disorders Disorders characterized by the experience of excessive anxiety in the absence of true danger.

arousal Term to describe psychological activation, such as increased brain activity, autonomic responses, sweating, or muscle tension.

assessment In psychology, examination of a person's mental state in order to diagnose possible mental illness.

assimilation The process by which a new experience is placed into an existing schema.

attachment A strong emotional connection that persists over time and across circumstances.

attention-deficit/hyperactivity disorder (ADHD) A disorder characterized by restless, inattentive, and impulsive behaviors.

attitude The evaluation of objects, events, or ideas.

attributions People's causal explanations for why events or actions occur.

autism A developmental disorder involving deficits in social interaction, impaired communication, and restricted interests.

autonomic nervous system (ANS) A major component of the peripheral nervous system, which regulates the body's internal environment by stimulating glands and by maintaining internal organs such as the heart, gall bladder, and stomach.

autoreceptors A neuron's own neurotransmitter receptors, which regulate the release of the neurotransmitters.

availability heuristic Making a decision based on the answer that most easily comes to mind.

axon A long narrow outgrowth of a neuron by which information is transmitted to other neurons.

basal ganglia A system of subcorticial structures that are important for the initiation of planned movement.

behavior modification Treatment in which principles of operant conditioning are used to reinforce desired behaviors and ignore or punish unwanted behaviors.

behavioral approach system (BAS) The brain system involved in the pursuit of incentives or rewards.

behavioral inhibition system (BIS) The brain system that is sensitive to punishment and therefore inhibits behavior that might lead to danger or pain.

behaviorism A psychological approach that emphasizes the role of environmental forces in producing behavior.

binocular depth cues Cues of depth perception that arise from the fact that people have two eyes.

binocular disparity A cue of depth perception that is caused by the distance between a person's eyes.

biological preparedness The idea that animals are biologically programmed to learn to fear specific objects.

biological therapy Treatment based on the medical approach to illness and disease.

bipolar disorder A mood disorder characterized by alternating periods of depression and mania.

blindsight A condition in which people who are blind have some spared visual capacities in the absence of any visual awareness.

blocking The temporary inability to remember something that is known.

body mass index (BMI) A ratio of body weight to height used to measure obesity.

borderline personality disorder A personality disorder characterized by identity, affective, and impulse disturbances.

bottom-up processing A hierarchical model of pattern recognition in which data are relayed from one processing level to the next, always moving to a higher level of processing.

brainstem A section of the bottom of the brain that houses the most basic programs of survival, such as breathing, swallowing, vomiting, urination, and orgasm.

Broca's area The left frontal region of the brain that is crucial to the production of language.

buffering hypothesis The idea that other people can provide direct support in helping individuals cope with stressful events.

bulimia nervosa An eating disorder characterized by dieting, binge eating, and purging.

bystander intervention effect The failure to offer help by those who observe someone in need.

Cannon-Bard theory of emotion A theory that emotion-producing stimuli from the environment elicit both an emotional and a physical reaction.

case study A research method that involves the intensive examination of one person.

cell body In the neuron, where information from thousands of other neurons is collected and processed.

central nervous system (CNS) The brain and spinal cord.

central tendency A measure that represents the typical behavior of the group as a whole.

cerebellum A large convoluted protuberance at the back of the brainstem that is essential for coordinated movement and balance.

cerebral asymmetry An emotional pattern associated with unequal activation of the left and right frontal lobes.

cerebral cortex The outer layer of brain tissue that forms the convoluted surface of the brain.

cholecystokinin (CCK) The peptide found in highest concentration in the cerebral cortex; it plays a role in learning and memory, pain transmission, and exploratory behavior.

chromosomes Structures within the cell body that are made up of genes.

circadian rhythms The regulation of biological cycles into regular patterns.

circumplex model An approach to understanding emotion in which two basic factors of emotion are spatially arranged in a circle, formed around the intersections of the core dimensions of affect.

classical conditioning A type of learned response that occurs when a neutral object comes to elicit a reflexive response when it is associated with a stimulus that already produces that response.

client-centered therapy An empathic approach to therapy that encourages personal growth through greater self-understanding.

clozapine An antipsychotic medication that acts on multiple neurotransmitter receptors and is beneficial in treating both the negative and positive symptoms of schizophrenia.

cochlea (inner ear) A fluid-filled tube that curls into a snail-like shape. The cochlea contains the basilar membrane, which in turn contains auditory receptor cells called hair cells. These transduce the mechanical energy of the sound wave into neural impulses.

cocktail party phenomenon The ability to focus on a single conversation in the midst of a chaotic cocktail party or other similarly noisy situation.

cognition Mental activity such as thinking or representing information.

cognitive-behavioral approach A diagnostic model that views psychopathology as the result of learned, maladaptive cognitions.

cognitive-behavioral therapy (CBT) A therapy that incorporates techniques from behavioral therapy and cognitive therapy to correct faulty thinking and change maladaptive behaviors.

cognitive dissonance The perceptual incongruity that occurs when there is a contradiction between two attitudes or between an attitude and a behavior.

cognitive map A visual/spatial mental representation of the environment.

cognitive restructuring A therapy that strives to help patients recognize maladaptive thought patterns and replace them with ways of viewing the world that are more in tune with reality.

cognitive therapy Treatment based on the idea that distorted thoughts produce maladaptive behaviors and emotions.

compliance The tendency to agree to do things requested by others.

concept A mental representation that groups or categorizes objects, events, or relations around common themes.

concrete operational stage The third stage in Piaget's theory of cognitive development, during which children begin to think about and understand operations in ways that are reversible.

conditioned response (CR) A response that has been learned.

conditioned stimulus (CS) A stimulus that elicits a response only after learning has taken place.

confabulation The false recollection of episodic memory.

confirmation bias A tendency to search for and believe evidence that fits our existing views.

conformity The altering of one's opinions or behavior to match those of others or to match social norms.

confound Anything that affects a dependent variable that may unintentionally vary between the different experimental conditions of a study.

consolidation A hypothetical process involving the transfer of contents from immediate memory into long-term memory.

continuous reinforcement A type of learning in which the desired behavior is reinforced each time it occurs.

conventional level The stage of moral reasoning that reflects conformity to rules of law and order that are learned from others.

coping response Any response an organism makes to avoid, escape from, or minimize an aversive stimulus.

corpus callosum A fiber of axons that transmits information between the two cerebral hemispheres of the brain.

correlation A statistical procedure that provides a numerical value, between +1 and −1, indicating the strength and direction of the relation between two variables.

correlational study A research method that examines how variables are naturally related in the real world, without any attempt by the researcher to alter them.

creativity The capacity to generate or recognize ideas, alternatives, or possibilities that may be useful in solving problems, communicating with others, or entertaining ourselves and others.

critical period The time in which certain experiences must occur for normal brain development, such as exposure to visual information during infancy for normal development of the brain's visual pathways.

critical thinking A systematic way of evaluating information in order to reach reasonable conclusions.

cryptomnesia A type of misappropriation that occurs when people think they have come up with a new idea, yet have only retrieved a stored idea and failed to attribute the idea to its proper source.

crystallized intelligence Knowledge acquired through experience and the ability to use that knowledge.

culture The beliefs, values, rules, and customs that exist within a group of people who share a common language and environment and that are transmitted through learning from one generation to the next.

cyclothymia A less extreme form of bipolar disorder.

data Objective observations or measurements.

declarative memory The cognitive information retrieved from explicit memory, knowledge that can be declared.

deductive reasoning A form of reasoning in which logic is used to draw a specific conclusion from given premises.

defense mechanisms Unconscious mental strategies the mind uses to protect itself from conflict and distress.

defining attribute model The idea that a concept is characterized by a list of features that are necessary to determine if an object is a member of a category.

deindividuation A phenomenon of low self-awareness in which people lose their individuality and fail to attend to personal standards.

delay of gratification When people transcend immediate temptations to successfully achieve long-term goals.

delusions False personal beliefs based on incorrect inferences about reality.

dendrites Branchlike extensions of the neuron that detect information from other neurons.

dependent variable In an experiment, the measure that is affected by manipulation of the independent variable.

descriptive study A research method that involves observing and noting the behavior of people or other animals in order to provide a systematic and objective analysis of behavior.

developmental psychology The study of changes in physiology, cognition, and social behavior over the life span.

Diagnostic and Statistical Manual of Mental Disorders (DSM) A handbook of clinical disorders used for diagnosing psychopathology.

dialectical behavior therapy (DBT) A treatment for borderline personality disorder that combines elements of behavioral, cognitive, and psychodynamic approaches.

diathesis-stress model A diagnostic model that proposes that a disorder may develop when an underlying vulnerability is coupled with a precipitating event.

difference threshold The minimum amount of change required in order to detect a difference between intensities of stimuli.

discrimination The inappropriate and unjustified treatment of people solely on the basis of their group membership.

display rules Cultural rules that govern how and when emotions are exhibited.

dizygotic twins Twin siblings who result from two separately fertilized eggs (i.e., fraternal twins).

dominant gene A gene that is expressed in the offspring whenever it is present.

dopamine A monoamine neurotransmitter involved in reward, motivation, and motor control.

dreams The product of an altered state of consciousness in which images and fantasies are confused with reality.

drive Psychological state that motivates an organism to satisfy its needs.

dualism The philosophical idea that the mind exists separately from the physical body.

dysthymia A form of depression that is not severe enough to be diagnosed as major depression.

eardrum (tympanic membrane) A thin membrane, which sound waves vibrate, that marks the beginning of the middle ear.

early selection theory A theory that we can choose the stimuli to which we will attend before we process their basic features.

ego In psychodynamic theory, the component of personality that tries to satisfy the wishes of the id while being responsive to the dictates of the superego.

elaboration likelihood model A theory of how persuasive messages lead to attitude changes.

elaborative rehearsal The encoding of information in a more meaningful fashion, such as linking it to knowledge in long-term memory.

electroconvulsive therapy (ECT) A procedure used to treat depression that involves administering a strong electrical current to the patient's brain.

electroencephalography (EEG) A method for measuring the electrical activity of the brain. Electrodes placed on the scalp are able to detect weak electrical signals produced by neural activity.

electrophysiology A method of data collection that measures electrical activity in the brain.

emotion Feelings that involve subjective evaluation, physiological processes, and cognitive beliefs.

emotion-focused coping A type of coping in which people try to prevent having an emotional response to a stressor.

emotional intelligence (EQ) A form of social intelligence that emphasizes the ability to perceive, understand, manage, and use emotions to guide thoughts and actions.

encoding The processing of information so that it can be stored.

encoding specificity principle Any stimulus that is encoded along with an experience can later trigger memory for the experience.

endocrine system A communication system that uses hormones to influence thoughts, behaviors, and actions.

endorphins Peptides involved in natural pain reduction and reward.

enzyme deactivation The process whereby the neurotransmitter is destroyed by an enzyme, thereby terminating its activity.

epinephrine A monoamine, found primarily in the body, which causes a burst of energy after an exciting event.

episodic memory Memory for one's personal past experiences.

evolutionary theory In psychological science, a theory that emphasizes the inherited, adaptive value of behavior and mental activity throughout the entire history of a species.

excitation transfer A form of misattribution in which residual physiological arousal caused by one event is transferred to a new stimulus.

expected utility theory A model of how humans should make decisions if they were to follow pure reason in their decision making.

experiment A study that tests causal hypotheses by measuring and manipulating variables.

experimenter expectancy effect Actual change in the behavior of the people or animals being observed that is due to observer bias.

explicit memory The processes involved when people remember specific information.

exposure A behavioral therapy technique that involves repeated exposure to an anxiety-producing stimulus or situation.

expressed emotion A pattern of interactions that includes emotional over-involvement, critical comments, and hostility directed toward a patient by family members.

extinction A process in which the conditioned response is weakened when the conditioned stimulus is repeated without the unconditioned stimulus.

extrinsic motivation Motivation to perform an activity because of the value or pleasure associated with that activity, rather than for an apparent biological goal or purpose.

facial feedback hypothesis The idea that facial expressions trigger the experience of emotion.

family systems model A diagnostic model that considers symptoms within an individual as indicating problems within the family.

fight-or-flight response The physiological preparedness of animals to deal with danger.

filter theory A theory that people have a limited capacity for sensory information and thus screen incoming information, letting in only the most important.

five-factor theory The idea that personality can be described using five traits: openness to experience, conscientiousness, extraversion, agreeableness, and neuroticism.

fixed schedule A schedule in which reinforcement is consistently provided upon each occurrence.

flashbulb memories Vivid memories for the circumstances in which one first learned of a surprising, consequential, and emotionally arousing event.

fluid intelligence Information processing in novel or complex circumstances.

forgetting The inability to retrieve memory from long-term storage.

formal operational stage The final stage in Piaget's theory of cognitive development; it involves the ability to think abstractly and to formulate and test hypotheses through deductive logic.

fovea The center of the retina where cones are densely packed.

framing The effect of presentation on how information is perceived.

frontal lobes The region at the front of the cerebral cortex concerned with planning and movement.

frustration-aggression hypothesis The extent to which people feel frustrated predicts the likelihood that they will act aggressively.

functional fixedness A tendency in problem solving to think of objects only as they are most commonly used.

functional magnetic resonance imaging (fMRI) An imaging technique used to examine changes in the activity of the working human brain.

functionalism An approach to psychology concerned with the adaptive purpose, or function, of mind and behavior.

fundamental attribution error The tendency to overemphasize personal factors and underestimate situational forces in explaining behavior.

GABA (gamma-aminobutyric acid) The primary inhibitory transmitter in the nervous system.

gender A term that refers to the culturally constructed differences between males and females.

gender identity Personal beliefs about whether one is male or female.

gender roles The characteristics associated with men and women because of cultural influence or learning.

gender schemas Cognitive structures that influence how people perceive the behaviors of men and women.

general adaptation syndrome A consistent pattern of responses to stress that consists of three stages: alarm, resistance, and exhaustion.

general intelligence (g) The idea that one general factor underlies all mental abilities.

generalized anxiety disorder A diffuse state of constant anxiety not associated with any specific object or event.

gene The unit of heredity that determines a particular characteristic in an organism.

genotype The genetic constitution determined at the moment of conception.

Gestalt theory A theory based on the idea that the whole of personal experience is much greater than simply the sum of its constituent elements.

glutamate The primary excitatory transmitter in the nervous system.

goal A desired outcome associated with some specific object of desire or some future behavioral intention.

gonads The main endocrine glands involved in sexual behavior: in males, the testes; in females, the ovaries.

gray matter A segment of the spinal cord that is dominated by the cell bodies of neurons.

group polarization A process in which group members conform to the initial attitudes of other members who already agree.

guilt A negative emotional state associated with an internal experience of anxiety, tension, and agitation, in which a person feels responsible for causing an adverse state.

habituation A decrease in behavioral response following repeated exposure to nonthreatening stimuli.

hallucinations False sensory perceptions that are experienced without an external source.

haptic sense The sense of touch.

hardiness A personality trait that enables people to perceive stressors as controllable challenges.

health psychology The field of psychological science concerned with the events that affect physical well-being.

heritability A statistical estimate of the fraction of observed measure of the overall amount of difference among people in a population that is caused by differences in heredity.

heuristics In problem solving, shortcuts used to minimize the amount of thinking that must be done when moving from step to step in a solution space.

hippocampus A brain structure important for the formation of certain types of memory.

homeostasis The tendency for bodily functions to maintain equilibrium.

hormones Chemical substances, typically released from endocrine glands, that travel through the bloodstream to targeted tissues, which are subsequently influenced by the hormone.

humanistic approaches Approaches to studying personality that emphasize personal experience and belief systems, and propose that people seek personal growth to fulfill their human potential.

hypothalamus A small brain structure that is vital for temperature regulation, emotion, sexual behavior, and motivation.

hypothesis A specific prediction of what should be observed in the world if a theory is correct.

id In psychodynamic theory, the component of personality that is completely submerged in the unconscious and operates according to the pleasure principle.

idiographic approaches Person-centered approaches to studying personality that focus on individual lives and how various characteristics are integrated into unique persons.

immune system The body's mechanism for dealing with invading microorganisms, such as allergens, bacteria, and viruses.

implicit attitudes Attitudes that influence our feelings and behavior at an unconscious level.

implicit memory The process by which people show an enhancement of memory, most often through behavior, without deliberate effort and without any awareness that they are remembering anything.

incentives External stimuli that motivate behaviors (as opposed to internal drives).

independent self-construals A view of the self as separate from others, emphasizing self-reliance and the pursuit of personal success.

independent variable In an experiment, the condition that is manipulated by the experimenter to examine its impact on the dependent variable.

inductive reasoning A form of reasoning in which we develop general rules after observing specific instances.

infantile amnesia The inability to remember events from early childhood.

inferential statistics A set of procedures used to make judgments about whether differences actually exist between sets of numbers.

informed consent A process in which people are given full information about a study, which allows them to make a knowledgeable decision about whether to participate.

ingroup favoritism The tendency for people to evaluate favorably and privilege members of the ingroup more than members of the outgroup.

insight (1) The sudden realization of a solution to a problem. (2) A goal of some types of therapy; a patient's understanding of his or her own psychological processes.

insomnia A sleep disorder characterized by an inability to sleep.

Institutional Review Boards (IRBs) Groups of people responsible for reviewing proposed research to ensure that it meets the accepted standards of science and provides for the physical and emotional well-being of research participants.

intelligence The human ability to use knowledge, solve problems, understand complex ideas, learn quickly, and adapt to environmental challenges.

intelligence quotient (IQ) The number computed by dividing a child's estimated mental age by the child's chronological age, and then multiplying this number by 100.

interactionists Theorists who believe that behavior is jointly determined by underlying dispositions and situations.

interdependent self-construals Self-concepts that are determined largely by social roles and personal relationships.

interneurons One of the three types of neurons, these neurons communicate only with other neurons, typically within a specific brain region.

interval schedule A schedule in which reinforcement is based on a specific unit of time.

intracranial self-stimulation (ICSS) A procedure in which animals are able to self-administer electrical shock to specific areas of the brain.

intrinsic motivation Motivation to perform an activity because of the value or pleasure associated with that activity, rather than for an apparent biological goal or purpose.

introspection A systematic examination of subjective mental experiences that requires people to inspect and report on the content of their thoughts.

James-Lange theory of emotion A theory that suggests that the experience of emotion is elicited by a physiological response to a particular stimulus or situation.

joint attentional engagement A process whereby caregivers make reference to objects that are part of a child's ongoing actions.

kin selection The tendency to be altruistic toward those who share a genetic bond.

late selection theory A theory that people take in sensory information, process it, and then select which aspects of the stimuli should be attended after processing.

latent content What a dream symbolizes, or the material that is disguised in a dream to protect the dreamer.

latent learning Learning that takes place in the absence of reinforcement.

lateral geniculate nucleus (LGN) A region of the thalamus where visual information first travels, and then relays the information to the visual cortex.

lateral inhibition A visual process in which adjacent photoreceptors tend to inhibit one another.

law of effect Thorndike's general theory of learning, which states that any behavior that leads to a "satisfying state of affairs" is more likely to occur again, and that those that lead to an "annoying state of affairs" are less likely to recur.

learned helplessness model A cognitive model of depression in which people feel unable to control events around them.

learning An enduring change in behavior that results from experience.

lithium A psychotropic medication used to treat bipolar disorder.

longitudinal studies A research design that examines the same individuals over time.

long-term memory (LTM) The relatively permanent storage of information.

long-term potentiation (LTP) The strengthening of a synaptic connection so that postsynaptic neurons are more easily activated.

loosening of associations A speech pattern among schizophrenic patients in which their thoughts are disorganized or meaningless.

loss aversion An unequal weighting of costs and benefits such that potential costs weigh more heavily than potential benefits.

lymphocytes Specialized white blood cells known as, B cells, T cells, and natural killer cells that make up the immune system.

magnetic resonance imaging (MRI) A method of brain imaging that produces high-quality images of the brain.

maintenance rehearsal A type of encoding that involves continually repeating an item.

major depression A disorder characterized by severe negative moods and a lack of interest in normally pleasurable activities.

manifest content The plot of a dream; the way a dream is remembered.

MAO inhibitors A category of antidepressant drugs that inhibit the action of monoamine oxidase.

mean A measure of central tendency that is the arithmetic average of a set of numbers.

median A measure of central tendency that is the value in a set of numbers that falls exactly in the halfway point between the lowest and highest values.

meme The knowledge transferred within a culture.

memory The capacity of the nervous system to acquire and retain usable skills and knowledge, allowing living organisms to benefit from experience.

mental age An assessment of a child's intellectual standing relative to that of his or her peers; determined by a comparison of the child's test score with the average score for children of each chronological age.

mental set A problem solving strategy that has worked in the past.

mesolimbic dopamine system The major brain system involved in reward, it connects the ventral tegmental area (VTA) to the nucleus accumbens.

methylphenidate A central-nervous-system stimulant medication used to treat ADHD.

microsleeps Brief, unintended sleep episodes, ranging from a few seconds to a minute, caused by chronic sleep deprivation.

mind-body problem A fundamental psychological issue that considers whether mind and body are separate and distinct or whether the mind is simply the subjective experience of the physical brain.

mirror neurons Neurons in the premotor cortex that are activated during observation of others performing an action.

modal memory model The three-stage memory system that involves sensory memory, short-term memory, and long-term memory.

mode A measure of central tendency that is the most frequent score or value in a set of numbers.

modeling The imitation of behavior through observational learning.

monoamines A group of neurotransmitters synthesized from a single amino acid that are involved in a variety of psychological activities.

monocular depth cues Cues of depth perception that are available to each eye alone.

monozygotic twins Twin siblings who result from one zygote splitting in two, and therefore share the same genes (i.e., identical twins).

mood A diffuse and long-lasting emotional state that influences rather than interrupts thought and behavior.

moral development Concerns the way in which people decide between behaviors with competing social outcomes.

morpheme The smallest unit of speech that has meaning.

motivation Factors that energize, direct, or sustain behavior.

motor neurons One of the three types of neurons, these efferent neurons direct muscles to contract or relax, thereby producing movement.

multiaxial system The system used in the DSM that provides assessment along five axes describing important mental health factors.

multiple intelligences The idea that people can show different skills in a variety of different domains.

myelin sheath A fatty material, made up of glial cells, that insulates the axon and allows for the rapid movement of electrical impulses along the axon.

natural selection Darwin's theory that those who inherit characteristics that help them adapt to their particular environment have a selective advantage over those who do not.

naturalistic observation A passive descriptive study in which observers do not change or alter ongoing behavior.

nature-nurture debate The arguments concerning whether psychological characteristics are biologically innate or acquired through education, experience, and culture.

need A state of biological or social deficiency within the body.

need hierarchy Maslow's arrangement of needs, in which basic survival needs are lowest and personal growth needs are highest in terms of priority.

need to belong theory The need for interpersonal attachments is a fundamental motive that has evolved for adaptive purposes.

negative feedback model The body's response to deviations from equilibrium.

negative punishment Punishment that occurs with removal of a stimulus that decreases the probability of a behavior's recurring.

negative reinforcement The increase in the probability of a behavior's being repeated through the removal of an aversive stimulus.

negative symptoms Symptoms of schizophrenia marked by deficits in functioning such as apathy, lack of emotion, and slowed speech and movement.

neuron The basic unit of the nervous system that operates through electrical impulses, which communicate with other neurons through chemical signals. Neurons receive, integrate, and transmit information in the nervous system.

neurotransmitter A chemical substance that carries signals from one neuron to another.

nodes of Ranvier Small gaps of exposed axon, between the segments of myelin sheath, where action potentials are transmitted.

nomothetic approaches Approaches to studying personality that focus on characteristics that are common to all people, although there is individual variation.

nonverbal behavior The facial expressions, gestures, mannerisms, and movements by which one communicates with others.

norepinephrine A monoamine neurotransmitter involved in states of arousal and vigilance.

obedience The willingness to follow an order given by an authority.

object permanence The understanding that an object continues to exist even when it cannot be seen.

objective measures Relatively unbiased assessments of personality, usually based on information gathered through self-report questionnaires or observer ratings.

observational learning Learning that occurs when behaviors are acquired or modified following exposure to others performing the behavior.

observational technique A research method of careful and systematic assessment and coding of overt behavior.

observer bias Systematic errors in observation that occur due to an observer's expectations.

obsessive-compulsive disorder (OCD) An anxiety disorder characterized by frequent intrusive thoughts and compulsive actions.

occipital lobes A region of the cerebral cortex at the back of the brain that is important for vision.

olfactory bulb The brain center for smell, located below the frontal lobes.

operant conditioning A learning process in which the consequences of an action determine the likelihood that it will be performed in the future.

operational definition The quantification of a variable that allows it to be measured.

orienting reflex The tendency for humans to pay more attention to novel stimuli.

ossicles Three tiny bones, the incus (hammer), malleus (anvil), and stapes (stirrup), in the middle ear that transfer the vibrations of the eardrum to the oval window.

outer ear The structure of the ear at which the sound wave arrives.

panic disorder An anxiety disorder characterized by sudden, overwhelming attacks of terror.

parallel play The type of play characteristic of two-year-olds, usually limited to sitting side by side and playing independently.

parasympathetic division of ANS A division of the autonomic nervous system that returns the body to its resting state.

parietal lobes A region of the cerebral cortex lying in front of the occipital lobes and behind the frontal lobes that is important for the sense of touch and the spatial layout of an environment.

Parkinson's disease A neurological disorder that seems to be caused by dopamine depletion, marked by muscular rigidity, tremors, and difficulty initiating voluntary action.

partial reinforcement A type of learning in which behavior is reinforced intermittently.

partial-reinforcement extinction effect The greater persistence of behavior under partial reinforcement than under continuous reinforcement.

participant observation A type of descriptive study in which the researcher is actively involved in the situation.

peptides Chains of two or more amino acids found in the brain and the body; they act like classic neurotransmitters or modify the quality of the neurotransmitter with which they are released.

perception The processing, organization, and interpretation of sensory signals that result in an internal representation of the stimulus.

perceptual constancy People correctly perceive objects as constant in their shape, size, color, and lightness despite raw sensory data that could mislead perception.

peripheral nervous system (PNS) All nerve cells in the body that are not part of the central nervous system. The PNS includes the somatic and autonomic nervous systems.

personal attributions Explanations that refer to internal characteristics, such as abilities, traits, moods, and effort.

personality Characteristics, emotional responses, thoughts, and behaviors that are relatively stable over time and across circumstances.

personality disorder A class of mental disorders marked by inflexible and maladaptive ways of interacting with the world.

personality trait A characteristic; a dispositional tendency to act in a certain way over time and across circumstances.

personality types Discrete categories based on global personality characteristics.

persuasion The active and conscious effort to change attitudes through the transmission of a message.

phenotype Observable physical characteristics that result from both genetic and environmental influences.

pheromones Chemicals released by animals and humans that trigger physiological or behavioral reactions in other members of the same species.

phobia An irrational fear of a specific object or situation.

phonology The study of the set of meaningless sounds and the rules by which we combine them to make words and sentences.

phrenology An early method of assessing personality traits and mental abilities by measuring bumps on the skull.

physical dependence Synonymous with addiction, the physiological state in which failing to ingest a specific substance leads to bodily symptoms of withdrawal.

pituitary gland Located at the base of the hypothalamus, the gland that sends hormonal signals that control the release of hormones from endocrine glands.

place coding A mechanism for encoding high-frequency auditory stimuli in which the frequency of the sound wave is encoded by the location of the hair cells along the basilar membrane.

plasticity A property of the brain that allows it to change as a result of experience, drugs, or injury.

pop-out The phenomenon whereby, when simple stimuli were used, subjects take the same amount of time to find the target, whether there are a few or many distracters.

positive punishment Punishment that occurs with administration of a stimulus that decreases the probability of a behavior's recurring.

positive reappraisal A cognitive process in which people focus on possible good things in their current situation.

positive reinforcement The increase in the probability of a behavior's being repeated following the administration of a pleasurable stimulus, referred to as a reward.

positive symptoms Symptoms of schizophrenia, such as delusions and hallucinations, that are excesses in behavior.

positron emission tomography (PET) A method of brain imaging that assesses metabolic activity by using a radioactive substance injected into the bloodstream.

posttraumatic stress disorder (PTSD) A mental disorder that involves frequent nightmares, intrusive thoughts, and flashbacks related to an earlier trauma.

pragmatics The way people use language to get what they want and to influence their listeners.

prefrontal cortex A region of the frontal lobes, especially prominent in humans, important for attention, working memory, decision making, appropriate social behavior, and personality.

prejudice The affective or attitudinal responses associated with stereotypes.

preoperational stage The second stage in Piaget's theory of cognitive development during which children think symbolically about objects, but reason is based on appearance rather than logic.

primacy effect In a list, the better memory for items presented first.

primary appraisal Part of the coping process that involves making decisions about whether a stimulus is stressful, benign, or irrelevant.

primary auditory cortex (A1) The region of the temporal lobe concerned with hearing.

primary emotions Evolutionarily adaptive emotions that humans share across cultures; they are associated with specific biological and physical states.

primary motor cortex The region of the frontal lobe concerned with movement.

primary reinforcers Reinforcers that are innately reinforcing, such as those that satisfy biological needs.

primary visual cortex (V1) The largest area in the occipital lobe, where the thalamus projects the image.

proactive interference When prior information inhibits the ability to remember new information.

problem-focused coping A type of coping in which people take direct steps to confront or minimize a stressor.

procedural memory A type of implicit memory that involves motor skills and behavioral habits.

projective measures Personality tests that examine unconscious processes by having people interpret ambiguous stimuli.

prosocial Tending to benefit others.

prototype model An approach to object categorization that is based on the premise that within each category, some members are more representative than others.

psychoanalysis A method developed by Sigmund Freud that attempts to bring the contents of the unconscious into conscious awareness so that conflicts can be revealed.

psychodynamic theory Freudian theory that unconscious forces, such as wishes and motives, influence behavior.

psychological dependence Habitual substance use, despite consequences, and a compulsive need to continue using the drug.

psychological practitioners Those who apply findings from psychological science in order to assist people in their daily lives.

psychological science The study of mind, brain, and behavior.

psychological scientist One who uses the methods of science to study the interplay between brain, mind, and behavior and how the social environment affects these processes.

psychomotor stimulants Drugs that activate the sympathetic nervous system and increase behavioral and mental activity.

psychopathology A disorder of the mind.

psychophysiological assessment A research method that examines how changes in bodily functions are associated with behavior or mental state.

psychosexual stages According to Freud, the developmental stages that correspond to the pursuit of satisfaction of libidinal urges.

psychotherapy The generic name given to formal psychological treatment.

psychotropic medications Drugs that affect mental processes.

punishment A stimulus following a response that decreases the likelihood that the response will be repeated.

qualia The properties of our subjective, phenomenological awareness.

quantum change A transformation of personality that is sudden, profound, enduring, and affects a wide range of behaviors.

random assignment The procedure for placing research participants into the conditions of an experiment in which each participant has an equal chance of being assigned to any level of the independent variable.

ratio schedule A schedule in which reinforcement is based on the number of times the behavior occurs.

reaction time A quantification of performance behavior that measures the speed of a response.

reactivity The effect that occurs when the knowledge that one is being observed alters the behavior being observed.

recency effect In a list, the better memory for words presented later in the list.

receptive field The region of visual space to which neurons in the primary visual cortex are sensitive.

receptors In neurons, specialized protein molecules on the postsynaptic membrane that neurotransmitters bind to after passing across the synaptic cleft.

recessive gene A gene that is expressed only when it is matched with a similar gene from the other parent.

reciprocal helping The tendency to help another because the recipient may return the favor.

reinforcer A stimulus following a response that increases the likelihood that the response will be repeated.

relative risk An important component of the ethical review in which the potential for possible harm to the participant is considered.

reliability The extent to which a measure is stable and consistent over time in similar conditions.

REM sleep The stage of sleep marked by rapid eye movements, dreaming, and paralysis of motor systems.

repetition priming The improvement in identifying or processing a stimulus that has previously been experienced.

replication Repetition of an experiment to confirm the results.

representativeness heuristic A rule for categorization based on how similar the person or object is to our prototypes for that category.

Rescorla-Wagner model A cognitive model of classical conditioning that states that the strength of the CS-US association is determined by the extent to which the unconditioned stimulus is unexpected.

research Scientific process that involves the systematic and careful collection of data.

response performance A research method in which researchers quantify perceptual or cognitive processes in response to a specific stimulus.

resting membrane potential The electrical charge of a neuron when it is not active.

restructuring A new way of thinking about a problem that aids its solution.

reticular formation A large network of neural tissue within the brainstem involved in behavioral arousal and sleep-wake cycles.

retina The thin inner surface of the back of the eyeball. The retina contains the photoreceptors that transduce light into neural signals.

retinotopic organization The systematic ordering of the neuronal pathway from the retina to the occipital lobe; this organization preserves spatial relationships, so that adjacent areas of the retina correspond to adjacent areas in the primary visual cortex.

retrieval The act of recalling or remembering stored information in order to use it.

retroactive interference When new information inhibits the ability to remember old information.

retrograde amnesia The condition in which people lose past memories, such as memories for events, facts, people, or even personal information.

reuptake The process whereby the neurotransmitter is taken back into the presynaptic terminal buttons, thereby stopping its activity.

rumination Thinking about, elaborating, and focusing on undesired thoughts or feelings, which prolongs, rather than alleviates, a negative mood.

schema A hypothetical cognitive structure that helps us perceive, organize, process, and use information.

schizophrenia A mental disorder characterized by alterations in perceptions, emotions, thoughts, or consciousness.

seasonal affective disorder (SAD) A disorder in which periods of depression occur during the times of year with less sunlight.

secondary appraisal Part of the coping process during which people evaluate their options and choose coping behaviors.

secondary emotions Blends of primary emotions, including states such as remorse, guilt, submission, and anticipation.

secondary reinforcers Events or objects that become reinforcers through their repeated pairings with primary reinforcers.

selective serotonin reuptake inhibitors (SSRIs) A category of antidepressant medications that prolong the effects of serotonin in the synapse.

self-actualization A state that is achieved when one's personal dreams and aspirations have been attained.

self-awareness A state in which the sense of self is the object of attention.

self-concept The full store of knowledge that people have about themselves.

self-efficacy The expectancy that one's efforts will lead to success.

self-esteem The evaluative aspect of the self-concept.

self-fulfilling prophecy The observation that people may come to behave in ways that confirm their own or others' expectations.

self-regulation The process by which people initiate, adjust, or stop actions in order to promote the attainment of personal goals or plans.

self-report method A method of data collection in which people are asked to provide information about themselves, such as in questionnaires or surveys.

self-schema The cognitive aspect of the self-concept, consisting of an integrated set of memories, beliefs, and generalizations about the self.

self-serving bias The tendency for people to take personal credit for success but blame failure on external factors.

semantic memory Memory for knowledge about the world.

sensation How sense organs respond to external stimuli and transmit the responses to the brain.

sensitization An increase in behavioral response following exposure to a threatening stimulus.

sensorimotor stage The first stage in Piaget's theory of cognitive development during which infants acquire information about the world through their senses and respond reflexively.

sensory adaptation When an observer's sensitivity to stimuli decreases over time.

sensory memory Memory for sensory information that is stored briefly in its original sensory form.

sensory neurons One of the three types of neurons, these afferent neurons detect information from the physical world and pass that information along to the brain.

serial position effect The ability to recall items from a list depends on order of presentation, with items presented early or late in the list remembered better than those in the middle.

serotonin A monoamine neurotransmitter important for a wide range of psychological activity, including emotional states, impulse control, and dreaming.

sexual response cycle A pattern of physiological responses during sexual activity.

sexual strategies theory Evolutionary theory that suggests men and women look for different qualities in relationship partners due to the gender-specific adaptive problems they've faced throughout human history.

shaping A process of operant conditioning that involves reinforcing behaviors that are increasingly similar to the desired behavior.

short-term memory (STM) A limited-capacity memory system that holds information in awareness for a brief period of time.

situational attributions Explanations that refer to external events, such as the weather, luck, accidents, or the actions of other people.

situationism The theory that behavior is determined as much by situations as by personality traits.

social comparison The evaluation of one's own actions, abilities, and beliefs by contrasting them with those of others.

social development The maturation of skills or abilities that enable people to live in a world with other people.

social dilemma A situation in which we feel a motivational conflict between cooperating and being selfish.

social facilitation A situation in which the mere presence of others enhances performance.

social loafing The tendency for people to work less hard in a group than when working alone.

social norms Expected standards of conduct, which influence behavior.

social psychology The branch of psychology concerned with how others influence the way a person thinks, feels, and acts.

social support A network of other people who can provide help, encouragement, and advice.

socially desirable responding When people respond to a question in a way that is most socially acceptable or that makes them look good.

social-skills training Treatment designed to teach and reinforce appropriate interpersonal behavior.

sociocultural model A diagnostic model that views psychopathology as the result of the interaction between individuals and their cultures.

sociometer An internal monitor of social acceptance or rejection.

sodium-potassium pump A mechanism of the neuron that keeps the resting membrane potential at a constant -70 mV, which sets the stage for electrical action.

somatic markers Bodily reactions that arise from the emotional evaluation of an action's consequences.

somatic nervous system A major component of the peripheral nervous system, which transmits sensory signals to the CNS via nerves.

sound wave The pattern of the changes in air pressure through time that results in the percept of a sound.

source amnesia A type of amnesia that occurs when a person shows memory for an event but cannot remember where he or she encountered the information.

source misattributions Memory distortions that occur when people misremember the time, place, person, or circumstances involved with a memory.

spatial memory Memory for the physical environment and includes such things as location of objects, direction, and cognitive maps.

spinal cord Part of the central nervous system. A rope of neural tissue that runs inside the hollows of the vertebrae from just above the pelvis and into the base of the skull.

split brain A condition in which the corpus callosum is surgically cut and the two hemispheres of the brain do not receive information directly from each other.

spontaneous recovery A process in which a previously extinguished response reemerges following presentation of the conditioned stimulus.

standard deviation A statistical measure of how far away each value is on average from the mean.

stereotypes Cognitive schemas that allow for easy and efficient organization of information about people based on their membership in certain groups.

stimulus discrimination A learned tendency to differentiate between two similar stimuli if one is consistently associated with the unconditioned stimulus and the other is not.

stimulus generalization Occurs when stimuli that are similar but not identical to the conditioned stimulus produce the conditioned response.

storage The retention of encoded representations over time that corresponds to some change in the nervous system that registers the event.

stream of consciousness A phrase coined by William James to describe one's continuous series of ever-changing thoughts.

stress A pattern of behavioral and physiological responses to events that match or exceed an organism's abilities.

stressor An environmental event or stimulus that threatens an organism.

structuralism An approach to psychology based on the idea that conscious experience can be broken down into its basic underlying components or elements.

Substance P A peptide that acts as a neurotransmitter and is involved in pain perception.

subtractive color mixing A way to produce a given spectral pattern in which the mixture occurs within the stimulus itself and is actually a physical, not psychological, process.

suggestibility The development of biased memories when people are provided with misleading information.

superego In psychodynamic theory, the internalization of societal and parental standards of conduct.

symbolic representation An abstract mental representation that does not correspond to the physical features of an object or idea.

sympathetic division of ANS A division of the autonomic nervous system that prepares the body for action.

synapse The site for chemical communication between neurons.

synaptic cleft The small space between neurons that contains extracellular fluid.

synaptic pruning A process whereby the synaptic connections in the brain that are frequently used are preserved, and those that are not are lost.

systematic desensitization An exposure technique that pairs the anxiety-producing stimulus with relaxation techniques.

tardive dyskinesia A side effect of some antipsychotic medications that produces involuntary movements of the lips, tongue, face, legs, or other parts of the body.

taste buds Sensory receptors that transduce taste information.

TAT (Thematic Apperception Test) A projective measure of personality where a person is shown an ambiguous picture and asked to tell a story about the picture.

telegraphic speech The tendency for children to speak using rudimentary sentences that are missing words and grammatical markings but follow a logical syntax.

temperaments Biologically based tendencies to feel or act in certain ways.

temporal coding A mechanism for encoding the low-frequency auditory stimuli in which the frequency of the sound wave is encoded by the frequency of firing of the hair cells.

temporal lobes The lower region of the cerebral cortex that is important for processing auditory information and also for memory.

tend-and-befriend response The argument that females are more likely to protect and care for their offspring and form social alliances than flee or fight in response to threat.

teratogens Environmental agents that harm the embryo or fetus.

terminal buttons Small nodules at the ends of axons, that release chemical signals from the neuron to an area called the synapse.

thalamus The gateway to the brain that receives almost all incoming sensory information before it reaches the cortex.

theory A model of interconnected ideas and concepts that explains what is observed and makes predictions about future events.

theory of mind The term used to describe the ability to explain and predict other people's behavior as a result of recognizing their mental state.

theory of multiple intelligences A theory that attempts to provide practical definitions of intelligence, including musical, verbal, mathematical/logical, spatial, kinesthetic (or body control), intrapersonal (or self-understanding), and interpersonal (or social understanding).

third-variable problem When the experimenter cannot directly manipulate the independent variable and therefore cannot be confident that another, unmeasured variable is not the actual cause of differences in the dependent variable.

tip-of-the-tongue phenomenon When people experience great frustration as they try to recall specific words that are somewhat obscure.

top-down processing A hierarchical model of pattern recognition in which information at higher levels of processing can also influence lower, "earlier" levels in the processing hierarchy.

TOTE model A model of self-regulation in which people evaluate progress in achieving goals.

trait approach An approach to studying personality that focuses on the extent to which individuals differ in personality dispositions.

transcranial magnetic stimulation (TMS) A procedure that transmits pulses of high-intensity magnetism to the brain.

transduction A process by which sensory receptors produce neural impulses when they receive physical or chemical stimulation.

transience The pattern of forgetting over time.

triangular theory of love Proposes that love is made up of differing combinations of passion, intimacy, and commitment.

tricyclic antidepressants A category of antidepressant medications that inhibit the reuptake of a number of different neurotransmitters.

two-factor theory of emotion A theory that a situation evokes both a physiological response, such as arousal, and a cognitive interpretation.

Type A behavior pattern A pattern of behavior characterized by competitiveness, achievement orientation, aggressiveness, hostility, restlessness, inability to relax, and impatience with others.

Type B behavior pattern A pattern of behavior characterized by relaxed, noncompetitive, easygoing, and accommodative behavior.

unconditioned response (UR) A response that does not have to be learned, such as a reflex.

unconditioned stimulus (US) A stimulus that elicits a response, such as a reflex, without any prior learning.

unconscious Those processes that are outside the realm of conscious awareness.

validity The extent to which the data collected address the research hypothesis in the way intended.

variability In a set of numbers, how widely dispersed the values are from each other and from the mean.

variable Something in the world that can be measured and that can vary.

variable schedule A schedule in which reinforcement is applied at different rates or at different times.

vicarious learning Learning that occurs when people learn the consequences of an action by observing others being rewarded or punished for performing the action.

visual search task An experiment used to study form perception, in which an observer tries to detect a target stimulus among an array of distracter stimuli.

white matter A segment of the spinal cord that consists mostly of axons and the fatty sheaths that surround them.

working memory An active processing system that keeps different types of information available for current use.

Yerkes-Dodson law A psychological principle that dictates that behavioral efficiency increases with arousal up to an optimum point, after which it decreases with increasing arousal.

Abramson, L. Y., Metalsky, G., & Alloy, L. (1989). Hopelessness depression: A theory-based subtype of depression. *Psychological Review, 96*, 358–372.

Ackerman, P. L., Beier, M. E., & Boyle, M. O. (2005). Working memory and intelligence: The same or different constructs? *Psychological Bulletin, 131*, 30–60.

Adams, C. E., Fenton, M., Quraishi, S., & David, A. S. (2001). Systematic meta-review of depot antipsychotic drugs for people with schizophrenia. *British Journal of Psychiatry, 179*, 290–299.

Adams, H. E., Wright, L. W., & Lohr, B. A. (1996). Is homophobia associated with homosexual arousal? *Journal of Abnormal Psychology, 105*, 440–445.

Adams, R. B., Jr., Gordon, H. L., Baird, A. A., Ambady, N., & Kleck, R. E. (2003). Effects of gaze on amygdala sensitivity to anger and fear faces. *Science, 300,* 1536–1537.

Adolphs, R. (2003). Cognitive neuroscience of human social behavior. *Nature Reviews Neuroscience, 1,* 165–178.

Adolphs, R., Gosselin, F., Buchanan, T. W., Tranel, D., Schyns, P., & Damasio, A.R. (2005). A mechanism for impaired fear recognition after amygdala damage. *Nature, 433,* 68–72.

Adolphs, R., Sears, L., & Piven, J. (2001). Abnormal processing of social information from faces in autism. *Journal of Cognitive Neuroscience, 13*, 232–240.

Adolphs, R., Tranel, D., & Damasio, A. R. (1998). The human amygdala in social judgement. *Nature, 393,* 470–474.

Alicke, M. D., Klotz, M. L., Breitenbecher, D. L., Yurak, T. J., & Vredenburg, D. S. (1995). Personal contact, individuation, and the better-than-average effect. *Journal of Personality and Social Psychology, 68*, 804–825.

Allport, G. W. (1961). *Pattern and growth in personality.* New York: Holt, Rinehart & Winston.

Amato, P. R. (2001). Children of divorce in the 1990s: An update of the Amato and Keith (1991) meta-analysis. *Journal of Family Psychology, 15*, 355–370.

Amato, P. R., Johnson, D., Booth, A., & Rogers, S. J. (2003). Continuity and change in marital quality between 1980 and 2000. *Journal of Marriage and Family, 65*, 1–22.

Amato, P. R., & Keith, B. (1991). Parental divorce and the well-being of children: A meta-analysis. *Psychological Bulletin, 110,* 26–46.

Ambady, N., Hallahan, M., & Conner, B. (1999). Accuracy of judgments of sexual orientation from thin slices of behavior. *Journal of Personality and Social Psychology, 77*, 538–547.

Ambady, N., & Rosenthal, R. (1993). Half a minute: Predicting teacher evaluations from thin slices of nonverbal behavior and physical attractiveness. *Journal of Personality and Social Psychology, 64*, 431–441.

American Psychiatric Association. (1994). *Diagnostic and statistical manual of mental disorders* (4th ed.). Washington, DC: Author.

American Psychiatric Association. (2000). Practice guidelines for the treatment of patients with eating disorders (revised). *American Journal of Psychiatry, 157* (Suppl.), 1–39.

Amminger, G. P., Pape, S., Rock, D., Roberts, S. A., Ott, S. L., Squires-Wheeler, E., et al. (1999). Relationship between childhood behavioral disturbance and later schizophrenia in the New York High-Risk Project. *American Journal of Psychiatry, 156*, 525–530.

Anderson, A. K., Christoff, K., Stappen, I., Panitz, D., Ghahremani, D. G., Glover, G., et al. (2003). Dissociated neural representations of intensity and valence in human olfaction. *Nature Neuroscience, 6,* 196–202.

Anderson, A. K., & Phelps, E. A. (2000). Expression without recognition: Contributions of the human amygdala to emotional communication. *Psychological Science, 11*, 106–111.

Anderson, A. K., & Phelps, E. A. (2001). Lesions of the amygdala impair enhanced perception of emotionally salient events. *Nature, 411,* 305–309.

Anderson, I. M. (2000). Selective serotonin reuptake inhibitors versus tricyclic antidepressants: A meta-analysis of efficacy and tolerability. *Journal of Affective Disorders, 58*, 19–36.

Anderson, S. W., Bechara, A., Damasio, H., Tranel, D., & Damasio, A. R. (1999). Impairment of social and moral behavior related to early damage in human prefrontal cortex. *Nature Neuroscience, 2,* 1032–1037.

Andreasen, N. C. (1984). *The broken brain: The biological revolution in psychiatry.* New York: Harper & Row.

Anfang, S. A., & Appelbaum, P. S. (1996). Twenty years after Tarasoff: Reviewing the duty to protect. *Harvard Review of Psychiatry, 4* (2), 67–76.

Angold, A., & Costello, E. J. (2001). The epidemiology of depression in children and adolescents. In I. M. Goodyer (Ed.), *The depressed child and adolescent* (2nd ed., pp. 143–178). New York: Cambridge University Press.

Antonuccio, D., & Burns, D. (2004). Adolescents with depression (Letter to the editor). *Journal of the American Medical Association, 292,* 2577.

Areni, C. S., & Kim, D. (1993). The influence of background music on shopping behavior: Classical versus top-forty music in a wine store. *Advances in Consumer Research, 20,* 336–340.

Arias, E., MacDorman, M. F., Strobino, D. M., & Guyer, B. (2003). Annual summary of vital statistics—2002. *Pediatrics, 112,* 1215–1230.

Aronson, E., & Mills, J. (1959). The effects of severity of initiation on liking for a group. *Journal of Abnormal and Social Psychology, 59,* 177–181.

Asberg, M., Shalling, D., Traskman-Bendz, L., & Wagner, A. (1987). Psychobiology of suicide, impulsivity, and related phenomena. In H. Y. Melzer (Ed.), *Psychopharmacology: The third generation of progress* (pp. 655–668). New York: Raven Press.

Asch, S. E. (1955). Opinions and social pressure. *Scientific American, 193,* 31–35 (offprint 450).

Ashby, F. G., Isen, A. M., & Turken, A. U. (1999). A neuropsychological theory of positive affect and its influence on cognition. *Psychological Review, 106,* 529–550.

Averill, J. R. (1980). A constructivist view of emotion. In R. Plutchik & H. Kellerman (Eds.), *Theories of emotion* (pp. 305–339). New York: Academic Press.

Aylward, E. H., Reiss, A. L., Reader, M. J., & Singer, H. S. (1996). Basal ganglia volumes in children with attention-deficit hyperactivity disorder. *Journal of Child Neurology, 11,* 112–115.

Baddeley, A. D. (2001). Is working memory still working? *American Psychologist, 56,* 851–864.

Bagby, R. M., Levitan, R. D., Kennedy, S. H., Levitt, A. J., & Joffe, R. T. (1999). Selective alteration of personality in response to noradrenergic and serotonergic antidepressant medication in a depressed sample: Evidence of non-specificity. *Psychiatry Research, 86,* 211–216.

Bailey, A., Le Couteur, A., Gottesman, I., Bolton, P., Simonoff, E., Yuzda, E., et al. (1995). Autism as a strongly genetic disorder: Evidence from a British twin study. *Psychological Medicine, 25,* 63–78.

Baillargeon, R. (1995). Physical reasoning in infancy. In M. S. Gazzaniga (Ed.), *The cognitive neurosciences* (pp. 181–204). Cambridge, MA: MIT Press.

Baldwin, D. A. (1991). Infants' contribution to the achievement of joint reference. *Child Development, 62,* 875–890.

Baldwin, D. A., & Baird, J. A. (2001). Discerning intentions in dynamic human action. *Trends in Cognitive Sciences, 5,* 171–178.

Baltimore, D. (2001). Our genome unveiled. *Nature, 409,* 814–816.

Banaji, M. R., & Greenwald, A. G. (1995). Implicit gender stereotyping in judgments of fame. *Journal of Personality and Social Psychology, 68,* 181–198.

Bandura, A. (1977). *Social learning theory.* Englewood Cliffs, NJ: Prentice-Hall.

Bandura, A., Ross, D., & Ross, S. (1961). Transmission of aggression through imitation of aggressive models. *Journal of Abnormal and Social Psychology, 66,* 3–11.

Bandura, A., Ross, D., & Ross, S. (1963). Vicarious reinforcement and imitative learning. *Journal of Abnormal and Social Psychology, 67,* 601–607.

Barch, D. M., Sheline, Y. I., Csernansky, J. G., & Snyder, A. Z. (2003). Working memory and prefrontal cortex dysfunction: Specificity to schizophrenia compared with major depression. *Biological Psychiatry, 53,* 376–384.

Bargh, J. A., Chen, M., & Burrows, L. (1996). Automaticity of social behavior: Direct effects of trait construct and stereotype activation on action. *Journal of Personality and Social Psychology, 71,* 230–244.

Bargh, J. A., & Ferguson, M. J. (2000). Beyond behaviorism: On the automaticity of higher mental processes. *Psychological Bulletin, 126,* 925–945.

Barkley, R. A. (1997). *ADHD and the nature of self-control.* New York: Guilford Press.

Barlow, D. H. (1988). *Anxiety and its disorders: The nature and treatment of anxiety and panic.* New York: Guilford Press.

Barlow, D. H. (2002). *Anxiety and its disorders: The nature and treatment of anxiety and panic* (2nd ed.). New York: Guilford Press.

Barlow, D. H. (2004). Psychological treatments. *American Psychologist, 59,* 869–878.

Barlow, D. H, Gorman, J. M., Shear, M. K., & Woods, S. W. (2000). Cognitive-behavioral therapy, imipramine, or their combination for panic disorder: A randomized controlled trial. *Journal of the American Medical Association, 283,* 2529–2536.

Baron-Cohen, S., Lutchmaya, S., & Knickmeyer, R. (2004). *Prenatal testosterone in mind: Amniotic fluid studies.* Cambridge, MA: MIT Press.

Baron-Cohen, S., Wheelwright, S., & Jolliffe, T. (1997). Is there a "language of the eyes"? Evidence from normal adults and adults with autism or Asperger Syndrome. *Visual Cognition, 4,* 311–332.

Bartoshuk, L. M. (2000). Comparing sensory experiences across individuals: Recent psychophysical advances illuminate genetic variation in taste perception. *Chemical Senses, 25,* 447–460.

Basbaum, A. I., & Fields, H. L. (1984). Endogenous pain control systems: Brainstem spinal pathways and endorphin circuitry. *Annual Review of Neuroscience, 7,* 309–338.

Batson, C. D., Dyck, J. L., Brandt, J. R., Batson, J. G., Powell, A. L., McMaster, M. R., et al. (1988). Five studies testing two new egoistic alternatives to the empathy-altruism hypothesis. *Journal of Personality and Social Psychology, 55,* 52–77.

Batson, C. D., Turk, C. L., Shaw, L.L., & Klein, T. (1995). Information function of empathic emotion: Learning that we value the other's welfare. *Journal of Personality and Social Psychology, 68,* 300–313.

Baumeister, R. F. (1991). *Escaping the self: Alcoholism, spirituality, masochism, and other flights from the burden of selfhood.* New York: Basic Books.

Baumeister, R. F. (2000). Gender differences in erotic plasticity: The female sex drive as socially flexible and responsive. *Psychological Bulletin, 126,* 347–374.

Baumeister, R. F., Campbell, J. D., Krueger, J. I., & Vohs, K. D. (2003). Does high self-esteem cause better performance, interpersonal success, happiness, or healthier lifestyles? *Psychological Science in the Public Interest, 4,* 1–44.

Baumeister, R. F., Campbell, J. D., Krueger, J. I., & Vohs, K. D. (2005). Exploding the self-esteem myth. *Scientific American, 292,* 84–91.

Baumeister, R. F., Catanese, K. R., & Vohs, K. D. (2001). Is there a gender difference in strength of sex drive? Theoretical views, conceptual distinctions, and a review of the relevant literature. *Personality and Social Psychology Review, 5,* 242–273.

Baumeister, R. F., Dale, K., & Sommers, K. L. (1998). Freudian defense mechanisms and empirical findings in modern social psychology: Reaction formation, projection, displacement, undoing, isolation, sublimation, and denial. *Journal of Personality, 66,* 1081–1124.

Baumeister, R. F., & Heatherton, T. F. (1996). Self-regulation failure: An overview. *Psychological Inquiry, 7,* 1–15.

Baumeister, R. F., & Leary, M. R. (1995). The need to belong: Desire for interpersonal attachments as a fundamental human motivation. *Psychological Bulletin, 117,* 497–529.

Baumeister, R. F., Smart, L., & Boden, J. M. (1996). Relation of threatened egotism to violence and aggression: The dark side of high self-esteem. *Psychological Review, 103,* 5–33.

Baumeister, R. F., Stillwell, A. M., & Heatherton, T. F. (1994). Guilt: An interpersonal approach. *Psychological Bulletin, 115,* 243–267.

Baumeister, R. F., & Tice, D. M. (1990). Anxiety and social exclusion. *Journal of Social and Clinical Psychology, 9,* 165–195.

Baumrind, D., Larzelere, R. E., & Cowan, P. A. (2002). Ordinary physical punishment: Is it harmful? Comment on Gershoff (2002). *Psychological Bulletin, 128,* 580–589.

Baver, J. J., McAdams, D. P., & Sakaeda, A. R. (2005). Interpreting the good life: Growth memories in the lives of mature, happy people. *Journal of Personality and Social Psychology, 88,* 203–217.

Baxter, L. R. (2000). Functional imaging of brain systems mediating obsessive-compulsive disorder. In D. S. Charney, E. J. Nestler, & B. S. Bunney (Eds.), *Neurobiology of mental illness* (pp. 534–547). New York: Oxford University Press.

Baxter, L. R., Schwartz, J. M., Bergman, K. S., Szuba, M. P., Guze, B., Mazziota, J. C., et al. (1992). Caudate glucose metabolic rate changes with both drug and behavior therapy for obsessive-compulsive disorder. *Archives of General Psychiatry, 49,* 681–689.

Beck, A. T. (1967). *Depression: Clinical, experimental and theoretical aspects.* New York: Harper & Row.

Beck, A. T. (1976). *Cognitive therapy and the emotional disorders.* New York: International Universities Press.

Beck, A. T., Brown, G., Seer, R. A., Eidelson, J. L., & Riskind, J. H. (1987). Differentiating anxiety and depression: A test of the cognitive content-specificity hypothesis. *Journal of Abnormal Psychology, 96,* 179–183.

Beck, A. T., Freeman, A., & Associates (1990). *Cognitive Therapy of Personality Disorders.* New York: Guilford Press.

Beck, A. T., & Rector, N. A. (2005). Cognitive approaches to schizophrenia: Theory and therapy. *Annual Review of Clinical Psychology, 1,* 577–606.

Beck, A. T., Rush, A. J., Shaw, B., & Emery, G. (1979). *Cognitive therapy of depression.* New York: Guilford Press.

Beck, A. T., Steer, R. A., & Brown, G. K. (1996). *Beck depression inventory manual.* San Antonio, TX: The Psychological Corporation.

Beck, A. T., Ward, C. H., Mendelson, M., Mock, J., & Erbaugh, J. (1961). An inventory for measuring depression. *Archives of General Psychiatry, 4,* 561–571.

Beggan, J. K. (1992). On the social nature of nonsocial perception: The mere ownership effect. *Journal of Personality and Social Psychology, 62,* 229–237.

Beggs, J. M., Brown, T. H., Byrne, J. H., Crow, T., LeDoux, J. E., LeBar, K., et al. (1999). Learning and memory: Basic mechanisms. In M. J. Zigmond, F. E. Bloom, S. C. Landis, J. L. Roberts, & L. R. Squire (Eds.), *Fundamentals of neuroscience* (pp. 1411–1454). San Diego, CA: Academic Press.

Behne, T., Carpenter, M., Call, J., & Tomasello, M. (2005). Unwilling versus unable: Infants' understanding of intentional action. *Developmental Psychology, 41,* 328–337.

Békésy, G. Von. (1957). The ear. *Scientific American, 197,* 66–78.

Bellak, L., & Black, R. B. (1992). Attention-deficit hyperactivity disorder in adults. *Clinical Therapeutics, 14,* 138–147.

Belsky, J. (1990). Children and marriage. In F. D. Fincham & T. N. Bradbury (Eds.), *The psychology of marriage: Basic issues and applications* (pp. 172–200). New York: Guilford.

Bem, D. (1967). Self-perception: An alternative explanation of cognitive dissonance phenomena. *Psychological Review, 74,* 183–200.

Bem, D. J. (1996). Exotic becomes erotic: A developmental theory of sexual orientation. *Psychological Review, 103,* 320–335.

Bem, D. J., & Honorton, C. (1994). Does psi exist? Replicable evidence for an anomalous process of information transfer. *Psychological Bulletin, 115,* 4–18.

Bem, S. L. (1975). Sex role adaptability: One consequence of psychological androgyny. *Journal of Personality and Social Psychology, 31,* 634–643.

Bem, S. L., Martyna, W., & Watson, C. (1976). Sex typing and androgyny: Further explorations of the expressive domain. *Journal of Personality and Social Psychology, 34,* 1016–1023.

Benedetti, F., Serretti, A., Colombo, C., Campori, E., Barbini, B., di Bella, D., et al. (1999). Influence of a functional polymorphism within the promoter of the serotonin transporter gene on the effects of total sleep deprivation in bipolar depression. *American Journal of Psychiatry, 156,* 1450–1452.

Benjamin, L. T. (2005). A history of clinical psychology as a profession in America (and a glimpse at its future). *Annual Review of Clinical Psychology, 1,* 1–30.

Bentler, P. M., & Newcomb, M. D. (1978). Longitudinal study of marital success and failure. *Journal of Consulting and Clinical Psychology, 46,* 1053–1070.

Berger, K. S. (2004). *The developing person through the life span* (6th ed.). New York: Worth.

Berkman, L. F. (1984). Assessing the physical health effects of social networks and social support. *Annual Review of Public Health, 5,* 413–432.

Berkowitz, L. (1990). On the formation and regulation of anger and aggression: A cognitive-neoassociationistic analysis. *American Psychologist, 45,* 494–503.

Bernhardt, P. C., Dabbs, J. M., Fielden, J. A., & Lutter, C. D. (1998). Testosterone changes during vicarious experiences of winning and losing among fans at sporting events. *Physiology & Behavior, 65,* 59–62.

Bernheim, K. F. (Ed.). (1997). *The Lanahan cases and readings in abnormal behavior.* Baltimore: Lanahan Publishers.

Berns, G. S., Chappelow, J., Zink, C. F., Pagnoni, G., Martin-Skurski, M. E., & Richards, J. (2005). Neurobiological correlates of social conformity and interdependence during mental rotation. *Biological Psychiatry, 58,* 245–253.

Berscheid, E., & Regan, P. (2005). *The psychology of interpersonal relationships.* New York: Prentice-Hall.

Bickel, W. K., Odum, A. L., & Madden, G. J. (1999). Impulsivity and cigarette smoking: Delay discounting in current, never, and ex-smokers. *Psychopharmacology, 146,* 447–454.

Bickerton, D. (1998). The creation and re-creation of language. In C. B. Crawford & D. L. Krebs (Eds.*), Handbook of evolutionary psychology: Ideas, issues, and applications* (pp. 613–634). Mahwah, NJ: Lawrence Erlbaum Associates, Inc.

Bidell, T. R., & Fischer, K. W. (1995). Between nature and nurture: The role of agency in the epigenesis of intelligence. In R. Sternberg & E. Grigorenko (Eds.), *Intelligence: Heredity and environment.* New York: Cambridge University Press.

Biederman, I. (1987). Recognition-by-components: A theory of human image understanding. *Psychological Review, 94,* 115–147.

Biederman, J., Faraone, S. V., Keenan, K., Knee, D., & Tsuang, M. T. (1990). Family-genetic and psychosocial risk factors, in DSM-III attention deficit disorder. *Journal of the American Academy of Child and Adolescent Psychiatry, 29,* 526–633.

Biederman, J., Faraone, S. V., & Lapey, K. (1992). Comorbidity of diagnosis in attention-deficit hyperactivity disorder. In G. Weiss (Ed.*), Child and adolescent psychiatry clinics of North America: Attention deficit hyperactivity disorder* (pp. 335–360). Philadelphia: Saunders.

Biederman, J., Hirshfeld-Becker, D. R., Rosenbaum, J. F., Herot, C., Friedman, D., Snidman, N., et al. (2001). Further evidence of association between behavioral inhibition and social anxiety in children. *American Journal of Psychiatry, 158,* 1673–1679.

Bierut, L. J., Saccone, N. L., Rice, J. P., Goate, A., Foroud, T., Edenberg, H., et al. (2002). Defining alcohol-related phenotypes in humans: The collaborative study on the genetics of alcoholism. *Genetic Technology in Alcohol Research, 26,* 208–213.

Biglan, A., & Lichtenstein, E. (1984). A behavior-analytic approach to smoking acquisition: Some recent findings. *Journal of Applied Social Psychology, 14,* 207–224.

Bigler, R. S., & Liben, L. S. (1993). A cognitive-development approach to racial stereotyping and reconstructive memory in Euro-American children. *Child Development, 64,* 1507–1518.

Birbaumer, N., Grodd, W., Diedrich, O., Klose, U., Erb, M., Lotze, M., et al. (1998). fMRI reveals amygdala activation to human faces in social phobics. *Neuroreport, 9,* 1223–1226.

Bisiach, E., & Luzzatti, C. (1978). Unilateral neglect and representational space. *Cortex, 14,* 129–133.

Blagys, M. D., & Hilsenroth, M. J. (2000). Distinctive feature of short-term psychodynamic-interpersonal psychotherapy: A review of the comparative psychotherapy process literature. *Clinical Psychology: Science and Practice, 7,* 167–188.

Blair, I. V. (2002). The malleability of automatic stereotypes and prejudice. *Personality and Social Psychology Review, 6,* 242–261.

Blair, R. J. (2003). Neurobiological basis of psychopathy. *British Journal of Psychiatry, 182,* 5–7.

Blakemore, C. (1983). *Mechanics of the mind.* Cambridge, UK: Cambridge University Press.

Blakemore, S. J., Wolpert, D. M., & Frith, C. D. (1998). Central cancellation of self-produced tickle sensation. *Nature Neurosciences, 1,* 635–640.

Blakemore, S. J., Wolpert, D. M., & Frith, C. D. (2000). Why can't you tickle yourself? *Neuroreport, 3,* 11–16.

Blanchard, R., & Ellis, L. (2001). Birth weight, sexual orientation, and the sex of preceding siblings. *Journal of Biosocial Science, 33,* 451–467.

Blitstein, J. L., Robinson, L. A., Murray, D. M., Klesges, R. C., & Zbikowski, S. M. (2003). Rapid progression to regular cigarette smoking among nonsmoking adolescents: Interactions with gender and ethnicity. *Preventive Medicine, 36,* 455–463.

Blood, A. J., & Zatorre, R. J. (2001). Intensely pleasurable responses to music correlate with activity in brain regions implicated in reward and emotion. *Proceedings of the National Academy of Science, 98,* 11818–11823.

Blumstein, P., & Schwartz, P. (1983). *American couples.* New York: Simon & Schuster.

Bohus, M., Haaf, B., Simms, T., Limberger, M. F., Schmahl, C., Unckel, C., et al. (2004). Effectiveness of inpatient dialectical behavioral therapy for borderline personality disorder: A controlled trial. *Behavioral Research and Therapy, 42,* 487–499.

Bohus, M., Haaf, B., Stiglmayr, C., Pohl, U., Boehme, R., & Linehan, M. M. (2000). Evaluation of inpatient dialectical-behavioral therapy for borderline personality disorder—A prospective study. *Behaviour Research and Therapy, 38,* 875–887.

Bolles, R. C. (1970). Species-specific defense reactions and avoidance learning. *Psychological Review, 77,* 32–48.

Bornstein, R. F. (1999). Criterion validity of objective and projective dependency tests: A meta-analytic assessment of behavioral prediction. *Psychological Assessment, 11,* 48–57.

Bouchard, C., Tremblay, A., Despres, J. P., Nadeau, A., Lupien, J. P., Theriault, G., et al. (1990). The response to long-term overfeeding in identical twins. *New England Journal of Medicine, 322,* 1477–1482.

Bouchard Jr., T. J., Lykken, D. T., McGue, M., Segal, N. L., & Tellegen, A. (1990). Sources of human psychological differences: The Minnesota study of twins reared apart. *Science, 250,* 223–228.

Bourin, M., Baker, G. B., & Bradwejn, J. (1998). Neurobiology of panic disorder. *Journal of Psychosomatic Research, 44,* 163–180.

Bouton, M. E. (1994). Context, ambiguity, and classical conditioning. *Current Directions in Psychological Science, 3,* 49–53.

Bouton, M. E., Nelson, J. B., & Rosas, J. M. (1999). Stimulus generalization, context change, and forgetting. *Psychological Bulletin, 125,* 171–186.

Bradbury, T. N., & Fincham, F. D. (1990). Attributions in marriage: Review and critique. *Psychological Bulletin, 107,* 3–33.

Bramlett, M. D., & Mosher, W. D. (2002). *Cohabitation, marriage, divorce, and remarriage in the United States* (Vital and Health Statistics, Series 23, No. 22). Hyattsville, MD: National Center for Health Statistics, Centers for Disease Control and Prevention.

Bransford, J. D., & Johnson, M. K. (1972). Contextual prerequisites for understanding: Some investigations of comprehension and recall. *Journal of Verbal Learning and Verbal Behavior, 11,* 717–726.

Modified by E. B. Zechmeister & S. E. Nyberg, 1982. *Human memory* (p. 305). Pacific Grove, CA: Brooks Cole.

Braun, A. R., Balkin, T. J., Wesensten, N. J., Gwadry, F., Carson, R. E., Varga, M., et al. (1998). Dissociated pattern of activity in visual cortices and their projections during human rapid eye movement sleep. *Science, 279,* 91–95.

Breland, K., & Breland, M. (1961). The misbehavior of organisms. *American Psychologist, 16,* 681–684.

Brent, D. A. (2004). Antidepressants and pediatric depression—the risk of doing nothing. *New England Journal of Medicine, 351,* 1598–1601.

Brewer, J. B., Zhao, Z., Glover, G. H., & Gabrieli, J. D. E. (1998). Making memories: Brain activity that predicts how well visual experiences will be remembered. *Science, 281,* 1185–1187.

Brewer, M. B., & Caporael, L. R. (1990). Selfish genes vs. selfish people: Sociobiology as origin myth. *Motivation and Emotion, 14,* 237–243.

Brigham, J. C., & Malpass, R. S. (1985). The role of experience and contact in the recognition of faces of own- and other-races persons. *Journal of Social Issues, 41,* 139–155.

Broadbent, D. A. (1958). *Perception and communication.* New York: Pergamon.

Brody, A. L., Saxena, S., Fairbanks, L. A., Alborzian, S., Demaree, H. A., Maidment, K. M., et al. (2000). Personality changes in adult subjects with major depressive disorder or obsessive-compulsive disorder treated with paroxetine. *Journal of Clinical Psychiatry, 61,* 349–355.

Brody, A. L., Saxena, S., Stoessel, P., Gillies, L. A., Fairbanks, L. A., Alborzian, S., et al. (2001). Regional brain metabolic changes in patients with major depression treated with either paroxetine or interpersonal therapy: Preliminary findings. *Archives of General Psychiatry, 58,* 631–640.

Brown, A. S. (1991). A review of the tip-of-the-tongue phenomenon. *Psychological Bulletin, 109,* 204–223.

Brown, B. B., Mounts, N., Lamborn, S. D., & Steinberg, L. (1993). Parenting practices and peer group affiliations in adolescence. *Child Development, 64,* 467–482.

Brown, G. W., & Harris, T. O. (1978). *Social origins of depression: A study of psychiatric disorders in women.* New York: The Free Press.

Brown, J. D., & Kobayashi, C. (2002). Self-enhancement in Japan and America. *Asian Journal of Social Psychology, 5,* 145–168.

Brown, J. L., & Pollitt, E. (1996). Malnutrition, poverty and intellectual development. *Scientific American, 274,* 38–43.

Brownell, C. A., & Brown, E. (1992). Peers and play in infants and toddlers. In V. Van Hasselt & M. Hersen (Eds.), *Handbook of social development: A lifespan perspective* (pp. 183–200). New York: Plenum.

Bruck, M. L., & Ceci, S. (1993). Amicus brief for the case of State of New Jersey v. Michaels. Presented by Committee of Concerned Social Scientists. Supreme Court of New Jersey docket no. 36,633. (Reprinted from *Psychology, Public Policy and Law* 1, 1995, 272–322.)

Bruer, J. (1999). *The myth of the first three years: A new understanding of early brain development and lifelong learning.* New York: Free Press.

Buckner, R. L., Kelley, W. M., & Petersen, S. E. (1999). Frontal cortex contributes to human memory formation. *Nature Neuroscience, 2,* 311–314.

Burian, S. E., Hensberry, R., & Liguori, A. (2003). Differential effects of alcohol and alcohol expectancy on risk-taking during simulated driving. *Clinical and Experimental Human Psychopharmacology Clinics, 18,* 175–184.

Burke, B. L., Arkowitz, H., & Menchola, M. (2003). The efficacy of motivational interviewing: A meta-analysis of controlled clinical trials. *Journal of Consulting and Clinical Psychology, 71,* 843–861.

Burman, B., & Margolin, G. (1992). Analysis of the association between marital relationships and health problems: An interactional perspective. *Psychological Bulletin, 112,* 39–63.

Bush, E. C., & Allman, J. M. (2004). The scaling of frontal cortex in primates and carnivore. *Proceedings of the National Academy of Sciences, 101,* 3962–3966.

Bushman, B. J., & Anderson, C. A. (2001). Media violence and the American public: Scientific facts versus media misinformation. *American Psychologist, 56,* 477–489.

Bushman, B. J., & Huesmann, L. R. (2001). Effects of televised violence on aggression. In D. G. Singer & J. L. Singer (Eds.), *Handbook of children and the media* (pp. 223–254). Thousand Oaks, CA: Sage.

Buss, A. H., & Plomin, R. (1984). *Temperament: Early developing personality traits.* Hillsdale, NJ: Erlbaum.

Buss, D. M. (1989). Sex differences in human mate preferences: Evolutionary hypotheses tested in 37 cultures. *Behavioral and Brain Sciences, 12,* 1–49.

Buss, D. M. (1995). Evolutionary psychology: A new paradigm for psychological science. *Psychological Inquiry, 6,* 1–30.

Buss, D. M. (1999a). Human nature and individual differences: The evolution of human personality. In L. A. Pervin & O. P. John (Eds.), *Handbook of personality: Theory and research* (pp. 31–56). New York: Guilford.

Buss, D. M. (2000). *The dangerous passion: Why jealousy is as necessary as love and sex.* New York: Free Press.

Buss, D. M., & Greiling, H. (1999). Adaptive individual differences. *Journal of Personality, 67,* 209–243.

Buss, D. M., & Schmitt, D. P. (1993). Sexual strategies theory: An evolutionary perspective on human mating. *Psychological Review, 100,* 204–232.

Cacioppo, J. T., Berntson, G. G., Sheridan, J. F., & McClintock, M. K. (2000). Multilevel integrative analyses of human behavior: Social neuroscience and the complementing nature of social and biological approaches. *Psychology Bulletin, 126,* 829–843.

Cacioppo, J. T., Klein, D. J., Berntson, G. C., & Hatfield, E. (1993). The psychophysiology of emotion. In M. Lewis & J. M. Haviland (Eds.), *Handbook of emotions* (pp. 119–142). New York: Guilford Press.

Cahill, L. (2003). Sex-related influences on the neurobiology of emotionally influenced memory. *Annals of the New York Academy of Sciences, 985,* 163–167.

Cahill, L., Haier, R. J., Fallon, J., Alkire, M. T., Tang, C., Keator, D., et al. (1996). Amygdala activity at encoding correlated with long-term, free recall of emotional information. *Proceedings of the*

National Academy of Sciences of the United States of America, 93, 8016–8021.

Cahill, L., Haier, R. J., White, N. S., Fallon, J., Kilpatrick, L., Lawrence, C., et al. (2001). Sex-related difference in amygdala activity during emotionally influenced memory storage. *Neurobiology of Learning and Memory, 75,* 1–9.

Cairns, R. B., & Cairns, B. D. (1994). *Lifelines and risks: Pathways of youth in our times.* Cambridge: Cambridge University Press.

Callaghan, T., Rochat, P., Lillard, A., Claux, M. L., Odden, H., Itakura, S., et al. (2005). Synchrony in the onset of mental-state reasoning: Evidence from five cultures. *Psychological Science, 16,* 378.

Campbell, W. K., & Sedikides, C. (1999). Self-threat magnifies the self-serving bias: A meta-analytic integration. *Review of General Psychology, 3,* 23–43.

Canli, T. (2004). Functional brain mapping of extraversion and neuroticism: Learning from individual differences in emotion processing. *Journal of Personality, 72,* 1105–1132.

Canli, T., Desmond, J. E., Zhao, Z., Gabrieli, J. D. (2002). Sex differences in the neural basis of emotional memories. *Proceedings of the National Academy of Sciences, 99,* 10789–10794.

Caporael, L. R. (2001). Evolutionary psychology: Toward a unifying theory and a hybrid science. *Annual Review of Psychology, 52,* 607–628.

Carmena, J. M., Lebdev, M. A., Crist, R. E., O'Doherty, J. E., Santucci, D. M., Dimitrov, D. F., et al. (2003). Learning to control a brain-machine interface for reaching and grasping by primates. *PLOS Biology, 1,* 193–208.

Carmody, T. P. (1993). Nicotine dependence: Psychological approaches to the prevention of smoking relapse. *Psychology of Addictive Behaviors, 7,* 96–102.

Caro, T. M., & Hauser, M. D. (1992). Is there teaching in nonhuman animals? *Quarterly Journal of Biology, 67,* 151–174.

Carstensen, L. L. (1995). Evidence for a life-span theory of socioemotional selectivity. *Current Directions in Psychological Science, 4,* 151–156.

Carter, C. S. (2003). Developmental consequences of oxytocin. *Physiology & Behavior, 74,* 383–397.

Caruso, S., Intelisano, G., Farina, M., Di Mari, L., & Agnello, C. (2003). The function of sildenafil on female sexual pathways: A double-blind, cross-over, placebo-controlled study. *European Journal of Obstetrics & Gynecology and Reproductive Biology, 110,* 201–206.

Carver, C. S., & Scheier, M. F. (1981). *Attention and self-regulation: A control theory approach to human behavior.* New York: Springer-Verlag.

Carver, C. S., & Scheier, M. F. (1998). *On the self-regulation of behavior.* New York: Cambridge University Press.

Case, R. (1992). The role of the frontal lobes in development. *Brain and Cognition, 20* (1), 51–73.

Caspi, A. (2000). The child is father of the man: Personality continuities from childhood to adulthood. *Journal of Personality and Social Psychology, 78,* 158–172.

Caspi, A., & Herbener, E. S. (1990). Continuity and change: Assortative marriage and the consistency of personality in adulthood. *Journal of Personality and Social Psychology, 58,* 250–258.

Caspi, A., McClay, J., Moffit, T. E., Mill, J., Martin, J., Craig, I. W., et al. (2002). Role of genotype in the cycle of violence in maltreated children. *Science, 29,* 851–854.

Castellanos, F. X., Giedd, J. N., Eckberg, P., & Marsh, W. L. (1998). Quantitative morphology of the caudate nucleus in attention deficit hyperactivity disorder. *American Journal of Psychiatry, 151,* 1791–1796.

Cattell, R. B. (1971). *Abilities: Their structure, growth, and action.* Boston: Houghton Mifflin.

Ceci, S. J. (1999). Schooling and intelligence. In S. J. Ceci & Wendy M. Williams (Eds.), *The nature-nurture debate: The essential readings* (pp.168–175). Oxford, UK: Blackwell.

Ceci, S. J., & Bruck, M. (1995). *Jeopardy in the courtroom: A scientific analysis of children's testimony.* Washington, DC: American Psychological Association.

Chabris, C. (1999). Prelude or requiem for the "Mozart effect"? *Nature, 400,* 826–827.

Chambers, D. W. (1983). Stereotypic images of the scientist: The Draw-a-Scientist-Test. *Science Education, 67,* 255–265.

Chapman, P. R., & Underwood, G. (1998). Visual search of driving situations: Danger and experience. *Perception, 27,* 951–964.

Charles, S. T., Mather, M., & Carstensen L. L. (2003). Aging and emotional memory: The forgettable nature of negative images for older adults. *Journal of Experimental Psychology: General, 132,* 310–324.

Chase, W. G., & Simon, H. A. (1973). Perception in chess. *Cognitive Psychology, 4,* 55–81.

Chassin, L., Presson, C. C., & Sherman, S. J. (1990). Social psychological contributions to the understanding and prevention of adolescent cigarette smoking. *Personality and Social Psychology Bulletin, 16,* 133–151.

Cherry, E. C. (1953). Some experiments on the recognition of speech, with one and two ears. *Journal of the Acoustic Society of America, 25,* 975–979.

Chesher, G., & Greeley, J. (1992). Tolerance to the effects of alcohol. *Alcohol, Drugs, and Driving, 8,* 93–106.

Chess, S., & Thomas, A. (1984). *Origins and evolution of behavior disorders: From infancy to early adult life.* Cambridge, MA: Harvard University Press.

Childress, A. R., Mozley, D., McElgin, W., Fitzgerald, J., Reivich, M., & O'Brien, P. C. (1999). Limbic activation during cue-induced cocaine craving. *American Journal of Psychiatry, 156,* 11–18.

Chistyakov, A. V., Kaplan, B., Rubichek, O., Kreinin, I., Koren, D., Feinsod, M., et al. (2004). Antidepressant effects of different schedules of repetitive transcranial magnetic stimulation vs. clomipramine in patients with major depression: Relationship to changes in cortical excitability. *International Journal of Neuropsychopharmacology, 8,* 223–233.

Choi, I., Dalal, R., Kim-Prieto, C., & Park, H. (2003). Culture and judgment of causal relevance. *Journal of Personality and Social Psychology, 84,* 46–59.

Choleris, E., Gustafsson, J. A., Korach, K. S., Muglia, L. J., Pfaff, D. W., & Ogawa, S. (2003). An estrogen-dependent four-gene micronet regulating social recognition: A study with oxytocin and estrogen receptor-alpha and -beta knockout mice. *Proceedings of the National Academy of Sciences, 100,* 6192–6197.

Christianson, S. (1992). Emotional stress and eyewitness memory: A critical review. *Psychological Bulletin, 112,* 284–309.

Cialdini, R. B., Shaller, M., Houlihan, D., Arps, K., Fultz, J., & Beaman, A. L. (1987). Empathy-based helping: Is it selflessly or selfishly motivated? *Journal of Personality and Social Psychology, 52,* 749–758.

Clark, A. C., & Watson, D. (1999). Temperament: A new paradigm for trait psychology. In L. A. Pervin & O. P. John (Eds.), *Handbook of personality: Theory and research* (pp. 399–423). New York: Guilford.

Clark, R. D., & Hatfield, E. (1989). Gender differences in receptivity to sexual offers. *Journal of Psychology and Human Sexuality, 2,* 39–55.

Clarke-Stewart, K. A., Vandell, D. L., McCartney, K., Owen, M. T., & Booth, C. (2000). Effects of parental separation and divorce on very young children. *Journal of Family Psychology, 14,* 304–326.

Cloninger, C., Adolfsson, R., & Svrakic, N. (1996). Mapping genes for human personality. *Nature and Genetics, 12,* 3–4.

Cohen, D., Nisbett, R. E., Bowdle, B. F., & Schwarz, N. (1996). Insult, aggression, and the southern culture of honor: An "experimental ethnography." *Journal of Personality and Social Psychology, 70,* 945–960.

Cohen, S., Tyrrell, D. A. J., & Smith, A. P. (1991). Psychological stress and susceptibility to the common cold. *The New England Journal of Medicine, 325,* 606–612.

Cohen, S., & Wills, T. A. (1985). Stress, social support, and the buffering hypothesis. *Psychological Bulletin, 98,* 310–357.

Colcombe, S. J., Kramer, A. F., Erickson, K. I., Scalf, P., McAuley, E., Cohen, N. J., et al. (2004). Cardiovascular fitness, cortical plasticity, and aging. *Proceedings of the National Academy of Sciences, 101,* 316–321.

Conway, A. R. A., Kane, M. J., & Engle, R. W. (2003). Working memory capacity and its relation to general intelligence. *Trends in Cognitive Sciences, 7,* 547–552.

Conway, M. A., Anderson, S. J., Larsen, S. F., Donnelly, C. M., McDaniel, M. A., McClelland, A. G. R., et al. (1994). The formation of flashbulb memories. *Memory and Cognition, 22,* 326–343.

Conway, M., & Ross, M. (1984). Getting what you want by revising what you had. *Journal of Personality and Social Psychology, 47,* 738–748.

Cook, M., & Mineka, S. (1989). Observational conditioning of fear to fear-relevant versus fear-irrelevant stimuli in rhesus monkeys. *Journal of Abnormal Psychology, 98,* 448–459.

Cooney, J., & Gazzaniga, M.S. (2003). Neurological disorders and the structure of human consciousness. *Trends in Cognitive Sciences, 7,* 161–165.

Cooper, L. A., & Shepard, R. N. (1973). Chronometric studies of the rotation of mental images. In W. G. Chase (Ed.), *Visual information processing* (pp. 75–176). New York: Academic Press.

Coopersmith, S. (1967). *The antecedents of self-esteem.* San Francisco: Freeman.

Corder, E. H., Saunders, A. M., Strittmatter, W. J., Schmechel, D. E., Gaskell, P. C., Small, G. W., et al. (1993). Gene dose of apolipoprotein E type 4 allele and the risk of Alzheimer's disease in late onset families. *Science, 261,* 921–923.

Corkin, S., Amaral, D. G., Gonzalez, R. G., Johnson, K. A., & Hyman, B. T. (1997). H. M.'s medial temporal lobe lesion: Findings from magnetic resonance imaging. *Journal of Neuroscience, 17,* 3964–3979.

Correll, C. U., Leucht, S., & Kane, J. M. (2004). Lower risk for tardive dyskinesia associated with second-generation antipsychotics: A systematic review of 1-year studies. *American Journal of Psychiatry, 161,* 414–425.

Cosmides, L., & Tooby, J. (2000). The cognitive neuroscience of social reasoning. In M. S. Gazzaniga (Ed.), *The new cognitive neurosciences* (pp.1259–1270). Cambridge, MA: MIT Press.

Cosmides, L., & Tooby, J. (2001). Evolutionary psychology: A primer. Retrieved May 24, 2002 from http://www.psych.ucsb.edu/research/cep/primer.html

Costa, P. T., & McCrae, R. R. (1992). *Revised NEO Personality Inventory (NEO-PI-R) and NEO Five-Factor Inventory (NEO-FFI) professional manual.* Odessa, FL: Psychological Assessment Resources.

Courchesne, E., Redcay, E., & Kennedy, D. P. (2004). The autistic brain: Birth through adulthood. *Current Opinion in Neurology, 17,* 489–496.

Cowan, N. (2001). The magical number 4 in short-term memory: A reconsideration of mental storage capacity. *Behavioral and Brain Sciences, 24,* 87–114.

Cowley, J. J., & Brooksbank, L. B. W. (1991). Human exposure to putative pheromones and changes in aspects of social behavior. *Journal of Steroid Biochemistry and Molecular Biology, 39,* 647–659.

Craft, L. L., & Perna, F. M. (2004). The benefits of exercise for the clinically depressed. *Journal of Clinical Psychiatry, 6,* 104–111.

Crocker, J., & Major, B. (1989). Social stigma and self-esteem: The self-protective properties of stigma. *Psychological Review, 96,* 608–630.

Crosnoe, R., & Elder, G. H. (2002). Successful adaptation in the later years: A life-course approach to aging. *Social Psychology Quarterly, 65,* 309–328.

Crowe, R. R. (2000). Molecular genetics of anxiety disorders. In D. S. Charney, E. J. Nestler, & B. S. Bunney (Eds.), *Neurobiology of mental illness* (pp. 451–462). New York: Oxford University Press.

Crundall, D., Chapman, P., Phelps, N., & Underwood, G. (2003). Eye movements and hazard perception in police pursuit and emergency response driving. *Journal of Experimental Psychology: Applied, 9,* 163–174.

Culler, E. A., Coakley, J. D., Lowy, K., & Gross, N. (1943). A revised frequency-map of the Guinea-pig cochlea. *American Journal of Psychology, 56,* 475–500.

Cunningham, M. R., Barbee, A. P., & Druen, P. B. (1996). Social allergens and the reactions they produce: Escalation of annoyance and disgust in love and work. In R. M. Kowalski (Ed.), *Aversive interpersonal behaviors* (pp. 189–214). New York: Plenum Press.

Cunningham, M. R., Roberts, A. R., Barbee, A. P. Druen, P. B., & Wu, C. (1995). Their ideas of beauty are, on the whole, the same as ours: Consistency and variability in the cross-cultural perception of female physical attractiveness. *Journal of Personality & Social Psychology, 68,* 261–279.

Cunningham, W. A., Johnson, M. K., Raye, C. L., Gatenby, J. C., Gore, J. C., & Banaji, M. R. (2004). Separable neural components in the processing of black and white faces. *Psychological Science, 15,* 806–813.

Cupach, W. R., & Metts, S. (1990). Remedial processes in embarrassing predicaments. In J. Anderson (Ed.), *Communication yearbook* (pp. 323–352). Newbury Park, CA: Sage.

Curtis, C. E., & D'Esposito, M. (2003). Persistent activity in the prefrontal cortex during working memory. *Trends in Cognitive Sciences, 7,* 415–423.

Curtiss, S. (1977). *Genie: a psycholinguistic study of a modern day "wild child."* New York: Academic Press.

Cutler, W. B., Friedmann, E., & McCoy, N. L (1998). Pheromonal influences on sociosexual behavior in men. *Archives of Sexual Behavior, 27,* 1–13.

Dabbs, J. M., & Morris, R. (1990). Testosterone, social class, and antisocial behavior in a sample of 4462 men. *Psychological Science, 1,* 209–211.

Dalton, M. A., Bernhardt, A. M., Gibson, J. J., Sargent, J. D., Beach, M. L., Adachi-Mejia, A. M., et al. (2005). "Honey, have some smokes." Preschoolers use cigarettes and alcohol while role playing as adults. *Archives of Pediatrics & Adolescent Medicine, 159,* 854–859.

Dalton, M. A., Sargent, J. D., Beach, M., Ahrens, M. B., Tickle, J., & Heatherton, T. F. (2003). Effect of viewing smoking in movies on adolescent smoking initiation: A cohort study. *Lancet, 362,* 281–285.

Damasio, A. R. (1994). *Descartes' error*. New York: Avon Books.

Damasio, H., Grabowski, T., Frank, R., Galaburda, A. M., & Damasio, A. R. (1994). The return of Phineas Gage: Clues about the brain from the skull of a famous patient. *Science, 264,* 1102–1105.

Darley, J. M., & Batson, C. D. (1973). "From Jerusalem to Jericho": A study of situational and dispositional variables in helping behavior. *Journal of Personality and Social Psychology, 27,* 100–108.

Darwin, F. (Ed.). (1887). *The life and letters of Charles Darwin*. London: Murray.

Dasgupta, A. G., & Greenwald, A. G. (2001). Exposure to admired group members reduces automatic intergroup bias. *Journal of Personality and Social Psychology, 81,* 800–814.

Davidson, J. R., Foa, E. B., Huppert, J. D., Keefe, F. J., Franklin, M. E., Compton, J. S., et al. (2004). Fluoxetine, comprehensive cognitive behavioral therapy, and placebo in generalized social phobia. *Archives of General Psychiatry, 61,* 1005–1013.

Davidson, R. J. (2000a). Affective style, psychopathology, and resilience: Brain mechanisms and plasticity. *American Psychologist, 55,* 1196–1214.

Davidson, R. J. (2000b). The functional neuroanatomy of affective style. In R. D. Lane & L. Nadel (Eds.), *Cognitive neuroscience of emotion* (pp. 371–388). New York: Oxford University Press.

Davis, J. O., Phelps, J. A., & Bracha, H. S. (1995). Prenatal development of monozygotic twins and concordance for schizophrenia. *Schizophrenia Bulletin, 21,* 357–366.

Davis, K. L., Stewart, D. G., Friedman, J. I., Buchsbaum, M., Harvey, P. D., Hof, P. R., et al. (2003). White matter changes in schizophrenia: Evidence for myelin-related dysfunction. *Archives of General Psychiatry, 60,* 443–456.

Davis, M. (1997). Neurobiology of fear responses: The role of the amygdala. *Journal of Neuropsychological and Clinical Neuroscience, 9,* 382–402.

Davison, K., & Pennebaker, J. (1996). Social psychosomatics. In E. T. Higgins & A. W. Kruglanski (Eds.), *Social psychology: Handbook of basic principles* (pp. 102–130). New York: Guilford.

Deacon, B. J., & Abramowitz, J. S. (2004). Cognitive and behavioral treatments for anxiety disorders: A review of meta-analytic findings. *Journal of Clinical Psychology, 60,* 429–441.

Deary, I. J. (2000). *Looking down on human intelligence*. New York: Oxford University Press.

Deary, I. J. (2001). *Intelligence: A very short introduction*. New York: Oxford University Press.

Deary, I. J., & Caryl, P. G. (1997). Neuroscience and human intelligence differences. *Trends in Neuroscience, 20,* 365–371.

Deary, I. J., & Der, G. (2005). Reaction time explains IQ's association with death. *Psychological Science, 16,* 64–69.

Deaux, K., & Major, B. (1987). Putting gender into context: An interactive model of gender-related behavior. *Psychological Review, 94,* 369–389.

Debiec, J., LeDoux, J. E., & Nader, K. (2002). Cellular and systems consolidation in the hippocampus. *Neuron, 36,* 527–538.

DeCasper, A. J., & Fifer, W. P. (1980). Of human bonding: Newborns prefer their mothers' voices. *Science, 208,* 1174–1176.

DeCasper, A. J., & Spence, M. J. (1986). Prenatal maternal speech influences newborn's perception of speech sounds. *Infant Behavior and Development, 9,* 133–150.

Deci, E. L., & Ryan, R. M. (1987). The support of autonomy and the control of behavior. *Journal of Personality and Social Psychology, 53,* 1024–1037.

Dejong, W., & Kleck, R. E. (1986). The social psychological effects of overweight. In C. P. Herman, M. P. Zanna, & E. T. Higgins (Eds.), *Physical appearance, stigma and social behavior: The Ontario Symposium* (pp. 65–87). Hillsdale, NJ: Erlbaum.

Demir, E., & Dickson, B. J. (2005). *Fruitless*. Splicing specifies male courtship behavior in *Drosophila. Cell, 121,* 785–794.

Dennerstein, L., & Burrows, G. D. (1982). Hormone replacement therapy and sexuality in women. *Clinics in Endocrinology and Metabolism, 11,* 661–679.

Denys, D., Zohar, J., & Westenberg, H. G. (2004). The role of dopamine in obsessive-compulsive disorder: Preclinical and clinical evidence. *Journal of Clinical Psychiatry, 65,* 11–17.

Depue, R. A., & Collins, P. F. (1999). Neurobiology of the structure of personality: Dopamine, facilitation of incentive motivation, and extraversion. *Behavioral and Brain Sciences, 22,* 491–569.

Devine, P. G. (1989). Stereotypes and prejudice: Their automatic and controlled components. *Journal of Personality and Social Psychology, 56,* 5–18.

Diamond, A., & Doar, B. (1989). The performance of human infants on a measure of frontal cortex function, delayed response task. *Developmental Psychobiology, 22,* 271–294.

Dickson, P. R., & Vaccarino, F. J. (1994). GRF-induced feeding: Evidence for protein selectivity and opiate involvement. *Peptides, 15*, 1343–1352.

Diener, E. (1979). Deindividuation, self-awareness, and disinhibition. *Journal of Personality and Social Psychology, 37*, 1160–1171.

Diener, E. (2000). Subjective well-being: The science of happiness and a proposal for a national index. *American Psychologist, 55*, 34–43.

Diener, E., Wolsic, B., & Fujita, F. (1995). Physical attractiveness and subjective well-being. *Journal of Personality and Social Psychology, 69*, 120–129.

Dijksterhuis, A. (2004). Think different: The merits of unconscious thought in preference development and decision making. *Journal of Personality and Social Psychology, 87*, 586–598.

Dijksterhuis, A., & van Knippenberg, A. (1998). The relation between perception and behavior, or how to win a game of trivial pursuit, *Journal of Personality & Social Psychology, 74*, 865–877.

Docherty, N. M. (2005). Cognitive impairments and disordered speech in schizophrenia: Thought disorder, disorganization, and communication failure perspectives. *Journal of Abnormal Psychology, 114*, 269–278.

Dohrenwend, B. P., Shrout, P. E., Link, B. G., Skodol, A. E., & Martin, J. L. (1986). Overview and initial results from a risk factor study of depression and schizophrenia. In J. E. Barrett (Ed.), *Mental disorders in the community: Progress and challenge*. New York: Guilford Press.

Dolan, R. J. (2000). Emotion processing in the human brain revealed through functional neuroimaging. In M. S. Gazzaniga (Ed.), *The new cognitive neurosciences* (pp. 115–131). Cambridge, MA: MIT Press.

Dolcos, F., LaBar, K. S., & Cabeza, R. (2004). Dissociable effects of arousal and valence on prefrontal activity indexing emotional evaluation and subsequent memory: An event-related fMRI study. *Neuroimage, 23*, 64–74.

Dolcos, F., Labar, K. S., & Cabeza, R. (2005). Remembering one year later: Role of the amygdala and the medial temporal lobe system in retrieving emotional memories. *Proceedings of the National Academy of Sciences, 102*, 2626–2631.

Donahue, A. B. (2000). Electroconvulsive therapy and memory loss: A personal journey. *Journal of ECT, 16*, 133–143.

Dovidio, J. F., ten Vergert, M., Stewart, T. L., Gaertner, S. L., Johnson, J. D., Esses, V. M., et al. (2004). Perspective and prejudice: Antecedents and mediating mechanisms. *Personality and Social Psychology Bulletin, 30*, 1537–1549.

Drummond, S. P., Brown, G. G., Gillin, J. C., Stricker, J. L., Wong, E. C., & Buxton, R. B. (2000). Altered brain response to verbal learning following sleep deprivation. *Nature, 403*, 655–657.

Dugatkin, L. A. (2004). *Principles of animal behavior*. New York: Norton.

Duncan, J., Burgess, P., & Emslie, H. (1995). Fluid intelligence after frontal lobe lesions. *Neuropsychologia, 33*, 261–268.

Duncan, J., Seitz, R. J., Kolodny, J., Bor, D., Herzog, H., Ahmed, A., et al. (2000). A neural basis for general intelligence. *Science, 289*, 457–460.

Duncker, K. (1945). On problem solving. *Psychological Monographs, 58*, (5, Whole No. 70).

Dunn, J. (2004). Annotation: Children's relationships with their nonresident fathers. *Journal of Child Psychology and Psychiatry, 45*, 659–671.

Dutton, D. G., & Aron, A. P. (1974). Some evidence for heightened sexual attraction under conditions of high anxiety. *Journal of Personality and Social Psychology, 30*, 510–517.

Dykman, B. M., Horowitz, L. M., Abramson, L. Y., & Usher, M. (1991). Schematic and situational determinants of depressed and nondepressed students' interpretation of feedback. *Journal of Abnormal Psychology, 100*, 45–55.

Eacott, M. J. (1999). Memory for the events of early childhood. *Current Directions in Psychological Science, 8*, 46–49.

Eaker, E. D., Sullivan, L. M., Kelly-Hayes, M., D'Agostino, R. B., Sr., & Benjamin, E. J. (2004). Anger and hostility predict the development of atrial fibrillation in men in the Framingham Offspring Study. *Circulation, 109*, 1267–1271.

Eberhardt, J. L., Goff, P. A., Purdie, V. J., & Davies, P. G. (2004). Seeing black: Race, crime, and visual processing. *Journal of Personality and Social Psychology, 87*, 876–893.

Egeland, J. A., Gerhard, D. S., Pauls, D. L., Sussex, J. N., Kidd, K. K., Allen, C. R., et al. (1987). Bipolar affective disorders linked to DNA markers on chromosome 11. *Nature, 325*, 783–787.

Eich, J. E., Weingartner, H., Stillman, R. C., & Gillin, J. C. (1975). State-dependent accessibility of retrieval cues in the retention of a categorized list. *Journal of Verbal Learning and Verbal Behavior, 14*, 408–417.

Eichenbaum, H. (2001). The hippocampus and declarative memory: Cognitive mechanisms and neural codes. Behavioural *and Brain Research, 127,* 199–207.

Eichenbaum, H. B., Cahill, L., Gluck, M., Hasselmo, M., Keil, F., Martin, A., et al. (1999). Learning and memory: Systems analysis. In M. J. Zigmond, F. E. Bloom, S. C. Landis, J. L. Roberts, & L. R. Squire (Eds.), *Fundamental neuroscience* (pp. 1455–1486). San Diego, CA: Academic Press.

Eimas, P. D., Siqueland, E. R., Jusczyk, P., & Vigorito, J. (1971). Speech perception in infants. *Science, 171*, 303–306.

Eisenberg, N. (2000). Emotion, regulation, and moral development. *Annual Review of Psychology, 51*, 665–697.

Ekelund, J., Lichtermann, D., Jaervelin, M., & Peltonen, L. (1999). Association between novelty seeking and type 4 dopamine receptor gene in a large Finnish cohort sample. *American Journal of Psychiatry, 156*, 1453–1455.

Ekman, P., & Friesen, W. V. (1971). Constants across cultures in the face and emotion. *Journal of Personality and Social Psychology, 17*, 124–129.

Ekman, P., & Friesen, W. V. (1975). *Unmasking the face: A guide to recognizing emotions from facial clues*. Englewood Cliffs, NJ: Prentice Hall.

Ekman, P., Levenson, R. W., & Friesen, W. V. (1983). Autonomic nervous system activity distinguishes among emotions. *Science, 221*, 1208–1210.

Ekman, P., Sorenson, E. R., & Friesen, W. V. (1969). Pan-cultural elements in facial displays of emotions. *Science, 164*, 86–88.

Ekselius, L., & von Knorring, L. (1999). Changes in personality traits during treatment with sertraline or citalopram. *British Journal of Psychiatry, 174*, 444–448.

Elfenbein, H. A., & Ambady, N. (2002). On the universality of cultural specificity of emotion recognition: A meta-analysis. *Psychological Bulletin, 128,* 203–235.

Ellis, B. J., Bates, J. E., Dodge, K. A., Fergusson, D. M., Horwood, L. J., Pettit, G. S., et al. (2003). Does father absence place daughters at special risk for early sexual activity and teenage pregnancy? *Child Development, 74,* 801–821.

Emslie, G. J., Rush, A. J., Weinberg, W. A., Kowatch, R. A., Hughes, C. W., Carmody, T., et al. (1997). A double-blind, randomized, placebo-controlled trial of fluoxetine in children and adolescents with depression. *Archives of General Psychiatry, 54,* 1031–1037.

Endo, Y., & Meijer, Z. (2004). Autobiographical memory of success and failure experiences. In Y. Kashima, Y. Endo, E. S. Kashima, C. Leung, & J. McClure (Eds.), *Progress in Asian social psychology: Vol. 4* (pp. 67–84). Seoul, Korea: Kyoyook-Kwahak-Sa Publishing Company.

Engle, R. W., & Kane, M. J. (2004). Executive attention, working memory capacity, and a two-factor theory of cognitive control. In B. Ross (Ed.), *The psychology of learning and motivation* (pp. 145–199). New York: Academic Press.

Engle, R. W., Tuholski, S. W., Laughlin, J. E., & Conway, A. R. A. (1999). Working memory, short-term memory, and general fluid intelligence: A latent variable approach. *Journal of Experimental Psychology: General, 128,* 309–331.

Enns, J. (2005). *The thinking eye, the seeing brain.* New York: Norton.

Epperson, C. N., McDougle, C. J., Brown, R. M., Leckman, J. F., Goodman, W. K., & Price, L. H. (1995). OCD during pregnancy and the puerperium [Abstract]. *American Psychiatric Association New Research Abstracts, 84,* NR112.

Era, P., Jokela, J., & Heikkinen, E. (1986). Reaction and movement times in men of different ages: A population study. *Perceptual and Motor Skills, 63,* 111–130.

Erikson, E. H. (1968). *Identity: Youth and crisis.* New York: Norton.

Eriksson, P. S., Perfilieva, E., Bjork-Eriksson, T., Alborn, A. M., Nordborg, C., Peterson, D. A., et al. (1998). Neurogenesis in the adult human hippocampus. *Nature Medicine, 4,* 1313–1317.

Erk, S., Spitzer, M., Wunderlich, A. P., Galley, L., & Walter, H. (2002). Cultural objects modulate reward circuitry. *Neuroreport, 13,* 2499–2503.

Eron, L. D. (1987). The development of aggressive behavior from the perspective of a developing behaviorism. *American Psychologist, 42,* 435–442.

Evers, S., & Suhr, B. (2000). Changes of the neurotransmitter serotonin but not of hormones during short time music perception. *European Archives of Psychiatry and Clinical Neuroscience, 250,* 144–147.

Eysenck, M. W., Mogg, K., May, J., Richards, A., & Matthews, A. (1991). Bias in interpretation of ambiguous sentences related to threat in anxiety. *Journal of Abnormal Psychology, 100,* 144–150.

Fagerström, K. O., & Schneider, N. G. (1989). Measuring nicotine dependence: A review of the Fagerström Tolerance Questionnaire. *Journal of Behavioral Medicine, 12,* 159–181.

Fallon, A. E., & Rozin, P. (1985). Sex differences in perceptions of desirable body shape. *Journal of Abnormal Psychology, 94,* 102–105.

Fantz, R. L. (1966). Pattern discrimination and selective attention as determinants of perceptual development from birth. In A. H. Kidd & L. J. Rivoire (Eds.), *Perceptual development in children.* New York: International Universities Press.

Farah, M. J. (1996). Is face recognition "special"? Evidence from neuropsychology. *Behavioural Brain Research, 76,* 181–189.

Farah, M. J., Levine, D. N., & Calvanio, R. (1988). A case study of mental imagery deficit. *Brain and Cognition, 8,* 147–164.

Fawcett, J. (1992). Suicide risk factors in depressive disorders and in panic disorders. *Journal of Clinical Psychiatry, 53,* 9–13.

Fazio, R. H. (1995). Attitudes as object-evaluation associations: Determinants, consequences, and correlates of attitude accessibility. In R. E. Petty & J. A. Krosnick (Eds.), *Attitude strength: Antecedents and consequences* (pp. 247–282). Hillsdale, NJ: Erlbaum.

Fazio, R. H., Eisner, J. R., & Shook, N. J. (2004). Attitude formation through exploration: Valence asymmetries. *Journal of Personality and Social Psychology, 87,* 293–311.

Feldman Barrett, L., Lane, R. D., Sechrest, L., & Schwartz, G. E. (2000). Sex differences in emotional awareness. *Personality and Social Psychology Bulletin, 26,* 1027–1035.

Ferguson, J. N., Young, L. J., Hearn, E. F., Matzuk, M. M., Insel, T. R., & Winslow, J. T. (2000). Social amnesia in mice lacking the oxytocin gene. *Nature Neuroscience, 25,* 284–288.

Ferguson, M. J., & Bargh, J. A. (2004). How social perception can automatically influence behavior. *Trends in Cognitive Science, 8,* 33–39.

Ferguson, T. J., & Stegge, H. (1995). Emotional states and traits in children: The case of guilt and shame. In J. P. Tangney & K. W. Fischer (Eds.), *Self-conscious emotions* (pp. 174–197). New York: Guilford.

Ferrari, P. F., Gallese, V., Rizzolatti, G., & Fogassi, L. (2003). Mirror neurons responding to the observation of ingestive and communicative mouth actions in the monkey ventral premotor cortex. *European Journal of Neuroscience, 17,* 1703–1714.

Festinger, L. (1954). A theory of social comparison processes. *Human Relations, 7,* 117–140.

Festinger, L. (1987). A personal memory. In N. E. Grunberg, R. E. Nisbett, J. Rodin, & J. E. Singer (Eds.), *A distinctive approach to psychological research: The influence of Stanley Schachter* (pp. 1–9). New York: Erlbaum.

Festinger, L., & Carlsmith, J. M. (1959). Cognitive consequences of forced compliance. *Journal of Abnormal and Social Psychology, 58,* 203–210.

Festinger, L., Schachter, S., & Back, K. W. (1950). *Social pressures in informal groups.* New York: Harper.

Field, T., Fox, N. A., Pickens, J., & Nawrocki, T. (1995). Relative right frontal EEG activation in 3- to 6-month-old infants of "depressed" mothers. *Developmental Psychology, 31,* 358–363.

Fillipek, P. A., Semrud-Clikeman, M., Steingard, R. J., Renshaw, P. F., Kennedy, D. N., & Biederman, J. (1997). Volumetric MRI analysis comparing subjects having attention deficit hyperactivity disorder with normal controls. *Neurology, 48,* 589–600.

Fine, I., Wade, A. R., Brewer, A. A., May, M. G., Goodman, D. F., Boynton, G. M., et al. (2003). Long-term deprivation affects visual perception and cortex. *Nature Neuroscience, 6,* 915–916.

Finger, S. (1994). *Origins of neuroscience.* Oxford, UK: Oxford University Press.

Fink, M. (2001). Convulsive therapy: A review of the first 55 years. *Journal of Affective Disorders, 63* (1–3), 1–15.

Fire, A., Xu, S., Montgomery, M. K., Kostas, S. A., Driver, S. E., & Mello, C. C. (1998). Potent and specific genetic interference by double-stranded RNA in Canorhabditis elegans, *Nature, 391,* 806.

Fischer, K. (1980). A theory of cognitive development: The control and construction of hierarchies of skills. *Psychological Review, 87,* 477–531.

Fisher, W. A., Byrne, D., White, L. A., & Kelley, K. (1988). Erotophobia-erotophilia as a dimension of personality. *Journal of Sex Research, 25,* 123–151.

Fitzgerald, P. B., Brown, T. L., Marston, N. A., Daskalakis, Z. J., De Castella, A., & Kulkarni, J. (2003). Transcranial magnetic stimulation in the treatment of depression: A double-blind, placebo-controlled trial. *Archives of General Psychiatry, 60,* 1002–1008.

Flynn, J. R. (1981). The mean IQ of Americans: Massive gains 1932 to 1978. *Psychological Bulletin, 95,* 29–51.

Flynn, J. R. (1987). Massive IQ gains in 14 nations: What IQ tests really measure. *Psychological Bulletin, 101,* 171–191.

Foa, E. B., Liebowitz, M. R., Kozak, M. J., Davies, S., Campeas, R., Franklin, M. E., et al. (2005). Randomized, placebo-controlled trial of exposure and ritual prevention, clomipramine, and their combination in the treatment of obsessive-compulsive disorder. *American Journal of Psychiatry, 162,* 151–161.

Foley, K. M. (1993). Opioids. *Neurologic Clinics, 11,* 503–522.

Folkman, S., & Moskowitz, J. T. (2000). Positive affect and the other side of coping. *American Psychologist, 55,* 647–654.

Forgas, J. P. (1998). Asking nicely: Mood effects on responding to more or less polite requests. *Personality and Social Psychology Bulletin, 24,* 173–185.

Fouad, N. A., & Walker, C. M. (2005). Cultural influences on responses to items on the strong interest inventory. *Journal of Vocational Behavior, 66,* 104–123.

Fox, N. A., Henderson, H. A., Marshall, P. J., Nichols, K. E., & Ghera, M. M. (2005). Behavioral inhibition: Linking biology and behavior within a developmental framework. *Annual Review of Psychology, 56,* 235–262.

Fox, R., Aslin, R. N., Shea, S. L., & Dumais, S. T. (1980). Stereopsis in human infants. *Science, 207,* 323–324.

Fraley, R. C., & Shaver, P. R. (2000). Adult romantic attachment: Theoretical developments, emerging controversies, and unanswered questions. *Review of General Psychology, 4,* 132–154.

Frangou, S., Chitins, X., & Williams, S. C. (2004). Mapping IQ and gray matter density in healthy young people. *Neuroimage, 23,* 800–805.

Frank, E., Kupfer, D., Perel, I., Comes, C., Jarret, D., Mallinger, A., et al. (1990). Three-year outcomes for maintenance therapies in recurrent depression. *Archives of General Psychiatry, 47,* 1093–1099.

Franken, R. E. (1998). *Human motivation.* Pacific Grove, CA: Brooks Cole.

Fratiglioni, L., Paillard-Borg, S., & Winblad, B. (2004). An active and socially integrated lifestyle in late life might protect against dementia. *Lancet Neurology, 3,* 343–353.

Fredrickson, B. L. (2001). The role of positive emotions in positive psychology: The broaden-and-build theory of positive emotions. *American Psychologist, 56,* 218–226.

Freedman, J. L. (1984). Effects of television violence on aggression. *Psychological Bulletin, 96,* 227–246.

Frijda, N. H. (1994). Emotions are functional, most of the time. In P. Ekman & R. J. Davidson (Eds.), *The nature of emotion: Fundamental questions. Series in affective science* (pp. 112–122). New York: Oxford University Press.

Frincke, J. L., & Pate, W. E. (2004). Yesterday, today, and tomorrow. Careers in psychology: 2004. What students need to know. Presented at the Annual Convention of the Southeastern Psychology Association, March, Atlanta, GA. Available at http://research.apa.org/

Funder, D. C. (1995). On the accuracy of personality judgment: A realistic approach. *Psychological Review, 102,* 652–670.

Funder, D. C. (2001). Personality. *Annual Review of Psychology, 52,* 197–221.

Fung, H. H., & Carstensen, L. L. (2004). Motivational changes in response to blocked goals and foreshortened time: Testing alternatives to socioemotional selectivity theory. *Psychology and Aging, 19,* 68–78.

Fung, M. T., Raine, A., Loeber, R., Lynam, D. R., Steinhauer, S. R., Venables, P. D., et al. (2005). Reduced electrodermal activity in psychopathy-prone adolescents. *Journal of Abnormal Psychology, 114,* 187–196.

Gallistel, C. R. (2000). The replacement of general-purpose learning models with adaptively specialized learning modules. In M. S. Gazzaniga (Ed.), *The new cognitive neurosciences* (pp. 1179–1191). Cambridge, MA: MIT Press.

Gallup Organization (1995). *Disciplining children in America: A Gallup poll report.* Princeton, NH: Author.

Gangestad, S. W., Simpson, J. A., Cousins, A. J., Garver-Apgar, C. E., & Christensen, P. N. (2004). Women's preferences for male behavioral displays change across the menstrual cycle. *Psychological Science, 15,* 203–207.

Garcia, J., & Koelling, R. A. (1966). Relation of cue to consequence in avoidance learning. *Psychonomic Science, 4,* 123–124.

Gardner, H. (1983). *Frames of mind: The theory of multiple intelligences.* New York: Basic Books.

Gardner, W. L., & Martinko, M. J. (1996). Using the Myers-Briggs Type Indicator to study managers: A literature review and research agenda. *Journal of Management, 22,* 45–83.

Gardner, W. L., Pickett, C. L., & Brewer, M. B. (2000). Social exclusion and selective memory: How the need to belong affects memory for social information. *Personality and Social Psychology Bulletin, 26,* 486–496.

Garlick, D. (2002). Understanding the nature of the general factor of intelligence: The role of individual differences in neural plasticity as an explanatory mechanism. *Psychological Review, 109,* 116–136.

Gazette: Monkeys move matter, mentally. (2004). *Duke Magazine, 90.* Retrieved September 21, 2005, from http://www.dukemagazine.duke.edu/dukemag/issues/010204/depgaz8.html

Gazzaniga, M. S. (2000). Cerebral specialization and interhemispheric communication: does the corpus callosum enable the human condition? *Brain, 123*, 1293–1326.

Geddes, J. R., Burgess, S., Hawton, K., Jamison, K., & Goodwin, G. M. (2004). Long-term lithium therapy for bipolar disorder: Systematic review and meta-analysis of randomized controlled trials. *American Journal of Psychiatry, 161*, 217–222.

Geen, R. G. (1984). Preferred stimulation levels in introverts and extraverts: Effects on arousal and performance. *Journal of Personality and Social Psychology, 46*, 1303–1312.

George, M. S., Lisanby, S. H., & Sackheim, H. A. (1999). Transcranial Magnetic Stimulation: Applications in neuropsychiatry. *Archives of General Psychiatry, 56*, 300–311.

George, M. S., Wassermann, E. M., Williams, W. A., Callahan, A., Ketter, T. A., Basser, P., et al. (1995). Daily repetitive transcranial magnetic stimulation (rTMS) improves mood in depression. *Neuroreport, 6*, 1853–1856.

Gergely, G., & Csibra, G. (2003). Teleological reasoning in infancy: The naïve theory of rational action. *Trends in Cognitive Sciences, 7*, 287–292.

Gershoff, E. T. (2002). Parental corporal punishment and associated child behaviors and experiences: A meta-analytic and theoretical review. *Psychological Bulletin, 128*, 539–579.

Gershon, E. S., Berrettini, W. H., & Goldin, L. R. (1989). Mood disorders: Genetic aspects. In H. I. Kaplan & B. J. Sadock (Eds.), *Comprehensive textbook of psychiatry* (5th ed). Baltimore: Williams & Wilkins.

Geula, C., & Mesulam, M. (1994). Cholinergic systems and related neuropathological predilection patterns in Alzheimer disease. In R. D. Terry, R. Katzman, & K. Bick (Eds.), *Alzheimer disease* (pp. 263–291). New York: Raven Press.

Gibson, J. J. (1966). *The senses considered as perceptual systems.* Boston: Houghton Mifflin.

Gick, M. L., & Holyoak, K. J. (1983). Schema induction and analogical transfer. *Cognitive Psychology, 15*, 1–38.

Giedd, J. N. (2004). Structural magnetic resonance imaging of the adolescent brain. *Annals of the New York Academy of Sciences, 1021*, 105–109.

Gigerenzer, G. (2004). Dread risk, September 11, and fatal traffic accidents. *Psychological Science, 15*, 286–287.

Gigerenzer, G., Todd, P. M., & the ABC Research Group (1999). *Simple heuristics that make us smart.* New York: Oxford University Press.

Gijsman, H. J., Geddes, J. R., Rendell, J. M., Nolen, W. A., & Goodwin, G. M. (2004). Antidepressants for bipolar depression: A systematic review of randomized, controlled trials. *American Journal of Psychiatry, 161*, 1537–1547.

Gilberg, C. (1980). Maternal age and infantile autism. *Journal of Autism and Developmental Disorders, 10*, 293–297.

Gilbert, D. T. (2005, January 20). Four more years of happiness. *The New York Times*, p. A23.

Gilbert, D. T., Morewedge, C. K., Risen, J. L., & Wilson, T. D. (2004). Looking forward to looking backward: The misprediction of regret. *Psychological Science, 15*, 346–350.

Gilbert, D. T., Pinel, E. C., Wilson, T. D., Blumberg, S. J., & Wheatley, T. (1998). Immune neglect: A source of durability bias in affective forecasting. *Journal of Personality and Social Psychology, 75*, 617–638.

Gillihan, S. J, & Farah, M. J. (2005). Is self special? A critical review of evidence from experimental psychology and cognitive neuroscience. *Psychological Bulletin, 131*, 76–97.

Gillis, J. J., Gilger, J. W., Pennington, B. F., & DeFries, J. C. (1992). Attention deficit disorder in reading-disabled twins: Evidence for a genetic etiology. *Journal of Abnormal Child Psychology, 20* (3), 303–315.

Gilovich, T. (1991). *How we know what isn't so: The fallibility of human reason in everyday life.* New York: The Free Press.

Gilpin, E. A., Choi, W. S., Berry, C., & Pierce, J. P. (1999). How many adolescents start smoking each day in the United States? *Journal of Adolescent Health, 25*, 248–255.

Gladwell, M. (2005). *Blink.* New York: Little, Brown.

Glenn, N. (1998). The course of marital success and failure in five American 10-year marriage cohorts. *Journal of Marriage and the Family, 60*, 569–576.

Godden, D. R., & Baddeley, A. D. (1975). Context-dependent memory in two natural environments: On land and underwater. *British Journal of Psychology, 66*, 325–331.

Golby, A. J., Gabrieli, J. D. E., Chiao, J. Y., & Eberhardt, J. L. (2001). Differential responses in the fusiform region to same-race and other-race faces. *Nature Neuroscience, 4*, 845–850.

Gold, P. E. (1987). Sweet memories. *American Scientist, 75*, 151–155.

Goldapple, K., Segal, Z., Garson, C., Lau, M., Bieling, P., Kennedy, S., et al. (2004). Modulation of cortical-limbic pathways in major depression: Treatment-specific effects of cognitive behavior therapy. *Archives of General Psychiatry, 61*, 34–41.

Goldenberg, J. L., McCoy, S. K., Pyszczynski, T., Greenberg, J., & Solomon, S. (2000). The body as a source of self-esteem: The effects of mortality salience on identification with one's body, interest in sex, and appearance monitoring. *Journal of Personality and Social Psychology, 79*, 118–130.

Goldman-Rakic, P. S., Scalaidhe, S., & Chafee, M. (2000). Domain specificity in cognitive systems. In M. S. Gazzaniga (Ed.), *The new cognitive neurosciences* (pp. 733–742). Cambridge, MA: MIT Press.

Gong, Q., Sluming, V., Mayes, A., Keller, S., Barrick, T., Cezayirli, E., et al. (2005). Voxel-based morphometry and stereology provide convergent evidence of the importance of medial prefrontal cortex for fluid intelligence in healthy adults. *Neuroimage, 25*, 1175–1186.

Goodale, M. A., & Milner, A. D. (1992). Separate visual pathways for perception and action. *Trends in Neuroscience, 15*, 22–25.

Goodall, G. (1984). Learning due to the response-shock contingency in signaled punishment. *Quarterly Journal of Experimental Psychology, 36*, 259–279.

Goodman, R., & Stevenson, J. (1989). A twin study of hyperactivity-II. The aetiological role of genes, family relationships, and perinatal adversity. *Journal of Child Psychology and Psychiatry, 30*, 691–709.

Goodwin, D. W., Powell, B., Bremer, D., Hoine, H., & Stern, J. (1969). Alcohol and recall: State dependent effects in man. *Science, 163*, 1358.

Goodwin, R. D., Lieb, R., Hoefler, M., Pfister, H., Bittner, A., Beesdo, K., et al. (2004). Panic attack as a risk factor for severe psychopathology. *American Journal of Psychiatry, 161*, 2207–2214.

Gopnik, A., & Graf, O. (1988). Knowing how you know: Young children's ability to identify and remember the sources of their beliefs. *Child Development, 59*, 1366–1371.

Gosling, S. D. (1998). Personality dimensions in spotted hyenas (Crocuta crocuta). *Journal of Comparative Psychology, 112*, 107–118.

Gosling, S. D. (2001). From mice to men: What can we learn about personality from animal research? *Psychological Bulletin, 127*, 45–86.

Gosling, S. D., & John, O. P. (1999). Personality dimension in non-human animals: A cross-species review. *Current Directions in Psychological Science, 8*, 69–75.

Gosling, S. D., Kwan, V. S. Y., & John, O. P. (2003). A dog's got personality: A cross-species comparative approach to evaluating personality judgments. *Journal of Personality and Social Psychology, 85*, 1161–1169.

Gottesman, I. I. (1991). *Schizophrenia genesis: The origins of madness.* New York: Freeman.

Gottesman, I. I., & Hanson, D. R. (2005). Human development: Biological and genetic processes. *Annual Review of Psychology*, 56, 263-286

Gottfredson, G. D. (1999). John Holland's contributions to vocational psychology: A review and evaluation. *Journal of Vocational Behavior, 55*, 15–40.

Gottfredson, L. S. (1997). Why g matters: The complexity of everyday life. *Intelligence, 24*, 79–132.

Gottfredson, L. S. (2004a). Intelligence: Is it the epidemiologists' elusive "fundamental cause" of social class inequalities in health? *Journal of Personality and Social Psychology, 86*, 174–199.

Gottfredson, L. S. (2004b). Schools and the g factor. *The Wilson Quarterly, Summer*, 35–45.

Gottfredson, L., & Deary, I. J. (2004). Intelligence predicts health and longevity: But why? *Current Directions in Psychological Science, 13*, 1–4.

Gottman, J. (1994). *Why marriages succeed or fail.* New York: Simon & Schuster.

Gottman, J. M. (1983). How children become friends. *Monographs of the Society for Research in Child Development 48* (3, Serial No. 201).

Gottman, J. M. (1998). Psychology and the study of marital processes. *Annual Review of Psychology, 49*, 169–197.

Gould, E., & Tanapat, P. (1999). Stress and hippocampal neurogenesis. *Biological Psychiatry, 46*, 1472–1479.

Grandin, T. (1995). *Thinking in pictures: And other reports from my life with autism.* New York: Doubleday.

Gray, J. R., Chabris, C. F., & Braver, T. S. (2003). Neural mechanisms of general fluid intelligence. *Nature Neuroscience, 6*, 316–322.

Gray, J. R., & Thompson, P. M. (2004). Neurobiology of intelligence: Science and ethics. *Nature Reviews Neuroscience, 5*, 471–482.

Green, L., Myerson, J., Lichtman, D., Rosen, S., & Fry, A. (1996). Temporal discounting in choice between delayed rewards: The role of age and income. *Psychological Science, 11*, 79–94.

Greenberg, J., Solomon, S., & Pyszczynski, T. (1997). Terror management theory of self-esteem and cultural worldviews: Empirical assessments and conceptual refinements. In M. P. Zanna (Ed.), *Advances in Experimental Social Psychology: Vol. 29* (pp. 61–136). New York: Academic Press.

Greenwald, A. G., & Banaji, M. R. (1995). Implicit social cognition: Attitudes, self-esteem, and stereotypes. *Psychological Review, 102*, 4–27.

Greenwald, A. G., McGhee, D., & Schwartz, J. (1998). Measuring individual differences in implicit cognition: The implicit association test. *Journal of Personality and Social Psychology, 74*, 1464–1480.

Greenwald, A. G., Oakes, M. A., & Hoffman, H. (2003). Targets of discrimination: Effects of race on responses to weapons holders. *Journal of Experimental Social Psychology, 39*, 399–405.

Gregory, A. H., Worrall, L., & Sarge, A. (1996). The development of emotional responses to music in young children. *Motivation and Emotion, 20*, 341–348.

Grill-Spector, K., Knouf, N., & Kanwisher, N. (2004). The fusiform face area subserves face perception, not generic within-category identification. *Nature Neurosciences, 7*, 555–562.

Gross, C. G., Rocha Miranda, C. E., & Bender, D. B. (1972). Visual properties of neurons in inferotemporal cortex of the macaque. *Journal of Neurophysiology, 35*, 96–111.

Gross, J. J. (1999). Emotion and emotion regulation. In L. A. Pervin & O. P. John (Eds.), *Handbook of personality: Theory and research* (2nd ed., pp. 525–552). New York: Guilford Press.

Grossman, L. (2005, January 24). Grow up? Not so fast. *Time, 165*, 42–53.

Grossman, M., & Wood, W. (1993). Sex differences in intensity of emotional experience: A social role interpretation. *Journal of Personality and Social Psychology, 65*, 1010–1022.

Gruenewald, P. J., Millar, A. B., Treno, A. J., Yang, Z., Ponicki, W. R., & Roeper, P. (1996). The geography of availability and driving after drinking. *Addiction, 91*, 967–983.

Guerin, B. (1994). What do people think about the risks of driving? Implications for traffic safety interventions. *Journal of Applied Social Psychology, 24*, 994–1021.

Gunderson, J. G. (1984). *Borderline personality disorder.* Washington, DC: American Psychiatric Press.

Habib, R., Nybert, L., & Tulving, E. (2003). Hemispheric asymmetries of memory: The HERA model revisited. *Trends in Cognitive Sciences, 7*, 241–245.

Haier, R. J., Jung, R. E., Yeo, R. A., Head, K., & Alkire, M. T. (2004). Structural brain variation and general intelligence. *Neuroimage, 23*, 425–433.

Haier, R. J., Jung, R. E., Yeo, R. A., Head, K., & Alkire, M. T. (2005). The neuroanatomy of general intelligence: Sex matters. *Neuroimage, 25*, 320–327.

Halligan, P. W., Marshall, J. C. (1998). Neglect of awareness. *Consciousness and Cognition, 7*, 356–380.

Halpern, C. T., Udry, J. R., & Suchindran, C. (1997). Testosterone predicts initiation of coitus in adolescent females. *Psychosomatic Medicine, 59*, 161–171.

Hamann, S. B., Ely, T. D., Grafton, D. T., & Kilts, C. D. (1999). Amygdala activity related to enhanced memory for pleasant and aversive stimuli. *Nature Neuroscience, 2*, 289–293.

Hamann, S., Herman, R. A., Nolan, C. L., & Wallen, K. (2004). Men and women differ in amygdala response to visual sexual stimuli. *Nature Neuroscience, 7,* 411–416.

Hambrecht, M., Maurer, K., Hafner, H., & Sartorius, N. (1992). Transnational stability of gender differences in schizophrenia: Recent findings on social skills training and family psychoeducation. *Clinical Psychology Review, 11,* 23–44.

Hammen, C. (2005). Stress and depression. *Annual Review of Clinical Psychology, 1,* 293–319.

Hancock, P. J., Bruce, V. V., & Burton, A. M. (2000). Recognition of unfamiliar faces. *Trends in Cognitive Sciences, 4,* 330–337.

Handleman, J. S., Gill, M. J., & Alessandri, M. (1988). Generalization by severely developmentally disabled children: Issues, advances, and future directions. *Behavior Therapist, 11,* 221–223.

Haney, C., Banks, C., & Zimbardo, P. (1973). Interpersonal dynamics in a simulated prison. *International Journal of Criminology and Penology, 1,* 69–97.

Hansen, C. J., Stevens, L. C., & Coast, J. R. (2001). Exercise duration and mood state: How much is enough to feel better? *Health Psychology, 20,* 267–275.

Hansen, W. B., Graham, J. W., Sobel, J. L., Shelton, D. R., Flay, B. R., & Johnson, C. A. (1987). The consistency of peer and parental influences on tobacco, alcohol, and marijuana use among young adolescents. *Journal of Behavioral Medicine, 10,* 559–579.

Harding, C. M., Zubin, J., & Strauss, J. S. (1987). Chronicity in schizophrenia: Fact, partial fact, or artifact? *Hospital and Community Psychiatry, 38,* 477–486.

Hare, R. D. (1993). *Without conscience: The disturbing world of the psychopaths among us.* New York: Pocket Books.

Hare, R. D., McPherson, L. M., & Forth, A. E. (1988). Male psychopaths and their criminal careers. *Journal of Consulting and Clinical Psychology, 56,* 710–714.

Hariri, A. R., Mattay, V. S., Tessitore, A., Kolachana, B., Fera, F., Goldman, D., et al. (2002). Serotonin transporter genetic variation and the response of the human amygdala. *Science, 297,* 400–440.

Harlow, H. F., Harlow, M. K., & Meyer, D. R. (1950). Learning motivated by a manipulation drive. *Journal of Experimental Psychology, 40,* 228–234.

Harmer, C. J., Perrett, D. I., Cowen, P. J., & Goodwin, G. M. (2001). Administration of the beta-adrenoceptor blocker propranolol impairs the processing of facial expressions of sadness. *Psychopharmacology, 154,* 383–389.

Harper, S. Q., Staber, P. D., He, X., Eliason, S. L., Martins, I. H., Mao, Q., et al. (2005). RNA interference improves motor and neuropathological abnormalities in a Huntington's disease mouse model. *Proceedings of the National Academy of Sciences, 102,* 5820–5825.

Harpur, T. J., & Hare, R. D. (1994). Assessment of psychopathy as a function of age. *Journal of Abnormal Psychology, 103,* 604–609.

Harris, J. R. (1995). Where is the child's environment? A group socialization theory of development. *Psychological Review, 102,* 458–489.

Hartsough, C. S., & Lambert, N. M. (1985). Medical factors in hyperactive and normal children: Prenatal, developmental, and health history findings. *American Journal of Orthopsychiatry, 55,* 190–201.

Hauk, O., Johnsrude, I., & Pulvermüller, F. (2004). Somatotopic representation of action words in human motor and premotor cortex. *Neuron, 41,* 301–307.

Haydon, P. G. (2001). Glia: Listening and talking to the synapse. *Nature Reviews: Neuroscience, 2,* 185–193.

Hazan, C., & Shaver, P. R. (1987). Romantic love conceptualized as an attachment process. *Journal of Personality and Social Psychology, 52,* 511–524.

Heatherton, T. F., Herman, C. P., & Poliny, J. (1991). Effects of physical threat and ego threat on eating behavior. *Journal of Personality and Social Psychology, 60,* 138–143.

Heatherton, T. F., & Baumeister, R. F. (1991). Binge eating as escape from self-awareness. *Psychological Bulletin, 110,* 86–108.

Heatherton, T. F., & Nichols, P. A. (1994). Personal accounts of successful versus failed attempts at life change. *Personality and Social Psychology Bulletin, 20,* 664–675.

Heatherton, T. F., & Vohs, K.D. (2000). Interpersonal evaluations following threats to self: Role of self-esteem. *Journal of Personality and Social Psychology, 78,* 725–736.

Heatherton, T. F., & Weinberger, J. L. (1994). *Can personality change?* Washington, DC: American Psychological Association.

Hebl, M. R., & Heatherton, T. F. (1998). The stigma of obesity in women: The difference is black and white. *Personality and Social Psychology Bulletin, 24,* 417–426.

Hegarty, J., Baldessarini, R., Tohen, M., Waternaux, C., & Oepen, G. (1994). One hundred years of schizophrenia: A meta-analysis of the outcome literature. *American Journal of Psychiatry, 151,* 1409–1416.

Heine, S. J. (2003). An exploration of cultural variation in self-enhancing and self-improving motivations. In V. Murphy-Berman & J. J. Berman (Eds.), *Nebraska symposium on motivation: Vol. 49. Cross-cultural differences in perspectives on the self* (pp. 101–128). Lincoln, NE: University of Nebraska Press.

Heine, S. J. (2005). Where is the evidence for pancultural self-enhancement? A reply to Sedikides, Gaertner, & Toguchi. *Journal of Personality and Social Psychology.*

Heine, S. J., Lehman, D. R., Markus, H. R., & Kitayama, S. (1999). Is there a universal need for positive self-regard? *Psychological Review, 106,* 766–794.

Heishman, S. J., Taylor, R. C., & Henningfield, J. E. (1994). Nicotine and smoking: A review of effects on human performance. *Experimental and Clinical Psychopharmacology, 2,* 345–395.

Helmholtz, H. von. (1909–1911). *Treatise on physiological optics* (3rd ed., vols. 2–3, J. P. Southall, Ed. and Trans.). Rochester, NY: Optical Society of America. (Original work published 1866)

Helmreich, R., Aronson, E., & LeFan, J. (1970). To err is humanizing sometimes: Effects of self-esteem, competence, and a pratfall on interpersonal attraction. *Journal of Personality and Social Psychology, 16,* 259–264.

Henderson, L., & Zimbardo, P. G. (1998). Shyness. *Encyclopedia of Mental Health, 3,* 497–509.

Hering, E. (1964). *Outlines of a theory of the light sense* (L. M. Hurvich & D. Jameson, Trans.). Cambridge, MA: Harvard University Press. (Original work published 1878)

Hernstein, R. J., & Murray, C. (1994). *The bell curve: Intelligence and class structure in American life*. New York: Free Press.

Herz, R. S., & Cahill, E. D. (1997). Differential use of sensory information in sexual behavior as a function of gender. *Human Nature, 8*, 275–286.

Hetherington, E. M., Bridges, M., & Insabella, G. M. (1998). What matters? What does not? Five perspectives on the association between marital transitions and children's adjustment. *American Psychologist, 53*, 167–184.

Higgins, E. T. (1987). Self-discrepancy: A theory relating self and affect. *Psychological Review, 94*, 319–340.

Higley, J. D., Mehlman, P. T., Higley, S. B., Fernald, B., Vickers, J., Lindell, et al. (1996). Excessive mortality in young free-ranging male nonhuman primates with low cerebrospinal fluid 5-hydroxyindoleacetic acid concentrations. *Archives of General Psychiatry, 53*, 537–543.

Hill, J. (2002). High-speed police pursuits: Danger, dynamics, and risk reduction. *FBI Law Enforcement Bulletin, 71*, 14–18.

Hingson, R., Heeren, T., Levenson, S., Jamanka, A., & Voas, R. (2002). Age of drinking onset, driving after drinking, and involvement in alcohol related motor vehicle crashes. *Accident Analysis and Prevention, 34,* 85–92.

Ho, B. C., Andreasen, N. C., Nopoulos, P., Arndt, S., Magnotta, V., & Flaum, M. (2004). Progressive structural brain abnormalities and their relationship to clinical outcome: A longitudinal magnetic resonance imaging study early in schizophrenia. *Archives of General Psychiatry, 60*, 585–594.

Hobson, J. A. (1995). *Sleep*. New York: Scientific American Library.

Hobson, J. A. (1999). Sleep and dreaming. In M. J. Zigmond, F. E. Bloom, S. C. Landis, J. L. Roberts, & L. R. Squire (Eds.), *Fundamentals of neuroscience* (pp. 1207–1225). San Diego, CA: Academic Press.

Hobson, J. A., Pace-Schott, E. F., & Stickgold, R. (2000). Consciousness: Its vicissitudes in waking and sleep. In M. S. Gazzaniga (Ed.), *The new cognitive neurosciences* (pp. 1341–1354). Cambridge, MA: MIT Press.

Holland, J. L. (1997). *Making vocational choices: A theory of vocational personalities and work environments* (3rd ed.). Odessa, FL: Psychological Assessment Resources.

Holland, P. C. (1977). Conditioned stimulus as a determinant of the form of the Pavlovian conditioned response. *Journal of Experimental Psychology: Animal Behavior Processes, 3*, 77–104.

Hollander, E., Novotny, S., Hanratty, M., Yaffe, R., DeCaria, C. M., Aronowitz, B. R., et al. (2003). Oxytocin infusion reduces repetitive behaviors in adults with autistic and Asperger's disorders. *Neuropsychopharmacology, 28*, 193–198.

Hollis, K. L. (1997). Contemporary research on Pavlovian conditioning: A "new" functional analysis. *American Psychologist, 52*, 956–965.

Hollon, S. D., Thase, M. E., & Markowitz, J. C. (2002). Treatment and prevention of depression. *Psychological Science in the Public Interest, 3*, 39–77.

Hooley, J. M., & Gotlib, I. H. (2000). A diathesis-stress conceptualization of expressed emotion and clinical outcome. *Applied and Preventive Psychology, 9*, 135–152.

Horn, J. L., & Hofer, S. M. (1992). Major abilities and development in the adult period. In R. J. Sternberg & C. A. Berg (Eds.), *Intellectual development* (pp. 44–99). New York: Cambridge University Press.

Hoshino, Y., Kumashiro, H., Yashima, Y., Tachibana, R., Watanabe, M., & Furukawa, H. (1980). Early symptoms of autism in children and their diagnostic significance. *Japanese Journal of Child and Adolescent Psychiatry, 21*, 284–299.

Hothersall, D. (1995). *History of psychology*. New York: McGraw-Hill.

House, J. S., Landis, K. R., & Umberson, D. (1988). Social relationships and health. *Science, 241*, 540–545.

Howlin, P., Mawhood, L., & Rutter, M. (2000). Autism and developmental receptive language disorder—A follow-up comparison in early adult life. II: Social, behavioural, and psychiatric outcomes. *Journal of Child Psychology and Psychiatry and Allied Disciplines, 41*, 561–578.

Hubel, D. H., & Wiesel, T. N. (1962). Receptive fields, binocular interaction, and functional architecture in the cat's visual cortex. *Journal of Physiology (London), 160*, 106–154.

Huesmann, L. R. (1998). The role of social information processing and cognitive schemas in the acquisition and maintenance of habitual aggressive behavior. In R. G. Geen & E. Donnerstein (Eds.), *Human aggression: Theories, research, and implications for policy* (pp. 73–109). New York: Academic Press.

Hughes, H. C. (2000). *Sensory exotica*. Cambridge, MA: MIT Press.

Hull, J. G., & Bond, C. F. (1986). Social and behavioral consequences of alcohol consumption and expectancy: A meta-analysis. *Psychological Bulletin, 99*, 347–360.

Hwang, W. S., Roh, S. I., Lee, B. C., Kang, S. K., Kwon, D. K., et al. (2005). Patient-specific embryonic stem cells derived from human SCNT blastocysts. *Science, 308*, 1777–1783.

Hynd, G. W., Hern, K., & Novey, E. S. (1993). Attention deficit-hyperactivity disorder and asymmetry of the caudate nucleus. *Journal of Child Neurology, 8*, 339–347.

Ilan, A. B., Smith, M. E., & Gevins, A. (2004). Effects of marijuana on neurophysiological signals of working and episodic memory. *Psychopharmacology, 176*, 214–222.

Insel, T. R. (1992). Oxytocin and the neurobiology of attachment. *Behavioral and Brain Sciences, 15*, 515–516.

Insel, T. R., & Young, L. J. (2001). The neurobiology of attachment. *Nature Reviews Neuroscience, 2*, 129–136.

Isen, A. M. (1993). Positive affect and decision making. In M. Lewis & J. M. Haviland (Eds.), *Handbook of emotions* (pp. 261–277). New York: Guilford Press.

Ivanovic, D. M., Leiva, B. P., Perez, H. T., Olivares, M. G., Diaz, N. S., Urrutia, M. S., et al. (2004). Head size and intelligence, learning, nutritional status and brain development. Head, IQ, learning, nutrition and brain. *Neuropsychologia, 42*, 1118–1131.

Iyengar, S. S., & Lepper, M. R. (2000). When choice is demotivating: Can one desire too much of a good thing? *Journal of Personality and Social Psychology, 79*, 995–1006.

Izard, C. E., & Malatesta, C. Z. (1987). Perspectives on emotional development. In J. Osofsky (Ed.), *Handbook of infant development* (pp. 494–554). New York: Wiley.

Jablensky, A. (1989). Epidemiology and cross-cultural aspects of schizophrenia. *Psychiatric Annals, 19*, 516–524.

Jacoby, L. L., Kelley, C., Brown, J., & Jasechko, J. (1989). Becoming famous overnight: Limits on the ability to avoid unconscious influences of the past. *Journal of Personality and Social Psychology, 56*, 326–338.

Jamison, K. R. (1995). *An unquiet mind.* New York: Vintage Books.

Jamison, K. R. (2004). Behavior: Essay by Kay Redfield Jamison. Johns Hopkins Public Health. Retrieved September 21, 2005 from http://www.jhsph.edu/publichealthnews/Mag_Spring04/The_Book/behavior/essay.html

Jang, K. L., Hu, S., Lively, W. J., Angleitner, A., Riemann, R., Ando, J., et al. (2001). Covariance structure of neuroticism and agreeableness: A twin and molecular genetic analysis of the role of the serotonin transporter gene. *Journal of Personality and Social Psychology, 81*, 295–304.

Janssen, E., Carpenter, D., & Graham, C. A. (2003). Selecting films for sex research: Gender differences in erotic film preference. *Archives of Sexual Behavior, 32*, 243–251.

Jencks, C. (1979). *Who gets ahead? The determinants of economic success in America.* New York: BasicBooks.

Jensen, A. R. (1998). *The g factor: The science of mental ability.* Westport, CT: Praeger.

Jensen, P. S., Hinshaw, S. P., Swanson, J. M., Greenhill, L. L., Conners, C. K., Arnold, L. E., et al. (2001). Findings from the NIMH Multimodal Treatment Study of ADHD (MTA): Implications and applications for primary care providers. *Journal of Developmental and Behavioral Pediatrics: Special Issue, 22*, 60–73.

Jessell, T. M., & Kelley, D. D. (1991). Pain and analgesia. In E. R. Kandel, J. H. Schwartz, & T. M. Jessell (Eds.), *Principles of neural science* (3rd ed., pp. 385–399). New York: Elsevier.

John, O. P. (1990). The "Big Five" factor taxonomy: Dimensions of personality in the natural language and in questionnaires. In L. A. Pervin & O. P. John (Eds.), *Handbook of personality: Theory and research* (pp. 66–100). New York: Guilford Press.

John, O. P., & Srivastava, S. (1999). The Big Five trait taxonomy: History, measurement, and theoretical perspectives. In L. A. Pervin & O. P. John (Eds.), *Handbook of personality: Theory and research* (2nd ed., pp. 102–138). New York: Guilford Press.

Johns, M., Schmader, T., & Martens, A. (2005). Knowing is half the battle. *Psychological Science, 16*, 175–179.

Johnson, D. L., Wiebe, J. S., Gold, S. M., Andreasen, N. C., Hichwa, R. D., Watkins, G. L., et al. (1999). Cerebral blood flow and personality: A positron emission tomography study. *American Journal of Psychiatry, 156*, 252–257.

Joiner, T. E., Coyne, J. C., & Blalock, J. (1999). On the interpersonal nature of depression: Overview and synthesis. In T. E. Joiner & J. C. Coyne (Eds.), *The interactional nature of depression: Advances in interpersonal approaches* (pp. 3–19). Washington, DC: American Psychological Association.

Joint Statement. (2000). *Joint statement on the impact of entertainment violence on children.* Congressional Public Health Summit. July 26, 2000.

Jones, R. A., & Ellis, G. D. (1996). Effect of variation in perceived risk on the secretion of beta-endorphin. *Leisure Sciences, 18*, 277–291.

Jones, S. S., Collins, K., & Hong, H. (1991). An audience effect on smile production in 10-month-old infants. *Psychological Science, 2*, 45–49.

Jope, R. S. (1999). Anti-bipolar therapy: Mechanism of action of lithium. *Molecular Psychiatry, 4*, 117–128.

Jorde, L. B., Mason-Brothers, A., Waldman, R., Ritvo, E. R., Freeman, B. J., Pingree, C., et al. (1990). The UCLA-University of Utah epidemiologic survey of autism: Genealogical analysis of familial aggregation. *American Journal of Medical Genetics, 36*, 85–88.

Jureidini, J. N., Doecke, C. J., Mansfield, P. R., Haby, M., Menkes, D. B., & Tonkin, A. L. (2004). Efficacy and safety of antidepressants for children and adolescents. *British Medical Journal, 328*, 879–883.

Kagan, J., & Snidman, N. (1991). Infant predictors of inhibited and uninhibited profiles. *Psychological Science, 2*, 40–44.

Kahneman, D., & Tversky, A. (1984). Choices, values, and frames. *American Psychologist, 39*, 341–350.

Kanayama, G., Pope, H. G., Cohane, G., & Hudson, J. L. (2003). Risk factors for anabolic-steroid use among weightlifters: A case-control study. *Drugs and Alcohol Dependent, 71*, 77–86.

Kanazawa, S. (2004). General intelligence as a domain-specific adaptation. *Psychological Review, 111*, 512–523.

Kandel, E. R., Schwartz, J. H., & Jessell, T. M. (1995). *Essentials of neural science and behavior.* Norwalk, CT: Appleton & Lange.

Kane, M. J., Hambrick, D. Z., & Conway, A. R. (2005). Working memory capacity and fluid intelligence are strongly related constructs: Comment on Ackerman, Beier, and Boyle (2005). *Psychological Bulletin, 131*, 66–71.

Kanwisher, N., Tong, F., & Nakayama, K. (1998). The effect of face inversion on the human fusiform face area. *Cognition, 68*, 1–11.

Kapur, S. E., Craik, F. I. M., Tulving, E., Wilson, A. A., Houle, S., & Brown, G. R. (1994). Neuroanatomical correlates of encoding in episodic memory: Levels of processing effects. *Proceedings of the National Academy of Sciences, 91*, 2008–2011.

Karney, B. R., & Bradbury, T. N. (1995). The longitudinal course of marital quality and stability: A review of theory, methods, and research. *Psychological Bulletin, 118*, 3–34.

Kassin, S. (2005). On the psychology of confessions: Does innocence put innocents at risk? *American Psychologist, 60*, 215–228.

Kassin, S. M., & Kiechel, K. L. (1996). The social psychology of false confessions: Compliance, internalization, and confabulation. *Psychological Science, 7*, 125–128.

Kassin, S. M., Goldstein, C. G., & Savitsky, K. (2003). Behavioral confirmation in the interrogation room: On the dangers of presuming guilt. *Law and Human Behavior, 27*, 187–203.

Kawakami, K., Dovidio, J. F., Moll, J., Hermsen, S., & Russin, A. (2000). Just say no (to stereotyping): Effects of training in the negation of stereotypic associations on stereotype activation. *Journal of Personality and Social Psychology, 78*, 871–888.

Kazdin, A. E. (1994). Methodology, design, and evaluation in psychotherapy research. In A. E. Bergin & S. L. Garfield (Eds.), *International handbook of behavior modification and behavior change* (4th ed., pp. 19–71). New York: Wiley.

Kazdin, A. E., & Benjet, C. (2003). Spanking children: Evidence and issues. *Current Directions in Psychological Science, 12*, 99–103.

Keane, M. (1987). On retrieving analogues when solving problems. *Quarterly Journal of Experimental Psychology, 39A*, 29–41.

Keel, P. K., & Mitchell, J. E. (1997). Outcome in bulimia nervosa. *American Journal of Psychiatry, 154*, 313–321.

Keith, S. J., Regier, D. A., & Rae, D. S. (1991). Schizophrenic disorders. In L. N. Robins & D. A. Regier (Eds.), *Psychiatric disorders in America: The epidemiological catchment areas study*. New York: The Free Press.

Keller, M. B., & Baker, L. A. (1991). Bipolar disorder: Epidemiology, course, diagnosis, and treatment. *Bulletin of the Menninger Clinic, 55*, 172–181.

Keller, M. B., McCullough, J. P., Klein, D. N., Arnow, B., Dunner, D. L., Gelenberg, A. J., et al. (2000). A comparison of nefazodone, a cognitive behavioral analysis system of psychotherapy, and their combination for the treatment of chronic depression. *New England Journal of Medicine, 342*, 1462–1470.

Keller, M. B., Shapiro, R. W., Lavori, P. W., & Wolfe, N. (1982). Recovery in major depressive disorder. *Archives of General Psychiatry, 39*, 905–910.

Kelley, W. M., Miezin, F. M., McDermott, K. B., Buckner, R. L., Raichle, M. E., Cohen, N. J., et al. (1998). Hemispheric specialization in human dorsal frontal cortex and medial temporal lobe for verbal and nonverbal memory encoding. *Neuron, 20*, 927–936.

Kelley, W. T., Macrae, C. N., Wyland, C., Caglar, S., Inati, S., & Heatherton, T. F. (2002). Finding the self? An event-related fMRI study. *Journal of Cognitive Neuroscience, 14,* 785–794.

Kellman, P. J., Spelke, E. S., & Short, K. R. (1986). Infant perception of object unity from translatory motion in depth and vertical translation. *Child Development, 57*, 72–86.

Keltner, D., & Anderson, C. (2000). Saving face for Darwin: The functions and uses of embarrassment. *Current Directions in Psychological Science, 9*, 187–192.

Keltner, D., & Bonanno, G. A. (1997). A study of laughter and dissociation: Distinct correlates of laughter and smiling during bereavement. *Journal of Personality and Social Psychology, 73*, 687–702.

Keltner, D., Young, R. C., Heerey, E. A., Oemig, C., & Monarch, N. D. (1998). Teasing in hierarchical and intimate relations. *Journal of Personality and Social Psychology, 75*, 1231–1247.

Kennedy, Q., Mather, M., & Carstensen, L. L. (2004). The role of motivation in the age-related positivity effect in autobiographical memory. *Psychological Science, 15*, 208–214.

Kenrick, D. T., & Funder, D. C. (1991). The person-situation debate: Do personality traits really exist? In V. J. Derlega, B. A. Winstead, & W. H. Jones (Eds.), *Personality: Contemporary theory and research* (pp. 149–174). Chicago, IL: Nelson Hall.

Kessler, R. C., McGonagle, K. A., Zhao, S., Nelson, C. B., Hugh, M., Eshleman, S. et al. (1994). Lifetime and 12-month prevalence of DSM-III-R psychiatric disorders in the United States: Results from the National Comorbidity Study. *Archives of General Psychiatry, 51*, 8–19.

Keys, A., Brozek, J., Henschel, A. L., Mickelsen, O., & Taylor, H. L. (1950). *The biology of human starvation*. Minneapolis: University of Minnesota Press.

Kiecolt-Glaser, J. K., & Glaser, R. (1988). Immunological competence. In E. A. Blechman & K. D. Brownell (Eds.), *Handbook of behavioral medicine for women* (Vol. 149, pp. 195–205). Elmsford, NY: Pergamon Press.

Kiecolt-Glaser, J. K., Malarkey, W. B., Chee, M., & Newton, T. (1993). Negative behavior during marital conflict is associated with immunological down-regulation. *Psychosomatic Medicine, 55*, 395–409.

Kihlstrom, J. R. (2005). Dissociative disorders. *Annual Review of Clinical Psychology, 1,* 227–253.

Kite, M. E., & Deaux, K. (1986). Attitudes toward homosexuality: Assessment and behavioral consequences. *Basic and Applied Social Psychology, 7*, 137–162.

Klauer, M. H., Musch, J., & Naumer, B. (2000). On belief bias in syllogistic reasoning. *Psychological Review, 107*, 852–884.

Kleinmuntz, B., & Szucko, J. J. (1984). Lie detection in ancient and modern times: A call for contemporary scientific study. *American Psychologist, 39*, 766–776.

Klin, A., Jones, W., Schultz, R., & Volkmar, F. (2003). The enactive mind, or from actions to cognition: Lessons from autism. *Philosophical Transactions of the Royal Society*, Series B, *358*, 345–360.

Klingemann, H. K. (1991). The motivation for change from problem alcohol and heroin use. *British Journal of Addiction, 86*, 727–744.

Knight, R. (1953). Borderline states. *Bulletin of the Menninger Clinic, 17*, 1–12.

Knight, R. T., & Grabowecky, M. (1995). Escape from linear time: Prefrontal cortex and conscious experience. In M. S. Gazzaniga (Ed.), *The cognitive neurosciences* (pp. 1357–1371). Cambridge, MA: MIT Press.

Knutson, B., Fong, G. W., Adams, C. M., Varner, J. L., & Hommer, D. (2001). Dissociation of reward anticipation and outcome with event-related fMRI. *NeuroReport 12,* 3683–3687.

Knutson, B., Wolkowitz, O. M., Cole, S. W., Chan, T., Moore, E. A., Johnson, R. C., et al. (1998). Selective alteration of personality and social behavior by serotonergic intervention. *American Journal of Psychiatry, 155*, 373–379.

Kobasa, S. C. (1979). Personality and resistance to illness. *American Journal of Community Psychology, 7*, 413–423.

Koch, J. L. (1891). *Die psychopathischen Minderwertigkeiten*. Ravensburg, Germany: Maier.

Kocsis, J. H., Rush, A. J., Markowitz, J. C., Borian, F. E., Dunner, D. L., Koran, L. M., et al. (2003). Continuation treatment of chronic depression: A comparison of nefazodone, cognitive behavioral analysis system of psychotherapy, and their combination. *Psychopharmacology Bulletin, 37,* 73–87.

Kocsis, R. N. (2004). Psychological profiling in serial arson offenses: A comparative assessment of skills and accuracy. *Criminal Justice and Behavior, 31*, 341–361.

Kocsis, R. N., Hayes, A. F., & Irwin, H. J. (2002). Investigative experience and accuracy in psychological profiling of a violent crime. *Journal of Interpersonal Violence, 17*, 811–823.

Kolar, D. W., Funder, D. C., & Colvin, C. R. (1996). Comparing the accuracy of personality judgments by the self and knowledgeable others. *Journal of Personality, 64*, 311–337.

Konishi, M. (1993). Listening with two ears. *Scientific American, 268*, 66–73.

Kontsevich, L. L., & Tyler, C. W. (2004). What makes Mona Lisa smile? *Vision Research, 44*, 1493–1498.

Koob, G. F. (1999). Drug reward and addiction. In M. J. Zigmond, F. E. Bloom, S. C. Landis, J. L. Roberts, & L. R. Squire (Eds.), *Fundamentals of neuroscience* (pp. 1261–1279). San Diego, CA: Academic Press.

Koole, S. L., Dijksterhuis, A., & van Knippenberg, A. (2001). What's in a name: Implicit self-esteem and the automatic self. *Journal of Personality and Social Psychology, 80*, 669–685.

Korn, M. L., Kotler, M., Molcho, A., Botsis, A. J., Grosz, D., Chen, C., et al. (1992). Suicide and violence associated with panic attacks. *Biological Psychiatry, 31*, 607–612.

Koshland, D. E. (1989). Drunk driving and statistical mortality. *Science, 244*, 513.

Kosslyn, S., & Koenig, O. (1995). *Wet mind: The new cognitive neuroscience.* New York: Free Press.

Kosslyn, S. M., Thompson, W. L., Kim, I. J., & Alpert, N. M. (1995). Topographical representations of mental images in primary visual cortex. *Nature, 378*, 496–498.

Kovaleski, S. F., & Sheridan, M. B. (2003, January 12). A boy of bright promise and no roots; after transient childhood, sniper suspect latched on to strong father figure. *The Washington Post*, p. C.01.

Kozorovitskiy, Y., & Gould, E. (2004). Dominance hierarchy influences adult neurogenesis in the dentate gyrus. *Journal of Neuroscience, 24*, 6755–6759.

Krongrad, A., Lai, H., Burke, M. A., Goodkin, K., & Lai, S. (1996). Marriage and mortality in prostate cancer. *Journal of Urology, 156*, 1696–1700.

Kruesi, M. J., Hibbs, E. D., Zahn, T. P., Keysor, C. S., Hamburger, S. D., Bartko, J. J., et al. (1992). A 2-year prospective follow-up study of children and adolescents with disruptive behavior disorders. Prediction by cerebrospinal fluid 5-hydroxyindoleacetic acid, homovanillic acid, and autonomic measures. *Archives of General Psychiatry, 49*, 429–435.

Krumhansl, C. (2002). Music: A link between cognition and emotion. *Current Directions in Psychological Science, 11*, 45–50.

Kuhl, P. K. (2004). Early language acquisition: Cracking the speech code. *Nature Reviews Neuroscience, 5*, 831–843.

Kulhara, P., & Chakrabarti, S. (2001). Culture and schizophrenia and other psychotic disorders. *Psychiatric Clinics of North America, 24*, 449–464.

Kuncel, N. R., Hezlett, S. A., & Ones, D. S. (2004). Academic Performance, career potential, creativity, and job performance: Can one construct predict them all? *Journal of Personality and Social Psychology, 86*, 148–161.

Kunda, Z., & Spencer, S. J. (2003). When do stereotypes come to mind and when do they color judgment? A goal-based theoretical framework for stereotype activation and application. *Psychological Bulletin, 129*, 522–544.

Kyllonen, P. C., & Christal, R. E. (1990). Reasoning ability is (little more than) working-memory capacity?! *Intelligence, 14*, 389–433.

LaFrance, M., & Banaji, M. (1992). Toward a reconsideration of the gender-emotion relationship. In M. Clarke (Ed.) *Review of personality and social psychology* (pp. 178–201). Beverly Hills, CA: Sage.

Laible, D. J., & Thompson, R. A. (2000). Attachment and self-organization. In M. D. Lewis & I. Granic (Eds.), *Emotion, development, and self-organization: Dynamic systems approaches to emotional development* (pp. 298–323). New York: Cambridge University Press.

Lambert, J., Fernandez, S., & Frick, K. (2005). Different types of environmental enrichment have discrepant effects on spatial memory and synaptophysin levels in female mice. *Neurobiology of Learning and Memory, 83*, 206–216.

Landau, B. (1994). Where's what and what's where: The language of objects in space. In L. E. Gleitman and B. Landau (Eds.), [special issue] *Lexical acquisition, Lingua, 92*, 259–296.

Lane, R. D., Reiman, E. M., Ahern, G. L., & Schwartz, G. E. (1997). Neuroanatomical correlates of happiness, sadness, and disgust. *American Journal of Psychiatry, 154*, 926–933.

Langleben, D. D., Schroeder, L., Maldjian, J. A., Gur, R. C., McDonald, S., Ragland, J. D., et al. (2002). Brain activity during simulated deception: An event-related functional magnetic resonance study. *Neuroimage, 15*, 727–732.

Langlois, J. H., Kalakanis, L., Rubenstein, A. J., Larson, A., Hallam, M., & Smoot, M. (2000). Maxims or myths of beauty? A meta-analytic and theoretical review. *Psychological Bulletin, 126*, 390–423.

Langlois, J. H., Ritter, J. M., Casey, R. J., & Sawin, D. B. (1995). Infant attractiveness predicts maternal behaviors and attitudes. *Developmental Psychology, 31*, 464–472.

Langlois, J. H., & Roggman, L. A. (1990). Attractive faces are only average. *Psychological Science, 1*, 115–121.

Larsen, J. T., McGraw, A. P., & Cacioppo, J. T. (2001). Can people feel happy and sad at the same time? *Journal of Personality and Social Psychology, 81*, 684–696.

Lasagna, L., Mosteller, F., von Felsinger, J., & Beecher, H. (1954). A study of the placebo response. *American Journal of Medicine, 16*, 770–779.

Latané, B., & Darley, J. M. (1968). Group inhibition of bystander intervention in emergencies. *Journal of Personality and Social Psychology, 10*, 215–221.

Latané, B., Williams, K., & Harkins, S. G. (1979). Many hands make light the work: The causes and consequences of social loafing. *Journal of Personality and Social Psychology, 37*, 822–832.

Lazarus, R. S. (1993). From psychological stress to the emotions: A history of changing outlooks. *Annual Review of Psychology, 44*, 1–21.

Leary, M. R. (2004). The function of self-esteem in terror management theory and sociometer theory: Comment on Pyszczynski et al. *Psychological Bulletin, 130*, 478–482.

Leary, M. R., & MacDonald, G. (2003). Individual differences in self-esteem: A review and theoretical integration. In M. R. Leary & J. P. Tangney (Eds.), *Handbook of self and identity* (pp. 401–418). New York: Guilford Press.

Leary, M. R., Tambor, E. S., Terdal, S. K., & Downs, D. L. (1995) Self-esteem as an interpersonal monitor: The sociometer hypothesis. *Journal of Personality and Social Psychology, 68*, 518–530.

Leckman, J. F., Elliott, G. R., Bromet, E. J., Campbell, M., Cicchetti, D., Cohen, D. J., et al. (1995). Report card on the National Plan for Research on Child and Adolescent Mental Disorders: The midway point. *Archives of General Psychiatry, 34,* 715–723.

Leckman, J. F., Goodman, W. K., North, W. G., Chappell, P. B., Price, L. H., Pauls, D. L., et al. (1994). The role of central oxytocin in obsessive compulsive disorder and related behavior. *Psychoneuroendocrinology, 19,* 723–749.

LeDoux, J. E. (1996). *The emotional brain: The mysterious underpinnings of emotional life.* New York: Simon & Schuster.

LeDoux, J. E. (2002). *Synaptic self.* New York: Viking.

Leff, J., Sartorius, N., Jablensky, A., Korten, A., & Ernberg, G. (1992). The International Pilot Study of Schizophrenia: Five-year follow-up findings. *Psychological Medicine, 22,* 131–145.

Leibowitz, H. (1996). The symbiosis between basic and applied research. *American Psychologist, 51,* 366–370.

Leichsenring, F., Rabung, S., & Leibing, E. (2004). The efficacy of short-term psychodynamic psychotherapy in specific psychiatric disorders: A meta-analysis. *Archives of General Psychiatry, 61,* 1208–1216.

Leigh, B. C., & Schafer, J. C. (1993). Heavy drinking occasions and the occurrence of sexual activity. *Psychology of Addictive Behaviors, 7,* 197–200.

Lenneberg, E. (1967). *The biological foundations of language.* New York: Wiley.

Lepper, M. R., Greene, D., & Nisbett, R. E. (1973). Undermining children's intrinsic interest with extrinsic reward: A test of the "overjustification" hypothesis. *Journal of Personality and Social Psychology, 28,* 129–137.

Lesniak, K. T., & Dubbert, P. M. (2001). Exercise and hypertension. *Current Opinion in Cardiology, 16,* 356–359.

Leuchter, A. F., Cook, I. A., Witte, E. A., Morgan, M., & Abrams, M. (2002). Changes in brain function of depressed subjects during treatment with placebo. *American Journal of Psychiatry, 159,* 122–129.

LeVay, S. (1991). A difference in hypothalamic structure between heterosexual and homosexual men. *Science, 253,* 1034–1037.

Levenson, R. W., Ekman, P., Heider, K., & Friesen, W. V. (1992). Emotion and autonomic nervous system activity in the Minangkabau of West Sumatra. *Journal of Personality and Social Psychology, 62,* 972–988.

Leventhal, H., & Cleary, P. D. (1980). The smoking problem: A review of research and theory in behavioral risk modification. *Psychological Bulletin, 88,* 370–405.

Levin, J. M., Ross, M. H., Mendelson, J. H., Kaufman, M. J., Lange, N., Maas, L. C., et al. (1998). Reduction in BOLD fMRI response to primary visual stimulation following alcohol ingestion. *Psychiatry Research, 82,* 135–146.

Levitin, D. J., & Rogers, S. E. (2005). Absolute pitch: Perception, coding, and controversies. *Trends in Cognitive Science, 9,* 26–33.

Lewinsohn, P. M., Allen, N. B., Seeley, J. R., & Gotlib, I. H. (1999). First onset versus recurrence of depression: Differential processes of psychosocial risk. *Journal of Abnormal Psychology, 108,* 483–489.

Lewinsohn, P. M., Rodhe, P. D., Seeley, J. R., & Hops, H. (1991). Comorbidity of unipolar depression: I. Major depression with dysthymia. *Journal of Abnormal Psychology, 98,* 107–116.

Lewontin, R. C. (1976). Race and intelligence. In N. J. Block & G. Dworkin (Eds.), *The IQ controversy* (pp. 78–92). New York: Pantheon Books.

Lieb, K., Zanarini, M. C., Schmahl, C., Linehan, M. M., & Bohus, M. (2004). Borderline personality disorder. *Lancet, 364,* 453–461.

Lieberman, M. D. (2000). Intuition: A social cognitive neuroscience approach. *Psychological Bulletin, 126,* 109–137.

Lieberman, M. D., Ochsner, K. N., Gilbert, D. T., & Schacter, D. L. (2001). Do amnesics exhibit cognitive dissonance reduction? The role of explicit memory and attention in attitude change. *Psychological Science, 121,* 135–140.

Lindemann, B. (2001). Receptors and transduction in taste. *Nature, 413,* 219–225.

Linehan, M. M. (1987). Dialectical behavior therapy for borderline personality disorder: Theory and method. *Bulletin of the Menninger Clinic, 51,* 261–276.

Linehan, M. M., Armstrong, H. E., Suarez, A., Allmon, D., & Heard, H. (1991). Cognitive behavioral treatment of chronically parasuicidal borderline patients. *Archives of General Psychiatry, 48,* 1060–1064.

Linehan, M. M., Heard, H., & Armstrong, H. E. (1993). Naturalistic follow-up of a behavioral treatment for chronically parasuicidal borderline patients. *Archives of General Psychiatry, 50,* 971–974.

Liu, J., Raine, A., Venables, P. H., & Mednick, S. A. (2004). Malnutrition at age 3 years and externalizing behavior problems at ages 8, 11, and 17 years. *American Journal of Psychiatry, 161,* 2005–2013.

Ljungberg, T., Apicella, P., & Schultz, W. (1992). Responses of monkey dopamine neurons during learning of behavioral reactions. *Journal of Neurophysiology, 67,* 145–163.

Lledo, P. M., Gheusi, G., & Vincent, J. D. (2005). Information processing in the mammalian olfactory system. *Physiological Review, 85,* 281–317.

Locke, E. A., & Latham, G. P. (1990). *A theory of goal setting and task performance.* Englewood Cliffs, NJ: Prentice-Hall.

Loehlin, J. C., & Nichols, R. C. (1976). *Heredity, environment, and personality: A study of 850 sets of twins.* Austin, TX: University of Texas Press.

Loewenstein, G. F., Weber, E. U., Hsee, C. K., & Welch, N. (2001). Risk as feelings. *Psychological Bulletin, 127,* 267–286.

Loftus, E. (1993). The reality of repressed memories. *American Psychologist, 48,* 518–537.

Loftus, E. F. (2003). Make-believe memories. *American Psychologist, 58,* 867–873.

Loftus, E. F., & Palmer, J. C. (1974). Reconstruction of automobile destruction: An example of the interaction between language and memory. *Journal of Learning and Verbal Behavior, 13,* 585–589.

Logan, J. M., Sanders, A. L., Snyder, A. Z., Morris, J. C., & Buckner, R. L. (2002). Under-recruitment and nonselective recruitment: Dissociable neural mechanisms associated with aging. *Neuron, 33,* 1–20.

Lovaas, O. I. (1987). Behavioral treatment and normal educational and intellectual functioning in young autistic children. *Journal of Consulting & Clinical Psychology, 55,* 3–9.

Lubinski, D. (2004). Introduction to the special section on cognitive abilities: 100 years after Spearman's (1904) "'General Intelligence,' objectively determined and measured." *Journal of Personality and Social Psychology, 86,* 96–111.

Lubinski, D., & Benbow, C. P. (2000). States of excellence, *American Psychologist, 55,* 137–150.

Luborsky, L., Crits-Christoph, P., McLellan, T., Woody, G., Piper, W., Liberman, B., et al. (1986). Do therapists vary much in their success? Findings from four outcome studies. *American Journal of Orthopsychiatry, 56,* 501–512.

Lucas, R. E., Diener, E., Grob, A., Suh, E., & Shao, L. (2000). Cross-cultural evidence for the fundamental features of extraversion. *Journal of Personality and Social Psychology, 79,* 452–468.

Luchins, A. S., (1942). Mechanization in problem solving. *Psychological Monographs, 54.* Whole No. 248.

Lykken, D. T. (1957). A study of anxiety in the sociopathic personality. *Journal of Abnormal Social Psychology, 55,* 6–10.

Lykken, D. T. (1995). *The antisocial personalities.* Hillsdale, NJ: Erlbaum.

Lykken, D. T. (2000). The causes and costs of crime and a controversial cure. *Journal of Personality, 68,* 559–605.

Lykken, D. T., McGue, M., Tellegen, A., & Bouchard, T. J., Jr. (1992). Emergenesis: Genetic traits that may not run in families. *American Psychologist, 47,* 1565–1577.

Lyubomirsky, S., & Nolen-Hoeksema, S. (1995). Effects of self-focused rumination on negative thinking and interpersonal problem solving. *Journal of Personality and Social Psychology, 69,* 176–190.

Maas, L. C., Lukas, S. E., Kaufman, M. J., Weiss, R. D., Daniels, S. L., Rogers, et al. (1998). Functional magnetic resonance imaging of human brain activation during cue-induced cocaine craving. *American Journal of Psychiatry, 155,* 124–126.

MacKay, D. G. (1973). Aspects of a theory of comprehension, memory and attention. *Quarterly Journal of Experimental Psychology, 25,* 22–40.

Macrae, C. N., Alnwick, K. A., Milne, A. B., & Schloerscheidt, A. M. (2002). Person perception across the menstrual cycle: Hormonal influences on social-cognitive functioning. *Psychological Science, 13,* 532–536.

Macrae, C. N., Bodenhausen, G. V., & Calvini, G. (1999). Contexts of cryptomnesia: May the source be with you. *Social Cognition, 17,* 273–297.

Macrae, C. N., Moran, J. M., Heatherton, T. F., Banfield, J. F., & Kelley, W. M. (2004). Medial prefrontal activity predicts memory for self. *Cerebral Cortex, 14,* 647–654.

Madden, G. J., Petry, N. M., Badger, G. J., & Bickel, W. K. (1997). Impulsivity and self-control choices in opioid-dependent patients and non-drug-using control participants: Drug and monetary rewards. *Experimental and Clinical Psychopharmacology, 5,* 256–262.

Maguire, E. A., Spiers, H. J., Good, C. D., Hartley, T., Frackowiak, R. S., & Burgess, N. (2003). Navigation expertise and the human hippocampus: A structural brain imaging analysis. *Hippocampus, 13,* 250–259.

Maier, N. R. F. (1931). Reasoning in humans II: The solution of a problem and its appearance in consciousness. *Journal of Comparative Psychology, 12,* 181–194.

Main, M., & Solomon, J. (1986). Discovery of a new, insecure-disorganized/disoriented attachment pattern. In T. B. Brazelton & M. Yogman (Eds.), *Affective development in infancy* (pp. 95–124). Norwood, NJ: Ablex.

Manderscheid, R. W., Witkin, M. J., Rosenstein, M. J., Milazzo-Sayre, L. J., Bethel, H. E., & MacAskill, R. L. (1985). In C. A. Taube & S. A. Barrett (Eds.), *Mental health, United States, 1985.* Washington DC: National Institute of Mental Health.

Maner, J. K., Luce, C. L., Neuberg, S. L., Cialdini, R. B., Brown, S., & Sagarin, B. J. (2002). The effects of perspective taking on motivations for helping: Still no evidence for altruism. *Personality and Social Psychology Bulletin, 28,* 1601–1610.

Mannuzza, S., Klein, R. G., Bonagura, N., Malloy, P., Giampino, T. L., & Addalli, K. A. (1991). Hyperactive boys almost grown up. Replications of psychiatric status. *Archives of General Psychiatry, 48,* 77–83.

Marcus, G. (2004). *The birth of the mind.* New York: Basic Books.

Marcus, G. F. (1996). Why do children say "breaked"? *Current Directions in Psychological Science, 5,* 81–85.

Marcus, G. F., Pinker, S., Ullman, M., Hollander, M., Rosen, T. S., & Xu, F. (1992). Overregularization in language acquisition. *Monographs of the Society of Research and Child Development, 57,* 181.

Marcus, G. F., Vijayan, S., Bandi Rao, S., & Vishton, P. M. (1999). Rule learning by seven-month-old infants. *Science, 283,* 77–80.

Markon, J. (2001, October 8). Elderly Judges Handle 20 Percent of U.S. Caseload. *The Wall Street Journal,* p. A.15.

Markowitz, J. C., & Weissman, M. M. (1995). Interpersonal psychotherapy. In E. E. Beckham & W. R. Leber (Eds.), Handbook of depression (2nd ed., pp. 376–390). New York: Guilford Press.

Markus, H. R. (1977). Self-schemata and processing information about the self. *Journal of Personality and Social Psychology, 35,* 63–78.

Markus, H. R., & Kitayama, S. (1991). Culture and the self: Implications for cognition, emotion, and motivation. *Psychological Review, 98,* 224–253.

Marlatt, G. A. (1999). Alcohol, the magic elixir? In S. Peele & M. Grant (Eds.), *Alcohol and pleasure: A health perspective* (pp. 233–248). Philadelphia: Brunner/Mazel.

Marr, D. (1982). *Vision: A computational investigation into the human representation and processing of visual information.* San Francisco: Freeman.

Marshall, E. (2004). Forgetting and remembering. A star-studded search for memory-enhancing drugs. *Science, 304,* 36–38.

Martin, N. G., Eaves, L. J., Heath, A. R., Jardine, R., Feingold, L. M., & Eysenck, H. J. (1986). Transmission of social attitudes. *Proceedings of the National Academy of Science, 83,* 4364–4368.

Maruta, T., Colligan, R. C., Malinchoc, M., & Offord, K. P. (2002). Optimism-pessimism assessed in the 1960s and self-reported health status 30 years later. *Mayo Clinic Proceedings, 77,* 748–753.

Maslow, A. (1968). *Toward a psychology of being.* New York: Van Nostrand.

Masten, A. S. (2001). Ordinary magic: Resilience processes in development. *American Psychologist, 56,* 227–238.

Mather, M., & Carstensen, L. L. (2003). Aging and attentional biases for emotional faces. *Psychological Science, 14,* 409–415.

Mayer, J. D., Caruso, D., & Salovey, P. (1999). Emotional intelligence meets traditional standards for an intelligence. *Intelligence, 27,* 267–298.

Mazur, A., & Booth, A. (1998). Testosterone and dominance in men. *Behavioural and Brain Science, 21,* 353–397.

McAdams, D. P. (1999). Personal narratives and the life story. In L. A. Pervin & O. P. John (Eds.), *Handbook of personality: Theory and research* (2nd ed., pp. 478–500). New York: Guilford Press.

McAdams, D. P. (2001). The psychology of life stories. *Review of General Psychology, 5,* 100–122.

McCarthy, G., Puce, A., Gore, J. C., & Allison, T. (1997). Face-specific processing in the human fusiform gyrus. *Journal of Cognitive Neuroscience, 9,* 605–610.

McClelland, D. C. (1987). *Human motivation.* New York: Cambridge University Press.

McClelland, D. C., Koestner, R., & Weinberger, J. (1989). How do self-attributed and implicit motives differ? *Psychological Review, 96,* 690–702.

McClintock, M. K. (1971). Menstrual synchrony and suppression. *Nature, 229,* 244–245.

McClure, S. M., Li, J., Tomlin, D., Cypert, K. S., Montague, L. M., & Montague, P. R. (2004). Neural correlates of behavioral preference for culturally familiar drinks. *Neuron, 14,* 379–387.

McCormick, D. A. (1999). Membrane potential and action potential. In M. J. Zigmond, F. E. Bloom, S. C. Landis, J. L. Roberts, & L. R. Squire (Eds.), *Fundamentals of neuroscience* (pp. 129–154). San Diego, CA: Academic Press.

McCrae, R. R., & Costa, P. T., Jr. (1990). *Personality in adulthood.* New York: Guilford Press.

McCrae, R. R., & Costa, P. T., Jr. (1999). A five-factor theory of personality. In L. A. Pervin & O. P. John (Eds.), *Handbook of personality: Theory and research* (2nd ed., pp. 139–153). New York: Guilford Press.

McCrae, R. R., Costa, P. T., Ostendorf, F., Angleitner, A., Hrebickova, M., Avia, M. D., et al. (2000). Nature over nurture: Temperament, personality, and life span development. *Journal of Personality and Social Psychology, 78,* 173–186.

McCrink, K., & Wynn, K. (2004). Large-number addition and subtraction in infants. *Psychological Science, 15,* 776–781.

McCullough, J. P. (2000). *Treatment for chronic depression: Cognitive Behavioral Analysis System of Psychotherapy (CBASP).* New York: The Guilford Press.

McDaniel, M.A. (2005). Big-brained people are smarter: A meta-analysis of the relationship between in vivo brain volume and intelligence. *Intelligence, 33,* 347–346.

McDougle, C. (1997). Psychopharmacology. In D. Cohen & R. Volkmar (Eds.), *Handbook of autism and pervasive developmental disorders* (2nd ed., pp. 707–729). New York: Wiley.

McEwen, B. S. (2000). The effects of stress on structural and functional plasticity in the hippocampus. In D. S. Charney, E. J. Nestler, & B. S. Bunney (Eds.), *Neurobiology of mental illness* (pp. 475–493). New York: Oxford University Press.

McGaugh, J. L. (2002). Memory consolidation and the amygdale: A systems perspective. *Trends in Neurosciences, 25,* 456–461.

McGlashan, T. H. (1988). A selective review of recent North American long-term follow-up studies of schizophrenia. *Schizophrenia Bulletin, 14,* 515–542.

McGough, J. J., & Barkley, R. A. (2004). Diagnostic controversies in adult attention deficit hyperactivity disorder. *American Journal of Psychiatry, 161,* 1948–1956.

McGue, M., Bacon, S., & Lykken, D. T. (1993). Personality stability and change in early adulthood: A behavioral genetic analysis. *Developmental Psychology, 29,* 96–109.

McGue, M., Bouchard, T. J., Jr., Iacono, W. G., & Lykken, D. T. (1993). Behavioral genetics of cognitive ability: A life-span perspective. In R. Plomin & G. E. McClearn (Eds.), *Nature, nurture, and psychology* (pp. 59–76). Washington, DC: American Psychological Association.

McInnis, M. G., McMahon, F. J, Chase, G. A., Simpson, S. G., Ross, C. A., & DePaulo, J. R. (1993). Anticipation in bipolar affective disorder. *American Journal of Human Genetics, 53,* 385–390.

McNally, R. J. (2003). Recovering memories of trauma: A view from the laboratory. *Current Directions in Psychological Science, 12,* 32–35.

McNally, R. J., Lasko, N. B., Clancy, S. A., Macklin, M. L., Pitman, R. K., & Orr, S. P. (2004). Psychophysiological responding during script-driven imagery in people reporting abduction by space aliens. *Psychological Science, 15,* 493–497.

McQuarrie, E. F., & Mick, D. G. (2003). Visual and verbal rhetorical figures under directed processing versus incidental exposure to advertising. *Journal of Consumer Research, 29,* 579–587.

Meddis, R. (1977). *The sleep instinct.* London: Routledge & Kegan Paul.

Mednick, S. A., Gabrielli, W. F., & Hutchings, B. (1987). Genetic factors in the etiology of criminal behavior. In S. A. Mednick, T. E. Moffitt, & S. A. Stacks (Eds.), *The causes of crime: New biological approaches* (pp. 267–291). Cambridge, MA: Cambridge University Press.

Mednick, S. A., Huttunen, M. O., & Machon, R. A. (1994). Prenatal influenza infections and adult schizophrenia. *Schizophrenia Bulletin, 20,* 263–267.

Mednick, S., Nakayama, K., & Stickgold, R. (2003). Sleep-dependent learning: A nap is as good as a night. *Nature Neuroscience, 6,* 697–698.

Medvec, V. H., Madey, S. F., & Gilovich, T. (1995). When less is more: Counterfactual thinking and satisfaction among Olympic medalists. *Journal of Personality and Social Psychology, 69,* 603–610.

Mehl, M. R., & Pennebaker, J. W. (2003). The sounds of social life: A psychometric analysis of students' daily social environments and natural conversations. *Journal of Personality and Social Psychology, 84,* 857–870.

Mehler, J., & Bever, T. G. (1967). Cognitive capacity of very young children. *Science, 158,* 141–142.

Mehler, J., Jusczyk, P. W., Lambertz, G., Halsted, N., Bertoncini, J., & Amiel-Tison, C. (1988). A precursor of language acquisition in young infants. *Cognition, 29,* 143–178.

Melcher, J. M., & Schooler, J. W. (1996). The misremembrance of wines past: Verbal and perceptual expertise differentially mediate verbal overshadowing of taste memory. *Journal of Memory and Language, 35,* 231–245.

Meltzoff, A. N. (1995). Understanding the intentions of others: Re-enactment of intended acts by 18-month-old children. *Developmental Psychology 31,* 838–850.

Melzack, R., & Wall, P. D. (1982). *The Challenge of pain.* New York: Basic Books.

Merckelbach, H., Devilly, G. J., & Rassin, E. (2002). Alters in dissociative identity disorders: Metaphors or genuine entities? *Clinical Psychology Review, 22,* 481–497.

Messias, E., Kirkpatrick, B., Bromet, E., Ross, D., Buchanan, R. W., Carpenter, W. T., Jr., et al. (2004). Summer birth and deficit schizophrenia: A pooled analysis from 6 countries. *Archives of General Psychiatry, 61,* 985–989.

Meston, C. M., & Frohlich, P. F. (2000). The neurobiology of sexual function. *Archives of General Psychiatry, 57,* 1012–1030.

Metcalfe, J., & Mischel, W. (1999). A hot/cool-system analysis of delay of gratification: Dynamics of willpower. *Psychological Review, 106,* 3–19.

Mezulis, A. H., Abramson, L. Y., Hyde, J. S., & Hankin, B. L. (2004). Is there a universal positivity bias in attributions? A meta-analytic review of individual, developmental, and culture differences in the self-serving attributional bias. *Psychological Bulletin, 130,* 711–747.

Mickelson, K. D., Kessler, R. C., & Shaver, P. R. (1997). Adult attachment in a nationally representative sample. *Journal of Personality and Social Psychology, 73,* 1092–1106.

Miller, B. C., & Benson, B. (1999). Romantic and sexual relationship development during adolescence. In W. Furman, B. B. Brown, & C. Feiring (Eds.), *The development of romantic relationships in adolescence* (pp. 99–121). New York: Cambridge University Press.

Miller, G. A., Galanter, E., & Pribram, K. H. (1960). *Plans and the structure of behavior.* New York: Holt.

Miller, G. E., Freedland, K. E., Carney, R. M., Stetler, C. A., & Banks, W. A. (2003). Cynical hostility, depressive symptoms, and the expression of inflammatory risk markers for coronary heart disease. *Journal of Behavioral Medicine, 26,* 501–515.

Miller, I. W., Norman, W. H., & Keitner, G. I. (1989). Cognitive-behavioral treatment of depressed inpatients: Six- and twelve-month follow-up. *American Journal of Psychiatry, 146,* 1274–1279.

Miller, L. C., & Fishkin, S. A. (1997). On the dynamics of human bonding and reproductive success: Seeking windows on the adapted-for human-environmental interface. In J. Simpson & D. T. Kenrick (Eds.), *Evolutionary social psychology* (pp. 197–236). Mahwah, NJ: Lawrence Erlbaum.

Miller, M. B., & Wolford, G. L. (1999). Theoretical commentary: The role of criterion shift in false memory. *Psychological Review, 106,* 398–405.

Miller, R. S. (1996). *Embarrassment: Poise and peril in everyday life.* New York: Guilford Press.

Miller, R. S. (1997). We always hurt the ones we love: Aversive interactions in close relationships. In R. M. Kowalski (Ed.), *Aversive interpersonal behaviors* (pp. 11–29). New York: Plenum Press.

Miller, W. R., & C'de Baca, J. (2001). *Quantum changes: When epiphanies and sudden insights transform ordinary lives.* New York: Guilford Press.

Miller, W. T. (2000). Rediscovering fire: Small interventions, large effects. *Psychology of Addictive Behaviors, 14,* 6–18.

Milton, J., & Wiseman, R. (2001). Does pi exist? Reply to Storm and Ertel (2001). *Psychological Bulletin, 127,* 434–438.

Mineka, S., Davidson, M., Cook, M., & Keir, R. (1984). Observational conditioning of snake fear in rhesus monkeys. *Journal of Abnormal Psychology, 93,* 355–372.

Mirsky, A. F., Bieliauskas, L. A., French, L. M., Van Kammen, D. P., Jonsson, E., & Sedvall, G. (2000). A 39-year followup of the Genain quadruplets. *Schizophrenia Bulletin, 26,* 699–708.

Mischel, W., & Shoda, Y. (1995). A cognitive-affective system theory of personality: Reconceptualizing situations, dispositions, dynamics, and invariance in personality structure. *Psychological Review, 102,* 246–268.

Mischel, W., Shoda, Y., & Rodriguez, M. L. (1989). Delay of gratification in children. *Science, 244,* 933–938.

Mitelman, S. A., Shihabuddin, L., Brickman, A. M., Hazlett, E. A., & Buchsbaum, M. S. (2005). Volume of the cingulate and outcome in schizophrenia. *Schizophrenia Research, 72,* 91–108.

Mittleman, M. A., Lewis, R. A., Maclure, M., Sherwood, J. B., & Muller, J. E. (2001). Triggering myocardial infarction by marijuana. *Circulation, 103,* 2805–2809.

Miyamoto, Y., & Kitayama, S. (2002). Cultural variation in correspondence bias: The critical role of attitude diagnosticity of socially constrained behavior. *Journal of Personality and Social Psychology, 83,* 1239–1248.

Mizerski, R. (1995). The relationship between cartoon trade character recognition and attitude toward product category in young children. *Journal of Marketing, 59,* 58–70.

Mobbs, D., Greicius, M. D., Abdel-Azim, E., Menon, V., & Reiss, A. L. (2003). Humor modulates the mesolimbic reward centers. *Neuron, 40,* 1041–1048.

Moffitt, T. E., Brammer, G. L., Caspi, A., Fawcett, J. P., Raleigh, M., Yuwiler, A., et al. (1998). Whole blood serotonin relates to violence in an epidemiological study. *Biological Psychiatry, 43,* 446–457.

Moises, H. W., & Gottesman, I. I. (2004). Does glial asthenia predispose to schizophrenia? *Archives of General Psychiatry, 61,* 1170.

Monteith, M. J. (1993). Self-regulation of prejudiced responses: Implications for progress in prejudice reduction efforts. *Journal of Personality and Social Psychology, 65,* 469–485.

Monteith, M. J., Ashburn-Nardo, L., Voils, C. I., & Czopp, A. M. (2002). Putting the brakes on prejudice: On the development and operation of cues for control. *Journal of Personality & Social Psychology, 83,* 1029–1050.

Montepare, J. M., & Vega, C. (1988). Women's vocal reactions to intimate and casual male friends. *Personality and Social Psychology Bulletin, 14,* 103–113.

Morris, N. M., Udry, J. R., Khan-Dawood, F., & Dawood, M. Y. (1987). Marital sex frequency and midcycle female testosterone. *Archives of Sexual Behavior, 16,* 27–37.

Morris, W. N. (1992). A functional analysis of the role of mood in affective systems. In M. S. Clark (Ed.), *Emotion: Review of personality and social psychology* (Vol. 13, pp. 256–293). Newbury Park, CA: Sage.

Mortensen, E. L., Michaelsen, K. F., Sanders, S. A., & Reinisch, J. M. (2002). The association between duration of breastfeeding and adult intelligence. *Journal of the American Medical Association, 287,* 2365–2371.

Morton, J., & Johnson, M. H. (1991). CONSPEC and CONLERN: A two-process theory of infant face recognition. *Psychological Review, 98,* 164–181.

Moscovitch, M. (1995). Confabulation. In D. L. Schacter (Ed.), *Memory distortions: How minds, brains, and societies reconstruct the past* (pp. 226–251). Cambridge, MA: Harvard University Press.

Moskowitz, A. K. (2004). "Scared stiff": Catatonia as an evolutionary-based fear response. *Psychological Bulletin, 111,* 984–1002.

Moskowitz, H., & Fiorentino, D. A. (2000). *Review of the literature on the effects of low doses of alcohol on driving-related skills.* Washington, DC: National Highway Traffic Safety Administration.

Mowery, P. D., Brick, P. D., & Farrelly, M. (2000). *Pathways to Established Smoking: Results from the 1999 National Youth Tobacco Survey* (Legacy First Look Report 3). Washington, DC: American Legacy Foundation.

Mroczek, D. K., & Kolarz, C. M.(1998). The effect of age on positive and negative affect: A developmental perspective on happiness. *Journal of Personality and Social Psychology, 75,* 1333–1349.

Mufson, L., Dorta, K. P., Wickramaratne, P., Nomura, Y., Olfson, M., & Weissman, M. M. (2004). A randomized effectiveness trial of interpersonal psychotherapy for depressed adolescents. *Archives of General Psychiatry, 61,* 577–584.

Muhle, R., Trentacoste, S. V., & Rapin, I. (2004). The genetics of autism. *Pediatrics, 113,* 472–486.

Munson, M. L., & Sutton, P. D. (2004). *Births, marriages, divorces, and deaths: Provisional data for May 2004* (National Vital Statistics Reports, Vol. 53, No. 8). Hyattsville, MD: National Center for Health Statistics, Centers for Disease Control and Prevention.

Muraven, M., & Baumeister, R. F. (2000). Self-regulation and depletion of limited resources: Does self-control resemble a muscle? *Psychological Bulletin, 126,* 247–259.

Mustanski, B. S., Chivers, M. L., & Bailey, J. M. (2002). A critical review of recent biological research on human sexual orientation. *Annual Review of Sex Research, 13,* 89–140.

National Research Council, Committee on Educational Interventions for Children with Autism (2001). *Educating young children with autism.* Washington, DC: National Academy Press.

Neidemeyer, E., & Naidu, S. B. (1997). Attention deficit hyperactivity disorder (ADHD) and frontal-motor cortex disconnection. *Clinical Electroencephalography, 28,* 130–135.

Neisser, U., & Harsch, N. (1993). Phantom flashbulbs: False recollections of hearing the news about Challenger. In E. Winograd & U. Neisser (Eds.), *Affect and accuracy in recall: Studies of "flashbulb" memories* (pp. 9–31). New York: Cambridge University Press.

Neisser, U., Boodoo, G., Bouchard, T. J. Jr., Boykin, A. W., Brody, N., Ceci, S. J., et al. (1996). Intelligence: Knowns and unknowns. *American Psychologist, 51,* 77–101.

Nelson, K. B., Grether, J. K., Croen, L. A., Dambrosia, J. M., Dickens, B. F., Jelliffe, L. L., et al. (2001). Neuropeptides and neurotrophins in neonatal blood of children with autism or mental retardation. *Annals of Neurology, 49,* 597–606.

Neuberg, S. L., Smith, D. M., & Asher, T. (2000). Why people stigmatize: Toward a biocultural framework. In T. F. Heatherton, R. E. Kleck, M. Hebl, & J. G. Hull (Eds.), *The social psychology of stigma* (pp. 31–61). New York: Guilford.

Neylan, T. C., Canick, J. D., Hall, S. E., Reus, V. I., Spolosky, R. M., & Wolkowitz, O. M. (2001). Cortisol levels predict cognitive impairment induced by electroconvulsive therapy. *Biological Psychiatry, 50,* 331–336.

Ng, D. M., & Jeffrey, E. W. (2003). Relationships between perceived stress and health behaviors in a sample of working adults. *Health Psychology, 22,* 638–642.

NIH Technology Assessment Conference Panel. (1993). Methods for voluntary weight loss and control. *Annals of Internal Medicine, 199,* 764–770.

Nisbett, R. E. (2003). *The geography of thought.* New York: Free Press.

Nisbett, R. E., Peng, K., Choi, I., & Norenzayan, A. (2001). Culture and systems of thought: Holistic versus analytic cognition. *Psychological Review, 108,* 291–310.

Nisbett, R. E., & Wilson, T. D. (1977). Telling more than we can know: Verbal reports on mental processes. *Psychological Review, 84,* 231–259.

Norem, J. K. (1989). Cognitive strategies as personality: Effectiveness, specificity, flexibility and change. In D. M. Buss & N. Cantor (Eds.), *Personality psychology: Recent trends and emerging issues* (pp. 45–60). New York: Springer-Verlag.

North, A. C., Hargreaves, D. J., & O'Neill, S. A. (2000). The importance of music to adolescents. *British Journal of Educational Psychology, 70,* 255–272.

Novotny, S. L., Hollander, E., Allen, A., Aronowitz, B. R., DeCaria, C., Cartwright, C., et al. (2000). Behavioral response to oxytocin challenge in adult autistic disorders. *Biological Psychiatry, 47,* 523.

Noyes, R. (1991). Suicide and panic disorder: A review. *Journal of Affective Disorders, 22,* 1–11.

Nurnberger, J. J., Goldin, L. R., & Gershon, E. S. (1994). Genetics of psychiatric disorders. In G. Winokur & P. M. Clayton (Eds.), *The medical basis of psychiatry* (pp. 459–492). Philadelphia: W. B. Saunders.

Oberauer, K., Schulze, R., Wilhelm, O., Süss, H. M. (2005). Working memory and intelligence—their correlation and their relation: Comment on Ackerman, Beier, and Boyle (2005). *Psychological Bulletin, 131,* 61–65.

Ochsner, K. N. (2000). Are affective events richly recollected or simply familiar? The experience and process of recognizing feelings past. *Journal of Experimental Psychology: General, 129,* 242–261.

Ochsner, K. N., Bunge, S. A., Gross, J. J., & Gabrieli, J. D. E. (2002). Rethinking feelings: An fMRI study of the cognitive regulation of emotion. *Journal of Cognitive Neuroscienc* e, *14*, 1215–1299.

Ogbu, J. U. (1994). From cultural differences to differences in cultural frames of reference. In P. M. Greenfield & R. R. Cocking (Eds.), *Cross cultural roots of minority child development* (pp. 365–392). Hillsdale, NJ: Erlbaum.

O'Kane, G. O., Kensinger, E. A., & Corkin, S. (2004). Evidence for semantic learning in profound amnesia: An investigation with the patient H. M. *Hippocampus, 14,* 417–425.

Olanow, C. W., Goetz, C. G., Kordower, J. H., Stoessl, A. J., Sossi, V., Brin, M. F., et al. (2003). A double-blind controlled trial of bilateral fetal nigral transplantation in Parkinson's disease. *Annals of Neurology, 54,* 403–414.

O'Leary, S. G. (1995). Parental discipline mistakes. *Current Directions in Psychological Science, 4,* 11–13.

Olds, J. (1962). Hypothalamic substrates of reward. *Psychological Review, 42,* 554–604.

Olds, J., & Milner, P. (1954). Positive reinforcement produced by electrical stimulation of the septal area and other regions of the rat brain. *Journal of Comparative and Physiological Psychology, 47,* 419–428.

Olfson, M., Marcus, S. C., Druss, B., Elinson, L., Tanielian, T., & Pincus, H. A. (2002). National trends in the outpatient treatment of depression. *Journal of the American Medical Association, 287,* 203–209.

Olfson, M., Shaffer, D., Marcus, S. C., & Greenberg, T. (2003). Relationship between antidepressant medication treatment and suicide in adolescents. *Archives of General Psychiatry, 60,* 978–982.

Oltmans, T. F., Neale, J. M., Davison, G. C. (Eds.). (1999). *Case studies in abnormal psychology.* New York: John Wiley & Sons, Inc.

O'Neal, J. M. (1984). First person account: Finding myself and loving it. *Schizophrenia Bulletin, 10,* 109–110.

O'Neil, J. (2004, December 29). Slow-motion miracle: One boy's journey out of autism's grasp. *The New York Times,* p. B8.

Osterling, J., & Dawson, G. (1994). Early recognition of children with autism: A study of first birthday home videotapes. *Journal of Autism and Developmental Disorders, 24,* 247–257.

Ottieger, A. E., Tressell, P. A., Inciardi, J. A., & Rosales, T. A. (1992). Cocaine use patterns and overdose. *Journal of Psychoactive Drugs, 24,* 399–410.

Packard, M. G., & Knowlton, B. J. (2002). Learning and memory functions of the basal ganglia. *Annual Review of Neuroscience, 25,* 563–593.

Paller, K. A., & Wagner, A. D. (2002). Observing the transformation of experience into memory. *Trends in Cognitive Science, 6,* 93–102.

Panksepp, J. (1992). Oxytocin effects on emotional processes: Separation distress, social bonding, and relationships to psychiatric disorders. *Annals of the New York Academy of Sciences, 652,* 243–252.

Papadimitrious, G. N., Zervas, I. M., & Papakostas, Y. G. (2001). Unilateral ECT for prophylaxis in affective illness. *Journal of ECT, 17,* 229–231.

Paquette, V., Levesque, J., Mensour, B., Leroux, J. M., Beaudoin, G., Bourgouin, P., & Beauregard, M. (2003). "Change the mind and you change the brain": Effects of cognitive-behavioral therapy on the neural correlates of spider phobia. *Neuroimage, 18,* 401–409.

Pascual-Leone, A. Catala, M. D., & Pascual-Leone, P. A. (1996). Lateralized effect of rapid-rate transcranial magnetic stimulation of the prefrontal cortex on mood. *Neurology, 46,* 499–502.

Pasupathi, M., & Carstensen, L. L. (2003). Age and emotional experience during mutual reminiscing. *Psychology and Aging, 18,* 430–442.

Patterson, C. M., & Newman, J. P. (1993). Reflectivity and learning from aversive events: Toward a psychological mechanism for the syndromes of disinhibition. *Psychological Review, 100,* 716–736.

Paykel, E. S. (2003). Life events and affective disorders. *Acta Psychiatrica Scandinavica, 108,* 61–66.

Payne, B. K. (2001). Prejudice and perception: The role of automatic and controlled processes in misperceiving a weapon. *Journal of Personality and Social Psychology, 81,* 181–192.

Paz-Elizur, T., Krupsky, M., Blumenstein, S., Elinger, D., Schechtman, E., & Livneh, Z. (2003). DNA repair activity for oxidative damage and risk of lung cancer. *Journal of the National Cancer Institute, 95,* 1312–1331.

Pegna, A. J., Khateb, A., Lazeyras, F., & Seghier, M. L. (2005). Discriminating emotional faces without primary visual cortices involves the right amygdala. *Nature Neuroscience, 8,* 24–25.

Pelham, W. E., McBurnett, K., Harper, G. W., Milich, R., Murphy, D. A., Clinton, J., et al. (1990). Methylphenidate and baseball playing in ADHD children: Who's on first? *Journal of Consulting and Clinical Psychology, 58,* 130–133.

Pelham, W., & Bender, M. E. (1982). Peer relationships in hyperactive children: Description and treatment. In K. D. Gadow & I. Bailer (Eds.), *Advances in learning and behavioral disabilities: A research annual.* Greenwich, CT: JAI Press.

Pennebaker, J. W. (1990). *Opening up: the healing power of confiding in others.* New York: William Morrow & Co., Inc.

Pennebaker, J. W. (1995). *Emotion, Disclosure, & Health.* Washington, DC: American Psychological Association.

Penton-Voak, I. S., Perrett, D. I., Castles, D., Burt, M., Koyabashi, T., & Murray, L. K. (1999). Female preference for male faces changes cyclically. *Nature, 399,* 741–742.

Peretz, I. (1996). Can we lose memory for music? A case of music agnosia in a nonmusician. *Journal of Cognitive Neuroscience, 8,* 481–496.

Peretz, I., & Zatorre, R. J. (2005). Brain organization for music processing. *Annual Review of Psychology, 56,* 89–114.

Perrett, D. I., May, K. A., & Yoshikawa, S. (1994). Facial shape and judgments of female attractiveness. *Nature, 368,* 239–242.

Perrett, D. I., Mistlin, A. J., & Chitty, A. J. (1987). Visual neurons responsive to faces. *Trends in Neurosciences, 10,* 358–364.

Petitto, L. A. (1988). "Language" in the pre-linguistic child. In F. Kessel (Ed.), *Development of Language and Language Researchers: Essays in Honor of Roger Brown* (pp. 187–221). Hillsdale, NJ: Lawrence Erlbaum Associates.

Petitto, L. A. (2000). On the biological foundations of human language. In H. Lane & K. Emmorey (Eds.), *The signs of language revisited* (pp. 447–471). Mahwah, NJ: Lawrence Erlbaum Associates.

Petitto, L. A., Holowka, S., Sergio, L., & Ostry, D. (2001). Language rhythms in babies' hand movements. *Nature, 413*, 35–36.

Petrie, K. J., Fontanilla, I., Thomas, M. G., Booth, R. J., & Pennebaker, J. W. (2004). Effect of written emotional expression on immune function in patients with human immunodeficiency virus infection: A randomized trial. *Psychosomatic Medicine, 66*, 272–275.

Petronis, A., & Kennedy, J. L. (1995). Unstable genes—Unstable mind? *American Journal of Psychiatry, 152*, 164–172.

Pett, M. A., Wampold, B. E., Turner, C. W., & Vaughan-Cole, B. (1999). Paths of influence of divorce on preschool children's psychosocial adjustment. *Journal of Family Psychology, 13*, 145–164.

Petty, R. E., & Cacioppo, J. T. (1986). *Communication and persuasion: Central and peripheral routes to attitude change.* New York: Springer-Verlag.

Pezdek, K., & Hodge, D. (1999). Planting false childhood memories in children: The role of event plausibility. *Child Development, 70*, 887–895.

Phelps, E. A. (2004). Human emotion and memory: Interactions of the amygdala and hippocampal complex. *Current Opinion in Neurobiology, 14*, 198–202.

Phelps, E. A., O'Connor, K. J., Cunningham, W. A., Funayama, E. S., Gatenby, J. C., Gore, J. C., et al. (2000). Performance on indirect measures of race evaluation predicts amygdala activation. *Journal of Cognitive Neuroscience, 12*, 729–738.

Phillips, M. L., Young, A. W., Senior, C., Brammer, M., Andrew, C., Calder, A. J., et al. (1997). A specific neural substrate for perceiving facial expressions of disgust. *Nature, 398*, 495–498.

Phinney, J. S. (1990). Ethnic identity in adolescents and adults: Review of research. *Psychological Bulletin, 108*, 499–514.

Piggott, S., & Milner, B. (1993). Memory for different aspects of complex visual scenes after unilateral temporal- or frontal-lobe resection. *Neuropsychologia, 31*, 1–15.

Pinker, S. (1984). *Language learnability and language development.* Cambridge, MA: Harvard University Press.

Pinker, S. (1994). *The language instinct.* New York: William Morrow and Company.

Pinker, S. (1997). *How the mind works.* New York: Norton.

Pitman, R. K., Sanders, K. M., Zusman, R. M., Healy, A. R., Cheema, F., Lasko, N. B., et al. (2002). Pilot study of secondary prevention of posttraumatic stress disorder with propranolol. *Biological Psychiatry, 51*, 189–192.

Plakun, E. M., Burkhardt, P. E., & Muller, A. P. (1985). Fourteen-year follow-up of borderline and schizotypal personality disorders. *Comprehensive Psychiatry, 26*, 448–455.

Plant, E. A., Hyde, J. S., Keltner, D., & Devine, P. G. (2000). The gender stereotyping of emotions. *Psychology of Women Quarterly, 24*, 81–92.

Plant, E. A., & Peruche, M. (2005). The consequences of race for Police Officers' responses to criminal suspects. *Psychological Science, 16*, 180–183.

Plomin, R., & Caspi, A. (1999). Behavioral genetics and personaliity. In L. A. Pervin & O. P. John (Eds.), *Handbook of personality: Theory and research* (2nd ed., pp. 251–276). New York: Guilford Press.

Plomin, R., & Spinath, F. M. (2002). Genetics and general cognitive ability (g). *Trends in Cognitive Sciences, 6*, 169–176.

Plomin, R., & Spinath, F. M. (2004). Intelligence: Genetics, genes, and genomics. *Journal of Personality and Social Psychology, 86*, 112–129.

Polivy, J., & Herman, C. P. (1985). Dieting and bingeing: A causal analysis. *American Psychologist, 40*, 193–201.

Pollock, K. M. (2004). Exercise in treating depression: Broadening the psychotherapist's role. *Journal of Clinical Psychology, 57*, 1289–1300.

Pomerleau, O., Pomerleau, C., & Namenek, R. (1998). Early experiences with tobacco among women smokers, ex-smokers, and never-smokers. *Addiction, 93*, 595–599.

Pope, H. G., Jr., Kouri, E. M., & Hudson, J. I. (2000). Effects of supraphysiologic doses of testosterone on mood and aggression in normal men: A randomized controlled trial. *Archives of General Psychiatry, 57*, 133–140.

Posner, M. I., & DiGirolamo, G. J. (2000). Cognitive neuroscience: Origins and promise. *Psychological Bulletin, 126*, 873–889.

Premack, D. (1970). Mechanisms of self-control. In W. A. Hunt (Ed.), *Learning mechanisms in smoking* (pp. 107–123). Chicago: Aldine.

Pylyshyn, Z. (1984). *Computation and cognition.* Cambridge, MA: MIT Press.

Pylyshyn, Z. W. (1999). Is vision continuous with cognition? The case for cognitive impenetrability of visual perception. *Behavioral and Brain Sciences, 22*, 341–365.

Pyszczynski, T., Greenberg, J., Solomon, S., Arndt, J., & Schimel, J. (2004). Why do people need self-esteem? A theoretical and empirical review. *Psychological Bulletin, 130*, 435–468.

Raesaenen, S., Pakaslahti, A., Syvaelahti, E., Jones, P. B., & Isohanni, M. (2000). Sex differences in schizophrenia: A review. *Nordic Journal of Psychiatry, 54*, 37–45.

Raine, A. (1989). Evoked potentials and psychopathy. *International Journal of Psychopathology, 8*, 1–16.

Raine, A., Mellingen, K., Liu, J., Venables, P., & Mednick, S. A. (2003). Effects of environmental enrichment at ages 3–5 years on schizotypal personality and antisocial behavior at ages 17 and 23 years. *American Journal of Psychiatry, 160*, 1627–1635.

Rakic, P. (2000). Molecular and cellular mechanisms of neuronal migration: Relevance to cortical epilepsies. *Advances in Neurology, 84*, 1–14.

Raleigh, M. J., McGuire, M. T., Brammer, G. L., Pollack, D. B., & Yuwiler, A. (1991). Serotonergic mechanisms promote dominance in adult male vervet monkeys. *Brain Research, 559*, 181–190.

Ramachandran, V. S. (1993). Behavioral and magnetoencephalographic correlates of plasticity in the adult human brain. *Proceedings of the National Academy of Sciences, 90*, 10413–10420.

Rampon, C., Jiang, C. H., Dong, H., Tang, Y., Lockhart, D. J., Schultz, P. G., et al. (2000). Effects of environmental enrichment on gene expression in the brain. *Proceedings of the National Academy of Sciences, 97*, 12880–12884.

Rapee, R. M., Brown, T. A., Antony, M. M., & Barlow, D. H. (1992). Response to hyperventilation and inhalation of 5.5% carbon dioxide-enriched air across the DSM III-R anxiety disorders. *Journal of Abnormal Psychology, 101*, 538–552.

Rapoport, J. (1990). *The boy who couldn't stop washing: The experience and treatment of obsessive-compulsive disorder*. New York: Penguin Books.

Rapoport, J. L. (1989). The biology of obsessions and compulsions. *Scientific American, 260,* 83–89.

Rapoport, J. L. (1991). Recent advances in obsessive-compulsive disorder. *Neuropsychopharmacology, 5,* 1–10.

Rauch, S. L., van der Kolk, B. A., Fisler, R. E., & Alpert, N. M. (1996). A symptom provocation study of posttraumatic stress disorder using positron emission tomography and script-driven imagery. *Archives of General Psychiatry, 53,* 380–387.

Rauscher, F. H., Shaw, G. L., & Ky, K. N. (1993). Music and spatial task performance, *Nature, 365,* 611.

Rayner, K., Foorman, B. R., Perfetti, C. A., Pesetsky, D., & Seidenberg, M. S. (2001). How psychological science informs the teaching of reading. *Psychological Science in the Public Interest, 2,* 31–74.

Read, J. P., & Brown, R. A. (2003). The role of exercise in alcoholism treatment and recovery. *Professional Psychology: Research and Practice, 34,* 49–56.

Recarte, M., & Nunes, L. M. (2003). Mental workload while driving: Effects on visual search, discrimination, and decision making. *Journal of Experimental Psychology: Applied, 9,* 119–137.

Reeves, L. M., & Weisberg, R. W. (1994). The role of content and abstract information in analogical transfer. *Psychological Bulletin, 115,* 381–400.

Regard, M., & Landis, T. (1997). "Gourmand syndrome": Eating passion associated with right anterior lesions. *Neurology, 48,* 1185–1190.

Reichelt, K. L., Knivsberg, A. M., Lind, G., & Nodland, M. (1991). Probable etiology and possible treatment of childhood autism. *Brain Dysfunction, 4,* 308–319.

Reinders, A. A., Nijenhuis, E. R., Paans, A. M., Korf, J., Willemsen, A. T., & den Boer, J. A. (2003). One brain, two selves. *Neuroimage, 20,* 2119–2125.

Reis, H. T., Collins, W. A., & Berscheid, E. (2000). The relationship context of human behavior and development. *Psychological Bulletin, 126,* 844–872.

Renfrow, P. J., & Gosling, S. D. (2003). The do re mi's of everyday life: The structure and personality correlates of music preferences. *Journal of Personality and Social Psychology, 84,* 1236–1256.

Repetti, R. L. (1997). *The effects of daily job stress on parent behavior with preadolescents.* Paper presented at the biennial meeting of the Society for Research in Child Development, April, Washington, DC.

Rescorla, R. (1966). Predictability and number of pairings in Pavlovian fear conditioning. *Psychonomic Science, 4,* 383–384.

Rescorla, R. A., & Wagner, A. R. (1972). A theory of Pavlovian conditioning: Variations in the effectiveness of reinforcement and nonreinforcement. In A. H. Black & W. F. Prokosy (Eds.), *Classical conditioning II: Current research and theory* (pp. 64–99). New York: Appleton-Century-Crofts.

Ressler, K. J., Rothbaum, B. O., Tannenbaum, L., Anderson, P., Graap, K., Zimand, E., Hodges L, & Davis M. (2004). Cognitive enhancers as adjuncts to psychotherapy: use of D-cycloserine in phobic individuals to facilitate extinction of fear. *Archives of General Psychiatry, 61,* 1136-1144.

Reynolds, D. V. (1969). Surgery in the rat during electrical analgesia induced by focal brain stimulation. *Science, 164,* 444–445.

Rhodes, G., Byatt, G., Michie, P. T., & Puce, A. (2004). Is the fusiform face area specialized for faces, individuation, or expert individuation? *Journal of Cognitive Neuroscience, 16,* 189–203.

Richeson, J. A., Baird, A. A., Gordon, H. L., Heatherton, T. F., Wyland, C. L., Trawalter, S., et al. (2003). An fMRI investigation of the impact of interracial contact on executive function. *Nature Neuroscience, 6,* 1323–1328.

Ridley, M. (2003). *Nature versus nurture: Genes, experience, and what makes us human.* New York: HarperCollins.

Rifkin, A., & Rifkin, W. (2004). Adolescents with depression. *Journal of the American Medical Association, 292,* 2577–2578.

Rinck, M., Reinecke, A., Ellwart, T., Heuer, K., & Becker, E. S. (2005). Speeded detection and increased distraction in fear of spiders: Evidence from eye movements. *Journal of Abnormal Psychology, 114,* 235–248.

Rizzolatti, G., & Arbib, M. A. (1998). Language within our grasp. *Trends in Neuroscience, 21,* 188–194.

Rizzolatti, G., & Craighero, L. (2004). The mirror-neuron system. *Annual Reviews in Neuroscience, 27,* 169–192.

Rizzolatti, G., Fadiga, L., Gallese, V., & Fogassi, L. (1996). Premotor cortex and the recognition of motor actions. *Cognitive Brain Research, 3,* 131–141.

Roberts, B. W., & Friend-DelVecchio, W. (2000). The rank-order consistency of personality traits from childhood to old age: A quantitative review of longitudinal studies. *Psychological Bulletin, 126,* 3–25.

Roberts, D. F. (2000). Media and youth: Access, exposure, and privatization. *Journal of Adolescent Health 27* (Suppl.), 8–14.

Robins, L. N., Helzer, J. E., & Davis, D. H. (1975). Narcotic use in Southeast Asia and afterward: An interview study of 898 Vietnam returnees. *Archives of General Psychiatry, 32,* 955–961.

Robins, L. N., & Regier, D. A. (1991). *Psychiatric disorders in America: The epidemiological catchment areas study.* New York: The Free Press.

Rock, I. (1984). *Perception.* New York: Scientific American Books.

Roediger, H. L., & McDermott, K. B. (1995). Creating false memories: Remembering words not presented in lists. *Journal of Experimental Psychology: Learning, Memory, and Cognition, 21,* 803–814.

Rogan, M. T., Stäubli, U. V., & LeDoux, J. E. (1997). Fear conditioning induces associative long-term potentiation in the amygdala. *Nature, 390,* 604–607.

Rogers, T. B., Kuiper, N. A., & Kirker, W. S. (1977). Self-reference and the encoding of personal information. *Journal of Personality and Social Psychology, 35,* 677–688.

Rolls, E. T., Burton, M. J., & Mora, F. (1980). Neurophysiological analysis of brain-stimulation reward in the monkey. *Brain Research, 194,* 339–357.

Rolls, E. T., Murzi, E., Yaxley, S., Thorpe, S. J., & Simpson, S. J. (1986). Sensory-specific satiety: Food-specific reduction in responsiveness of ventral forebrain neurons after feeding in the monkey. *Brain Research, 368,* 79–86.

Rosenbluth, M., & Silver, D. (1992). The inpatient treatment of borderline personality disorder. In D. Silver & M. Rosenbluth, *Handbook of borderline disorders.* Madison, CT: International Universities Press.

Rosenfeld, J. P. (2001). Event-related potentials in detection of deception. In M. Kleiner (Ed.), *Handbook of Polygraph* (pp. 265–286). New York: Academic Press.

Rosenman, R. H., Brand, R. J., Jenkins, C. D., Friedman, M., Straus, R., & Wurm, M. (1975). Coronary heart disease in the Western Collaborative Group Study: Final follow-up experience of 8½ years. *Journal of the American Medical Association, 233,* 872–877.

Rosenstein, D., & Oster, H. (1988). Differential facial responses to four basic tastes in newborns. *Child Development, 59,* 1555–1568.

Rosenthal, D., (Ed). (1963). *The Genain quadruplets.* New York: Basic Books.

Rosenzweig, M. R., Bennett, E. L., & Diamond, M. C. (1972). Brain changes in response to experience. *Scientific American, 226,* 22–29.

Ross, D. M., & Ross, S. A. (1982). *Hyperactivity: Research, theory, and action.* New York: Wiley.

Rothbaum, B. O., Hodges, L., Alarcon, R., Ready, D., Shahar, F., Graap, K., et al. (1999). Virtual reality exposure therapy for PTSD Vietnam veterans: A case study. *Journal of Traumatic Stress, 12,* 263–271.

Rovee-Collier, C. (1999). The development of infant memory. *Current Directions in Psychological Science, 8,* 80–85.

Rowe, D. C., Chassin, L., Presson, C., & Sherman, S. J. (1996). Parental smoking and the "epidemic" spread of cigarette smoking. *Journal of Applied Social Psychology, 26,* 437–445.

Rozin, P. (1996). Sociocultural influences on human food selection. In E. D. Capaldi (Ed.), *Why we eat what we eat: The psychology of eating* (pp. 233–263). Washington, DC: American Psychological Association.

Rozin, P., & Kalat, J. W. (1971). Specific hungers and poison avoidance as adaptive specializations of learning. *Psychological Review, 78,* 459–486.

Rubenstein, A. J., Kalakanis, L., Langlois, J. H. (1999). Infant preferences for attractive faces: A cognitive explanation. *Developmental Psychology, 35,* 848–855.

Rudman, L.A., & Goodwin, S.A. (2004). Gender differences in automatic in-group bias: Why do women like women more than men like men? *Journal of Personality and Social Psychology, 87,* 494–509.

Rusbult, C. E., & Van Lange, P. A. M. (1996). Interdependence processes. In E. T. Higgins & A. Kruglanski (Eds.), *Social psychology: Handbook of basic principles* (pp. 564–596). New York: Guilford Press.

Russell, J. A. (1980). A circumplex model of affect. *Journal of Personality and Social Psychology, 39,* 1161–1178.

Russell, J. A. (1994). Is there universal recognition of emotion from facial expressions? A review of the cross-cultural studies. *Psychological Bulletin, 115,* 102–141.

Russell, J. A., & L. Feldman Barrett. (1999). Core affect, prototypical emotional episodes, and other things called emotion: Dissecting the elephant. *Journal of Personality and Social Psychology, 76,* 805–819.

Russell, M. A. H. (1990). The nicotine trap: A 40-year sentence for four cigarettes. *British Journal of Addiction, 85,* 293–300.

Rutter, M. (2005). Incidence of autism disorders: Changes over time and their meaning. *Acta Paediatrica, 94,* 2–15.

Rymer, R. (1993). *Genie: A scientific tragedy.* New York: HarperCollins.

Sabol, S. Z., Nelson, M. L., Fisher, C., Gunzerath, L., Brody, C. L., Hu, S., et al. (1999). A genetic association for cigarette smoking behavior. *Health Psychology, 18,* 7–13.

Sachs, J. (1967). Recognition memory for syntactic and semantic aspects of connected discourse. *Perception and Psychophysics, 2,* 437–442.

Sacks, O. (1995). *An anthropologist on Mars: Seven paradoxical tales.* New York: Knopf.

Salfati, C. G. (2000). The nature of expressiveness and instrumentality in homicide and its implications for offender profiling. In P. H. Blackman, V. L. Leggett, B. L. Olson, & J. P. Jarvis (Eds.), *The varieties of homicide and its research: Proceedings of the 1999 meeting of the Homicide Research Working Group.* Washington, DC: Federal Bureau of Investigation.

Salovey, P., & Mayer, J.D. (1990). Emotional intelligence. *Imagination, Cognition, and Personality, 9,* 185–211.

Salthouse, T. (1992). The information-processing perspective on cognitive aging. In R. Sternberg & C. Berg (Eds.), *Intellectual development.* Cambridge, MA: Cambridge University Press.

Sanderson, W. C., & Barlow, D. H. (1990). A description of patients diagnosed with DSM-III-R generalized anxiety disorder. *The Journal of Nervous and Mental Disease, 178,* 588–591.

Sapolsky, R. M. (1994). *Why zebras don't get ulcers.* New York: Freeman.

Savic, I., Berglund, H., & Lindström, P. (2005). Brain responses to putative pheromones in homosexual men. *Proceedings of the National Academy of Sciences, 102,* 7356–7361.

Savitz, J. B., & Ramesar, R. S. (2004). Genetic variants implicated in personality: A review of the more promising candidates. *American Journal of Medical Genetics, 15,* 20–32.

Sayette, M. A. (1993). An appraisal-disruption model of alcohol's effects on stress responses in social drinkers. *Psychological Bulletin, 114,* 459–476.

Scarr, S., & McCarthy, K. (1983). How people make their own environments: A theory of genotype l environment effects. *Child Development, 54,* 424–435.

Schachter, S. (1959). *The psychology of affiliation.* Stanford, CA: Stanford University Press.

Schachter, S. (1982). Recidivism and self-cure of smoking and obesity. *American Psychologist, 37,* 436–444.

Schachter, S., & Singer, J. (1962). Cognitive, social, and physiological determinants of emotional state. *Psychological Review, 69,* 379–399.

Schacter, D. L. (1996). *Searching for memory: The brain, the mind, and the past.* New York: Basic Books.

Schacter, D. L. (1999). The seven sins of memory: Insights from psychology and cognitive neuroscience. *American Psychologist, 54,* 182–203.

Schacter, D. L., & Buckner, R. L. (1998). On the relations among priming, conscious recollection, and intentional retrieval: Evidence from neuroimaging research. *Neurobiology of Learning and Memory, 70*, 284–303.

Schaie, K. W. (1990). Intellectual development in adulthood. In J. E. Birren & K. W. Schaie (Eds.), *Handbook of the psychology of aging* (3rd ed.). New York: Van Nostrand Reinhold.

Schank, R. C., & Abelson, R. P. (1977). *Scripts, plans, goals, and understanding.* Hillsdale, NJ: Erlbaum.

Scheerer, M. (1963). Problem-solving. *Scientific American, 208*, 118–128.

Schiffman, J., Walker, E., Ekstrom, M., Schulsinger, F., Sorensen, H., & Mednick, S. (2004). Childhood videotaped social and neuromotor precursors of schizophrenia: A prospective investigation. *American Journal of Psychiatry, 161*, 2021–2027.

Schmahmann, J. D, & Sherman, J. C. (1998). The cerebellar cognitive affective syndrome. *Brain, 121*, 561–579.

Schmajuk, N. A., Lamoureux, J. A., & Holland, P. C. (1998). Occasion setting: A neural network approach. *Psychological Review, 105*, 3–32.

Schmidt, F. L., & Hunter, J. (2004). General mental ability in the world of work: Occupational attainment and job performance. *Journal of Personality and Social Psychology, 86*, 162–173.

Schmitt, D. P., Alcalay, L., Allik, J., Angleitner, A., Ault, L., Austers, I., et al. (2003). Universal sex differences in the desire for sexual variety: Tests from 52 nations, 6 continents, and 13 islands. *Journal of Personality & Social Psychology, 85*, 85–104.

Schoenemann, P. T., Sheehan, M. J., & Glotzer, L. D. (2005). Prefrontal white matter volume is disproportionately larger in humans than in other primates. *Nature Neuroscience, 8*, 242–252.

Schooler, J. W. (2002). Verbalizaton produces a transfer inappropriate processing shift. *Applied Cognitive Psychology, 16*, 989–997.

Schooler, J. W., & Engstler-Schooler, T. Y. (1990). Verbal overshadowing of visual memories: Some things are better left unsaid. *Cognitive Psychology 22*, 36–71.

Schreiber, F. R. (1974). *Sybil: The true story of a woman possessed by sixteen personalities.* London: Penguin.

Schuckit, M. A., Edenberg, H. J., Lakmijn, J., Flury, L., Smith, T. L., Reich, T., et al. (2001). A genome-wide search for genes that relate to a low level of response to alcohol. *Alcoholism: Clinical and Experimental Research, 25*, 323–329.

Schulz, K. P., Fan, J., Tang, C. Y., Newcorn, J. H., Buchsbaum, M. S., Cheung, A. M., et al. (2004). Response inhibition in adolescents diagnosed with attention deficit hyperactivity disorder during childhood: An event-related fMRI study. *American Journal of Psychiatry, 161*, 1650–1657.

Schwartz, B. (2004). *The paradox of choice: Why more is less.* New York: Ecco.

Schwartz, C. E., Wright, C. I., Shin, L. M., Kagan, J., & Rauch, S. L. (2003). Inhibited and uninhibited infants "grown up": Adult amygdalar response to novelty. *Science, 300*, 1952–1953.

Schwartz, J. M., Stoessel, P. W., Baxter, L. R., Martin, K. M., & Phelps, M. E. (1996). Systematic changes in cerebral glucose metabolic rate after successful behavior modification treatment of obsessive-compulsive disorder. *Archives of General Psychiatry, 53*, 109–113.

Schwarz, N., & Clore, G. L. (1983). Mood, misattribution, and judgments of well-being: Informative and directive functions of affective states. *Journal of Personality and Social Psychology, 45*, 513–523.

Sclafani, A., & Springer, D. (1976). Dietary obesity in adult rats: Similarities to hypothalamic and human obesity syndromes. *Physiology and Behavior, 17*, 461–471.

Sedikides, C., Gaertner, L., & Toguchi, Y. (2003). Pancultural self-enhancement. *Journal of Personality and Social Psychology, 84*, 60–79.

Segerstrom, S. C., & Miller, G. E. (2004). Psychological stress and the human immune system: A Meta-analytic study of 30 years of inquiry. *Psychological Bulletin, 130,* 601–630.

Seguin, J. R. (2004). Neurocognitive elements of antisocial behavior: Relevance of an orbitofrontal cortex account. *Brain and Cognition, 55*, 185–197.

Seligman, M. (1970). On the generality of the laws of learning. *Psychological Review, 77*, 406–418.

Seligman, M. E. P. (1974). Depression and learned helplessness. In R. J. Friedman & M. M. Katz (Eds.), *The psychology of depression: Contemporary theory and research.* Washington, DC: V. H. Winston.

Seligman, M. E. P. (1975). *Helplessness: On depression, development, and death.* San Francisco: W. H. Freeman.

Seligman, M. E. P., & Csikszentmihalyi, M. (2000). Positive psychology: An introduction. *American Psychologist, 55*, 5–14.

Seligman, M. E. P., Walker, E. F., & Rosenhan, D. L. (2001). *Abnormal psychology.* New York: Norton.

Shallice, T., & Warrington, E. (1969). Independent functioning of verbal memory stores. *Quarterly Journal of Experimental Psychology, 22*, 261–273.

Shankar, P., Manjunath, N., & Lieberman, J. (2005). The prospect of silencing disease using RNA interference. *Journal of the American Medical Association, 293*, 1367–1373.

Shapiro, E., Shapiro, A. K., Fulop, G., Hubbard, M., Mandell, J., Nordlie, J., et al. (1989). Controlled study of haloperidol, pimozide, and placebo for the treatment of Gilles de la Tourette's syndrome. *Archives of General Psychiatry, 46*, 722–730.

Shedler, J., & Block, J. (1990). Adolescent drug use and psychological health: A longitudinal inquiry. *American Psychologist, 45*, 612–630.

Sheese, B. E., Brown, E. L., & Graziano, W. G. (2004). Emotional expression in cyberspace: Searching for moderators of the Pennebaker disclosure effect via e-mail. *Health Psychology, 23*, 457–464.

Sheffield, F. D., & Roby, T. B. (1950). Reward value of a non-nutritive sweet taste. *Journal of Comparative and Physiological Psychology, 43*, 471–481.

Shenkin, S. D., Starr, J. M., & Deary, I. J. (2004). Birth weight and cognitive ability in childhood: A systematic review. *Psychological Bulletin, 130*, 989–1013.

Sherman, D. K., McGue, M. K., & Iacono, W. G. (1997). Twin concordance for attention deficit hyperactivity disorder: A comparison of teacher's and mother's reports. *American Journal of Psychiatry, 154,* 532–535.

Sherman, S. J., Presson, C., Chassin, L., Corty, E., & Olshavsky, R. (1983). The false consensus effect in estimates of smoking prevalence: Underlying mechanisms. *Personality and Social Psychology Bulletin, 9,* 197–207.

Sherwin, B. B. (1988). A comparative analysis of the role of androgen in human male and female sexual behavior: Behavioral specificity, critical thresholds, and sensitivity. *Psychobiology, 16,* 416–425.

Sherwin, B. B. (1994). Sex hormones and psychological functioning in postmenopausal women. *Experimental Gerontology, 29,* 423–430.

Shettleworth, S. J. (2001). Animal cognition and animal behaviour. *Animal Behaviour, 61,* 277–286.

Shih, M., Pittinsky, T. L., & Ambady, N. (1999). Stereotype susceptibility: Identity salience and shifts in quantitative performance. *Psychological Science, 10,* 80–83.

Siegel, S. (1984). Pavlovian conditioning and heroin overdose: Reports by overdose victims. *Bulletin of the Psychonomic Society, 22,* 428–430.

Siegel, S., Hinson, R. E., Krank, M. D., & McCully, J. (1982). Heroin "overdose" death: Contribution of drug-associated environmental cues. *Science, 216,* 436–437.

Siegler, I. C., Costa, P. T., Brummett, B. H., Helms, M. J., Barefoot, J. C., Williams, R. et al. (2003). Patterns of change in hostility from college to midlife in the UNC Alumni Heart Study predict high-risk status. *Psychosomatic Medicine, 65,* 738–745.

Silva, P. A., & Stanton, W. (1996). *From child to adult: The Dunedin study.* Oxford, UK: Oxford University Press.

Silver, R. L., Cirincione, C., & Steadman, H. J. (1994). Demythologizing inaccurate perceptions of the insanity defense. *Law and Human Behavior, 18,* 63–70.

Simons, D. J., & Levin, D. T. (1998). Failure to detect changes to people during a real-world interaction. *Psychonomic Bulletin and Review, 5,* 644–649.

Sims, H. E. A., Goldman, R. F., Gluck, C. M., Horton, E., Kelleher, P., & Rowe, D. (1968). Experimental obesity in man. *Transactions of the Association of American Physicians, 81,* 153–170.

Singer, T., Seymour, B., O'Doherty, J., Kaube, H., Dolan, R. J., & Frith, C. D. (2004). Empathy for pain involves the affective but not sensory components of pain. *Science, 303,* 1157–1162.

Sirois, B. C., & Burg, M. M. (2003). Negative emotion and coronary heart disease: A review. *Behavior Modification, 27,* 83–102.

Skodol, A. E., Siever, L. J., Livesley, W. J., Gunderson, J. G., Pfohl, B., & Widiger, T. A. (2002). The borderline diagnosis II: Biology, genetics, and clinical course. *Biological Psychiatr y, 51,* 951–963.

Sloane, R. B., Staples, F. R., Whipple, K., & Cristol, A. H. (1977). Patients' attitudes toward behavior therapy and psychotherapy. *American Journal of Psychiatry, 134,* 134–137.

Slovic, P., Finucane, M., Peters, E., & MacGregor, D. (2002). The affect heuristic. In T. Gilovich, D. Griffin, & D. Kahneman (Eds.), *Heuristics and biases: The psychology of intuitive judgment* (pp. 397–420). New York: Cambridge University Press.

Smith, C., & Lapp, L. (1991). Increases in number of REMs and REM density in humans following an intensive learning period. *Sleep, 14,* 325–330.

Smith, C. A., & Ellsworth, P. C. (1985). Patterns of cognitive appraisal in emotion. *Journal of Personality and Social Psychology, 48,* 813–838.

Smith, S. M., Glenberg, A. M., & Bjork, R. A. (1978). Environmental context and human memory. *Memory and Cognition, 6,* 342–353.

Smith, T. W., Orleans, C. T., & Jenkins, C. D. (2004). Prevention and health promotion: Decades of progress, new challenges, and an emerging agenda. *Health Psychology, 23,* 126–131.

Snider, L. A., & Swedo, S. E. (2004). PANDAS: Current status and directions for research. *Molecular Psychiatry, 9,* 900–907.

Snyder, E. E., Walts, B. M., Chagnon, Y. C., Pérusse, L., Weisnagel, S. J., Chagnon, Y. C., et al. (2004). The human obesity gene map: The 2003 update. *Obesity Research, 12,* 369–438.

Snyder, M., & Cantor, N. (1998). Understanding personality and personal behavior: A functionalist strategy. In D. T. Gilbert, S. T. Fiske, & G. Lindzey (Eds.), *Handbook of social psychology* (pp. 635–679). New York: McGraw-Hill.

Solms, M. (2000). Dreaming and REM sleep are controlled by different brain mechanisms. *Behavioral and Brain Sciences, 23,* 793.

Somerville, L. H., Kim, H., Johnstone, T., Alexander, A. L., & Whalen, P. J. (2004). Human amygdala responses during presentation of happy and neutral faces: Correlations with state anxiety. *Biological Psychiatry, 55,* 897–903.

Sommerville, J. A., & Woodward, A. L. (2005). Pulling out the intentional structure of action: The relation between action processing and action production in infancy. *Cognition, 95,* 1–30.

Sorensen, T., Holst, C., Stunkard, A. J., & Skovgaard, L. T. (1992). Correlations of body mass index of adult adoptees and their biological and adoptive relatives. *International Journal of Obesity and Related Metabolic Disorders, 16,* 227–236.

Spangler, W. D., & House, R. J. (1991). Presidential effectiveness and the leadership motive profile. *Journal of Personality and Social Psychology, 60,* 439–455.

Spearman, C. (1904). "General intelligence," objectively determined and measured. *American Journal of Psychology, 15,* 201–293.

Spence, S. A., & Frith, C. D. (1999). Towards a functional anatomy of volition. *Journal of Consciousness Studies, 6,* 11–29.

Spencer, H. (1872). *The principles of psychology.* London, England: Williams & Norgate.

Spencer, M. B., & Markstrom-Adams, C. (1990). Identity processes among racial and ethnic minority children in America. *Child Development, 56,* 564–572.

Spencer, S. J., Steele, C. M., & Quinn, D. M. (1999). Stereotype threat and women's math performance. *Journal of Experimental Social Psychology, 35,* 4–28.

Sperling, G. (1960). The information available in brief visual presentations. *Psychological Monographs, 74,* 1–29.

Spitzer, R. L., Skodol, A. E., Gibbon, M., & Williams, J. B. W. (1983). *Psychopathology, a case book.* New York: McGraw-Hill.

Spitzer, R. L., Williams, J. B., Gibbon, M., & First, M. B. (1992). The Structured Clinical Interview for DSM-III-R (SCID). I: History, rationale, and description. *Archives of General Psychiatry, 49,* 624–629.

Sprecher, S., Barbee, A., & Schwartz, P. (1995). "Was it good for you, too?": Gender differences in first sexual experiences. *Journal of Sex Research, 32,* 3–15.

Squire, L. R., Stark, C. E. L., & Clark, R. E. (2004). The medial temporal lobe. *Annual Review of Neuroscience, 27,* 279–306.

Srivastava, S., John, O. P., Gosling, S. D., & Potter, J. (2003). Development of personality in early and middle adulthood: Set like plaster or persistent change? *Journal of Personality and Social Psychology, 84,* 1041–1053.

Starcevic, V., Linden, M., Uhlenhuth, E. H., Kolar, D., & Latas, M. (2004). Treatment of panic disorder with agoraphobia in an anxiety disorders clinic: Factors influencing psychiatrists' treatment choices. *Psychiatry Research, 125,* 41–52.

Stark, S. (2000, December 22). "Cast Away" lets Hanks fend for himself. *The Detroit News.* Retrieved June 27, 2005, from http://www.detnews.com/2000/entertainment/1222/mcastaway/mcastaway.htm

Steele, C. M. (1997). A threat in the air: How stereotypes shape intellectual identity and performance. *American Psychologist, 52,* 613–629.

Steele, C. M., & Aronson, J. (1995). Stereotype threat and the intellectual test performance of African Americans. *Journal of Personality and Social Psychology, 69,* 797–811.

Steffenburg, S., Gillberg, C., Helgren, L., Anderson, L., Gillberg, L., Jakobsson, G., et al. (1989). A twin study of autism in Denmark, Finland, Iceland, Norway, and Sweden. *Journal of Child Psychological Psychiatry, 30,* 405–416.

Stein, J., & Richardson, A. (1999). Cognitive disorders: A question of misattribution. *Current Biology, 9,* R374-R376.

Steinberg, L., & Scott, E. S. (2003). Less guilty by reason of adolescence: Developmental immaturity, diminished responsibility, and the juvenile death penalty. *American Psychologist, 12,* 1009–1018.

Steiner, J. E. (1977). Facial expressions of the neonate infant indicating the hedonics of food-related chemical stimuli. In J. M. Weiffenbach (Ed.), *Taste and development* (pp. 173–189). Bethesda, MD: U.S. Department of Health, Education, and Welfare.

Stellar, J. R., Kelley, A. E., & Corbett, D. (1983). Effects of peripheral and central dopamine blockade on lateral hypothalamic self-stimulation: Evidence for both reward and motor deficits. *Pharmacology, Biochemistry, and Behavior, 18,* 433–442.

Steriade, M. (1992). Basic mechanisms of sleep generation. *Neurology, 42* (Suppl.), 9–18.

Sternberg, E. M. (2000). *The balance within.* New York: Freeman.

Sternberg, R. J. (1986). A triangular theory of love. *Psychological Review, 93,* 119–135.

Sternberg, R. J. (1999). The theory of successful intelligence. *Review of General Psychology, 3,* 292–316.

Sternberg, R. J., & Davidson, J. E. (1983). Insight in the gifted. *Educational Psychologist, 18,* 51–57.

Stickgold, R., Whidbee, D., Schirmer, B., Patel, V., & Hobson, J. A. (2000). Visual discrimination task improvement: A multi-step process occurring during sleep. *Journal of Cognitive Neuroscience, 12,* 246–254.

Stokstad, E. (2001). New hints into the biological basis of autism. *Science, 294,* 34–37.

Stoleru, S., Gregoire, M. C., Gerard, D., Decety, J., Lafarge, E., Cinotti, L., et al. (1999). Neuroanatomical correlates of visually evoked sexual arousal in human males. *Archives of Sexual Behavior, 28,* 1–21.

Stone, A. A., Neale, J. M., Cox, D. S., & Napoli, A. (1994). Daily events are associated with a secretory immune response to an oral antigen in men. *Health Psychology, 13,* 440–446.

Stone, M. H., Stone, D. K., & Hurt, S. W. (1987). The natural history of borderline patients treated by intensive hospitalization. *Psychiatric Clinics of North America, 10,* 185–206.

Stone, V. E., Baron-Cohen, S., & Knight, R. T. (1998). Frontal lobe contributions to theory of mind. *Journal of Cognitive Neuroscience, 10,* 640–656.

Strange, B. A., & Dolan, R. J. (2004). Beta-adrenergic modulation of emotional memory-evoked human amygdala and hippocampal response: An emotion-induced retrograde amnesia in humans is amygdala- and beta-adrenergic-dependent. *Proceedings of the National Academy of Sciences, 101,* 11454–11458.

Strayer, D. L., Drews, F. A., & Johnston, W. A. (2003). Cell phone-induced failures of visual attention during simulated driving. *Journal of Experimental Psychology: Applied, 9,* 23–32.

Strentz, T., & Auerbach, S. M. (1988). Adjustment to the stress of simulated captivity: Effects of emotion-focused versus problem-focused preparation on hostages differing in locus of control. *Journal of Personality and Social Psychology, 55,* 652–660.

Stunkard, A. J. (1996). Current views on obesity. *American Journal of Medicine, 100,* 230–236.

Stuss, D. T. (1991). Self, awareness, and the frontal lobes: A neuropsychological perspective. In J. Strauss & G. R. Goethals (Eds.), *The self: Interdisciplinary approaches* (pp. 255–278). New York: Springer-Verlag.

Stuss, D. T., Gow, C. A., & Hetherington, C. R. (1992). "No longer Gage": Frontal lobe dysfunction and emotional changes. *Journal of Consulting and Clinical Psychology, 60,* 349–359.

Sulin, R. A., & Dooling, D. J. (1974). Intrusion of a thematic idea in retention of prose. *Journal of Experimental Psychology, 103,* 255–262.

Suls, J., & Rothman, A. (2004). Evolution of the biopsychosocial model: Prospects and challenges. *Health Psychology, 23,* 119–125.

Süß, H. M., Oberauer, K., Wittmann, W. W., Wilhelm, O., & Schulze, R. (2002). Working-memory capacity explains reasoning ability—and a little bit more. *Intelligence, 30,* 261–288.

Svenson, O. (1981). Are we all less risky and more skillful than our fellow drivers? *Acta Psychologica, 47,* 143–148.

Swartz, M. S., Blazer, D., George, L., & Winfield, I. (1990). Estimating the prevalence of borderline personality disorder in the community. *Journal of Personality Disorders, 4,* 257–272.

Swenson, C. R., Sanderson, C., Dulie, R. A., & Linehan, M. M. (2001). The application of dialectical behavior therapy for patients with borderline personality disorder on inpatient units [special issue]. *Psychiatric Quarterly, 72,* 307–324.

Sylva, K., Bruner, J. S., & Genova, P. (1976). The role of play in the problem-solving of children 3–5 years old. In J. S. Bruner,

A. Jolly, & K. Sylva (Eds.), *Play: Its role in development and evolution* (pp. 244–257). New York: Penguin.

Szatzmari, P., Jones, M. B., Tuff, L., Bartolucci, G., Fisman, S., & Mahoney, W. (1993). Lack of cognitive impairment in first-degree relatives of children with pervasive developmental disorders. *Journal of the American Academy of Child and Adolescent Psychiatry, 32,* 1264–1273.

(TADS) Treatment for Adolescents with Depression Study Team (2004). Fluoxetine, cognitive-behavioral therapy, and their combination for adolescents with depression: Treatment for Adolescents with Depression Study (TADS) randomized controlled trial. *Journal of the American Medical Association, 292,* 807–820.

Tajfel, H., & Turner, J. C. (1979). An integrative theory of intergroup conflict. In W. G. Austin & S. Worchel (Eds.), *The social psychology of intergroup relations* (pp. 33–47). Monterey, CA: Brooks/Cole.

Talley, P. R., Strupp, H. H., & Morey, L. C. (1990). Matchmaking in psychotherapy: Patient-therapist dimensions and their impact on outcome. *Journal of Consulting & Clinical Psychology, 58,* 182–188.

Tang, Y. P., Wang, H., Feng, R., Kyin, M., Tsien, J. Z. (2001). Differential effects of enrichment on learning and memory function in NR2B transgenic mice. *Neuropharmacology, 41,* 779–790.

Tateyama, M., Asai, M., Kamisada, M., Hashimoto, M., Bartels, M., & Heimann, H. (1993). Comparison of schizophrenic delusions between Japan and Germany. *Psychopathology, 26,* 151–158.

Taylor, S. E., & Brown, J. D. (1988). Illusion and well-being: A social psychological perspective on mental health. *Psychological Bulletin, 103,* 193–210.

Taylor, S. E., Klein, L. C., Lewis, B. P., Gruenewald, T. L., Gurung, R. A., & Updegraff, J. A. (2000). Biobehavioral responses to stress in females: Tend-and-befriend, not fight-or-flight. *Psychological Review, 107,* 411–429.

Teller, D. Y., Morse, R., Borton, R., & Regal, C. (1974). Visual acuity for vertical and diagonal gratings in human infants. *Vision Research, 14,* 1433–1439.

Tesser, A. (1988). Toward a self-evaluation maintenance model of social behavior. *Advances in Experimental Social Psychology, 21,* 181–227.

Tettamanti, M., Buccino, G., Saccuman, M. C., Welshman, V., Damn, M., Perani, D., et al. (2002). Sentences describing actions activate visuomotor execution and observation systems. 8th Annual HBM Conference.

Thigpen, C. H., & Cleckley, H. (1954). A case of multiple personality. *Journal of Abnormal Psychology, 49,* 135–151.

Thompson, P. (1980). Margaret Thatcher: A new illusion. *Perception, 9,* 483–484.

Thompson, P. M., Cannon, T. D., Narr, K. L., van Erp, T., Poutanen, V.P., Huttunen, M., et al. (2001). Genetic influences on brain structure. *Nature Neuroscience, 4,* 1253–1258.

Thompson, W. F., Schellenberg, E. G., & Husain, G. (2001). Arousal, mood, and the Mozart effect. *Psychological Science, 12,* 248–251.

Tickle, J. J., Sargent, J. D., Dalton, M. A., Beach, M. L., & Heatherton, T. F. (2001). Favorite movie stars, their tobacco use in contemporary movies and its association with adolescent smoking. *Tobacco Control, 10,* 16–22.

Tienari, P., Lahti, I., Sorri, A., Naarala, M., Moring, J., Kaleva, M., et al. (1990). Adopted-away offspring of schizophrenics and controls: The Finnish adoptive family study of schizophrenia. In L. Robins & M. Rutter (Eds.), *Straight and devious pathways from childhood to adulthood.* New York: Cambridge University Press.

Tienari, P., Wynne, L. C., Moring, J., Lahti, I., Naarala, M., Sorri, A., et al. (1994). The Finnish adoptive family study of schizophrenia: Implications for family research. *British Journal of Psychiatry Supplement, 23,* 20–26.

Tollesfson, G. D. (1995). Selective serotonin reuptake inhibitors. In A. F. Schatzberg & C. B. Nemeroff (Eds.), *The American psychiatric press textbook of psychopharmacology* (pp. 161–182). Washington, DC: American Psychiatric Press.

Tomasello, M. (1999). The *cultural origins of human cognition.* Cambridge, MA: Harvard Press.

Tong, F., Nakayama, K., Vaughan, J. T., & Kanwisher, N. (1998). Binocular rivalry and visual awareness in human extrastriate cortex. *Neuron, 21,* 753–759.

Tooby, J., & Cosmides, L. (1990). On the universality of human nature and the uniqueness of the individual: The role of genetics and adaptation. *Journal of Personality, 58,* 17–68.

Torgersen, S., Kringlen, E., & Cramer, V. (2001). The prevalence of personality disorders in a community sample. *Archives of General Psychiatry, 58,* 590–596.

Torrey, E. F. (1999). Epidemiological comparison of schizophrenia and bipolar disorder. *Schizophrenia Research, 39,* 101–06.

Torrey, E. F., Torrey, B. B., & Peterson, M. R. (1977). Seasonality of schizophrenic births in the United States. *Archives of General Psychiatry, 34,* 1065–1070.

Treisman, A. (1988). Features and objects: The Fourteenth Bartlett Memorial Lecture. *Quarterly Journal of Experimental Psychology, 40A,* 201–237.

Treisman, A., & Gelade, G. (1980). A feature-integration theory of attention. *Cognitive Psychology, 12,* 97–136.

Triandis, H. C. (1989). The self and social behavior in differing cultural contexts. *Psychological Review, 96,* 506–520.

Trivers, R. L. (1971). The evolution of reciprocal altruism. *Quarterly Review of Biology, 46,* 35–57.

Tsien, J. Z. (2000). Building a brainier mouse. *Science, 282,* 62–68.

Tuchfeld, B. S. (1981). Spontaneous remission in alcoholics: Empirical observations and theoretical implications. *Journal of Studies on Alcohol, 42,* 626–641.

Tugade, M. M., & Fredrickson, B. L. (2004). Resilient individuals use positive emotions to bounce back from negative emotional experiences. *Journal of Personality and Social Psychology, 86,* 320–333.

Tulving, E. T., Kapur, S., Craik, F. I. M., Moscovitch, M., & Houle, S. (1994). Hemispheric encoding/retrieval asymmetry in episodic memory: Positron emission tomography findings. *Proceedings of the National Academy of Sciences, 91,* 2016–2020.

Uchino, B. N., Cacioppo, J. T., & Kiecolt-Glaser, J. K. (1996). The relationship between social support and physiological processes:

A review with emphasis on underlying mechanisms and implications for health. *Psychological Bulletin, 119,* 488–531.

Ungerleider, L. G., & Mishkin, M. (1982). Two cortical visual systems. In D. J. Ingle, R. J. W. Mansfield, & M. S. Goodale (eds.), *The analysis of visual behavior* (pp 549–586). Cambridge, MA: MIT Press.

United States Department of Health and Human Services. (1993). *Alcohol and health.* Washington, DC: U.S. Government Printing Office.

Upton, N. (1994). Mechanisms of action of new antiepileptic drugs: Rational design and serendipitous findings. *Trends in Pharmacological Sciences, 15,* 456–463.

U.S. Department of Health and Human Services. (1999). *Mental health: A report of the Surgeon General.* Washington, DC: Department of Health and Human Services.

U.S. Department of Health and Human Services. (2004). *The health consequences of smoking: A report of the Surgeon General.* Department of Health and Human Services, Public Health Center, Centers for Disease Control and Prevention, National Center for Chronic Disease Prevention and Health Promotion, Office on Smoking and Health.

Valzelli, L. (1973). The "isolation syndrome" in mice. *Psychopharmacologia, 31,* 305–320.

Vargha-Khadem, F., Gadian, D. G., Watkinds, K., Connelly, A., Can Paesschen, W., & Mishkin, M. (1997). Differential effects of early hippocampal pathology on episodic and semantic memory. *Science, 277,* 376–380.

Varley, C. K. (1984). Attention deficit disorder (the hyperactivity syndrome): A review of selected issues. *Developmental and Behavioral Pediatrics, 5,* 254–258.

Vernon, P. A., Wickett, J. C., Bazana, P. G., Stelmack, R. M., & Sternberg, R. J. (2000). The neuropsychology and psychophysiology of human intelligence. In R.J. Sternberg (Ed.). *Handbook of Intelligence* (pp 245–264). Cambridge: Cambridge University Press.

Vohs, K. D., & Heatherton, T. F. (2004). Ego threat elicits different social comparison processes among high and low self-esteem people: Implications for interpersonal perceptions. *Social Cognition, 22,* 168–190.

Volkman, F., Chawarska, K., & Klin, A. (2005). Autism in infancy and early childhood. *Annual Review of Psychology, 56,* 315–336.

von Neumann, J., & Morgenstern, O. (1947). *Theory of games and economic behavior.* Princeton, NJ: Princeton University Press.

Wadhwa, P. D., Sandman, C. A., & Garite, T. J. (2001). The neurobiology of stress in human pregnancy: Implications for prematurity and development of the fetal central nervous system. *Progress Brain Research, 133,* 131–142.

Wager, T. D., & Smith, E. E. (2003). Neuroimaging studies of working memory: A meta-analysis. *Cognitive, Affective, and Behavioral Neuroscience, 3,* 255–274.

Wagner, A. D., Schacter, D. L., Rotte, M., Koutstaal, W., Maril, A., Dale, A. M., et al. (1998). Building memories: Remembering and forgetting of verbal experiences as predicted by brain activity. *Science, 281,* 1188–1191.

Wagner, U., Gals, S., Haider, H., Verleger, R., & Born, J. (2004). Sleep inspires insight. *Nature, 427,* 352–356.

Walker, E., Kestler, L., Bollini, A., & Hochman, K. M. (2004). Schizophrenia: Etiology and course. *Annual Review of Psychology, 55,* 401–430.

Waltrip, R. W., Buchanan, R. W., Carpenter, W. T., Kirkpatrick, B., Summerfelt, A., Breier, A., et al. (1997). Borna disease virus antibodies and the deficit syndrome of schizophrenia. *Schizophrenia Research, 23,* 253–257.

Warburton, D. M. (1992). Nicotine as a cognitive enhancer. *Progress in Neuro-Psychopharmacology and Biological Psychiatry, 16,* 181–191.

Watson, D., & Clark, L. A. (1997). Extraversion and its positive emotional core. In R. Hogan, J. Johnson, & S. Briggs (Eds.), *Handbook of personality psychology* (pp. 767–793). San Diego, CA: Academic Press.

Watson, D., Wiese, D., Vaidya, J., & Tellegen, A. (1999). The two general activation systems of affect: Structural findings, evolutionary considerations, and psychobiological evidence. *Journal of Personality and Social Psychology, 76,* 820–838.

Watson, J. B. (1924). *Behaviorism.* New York: Norton.

Wegner, D. M., & Bargh, J. A. (1998). Control and automaticity in social life. In D. T. Gilbert, S. T. Fiske, & L. Gardner (Eds.), *Handbook of social psychology* (pp. 446–496). New York: Oxford University Press.

Wegner, D., Shortt, J., Blake, A., & Page, M. (1990). The suppression of exciting thoughts. *Journal of Personality and Social Psychology, 58,* 409–418.

Weiner, B. (1974). *Achievement motivation and attribution theory.* Morristown, NJ: General Learning Press.

Weiss, G., & Hechtman, L. T. (1993). *Hyperactive children grown up.* New York: Guilford Press.

Weissman, M. M., Bland, R. C., Canino, G. J., Greenwald, S., Hwu, H. G., Lee, C. K., et al. (1994). The cross national epidemiology of obsessive compulsive disorder. The Cross National Collaborative Group. *Journal of Clinical Psychiatry, 55,* 5–10.

Wells, G. L., Small, M., Penrod, S., Malpass, R. S., Fulero, S. M., & Brimacombe, C. A. E. (1998). Eyewitness identification procedures: Recommendations for lineups and photospreads. *Law and Human Behavior, 22,* 603–647.

Welsh, D. K., Logothetis, D. E., Meister, M., & Reppert, S. M. (1995). Individual neurons dissociated from rat suprachiasmatic nucleus express independently phased circadian firing rhythms. *Neuron, 14,* 697–706.

Werker, J. F., Gilbert, J. H., Humphrey, K., & Tees, R. C. (1981). Developmental aspects of cross-language speech perception. *Child Development, 52,* 349–355.

Westen, D. (1998). The scientific legacy of Sigmund Freud: Toward a psychodynamically informed psychological science. *Psychological Bulletin, 124,* 333–371.

Westen, D., Novotny, C. M., & Thompson-Brenner, H. (2004). The empirical status of empirically supported psychotherapies: Assumptions, findings, and reporting in controlled clinical trials. *Psychological Bulletin, 130,* 631–663.

Wexler, N. S., U.S.-Venezuela Collaborative Research Project et al. (2004). Venezuelan kindreds reveal that genetic and environmental factors modulate Huntington's disease age of onset. *Proceedings of the National Academy of Sciences, 101,* 3498–3503.

Whalen, C. K. (1989). Attention deficit and hyperactivity disorders. In T. H. Ollendick & M. Herson (Eds.), *Handbook of child psychopathology* (2nd ed., pp. 131–169). New York: Plenum.

Whalen, P. J., Kagan, J., Cook, R. G., Davis, F. C., Kim, H., Polis, S., et al. (2005). Human amygdala responsivity to masked fearful eye-whites. *Science, 306,* 2061.

Whalen, P. J., Rauch, S. L., Etcoff, N. L., McInerney, N. L., Lee, M. B., & Jenike, M. A. (1998). Masked presentations of emotional facial expressions modulate amygdala activity without explicit knowledge. *Journal of Neuroscience, 18,* 411–418.

Whalen, P. J., Shin, L. M., McInerney, S. C., Fischer, H., Wright, C. I., & Rauch, S. L. (2001). A functional MRI study of human amygdala responses to facial expressions of fear versus anger. *Emotion, 1,* 70–83.

Wheeler, M. E., Petersen, S. E., & Buckner, R. L. (2000). Memory's echo: Vivid remembering reactivates sensory-specific cortex. *Proceedings of the National Academy of Sciences, 97,* 11125–11129.

White, D., & Pitts, M. (1998). Educating young people about drugs: A systematic review. *Addiction, 93,* 1475–1487.

Whiteside, S. P., Port, J. D., & Abramowitz, J. S. (2004). A meta-analysis of functional neuroimaging in obsessive-compulsive disorder. *Psychiatry Research, 15,* 69–79.

Widiger, T. A., & Corbitt, E. M. (1995). Are personality disorders well-classified in DSM-IV? In W. J. Lively (Ed.), *The DSM-IV personality disorders* (pp. 103–126). New York: Guilford Press.

Widom, C. S. (1978). A methodology for studying noninstitutionalized psychopaths. In R. D. Hare & D. A. Schalling (Eds.), *Psychopathic behavior: Approaches to research* (pp. 72ff). Chichester, England: John Wiley.

Wiesel, T. N., & Hubel, D. H. (1963). Single-cell responses in striate cortex of kittens deprived of vision in one eye. *Journal of Neurophysiology, 26,* 1003–1017.

Wilens, T. E., Faraone, S. V., & Biederman, J. (2004). Attention-deficit/hyperactivity disorder in adults. *Journal of the American Medical Association, 292,* 619–623.

Wilke, M., Sohn, J.H., Byars, A.W., & Holland, S.K. (2003). Bright spots: correlations of gray matter volume with IQ in a normal pediatric population. *Neuroimage, 20,* 202–215

Williams, J. M. G., Mathews, A., & MacLeod, C. (1996). The emotional Stroop task and psychopathology. *Psychological Bulletin, 120,* 3–24.

Williams, P., Fitzsimons, G. J., & Block, L. G. (2004). When consumers don't recognize "benign" intentions questions as persuasion attempts. *Journal of Consumer Research, 31,* 540–550.

Williams, R. B., Jr. (1987). Refining the type A hypothesis: Emergence of the hostility complex. *American Journal of Cardiology, 60,* 27J–32J.

Williams, R. B., Barefoot, J. C., Califf, R. M., Haney, T. L., Saunders, W. B., et al. (1992). Prognostic importance of social and economic resources among medically treated patients with angiographically documented coronary artery disease. *Journal of the American Medical Association, 267,* 520–524.

Wills, T. A., DuHamel, K., & Vaccaro, D. (1995). Activity and mood temperament as predictors of adolescent substance use: Test of

a self-regulation mediational model. *Journal of Personality and Social Psychology, 68,* 901–916.

Wilson, A. E., & Ross, M. (2001). From chump to champ: People's appraisals of their earlier and present selves. *Journal of Personality and Social Psychology, 80,* 572–584.

Wilson, M. A., & McNaughton, B. L. (1994). Reactivation of hippocampal ensemble memories during sleep. *Science, 265,* 676–679.

Wilson, T. D., & Gilbert, D. T. (2003). Affective forecasting. In M. Zanna (Ed.), *Advances in experimental social psychology: Vol. 35* (pp. 345–411). New York: Elsevier.

Wilson, T. D., Lindsey, S., & Schooler, T. Y. (2000). A model of dual attitudes. *Psychological Review, 107,* 101–126.

Wilson, T. D., & Schooler, J. W. (1991). Thinking too much: Introspection can reduce the quality of preferences and decisions. *Journal of Personality and Social Psychology, 60,* 181–192.

Wilson, T. W., & Grim, C. E. (1991). Biohistory of slavery and blood pressure differences in Blacks today. *Hypertension, 17* (Suppl. 1), I122–I128.

Winberg, J., & Porter, R. H. (1998). Olfaction and human neonatal behaviour: Clinical implications. *Acta Paediatrica, 87,* 6–10.

Wise, R. A., & Rompre, P. P. (1989). Brain dopamine and reward. *Annual Review of Psychology, 40,* 191–225.

Wiseman, C. V., Harris, W. A., & Halmi, K. A., (1998). Eating disorders. *Medical Clinics of North America, 82,* 145–159.

Wishaw, I. Q., Drigenberg, H. C., & Comery, T. A. (1992). Rats (rattus norvegicus) modulate eating speed and vigilance to optimize food consumption: Effects of cover, circadian rhythm, food deprivation, and individual differences. *Journal of Comparative Psychology, 106,* 411–419.

Wolford, G. L., Miller, M. B., & Gazzaniga, M. (2000). The left hemisphere's role in hypothesis formation. *Journal of Neuroscience, 20,* 1–4.

Wolpe, J. (1997). Thirty years of behavior therapy. *Behavior Therapy, 28,* 633–635.

Wood, J. M., Garb, H. N., Lilienfeld, S. O., & Nezworski, M. T. (2002). Clinical assessment. *Annual Review of Psychology, 53,* 519–543.

Woodruff, G. N., & Hughes, J. (1991). Cholecystokinin antagonists. *Annual Review of Pharmacology & Toxicology, 31,* 469–501.

Woods, S. C., & Stricker, E. M. (1999). Food intake and metabolism. In M. J. Zigmond, F. E. Bloom, S. C. Landis, J. L. Roberts, & L. R. Squire (Eds.), *Fundamentals of neuroscience* (pp. 1091–1109). San Diego, CA: Academic Press.

Woodward, S. A., McManis, M. H., Kagan, J., Deldin, P., Snidman, N., Lewis, M., et al. (2001). Infant temperament and the brainstem auditory evoked response in later childhood. *Developmental Psychology, 37,* 533–538.

World Health Organization (2002). *The World Health report.* Geneva: World Health Organization.

Wynn, K. (1992). Addition and subtraction by human infants. *Nature, 358,* 749–750.

Yates, W. R., Perry, P., & Murray, S. (1992). Aggression and hostility in anabolic steroid users. *Biological Psychiatry, 31,* 1232–1234.

Yuille, J. C., & Cutshall, J. L. (1986). A case study of eyewitness memory of a crime. *Journal of Applied Psychology, 71,* 291–301.

Zahn-Waxler, C., & Radke-Yarrow, M. (1990). The origins of empathic concern. *Motivation and Emotion,* 14, 107–130.

Zahn-Waxler, C., & Robinson, J. (1995). Empathy and guilt: Early origins of feelings of responsibility. In J. P. Tangney & K. W. Fischer (Eds.)*, Self-conscious emotions: The psychology of shame, guilt, embarrassment, and pride* (pp. 143–173). New York: Guilford.

Zajonc, R. B. (1965). Social facilitation. *Science 149,* 269–274.

Zajonc, R. B. (1968). Attitudinal effects of mere exposure. *Journal of Personality and Social Psychology Monographs, 9,* 1–27.

Zajonc, R. B. (1980). Feeling and thinking: Preferences need no inferences. *American Psychologist, 35,* 151–175.

Zajonc, R. B. (2001). Mere exposure: A gateway to the subliminal. *Current Directions in Psychological Science 10,* 224–228.

Zajonc, R. B., Murphy, S. T., & Inglehart, M. (1989). Feeling and facial efference: Implications of the vascular theory of emotions. *Psychological Review, 96,* 395–416.

Zametkin, A. J., Nordahl, T. E., Gross, M., King, A. C., Stemple, W. E., Rumsey, J., et al. (1990). Cerebral glucose metabolism in adults with hyperactivity of childhood onset. *New England Journal of Medicine, 323,* 1361–1366.

Zatorre, R. J. (1989). On the representation of multiple languages in the brain: Old problems and new directions. *Brain and Language, 36,* 127–147.

Zatorre, R. J. (2003). Absolute pitch: A model for understanding the influence of genes and development on neural and cognitive function. *Nature Neuroscience, 6,* 692–695.

Zentall, S. S., Sutton, J. E., & Sherburne, L. M. (1996). True imitative learning in pigeons. *Psychological Science, 7,* 343–346.

Zihl, J., von Cramon, D., & Mai, N. (1983). Selective disturbance of movement vision after bilateral brain damage. *Brain, 106,* 313–340.

Zuckerman, M. (1995). Good and bad humors: Biochemical bases of personality and its disorders. *Psychological Science, 6,* 325–332.

Every effort has been made to contact the copyright holders of the material used in *Psychological Science*. Rights holders of any material not credited should contact W. W. Norton & Company, Inc., 500 Fifth Avenue, New York, NY 10110 for a correction to be made in the next reprinting of our work.

Photos

CHAPTER 1: p. 2: Aydelotte Rod/Corbis Sygma; **p. 4, 1.1:** AP/Wide World Photos; **p. 5, 1.2:** From Phelps, E. A., O'Connor, K. J., Cunningham, W. A., Funayama, E. S., Gatenby, J. C., Gore, J. C., et al. (2000). Performance on indirect measures of race evaluation predicts amygdala activation. *Journal of Cognitive Neuroscience, 12,* 729–738. Images courtesy Elizabeth A. Phelps, Phelps Lab; **p. 9:** The Far Side ® by Gary Larson © 1982 FarWorks, Inc. All Rights Reserved. Used with permission; **p. 11, 1.3:** Courtesy Professor Joseph J. Campos, University of California, Berkeley; **p. 17, 1.5:** The Granger Collection, New York; **p. 18, 1.6 and 1.7:** Bettmann/Corbis; **p. 20, 1.9:** Archives of the History of American Psychology, University of Akron; **p. 21, 1.10:** Archives of the History of American Psychology, University of Akron; **p. 22, 1.11:** Archives of the History of American Psychology; **p. 23, 1.12:** From *American Journal of Psychology.* Copyright 1974 by the Board of Trustees of the University of Illinois. Used with permission of the University of Illinois Press; **p. 23, 1.13:** From *Mind sights,* by Roger N. Shepard. © 1990 by Roger N. Shepard. Henry Holt and Company, LLC; **p. 24, 1.14:** Corbis; **p. 25, 1.15:** Archives of the History of American Psychology, University of Akron; **p. 26, 1.16:** Courtesy George Miller, Princeton University. © 2001, Pryde Brown Photographs, Princeton, NJ; **p. 27, 1.17:** Archives of the History of American Psychology, University of Akron; **p. 29, 1.19:** Courtesy James Carpenter/Gitchell's Studio; **p. 30:** © The New Yorker Collection 1998 Sam Gross from cartoonbank.com. All Rights Reserved; **p. 32, 1.20:** Lea-Dann Tardif/Corbis.

CHAPTER 2: p. 36: Laura Dwight/Corbis; **p. 49, 2.3:** Karl Ammann/Corbis; **p. 50, 2.4:** Courtesy Robert Rosenthal, University of California, Riverside; **p. 52:** © The New Yorker Collection 1998 Roz Chast from cartoonbank.com. All Rights Reserved; **p. 54, 2.6:** (left) Reuters/Corbis; (right) The Oregonian/Corbis; **p. 57, 2.10:** Photo Researchers, Inc.; **p. 58, 2.11:** Fig. 1–1 (B), (C), and (D), Greenberg, J. O., and Adams, R. D. (Eds.), *Neuroimaging: A companion to Adams and Victor's principles of neurology.* New York: McGraw-Hill, Inc., 1995; **p.**

59, 2.12: Courtesy Cathy J. Price, Institute of Neurology, University College, London. From Delineating necessary and sufficient neural systems with functional imaging studies of neuropsychological patients. *Journal of Cognitive Neuroscience.* (1999). 11(4): 377, Figure 2; **p. 65:** (bottom) © 2005 Sidney Harris from cartoonbank.com. All Rights Reserved; **p. 68, 2.17:** Images.com/Corbis.

CHAPTER 3: p. 72: Mario Tama/Getty Images; **p. 77, 3.1:** CNRI/Science Photo Library/Photo Researchers, Inc.; **p. 81, 3.3:** Courtesy Hereditary Disease Foundation; **p. 83, 3.4:** (top row, second from left) Harry B. Clay, Jr., photographer, Bernardsville, NJ; **p. 84, 3.5:** Bob Sacha; **p. 91, 3.9:** (b) James Stevenson, Science Photo Library/Photo Researchers, Inc.; **p. 94, 3.13:** James Stevenson/Science Photo Library/Photo Researchers, Inc.; **p. 101, 3.16:** From Widner, H., Rehncrona, S., Snow, B., Brudin, P., Gustavii, B., Bjorklund, A., et al. (1992). Bilateral fetal mesencephalic grafting in two patients with Parkinsonism induced by 1-methyl-4-phenyl-1,2,3,6 tetrahydropyridine (MPTP). *The New England Journal of Medicine, 327, (22).* Copyright © 1992 Massachusetts Medical Society. All Rights Reserved; **p. 102, 3.17:** From Jon Palfreman and J. William Langston, *The case of the frozen addicts.* Photograph by Russ Lee, © Pantheon Books, New York, 1995; **p. 109:** © The New Yorker Collection 1999 William Haefeli from cartoonbank.com. All Rights Reserved; **p. 111, 3.21:** Hekimian Julien/Corbis Sygma.

CHAPTER 4: p. 116: Ron Sachs/Corbis; **p. 118, 4.1:** From Penfield, Wilder (1958). *The excitable cortex in conscious man.* Liverpool University Press; **p. 119, 4.2:** From Spurzheim, J. (1825). *Phrenology, or, the doctrine of the mind; and the relations between its manifestations and the body,* London: C. Knight; **p. 120, 4.3:** From the Musée Dupuytren. Courtesy Assistance Publique, Hopitaux de Paris; **p. 127, 4.10:** Ramachandran, V. S. and Blakeslee, S., Fig. 6.1, Drawing made by a neglect patient, from *Phantoms in the brain.* Copyright © 1998 by V. S. Ramachandran and Sandra Blakeslee. Reprinted by permission of HarperCollins Publishers Inc.; **p. 128, 4.11:** Warren Anatomical Museum, Francis A. Countway Library of Medicine; **p. 133, 4.14:** © Duke University Photography, by Jim Wallace; **p. 135, 4.15:** (left) Peter Macdiarmid/Reuters/Corbis; **p. 135, 4.15:** (right) Reuters/Corbis; **p. 141:** (top) © Sidney Harris; **p. 142, 4.21:** © August Bullock. SubliminalSex.com. All rights reserved; **p. 152, 4.29:** Braun, A. R., Balkin, T. J., Wesensten, N. J., Gwadry, F., Carson, R. E., Varga, M., et al. (1998). Dissociated pattern of activity in visual cortices and their projections during human rapid eye movement sleep. *Science,* 279,

91–95. Images courtesy Allen R. Braun, NIH; **p. 153:** © 2005 Robert Mankoff from cartoonbank.com. All Rights Reserved.

CHAPTER 5: p. 158: Stone/Getty Images; **p. 160, 5.1:** Bettmann/Corbis; **p. 181, 5.16:** Courtesy of Todd Heatherton/Dartmouth; **p. 183:** © The New Yorker Collection 2001 Pat Byrnes from cartoonbank.com. All Rights Reserved; **p. 190, 5.26:** From McCarthy, G., Price, A., Allison, T. (1997). Face specific processing in the human fusiform gyrus. *Journal of CognitiveNeuroscience, 9,* 605–610, Images courtesy Dr. Gregory McCarthy, The Duke-UNC Brain Imaging and Analysis Center; **p. 190, 5.27:** Courtesy Peter Thompson, University of York; **p. 191, 5.29:** www.news.bbc.co.uk; **p. 192, 5.30:** AP/Wide World Photos; **p. 193, 5.32:** © 2002 Magic Eye Inc. (www.magiceye.com); **p. 194, 5.33:** David Muench/Corbis; **p. 195, 5.35:** Courtesy of Todd Heatherton; **p. 195, 5.36:** © Exploratorium, www.exploratorium.edu; **p. 198, 5.41:** From *Psychology,* 6th edition, by Henry Gleitman, Alan J. Fridlund, Daniel Reisberg. Copyright © 2004 by W. W. Norton & Company, Inc. Used by permission of W. W. Norton & Company Inc.; **p. 204, 5.46:** The Image Bank/Getty Images.

CHAPTER 6: p. 208: Gideon Mandel/Corbis; **p. 212, 6.1:** Culver Pictures; **p. 213, 6.2:** Bettmann/Corbis; **p. 214:** (top) © The New Yorker Collection 1999 Edward Koren from cartoonbank.com. All Rights Reserved; **p. 218, 6.7:** From Childress, A. R., Mozey, P. D., McElgin, W., Fitzgerald, J. Reivich, M., O'Brien, C. P. (1999). Limbic activation during cue-induced cocaine craving. *American Journal of Psychiatry, 156,* 11–18. Copyright © 1999 by American Psychiatric Association. Images courtesy Anna Rose Childress, University of Pennsylvania; **p. 219, 6.8:** Benjamin Harris/University of New Hampshire; **p. 220:** © The New Yorker Collection 1993 Tom Cheney from cartoonbank.com. All Rights Reserved; **p. 223, 6.10:** Nina Leen/Time Pix/Getty Images; **p. 224, 6.11:** AP/Wide World Photos; **p. 232, 6.15:** Albert Bandura, Department of Psychology, Stanford University; **p. 233, 6.16:** Albert Bandura, Department of Psychology, Stanford University; **p. 233, 6.17:** Susan Mineka, Northwestern University; **p. 236, 6.18:** Corbis Sygma; **p. 240, 6.20:** McGill Reporter, PR050904; **p. 240, 6.21:** Biophoto Associates/Photo Researchers, Inc.; **p. 242, 6.23:** AP/Wide World Photos.

CHAPTER 7: p. 248: Photofest; **p. 256:** © The New Yorker Collection 1998 Mick Stevens from cartoonbank.com. All Rights Reserved; **p. 258:** © Sidney Harris; **p. 269, 7.11:** From Wheeler, M. E., Petersen, S. E., & Buckner, R. L. (2000). Memory's echo: Vivid remembering reactivates sensory-specific cortex. *Proceedings of the National Academy of Sciences, 97,* 11125–11129; **p. 275, 7.16:** Photofest; **p. 280, 7.18:** AP/Wide World Photos; **p. 282, 7.19:** AP/Wide World Photos; **p. 283, 7.20:** Courtesy Elizabeth Loftus, University of Washington; **p. 285, 7.21:** Courtesy Daniel Schacter, Harvard University; **p. 287, 7.22:** AP/Wide World Photos.

CHAPTER 8: p. 292: CBS Archives/Getty Images; **p. 310, 8.9:** AP/Wide World Photos; **p. 317:** © The New Yorker Collection 1998 Bruce Eric Kaplan from cartoonbank.com. All Rights Reserved; **p. 320, 8.14:** The Granger Collection, New York; **p. 322:** © The New Yorker Collection 2002 David Sipress from cartoonbank.com. All Rights Reserved; **p. 324, 8.17:** (a) Duomo/Corbis (b) Reuters New Media Inc./Corbis (c) AP/Wide World Photos (d) AP/Wide World Photos; **p. 325, 8.19:** © BBC Picture Archives; **p. 334, 8.26:** AP/Wide World Photos.

CHAPTER 9: p. 340: AP Wide World Photos; **p. 342, 9.1:** Vince Bucci/Getty Images; **p. 346, 9.5:** Archives of the History of American Psychology, University of Akron; **p. 347, 9.7:** Jacob E. Steiner, PhD, Laboratory of Oral Physiology, The Hebrew University; **p. 349:** © 2005 Bob Zahn from cartoonbank.com. All Rights Reserved; **p. 356, 9.10:** Photo Services, Harvard University; **p. 366, 9.14:** Bettmann/Corbis; **p. 369, 9.15:** AP/Wide World Photos; **p. 375, 9.17:** Courtesy David Buss, University of Texas at Austin; **p. 376:** © The New Yorker Collection 1997 Barbara Smaller from cartoonbank.com. All Rights Reserved.

CHAPTER 10: p. 382: David Leeson/Dallas Morning News/Corbis Sygma; **p. 387, 10.1:** From Izard, C. E., Fantauzzo, C. A., Castle, J. M., Hayes, O. M., Rayias, M. F., Putnam, P. H. (1995). The ontogeny and significance of infants' facial expressions in the first nine months of life, *Developmental Psychology, 31,* 997–1013. Photographs courtesy Carroll Izard, University of Delaware; **p. 388, 10.3:** © Ekman 1972–2004; **p. 396, 10.6:** Edgar Fahs Smith Collection; **p. 397, 10.8:** Photo by Bill Apple; **p. 398, 10.10:** Chris Lisle/Corbis; **p. 399:** © The New Yorker Collection 1989 George Price from cartoonbank.com. All Rights Reserved; **p. 401, 10.11:** From Lane, R. D., Reiman, E. M., Ahern, G. L., Schwatz, G. E., Davidson, R. J. (1997). Neuroanatomical correlates of happiness, sadness, and disgust. *American Journal of Psychiatry, 154,* 926–933. Copyright © 1997 by American Psychiatric Association; **p. 405, 10.14:** Photo by James Prince; **p. 405, 10.15:** From Dolan, R. J. Emotion processing in the human brain revealed through functional neuroimaging. In M. S., Gazzaniga (Ed.) *The New Cognitive Neurosciences.* Cambridge, MA: MIT Press; **p. 407, 10.17:** Courtesy Richard J. Davidson, University of Wisconsin; **p. 407, 10.18:** (a) American Psychological Association; **p. 409, 10.20:** Courtesy Shelley Taylor, UCLA; **p. 409, 10.21:** Archives of the History of American Psychology, University of Akron; **p. 412:** © The New Yorker Collection 1987 Donald Reilly from cartoonbank.com. All Rights Reserved; **p. 422:** The Far Side ® by Gary Larson © 1982 FarWorks, Inc. All Rights Reserved. Used with permission; **p. 423, 10.27:** AP/Wide World Photos.

CHAPTER 11: p. 430: Jose Fuste Raga/Corbis; **p. 438, 11.4:** Robert Marvin, Estate of Mary Ainsworth; **p. 439, 11.5:** Nina Leen/TimePix/Getty Images; **p. 439, 11.6:** Harlow Primate Laboratory, University of Wisconsin; **p. 440, 11.7:** Robert Marvin, Estate of Mary Ainsworth; **p. 442:** © The New Yorker Collection 2003 Donald Reilly from cartoonbank.com. All Rights Reserved; **p. 445, 11.9:** Stock Boston, LLC/Spencer Grant; **p. 446, 11.10:** Courtesy Velma Dobson, University of Arizona; **p. 447, 11.12:** Bettmann/Corbis; **p. 449, 11.14:** Michael Newman/PhotoEdit; **p. 452, 11.19:** © Dr. Carolyn Rovee-Collier, Director, Rutgers Early Learning Project; **p. 457, 11.22:** AFP/Getty Images; **p. 459, 11.23:** Courtesy of Laura Ann Petitto; **p. 460, 11.24:** Gaetano/Corbis; **p. 462:** © The New Yorker Collection 2001 Edward Koren from cartoonbank.com. All Rights Reserved; **p. 463, 11.25:** Corbis Sygma; **p. 464, 11.26:** Photo Courtesy David Reimer. From Colapinto, John, *As nature made him: The boy who was raised as a girl,*

(2000), HarperCollins Publishers Inc.; **p. 464, 11.27:** Reuters Newsmedia Inc./Corbis; **p. 469, 11.28:** Sarah Putnam/Index Stock Imagery, Inc.; **p. 470:** © The New Yorker Collection 1994 Sidney Harris from cartoonbank.com. All Rights Reserved; **p. 473, 11.29:** (left) Stephanie Maze/Corbis.

CHAPTER 12: p. 480: Tom Wagner/Corbis; **p. 483, 12.1:** Dan McAdams, Northwestern University; **p. 484, 12.2:** Bettmann/Corbis; **p. 487, 12.4:** Courtesy Carl Rogers Memorial Library; **p. 492, 12.6:** (top) Royalty-Free/Corbis; (bottom) Ralph A. Clevenger/Corbis; **p. 495, 12.7:** Adapted from Norman, W.T. (1963). Toward an adequate taxonomy of personality attributes: replicated factor structure in peer nomination personality rating, *Journal of Abnormal and Social Psychology, 66,* 5770; **p. 497, 12.8:** Columbia University; **p. 502:** © The New Yorker Collection 1999 Barbara Smaller from cartoonbank.com. All Rights Reserved; **p. 503:** © The New Yorker Collection 1996 J. B. Handelsman from cartoonbank.com. All Rights Reserved; **p. 505, 12.11:** Hulton Archive/Getty Images; **p. 513, 12.16:** (left) Crabtree/Reuters/Corbis; (right) Corbis Sygma.

CHAPTER 13: p. 518: Kat Wade/San Fransisco Chronicle/Corbis; **p. 520, 13.1:** Edna Morlok; **p. 522, 13.2:** The Granger Collection, New York; **p. 527, 13.3:** *Abnormal Psychology* 4th Edition, by Seligman, Walker, and Rosenhan. Copyright W. W. Norton & Company, Inc. Used by permission of W. W. Norton & Company, Inc.; **p. 529, 13.4:** Joe McNally; **p. 531, 13.5:** Bettmann/Corbis; **p. 532, 13.6:** (top) Manchester Scott/Corbis Sygma; (bottom) Denver Post/Kent Meireis/Corbis Sygma; **p. 535:** © The New Yorker Collection 2003 Michael Shaw from cartoonbank.com. All Rights Reserved; **p. 536, 13.7:** Courtesy Dr. Lewis Baxter, UAB; **p. 542, 13.11:** © Richard Wyatt; **p. 553, 13.13:** Peter Aprahamian/Corbis; **p. 557, 13.14:** From Osterling, J., & Dawson, G. (1994). Early recognition of children with autism. A study of first birthday home videotapes. *Journal of Autism and Developmental Disorders, 24,* 247–257. Photographs courtesy Geraldine Dawson; **p. 557, 13.15:** Courtesy of Dr. Ami Klin, (2003) *The enactive mind from actions to cognition: Lessons from autism.* Philosophical Transactions of the Royal Society; **p. 559, 13.16:** From Zametkin, A. J., Nordhal, T. E., Gross, M. et al., (1990). Cerebral glucose metabolism in adults with hyperactivity of childhood onset. *New England Journal of Medicine, 323(20),* 1361–1366. Images courtesy Alan Zametkin, NIH; **p. 560:** © The New Yorker Collection 1997 Robert Mankoff from cartoonbank.com. All Rights Reserved.

CHAPTER 14: p. 564: Jeffrey L. Rotman/Corbis; **p. 568, 14.1:** Bettmann/Corbis; **p. 569:** © The New Yorker Collection 1989 Danny Shanahan from cartoonbank.com. All Rights Reserved; **p. 570, 14.2:** © 1983 Erika Stone; **p. 570, 14.3:** Courtesy Barbara A. Marinelli; **p. 575, 14.6:** Courtesy James Pennebaker, University of Texas at Austin; **p. 580, 14.8:** AP/Wide World Photos; **p. 582, 14.9:** From Baxter, L. R., et al. (1992). Caudate glucose metabolic rate changes with both drug and behavior therapy for obsessive-compulsive disorder. *Archives of General Psychiatry, 49,* 681–689, Copyright © American Medical Association. Images courtesy Dr. Lewis Baxter, UAB; **p. 583:** © The New Yorker Collection 1993 Lee Lorenz from cartoonbank.com. All Rights Reserved; **p. 586, 14.13:** © Pascal Goetheluck/Scienve Photo Library/Photo Researchers, Inc.; **p. 586, 14.14:** © Will McIntyre/Photo Researchers, Inc.; **p. 594, 14.18:** Courtesy Marsha Linehan, University of Washington; **p. 602, 14.21:** Richard Perry/*The New York Times.*

CHAPTER 15: p. 606: Kumar/AFP/Getty Images; **p. 609, 15.1:** © Philip G. Zimbardo, PhD; **p. 618:** © The New Yorker Collection 1985 Michael Maslin from cartoonbank.com. All Rights Reserved; **p. 621, 15.18:** Najlah Feanny/Corbis; **p. 622, 15.9:** © 1982 Karen Zabuion, Courtesy New School Public Relations Department; **p. 629:** © New Yorker Collection 1996 Tom Cheney from cartoonbank.com. All Rights Reserved; **p. 630, 15.13:** Courtesy Keith Payne, Washington University; **p. 637, 15.16:** Photos by William Vandivert; **p. 639, 15.17 and 15.18:** Courtesy Alexandra Milgram; **p. 645, 15.23:** New York Times Pictures; **p. 649, 15.25:** From Langlois, J. H., & Ruggerman, L. A., (1990). Attractive faces are only average. *Psychological Science 1,* 115–121. Photographs courtesy Judith Hall Langlois, University of Texas at Austin; **p. 649, 15.26:** From Perrett, D. I., May, K. A., Yoshikawa, S. (1994). Facial shape and judgments of female attractiveness. Reprinted by permission from *Nature,* 1994, vol. 368, 239–242. Copyright 2002 Macmillan Publishers Ltd. Images courtesy D. I. Perrett, University of St. Andrews; **p. 650, 15.27:** (top) Courtesy Elaine Hatfield, University of Hawaii at Manoa; (bottom) Courtesy Ellen Berscheid, University of Minnesota.

Figures

CHAPTER 1: p. 19, 1.8: Grant, Peter R.; *Ecology and evolution of Darwin's finches.* © 1986 Princeton University Press. Reprinted by permission of Princeton University Press; **p.28, 1.18:** The Subfields Doctoral Psychologist.

CHAPTER 3: p. 92, 3.11: From Pinel, John P. J. *Biopyschology* 4/e © 2000. Published by Allyn and Bacon, Boston, MA. Copyright © 2000 by Pearson Education. Reprinted by permission of the publisher.

CHAPTER 4: p. 151, 4.28: Aston-Jones, G. and Bloom, F. E. (1981), *The Journal of Neuroscience, 1,* 876–886. Copyright © 1981 by The Society for Neuroscience.

CHAPTER 5: p. 165, 5.3 and p. 179, 5.14: From Zimbardo, P. G. & Gerrig, R. J. *Psychology and life,* 15/e © 1999. Published by Allyn and Bacon, Boston, MA. Copyright © 1999 by Pearson Education. Reprinted by permission of the publisher; **p. 179, 5.15:** Bear, *Neuroscience* 2E. Reprinted by permission of Lippincott Williams & Wilkins; **p. 186, 5.19:** Psychology by Peter Gray. © 1991, 1994, 1999 by Worth Publishers. Used with permission; **p. 187, 5.23:** Kuhl, Jerome, Subjective contours, *Scientific American 234* (1976), 44–52; **p. 188, 5.24:** Osherson, Daniel, adapted from Biedermann, *An invitation to cognitive science* 2nd ed., Vol. 2. Reprinted with the permission of MIT; **p. 199, 5.42:** Turning the tables diagram from *Mind sights* by Roger N. Shepard, © 1990 by Roger N. Shepard.

CHAPTER 6: p. 225, 6.12: *Psychology by Peter Gray.* © 1991, 1994, 1999 by Worth Publishers. Used with permission.

CHAPTER 7: **p. 263, 7.7:** Adapted from Craik, F. I. M., & Tulving, E. (1975). Depth of processing and the retention of words in episodic memory. *Journal of Experimental Psychology: General, 104,* 268–294; **p. 265, 7.8:** Adapted from Collins, A. M., & Loftus, E. F. (1975). A spreading-activation theory of semantic processing. *Psychological Review, 82,* 407–428; **p. 266, 7.9:** Adapted from Godden, D. R., & Baddeley, A. D. (1975). Context-dependent memory in two natural environments: On land and underwater. *British Journal of Psychology, 66,* 325–331; **p. 271, 7.14:** Adapted from Wagner, A. D., Schacter, D. L., Rotte, M., Koutstaal, W., Maril, A., Dale, A. M., et al. (1998). Building memories: remembering and forgetting of verbal experiences as predicted by brain activity. *Science, 281,* 1188–1191.

CHAPTER 8: **p. 297, 8.1:** Eysenck, M. W., figures 7.6 and 7.7, *Cognitive psychology: A student's handbook,* 2nd Edition, Lawrence Erlbaum Associates. Copyright © 1990; **p. 300, 8.5:** Eysenck, M. W., figure 8.3, *Cognitive psychology: A student's handbook,* 2nd Edition, Lawrence Erlbaum Associates. Copyright © 1990; **p. 309, 8.8:** Plous, S., figure 9.1, *Psychology of judgement and decision making.* Copyright © 1993 by The McGraw-Hill Companies; **p. 331, 8.22:** Plomin from *Journal of Personality and Social Psychology 86;* **p. 331, 8.23:** McGue, Behavioral Genetics of Cognitive Ability from Nature, Nurture.

CHAPTER 9: **p. 353, 9.8:** Adapted from Schachter, S. (1959). The psychology of affiliation. Stanford, CA: Stanford University Press; **p.357, 9.11:** Adapted from Miller, G. A., Galanter, E., & Pribram, K. H. (1960). *Plans and the structure of behavior.* New York: Holt. **p. 375, 9.18:** Adapted from Clark, R. D., & Hatfield, E. (1989). Gender differences in receptivity to sexual offers. *Journal of Psychology and Human Sexuality, 2,* 39–55.

CHAPTER 10: **p. 394, 10.4:** Adapted from Russell, J. A., & Feldman Barrett, L. (1999). Core affect, prototypical emotional episodes, and other things called emotion: Dissecting the elephant. *Journal of Personality and Social Psychology, 76,* 805–819; **p. 396, 10.7:** From *Introduction to psychology* (with Info Trac) 5th edition by Kalat. © 1999. Reprinted with permission of Wadsworth, a division of Thomson Learning: www.thomsonrights.com. Fax 800-730-2215; **p. 417, 10.24:** Bray, George A., Nomogram for determining body mass index. Copyright © 1978 George A. Bray; **p. 418, 10.25:** Fallon, A. E. (1985). Sex differences in perceptions of desirable body shape, *Journal of Abnormal Psychology, 94,* 102–105; **p. 419, 10.26:** Adapted from Hibscher, J., & Herman, C. P. (1977). Obesity, dieting, and the expression of "obese" characteristics. *Journal of Comparative and Physiological Psychology, 91,* 374–380.

CHAPTER 11: **p. 450, 11.16:** Reprinted from *Cognition,* vol. 47 (2) May 1993, Needham, Amy, and Baillargeon, Renee, Intuitions about support in 4.5 month-old infants, 121–148, Copyright © 1993, with permission from Elsevier Science; **p. 455, 11.21:** Nairne, J. S., figure 9.2 from *Psychology: The adaptive mind,* Wadsworth Group; **p. 475, 11.30:** Sternberg, Robert J., Major abilities and development in the adult period, Intellectual development.

CHAPTER 12: **p. 509, 12.14:** Adapted from McCrae, R. R., Costa, P. T., Ostendorf, F., Angleitner, A., Hrebickova, M., Avia, M. D., et al. (2000). Nature over nurture: Temperament, personality, and lifespan development. *Journal of Personality and Social Psychology, 78,* 173–186; **p. 510, 12.15:** Adapted from McCrae, R. R., & Costa, P. T., Jr. (1999). A five-factor theory of personality. In L. A. Pervin and O. P. John (Eds), *Handbook of Personality: Theory and research* (2nd ed., p. 139–153). New York: Guilford Press.

CHAPTER 13: **p. 537, 13.8:** Adapted from Rapee, R. M., Brown, T. A., Anthony, M. M., & Barlow, D. H. (1992). Response to hyperventilation and inhalation of 5.5 % carbon dioxide enriched air across the DSM-III-R anxiety disorders. *Journal of Abnormal Psychology, 101,* 538–552; **p. 540, 13.9:** Rosenthal, Sack, Gillin, Lewy, Goodwin, Davenport, Mueller, Newsome, Wehr, Depression and length of daylight in seasonal affective disorder. *Archives of General Psychiatry, 41,* [1984], 72–80; **p. 541, 13.10:** Adapted from Brown & Harris (1978). *Social origins of depression A study of psychiatric disorders in women.* New York: The Free Press; **p. 547, 13.12:** Gottesman, *Schizophrenia Genesis: The origins of madness,* W. H. Freeman. Copyright ©1991.

CHAPTER 14: **p. 571, 14.4:** Vaughn, C. E. (1976). Relapse rates in schizophrenia patients, *British Journal of Psychiatry, 129;* **p. 579, 14.7:** Rudestam, Kjell Erik, *Anxiety Hierarchy, Methods of Self-Change: An ABC Primer,* 1980, Monterey, CA: Brooks/Cole; **p. 583, 14.10:** Reprinted with permission from the *American Journal of Psychiatry,* Copyright 2005. American Psychiatric Association; **p. 585, 14.11:** Nolen-Hoeksema, S., figure 5.16 from *Abnormal Psychology* (1998), The McGraw Hill Companies; **p. 589, 14.15:** Adapted from Kane, J. M., Honingfield, G., Singer, J., & Meltzer, N. (1988). Clozapine for the treatment-resistant schizophrenic. *Archives of General Psychiatry, 45,* 789–796; **p. 590, 14.16:** Adapted from Hogarty, G. E., Anderson, D. M., Reiss, D. J., Kornblith, S. J., Greenwald, D. P., Jaund, D. D., et al. (1986) Family psychoeducation, social skills training, and maintenance chemotherapy in the aftercare treatment of schizophrenia: One-year effects of a controlled study on relapse and expressed emotion. *Archives of General Psychiatry, 43,* 633–642; **p. 596, 14.19:** Adapted from Hare, R. D., McPherson, L. M., & Forth, A. E. (1998). Male psychopaths and their criminal careers. *Journal of Consulting and Clinical Psychology, 56,* 710–714; **p. 598, 14.20:** Adapted from Pelham, W. E., Jr. (1993). Pharmocotherapy for children with attention-deficit hyperactivity disorder. *School Psychology Review, 22,* 199–227.

CHAPTER 15: **p. 616, 15.6:** Adapted from Johnson, M. M. S. (1986). The initial letter effect: Ego-attachment or mere exposure? Unpublished doctoral dissertation, Ohio State University. Reported in Greenwald, A. G., & Banaji, M. R., (1995). Implicit social cognition: Attitudes, self-esteem, and stereotypes. *Psychological Review, 102,* 4–27; **p. 635, 15.14:** Adapted from Zajonc, R. B. (1965). Social facilitation. *Science, 149,* 269–274; **p. 637, 15.15:** Adapted from Asch, S. E. (1955). Opinions and social pressure. *Scientific American, 193,* 31–35 (offprint 450); **p. 640, 15.19:** Adapted from Milgram, S. (1974). *Obedience to authority: An experimental view.* New York: Harper & Row; **p. 642, 15.20:** Adapted from Raleigh, M. J., McGuire, M. T., Brammer, G. L., Pollack, D. B., & Yuwiler, A. (1991). Serotonergic mechanisms promote dominance in adult male vervet monkeys. *rain Research, 559,* 181–190; **p. 643, 15.21:** Data from United Nations, 1991; **p. 644, 15.22:** Adapted from Cohen, D., Nisbett, R. E., Bowdle, B. F., & Schwartz, N. (1996). Insult, aggression, and the southern culture of honor: An "experimental ethnography." *Journal of Personality and Social Psychology, 70,* 945–960; **p. 646, 15.24:** Adapted from Latané, B., & Darley, J. M. (1968). Group inhibition of bystander intervention in emergencies. *Journal of Personality and Social Psychology, 10,* 215–221.

Tables

p. 278, Table 7.1: Adapted from Schacter, D. L. (2001). *The seven sins of memory: How the mind forgets and remembers.* Boston: Houghton Mifflin; **p. 421, Table 10.1:** Adapted from *Diagnostic and Statistical Manual of Mental Disorders DSM-IV,* American Psychiatric Association, 1994; **p. 511, Table 12.4:** Adapted from McAdams. (2000). *The person: an integrated introduction to personality psychology.* Orlando, FL: Harcourt; **p. 523, Table 13.1:** Adapted from *Diagnostic and Statistical Manual of Mental Disorders DSM-IV,* American Psychiatric Association, 1994; **p. 530, Table 13.2:** Adapted from Silver, E., Cirincione, C., & Steadman, H. J. (1994). Demythologizing inaccurate perceptions of the insanity defense. *Law & Human Behavior, 18,* 63–70; **p. 544, Table 13.3:** Adapted from *Diagnostic and Statistical Manual of Mental Disorders DSM-IV,* American Psychiatric Association, 1994; **p. 551, Table 13.6:** Adapted from *Diagnostic and Statistical Manual of Mental Disorders DSM-IV,* American Psychiatric Association, 1994.

Boden, J. M., 616
Bodenhausen, G. V., 372
Bohus, M., 552, 594, 595
Bolles, Robert, 229
Bollini, A., 547, 589
Bonagura, N., 560
Bonanno, George, 399
Bond, Charles, 369–370
Boodoo, G., 322, 330, 332, 334
Booth, A., 110, 471
Booth, C., 443, 444
Booth, R. J., 575
Borian, F. E., 585
Born, J., 146
Bornstein, R. F., 495
Borton, R., 445–446
Bosch, E. O., 329
Boston, P., 557
Botsis, A. J., 534
Bouchard, Claude, 386, 417, 418
Bouchard, T. J. Jr., 84, 83, 322, 330, 332, 334, 417, 501
Bourgouin, P., 579
Bourin, M., 103
Bouton, M. E., 215
Bowdle, B. F., 643
Bowlby, John, 433, 438, 440
Boykin, A. W., 322, 330, 332, 334
Boyle, M. O., 328
Bozarth, Michael, 344
Bracha, H. S., 549
Bradbury, T. N., 497, 652
Bradwejn, J., 103
Bramlett, M. D., 442
Brammer, G. L., 642
Brammer, M., 401
Brand, R. J., 412
Brandt, J. R., 644
Bransford, J. K., 264
Branson, Richard, 325
Braun, A. R., 152
Breier, A., 548
Breitenbecher, D. L., 616
Breland, J. B., 229
Breland, M., 229
Bremer, D., 266
Brent, D. A., 592
Breuer, Josef, 521, 568
Brewer, J. B., 271
Brewer, M. B., 352
Brewster, David, 193
Brick, P. D., 422
Brickman, A. M., 547
Bridges, M., 443
Brigham, J. C., 191
Brin, M. F., 101
Broadbent, Donald, 202–203
Broca, Paul, 119, 120
Brody, A. L., 512, 585
Brody, C. L., 422
Brody, N., 322, 330, 332, 334
Bromet, E., 546
Brooksbank, L.B.W., 373
Brown, Alan, 277
Brown, B. Bradford, 466
Brown, E., 465
Brown, E. L., 575
Brown, G. G., 149
Brown, G. K., 525
Brown, G. R., 263
Brown, G. W., 540, 541
Brown, J., 261
Brown, J. D., 618, 619

Brown, Jonathan, 616–617
Brown, R. A., 424
Brown, R. M., 581
Brown, Roger, 277, 280, 456
Brown, S., 644
Brown, T. A., 537
Brown, T. H., 241
Brown, T. L., 587
Brownell, C. A., 465
Brozek, J., 419
Bruce, V. V., 190
Bruck, M., 285
Bruck, M. L., 452
Bruer, John, 33
Brummett, B. H., 412
Bruner, J. S., 348
Buchanan, R. W., 546, 548
Buchanan, T. W., 124
Buchsbaum, M. S., 547, 559
Buckner, R. L., 252, 269, 271, 359, 475
Bucy, Paul, 642
Burg, M. M., 412, 413
Burge, S. A., 399
Burgess, N., 124
Burgess, P., 329
Burgess, S., 587
Burian, S. E., 43
Burke, B. L., 569
Burke, M. A., 471
Burkhardt, P. E., 594
Burrows, G. D., 109
Burrows, L., 143
Burt, M., 372
Burton, A. M., 190
Bush, E. C., 127
Bushman, B. J., 236
Buss, Arnold, 503
Buss, David, 6, 10, 374, 375, 392–393, 506–507
Buxbaum, J., 547
Buxton, R. B., 149
Byars, A. W., 329
Byatt, G., 127
Byrne, D., 374
Byrne, J. H., 241
Cabeza, R., 273, 405
Cacioppo, J. T., 352, 395, 401, 415
Cacioppo, John, 624
Cade, John, 587
Caglar, S., 613
Cahill, E. D., 373
Cahill, L., 273, 405
Cairns, Beverly, 466
Cairns, Robert, 466
Calder, A. J., 401
Calkins, Mary Whiton, 22
Call, J., 453
Callaghan, T., 454
Callahan, A., 587
Calvanio, R., 298
Calvini, G., 281
Campbell, J. D., 615, 616
Campbell, W. K., 618
Campeas, R., 582
Canick, J. D., 586
Canino, G. J., 534
Canli, T., 273, 506
Cannon, Walter B., 342, 345, 363, 384, 395–396, 400, 408–409
Cantor, Nancy, 491
Caporael, L. R., 352, 507
Carey, Susan, 434
Carlsmith, Merrill, 622–623

Carmena, J. M., 133
Carmody, T., 420, 591
Carnevale, Amy, 109, 110, 111
Carney, R. M., 412
Caro, T. M., 233
Carpenter, D., 373
Carpenter, M., 453
Carpenter, W. T. Jr., 546, 548
Carson, R. E., 152
Carstensen, Laura, 434, 474
Carter, C. S., 441
Cartwright, C., 558
Caruso, S., 372
Carver, C. S., 357
Caryl, P. G., 327
Case, R., 449
Casey, R. J., 649
Caspi, A., 500, 501, 504, 642, 648
Caspi, Avshalom, 85
Castellanos, F. X., 560
Castles, D., 372
Catala, M. D., 587
Catanese, K. R., 374
Cattell, Raymond, 294, 323, 488–489
C'de Baca, Janet, 510
Ceci, Stephen, 285, 322, 330, 332, 334, 452
Cezayirli, E., 329
Chabris, Christopher, 32
Chafee, M., 272
Chagnon, Y. C., 418
Chakrabarti, S., 543
Chambers, D. W., 302
Chan, T., 512, 642
Chapman, P. R., 203, 204
Chappell, P. B., 581
Chappelow, J., 638
Chase, G. A., 541
Chase, W. G., 254
Chassin, L., 365, 422
Chawarska, K., 556
Chee, M., 415
Cheema, F., 274, 391
Chen, C., 534
Chen, M., 143
Cherry, E. C., 202
Chesher, G., 44
Chess, Stella, 441–442
Cheung, A. M., 559
Chiao, J. Y., 191, 281
Childress, A. R., 218
Chistyakov, A. V., 587
Chitins, X., 329
Chivers, M. L., 375
Choi, I., 187, 628
Choi, W. S., 421
Choleris, E., 86
Chomsky, Noam, 432, 456–457, 459, 477
Christensen, P. N., 372
Christianson, S., 280
Cialdini, Robert B., 638, 644–645
Clark, A. C., 490
Clark, Beverly, 53
Clark, Lee Anna, 394
Clark, R. D., 374
Clark, R. E., 269
Clarke-Stewart, K. S., 443, 444
Claux, M. L., 454
Cleary, P. D., 422
Cleckley, H., 527
Clinton, J., 598
Cloninger, C., 502

Clore, G. L., 389
Coakley, J. D., 172
Coast, J. R., 424
Cohane, G., 111
Cohen, B. M., 57
Cohen, D., 643
Cohen, N. J., 271, 424
Cohen, S., 416
Colapinto, John, 463–464
Colcombe, S. J., 424
Cole, S. W., 512, 642
Colligan, R. C., 413
Collins, Allan, 264
Collins, K., 387
Collins, P. F., 506, 512
Collins, W. A., 352
Colombo, C., 150
Colvin, C. R., 496
Comery, T. A., 231
Comes, C., 584
Compori, E., 150
Compton, J. S., 580
Conneally, P. M., 56
Conners, C. K., 599
Connor, B., 627
Connor, K. M., 580
Conway, A. R. A., 326, 328
Conway, Martin, 280
Conway, Michael, 286
Cook, I. A., 584
Cook, M., 220, 233
Cook, R. G., 124, 144
Cooney, J., 145
Cooper, L. A., 297
Coopersmith, S., 615
Corbett, D., 238
Corbitt, E. M., 553
Corder, E. H., 473
Corkin, Sue, 268, 278–279
Correll, C. U., 589
Corty, E., 422
Cosmides, Leda, 6, 10, 11, 354, 506
Costa, P. T., 412, 495
Costa, P. T. Jr., 490, 508, 509
Costa, Paul, 484, 509
Costello, E. J., 591
Courchesne, E., 558
Cousins, A. J., 372
Cowan, N., 253
Cowan, P. A., 226
Cowen, P. J., 391
Cowley, J. J., 373
Coyne, J. C., 540
Cox, D. S., 413
Craft, L. L., 424
Craighero, L., 235
Craik, Fergus, 251, 262–263, 271
Cramer, V., 551
Crist, R. E., 133
Cristal, R. E., 328
Cristol, A. H., 574
Crits-Christoph, P., 574
Crocker, Jennifer, 618
Croen, L. A., 558
Crosnoe, R., 473
Crow, T., 241
Crowe, R., 56
Crowe, R. R., 536, 537
Crundall, D., 204
Csernansky, J. G., 547
Csibra, G., 453
Csikszentmihalyi, M., 488
Culler, E. A., 172

filling-in process, 185
filter theory, 202–203
five-factor theory, 490
fixation, 485
fixed-interval reinforcement, 226
fixed schedules, 226
flashbulb memories, 280, 288, 290
fluid intelligence, 323, 326, 329, 336, 337, 475, 477
fluoxetine hydrochloride. *See* Prozac
Flynn effect, 332
fMRI, and mental disorders, 529
focusing, 328, 359
    See also attention
Fogle, Jared, 422–423, 424
Food and Drug Administration (FDA), U.S., 591, 593
foot-in-the-door effect, 638, 641, 656
foraging, study of animal, 230–231
forebrain, 123, 435
forecasting, affective, 309
forensic psychology, 531–532
forgetting, 248, 250, 274–279, 285, 289, 473
formal operation stage, 448–449, 477
Foster, Jodie, 531
fovea, 173
Fox, Michael J., 116
frame of reference effect, 198, 206
framing, 308–309, 337, 399
free association, 24, 213, 568
free will, 210
freezing, 242
Freudianism, 213, 218, 391, 439, 482, 485, 486, 528, 578
    and overview of psychological science, 4
    and scientific foundations of psychology, 24, 26
Freudian slips, 143, 484
friendships
    and development, 465–466, 476, 477
    and identity, 465–466, 470, 477
    and mental disorders, 541, 558
    and quality of relationships, 647–650, 654, 656
frontal lobes
    and aging, 472, 474
    and basic structure and functions of brain, 125, 127, 129, 155
    and development, 452, 453, 476, 477
    and eating, 362
    and emotions, 383–384, 390, 403, 407, 467
    functions of, 54, 358–359, 379
    and intelligence, 296, 329, 330–331, 338
    and learning, 453
    and memory, 271–272, 275, 283, 289, 290, 452, 474, 475, 477
    and mental disorders, 524, 536, 547, 554, 559, 562, 579–580, 587
    and motivation, 358–359, 360, 362, 376, 379
    pathology of, 118
    and personality, 505, 511
    and research methodology, 38
    See also prefrontal cortex
    and self-knowledge, 612, 613
    and sensation, 167
    and sexual behavior, 376

and sleep, 153
    and stereotypes, 630
Frost, Robert, 209
"frozen addicts," 101–102
frustration-aggression hypothesis, 642, 656
fugue states, 525
Fuller, Jamie, 109–111
fully functioning person, 487
functional fixedness, 314, 315, 337
functionalism, 21, 24, 27, 34
functional magnetic resonance imaging (fMRI), 5, 58, 59, 61, 120, 122, 329, 529, 547, 597
fundamental attribution error, 608, 609, 655
fusiform face area, 127, 281–282
fusiform gyrus, 190, 191

g. See general intelligence
GABA (gamma-aminobutyric acid), 98, 102–103, 105, 113, 370, 572, 603
Gage, F. H., 131
Gage, Phineas, 128–129, 511
Gallup, 225
gametes, 80
Gandhi, Mahatma, 606
ganglion cells, 173–174, 175, 176, 179–180, 185
gate-control theory, 169–170, 206
Gates, Bill, 325
Genain quadruplets, 519–520, 521, 528, 547, 561
gender
    and biology, 463, 477
    and brain, 123, 124–125, 463
    and cognition, 477
    and culture, 463, 477
    and development, 434, 461–464, 468, 477
    and emotions, 388–89, 427
    and environment, 463–464
    and genetics, 463–464
    and identity, 461–464, 468, 477
    and impressions, 629
    and ingroup-outgroup bias, 632
    and intelligence, 335
    and memory, 273
    and mental disorders, 534, 539, 546, 551, 553, 556, 581, 591
    and moral reasoning, 433
    and motivation, 374, 378, 380
    and norms, 477
    and personality, 503–504
    roles, 434, 462, 463, 477
    schemas, 462
    and sexual behavior, 109, 374, 378, 380
    and situation, 463
    and socialization, 462, 464
    and social psychology, 610, 629, 632
    and stress, 409, 415
gender typed, 462
general adaptation theory, 384, 409–410, 416, 428
general intelligence, 294, 295, 296, 323–327, 328, 336, 337
generalization, and learning, 215–217, 244
generalized anxiety disorder, 534, 561
generalized learned behavior, 599, 601

genetics/genes
    and adaptation, 10
    and addictions, 365, 422, 428
    and aging, 473
    and alcoholism, 56–57
    as basis of psychological science, 73–87, 112–113
    and behavior, 9, 76, 82–85, 113, 386, 417–418, 419, 422, 426, 428
    and brain, 129–131, 155, 329, 562
    definition of, 76, 77
    and development, 432, 433, 434, 435, 437, 438, 442, 443, 444
    dominant, 74, 79, 80–81, 113
    and environment, 75, 77, 79, 82–86, 113, 333
    functions of, 112–113
    and gender, 463–464
    and group differences, 333–334
    and harming and helping others, 645
    and heredity, 78–79
    and identity, 461, 463–464
    importance of, 72, 113
    and intellectual origins of psychology, 16–17
    and intelligence, 295, 320, 329, 330–334, 336, 338
    and learning, 220, 242–243
    and levels of analysis, 15
    and memory, 76, 274
    Mendel's studies as basis of, 74
    and mental disorders, 75, 100, 521, 522, 529, 530, 536, 537, 539–540, 541, 546–547, 549, 552, 554, 557, 558, 559, 561, 562, 581
    modification of, 76, 86–87, 113
    and mood, 182
    and motivation, 359, 365, 377
    mutations of, 10
    natural selection at level of, 645
    and nervous system, 94
    and obesity, 386, 417–418, 419, 426, 428
    overview about, 112–113
    and personality, 76, 490, 500–502, 506, 509, 514, 515
    recessive, 74, 79, 80, 113
    and research methodology, 40, 59–60
    and RNA, 76
    and scientific foundations of psychology, 21
    and sensation, 167
    and sexual behavior, 377
    and smoking, 422, 428
    and themes of psychological science, 9, 10, 33, 34
    See also DNA; genotypes; phenotypes; RNA
Genie (case study), 431–432, 437, 454, 458
genital stage, 485
genotypes, 79–80, 83, 113
Genovese, Kitty, 645
geon theory, 188
Gestalt psychologists, 29
Gestalt psychology
    and application of psychological science, 29
    definition of, 22
    emergence of, 5
    and learning, 23, 34

and perception, 5, 27, 34, 161, 186–187, 198, 199–200, 206
    and scientific foundations of psychology, 23, 25, 27, 34
Gilmore, Gary (case study), 553
glial cells, 93–94, 103, 547
globalization, 12
glucose, 273, 363, 380
glucostatic theory, 363
glutamate, 98, 103, 105, 113
gluten, 600, 604
goals
    achievement of personal, 355–360, 379
    and aging, 474
    definition of, 355
    and emotions, 389
    and ingroup-outgroup bias, 633
    and memory, 272
    and motivation, 343, 351, 355–360, 379
    and organization of subgoals, 311–312
    and personality, 491, 510, 511
    and problem solving, 311–319, 337
    of psychological science, 42
Golgi stain, 74
gonads, 109
"good person," 619
Graham, Martha, 325
Grandin, Temple, 556
gratification, delayed, 230, 343, 358, 360, 379
gray matter, 121, 124, 134, 137, 329
groups
    collective memory of, 286
    control, 39
    decision making by, 636
    and environment, 333–334
    and genes, 333–334
    and harming and helping others, 644
    influence on individual behavior of, 635–636, 655–656
    and intelligence, 333–334, 336
    polarization in, 636
    and scientific foundations of psychology, 26
    See also ingroup-outgroup bias
group socialization theory, 465
group therapy, 570–571, 594, 595, 603
groupthink, 636
growth hormone (GH), 112, 149
growth hormone releasing factor (GRF), 112
Gueye, Nogaye, 191–192
guilt, 386, 391–392, 427, 442, 466, 467, 477, 538
gut feelings, 390

habits, 131, 260, 346, 380
    and scientific foundations of psychology, 26
habitual response level, 489
habituation, 240, 241, 244, 245, 445, 446, 450, 454, 477, 580
Halbrook, Diana, 285
Hale, Fred, 472
hallucinations, 100, 545, 551, 562, 572, 588, 590
haloperidol, 588, 589
Hamm, Mia, 324
handwriting, 527, 597

Hanks, Tom, 481, 482, 494, 496, 652
haptic sense. *See* touch
hardiness, 415, 428
harming others, 641–647, 655, 656
Harrison, George, 281
Hawthorne effect, 50
hazing study, 623
head, size of, 329
health
    behaviors affecting, 416–426, 428
    and emotions, 399
    and general intelligence, 326
    overview about, 427
    and personality, 412
    and stress, 382, 384–385, 411–413,
        425–426, 428
health psychology, 385, 386, 416
hearing
    and aging, 474
    as basic sensory process, 166,
        170–172, 206
    and basic structure and functions
        of brain, 127, 155
    and development, 436, 446, 477
    and how we sense the world, 161
    and language, 455
    and learning, 220
    and location of sound, 172
    and memory, 152–153, 268–269, 289
    and perception, 182–183, 200, 206
    theory of, 161
heart disease, 46–47, 135, 411–413, 418,
    425, 427
Heatherton, James, 195
Heatherton, Sarah, 195
Hebbian learning, 131
hedonism, 348
helping others, 641–647, 655, 656
hemineglect, 126–127, 145
Hemingway, Ernest, 543
hemispherical encoding retrieval
    asymmetry (HERA), 271
heredity, 78–79, 84, 113
    See also genetics/genes
heritability, 84–85, 87, 500–501, 541
Hermann Grid, 177
heroin, 101–102, 104, 106, 218, 230,
    238, 367, 368
heuristics, 306–310, 319, 336, 337,
    389, 634
hierarchy
    of fears, 578, 579
    model of personality, 489–490, 515
    and perception, 183
    and storage of memory, 264, 266
Higazy, Abdallah, 286–287, 288
Hinckley, John Jr. (case study), 529–531
hindbrain, 435
hippocampus
    and addiction, 367
    atrophy of, 533
    and basic structure and functions
        of brain, 123, 124–125, 127, 129,
        155, 329
    and development of brain, 131, 132
    and emotions, 405
    and learning, 241, 245
    and memory, 249–250, 268, 269,
        270, 272, 275, 289
    and mental disorders, 533
    and motivation, 358, 367
    size of, 124, 329
    and stress, 411

histamine, 572, 583, 589
histrionic personality, 550
Hitler, Adolph, 494
H. M. (case study), 5, 249–250, 251,
    254, 256, 267, 268, 277–278,
    279
homeostasis, 342, 344, 345–346, 351,
    363, 379, 396
homosexuality, 370, 376–378, 486
homunculus, 132, 183
honor, culture of, 643–644
hormone replacement therapy, 577
hormones
    and basic structure and functions
        of brain, 129
    definition of, 108
    and development, 435, 444
    and gender, 464
    and harming and helping others,
        656
    and mental disorders, 521
    and motivation, 371–372, 377,
        378, 380
    and neuron integration into
        communication systems, 76,
        108–112, 114
    and sexual behavior, 109, 371–372,
        377, 378, 380
    and stress, 409–410
    See also specific hormone
hostage study, 414
HPA (hypothalamic-pituitary-
    adrenal) system, 410
human genome, and themes of
    psychological science, 9, 16, 33
Human Genome Project, 76, 78,
    87, 113
humanistic approach
    and motivation, 344
    to personality, 483, 487–488, 493,
        495, 515
    and scientific foundations of
        psychology, 26–27
    and treatment of mental disorders,
        568–569, 603
humor, 399, 400
humoral theory, 482, 520
Huntington's disease, 80–82, 87, 125,
    134, 135, 136
H. W. (patient), 284
hyperpolarization, 92, 93, 95, 96, 97,
    102, 105
hypertension, 533
hypnosis, 527
hypomanic episodes, 539
hypothalamus
    and basic structure and functions
        of brain, 123, 124, 129, 155
    and development, 435
    and eating, 362, 363, 380
    and emotions, 401
    functions of, 111
    and harming and helping others,
        642
    and motivation, 343, 362, 363, 372,
        377, 378
    and neuron integration into
        communication systems,
        111–112, 114
    and sexual behavior, 372, 377, 378
    size of, 378
    and sleep, 150–151
    and stress, 410

hypotheses, and research
    methodology, 39, 41–42, 52
iconic memory, 252–253, 289
id, 485, 514
identity
    adolescent, 461–468, 477
    and biology, 463
    and culture, 461–463, 468, 477
    and development, 461–468, 476, 477
    and environment, 463–464
    and friendships, 465–466
    gender, 461–464, 468, 477
    and genetics, 461, 463–464
    and mental disorders, 525–528,
        530, 551, 552, 554, 561, 562, 594
    and moral values, 466–467
    multiple, 525–528, 561
    and norms, 461–463, 477
    race/ethnicity, 467–468, 477
    sexual, 123, 343, 435, 468, 632
    and situation, 463
    and social influence, 655–656
    and socialization, 462, 464
    stages of, 433, 469–470
idiographic approach, 494, 515
illusions, 187, 199, 201, 206, 285
images
    and memory, 252, 258
    See also representations, mental
imaging studies, and themes of
    psychological science, 16
imipramine, 580, 581, 583
imitation, 226, 234–235, 237, 245
    See also modeling
immediate memory. *See* short-term
    memory
immune system, 95, 149, 413, 425, 427,
    536, 575
implicit attitudes, 621–622, 655
implicit attitudes test (IAT), 5,
    622, 630
implicit memory, 260–261, 262, 267,
    289, 622
implicit personality theory, 488
impressions
    first, 626
    formation of, 625–634, 655
imprinting, 439
impulsivity
    and basic structure and functions
        of brain, 127, 128
    and brain, 560
    and influence of
        neurotransmission, 100, 113
    and mental disorders, 5, 536, 551,
        552, 554, 558, 560, 562, 594, 595
    and personality, 489, 512
incentives, 346, 348
    See also motivation; punishment;
        rewards
inclusive fitness, 645, 656
independent self, 613–614
independent variables, 43, 44, 48
individual differences. *See*
    uniqueness, individual
individual differences
    and evolution, 34
    and intellectual origins of
        psychology, 19, 34
individuals
    and research methodology, 48–49
    See also levels of analysis

induced movement illusion, 198
inductive reasoning, 305, 319, 337
industrial melanism, 80
infantile amnesia, 451–452
inferences, and perception, 199–200
inferential statistics, 66–67
influence, social, 634–641
information processing
    and perception, 199–200, 206
    and study of consciousness, 141
    See also neurotransmission
information-processing theories, and
    scientific foundations of
    psychology, 25–26, 34
informed consent, 60–61
ingroup favoritism, 632, 633
ingroup-outgroup bias, 631–632,
    633, 655
ingroups, 12
inhibiting stereotypes, 629–630
inhibition
    centers of, 343, 362
    and eating, 362
    lateral, 176, 177
    and learning, 244, 505
    and mental disorders, 568
    and motivation, 343, 362
    and nervous system, 92, 93, 96, 98,
        102–103, 105, 113
    and personality, 484, 503–504,
        505, 506
    and sensation, 176, 177
innate knowledge, 434, 449–451,
    461, 477
insanity defense, 530–531, 561
insight, 230, 294, 312–313, 316, 337,
    567–568, 569, 571, 574, 577,
    596, 603
insomnia, 102, 148, 149, 151
inspection time tasks, 327
instincts, 231, 342, 376, 484–485, 532
    See also intuition
Institutional Review Boards (IRBs),
    60, 61
instrumental conditioning. *See*
    operant conditioning
intelligence
    and adaptation, 295, 326–327, 337
    and aging, 475, 476, 477
    biological approach to, 320
    and brain, 296, 320, 327–331, 338
    cognitive approach to, 320,
        327–330, 337–338
    and culture, 322–323, 337
    and decision making, 328, 336
    definition of, 294, 319
    early efforts to study, 320
    and environment, 320, 326, 329,
        330–334, 336, 337, 338
    and gender, 335
    and genes, 295, 320, 329, 330–334,
        336, 338
    and group differences, 333–334,
        336
    measurement of, 320–323
    and memory, 250, 260, 296,
        336, 337
    and mental disorders, 556, 590, 601
    and Mozart Effect, 32–33
    multiple, 296, 323–325, 337
    overview about, 292, 293–295,
        319–320, 336–338
    and personality, 489

intelligence (*continued*)
    and problem solving, 328, 336, 337
    psychometric approach to, 320–323
    and race, 295, 333–334, 335, 338
    and reasoning, 336
    and scientific foundations of psychology, 25, 32–33
    See also IQ; *type of intelligence*
    and sensory/perceptual system, 294, 320
    and social engagement, 475, 477
    and speed of mental processing, 327, 336, 337, 475, 476, 477
    testing of, 294, 320–323, 327, 329, 333, 334–336, 337, 475
    and unconscious, 295
    understanding of, 319–338
    and working memory, 328, 337–338
intentionality, 453
    See also theory of mind
interactionist approach, to personality, 497–498, 500, 514, 515
interdependent self, 613–614
interference, and memory, 279, 289
The International Society of Sports Psychology, 30
International Society of Sports Psychology, 30
interneurons, and nervous system, 89–90
interpersonal psychotherapy, 568, 569, 593
interpersonal relations. *See* relationships; social bonds; social support
interpreter, brain, 139–140, 143, 145, 155, 284, 317
interval schedules, 226
interviews
    clinical, 524, 533, 561
    motivational, 569
    and research methodology, 51
intracranial self-stimulation (ICSS), 237–238
intrinsic motivation, 344, 348–350, 351
introspection, 20–21, 24, 34
introversion-extraversion trait, 489
introverts, 483, 484, 488, 489, 498, 504–506, 508, 515
intuition, 31, 34, 38, 42, 295, 316, 532, 608, 628
    See also instincts
I-O (industrial and organizational psychology), 350–351
ions, 90–91
    See also type of ion
iproniazid, 583
IQ (intelligence quotient)
    and aging, 475
    and behavior genetics, 330
    and brain, 329
    definition of, 321
    development of, 294
    and environment, 332
    and measurement of intelligence, 321, 322–323, 337
    and memory, 250, 260
    and mental disorders, 590, 601
    and self-fulfilling prophecy, 631
iris, 173
isolation, 415, 432, 454, 546, 556

Jackson, William, 281, 282
James-Lange theory of emotion, 395, 400
Jamison, Kay Redfield, 542–543, 588
jealousy, 392–393, 651, 656
Jensen, Jay (case study), 518
"Jim Twins" (case study), 83–84
job
    motivation on the, 350–351
    See also careers
John Paul II (pope), 135
Jordan, Michael, 629
Joyner-Kersee, Jackie, 310
justifying effort, 623–624
just world hypothesis, 627

Kaczynski, Theodore (case study), 531–532
k-complexes, 147–148
Keller, Helen, 159–160, 166, 168, 263
Kemper, Edmund E. III (case study), 532
Kennedy, John F., 280
killers, 53–54
Kinkel, Kip, 53–54
kin selection, 645, 656
Kluver-Bucy syndrome, 642
knock-out/knock-in studies, 40, 60, 331–332
knowledge
    and application of psychological science, 30–31, 33, 34
    innate, 449–451, 461, 477
Korsakoff's syndrome, 279, 370

language
    and aging, 473
    and brain, 138, 139, 140, 155, 432, 454, 458
    and cognition, 457, 458
    and critical learning periods, 458, 461, 477
    and culture, 457, 458
    and development, 432
    development of, 432, 433, 436, 437, 438, 454–459, 461, 476, 477
    and environment, 457
    errors in, 456
    and hearing, 455
    as innate, 461
    and isolation, 454
    learning of, 235, 237, 454–459
    and mental disorders, 556–557, 591, 601, 604
    and scientific foundations of psychology, 25, 27
    and sensation, 170
    sign, 458, 459, 477
    surface vs. deep structure of, 457
    and universal grammar, 432, 456–458, 477
latency stage, 485
latent learning, 230, 245
lateral inhibition, 176, 177
late selection theory, 203
law of conservation, 448, 449
law of effect, 210, 222
laws of nature
    and animal research, 59
    understanding the, 450–451, 461, 476, 477
L-DOPA, 100
learned helplessness model, 541

learning
    and adaptation, 12, 215, 220, 229, 245
    behavioral study of, 212–221, 244–245
    and behaviorism, 5
    and biology, 228–230, 231, 245
    and brain, 125, 129, 131, 155, 217, 229, 237–238, 239, 241, 243–244, 245, 289, 453–454, 476
    cellular basis of, 241–243
    and cognition, 211, 220–221, 228–230, 231, 245
    computerized neural networks for, 212, 243–244, 245
    and culture, 232, 244, 245, 461
    definition of, 212
    demonstration, 233, 237
    and development, 436–438, 444–461, 476, 477
    and drugs, 274
    and emotions, 244
    and environment, 210, 212, 213, 332, 461
    and evolution, 211, 220, 223, 229
    facilitation of, 149, 150, 155
    and fear, 217, 218–219, 220, 225, 232–233, 242, 245, 267, 268, 529, 576, 578
    generalized, 599, 601
    and genes, 220, 242–243
    and Gestalt psychology, 23, 34
    Hebbian, 131
    and imitation, 226, 234–235, 237, 245
    importance of, 212
    and influence of neurotransmission, 99, 103, 113
    and intellectual origins of psychology, 16
    and learning curves, 227
    and levels of analysis, 15
    and memory, 241, 242, 257, 258, 269, 270, 271, 279, 289
    and mental disorders, 155, 537, 561, 600
    and motivation, 342, 349
    at neuronal level, 240–244, 245
    observational, 212, 231–237, 245, 491
    over-, 256, 258
    overview about, 209–212, 244
    and perception, 199, 461
    and personality, 490–491, 505, 515
    and pleasure, 237–238, 239, 245
    and punishment, 210, 211, 224–226, 231, 237, 245
    reading, 459–460
    and reinforcement, 208, 211, 222–226, 227–228, 231, 238, 245
    and research methodology, 40, 59, 244
    and rewards, 230, 237–239, 245
    rote, 21
    rules for, 243
    and scientific foundations of psychology, 21, 23, 24, 25, 26, 34
    and sensory information, 213
    simple models of, 240–241, 244, 245
    and situations, 26
    and sleep, 149, 150, 155
    and social influence, 655

    and social learning theory, 211
    and synaptic alteration, 211, 240–242, 244, 245
    and themes of psychological science, 12
    vicarious, 234, 237, 245
    See also conditioning; language; *type of learning*
left hemisphere
    and development, 435
    and emotions, 407–408, 427
    and memory, 271, 475
    and mental disorders, 540
legal system, and mental disorders, 530–531, 533, 561
lens, 173, 174, 206
leptin, 363, 380
levels of analysis
    and application of psychological science, 28–29, 33, 34
    and research methodology, 48–49, 59–60
    and themes of psychological science, 13–15, 16, 33, 34
libido, 439, 484, 485, 486
lie-detector tests, 55–56, 402–404
life instinct, 484
life span, 469–476, 477, 560
life stories, 494, 510, 511, 514, 516
light
    color of, 176–177
    nature of, 160
limbic system
    and basic structure and functions of brain, 123
    definition of, 404
    and emotions, 386, 404
    and learning, 218
    and mental disorders, 559
    and motivation, 344, 359, 372
    and sexual behavior, 372
    and sleep, 152, 154
lipostatic theory, 363
listening, selective, 202–203, 206
lithium, 542–543, 573, 587–588, 593, 595, 603
Little Albert, 529
lobotomies, 128, 567, 586, 588
locus of control, 483, 491
London taxi drivers, study of, 124, 132, 329
longitudinal studies
    and mental disorders, 521, 547, 560
    and treatment of mental disorders, 597
long-term memory
    and aging, 474
    and brain, 268, 272
    and forgetting, 277–278, 279, 289
    organization of information in, 262–266, 289, 629
    retrieval from, 251, 262, 264, 265–266, 271, 272, 276, 289
    short-term memory distinguished from, 255–256, 259
    as stage of memory, 251, 254, 255–257, 259, 289
    storage in, 250, 251, 256, 259, 262–266, 268–269, 271, 272, 273, 275, 279, 289, 629
long-term potentiation, 241, 244, 245, 258
loosening of associations, 545–546

mind (*continued*)
and physiological psychology, 5
rational, 18
representations of, 296–303, 337
and research methodology, 38
and scientific foundations of
psychology, 20, 21, 23, 26, 27,
34
See also mental disorders; mind-
body problem; theory of mind
and situations, 26
and stereotypes, 654–655
and study of consciousness,
140–141
as subjective interpreter, 139–140,
155
and themes of psychological
science, 7, 9, 10–13, 16, 34
topographical model of, 484
mind-body problem, 17–18, 19
Minnesota Multiphasic Personality
Inventory (MMPI), 521, 525
mirror neurons, 212, 235, 237, 245
misattribution of arousal, 398
misattributions, source, 278, 280–281,
290
misinformation, 282–283, 290
miximizing, 318–319
mnemonics, 257–258
modal memory model, 250, 251–259
mode, 64
modeling, 237, 245, 569
See also imitation
monoamine oxidase (MAO)
inhibitors, 85, 99, 572, 583, 603
monoamines, 98, 99–101, 105, 113
See also specific monoamine
monocular depth perception, 192, 193,
194, 196, 206
moods
and addiction, 380
and application of psychological
science, 32
and cognition, 389
and decision making, 389–390
definition of, 385–386
and exercise, 424
and genetics, 182
and influence of
neurotransmission, 100, 104
and levels of analysis, 14, 15
and memory, 266
and mental disorders, 393,
538–543, 548, 551, 552,
561–562, 570, 573, 577, 593
and neurophysiological basis of
emotions, 400
and personality, 489, 512
regulation of, 398–400, 427
and social influence, 638, 656
See also emotions; *specific
disorder*
moon illusion, 195, 196–197, 206
moral dilemmas, 433, 467
moral values, 433, 466–467, 468,
476, 477
morphemes, 454, 455
morphine, 104, 170, 367, 368
mothers
and mental disorders, 557, 558, 561
surrogate, 432, 439
See also attachment; parenting
style; parents

motion
aftereffects of, 197
and perception, 194, 197–198,
200, 206
motion parallax, 194
motivation
and adaptive behavior, 347–348,
349, 351, 359–360, 376, 379
and addiction, 364–370
and application of psychological
science, 29
and arousal, 379
and behaviors for their own sake,
348–350, 379
and biology, 377, 379
and brain, 358–359, 360, 362–363,
367, 370, 372, 376, 377–378,
379, 407
and cognition, 379
and control theory, 349–350
and culture, 376
definition and characteristics of,
343
and development, 438
and drives, 342, 344–347, 348,
351, 379
and eating, 360–364, 380
and emotions, 384, 395, 427
and environment, 365, 376–377, 378
and evolution, 349, 359, 374,
375–376, 379
and exercise, 424
and gender, 378
and genes, 359, 365, 377
and goals, 343, 351, 355–360, 379
and impressions, 627, 634
and incentives, 346, 348
and influence of
neurotransmission, 100,
105, 113
and intelligence, 322
job, 350–351
and memory, 367
and needs, 342, 343, 344–347, 351,
355, 379
overview about, 341–343, 379
pain as, 395
and personality, 484, 487, 491, 493,
495, 505, 510
pleasure as, 344, 347–348, 351,
364–370, 379, 395
and self-knowledge, 611, 619
and self-perception, 349–350
and self-regulation, 343, 344, 355,
356–359, 360, 379
and sexual behavior, 370–378,
379, 380
and social influence, 634, 655
and social needs, 351–355, 379
and social psychology, 610, 611, 619,
627, 630, 634, 655
and stereotypes, 630
and survival, 379
and treatment of mental disorders,
569, 595, 603
understanding, 344–351
See also incentives; rewards; *type of
motivation*
motivational interviewing, 569
motor functions
and brain, 122–123, 125, 127, 129, 133,
155, 559, 560
and development, 434

and memory, 250, 258, 260,
267, 289
and mental disorders, 534, 544,
546, 548, 556, 559, 560, 562,
581, 589, 600
and nervous system, 93–94, 98–99,
100, 103, 105, 113
and sleep, 153
motor memory. *See* procedural
memory
motor neurons, 89–90
Mozart Effect, 32–33
M. P. (case study), 197
MPTP, 102
Muhammad, John Allen, 54
multiaxial system, 522, 523, 561
multimodal intelligence, 296, 337
Multimodal Treatment of Attention-
Deficit Hyperactivity
Disorder (MTA), 599
multiple intelligence, 296, 337
multiple personality disorder, 52,
525–528, 561
multiple sclerosis, 94–95
music, 14–15, 28, 32–33, 182
mutations, 80, 113
myelination, 93–95, 96, 103, 113, 169,
435, 436, 437, 547
Myers-Briggs Type Indicator
(MBTI), 498

Nagle, Matthew, 134
narcissistic personality, 550
National Academy of Sciences, 403
National Advisory Mental Health
Council, 597
National Institute of Drug Abuse, 366
National Institute of Health, 30
National Institute of Mental Health,
536, 577, 599
National Institutes of Health, 423,
522, 592
National Research Council, 601
naturalistic observation, 47
natural killer cells, 413
natural reinforcement, 238, 239
natural selection
and dreams, 154
and emotions, 384
at gene level, 645
and harming and helping
others, 645
as integral to psychological
science, 33
and intellectual origins of
psychology, 18–19, 34
and learning, 211
and motivation, 376
and overview of psychological
science, 4
and personality, 506
and themes of psychological
science, 10
nature-nurture debate, 16–17, 19, 24, 34
needs
hierarchy of, 344, 345, 351, 379
and motivation, 342, 343, 344–347,
351, 355, 379
and personality, 488
See also type of need
need to belong, 10, 351–352, 355, 379,
638, 641, 655
negative activation, 394–395
negative affect, 643, 647

negative feedback model, 345, 363
negative punishment, 224, 225
negative reinforcement, 224, 225
negative symptoms, of schizophrenia,
546, 562, 589, 603
neo-Freudians, 482, 486, 514–515
NEO Personality Inventory, 495
neophobia, 361, 364, 648
nervous system
and basic structure and functions
of brain, 123, 129
and biological basis of psychological
science, 74, 87–96
and development, 435
and development of brain, 134
diseases of central, 120
and endocrine system, 108–112, 114
and environment, 94
and genetics, 94
and influence of
neurotransmission on
emotion, thought, and
behavior, 95–106
major divisions of, 106
and neuron integration into
communication systems,
105–112, 113
operation of, 87–96, 113
See also central nervous system
(CNS); memory; peripheral
nervous system (PNS)
and stem cell research, 136
network models, of memory, 252, 264,
266, 272, 275, 289
neurochemistry
of emotion, 273–274
and levels of analysis, 15
and memory, 251, 252, 262, 267,
268, 270, 272–274, 275, 289
and mental disorders, 6, 16, 27, 529,
549, 562
and scientific foundations of
psychology, 27
and themes of psychological
science, 8, 16, 34
and treatment of mental disorders,
572, 584, 603
neurogenesis, 120, 131
neuroimaging, 407, 521
neuroleptics, 572
neuronal firing. *See* action potential
neuronal workspace model, 145, 155
neurons
and basic structure and functions
of brain, 119, 121, 122
as basic units of nervous system,
88, 96
definition of, 88
and development, 436, 437, 477
and development of brain, 130–131,
132, 133–134, 137
and eating, 362–363, 380
and emotions, 385
and Golgi stain, 74
integration into communication
systems of, 105–112, 113
and intelligence, 332
and learning, 212, 239, 240–244, 245
and mental disorders, 537, 540
mirror, 212, 235, 237, 245
and motivation, 344, 362–363
and operation of nervous system,
88–96

social regard, 614–616, 655
social-skills training, 237, 569, 590, 593, 602, 603
socio-cognitive theories, of personality, 483, 491, 493
sociocultural model, and mental disorders, 528
socioemotional selective theory, 434, 474, 477
sociometer theory, 615, 655
sodium, and nervous system, 75, 90–91, 92–93, 96, 103, 113
somatic markers, 390, 406, 467
somatic nervous system, 106–108, 114
somatosensory hallucinations, 545
somatosensory homunculus, 126
somatosensory signals, 90, 106
sonar senses, 180
sound waves, 170, 171, 172, 206
source amnesia, 283, 452, 477
source misattributions. See misattributions, source
spankings, 225, 226
spatial memory, 270, 271, 289
spatial relationships, 126, 138, 140, 155, 160, 183, 184, 192–194, 298
Spears, Britney, 513
species, attachment across, 438–439
specific response level, 489
speech, 155, 235, 408, 455–458, 477, 546, 556–557
spinal cord
   and basic structure and functions of brain, 121, 129, 155
   and development, 436
   and development of brain, 133–134
   function of, 105–106
   and influence of neurotransmission, 112
   injuries to, 133–134, 135
   and neuron integration into communication systems, 105–106, 114
   as part of central nervous system, 105–106, 112, 114
   and sensation, 169, 206
split brain, 120, 137, 138, 140, 155, 284, 317, 348–349
spontaneous recovery, and learning, 215
sports psychologists, 29–30
spreading activation models, 252, 264, 266, 289
Springsteen, Bruce, 472
SSRIs. See Prozac; selective serotonin reuptake inhibitors
standard deviation, 64
Stanford prison study, 608–609, 610, 636
startle response, 533
state-dependent memory, 266
state hospital system, 566
statistical procedures, 39, 46, 62, 64–67
stem cells, 74, 101, 120, 134, 135–136, 155
stereograms, 446
stereoscopic vision, 160, 193
stereotypes
   of aging, 472
   and aging, 475
   and attitudes, 622
   automatic categorization as basis of, 628–631, 634, 654–655

and brain, 654
and decision making, 308
and development, 434, 477
and emotions, 388
and expectations, 189
and gender, 463, 477
and heuristics, 308
and identity, 462, 463, 468
and impressions, 628–631, 634
and ingroup-outgroup bias, 631–634
inhibiting, 629–630
and insight, 312
and mental disorders, 600
and mind, 654–655
and perception, 189, 630–631
and personality, 492, 493, 509
and prejudice, 631–632, 634, 655
and problem solving, 312
and race, 189, 629, 630–631
and race/ethnicity, 468
and relationships, 649, 650
stereotype threat, 335
steroids, 109–111, 275
stimulants, and addiction, 366
stimulus
   and perception, 206
   and scientific foundations of psychology, 24–25
   See also sensation
stimulus discrimination, 216, 217, 244
stimulus generalization, 215–216, 217, 244
stimulus judgments, 55
stimulus processing, 54–55
storage, of memory, 251, 256, 259, 262–266, 268–269, 271, 272, 273, 275, 279, 289
Strange Situation Test, 440
strategies, and motivation, 344
stream of consciousness, 21
streptococcal infections, 536
stress
   and adaptation, 409
   advantages and disadvantages of, 382
   and behaviors affecting health, 416–426
   coping with, 385, 386, 408–416, 424, 425, 426, 427, 428
   in daily life, 382, 410–411, 416–426, 428
   definition of, 386
   and development, 435
   and evolution, 408, 409
   and exercise, 424, 425, 426
   and gender, 409, 415
   and health, 382, 384–385, 411–413, 425–426, 428
   and lying, 402
   and major life stressors, 410–411, 416, 428
   and memory, 273, 280, 283, 288, 391, 411
   and mental disorders, 529–530, 533–534, 540, 541, 548, 561, 566, 586, 590
   and perception, 204
   and personality, 488
   and research methodology, 45
   and social support, 426, 427, 428
stressors, 408
   See also stress

stretch reflex, 121
stroboscopic motion perception, 197, 198
stroke patients, 126, 134, 141, 144, 151
Strong Interest Inventory, 498–499
Stroop effect, 55
structuralism, 20–21, 23, 24, 27, 34
structural model of personality, 485–486
Structured Clinical Interview for DSM (SCID), 524
study-skills course study, 286
subcortical structures
   and basic structure and functions of brain, 123–125, 155
   and emotions, 396, 404
   and memory, 267, 272, 279
   and mental disorders, 559–560, 562
   See also specific structure
subjective well-being, 488
subjectivity, 20, 141, 393–395, 400, 427
subliminal perception, 142–143
substance abuse, 594
   See also type of abuse
substance P, 98, 103, 104, 114
subtractive color mixing, 177–178
subtyping, 629
suggestibility, 278, 282–283, 285, 290
suicide, 538, 539, 543, 552, 585, 586, 591, 592, 594, 595, 642
Sullivan, Anne, 159–160
superego, 485, 514
support, social
   and stress, 415–416, 426, 427, 428
   and treatment of mental disorders, 570–571, 586, 591, 594
suppression, thought, 399–400
suprachiastic nucleus (SCN), 150–151
surgery, and mental disorders, 572, 588
survival
   and adaptation, 10–11, 12, 13
   and basic structure and functions of brain, 121–122, 129, 155
   and development, 433, 438–441, 477
   and eating, 364
   and emotions, 387, 390, 391
   and harming and helping others, 644, 656
   and ingroup-outgroup bias, 632
   and intellectual origins of psychology, 34
   and learning, 220, 245
   and memory, 248, 257, 288
   and mental disorders, 561
   and motivation, 343, 348, 349, 351, 364, 379
   and perception, 190, 205
   and personality, 506, 515
   and self-knowledge, 615
   and sensation, 161, 205
   and stress, 408
   and themes of psychological science, 10–11, 12, 34
survival of the fittest, 18
Sybil (case study), 52–53
syllogisms, 304–305, 337
symbolic knowledge, 337
symbolic representations, 296, 299–301, 303
symbolism, and Piaget's cognitive development stages, 448, 449

sympathetic division, 107–108, 114
sympathetic nervous system, 410, 412, 537
synapse/synapses
   definition of, 89
   and development, 436–437, 476
   and exercise, 424
   and intelligence, 332
   and learning, 211, 240–242, 244, 245
   and memory, 272
   and mental disorders, 572, 573
   and nervous system, 75, 89, 95–96, 98, 100, 102, 103, 112, 113
   and personality, 512
   and sensation, 175
   and termination of synaptic transmission, 96
synaptic cleft, 95, 96, 97, 103–104, 105
synaptic pruning, 436–437, 476
synaptic transmission, 131, 141
systematic desensitization, 217, 569, 578–579, 603
systematic errors, 63
systems approach, 571

"talk" psychotherapy, 578
Tan (case study), 38
tardive dyskinesia, 572, 589, 603
taste, 166–167, 182, 200, 205, 380, 436
T cells, 413
technology, 7, 16, 40
telegraphic speech, 456
temperament
   definition of, 441
   and development, 441, 443, 477
   and divorce, 443
   and mental disorders, 535, 560
   and personality, 482, 484, 502–504, 507, 508, 511, 514, 515
temporal coding, 171–172
temporal lobes
   and basic structure and functions of brain, 125, 127, 129, 155
   and memory, 249–250, 256, 267, 268–270, 272, 273, 275, 279, 289
   and mental disorders, 547, 562
   and perception, 182–183, 184, 190
   and personality, 511
   and representations, 298
tend-and-befriend response, 408, 409, 427
teratogens, 435–436, 476
terminal buttons, 89, 95, 97, 98, 99
terrorism, 280, 641
terror management theory, 615
testing
   aptitude, 320, 334–336
   intelligence, 327, 329, 333, 334–336, 337, 475
   as measurement of intelligence, 320–323
   and mental disorders, 521, 524–525, 533, 553, 561
   neuropsychological, 524
   for personality, 521
   psychological, 521, 524–525, 533, 553, 561
   validity of, 321–322, 337
   See also type of test
testosterone, 109, 110, 123, 371–372, 373, 409, 435
texture gradient, 194

Western Collaborative Group, 412
white matter, 121
Whitman, Charles, 53
whole-language approach, 459–460
will, illusion of conscious, 143–144
Wilson, Rita, 652
Wiltshire, Stephen, 324, 325
Winfrey, Oprah, 341–342, 345, 362, 363
withdrawal, 217, 245, 364, 546, 562, 589
women, as scholars, 22–23

Woods, Tiger, 234, 333
Woodward, Joanne, 652
working backwards, 315, 319
working memory
    and basic stages of memory,
        254–255, 259, 289
    and brain processes involved in
        memory, 271, 272, 275
    and brain structure and functions,
        329, 359

definition of, 328
and development, 474
and forgetting, 279
importance of, 359
and intelligence, 328, 336, 337–338
and motivation, 359
and organization of information,
    264
working self-concept, 613, 655
World Health Organization, 411

Xanax, 572

Yerkes-Dodson law, 342, 346, 348

Zilstein study, 353
zygotes, 80
Zyprexa, 572